CATHOLIC KOREA

YESTERDAY
AND
TODAY

CATHOLIC KOREA

YESTERDAY AND TODAY

Compiled and Edited

By

Father Joseph Chang-mun Kim
Catechist John Jae-sun Chung

CATHOLIC KOREA PUBLISHING CO.
Seoul, Korea

NIHIL OBSTAT

Paulus Kim, Censor

IMPRIMATUR

die 15 Aug. 1964

✝Paulus M. Ro

Archiep. Seoulensis

Printed in the Republic of Korea

Pope Paul VI

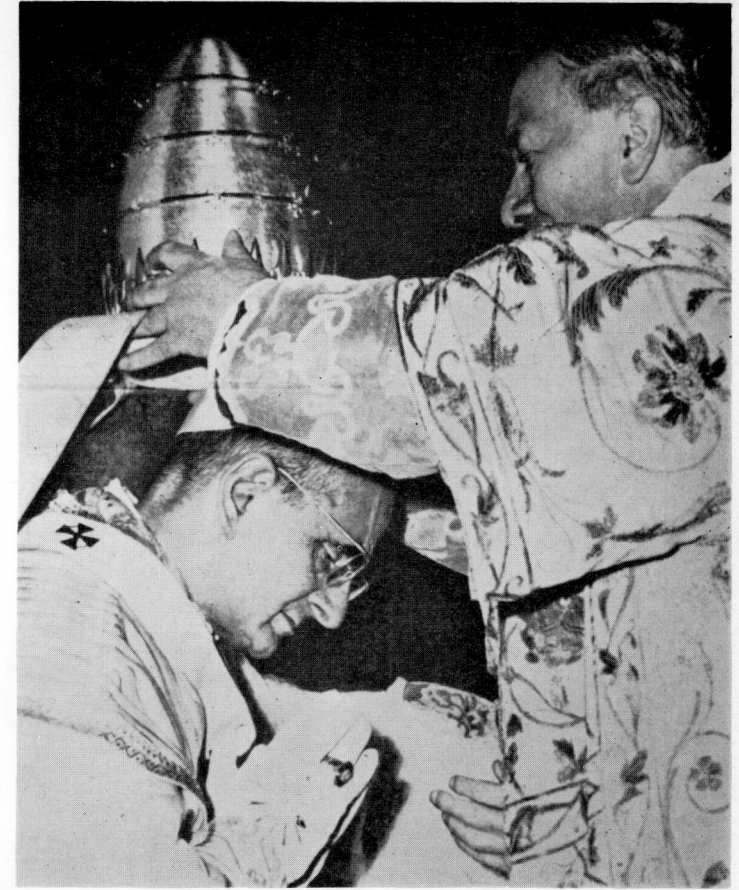

The Coronation

His First Benediction to the world

His Parents

The Pope in his infancy in grandma's arms and his brother

Birthplace of the Pope

The Last Journey

Through a dense crowd hushed by sorrow and respect, the body of Pope John XXIII is carried in procession from the Apostolic Palace to St. Peter's Basilica to lie in state before the high altar.

Birthplace of the late Pope

Sister Angela, Brothers Giuseppe and Zaverio Roncalli

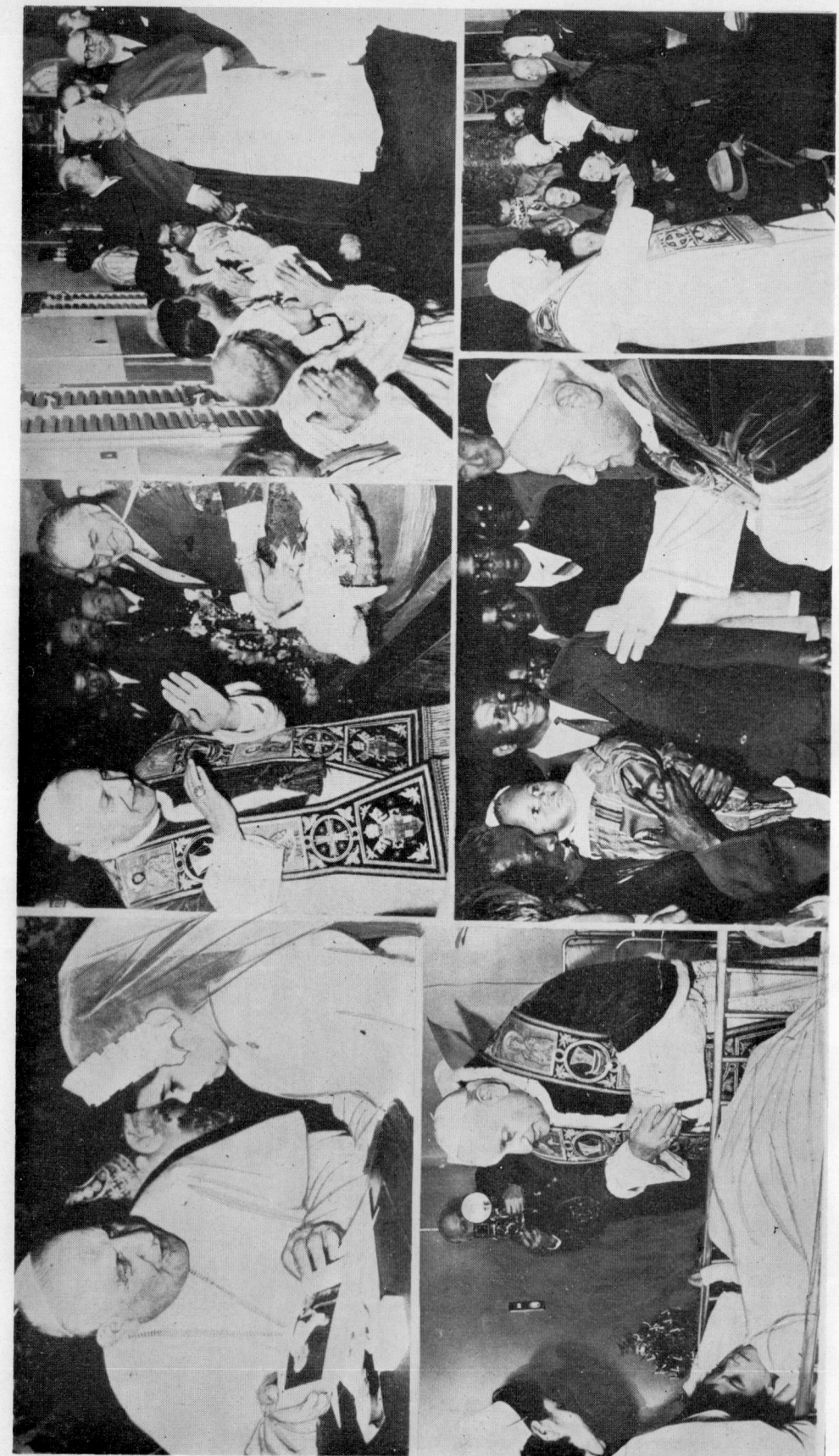

Warmth, humor and compassion distinguished Pope John XXIII

Congratulations

on the Publication of
"Catholic Korea—Yesterday and Today"

On the occasion of publishing "Catholic Korea—Yesterday and Today," I feel highly honored to have an opportunity for offering my congratulations.

To commemorate the establishment of the Catholic Hierarchy in Korea, over which it was my honor and privilege to preside, the Reverend Joseph Ch'ang-mun Kim and Catechist John Jae-sŭn Chŭng have published a book on the history of the Catholic Church in Korea, together with a unique and complete collection of photographs depicting Catholic life in this country.

The Church in Korea has now attained its full ecclesiastical jurisdiction. Its history, however, is one of suffering and hardship, and even of frequent martyrdom, as the devoted Korean Catholics strove to practice their Faith in an environment which was often hostile.

One of the most recent in the glorious procession of the Catholic martyrs of Korea was the first resident Apostolic Delegate to Korea, His Excellency The Most Reverend Patrick J. Byrne of Maryknoll, who, in 1950, refused to flee the Communist invasion from the north, and died a victim of the infamous Death March.

"Catholic Korea—Yesterday and Today" should prove to be of interest to the people of Korea, who, especially in these recent years, have palpably demonstrated their desire to know more about the Catholic Church. It should also arouse considerable interest abroad, illustrating as it does the progress of the Catholic Church in this land.

I close my message with appreciation for various endeavors by the Reverend Joseph Ch'ang-mun Kim, Catechist John Jae-sŭn Chŭng and other editorial members in compiling the unparalleled book. God bless them.

Monsignor Charles Burton Mouton, J.C.D.,
Ex-Chargé d'Affaires *ad int.*,
The Apostolic Delegation in Korea

Congratulations

on the Publication of
"Catholic Korea—Yesterday and Today"

I am very happy to have this opportunity to make known to the people at home and abroad an aspect of the magnificent development of the Korean Catholic Church by means of the publication of "Catholic Korea—Yesterday and Today" in both English and Korean, compiled and edited by Father Joseph Ch'ang-mun Kim and Catechist John Jae-sŭn Chŭng.

The Church of Our Lord, which was established for the testimony of the truth and for the enlightenment and salvation of the people all over the world, has achieved a triumph always and everywhere, whatever persecution it confronted and in the face of the tyrants. The histories of the world Churches speak eloquently of this fact. Especially the Catholic Church in Korea notwithstanding the suffering of her myriads of martyrs, through the incessant persecutions in her infancy, has never ceased to develop and has finally come to the erection of the Hierarchy of the Church in Korea.

This happy consummation, I firmly believe, will be a most eloquent proof, first, in sustaining a unique origin of the Korean Catholic Church, that is to say, by the special grace of God, our Korean forefathers embraced the Catholic religion not in a passive response to the teaching of foreign missionaries but as an active and positive result of their zeal in their search for truth and, having been baptized in Peking, spread the Gospel among their fellow countrymen and established the Church; second, that the heroic deeds of martyrdom of the priests of the foreign missions, the native-born priests and the devout Christians will not be forgotten; third, that the blessings of God are still as abundant as in her infancy.

I do also firmly believe that through this book our gratitude toward God and those innumerable foreign missionaries and our forefathers who shed their blood to make the Korean Catholic Church brilliant and prosperous will be represented forever.

Finally I extend my heartfelt thanks to Father Joseph Ch'ang-mun Kim, Catechist John Jae-sŭn Chŭng and the many others who dedicated themselves to the work of bringing the book through the press.

The Most Reverend Paul M. Ro, D.D.
Archbishop of Seoul, Korea

Congratulations

on the Publication of
"Catholic Korea—Yesterday and Today"

In the history of no country has the road to the Church been a smooth and pleasant one. The road was always a blood-stained and thorny one and also an extremely desolate one. Nevertheless valiantly following the path the Church has improved its lot through the years and at last has established an imperishable monument of mankind.

We note especially that the scholars of our country embraced the Catholic religion not in a passive response to the teaching of foreign missionaries but as an active and positive result in their zealous quest for the true religion. They established the Church and brought in priests from Peking. From that time on our Church had produced countless martyrs in the vortex of continuous persecutions lasting for more than a hundred years, and it is beyond doubt that the record of those who gladly sacrificed themselves, undergoing decapitation, hanging and laceration, will inspire in the Christians of today and tomorrow a desire for praying with more fervent zeal for the future of the Korean Catholic Church.

It is unimaginable that, without the grace of God, our forefathers could possibly have propagated the Gospel among their compatriots shivering in the darkness of death with such courage to fight against such hardships and with such passion for the salvation of souls.

In commemoration of this occasion Father Joseph Ch'ang-mun Kim and Catechist John Jae-sŭn Chŭng had planned the publication of "Catholic Korea—Yesterday and Today." On this occasion I earnestly hope that our Catholic Church in Korea will prosper and every Christian will exert all his power, to enable the grace of God to prevail throughout the world.

In conclusion I tender my heartfelt thanks to Father Joseph Ch'ang-mun Kim, Catechist John Jae-sŭn Chŭng and their editorial staff for their assiduous efforts.

The Most Reverend John Sŭh, D.D.,
Archbishop of Tae-gu, Korea

Congratulations

on the Publication of
"*Catholic Korea—Yesterday and Today*"

On the occasion of the publication of "Catholic Korea—Yesterday and Today" it is not only a great privilege but a pleasure for me to congratulate you Father Joseph Ch'ang-mun Kim and Catechist John Jae-sŭn Chŭng on a masterpiece. The history of the introduction of Christianity into the land of my adoption is unique in the missionary annals of the Church. Because our Korean people brought the Faith to themselves, I have always referred to them as the Do-It-Yourself Catholics.

This edition of "Catholic Korea—Yesterday and Today" will be instrumental in bringing to the knowledge and attention of others the great progress made by the Church, especially during the last few years, and of the opportunities there. I hope it will be instrumental in interesting many Communities of priests, Brothers, Sisters to come to this land of promise.

I ask God to reward and bless you for your valiant efforts.

+ Harold W. Henry

The Most Reverend Harold W. Henry, S.S.C., D.D.
Archbishop of Kwang-ju, Korea

Preface

The Catholic Church in Korea is marked by its unique origin, its horrifying persecutions, and its amazingly rapid growth.

Unlike other nations, the initial seeds of the Gospel were brought into the land by the Koreans themselves in the 18th century (1784) and the Church was thus established through the zealous efforts of lay apostles, who baptized more than 4,000 converts before any missionary priest had ever set foot in this kingdom.

When Father James Chou, a Chinese priest and the first missionary, entered Korea in 1795, he discovered to his amazement that the Faith had already been well spread, especially among the best-known scholars of the land. The whirlwind of persecution was also sweeping over the country, bringing death to many of the gallant Christians. After five years of strenuous labor Father Chou also met his death by martyrdom, leaving behind more than 10,000 faithful without a shepherd for more than thirty-three years.

To the eyes of the government at that time, the strange new religion was nothing but a downright heresy, contradictory to the ancestral traditions and a possible pathway to foreign encroachment, to the detriment of the nation. Accordingly, strong repressive measures were taken to uproot the Christian faith completely from the land through a series of persecutions.

Outstanding among these were the Four Great Persecutions (in 1801, 1839, 1846, and 1866). Each of these was marked by unparalleled atrocities. Every Christian was exposed to the constant peril of torture and death, but the Faith survived miraculously under the sword of the executioners.

Korean Catholics may well take pride in the history of their Church, the glory of which shines forth in splendor, comparable to that of ancient Rome. Among ten thousand known martyrs, seventy-nine were declared Blessed in 1925, and a new group of twenty-six are expected to be beatified before long.

"Florete Flores Martyrum" was the motto of the late Archbishop Mutel of Seoul, and the venerable shepherd's wishes are now being fulfilled. The fragrant flowers of the Martyrs are in full bloom today, thanks to the heroic labors of the Fathers of the Paris Foreign Mission Society, the Benedictines, the Maryknoll Fathers, the Columban Fathers, and the Korean clergy who have brought about the present thriving condition of the Church.

Recognizing this marvelous development, the Holy See saw fit to establish the Hierarchy of the Church in Korea in 1962, comprising three archdioceses and eight dioceses, with over six hundred thousand faithful.

It is most gratifying that this volume has now appeared at such an opportune moment, covering as it does every detail of the history of the Church in Korea with the specific purpose of making it known to the world and of showing how the hand of the Almighty, through the supreme sacrifice of His noble martyrs, has wrought miraculous achievements in this land.

EDITOR'S FOREWORD

For the glory of God, the renown of the Korean Catholic Church and the victorious faith of our martyred forefathers we began planning a book, "Catholic Korea—Yesterday and Today."

Superficial and shallow though our knowledge is, we have done our best to present, in this book, clear and accurate information on every aspect of the Korean Catholic Church from its infancy to the present. There are numerous photographs and other illustrations; the book is in royal octavo format of more than a thousand pages edited separately both in Korean and in English.

Six years have elapsed since we set foot in this field of untamed wilderness, and now by the grace of God we are finally able to publish this book.

In spite of formidable obstacles, we have finally completed this task, by the grace of God. Once again we sincerely tender our heartfelt thanks to Our Lord, to our martyred forefathers, and to those who were unsparing of their time and labor on our behalf regardless of their busy life both public and private.

In the collection of historical records and pictures, we are deeply indebted to the following persons for their efforts and cooperation.

The Most Rev. Antonio del Giudice, Apostolic Internuncio to Korea; the Right Rev. Msgr. Charles Burton Mouton, J.C.D., former Chargé d'Affaires *ad int.*, the Apostolic Delegation in Korea; the Most Rev. Paul M. Ro, D.D., Archbishop of Seoul; the Most Rev. John Sŭh, D.D., Archbishop of Tae-gu; the Most Rev. Harold W. Henry, S.S.C., D.D., Archbishop of Kwang-ju; the Most Rev. Adrien Larribeau, M.E.P., D.D., Bishop of Tae-jŏn; the Most Rev. Thomas Quinlan, S.S.C., D.D., Bishop of Ch'un-ch'ŏn; the Most Rev. James V. Pardy, M.M., D.D., Bishop of Ch'ŏng-ju; the Most Rev. John Ch'oe, D.D., Bishop of Pu-san; the Most Rev. Peter Han, D.D., Bishop of Chŏn-ju; the Most Rev. William J. McNaughton, M.M., D.D., Bishop of In-ch'ŏn; the Most Rev. Victorinus Youn, S.T.D., Bishop of Su-won; the Right Rev. Msgr. George Carroll, M.M., Administrator of P'yŏng-yang Diocese; the Right Rev. Msgr. Timothy Bitterli, O.S.B., Administrator of Ham-heung Diocese; the Right Rev. Msgr. Paul Kim, Vicar General of Archdiocese of Kwang-ju; the Right Rev. Msgr. Joseph Chang, Vicar General of Diocese of Pu-san; the Right Rev. Msgr. John V. Bulaitis, Secretary to the Apostolic Internunciature in Korea; the Very Rev. Laurent Youn, Ph.D., Vicar General of Archdiocese of Seoul; the Very Rev. Regional Superior of the Paris Foreign Mission Society; the Very Rev. Regional Superior of Columban Fathers; the Very Rev. Regional Superior of Maryknoll Fathers; the Rev. Paul Chu Chae-yong, Spiritual Director of the Sisters of Our Lady of Perpetual Help; the Rev. Superior of the Congregation of the Sisters of St. Paul de Chartres; the Most Rev. Abbot of the Order of St. Benedict; the Rev. Superior of the Sisters of Our Lady of Perpetual Help; the Rev. Superior of the Missionary Benedictine Sisters; the Rev. Superior of the Sisters of St. Benedict; the Rev. Superior of the Handmaids of the Sacred Heart of Jesus; the Very Rev. Superior of the Order of Friars Minor; the Rev. Superior of the Maryknoll Sisters of St. Dominic; the Rev. Superior of the Discalced Carmelites of the Annunciations; the Rev. Superior of Order of Discalced Carmelites; the Rev. Superior of the Holy Family Sisters; the Rev. Superior of Brothers of the Blessed Korean Martyrs; the Rev. Superior of the Convent of the Korean Martyrs; the Very Rev. Superior of the Salesian Society; the Very Rev. Superior of the Society of Jesus; the Rev. Superior of the Caritas Sisters of the Blessed Sacrament; the Rev. Superior of the Mission-ary Sisters of St. Columban; the Rev. Superior of the Society of the Sacred Heart; Team Leader of the Korean Branch of the International Catholic Auxil-iaries; the Rev. Superior of the Salesian Sisters of St. John Bosco; the Very Rev. Superior of the John of God Brothers; the Rev. Superior of the Franciscan Missionaries of Mary; the Rev. Superior of the Society of Mary (Marianists); the Rev. Superior of the Miyasaki Caritas Sisters; the Rev. Superior of the Sisters of Charity of Mother Seton; the Rev. Superior of the Daughters of Paul; the Rev. Superior of the Society of Paul; the Rev. Petite Soeur of the Fraternity of the Little Sisters of Jesus; the Rev. Superior of the Institute of the Blessed Virgin Mary; the Very Rev. John Lee, Ph.D., Dean of Theological Department, Catholic College; the Very Rev. Andrew Bachhuber, S.J., Rector of Tae-kŏn Major Seminary; the Very Rev. John P. Daly, S.J., Ph.D., President of Sŏ-kang Jesuit College; the Very Rev. Ignatius Chŭn, Dean of Hyo-sŏng Women's College; the Very Rev. Peter Cho, Principal of the Holy Ghost Middle and High School; the Rev. John Heisse, M.M., Executive Secretary of the Catholic Commit-tee of Korea; the Rev. Paul Ch'oe, Book Censor of the Catholic Publishing Co.; the Rev. Cyril Shin, Director of the Catholic Times; the Rev. Kim, Director of the Tae-gu Daily News; the Rev. Patrick Burke, S.S.C., N.C.W.C. Correspondent; all parish priests and members of religious communities, and all Christians.

In the compilation, editing and proofreading, the editors are greatly indebted to the following persons for their assiduous efforts and cooperation.

Dr. John M. Chang LL.D.; Prof. Ryu Hong-ryŏl, Litt.D., College of Liberal Arts and Sciences, Seoul National University; the Rev. Andrew Ch'oe, S.T.D., Professor of the Theological Department, Catholic College; Prof. Ko Kwang-man, former Dean of Education College, Seoul National University; the Rev. John Heisse, M.M., Executive Secretary of the Catholic Committee of Korea; the Rev. Kenneth Killoren, S.J., former President, Sŏ-kang College; the Rev. John P. Daly, S.J., President of Sŏ-kang College; the Rev. John E. Bernbrock, S.J., Professor of Sŏ-kang College; Prof. Chang Pal, former Dean of College of Fine Arts, Seoul National University; the Rev. Paul Kim Ch'ang-yŏl, Assistant Dean of the Theological Department, Catholic College.

We take special pride in announcing that Mr. George Rainer, former professor at Wuhan National University (1938-1946) and Anhwei National University (1947-1951) in China, and now lecturing at the Graduate School and College of Liberal Arts and Sciences, Seoul National University, exerted himself in a kindly spirit in the compilation, copyreading and proofreading of the book over a period of three years.

Our wholehearted thanks are sincerely tendered to him for his assiduous and indefatigable efforts.

We owe a great deal to the writers and publishers at home and abroad for permission to quote and reproduce some articles and pictures, especially to Didde Printing Company of the United States in using *The Story of Chaplain Kapaun*.

Special acknowledgment is also expressed for the generous cooperation of the Ministries of Foreign Affairs and Public Information of the Republic of Korea.

We express our thanks also to the following persons for various kinds of work on the book; the Rev. Kim Yang-sun, professor of Union Christian College; the Rev. Hong Tong-keun, Assistant Pastor of the Yŏng-rak Presbyterian Church; Mr. Chung Young-tek; Mr. Im Tae-bin; Mr. Lee Hyŏk-jong; Miss Lee Kye-hee; Catechist Joseph Kim Kyŏng-sik; Mr. Joseph Chŭng Shin-nam; Mr. Chŭng Shin-ch'ŏl; Mr. John Chŭng Shin-su, and all of the editorial staff members. We also tender our gratitude to the Sam-hwa Printing Co. for its efforts in photogravure and typography, and also to the I-u Bindery.

Finally we shall be very happy if this book should contribute to the glory of God, the renown of the Korean Catholic Church, and the victorious faith of our martyred forefathers. And if God bless this task and grant us a plentiful of harvest, we will endeavor to erect Memorial Museum, Church, and Monument, as the work commemorative of martyrs, and set up a "Catholic Center" including the Catholic Student Guidance Division, International Catholic Cultural Research Division, Book Publication Division, Institute for Catechists, Catholic Self-Sustenance Plant, Catholic Self-Sustenance Farm and so on.

These projects will require a fund of ten million dollars. In due time we intend to make an accurate and detailed plan and carry it out as soon as the fund is secured.

We sincerely hope that those who give their good wishes to the development of the Korean Catholic Church will furnish aid spiritually and materially to this enterprise so that the glory of God and the Catholic Church in Korea will be further enhanced.

Though we have done our best, taking advantage of many helpful suggestions, it is realized that imperfections of several types must still exist. Therefore additional constructive criticism is welcomed to the end that such defects may be remedied when the opportunity presents itself, so that the needs of readers may be met more adequately.

December 8, 1964   Father Joseph Ch'ang-mun Kim
                            Catechist John Jae-sŭn Chŭng

Explanatory Note on Romanization

The romanization system we have adopted purports to transliterate the Korean proper nouns used in this historical book—the only one in this domain at home and abroad—in such a way as to differentiate each Korean sound as clearly as possible and thus enable readers to recognize inductively both the original Korean sounds and the corresponding Chinese characters.

Our system, we are confident, enjoys advantages over others, but we must admit that it is virtually impossible to devise one that will be perfect for every purpose. It is derived in large part from the widely-used McCune-Reischauer system, and incorporates several useful features from that of Homer Hulbert (1863-1949).

In conformity with common practice we have, in cases where personal preference or long-established usage has given rise to divergent spellings, used these instead of the forms shown in the tables below. *e.g.* Tae-gu (instead of Tae-ku), Ahn (instead of An), Hŭh (instead of Hŭ), Sŭh (instead of Sŭ), Park (instead of Pak), Lee (instead of Yi, although Yi is used in referring to Yi Dynasty), Oh (instead of O), Ro (instead of No), Shin (instead of Sin), and Ryu (instead of Yu).

Personal names are transliterated in the traditional way, with the surname first, followed by the given name, which, unless monosyllabic, is hyphenated. The Christian name, if any, precedes the surname. *e.g.* Andrew Kim Tae-kŏn; Lee Pyŏk.

Geographical names are hyphenated, each syllable usually representing one of the component Chinese characters. *e.g.* Pu-san, P'yŏng-an, Sin-eui-ju.

We have emphasized the hyphenation of geographical and personal names in order to facilitate the tracing of the original Korean sounds and their corresponding Chinese characters.

The reverse apostrophe (') represents the '*spiritus asper*' and is used in transliterating the aspirated Korean sounds ch' ㅊ, k' ㅋ, t' ㅌ, and p' ㅍ.

The micron (˘) is used in transliterating the Korean vowels ŏ (어), yŏ (여), ŭ (으), and yŭ (으). The latter, ŭ and yŭ, are used only in special cases.

In geographical names ju is used in place of chu when not at the beginning of a word. *e.g.* Che-ju-do, Chin-ju.

The unfamiliar appearance of pages bespattered with diacritical marks might at first annoy some of our readers, but we maintain that it is only by retaining them for the sake of accuracy and convenience in tracing the sounds and the Chinese characters that we can best serve our readers' interests.

In romanizing the tense consonants ㄲ, ㄸ, ㅃ, ㅆ, and ㅉ, we use k, t, p, s, and ch, just as in romanizing the consonants ㄱ, ㄷ, ㅂ, ㅅ, and ㅈ. We consider it unnecessary for our purpose to use the doubled forms kk, tt, pp, ss, and chch, as in the McCune-Reischauer system.

리 (里), when part of a place name, or the name of an administrative division, is spelled ri in our system. When, however, it refers to the Chinese or Korean unit of distance (usually equal to about a quarter of a mile) it is spelled li; in this form it has long been established as an English loanword.

Juxtapositional Assimilation: Care has been taken to retain certain apparently anomalous spellings in consideration of the assimilated sounds which they represent. We have done our best to keep the number of these as few as possible so as not to harass our readers and the few that we retain are indispensable.

As in English, it often happens in Korean that a particular sequence of two sounds involves a change in one of them. In English the pb in cupboard becomes b: in the Korean geographical name 전라(全羅) (Chŏn+La) the n becomes l under the influence of the succeeding phoneme, and we show this by using the spelling Chŏl-la, rather than Chŏn-la. The assimilated form Chŏl-la is absolutely established and is in current use throughout the country.

To translate the word 도 〔島, island(s)〕, we use the spelling do; all other words written in Korean 도 are transliterated as to.

English loanwords, the titles of literary works and other publications, and foreign words other than names of persons or places are italicized.

TABLE NO. I
VOWELS

Korean	ㅏ	ㅑ	ㅓ	ㅕ	ㅗ	ㅛ	ㅜ	ㅠ	ㅡ	ㅣ	ㅐ	ㅒ	ㅔ	ㅖ	ㅚ	ㅟ	ㅢ	ㅘ	ㅝ	ㅙ	ㅞ
Roman	a	ya	ŏ	yŏ	o	yo	u	yu	eu	i	ae	yae	e	ye	oe	wi	eui	wa	wo	wae	we
IPS	a	ja	ʌ	jʌ	o	jo	u	ju	u①	i	æ	jæ	e	je	oe	wi	ui①	wa	wʌ	wæ	we

TABLE NO. II
CONSONANTS

Korean	ㄱ	ㄴ	ㄷ	ㄹ	ㅁ	ㅂ	ㅅ	ㅇ	ㅈ	ㅊ	ㅋ	ㅌ	ㅍ	ㅎ
Roman	k	n	t	l,r	m	p	s	ng②	ch,j	ch'	k'	t'	p'	h
IPS	k	n	t	l,r	m	p	s	ŋ	z	ts	k③	t③	p③	h

Remarks:　① u is pronounced as the sound u in such English words as book [buk] or good [gud].
　　　　　　② The initial Korean sound "o" of a syllable is ignored in the transliteration.
　　　　　　③ k, t, and p have the sound values of the aspirated sounds k, t and p, respectively.

TABLE OF CONTENTS

Martyrology

BOOK ONE

THE DAWN OF THE CHURCH IN KOREA

BOOK TWO

THE ESTABLISHMENT OF THE VICARIATE APOSTOLIC OF KOREA AND THE GREAT PERSECUTION

BOOK THREE
THE ERA OF RELIGIOUS LIBERTY

APPENDIX

APPENDIX A

APPENDIX B

The Catholic Church in Korea Today

THE APOSTOLIC INTERNUNCIATURE 571

THE SHORT HISTORY OF THE DIOCESES OF KOREA

THE MISSIONARY SOCIETIES, THE RELIGIOUS ORDERS AND OTHERS

TABLE OF CONTENTS

LIST OF PICTURES

Martyrology

APPENDIX

APPENDIX A

The Catholic Church in Korea Today

THE SHORT HISTORY OF THE DIOCESES OF KOREA

THE MISSIONARY SOCIETIES, RELIGIOUS ORDERS AND OTHERS

APPENDIX

Korea
Glancing Through Pictures

CATHOLIC KOREA

Yesterday and Today

The Papal Brief

Establishing the Hierarchy of the Church in Korea

Facsimile of the Papal Brief

John Bishop, Servant of the Servants of God, in perpetual memory

The fruitful seed of the Gospel which the holy preachers of divine truth by the command of Christ have undertaken to bring to the very ends of the earth, is, by the work of the Holy Spirit and through the efforts of apostles, not only disseminated throughout all races, peoples, and nations; but indeed among some nation it has taken such deep roots that, sending forth foliage and branches, it has grown into a wide-spreading tree laden with fruit. Among these places is noble Korea, a people eager to embrace the truth. Therefore, since it seemed good to the Sacred Congregation for the Propagation of the Name of Christ to establish a Catholic hierarchy in the land of Korea, we, judging that this would spread wider the boundaries of Christ's most holy religion, after asking the opinion of Our Venerable Brothers, the Holy Roman Cardinals in charge of that Sacred Congregation, and having sought the advice of Our Venerable Brother Xavier Zupi, Titular Archbishop of Serren in Proconsulari, and formerly Apostolic Delegate to Korea, decree and command the following:

By this letter We erect a holy hierarchy in Korea, ordaining that there shall be three ecclesiastical provinces altogether, namely:

(1) **The Province of Seoul** which will consist of the metropolitan residential Church of Seoul, previously a Vicariate Apostolic, whose Cathedral will be the one dedicated to the Immaculate Conception; and the suffragan dioceses of P'yŏng-yang, formerly a Vicariate Apostolic; Ham-heung, formerly a Vicariate Apostolic; Ch'un-ch'ŏn, formerly a Vicariate Apostolic, whose Cathedral will be the one dedicated to the Most Sacred Heart of Jesus; Tae-jŏn, formerly a Vicariate Apostolic, whose Cathedral will be the one dedicated to St. Theresa of the Child Jesus; In-ch'ŏn, formerly a Vicariate Apostolic, whose Cathedral will be the one dedicated to St. Paul the Apostle.

(2) **The Province of Tae-gu** which will consist of the metropolitan residential Church of Tae-gu, until now a Vicariate Apostolic, whose Cathedral will be the one dedicated to the Apparition of the B. V. M.; and the suffragan dioceses which follow: Chŏng-ju, until now a Vicariate Apostolic, whose Cathedral will be the one dedicated to the Holy Family of Jesus, Mary and Joseph; Pu-san, until now a Vicariate Apostolic, whose Cathedral will be the one dedicated to the Holy Family of Jesus, Mary, and Joseph.

(3) **The Province of Kwang-ju** which will consist of the metropolitan residential Church of Kwang-ju, until now a Vicariate Apostolic, whose Cathedral will be the one dedicated to the Most Sacred Heart of Jesus, and the suffragan diocese of Chŏn-ju, formerly a Vicariate Apostolic, whose Cathedral will be the one dedicated to the Most Sacred Heart of Jesus. All these divisions, We determine, fall under the authority of the Sacred Congregation of the Propagation of the Faith.

Since the Reverend Vicars Apostolic who until now have been in charge of the Vicariates have labored so hard in every way to spread the Faith, we not only publicly render thanks to them, but We are pleased to transfer them to residential Sees.

Thus, **in the Province of Seoul,** Our Venerable Brother Paul Ro Ki-nam is transferred from the titular See of Colbase to the metropolitan Church of Seoul; Our Venerable Brother Francis Hong Yong-ho is transferred from the titular See of Auzien to the Cathedral Church of P'yŏng-yang; Our Venerable Brother Thomas Quinlan is transferred from the titular See of Furnitan Major to the Cathedral Church of Ch'un-ch'ŏn; Our Venerable Brother Adrien Larribeau from the titular See of Dusen to the Cathedral Church of Tae-jŏn; Our Venerable Brother William J. McNaughton from the titular

4

See of Thuburbitana to the Cathedral Church of In-ch'ŏn.

In the Province of Tae-gu, Our Venerable Brother John-Baptist Sŭh Pong-kil is transferred from the titular See of Chomatitina to the metropolitan Church of Tae-gu; Our Venerable Brother James Vincent Pardy is transferred from the titular See of Irenopolis in Isauris to the Cathedral Church of Ch'ŏng-ju; Our Venerable Brother John Ch'oe Chae-sŏn from the titular See of Fussali to the Cathedral Church of Pu-san.

In the Province of Kwang-ju, Our Venerable Brother Harold Henry is transferred from the titular See of Corydale to the metropolitan Church of Kwang-ju; Our Venerable Brother Peter Han Kong-ryŏl is transferred from the titular See of Sagalassa to the Cathedral Church of Chŏn-ju. With regard to the See of P'yŏng-yang, because the Reverend Vicar Apostolic, Our Venerable Brother Francis Hong Yong-ho, was lost in the recent Korean War, We name Our Beloved Son George M. Carroll of the Society of Maryknoll for the Foreign Missions as Apostolic Administrator of the diocese. He has been up until now Apostolic Administrator of the Vicariate of the same name. He will continue in this appointment at Our pleasure and that of the Roman See until We shall by Our authority make other arrangements. And also, because circumstances do not permit a bishop to be named to the See of Ham-heung, we appoint Our Beloved Brother Timothy Bitterli as Apostolic Administrator at the pleasure of the Holy See. Msgr. Bitterli is of the Ottilien Congregation of the Order of St. Benedict for Foreign Missions and has been up until now Apostolic Administrator of the Vicariate of Ham-heung. Concerning the college of canons to be set up in every diocese, the seminary, the episcopal board, as it is called, the rule and election of capitular vicars when the See is vacant, we decree what the ecclesiastical laws provide or what the Sacred Congregation of Propagation of the Faith rules. Furthermore the carrying out completely of Our letter rests with him who at the time of its publication is performing the duties of Apostolic Delegate in Korea and who has every faculty necessary to see to its complete fulfillment. Let him see to things himself, though it can be done by another if he has ecclesiastical dignity. When the business is taken care of, let the signed and sealed documents be sent without delay to the Sacred Congregation for the Propagation of the Name of Christ. This decree We wish to be effective now and henceforth in such a way that what We have decreed be religiously observed by those whom it concerns. No contrary prescript of any kind can affect the power of this decree since this decree supersedes all others. So if anyone, no matter with what authority, whether knowingly or inadvertently, acts against the things We have decreed, We order his actions to be considered as null and void. No one, furthermore, is allowed to mutilate or destroy this document expressing Our will; and every copy of this decree, whether printed or handwritten, which shall have affixed to it the seal of the person in charge who is the Church dignitary and which at the same time shall be published on any public bulletin board, shall have the same respect as this original would merit if it were presented. If anyone ignores or opposes this Our decree he shall incur the statutory penalties applicable to those who violate the commands of the Supreme Pontiff.

Given at Rome at St. Peter's, the 10th day of March, in the year 1962, the fourth of Our pontificate.

Jacobus Aloysius Cardinal Copello
Chancellor of the Apostolic Chancery

Msgr. Francesco Tinello, Regent

Gregoire Pierre Cardinal Agagianian, Prefect of the Sacred Congregation of the Propagation of the Faith
Msgr. Caesar Federici, Msgr. Josephus Rossi

Ceremonial Proclamation of the Execution of the Papal Brief
Establishing the Hierarchy

*Held at the Cathedral, of the Immaculate Conception, on June 29, 1962, by the Very Rev.
Msgr. Charles Burton Mouton, Chargé d'Affaires ad int., the Apostolic Delegation in Korea*

The faithful listening to the message of Pope John XXIII

*The Episcopate of the
Korean Church*

The Solemn Mass after the reading of the Papal Brief

The three Archbishops receiving the Papal Order of their appointment

The Episcopate of the Church of Korea and the Second Ecumenical Council of the Vatican

↑ The Basilica of St. Peter, Rome

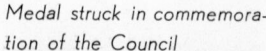

Medal struck in commemoration of the Council

The Inaugural Session of the Second Ecumenical Council of the Vatican

The Episcopate of the Church in Korea received in audience by Pope John XXIII during the Council

The great dome of the Basilica of St. Peter

MARTYROLOGY

The Seventy-nine Korean and French Martyrs, beatified in 1925 (The original of this painting was hung then in the Vatican).

The Seventy-nine Blessed Martyrs of Korea (a Korean painting)

15

BOOK ONE

THE DAWN OF THE CHURCH IN KOREA

CHAPTER ONE

THE DAWN OF CHRISTIANITY IN KOREA

1. The Special Characteristics of the Foundation of the Church in Korea

The Catholic religion was first embraced by our Korean forefathers not in a passive response to the teaching of foreign missionaries but as an active and positive result of their zeal in the search for truth.

It was through the devotion of St. Francis Xavier (1506-1552) that Catholicism took root in India and Japan: it was his fellow-Jesuits, Matteo Ricci (1552-1610) and his companions, who introduced it into China. A thousand years earlier, it had been through the vigorous efforts of the Irish missionaries, St. Columba and others, that Catholicism spread in the British Isles and western Europe, and through the genius of St. Benedict at Monte Cassino that it continued to be propagated and organized.

Korea was unique: from the reign of Sŏn-jo (1568-1608) Catholic books were brought back to Korea by members of the annual embassies to the court of the Chinese emperor at Peking, and became the object of great interest and intense study on the part of Korean scholars in their zealous quest for the true religion.

Prominent among them were the Confucianists Hŭh Kyun, Lee Su-kwang, Lee Ik and Ahn Chŏng-pok. Though their conception of the Catholic religion was extremely vague, their understanding of it was enough to lead the more humble and modest of them to accept it. Hong Yu-han, a disciple of Lee Ik, read Catholic books for the first time in 1770, and was so deeply impressed that he gave up all other reading. He had no knowledge of the Gregorian calendar, but kept the 7th, 14th, 21st and 28th days of each lunar month as fasts devoted to prayer and meditation, and abstention from mundane activities. When his rule of life aroused the curiosity of his friends and neighbors he would piously teach and exhort them, but it is not known whether he succeeded in making any converts to Catholicism: what is known is that many were led to follow his way of life. Among them were Lee Pyŏk, Kwon Ch'ŏl-sin, Chŭng Yak-jŏn, and Lee Seung-hun. When they had learnt the truths from Catholic books, they realized the necessity for making them more widely known: they felt their responsibility, as pioneer teachers of Christianity in Korea, for saving the souls of their compatriots shivering in the darkness of pagan ignorance.

Despite the suspicion that their way of life drew upon them from non-Christians, they abandoned all superstitious pagan rites, and preached the Gospel openly. After instructing their converts in the catechism, they gave them Christian Baptism.

This continued for more than ten years, before a regularly ordained priest ever came to Korea. It was in 1794 that Father James

Chou Wen-mo (Chu Mun-mo) came to Korea, the first Catholic priest to be invited to enter the country, to find four thousand Catholics already baptized and awaiting his instruction. Such a fact is believed to be unique in the history of Catholic foreign missions, and is a source of pride to Korean believers.

2. Propagation of Catholicism in the Orient

In the thirteenth century the rise of the Franciscans and Dominicans brought new vigor to Christian missionary endeavor. In the new empire of the Mongols travel was easier than before, and a considerable number of Genoese and Venetian merchants reached China.

In 1245-1247 the Franciscan, Giovanni da Piano di Carpine made the round trip to Karakorum, the new capital established by Genghis Khan, as diplomatic envoy of Pope Innocent IV and King Louis IX of France (Saint Louis).

In 1253-1255 another Franciscan, the Flemish missionary Guillaume de Rubruc (1220-1293) made the journey under the same auspices and wrote accounts of his travels in the Orient.

In 1294 the Franciscan, Joannes a Monte Corvino reached Cambaluc (Peking) by way of India and gained the favor of Kublai Khan and succeeding emperors. During the remaining thirty-four years of his life he made over thirty thousand converts to Christianity.

Pope Clement V appointed him Archbishop of Cambaluc and sent more friars to China to assist him. Franciscan houses were set up at Zaitun (the modern Ch'uanchow), Hangchow and Yangchow.

In 1342 the Papal Legate, Joannes de Marignolli, reached Cambaluc, returning in 1353. Shortly afterward the fall of the Yuan Dynasty caused all communication with China to be cut off, and very soon nothing remained of these missions.

In 1534 St. Ignatius de Loyola founded the Society of Jesus, which was charged by Pope Paul III with the education of youth and the missions to the Orient in 1540. St. Francis Xavier, after his apostolate in India and the East Indies, arrived in Japan in 1549, and during his epic stay of two years and three months made more than three thousand converts. Desiring to extend his apostolate to China, he came as far as the little island of Sancian, near the Portuguese colony of Macao, and looking with dying eyes on the Chinese coast, bolted and barred to him, tranquilly died there in 1552 at the age of forty-seven.

St. Francis Xavier was followed by other missionaries and in 1557 Macao became an episcopal see and the seat of several churches and religious houses from which many missionaries sought to extend their apostolic labors into the regions beyond.

The first really successful mission outside Macao was established by the Jesuits, and its leading figure was an Italian, Father Matteo Ricci, who arrived in China in 1582 and died in Peking in 1610. In twenty-eight years he did more than any other man to win a hearing for the faith and to develop the methods used by his colleagues and successors. He won the respect of the scholars by adopting their dress and studying the Confucian classics, and by his knowledge of mathematics and astronomy, and was summoned by the Ming Emperor Shintsung (Wanli) to the court at Peking, where he was able to convert two members of the Hanlin Academy to Catholicism. Thanks to his efforts and those of his colleagues, the number of Catholics rose to two thousand five hundreds by 1610.

Hsu Kwang-chi (1562-1633), scholar and official, met Father Ricci at Nanking in 1600. In 1603 he was baptized under the name of Paul.

Li Chih-tsao (d. 1630), scholar and official, met Father Ricci at Peking in 1601, and saw the map of the world that Father Ricci had made, as well as new forms of sundial and astrolabe. From 1604 he and Paul Hsu Kwang-chi received instruction from Father Ricci translating works on geography, mathematics, hydraulics and astronomy until the latter's death on May 11, 1610. Efforts were also made by the priests in China to spread the faith in Korea, and others tried to do the same in Japan through Korean Catholics residing in Japan who had been taken to that country as prisoners of war in the Hideyoshi Invasion of 1592. These Catholics numbered some two thousand persons, not a few of whom indeed volunteered to spread Catholicism in Korea in collaboration with Jesuit missionaries.

Father Gaspar Vilela, a Jesuit, had drafted a plan for the evangelization of Korea, and the Dominican Fathers in Manila also planned a mission to Korea and sent Father Juan de Domingo to prepare the way, in 1616, but he was unable to land, and returned to Japan. He was arrested by the persecutors and died in jail at Omura, Japan in 1619.

There were nine Koreans among the two hundred and five Blessed Martyrs in Japan. Friar Vincent Kwon, one of the nine, tried to propagate the Gospel in Korea, traveling between Japan and China for the space of seven years. In 1614, he tried to return to Korea, after having been sent there by the provincial of the Jesuit Order in Japan, but owing to the tense situation between Korea and Japan, the entire coast was closely guarded, and it was impossible for him to effect an entry into the country. Thereupon, in an attempt to smuggle himself into Korea via the land route, he went to Peking and awaited a chance to cross the frontier. But this was also prevented by the war which broke out between the Manchus and the Ming Empire in 1616. As a result he was obliged to return to Japan in 1620. He was martyred at Nagasaki in 1626 after five years' propagation for Koreans in Japan. After his abduction to Japan at the age of fifteen he had entered the Kyoto Seminary and then devoted the rest of his life to the salvation of the souls of Koreans in Japan.

On the other hand, the project of the Chinese Catholic Church founded by Father Matteo Ricci was to propagate the faith in Korea. After the war between Korea and Japan in 1592, he remained on the lookout for an opportunity to achieve this aim.

When the Manchus captured Fushun in 1618, Paul Hsu Kwang-chi was called to Peking and appointed Supervisor of Instruction and concurrently a censor. On August 7, 1620 he petitioned the Ming Emperor to dispatch him to Korea as a special envoy to advise the Korean government in its struggle against the Manchus. Though the petition was disallowed, Paul was put in charge of training troops, and ordered from Macao four cannons of Western design. The Manchus captured Shenyang and Liaoyang in 1621 and Paul Hsu once more petitioned the Ming Emperor to send him to Korea, but his petition was again denied.

In 1650 Father Antoine de Sainte-Marie, a Franciscan, approached the Korean border via Manchuria but as King Hyo-jong was planning a northern expedition against the invaders the frontier was closed, and Father Sainte-Marie returned to Peking.

In 1703 Father Noel wrote on the subject of evangelizing Korea, "If a solid Church were founded at Shenyang it could serve as a springboard for rapid propagation of the Gospel in Korea. This country of Korea is actually larger than it is shown on the maps, and being separated from Japan only by a narrow strait, could well become a bridge between China and Japan."

3. Dawn of the Catholic Church in Korea

Of the four Catholic Churches in Peking it was the East and South Church that the Korean envoys used to visit most frequently. The following realist scholars are known to have stayed near the Yu-ho-kuan in the capital, visiting nearby churches where by associating with Catholic priests, they endeavored to learn about Christianity: Sŭh Myŏng-yong, Hong Yang-ho, Hong Tae-yong, Park Che-ka, Lee Tŏk-mu, and Ryu Teuk-kong. *Tam-hŏn's Tour to Peking*, by Hong Tae-yong (1731-1783), reads in part as follows: "I visited a Catholic Church in Peking and met a European priest during the reign of the Emperor Kang-heui (*sc.* Kang-hsi 1661-1722). He was pleased to see me and showed me exotic paintings and images, several of which he presented to me." Hong Tae-yong visited the East and South Church on several occasions and met Father Augustinus von Hallerstein (1703-1774) and Father Antonius Gogeisl (1701-1771), director of the Imperial Board of Astronomy, Peking, and recorded his astonishment and admiration in his diary.

During the reign of King Suk-jong (1675-1720) the legate Lee I-myŏng visited Peking and met Fathers Ignatius Koegler (1680-1746) and Joseph Suarez.

Park Chi-won, known as Yŏn-am, also discussed Catholicism with the scholar Wang Min-hao.

Prince So-hyŏn and Father Johann Adam Schall von Bell (1591-1666)

So-hyŏn, the Crown Prince during the reign of King In-jo (reigned 1623-1649), was taken captive by the Ch'ing (Manchu) court following the Northern Disturbance of 1637 and stayed there for 'eight agonizing years'. During his stay in China, the prince saw much of Father Johann Adam Schall von Bell who had been one of the translators of Western books on astronomy and the calendar at the Ming court with Paul Hsu Kwang-chi, and had remained in Peking after the fall of the Ming Dynasty. In August 1644, Father Schall was asked by the Regent Dorgon (1612-1650), the first Prince Jui, to prepare for the new regime a calendar based on Western mathematical calculations, which became known as *Shih Hsien Li*. In 1650 he was permitted to build a church near the Calendrical Bureau which became known as the Nant'ang or South Church.

Father Schall received the prince with joy, treating him with kindness and giving him books and religious pictures. The following is a passage from a letter from Prince So-hyŏn to Father Schall:

"Yesterday, looking at your unexpected gift of the image of our Divine Saviour, of the globe and the books on astronomy and other European sciences, I was moved by such extreme pleasure that I could hardly believe it to be true. For everything I am deeply indebted to you. Glancing through some of the books I noted that they bring us a doctrine which is quite new to us, and well fitted to improve our minds and develop our virtues. In our territories, so cut off from intellectual matters, it has been quite unknown until now. The holy image possesses such majesty that, hanging on the wall, it calms the mind and drives out even the slightest thought of evil. As for the globe and the books on mathematics, they are of such great value that they are indispensable to our age and I don't know how I am so lucky as to have them in my kingdom. It is true that we have books on the subject, but they are teeming with blunders and have not been revised for centuries. Once I have returned to the court I shall have them published for the use of our scholars—they will be astonished to see how they will step from the desert of ignorance into the world of enlightenment. My subjects will come to know that they owe all that to the Europeans. We two come from different countries so distant from each other, yet ever since we met on foreign soil we have felt like brothers. I don't know what hidden force of nature is responsible for it but I feel convinced that men are drawn to one another by fellowship of learning, even though vast continents lie between them.

"I should like very much to take these books and the holy image with me to my country, but when I consider that my subjects who know nothing about the cult of the divine may fall unwittingly into the sin of sacrilege, I am full of anxiety. Let me therefore return the holy image to you that I may not be the occasion of sin in others by taking it with me."

Father Schall remarks that the words 'return the holy image' are merely a polite formula, in proof of which he tells us that the prince accepted it with great joy, and also manifested the desire to be accompanied by a European priest, so that the prince and his subjects could be taught by him rather than by the intermediation of one of his own baptized eunuchs whom the Jesuits proposed to train for the purpose. Father Schall accordingly requested the Superior to send a priest to accompany the prince to Korea, but the request was refused.

With the permission of Prince Dorgon the Imperial Regent, uncle of the first Ch'ing Emperor, the prince brought five Chinese Catholic eunuchs to Korea, namely: Li Pang-shao, Chang San-wei, Liu Chung-lin, Ku Feng-teng, and Tou Wen-fang, as well as three Chinese Catholic court ladies.

Upon arrival the prince was received in audience by his father King In-jo on the eighteenth of the second lunar moon of 1645. Sixty days later he was dead, and his Chinese entourage all had to return to their native land.

In this way the Peking Church once more lost a very good opportunity to propagate the Gospel in Korea. Bitterly regretting his failure, the Bishop of Peking now approached the members of the French Order of the Blessed Sacrament, and in response the order took steps to send a priest to Korea.

A document of the order reads: "The King of Korea (sc. Crown Prince So-hyŏn) during his stay at Peking associated with Jesuit Fathers who, however, were unable to furnish a priest to Korea owing to shortage of staff. Thus the order lost a good opportunity to spread the faith in that country. At the time there were only fifteen priests in China, four in Tonkin, and one in Cochin-China."

World attention began to be directed toward Korea, and further evangelistic efforts were made.

Lee Su-kwang (1563-1628), better known as Chi-pong, had visited China during the previous dynasty, and had learnt something about European science and the Catholic religion. In one of his essays he says, "In T'ien Chu Shih I (True Doctrine of God), by the European scholar Matteo Ricci, is set forth the creation and control of the world by God, the falsity of the doctrine of Karma is shown, and the Christian doctrine of Heaven and Hell is explained. The book teaches reverence for the divine will and the necessity for repentance. The Pope is childless as he is vowed to lifelong chastity. When he dies, a wise man is selected to succeed him." (The Essays of Chi-pong by Lee Su-kwang, the first mention of Catholicism by a Korean scholar.)

Chi-pong's work was very popular and had wide influence on succeeding generations. During the reign of King Sŏn-jo, Ryu Mong-in (1559-1623) mentioned Catholicism in his book, Ŏ-u's Talks on History and Tradition. He also recorded that Hŭh Kyun visited China during the Ming Dynasty and acquired a copy of Twelve Hymns. During the reign of King Chŏng-jo two writers, Ahn Chŏng-pok (Sun-am) and Park Chi-won (Yŏn-am) referred to Hŭh Kyun as a Catholic.

Lee Ik took up their studies of Catholic doctrine in the reign of King Chŏng-jo. His disciples included Chŭng Yak-yong, Chŭng Yak-jong, Chŭng Yak-jŏn, Lee Ka-hwan, Lee Pyŏk, Lee Seung-hun, Hwang Sa-yŏng, Kwon Ch'ŏl-sin, Kwon Il-sin, Lee Ki-yang and Lee Yun-ha, all of whom later became devout Catholics. Besides these, other disciples of his, namely Lee Hŏn-kyŏng, Shin Hu-tam and Hong Yu-han made an intensive study of Catholicism and the last, Hong Yu-han, practiced its precepts to some degree.

The Royal History of the Yi Dynasty records that in the twelfth year of the reign of King Suk-jong (1686) Catholicism had become so widespread that it was directed that foreigners entering the country be apprehended and deported.

In the thirty-fourth year of the reign of King Yŏng-jo (1758) Catholicism was becoming so prevalent in the Provinces of Hwang-hae and Kang-won that many of the inhabitants had abandoned the observance of the traditional rites of ancestor worship.

Evidently the Catholic teaching was being obeyed in those days, and it is clear that it had become widely known by 1760.

CHAPTER TWO

THE FOUNDATION AND DEVELOPMENT
OF THE CHURCH IN KOREA

4. The Baptism of Lee Seung-hun (1784)

In the year of Our Lord 1784 the day of salvation at last dawned in Korea. It was then that God in His mercy planted the Christian faith and founded this glorious Church which ever since has grown and strengthened itself under persecution and oppression.

The principal agent of Providence to introduce the Gospel into Korea was Lee Pyŏk, surnamed Tŏk-jo, the descendant of Lee Chŏng-hyŏng, whose forerunners had devoted themselves to the military career for many generations. As Lee Pyŏk was endowed with fine physical and intellectual qualities his father wanted him to practice archery and swordsmanship, but the boy steadfastly refused to take any interest in these pursuits, and preferred reading and study.

In 1777, when King Chŏng-jo ascended the throne, there was a group of scholars, led by Kwon Ch'ŏl-sin and Chŭng Yak-jŏn, who, wishing to pursue advanced studies without interruption or distraction, went to live in retirement at a lonely mountain temple. Lee Pyŏk resolved to join them.

It was winter, all the roads were deep in snow, and the temple lay at a distance of nearly forty miles. These difficulties could not daunt his ardent spirit. He set off at once, through almost impassable roads. Plodding forward through the thick darkness, Lee Pyŏk finally reached the spot.

His arrival at that isolated little temple hidden in the mountains, at that late hour and with so many companions, filled the occupants with terror. For what purpose could a large band of strangers want to come there in the middle of the night? But soon all became clear: their fear changed to joy, and in their emotion and excitement at this happy meeting, they hardly noticed that it was already dawn.

There they entered upon an intensive study of Catholicism and after a ten-day debate decided that the truth they were seeking lay in this faith. Their next step was to put the Catholic religion into practice and try to live in accordance with its precepts. This they did to the best of their ability, though their only source of information and enlightenment was the books brought back from Peking over the years by the members of the annual embassies. These included treatises on mathematics, astronomy, philosophy, and religion, and in especial the works of Father Matteo Ricci, including *True Doctrine of God*, by which they regulated their conduct, tried to combat *The Seven Mortifications*, and held morning and evening services of prayer, consecrating every seventh day of the lunar month to the worship of God, and observing each *neomenia* as a day of fasting and meditation though they had no knowledge of the exact nature of the Christian Sabbath.

Lee Pyŏk became an ardent follower of the Christian principles and longed to go to Peking in one of the annual embassies to find out more about the Catholic religion. It was God's will that the fervent prayers of this upright soul who so zealously sought the truth should be answered, and answered they were. Learning that Lee Tong-uk had been appointed third secretary to the embassy, and that his son Lee Seung-hun was to accompany him to Peking, he asked Seung-hun to get in touch with the European missionaries there and learn more about Christianity.

Here, according to contemporary records, is an account of the remarkable discourse that took place:

"Your journey to Peking is a heaven-sent opportunity for us to learn the true religion. This doctrine of the true saints, as well as the true way to serve the All-Highest, Creator of all, is developed to the highest degree among the Europeans. Without this doctrine we can do nothing. Without it we can improve neither in spirit nor in character. Without it, how can we know the various laws of the kings and their people? Without it, there can be no basic rule in life. Without it, the creation of Heaven and earth, the laws of the celestial and terrestrial poles and the annual and diurnal movements of the heavenly bodies, the distinction between good and evil spirits, the origin and the purpose of the world, the relation between the body and the soul, the problem of good and evil, the Incarnation of the Son of God for the remission of sins, the rewards for the good in Heaven and the punishments of the wicked in hell, all this will remain unknown to us.

"Since you are going to Peking, this is a sign that God the All-Highest is taking pity on our country and wishes to save it. As soon as you arrive, go at once to the temple of the Lord of Heaven (*sc.* the Catholic Cathedral), discuss the matter with the European sages, inquire of them about everything, investigate the doctrine with them, inform youself in detail of all the rites of the religion, and bring us the necessary books. This is a matter of life and death, the all-important business of eternity is in your hands: go, and above all proceed with prudence."

Lee Seung-hun was born in 1756 at P'yŏng-ch'ang in the Province of Kang-won. His precocious ability revealed itself at the age of ten, and at twenty he had already made a name for himself in the world of letters. He passed the first state examination at twenty-four, and gaining the favor of King Chŏng-jo, was appointed district magistrate of P'yŏng-t'aek. Lee Pyŏk's request to him shows him as thirsting more for religious than for scientific knowledge, and it penetrated deeply into the soul of Lee Seung-hun. He promised to do all he could to realize their common desire.

Lee Seung-hun left for Peking late in 1783. Upon his arrival, we are told, he went to the Nant'ang (the South Church) and was warmly received by some priests there. He plunged zealously into the study of Christian doctrine and was soon ready for Baptism. Early in 1784 he was baptized by Father Louis de Grammont and as it was hoped that he would become the first stone of the Church of Korea, he was given the name of Peter (Dallet: *Histoire de l'Église de Corée*).[1]

This is how Father Jean-Matthieu de Ventavon, S. J., (Wan Ta-hong in Chinese), writing in 1784, announced this happy event to his friends in Europe:

---

[1] This account, however, has recently been refuted by Father Andrew Ch'oe Sŏk-u, who points out, among other discrepancies, that it was the North, and not the South, Church, to which he went, and that there was no Bishop at Peking at the time, for Msgr. de Salusti, the Bishop of Peking, had died in 1780 and his successor, Bishop de Gouvêa, did not arrive until 1785. (*Andrew Ch'oe, L'Érection du Premier Vicariate Apostolique et les Origines du Catholicisme en Corée, 1592-1837*, Schöneck-Beckenried, Switzerland, 1961, p. 26)

"...You will undoubtedly be gratified to learn of the conversion of a person whom God has perhaps raised up to spread the light of the Gospel, in a kingdom where it is not known that any missionary has ever penetrated: it is Korea, a peninsula located to the east of China. The king of this country sends ambassadors to the emperor of China every year, for he regards himself as his vassal. He loses nothing by it, for if he goes to considerable expense in sending him presents, the emperor gives him as much or more in return. These Korean ambassadors came, they and their suite, at the end of last year, to visit our Church; we gave them some religious books. The son of one of these nobles, aged twenty-seven and a very good scholar, read them eagerly; he saw the truth in them, and grace working in his heart, he resolved to embrace the faith as soon as he had received instruction. Before admitting him to Holy Baptism, we asked him many questions, all of which he answered satisfactorily.

"We asked him, among other things, what he would propose to do if the king should disapprove this step, and should wish to force him to renounce his faith: he replied, without hesitation, that he would suffer every torment, and death, rather than give up the religion which he clearly recognized as true. We did not fail to warn him that the purity of the evangelic law would not permit a plurality of women. He replied, 'I have no one but my legitimate wife and shall never have any others.' Finally, before his departure to return to Korea, with the consent of his father, he was admitted to Baptism, which Louis de Grammont administered to him, giving him the name of Peter. His surname is Lee. He is said to be related to the royal family. He declared that on his return he wished to retire from public life, with his family, and devote himself entirely to his salvation. He promised to send us his news every year. The ambassadors also promised to propose to the king that he should summon Europeans to his lands. From Peking to the capital of Korea is a journey of

about three months.

"For the rest we can communicate with the Koreans only by writing. Their writing and that of the Chinese is the same, as regards its appearance and meaning, but their pronunciation is quite different. The Koreans put in writing what they want to say: on seeing the characters, we understand the meaning, and they also understand the meaning of what we write in reply." (*Nouvelles Lettres Édifiantes*, Paris, 1818, Vol. II, p. 120)

In the spring of 1784 Peter Lee Seung-hun returned to Seoul bringing with him large numbers of books, crucifixes, images, and sundry presents which he had been given in Peking. Nothing was more pressing than to seek out Lee Pyŏk and share these treasures with him. The latter had been counting the days until his return, and now he rented a secluded dwelling-house and shut himself up in it so as to be able to concentrate on reading and thinking over all this material. At last he had in his hands proof positive of the truth of this religion, the most complete refutation of the superstitious cults of China and Korea, the explanations of the Seven Sacraments, catechisms, commentaries on the Gospels, lives of the saints for each day, and prayer books. As he went on reading he felt new life entering into his soul. His faith in Christ grew stronger, and with his faith, the desire to make God's gift known to his fellow-countrymen. He began at once to announce the good news, first to his friends in the middle class, distinguished for their knowledge and good character. He soon won over a number of them by his lively and penetrating preaching. He also preached to the nobles with success, and without relaxing his efforts began itinerant preaching.

Lee Pyŏk and Peter Lee Seung-hun are indeed the ones who laid the foundations for Catholicism in our country, and they deserve our gratitude and admiration.

5. Propagation Activities of Lee Pyŏk

The success of Lee Pyŏk's preaching of the Gospel to all levels of society aroused enough comment to offend the susceptibilities of the pagan scholars, who felt instinctively that the new doctrine would undermine their power and prestige and disturb their way of life. Foremost among them was Lee Ka-hwan, a celebrated scholar. Learning of Lee Pyŏk's preaching he said: "This is a serious matter. Though the foreign doctrine sounds quite reasonable, it is not our Confucianism, and if Lee Pyŏk wants to change the world by such means, I cannot just sit idle. I must go and bring him back to the right way of thinking."

A date was set for a formal discussion of the matter with Lee Pyŏk. The friends of the two scholars and a large number of interested spectators listened to the solemn debate, which lasted three days. Ka-hwan first tried to bring Lee Pyŏk to give up what he called the errors of the foreign teaching. He felt sure of success, but each of his assertions was taken up by his adversary and refuted point by point, one after another. In vain did he try to save the structure of his reasoning: every part of Lee Pyŏk's rebuttal struck home like a blow. Always consistent in his utterances, he made no assertion without proving its truth. His clear and lucid doctrine, the Korean accounts tell us, "brought always light and conviction; his arguments were as brilliant as the sun; they struck like a hurricane and they cut like a sword."

The onlookers followed the debate with delight. There was this coryphaeus of the old school at grips with the champion of evangelic enlightenment. The latter, backed by the truth, was unshakable. The Christian faith triumphed, and made a conquest of many upright and sincere souls, strengthening its empire in the hearts of the neophytes. At the end of three days, Ka-hwan, completely defeated, pronounced these memorable words:

"Christianity is magnificent, and it is true. But Christianity brings pain and suffering to its partisans. What is to be done?"

So saying he withdrew, and never again opened his mouth on the subject of religion or gave it another thought.

Lee Pyŏk now set about gaining converts from among the *literati*, whose prestige, knowledge and experience would qualify them as leaders of the new Christian community. There were five brothers named Kwon who were so learned that they had a large following of disciples who came from all parts of the kingdom to their houses at Kal-san in Yang-keun (now Yang-p'yŏng county), Kyŏng-ki Province. In the autumn of 1784 Lee Pyŏk visited them, and conferences on religion recommenced. Soon the truth shone out in all its brilliance. The eldest brother, Kwon Ch'ŏl-sin, aged about fifty years, had devoted his life to the study of Confucian ethics and philosophy. At first he hesitated to jettison all the fruits of the immense labor that had made his reputation, but he could not reject the light of the Gospel, and was baptized under the name of Ambrose. The third brother Kwon Il-sin was at once converted and his extraordinary fervor and enlightened zeal fully justified the hopes of Lee Pyŏk. Not content with practicing the religion himself he instructed the members of his family and began to preach the faith to his friends and acquaintances, with all the success which the authority of his name, his knowledge and his virtues assured. At about this time Peter Lee Seung-hun baptized Lee Pyŏk and Kwon Il-sin: the choice of baptismal names was not a matter of chance. As Lee Pyŏk had begun the work and prepared the way it was decided that he should be called John-Baptist. Kwon Il-sin, wishing to devote his life to preaching, took as his patron, St. Francis Xavier, the Apostle of the Orient.

Other leading members of the circle were the three brothers, Chŭng Yak-jong, Chŭng Yak-jŏn, and Chŭng Yak-yong. Chŭng Yak-jŏn was later banished to Heuk-san Island, during the Church catastrophe, and during his exile produced a work on ichthyology entitled *Cha-san-ŏ-po* (Cha-san's Book on Fish). Chŭng Yak-yong, whose pen name was Ta-san, was the author of more than four hundred books. The eldest brother, Chŭng Yak-jong was to win the glory of martyrdom, with his entire family. God so blessed the efforts of this group that Yang-keun could justly be called the cradle of the Korean Church.

Lee Tan-won, a disciple of Francis-Xavier Kwon Il-sin, after being baptized by him under the name of Louis-Gonzaga, returned to his home town of Nae-p'o, where he preached the Gospel with such diligence and success that after his martyrdom he became known as the "Apostle of Nae-p'o". Conversions multiplied: Luke Hong Nak-min, Matthias Ch'oe In-kil, Sabas Chi Hwang, John Ch'oe Ch'ang-hyŏn, Thomas Kim Pŏm-u and Augustine Ryu Hang-kŏm, all of them were persons of high standing, and received into the Church and were to set an admirable example to society.

6. Thomas Kim Pŏm-u, Protomartyr

Some days before His death, Our Lord Jesus Christ said, "The time has now come for the Son of Man to achieve his glory. Believe me when I tell you this; a grain of wheat must fall into the ground and die, or else it remains nothing more than a grain of wheat; but if it dies, then it yields rich fruit. He who loves his life will lose it; he who is an enemy to his own life in this world will keep it, so as to live eternally. If anyone is to be my servant, he must follow my way; so shall my servant too be where I am. If anyone serves me, my Father will do him honour." (St. John, 12:23-26)

These divine words are true for everybody, everywhere and always. The faith of the individual Christian cannot take root and live unless he undergoes mortification and suffering, and the faith of the people cannot thrive and develop unless watered with the blood of the martyrs.

The new Church of Korea was soon to have experience of this. At the beginning of 1785 the Minister of Justice, Kim Hwa-jin, wishing to put a stop to spread of Christianity but not daring to challenge its influential leaders openly, ordered the arrest and trial of Thomas Kim Pŏm-u, an interpreter, who had been converted by John-Baptist Lee Pyŏk in 1784 and had himself instructed and converted not only his entire family but also some of his friends, principally among the interpreters.

Summoned before the Minister of Justice and called upon to renounce his religion, Thomas, sustained by divine grace, stoutly refused to apostatize. He was put to several different kinds of torture, but never gave way. Francis-Xavier Kwon Il-sin, hearing what had happened, appeared before the minister with several other Christians.

"All of us profess the same religion as Thomas Kim Pŏm-u. We wish to share the fate that you are reserving for him."

The minister thought it prudent not to attack such powerful and distinguished personages. He dismissed them, but did not lessen his persecution of Thomas. After several bouts of severe torture Thomas was exiled to Tan-yang, where he continued the public practice of his religion, saying his prayers in a loud voice and teaching all who cared to listen. His courage and patience never wavered, but the injuries he sustained during torture brought about his death. Such was the end of the first martyr who, on Korean soil, gave his life for Christ.

This served as a lesson and an example for the other Christians.

A number of Sŏng-kyun-kwan (Confucian College) students published a violent circular against the Christians, calling on their relatives and friends to break off relations with them. This document, dated the third lunar month of 1785, is the first public document known, in which Christianity is publicly attacked. Several families tried hard by entreaties and threats to bring about the apostasy of those of their members who had embraced the faith. There were glorious confessions of faith as a result, but there were also some deplorable defections, even among those regarded as pillars of the Church. Peter Lee Seung-hun and John-Baptist Lee Pyŏk were pointed out as the principal leaders of Christianity, so their relatives who had not embraced the faith, terrified by the sufferings of Thomas Kim Pŏm-u, tried by every means to make them renounce the religion which would bring misfortune to them and to their families. They were only too success-

28   CATHOLIC KOREA—YESTERDAY AND TODAY

ful in their disastrous plan.

The younger brother of Peter Lee Seung-hun, named Ch'i-hun, manifested violent hostility to the religion, and exerted pressure on Peter to make him change his mind. Harassed by incessant domestic persecution, Peter yielded. He burnt his religious books and wrote an open letter to justify himself for having been a Christian.

John-Baptist Lee Pyŏk's father, also, did everything he could to bring about his son's apostasy. Unable to succeed, he attempted to commit suicide. Lee Pyŏk finally yielded. From that time on he was terribly afflicted with remorse: he had no further contact with Christians, and would be heard weeping and groaning at all hours of the day and night. In the spring of 1786 he fell ill of the plague (a form of typhus) and died at the age of thirty-three, after an illness of eight days.

Let us trust that a man who had done so much to introduce the faith into Korea would no doubt have had the grace to repent of his apostasy, and obtain forgiveness at the last moment.

7. The False Ecclesiastical Hierarchy

The faith of the little band of Christians, which had received such violent shocks, was by no means destroyed. If they were saddened by the defection of some of their fellow-members, they were at the same time consoled by the constancy of the majority, in the face of domestic persecution often harder to bear than that of the judges and executioners. The Church regained its vigor, as if the persecution had given it a new lease of life. Louis-Gonzaga Lee Tan-won continued to preach the Gospel in Nae-p'o, and his great talents attracted more and more converts. Francis-Xavier Kwon Il-sin, for his part, felt the need of a spiritual retreat after the catastrophe. With a single friend Justin Cho, he agreed to leave the society of his friends and family and, observing strict silence, go to live for a time at a deserted temple among the Yong-mun Mountains of the Province of Kyŏng-ki. There they spent eight whole days employed solely on religious exercises, not speaking a single word throughout the whole course of the retreat.

The following year, 1787, the clamor against the faith had somewhat calmed down, and Francis-Xavier Kwon Il-sin, with the repentant Peter Lee Seung-hun, the brothers Chŭng Yak-yong, Yak-jong and Yak-jŏn, discussed ways and means to develop the Church, and with other influential Christians resolved to establish a 'sacred hierarchy'. This thought, surprising as it was, was nevertheless very natural. Not having the good fortune of their models, the Chinese, of possessing duly-ordained priests, the Christians of Korea nevertheless realized that no Church can subsist without a chief. In their ignorance of the nature of Holy Orders, they thought they could do nothing better than make a 'bishop' and 'priests' of themselves. In this way, Francis-Xavier Kwon became 'bishop', while Peter Lee Seung-hun, Louis-Gonzaga Lee Tan-won, Augustine Ryu Hang-kŏm, and John Ch'oe Ch'ang-hyŏn became 'priests'. They proceeded to carry out the duties of their ministry, preaching the Gospel with great success, and administering the Seven Sacraments. This they did in good faith and their work bore substantial results for two years, until in 1789 certain passages in the religious books began to arouse serious doubts in the minds of this self-styled clergy, and a consultative letter was sent to Peking.

In his letter to the French missionaries of Pei-t'ang (North Church) at Peking, Peter Lee explains the state of religion in his country, and gave details concerning the administration of the Sacraments and their validity:

Korea, late in 1789.

"I, Peter Lee, prostrate myself upon the ground and beating my breast in token of my submission and prayers for mercy, confess to my reverend Fathers that since the year 1784 when, during the spring, I received Holy Baptism, I have committed grievous sins whereby I have forfeited the grace of God and put myself in the power of the devil, inasmuch as I have not only lost my own soul but have also been the cause of others' damnation. Alas! Is there any corner of the world that might tolerate my presence? What is left for me now but that infinite mercy which has never yet been withheld from me? All these thoughts fill me with fear and enfeeble my consciousness of the great debt of gratitude that I owe. A full account of my sins, and of what has occurred here in this young community of Christians will move you to beg God's forgiveness of my sins, and to show me the true road to redemption, not only for myself but also for my compatriots who number more than a thousand, and who go on performing the duties of our Holy Religion, borne down by the weight of their sins with no means to free themselves; living in darkness yet not knowing where to seek the light; deprived of the Sacrament of Penance without being able to find any priests; these Christians are already in a state of continual anxiety. Well do we know of the blessing of the redemption, but who will make it available to us? Only imagine then, reverend Fathers, what sorrow and affliction we are in. Have pity upon us, we beseech you, allow yourselves to be moved by our appeal and extend a helping hand to rescue us, poor shipwrecked souls in danger of drowning. The following are my sins, with an account of the present conditions of this new Christian community.

"1. At the time of my Baptism I possessed only a rudimentary knowledge of my responsibilites as a Christian. Is my Baptism valid? Ought I to be rebaptized? I await your instructions.

"2. I cherished a sincere desire to become a Christian but this desire was accompanied by the selfish motive of acquiring more knowledge of mathematics.

"3. During my journey from Peking back to my country, I handed over the sacred images to the custody of non-believers, who afterward returned them to me: does this not constitute a profanation of the sacred objects?

"4. Immediately upon my arrival in my country I felt it my most pressing duty to study my religion as set forth in the books which I had brought with me and to preach it to my relatives and friends. In the course of this work I became acquainted with a scholar who had come into possession of a book of our religion, to the study of which he had devoted himself for several years. His efforts had not been unavailing, for he had gained some knowledge of the less easily-comprehended points of our religion, but his faith and his fervor far surpassed his knowledge. It was he who taught and encouraged me; we helped each other to serve God and to lead others to serve Him, to the number of a thousand who embraced the faith and earnestly pleaded to be baptized; at the unanimous desire of all, I baptized several of them according to the rite observed at my own Baptism in Peking. In the meantime the persecution broke out; my family was the worst to suffer, and I was obliged to withdraw from the companionship of my Brothers in Christ. In order not to bring about a discontinuance of Baptism, I delegated two other persons to take my place. One of them was the above-mentioned scholar, and the other was the one who suffered greatly in the persecution, and who died in the autumn of 1785, a year after his arrest.

"5. During the spring of 1786, the Christians held an assembly to discuss how to confess and hear confessions, and it was decided that A and B might confess to C, but that A and B or B and C must not confess to each other. Toward autumn of that year a second assembly was held, at which it was decided that I should celebrate Holy Mass and that I should confer the Sacrament of Confirmation: not only did I yield to their request, but I conferred the same power to celebrate Holy Mass on ten other persons. For these ceremonies I followed the procedure laid down in various books, both prayer books and books of hours (primers), adding certain parts and omitting others. For the prayers I made selections from our prayer books. I did not realize that I was guilty of sacrilege until 1786. Toward spring, one of the ten, finding himself invested with the priestly dignity, began a careful and assiduous study of a book entitled *Sheng Chiao Chieh Yao* or Indispensable Points of the Holy Religion, whereby he discovered all the crimes of which I was guilty. He at once wrote to warn me —I attach a copy of his letter—such horrible crimes that I trembled to the very marrow of my bones: I made haste to put an end to the administration of the Sacraments in all the various localities where it was being carried on, and to give due warning to all the Christians of my acts of sacrilege."

"6. Toward the end of 1784 I wrote to Father Louis de Grammont requesting him to send certain books to me by a messenger whom I indicated to him: this man did not arrive until about the fourth month of 1785. The persecution was by then already at its height; the man was caught and the books and Father Louis de Grammont's reply were intercepted, but fortunately he was not sentenced to death. From that time on all the roads have been under strict surveillance and all travelers closely questioned. It is for this reason that I have written these letters on silk which I have enclosed in cotton-wool garment-wadding lest they be discovered. For if a single one of my courier's fellow-travelers should come to know of their existence, this entire new Christian community would be subjected to renewed persecution and there would be an end to our correspondence with you by letter. I humbly beg my reverend Fathers to extend their good offices to the bearer of this letter and protect him from the various dangers to which he may be exposed. It is essential to be warned and to be on guard and to take every precaution to ensure that we may continue to enjoy the happiness of receiving news of you.

"Since 1784 the number of those who listen to our preaching has gone on increasing: those who worship God within a thousand li (about 250 miles) amount to a thousand persons; the persecution goes on in five or six districts, many Christians have been arrested, thrown into jail, beaten, threatened, won over by promises; in short no means has been spared to make them renounce their religion. The number of outstanding cases of constancy, resolution and courage is also very great, more than ten among them having sealed their faith with their blood. This good record is not being maintained: after the discontinuance of the Sacraments we are as it were without succor, every day spent in sorrow and anxiety, longing night and day for relief. Toward whom should we direct our cries for help if not to you missionaries who have come from Europe? Hear our prayers, do not abandon us but take steps to procure us the means of grace and redemption.

"If I have not sent you this news earlier, it is because the persecution placed obstacles in our way, and our poverty could not furnish us with the means to do so, to which I must add that dispersal of the Christians, who now live exposed to all the fury of the enemies of salvation, deprived of the Sacrament of Penance, has gradually changed their earlier fervor into remissness. Every country under the sun has received the grace of the redemption and the whole world is full of bishops and priests! Why should this little strip of land we live in be the only one excluded from the benefit of the redemption? We prostrate ourselves on the ground before you priests and ministers of Our Lord, and we solemnly appeal to you in the name of God to have regard for the precious blood. His son shed for us, to imitate the virtues of the Apostles, to take pity on us and to do everything possible to ensure that people bowed down under the weight of their own iniquities, people to whom every avenue of escape is closed, may have some means of renewal and revival. This is the favor we entreat. If my report to you becomes known to the authorities, it will be the deathblow to this community of Christians. No one must know of it but the priests of our Church."①

---

① Archives of the Sacred Congregation *De Propaganda Fide*, original documents relating to private religious congregations in the East Indies and in China, 1791-1792, f. 456-457, (translation) in *"L'Érection du Premier Vicariate Apostolique et les Origines du Catholicisme en Corée by Andrew Ch'oe*, 1961, Schöneck-Beckenried, Switzerland, p. 90f.

A disciple of Francis-Xavier Kwon, named Paul Yun Yu-il, accepted this letter and, disguised as a merchant, left for Peking in the tenth lunar month of 1789. Upon his arrival in Peking he went straight to Bishop Gouvéa. He handed the letter he brought with him to the Bishop, and told him what had been happening in Korea. The unexpected visit of Paul Yun from a country in which no priest had ever set foot to preach, and explaining to them how the faith had been propagated was one of the most rewarding experiences for the missionaries and the Bishop. In the spring of 1790, Paul returned to Korea, bringing the Bishop's reply. In Peking he had received the Sacraments of Baptism, of the Eucharist, and of Confirmation.

The Bishop's reply, written on a piece of silk, so as to be easily concealed, began by exhorting the neophytes to render thanks to God for their vocation, and encouraging them to persevere. There followed a brief explanation of the doctrine and of Christian morals. Peter and Francis-Xavier were rebuked for assuming the priestly ministry. The Bishop explained to them that they had no power to administer any of the Sacraments except Baptism, because they had not received the Sacrament of Holy Orders themselves, but that in converting and instructing the pagans they were doing work most pleasing to God. He exhorted them to persevere along these lines.

This long-awaited reply left the Korean Catholics in no doubt, and they duly abolished their false ecclesiastical hierarchy without delay.

8. The Rites Controversy—"Ancestor-Worship"

In May 1790 they sent Paul Yun Yu-il to Peking again with a letter of thanks to the Bishop, in which they appealed to the Church of Peking to send a priest to Korea as soon as possible, and inquired about the traditional rites of ancestor-worship and other difficult points.

Paul Yun soon returned with the Bishop's reply, instructing them to make preparation to receive a priest whom he promised to send and declaring the practice of the traditional rites of ancestor-worship to be heretical.

The fledgling Church in Korea was greatly encouraged by the promise of a priest in the near future, but many Korean Catholics were embarrassed by the ban on ancestor-worship. With its ancient tradition extending back for so many generations, during which the rites had been faithfully observed, ancestor-worship was indeed the foundation of national morals and state discipline, and any failure to comply with its requirements, or even criticism of it, would be considered as treason and blasphemy for which no punishment would be too severe. Enemies of the Church could now take advantage of this fact to provoke persecution of the Catholics and perhaps bring about the destruction of the Church. Several of the weaker-minded Catholics were so shocked by this vital issue that they abandoned the practice of their faith. It was at this juncture that Peter Lee Seung-hun, one of their stragglers, apostatized for the second time.

9. Martyrdom of Paul Yun Chi-ch'ung and James Kwon Sang-yŏn

The first martyrs in the persecution touched off by the Confucianists and politicians with the ban on ancestor-worship as their pretext were Paul Yun Chi-ch'ung and James Kwon Sang-yŏn. Known as the Chin-san incident, this martyrdom was the beginning of the persecution of the year Sin-hae (1791).

Yun Chi-ch'ung was born in Chin-san, Chŏl-la Province, in 1759. He gained his *Chin-sa* degree at the age of twenty-five and in the following year, on reading Father Matteo Ricci's *True Doctrine of God* and *Ch'i Ko* (The Seven Mortifications) he was greatly impressed and made copies of them for his personal use. Three years later, he was converted, and baptized by his cousin, Chŭng Yak-jŏn, and became a devout Christian.

At the height of the persecution he became so frightened that he burned some of his religious books, while steadfastly retaining his faith in secret. His mother died, and pursuant to tradition he wore mourning dress and carried out the funeral ceremony but without bowing before his mother's memorial tablet as the rite prescribed. His cousin, James Kwon Sang-yŏn loyally followed his example in refusing to perform the act of worship to the dead. This triggered a thunderstorm of horrified denunciation, first among his neighbors, who humiliated him in public as an unfilial son. The news spread, from an anti-Christian named Hong Nak-an, who had circulated a violent anti-Catholic manifesto and had even petitioned the throne for a decree of proscription of the Catholic religion. On hearing of the incident, Hong wrote a long letter to the Counselor of the Left Ch'ae Che-kong, requesting the death penalty for Paul Yun. At the same time he demanded that the local magistrate arrest Paul and search his house. The magistrate complied, and as the search revealed that there was no memorial tablet for the defunct parent, he at once ordered the arrest of Paul and James. Forewarned, they had fled, and Paul Yun's uncle was taken into custody as a hostage.

As soon as they heard of this they set off together to deliver themselves into the hands of the magistrate, and arrived at the county of Chin-san on the evening of the twenty-sixth of the tenth lunar month, 1791. The interrogations began at once.

Dallet reproduced them in full, from Paul's notes in Chinese, because they are the first of their kind extant, and because they show what the Korean people thought of ancestor-worship in those days:

"Toward evening on the twenty-sixth of the tenth moon in 1791, I arrived at the Chin-san magistracy and soon after supper Magistrate Shin Sa-won summoned me to his presence.

"'In what state do I see you and how did you get here?'

"'I don't quite understand your question.'

"'I am saying that there are very grave rumors about you. Can they be true? Have you abandoned yourself to superstition?'

"'I am in no way given over to superstition. It is true that I profess the religion of the Lord of Heaven.'

"'Isn't that a superstition?'

"'No, it is the true doctrine.'

"'Do you mean to say, then, that all that has been practiced since the days of Fu Hsi, (first emperor of China, B.C. 2852) right up to the great masters of the Sung Dynasty, is false?'

"'In our religion, among the commandments, there is one that forbids us to judge or condemn others. As for me, I am content to profess the religion of the Lord of Heaven, without dreaming of criticizing anybody, or of making comparisons.'

"'You refuse to offer sacrifices to your ancestors; take the wolf, doesn't it give proof itself of its gratitude toward the authors of its being! Some kinds of birds, too, know how to offer up sacrifices; how much the more, then, ought man to do so. Haven't you read that passage in Confucius which runs: he who, during the life of his parents, has served them according to all the rules, who, after their death, has conducted their funerals in accordance with all the rules, and finally offers sacrifices according to the prescribed rites; only he can be said to possess filial piety.'

"'All that,' I replied, 'is not written in the Christian religion.'

Thereupon the magistrate, quoting other passages from the Confucian canon, earnestly exhorted me to change my conduct, adding with a sigh:

"'What a pity! After so many generations of renown that has never ceased to increase until now, your family has been brought to ruin and disgrace. You, yourself, have the reputation of a talented man of letters, but your spirit lacks maturity and reflection, and you have come to the point of giving up the cult of your fathers. If I had known earlier what you were doing, I would have gone at once to you to exhort you to open your eyes, and I would have prevented you from going to this extremity. In the meantime, all is not yet lost. There have been cases in the past of great men who have returned, after having been long misled by the teachings of Buddha and of Laotse. If then from now on you purpose to change, you will still be able to tread in the path of honor.'

"'If I had intended to change, I would have done so at once, and not come here.'

"'Is there no way, then, to try to bring you back to better feelings? As for me, I have no desire to decide your fate, or to interrogate you minutely on the matter. Once you are brought before the court for trial, you will have to give an account of your conduct. This body which you have received from your parents—do you then in your folly wish to have it suffer torture and death? And another thing: you are the cause of your uncle being arrested in his old age; is that what you call fulfilling the duties of filial piety?'

"'To acquire virtue in spite of torture and death—isn't that filial piety? As soon as I heard of my uncle's arrest, I came here as quickly as possible to deliver myself into your hands—isn't that fulfilling the duties of filial piety?'

"The magistrate then ordered that I should be dealt with according to the law, and immediately a heavy cangue was fastened round my neck, whereupon he said with a sigh:

"'Look at yourself now! To die under the cangue and the irons is to die a criminal's death.'

"He had me put in prison, but the cell intended for me was in ruins, and as it had not been possible to repair it, I was put in another. My journey was ended.

"The twenty-seventh passed without incident. On the twenty-eighth, at breakfast-time, I saw my cousin James Kwon come into the prison. He had come to undergo his interrogation. The same questions were asked, and he answered them in the same way as I. At noon, the magistrate sent for my uncle, and, after having expressed his condolences at great length, he went on:

"'Can you, then, not do like so-and-so, and so-and-so, whom you know well, and prevent these young fellows from giving themselves up to bad habits?'

"My uncle did not answer a word, left the court, and was, I believe, at once released. Toward evening we were summoned again, my cousin and I; the heavy cangue was removed and replaced by a lighter one.

"'You are going,' the magistrate told us, 'to Chŏn-ju, the home of Chŭng Min-si, governor of the province. But what manner of behavior is this of yours? Not to follow the doctrine of the scholars, which would afford you a life of comfort and ease, but to go and throw yourself into misery and misfortune—where's the sense in that?' Then, looking at my cousin Kwon, he said,

"'You who have been living in the bosom of your family, have you spread your superstitions among them?'

"We both remained silent, and the magistrate receiving no answer, sent us on our way. We were accompanied by a guard of three. They had been ordered to set off with us at once, but it was nightfall before we left the court, and it was impossible to start, so we spent the night at the house of the county correspondent.①

"On the twenty-ninth, at cockcrow, we were on our way. We made our first stop at the tavern of Sin-ke-ren for breakfast, and a second, at Kae-pa-hae to bait the horses. At nightfall after passing near the guest house for distinguished visitors, at An-tŏk, we crossed a small hill and met the group of criminal-court attendants that was waiting for us. A number of menservants were standing by, and these rushed up to us shouting and yelling and kicking up such a shindy that one might have thought we were a couple of notorious bandits. We were conducted to the prefecture, and outside the south entrance where, as it was now quite dark, torches were lit on our right and on our left, we were brought before the tribunal.

"'What are your names?' asked the criminal judge.

"'We decline to give them.'

"'Do you know the crime of which you are

---

① This is the title of the representative which each district officer must have at the capital.

accused?'

"'I do not know which one you refer to. Our magistrate having sent us to the judge, we are here at his order, and contrary to all our expectations we have been seized, on our way here, like thieves.'

"'What are your customary occupations?'

"'I am a student.'

"'Of what?'

"'Of religion.'

"'Where were each of you?'

"'I was at Kwang-ju,' I replied, 'And I at Han-san,' said my cousin James Kwon. 'Having learnt of the orders of the magistrate, we came at once, not stopping our journey, at night, in order to deliver ourselves into his hands.'

"A little later each of us had a large cangue fastened round his neck, and we were fastened together with an iron chain.

"Our right hands were fastened to the edge of our cangues with a wooden hook.

"The judge having given the order for us to be taken to the prison, we were led there. On arrival we sat down on a bench outside the door. Afterward, when everybody had left, we were obliged to take our place among thieves. Fortunately, the warden soon came and took us to the guards' quarters. This apartment had the disadvantage of being rather too near the thieves' prison, but on the other hand it was lofty and the floor was fairly warm. It was just like an ordinary room. We spent the night there, either lying down and dozing, or else sitting up. On the thirtieth at dawn we were taken away, and by mid-morning conducted to the governor's prison, where we were summoned to the bar and the following interrogation took place:

"'Which of you is named Yun? and which is Kwon?'

"Each of us anwered, declaring his name.

"'What is your usual occupation?'

"'In my youth,' I replied, 'I studied literature in order to pass the examinations; after some time, I took up those studies which regulate the heart and the conduct of man.'

"'You have studied the Confucian canon?'

"'I have.'

"'If you wish to regulate your heart and your conduct, are our sacred classics not enough? Why did you have to ruin yourself with superstitions?'

"'I am in no way ruined with superstition.'

"'And this religion they call Lord of Heaven: isn't that a superstition?'

"'God is the supreme Father, Creator of Heaven and earth, and of angels, of men, and of all the creatures; can His service be called superstition?'

"'Give me a simple summary of this doctrine.'

"'The place where we now are is a fit and proper one for the examination of criminal cases but not for unfolding a doctrine. What we practice can be reduced to the Ten Commandments and *The Seven Mortifications*.

"'From whom did you receive these books?

"'I could tell you his name, but when he lent them to me, the king's ban was not yet in force, so the lender is not guilty. Now that there is this strict prohibition, he would be exposed, without any guilt on his part, to violent tortures; what can I do? It would be an infringement of the precept that forbids us to harm our fellow-man. I cannot, therefore, denounce him.'

"'That is not the case; even though you declare it, this man who lent you the books before the prohibition will certainly not be inculpated. Do not, then, be so reserved on account of this vain fear. The king having ordered an investigation into the exact facts, if you declare nothing, how can I make my report? It would be an infringement of the king's order, which is absolutely not permitted. Make your declaration, then, and don't wait till you are forced by torture to do so.'

"I remained silent for a fairly long time, and as my cousin James pressed me to answer, I said first:

"'This is a thing that goes back a long time and I find it difficult to remember.' Then I added, 'In the winter of 1784 I went by chance to the home of Thomas Kim Pŏm-u of the middle-class, and finding these books, I borrowed them, copied them, and returned them to their owner. Later when I heard of the king's prohibition, I burnt that which was written on Chinese paper, and washed off what was written on Korean paper. It is now already several years since the treatises on the Ten Commandments and *The Seven Mortifications* have not been in my house.'

"'The order of the king commands that, if there are these books, they must be burnt. If, then, you have any others, it is only right for you to hand them over at once.'

"'The magistrate of my district visited my house, and did not find a single page.'

"'You are guilty of a sin so great that heaven and earth cannot contain it, and as the order of the king requires things to be examined to the bottom, here are the questions to which you must answer frankly, article by article.' At this the governor placed before us a list of questions of which the following is the contents:

"'You who do not follow the true way and foolishly repose your faith in deceiving words, you are infatuating the whole world and corrupting the people, you are destroying and falsifying the natural relations of man. Declare, then, what books you have been studying, and with whom. In spite of a strict prohibition you dare to permit yourself a great freedom of thought, and you most foolishly join your practice to your theory. It is a great impiety. But that fault is relatively light. It is stated in the royal dispatch that you no longer make sacrifices. And this is not all: you burn the tablets and do not allow visitors to come to pay their respects to the dead. Finally you do not allow even your parents the honors of burial, and that unblushingly and without the slightest desire to return to better ways. This conduct is worthy of a beast. Deliver up your books at once.

"'Declare the names of your coreligionists. Furthermore, it is said that there are bishops among you, who give you secret orders, and spread abroad this religion: you cannot say you do not know them. Declare everything, then, without concealing anything.'

"After having read this through to the end, I replied:

"'I have, it is true, given up the sacrifices, I have also destroyed the tablets, but I have received visitors who came to make their condolences, and I never prevented them from entering. I have also rendered my father and mother full honors of burial. As for books, I have already explained what there were; I have nothing to deliver up. As for bishops, the word does not exist here. In Europe, this dignity exists, and it is said that they deal with religious affairs. If you wish to make inquiries, you should do so in Europe. Finally in religion there is no master, nor disciple, in the sense that is attached to the words here.'

"The governor then turned to James Kwon.

"'And you,' he asked, 'what books have you studied?'

"'I have studied the book of *True Doctrine of God*, and that of *The Seven Mortification*.'

"'Where did you get them?'

"'I read them with my cousin Yun Chi-ch'ung, who lent them to me.'

"'Did you also make copies of them?'

"'I did not.'

"'Have you omitted the sacrifices?'

"'I have.'

"'And burnt the tablets?'

"'I have the boxes at home still, which the magistrate noted on his visit.'

"The governor then asked his relationship with various other persons, and continued,

"'One of your relatives has spread the rumor, at the capital, that you have burnt the tablets—what is one to believe?'

"'Since I gave up sacrificing, my relatives regard me as an enemy, and reprimand me, saying "This fellow will surely go so far as to burn his tablets." Their words of blame, in spreading, become news, and that is the way they conclude that I must undoubtedly have burnt my tablets.'[1]

"Turning to me again the governor said,

---

[1] At this point, as in the two defenses that follow, the confessors try to hide the fact of their having burnt the tablets of their ancestors, before burying them. It is a (continued on page 36)

"'Do you know Hong Nak-an?'

"'I know the name, but I have never seen him.'

"'Hong Nak-an and his friends have made a report to the councilor about you, and he has sent me orders. That is the cause of your affair. But the rumor, that you have not conducted funeral rites of your parents, must have some base; how could anyone talk so wildly?'

"'I really do not know the cause of these rumors. At the moment of burial, the plague had entered my house, and my relatives and friends did not come, and not being in touch with strangers, I performed the whole ceremony with only the men of the village. Is it from this that the rumor arose? I really don't know the cause.'

"'Among you there are certainly masters, with whom you discuss, and whom you consult: who are they?'

"'In the religion (of Christianity) as I have already said, there is no master, no disciple, as the words are understood here; even more so in this kingdom, where no one has been able to do more than read a few books, who is there that would dare to set himself up as a master and pretend to have plumbed the doctrine to its depths?'

"'What extraordinary being are you to have been able to learn without having been taught?'

"'As I know a few characters, it was enough for me to open a book and read it.'

"'Have you the degree of Chin-sa (licentiate of the state examinations)?'

"'I have.'

"'In what year did you obtain it?'

"'In the spring of 1783.'

"Thereupon, after having interrogated me on my relationship to certain other persons, he said:

"'They say that in your religion, you rejoice in suffering and torture, and that you are glad to die by the sword—is this to be believed?'

"'The desire to live and the fear of death are sentiments common to all; how can we be as you say?'

"We were dismissed, and when we returned to prison, it was already night.

"On the first day of the eleventh moon, at dawn, our own magistrate called for us, told us to be seated in a kind of vestibule, and told a guard to have us recite the Ten Commandments and *The Seven Mortifications*. We recited them to him; he took down our words in writing and sent them to the governor. A little later, this magistrate sent for us and after some exhortations said, 'What you have declared here is not the truth, and is not enough to permit judgment. And furthermore, this religion, in spite of its Ten Commandments, says nothing about the relationship between the king and his subjects. It is what might be called a doctrine without king, or one which disowns the king.'

"'It is not so,' I replied, 'the king is the father of the whole kingdom, and the magistrate, the father of his district; we must therefore render them the duties of piety; now, all that is comprised in the Fourth Commandment.'

"'If it is indeed so, the Fourth Commandment should be annotated to this effect, and be presented in its annotated form. From our point of view the religion of the Europeans is a superstition. But you people, if you follow it because you think it is true, and because you know it is different from that of the Buddha, which disowns parents and king, what reason have you for not setting up tablets, and for not making the sacrifices to your deceased parents? Even if you don't offer them food, you have no doubt some other way of showing your filial piety. If all this does in fact exist among you, you must state it in detail. Furthermore, yesterday you said that the desire to live and the fear of death are sentiments common to all; it is therefore only right to reflect, and, in

temporary weakness, caused, no doubt, by traces of respect, not easily understood by foreigners. Further on, we shall see them courageously avow that they have burnt them, and go to the torture after the avowal. These passages from Paul's report, though they saw him in an unfavorable light, are examples of the loyalty and exactitude with which he recounts what happened.

making these declarations, to emphasize, and give first place to the principles of loyalty to the king and filial piety, in order, by doing so, to save your life.'

"The magistrate of Im-p'i, charged with the investigation, came closer to me and in a calm voice spoke to me like a counselor. I replied:

"'All that you say is in accordance with my desire, only I cannot explain it all by word of mouth. If you will allow me a guard and a few brush-pens, I will write it all out in detail.' He then had me taken to another apartment, with orders to write my defense and submit it. I sat dawn, and dictated the following:

DEFENSE STATEMENT OF PAUL YUN

In the case of the accused Yun

"Early in life I began to study for the examinations, planning to enter an official life. My humble desires were limited to satisfaction of my duties of loyalty to my sovereign, piety toward my parents, and amity toward my friends. In the spring of the year Kye-myo (1783), I obtained the degree of *Chin-sa*. The following year, while spending the winter at the capital, I went by chance to the home of Kim Pŏm-u, of the middle-class, in the Myŏng-rye-pang-kol quarter. He had in his house two books, one of which was *True Doctrine of God* and the other, *The Seven Mortifications*. In looking through them, I saw that the Lord of Heaven is our common Father, Creator of Heaven and earth, the angels, men and all creatures. He is what the Chinese books call Shang Ti. Man is born between heaven and earth, and what he receives from his parents by way of flesh and blood is at bottom a gift from God. A soul is united to its body, but the one who unites them is, again, God. The basis of loyalty to the sovereign is the order of God, the basis of piety toward one's parents is again the order of God. In comparing the whole with the sacred books of the Chinese Confucian canon, of serving Shang Ti with all one's heart and with the greatest care and pains, I believed I had found a good deal of agreement. The practice is comprised in the Ten Commandments, and *The Seven Mortifications*.

The Ten Commandments are:

1. To worship one God only above all other things.
2. Not to take the name of God in vain for making false oaths.
3. To observe the feast days.
4. To honor father and mother. (The gloss says that the king being the father of the realm and the magistrate being the father of his district, they must likewise be honored).
5. Not to commit murder.
6. Not to commit impurity.
7. Not to steal.
8. Not to bear false witness.
9. Not to desire one's neighbor's wife.
10. Not to covet one's neighbor's goods.

The Seven Mortifications are:

1. Humility, with which to conquer Pride.
2. Charity, with which to conquer Jealousy.
3. Patience, with which to conquer Anger.
4. Compassion, with which to conquer Avarice.
5. Temperance, with which to overcome Gluttony.
6. Continence, with which to conquer Luxury.
7. Diligence, with which to conquer Sloth.

"All this being clear, precise and simple for an aid to the practice of virtue, I borrowed these two books, put them in my sleeve and on my return home in the country, I transcribed them.

"In the spring of the year Eul-sa (1785) I returned them to their owner. It was only three years later when, having studied and thought over the contents of these books, I began the serious practice of them. Two years later, I learnt that this doctrine was strictly prohibited, and I burnt or washed these volumes and did not keep them in my possession.

"I have thus not learnt the Christian doctrine in person, as also I have not communicated it to any other person. But, once having recognized God as my Father, I cannot allow myself to disobey His orders. Now, the tablets in use in the homes of the nobles being prohibited by the religion of the Lord of Heaven, I cannot, since I belong to this religion, do anything but obey and conform to what it prescribes. The Fourth Commandment orders us to honor father and mother so that if in fact our parents were in these tablets every man who professes religion would have to honor them. But these tablets are made of wood. They have with me no relationship of flesh, blood or life. They took no part in the labors of my birth and education. The soul of my father and my grandfather once having left this world, cannot remain attached to these material objects. Now, the name of father and mother being so great and venerable how could I dare to take an artificial thing made by a workman and make it my father or my mother and treat it as such?

"This is not founded on right reason, nor could my conscience accept it and even if I ought, according to you, to recognize my obligations as noble, I cannot make myself guilty before God. I have therefore buried my tablets in the ground under my house. The rumor has spread that I have burnt them, but as the religion gives us on this point no formal precept, I do not know what mouths have formulated the accusation, nor what ears have heard it.

"As for the offerings of meat and wine to the dead or to their tablets, that is also a thing forbidden by the religion of the Lord of Heaven, and those who follow it must conform to its laws. In fact, when the Creator first made the different kinds of creatures it was His will that material creatures should use material things and spiritual creatures should use spiritual things. That is why virtue is the food of the soul as material aliments are the food of the body. No matter how excellent the wine or the meat, it cannot nourish the soul, for the reason that an immaterial being cannot get nourishment from material things. The ancients have said, 'One should serve the spirits as if they were really present,' and you admit that this is a fundamental maxim of the sacred books of

this country. Now, since during their lifetime their souls could get no nourishment from wine and meat, how much stronger is our reason for declaring them to be unable to do so after their death. No matter how pious a man may be toward his parents, he doesn't try to offer them food while they are asleep, because the time of sleeping is the time when one cannot eat. For the same and stronger reasons, when they are sleeping the long sleep of death, to offer them food is a vain thing and a false practice. Now, how can a child resolve to honor his parents with vain things and false practices?

"So, putting aside the use of food which has no true smell for the parents, to apply oneself to the practice of virtue to such an extent that the effects may reach them and at the same time nourish our own souls, there is the true way and the right doctrine. And, I repeat, if in that I must derogate from my nobility, I cannot render myself culpable in the eyes of God. Moreover, consider that the common people who do not set up tablets do not refrain from doing so in opposition to the government, and that the nobles who on account of their poverty, do not carry out the sacrifices according to the regulations, are not severely punished. It seems to me that, in my humble opinion, not to set up tablets and not to offer sacrifices to the dead, while carrying out in my own home the faithful observation of the religion of the Lord of Heaven, is in no way a violation of the laws of the state.

"I am also accused of forbidding condolences after the death of my parents. To make and receive such visits of condolence in such a case is a duty of humanity. How could a well-born child be opposed to it? If you do not believe me, there are persons who came to make visits to me of this nature, and you have but to order an investigation, and you will recognize the truth of what I say.

"It is said in addition that I did not bury my parents. The death of my mother took place this year, in the fifth moon, and I performed the ceremonies of interment on the last day of the eighth moon. As regards the burial, the grave, the weeping, the mourning clothes and so on the Christian religion recommends that all be done with the greatest care and attention. I performed these ceremonies and chose a suitable site, like everyone else. The plague had entered my house, and I could not, it is true, get in touch with strangers, and not all my relatives and friends were able to take part in the funeral procession, but all the village people, old and young, came and took part. Here again you have only to obtain information in order to see that the rumors are false and calumnious. This word, Christian religion, is a weapon they use in order to impute every kind of blame. One speaks to another, the latter to a third, one lie begets another, and so little by little it comes to such a point that they say I refused to receive the usual condolences, and even that I left my parents unburied. The accusation of having burnt my tablets is also wild talk lacking in foundation. They say that I am the *Bishop* of the Christians. In all the countries of Europe it is true that there is this episcopal rank, but it is not given to children or novices, still less would they give it to me, a man who has lived a retired life in the depths of the country. I who have seen and heard nothing, and who alone, by means of two or three books, have striven for my personal sanctification, who have never received lessons from anybody, and who have never propagated the doctrine, am the least likely to be selected for consecration as Bishop.

"To call me a *Bishop* is too ridiculous and calls for no answer. Born of noble parents, having discovered more or less the origin of Heaven and earth, and of man, and the commandments of loyalty to the sovereign and of filial piety, my feeble desires are limited to the cultivation of virtue, and the task of fitly serving God. Beyond this I have nothing to say."

DEFENSE STATEMENT OF JAMES KWON

In the case of the accused Kwon

"Being cousin german to Yun Chi-ch'ung by his mother, and living in the vicinity, I saw in his home and borrowed from him two books entitled *True Doctrine of God* and *The Seven Mortifications*. It was several years ago. It was before Paul Yun Chi-ch'ung buried or washed the books. I did not copy them, but merely read them. I have, it is true, ceased to offer the sacrifices, but I have neither burnt nor destroyed the tablets, the boxes are still in my house, and the magistrate of Chin-san having noted everything in the inventory which he made, it is useless to say anything more. From the moment when I began to practice religion, all my kindred looked on me with hostility and poured out upon me all sorts of blame. Then, seeing that I no longer offered sacrifices, they cried out in one voice: 'Since he no longer sacrifices, the tablets are of no further use, and assuredly he must have burnt them.'

To this wild talk everyone added his contribution and spread the rumor abroad, and that is why I am a prisoner today. For the rest, having lost my father and my mother early in life, I have not had occasion, since I began to practice religion, to perform the ceremonies of interment for my parents. Except for this, all that I have to say is no different from what Chi-ch'ung has declared, and I have nothing more to add.

"Through the guard, I sent these two defenses up to the magistrate of Im-p'i. He read them attentively, put them in his sleeve, and went to the criminal tribunal of the governor, giving orders that we should wait outside. It was now midday and we sat down to wait. After a long time we were called and the governor at once asked James Kwon.

"'Have you really kept the tablets? Not long ago you said you had them, and in the meantime the magistrate of Chin-san, in his report, says that he saw only four empty boxes and no tablets: what is this?'

"'When I came from Chin-san to the prefecture,' James replied, near to the governor, 'I was told to declare everything as it was stated on the report of the magistrate. Fearing that if I said too much, the magistrate might get into trouble, I simply told the governor that I had kept the boxes, but in fact the tablets are not in them: I buried them.'

"'Where did you bury them?' the governor demanded.

"James told him the place, but added that a landslip having taken place one could not be sure of finding them in the same place.

"'You did not bury them alone, I suppose. There must have been a man to dig the hole, he can be your witness.'

"'As I was afraid of being seen by anybody, I did not send for a man, and buried them single-handed.'

"Turning to me, the governor said,

"'And you? How did you proceed?'

"'I have told you all in my report—please don't question me any more.'

"'Did you bury the tablets entire, or after you had burned them? The extent of your guilt will depend on whether you burnt them or not. In any case, a delay of a few days will be sufficient for me to find out which it was. What is the use?'

"'I burnt them, and then buried them.

"'If I had believed that they were my parents, how could I have resolved to burn them? But knowing very well that these tablets have nothing in them of my parents, I burnt them. For that matter, whether one buries them or burns them, they come to dust; there is nothing that makes either of these acts graver than the other.'

"The governor, having ordered us to get up and sit on the torture table, signed our judgment warrant and said to me,

"'Do you recognize that you are being justly condemned for having burned the tablets of the dead?'

"'If I had burnt any tablet believing that my parents were in it, the tortures would be just; but in the way I did it, knowing full well that there was nothing of my parents in them, what fault have I committed?'

"'If you were in Europe, these words might be acceptable, but here in our kingdom you must be punished according to the law.'

"'In our country, after five generations, all, even the nobles, bury the tablets, do you punish them for that?'

"'According to the decision of the saints,

five generations is the period after which a man's duty to his ancestors ends.'

"With these words the governor gave orders for the beating to begin. I received ten blows. The governor then said,

"'You who are noble don't you feel any pain in this punishment?'

"'How can I but suffer, who am of flesh and blood like you?'

"'Have you no regret?'

"'As the Christian religion does not specifically order the *burning* of a tablet, I might, to stretch a point, regret having lightly done so; apart from that, I have nothing that I could regret.'

"The governor ordered another man to beat me, and he gave me ten blows more. Then the governor said,

"'When you are about to die under the blows, will you not renounce this religion?'

"'If I come to deny my supreme Father living or dead, to what place can I go?'

"'If your parents or your king pressed you, wouldn't you yield to their voice?'

"'To this question I made no answer.

"'You, you know neither parents nor king.

"'I know very well both parents and king.'"

Here Paul's report ends. It has been remarked that he gave no answer to the last question but one. This was by no means due to hesitation. but so as not to offend the usage of his country which would not permit a negative answer to a question concerning the king. Besides, his silence was well understood by the judges. The governor then ordered him to be given ten more strokes which brought the total to the thirty strokes fixed by law.

After that Paul and James were dismissed and shut up in prison. Night had fallen. His interrogations being completed, the governor sent a report to the king. The king at this time was Chŏng-jo. He was forty years old, and had been fifteen years on the throne. History tells us that he was a sage ruler, moderate, prudent, a friend of learning and a just appreciator of the merits of his subjects. He received the governor's report, but seemed in no way disposed to push matters to the extreme. However, the enemies of religion showed themselves to be more threatening in their attitude: from all sides came addresses to the king, petitions to the councilors, demanding the punishment of the guilty and the extirpation of this new doctrine, which was upsetting all the foundations of society. More than thirty documents of this nature appeared from the ninth to the twelfth month of this year. Aghast at these manifestations, the Counselor of the Left Ch'ae Che-kong, although far from personally hostile to the Christians, adopted the views of their most violent accusers, and pressed the king to condemn Paul Yun and James Kwon to capital punishment. This conduct surprised many members of the public, for this counselor belonged to the *Nam-in* (South Party), as well as many of the principal figures among the Christians, and what is more, he was connected by ties of blood or friendship with the majority of them. But the fear of losing his credit and perhaps his dignity, the desire to safeguard his fortune and that of his family, turned him into a persecutor. We shall see later how he was punished by the justice of God, even in this world, for his cowardice.

Yielding to the instances of his counselor, King Chŏng-jo finally consented to sign the decree which condemned Paul Yun and James Kwon to be beheaded. Their heads would be exposed in public for five days, in order to strike terror into the neighboring regions and prevent the people from following the new religion. The decree, invested with the royal authority, was sent to the governor of Chŏn-ju. At the reception of the sentence, the confessors were at once taken to prison in lieu of torture. An immense crowd of pagans and Christians followed them. James, weakened by the blows he had received, was content to pronounce from time to time the names of Jesus and Mary. Paul, more robust, went forward with an air of gaiety, greeting death as if going to a party, and preaching Jesus Christ with such dignity that not only the Christians but the pagans were struck with admiration.

Arrived at the execution ground, the officer in charge inquired whether they were willing to obey the king, and render the ordinary service of the cult to the tablets of their ancestors, and renounce the foreign religion. Upon their answering in the negative, the officer commanded Paul Yun to read the sentence of death, confirmed by the king, and written on a board, following the usage of the kingdom. Paul took it at once and read it in a loud voice. He then placed his head on the block, repeated several times the holy names of Jesus and Mary, and with the greatest composure signed to the executioner to strike. His head was cut off at a single blow. Then came the turn of James who also never ceased to invoke Jesus and Mary. He was beheaded immediately after his cousin. It was three o'clock in the afternoon on the thirteenth day of the eleventh moon of the year Sin-hae (December 8, 1791). Paul Yun was aged thirty-three years and James Kwon forty-one years.

The king in the meantime had repented of having yielded to the instances of his councilor. He foresaw that after the custom of the country the first act would set a precedent and become the law of the state, and that those who followed the new religion would be put to death one after another. A special courier was sent at full speed to the governor of Chŏn-ju to stay the execution. But it was too late: Paul Yun and James Kwon had already gained the crown of martyrdom. The bodies of the two martyrs remained nine days without burial. To intimidate the Christians, guards were placed over them night and day. On the ninth day the relatives who had obtained royal permission to enshroud them and their friends who had come to their funerals were astonished to see the two bodies without the slightest sign of corruption, fresh-looking and supple as if they had been decapitated that very day. Their astonishment was redoubled when they saw the block on which they had been beheaded, and the board on which the sentence of death had been written, sprinkled with still-liquid blood as fresh as if it had just been shed. These circumstances seemed all the more surprising in that in the month of December the excessive rigor of the cold freezes all liquids in the vessels in which they are contained. The pagans, full of wonder, cried out against the injustice of the judges and proclaimed the innocence of the two confessors. Some of them, moved by the prodigy that they had so carefully examined, were converted. Their eyes bathed with happy tears, the Christians blessed the Lord. They dipped a large number of handkerchiefs in the blood of the martyrs, and sent several to the Bishop of Peking with a fully circumstantiated account of all that had happened. The neophytes maintained that a man whom the doctors had given up for dead and who was about to die had been cured in an instant by drinking the water in which the blood-spattered board had been dipped. They reported also that several moribund persons, who had been made to touch a handkerchief dyed with the same blood, were at once cured.

The example of Paul and James had a prodigious influence on the early Christians of Korea. Their names have remained celebrated and Paul, especially, is even today still venerated by the faithful. He left a daughter aged thirteen, who went to stay temporarily at the home of Thomas Kim, a guard and a former pupil of her father. Later she married into the family of Song, at Sutpang-i district of Kong-ju. Her mother followed her to her husband's home, and continued, it is said, to practice the religion. The Christians no longer kept in touch with the family.

Some days after the execution of Paul Yun and James Kwon, the government posted notices of their sentence and the news of their death in every town and village, in order to intimidate the people and prevent new conversions. But God was pleased to defeat the plans of His enemies. This official publication gave great publicity to the case of the two confessors and brought knowledge of Christianity to numbers of people who had never even heard of it before, and it contributed greatly to the propagation of the

faith. Today, as always, in Korea as in the rest of the world, these words are always true:

Sanguis martyrum semen Christianorum: The blood of the martyrs is the seed of Christians.
Tertullian

10. The Aftermath of the Sin-hae (1791) Persecution

While the Christian religion was being so gloriously upheld before the highest court of the southern part of Korea, many other Christians at the capital and in the neighboring provinces were also being called upon to profess their faith.

Francis-Xavier Kwon Il-sin had not been molested in 1785, in spite of his outspoken public preaching, but in 1791 he could not escape the enemies' malice. Everyone well knew that his name, his knowledge and his continual efforts for the propagation of the new doctrine had been of enormous influence in bringing about conversions and fortifying the faith of the believers. Accordingly, at the time of the Chin-san incident, Hong Nak-an, Mok Man-jung and several others denounced him as the principal fomenter of the Christian religion. Francis-Xavier Kwon was thereupon arrested and brought up for trial in the eleventh lunar month of 1791. Failing to make him retract, they repeatedly put him to the torture, but still he remained steadfast, and declared:

"It is impossible not to serve Almighty God, the Creator of Heaven and earth, of the angels and of mankind. Not for anything in the world will I deny Him: rather than fail in my duty to Him, I would gladly suffer death."

The torture had already reduced his body to a shocking state when the king, who was acquainted with Francis-Xavier Kwon Il-sin and held his fine qualities in high esteem, declined to sign his death-warrant, and tried by gentler means to bring about his apostasy. But kindly remonstrance, flattery, promises of future favors, and expressions of pity and affection were all of no avail. Much against his will, the king condemned him to exile in the Island of Che-ju, or Quelpart, and the governor of this island was ordered to put him to the torture three times a month until he recanted. Before he left, however, several officials called on him, at the instigation of the king, to inform him that his mother, now eighty years old, was ill and could not live long. Once sent to Che-ju Island, how could he bear the thought of having deprived her of the presence of her son during her last hours? Without mentioning apostasy, these officials suggested that he make a token submission to the king, in return for which he would be sent to a much less distant place of exile. Filial piety led him to make a vague gesture of submission, and his place of exile was changed to Ye-san, but before reaching his destination, he died of his injuries at a wayside inn.

Defection of Several Influential Catholics

After the death of Francis-Xavier Kwon Il-sin, his disciple, Louis-Gonzaga Lee Tan-won, the so-called Apostle of Nae-p'o, also renounced his faith under torture. On his release from prison, however, he repented of his weakness and remained a devout Catholic until his martyrdom.

There were others who apostatized during this stormy persecution, including Chŭng Yak-jŏn and Chŭng Yak-yong, of Yang-p'yŏng, but there were also great and glorious examples of courage and fidelity to console the growing Church in Korea. The case of Lawrence Park is an example: indignant at the way in which large numbers of Christians were being treated in the prison, he boldly entered the magistrate's room and said:

"All this flogging of innocent men and women, and holding them in jail for months on end: isn't it a horrible crime?"

The magistrate was furious, and had him seized, imprisoned, beaten and fastened into a heavy cangue, but nothing could break his spirit.

"This cangue is too light," he told the magistrate, "order me an iron one."

After a month and a few days, during which he underwent further beatings, an order came from the court for his release.

Another staunch Catholic was Pius Kim Chin-hu, the great-grandfather of Korea's first native Catholic priest, Blessed Andrew Kim Tae-kŏn. He showed the same constancy before the judges, but did not gain the crown of martyrdom.

The Martyrdom of Peter Won Si-jang

Peter Won Si-jang was more fortunate. He was a native of Hong-ju, and was a descendant of an honest family of considerable fortune. The savage violence of his character had earned him the sobriquet of the "Tiger." In 1788 or 1789 when he was about fifty-five years old, he first heard of the Christian religion. By the extraordinary grace of God, he was converted at once, but told nobody about it. He left his house, saying: "I have wasted fifty years of my life, and when I return you will know the cause of my departure. Do not worry about me and above all do not wait for me."

He left at once, and for more than a year there was no news of him. At last, Peter having reappeared, his relatives and friends ran to welcome him, asking him 'a thousand' questions, to some of which he smilingly replied:

"For more than fifty years I nearly died on a number of occasions, but now I have a medicine that prolongs life for thousands of years. I'll tell you about it tomorrow."

The next day, he called all his relatives together and proceeded to give them a complete explanation of first and last things; the existence of God, the Creator and preserver of all things; original sin, the Incarnation, the commandments of God; Heaven and hell, in short, everything he knew of the Christian religion.

"There you are," he said, "for all men of good will, these are the means of eternal life. O, all my dear ones, receive my words as my testamentary vows, and embrace with me this divine religion." Grace was in his words, and all promised to pledge themselves from that day on to the service of the great King and Father of all men.

But what gave Peter, more than his courage, his extraordinary power of bringing about conversions, was his good example; it was the victory that he had won over himself. Now that he was home again, his character was completely changed, and he showed in all circumstances an unalterable sweetness of temper. People were amazed at his ardent zeal in relieving the poor, and sharing his goods with them, and in exhorting the pagans among his acquaintance, more than thirty families of whom he converted. His fervor was so great that even in the presence of pagans he always carried out all his religious observances. About two years after his conversion, the rumor that his entire family had become Christian reached the ears of the magistrate. The latter sent a subordinate to seize a cousin of Peter named James, but, warned by his friends, James had fled. They asked Peter:

"Where is your cousin?"

"He is hiding for fear of death—how do you expect me to know where he is?"

"We have a warrant from the magistrate to arrest him as a Christian, but, since he is not here, we had better take you in his place."

"Be it so," replied Peter, and at once he was arrested and brought before a minor official at the tribunal, who asked him,

"Where has your cousin gone?"

"I don't know."

"They say your cousin is a practicing Christian; are you?"

"I am."

"Promise to stop practicing deny God, and I will report to the magistrate that all these rumors are mere calumny; you will be released at once."

"I cannot deny God."

He was shut up in a room and for several days incessantly urged to apostatize. But when Peter constantly refused to do so, the infuriated official sent him to the magistrate.

"Is it true," the magistrate asked him, "that you follow the religion of the Lord of Heaven?"

"That is true."

"Deny your God, denounce your accomplices, and tell me that you will follow it no more, and I will at once release you."

"Deny God! Never! Nor will I denounce other Christians either."

"Do you refuse to denounce your accomplices and tell me what books you have in your possession?"

"It is impossible for me to do so."

In a fury the magistrate made him undergo the torture of dislocation of the joints (of the fingers, and so on), and ordered him seventy strokes of the heavy rod used for punishing thieves and robbers. But Peter bore all patiently, never ceasing to declare his true faith in God, the duty of man toward God and his parents, the vanity of pagan superstitions, and so on. Returned to prison, he was called out again on the following day.

He made the same answers.

He underwent the torture of dislocation of the joints a second time, and was beaten again, more cruelly than on the previous day, with the "thieves' rod." His flesh was in ribbons, his shoulder-bones broken, and the bones of his back exposed to view beneath the torn, black and blue flesh. It was in this dreadful condition that he was sent back to prison. In spite of his sufferings, he maintained an expression of calm and contented joy on his face. He preached to the guards and jailers, and a few days later, a Christian having come to see him in prison, Peter received Baptism from him, for until then he had been only a catechumen. In the meantime the magistrate, having sent a report to the governor of the province, received the order to have Peter beaten to death. At the third interrogation before the criminal judge, a frightful-looking machine was brought in, and a number of subordinate guards placed around him to intimidate him. The judge then said to him,

"The desire to save your life made me employ every means to bring you to better feelings; but as you will not listen to anything that I say, and you obstinately wish to die, I have informed the governor, and the order has now come for you to be beaten to death; you may understand now that you are going to die."

"It is my fervent desire," replied Peter.

At these words, they tightened his bonds, and began to inflict a series of horrible tortures that lasted the whole day. Peter bore them bravely, but his body was so crushed and bruised that he could no longer use his limbs. They had to carry him back to prison, and put into his mouth the food he could no longer pick up himself.

Finally the criminal judge and the magistrate together made a last effort to win him over, by speaking of his children, who were constantly calling for him at home.

"This touches me very deeply," said Peter, "but it is God Himself who is calling me; how can I fail to respond to His voice?" Then he was served with the customary meal provided by law for those condemned to death. After that he was beaten again more violently than ever, in an attempt to kill him as quickly as possible. But he did not die. The magistrate, the guards and the executioners, exhausted with fatigue, said to each other:

"This culprit doesn't feel the blows; it's impossible to put an end to him."

"I feel the blows," replied Peter, "but God is there, Who speaks to me and Himself strengthens me."

On hearing these words, the magistrate said:

"This rascal must have the devil at his orders," and ordered them to strike harder, but in vain. Finally, abandoning the attempts to kill him by these means, he ordered them to fasten him down and expose him, drenched with water, to the freezing cold of the night, that he might freeze to death. Peter was then tied with a thick rope and buckets of water were poured over his whole body. Soon he was entirely covered with ice. In this suffering, he remembered the passion of Our Saviour, and repeated:

"O Jesus, scourged for me, and crowned with thorns for my salvation, see the ice with which my body is covered, for the honor of Your name." Then he offered his life to God in testimony of his love and gratitude. At the second cockcrow, he breathed his last. It was the seventeenth day of the

twelfth moon of the year Im-ja (January, 1793). Peter was sixty-one years of age.

At about this time, the persecution began to diminish in activity, especially in the capital. The king, naturally a temperate and moderate man, detested all violent measures. He preferred to deal with the Christians by means of blandishments, promises, and seductions of every kind, and too often this method succeeded in bringing about apostasies, especially among the nobles. In the provinces, things were left more or less to the governors' own will: they persecuted the Christians or left them in peace according to their own whim or personal prepossession. In this way, although some Christian communities might enjoy almost complete liberty, in others, such as Nae-p'o, the neophytes were constantly beset and maltreated.

Such was the first persecution that the Church in Korea underwent, such was the Baptism of blood and tears by which this young Christian community was consecrated. When one thinks that by a special disposition of God, perhaps unique in the history of Christianity, this Church had been founded, had grown and strengthened itself, all without the help of a single priest, the courage of its martyrs, the constancy of its confessors, the perseverance of its children, its very existence even, reveal themselves as an astounding prodigy.

Without doubt, not all of them could confess their faith. The first converts, the most celebrated propagators of the Gospel, have saddened us with the spectacle of their cowardice. In punishment perhaps of some secret pride arising from the success of their eloquence, they fell, and dragged many others with them in their fall. But it is not the defection of a few that ought to surprise us: what is really amazing is that they did not all apostatize. They had nothing more than a very incomplete knowledge of Christianity, they had no other teachers than a few Chinese books brought in by stealth, and possessed only by the most instructed among them; and above all, they were without the succor of the Sacraments. We see everyday what so many Christians are, even with this supernatural help, which they receive so often. What must have been those poor neophytes, who hardly knew even the name of the Sacrament!

Yet by the unique power of the grace of God, there were among these neophytes martyrs, confessors, and zealous preachers of the Gospel.

Ten years after the Baptism of Peter Lee Seung-hun at Peking, we find, in spite of the persecution, in spite of the successive defection of the most illustrious of their chiefs, more than four thousand Christians in Korea. We find among them the practice of the greatest virtues, charity toward one's neighbor, humility, chastity, all so strange to the pagans and so difficult to explain to them. The finger of God was there.

11. Efforts to Obtain a Priest for Korea

A period of comparative peace followed the abatement of the persecution. The community of Christians availed themselves of this to close their ranks and gather strength in silence and in prayer, and even to make new conquests. Their eminent leaders had disappeared. On the side of truth there remained Ambrose Kwon Ch'ŏl-sin, elder brother of Francis-Xavier Kwon Il-sin, and the illustrious Chŭng family, but by nature they took little part in the affairs of the Church and there is no evidence that they ever directed it. Those whom we find at the head now are John Ch'oe Ch'ang-hyŏn and Matthias Ch'oe In-kil, zealous and capable men, of the middle-class. They did not possess honors, but the progress of religion was in no way impeded on that account, and although they were less striking figures in the eyes of the pagans, they were more solid, and more real. It would seem that Providence, having made use of the scholars and nobles to bring about the first assault, allowed them to disappear, as if to show that the Gospel does not need them exclusively, and to let the Korean people understand that this was not a matter of one more fashionable philosophic

fad to the name of which the high position and education of its adepts would give for a few days a kind of artificial vitality, and which would die with its founders.

Non multi sapientes secundum carnem, non multi nobiles...ut non evacuetur crux Christi.

—Few "wise men", few great men, few nobles, lest the cross of Christ be reduced to nothing. (1 Corinthians, 1:26)

"Christ did not send me to baptize; he sent me to preach the gospel; not with an orator's cleverness, for so the cross of Christ might be robbed of its force." (1 Corinthians, 1:17)

The following is the picture of John Ch'oe Ch'ang-hyŏn as drawn in the Korean records. The chief catechist, John Ch'oe, was one of the first to embrace the faith. He was a calm, prudent, enlightened man, of noble and resolute heart. He taught the truth with exactitude. His words were without affectation of style, yet all listened to him with gentleness and pleasure and with profit to their souls. His humility and resignation to the will of God were natural to him, and although there is nothing extraordinary to report of his conduct, no man was ever more esteemed or more loved by the Christians.

The first care of John Ch'oe and companions was to seek and obtain the services of a priest. The difficulties arising from the persecution had been almost entirely overcome, and the desire of the faithful for a minister of God was more ardent than ever. It was therefore decided that Paul Yun Yu-il, who had already made the journey to Peking on two occasions, should lead an expedition, and that Sabas Chi Hwang should accompany him, with several others. During their absence, a house would be made ready at the capital to receive the priest, and the care of this house was entrusted to Matthias Ch'oe In-kil.

The courageous deputation, accordingly, left in the suite of the embassy, toward the end of the year 1793. God protected them on the journey, and they arrived safely at their destination.

Bishop Gouvéa was told of the ordeal the

Catholic Church of Korea had undergone, and decided to send a Chinese priest, Father James Chou Wen-mo (Chu Mun-mo) to Korea. Father Chou was a virtuous and scholarly product of the Peking seminary, of strong character and complete self-possession. He was forty-two years old.

He arrived at the border in February 1794, in the eighteenth year of King Chŏng-jo's reign. Owing to the surveillance, however, it was not until December that, disguised as a Korean, he was able to cross the Yalu River in the company of Paul Yun Yu-il and Sabas Chi Hwang. After a journey of twelve days they entered Seoul: it was now January 1795.

Father Chou found to his surprise that there were four thousand Catholics in Korea. He took lodgings in Puk-ch'on (north village), in a house prepared by Matthias Ch'oe. He began by getting ready everything necessary for the celebration of Holy Mass, and on Easter Sunday Mass was said in Korea for the first time, and Holy Communion was given to a number of Catholics who had confessed the previous day.

The occasion marked a milestone in the development of the Church in Korea, and we remember with gratitude the heroism of Paul Yun Yu-il and Sabas Chi Hwang, without whom the achievement would have been impossible.

CHAPTER THREE

THE PERSECUTION OF 1801

12. Father James Chou, Paul Yun Yu-il, Sabas Chi Hwang and Matthias Ch'oe In-kil

Father Chou Wen-mo: The first Catholic missionary who worked in Korea managed, in spite of cruel oppression and constant surveillance, to carry on his religious activities for six years.

For the first six months of his secret activities nothing serious occurred to disturb his missionary work. During that period he baptized many pagans and administered the Sacrament of Penance to many of the faithful. He celebrated Mass and administered Holy Communion to large numbers. His spare time he devoted to mastering the Korean language. His congregation grew in numbers day by day, and he received all visitors indiscriminately. He never denied the sacraments to those who had made the necessary preparations, and took no precautions against his numerous visitors but admitted them all without suspicions. Thus it was that a traitor was able to penetrate into the group of visitors, a man who was determined to frustrate Father Chou's work and overthrow the Church in Korea. His name was Han Yŏng-ik and, masquerading as a genuine convert, he called regularly on Father Chou. While conversing with the priest he tried his best to find out how he had evaded the border guards and entered Korea, and on these

occasions also was able to familiarize himself with the priest's features so as to be able to recognize him again.

He then went to see the brother of Lee Pyŏk who held high office in the government, and revealed the surprising information to him. Soon afterward King Chŏng-jo (reigned 1777-1800) and the Chwa-eui-jŏng or the Counselor of the Left came to hear of this news. An imperial order was handed down to the minister of justice to send constables to arrest the priest secretly. This was on June 27, 1795. Fortunately the Catholics had been forewarned, so that they could take him to a place of concealment, so as to ensure the continuance of the Christian ministry.

Matthias Ch'oe secretly took the priest to a safe place, and then, as he knew Chinese, decided to disguise himself as Father Chou and go on living in the same house. He put on a false queue and Chinese clothes, and allowed himself to be arrested in mistake for Father Chou. The police soon found out their mistake, and set out in search of him once more, but, failing to find him, arrested Sabas Chi Hwang and Paul Yun and imprisoned them together with Matthias Ch'oe. Torture began at night on the day of their capture in an endeavor to make them reveal the priest's whereabouts. Though they were beaten and had their arms and legs twisted and their ankles crushed, they would not betray their shepherd, but rather seemed to undergo

the excruciating pain with exultation and
joy. They were then sentenced to death and
executed the same night, their bodies being
thrown into the Han River. This was on
June 28, 1795. Sabas Chi was twenty-nine,
Paul Yun thirty-six, and Matthias Ch'oe
thirty-one years old.

13. Father Chou and Columba Kang Wan-suk

In his escape from the cruel hands of the
government authorities, Father Chou hid in
a woodshed in the house of Columba Kang
Wan-suk, a wealthy widow and the only
convert among the families of the nobility
(*yang-pan*). Columba was born in the Nae-p'o
district of Ch'ung-ch'ŏng Province. A bright,
eloquent and magnanimous girl, she had been
married to Hong Chi-yŏng of Tŏk-san in the
same province, as his second wife. When
the faith was brought to the district she was
the first to be converted, and not only
brought her family into the Church with her
but actively helped to spread the Gospel in
the locality.

During the persecution of 1791 she was
arrested while bringing food to imprisoned
Catholics and detained at the prison several
days. Her husband, Hong Chi-yŏng, a man
of weak character, fearing that his wife's
religion would endanger his safety, asked for
a separation, and Columba thereupon moved
with her mother-in-law, her daughter, and
her stepson Hong P'il-ju, to Seoul, where she
received Baptism at Father Chou's hands. He
found her shrewd, intelligent and devout,
and of great help to him in spreading the
faith. He appointed her a catechist, and she
became the first Korean woman to engage
in this work.

On hearing that Han Yŏng-ik had betrayed
the Father to the authorities, she hid him in
her woodshed and at first concealed his
whereabouts from everybody, including her
own family. At last, after three months, she

felt that she could confide in her mother-in-
law, and from then on she was able to lodge
him in one of the guestrooms. This became
the headquarters from which he governed
and commanded the Church in Korea for six
years.

In September 1796, Father Chou gave a
Catholic named Thomas Hwang Sim a
letter to convey to the Bishop of Peking.
Hwang was to accompany the Korean embassy to the Emperor of China.[1]

Hwang Sim arrived safely on January 28,
1797 and presented the letter to Bishop
Gouvéa, who, long anxious of the silence
of the Church in Korea, was delighted to
receive news of its condition.

During his first three years of concealed
activity the priest had made himself proficient in the Korean language and in Korean
domestic affairs and now felt confident that
he could undertake pastoral visits. He visited
the bereaved family of Paul Yun who had
given his life to bring him into Korea, and
also stayed at Ryu Hang-kŏm's in Chŏn-ju,
Chŏl-la Province. We have no record of the
exact date of his tour of Ko-san, Nam-p'o,
Kong-ju, On-yang and Nae-p'o, but it is
recorded that on this occasion he could not
always administer the Holy Eucharist to all
of the Catholics, owing to the necessity for
secrecy. In spite of difficulties, the number
of Catholics grew from 4,000 at his arrival
to 10,000 within five years.

Father Chou owed much to Columba's devotion and prudence. Taking advantage of
the provision of Korean law that exempted
noblewomen from undergoing punishment,
she disregarded the official ban on Catholicism and continued to spread the Gospel
both in Seoul and throughout the countryside. She gathered numbers of girls at her
house and taught them the Catholic doctrine, and these girls in turn brought in
more converts from their families and acquaintances, and from their husband's, once
they were married.

[1] *Jen Tsung Yung Yen*, Nov. 13, 1760—Sept. 2, 1820, the sixth emperor of the Ch'ing Dynasty, who ruled
from 1796 until his death, under the reign title *Chiaching*.

The King Chŏng-jo had a half-brother named Prince Eun-ŏn or In whose grandson was to ascend the throne in 1850 as King Ch'ŏl-jong (ruled 1850-1864). After Prince Eun-ŏn's son, Prince Sang-kye, was executed on the charge of conspiring against the king, Eun-ŏn was exiled to Kang-hwa Island. His wife, Song, and his widowed daughter-in-law Shin, continued to live in retirement in a house within the precinct of the secret palace. In 1791 or 1792 they were visited by a Catholic lady who began to teach them the Gospel. They became fervent Catholics, converting several of their women-servants and joining the Myŏng-to-hoe, a Catholic laymen's club, for the study of Holy Scripture and doctrine. They were glad to receive Father Chou in their house and were baptized by him, as Maria Song and Maria Shin. The Myŏng-to-hoe had as its first chairman Chŭng Yak-jong.

14. The Persecution in the Local Areas

While Father Chou continued his missionary work there were several cases of martyrdom for the faith. Among them we take especial pride in mentioning the following confessors and citing their achievements.

(1) Thomas Kim

One of their first victims was Thomas Kim, also known as Kim P'ung-hŏn, that is to say, "Kim the tax-collector". Born in the Province of Ch'ung-ch'ŏng in the district of Ch'ŏng-yang, of a middle class family, he had managed to gain an education. In the year 1796 he was arrested and taken to the Ch'ŏng-yang county, where he had to undergo the most violent tortures. They even went so far as to cauterize his anus with burning moxa, but nothing would make him deny his faith. They made a ploughshare red-hot and ordered him to take off his shoes and stand on it. He was going to obey when somebody stopped him, saying that he was mad; this was his holy enthusiasm. Thomas was condemned to death.

Three days before his execution, they daubed his face with lime and drummed him three times round the market place. In the meantime the magistrate of Ch'ŏng-yang was dismissed and Thomas's case had to await the arrival of his successor, in spite of Thomas's demands for the execution of his sentence. The new magistrate, however, after reviewing the case released the confessor from prison on bail, and a few days later ordered him to leave the district. Thomas, deeply disappointed at his failure to win the crown of martyrdom, went away groaning and telling everyone that he had been unfortunate, and that henceforth country, home, and family were nothing to him. He lived successively in the districts of Pu-yŏ, Keum-san, and Ko-san, devoting himself to teaching the Christians, and living in the utmost austerity. Whenever the faithful gave him clothing or a new pair of shoes he would declare that fine raiment led to the sin of pride, and he would change clothes with the first beggar he met. He never took more than one meal a day, and that always consisted of the coarsest food. He always cherished the hope of obtaining the grace of martyrdom, but God hearkened otherwise to his prayers. A few days later, in the seventh lunar month of the year 1801, he fell ill at An-ko-kae, in the district of Yong-tam. On the eve of his death, he predicted that he would die on the morrow. When the moment came, he had himself carried into the courtyard of the house where he was staying and knelt down, and it was in this humble posture that he breathed his last.

(2) Paul Lee

Paul Lee To-ki was arrested in Ch'ŏng-yang, Ch'ung-ch'ŏng Province in the sixth moon of 1797 and for the glory of God beaten to death by a mob on the twelfth of the sixth moon in the following year, after undergoing brutal torture. For over a year he was repeatedly tortured and continually brought before the rabble in the market place for public scorn and mistreatment, but his faith was never shaken.

The persecutors brought him back to the prison, and this time they put no restraint on their anger, until the martyr's soul took flight to Heaven. But the magistrate, fearing lest he should revive, had the tortures continued on the corpse. One of the constables put the end of the cangue on its chest and jumped on it: the ribs broke and the blood gushed out. The corpse no longer looked like a man. It was covered with a straw mat and guarded throughout the night. The next day it was buried by order of the magistrate. Seven or eight days later his wife came to take it away for honorable burial. The jailor, trying to console the widow, said to her:

"Don't be sad, for on the twelfth, during the night, I saw a great light surrounding the body of your husband."

(3) Lawrence Park

About the same time, but in another district, Lawrence Park gave the faithful an example of the same courage and perseverance. We have seen how in 1791 he boldly intervened in favor of the Christians, and was scourged for his faith. In 1797 when persecution broke out again in the Hong-ju area, orders were given for his arrest. Lawrence, in humble mistrust of his own strength, at first hid himself. But when his young son was taken captive in his place, his mother said to him, "Now you cannot avoid giving yourself up." He recognized God's Will in these words and relying on help from above he gave himself up at the prefectural office on the nineteenth of the eighth moon.

In the ensuing eighteen months he received no fewer than 1,400 strokes of the *ch'i-to-kon* and underwent torture on seventeen occasions. He was kept without drinking water for eight days on end, but remained faithful until death. He was strangled in 1799 at the age of thirty. His endurance seems almost miraculous, and even to the present day Catholics have never ceased to visit the place where he and Paul Lee were executed. Once again the blood of the martyrs proved to be the seed of the Church.

(4) James Won

James Won was an elder cousin of Peter Won, martyred in 1793. They used to live together in the village of Eung-chŏng-ri in the district of Hong-ju, and they were brought up in the faith together.

A strong friendship bound him to Lawrence Park; they were always together, and encouraged each other in the practice of the faith and the desire for martyrdom. James spent several years in this way until in 1798 he was seized by the constables of Tŏk-san and taken to prison, where he was kept for a month without being charged or interrogated. Thinking that the police were to blame for this, he pressed them either to bring him before the judge or else set him free. He was at length brought before the judge, who asked:

"Is it true that you practice the religion of the Lord of Heaven?"

"Yes," he replied, "I do indeed, in order to worship Him and save my soul."

"Denounce your accomplices."

"There are," he answered, "three other persons animated like me with the desire to worship God and to give their life for Him."

James said this in compliance with a mutual vow that he, Lawrence Park, Francis Pang and Peter Chŭng had made to denounce one another so that they could suffer martyrdom together. It does not appear, however, that James actually denounced them by name.

"Explain yourself more clearly."

"Even if I had to undergo ten thousand deaths, I could not put it more clearly than I have."

The judge then ordered him to be put to various kinds of torture including the dislocation of the bones at their joints, stabbing with pointed sticks, and floggings, but to no avail.

James was then transferred to the Hong-ju criminal court where he repeatedly explained the truths of the faith and had to undergo the most frightful torture two or three times more. He was then sent to Tŏk-san, where he was again cruelly beaten, and had his legs completely broken.

Finally, at the special order of the governor, he was sent to Ch'ŏng-ju, the military headquarters of the province. On his arrival at Ch'ŏng-ju he underwent interrogation. The judge tried to make him abjure the faith by promising to spare his life but James replied:

"For nine years I have been hoping to die a martyr for God." The judge, furious, made him undergo cruel torture for a whole day. On the following day this was repeated, and it went on day after day for a whole month. The rods, clubs, and planks of the torturers, the dislocation of bones, all were brought into use until at last on the thirteenth of the third lunar month of 1799 he died under the blows. He was seventy years old. After his death his body appeared to be bathed in extraordinary luminescence. Crowds of pagans witnessed this prodigy, and nearly fifty families were converted on this occasion.

(5) Peter Chŭng

Peter Chŭng belonged to a respectable family of Tŏk-san and before his conversion he was renowned far and wide for his violent temper and his extraordinary strength. He had the good fortune to be received into the Church and baptized by Father Chou, and thenceforward he became gentle, modest and friendly. It is believed that he spent some time in the priest's service. Later, appointed catechist in the district of Nae-p'o, he showed himself to be pious and devout, spending all his time in giving religious instruction to those who were confided to his care.

In 1798 or 1799, he was arrested and taken to the town of Tŏk-san, where he had to undergo repeated interrogation and torture; he bravely declared his faith and put his signature to his own death sentence without allowing the slightest sign of emotion to appear on his countenance. In prison he comforted and encouraged his fellow-prisoners and on the execution day, when the jailers brought him the meal customarily given to those condemned to death, he invited them to share it with him, saying: "For the last time, we must gratefully eat the food that God has created for mankind, and then we will go to Heaven together to enjoy eternal bliss." He was beheaded. It is believed that he was then about fifty or sixty years old.

(6) Francis Pang

Francis Pang was born in the district of Myŏn-ch'ŏn, and was major-domo to the provincial governor. Nothing is known of the circumstances or the date of his conversion. He was distinguished for his extraordinary fervor and his intense desire for martyrdom. In 1798 he was arrested at Hong-ju and for six months had to undergo repeated torture, the details of which have not come down to us. All that is told of him is that there were two other Christians who, like himself, had been condemned to death and that when in accordance with custom they were brought the last meal of the condemned, they burst into tears, but that Francis, his countenance radiant with joy, thanked God and the Blessed Virgin Mary, and said to his companions: "The creation, and salvation, are the benefits given by God, but such generous hospitality on the part of the magistrate: is this not also a providential gift? Why are you so sad and downcast? That is due to a temptation of the devil. If we lose this fortunate chance of winning to Heaven, what other opportunity can we hope for?" God made his words carry weight with them, and his two companions shared the meal with him in holy joy. The three were martyred in the same town of Hong-ju. It is not known whether Francis was beaten to death or strangled. It was the sixteenth of the twelfth lunar month (January, 1799).

(7) Francis Pae

Francis Pae, born at Chin-mok in the district of Tang-jin, had embraced the faith at the time when it was being preached by Lee Pyŏk.

Arrested for the first time in 1791, he had the weakness to apostatize in the presence of the judge. But very soon afterward, moved by sincere repentance, he resumed his fervent worship of God. Being obliged to leave his district he retired at first to Sŏ-san. Later, in the company of other Christians, he settled at Yang-che-ri in the district of Myŏn-ch'ŏn and it was there that, in 1798, he and his companions set up an oratory in preparation for the reception of a priest. Some time later an apostate named Cho Hwa-jin betrayed them to the magistrate and himself conducted the constables to the village. Francis Pae was arrested on the third of the tenth moon, and taken to Hong-ju. They attempted to force him to denounce the other Christians and to surrender his religious books but not even the most violent torture could drag their names from him. For several months he was repeatedly put to the question; he was then transferred to Ch'ŏng-ju, the military and judicial capital of the province, where he shared the sufferings of James Won and the other Christian prisoners. There are no details about the last months that he spent in this prison—all that is known is that he bore his tortures with heroic patience. All his flesh hung in shreds, his limbs were fractured, and his bones were laid bare. At last he died under the blows, at the age of about sixty years. A family tradition fixes the date of his martyrdom as the thirteenth of the twelfth moon of 1799.

(8) Francis Lee

Francis Lee Po-hyŏn was descended from a wealthy and respectable family of Hwang-mo-ri in the district of Tŏk-san. From childhood his strong and somewhat self-willed nature made him remarked among his companions. The death of his father, whom he lost in infancy, left him free to do as he liked, and led him to give rein to his passions, and he became so violent that nobody could control him. At the age of twenty-four, however, having been instructed in the faith by Thomas Hwang he was converted, and in a short time had succeeded so well in mastering his passions that his quiet and orderly behavior

soon became an edifying example to all.

When the persecution of the Christians began, Francis, far from being afraid, never ceased to exhort his family and his fellow-Christians in the village. He discoursed daily on the Passion of Our Lord, and urged them not to let slip this chance to confess the faith and win to Heaven.

Finally Francis was arrested and was subjected to the complete series of tortures. Being unable to get even a word of weakness from him, the magistrate presented him with the sentence, which he signed with such an air of satisfaction that everyone was struck dumb with astonishment. He was taken back to prison and on the following day the customary special meal for those condemned to death was brought to him. This he ate happily and then the jailers, having drummed him round the market place, began to beat him. These men each with a thick cloth tied in front of him like a butcher's apron, beat him till they were tired and then seeing that their victim was taking such a long time to die, turned him on his back, concentrated their blows on his private parts, and in this way on the fifteenth of the twelfth moon of 1799 put an end to his life.

Francis was then twenty-seven years of age. A few days later, his remains were recovered, and all the population of the village saw for themselves that his countenance was fresh and smiling. Several pagans, it is said, were converted at the sight.

(9) Martin In

Martin In Eun-min was a young noble who lived at Chu-rye in the district of Tŏk-san. Of a character at once firm and kind, Martin had done well in his studies, and was connected with the scholar Alexander Hwang, who taught him the faith. No sooner was he converted than he sealed up his ancestral tablets in a pot, which he threw into a pond. He then came to the capital, where he was baptized by Father James Chou. He left his eldest son named Joseph with the priest, arranged for his second son to marry into a family that enjoyed great esteem among the Christians; then, giving up his house and land he emigrated to the district of Kong-ju. His pagan relations could not understand such strange behavior, so he explained frankly to them his religious motive, without however succeeding in winning their hearts. Arrested by the constables of the Kong-ju magistracy, he went straight to the point and declared that he was a Christian who wished to give his life for God. Sent to Ch'ŏng-ju, he underwent violent tortures that rendered him incapable of walking. Sent back to the criminal court at Haemi, his home town, he had to be carried by relays of government post horses. His courage and constancy never left him for an instant, and the judge, provoked beyond endurance, condemned him, like Francis Lee, to be beaten to death. He was given the usual final repast, and then a score of constables proceeded to execute the sentence. During his suffering Martin kept on saying "Ah, yes, it is of my own free will that I give my life for God!" At last one of the executioners seizing a large rock struck it forcibly several times on Martin's chest. His lower jaw was dislocated, the ribs smashed, and the holy confessor died in this torture, on the same day as Francis Lee, at the age of sixty-three.

15. The Persecution of Sin-yu

On the seventeenth of the twelfth moon in 1800, Thomas Ch'oe P'il-kong was arrested, signaling the start of nationwide oppression of the Catholic Church, during which more than three hundred Catholics died either under sentence of death by official court ruling or under torture inflicted on them in prison.

King Chŏng-jo himself was a tender-hearted man and recoiled from taking harsh action against his Catholic subjects; moreover, he had great confidence in Ch'ae Che-kong, a member of the *Si* clique of the South Men Party which was in close relation with the Church. Ch'ae had held the post of Yŏng-eui-jŏng or the Admirable Counselor for six

years, and the king always agreed with him in deprecating the harsh measures against Catholics advocated by the rival faction. For this reason no widespread anti-Catholic measures were put into effect during his lifetime. But with the death of Ch'ae in 1799 and that of the king himself in 1800 everything changed.

King Sun-jo ascended the throne in 1800 at the age of eleven and Queen Regent Kim, his mother, administered the affairs of state from behind a screen. This touched off a series of radical changes, and as soon as the five-months' official period of mourning for the late king was over, the persecution commenced. On the seventeenth of the twelfth moon in 1800, Thomas Ch'oe P'il-kong was arrested; on the nineteenth his cousin Peter Ch'oe P'il-je suffered the same fate, and on the ninth day of the first moon in 1801, John Ch'oe Ch'ang-hyŏn was arrested. On the tenth day of the first moon of the new year the "Imperial Message Prohibiting the Evil Learning" was promulgated:

"His late Majesty always maintained that with proper elucidation of the True Learning (Confucianism) the Evil Learning would die out of itself. Now, however, we hear that the Evil Learning flourishes from the capital to the remotest provinces ···· Provincial governors and county magistrates must open the eyes of the ignorant and ensure that the followers of the Evil Learning abandon it with all sincerity, while those who do not follow it must be warned against coming under its influence. In this way the great achievements of His late Majesty in ensuring the prosperity of his people will not be imperiled. After the promulgation of this edict all who disobey will be considered as rebels, guilty of high treason. Every magistrate is to enforce the Five-Family System of Collective Responsibility and ensure that the head of each unit of five families shall immediately denounce any who persist in following the Evil Learning. All such persons are to receive condign punishment so as to root out the Evil Learning once and for all and leave no trace of it remaining. Such is our royal will: let it be made known and carried out, both in the capital and in the provinces."

This year of 1801 will be remembered as the one in which the Church in Korea came of age as a member of the family of the Catholic Church, and faith in Our Lord Jesus Christ became so deeply rooted in this land that neither time nor the devil shall destroy it.

16. The Particulars of the Sin-yu (1801) Persecution

The whirlwind swept through the country; persons were arrested on suspicion while walking along the roads, and soon the prisons at the capital and in every province were filled to overflowing. The following is a rough chronology by lunar calendar of some of the martyrdoms that ensued.

26th day, 2nd moon, 1801: Kwon Ch'ŏl-sin died under torture, and Chŭng Yak-jong, Ch'oe P'il-kong, Hong Kyo-man, Hong Nak-min, Ch'oe Ch'ang-hyŏn were beheaded outside the Small West Gate, and also beheaded was Lee Seung-hun. Chŭng Yak-jŏn was exiled to Sin-ji Island in South Province of Chŏl-la and Chŭng Yak-yong to Chang-ki district in South Province of Kyŏng-sang.

28th day: Lee Tan-won was executed.

13th day, 3rd moon: Lee Chung-pae, John Won, Im Heui-yŏng, Ch'oe Ch'ang-ju and Chŭng Chong-ho were executed in Yŏ-ju, and in Yang-keun Yu Han-suk and James Yun (whose brother Yun Yu-il died in 1795) were also beheaded. On the same day Maria Song, the wife of Prince Eun-ŏn and Maria Shin, the widow of Prince Sang-kye, were given poison by the orders of the young king.

2nd day, 4th moon: Charles Chŭng (son of Chŭng Yak-jong), Peter Ch'oe, Chŭng In-hyŏk and Lee Hap-kyu were executed, and at about the same time Barbara Sim and Hwang Il-kwang (manservant of Chŭng Yak-jong) were beheaded, the former in Kwang-ju and the latter in Hong-ju.

19th day, 4th moon: Father Chou was executed.

20th day: Kim Kŏn-sun, Kim Paek-sun and Lee Heui-yŏng were beheaded.

23rd day, 5th moon: The following were executed outside the Small West Gate:

Kang Wan-suk, Kang Kyŏng-pok, Mun Yŏng-in, Kim Yŏn-i, Han Sin-ae, Ch'oe In-ch'ŏl, Lee Hyŏn, Hong Chŏng-ho and Kim Hyŏn-u.

25th day: Chŭng Sun-mae and Yun Chŏm-hye were executed, the former in Yŏ-ju and the latter in Yang-keun.

27th day: Ko Kwang-sŏng, in P'yŏng-san, and Lee Kuk-seung, in Kong-ju.

17th day, 7th moon: Kim Kwang-ok and Kim Chŏng-teuk were beheaded in Ye-san.

18th day: Han Ch'ŏng-hyŏn, in Kim-je; Kim Chŏng-ae, in Chŏn-ju; Ch'oe Yŏ-kyŏm, in Mu-jang.

27th day, 8th moon: Hong P'il-ju and Kim Chong-jŏ were executed.

17th day, 9th moon: Ryu Hang-kŏm and his brother Ryu Kwan-kŏm were beheaded in Chŏn-ju, and also beheaded were Yun Chi-hŏn and Lee U-jip.

22nd day, 12th moon: Kim Sa-jip died under torture in Ch'ŏng-ju.

26th day: Lee Kyŏng-to

27th day: Leo Hong (son of Hong Kyo-man) in P'o-ch'ŏn, and on the same day Kwon Sang-mun in Yang-keun; Lee Kye-yŏn, Lee Po-ch'un and his son Lee Sŏk-jong were executed in Ch'ung-ju.

28th day: Lugartha Lee, Matthew Ryu, Lee's mother-in-law and aunt-in-law, in Chŏn-ju, and on the same day U Tŏk-un were executed in Kwang-ju.

Eleventh moon, 5th day: Hwang Sa-yŏng, the writer of the *Hwang Sa-yŏng Silk Letter* who had been arrested earlier and sentenced to death, was executed together with Ok Ch'ŏn-heui and Hyŭn Kye-heum.

Hwang Sim who was to have delivered the letter was put to death at Seoul prior to the execution of Hwang Sa-yŏng.

The persecutors, who had now abandoned themselves to their lust for blood, announced publicly that the families of the martyrs and exiles should also be sentenced to death on account of the *Hwang Sa-yŏng Silk Letter* incident. This was too much, however, for the young King Sun-jo. Invoking the royal prerogative with a courage beyond his years, he put an end to their plan to annihilate the Catholics. Queen Regent Kim was forced against her will to rescind the order for the searching-out of further Catholics, but in revenge issued the so-called *"Imperial Edict Calling for Suppression of the Heretical Doctrine."* This edict served as the legal basis for persecution of Catholics for the ensuing eighty years.

The imperial edict was circulated to every part of the country, with a proviso that Catholics who had already been sentenced to death should be executed before the end of the year, and that all further arrests of Catholics were forbidden. In accordance with this proviso the death sentence was carried out on several occasions toward the end of the twelfth moon.

17. Father Chou Wen-mo's Martyrdom

As recounted above Father Chou was once faced with a crisis when the Judas-like Han Yŏng-ik informed the authorities of his activities. Thanks, however, to Columba Kang Wan-suk, who concealed him in her house, he was able to carry on his missionary work for several years. The time came for him to be harassed again: this time by one Kim Yŏ-sam.

Of Kim Yŏ-sam, Hwang Sa-yŏng wrote the following paragraphs in his Silk Letter:

"Kim Yŏ-sam is a native of Ch'ung-ch'ŏng Province. After being baptized, he and his two brothers moved to Seoul to take refuge from persecution. Recently he apostatized and joined a gang of villains, ignoring his brothers' dissuasions. As a result Lee An-jŏng, a wealthy Catholic of Seoul, discontinued his financial support of the impoverished Kim, who began to nurse a grudge.

This led him to lay information against Father Chou with the police. Fortunately a Catholic discovered this in time and was able to warn Columba Kang Wan-suk, with whom he had been staying, and to enable him to escape. After that Kim went on associating with the gangsters and planning further mischief.

Another Catholic seeing danger ahead called on Columba Kang Wan-suk and asked her to introduce him to Father Chou. He had found two places in the country which would be safe to hide in during the coming trouble. Columba, however, told him that the priest had already departed, so the Catholic, six days later, also left with his family for a remote district.

Soon afterward Chŭng Yak-jong was arrested (on the eleventh of the second moon in 1801) and subjected to torture, but refused to disclose where the priest was staying. On the twenty-fourth of the same month Columba Kang and her son Hong P'il-ju were arrested and ordered to reveal the priest's whereabouts. They steadfastly refused, so Columba's maidservant was arrested and severely beaten also. The maid thereupon told what she knew, and when Columba was confronted with the maid's testimony she admitted that she had indeed sheltered the priest in the past, but was now no longer in touch with him and did not know where he was staying. A description of the priest was then circulated throughout the country and a reward offered for his capture.

Father Chou at this point seems to have considered that it was on account of his presence in Korea that the Korean Catholics were being subjected to so much ill-treatment, and that he had better return to China. With much skill and at the risk of his life he evaded the border guards that were on the lookout for him, and arrived safely at the border. Only one step from the safety of his native land, he experienced a revulsion of feeling at the thought of abandoning his flock, and went straight back to Seoul. Here he saw how the persecution was daily growing in ferocity, and resolved to give himself up to the authorities in the hope of mitigating their harsh treatment of his flock. On the sixteenth of the third lunar month he presented himself at the High Court of Justice and declared,

"I am a Catholic believer. I have heard of the government's ban on the Catholic religion, and of the killing of many innocent people, and I wish to join the ranks of death." As he was a Chinese subject there was a delay of a month in deciding his case, but he was finally sentenced to be decapitated, his head to be exposed to the public.

On the nineteenth of the fourth moon (May 31) Father Chou's execution took place at Sae-nam-t'ŏ: he was first made to read aloud the lengthy accusations against him, then each ear was pierced with an arrow, and he was beheaded. It was four o'clock in the afternoon of Trinity Sunday, and he was forty-eight years of age. As the executioner prepared to carry out the sentence the sky suddenly darkened, there was a sudden strong wind, and the sound of thunder was heard, but as soon as his head had fallen to the sword the clouds dispersed and a bright rainbow appeared high in the sky. It was as though the sky reflected the attitude of the Church, which both mourns and rejoices at the death of a martyr.

The body of the martyr was held in custody for five days, but it has not been possible to trace what happened to it afterward. Father James Chou Wen-mo, Korea's first priest, however, will remain in the hearts of Korean Catholics for ever.

18. The Silk Letter of Hwang Sa-yŏng

Hwang Sa-yŏng, a native of Ch'ang-won in Kyŏng-sang Province, was a son-in-law of Chŭng Yak-hyŏn and had been baptized by Father Chou with the name of Alexander. From childhood he had displayed remarkable intelligence, and had astonished the civil service examiners by obtaining the degree of *Chin-sa* at the age of seventeen.

On the outbreak of the persecution of 1801 he took refuge in an abandoned kiln in the mountains of Che-ch'ŏn. Aware that he was one of the leading figures in the Church, the Queen Regent issued a special proclamation for his arrest.

After consultation with Thomas Hwang Sim at their hideout in Che-ch'ŏn, he wrote to the Bishop of Peking on the twenty-second day of the ninth moon of 1801 (October 29), reporting the distressing circumstances of the Korean Church and appealing for help. The letter was written on a silk scroll 62cm long and 38cm wide, and contained thirteen thousand Chinese ideograms. The contents of the letter were:

(1) The present strength of the Church—the activities of Father Chou—a short biography of each of the martyrs.

(2) An account of the arrest of Father Chou and his martyrdom.

(3) Proposals to the Church at Peking, requesting definite measures to assist the missionary work during the critical domestic situation.

This letter was entrusted to Ok Ch'ŏn-heui for transmission to Peking, but he was caught on the twentieth of the ninth moon. The arrest of Hwang Sim followed on the twenty-sixth of the ninth moon, and that of Hwang Sa-yŏng himself three days later, and the letter was seized. Hwang Sa-yŏng was found guilty of high treason and beheaded, his body dismembered, his parents, wife and children exiled, and his estate and property confiscated.

The Silk Letter was preserved by the High Court of Justice for a hundred years, until at the time of the political reforms of 1894 it was discovered by Bishop Mutel who presented it to H.H. Pope Pius XI (reigned 1922-1939) on the occasion of the Beatification of the Seventy-nine Korean Martyrs at Rome on July 5, 1925.

19. Martyrs in 1801

Some of the most famous martyrs who died in the 1801 persecution are listed below. The Church records their merit with rejoicing and their eternal glory will always be remembered:

(1) Thomas Ch'oe P'il-kong

Born to a family of the middle-class, he

was unfortunately tricked into a temporary apostasy during the oppression of 1791.

He won the favor of King Chŏng-jo and held a government post. Summoned by the Ministry of Justice in August 1799 to clarify his attitude, he took this as a good opportunity to redeem his mistake. He made a firm confession of his faith and expounded the Catholic doctrine so clearly that all who heard him were impressed. Sentence of death was passed but King Chŏng-jo would not sanction it, and ordered his release. On the seventeenth of the twelfth moon of 1800 he was re-arrested, and became the first of the Catholics to be arrested during that year. He underwent severe torture but remained steadfast in the faith until the twenty-sixth of the second moon of 1801, when he, together with Chŭng Yak-jong and Ch'oe Ch'ang-hyŏn, was beheaded outside the Small West Gate. He was fifty-six years old. Two and a half months of severe torture had deprived the elderly man of his faculties, but he recovered full consciousness at the execution ground and underwent capital punishment in a serene and joyful mood. At the first stroke the executioner failed to sever the head, and the martyr, putting his hand to the wound and then regarding his blood-stained palm, exclaimed, "Oh! Precious blood!" It was indeed precious blood, and the second stroke of the executioner opened the gates of Heaven to him.

(2) Martin Lee Chung-pae

Born to a *yang-pan* (noble) family in Yŏ-ju he was converted to Catholicism through the influence of Kim Kŏn-sun. On Easter Day, 1800 he went for a picnic in the country with his fellow-believers, to celebrate the occasion, and they spent the day singing the Regina Caeli in chorus:

> *Regina caeli, laetare, alleluia!*
> *Quia quem meruisti portare, alleluia!*
> *Resurrexit sicut dixit, alleluia!*
> *Ora pro nobis Deum, alleluia!*
> *Gaude et laetare, Virgo Maria, alleluia!*
> *Quia surrexit Dominus vere, alleluia!*

(Joy to thee, O Queen of Heaven, alleluia;

For He whom thou wast meet to bear, alleluia;
As He promised, hath arisen, alleluia;
Pour for us to Him thy prayer, alleluia;
Rejoice and be glad, O Virgin Mary, alleluia;
For the Lord hath risen indeed, alleluia.)

This reached the ears of the authorities and all eleven were arrested. Undergoing torture in prison, Lee encouraged his weaker brethren with his ardent faith. With fiery zeal he helped his comrade, John Won, as the latter began to waver in his faith under the entreaties of his pagan family. Peter Cho also gained from Lee the strength to conquer the temptation to apostatize, and died a martyr. Lee had studied medicine, and whenever his fellow-prisoners or others in the prison asked for help in their sickness he would first pray and then administer herbal medicine or acupuncture, by way of treatment. In addition to this, he employed his time in prison in transcribing Catholic books, in prayer, and in preaching, and by so doing was able to convert one of the jailors.

On the thirteenth of the third moon, 1801, in the fiftieth year of his age, he was beheaded, outside the town of Yŏ-ju, together with Im Heui-yŏng and John Won.

(3) Ambrose Kwon Ch'ŏl-sin

He was a son of Kwon Heum, a *yang-pan* and provincial governor, and lived in Yang-keun, Kyŏng-ki Province. All the members of his family were converted to Catholicism. His brother, Francis-Xavier Kwon Il-sin, had been martyred in 1791. On first hearing of the Christian doctrine he thought it incredible, but resolved to study it from all aspects with prudence and wisdom. Once convinced of its truth he never slackened. The authority of his character and example brought many pagans to believe in the Gospel, though he never preached directly to the people, nor did he take part in the affairs of believers, but only devoted himself to study and worship. Abuse and calumny, whether in public or private, left him unmoved. Hearing that certain Catholics had defected under torture, he sighed, "Poor mortals! They have thrown away the merits they had acquired, and have forfeited the glorious crown of martyrdom." Arrested on the eleventh of the second moon of 1801, he died under torture on the twenty-sixth before sentence was passed upon him. He was sixty-six years old. His calmness and self-possession under torture won him the admiration of all.

(4) Augustine Chŭng Yak-jong

A son of the magistrate Chŭng Chae-won and elder of Chŭng Yak-yong and a firm believer, Augustine Chŭng served as chairman of Myŏng-to-hoe. To escape the attacks of the anti-Catholic faction he left Yang-keun for the capital in the fifth moon of 1800. He was the author of *Chu-kyo-yo-ji* (Main Tenets of Catholicism) in two volumes. This was written in the simplified *Ŏn-mun* script now known as *Han-keul* (Korean letters) in order to make it intelligible to the large proportion of the population unable to read *Han-mun*, the traditional Chinese ideographic script. This was the first Catholic book to be published in *Han-keul*. Foreseeing that the tide of Catholic persecution would rise after the death of King Chŏng-jo he packed his crucifix, Catholic manuals, and letters from the Chinese priest (Father Chou) in a wicker trunk, which he left with a friend for safe custody. This friend, however, became frightened, and decided to send it back secretly to its owner. On its way to Chŭng, it was intercepted by police, whose discovery of it led to Chŭng's arrest on the eleventh of the second lunar month, 1801, and his imprisonment at the High Court of Justice. The judge tried his best to elicit from Chŭng the whereabouts of Father Chou, but in vain. He even sent emissaries to Chŭng's family offering to release their father in exchange for information enabling them to find the priest. They answered that they knew nothing. The judge then characterized Chŭng as "most diabolic of the archtraitors," and on the twenty-sixth of the same month had him beheaded outside the Small West Gate. On his way to the execution ground he spread the faith among the bystanders, saying to them:

"It is only right and proper for a man to give his life for God, for 'He so loved mankind that He gave up His only begotten Son, so that those who believe in Him may not perish, but have eternal life.'① Our tears will turn to joy at the day of judgment." On arriving at the execution ground he addressed the crowd, saying:

"Dear people, have no fear. This is the consummation of my life's work. Cast away fear—follow my example—hold fast to the truth!"

At the first stroke of the executioner's sword his neck was half severed, but he rose to his feet and, shedding his holy blood in copious streams, made the sign of the cross. He was forty-two years old.

(5) John Ch'oe Ch'ang-hyŏn

He was a relative of Ch'oe In-kil, the martyr of 1795. Converted soon after the introduction of Catholicism into Korea, he devoted himself to missionary work, and served for twenty years as the chief catechist. He was by nature grave, just and diligent, and was able to draw many converts to him by his moral influence and to win their confidence. On the ninth of the first moon, 1801, the traitor Kim Yŏ-sam led a posse of constables to his house, and he was arrested while lying sick in bed. At his first interrogation he suffered thirteen strokes of the club and lost consciousness. In answer to the charges against him he invariably stood erect and recited the Ten Commandments in a dignified manner, after which he would explain the futility of ancestor-worship. He was beheaded with his fellow Catholics outside the Small West Gate on the twenty-sixth of the following month. He was forty-three years old.

---

① St. John 3:16

(6) Louis-Gonzaga Lee Tan-won

Known as "the Apostle of Nae-p'o", he distinguished himself in propagating the Gospel in Ch'ung-ch'ŏng Province. It helps us to understand the greatness of his achievement when we realize the fact that many of the Catholics of today are the descendants of those who were converted to Catholicism by his preaching. Although he deserted the Church for a brief period during the persecution of 1791, he soon repented bitterly and under the leadership of Father Chou, made a strenuous effort to spread the Gospel. Arrested again at the close of 1795, he was held prisoner in his native town of Ch'ŏn-an for six years, during which he was exposed to tribulation and temptation. Resolved never to repeat his past mistake, he steadfastly held to his faith. On the outbreak of the 1801 persecution he was transferred to the High Court of Justice with Chŭng Yak-jong and Ch'oe Ch'ang-hyŏn and sentenced to death. He was sent back to Kong-ju, his former missionary field, and executed on the twenty-eighth of the second moon. It took six blows of the executioner's sword to behead him. Eyewitnesses have related that when his relatives came to take away his body, they found the head united to the trunk, with only a thin white line round the neck where it had been cut off. He was over fifty years of age at his death.

The first two Catholic priests of Korean nationality were descended from Louis-Gonzaga Lee Tan-won, namely Blessed Andrew Kim Tae-kŏn, a grandson of his niece, and Father Thomas Ch'oe Yang-ŏp, a grandson of his sister's son.

(7) Francis-Xavier Hong Kyo-man

Hong Kyo-man was Kwon Ch'ŏl-sin's maternal uncle, and lived in P'o-ch'ŏn, Kyŏng-ki Province.

Having passed the examinaticn for *Chin-sa* at an early age, he abandoned official life, entered the Church, and devoted his life to preaching the Gospel. His daughter was married to a son of Chŭng Yak-jŏn and

this drew on him the hostility of the enemies of religion: he was beheaded at the age of sixty-four. The record of his trial contains the following account of his last moment:

"The prisoner has the audacity to declare that to die for the Catholic faith will be a joyful thing for him. He is more obstinate than a lump of stone or a log of wood. No conceivable punishment could be too severe for him."

(8) Luke Hong Nak-min

Hong Nak-min had held the position of *Chŏng-ŏn* or senior adviser to the Court of Remonstrance, but was converted to Catholicism under the influence of Chŭng Yak-yong and Lee Seung-hun. Yielding to the persuasion and veiled threats of King Chŏng-jo he made a public declaration of apostasy, but continued to practice his religion in secret, and, in obedience to the instructions of the Bishop of Peking, made no obeisance before his mother's ancestral tablet at her funeral. He was arrested during the persecution of 1801 and subjected to severe torture, but said afterward, while stanching the blood that flowed from his wounds, that he felt refreshed by it. On his way to execution he declared, from the cart in which he was being carried, that it was a just punishment for his apostasy, and appeared to be in ecstasy. He was beheaded outside the Small West Gate, at the age of fifty-one.

(9) Peter Ch'oe P'il-je

A cousin of Ch'oe P'il-kong, he was born to a poor family which his aged father, a medicine dealer, could hardly manage to support. Father Chou always spoke highly of his sincere, pious and gentle nature. His arrest brought his father to bed with serious illness caused by worry and anxiety, as a result of which his father already dying embraced the faith and was baptized just before he breathed his last. The son was granted permission to leave the prison on parole in order to attend his father's funeral, and was secretly advised by a friendly jailor to use the opportunity to make good his escape. Nevertheless he returned to the prison and was beheaded at the age of thirty-two.

(10) Josaphat Kim Kŏn-sun

He was a descendant of Kim Sang-hŏn, the famous minister of state who won distinction during the Manchu invasion of 1637, during the last years of the Ming Dynasty. This was during the reign of King In-jo (reigned 1623-1649). His home was in Yŏ-ju in the Province of Kyŏng-ki.

During his childhood he was fond of reading *Chi Jen Shih Pien* (1608, by Fr. Matteo Ricci, with preface by Li Chih-tsao, d. 1630) or Ten Ways of Practicing Catholic Life, 'an extraordinary man is extraordinary to other men but is ordinary to God.' As a youth he wrote *The Discourse on Heaven and Hell*. Hearing of his wisdom Father Chou wrote a letter to him, advising him to accept the Catholic faith. Surprised and delighted to receive the missionary's encouragement, he followed the advice and received Baptism at the age of twenty-two. His father and brothers tried every means to dissuade him, and for three or four years his family life was an ordeal of persecution. When this became known to the opposition faction they redoubled their efforts to harass him, and eventually persuaded his family council to strike out his name from the genealogical register.

This meant his exclusion from the rites in honor of his distinguished ancestor Kim Sang-hŏn and finally led to his arrest and imprisonment. He was condemned to death, and on the twentieth of the fourth lunar month of 1801 was beheaded at the execution ground outside the Small West Gate. On his way there he addressed the crowd, saying:

"High official rank and earthly honors are worthless and I care nothing for them. Only God is really good and true, and I regard it as the supreme honor to die for Him. Fellow-countrymen! Think over my words and follow my example." He gave his life for God at the age of twenty-six.

(11) Kim Paek-sun

Remotely related to Kim Kŏn-sun, he was in youth a brilliant scholar, ambitious for position and fame, and at times he slandered the Catholic Church. On getting to know some of the Catholics, however, after a series of hot debates with them lasting for several years, he became firmly convinced of the truth of the doctrine and was received into the Church. He encouraged his mother in her faith and she too was converted. His wife, on the other hand, was ambitious for her husband's worldly success, and heaped continual insults upon him, and his maternal uncle exerted every effort to persuade him to abandon his faith. He staunchly defended his position and declared, "I would far sooner break with my uncle than with God, for since I came to know Him I have enjoyed a sense of peace and security that is as unshakable as a mountain."

His conversion came too late for him to receive Baptism, for he was arrested soon afterward, and was beheaded together with Josaphat Kim. The blood that he shed in witness of his deep penitence and zealous piety was enough to baptize him and to win him the glory of martyrdom.

(12) Luke Lee Heui-yŏng

A close friend of Kim Kŏn-sun, he shared with him the glory of crowning his declaration of faith with martyrdom. He lived for some time at Yŏ-ju as a Catholic, later moving to Seoul. An artist by profession, he was able to make a valuable contribution to missionary work by his paintings of sacred subjects. These pictures led to his arrest, and he was beheaded with Kim Paek-sun on the same day.

(13) Philip Hong P'il-ju

Philip was the stepson of the first woman catechist in Korea, Columba Kang Wan-suk, who was married to Hong Chi-yŏng as his second wife. He had a forthright and tender nature, and following his stepmother's example became a convert to Catholicism. At first somewhat lukewarm in his faith, under Father Chou's pastoral care he became a devoted believer and regularly served at Mass for him. Arrested with his stepmother on the twenty-fourth of the second moon of 1801, he was imprisoned separately from her, and the cruel and harsh torture that he underwent almost shattered his faith. Once when he had been dragged before the court in a state of physical exhaustion, his stepmother came to him with words of encouragement, saying:

"Our Lord Jesus Christ is looking down at you from on high: why are you so blind as to run the risk of losing your soul? Stir up your courage! Think of your happiness and eternal joy in Heaven!" Regaining his fortitude, he was beheaded on the twenty-seventh of the eighth moon. He was twenty-eight years old.

(14) Peter Cho Yong-sam

Peter Cho was the son of a destitute family of Yang-keun. He spent his life helping his widowed father to till the soil, and was unable to take a wife until he was thirty years old. Under the influence of Chŭng Yak-jong he was converted to Catholicism and began to lead a devout Christian life. In the fourth moon of 1800 he and his father were arrested at a village near Yŏ-ju where Lee Chung-pae was living. While he was under torture he was told that unless he apostatized his father would be killed. The judge then proceeded to inflict merciless beatings on his father in his presence. Overcome by filial love he could not but obey the judge. Lee Chung-pae and other Catholics imprisoned with him rebuked him for this weakness, and exhorted him to hold fast to the faith. This aroused the anger of the judge who subjected him to torture of redoubled intensity. Peter then resolutely declared his faith, saying, "There cannot be two gods in Heaven, nor two minds in man." He was baptized in prison, and on the fourteenth day of the second moon of 1801, he died after eleven months of torture.

(15) Thomas Cho

Thomas Cho was a native of Yang-keun and the faithful son of Justin Cho Tong-sŏm.

When his father was arrested during the persecution of 1801 and imprisoned in a jail some three miles distant from his home, Thomas brought him food almost every day. When his father was removed to the prison in Seoul, Thomas accompanied him and attended on him day and night, and on his father's subsequent exile to Mu-san in Ham-kyŏng Province, Thomas escorted him thither and remained with him throughout the long and critical illness that resulted from the torture and the fatigue of the long journey, caring for him so assiduously that he was able to bring about his recovery. His filial piety aroused the admiration of the pagans of the district, who said they had never before seen such a devoted and dutiful son. The magistrate of Yang-keun, who had taken a personal animosity to Justin, seemed to resent the fact that he was not to execute sentence of death on him. He vented his spite on the son, and sent constables to Mu-san to arrest him. Father and son were both in fear of further danger, but when Justin asked his son, "Thomas, what do you plan to do?" Thomas answered, "I have no other plan than to follow Our Lord Jesus Christ along the Way of the Cross."

He was taken to Yang-keun and subjected to savage and inhuman torture. Two months of this, though it could not break his spirit, was too much for his body to bear, and he died in prison early in the tenth moon.

(16) Columba Kang Wan-suk

Upon her arrest the judge ordered the application of the *Chu-ri*, an instrument of torture described by Father Dallet as follows:

"**3. Dislocation and bending of the bones.** There are three degrees: the *Ka-wi-chu-ri* in which the prisoner's legs are tied together tightly at the knees and the big toe of each foot; into the space between them two wooden tommy bars are inserted, and these are turned in opposite directions until the bones become curved in an arc or bow, after which they are slowly allowed to return to their natural position. The *Chul-chu-ri* differs from the preceding in that the big toes of each foot are first tied together, and then a thick piece of wood is placed between the legs, after which two men pull in opposite directions on cords attached to each knee, until the knees are brought into contact with each other. The *P'al-chu-ri* is the dislocation of the arms. They are tied together behind the back above the elbows, after which two large wooden bars are used as levers to bring the shoulders together. The executioner then unties the arms, and placing one foot on the prisoner's chest, draws them toward himself in order to reset them in their place. If the executioner is an expert he is able to do this without breaking the bones, but a novice will break them at the first attempt, and the marrow will run out with the blood."[1]

Though this torture was inflicted on Columba no fewer than six times in an attempt to make her reveal the whereabouts of Father Chou she did not yield. With her four fellow-prisoners she prayed day and night, and devoted herself to the spiritual life of a *chŏng-pae* (ever-maiden spouse). After undergoing three months of agony in the prison they were taken to the execution ground outside the Small West Gate on the twenty-third of the fifth moon. On the way to the site, they comforted one another, and with an expression of holy joy on their faces they proclaimed the glory of God. Columba requested the executioner, in view of the fact that the five were all women, not to carry out the official regulation that condemned prisoners must be stripped to the waist when undergoing capital punishment. The executioner granted her request and Columba, making the sign of the cross, was the first to kneel and be beheaded. She was forty-one years old. Her four companions in martyrdom were:

Susanna Kang Kyŏng-pok, Kim Yŏn-i,

Han Sin-ae, and Bibiana Mun Yŏng-in.

All of them were converted to Catholicism under the influence of Columba Kang, and were baptized by Father Chou. They rendered distinguished service in missionary work; Susanna and Bibiana had previously been court ladies, and in co-operation with Father Chou were able to keep in touch with Catholic believers who were living in hiding during the persecution. They were in charge of a concealed store of crucifixes, rosaries, and other sacred objects.

(17) Bibiana Mun Yŏng-in

Born to a middle-class family, Bibiana Mun entered the royal palace service at the age of seven and became a court lady at the age of fifteen. One day she collapsed at the palace and became seriously ill. She was sent home to her family to receive medical treatment, and her mother, a devout Catholic, had her instructed in the faith and baptized. Mysteriously enough, the next day found her completely recovered in health. On account of her attractive looks and talent, the palace sent a doctor to visit her every day to provide her with medical treatment, but whenever he stepped inside her house she would become seriously ill and lose consciousness, so that she was eventually freed from further service in the palace and her name was struck out from the court register. Once free of obligation to the court she devoted herself to a religious life in the service of Father Chou. Not long afterward constables, conducting a domiciliary search at her house, discovered that she was now a Catholic, and arrested her. She had now reached the age of twenty-six. Strenuous efforts were made by officials of the court to persuade her to abandon her faith, but without result. She was thereupon condemned to death, and on her way to the execution ground, as the constables were attempting to disperse the large crowd of curious onlookers, she said:

"Let them be: people like to watch the butchers slaughter their livestock; so why

---

[1] Ch. Dallet, *Histoire de l'Église de Corée*, Paris, 1874, Introduction, Vol. 1, p. LXVI.

shouldn't they be allowed to see the killing of human beings?" She then stretched out her neck to the executioner's sword, and it is said that as her head was struck off, the officials were frightened to see that the blood which gushed out was as white as milk.

(18) Barbara Chŭng Sun-mae

Among those sentenced to death at the same time as Columba Kang, many were sent home to their native place for execution. Of such women the most famous are two virgins: Barbara Chŭng Sun-mae and Agatha Yun Chŏm-hye.

Barbara was an elder sister of Chŭng Kwang-su, and was born at Yŏ-ju. She told Father Chou that she had lived a virgin, and that in order to keep her virginity she used to say that she had already been married to a man named Hŭh. After being baptized by the priest she became a useful assistant to him and became known for her good works Sentenced to death in Seoul, she was sent to her native town of Yŏ-ju for execution, as a warning to the people of that place, and was beheaded on the twenty-fifth day of the fifth moon.

(19) Agatha Yun Chŏm-hye

A cousin of Yun Yu-il, Agatha was born to a *yang-pan* or noble family, as an illegitimate child. After learning the Catholic doctrine she made a vow of chastity and resolved to live a celibate life. Fearing that her family would oppose her plan she disguised herself as a young man and took refuge in her uncle's house. On moving to Seoul with her mother in 1795 she had to go into hiding without receiving Baptism, for the persecution began in that year. Her mother's death followed soon afterward, and she then went to live with Columba Kang, taking charge of the instruction of the women believers who were staying at Kang's. Observing the days of fasting and abstinence and practicing self-denial and constant prayer and meditation, she grew in moral stature and grace until, after many days of mourning for

her mother, who died without receiving the Sacrament, she had a vision in which she saw her mother in the company of the Blessed Virgin.

Early in the second moon of 1801 she was arrested with Columba Kang, and sentenced to death with her on the same day. Taken to her native town of Yang-keun, she was beheaded on the twenty-fifth day of the fifth moon, the expression on her face showing clearly her peaceful state of mind.

(20) Augustine Ryu Hang-kŏm

The Catholic Church in Chŏl-la Province had been steadily growing during the ten years that had elapsed since the Chin-san incident in 1791. Ryu Hang-kŏm, a wealthy man, was a prominent figure among the Catholics of the district. His family consisted of his aged mother, his wife, and six children. All of them were pious Catholics and his was an exemplary Christian family, so it was only natural that the celibate couple Lugartha Lee and Ryu Chong-sŏn should live together with them, fulfilling their vow to imitate the example of Saint Joseph and the Blessed Virgin Mary.

When the new wave of persecution swept across the Ho-nam district, Ryu Hang-kŏm was the first to be arrested. Together with his brother Ryu Kwan-kŏm, his relative Lee U-jip and Yun Chi-hŏn, brother of Korea's first martyr Yun Chi-ch'ung, he was taken to Seoul, where they all underwent harsh torture for a period of four months. The High Court of Justice finally pronounced them guilty of treason and sentenced them to death. A few days afterward they were returned to Chŏl-la Province where they were executed and their bodies dismembered in public, before a large crowd of spectators. Augustine's house and properties were confiscated. He was forty-six years old.

(21) Lugartha Lee Yu-hye and John Ryu Chong-sŏn

Lugartha was the daughter of Lee Yun, the eleventh-generation descendant of King T'aejong (the third king of Yi Dynasty 1401-1418). Her father died during her infancy, and she was brought up by her mother (née Kwon), who was a devout Catholic. Lugartha, in addition to her strong will, was endowed with exceeding talent and beauty. Since childhood she had cherished under her mother's influence a firm faith in her religion. When Father Chou came to Seoul she was fourteen years old, and she made special efforts to prepare herself to receive the Sacrament, withdrawing to her room for four days of prayer and meditation. She then made her vow to maintain perpetual virginity so as to be worthy of becoming the pure spouse of God. It was not possible for her to obtain permission to live as a single woman in the society of that time, and the thought of being compelled to marry and to break her vow caused her great distress until she learnt that John Ryu Chong-sŏn, the eldest son of the wealthy Catholic Augustine Ryu Hang-kŏm of Chŏn-ju, had made a similar vow of celibacy. Through Father Chou's good offices they were united in holy matrimony with the mutual agreement to respect the vow which each had made. Throughout their married life they overcame all temptation to break the vow and lived together like brother and sister, while at the same time outwardly conforming to the social custom which forbade a woman to remain unmarried. Thus they emulated the holy example of Saint Joseph and the Blessed Virgin Mary.

On the outbreak of the 1801 persecution John Ryu Chong-sŏn was executed together with his brother John Ryu Mun-ch'ŏl on the ninth day of the tenth moon. Lugartha and the three members of her family were also arrested and sentenced to exile, but on their way to their place of exile they were suddenly re-arrested and sentenced to death. Prior to their execution they underwent a form of torture apparently analogous to the Scottish 'boots' (OED s.v. sb. 3, 3) mentioned by Sir Walter Scott, whereby the bones of the feet were shattered.

On the twenty-eighth day of the twelfth moon (January 31, 1802) the death sentences pronounced upon her entire family were executed in Chŏn-ju. Matthew, her husband's cousin aged seventeen or eighteen years, preached to the bystanders on his way to the execution ground, and the twenty-year-old Lugartha Lee spoke words of encouragement to her grief-stricken mother-in-law and aunt-in-law and helped them open the gates to eternal bliss in Heaven. At the execution ground one of the executioners tried to strip them of their garments, but Lugartha dissuaded him and put off the upper garment by herself. She refused to have her hands tied, and was the first of her family to offer her outstretched neck to the executioner's sword.

Thus it was that she won the crown of a virgin martyr, followed by three members of her family who shared the glory of martyrdom with her.

Let us now introduce Lugartha's letter written in prison;

Letter of Lugartha

My dear sisters:

I pick up my pen but cannot find words to express what I want to say. Is my poor brother dead or alive? I received indirect news during the first few days of the ninth lunar month, but since then, being a prisoner myself, I have been sitting here unable to communicate with anybody. It almost breaks my heart to think of my brother. If sentence has been passed on him, all must be over by now, but before his death he cannot enter into possession of supreme happiness. And yet, what a situation for the whole family! How can mother and sister-in-law bear it? I should think they can hardly have a single heartbeat left. When I think of that, there is nothing but anxiety and worry; what words can tell my feelings? How could you bear all the distress of his death? And then, if all is not yet over, how can Charles bear to stay in that cold prison cell? Whether he is alive or dead, Mother cannot but remain in extreme anguish.

As for me, my sins are so heavy and the outlook is so dark that I don't know how to write what I feel, and cannot find anything to say. Here I am on the brink of death, and I cannot express myself, yet I dearly wish to say a few words to you about what has happened, and to make my farewell to this world for ever. This year, when I was already suffering extreme agony on account of all these irremediable calamities, I had to bear the further pain of being separated from my family. Since then no further desire to live remains with me, and I think only of giving my life to God when the time comes. I have firmly resolved to do this, and the more I think of it the more I try to become worthy of it.

Suddenly, when I least expected them, a large number of petty bailiffs and catchpolls came in and took me prisoner: just as I was thinking that I was without the opportunity everything fell out as I wished—thanks to Almighty God for His benefits! I was joyful and contented, but at the same time preoccupied and troubled. The catchpolls seized me; screams loud enough to shake the sky could be heard on every side; I was forced to part forever from Mother, and from my mother-in-law, my brothers and sisters, my neighbors, and my homeland. Natural affection being still alive in me it was hard to say a last farewell to them, and my eyes filled with tears; then, coming to myself, one sole desire remained, that I might make a good end to my life.

First of all I was imprisoned in a place called Su-keup-ch'ŏng where the humblest woman slaves live. Then, within an hour, I was carried off to another prison, where I found my mother-in-law, my aunt, and two of my brothers-in-law. As we regarded each other without a word our tears fell. Little by little the night came on: it was the fifteenth of the ninth lunar month and the moon was full, shining brightly in the calm clear sky: we could still see one another by the light that shone in through the window, and read on our faces what we were thinking and feeling. Whether seated or lying down all that we silently prayed for was the grace of martyrdom. Soon our hearts overflowed, and we began to speak in turn, and all five of us, of one mind, made a vow to be martyrs for God, which we swore to fulfil with resolution strong as steel and stone. This mutual vow was proof of our unanimity and close affection, and, of course, all regrets were forgotten. The further one advances on the road the more are the benefits and graces poured down by God; the spiritual joy increases in the soul, we become indifferent to all worldly affairs and our mind is in perfect peace.

Nevertheless my thoughts and feelings kept returning continually to John, my husband, shut up in another prison in the same town. How could I forget him, even for a moment? Before leaving the house, I had written to him, "What happiness if we could die together on the same day!" but the time was not right, and I put off sending the letter to him, and now that we are held incommunicado it is impossible. In spite of this it is my constant silent prayer that we may be able to die together, on the same day, as martyrs for God. Who could have guessed the adorable plans of our divine and sovereign Master? On the ninth day of the tenth moon, they carried off my brother-in-law, John, with what intention we know not. "Where is he going, then?," I asked. "It's the magistrate's order," replied the jailor. I felt as if cut in two, or stabbed with a thousand daggers. They took him away. "God's will be done," I said to him, "Go, and be with Him; do not forget us." Then I earnestly entreated him to tell John that my one desire was to die together with him, on the same day. I repeated this to him three or four times, and then, letting go of his hand, I returned.

There were four of us left, all deeply disturbed, with no other recourse but the Lord. Before a quarter of an hour had passed the news of their death came. The blow to my natural affection was but of secondary rank, for the happiness of John filled me with joy. I felt, nevertheless, some anxiety in the depths of my soul. Oh, God, what has happened? I asked myself; am I too to undergo a death as sudden as this? Ten thousand swords seemed to rend my heart, and I knew not where to turn my thoughts. About an hour passed before calm returned. "May not even this kind of death be a grace and favor from God? After all he was not without merits; could God, so good and so merciful, have rejected him?" My heart became less troubled, but my thoughts kept returning to him. I asked one of our relatives, who answered, "Rest assured, he had already made his firm resolution." At last a letter came; it said: "A letter was found in John's pocket, addressed to his sister" (that is how he always regarded me.) This letter said: "I exhort, encourage and console you: we shall meet again in Heaven." Only then was my heart completely at rest. Indeed, when I look back at his life, there is nothing to regret: he had renounced the world and could be said to be a true Christian. His diligence, fervor and uprightness won him general esteem.

When we came to understand together what I had longed for during so many years, he opened his heart to me and revealed that he had had the same desire even before our marriage. Our union was therefore especially blessed by God who approved of our carrying out our plans, and that is why we wanted to show our appreciation and recognition of so great a benefit, in giving our life for the faith in Jesus Christ. We had pledged each other that when the day came for them to hand over the administration of the house and the estate to us we would divide it into three or four parts, one for the poor, another, very large, for the young brothers, so that they might be able to look after our parents, and, if the times became better, we ought to separate and live each his or her own private life. And now after all neither of us would break this vow.

Last year in the twelfth moon I felt sorely tempted and my heart palpitated with fear as if I were walking on thin ice or the edge of a precipice.① With eyes uplifted to Heaven I earnestly prayed for grace to overcome it, and with God's help, after a long, long struggle, we conquered, and we still remained like children. Our mutual confidence became firm as a rock and strong as steel, our love and our faith as immovable as a mountain.

After this vow to live as brother and sister, four years passed until this year he was taken in the springtime. During the four seasons he never altered his mode of dress. Imprisoned for eight months he wore the heavy cangue up to the moment of his death. Might he not have renounced God? I used to ask myself, and I longed to go and die with him to give him courage. What should I have thought? Ought I not to have known that he would take the lead? It is indeed a great benefit given by God. Here below, wherever I turn, I see nothing that will attract my affection or preoccupy me from this day on. Henceforth let there be but one thought in my mind, the thought of God; if a sigh arises in my heart, it will be a sigh for Heaven.

On the thirteenth of the tenth moon I was sentenced to be degraded to the rank of prefectural slave, and condemned to a remote exile in the town of Pyŏk-tong, in P'yŏng-an Province. I presented myself before the magistrate with a thousand appeals: "All we who believe in God and honor Him ought, in accordance with Korean law, to be condemned to death; I desire, I also, to die for God like the rest of my family." He dismissed me and ordered me to be removed from his presence. I went closer to him, sat down before

him and said: "You who receive a salary as governor, why don't you obey the orders of the king?" and a thousand other things, but he pretended not to understand and had me thrown out by the attendants. Having no other resort I went on my way, and along the road I redoubled my earnest prayers to God. We had barely covered 25 miles when I was recalled and re-arrested. This was indeed an answer to my prayers, a grace above all graces. How could I ever show my gratitude? Even after death, I should have to go on thanking God for this benefit.

We had passed four villages, and I meditated on the four places Jesus passed through on His way to Calvary, and said to myself: "Is this a slight resemblance to Our Saviour that God is allowing me?" I received the bailiffs who came to arrest me with unspeakable delight as if I were meeting my own parents.

At the first interrogation that followed, I declared that I wished to die honoring God; thereupon a report was sent to the king, and, the reply coming back, I was brought before the criminal judge once more; my sentence was brought, and I signed it. The judge ordered me to be given the bastinado on my legs, a cangue was fixed round my neck, and I was sent back to prison. My flesh was all flayed and bleeding profusely but in the space of time enough for a meal it dried up and I felt no more pain. These were graces upon graces all unexpected; four or five days later it was completely cured; what could one think?

After this ordeal, twenty days passed, and I no longer felt the slightest pain. The others all said that I was suffering: this is not only wrong, but directly contrary to the fact, for I would say that I was in a state of peace and well-being. Who could even in his own home feel as tranquil and happy as I am here? When I think of this, it even troubles and frightens me. Can it be that God does not need me? Is it because I would not be able to bear torture? I tremble at the thought, and am full of shame. Since they sent a courier to the king more than twenty days have passed and there is still no news; moreover there are certain rumors that I may have a chance to live; I hope for nothing but the help of the Lord, who, I feel sure, will not entirely reject me. May the reply come quickly, as quickly as possible, I hope for

---

① A proverbial phrase, which appears in the Ch'ŏn-cha-mun, (Thousand-Character Classic) ll. 65-66: "as if approaching thin ice or the brink of an abyss."

nothing but death. Waiting here, sitting idly with nothing to occupy my mind, I can hardly manage to escape the eye of the jailor and seize a few moments to say goodby to you forever, on a sheet of paper which you will receive as my self portrait, and which I hope may be of some consolation to you. But there is so much to say and having to do it in a hurry I write disconnectedly. If you would follow my thoughts, read these lines as if I were present before your eyes.

When we parted we agreed to meet again the following year, and now four whole years have passed. Who would have thought it, even in a dream? But can one never foresee anything of the future? A separation of four years has seemed hard to us; what can we say of a final separation with no return here below? And how troubled you must be over your little good-for-nothing sister! However, you my eldest sister have a heart as large as the ocean, you are wise and prudent; will you not be quite capable of bearing it? Yes, you will, calmly, and I will no longer worry about that. In spite of everything, though, when I think of you, dear sister, I cannot but become preoccupied with useless thoughts. Love of one's neighbor is such a natural feeling that one only loses it with one's life. 'However,' I say to myself, 'If I possessed only a modicum of fervor, would I tire myself like this with useless worrying?' and then I reproach myself for these thoughts of mine. Your heart will suffer enough on my account, no doubt, but after all, if I have the good fortune to become a martyr, what is there to be sorry about? Do not afflict yourself, therefore, but congratulate yourself.

In thinking of the pain and affliction which overwhelms you, dear mother and sisters, I send you my last greetings as my testament. Receive them graciously; do not reject them. When you hear the news of my death, I dare to hope ten thousand times that you will not let it upset you too much. I, your vile and wretched daughter, I, your stupid sister devoid of proper feelings, if I can become a child of the great God and take part in the rejoicing of the just, and enjoy perfect happiness and share in the sacred banquet, what a glorious thing it will be! To wish to achieve this on one's own is to wish for the impossible. If a daughter or a sister becomes the object of the favors of the ruler, she has a perfect right to congratulate herself, but if a child becomes the object of the love of the great King of Heaven and earth, how can she express her joy? People strive with one another for the favors of earthly rulers: if one obtains the love of God without having intrigued for it, is that not an infinitely greater good?

In the whole universe I am one of the greatest of sinners. In the world's eyes, I am no longer able to wash away the shameful title of prefectural slave of Pyŏk-tong; in the eyes of God, I have by my sins a hundred times denied my divine Master and his benefits; if, however, in making a good end, I become a martyr, all my sins will be washed away and I shall repose on the breast of ten thousand joys; have I, then, any reason for anxiety? Between the title of sister of the slave of Pyŏk-tong Prefecture and that of sister of a martyr, which pleases you more? And you, dear Mother, if they call you mother of a martyr, what will you think of the title? If I do in fact become a martyr, will it not be an incomparable wonder? For the other saints, this would be quite right and proper, but for such a great honor to descend upon a wretched creature like myself, is there anything more extraordinary and amazing?

Look on my death as a true life, and my life as really a death. Do not distress yourself at losing me, but distress yourself at having lost God in the past, and go in fear lest you lose Him again in the future. Save all your regrets for the past and strive to efface and redeem it. Supported by the Holy Mother and with your heart at peace strive to reach the throne of the Lord.

If you will submit obediently to God's will, you will be fulfilling His intention, which is to purify you through sorrow, and to cherish and console you in Himself. You will have a good opportunity to obtain His most precious graces and acquire merit. If on the other hand you mourn uselessly, you will offend this same God: could anything be more deplorable than that?

In everything, therefore, submit yourself to His Providence and with calm mind and soul at peace avail yourself of your afflictions to satisfy His justice to the full. Devote yourself to good works and the acquisition of merit; no matter how small the fault, avoid it like a mortal sin, and repent it as deeply; in good works on the contrary no matter how trifling they may be, lose no opportunity to perform them. Rely entirely on the help of God, pray always that you may have the grace to make a good end, and strive always to perform acts of loving fervor. If you feel no love, no contrition, force yourself to bring these feelings to birth; when one asks for them earnestly God will give them.

If you slacken and backslide momentarily, pull yourself together at once and wake up to your danger; if you seek God with ardor, little by little you will draw near to Him. If God, fulfilling my desires, were to admit me to His presence, and if Brothers and Sisters, Mothers and Daughters could all meet together before Him, would not that be a beautiful thing? Each one of you, indulgent toward the others, ought to examine himself or herself with severity, and strive always for harmony and concord: in this way Mother, in her old age, will become completely united to the divine will and my sisters will become loving and dutiful daughters.

Dear sister-in-law, if my brother has been put to death, do not grieve too deeply, to no avail; but with a calm heart thank God for this benefit. He will sustain you from on high and will help you in the midst of your difficulties. Apply yourself to contrition, do your best, and employ all the faculties of your soul to follow in my brother's footsteps.

Here with me is my aunt with her son, the only one she has. They want to give their lives to God with us. They are perfectly calm and resigned. Take them as your model, and imitating Our Blessed Mother, the Virgin Mary, and all the saints, give no affection to vain things. My sister-in-law and my brother-in-law are in a position difficult to bear, but in order to advance in virtue and acquire merit, it is good to be in such trouble, and up to now they have shown exemplary patience. But if it is good to begin well, it is still better to end well; be, therefore, always on guard and do not lose the merit you have won. If you are in extreme sorrow, accept them with good grace, think of the divine will and have faith in the reward to come. If you will only repress these lively reactions of nature to pain, even the most painful things will lose their power to harm you. It seems to me that it would be of the utmost advantage to us if we could always keep our hearts in this disposition. All the virtues are well worth praying for, but faith, hope and charity are the principal ones; if only these three are in the soul, the others will come naturally.

How is my brother-in-law at present? When I think of the situation of my sister, my soul is deeply troubled. Although you may not always be in complete harmony with him, do your best to please him in every way which is not sinful, and try not to lose his affection. John and I, married for five years and having lived four years together, have never once had a single moment of disagreement, nor with anybody in the house did I ever have the slightest dissension.

I could say a thousand things more, but there is a frightful noise going on outside and I can write only with difficulty, but I wish to write separately to Mother. I should like, at last, to tell you one ten-thousandth part of what has happened during these four years, but each time the guards shout for one or other of the prisoners to appear. It seems that they are calling for me, and I stop writing; then, when I begin again, I have to stop once more. My words come tumbling out without order and perhaps are incomprehensible, but believing that you will be glad to have a few lines from me I seize every opportunity to put down a few words. If by His infinite goodness God does not reject me as a martyr and if my brother has already achieved martyrdom, you will have two children to precede you; can we do other than conduct you to a good place? Though I should die, can I ever forget you and my sisters? If I obtain the object of my desires, one day I shall see you again, but as I have no merit I had better not talk too much about that before I have made a good death.

My dear sister-in-law, if my brother dies do not listen only to your natural affections and abandon yourself to excessive grief. Husband and wife are one flesh, and if one mounts to Heaven he will easily take the other with him; do not then be faint-hearted in doing good, do not sadden your heart in vain, for you will only grieve God and my brother. Tong-won being the only scion of his branch of the family, he is the more precious: take good care of him, body and soul, and when he is grown up, find him a good wife and teach them how to live in holy wedlock.

As for me, during the twenty years of my life I have never spent a day without yielding to weaknesses, and have never fulfilled my duties as a daughter, so now you see me about to depart without leaving any sign of filial piety: dear sister, make up for this by taking all the more care of Mother and do in place of me what I have left undone. Piety toward the body is good but that of the heart is better. I, too, having lived with my husband's parents, have learnt that what pleases them most is for us to agree with all their views and sentiments. If you find that you cannot afford to take care of Mother as well as you would like to, at least enter into her plans and comfort her well: awaken always her dimming faculties, and if by chance, she happens to make a little mistake, do not merely address a few good words to her, but say them in a gay and kindly tone. If she is sad, hide your own sadness from her. Play the child to her even, and, with a few pleasant and good-humored remarks make her forget her troubles. After the death of our eldest brother, our younger brothers have no one but you to rely on: be both brother and elder sister to them, bring them up to be virtuous, and try to establish and maintain a family of fervent Christians.

If my brother achieves martyrdom, and I too, by the grace of God, make a good end, I dare to hope that we may meet again in another life. Above all, help Mother to spend her remaining years well and obtain the grace of a good death, so that Mother and children, brothers and sisters, husbands and wives, all of us may meet again in happiness; this I would urge upon you a thousand times. I know well that you will not neglect these things, but in thinking of my words you will do them twice as well. Whoever has parents must not allow them to fall into sadness but free them from their affliction; bear this in mind. I do not say these words out of mistrust in your good will, but because I know that you are somewhat prone to impatience.

As for John, they call him my husband, and I call him my faithful friend; if he has succeeded in making his way to Heaven, I believe he will not forget me. Here below he had such consideration for me and showed me so much kindness; living in the abode of bliss he will not fail to hear my cries of fear and pain nor will he forget our vows. Oh! our love (amity) will never be broken. When, then, leaving this prison, shall I meet our great King and common Father, the Queen of Heaven, my beloved Parents, and my faithful friend John, to share bliss with them? Being nothing but a sinner and without merit, it is presumptuous of me to hope, I know. Can my desires be fulfilled so soon?

Here, there are lots of people in distress, how can I tell you all? My sister-in-law, brought up in wealth and opulence, after having lost her parents, her brothers and all her property, has been obliged to give up her big house; she has withdrawn to a ruined cottage with one of her aunts and her grandmother weighed down with years. Recently married, she has not yet been escorted to the home of her husband, and it is said that her father-in-law is unwilling to receive her on account of the misfortunes of her family. What a deplorable situation! With what words can one describe it? My three brothers-in-law, aged nine, six and three, have all been sent into separate exile in Heuk-san Islands, Sin-ji Island, and the Kŏ-je Island; how can one bear to contemplate such a frightful thing? My mother-in-law, my aunt, and Matthew, the cousin german of my husband share with me one heart and one mind. They too have been put to the question, and have had to undergo cruel tortures. They are imprisoned here; I hope all goes well.

My eldest sister, among us five, has an especial affection for me, perhaps because, as she says, she nursed me in her arms as a baby and took care of my upbringing. You can be sure I have as strong an affection for her, but that is no reason for her to mourn my death. If, by the grace of God, I have the good fortune to go to Heaven, when, after having diligently acquired merit, you make a good end, I hope myself to lead you there and take you by the hand. Having taken up my pen to write you my eternal farewell I don't want to omit anything that I intended to say, and yet as there is so much, I am obliged to cut it short. I do hope you will live a good life and acquire merit: keep yourself healthy both in body and in soul, in order to enter Heaven, that we may all enjoy eternal happiness together. After my death, I shall earnestly pray for that without ceasing. But if by chance my prayers should remain unanswered, if I should be condemned to go on living, ah! how terrible it would be! But no! I trust in my Savior Jesus Christ.

After my arrest, fearing that my case might take a long time to decide, I wrote a few lines to mother; please read them, and after having read this letter, pass it on to the rest of the family so that when they read it they may think they are looking at me once more. What a long letter, with lots of words! Utterly without virtue as I am, I have the audacity to preach to others: am I not really just like those wooden *Chang-seung* (statues) that stand by the roadside, and point the way without following it themselves? However, it is said that the words of the dying carry weight; perhaps mine will—but they are too imperfect—read them with indulgence.

Yu-hye

This letter was sent from the prison by Lugartha Lee to her sister and sister-in-law, the wife of Charles Lee Kyŏng-to. It expressed her feelings, thoughts, memories and hopes, and might well be regarded as her testament. It was written on scraps of paper during the moments when she was alone, and could escape the vigilance of her jailors. Fortunately it was kept by a certain Catholic family, and reprinted in Father Dallet's *Histoire de l'Église de Corée*.

(22) Charles Lee Kyŏng-to

On the promulgation of the so-called *Imperial Edict Calling for Suppression of the Heretical Doctrine* on the twenty-first of the tenth moon, 1801, the government also issued an ordinance calling for all Catholics who had already been sentenced to death to be executed before the end of the year. In accordance with these harsh instructions eight Catholics, including Charles Lee, an elder brother of Lugartha Lee, the catechist Sohn Kyŏng-yun, and Simeon Kim Paek-sim were executed and achieved martyrdom on the twenty-sixth of the twelfth moon. Charles Lee Kyŏng-to was twenty-two years old. From childhood his nature had always been mild, generous, gentle and reserved. At an early age he became remarkable for his rapid progress in learning. At the age of seventeen he was married to a young woman of his own standing in society. Three months after his marriage his father died, and he did his best to shoulder his responsibilities as head of the family. He taught the Catholic faith to his servants and trained them never to behave in a manner that might bring shame or disgrace to themselves or to their religion. In his effort to withdraw from secular life he prayed that he might be afflicted with physical deformity. By always walking with a stoop he actually became a cripple, and when he was summoned for interrogation he had to be carried into court. Though at first cast down his determination grew stronger in captivity, and he met his death without wavering in his faith.

(23) Sohn Kyŏng-yun

He belonged to a middle-class family of Seoul and was converted to Catholicism before the coming of Father Chou to Korea. He was appointed a catechist and performed his duties with zeal and sincerity. He purchased a spacious house which he fitted up as a tavern, and soon had a large number of regular customers, mostly pagans. Their constant coming and going and their noisy drinking parties served to distract attention from the secret prayer meetings of Catholics which were held in the inner apartments, but as soon as the persecution began he was brought to the attention of the authorities. At first he fled, but learning that all his family were being held as hostages he gave himself up in order to secure their release. He was subjected to horrible torture, but by the grace of God he was able to overcome all temptations to recant, and won a martyr's crown at the age of forty-two.

(24) Kim Paek-sim

Born to a middle-class Seoul family, he worked for a time as a servant at one of the houses where Father Chou resided. This gave him a good opportunity to learn about the faith and to practice virtue. When the police began looking for him in the spring of 1801 he went into hiding, until he learnt that his father had been arrested and was being held in hostage for him. He gave himself up and courageously declared his faith in Jesus Christ. The judge, whom Simeon's friends had bribed to release him, granted him only three days' leave to return home on parole, hoping that he would recant in order to gain his liberty, but on the expiration of his leave he punctually presented himself at the prison. "Well, have you changed your mind at all?" asked the judge.

"Yes," he answered.

"Good," said the judge, "from now on you'll have nothing more to do with the evil religion, you understand?"

"On the contrary," said Kim, "I have undergone a complete change. I am now resolved to give my whole life up to following God's teachings, more devotedly than before."

This answer left the judge dumbfounded. Kim kept steadfastly to his decision, was sentenced to death, and won the glory of a martyr.

20. Church Reconstruction after Persecution

The year 1801 had dawned with horrible oppression, and drew to a close with heroic martyrdom. Now that the power of the Queen Regent Kim was in a decline, a struggle for power arose between two branches of her family, the Kyŏng-ju Kims and the An-tong Kims. Taking advantage of this, the Church began to recover strength and grow. As the persecution receded, Catholics began to come out of hiding and get in touch with one another: assemblies were held, and they encouraged one another to maintain the faith and spread the Gospel, and to set about rebuilding a new Church on the ashes of the old. The report written by Peter Shin Tae-po gives a vivid account of their efforts.:

"The persecution had at last subsided, it is true, but we were all dispersed and isolated, and had lost our prayer books. The surviving relatives of several of the martyrs were now living in the district of Yong-in and after protracted search I succeeded in finding them. There were only a few elderly women and some young people, little more than children, in all five households, related to one another. They were friendless and without means. They hardly dared to speak to strangers and trembled with fear at the mention of religion. They possessed several prayer books and copies of explanations of the Gospels, but all hidden away with the utmost care. When I asked to see them they immediately interrupted me, waving their hands rapidly as if to say 'Hush! Don't speak of that!' I could not bear to distress them by insisting. However, these poor women were all very glad to learn from their children that a Christian was among them, and, although etiquette forbade that I should see them, they wished to talk to me.[1] I told them some of the latest news, the present state of religion, and of our common circumstances, in which we were prevented both from serving God and from saving our souls. They were deeply moved; some of them even wept, and expressed a desire that we should meet again frequently to sustain each other in the faith.

"I was living about ten miles away, and from now on we visited each other regularly every eight or ten days. Our mutual affection was as lively and sincere as if we had been members of the same family. We took up our reading again and held regular meetings for worship and meditation on Sundays and feasts of devotion. These persons used formerly to receive the Sacraments at the hands of the priest, and when they described him to me and recounted the words of teaching and exhortation that he had addressed to them, he seemed to come to life before my eyes. My spirit was filled with holy joy; it was as if I had discovered a precious treasure. I felt toward these Christians a reverent love such as angels might evoke, but there were, living among pagans, those whose eyes were watching us incessantly from every direction. I had to make a ten-mile detour by night in order to bypass them. Shortly afterward the neighboring pagans began to ask my name; next they wanted to know where I lived, and whom I associated with. All this made us uneasy, and we conceived the plan of leaving the district together and migrating to some place where we might set up a separate village of our own. As for me, I had only my son and daughter, but our five families made up a total of more than forty persons, and as not one of them possessed anything but debts, the sale of their houses would not yield enough, once these debts were paid, to pay more than our bare traveling expenses, for the site that I had in view was located deep in the mountains of Kang-won Province, where there was

---

[1] In such cases, in order to comply with the rules of etiquette and maintain propriety, the visitor sits in an adjoining room, and speaks through a large grating (grille) which may be curtained, just as when conversing with inclosed nuns in their "parlor."

Lee Pyŏk on his epoch-making journey to the "Chu-ŏ-sa" Temple

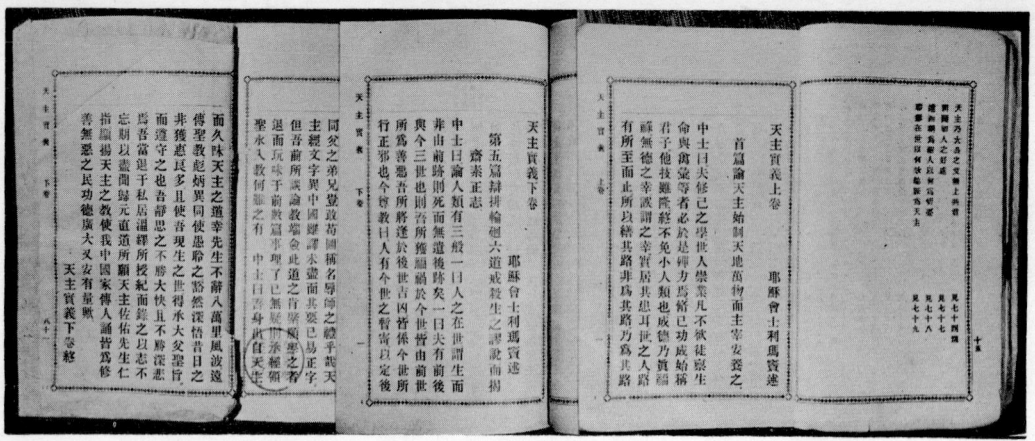

A copy of the Chinese original of Matteo Ricci's "T'ien Chu Shih I" (The True Doctrine of God)

A work of apologetics in the form of a dialogue between a Chinese and a European scholar. First published in 1603, it attracted the attention of a Confucian scholar in Korea, Lee Su-kwang (1563-1621).

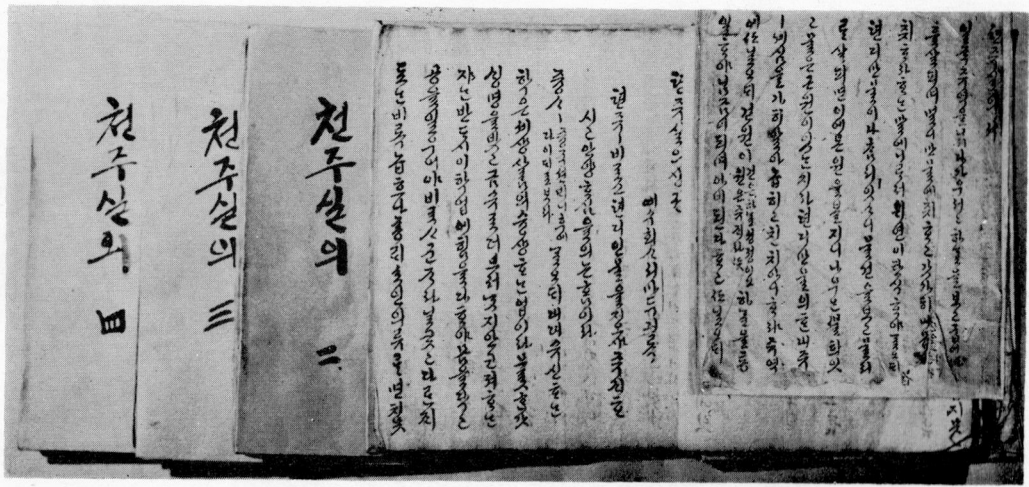

The Korean version of "The True Doctrine of God" dates from the nineteenth century

An early copy of the "Ch'i Ko" (The Seven Mortifications)

A Chinese work by the Jesuit Missionary Diego de Pantoja (1571-1618), the first Spaniard to work in China

"Ch'il-keuk-chin-hun"

An extract from the book shown at the right by Danicourt

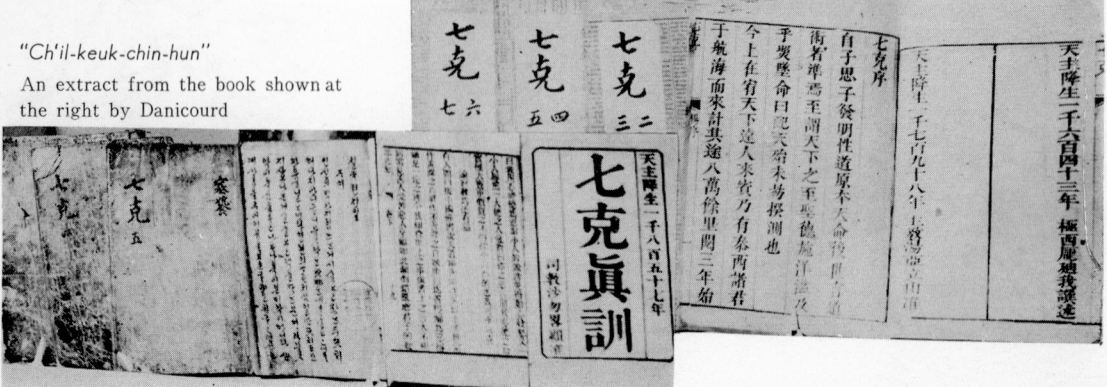

Portrait of the Jesuit Missionary Matteo Ricci (1552-1610)
Painted in 1610 by the Chinese Brother Emmanuel Pereira

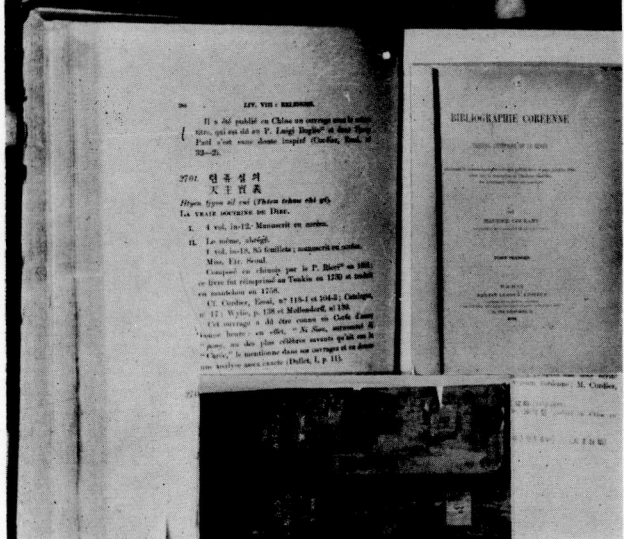

Bibliographie Coréenne Courant, Maurice:
3 vols., Paris, 1894-1896

Father Adam Schall von Bell

An early portrait of the German Jesuit missionary to China (1591-1666), who was one of the translators of Western books on astronomy and the calendar at the Ch'ing court.

The Baptism of Peter Lee Seung-hun

Peking.   Peitang Kathedrale. Peitang cathedral.

The North Church in Peking

Tomb of Francis-Xavier Kwon Il-sin

Tomb of Peter Lee Seung-hun at So-sa

A page from Lee Man-ch'ae's "Pyŏk-wi-p'yŏn" (The Confucian Ban on Christianity), 7 vols., Seoul, 1931. The Volume V mentions Alexander Hwang Sa-yŏng's "Silk Letter" of 1801.

闢衛編卷五

辛酉治邪元年 純祖

辛酉正月十一日 大王大妃殿傳曰 先王每謂正學明則

邪學自熄今聞邪學依舊自京至于圻沕而日益熾盛云此豈

不凜然子人之為人以有人倫國之為國以有教化今所謂邪

學無父無君毀壞人倫背反教化歸乎夷狄禽獸彼魚魚之氓

漸染詿誤若赤子之入井此豈不惻然惶然傷心甚字監司守令詳

細曉諭俾為邪學者翻然改悟而如是嚴禁之後猶有不悛之類當

以逆律從事各邑守令各枚其境內修明五家統之法其統內

如有邪學之類則統首告官懲治然猶不悛則國有法焉剿殄

滅之無俾遺種以此下教自廟堂知悉曉諭京外○時京外邪

類就捕者甚多 大妃聞之有此 下教

二月初九日憲府新啓 大諫申鳳朝執義閔命安延善正言御史 請

前判書李家煥前縣監李承薰前承旨丁若鏞亟令王府為先

嚴鞫得情快正典刑

大王大妃傳曰邪學事向進有下教者今此臺啓實合予意嚴

覈之道不容少緩臺啓中人令金吾今日內舉行○委官李東

橫禁堂徐鼎修李書九尹東晚韓用鐸

初十日 大王大妃傳曰推鞫其間已為舉行子輯葉催促入

之而各別嚴覈暴其端緒快為掃蕩俾無漏網之獎○罪人李

家煥李承薰丁若鏞原情○次對備堂李書九請李存昌令本

道還囚訊服衆 允○玉堂劄子曰蔡濟恭之自來負化云云入

雖以目下邪學言之指授徒黨華成淵教浸浸泯泯驅一遍入

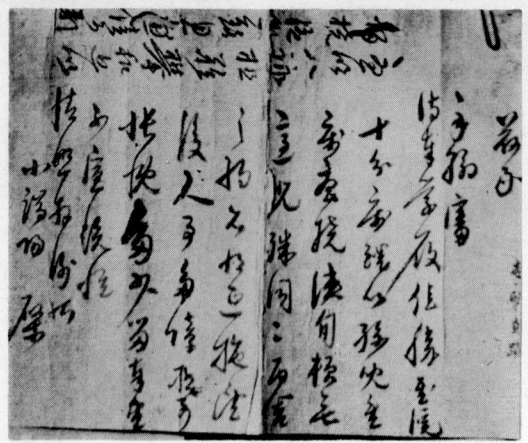

Handwriting of Lee Pyŏk

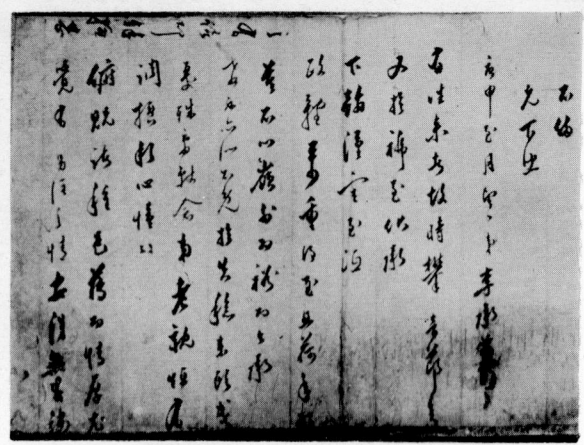

Handwriting of Peter Lee Seung-hun

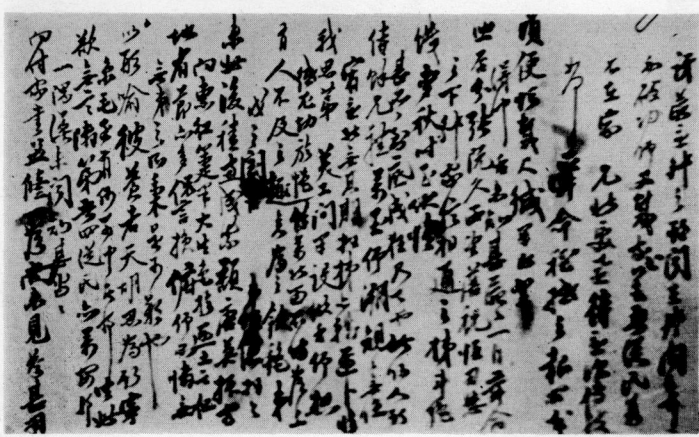

Handwriting of Augustine Ryu Hang-kŏm

Handwriting of Matthias Ch'oe In-kil

Handwriting of Lee I-myŏng

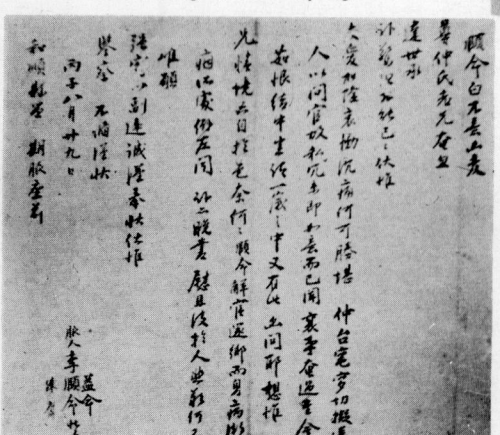

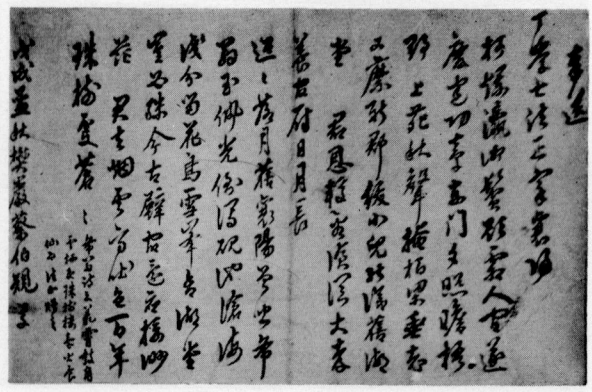

Handwriting of Ch'ae Che-kong

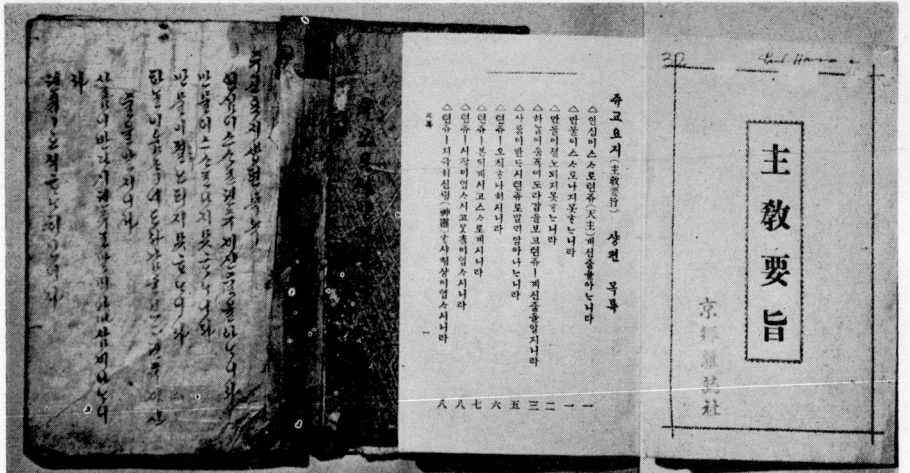

Chŭng Yak-jong's "Chu-kyo-yo-ji" (The Essence of Catholicism) Circulated in manuscript form from 1801. The first printed edition, illustrated here, appeared in 1864.

The memorial to Chŭng Yak-yong, with the pen-name Ta-san

A specimen of Ta-san's calligraphy

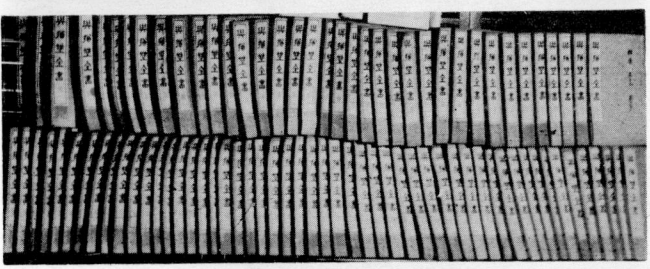

The complete works of Ta-san, in 467 volumes

Chŭng Yak-yong's "Mok-min-sim-sŏ" (A Treatise on Shepherding the People)

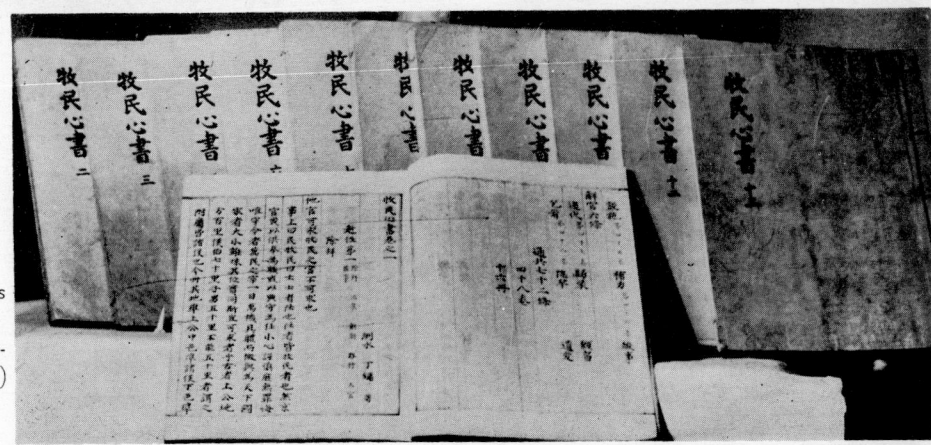

The execution of Father James Chou Wen-mo at Sae-nam-t'ŏ

Monument commemorating
the Martyrdom of Lugartha
Lee on "Martyrdom Hill"
in Chŏn-ju

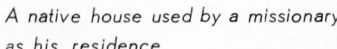

A native house used by a missionary
as his residence

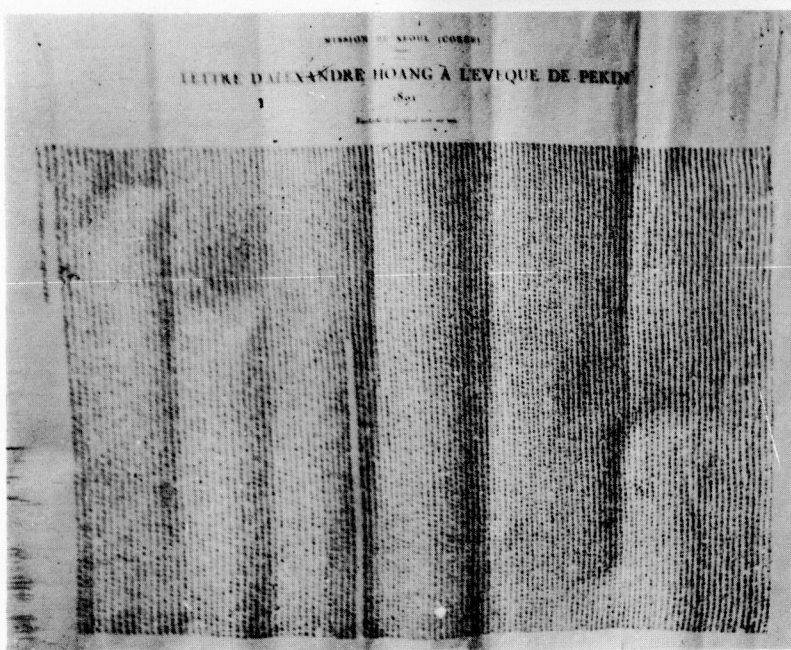

A facsimile of the Silk Letter
written on silk by Alexander
Hwang Sa-yŏng

Monument commemorating the Catholic
Martyrs of 1866
At Hae-mi, South Ch'ung-ch'ŏng Province

Monument commemorating Catholic Martyrs
At Sup-jŏng, the site of their martyrdom, often referred to as "the Second Sae-nam-t'ŏ", near Chŏn-ju

hardly a trace of human habitation. Nevertheless, we decided to set out regardless of success or failure.

"Two families were living in houses which were completely bare, and they never knew each morning what food they would be able to get for the evening. The three remaining families sold their houses with their few sticks of furniture, and received barely a hundred *taels*, (ounces of silver; about £ 10 sterling) out of which many debts had to be paid. When we were discussing the date for our departure each of these families had the same idea; to be the first to leave this inferno and set out on the search for paradise. They argued about it with such heat that they almost began to quarrel. What trouble I had to pacify them and make them listen to reason! As for myself, I entrusted the care of my son and daughter to my nephew, and it was decided that the departure of one of the families should be put off for the time being. But, not to mention the children, there were five women who could not possibly be left behind, and who would have to be provided with transportation. I managed to buy a couple of horses, and shortly afterward a third, which completely exhausted our little capital. I therefore sought out two wealthy friends in the village, who were kind enough to have five litters made for us, and to lend us two horses. Thus equipped we started on our way. The horses were good, and the horse-boys worked well but in spite of this the first day's journey was full of difficulty. Our little group of travelers aroused much curiosity and suspicion: we were obviously not a cortege of nobles, nor did we appear to belong to the class of common people; but above all the way our horses were harnessed looked very strange. On the second day we had to make a change. We discarded the five litters, and the women, muffling themselves up with their petticoats

over their heads to look like riding cloaks, had to ride on horseback. Our appearance now approximated to that of the ordinary people of the countryside, or perhaps of the hill districts, but nevertheless the passers-by and the innkeepers could be heard muttering to one another that we were from the capital. Some of them even said to us with a mischievous smile: 'You must belong to the families of the Christians.' At every step we were in mortal fear of being recognized and arrested.

"After eight days of arduous travel we at last arrived at our destination. More trouble! No house, and nobody we knew. We managed to borrow a tumble-down shack for the whole group to live in, and, the five horses now being a burden to us, I at once sold my own and used the money to buy food, and a small hut hardly big enough for one to lie down at full length. We had to return the two borrowed horses, but as we had no money we had to keep them with us for a month, and the cost of their feed came to almost as much as the price of one horse. However, we managed to return them, and, on the way back, to bring the family that had been left behind. Without our realizing it, the season for harvesting went by and winter was upon us; snow began to fall and all the roads became invisible.[1]

"In the whole neighborhood there was not a soul we knew, and as it was impossible to communicate with even our closest neighbors the entire group of more than forty persons was in danger of death by starvation. One of the horses which remained to us had gnawed away and almost devoured its enormous wooden drinking trough; the children cried incessantly and asked for food, and the grown-ups themselves grew impatient and irritable. Our provisions were almost at an end and the future looked blacker everyday, and we succumbed to the temptation of complaining

---

[1] In the Province of Kang-won the snowfall is of terrifying severity. Not only are all the roads rendered impassable, but often one is cut off from other houses even in the same village. Those who have not provided themselves with a store of food simply starve to death, and unless constant re is taken to prevent it, the houses may be completely buried and the inmates suffocated.

about our faith that had brought us to these straits, and in our weakness we even went so far as to curse ourselves for believing in God.

"In the end, by a miracle of divine mercy, we survived without quite knowing how. Winter was over and once the snows had melted it became possible to get out and about. Learning that a wealthy scholar named Ch'oe lived about 17 miles' distance from us, I went to his home, where I stayed two days. Having given him an account of the wretched circumstances of our families I was able through his intervention to obtain some twenty hectoliters (about fifty-five bushels) of paddy (rice in the husk). In order to save the cost of transport I arranged for the local people, who were very obliging, to husk it for me, after which I sold a part of it and had the rest transported. All this grain would have to be paid for on a fixed date. Having attended to this business I tried again to console our little community and only now would they listen to me; joy and charity reappeared among us. Our various debts now amounted to more than a hundred taels but I was afraid to mention this to them, for whenever I spoke of being thrifty and of rationing our food, all their faces would become downcast and sullen."

All the Catholics who took refuge in the mountains of Kang-won and Kyŏng-sang Provinces underwent a similar miserable fate. Those who were exiled to remote islands were even worse off, for they were deprived of liberty, kept under constant surveillance, and often forcibly deprived of the company of their nearest and dearest who had accompanied them to share their exile. Yet Providence brought it about that these wretched exiles and refugees, without being aware of it, became apostles. Villages grew up around their homes, their families grew into flourishing Christian communities, and the Gospel became known in even the remotest corner of the nation. New leaders arose, such as John Kwon Kye-in the nephew of Kwon Ch'ŏl-sin, Maurus Ch'oe, Peter Shin Tae-po,

John Lee Yŏ-jin, and Paul Chŭng Ha-sang and under their leadership a reconstruction movement began. Two letters were written by John Kwon, one to the Bishop of Peking himself, reporting on the persecution of the Korean Church and its present pitiable position, and beseeching him to dispatch a priest to Korea; the other was a petition addressed to the Pope in Rome, the first of its kind to be sent from Korea. In view of their significance they are transcribed hereunder. (The words "Francis and other believers" at the beginning of the letter to the Pope are believed to be an alias intended to put the authorities off the scent in the case that the letter should fall into their hands.)

Letter of the Christians to the Bishop of Peking

"Francis and other Korean believers, notwithstanding our knowledge that we are miserable sinners, nevertheless, heartbroken with sorrow and with our heads bowed to the ground before the episcopal throne, we tender our letter with the utmost respect to the supreme ecclesiastical ruler of the Diocese.

"The enormity of our sins has reached its height; we have forfeited the divine grace of the Lord. Alas! Our crimes have caused the death of our spiritual Father! Sadness and affliction have dispersed many of us, while in others all feeling for religion is dead or dying. It is now eleven years since we lost all those whose zeal and talents were of any avail. The rigor with which we have been unceasingly watched has prevented us from submitting our supplications at an earlier date. All that is told of the prophets of old and how eagerly they awaited the coming of the Messiah, all that the sacred tradition teaches regarding the loving kindness with which Our Savior hearkens to the ardent prayers of His saints; all is proof enough that just as in the animal world breathing in and breathing out exactly correspond to one another, so also in the spiritual domain a fervent prayer which issues from the depths of the heart is a sure means to reach the Lord and obtain His mercy in return.

"In thinking of the enormity of our sins, now at its height, we humbly confess that they are enough to close the doors of the divine mercy against us and cut us off from grace. His justice has manifested itself with such terrifying power that we are like little children who on hearing a clap of thunder are dismayed and run about not knowing where to hide. Like a flock of sheep attacked and with no shepherd to take care of them we are in panic and without any means of succor. Ah, what else can have caused our disasters but our own iniquity? We are utterly abased and dejected at the heart-rending violence of our sorrows, which strikes our very entrails and makes us weep tears of blood. Nevertheless, great as our sins are, the mercy of God is infinitely greater. Oh! If the Lord would but deign to defer these blows of His justice, and bear with us, and hear our cries of penitence! Oh! If He would but stretch out His hand to raise us from the deplorable state to which we have fallen! This is our prayer by day and by night, through ceaseless sobs and tears. If we desire to escape an early death, it is solely in order to be able to receive the Sacraments and confess our sins; though we were to die immediately afterward, we should be satisfied—nay, rather, transported with joy.

"Moreover when we remember that the Holy Mother of God in former times designed to look favorably upon a sinner who redeemed his apostasy with his blood, and when we recall the remarkable conversion of the impious prince who was miraculously affected by the presence of the Holy Sacrament[1], great sinners though we be, we dare to hope that the Mother of Mercy will little by little also appease the divine anger on our behalf, and temper His justice so that we may come to share in the benefits of the Seven Sacraments, and find a sure refuge in the Five Wounds of our crucified Lord. Prostrate at the feet of our pastor who is invested with the authority of God Himself, we hope that in consideration of the dreadful responsibility with which He is charged, He will let Himself be moved to pity at the sight of the anguish which afflicts us, and will in good time vouchsafe to us the benefits of the sacred ministrations. We are emboldened in this hope by our faith in the holy grace of the redemption, common to the whole human race, and we maintain our hope by virtue of the Holy Name of God and the glory of the martyrs of our nation. Amen."

The letter goes on to give an abridged account of all that had happened since the death of the king in 1800, and a note on each of the principal martyrs, after which the letter continues:

"There are still a great number of others who in their efforts to respond to the grace of the Lord have consummated their merits with martyrdom. Their families conserve documents concerning them. Whenever a missionary comes he will be able to compile a complete account, beginning with Paul Yun Chi-ch'ung (martyred in 1791).

"We may read in the Gospel of Saint Matthew, 'At that time Jesus said openly, Father, who art Lord of heaven and earth, I give thee praise that thou hast hidden all this from the wise and the prudent, and revealed it to little children.' (St. Matthew, 11:25) This holy word is being fulfilled, generation after generation, and is confirmed at this moment in our country. Among the long-established families of the great and noble, among the descendants of the mandarins or state officials who are at present in power, there are a fair number of persons who are well disposed toward the faith, but they are held back by their desire to rise in the world, or by their fear of ridicule. Among the wealthy it is the thirst for gold that stifles the voice of conscience. Those who turn to religion and seek for justice are

---

[1] An allusion to Saint Theophilus the Penitent (c. 538), recorded in a book of lives of the Saints translated from Chinese into Korean.

the poor and the oppressed, those who are destitute and ruined. Moreover all the ways of doing business in our country, all our social institutions, have long been riddled with superstition and malpractice. Christians who wish to devote themselves to commerce in order to gain are *ipso facto* excluded from the merchants' guilds and business circles. In this way the wealthy Christians are reduced to poverty and the poor ones become homeless, wandering beggars, and only with the utmost difficulty can they manage to live. Yet not a word of resentment or complaint is heard from them: they are content to beg their way from place to place and to endure these sufferings if only they can be free to practice their religion. Is it not evident that we are animated and sustained by some especial favor of the Lord? We are undoubtedly indebted to the saints and angels and to the entire Church for their intercession on our behalf.

"Those among us who were endowed with talents for social leadership and the management of affairs in the world have all died under the great persecution. Those who escaped torture and are still in hiding are seized with terror and their souls are paralyzed with fear. Having lost all their land and personal possessions, they are compelled to beg for a living: there is not one among them able to be self-supporting. Moreover their sufferings have in many cases brought about a change of character in them: they seem to have lost their nerve, and to have become timid and reluctant to play their part in society. More than ten years have passed since the terror was at its height; circumstances have changed, and the crisis is less violent. Little by little the broken-spirited begin to regain their courage and take up their former way of life. If only we had the benefit of the Sacraments, our religion could rise again with renewed splendor. But we

seem to have no talented men among us nowadays; all the survivors are simple, uneducated people. We have good intentions, but we are without the means to carry them out: even if one of us should show some ability in business matters, our warehouses are empty and our markets without purchasing power and, not knowing where to turn, what is left for us to do except to sigh and groan and deplore our wretched condition?

"This is why we have sent nobody to Peking for the last ten years. In vain do we stand on tiptoe and lift up our heads; in vain do we look toward the north,[1] weeping and wailing; it was not the difficulty of the journey that prevented us, nor were we daunted by the danger to our lives: we simply could not scrape together the few hundred *taels* necessary for the expenses of the journey. From the beginning a close watch was set up along the frontier and the guards seemed as numerous as the trees of the forest: the smallest border village was garrisoned as strongly as a town in wartime. After a time this strictness was somewhat relaxed and it became possible to take action, but, on the one hand, our lack of funds completely immobilized us, and on the other, the fact that we were all dispersed in remote parts of the country made it impossible for us to meet and carry out our plans. Broken-hearted with sorrow and grief, we could only sigh and groan without knowing what to do.

"The whole country was involved in the persecution: it was for long the sole topic of conversation. The excellent doctrine and the good example of the Christians filled all the eyes and ears of the people, and their pathetic last words touched all hearts. Everyone was astonished at the way in which religion showed its superiority to worldly materialistic science; all were moved to wonder and respect by the charity of the Christians[2] and

[1] 'Look toward the north' here signifies 'look toward the Emperor' just as 'to sit facing the south' means 'to occupy the Imperial throne.'
[2] By 'charity' the writer means the virtue which enabled the Christians to love God above all things for His own sake, and to love for God's sake all men of good will. (Continued on page 87)

nearly all hearts were softened. Public opinion condemns as unjust the death sentences on those of us who are no more, and extends pity toward those of us who remain. Well has it been said that the light of Heaven cannot be extinguished nor the voice of conscience rendered mute. This feeling is natural to all mankind, but without the help that comes from the Sacraments, no effect is produced upon the will. Scoffed at, reviled, with torture and death always before their eyes, we may well be said to be under persecution. The heart is always the same, but there is the fear of making a rash decision; we want to understand, but no one tells us what to do: this is really a pitiful plight to be in. However, the present moment is propitious, for you will not withhold such a great benefit from us.

"We have heard that in 1804 there was a violent persecution in Peking and that entry into the Churches was strictly forbidden and many of the Christians were put to death, and that the European missionaries were imprisoned. This news caused us the greatest consternation and bitter sorrow. Until now we have been unable to verify the truth of these rumors, so that we are still anxious, and we beg you to inform us on this point. The Church being under such strict surveillance in Peking, and our foreign affairs requiring the greatest secrecy, we beg you to tell us what is the best thing for us to do, and we implore you to consider what means would be efficacious to deliver us from the frightful conditions in which we are now living.

"After the great persecution, everything concerning our religion, its laws and its doctrine, has become known throughout the country. It would be futile for us to try to conceal or dissimulate the laws which forbid us to sacrifice to our ancestors or to idols. Those which prescribe our fasts and abstinences make us known to the pagans. Now as to the first commandment of God and that which our religion rigorously prescribes (sc. worship of idols), even at the cost of one's life, it must never be broken. It is not the same with regard to fasts and abstinences, for we have seen that dispensations are often granted. Would it be possible to grant a general dispensation to (Christian) travelers and domestic servants?

"All the books and sacred objects that were taken to the lower courts have been destroyed by fire. All that was at the High Court of Justice is being kept under lock and key. It includes writings by the missionary Alexander Hwang which we have already mentioned. Today nothing can be found but scraps and stray sheets of paper. His images, books and chalice have disappeared. Nothing remains but a couple of small volumes in the possession of a Christian woman. The books printed in China, which we saw, are of large format and would be difficult to hide. If you could have them reprinted in a smaller format you could send them to us more easily and it would be easier for us to conceal them. We beg you to take this point into consideration.

"Now that we are deprived of all means of receiving the Sacraments, it is a cause of great anxiety to us to lack the spiritual succor of the viaticum when on the point of death. If we could be provided with the sacred objects and the holy oils and the accompanying plenary indulgences it would be a great source of strength and comfort to us, especially in confirming and encouraging us in the virtues of faith, hope, and charity.

"Since we have been unable to communicate with you for the last ten years we do not know the name of the present Supreme Pontiff; we also lack information about the priests in Peking, how many there are, besides the Bishop, what progress the religion

Its range is much wider than in its common sense of good works and general amiability; these are the fruits of charity rather than charity itself. "I may speak with every tongue that men and angels use; yet, if I lack charity, I am no better than echoing bronze or the clash of cymbals." (1 Corinthians, 13:1) has made in China, and in how many countries of the Orient it is being publicly preached and practiced. We beg you to provide us with some information regarding these different points.

"No one among us survivors of the persecution is fully informed of the matters which were dealt with secretly in the year Kyŏng-sin, 1800. Simon Kim and Lee Yŏ-jin,[1] it is true, wrote to us from their prison, but they told us only about matters in general and did not dare to go into details. They told us that in ten years' time a large ship would arrive; that the numerous sectaries were causing a great deal of trouble in Nanking. They assured us that the priests of the Church in Peking had decided to come to the Orient to work for the salvation of our souls. But the great persecution prevented us from going to receive these missionaries. We underwent the most bitter disappointment, and were disconsolate at not knowing what had become of them. If the Lord had kept them safe and sound, as soon as they saw the representatives that we sent to Peking, they would doubtless have begun to think about fulfilling their promise. We earnestly beg them to do so: we yearn for them as an infant does for its mother. Prostrating ourselves on the ground we implore, above all, the mercy and the infinite goodness of God, Who is our only support. We are confident that the zeal and virtue of the priests will bring us the words of salvation with the speed of a shooting star and redeem us all. If that shop that used to be situated near the entrance to one of the houses that the Europeans have in Peking could be repaired, it would greatly help us in communicating with the Church in Peking. We humbly request that this amenity be graciously provided for us.

"In the year Sin-yu, 1801, after the priest and a great number of Christians had been put to death, our government reported the matter to the emperor of China. The Church

in Peking will no doubt have heard of this. Since then, it has frequently happened that various compatriots of ours have pretended to become Christians in order to spy on us. These are the apostates and traitors to the faith, who act in this way in order to demonstrate their loyalty (to the government) and to gain some reward. We trust that you will have realized their duplicity and that you will not allow yourselves to be cheated. If communications between you and us are interrupted would it not be a good idea to agree upon a certain Christian house in the town, which could serve as our place of rendezvous?

"Our king is gravely ill, and his life seems to be near its end, for medicine seems to have no effect. We beseech our Church (the Church in Peking) to pray to God for his safety and the recovery of his health.

"In writing to the Sovereign Pontiff[2] we have taken a great liberty. Forced by the distressing circumstances in which we are situated we could not do otherwise. We beg you to translate our letter and forward it: it is a slight testimony of affection which in our lowly position we tender to him who is the Vicar of God on earth and the source of our happiness. We trust that our affairs will be communicated in faithful detail, in the hope that he will be touched with pity for us.

"There are many other things that we are unable to write about on this piece of silk. The bearer will inform you of them as fully as possible.

"We earnestly beg you to keep us in mind, and to render us your support in our appeal and to give us your blessing, in the holy name of God and the redemption. Amen.

"The third of the eleventh moon of the year Sin-mi (December 18, 1811)."

In their letter to the Pope, the neophytes described their pitiful situation and entreated his spiritual help in even stronger terms.

---

[1] These were the two couriers sent to China by Father Chou. They were seized on their return from Peking, and the Bishop's letter was found in their possession.

[2] Pius VII (Chiaramonti); reigned 1800-1823.

Letter from the Christians of Korea
To the Sovereign Pontiff

"Francis and the other Christians of Korea prostrate on the ground and beating the breast offer this letter to the chief of the entire Church, the supreme and greatest Father.

"It is with the utmost earnestness and the sincerest fervor that we supplicate Your Holiness to have compassion on us and to give us testimony of the mercy which fills your heart by according us as speedily as may be possible the benefits of the redemption. We live in a small kingdom, and have had the good fortune to receive the sacred doctrine, at first through the medium of books and, ten years later, through sermons and participation in the Seven Sacraments. Seven years afterward a persecution began; the missionary who had come to us was put to death together with a large number of Christians, and all the others, bowed down under affliction and terror, have gradually become dispersed. They cannot assemble for religious exercises, and each one remains in hiding. Nothing is left to us but our firm trust in the infinite mercy of God and the great compassion of Your Holiness, who will certainly be willing to rescue and succor us without delay; this is the object of our prayers and lamentations. After ten years we are overcome with sorrow and affliction; many of us have died of old age or various diseases, and we do not even know their number, while those who remain do not know when they will receive the sacred teaching. They earnestly desire this grace as a thirsty man seeks what will assuage his distress; they call for it as during a time of drought we call for rain. But Heaven is high and our cries do not reach it; the ocean is broad and we are without means to go and seek it for ourselves. We have read some of the sacred books. The holy religion is being preached throughout the world; it is only in our eastern kingdom that it has been announced without the help of missionaries and solely by means of books. Yet several hundred martyrs have given their life for God, both before and after the advent of the missionary, and the actual number of converts at present is not less than ten thousand.

"We, miserable sinners, cannot express to Your Holiness with what sincerity, with what fervor we yearn for your aid. But our kingdom is small, remote, and situated in a corner of the ocean, and no ships or vehicles come, by means of which we might receive your instructions and your orders; and what can the cause of our privation be but our spiritual sloth and the gravity of our sins? This is the reason why, beating the breast in profound fear and sincere sorrow, we most humbly pray to the great God of the Incarnation, Who died on the cross, Who cares even more for the repentant sinners than for the just, and to Your Holiness who are the representative of God, Who cares for all and truly redeems the sinners. We have been redeemed and have left the darkness, but our bodies still suffer in this world: sin and malice oppress our souls. We have no means of receiving the benefit of Baptism,[1] and of confession; we are unable to share in the sacrifice of the most Holy Body of Jesus Christ; our desire is great, but when can it be fulfilled? Our tears and moans and our afflictions are of small worth but we believe that the mercy of Your Holiness is infinite and immeasurable, and that in consequence, you will take pity on your flocks in this realm who have lost their shepherd, and will send us missionaries without delay, so that our souls may be succored and redeemed, and merits of the Saviour Jesus be proclaimed, and the Holy Name of God may be glorified everywhere and forever.

"1. Formerly we had heard nothing relating to foreign countries but during the last few years on the occasion of the propagation of the holy religion we have come to learn a little about Europe. We are most gratified to speak of this. Our entire nation admires the Europeans for their knowledge of mathe-

---

[1] Evidently it is Solemn Baptism which is referred to.

matics, and the ability of their painters. On the other hand the population has been rapidly increasing over a considerable period of time and in consequence we have poverty, famine and destitution. Except for a few stubborn converts to Buddhism, the whole population exhausted by so many calamities, groaned in distress and craved for instruction in the holy law. In spite of this, the natural weakness of spirit and the lack of means impeded any great progress in religion until suddenly the great persecution began. All of the better educated and more virtuous were put to death. The sufferings which the survivors have undergone are proof that they have not changed, but the official ban, the tortures and death with which they are threatened and of which they have witnessed such terrible examples, have intimidated them. If a man of courage should arise before them with words of encouragement it seems certain that they would hasten to practice the religion, and they would show their capacity for energetic action, just like a mountain stream which, coming down from the mountains, throws itself into the valleys and overcomes all obstacles in its path.

"2. Our kingdom, contiguous to the empire of China, of which it is a tributary state, is situated at the world's end, and it maintains certain national habits and customs to which it is particularly attached. Entry and exit are strictly forbidden, especially during the persecution, and the border guards are a hundred times more vigilant than ever before. Moreover, we have heard that there is also a persecution going on in Peking. If, then, our souls are to be saved priest must come by sea, for no other route is practicable. The only way to enter our country by land is by way of the north, for the other three sides are bounded by the ocean. From our coasts to the province of Shantung in China is not more than three hundred miles, so that with a favorable wind a cockcrow is almost within earshot.[1] The southern part of our country is only a few hundred leagues from Nanking, and only three or four hundred leagues from Macaó, where our sacred religion is public. If a ship could be sent from Macao to Korea, sailing between Nanking Province and the Ryukyu Islands toward the north, in a few days it would arrive at the south (sic) coast of our country. From there the distance to the capital is no more than ten leagues. Although this western sea is rather shallow it can be easily navigated by small ships. It is only to this side that we can look for succor, which is why we humbly beg Your Holiness to give your attention to our request as soon as possible.

"3. Whenever foul weather forces foreign ships to touch at our coasts, they are never allowed to prolong their stay. They are never left alone, but kept under constant surveillance and forced to depart as quickly as possible. For this reason it is necessary to have, on board the vessel which we are asking for, a prudent, capable and experienced man, able to write Chinese characters well, in order that by this means we can understand one another. Moreover it would be well for the Sovereign Pontiff and the king[2] to send presents and letters of amity, couched in terms of propriety, to our king. They would be well advised to make it perfectly clear in their letters that their sole intention is that only the one God proclaimed by our holy religion should be worshiped, that all men should be free, that the kingdoms should be maintained in their integrity, and that peace should reign among all the peoples of the world. The Christian doctrine should also be clearly set forth in the letters, stating with all sincerity and in the most convincing manner that the priests have no designs upon the

---

[1] A popular Chinese phrase, occurring in the *Tao-te-king* and other classics, signifying nearness.
[2] King John VI of Portugal, Regent 1792—1816, King 1816—1826, of whose territory the colony of Macao (*Cidade do Santo Nome de Deus de Macau, Não Ha Outra Mais Leal* 'City of the Name of God, Macao, Most Loyal of the Colonies') had formed part since its foundation in 1557. The Diocese of Macao formerly embraced the whole of China and Japan as well as Malacca and the East Indies.

independence of the country or its territory, but seek only to practice charity. Perhaps by this method it may be possible to open the eyes and allay the suspicions of our king's advisers, so that they may see the truth. They have known for a long time that the Europeans are very skilful in the arts, and sciences, and are endowed with prudence and other virtues. They are too honest to measure themselves against the Europeans or to offend them. They know very well that the European preachers travel to every part of the world without any of them ever thinking of making themselves masters of foreign countries. But our little country is full of suspicion and fear. They cannot make up their own minds, and will certainly have recourse to Peking, to warn the emperor and await his order, in order to be sure of his protection, and to avoid being punished. Now, how can the Emperor compel our government not to receive someone who brings compliments and presents? Our king and his ministers will then have nothing to fear and their minds being at rest they will not fail to accord a kindly reception to this envoy.

"4. In the seas to the south of Korea which lie near Nanking Province and not far from Macao, there are thousands of small islands, which belong to nobody, and which are capable of being tilled and inhabited. Our kingdom maintains no communication with other countries either by sea or by land;① that is why our nation is so lacking in culture and so weak. As we have not developed our talents or enlarged our knowledge, we make no effort to undertake long sea voyages to distant countries. We even have a custom in our country of cursing a man by saying 'go to sea.' A ship, then, might very well be sent from Macao to explore these uninhabited islands and to establish settlements on such of them as seem most suitable, or, if they prove to be inhabited, to convert the people, and make them Christians. By these means we might well be able to extricate ourselves from our sorry predicament; but this would in any case be a desperate remedy, for it would take far too long a time. The best thing would be to send a vessel direct to us without delay.

"5. There is not much ability or intelligence to be found in this country. We are far from being endowed with such talents as other peoples possess; the most essential tools for gaining a living are so crude as to be almost worthless: our poverty is extreme. Neither the nobles nor the common people enjoy an assured income sufficient to supply them with enough food and clothing whenever, in consequence of the frequent floods and droughts, there ensues a year of famine. As for the Christians, on account of the persecution, they are wandering about in confusion to the east and to the west; they cannot stay unmolested in any place, nor avail themselves of any such resources as they formerly relied upon for their living. They are almost all reduced to a life of beggary. Usually the mind governs the body and the body nourishes the mind: it is a natural relationship. But now, as our bodies lack the means necessary to conserve life, our minds are deprived of the strength necessary to maintain our virtue. Those who were educated and who had the gift of eloquence were all killed in the persecution, and there have not been enough converts possessed of talents qualifying them to take their place. There are now only women and children, and men so ignorant that they cannot distinguish between the characters lo and yo. Great though the number of Christians may be, they are all far too ignorant; they know of the existence of God, the soul, reward, and punishment; but as for the other articles of religion they know nothing at all about them. Moreover they are in the grip of terror of persecution

---

① China was no exception, for the communications between this country and Korea were extremely restricted. They were limited, as we have seen, to a few official embassies, and one or two fairs a year at the frontier post between the two countries, on the occasions when the embassy was in transit.

and of the civil authorities. Tormented by hunger and cold, worn out with hard labor, they cannot help one another; they are dispersed like sheep that have lost their shepherd; they have fled from all sides and cannot reassemble for religious exercises, but all of them hope and trust that the Lord will take pity on them and will not leave them unprotected.

"6. We have heard that as a general rule when there are more than a thousand Christians in a given locality, a priest must be sent to them, and that when there are more than ten thousand, they should be governed by a bishop. It is true that we are very poorly instructed in religion; we know only how to fast and pray, and indeed we are unworthy to be called Christians. However, there are more than ten thousand of us who know of the existence of God, and yet we have not succeeded in being governed by a bishop. We are weighed down with sorrow when we think that the object of our hopes is so far beyond our reach; we most earnestly beg, by the mercy of Jesus Christ, that Your Holiness will send us as soon as possible a spiritual director for the salvation of our souls.

"7. It was not yet twenty years since our conversion, and not yet seven since the arrival of the missionary, when the great persecution broke out. In the preceding years there had been few martyrs. But the year 1801 came with a great commotion and our Church gained greater renown. At that time there were more than a hundred martyrs,[1] and about four hundred sentenced to exile. The spiritual benefit of the Sacraments and the augmentation of divine grace had given them strength. As for the less instructed prisoners and those not given to regular prayer, as they belonged to the uncultivated lower classes, the government considered that it was of little consequence whether they were Christians or not, and set them at liberty. They went out like a shoal of fish and it is im-

possible to estimate their number.

As for those who, although they never became acquainted with the missionary and were never accused, took to flight and went into hiding, and are still displaced, without home or family, their number is also unknown. Have pity on these innumerable souls who, deprived of all means of salvation, have nothing to look forward to but death. If there is no pity for us in Europe, and no aid is sent to us, and if we can expect none from Peking, we shall fall into despair and everything will come to an end. If help is delayed for a single day, our sufferings are prolonged for another day; if for two days, we suffer two days more: if we see no ship arrive from Europe, then the precept of Jesus Christ to teach and baptize all the nations, the words of the Holy Gospel regarding love of one's neighbors and the care of souls, all that will be cast away like an old hat or so much useless rubbish. We shall lose all hope, like a castaway washed overboard in a storm who at first tries hard to keep afloat, confident that he would be rescued eventually, but finally realizes that he is mistaken and that all his efforts will be in vain. We humbly beg Your Holiness to forgive us for troubling you with these cries for help, these outbursts of frenzied appeal, this disorderly expression of our bewilderment occasioned by our dismay at the contemplation of our peril. Like drowning men or people imprisoned in a burning building, we are no longer masters of ourselves and the loss of self-possession makes us become confused.

"8. The continuance of the state of permanent persecution obliges us to write this letter on a piece of silk, so as to enable the bearer to conceal it in his clothing. The chances that he will lose his life in the attempt to convey it are ten thousands to one. This is why it is impossible for us to send you any bulky volumes of records; we are sending

---

[1] We have seen above that the number was actually much greater, and was at least two hundred or more. In view of the state of isolation to which the Christians had been reduced by dispersal, it is easy to understand that the authors of this letter must have been unable to know the exact number.

only those of the martyrdom of the missionary, of the catechist, Columba Kang, and a
few others, about ten in all, with the names
and surnames of forty-five of the most outstanding among the remainder. A complete
account of all of them would fill many volumes, which we shall take the liberty of for-
warding to you in due course: our martyred
compatriots, though they were subjects of a
petty foreign kingdom, have all had the
honor of being received into the Church and
their names are inscribed in the register of
those who gave their lives for truth and justice.
They are indeed pleasing to God and beloved
by the Blessed Virgin Mary and all the
saints and angels; they will be no less pleasing to Your Holiness than they are to God.
Through the merits of our martyrs we hope
to receive without delay the spiritual succor
we beg for, shedding a thousand, nay, ten
thousand tears of blood.

"The twenty-fourth day of the tenth moon
of the year Sin-mi (December 9, 1811)."

These two letters were safely conveyed to
the Bishop of Peking by John Lee Yŏ-jin,
who managed to accompany the Korean
winter embassy to China, by obtaining the
post of personal servant to one of the members of the ambassador's suite.

Bishop Gouvéa had died on July 6, 1808. The
Most Rev. Joachim de Souza-Saraiva, Bishop of Tipase, who had been consecrated at
Macao in 1804, as Coadjutor to the Diocese of
Peking with the right of succession, was never
able to enter and take possession of his see,
and died at Macao in 1818. During the whole
of this episcopate the Diocese was administered by the Vicar General, Father José
Ribeiro Nunes (1767–1826).

The missionaries of Peking received the two
letters in 1812 and forwarded them the same
year to the Bishop of Peking, resident at Macao[1]. The letter to Pope Pius VII was forwarded to him while he was being held at

Fontainebleau by the Emperor Napoleon, who
was about to march on Moscow. Owing to
the persecution in China and the danger and
difficulty it was for the time being impossible to send a missionary. When this was
told to John Lee Yŏ-jin he blamed himself
for the failure of his mission, and retired from
public life. He died in 1830.

John Kwon Kye-in also thought that the
failure to obtain a missionary for Korea was
due in part to his own shortcoming, and went
to live in retirement among the mountains
in order to cultivate his faith and virtue. He
died in March, 1814 at the age of forty-seven.

Succeeding John Kwon and John Lee as
outstanding Catholic figures were Paul Chŭng
Ha-sang and Charles Hyŭn Sŏk-mun.

They were assisted by Augustine Yu Chin-
kil and Charles Cho Sin-ch'ŏl.

Chŭng Ha-sang was the son of the famous
Chŭng Yak-jong, chairman of the *Myŏng-
to-hoe.*

After his father's martyrdom he had taken
refuge with his elder sister in Yang-keun,
where he quietly devoted himself to the study
of Catholic doctrine. As a result of the indefatigable efforts of Chŭng Ha-sang and Yu
Chin-kil who continued to impress the Korean
Church's needs every year upon the Church
in Peking, the way was paved for the invitation of a missionary to Korea. Communication was established with Peking and then
with the Vatican, insuring an eventual far-
flung development of the Church in Korea.

The rebirth of Catholic community life
proceeded principally in the three provinces
of Kyŏng-ki, Ch'ung-ch'ŏng and Chŏl-la. The
seed of religion spread to Kyŏng-sang and
Kang-won Provinces as well. The fact that
cases of oppression continued to occur in the
Province of Ch'ung-ch'ŏng long after the persecution of 1801 had abated in the rest of
the country indicates that the Catholics were
probably most active and most numerous in
this province.

---

[1] Letter from Bishop Souza-Saraiva to the *Propaganda* dated Dec. 29, 1815, in the Archives of the Sacred
Congregation *De Propaganda Fide*, section *Scritture originali delle Congregazioni particolari dell' Indie Orientali e
Cina,* 1871, f. 379-380, quoted by Fr. Andrew Cho'e Sŏk-u, op. cit. p. 64, pp. 112-114 (text of letter).

CHAPTER FOUR

CONTINUED CHURCH SUFFERINGS
IN PROVINCIAL AREAS

21. Sporadic Cases in Ch'ung-ch'ŏng Province

After the sending of the two letters to the Bishop of Peking and to Pope Pius VII things became relatively calm and peaceful for a few years. Nationwide persecution, however, did not completely cease. The official ban on the religion of Catholicism had never been lifted, and the fate of our Christians lay in the hands of the coercive provincial governments. From time to time cases of martyrdom continued to occur in various parts of the country.

On the third of third moon, 1811, the government promulgated the Decree Calling for the Singling Out of Catholics in all eight provinces, and beginning with the three cities, Kae-sŏng, Su-won and Kwang-ju. At the time, Catholicism was particularly active in the Province of Ch'ung-ch'ŏng and many Catholics gave up their lives as a result of this decree.

At Kong-ju, Park Ok-kwi and Ahn Chŏng-ku died for the faith on the twenty-third of fifth moon, and more than ten other Catholics were exiled. On the fifteenth of tenth moon, Chang Ŏ-tun-nam and Kim Tŏk also gave their lives as martyrs.

In the following year Paul Lee Yŏ-sam was beaten to death after months of torture.

In 1813 Paul Hwang, Peter Won and Matthias Chang died martyrs for the faith, and in 1814 Pius Kim Chin-hu and Simeon Yu Keun-myŏng met the same end.

(1) Paul Lee Yŏ-sam

Exiled for the faith in 1802 he had been able to obtain pardon, and permission to return to his native place. For some unknown reason the magistrate later arrested several of his relatives, who denounced him. One of them conducted the constables to the village of Kae-chi-ki in Keum-san, Chŏl-la Province, where he was in hiding. He was arrested and imprisoned for the third time. He underwent severe torture for six months in Hong-ju, and many of his pagan friends continually urged him to save his life by uttering a few words of submission to the authorities, but he always answered firmly that he had made up his mind to give up his life for God. Finally, one market day, during the eleventh moon, the magistrae decided to get rid of him, and ordered two executioners to beat him with heavy three-edged wooden bars. After a long series of blows, Paul lay motionless and the magistrate told them to find out whether he was still alive. Suddenly to the amazement of all he got up, seated himself formally on his heels, as was the custom on a ceremonial occasion, and asked for water, which was at once brought to him. Then, as he was still only a catechumen, he crossed himself and poured the water over his head, as if to baptize himself.[1]

After that, turning his gaze toward the astonished magistrate he said, "I am a very great sinner, and if you go on beating me in the way you have been doing up to now, it will take too long to put me to death; if you want me to die, strike here," and with his finger he pointed to a spot on the side of his body. Two strokes on the place he had indicated were enough, and he gave up the ghost. He was about forty-three years old when he died.

It is said that at the moment of the consummation of his martyrdom three young men passing not far from that place saw a bright light ascending into the sky. They said to one another, "What can that be? It is not a fire. It's extraordinary!" and they went on their way. One of them, who was a Christian, on returning home three days later heard of the death of Paul and on working out the exact time and date he verified that the time of the phenomenon they had observed coincided exactly with that of the Paul's martyrdom, and in his exultation began to praise God for this prodigy. The relatives and pagan friends of Paul took away his body to prepare it for burial and were amazed to see that his beaten and battered body now showed no sign of injury, but on the contrary seemed to be radiant with unearthly splendor. One of them, struck by the strangeness of this circumstance, was converted on the spot. An eyewitness of the light that had appeared at the moment of Paul's death was still living in 1870, as well as many others who heard it on the same day, and

later the testimony of a pagan whose mother and father saw the unblemished body at the time of burial was also received.[2] The name of Yŏ-sam became proverbial for a long time among the constables of the Hong-ju law court. They used to say to the Christians undergoing torture, "You must bear these blows like Yŏ-sam," and after the death of the confessors, seeing no such strange light, they would say, "That one, no doubt, was no Yŏ-sam."

(2) Paul Hwang

Paul Hwang first had the glory of confessing his faith in Jesus Christ in 1794. It seems certain that at this time he underwent a severe persecution in his own home. His father, an implacable enemy of all who bore the name of Christian, is said to have gone the length of putting red-hot charcoal between his son's fingers and upon the most sensitive parts of his body, without being able to bring about his son's apostasy. Arrested on the fifteenth of the fourth moon, 1813 at Po-ryŏng county, he was thrown into jail at Hae-mi. Many other Christians were arrested at the same time and imprisoned together with him. Asked to reveal who had taught him the Catholic faith, he said, "The one who taught me is dead, and those whom you call my accomplices are all here with me." Dissatisfied with this answer the magistrate pressed him to reveal the names of other Christians of his acquaintance, and subjected him three times to the torture of dislocation of the joints of the leg bones.

Under this horrible torture he held firmly to his faith and after several months of suffering was transferred in the eighth moon to the court of the governor of Kong-ju. In the prison of Kong-ju he met many other Christians,

---

[1] It goes without saying that such a form of Baptism is null and void, and that nobody can baptize himself by water. This is not true of Baptism by desire, or by blood (martyrdom). Paul acted in good faith. In no more convincing manner could he manifest his desire for the Sacrament of Baptism, and the teaching of the Church is that in case of absolute impossibility, desire is enough. With still stronger reason is this true when to Baptism by desire there is conjoined the Baptism of blood.

[2] Dallet, op. cit., p. 267

among them Peter Won and Matthias Chang.

(3) Peter Won

Peter Won came from a village in Kyŏl-sŏng county in the Province of Ch'ung-ch'ŏng. He was a potter and became converted together with his elder brother. In order to be free to practice their religion the two brothers emigrated to Kong-ju, where they were arrested by the magistrate and put to the torture. They were released and moved to Yŏn-san county in the same province where they found work in a pottery owned by a Christian. Re-arrested, Peter Won was transferred to Kong-ju for interrogation. There his elder brother had the weakness to abjure but Peter remained firm. He died a martyr in the beginning of the tenth moon.

(4) Matthias Chang Tae-won

From a poor family of the same village as Peter Won, his life was so hard that for a time he joined a troupe of wandering actors. Having had the good fortune to embrace the faith he reformed his life and went to work at Sol-t'i in Keum-san county. He was arrested in the eighth moon at Kong-ju in the district of Yŏn-san and taken to Kong-ju. He, too, bore unflinchingly the most horrible tortures and succeeded in maintaining his faith.

Paul Hwang and Matthias Chang shared the same sufferings at Kong-ju prison and died together for their faith on the nineteenth day of the tenth moon of the year 1813. As he was being taken to the execution ground the onlookers jeered at him, but he replied, "You ought not to laugh at me but rather to weep, for assuredly your fate is more wretched than mine." He was fifty-five years old.

(5) Pius Kim Chin-hu

Born at Sol-moe in the district of Myŏn-ch'ŏn of a family of good standing, he was at first too fond of all kinds of superstition, magic and geomancy. He was about fifty when he first heard of the Christian religion, but his heart being still set on worldly honors and riches he remained deaf to the

voice of grace. He held a minor post in the provincial government, but finally resigned and embraced the faith. Brought before the court for the first time in 1791 he bravely confessed himself a Christian. He escaped and was re-arrested and released four or five times until he came to suffer the tortures of Hong-ju, Chŏn-ju and Kong-ju. It is believed that during the great persecution he could hardly have escaped except by apostasy. Sent into exile at this time, he was re-arrested shortly after his return in 1805 and thrown into Hae-mi jail. This time he behaved like a true Christian. He was not condemned to death but his case dragged interminably, and he was left in prison without trial for an indefinite period. His grave and dignified character won him the respect of the constables and jailors, and he openly practiced his religion. At last, after ten years of imprisonment borne with exemplary patience, he died at the age of seventy-six on the twentieth day of the second moon. It is not exactly known whether he died of hunger, of old age, or under the executioner's blows; but the protracted persecution that preceded his death has remained a memory cherished by all Christendom. Among his descendants there were many martyrs, among others the first Korean priest, Father Andrew Kim.

(6) Simeon Yu Keun-myŏng

Let us mention also the edifying life and death of Simeon Yu Keun-myŏng, a provincial noble, native of So-yak-kol in the district of Myŏn-ch'ŏn. His character was natural, gentle and frank. He spoke little, and never of useless or mundane matters. He was noted for his filial piety both during his parents' lifetime and after their death. At the age of fifty-nine he embraced Christianity, and abandoned pagan superstitions, honoring and serving God alone. Baptized by Louis-Gonzaga Lee Tan-won he set a good example among his brothers, always sharing his goods with the poor and unfortunate. He emancipated his slaves and spent his time instructing his friends in Christian doctrine. He was arrested in the fifth moon of the year 1801 and underwent torture several times without flinching. Later he was weak enough to declare where his books of religion were concealed, but he never denounced a fellow-Christian and refused right up to the end to give the slightest sign of apostasy. Condemned to exile in a distant province, he kept up the practice of his religion, showing only regret at possessing no religious books. At length after long suffering bravely borne he died while praying, on his knees, seated on his heels, to the great wonder and admiration of the local inhabitants. He was eighty-two years old.

22. The Eul-hae (1815) Persecution

We have seen already that many Catholics took refuge among the mountains in Kang-won and Ch'ung-ch'ŏng Provinces: they now began to penetrate into the remote valleys of the T'ae-paek mountains, where they built a peaceful little Christian village. In the year 1814, the fourteenth year of the reign of King Sun-jo there was a famine, but this village was unaffected. This was brought to the notice of the government by a backslider named Chŭn Ch'i-su and the hungry officials eagerly rushed to the village. This was at Easter-tide, the twenty-second day of the second moon by the lunar calendar. The village of Mo-rae-san in Ch'ŏng-song county, and a few days later that of Mŏ-ru-san in Chin-po county was ransacked and turned into a shambles, and the prisons of An-tong, Kyŏng-ju and other places in the vicinity were filled with Catholics. Some of these, unable to bear the hunger and persecution, apostatized, but the majority of them remained faithful to the end. Some died in captivity, and some were transferred to the prisons of the provincial capital of Tae-gu. It is not known how many Christians died in the Eul-hae (1815) catastrophe, but in Tae-gu prison alone the prisoners numbered more than one hundred.

Among those who died before being transferred to the Tae-gu prison were Paul Park, his cousin John Park Kwan-sŏ and five others in the Kyŏng-ju prison; Kim Myŏng-suk and

his son, who were baptized in the An-tong prison, were killed and Andrew Ch'oe and his brother Martin Ch'oe died of hunger. Catholics who died in Tae-gu prison before being sentenced include:

(1) Andrew Sŭh and His Family

Andrew Sŭh, after having undergone torture with unshaken constancy, died in prison before the sentence of death which had been pronounced upon him could be executed. His wife, Barbara Ch'oe, and his son-in-law Francis Ch'oe Yŏ-ok, managed to survive the persecution for some time, but the mother was arrested on Easter Day, and beaten so cruelly with the three-edged club that her resolution almost failed. Her son-in-law, however, joined her in prison, comforted her and encouraged her to maintain her faith until her death. Francis Ch'oe Yŏ-ok known to many under the name of Chin-kang, his childhood name, was the son-in-law of the couple mentioned above. He was born at Ta-rae-kol in the districts of Hong-ju, and was converted together with his mother, after which he came to live among the hills of Mu-sŏng-san. As soon as he heard that Father Chou was staying in the capital he went with his mother and sister to visit him. His mother was able to receive the Sacraments, including Extreme Unction at the time of her death. His sister then went to stay at the home of Augustine Chŭng, while he himself withdrew to the country. He had at first intended to live a celibate life, but the example of his cousin german and the exhortations of some of his other relations made him change his mind, and he married the daughter of Andrew Sŭh. Later he regretted not having carried out his former project, though this did not prevent his living very happily with his wife and children. As soon as he was arrested, he told his companions to refer all the magistrates' questions to him, which drew upon him especially violent torture, but he never weakend for an instant. Taken to Tae-gu he had to bear, blow by blow, torments so atrocious that several times he fainted but his courage and fervor remained unshaken. He was condemned to death but before the day fixed for his execution he died in prison, of the injuries which he had received: this was during the fifth moon of the year 1815. He was a little over thirty years of age.

(2) Alexis Kim Si-u

Alexis Kim Si-u was of a noble but impoverished family of Ch'ŏng-yang county in Ch'ung-ch'ŏng Province. He was semi-paralyzed but used to write copies of Christian books with his left hand and distribute them among his fellow-Christians, who supported him with their alms. Arrested in the Easter season of 1815, he was sent to Tae-gu Prison, where the provincial governor, moved to pity at the sight of his crippled body, tried to make him abjure his faith. Alexis in reply exhorted the governor to worship Jesus Christ, which so angered him that he ordered Alexis to be put to further torture, which was inflicted on him with such ferocity that his jaw was broken. He was sentenced to death, but, unable to support himself in prison by making straw-sandals as all the other prisoners did, he starved to death before the sentence was executed. He was thirty-four years old.

Of the twenty-nine Christians sentenced to death at the Tae-gu prison, twenty-two died in prison while awaiting execution. The seven who survived the ordeal of hunger and torture to meet their death on the execution ground were:

Peter Ko Sŏng-tae, Joseph Ko Sŏng-un, Barbara Ch'oe Sŏng-yŏl, Anna Lee Si-im, Francis Kim Kyŏng-sŏ, James Kim Hwa-ch'un, Andrew Kim Kye-won.

(3) The brothers Peter Ko Sŏng-tae and Joseph Ko Sŏng-un

These two brothers were born at Pyŏl-am-kol, Tŏk-san, in Ch'ung-ch'ŏng Province, and were brought up as Christians by their parents, becoming staunch Catholics as they grew up. In 1801, Peter, the elder, was arrested at Ko-san county in Chŏl-la Province, and imprisoned at the Chŏn-ju jail. The punishments he had to endure were so cruel that he could not bear them, and promised to give up his faith, but as soon as he was released he resumed his preaching of the Catholic religion at Mo-rae-san, Ch'ŏng-song county, Kyŏng-sang Province where, while engaged on building a community village for refugee Catholics, he was re-arrested together with his brother.

(4) Barbara Ch'oe Sŏng-yŏl

She was born at Hong-ju in Ch'ung-ch'ŏng Province, converted in 1801, and after her first husband died she married Andrew Sŭh. She was beheaded at the age of forty.

(5) Anna Lee Si-im

Anna Lee was the beautiful and talented daughter of a distinguished family of Tŏk-san, Ch'ung-ch'ŏng Province. Her father was Lee Sŏng-sam who died in Chŏn-ju prison in 1827. A pious Catholic, she made a vow of perpetual virginity and decided to join a community of unmarried women who had also resolved to live celibate lives. On her way to their house, which was situated in a remote region far from her home, she met a fellow-Catholic named Park, an educated man holding the degree of licentiate or *Chin-sa*. She changed her mind, married Park, and bore him a son. After her husband's death she lived as a pious Catholic widow. She was arrested in 1815 at Chin-po in Kyŏng-sang Province and sent to prison at Tae-gu where she died at the age of thirty-five. Her son predeceased her, his death having resulted from the hunger and hardships he underwent.

(6) Francis Kim Kyŏng-sŏ

Born of a wealthy and elevated family of Ye-san in Ch'ung-ch'ŏng Province, Francis Kim was brought up as a good Catholic by his father, Andrew Kim Kwang-ok, a fervent Christian. Of somewhat excitable nature, he overcame this shortcoming by diligent practice of his religion and the virtue of perseverance in particular. His father gave his life for the faith, as we have seen above, and Francis took refuge in the mountains in Kyŏng-sang Province, where he was reduced to living on acorns and herbs. In the third moon of 1815 the apostate Chŭn Ch'i-su led the police to his home in the hills. He received them with kindly hospitality, took an affectionate farewell of his wife and family, and with parting words of blessing and good advice accompanied the police with a joyous and smiling air. He endured the tortures with a courage, was sentenced to death, and gave his life for the faith on the first day of eleventh moon 1816. He was fifty-two years old.

(7) James Kim Hwa-ch'un

James Kim Hwa-ch'un, regarding whom very little information has come down to us, belonged to a family in Ch'ŏng-yang county, Ch'ung-ch'ŏng Province. He was of a gentle and resigned disposition, but he knew how to display great energy when it was a matter that concerned the service of God and the salvation of his soul, and, being a faithful follower of the rules of the Church, he distinguished himself by his devotion to prayer and the reading of religious books. Arrested in 1815 (it is not known on what date) he was taken to An-tong, whence, indifferent to all the solicitations and promises of the magistrates, as well as to the violent torture that was inflicted on him, he was sent to Tae-gu and condemned to death.

(8) Andrew Kim Kye-won

Andrew was the son of Pius Kim Chin-hu of Sol-moe, Myŏn-ch'ŏn county, Ch'ung-ch'ŏng Province. For over twenty years he witnessed the continual persecution of Catholics, until he decided to take refuge, taking leave of his family in a remote village near An-tong in Kyŏng-sang Province. There he lived for seventeen years on mountain fruits, nuts and wild herbs. He transcribed the Holy Bible and distributed the copies to his fellow-Christians and others, and strove to spread the faith. Arrested and taken to Tae-gu prison, he saw Agatha-Magdalene Kim em-

erge from the prison gate just as he was about to enter. Learning that she had that very day gained her freedom by abjuring Christianity, he remonstrated with her so convincingly that she saw the light once more and returned to prison. The magistrate was so enraged at her constancy that he ordered her to be beaten so severely that the flesh was torn away from her body and the bones exposed. She died soon afterward in her prison cell, at the age of fifty. This was in the early part of the fifth moon. Andrew was interrogated and kept in prison over a period of twenty months but his faith never wavered. In two letters which he wrote to his brother during this period of imprisonment he says that more than a hundred Catholics were imprisoned in Kyŏng-sang Province at the time.[1]

These seven Catholics were put to death and sowed the seeds of the faith with their blood on the first day of the eleventh moon of 1816. Andrew Kim was the first, and the executioner was so maladroit as to take ten blows of the sword to strike off his head. The four men including Joseph Ko were the next, and then the magistrate, wishing to shake the faith of the two women who awaited their turn to cull the palm of martyrdom, said to them:

"These men have now been put to death, but you are women; why do you wish to die? Compared to theirs, your guilt is light. Come on, now; there is still time. Say the word, and I will set you free."

"How can you still go on misunderstanding the principles?" Anna asked in reply, "According to you, men must honor God the Father, but women are not to be allowed to follow their example! Words are a waste of time: I am merely waiting to be dealt with according to the law."

The two women then called out in a loud voice:

"When Jesus and Mary are calling to us to join them in Heaven, how can we apos-

---

[1] Dallet. op, ci t. vol. I, pp. 289-293

tatize, and by choosing this transitory existence lose eternal bliss?"

Accordingly the order was given and the two women were beheaded. Anna Lee was thirty-five and Barbara Ch'oe forty: the ages of the others are unknown.

These seven martyrs sowed the seeds of the faith in the Kyŏng-sang region: in Won-ju, Kang-won Province, the following martyrs are among the most noteworthy.

(9) Simon Kim

Simon Kim was of a wealthy and distinguished family in Sŏ-san county and was known for his righteous and vigorous personality. Converted before the arrival of Father Chou Wen-mo (Fr. James Chou) he relinquished all his property to his serfs, left his family and friends and withdrew with his brother Thaddaeus to the district of Ko-san in the Province of Chŏl-la. It was there that he first met Father Chou, and established a firm friendship with him. During the Sin-yu persecution of 1801 he was marked out as one of the principal leaders of the Christians, and numerous police constables were put on his trail. They searched everywhere for him and it would be difficult to tell of all the privation and suffering that Simon had to undergo for over a year to evade their search. His wife had already been seized and was not released until a year later, after payment of a large sum of money. In order to conceal his whereabouts and at the same time make a living, Simon disguised himself as a peddler, and was brave enough to preach the Gospel to the pagan peddlers who associated with him in his daily life. Finding, however, that this way of life left him insufficient time for the practice of his religion he took up a more contemplative life at Mŏ-ru-san in Kyŏng-sang Province. He was joined by several of his proselytes and their families and they set up a Catholic village community. He made several more converts here but was eventually forced to move to Ul-jin county in Kang-won Province. When the 1815 persecution began in Kyŏng-sang Province his whereabouts was made known by a former servant

of his, a Christian who had been arrested at An-tong, and in the fourth moon of that year he was arrested and most of his property was confiscated.

In prison he found many Christians who were suffering horribly from hunger. He petitioned the magistrate to order the return of his confiscated property so that it might be sold to provide food for his starving fellow-prisoners, and in this way he was able to bring them some relief. After steadfastly refusing to abjure the faith he was transferred to Won-ju prison where he met six or seven other Catholics. Here the torture was so inhuman that all except Simon were forced to renounce their religion. Simon remained faithful to the end, and while his sentence of death was awaiting the royal assent he died of dysentery and injuries received while under torture, on the fifth day of the eleventh moon, 1815. He was more than fifty years of age.

Notable differences between the great persecution of 1801 and that of 1815 are that the former was general, while the latter was largely concentrated upon the newly formed Christian communities in Kang-won and Kyŏng-sang Provinces: during the former, political animosity and party jealousy played a considerable role, whereas this time the converts were imprisoned simply for being Christians, and put to death for the same reason: the first persecution had commenced with a solemn decree and terminated by a royal proclamation announcing to all that the work was completed, but now there was no need for new edicts, for the old laws against religion were still in force. There was no official end to it, for it went on, and, as Dallet says, was still going on when he wrote in 1874, increasing or decreasing at the whim of the magistrate.

Moreover in 1801 few women were seized, and then only in the elevated classes most feared by the government; most of the others were neither arrested nor prosecuted. What they had to endure was the aftereffects; they were ruined by confiscation or pillage of their property but could usually withdraw with their children to other districts. In 1815, on the other hand, the constables had a free hand and the number of women arrested and put to death seems to have been proportionately much greater.

23. The Martyrdom of Peter Cho Myŏng-su and His Virgin Wife Theresa Kwon

Peter Cho Myŏng-su, better known under his legal name of Suk, was a close relative of Justin Cho, a celebrated figure of Yang-keun. A child at the outbreak of the persecution of 1801, he went to live with his maternal relatives in Kang-won Province for several years. As he grew up he showed remarkable talent, a kindly nature and a gravity beyond his years. Unfortunately the neglect of his studies and the constant fear under which the refugees lived had prevented the regular practice of his religion until, his marriage to Theresa Kwon having been concluded, her exhortations and example made him once again a good Christian.

Theresa Kwon was the daughter of one of the earliest and most zealous propagators of the faith, the famous Francis-Xavier Kwon Il-sin. At the age of seven she lost her mother and two years later she saw her father perish in the persecution of 1791. In bearing this double loss for God, in bringing up the family as the eldest of four orphans, and supporting them, her virtue developed to the point that, in spite of her fine qualities of wit and beauty which attracted the admiration of all, she despised these temporal advantages and vowed to live a life of perpetual virginity devoted to God, a vow which she confirmed when receiving the Sacraments at the hand of Father Chou. Theresa was eighteen years of age when as a result of the persecution her brothers were sent into exile and her family ruined. She made no complaint but withdrew to the capital with her nephew, determined not to marry. Before long her family, seeing her without means and fearing the adverse comments that must arise among the pagan community if she remained single, earnestly advised her to mar-

ry and she reluctantly consented. She married Peter Cho Myŏng-su, whom she knew to be a somewhat lukewarm Catholic, and on the wedding night when they were alone together for the first time, she tendered him a letter extolling the virtue of virginity, and exhorting him to maintain, like herself, perpetual continence. Peter, surprisingly enough, underwent a sudden change and acceded to her proposal, promising that they should live their married life as brother and sister.

Theresa saw in this clear proof of God's Providence and never ceased to thank Him. The two lived in perfect harmony and Peter's faith was revived so that he soon became another man.

As soon as things had quieted down he moved his family to the capital where he devoted himself to good works. They were very poor but bore their privations with joy and by practicing economy were able to help those even poorer than they. Peter, devoted to prayer and meditation, often wept at the thought of his sins. If he met a Christian who was lax or indifferent he would be so upset, and would rouse his friend from his lethargy so earnestly, that God nearly always crowned his efforts with success. He instructed and converted many pagans and by his zeal in baptizing children on the point of death brought eternal salvation to many of these unfortunates. Both Christians and pagans liked to listen to him and came in crowds to his lessons. His principal aim was to do all he could to help bring a priest into Korea, and when Paul Chŭng Ha-sang set off for Peking on this errand it was Peter who did all the preparatory work. The troubles and frustrations that he overcame, without ever becoming discouraged or impatient, were innumerable.

Theresa, for her part, was no less assiduous in doing all the good that lay within her power. Eager for spiritual advancement she subjected herself to the practice of acts of self-discipline and spiritual mortification, fasting twice a week and secretly mixing ashes and dust with her daily meal of rice. All who resorted to her for instruction, comfort or consolation were touched and edified by her counsel.

It was while this holy couple awaited the return of Paul Chŭng from Peking, toward the end of the third moon of the year 1817, that the police discovered a copy of the Church calendar① on Peter's person, or, according to other reports, on that of one of his catechumens whom he had been teaching and who had denounced him. Peter was arrested. With her maidservant Barbara-Magdalene Ko, Theresa insisted on being imprisoned with him. Peter was then interrogated and in accordance with usage called upon to apostatize, surrender his religious books, and denounce his coreligionaries. He remained firm under torture and did not let fall a single word that might compromise anybody. The judge wished Theresa to apostatize in order to save her life. She replied, firm and calm as ever:

"Since God is the Father of all mankind and Lord of the universe, how can you expect me to deny Him? In this world, to deny one's parents is an unpardonable crime: how much greater a crime it would be to deny the One Who is Father of all!" She was put to the torture, but bore it with joy: her countenance did not even change color, and the magistrate saw at once that it would not be easy to obtain her submission. In the interrogations to which the couple were subjected, she was always the first to answer, without giving her husband time to speak, as a result of which she underwent even more violent torture.

Barbara-Magdalene Ko was the faithful companion of Peter and Theresa in prison, and shared all their sufferings. She was a woman of the people, of the district of Chae-ryŏng in the Province of Hwang-hae. While still a pagan she followed her hus-

band into exile at the town of Mu-san, where she met Justin Cho Tong-sŏm and was instructed by him in the faith. Her husband having died, Barbara-Magdalene made a journey to the tomb of her parents, then, confident that nothing here below is comparable to the service of God, and the salvation of the soul, she went to the capital, where, after a long search, she found Peter, whom she had met at Mu-san. She stayed with him as his attendant, assiduously studying and practicing religion. When Peter and Theresa were arrested she followed them to prison and shared their fate to the end.

The three Catholics underwent every kind of torture and humiliation in the filthy prison for two years. On the twenty-first day of the fifth moon of the year 1819, after twenty-seven months of imprisonment, they were beheaded. Peter was thirty-three years old, Theresa thirty-six years old, and their attendant Barbara-Magdalene sixty.

The authorities did not allow their bodies to be removed until after one month, by which time only the skeletons remained. Theresa's hair was kept in a box by Sebastian Nam I-kwan, who was to die a martyr in 1839, and according to witnesses whenever the box was opened a strong fragrance would fill the room.

The three martyrs mentioned above having refused to make any denunciation, no one else was compromised in the proceedings relating to them, and there were no further arrests in the capital but we have to mention several others that took place in the provinces. In 1817, in the tenth moon, the constables of Hae-mi, for some unknown reason, suddenly appeared in the village of Pae-na-teu-ri in the district of Tŏk-san, bound some thirty Christians in

---

① Liturgical Calendar: A copy of a collection of rules to show how to deal (under each of the 35 possible variations in the date of Easter) with the concurrence of more than one office on the same day, accurately indicating the manner of commemorating, or of putting off till another time, the Saints' days, etc., occurring in the ever-changing times of Lent, Easter, Whitsuntide, and the Octave of the Trinity; formerly called the Pye (OED s.v. Pie), and banned in England also during penal times.

chains, and took them to Hae-mi. Most of them immediately regained their liberty by apostasy. A few others remained firm and had the grace to remain faithful with death. The following is what is known with more certainty about the chief ones among them.

(1) Peter Min Ch'ŏm-ji

Born in Kyŏl-sŏng, Ch'ung-ch'ŏng Province, Peter Min became a devout Catholic. While living at Soe-ak-kol he was arrested together with his widowed sister-in-law, Anna, in the tenth moon of the year 1817. The two martyrs died of starvation in the prison. They were over sixty years of age.

(2) Joseph Song Ch'ŏm-ji

Joseph was also an old man when he was arrested. A gentle and honest man, with no kinsmen, he spent his life in the service of others, and chose martyrdom rather than to renounce his faith.

(3) Joseph Sohn Yŏn-uk

A native of Hong-ju county, for seven long years he steadfastly resisted the jailors' demands that he renounce his faith, surrender his Catholic books, and denounce his fellow-Christians. He was finally released, but died a few weeks later. On the eve of his death he spent the night in prayer, reciting the prayers of the Sacrament of Extreme Unction. Next morning he went to a nearby fountain, washed his face, and, sitting down on the rock, breathed his last so peacefully that none of the other persons present realized that he had died. A strong fragrance emanated from his body, which did not stiffen for many days. This was in the year 1824.

24. The Chŏng-hae (1827) Persecution

During 1826 there was little to relate. According to a rumor that spread among the Christians, the emperor of Japan wrote a letter to the king of Korea during that year, stating that six Japanese, professing Christianity, had escaped in a small boat, and re-

questing their return if they should arrive in Korea, but it had not been possible to confirm the fact.

Except for a few sporadic cases of harassment the Church remained in peace, until, in the year Chŏng-hae,1827, the imprudence and misconduct of some Catholics gave rise to a horrible disaster. As we have seen, in 1815 the storm of persecution broke out in the Province of Kyŏng-sang: this time, the principal area affected was the Province of Chŏl-la, so cruelly put to the test already in 1801. Long years of tranquillity had attracted a large number of Catholics to go and live there, and little by little many converts joined them.

In the village of Tŏk-sil in the district of Kok-sŏng toward the southeasterly part of Chŏl-la Province there was a pottery works, where the workers were all Christians. A new convert named Chŭn had set up a wineshop to supply the needs of the village. Han Paek-kyŏm, son of the famous martyr Thomas Han, and a man only too well-known for his violent temper and unedifying conduct, lived in this village, and by his behavior gave good reason to the Catholics to ask one another, "Need such a noble martyr have left us such a bad son?" One day when the pots were being removed from the kilns there was the customary celebration and, as usual, a lot of drinking going on. Han Paek-kyŏm, already excited by the wine, complained sharply that the winecups were too small, and after a dispute with the tavern-keeper, turned to the latter's wife and insulted and violently struck her. The tavern-keeper, not yet well established in the tenets of the faith, resented this deeply and swore to have his revenge. He took some religious books and, no doubt without reflecting on the consequence of his act, went to the magistrate and denounced Han Paek-kyŏm and several others against whom he bore a grudge, as owners of them. It is most distressing to observe how this wretched quarrel among Christians led to so much devastation, so many cases of apostasy, and brought ruin to so many souls that had been redeemed by the blood of Jesus Christ.

Possessed of this evidence the magistrate of Kok-sŏng issued immediate orders for the arrest of the Christians. This was in the second moon of the year 1827. Once again the faithful were at the mercy of the cruel and greedy police; men, women and children were plundered of all they possessed, thrown into the jails, put to the question and tortured without mercy. Little by little, either by means of denunciations wrested by force from the weaker Christians, or because a conflagration spread naturally to every place around it, the persecution extended from district to district throughout the entire province.

Many of the Christians took refuge in flight; others waited in their homes or in the surrounding hills for the fate that God had destined for them, but none of them could evade the police who searched everywhere and watched all the roads. Those who were thought not worth imprisoning could not congratulate themselves on being spared, for, left by pillage without food or other resources, nothing awaited them but a slow death by starvation.

Some two hundred and forty Christians were held captive in the prisons of Chŏn-ju. The governor of Chŏn-ju followed a system different from those of previous persecutions. Perhaps he personally was less hostile to religion, or perhaps, seeing that among all these prisoners there was no personage of distinction, he decided to attain the same end by different means. He avoided wherever possible the infliction of capital punishment, confining himself to banishing all those who remained firm under torture and refused to denounce their fellow-Christians; or, if compelled by the circumstances to pronounce a sentence of death, he left the victims to rot in jail and die eventually of hunger or distress. This method succeeded beyond his hopes. Christianity in Chŏl-la fell into almost complete discontinuance, and when we consider the number of defections it occasioned, we may well say that this persecution of 1827 was the most deplorable of all. Never before had the cases of apostasy been so numerous. A few staunch Catholics, however, kept their

faith and maintained the honor of the Church. We will here give an account of most famous among them.

(1) Magdalene Lee

Magdalene Lee was the sister of Paul Lee of Chang-ki in Kyŏng-sang Province. She married Andrew Lee at Nae-p'o at the age of seventeen, and had seven children. A pious Catholic, she steadfastly refused, under severe torture, to reveal the whereabouts of her brothers, and was banished to Paek-ch'ŏn in Hwang-hae Province. Here she was subjected to public ridicule for her faith but bore it meekly. Being illiterate, she kept count, on her fingers of the days on which Sunday fell. After four years of poverty and ill-health she passed away peacefully while saying her rosary. This was on the twelfth day of the eleventh moon of the year 1830, the fifty-third year of her age.

(2) Andrew Kim To-myŏng

Born at Myŏn-ch'ŏn in Ch'ung-ch'ŏng Province, Andrew Kim was brought up as a Catholic by his parents and led a peaceful and quiet life of piety until his arrest in the second moon of 1827 in Sun-ch'ang county, when he was thrown into jail at Chŏn-ju. Put to the torture, he unswervingly maintained his faith and firmly refused either to give it up or to reveal the names of his fellow-Christians. He died in prison in the early part of 1832, over fifty years of age.

(3) John Lee Sŏng-ch'i

John Lee belonged to a family of distinction, ranking high in the annals of military service, the Ham-p'yŏng clan of the Lee family, in Chŏl-la Province. As the eldest of three brothers he was responsible for their welfare. Though he had taken interest in Christian teachings since the age of twenty-four, he did not feel free to profess the religion among his pagan neighbors, so he migrated to the mountains, where he and his family had to suffer hunger and privation for a long time. His father was hostile to Catholicism, which he regarded as the cause of their poverty, but eventually embraced the faith, and twenty years later reaped the fruits. John traveled from province to province and finally settled in Ko-san county, Chŏl-la Province, where he led a Christian life consoling the sick and helping the poor. He buried the bodies of those who died by the roadside during famine years, like the father of Tobias (Tobias 1: 20). On the twenty-third of the third moon of 1827 the police descended on his village and carried off thirteen members of his family, imprisoning some and holding others in private homes as hostages under house arrest. John was severely punished for having buried his ancestral tablets. He underwent the bone-bending and dislocation tortures and received more than three hundred blows of the heavy club. After nine years' sickness and privation he died in prison on the eleventh of the fourth moon, 1835: he was then aged fifty-eight.

(4) John Lee Sŏng-sam

John Lee Sŏng-sam was the youngest brother of the foregoing. Denounced by weaker brethren imprisoned with him in 1827 as a distributor of the Holy Scriptures, John Lee underwent especially heavy punishment. He died in the ninth moon of the same year, in the prison, at the age of thirty-three.

(5) Paul Chŭng Man-po

A native of Tŏk-san in the Province of Ch'ung-ch'ŏng, Paul Chŭng was a cousin of the martyr, Peter Chŭng, who died for the faith in 1801. Orphaned in infancy, he became almost a slave in the home of a remote relative, but bore all hardship with humility and resignation. Once old enough to support himself he left Nae-p'o and went to live in Yong-tam county in the Province of Chŏl-la. He stayed there three years, until the outbreak of the persecution of 1827. He had always been a zealous Christian, so eager to fulfil his duties that whenever he opened a religious book he would not put it down until he had read it from cover to cover. He yearned for martyrdom, and more than once, placing his

head upon a block of wood like the execution block he would say, "If only the executioner's sword could fall upon me now, perhaps I might save my soul." Nevertheless, to avoid acting with undue temerity, he went into hiding at first. As he often went back to his house, he was soon caught by the police, who had a warrant for his arrest issued by the court as a result of his denunciation by an apostate. This warrant bore a name different from his own, and it would have been easy for Paul to evade it, but he would not let slip this favorable opportunity and went with the police to Yong-tam. After interrogation and beating he was sent to Chŏn-ju, the provincial capital, and there twice underwent the bone-bending and other tortures. He was then left to rot in jail of hunger, privation, and disease for thirteen years, at the end of which he died.

(6) Job Lee Il-ŏn

Job Lee Il-ŏn, surnamed T'ae-mun and better known under his name of Lee Tan, was a native of T'ae-p'ul in the district of Hong-ju. Brought up as a Christian by his parents, he was already a practising Catholic before the persecution of 1801. At that time he was arrested and exiled to An-eui in Kyŏng-sang Province. There, the object of the magistrate hostility and of that of his subordinates, he was imprisoned, which was unusually harsh treatment for an exile. There he was given only one meal a day, and sometimes only every other day, and sometimes deprived of food and water. There he remained for more than ten years, exposed to every kind of humiliation and ill-treatment. He seemed not to hear the insults or resent the outrages. His invariable resignation finally won him the respect of his jailors, who began to treat him less cruelly and eventually allowed him out on bail to live in a private home, where his wife came to join him in 1815. They lived together at An-eui until the fifth moon of 1826, when he was set free, and went to live at Tae-p'an in Im-sil county in the Province of Chŏl-la. They had just settled down here when the 1827 persecution broke out. His wife

counseled flight but he seemed deaf to her entreaties. One day he disappeared, and after
seeking him everywhere, they found him at
last, weeping bitterly in a secluded place.
Asked why he wept, he replied, "Last time
I missed a good opportunity of becoming a
martyr, and I deeply regret having foregone
it to become an exile. Am I not indeed unfortunate to be here with no chance to sacrifice my life for God?" His sighs must have
been heard in Heaven for three days later
the police came to arrest him. He went joyfully into their custody and the judge, knowing his past, had him tortured and beaten
with more cruelty than usual, and, a few days
later, sentenced him to death. Job was a man
of small stature and puny physique but his
constancy and steadfastness under torture had
gained him the respect of the employees of
the judiciary and they used to tell one another. "We shouldn't have judged him by his
appearan. This man is the true leader of
the Christians." Job, too, was left to await
execution in jail.

(7) Peter Kim Tae-kwon

The eldest brother of James Kim, the
martyr of 1816, and a Christian from infancy
but it was not until after the death of his
parents that, by the grace of God, Peter Kim
began to take his religion seriously. He worked
at the Kong-ju pottery, where he frequently
quarreled with his wife. One day, after an
angry dispute, he shut himself in the inner
room while his wife went to bed in the kitch-
en. Peter had fallen asleep when, awakened
by what he believed to be the voice of
God calling him, he leapt out of bed and
saw a tiger carrying off his wife. He at once
chased the beast with loud cries and succeeded
in rescuing his wife, who had sustained a
deep wound in the leg. The following morning he said, "This is all due to our constant
quarrels, but since God has permitted you to
escape with your life, the first thing to do is
to render thanks to Him, and, profiting by
this warning, to mend our ways and lead a
good life, in complete understanding with one
another until death." They kept their vow

and lived happily together for the rest of their
lives. Every Sunday Peter held a prayer and
instruction meeting for his family and for the
villagers, and never missed spending Christmas
in one of the neighboring mountains, where
he would spend the night in pious exercises.
During Lent, Peter devoted himself all the
more, to prayer and meditation, taking only
one meal a day consisting of half a spoonful
of rice, which he ate with cold water and no
seasoning except a little salt. His bodily vig-
or was in no way impaired by this extreme
asceticism. He cherished a sincere desire for
martyrdom, and after the execution of
his younger brother in 1816, having taken
possession of the executioner's block on which
James had been decapitated, he often put it
under his own chin at night, so as to be able to
think more clearly about death.

Peter had moved to Ko-san, when he learnt,
in 1827, that the persecution was about to begin.
He urged the others to flee but remained
in peace to await God's will. A band of
more than a hundred policemen surrounded
the village where he was staying and flung
themselves at the poor Christians. Peter,
unmoved, went smilingly to receive them,
and was at once bound with a red cord like
a criminal and led off to the court. He walked
like one going to a banquet.

"Do you profess the evil religion?" asked
the magistrate.

"I profess no evil religion, but worship
the true God of Heaven and earth." A
heavy cangue was fixed round his neck, and
he was sent off to the governor of Chŏn-ju,
who said,

"You too belong to this evil sect prohibited
by the king and his government; if you
will deny God, I will release you, and your
children too: if not, you will be put to death."

Peter then, in a clear and loud voice, made
this admirable answer, which has been recorded by eyewitnesses of his trial:

"Though I should die under the blows of
the executioner, I cannot deny my God.
These feelings have penetrated right into my
very flesh and blood. Though you cut off
my limbs, each part is thoroughly imbued

with them; though you burn my bones, each cinder will conserve them intact; no, a thousand times no, I cannot deny my God."

Peter feared the judges as little as he had feared the tigers. The magistrate, infuriated at his words, had him stripped and flogged, with the utmost violence of which his men were capable. As the blood streamed from his body, Peter fervently invoked the Holy Names of Jesus and Mary, and maintained a smiling and joyful expression on his face.

Taken to an adjoining room, he underwent even more cruel tortures, but his faith remained unshaken. On the following day he was brought before the judge again, and ordered to surrender his religious books and denounce his coreligionaries. On his refusal he was beaten three times. He fainted and was taken back to jail. Little by little he regained consciousness and seeing his body so badly injured he said, "Can this suffice to pay even the one ten-thousandth part of my debt to Almighty God for all the benefits that I have received from Him?" Then with a gush of tears of penitence and gratitude, he calmly prepared to die. His imprisoned son was brought to him, and a knife was held at the boy's throat, with the threat that they would cut off the boy's head unless Peter immediately apostatized. "If my son has his head cut off for such a cause it will be a great glory for him and for me: no, I shall not apostatize." The son was banished.

After further futile attempts to make him apostatize Peter was subjected to the bone-bending and other tortures, and then sent to the governor. The latter, surrounded by eighty men, all armed with clubs, put him to the question for two successive days, but under renewed torture Peter maintained the same firmness, the same air of tranquillity, and invoked always the name of the Lord, saying, "How can I ever repay even with the equivalent of a single hair, the manifold blessings of the Passion of Jesus Christ?" The governor, abandoning all hope of making

him change his mind, had him thrown back into jail. It was not until thirteen years later, the twelfth of the fourth moon, (May 29, 1839) that he was beheaded.[1]

(8) Peter Lee Sŏn-hwa

When the 1827 persecution began Peter Lee at first thought of taking flight, but all the roads were so strictly guarded that, with his aged mother, his wife, and children to take care of, it was impossible. He decided to stay and await God's will, sending only his younger brother off to try and make his way through the mountains. Arrested and brought before the Chŏn-ju court for the third time, he was denounced by a few renegade Catholics as a distributor of religious reading matter. It does not appear that he actually apostatized, but he is said to have confessed later that he had, been weak enough, during the tortures, to surrender some books and give the name of a Christian to the authorities. In spite of this fault he remained unshaken in his faith and earned this expression of respect from the magistrate: "If this man goes on talking and acting like this, he must not be allowed to live."

He was sent back to jail, where he died after thirteen years.

The persecution of 1827 after its outbreak in Chŏl-la Province spread to the Provinces of Kyŏng-sang and Ch'ung-ch'ŏng and even extended to the capital. In Kyŏng-sang the great Church leader Peter Shin Tae-po was arrested, and in Seoul Paul Lee Kyŏng-pyŏn met the same fate.

(9) Peter Shin Tae-po

Peter Shin Tae-po (already mentioned above) after working hard to raise funds for the journey to Peking, took no further part in Church management and went to live in retreat in the district of Sang-ju in Kyŏng-sang Province, until, learning of the outbreak of the persecution in 1827 and realizing that his name was well-known to the authorities and that the great number of Catholic books

[1] Dallet. *op. cit.*, vol. ii, p. 155

he had transcribed and distributed would no doubt draw their attention to him, he made preparations for flight, but his house was suddenly surrounded by police and he was arrested. On the way to Chŏn-ju they met another band of police escorting a number of prisoners from Chŏn-ju to their homes, to fetch their self-confessed religious books to the judge. The prisoners were so badly injured by the tortures they had undergone that they could not walk, and were being carried on the backs of oxen and horses. The two bands of police took the opportunity to feast and get drunk at the expense of the local villagers, and during the night Peter was able to talk to his fellow-Catholics. He learnt that many of the books they were going to surrender were in his own handwriting, so that there was no further point in concealment. On the following day he was brought before the court. It is from Peter himself that we learn these details, in the memoirs that he later wrote in prison at the request of Father Chastan. Let us hear the description of his trial in his own words.

" 'First of all', the judge asked me, 'are you a nobleman?'

" 'Once I am here, there is no difference between noble and commoner.'

" 'It is said that you are spreading a perverse doctrine throughout three provinces, and deluding the people: is it true?'

" 'I have no perverse doctrine, but solely the religion of the Lord of Heaven.'

" 'He will not admit that it is a perverse doctrine! He calls it the religion of the Lord of Heaven! Well! In following the perverse doctrine of the Lord of Heaven, did you know that it is strictly prohibited?'

" 'How could I not be aware of it? What I have done, I have done knowingly.'

" 'Having knowingly contravened the orders of the king, do you not deserve to die?'

" 'I know well that I am to be killed.'

" 'Now that the king commands that all of you are to be put to death, will you not change your mind?'

" 'A man who, after serving his king in times of peace and prosperity, disobeys him in time of danger is a coward; he who teaches the truth when all receive it smilingly and abandons it in time of danger is a greater coward. Proceed according to the law: I will proceed according to my convictions.'

" 'This fellow is insolent. No doubt he is one of the leaders of the sect. Well, since you wish to be dealt with according to the law, your wish will be granted.'

"He then ordered me to be put to the most severe torture. My crossed arms were tied behind my back, and then between them and my back they inserted a wooden bar which one of the men held. Then, with a horsehair cord they tied my legs together at the knees and just above the ankle-bones, and inserted between them two thick bars on each of which a man would press from either side.

"Then as they pulled the bar attached to my back and at the same time twisted the bars between my legs, I felt my body lifted up and I thought my chest would burst and that all my bones would be broken. I lost consciousness, and the judge, seeing that I could no longer answer his questions, ordered them to loose my bonds. Little by little I regained my senses: the rays of the sun seemed like burning torches to me; I felt as if I had no arms or legs any more, while my whole body seemed to be on fire.

"Two men stabbed me in the sides with pointed sticks to make me talk. With the utmost difficulty I managed to tell them that I had been instructed by an old Christian who had long ago died a martyr for the faith, and that I had no followers. 'You vile liar!' shouted the judge, 'Do you want us to put you to further torture to make you talk?'

" 'When the answer is yes, I say yes. When it is no I say no. I am already half dead, and if you go on like this I shall soon be quite dead. Do you think I would try to deceive you when I am on the point of death?'

" 'No, no, you're not going to die, but you'll

have to suffer a lot more pain; just wait and see.'

"They then lifted up my legs and pressed hard on the two bars. My whole body became lifeless, all saliva drained away, my tongue protruded far out of my mouth and my eyeballs started from their sockets.

"'Tell all!' shouted the men. But I could not speak; I prayed only that God would let me die at once. It was the last day of the fourth moon. Night had fallen, and the judge said,

"'It's getting late. As this is the first day, we have shown you only a sample: tomorrow you'll have some real tortures to put up with. Think things over tonight, then, and make up your mind how to save your life.'

"They untied me, and two men, passing a pole between my legs, carried me into the prison, where supper was soon brought. But I could neither sit nor move my arms: the smell of the food made me sick. Someone held a bowl of rice wine to my lips, which I drank sip by sip, and only then did I seem to recover my senses.

"It was late at night when the chief of the constables who had brought me to Chŏn-ju came and said,

"'You deserve to be pitied. The judge is convinced that Lee Yŏ-jin is in your house, or, if not, that you know where he is. Tomorrow you will have the most frightful tortures to undergo on account of this. It seems to me that the best thing you can do is to tell the judge everything and save your life.'

"'I have no idea who the man is. If I see him, I shall be able to say whether I know him or not, but as he is neither my father nor my brother, what reason have I to conceal him at the risk of my life? But you who have seen my house ought to know where he is. Is he hiding there?—If not, how can I possibly know where he has got to by now? It seems to me that the whole outcome of this affair depends on what you are going to say.'

"'On account of Lee Yŏ-jin,' he answered, 'the judge and the officials are accusing me of incapacity, for not having been able to catch him up to now. I don't want to say anything more, but you surely must know something about him. Do something about it! They are blaming me for not having seized a single book in your house. I told them that I had searched everywhere, but had found nothing. They will question you on this point; tell them that you didn't have any.'

"So saying, he proceeded to tie up the heavy cangue, which was fixed around my neck, so as to take the weight off my body, and ordered the jailor to give me a wash and attend to matters of sanitation in a manner suitable for a man of my position, adding that he would bear in mind, later on, to let me have some rice wine. What he did was a great comfort to me and I was deeply touched by these marks of his pity.

"Soon the doors of the court opened and men came out to take me there. The judge, in a loud voice, cried:

"'Remember what I said yesterday, and make your confession once more as ordered!'

"'Yesterday,' I replied, 'I lost consciousness and can not recall your orders. As for confessing, if I had anything to confess, I would not have waited till now.'

"'Lee Yŏ-jin was certainly at your house, and you know all about him: if you don't confess it, it will go hard with you!'

"'I don't know this man Lee, but even if I hid him before, how can I know where he has gone now? I can tell you nothing about him. He is neither my father nor my brother; is it likely that I would let myself be killed on his account? If you want to put me to death, let it be for my own crimes.'

"'It seems you found our tortures too light yesterday, and you wish to enjoy something a little more violent. Very well! If you insist, be it so!' He at once called out the executioners and said. 'This convict, although elderly, is the most obstinate of all. Do not spare him!'

"Once again I underwent the bending of

the leg-bones. They bound me as before and already I was almost fainting with pain when, under the strain, one of the wooden bars broke. At the sound, I thought my leg was broken and I looked at it in terror. I heard someone talking to me but I was unable to speak. They brought some rice wine and put it to my lips but I could not swallow. After a few moments' rest they brought it to me again and I was able to drink it. The judge said in a somewhat more kindly tone: 'You are determined to die on account of someone else. I really cannot understand you.' He then called for his escort, mounted his horse, and rode off to his superior official.

"As he had not had me untied, I lay there in the blazing sun. Nevertheless I could not feel the heat: even the air seemed cold to me. After a fairly long time the judge returned and said in an angry tone: 'Since you refuse to confess, either you will have to die or I shall have to lose my position. There is no third way. So, on with the tortures!' They obeyed; the pain was neither greater nor less; they merely changed their methods from time to time, but it was all one to me. Evening came and they untied me and took me back to prison. I could not eat the rice: I was given a cup of rice wine, and spent the night thus. Next morning I heard once more the shouts as they opened the court house doors. The sound dismayed me, and I imagined I could hear the cries of the prisoners. The men were not long in coming to fetch me. They shouted insults and thrusting me roughly upon a horse, carried me before the judge.

"'You see here a number of books written by you. You are considered to be the chief of three provinces, and have been supplying these books in great numbers to all the Christians. Confess it frankly, and don't be so obstinate as to let yourself be killed by the tortures.'

"I had not strength enough to utter a single word in reply. They brought me a little rice wine to sip, and with the utmost difficulty I managed to say a few words. In this examination, in accordance with the information the Christians whom I had met on the road had given me, I confessed to having copied a few volumes for them. I added that there were none in my house, as could be easily confirmed by the constables who had ransacked it. 'When I did the copying,' I continued, 'it was at the homes of those Christians, and from old examples in their possession.' Soon afterward I was taken away, without undergoing any further torture.

"That night I was put with the subordinates. They all gathered closely round me, saying, 'You pass yourself off as a noble but you don't speak frankly to the magistrate. While Lee Yŏ-jin is still at liberty the case cannot be closed. It is certain that he was in your village, and if he has left it must have been you who warned him. To say that you don't know him and to lie about the books is simply to bring still worse punishment upon yourself. What do you intend to do about it? Tomorrow the questioning will begin again; confess everything to us here, and we'll let the judge know in advance.'

"'The love of life and the fear of death,' I answered, 'is common to all, and who would wish to throw himself into danger for the fun of it? But all you know how to do is to inflict torture, without paying attention to the root of the matter. Do you call this justice?'

"'Why do you take our words amiss? We only want to spare you pain. Only denounce Lee, and nothing more will be said. They have authorized us to promise you this. Why are you so obstinate?'

"'I have said all that I had to say, and have nothing further to confess. If I die, that will put an end to it. If I am allowed to live, it will be by God's will, but I have hardly any desire to go on living. Take me back quickly to where I was before.'

"The whole thing had been done at the magistrate orders. I was taken into court again as soon as the doors opened and soon brought before the judge, who cried out in anger, 'I wanted to finish this case quickly, but your declarations are so confused that I cannot find out the facts.' Then, briefly, he accused me of being guilty of having copied out all those books. What could I say in rebuttal? That was not all. A large number of images and religious articles, many of them imported from abroad, had been seized in the homes of the Christians, who, to evade responsibility, put the blame on me. The judge said, 'There is no way for you to justify yourself, so tell us where these images and other things come from.'

" 'I have told you the truth about the books. As for the other things, ask the persons to whom they belong.'

" 'Everyone accused you and only you.'

"Not knowing what to say, I remained silent. The judge asked the Christian prisoners once more whether the objects belonged to me, and they all answered in the affirmative. I then said, 'I was told some time ago that after the year Sin-yu (1801) a certain person, having purchased the house of someone who had recently been executed, found, on pulling it down, some of these objects in the walls. They were distributed and passed around from one place to another. No doubt this is where they came from.' Infuriated at my words, the judge cried: 'This is getting us nowhere. We shall have to torture the Christians.'

"They were at once tied up with cords and immediately all of them began putting the blame on me, more insistently than before. As I was not disposed to speak the judge put me to the same torture, crying 'Tie him up, tie him up, we must put an end to this.' The torturers were too excited to spare me pain but, by the grace of God, I suffered less than before.

" 'Now, are you willing to make a clean breast of it or not?' cried the judge.

" 'I have told you everything.'

" 'Who first received these objects, and to whom were they passed on?'

" 'Of those who were living in 1801 few remain, and those who are still living are not Christians.'

" 'Who were the first to receive them? To whom did they give them?'

" 'I do not know. These things, like everything else, change their owners by death, gift, or purchase. Who can possibly know through whose hands they have passed?'

" 'Tell what you know.'

" 'I then gave the names of four or five Christians already dead and added, 'As for the others, I know nothing.'

" 'Among so many, you knew only four or five? You are trying to make a mockery of these proceedings.'

"They then tightened my bonds again, until I felt as if I was going to die. The judge then told a court official to read out a list of names, and ordered me to say, as each name was read out, whether I knew him or not. No longer able to speak, I was ordered to answer either by nodding or shaking my head, and I gave a negative answer for all of them, whether I knew them or not. The judge then added. Don't you even know *Ya-so*?' I gave the same negative sign. Night came, and I was unbound, but the cords had sunk so tightly into my flesh that they dare not remove them, and I fainted with pain under the operation. They carried me back to prison and as I was unable to eat they laid me down with my head resting on my cangue.

"The frightful shouting during the trial still re-echoed in my ears, the pain prevented me from sleeping, and, as I revived, the words of the judge occurred to my mind 'Don't you even know *Ya-so*?' Only then did I realize that the Chinese characters representing the holy name of Jesus (耶穌)[1] are pronounced *Ya-so* in Korean. I was aghast at what had happened, and in my agitation of mind began to tremble with fear. I could hardly

---

[1] The characters (耶穌) are pronounced *Yeh-su* in China, and the Christians of Korea have traditionally conserved this pronunciation, but the pagans, recognizing only the separate characters, read them as *Ya-so* according to the rules of Korean pronunciation. One can well understand how a poor victim of the torturers might not connect the sounds with their meaning.

breathe. Those who came to press me to take some nourishment I pushed away, desperate at the thought that my slowness of apprehension had deprived my death of any value. I swallowed only a few mouthfuls of rice wine. Then I began to take heart, and said to myself 'What the judge intended to designate Jesus, you understood as *Ya-so* and nothing more. Will God forgive me?' I resolved to make a clear retraction on the morrow; but having already been brought before the civil court I would be unable to make the retraction, and the thought of this made my blood run cold.

"The following day, the fifth day of the fifth moon, I was brought before the civil court. On the bench were the magistrates of Mu-ju, Ko-san and Ik-san. The last, accompanied by a court official, stood at the bar and said,

"'If you will only live your life in accordance with the principles of sound morality, the books of Confucius, Mencius and the other holy sages will be amply sufficient. Hitherto, in contravention of the royal prohibition, you have been following an alien doctrine, and now you have been arrested; doesn't your crime deserve death?'

"I realized at once that I was no longer before the criminal court. The magistrate of my own district seemed irritated, but all the others looked friendly. They showed signs of pity for me, and of regret at the frightful sufferings I had undergone. Their attendants no longer shouted, but spoke in moderate tones. It was more like a private house than a court of law. I replied with all the more respect. 'Our religion is forbidden, simply because it comes from a foreign country. But I see in your homes all sorts of things from abroad; books, clothing, furniture, and so on....' 'These are things used in all countries, and there is no point in banning their use,' was the reply, 'aren't Con-

fucius and Mencius enough?'

"'For diseases of the body,' I answered, 'when our Korean medicine has no effect, we resort to Chinese medicine which is often efficacious. Every man has seven vices, which are diseases of the soul. Now, without our religion, these are incurable. It is not that I have not studied Confucius and Mencius; but you know as well as I do that in the temples of these sages and their like, they are ready to fight over a spoonful of rice or a bit of meat, at the same time exchanging the foulest of insults; not only do they care very little for the teaching and actions of these sages, but they often profane them, and the temples, instead of being schools of virtue, have become schools of disorder. There are a few who know how to control themselves, at least outwardly, and behave decently, but at the bottom of their hearts they too are evil. Our doctrine, on the other hand, attends primarily to the inward man, controls the seven passions (emotions) and by means of the Ten Commandments regulates both the inward and outward conduct of life. It is in fact the perfecting and completion of Confucianism.'

"'If you are speaking the truth, the doctrine is not a perverse one, but since the king has forbidden it, are you suggesting that the king is in error?'①

"'Just as there is but one sun in the sky, you would permit but one doctrine in the kingdom: well and good. The king does no wrong in laying a temporary ban on the religion of the Lord of Heaven (Catholicism), until its truth or falsity has been determined. On the other hand, those who follow our religion because they know that it is the only true one, also commit no error in doing so.'

"'What's that you say? A false thing is false, and a true thing is true. Now, according to you, a thing can be both true and false at

---

① In Korea, out of respect for the crown, it was not permitted to allege that the king could do wrong. It is for this reason that Christians on trial always tried to avoid answering such questions as the above.

the same time.'

" 'In all things reason is supreme. Now, when by means of reason we try to distinguish between true and false, there is a stage at which nothing is yet decided. In discussion, some reveal the truth to others, and in matters of doctrine, an individual subject of His Majesty might well be able to perceive the truth before the government had even come to hear of it. This is precisely the state of affairs in the kingdom today.'

" 'According to you all those who were legally executed were in the right?'

" 'The doctrine being true, they were in the right: if it had been false, they would have been in the wrong.'

" 'The district magistrate rose in fury, saying,

" 'Such talk is a waste of time,' and brought the records of the civil court, saying something else that I did not quite understand. The magistrate of Mu-ju began to read from it, and ejaculated in surprise.

" 'So you have decided in favor of execution?'

" 'Yes,' was the answer.

" 'But,' went on the other, with a worried look on his face, 'in cases like this, it is not always reasonable to apply capital punishment.'

"At this the magistrate of Ik-san turned to me and said,

" 'Report everything that you said to the criminal judge, and explain fully what you meant when you spoke of the seven passions.' I then repeated all that I had said at the criminal court, and explained that the seven passions could each be overcome by the corresponding virtues, their opposites. A court official took notes of all that I said.

" 'When I think of all the tortures you underwent,' said the magistrate 'and when I look at you now and see the pitiful condition to which you have been reduced, I am quite convinced that you have been punished too severely. It will be too hard for you to read the summary of your case for yourself. I will have the court-official read it out.' It was merely a summary of the proceedings, without any details. Some of the language

had been softened, and gave the impression that I was to be allowed to live.

" 'It appears that you have been moved to pity,' said I; 'your judgment will be a triumph over the law itself.' This infuriated the district magistrate who cried angrily.

" 'We would have done well to sentence him to death. They all wanted us to do so.'

" 'According to his own words you would not have been wrong,' said the Ik-san magistrate to him, then, turning to me, 'You have contravened the royal prohibition, and I have been deputed to pronounce sentence on you. Perhaps you might have been acquitted elsewhere, but 'other lands, other laws,' here, in Korea, there is nothing we can do but commit you. They sent for a warder to take charge of me, and I was carried off to a private house. After a few days I was able to get up, but was still unable to walk. My stomach refused all food, and I could drink only very little rice wine.

"A few days later, they brought me before the governor. All the Christian prisoners were assembled. I waited outside the door, seated, and leaning on my cangue. All the servingmen and constables were jeering at me; some of them kicked my cangue, and the more hostile among them climbed onto it to make it press more heavily on me; none had a kind word for me. I was called first. 'Are you of the nobility?' 'What does that matter?' I answered, 'what difference is there between noble and commoner here?' 'If all you Christians want to follow your religion, why can't you do it secretly?' He went on to order me to state the name of the owner of each separate book, image and other religious article. 'In the examination,' I replied, 'all the prisoners blamed the whole thing on me; I was pressed to declare what I knew, and when I answered that I knew nothing, the torture was redoubled, with the insistent demand that I should accept responsibility for everything. Unable to do otherwise, I accepted the responsibility. Now you want me to tell you to whom each object belongs. How on earth can I do it?'

" 'Do you have your ancestral tablets?' 'No,

I do not.' 'And why not?' 'As I am the last descendant and sole remaining representative of a ruined family, without a home, and always wandering from one place to another, I have nowhere to set them up, so I don't have any.' 'Don't you perform the sacrifices to your ancestors?' 'On their anniversaries, I prepare the simplest dishes according to my means, and share them with my neighbors.' 'Do you then eat without making the customary genuflections?' 'I never genuflect.' Thereupon, without further questioning, I was taken back to prison.

"The next day, I was brought before the district officer. All the other Christians were present. We were called out in groups of five, and beaten, but although they beat us severely, it was nothing compared to the bone-bending torture. Next, the accused were unbound, the cangue was placed around their necks, and they were put in irons hand and foot. I was the only one unfettered, for my legs were too swollen for the fetters to be put on. When we were taken back to prison, the magistrate, seeing my condition, ordered them to take off my cangue and replace it with a lighter one, and for the first time it was taken off. My legs were so lacerated that the bones were visible, and I could still neither take food nor sit down. All I took was two or three bowls of rice wine a day. Gangrene had set in, and my wounds emitted an unbearably nauseating odor. What is more, my cell was so full of worms and vermin that nobody dared come near me. Luckily a few able-bodied Christians helped me to get about a little, and were kind enough to clean up my cell from time to time. How can I ever thank them enough for this act of charity?"

Such was the condition in which Peter Shin had to wait for thirteen long years in prison until he gained the crown of martyrdom on April 12, 1839. We have recounted these particulars in detail because nothing else could give a more correct idea of the cruelty with which the Christians were treated.

(10) Paul Lee Kyŏng-pyŏn

Paul Lee was the younger brother of Charles and Lugartha Lee, martyred in 1801. Like them he received a thoroughly Christian education. He was frail and delicate of body, and gentle but firm of spirit, and distinguished for his kindly nature and brilliant intellect. He was a descendant of Lee Sŏng-kye, the founder of the Yi Dynasty (reigned 1392–1398), and his ancestors held high office, but after his brother and sister were beheaded, all the family property was confiscated and from the age of nine he lived in poverty with his mother, and sister-in-law in Seoul until in 1815, at the age of 23, he sent them to live with his elder brother in Yŏn-p'ung county and began to support himself by copying books of religion and holy pictures for sale. He collected funds for the projected dispatch of an emissary to Peking, and worked hard at the training of catechists. His house was for years the center for Sunday meetings but on the twenty-first in the fourth moon of 1827 he was arrested and taken to Chŏn-ju, the site of his sister Lugartha's martyrdom.

He underwent torture and hardship with fortitude, like his brother, but though his will power was strong his physique was not, and on the fifth of the fifth moon, 1827 he succumbed to the injuries received in jail, at the age of thirty-six. Like his sister, he wrote lengthy letters to his faimily and the members of the Myŏng-to-hoe, the texts of which are carried in Dallet's *Histoire de l'Église de Corée*. In his letter to his mother he begs her forgiveness for not being able to take better care of her, and rejoices at her being the mother of three martyrs. The letter to his wife expresses his regret at the hardship in her married life, and exhorts her to have the children baptized and brought up in the faith. To the Myŏng-to-hoe, which played a leading role in the guidance of the faithful, he wrote stressing the special characteristics of the Church's history in Korea, and invoking the protection of the Blessed Virgin Mary for this small Catholic organization. Other letters reported the defection of many of the Catholic prisoners held in Chŏn-ju prison, and stressed the importance of redoubled effort to further the advancement of the Church in the years to come.

For more than two months the persecution, though extremely violent in the Province of Chŏl-la, remained, so to speak, concentrated in this province. All the other Christian communities enjoyed peace, until the twenty-second day of the fourth moon of this year (1827). Then it was that the constables of Chŏn-ju crossed the borders of Kyŏng-sang Province and seized Peter Shin, in the district of Sang-ju. Two days later, other constables were sent to the same district, to the village of Eng-mu-tang, to arrest other Christians who had been denounced. But news of the arrest of Peter Shin had already spread and all the Christians had taken flight; as a result it was impossible for the police to arrest anybody on that day. We do not know exactly what happened then at Sang-ju, but the sequence of events seems to show that both the civil and the criminal magistrate, thus officially warned of the presence of Christians in their district, and no doubt stimulated by the example of their colleagues of the Province of Chŏl-la, also wished to ingratiate themselves by tormenting the disciples of Jesus Christ.

Whatever the case may have been, toward the end of the fourth moon five or six fairly large Christian villages in the district of Sang-ju were suddenly invaded by constables. The more alert or the more adroit of the neophytes found safety in flight, while a great number, seized in their homes or on the highways, were thrown into the jails of Sang-ju. Here again we have to deplore the numerous cases of apostasy: nevertheless, courageous defenders and eloquent champions of the faith were not lacking.

Among them were Paul Park Kyŏn-hwa and his son Andrew Park Sa-sim, Andrew Kim Sa-kŏn, Richard Ahn Kun-sim, Andrew Lee Ch'ŏng-il, and Ambrose Kim Kun-mi. Let us now glance at these confessors:

(11) Paul Park Kyŏn-hwa

Paul Park Kyŏn-hwa was of a noble and well-to-do family at Hong-ju. In 1792, at the age of thirty-three, he became a Christian, and was still a catechumen two years later when he was arrested. He obtained his release by promising to give up his Christian faith, but soon repented of his apostasy and, abandoning his property and taking leave of his relatives, he went to live a pious Christian life among the mountains. After Father James Chou Wen-mo's arrival in Korea he received the Sacrament of Baptism and continued his secluded life of prayer and meditation, preaching sermons, and educating the young until 1827, when the Chŏng-hae persecution broke out. He then counseled his fellow-Christians to go into hiding, but himself remained ready to suffer martyrdom. He gave up his mountain life and removed with his family to Mŏng-e-mok, Sang-ju county. On Ascension Day he was holding a prayer-meeting in his house when an apostate led a band of policemen to the place, who arrested the Catholics. Accused of being their leader, Paul was tortured and otherwise mistreated in many ways, but refused to give up his faith. Taken to the provincial capital of Tae-gu, he was further tortured, and then sentenced to death, but before the sentence could be carried out he died in prison, on the twenty-seventh in the ninth moon of 1827 at the age of seventy-one.

(12) Andrew Park Sa-sim

Although the law at that time forbade father and son being called upon to testify against each other, Paul's son Andrew Park Sa-sim, who had asked permission to accompany his father to jail in order to take care of him, was put to the torture simultaneously with his father at Tae-gu, and sentenced to death together with him. During their imprisonment Andrew was indefatigable: he used to stand holding up the wooden cangue which was locked around his father's neck, so as to relieve him of the heavy weight. He was executed twelve years after his father, on the twenty-sixth in the fifth moon of 1839, together with Andrew Kim Sa-kŏn.

(13) Andrew Kim Sa-kŏn.

A native of Sŏ-san county, Andrew had been a proud and irascible youth, but the Christian education which his parents gave him brought about a change in his character, and he became humble and philanthropic. He had already been arrested in 1815 at the time of his uncle Simon's martyrdom, when his father Thaddaeus was banished, but he was freed in consideration of his youth. He used frequently to visit his father in exile, and spent his time distributing religious books among his fellow-Catholics, preaching sermons, and reading. On the outbreak of the 1827 disaster, he was arrested as he had expected, and, accused of being the leader of the Church, was called upon to divulge the names of his fellow-Christians. After many and various cruel tortures, which left his flesh lacerated and the bones of his body exposed, he still held to his firm refusal to act as informer and betray his associates. He was accordingly transferred to the provincial court at Tae-gu, where he was sentenced to death. The sentence was confirmed by the King Sun-jo (reigned 1801-1834) but in the meantime further accusation, of distributing religious objects, was brought against him by a Catholic imprisoned at Chŏn-ju, and this led to further cruel torture, which left him completely crippled. He was then carried to Chŏn-ju on horseback for further torture, after which he was brought back to Tae-gu, a journey of more than two hundred and fifty miles. In his condition, this could have meant only agony alternating with periods of unconsciousness brought on by pain and exhaustion.

(14) Richard Ahn Kun-sim

Richard Ahn Kun-sim was a native of Po-ryŏng. He was a good-humored man, frank and unpretentious. After being received into the Church as a young man he left his home town in order to be able to practice his religion more freely. The care he took in the upbringing of the children and the kindness he showed to his neighbor were admirable. Assiduous in prayer and meditation, he was never slack in his religious duties: he fasted regularly three times a week. He spent a great part of his time in transcribing religious books, in order to support himself and his family, and took delight in explaining them to the Christians and even to the pagans. In 1827, realizing that he was sure to get into trouble over a number of books transcribed in his handwriting, and remembering that Our Lord Himself had several times fled from His enemies, he went into hiding for a time, in order to prepare himself in retreat to take up the fight with redoubled fervor. The constables of Sang-ju finally found him and took him to that town. The magistrate asked him:

"Is it true that you follow the Christian religion?"

"It is true," he replied.

"Tell me, then, what the doctrine says about God."

Richard did his best to give him a clear and succinct exposition of the Christian religion.

"What you say is all very fine, but you are committing a breach of the law: aren't you being disloyal to the king?"

To this question Richard gave the same answer that we have heard from nearly all the martyrs, and in the same terms, for it is found in the text of the shorter catechism which nearly everyone could repeat by heart. It runs:

"God being the great King of the universe and the Father of all men, we honor Him above all. The king, the officials, and our parents ought not to be honored except as subordinate to God."

"Renounce this God and tell us the names of your accomplices."

Upon his refusal, he was violently beaten, but he remained constant in his profession of faith and was taken back to prison. For several days in succession the magistrate had him repeatedly tortured but to no avail, and after spending some time in these vain efforts, sent him to Tae-gu, the seat of the governor. There Richard had to undergo renewed torture; though his body was nothing but a mass of bruises and wounds his sufferings only intensified the ardor of his love for God. Finally he was condemned to death and sent back to jail, where he died of dysentery in 1835.

(15) Andrew Lee Ch'ŏng-il

Andrew Lee Ch'ŏng-il, a native of Sang-ju district, was a man of strong character, upright and charitable, and respected by all. He was not instructed in the faith until his twenties, but his conversion was so sincere and so thorough that, not finding freedom to practice the Christian religion in his home town, he left his family, property, and friends, and withdrew to the hills. Forced by circumstances to move from place to place, in various provinces, he soon found himself without means of support, and took to manual labor. Andrew's resignation during his life of poverty and privation, his patience under insult, his sparing use of words, the care he devoted to bringing up his family, and the many other virtues he manifested, were the admiration of all. Although kept constantly busy by his family cares he never neglected prayer and pious reading.

As soon as the persecution began in 1827, he prepared for martyrdom by withdrawing from worldly life and by redoubling his fervor. He heartened his family with the words:

"Each of us must prepare to die, but, as we cannot know God's will for certain, let us try to escape the persecutors if we can."

He lived at Kom-ch'ik, in the district of Sun-heung, and there constables went to arrest him. He received them gaily, and they took him to An-tong. The judge asked: "Is it true that you follow an evil doctrine?" "The God of Heaven," replied Andrew, "is the Creator of all things: He is the great King Who governs all, the Supreme Father Who cares for all; it is He Who rewards the good and punishes the evil. As it is the duty of everyone to worship Him, I worship Him and serve Him. As for any evil doctrine, I know of none."

"That is a thoroughly insolent answer," shouted the magistrate, "apostatize at once."

He ordered Andrew to be given a cruel beating. With a calm expression on his face, he said in a firm voice: "Though you ask me ten thousand times, I will never renounce my faith in my God. Do not ask me any more questions." The magistrate, angered, had the torture kept up for several days, but the love of God sustained Andrew until the end. He was then sent to the governor, who said: "I am told that you are unwilling to renounce your faith. We shall see." He then subjected Andrew three times to the most atrocious torture. They then tried to win him over by kindness and gentle means, but it was all in vain, and he was finally condemned to death and thrown into jail with the other confessors. His sentence of death was executed thirteen years later, on the twenty-sixth in the fifth moon of 1839.

(16) Ambrose Kim Kun-mi

Ambrose Kim Kun-mi was descended from a family of interpreters at the capital, and was a distant relative of Thomas Kim Pŏm-u, a confessor of the faith in 1785. No sooner had the faith been introduced into Korea than he embraced it heart and soul, and taught it to his wife and children. These, however, would not listen to him, and not content with merely refusing to imitate him, they sought by a thousand annoyances to bring him back to idolatry.

His wife especially, a violent and cross-tempered woman, would not leave him in peace. She wished, among other things, to prevent him from keeping the fasts and abstinences of the Church, and often shouted out insulting remarks about the Catholic faith. Ambrose, worn-out with so much troublesome and persistent annoyance, decided to live separately, and taking leave of his family, a little after 1791, stayed with various Christian families of the province in succession, teaching all who were willing to listen, and copying out religious books in order to gain a livelihood. He had the good fortune to meet with Father Chou, with whom he appears to have stayed for some time, strengthening his faith and virtue. Having no home of his own, from time to time he would go off by himself and live in the hills, in order to devote himself to pious exercises without disturbance. He loved most of all to teach children, and constantly exhorted them to the practice of virtue, even more by his example than by his words. Every night, even during the depth of winter, he would get up at midnight to pray. He ate sparingly, prescribing for himself strict limits which he never transgressed, no matter whether the quality of the food was good or bad.

Ambrose had escaped the persecutions of 1801 and 1815. In 1827, all his Christian friends were in flight, and every day several of them were being arrested. The head of the family with whom he was staying also fled, and took refuge in the home of a pagan. Ambrose, who now had nowhere to stay, and who could see no way to avoid the searches, decided to give himself up to the authorities. He accordingly presented himself at An-tong during the fifth lunar month, and, putting his small bundle of personal belongings into the jailer's hands, asked to be brought before the judge of criminal cases. The doorkeeper of the court-house tried to dissuade him, but Ambrose answered: "I am a Christian: go and report to the judge that I am here." The constables would not take him seriously, and pushed him away, but he cried out at the top of his voice: "I am not mad; I am indeed a Christian." There was nothing for it but go and tell the judge, who sent for him and asked him several questions. Ambrose refused to reveal either his dwelling-place or the place where his books were hidden. A month later, he was sent to Tae-gu where the other confessors were, all of them his close friends. In the presence of the governor he was three times subjected to violent beatings and then put to varied tortures, all of which he bore with resolute courage and patience. Finally he was condemned to death and thrown into prison to await the confirmation of his sentence.

During his life he always regretted having been a burden to those with whom he sought asylum. Having learnt that the cost of feeding the prisoners who, like himself, were without means, was met by a tax imposed on the neighboring households, he began to feel worried again at being a burden on the local people. It was no doubt this that made him decide to go on a hunger strike. Many Christians, however, attribute this strange decision to divine inspiration. He began by observing almost complete abstinence, on seeing which, the other prisoners said: "Master, if you don't eat, we shall have to do the same as you."

He rebuked them sharply, saying:

"Although I do this, without being able to reveal my motive to you, similar conduct on your part would be tantamount to suicide." Some say that he lingered on in this way for some time and then died peacefully. According to other testimony, to avoid scandal he began to eat sparingly. He died at the age of sixty-eight, on the twenty-seventh of the tenth moon of the year 1828.

(17) Lawrence Ryu Sun-ch'i

The last case of martyrdom to which we shall refer in our review of the Chŏng-hae persecution occurred at the southeastern tip of Ch'ung-ch'ŏng Province.

Lawrence Ryu Sun-ch'i moved to the remote village of Kip-keun-kol, Tan-yang county, Ch'ung-ch'ŏng Province early in 1827. When the persecution erupted in the Province of Kyŏng-sang, many of his relatives and friends flocked to this village to escape arrest, among whom was a pagan who for monetary reward informed the authorities at Tan-yang. Lawrence's house was surrounded by police and some twenty Catholics were arrested on the spot, all of whom gained their release by making a formal undertaking to the magistrate to abandon their faith in Christianity. Lawrence, however, remained steadfast, despite severe torture. This infuriated the magistrate who told the

Catholics who were under arrest:

"I want to dismiss the case against all of you, but as long as this man obstinately holds out I cannot do so."

The renegades then became angry with Lawrence, who was at last obliged by their resentment and clamorous protests to make a formal act of apostasy so as to free them all *en bloc*. As soon as they had gained their liberty by this means, however, he told them all to make off and returned alone to the prison, where he at once confronted the magistrate with the retractation of his earlier declaration of apostasy. This led to further torture, followed by his transfer to the provincial court at Ch'ŏng-ju, where he was sentenced to death. King Sun-jo commuted the sentence to exile, but Lawrence insistently called for execution of the capital sentence. As the governor, in compliance with the royal command, was sending Lawrence into exile to Mu-san, the latter defiantly shouted, "I plan to bring ten thousand souls into the Church!" At Mu-san he not only practiced his religion openly but preached the Gospels to all, policemen, countryfolk, and chance acquaintances. His courageous behavior led to his loss of liberty in exile, and he was kept closely shut up in a house, without food. Not even hunger could break the indomitable spirit that had withstood the severest torture without yielding, and the brave Lawrence died of starvation at the age of thirty-five or forty. His death occurred either in the twelfth moon, 1827 or in the third moon, 1828, but the exact date is not recorded.

So it was that this persecution of 1827, like a violent tempest, finally spent itself. All the Christian communities of Chŏl-la Province were ravaged, but except for a few districts in Kyŏng-sang Province and one village in Ch'ung-ch'ŏng, there is no record of the faithful in the remaining five provinces having been molested. This persecution differs from the preceding ones in several respects which it is worth while to note. It was comparatively short. The first arrests took place toward the end of the second lunar month; three months later, they had ceased. It seems evident that the central government took no part in the seizures. The greed of the magistrates and their subordinates and hangers-on, popular rancor and individual denunciations were at the bottom of all the trouble. Another difference was that the government, far from indulging in the prodigal bloodshed of Christians as on previous occasions, did not permit the execution of any one of the death sentences passed by the provincial courts, but left the condemned to languish in prison indefinitely. This relatively indulgent policy was probably due, as we have already pointed out, to the personal opposition of the king to his ministers' and magistrates' rigorous proposals. Finally what distinguishes the persecution of 1827 in a most distressing manner from all others previous or subsequent to it is the high proportion of apostates. There were approximately five hundred arrests, and the only ones who remained faithful are the few cited above.

(1) Paul Kim Ho-yŏn

After the persecution of 1827 the Church in Korea enjoyed a comparatively peaceful time for some time and was preparing for laying a sound foundation.

In the year 1830 in the north of Kyŏng-sang Province the grace of God brought about wonders in the person of a young man named Kim Ho-yŏn. The descendant of a family belonging to the district of An-tong, celebrated for the rare virtue of one of its forebears, he himself was a good-natured simple and thoughtful man. From childhood he had been accustomed to say very little, and not to take part in the games and amusements of the other children. At first some thought that this was due to mental deficiency, but they were very soon enlightened. At the age of twenty, Ho-yŏn had acquired exact knowledge of the greater part of the sacred books of the country; he was versed in all kinds of sciences, in moral philosophy, mathematics, astronomy, geomancy, and the most abstruse doctrines of

Buddhism and Taoism. The world, however, had no attraction for him, and he cared so little for glory or fame that he would not even go to the trouble of sitting for the public examinations. Always withdrawn, humbly seated in a corner, plunged in some profound meditation or other, he hardly bothered to speak to his friends, and paid no attention to their joking remarks. Thus he came to be looked upon throughout the country as a sage and his reputation for wisdom and virtue was so widespread that many people used to bring their personal problems to him for solution.

Annoyed by these importunate visitors he secretly left his home and went to live in retirement among the foothills of T'ae-paek-san, a mountain in the district of Sun-heung, to enjoy solitude and tranquillity and to continue his studies. There it was that grace awaited him. Hardly had he settled there when he made the acquaintance of an instructed and capable Christian, who lived among these mountains. Their talk ranged through the sciences and he soon conceived a high esteem for this Christian whom the light of truth had put in a position to deal with and solve problems unknown to the pagans. The more Ho-yŏn consulted him the more highly he came to esteem his Christian friend. Little by little Ho-yŏn led him on to speak of his religion, and no sooner had he set forth its basic principles than Ho-yŏn, leaping with joy, exclaimed: "This is just what I have been looking for! All my life I have believed that man should have some end or aim worthy of him, but as I could never find anything written in our sacred books I was always in doubt: now at last I have discovered the true doctrine."

Without wasting time, he set himself to study several religious books, broke off at once with all the pagan superstitions, and conceiving a profound disgust for all the errors under which his soul had hitherto been laboring, sought for nothing but the knowledge and the grace of God. Eagerly occupied in this preparation he took no

sleep. He spent twenty days in penitential exercises to purify his soul, and then he invited the Christian to go for a walk with him. They chatted together on various topics until, having come to the bank of a little stream, Paul went down on his knees and asked to be baptized, with such fervor that his friend could not refuse, and administered to him the sacrament of regeneration. Ho-yŏn took the name of Paul. All this day he wept freely, and in the excess of joy said, "To thank God for these inestimable benefits, there is no other way than to suffer martyrdom." From that day his fervor steadily grew. His entire life was occupied with pious exercises and the fulfilment of his duties.

He soon returned to his father's roof, instructed his brother, and soon afterward showed his father some religious books. The latter was immediately captivated and at once recognized the truth of Christianity, but on looking more deeply into the consequences of its dogmas, he burst into anger and, pronouncing those words which so well expressed the idolatry of the country, and the principal superstitions that obstructed the Gospel, he exclaimed: "If we follow this new religion, the temple of the tutelary spirit of our kingdom, the ancestral temples of the royal family, the temples of Confucius, our ancestors' tablets, and all our sacrifices will become useless and will have to disappear. Now I clearly see how right our king is in strictly forbidding this religion and punishing its followers." Then he roundly rebuked his son, ordered him to break off at once all relations with the Christians and to burn all his books, and never ceased maltreating him in their efforts to prevent him from practicing his faith. Paul's brother, a violent and brutal man, even went so far as to beat him several times with a cudgel. But our brave neophyte, strengthened by the grace that he had received on the day of his Baptism, put up an inflexible resistance.

However, as he was by nature of a somewhat delicate constitution, he was afraid that this continued ill-treatment might be too much for him to bear with safety. This is why he secretly left his home, and went to live among the poor Christians, where he spent several months in complete destitution, among privations difficult to describe. He had chosen a place which he wished never to leave again. There, squatting on his heels, he devoted himself to prayer, reading, and meditation, in this way spending the whole day and part of the night. Only at cockcrow would he seem to snatch some sleep. What is more, he regularly fasted on Fridays and Saturdays, until the Christians said to one another that Paul seemed to be a man without a body. During the great heat in the height of summer he made no change in this rule of life, and he was never seen to leave his room to take the air. In spite of this, he seemed to be very well, nor could one discern on his countenance the slightest sign of fatigue, which all attributed to a miracle of Providence.

Paul's father, seeing that his son had not returned for several months, guessed that he must be somewhere among the Christians, and was thinking of denouncing some of them to the magistrate, so that he might get back his son. This could have led to grave consequences. Paul was warned, and decided to return to his home. He gave the Christians a book that he had composed on the subject of religion, together with the few religious objects that he possessed, and took leave of them saying: "Let us meet again in our true Fatherland." When he arrived home, his father at first gave him a kindly reception, but a few days later he said:

"While you were away, people came from all sorts of places looking for you; your reputation for knowledge has spread far and wide; next time they come to consult you, if you persist in this religion, how are you going to answer the questions that they put to you? Why are you still so obstinate? I know how to cure your madness," and he then began to beat him cruelly. The same thing was repeated day after day. Paul bore it all with patience, without

giving up his pious exercises, but after a few weeks of this treatment he fell seriously ill. His strength was exhausted, and he became shockingly thin.

About two months had passed in this way without this unnatural father's anger being appeased, and without the slightest diminution in Paul's religious fervor. He was almost at his last breath when his father came to look for him, holding a dagger, and said: "You are evidently going to die very soon: if you die after having apostatized, I will recognize you as my son; but if you refuse to apostatize, I will kill you now with this dagger, and then, with the same weapon, I will kill myself." Paul answered: "In order to obey one's father, one may not disobey the king's orders: with how much the more reason, God being the sovereign ruler of the universe and the Father of all men, rewarding the good and punishing the evil, ought we to obey Him in spite of everything! You wish to force me to deny my God; is that the duty of a father?" He had hardly finished when his father, exasperated, rushed at him to stab him with the dagger, but his mother and brothers threw themselves on their father and restrained him.

Unable to free himself and get at his son he attempted to cut his own throat. This they also prevented. Paul, however, speaking in a gentle voice said: "Father, even though you go so far beyond reason to make me obey you, I cannot break the commandments of our Heavenly Father."

Next day at daybreak Paul devoted himself as usual to prayer and meditation. During the morning he inquired repeatedly whether it was noon or not, and as soon as the hour arrived he devoutly recited the Angelus: then at once knelt down and rendered up his soul to God so tranquilly that those around him did not realize that he had breathed his last. It was in the eighth moon (September), 1831.

Barely a year had passed since his conversion and he was only thirty-six years old. It is said that after his death, his parents wished to perform the traditional sacrifice but the altar set up for the purpose, suddenly and for no apparent reason, collapsed in ruins.

The Christians of Korea count Paul among their most glorious martyrs, and God will no doubt have ratified their judgment. Paul's conduct was admirable, especially for a Korean. Let us not forget that we have already seen several cases in which confessors after valiantly braving the magistrates and overcoming the pains of torture, have succumbed miserably to the assaults of parental tenderness. This sentiment of filial piety, so holy in itself, is all powerful in this country, to the point of often making even Christians forget that the law of God comes before everything else, and His love before all other love. Honor then to Paul for having, in such circumstances, kept his faith with such heroism!

(2) Peter Hwang Sa-yun

The general amnesty granted to the exiled Christians seemed to be proof of a certain spirit of tolerance on the part of the government, and served to tranquilize the faithful. But almost every page of this book has already shown us what a precarious peace it is that the disciples of Jesus Christ are able to enjoy in Korea.

On the tenth in the ninth moon of 1832, when they were least expected, the constables from the capital forced their way into the house of Andrew Hwang, a devout and fervent Christian, long noted for his various journeys to Peking and for other general works in favor of his brothers in the faith. It does not appear that this incident was the result of orders from the superior authorities: it seems rather to have been motivated either by the rancor and cupidity of a subordinate official or else by the constables' fondness for pillage. As Andrew was not at home at the time, they failed to arrest him, but his uncle Peter Hwang was seized together with other members of the household, as well as several Christians who lived near by. Ten persons in all were taken prisoner. Only Peter had the spirit to admit

that he was a Christian.

Peter Hwang, descended from a noble family of the province, lived in the village where he was born, Saem-kol, Su-won district. He was a man of grave and austere character, respected by all his relations and neighbors, and in whose presence no one would dare to let fall a frivolous or improper remark. At the age of forty he was instructed in the faith and converted together with his entire family, and from that day he practiced the Christian faith with perseverance and fervor, in spite of all difficulties. "Before my conversion," he often used to say, "I could see nothing in the desire for martyrdom manifested by several Christians except the illusion of enthusiasm and the delirium of a heated imagination, but I was completely mistaken." He determined to overcome his somewhat too severe and dominating character, and to correct his other defects. Having resolved to drink no more wine, which he had been too fond of in former times, he never allowed another drop to touch his lips. He lost four children one after another and then his wife, but in the midst of these afflictions he showed no undue emotion, nor did he utter any complaint unworthy of a Christian.

On the contrary, he thanked God for having called them all to Him while they were still fit to appear before Him. After his family had died out in this way, and his small fortune was all spent, he was all the more given to prayer. He sought and found in the practice of virtue his only true comfort. His equanimity, and the calm resignation with which he bore his misfortunes, were the admiration of all.

He had withdrawn to the capital for some time and was staying with his nephew Andrew when, as already related, he was unexpectedly arrested. The judge of the criminal court having heard his confession of faith, touched perhaps with pity at the sight of his gray hair, promised to spare his life if he would only pronounce a word of formal apostasy. The confessor declined with dignity. "Who then are you," said the judge in rebuke, "to infringe the king's laws in this way?" At the same time he had him put to the torture, but in vain. Peter remained firm and was sent to jail, where he had to undergo the insolence and the cruelty of the warders. He had been arrested without a single object of religious significance in his possession, which would have facilitated his release, but wishing for death rather than fearing it, wishing also to relieve the other Christians arrested with him from their embarrassment, he offered to declare himself the owner of all the sacred objects that had been found in their possession and seized. We have often seen, in fact, that in similar circumstances the better Christians would assume the responsibility for sacred objects belonging to others, either to save the latter from the compromising denunciations which their possession might provoke on the part of their weaker brethren, or else to lighten, at their own risk, the burden of their fellow-captives. They were no doubt unaware that lying is absolutely forbidden by the law of God, in this case as in all others, and their good faith as well as their charity will have been their excuse.

They accordingly let Peter pass himself off as the owner of the seized objects, as a result of which he drew upon himself long interrogations and severer torture than the others. In the course of the trial the judge, suspecting fraud of some kind, denied that the objects really belonged to Peter, but the latter loudly protested and maintained his former affirmation. After many questionings in the common thieves' court, Peter, always firm, was transferred to the High Court of Justice. There he scorned to save his life at the cost of his faith, and had to undergo further torture. While they were engaged in cruelly torturing him he cried: "What! I am soon going to die of old age in any case; for thirty years I have kept the commandments of the Lord Who is Creator of Heaven and earth: do you think that now, by a word of infamy, I am willing to forfeit in a moment the love of God?" we may recall the words of St. Polycarp, a disciple of

St. John, in similar circumstances: "For ninety years have I served the Christ and never did He harm me: am I now to revile Him?" The sentiments are similar, for the same Holy Spirit inspired the two martyrs.

After his glorious confession Peter had the joy of hearing himself condemned to death. He gladly put his signature to his death sentence, after which, loaded with a heavy cangue, he was sent to solitary confinement in the jail. On his arrival the pagan prisoners, among whom was a scholar named Kim, were all astonished at the holy joy that showed itself on the countenance of the Christian. "Everyone must pay for his sins," they said, "but how can this old man, far from fearing death, seem to be so happy to die? Master, why are you so happy?" "Because," replied Peter, "the God whom I serve is the great King of Heaven and earth, Father of all creatures, and rather than deny Him I would die ten thousand times for Him." "If that's the case," replied the prisoners, "please let us know more about this doctrine." Peter did not wait for further invitation but, from that day on, he frequently explained the truths of religion and the commandments of God to them. In this way he spent more than eight months, fearing only that his sacrifice might not be accepted, and incessantly imploring the intercession of Our Blessed Lady. Suddenly he fell ill and in a few days peacefully gave up his soul into God's hands, at the beginning of the fifth lunar month of the year 1833 (June 1833). He was nearly seventy, and had undergone the same tortures as the worst criminals no fewer than five times, without counting the other tortures.

The members of his family were informed of his death, and when they came to receive his remains the pagan scholar Kim said: "At the moment when Peter Hwang died, a bright light appeared throughout the prison. All of us, his fellow-prisoners, came out to see what it was. A bright fire shone in his cell: we entered and saw a dove which circled over his bed and, a few minutes later, he died." Thus it is that God is pleased even here below to glorify those who die for His glory.

(3) Justin Cho Tong-sŏm

While John Chŭng Yak-yong was regaining his rank among the high nobility of the kingdom, another Christian nobleman, like him in exile since the great persecution, died at Mu-san, at the extremity of the northernmost province, after thirty years of privation and suffering. This was Justin Cho Tong-sŏm. Arrested at Yang-keun, at the end of 1800, and taken to the capital, he was sentenced to exile, although most probably he had never given the slightest sign of apostasy. He continued always to practice the Catholic religion, and bore with heroic calm the departure of his son who was taken from him, condemned to torture, and sentenced to death. In 1819, as a result of the arrest of Peter Cho Myŏng-su, one of his relations, in 1817, Justin was subjected once more to interrogation. The magistrate asked him if he still went on practicing his religion; Justin answered: "If I didn't, would I be here now?"

"If you persist in resisting the orders of the king, you will be put to death together with all members of your family that we succeed in laying our hands on."

"That doesn't frighten me; do as you please."

From this moment Justin was to be kept incommunicado by order of the magistrate, and most of those who used to visit him obeyed this order, but a number of his students, whom he had been instructing in the study of Chinese characters, and who were bound to him by ties of affection, paid no heed to the order. Under the eyes of the guards they clambered over walls and through hedges to attend his lessons, and were so numerous and so resolute that the magistrate thought it wise to ignore their behavior.

During his thirty years of exile, Justin bore the hardships of his situation with exemplary patience and resignation. He was glad to suffer for Jesus Christ, and the Savior, accepting his sacrifice, accorded him the grace of a holy death on the fourteenth of the sixth moon of the year Kyŏng-in (August 2, 1830). Justin Cho was then ninety-two years of age. In the following years, some of his disciples would travel as far as five or six hundred miles into country unknown to them, in order to get into touch with the faithful and complete the religious instruction they had received from Justin and be received into the Church. Unfortunately, the fear of being compromised prevented those to whom they addressed themselves from admitting that they were Christians, so that these unfortunate people had to return to their homes without having received Holy Baptism. One hears no more of them after this, for the Christians were out of touch with this remote province. It is however impossible for us to believe that these brave men, who were not afraid to make such extraordinarily long journeys in search of salvation, could have been entirely abandoned.

God Himself has said: "Ask, and the gift will come; seek, and you shall find; knock, and the door shall be opened to you," (St. Matthew 7:7) and our God always keeps His promises.

BOOK TWO

THE ESTABLISHMENT OF THE VICARIATE APOSTOLIC OF KOREA AND THE GREAT PERSECUTION

CHAPTER FIVE

THE ESTABLISHMENT OF THE KOREAN
VICARIATE APOSTOLIC

25. The Missionary Invitation Campaign of Chŭng Ha-sang and Others

Since the martyrdom of its first shepherd, Father Chou Wen-mo, in 1801, the Church in Korea had been left abandoned like an unwanted child for thirty-three years. Without a priest during that period, fervent Korean Catholics, though deprived of the Sacraments, encouraged one another in their faith and, at the same time, went on sending emissaries to Peking one after another with their request that a missionary be sent to Korea.

Owing to the decline of Portugal's power as a result of the Napoleonic wars, she was no longer able to render the generous support she had given to the missionaries during the sixteenth, seventeenth and eighteenth centuries, and the turmoil in Europe also led to a general diminution of aid to foreign missions. Under the Emperor Kaotsung (Ch'ienlung, reigned 1736-1795) the Church in China had been steadily losing ground, and now in its sad plight it was unable to send a single missionary to Korea, in spite of repeated requests from Korean believers during the reign of his successor Jentsung (Chiach'ing, reigned 1796-1820), in the years 1811 and 1813. Nevertheless the Korean

Catholics refused to give up hope, and in the winter of 1816 they sent the twenty-three-year-old Paul Chŭng Ha-sang to Peking in a renewed attempt to persuade the Church in Peking to dispatch a priest to Korea. Paul Chŭng was the second son of Chŭng Yak-jong, who died a martyr in 1801, and this was his first visit to Peking. The sum of eleven hundred taels of silver had been collected from poor Korean Catholics to provide for his travelling expenses, and after a journey of thirteen hundred miles on foot he arrived safely in Peking and was received by the Bishop. The Korean youth earnestly besought him to dispatch a priest to Korea, but the complicated situation of the Church in China rendered it impossible for the Bishop to accede to his request, and he returned to Korea empty-handed in the spring of the following year.

During the next ten years Paul Chŭng made no fewer than nine such journeys between the two capital cities, devoting himself body and soul to God and rendering incalculable service to the development of the Korean Church. In his twenties Paul was in fact performing all the duties of a secretary-general to the Church in Korea. In co-operation with Charles Hyŭn Sŏk-mun, author of the *Ki-hae Diary*—an early record of Korean martyrs—Paul Lee Kyŏng-pyŏn, the youngest brother of the royal descendant Charles Lee Kyŏng-to, and several others, he taught and led his fellow-believers and, while the Church in Korea remained without a priest, provided many of them with the opportunity to receive the Sacraments of Baptism, Confirmation, Penance and Holy Communion by conducting parties of them to Peking every year. Among one of these groups was the famous translator Yu Chin-kil who was converted to Catholicism in 1823. Yu, who had first gone to Peking in the guise of translator in the service of the winter-solstice embassy in 1824, on which occasion he received Baptism at the hands of Bishop Pires, taking the name of Augustine, was able to have access to the Church authorities on his subsequent visits, and also asked repeatedly for a priest to be sent to Korea as soon as possible, but his efforts were also fruitless.

In the following year 1825, a group of prominent Catholics in Korea, including Chŭng Ha-sang, Lee Yŏ-jin and Yu Chin-kil, held a protracted conference as a result of which a letter was addressed to the Pope in Rome explaining the situation of the Korean Church and entreating him to send a priest to Korea as soon as possible, and it was really this letter which brought about the establishment of the Korean Vicariate Apostolic and simultaneous dispatch of Bishop Bruguière by the Vatican.

Chŭng Ha-sang and Yu Chin-kil now held a private conference between themselves, to make the necessary arrangements for the prospective entry of a missionary into Korea, which was now regarded as imminent.

They selected Cho Sin-ch'ŏl as the most dutiful and selfless man among the staff of the winter-solstice embassy and the most deserving of an invitation to become a Catholic, and in due course he was baptized in Peking, with the name of Charles, later playing a great role as a guide in bringing a missionary into Korea, and eventually attaining martyrdom.

On Paul Chŭng's fifth visit to Peking Bishop Pires was so deeply impressed with his zeal that he finally promised to send a missionary to Korea during the following year. This was the occasion for great rejoicing on the part of Paul Chŭng and his fellow Catholics, and they made all preparations for receiving their new priest. When, however, they went to the border to receive him in 1826, they were disappointed, for although they waited until long after the appointed time no priest emerged from Chinese territory before them. Tired of waiting, Paul Chŭng proceeded toward Peking. where he learnt to his great surprise that the priest, Father Sim, had died of an illness on his journey to Korea.

The following year Paul made another fruitless journey to Peking. Realizing that the time was not propitious, Paul then decided to postpone further attempts, and returned to his home at Yang-keun, to live with his family. He devoted himself to spreading the Gospel, and other Church work for six years, when he returned once more to Seoul. His personality and scholastic attainments won him the admiration and respect of all his fellow-Catholics, who indeed regarded him as their leader and shepherd. It is most gratifying to record that he was a worthy son of his father, Augustine Chŭng, and inherited his father's virtues.

26. The Establishment of the Korean Vicariate Apostolic

Owing to the unflagging efforts of such persistent and indefatigable Catholics as Chŭng Ha-sang, their letter to the Pope, through the intermedium of the Peking Church, finally reached its destination and was brought to Pope Leo XII in 1827. The grief-stricken message moved the Pope and the Sacred College to take immediate measures. Accordingly Cardinal Capellari, who was then Prefect of the Sacred Congregation for the Propagation of the Faith, wrote to Father Langlois, dean of the theological seminary of the *Société des Missions-Étrangères de Paris*[1] on September 1, 1827, in accordance with the decision of the Cardinals' conference, asking him to take "immediate and permanent" action to relieve the Korean Church from its spiritual distress. Cardinal Capellari's wish, however, was not immediately fulfilled. The dean of the theological seminary pointed out such difficulties as the shortage of priests, the lack of missionary funds, the prohibition of the entry of foreigners by the Korean government, doubts as to whether episcopal consent would be forthcoming, and so forth.

At this juncture there fortunately appeared a priest in a remote corner of the Orient who expressed his desire to go to Korea and save the Church. This was Bishop Barthélemy Bruguière, already on the point of being consecrated as coadjutor in Siam who, not content with writing to the *Missions-Étrangères*, also wrote directly to the Pope, offering himself as the one to make the first attempt.

Pope Leo XII died in 1829 and his successor Pope Pius VIII died in the following year; Fra Mauro Capellari was now elected to the Holy See, choosing the name of Gregory XVI. On September 9, 1831, within a year of his enthronement, he issued two messages, one of which removed the territory of Korea from the ecclesiastical jurisdiction of the Bishop of Peking and simultaneously established it as a Vicariate Apostolic, while the other announced the appointment of Bishop Bruguière as the first Vicar Apostolic of the mission in Korea.[2]

The messages were as follows:

POPE GREGORY XVI
In Perpetual Memory

1. Although the Providence of God has placed on Our shoulders the shepherd's task of caring for the whole flock of the Lord, nevertheless We believe that Our office demands an even greater care for those sheep especially who dwell in regions far from Our Apostolic See, which is the center of Catholic unity. The object of this greater attention paid to them in particular is to see that when the Eternal Shepherd comes they may be found where they belong, among the true flock—thanks to Our apostolic concern for them. We want them to be called to the Heavenly pastures and happily enter in.

2. Since there is no little hope that apostolic missionaries may eventually be able to enter the kingdom of Korea and help the Christians in their needs who are already living there, and cultivate that part of the vineyard of the Lord by teaching catechism and administering the Sacraments; and since the natives of that country are able to communicate with the rest of the Orient only rarely and with great difficulty, We have consulted Our venerable Brothers of the Holy Roman Church, the cardinals in charge of the affairs of "Propagation of the Faith," and We think it opportune to constitute the kingdom of Korea from henceforth, a new Vicariate Apostolic entirely independent of the Bishop of Peking.

3. Therefore, of Our own accord and with full knowledge and mature deliberation, by Our full apostolic authority, We hereby

---

[1] Founded in 1658 by Msgr. François Pallu and Msgr. Pierre de la Mothe-Lambert to prepare priests for service as missionaries.   Approved by Louis XIV (1664), by Louis XV (1775), it had been suppressed in 1791 but was re-established by Napoleon in 1805. It was again suppressed in 1809 in consequence of Napoleon's impious conflict with the Holy See, but re-established in 1815, since when it has never ceased to supply the foreign missions with apostolic workers in ever-increasing numbers, and serves no fewer than thirty-seven Catholic missions in the Far East.

[2] A Vicar Apostolic is a titular bishop who rules a territory called a vicariate apostolic as delegate of the Holy See. Vicars Apostolic have no territorial diocese, cathedral Church or chapter of canons and their name is not mentioned in the canon of the Mass; but they usually exercise by delegation the same powers as diocesan bishops.

declare and announce by this apostolic letter that the kingdom of Korea is henceforth a new Vicariate Apostolic, entirely independent of the Bishop of Peking. By this decree of the Holy See about the said Vicariate, and by Our authority, we hereby bestow each and all the faculties which are customarily granted to Vicariates Apostolic in China or in the neighboring regions.

4. We decree that this document be in effect, valid, and operative now and henceforth, to achieve its full effect; and that everyone whom it concerns, or whom in the future it shall concern, obey it with complete conformity.

5. This order supersedes any other Apostolic Constitutions and sanctions, and other orders, even special ones, no matter what they say to the contrary.

Given at Rome St. Mary Major under the seal of the Fisherman on the ninth day of September, 1831; the first year of Our pontificate.

A LETTER OF POPE GREGORY XVI TO MSGR. BARTHÉLEMY BRUGUIÈRE, BISHOP OF CAPSE

Venerable Brother, Greetings and Apostolic Benediction

The pastoral office which has been committed to Us from above especially demands that Christians be directed in the way of the commands of God, and that they be helped to achieve the eternal salvation of their souls by every means which, with God's help, We can provide. And therefore, since you, Venerable Brother, Coadjutor of the Bishop of Sozopolis, Vicar Apostolic of Siam, have petitioned that you be permitted to enter the kingdom of Korea and assume the care of the Korean neophytes, upon the advice of Our Venerable Brothers, the Cardinals of the Holy Roman Church, We gladly grant your request. We are moved to do this because of the same need on the part of the Korean Christians, and because We realize,

besides, that the Vicar Apostolic of Siam can with little trouble find another suitable priest whom he can choose for his coadjutor. If nothing hinders you, therefore, you may set out for the new mission. And so that from the start it might proceed well and successfully, forthwith We appoint and depute, make and constitute you the Vicar Apostolic of Korea with all the faculties of Vicar Apostolic. We do this by the authority in Us and the Holy See, if this shall so please the Congregation of Cardinals. We order, furthermore, that each and everyone whom this concerns in the future, give you prompt obedience in the aforementioned arrangements and receive humbly your salutary admonitions and commands and see that they are fulfilled to the letter. If anyone fails, We ratify the sentence or penalty which you place or decree against the recalcitrant, and We decree by the authority of the Lord that it be inviolably observed until condign satisfaction has been made. This supersedes all previous orders, etc.

Given at Rome St. Mary Major under the seal of the Fisherman on the ninth day of September, 1831; the first year of Our pontificate.

Thomas Cardinal Bernetti

The text of the messages was as follows:

GREGORIUS PP. XVI.

Ad Perpetuam Rei Memoriam.

(1) Ex debito pastoralis officii superna Dei providentia humeris Nostris impositi onus ferentes totius gregis Dominici, illis praecipue ovibus, quae regiones a Sede hac Apostolica, ubi catholicae centrum est unitatis, longe dissitas incolunt, majori consulendum sedulitate censemus, ut in adventu pastoris aeterni repertae sicut oportet, per apostolicam curam intra verum ovile, ad pascua coelestia vocari valeant, feliciterque perduci.

(2) Quum non minima spes fulgeat, ut tandem aliquando in Coreae regnum missionarii apostolici ingredi queant, qui Christianorum illic degentium necessitatibus subveniant, eamque vineae Domini partem catechesibus excolant et sacramentorum

administratione; quumque praefati regni incolae nonnisi rarò et difficillime cum caeteris Sinarum regionibus communicare possint, Nos, de venerabilium fratrum Nostrorum Sanctae Romanae Ecclesiae Cardinalium negotiis Propagandae Fidei praepositorum consilio, opportunum ducimus regnum Coreanum, nunc pro tunc in novum vicariatum apostolicum erigere, et in eum Vicarium Apostolicum constituere ab episcopo Pekinensi omnino independentem.

(3) Motu igitur proprio atque ex certa scientia et matura deliberatione Nostris, deque apostolicae potestatis plenitudine, vi praesentium litterarum apostolicarum, Coreanum regnum in novum vicariatum apostolicum nunc pro tunc erigimus, et in eo vicarium apostolicum constituendum ab episcopo Pekinensi omnino independentem declaramus, ac hujusmodi vicario ab hac Sancta Sede eligendo omnes et singulas facultates vicariis apostolicis in regionibus Sinarum, vel Sinis adjacentibus concedi solitas dicta Nostra auctoritate concedimus et impertimur.

(4) Decernentes has praesentes litteras firmas, validas et efficaces existere et fore, suosque plenarios et integros effectus sortiri et obtinere, ac iis ad quos spectat ac in futurum spectabit plenissime suffragari, et ab omnibus inviolabiliter observari; sicque in praemissis per quoscumque judices ordinarios et delegatos etiam causarum palatii Nostri Apostolici auditores judicari et definiri debere, ac irritum et inane si secus super his à quoquam quavis auctoritate scienter vel ignoranter contigerit attentari.

(5) Non obstantibus constitutionibus et sanctionibus Apostolicis, caeterisque etiam speciali et expressa mentione et derogatione dignis, contrariis quibuscumque.

Datum Romae apud Sanctam Mariam Majorem sub annulo Piscatoris die nona septembris millesimo octingentesimo trigesimo primo, pontificatus Nostri anno primo.

(II) VEN. FRATRI BARTHOLOMAEO BRUGUIÈRE EPISCOPO CAPSENSI.

Gregorius Papa XVI.

Venerabilis Frater, Salutem et Apostolicam Benedictionem.

Pastorale officium Nobis ex alto commissum

nihil Nos magis solicitat quam Christi fidelibus ut in viam mandatorum Dei dirigantur, atque ad aeternam animarum suarum assequendam salutem opportunis praesidiis adjuventur, omni quo cum Deo possumus studio providere. Quum itaque tu, Ven. Frater, qui coadjutor Episcopi Sozopolitani vicarii apostolici Siamensis, humiliter petieris, ut tibi liceat Coreanum regnum ingredi, et Coreanorum neophytorum curam suscipere, Nos perpensis Coreanorum christianorum necessitatibus, habitaque insuper ratione quod vicarius apostolicus Siamensis facili negotio alium idoneum presbyterum invenire possit, quem in coadjutorem sui eligat, de consilio Ven. Fratrum Nostrorum S. R. E. Cardinalium tuis precibus benigne annuentes, tibi permittimus, ut, si nihil obstet, ad novam missionem proficiscaris, qua quidem ad exitum prospere feliciterque perducta, etiam nunc te in vicarium apostolicum pro regno Coreae cum omnibus facultatibus vicariis apostolicis in regionibus Sinarum, vel Sinis adjacentibus concedi solitis, ad Nostrum et Sedis Apostolicae beneplacitum, auctoritate Apostolica tenore praesentium eligimus, et deputamus, facimus et constituimus, salva tamen semper in praemissis Congregationis eorumdem Cardinalium auctoritate. Mandamus propterea omnibus et singulis ad quos spectat ac spectabit in posterum, ut tibi in praemissis prompte pareant et obediant, tuaque salubria monita et mandata humiliter suscipiant, et efficaciter adimplere procurent, alioquin sententiam sive poenam, quam rite tuleris, seu statueris in rebelles ratam habebimus, et faciemus auctorante Domino usque ad satisfactionem condignam inviolabiliter observari. Non obstantibus, etc. quibuscumque.

Datum Romae apud S. M. M. sub annulo Piscatoris die 9 septembris 1831, pontificatus Nostri anno primo.

Th. card. Bernetti

27. The Entry of Missionaries Sent by the Société des Missions-Étrangères de Paris

As soon as Bishop Bruguière learnt of the decision of the Holy See, he received a letter from the Bishop of Nanking, who was administering the Diocese of Peking, to the following effect:

"...I have announced to the Christians

from Korea, who came to Peking this year with the Korean embassy, that a European missionary wished to go to their homeland. At the news, these good men wept with joy: they send their greetings to this missionary who has taken pity on them. They admit that it would be difficult to introduce a European into their kingdom, but they do not say it is impossible."

On the receipt of this news Bishop Bruguière, without waiting for official documents or funds for his expenses, set off at once for Korea on September 12, 1832, accompanied only by a young Chinese.

A missionary from the Siam mission had wished to accompany Bishop Bruguière: he was Father Jacques-Honoré Chastan, who had been zealously working at Penang for several years. He had been assured that if the *Société des Missions-Étrangères de Paris* should be entrusted with the Korean mission, he could be sent there, and from then on this was the object of all his desires. It was agreed that he should set out at the first summons.

In the meantime Bishop Bruguière's only assistant had to be a Chinese priest, furnished directly by the Sacred Congregation. He had been trained in Naples, in a college founded for Chinese candidates for the priesthood. As soon as it was known in this college that the Sacred Congregation wished to send priests to Korea two of the collegians had volunteered, but one of them withdrew. The other, Father Pacificus Liu Fang-chi, was more persevering. He left Europe at once, and when Bishop Bruguière started Father Pacificus had already arrived in China and was seeking a way to penetrate into Korea.

The next to be sent was Father Pierre-Philibert Maubant, born at Vassy (Calvados) in 1803. He had been deeply moved by the appeals from the Korean Christians and the missionaries, and he thought of the Master's words:

"The harvest is plentiful enough, but the laborers are few." (St. Matthew, 9:37). This led him to join the *Société des Missions-Étrangères de Paris* in 1831. A few months later he set out for China. He was to have

gone to Szechwan Province, but on the way he met Bishop Bruguière, and obtained permission from his Vicar Apostolic, Bishop Fontana, to go to Korea instead.

In those days it was imprudent for two Europeans to travel together across China, which was strictly closed to foreigners; the Bishop decided to go by the west and then turn north, while the missionary would go via Peking. The two were to meet at Siwantse, in Jehol Province, Inner Mongolia.

Father Maubant followed the route indicated. After a journey during which he ought to have been arrested twenty times, but which passed almost without incident, he entered Peking in broad daylight, the first foreigner to do so without an imperial passport for several hundred years.

The astonishment of Bishop Gouvéa was such that he kept Father Maubant close hidden for two months; he then sent him on his way to Manchuria where Father Mouly of the Congregation of the Mission received him with brotherly kindness.

The priest went to rejoin Bishop Bruguière, but alas! in less than a fortnight, in the little village of Machiatse, near Piehlikou, Bishop Bruguière fell suddenly ill and died within a few hours, in the presence of a Chinese priest.

On hearing this sad news Father Maubant resolved to proceed on his way to Korea, and to go to the Christians who were awaiting the Bishop on the frontier.

At midnight on January 12, 1836, in the company of five Korean Catholics, he got safely through the barrier, crossed the plains and forests between Manchuria and Korea, and reached the neighborhood of the Yalu River, the boundary between the two countries, which, with the utmost precautions, they crossed, and entered Eui-ju. Fifteen days later they came to the Han River, and were in sight of Seoul, the capital of the country which the apostle had come to conquer for Jesus Christ. (At this date the population of the city was about 120,000.) He was conducted to the house where Father Pacificus Liu was living, and received with the greatest respect by a score of Christians, who knelt to receive his blessing.

Such was the way in which the first French missionary entered Korea, more like a malefactor than a conqueror, and yet this humble priest was indeed a conqueror who would firmly plant the cross of Christ in this remote country, bring it to the notice of savants and statesmen, and startle the whole world with the account of his work and his heroic death.

The second to arrive was Father Jacques-Honoré Chastan. Born on October 7, 1803, at Marcoux in Basse-Alpes, he had long thought of the foreign missions: it seemed to him that he heard the words.

Surge: exi: vade: veni. "Arise! Come out! Set off! Come!" When they told him of the hardships he would have to undergo, he merely said that the Lord would give him strength to bear them. On the eve of his departure for Korea, the young priest knelt at his mother's feet to ask her blessing.

"No," she cried, "no, you bad son, I have no blessing for you. Ingrate that you are, is this how you repay me for all my sacrifices on you behalf? What! You are going to desert us, after all the privations we have undergone in the hope that you would be the consolation of our old age! Oh, we cannot let you go: surely you have not the heart to leave us to die alone."

This soul-searing scene distressed the son, without shaking his resolution. He tried to explain that it was God's will that he should go to this distant land, but no one would listen to him. At last, he knelt once more before her, and repeated:

"Bless me! Mother!"

With her deeply troubled motherly instinct suppressed, in a voice broken with sobs, she murmured:

"Yes, my child, since it is God's will, and may all the holy angels of Heaven accompany you."

In May 1833 he arrived in Macao, whence he sailed for Fukien Province, and then to Kiangnan Province, where with three Christians he set sail across the gulf of Pechili toward the coast of Manchuria. At the sight of the wild and deserted terrain

two of his guides deserted him, but he went on his way with the one faithful Fukienese, and after a month's hard going reached the Korean border, but having no one to help him he was forced to return to Shantung, where he stayed two years. In the meantime he told Father Maubant of his whereabouts, and asked him to send couriers. This was done, and on Christmas day, 1836, he arrived at the barrier.

"Can you walk like a poor man with a pack on your back?"

"Yes, indeed, all the more so because I am not a very rich one."

They set out at midnight on December 31. Luckily they got through safely, and then there was a second apostle in Korea. Fifteen days later the two missionaries joined one another in a little house in Seoul, to give thanks to God and renew their offer of their life.

Father Maubant was not able to spend much time learning the Korean language: the Christians were so eager for his ministration and instruction. As he could read Chinese, those who could write made their confessions in Chinese writing: those who could not had them written by those who could, or else asked to be allowed to confess through an interpreter.

After the arrival of Father Chastan, Father Maubant went to live at Yang-keun, near Yang-p'yŏng, while Father Chastan remained at the capital, where he learnt the rudiments of Korean, heard at least a hundred confessions, and then rejoined Father Maubant at Yang-keun, where they celebrated the Easter Mass together.

They always wore the dress of Korean mourners which they had adopted on their entry into the country; they always traveled by the less-frequented routes and lived, like the poorer Christians, on roots and vegetables cooked in salt water. During the night, they celebrated the Mass, heard confessions, and gave instruction in Christian doctrine: during the day, they rested, lying on the bare earth or on a worn straw mat. They never stayed more than two or three days in one place, in order not to arouse the suspicions of pagans.

A hard life, which though easy to describe

could not have been easy to bear with such indomitable fortitude and unchanging patience except by the grace of God.

Weakened by his labors, Father Maubant became seriously ill, and was at the point of death. He was taken to Seoul and received the last Sacraments, but as soon as the Holy Eucharist appeared at the threshold of his room he felt assured of his recovery. This intuition was correct, for after a convalescence of three months he was able to resume his labors.

With Father Chastan he made a census of the Catholics, a number of whom were hidden in the mountains and far separated from one another. They appointed catechists, set up communities of Christians, prescribed rules for infant Baptism, marriages, funerals, meetings on Sundays and feast days, and for the settlement of disputes; in short, they founded the organization of this Church which had practically formed itself. The result of their work was shown in 1837 in the following figures: 1,237 Baptisms of adults and of children of pagans, 2,078 confessions, 1,950 communions.

Since the end of 1836, Father Maubant had sent three students to Macao: Francis-Xavier Ch'oe, Andrew Kim, and Thomas Ch'oe. After a journey of eight months through Manchuria, Inner Mongolia and China, these young men arrived at the Procuration of the *Société des Missions-Étrangères de Paris* and began their studies under Father Legrégeois.

It was necessary, however, for this Church of Korea to have a chief to take the place of Bishop Bruguière, and Rome chose one.

In 1830 a missionary of Szechwan Province, Father Laurent-Joseph-Marie Imbert, had offered to serve in Korea. His offer was declined as it was thought that he would be more useful in the Moupin seminary, of which he was the director. On the death of Bishop Bruguière, however, it was decided to entrust the Vicariate to him.

The childhood and youth of Bishop Imbert are worth recording, for they were distinguished by piety, generosity and activity.

He was born on April 15, 1797, at Marignane, in Bouches-du-Rhône, where his mother was on a visit, but his family lived in Calas, a village on a hill overlooking the plain of Aix-en-Provence. His parents were too poor to give him an education. One day, which remained in his memory all his life, he found a penny in the road. He was only eight years old, and might well have been expected to spend it on lollipops, but he ran off to buy a primer, and then went to an old woman of the village known as Aunt Marguerite, and asked her to teach him the names of the letters. The good lady obliged; the child listened, repeated, and reviewed what he learned; he came again to his make-shift teacher, and before very long he had learnt to read.

His ambition grew with his progress; he found a bit of charcoal and copied the letters on the walls. Touched by his diligence, Aunt Marguerite gave her pupil a pen and a copybook, in which he traced the letters in their written form. That is how the future martyr learned to read and write. His parish priest gave him some lessons in grammar, and sent him to Aix, to study at the St. Joachim School maintained by the Brothers of the Christian Retreat. Tuition fees were waived, and all the child needed to pay for was his clothing, but his parents were in no condition to meet this little expense so he raised the money himself; he had seen how the Brothers made rosaries, and he imitated them. With a coil of wire over his shoulder and his pliers in hand during the morning break (his fellow-students told, fifty years later) he would make rosaries every day, and they never saw him play games. He sold these rosaries and with the money paid for his textbooks, exercise books, and clothing; what was left over he gave to his father who in this way received a monthly income of fifteen francs.

This manual labor in no way interfered with either his piety or his application to his studies.

He obtained his baccalaureate and entered the Major Seminary of Aix. He had already resolved to go and preach to the pagans. To strengthen his body for the work of the apostolate he exposed himself to cold and heat, and practiced going without food and sleep. As he finished his studies before reaching the required age for the subdiaconate he became a private tutor in a family of Givors, where he won the affection of his pupils, who kept up a lifelong correspondence with him.

However, the thought of the missions never left him. He made a retreat at the Trappe d'Aiguebelle. The abbot of the monastery, to whom he confided his desire, at once recognized his vocation and approached the seminary of the *Société des Missions-Étrangères* on his behalf.

Father Imbert arrived on October 8, 1818, in this house which his death and that of many of his friends were to glorify with the name of the Seminary of the Martyrs. A subdeacon on March 27, 1819, he was ordained a priest on December 18 of the same year. Destined for the mission in Szechwan Province he left Paris on March 20, 1820, and embarked at Bordeaux on May 1.

We need not recount here his labors at his first mission, his zeal under persecution, his founding of the seminary of Moupin; these details belong to the history of the apostolate of Szechwan Province.

As soon as the seminary of the *Missions-Étrangères* received news of the death of Bishop Bruguière they proposed him to the Holy See as a fitting successor. The missionary was consecrated Bishop of Capse on May 14, 1837 by the Vicar Apostolic of Szechwan Province, Bishop Fontana, who paints his portrait in the following terms:

"If the dispatch of Bishop Imbert to Korea gives us pleasure on account of the benefit which it will bring to that poor mission, his departure from Szechwan Province will grieve all. He is loved by everybody; he has made himself very useful; he speaks Chinese well, and he has a good knowledge of Chinese characters. He is good-natured, kind, gentle, gay, and courageous: he has experience in the sacred ministry, which he exercised for twelve years with zeal and success in the Vicariate of Szechwan Province. He is only forty-two years old, and he has a gift for learning foreign languages. His health is not as robust as it ought to be in order to bear the hardships of travel and other inconveniences; however, during the last few years it has improved, and he is convinced that God has endowed him with strength more than enough to cope with a sedentary life devoted to study."

The new Bishop crossed China safely and arrived at Siwantse at the end of October; he stayed a fortnight in the house where two years before Bishop Bruguière and Father Maubant had received the hospitality of the Lazarist Father. The heavy snow that accumulates from November on made the route which his predecessors had taken seem too dangerous and he decided to go by the imperial route via Peking and Mukden.

In order to avoid arrest at the customs barrier of Shanhaikuan, the Bishop had the Christians look for a smuggler who, for ten francs, promised to lead them by roundabout paths to a breach in the Great Wall of China; some hours later, they were being sheltered in the home of a Catholic family. On December 4 they arrived at Mukden, and on the 16th at Pienmen.

That evening the ambassadorial *cortege* arrived on its way to Peking. Five Catholics formed part of it and it was these who were to conduct the Bishop to Seoul.

Bishop Imbert set out on the morning of December 17. He had to run the same risks as Fathers Maubant and Chastan; he escaped them by the same means, and thirteen days later he entered the capital of Korea.

"God be praised!" he wrote at the time, "God be praised! What does all the fatigue matter? I am among my children, and the joy I feel at seeing them makes me forget all the difficulty and danger I had to undergo in order to join them. I spent the New Year's Day (1838) in a Christian home. In the evening, Father Maubant, who welcomed me on my arrival, rejoined me..."

Father Chastan was traveling in the southern provinces and it was not until May 1838 that he was able to meet the Bishop.

After three months' study of the Korean language, the Bishop was able to hear confessions. More than three hundred of the faithful were presented to him at Easter, and received the Sacraments at his hands. In the month of May, Fathers Maubant and Chastan, having concluded their visits to the Christian communities in the provinces, came to help him for a few weeks at the capital, where there were now a thousand neophytes. By the month of November, the three baptized 1,994 adults. The work of baptizing pagan children at the point of death now began to develop; in the first eight months of 1838, 192 such children were given this Sacrament. The six thousand Catholics whom Father Maubant had found on his arrival had grown to nine thousand at the beginning of 1839. In a word, on a soil only just recently brought into cultivation, tempest-tossed and watered with the blood of its children, the Church of Korea felt, under the action of its pastors, that the sap was rising vigorously and that there was promise of a most abundant harvest.

Such gratifying results could be obtained only at the cost of continual hard work.

"I am tired out," wrote Bishop Imbert, "and I am exposed to constant danger. Every day I get up at half past two in the morning. At three I hold family prayers, and at half past three begin the duties of my ministry, with Baptism if there are any catechumens, or with confirmation; then come Mass and Holy Communion, and thanksgiving. Thus the fifteen or twenty persons who have received the Sacraments may withdraw before daybreak; during the day about as many come in one by one for confession, and they do not leave until the next morning, after communion. I never stay more than two days in the house where I meet the Christians, and before daybreak I move to another house. I suffer a good deal from hunger, for after having risen at half past two in the morning I have to wait until midday for a meager breakfast of the poorest food, in this cold, dry climate, which is no easy matter. After this meal I rest a little, then I hold a class in theology for my advanced scholars, then I hear a few confessions until nightfall. I go to bed at nine, sleeping on the ground covered with a mat and a Tartar blanket; in Korea there are no bedsteads or mattresses. I have always, in spite of a frail physique, led an active and busy life, but here I seem to have arrived at the superlative and *ne plus ultra* of hard labor. As you may well understand, living such a painful life we have no fear of the sword which is no doubt going to put an end to it."

CHAPTER SIX

THE PERSECUTION OF 1839

28. The Discovery of Three Priests and Their Missionary Work

Martyrdom of Blessed Peter Lee Ho-yŏng

It had been impossible to keep the presence of the missionaries secret. At first the only ones allowed to know of it were the Christians receiving the Sacraments; the possibility of betrayal or indiscretion made this necessary. Little by little all the faithful, and then the pagans heard the news. It began to be bruited about that there were men from a country some twenty-three hundred miles away in the kingdom of Korea. Two countrymen were talking about this one day; one of them declared that it was impossible for foreigners to enter the country. "In the Christian religion," replied the other, "there are secrets that we know nothing about. When Jesus sends His disciples anywhere, they always find a way to get there."

The hostility of the enemies of Christianity, though restrained by the Regent, was evident from the number of arrests. We shall speak here only of the confessors and martyrs beatified in 1925.

First among them is Peter Lee; he was a native of I-ch'ŏn and the son of recent converts. After the death of his father, he went to live in the capital with his mother and his sister Agatha, in the Mun-mak quarter on the north bank of the Han River.

Father Liu, a Chinese priest, of whose arrival we have already spoken, was impressed by Peter Lee's rectitude, and entrusted several delicate matters to him, which in spite of his youth, he was able to deal with in a satisfactory manner. When he was about thirty years old he was converted and married a young non-Christian woman. Shortly afterward, he had a dream. It seemed to him that a friend invited him to go and see the official examination results announced; he went there, and soon heard delightful music being played. "It's you who have been selected," his companion told him.

"But how," he asked, in astonishment, "how can that be?"

"It's because you have a very good friend at court."

He woke up, remembered the dream, and remained deeply impressed by it. "This is undoubtedly a portent of my martyrdom," he thought to himself. He was right. A few months later, one evening in February 1835, on returning home, he found at the door of his house a squad of police officers, who arrested him.

"Why are you arresting me?" he asked.

"Don't you know your crime? It's because you practice the Christian religion."

The officers also arrested his sister Agatha, and both were thrown into prison.

They were at once subjected to the 'bone-bending' torture.[①]

"If you are reluctant to deny God by word of mouth," the judge kept on saying, "I'll have one large Chinese character written for you, and if you will only make a *mark* on it, or *spit* on it, I will accept that as a token of your apostasy and set you free."

The sufferer replied:

"Ten thousand times no, I will never agree to that." After this torture, Peter underwent that of the rods. These rods, with more or less sharpened edges, are about five or five and a half feet long and about as thick as a man's arm. Four police officers beat the victim at the same time, on the buttocks and thighs.

"If you utter the slightest groan," said the judge to his victim, "I shall declare it an act of apostasy."

The Christian's flesh fell in shreds; some of his bones were laid bare, he was beaten on the arms until they were broken. Peter spoke not a single word, and uttered no cry of pain. To salute such heroism one could only bow to the ground; to reward it, there is only Heaven.

The martyr was condemned to death as guilty of following a false and perverted religion.

According to the law which requires that the criminal, before being executed, must sign a confession admitting his guilt, the judge presented the statement of the judgment.

"Sign this document," he said. To the statement of his guilt were appended a few lines of writing affirming the falsity of the Catholic religion.

"My religion is holy," replied Peter. "The doctrine which it teaches is true, and I cannot testify that it is false."

The judge then ordered an officer of the court to seize his hand and make him sign it by force, after which he was sent back to prison.

Peter Lee remained in prison for nearly four years. His rectitude of character, his kindliness and affability won the hearts of his jailors, and he succeeded in converting an elderly prisoner and preparing him for Baptism.

Peter and his sister Agatha encouraged each other in constancy and the love of God. They had vowed to undergo martyrdom on the same day, but Peter's strength was exhausted and he fell sick. He regretted only one thing, and was not this equivalent to an act of complete and holy resignation? "I had hoped," he said, "to die under the executioner's sword, but nothing happens except by God's will." He died on November 25, 1838, aged thirty-six years.

29. The Persecution in 1839 and Court Council—Persecution Order

The martyrdom in prison of Blessed Peter Lee Ho-yŏng seemed to presage a further outbreak of persecution, and in a few months this was confirmed in fact. The ailing and much weakened Regent finally resigned, and political power fell into the hands of a group of strongly anti-Catholic ministers. Their ill-will combined with the greed of petty officials and the general corruption of the time to start the new wave of persecution that now assailed the Catholics. Among the believers there were some who lacked a sound basis of doctrinal instruction and others who lacked the courage of their convictions. Indeed there were some who even played the part of Judas Iscariot and betrayed their fellow-Christians and their priest into the hands of the authorities. Many of the believers were arrested as a result. The new government, convinced that the Catholics constituted a

---

① The *bone-bending torture* is called in Korean *Ka-wi-chu-ri* or *Chul-chu-ri* according to the manner in which it is inflicted. The former consists in tying the legs tightly together at the knees and by the big toes of each foot, and inserting in the space between, two wooden bars which are turned in opposite directions until the bones become bent in an arc, and afterward are allowed to resume their original position. In the latter, the toes of each foot are tied together, a thick piece of wood is inserted between the calves, and two men pull cords tied to the knees until they bring the knees into contact.

danger to the state, began to take measures to suppress the new religion. At a cabinet meeting on April 18 the Senior Assistant Chief of Police, Nam Hŏn-kyo, warned the conferees that "the evil learning was rampant." Lee Chi-yŏn, the Admirable Counselor emphatically supported Nam. Queen Regent Kim, although she herself harbored no ill-will toward the Catholics, confessed that the rapid spread of the 'evil learning' throughout the country had caused her some misgiving, and asked for effective legislation to put a stop to its propagation. "The Senior and Junior Assistant Chiefs of Police and the ministers in charge of penal administration should appear to court and receive at the hands of His Majesty the royal decree on the action to be taken, and the Admirable Counselor should issue a rigorous order to carry it into effect." Her instructions resulted in the law which was promulgated on the following day, April 19, and the persecution which had already begun was now greatly intensified.

30. Blessed Protase Chŭng Kuk-po
(died in prison, May 20, 1839)

Protase Chŭng was the first to suffer martyrdom under the new law.

Protase had been converted to Christianity at the age of thirty, and was a faithfully practicing Catholic.

Put in charge of the hostel for Christians who came to the capital to receive the Sacraments, he acquitted himself of his duties with zeal tempered by kindness. The father of fourteen children who all died in infancy, he accepted their death with resignation.

Denounced in the month of April 1839, he was arrested together with his wife; he appeared before the Police Commissioner, who called upon him to apostatize: Protase refused. Cruelly tortured, he remained resolute, and was transferred to the criminal court. There he had a moment of weakness: overcome by the gentle means employed by the mandarin, seduced by his counsels, he apostatized and was set free.

But no sooner was he home than he began to repent his crime so bitterly that for several days he could neither eat nor sleep, and he wept continually. Finally, encouraged by the exhortations of one of his friends, he resolved to give himself up to the judges, and returned to the law court. "Ah! You are back again," said the police officers to him. "What brings you here?"

"To make amends for the crime I committed: I apostatized, and now I repent having done so. I have come to report the fact to the judge." So saying, he stepped across the threshold of the judgment hall.

"Pooh!" said the officers, pushing him back. "What you have said you have said; the case is closed. Go home."

Protase returned to the charge on three successive days, but was constantly refused admittance. He thereupon took his stand in the street and waited for the judge to come out. On seeing the latter approach, he prostrated himself and said, in tears:

"I have sinned," he cried. "My mouth has uttered words that my heart denies: I am a Christian, and I want to go on being one."

"I don't believe you," said the judge, going on his way.

Protase followed him, shouting: "I am a Christian, and I will die a Christian."

"What people these are! There's no dealing with them," grumbled the judge in annoyance.

He ordered them to take him away. Protase held out his hands to the police officers, who led him back to prison. He entered with his heart full of holy joy, which the congratulations of the Christians made still greater.

Called before the court which had heard his apostasy, he was given twenty-five blows with such force that he had to be removed dying to his dungeon. He died in a few hours, during the night of May 20, 1839, at the age of forty-one.

His fault had been followed by sincere repentance, his weakness by unshakable courage which God crowned with grace.

31. The Martyrdom of Nine Blessed Men and Women

(beheaded on May 24, 1839)

Agatha Lee, Anne Park, Magdalene Kim, Barbara Han, Agatha Kim, Peter Kwon, Damian Nam, Augustine Lee, Lucy Park

The arrest of these nine confessors of the faith took place over a space of three years.

The first, in the month of February, 1836, was that of Agatha Lee So-sa, aged 56; in April of the same year that of Anne Park Yŏ-a-ji, 57 years; in October those of Magdalene Kim Yŏ-a-ji, 66 years, Barbara Han Yŏ-a-ji, 48 years and Agatha Kim Yŏ-ŏp-i, 50 years; in 1839 the following were imprisoned; on January 16, Peter Kwon Teuk-in, 35 years; April 8, Damian Nam Myŏng-hyŏk, 38 years and Augustine Lee Kwang-hŏn, 53 years; on April 8 or 9, Lucy Park Heui-sun, 39 years.

Agatha Lee, for some years a widow, lived by hard work in poverty and humility.

A little hamlet situated near the Han River that flows past the town of Seoul was the birthplace of **Anne Park** whose parents were Christians. With a rebellious memory she only succeeded in learning the catechism and prayers with great difficulty. She consoled herself with the saying: "Since I cannot learn to know my God as well as I should like to, let me at least try my best to love Him with all my heart." Married at the age of eighteen to a Catholic, she brought up her children very piously. She cherished a particular devotion to the Passion of Our Lord. The thought of the Five Wounds of the Saviour invariably moved her to tears. When she heard people talking of the persecution her eyes would light up and the expression of her face would show the deep desire she felt to become a martyr. She was arrested together with her husband and her eldest son.

Magdalene Kim had, in her youth, wished to live a celibate life; her family forced her to marry. Having lost her husband and children, she lived in the Kam-na-mu-kol quarter of Seoul with her mother whose quarrelsome nature she bore with exemplary patience. When her mother died, the excellent woman devoted her spare time to baptizing pagan children on the point of death, and to teaching various Christian children.

Barbara Han belonged to a pious Christian family whose lessons and examples she long disdained. Without the spirit of the faith, fond of pleasure, she married a pagan. One day her mother was about to visit her when she met Magdalene Kim at her door. The two entered and earnestly besought the young woman to return to God. This was Barbara's moment of grace: she was converted and from that time on practiced the finest Christian virtues. At the age of thirty she lost her husband and children, and returned to live with her mother.

Animated by a lively zeal for the salvation of souls she preached to the pagans, baptized dying children and called upon sinners to repent; to draw down the blessing of God upon her works she frequently fasted and practiced prolonged mortification by acts of self-discipline.

Agatha Kim, born in a non-Christian *milieu* strongly imbued with superstition, followed the example of her husband for several years. Her elder sister, who was a Christian, explained to her the vanity of idolatry and the uselessness of the sacrifices she offered. "All these spirits are idle things," she would often repeat, "be careful not to believe in them." Agatha took her advice, and paying no attention to the reproaches of her husband she threw the images and statuettes that she had in her house into the fire. Though full of faith and piety, and in spite of all her efforts, she had such a weak memory that she could not manage to learn the morning and evening prayers.

Peter Kwon, of Christian origin, was a small shopkeeper barely able to make a living, but widely known for his piety and his obliging nature. He would rise at the first cockcrow, light his lamp, and pray until dawn. He was imprisoned together with his family, but the Korean annalists tell us nothing about the circumstances and the details of his case.

We are better informed about the following martyrs. Here is what the *Ki-hae Diary* edited by Charles Hyŭn, says about Augustine Lee:

Augustine Lee was descended from a distinguished family, he had a lofty and generous character and was given to a life of amusement and pleasure. At the age of thirty, he was converted; his brother and his wife followed his example. and all three practiced their religion with fervor.

The life of **Damian Nam,** who belonged to the nobility, resembled that of Augustine Lee: dissipation up to the age of twenty-five to twenty-eight, but afterward sincere and complete conversion.

Both of them, intelligent and well-educated, were appointed catechists. They gathered the Christians together in their homes for Catholic instruction and prayer, did their best to help them, visited the sick, assisted the poor, and baptized children in danger of death.

Lucy Park belonged to a rich family. Distinguished for her wit and beauty, she was presented at court and admitted to the number of maids of honor in attendance upon the queen.

At the age of thirty she heard of the Christian religion for the first time; she conceived the desire to practice it. But she belonged to the court and was a favorite of the queen's and had other maids of honor to wait upon her, and above all other impediments she was the vestal priestess in charge of the spirit tablet of the late king. These obstacles only intensified her desire, and, pretending to be sick, she obtained her release and, as her pagan father was extremely hostile to Catholicism, she went to live with one of her nephews.

Considering from that time on the number of years she had wasted in a life of luxury and pleasure, she redoubled her zeal in order to perform her duties to the full, devoting herself especially to mortification and self-discipline in the matter of food and clothing. By her words and her example, she soon succeeded in converting the family of her nephew. Having won this success, she withdrew to the home of an excellent Christian lady, Agatha Chŭng.

As soon as she saw the outbreak of the persecution, she bought a house in the K'eun-sal-li-mut-kol quarter in downtown Seoul, where she received several women of her acquaintance, among whom was Agatha Chŭng. A few days later, she was discussing with the latter what means to take in order to avoid the persecution when suddenly the constables burst in upon them.

"Nothing happens except by God's will," she said. And stepping forward toward them, she requested them to stop shouting, and offered them some cord, some wine, and some dishes of food. Then, joyously she surrendered herself to the authorities together with the other Christians, among whom was her sister Maria.

Here are a few details of the imprisonment and interrogation to which these faithful Christians were subjected.

From the time of her first interrogation Agatha Lee was severely beaten, and then forced to undergo the bone-bending torture. Powerless to overcome her steadfastness, the judge handed her over to the hangmen and executioners. These men, dressed in white or grey trousers, and black or blue vests, armed with enormous red clubs as thick as a man's arm and about eight feet long, seized their victim. They stripped her of her clothes, hung her up by the arms, and struck her with rods. Her entire body was covered with lesions, without her courage failing in the slightest degree.

"Anne Park was so cruelly beaten," says a witness, "that the bones of her legs were bared to the view, and her flesh pierced with gaping wounds as big as bull's eyes." Perhaps these tortures were not the worst that she had to bear. Every day her husband and one of her sons came and implored her to speak the one word that would set her free. They told her of the desolation of her family, of the sorrow of her aged mother, now at death's door, and the distress of her children who were calling for her. Her courage enabled her to resist this supreme temptation.

Magdalene Kim showed no less courage. She was not afraid to explain the principal Catholic truths to the magistrate, while her companion Barbara Han underwent the torture of the wooden clubs with joyful resignation.

Agatha Kim was just as brave. Here is the first dialogue between her and the magistrate.

"Is it true that you practice the Christian religion?"

"I only know Jesus and Mary: apart from that, I am ignorant of the rest."

"If we put you to the torture up to the point of death, would you not renounce Jesus and Mary?"

"Even if I were to die, I could not renounce them."

Put to the torture, she gave equally firm replies. The judge transferred her to the criminal court. As soon as she entered, the Christians greeted her with laughing countenance; "Ha, ha! Here is Agatha, who only knows Jesus and Mary, and nothing more." They praised her courage, taught her the essential truths, and baptized her. Having drawn new strength from the Sacrament of regeneration, she underwent further torture with the same fortitude.

Peter Kwon was equally inflexible.

"Why do you practice the religion of the Lord of Heaven?" asked the magistrate.

"The Lord of Heaven is the master of angels, men, and everything, and man, who lives in this world, makes use of all these things and receives from God an infinite number of benefits; would it be fair not to think about showing some gratitude to Him? It is, moreover, every man's duty to honor and serve God."

The infuriated judge ordered him to be beaten with redoubled force.

"Denounce your coreligionists," he shouted.

"Our religion strictly forbids us to kill our fellow-man or do him wrong: how dare I, by my words, expose men to the risk of being killed?"

To force him to apostatize, the judge handed Peter over to the criminal prisoners, telling them that they were permitted to torture him. The judge's wishes were satisfied: the wretches beat this faithful follower of Christ unmercifully and twice left him for dead.

The judge desired to intimidate them and chose Damian Nam as his victim.

"Renounce this foreign religion and save your life, and that of your wife and children."

"My religion, which you call foreign, belongs to all times and all places; it is eight years since I began to practice it, and I shall never renounce it."

"You know the Christians. Point out the houses where they live."

"Among the commandments of Our God there is one which forbids us to harm our fellow-men. I cannot denounce them."

The judge ordered them to break the bones of his legs, and to beat him unmercifully on the arms, the sides, and finally his whole body. His desire was to bring about the death of the neophyte in order to put an end to the affair, which was becoming an embarrassment to him.

Damian, broken under the torture, fell down in a faint, and for four days was given up for dead, but he finally recovered. God saved him for further battles.

The interrogations which Augustine Lee underwent were as long and his tortures as painful as those of his companion.

Let us relate part of them:

"Speak only one word," the magistrate ordered, "and I will set you free, you, your wife, your brother, and your children, and you shall also have your property back."

"What I hold dearest to me in this world," replied Augustine, "is my religion. I would rather lose everything else than renounce it."

They beat him on the legs with the sharp-edged rods. He bore the blows in silence.

"Ha!" said judge, "you count your life as nothing; but have you no pity for your wife and children?"

"I love my wife and children, and that is why I don't give them an example of weakness."

"Beat him to death."

The brutal executioners made him lie on the ground face downward: one of the strongest of them seized a hard oaken plank about five feet long, six or seven inches wide, and a little more than two inches thick, shaped at one end so as to form a handle. After a few heavy blows on the calves, the blood spurted out, and the flesh became detached and fell in shreds; at the tenth or twelfth blow, the plank resounded upon the exposed bone. The shocked witnesses averted their eyes in horror. The confessor of the faith remained silent. At a last injunction by the mandarin, who once more called upon him to apostatize, he replied: "Never."

Of Lucy Park, the last of this group to be arrested, here is what the witnesses relate. As soon as she appeared before the court for the first time, the police commissioner told her:

"A lady of the palace is in a class apart from other women: how then does it come about that you practice such a perverse and contemptible religion?"

"There is nothing contemptible about our religion," replied Lucy, "God created Heaven, earth, and all that is in them; all men owe their life to Him, and, as a consequence, praise and worship."

"Renounce your religion, and tell us the names of your accomplices."

"God is my Creator and my Father, I cannot deny Him, Who forbids me to hurt my brothers, so I cannot denounce them."

The magistrate had Lucy's hands tied behind her back, and sent her to the criminal court. Three times she was called up before her new judges, and each time received thirty strokes of the wooden bar. One of her legs was fractured, and she took her hair in her hands to cut away the marrow extruded from the broken bones. "Now at last I begin to understand a little of the sufferings of Our Lord and the Holy Virgin," she said.

In spite of her injuries, she was able to go on foot to her next interrogation, and all the witnesses regarded this as a most extraordinary thing. The judge attributed it to sorcery.

In the face of such constancy, the judges, by government order, condemned all the confessors of the faith to death. After a discussion in the Grand Council of State lasting three days, this sentence was confirmed.

On hearing this Damian Nam wrote to his imprisoned wife. "This world is nothing more than an inn, our true homeland is in Heaven. Die for God, and I hope to meet you in the abode of eternal glory."

The date and place of the beheading had been fixed for Friday, May 24, 1839, outside the Small West Gate of the city of Seoul.

Charles Cho, who was destined to follow these martyrs along the royal road of supreme sacrifice, has left us some details about the execution of these Christians whose heroism we recall to our minds:

"At dawn a wagon was brought in front of the prison. In the middle of it a cross had been set up, higher than a man of ordinary stature. When this was ready, an executioner entered the dungeon, lifted the condemned victim on to his shoulders, and fastened him to the cross by the arms and by the hair: to support part of the weight, he put a sort of stool under the victim's feet. Then he gave the signal to start. As soon as the procession reached the Small West Gate, which stands at the top of a steep slope, the executioner plucked away the stool and the driver goaded the oxen, which plunged down the slope at high speed. The road is of cobblestones and while the wagon bumped and swayed on its way the body of the victim, being held up only by the hair and the arms, was so violently shaken and thrown about that it caused horrible suffering. At the foot of the slope was the execution ground. The soldiers unfastened the victim and stripped him naked; the executioner seized his head and placed it on the block, and then decapitated him."

Augustine Lee's head fell at the fourth stroke, and on this occasion a witness records that Damian Nam said smilingly to Augustine: "As for me, I'm a puny fellow and they'll have no difficulty in cutting off my head: but you—you've got a neck so thick and strong that I feel quite sorry for the executioner who has to cut yours off."

Of Damian Nam they say: "He went to his execution full of joy, and never ceased praying until his head fell under the blows of the executioner's blade."

Of Peter Kwon: "He walked to his execution with redoubled joy. His severed head still kept its smiling air." Of Agatha Lee: "As she was carried along in the cart she had her usual kindly expression on her face, with lowered eyes. When she alighted she made the sign of the cross and received the blow of the saber with tranquillity." Of Lucy Park: "On her way to execution, she wore her usual peaceful and serene look, and never stopped saying her prayers until her head fell to the executioner's sword."

32. Blessed Joseph Chang, Barbara Lee and Barbara Kim

(died in prison, May 26–27, 1839)

In four days, the prisoners of Seoul saw one man and two women die as Christians, and although the lives of these three persons had been very different, their heroism, drawn from the same fountains of grace, was of equal grandeur.

Joseph Chang Sŏng-jip, aged fifty-four years, was born to a pagan family; **Barbara Lee**, aged fifteen, and **Barbara Kim**, thirty-five, belonged to Catholic families.

In the month of April 1838 **Joseph** received Baptism and Confirmation with remarkable fervor. He cheerfully learnt from the Christians how to be constant under torture and at the hour of death; and kindled with

a holy desire for martyrdom, he resolved to give himself up to the authorities. His godfather dissuaded him. A few days later, on May 18, 1839, he was denounced and arrested.

His neighbors and friends came to offer their condolences, and to advise him to obtain his freedom by apostasy, and the police officers added their persuasion in the same way. Far from following their counsels, he explained the Catholic teaching to them:

"There is one sovereign Master who created Heaven and earth and everything contained in them," he told them, "mankind is therefore under an obligation to honor Him; it is He Who gives us our life, feeds us, and takes care of us: it is He Who rewards the good in Heaven and punishes the wicked in hell: how could I, for the sake of this life which is so short, risk the loss of that greater prize which is eternal?"

Several hours passed in these debates. Finally, seeing that his will was unshakable, they took him to prison. Next morning, astonished at not having been brought before the court, he cried:

"Why do you leave me here like this without putting me to the torture, a man whom you have arrested in order to condemn him to death?" But he spoke in vain, for nobody answered him. He emerged from his cell and began shouting his question as loud as he could. The commissioner's assistant, who heard him, asked what was the matter: he was told that it was a sick man in delirium, and he ordered Joseph to be put back in his cell.

"No," said Joseph, "this is not delirium, it is from conviction that I say this."

They paid no attention to his words. A little later the commissioner interrogated him, and insisted on his making an act of apostasy. The prisoner replied by giving him a brief explanation of Catholic faith. He was given twenty strokes of the plank, but he did not falter in the slightest, and was locked up again in his cell, where he died soon afterward, on May 26.

Barbara Lee, a mere child of fifteen, was born in Seoul, in the Ch'ŏng-p'a district. Orphaned at an early age, she was brought up by her aunts Magdalene and Barbara Lee, two future martyrs. She appears to us like one of those whose destiny is to be given to the world to love God and win Heaven in the shortest possible time.

In *Procès Apostoliques* (Apostolic reports) we read that, "taken to the police headquarters, she underwent innumerable tortures."

Transferred to the criminal court, she resisted the judge "who tried by threats and by cajolery to get her to give up her faith," and who was unable to obtain either a single word or the slightest sign of weakness from her.

Touched with pity, he sent her back to the petty offenders' court, as too young to come before the criminal court.

Barbara and three other children of her own age with whom she was incarcerated "spent their time in exhorting and encouraging one another." She caught the plague, which at that time cruelly aggravated the sufferings of the prisoners; "it was a sort of putrid fever (jail fever) caused by overcrowding and by infection from the filthy state in which the prison cells were allowed to remain." The brave young girl succumbed to this scourge on May 27, 1839 after a week of intense pain.

On the same day, a widow, of upright and firm character, **Barbara Kim** died of the same scourge in the same prison. A domestic servant in a Catholic family, Barbara cherished the desire to live a celibate life. Her father came to see her, and letting her believe that he was speaking of a Christian youth, said to her:

"A desirable match has been proposed, and I have given my consent; get yourself ready for your wedding."

"My desire is to remain single, and to live a maiden," answered Barbara. Her father would not permit this.

The marriage was celebrated, but instead of a Christian, the bridegroom was a callous pagan, and Barbara tried unavailingly to convert him to Catholicism. She became the mother of several children, and baptized at least one of her daughters.

After becoming a widow she got in touch with the missionaries newly arrived in Korea, received the Sacraments, and from that time she evinced great fervor.

Arrested in April, 1839, with the owners of the house she occupied, she refused to apostatize or to divulge the names of the Christians whom the judge called "her accomplices." She underwent the bone-bending torture and was beaten with the wooden bar with such violence that her arms were broken: she continued to affirm her faith.

Two months later, lying naked on the floor of her cell, a victim of cholera, the poor young Korean woman "died a holy death" on May 27.

33. The Martyrdom of Eight Blessed Man and Women

Toward the end of June, 1839, nearly all governmental authority was in the hands of the Christians' greatest enemy, Cho Pyŏng-ku, the uncle of the young king. Thus, on July 5, in a royal council over which he presided, the Regent (Queen Dowager) asked: "At the present time, what is to be said of the way the minister of crime is conducting the repression of the perverse doctrine? Unless we exterminate this brood without delay it will continue to pullulate, and this is no small matter. How can we go on even for a moment temporizing in this neglectful manner?"

Several counselors spoke in support and the Regent concluded: "After the order has been given to search out and confiscate all the objects that the Christians keep in their homes, it is said that the police officers have not arrested anybody: did you ever see such a kingdom? This is not merely a personal matter but one that affects the entire court. In a short time who can say that even among the court dignitaries there will not be some who are infected with this doctrine? As soon as Your Excellency withdraws, let the Commissioners of Police be ordered to renew their efforts: it is indispensable."

Among the faithful the first to be executed after the publication of these orders were **Rose Kim, Magdalene Lee, Theresa Lee, Martha Kim, Lucy Kim, John Lee, Anne Kim** and **Mary Won.**

We will give a few details about them:

Rose Kim, born in Seoul about 1783, embraced the Catholic faith on the death of her husband. Happy in the possession of this treasure, she wished to share it with others, especially the members of her own family. She was arrested without warning, at her home, on January 16, 1839: she was then fifty-six years old. Quite unmoved, she called upon Jesus and Mary in a loud voice and went cheerfully to prison.

Magdalene Lee belonged to an impoverished family of the nobility. Her mother, Magdalene Hŭh, her sister Barbara, and her aunt **Theresa Lee** were fervent Catholics, but in secret. Her father, an obstinate infidel, abhorred Catholicism.

Martha Kim, a widow aged fifty, had, while still a pagan, left her husband on account of dissension and had married a blind man who was a professional sorcerer. It was at this time that she first heard of Catholicism and began to practice some of its precepts. After the death of the blind man, being left without support, she went to live with some Christians who received her out of charity and in return for their hospitality she tried to be of service to them in every possible way. Her life was often hard, and at times she bitterly resented having to be the recipient of alms, but she remained sweet-tempered and full of faith in God.

Lucy Kim, aged twenty-two years, was endowed with remarkable intelligence, sweetness of temper, and courage. On the death of her parents she sold her poor belongings in order to pay for their funeral. Wishing to consecrate herself to the service of God, she made a vow of chastity and resolved to live a celibate life in the home of a Catholic family.

One day, Magdalene, Theresa, Martha and Lucy were talking about the persecution, of the valor of the martyrs, and of the bliss of paradise; in a transport of holy enthusiasm, they resolved to give themselves up to the police and declare their faith.

On April 11, 1839, these heroines presented themselves at a police station and one of them, speaking on behalf of them all, said to the chief:

"You are angry with the Christians; chain us up and take us to prison."

Taken aback, the chief and his men refused to believe them.

"We are Christians," they repeated, "make no mistake. Here is the proof." They showed their chaplets.

Finally the police bound their hands behind their back and took them to prison.

From the life and virtues of these Christian women they might well be expected to display great courage under torture and during the interrogations in prison, and display it they did.

John Lee Kwang-ryöl, arrested on April 8, 1839, was the younger brother of Augustine Lee whose martyrdom we have already related. He had been converted at the same time, and was remarkable for his upright character, piety, and devotion, and for this reason the Christians enroled him, soon after his conversion, among the number of those entrusted with the important mission of the journeys to Peking. It was in this city that he was baptized. From the day of his return he subjected himself to strict abstinence from meat and vowed to live a celibate life. His habit of peaceful meditation aroused the admiration of all: nothing could distract him from his intimate and continual communion with God.

Anne Kim, aged 56 years and Mary Won, aged 22 years, were also imprisoned on April 8, 1839.

Belonging to a Catholic family, a quite young widow, Anne Kim lived with her mother a life of prayer and poverty.

Mary Won, born in 1819 at Yong-mŏ-ri in the district of Ko-yang, lost her mother early in life and followed her father who begged his living from place to place. At the age of nine she was taken into the home of one of her aunts, Lucy Won, an excellent Christian woman, who taught her the catechism, the prayers, and also embroidery, which enabled her to earn her living. Intelligent, docile, and pious, the young woman was a credit to her aunt through her fervor and hard work. At the age of fifteen she received Baptism. Shortly afterward, whenever anyone spoke to her of marriage, she would refuse, saying that she had resolved to dedicate her life to God. In the following year she began to wear her hair in the style of a married woman. When she was denounced by her neighbors she tried to run away, but was arrested. It is said that at the beginning of her incarceration she was somewhat upset, but very soon the thought that nothing happens without God's permission restored her to her customary calm demeanor.

As soon as Rose Kim, the first to be imprisoned, appeared before the court the magistrate had various instruments of torture set out before her.

"Before you get your legs broken," said he, "or your body torn to pieces, renounce the Lord of Heaven and divulge the names of your accomplices."

"I cannot deny my God," replied Rose, "I cannot denounce them." The judge had her tortured. She remained invincible. Sentenced to death by decapitation, she was kept in prison for several days, and was still there when the Christians arrested on April 11, 1839 were brought into the jail. The following is what is known of the dialogues between the judge and the four Christians, Magdalene and Theresa Lee, Martha and Lucy Kim:

"Do you believe that the Christian doctrine is true?" asked the presiding judge.

One of the prisoners answered,

"Certainly: if we had any doubt about that, we would not be here before you."

"Renounce this religion and hand over to me all the books that mention it."

"We would sooner die than deny our God."

Four times were they brutally beaten on the legs, but they were unshakable in their faith.

Five days later, the judge sent for them again.

"The tortures you have endured," he said, "and the horrors of the jail—have they not awakened you from your dreams?"

"You are wasting your time in trying to make us apostatize. It is in order to bear witness to Jesus Christ that we have been delivered into your hands, and now you wish us to deny Him? No, no, make no mistake, a true Christian lives and dies for his God. If the laws of the kingdom condemn us to death, we will die, but renounce our religion? Never."

They underwent the same torture as before.

Lucy Kim's air of distinction and her equanimity under torture especially attracted the attention of the presiding judge.

"How," he asked, "can a well-born person like you actually bring yourself to practice this religion?"

"Well, I do practice it."

"Give it up, and I will save your life."

"Our God is the one who created and governs everything; He is the Great King and the Father of all creatures. How can one deny one's king and one's father? Had I to die ten thousand times I would never consent to that."

"Have you ever seen the God of Heaven?"

"Do not the people in the countryside believe in the existence of the king of this country without ever having seen him? When I look at the sky, the earth, and all the living beings I believe in the Great King and Father of all who created them."

The judge tried for a long time to overcome her constancy, at first gently, and then by threats, but getting nothing but the shame of defeat by these means, he condemned her to further tortures. The officers who witnessed her composure believed that

Paul Chŭng Ha-sang submitting to the Bishop of Peking a petition addressed to the Pope

Pope Gregory XVI conferring on the Most Rev. Bruguière, Bishop of Capse, the papal appointment of first Vicar Apostolic of Korea in 1831

A Brief History of the Catholic Church in Korea, centennial publication, 1931, p. 14

Tomb of Bishop Bruguière, first Vicar Apostolic of Korea, at Piehlikou in Manchuria

십으발를서령사 께에六十 오리고레그황교 교주소

二、腥風肉泥의
窘難時代

지금부터 百년친인 一八
三一년(純祖辛卯)에 교황
그레고리오十六세께쓰는 우
리 조선 교우들이 애원하
는 간청을 하흫하사 그해
九월九일에 우금 북경교구
의 관할을 받아오든 조선
지방을 따로 「조선교구」로

파蘇主敎
「朝鮮敎區」의設定
조션교구 설졍

蘇公之墓

Seminary Chapel of the Paris Foreign Mission Society

Blessed Laurent Imbert, Bishop and
Martyr, second Vicar Apostolic of
Korea (1837-1839)

Blessed Pierre-Philibert Maubant, martyr

Blessed Jacques-Honoré Chastan, martyr

Korean mourning costume used as
a disguise by missionaries on entering Korea from 1836 until 1890

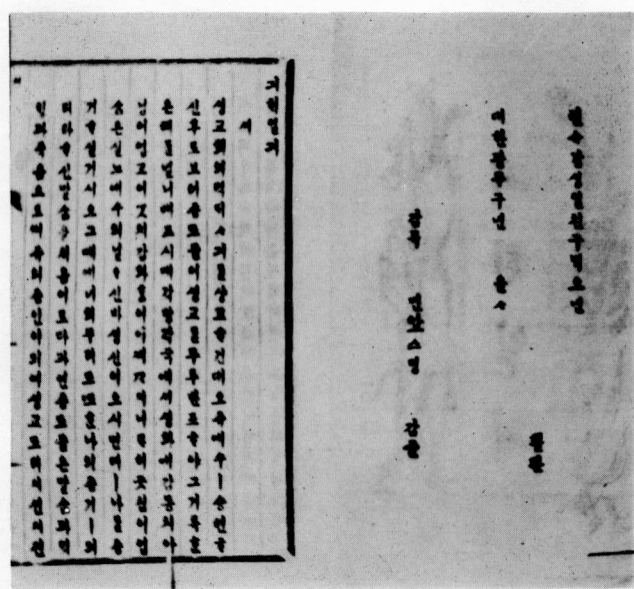

The execution of the Blessed Martyrs Laurent-Joseph-Marie Imbert, Pierre-Philippe Maubant and Jacques-Honoré Chastan at Sae-nam-t'ŏ (Sept. 21, 1839)

Facsimile of pages from the Korean book "Ki-hae-il-ki" (or the Ki-hae Diary on the Persecution of 1839) by Charles Hyŭn Sŏk-mun

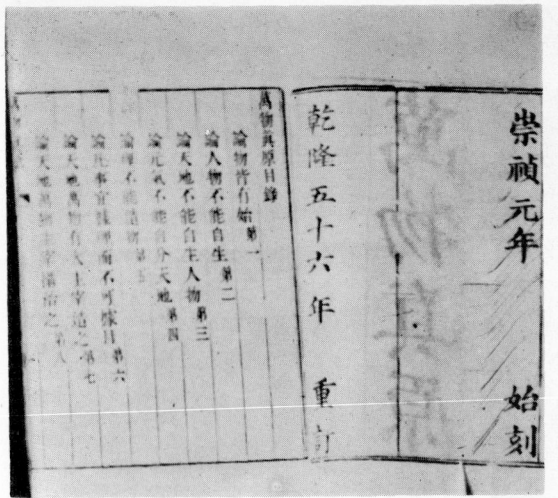

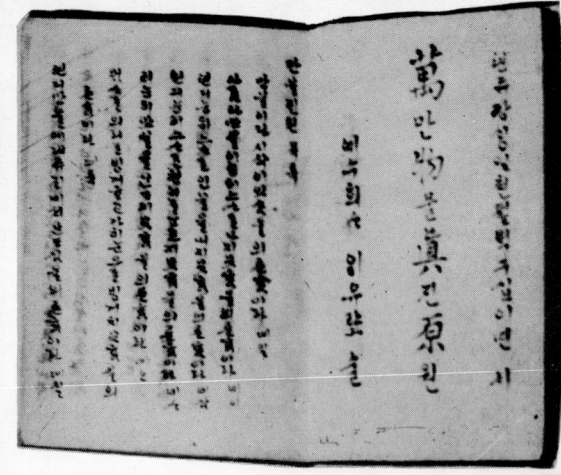

Korean version (right) of "Wan Wu Chen Yuan" (The True Origin of the Universe) by the Jesuit Father Aleni...a book on Christian doctrine

"Kyŏng-se-keum-sŏ" (Maxims for Renouncing Worldliness), an extremely popular book of Catholic doctrine

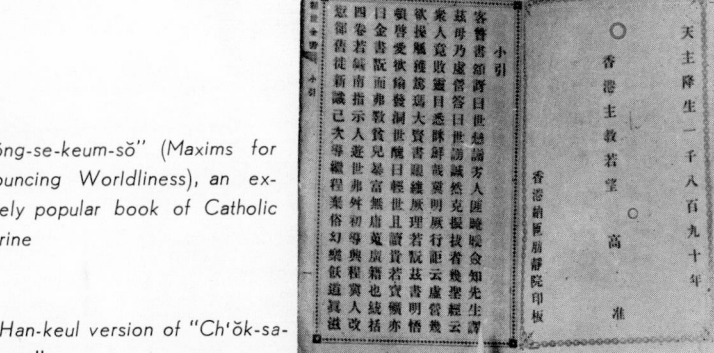

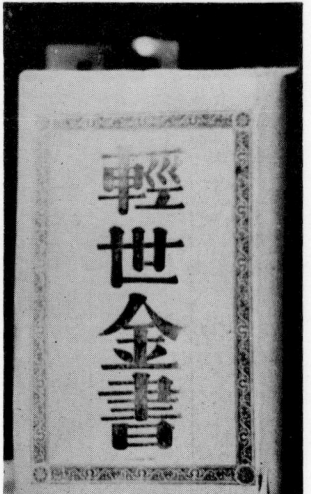

The Han-keul version of "Ch'ŏk-sa-yun-eum"

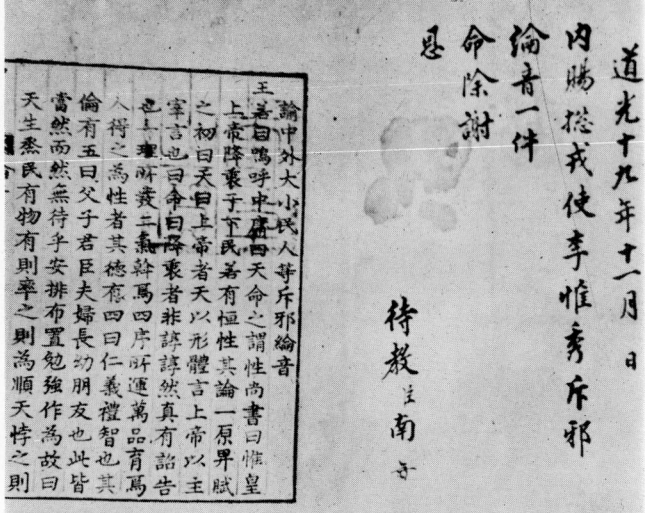

Facsimile of the "Ch'ŏk-sa-yun-eum" (Decree Calling for the Singling Out of Datholics)

The Royal Proclamation of King Hŏn-jong for the proscription of Christianity

Awaiting the executioner's sword
An old picture showing how the Christian victims, Blessed Columba Kim and companions, were conveyed to the scene of their execution.

Blessed Martyrs Columba Kim and Agnes Kim

The execution of Blessed Martyrs Columba Kim and Agnes Kim

152

An early portrait of the Blessed Martyr Peter Yu Tae-ch'ŏl

The torture undergone by the thirteen-year-old martyr,
Blessed Peter Yu Tae-ch'ŏl

Blessed Paul Chŭng Ha-sang

Blessed Paul Chŭng Ha-sang's "Letters to the Minister"

Written in prison before his execution in 1839, published in book form in 1889 (bottom, right). The original was written in Chinese characters (right, middle), and the date of the Korean version (bottom, left) is unknown.

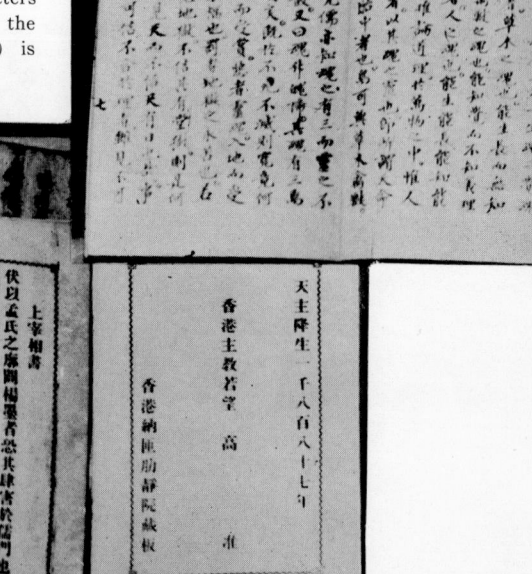

Father Dallet's "Histoire de l'Église de Corée" (2 vols.)
published in Paris in 1874

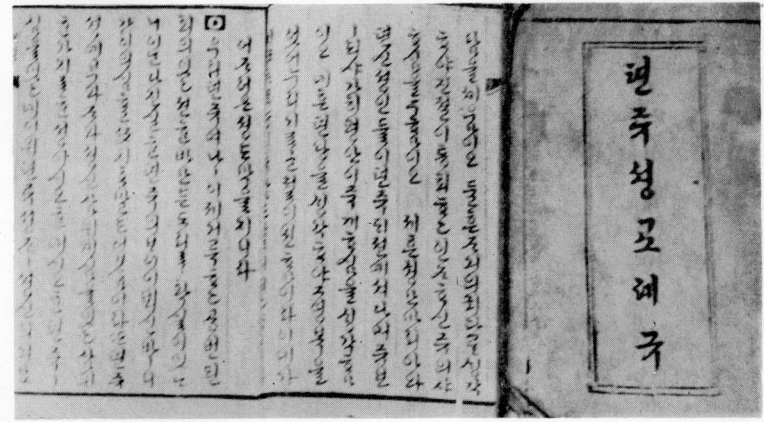

"Ch'ŏn-ju-sŏng-kyo-ye-kyu" (The Liturgy of the Holy Catholicism)
Published by the Catholic Publication Office, 1885

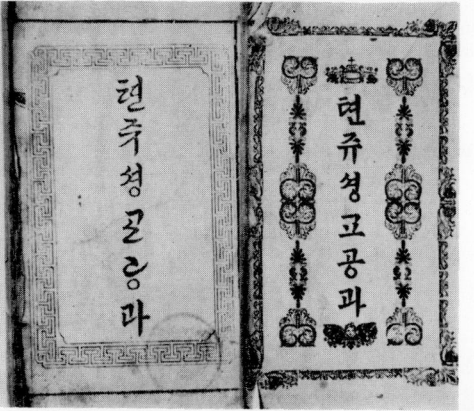

"Ch'ŏn-ju-sŏng-kyo-kong-kwa" (Catholic Prayer Book)
The earliest Korean Catholic prayer book, compiled in 1838 by Bishop Imbert, published 1862-1864

"Ch'ŏn-ju-sŏng-kyo Sa-cha-kyŏng-mun" (Catholicism Explained in Tetrameters)
A book of Catholic doctrine in the four-character style

Seminary of St. Joseph in the Portuguese Colony of Macao

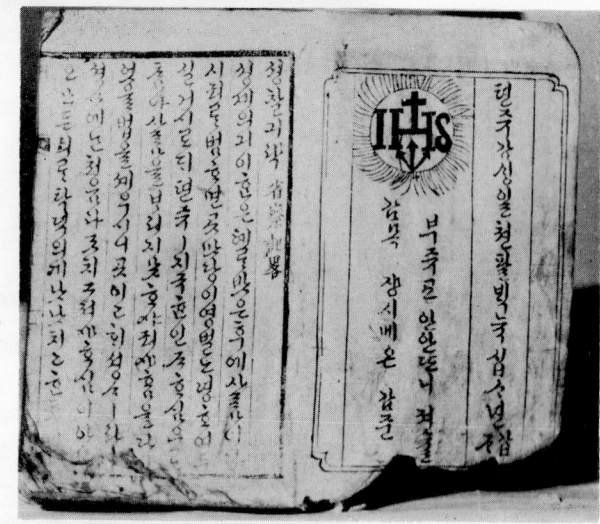

"Sŏng-ch'al-ki-ryak" (The Principal Points to Be Observed in the Examination of Conscience)

A manual for Catholics preparing to receive the Sacrament of Penance, compiled by Bishop Daveluy during his coadjutorship in Korea

A view of Pae-ron, Che-ch'ŏn, where the first seminary in Korea was founded

she must be possessed by some supernatural spirit.

John Lee was repeatedly subjected to the bone-bending torture, beaten with the wooden bar, and left for long weeks in prison. Called again before the court he underwent the tortures of 'the ruler' and 'the rods.'

The ruler is a strip of wood one meter long, five centimeters wide, and only a few millimeters thick. Usually the number of blows is limited to thirty at an interrogation, and as the executioner is supposed to break the ruler at each blow, thirty such rulers are supplied for beating each accused. The rods are bound three or four together, and form flexible bundles which in vigorous hands are capable of tearing the victim's flesh to pieces.

The confessor, without ever weakening, had declared his faith in Jesus Christ and affirmed that he would always keep it.

He was to have been beheaded at the same time as his elder brother, but as Korean law does not permit the simultaneous execution of brothers, he had been kept in prison, where he had edified his fellow-prisoners by his patience and piety.

Mary Won's turn also came. Here is her dialogue with the magistrate:

"You belong to the Christian sect?"

"You are right. I am a Christian."

"Give up your religion and save your life."

"I worship God, I wish to save my soul, my mind is made up; if I must die, I will die; but the salvation of my soul comes before everything else. In giving up my religion I should lose my soul."

They twisted her legs, they beat her with the bar, they kept up a series of interrogations; several of her bones were dislocated, but they could not shake her faith.

These brave Christian women were then sent to the criminal court. After two or three weeks they were brought before the judges who put the same questions to them as they had already answered at the police headquarters. The chief one was this:

"Do you believe that the religion of the Christians is true?"

"We believe it to be true, we worship God, and we are ready to shed our blood for Him."

The magistrate ordered them to be beaten more severely than the other Christians in order to punish them for taking the initiative in giving themselves up to the police, and being unable to overcome their resistance he condemned them to death.

For several weeks the confessors continued to endure the horrors of prison life, to which were added the sufferings of hunger and thirst. Lucy Kim, who had a most beautiful head of hair, cut it all off and sold it to "a Christian, and with the money, bought rice porridge which she shared with her fellow-prisoners." She wrote a letter to her friends, in which we may read the following brave and touching words:

"Until now, by the grace of God, I have never flinched under torture and hardship; now at last I am condemned to death; when will the Lord call me? I do not know, so please pray to God for us, and follow us as soon as possible; we are only waiting for God to call us."

The death sentence was executed on July 20, 1839. The eight confessors of the faith, taken to the Small West Gate, were beheaded, and this was the last of their sufferings. They bore it with the same patient courage that they had shown under torture and interrogation.

Caeduntur gladiis more bidentium: non murmur resonat, non querimonia, sed corde impavido mens bene conscia conservat patientiam.

(They were cut down like lambs brought to the slaughter, without complaint, but a heart without fear and clear conscience gave them the strength to bear it.)

34. Blessed Lucy Kim

(died in prison, in early Sept. 1839)

Lucy Kim, commonly known as "Hunchback Lucy" on account of her deformity, seems to have been Christian from early infancy. She was married to a pagan who did not allow her to associate with Catholics or to devote herself to the practice of her religion, and this made her so unhappy that she left her husband and took refuge with various families of the faithful who were willing to receive her. She paid for this hospitality with domestic service, looking after children, the sick and infirm, and she set an edifying example of religious fervor.

Loving God with all her heart, zealous for the salvation of souls, this poor woman whom one might have thought narrow-minded was in fact able to convert a number of pagans. She had her own arguments and answers which were remarkable for their sound common sense and originality. To one noble pagan who inquired, "If hell is as narrow as you say, how can it hold so many sinners?" she answered, "Your brain, which is so small, can hold ten thousand books; you never thought it was too small for that." Her interlocutor was at a loss for a reply and went off muttering to himself, "All these Christians, even the ignorant ones, can speak the language of reason."

Arrested and imprisoned, she desired, in spite of her weakness and her advanced age of seventy-one years, to help the sick prisoners and share her limited means with them. When asked by the magistrate to divulge the names and addresses of other Catholics, she simply answered that she would not do so, and was ready to die. "Don't keep on urging me like this any longer: I'm a Catholic: send me to my death, I'm quite ready and willing to go." She was given thirty blows with the rods which on her emaciated body, said a witness, "sounded like hitting bones."

After this torture she was sent back to prison. On arriving there, she lay down exhausted; she never rose again. Three or four days later, at the beginning of September, surrounded by her Christian fellow-prisoners, she died, with the holy names of Jesus and Mary on her lips.

35. Martyrdom of Six Blessed Man and Women
(beheaded, on Sept. 3, 1839)

All these confessors of the faith had been arrested in 1839: **Barbara Lee Chŏng-heui** on April 11; **Barbara Kwon Heui** and **Mary Lee Yŏn-heui** on April 7; **Mary Park Tae-a-ji** on April 15; **Agnes Kim Hyo-ju** and **John Park Hu-jae** on May 3, respectively.

Barbara Lee, born in 1799 in Pong-ch'ŏn, showed great faith and strength of character while still a young woman. Betrothed by her father to a pagan, but determined not to contract this marriage, which her conscience could not approve, she pretended to be ill and took to her bed for three years. Tired of waiting, the *fiancé* broke off the engagement, and Barbara married a Christian. Two years later she was a widow, and she went to live with her family, and afterward went to live in Seoul near her aunt Theresa Lee, in whose house, as we have seen, her sister Magdalene had taken refuge.

Barbara Kwon, aged forty-six years, of a pagan family, was converted to the Catholic faith at the same time as her husband. At the risk of her life she sheltered Bishop Imbert and his missionaries in her house, which she also permitted to be used as a Mass center and meeting place by the Catholics.

Mary Lee, an energetic and intelligent woman, followed Barbara Kwon's example. When there were meetings of Catholics in her home, she was assiduous and painstaking in waiting on the Bishop and the priests, full of zeal in teaching the faithful and preparing them to receive the Sacrament in a worthy and decorous manner. Her modesty and good example won all hearts.

Mary Park and Agnes Kim, whose names perhaps pale somewhat beside those of their sisters Lucy Park and Columba Kim, gave throughout their life and at the hour of their death beautiful examples of faith and magnanimity. Mary Park, aged fifty-four years, underwent the bastinado and the bone-bending tortures; condemned to death at the same time as Lucy, she was not executed, because, as we have said already, the law of Korea forbids the simultaneous execution of close relations.

Agnes Kim, born about 1814 in Seoul or its environs, was of a pagan family. After the death of the head of the family, her mother embraced Christianity together with her six children. Agnes and her two sisters, Columba and Clare, consecrated themselves to God. They lived at the home of their brother Anthony. Agnes, whose sweetness of temper was manifested in her looks, possessed solid virtues which concealed a character always completely modest.

John Park, born in 1798 or 1799 in the district of Yong-in, had migrated with his family to Seoul, where he plied the trade of a maker of straw-sandals. His wife had described many of his edifying traits.

We have described above how bravely Magdalene Lee and her companions gave themselves up to the authorities and bore imprisonment and torture: Barbara Lee, Magdalene's elder sister, showed the same valor and underwent the same torments.

Many were the sufferings of Barbara Kwon: incomparably more painful to her as a mother were those of her daughter Agatha, aged sixteen years, arrested at the same time, beaten repeatedly and with atrocious brutality, and cruelly put to the proof by hunger, thirst and cold.

On first entering the prison Mary Lee gave brisk and sharp retorts to the insolent remarks of the police officers. When her husband, Damian Nam, made the following comment to her, "A Christian ought to die for his God as meekly as a lamb: don't miss such a good opportunity as this," she bore all insults and ill-treatment without a murmur of complaint. Separated from her twelve-year-old son, she was afraid he had apostatized under the tortures which the officers had inflicted on him, and which they reported to her in detail with fiendish glee. But she quieted her heart, or rather lifted it up to God, saying: "It is to the greater glory of

God." She maintained an inalterably calm demeanor. "She truly loved God with all her heart," declares one of the witnesses. "All the desires of her heart were directed toward Heaven."

The most cruelly treated of all, however, was Agnes Kim. Besides the tortures that we have already described, those of dislocation of the joints of the bones and piercing of the body with sharpened sticks were inflicted upon her, and as her will still remained inflexible, the infuriated judge cried: "Stab her harder, stab her harder." From time to time the presiding judge would interrupt the torture and attempt to win her over with mild and friendly words, but threats, tortures, and flattery were all equally unavailing and left the young woman unmoved.

The executioners beat Agnes with unprecedented cruelty, pouring out a stream of insults and mockery as they did so. With redoubled fervor she offered her sufferings to God and said not a word.

The interrogation of John Park is still extant in part:

"Are your parents still living?" asked the judge, after having questioned him as to his name and profession.

"My mother died a few years ago: my father had his head cut off in 1801 for the same reason that now brought me here before you: I have no other relatives."

"Renounce your religion if you wish to live."

"My religion is dearer to me than my life; I would rather die than give it up."

He was given forty blows with the plank: his flesh fell in shreds, and his blood gushed out: the wood striking on the exposed bones produced a sound that caused excruciating anguish among the bystanders. The Christian remained unshakable in his faith. All these confessors of the faith were condemned to death, and beheaded on September 3, 1839.

Thus in the course of this persecution there were brought together group after group, sometimes entire families of those whom God gathered to Himself in order to crown them with heavenly glory.

36. Blessed Francis Ch'oe Kyŏng-hwan
(died in prison, Sept. 11—12, 1839)

Born at Ta-rae-kol in the district of Hong-ju in the Province of Ch'ung-ch'ŏng, Francis Ch'oe belonged to a rich and numerous family, one of the first to be converted at the end of the eighteenth century, and accordingly followed the Catholic way of life from early youth.

On July 31, 1839, police agents sent from Seoul arrived during the night at Su-ri-san (hill), in the Kwa-ch'ŏn district of Kyŏng-ki Province where he had migrated. With shouts and insults they broke down the doors and forced their way into Ch'oe's home.

The next day the captives were brought before the court. Numerous instruments of torture were displayed before them. The police commissioner addressed Francis Ch'oe:

"If you wanted to practice this religion, couldn't you have done it on your own, in your own way, without bewitching all these people?"

"Anyone who is ignorant of the religion of the Lord of Heaven," answered the Christian, "is bound to go to hell; what I did was out of pity toward those for whom such a fate was waiting, and also in order to serve God and save my own soul."

Guessing the strong attachment which Francis felt toward his religion the commissioner asked no more questions, but had him undergo the bone-bending torture twice, and then ordered them to pierce his flesh with the pointed sticks, and to go on torturing him until he consented to apostatize. The unfortunate man was immediately seized, partially stripped, and put to the question. Soon his blood was streaming, his flesh flying in shreds, and his bones exposed to view. Ch'oe did not give way but grew more inflexible with the pain, and let no sign of emotion appear.

Witnesses have declared that he was given three hundred and forty blows with the rods and a hundred and ten blows with the plank. To increase his sufferings, they chained a convict thief to him who overwhelmed him with jeers and insults and amused himself by kicking at Francis's wounds until they bled again.

On another occasion they brought the miter and chasuble belonging to Bishop Imbert and ordered the captive to put them on. Francis refused. They then made a pagan prisoner wear them. The Christian then prostrated himself before him.

"Whom are you worshiping?" asked one of the guards.

"The crucifix," he answered.

Irritated, the officer raised his fist to strike Ch'oe, but through some feeling of respect or fear he restrained himself.

On September 11 Francis was summoned before the deputy commissioner and given fifty blows of the plank. This was his last appearance in court, his last punishment, and his supreme profession of faith. When he returned to his cell, he lay down on the ground and knowing that he was about to die, said to the bystanders who surrounded him:

"It was my hope that I could give my life for Jesus, and that my head should fall to the executioner's axe, but since God wishes me to die in prison, His will be done."

Some hours later that night or early next morning (September 12, 1839) he died, leaving to the faithful the memory of a life full of good works, profound piety, and invincible courage.

Three days later his son Peter, accompanied by several Christians, fetched his body and carried it to Ae-u-kae, where it remained until the funeral which took place that autumn at Su-ri-san.

There was no flash of the executioner's sword at the passing of Francis Ch'oe, but his memory is radiant with the splendor of his heroic soul and with the glory of the chosen of God.

37. Blessed Laurent-Joseph-Marie Imbert, Martyr; Blessed Pierre-Philibert Maubant, Martyr; Blessed Jacques-Honoré Chastan, Martyr
(beheaded, Sept. 21, 1839)

During these days of persecution, what became of the Bishop and his missionaries? Bishop Imbert had left Seoul, and, led by a zealous Catholic, Andrew Sohn, he had taken refuge since June 3 in the district of Su-won, at Sang-kok, a remote little village situated at the tip of a peninsula extending some considerable distance to sea. Fathers Maubant and Chastan still kept up the administration of the missionary station in the country. Summoned by the Bishop toward the end of June they went to discuss with him this grave situation of their flock.

Should they leave Korea and by their departure perhaps appease the persecution?

Ought they to stay in order to hearten the faithful? Bishop Imbert offered to stay in Korea alone while the two missionaries took refuge in China. But to travel when traitors and spies were seeking Catholics, when police agents were on every highway and footpath, and soldiers stood guard along the frontier seemed almost impossible, and the idea was abandoned.

The Bishop recommended his missionaries to hide themselves very carefully and to be ready for any eventuality, and on July 3 the apostolic workers separated.

At this moment, thanks to the apostates, there was no one who did not know of the presence of the Europeans in Korea. The seizure of their persons was decreed by the Prince Regent and a large reward was offered for their arrest.

A false brother, Kim Sun-sŏng, (or Kim Yŏ-sam) offered to deliver them into the hands of the government if he were given the necessary men, and the government gladly agreed. Foreseeing, however, that the missionaries might well defy their search for a considerable time, he resolved to practice deceit. This is the favorite method of traitors such as he, and Kim was experienced in the role. He set out on a tour of the countryside, visited several of his old friends among the unsuspecting Christians, and gave them an account of the important changes which, according to him, were taking place in Seoul.

"At the capital, the more enlightened of our coreligionists have been explaining the truths of our religion to the officials. By the grace of God, the magistrates, and even the ministers themselves have begun to open their eyes, and if only the Gospel is properly explained to them they will no doubt embrace our faith. I am the bearer of a letter from Paul Chŭng to the Bishop; tell me where I can find him."

Two neophytes, deceived by these words, said that Andrew Chŭng probably knew his whereabouts, and the traitor, followed by his posse, was led to Andrew Chŭng's house. Andrew Chŭng Hwa-kyŏng, a native of Chŏng-san, was an excellent Christian who had lost his little all on leaving his hometown in order to be free to practice his religion. He was devoted to the service of the faithful. He had taken great pains, together with Andrew Sohn, to prepare a refuge for the Bishop, and he was in fact one of those who shared the secret. Unfortunately his artless trustfulness went beyond all bounds.

Kim's story, which he never dreamed of doubting, filled him with joy. However, after thinking it over all night, he began to have some fears, and decided to take precautions. He accordingly wished to go alone to make inquiries.

Pressed to allow the traitor and his posse of soldiers disguised as workmen to go with him, he at first consented, but when they had gone halfway he began to have his suspicions, told his companions to go away, and refused to proceed any further if they followed him. He set out accompanied only by Kim, and the latter stopped at a few miles' distance from the Bishop's residence, while Andrew went on ahead to find the Bishop and tell him the traitor's news.

"My son," said the prelate, who guessed the truth at once, "you have been deceived by the devil."

Then, realizing that Kim was near, and that

further flight would only serve to increase the persecutors' anger against the Christians, who, in a state of terror and consternation, pressed around him and urged him to save his life, he decided to give himself up.

This took place on the night of August 10, 1839.

In the morning, the Bishop said Mass for the last time, and wrote the following letter to Fathers Maubant and Chastan:

J. M. J. August 11

My dear confreres,

Praise the Lord, and may His Will be done! There is no retreat: it is no longer the police that they have sent to find us, but the Christians themselves: Andrew Chŭng arrived an hour after midnight. They have been telling him a lot of fine tales, and the poor fellow promised to fetch me. However, hide yourselves well until further notice if I can send you any. Pray for me.

Laurent-Joseph-Marie Imbert
Bishop of Capse

He made up a small bundle of his vestments, declined to be accompanied, and set off alone to the hamlet where the traitor Kim was waiting. On his way he met five of the men, and succeeded in persuading them to send back Andrew Chŭng, who insisted on accompanying him. On the journey he announced the word of God to his guards and to a score of others whose curiosity drew them to the wayside.

He was taken to the capital. On arriving at the city gates he was bound with the red cord which is used for state criminals. This cord, about six feet long, is ornamented with a dozen brass rings or balls, and has a little brass dragon at each end. One of the guards passed it round his shoulders, crossed it over his breast, and tied it with a double knot behind his back. The guard held the end of the cord by the brass dragon.

The Bishop was brought before the chief judge who ordered him to be detained in the thieves' prison.

Interrogation began almost at once. The bone-bending torture was inflicted on him in an endeavor to make him divulge the whereabouts of the other Europeans, after which he was asked:

"Why have you come here?"

"For the salvation of souls."

"How many persons have you instructed?"

"About two hundred."

"Deny God."

At these words the Bishop shivered with horror, and raising his voice said in firm tones: "No, I cannot deny my God."

Realizing that he was wasting his time the judge ordered him to be beaten and sent back to prison.

The trick having been successful the first time, the agents tried it again in their pursuit of Fathers Maubant and Chastan. They seized two Christians, Thomas Lee and Peter Ch'oe, and tried to persuade them that the Bishop enjoyed or would very soon enjoy full liberty. The Christians were not to be fooled with these lies, but knowing that their own safety depended on their pretending to believe them, they did not disobey. On the way Thomas managed to escape; Peter was taken to the home of one of the agents in Seoul, who treated him with the utmost kindness. To deceive him better, they hurriedly carpeted and decorated one of the halls of the prison and took him there. There he found Bishop Imbert who asked him:

"Do you know where the priests are?"

"I am sure it would not take me long to find them," he replied.

"I am afraid they have not received my letter; will you take them one for me?"

"I am at your service."

Without further words, Bishop Imbert wrote a few lines and handed him the letter. Peter took leave of the Bishop and withdrew. The agents, delighted, congratulated him, and would not stop talking about the honor with which the Bishop was being treated.

The faithful Peter knew what was to be done; he succeeded in escaping and handed the letter to some trustworthy Christians. This letter was in the following terms:

In extremis, bonus pastor dat vitam pro ovibus;

unde si nondum profecti estis, venite cum praefecto
Son-kie-tsong, sed nullus christianus vos sequatur.
                    Imbert Episcopus Capsensis

(As a last resort the good shepherd gives his life for his flock; if you have not yet set out, come with the officer Sohn Kye-ch'ang, but let no Christian follow you.)

Sohn Kye-ch'ang was a captain sent, with a hundred constables, to capture the missionaries.

The procedure of Bishop Imbert in first giving himself up and then ordering his missionaries to give themselves up as well, has aroused diverse comment.

It is true that as a general rule one must not offer oneself up to one's persecutors, especially when as a result the entire Church will be left without a shepherd, abandoned to the rage of the executioners, but it is also true that very often the Holy Spirit has inspired its faithful servitors to similar resolutions, in apparent contradiction to the ordinary dictates of prudence. The following remarks on the subject are those of the Promoter of the Faith[1]:

"Could the Bishop order or invite his missionaries to give themselves up, knowing full well that they would be martyred? Could the missionaries, ought they to, obey such an order or follow such a counsel, with the foreknowledge that it would lead inevitably to their death? It is to Your Eminences that the right to answer these questions belongs. As for me, it seems that the case presents no difficulty, when one recalls the very grave circumstances in which they were situated. The persecution was at its height. All, officials, judges, magistrates and people were aware of the presence of the three Europeans in Korea. It was without doubt with a view to discovering their hiding place and getting hold of them that they martyred so many Christians, a great number of whom,

unable to bear the tortures, fell into pitiful apostasy. In a word it might reasonably be supposed that it was solely on their account that the persecution was so terrible and that with their discovery, arrest and death it would at least be appreciably diminished. In such a state of things it seems to me that they will have said with the prophet Jonas: 'Take me up and throw me over the ship's side; doubt there is none, I am the cause of all this peril which has befallen you.' (Jonas 1:12) I therefore believe that the Bishop's order or counsel was neither imprudent nor worthy of blame; that the obedience of the missionaries was heroic, and that all three voluntarily sacrificed themselves in order to bring about the cessation, or at least a sensible diminution, of such an appalling calamity. In a word, they offered themselves for the salvation of their fellow-men, and put into practice the words of Our Lord. 'This is the greatest love a man can show, that he should lay down his life for his friends.' (John 15:13)"

Bishop Bonnand, that remarkable Vicar Apostolic of Pondichéry, who died while visitor to the missions of India, has well caught this aspect of the conduct of the Bishop and his missionaries, when he exclaims, on hearing of this appeal followed by martyrdom:

"Now I perceive the magnanimity of this shepherd, of this Bishop worthy of olden times, how he had the grandeur of temper not only to sacrifice himself for his flock, but to add further to the holocaust that of the two apostles whom he had been charged to lead to the fray. In my profound admiration I prostrate myself before his devotion and that of his valiant missionaries who have thus received in a single day the triple crown of Faith, Obedience, and Charity: a devotion unsurpassed in heroism by any deed in history, whether ancient or modern, which only the

---

[1] Lat. *Promotor Fidei*, commonly called the Devil's Advocate, an official of the congregation of rites whose business it is scrupulously to examine all evidence both of miracles and virtue in the processes of beatification and canonization in order that no person may through human enthusiasm or error receive the highest honors of the Church unless in every way worthy thereof. Every objection must be satisfactorily answered before the case is allowed to proceed.

example of God's own sacrifice of Himself for the salvation of mankind could inspire, and before which my own worthlessness is humbled and utterly annihilated."

To these noble and moving words we may be permitted to add this thought: the first Korean Catholics became martyrs; the first priest to evangelize Korea became a martyr; were not the first missionaries sent from France by the head of the Church under an obligation to join the ranks of those who had shed their blood for Jesus crucified, and to glorify by their martyrdom the God whom they proclaimed, and give irrefutable proof of their faith in the truth which they taught?

Father Maubant was the first to receive the Bishop's letter; he sent it to Father Chastan and wrote a few lines to the chief of the police agent, a translation of which flollows:

"Ra *sin-pu* (Father Maubant's Korean name and title) informs Sohn Kye-ch'ang that he is unable to proceed immediately to P'al-ke-mŏ-ri where he is awaited, because Chŭng *sin-pu*, (the Korean name and title of Father Chastan) is at present a long way from here; we will appear together in ten days. I trust you will experience a change of heart, and that after death you will find happiness."

On September 1 the two messages were sent to Father Chastan.

On arriving at the town of Hong-ju they were put in chains and carried on horseback to Seoul, immediately brought before the minister of crime and reunited with their Bishop. What profound and intimate joy for the hearts of these priest apostles to be together in irons for the sake of Jesus Christ!

Next day the three missionaries were Brought to trial. At the further end of the hall were the judges, seated on a kind of platform, and dressed in their ceremonial robes: blue silk gowns held by a belt ornamented with tortoise-shell, black horse-hair caps in the form of a miter with pendants. On each side there were soldiers and constables lined up, armed with rifles, sabers or truncheons; near them stood the group of executioners with their instruments of torture, some of which they held in their hands while others were set out on the ground. The *Court Journal* for September 12 reports part of Father Maubant's words, as follows:

"I am by birth a European; in the winter of 1835, wishing to preach the doctrine in a distant land, I was not deterred by distance from coming to Korea. At first I resided in the capital, at the home of Chŭng Ha-sang; later I traveled about the capital and the countryside, I know not how many different places. In principle the 'perverse religion' (*sic*) has for its aim not to deceive but to make itself profitable to others. That is why, if my divulging the names of my guides will result in harm to them, I shall say nothing; that is also a very grave precept, for in guarding oneself from harming others one puts oneself in danger: accordingly, though it should mean my death, I would still say nothing. As for converts made in preaching the doctrine, there is no region where I did not make any; but, as for their names and surnames and their addresses, I do not remember them exactly. Likewise as to the hills and water courses on my itinerary, I do not remember them, and as for pointing out any particular village or region, it is impossible for me to do so. No one is responsible for sending me to this country, since the initiative was my own, but from the Catholic mission money was sent to the home of the interpreter Yu and I used it to procure clothing. I now see that the person named Cho has himself declared that he came with me, I have nothing to say by way of excusing myself."

With regard to the depositions made on the same day by Father Chastan they are in part analogous to those of Father Maubant.

The following interrogations contain nothing special, but we cannot pass over in silence the firm and noble answers given by the first Vicar Apostolic of Korea:

"With regard to the entire body of Catholics, it is not only that they are very numerous, and that it is difficult for me to remember all their names and surnames, but that, not having quailed before the enormous distance of ten thousand miles, and having come here in order to engage in the salvation of souls, to proceed to denounce them all now and cause harm to them, in contravention of the Ten Commandments—we shall never do that, even if it means our death. Even with the swords and saws before us, and our flesh reduced to shreds, we shall say nothing."

After this session, order was given to transfer the accused to the High Court of Justice and to constitute a 'Supreme Court' for the Europeans, Pŏm Se-hyŏng and others, in order to examine them with severity.

The missionaries appeared before these new judges, who no doubt put the same questions to them as the previous ones. On this date of September 15, the *Annals of the Grand Council* contains the following mention: "The criminals: Pŏm Se-hyŏng (Bishop Imbert) interrogated anew was put to the torture on one occasion, the beating was stopped after the ninth round; Peter Ra (Father Maubant) interrogated anew and put to the torture once, the beating was stopped after the ninth round; Jacob Chŭng (Father Chastan) interrogated anew and put to the torture once, the beating was stopped after the thirteenth round."

On September 16, there was another interrogation accompanied with blows of the truncheon: the Bishop received five, Maubant thirteen, and Chastan eleven. On the occasion of their appearance before the court on September 19, each of the accused received five blows of the truncheon.

Finally, on September 21, all three were condemned to death and beheaded.

As state criminals the Bishop and his priests were put to death with extraordinary ceremony according to the special ritual called *Kun-mun-hyo-su*, culminating in the exposure of the decapitated persons' heads at the city gates, (similar to the English treatment of Catholics during penal times). The place of execution was not at the usual execution ground outside the Small West Gate, but at a more remote locality called Sae-nam-t'ŏ or No-ryang from the name of a nearby village, on the banks of the Han River

some three miles from the capital.

The condemned men, their hands tied behind their backs, in narrow chairs on the shoulders of bearers, and surrounded by a hundred soldiers, were conveyed to the execution ground.

Was there an enormous crowd lining the route? Did it follow them all the way to Sae-nam-t'ŏ? What were the people saying? What were they thinking of? No Korean annalist has told us.

The execution was presided over by the commanding general officer at the capital. The apostles were stripped to the waist. The soldiers then bound their hands together in front of the chest, and thrust two arrows from above downward through the ears of each, afterward throwing water in their faces, at which they then threw a handful of lime. Six of the men then carried them, by poles thrust under their armpits, three times around the execution ground, during which they were exposed to the derision and coarse mockery of the bystanders.

A soldier hoisted a flag to the top of a flagstaff; another read the sentence of death with all its preamble. The commander ordered the convicts to kneel. Immediately ten soldiers began running around the victims, and each one, as he passed, would give them a blow with his saber.

Father Chastan received the first blow which lightly grazed his shoulder. He rose instinctively but sank back to his knees. Bishop Imbert and Father Maubant remained motionless right up to the mortal blow. One of the soldiers picked up the three heads which rolled on the ground, placed them on a tray and held them out before the general. Pagan justice was satisfied, and the foundations of the Church of Korea were firm, for its stones were cemented with the blood of its first apostles.

The bodies of the Bishop and his priests were exposed for three days and then buried in the sands along the river bank. The neophytes longed to recover these precious relics, but a strict watch was kept over them by plainclothes police. On the fourth day after the execution, three Christians attempted to carry them away and one of them was caught and thrown into prison: there was nothing to do but wait until later. Some twenty days later, a group of seven or eight Christians, at the risk of death, made another attempt and succeeded in carrying away the bodies. After being placed in a large coffin they were buried on No-ko-san, outside the Small West Gate, where they remained for several years. In 1843, the faithful transferred the remains to Sam-sŏng-san, some four miles south of Seoul. Then happier days dawned for the Korean mission. On November 2, 1901 the holy relics were translated to the crypt of the cathedral at Seoul, newly built by Bishop Mutel, to await the hour, which has now finally struck, for them to be placed on the altars.

38. Blessed Paul Chŭng Ha-sang and Augustine Yu Chin-kil

(beheaded, Sept. 22, 1839)

Some of the Korean faithful preceded the French missionaries on the road to martyrdom: others of the faithful, in greater numbers, followed them. The two Catholics of whose virtue and courage we now have to speak belonged, Chŭng to the ancient nobility of the country, and Yu to a family of mandarins and employes of the state.

The first member to embrace the faith, Chŭng Yak-jong of the Chŭng family, received the baptismal name of Augustine. In 1801, with his eldest son Charles, he paid with his life for the honor of his conversion. His wife Cecile Ryu also died a martyr in 1839, and his two other children Paul and Elizabeth had been imprisoned together with him. After his death they recovered their liberty, but the government deprived them of all their property.

Without means of support, they went to the country town of Ma-jae in the district of Yang-keun to beg shelter of one of their relatives, the scholar Chŭng Yak-yong. "It would be difficult," says a witness, "to recount all the sufferings that they underwent." To be despised not only by the relatives under whose roof they sheltered, but even by servants and slaves of their hosts, seemed to have been quite natural in a country in which respect is paid only to wealth and rank.

They accepted this humiliating situation without complaint, but it was not easy for them to do so.

Paul Chŭng, while still young, had learnt the prayers and doctrine from his mother, but in that pagan *milieu* it was only with difficulty that he could practice his religion. At the age of twenty he left for Seoul and went to live at the home of an excellent Catholic, Barbara Cho, but he aimed at something higher than personal security and a tranquil life. What weighed upon this young man's mind was the thought of the Korean Church, fated to be without a priest since 1801; a trait of character that shows his noble spirit, his exceptionally high intelligence, and his deep-rooted faith.

The character and the career of **Augustine Yu** are analogous to those of Paul Chŭng, but this early life was different. Brought up in a family of officials and *literats* destined to suffer misfortune, Yu distinguished himself very early in life by a meditative spirit rare among Koreans. He had a pronounced leaning toward philosophical and religious studies. For more than ten years he devoted himself to a careful investigation into the teachings of Buddha and of Laotse, and this protracted research won him recognition as a remarkable scholar.

Ambroise Hong having explained Father Matteo Ricci's *True Doctrine of God* and lent him a number of books, the pagan read them over and over again, and felt that at last he had discovered the true religion which he had been seeking so long. He informed Ambroise of this, and from that day he began to practice the precepts of Catholicism to the best of his ability.

Shortly afterward he became acquainted with Paul Chŭng. From this same year he began to cherish the desire to go with him to Peking. He was enrolled on the list of embassy interpreters and, on arriving at the capital, visited Bishop Pires, and was baptized. He immediately requested that missionaries be sent to his country.

Surprising as it may seem, Augustine Yu, who was able to govern a Church almost like a priest, and who could enlighten and convince the scholars of Korea, could never succeed in persuading his wife and daughters to share his faith in the Catholic religion. He did however have the satisfaction of convincing his two sons, the elder of whom, aged thirteen years, was to follow his father to martyrdom.

In 1833, with the help of his friends, and in particular that of the future martyr Sebastian Nam, Paul Chŭng had succeeded in bringing Father Pacificus Liu into Korea, after which he became the priest's principal coadjutor. They lived in Seoul.

Some years later he rendered the same service to Fathers Maubant and Chastan, and Bishop Imbert.

Bishop Imbert considered him worthy of the priesthood and taught him some Latin and theology: he was about to ordain him when the persecution broke out.

On July 11, the police came to his house and arrested him together with his aged mother and his sister, bound him with the red cord, and brought him before the police court. They took down his name and those of his ancestors to the fourth generation, and threw him into jail.

On the following day he submitted his defense to the deputy commissioner. Three days later, the commissioner summoned him to court and asked him:

"Is it true that, setting aside the customs of Korea, you practice a foreign doctrine, and that you contaminate others with it?" He answered:

"We receive valuable things from abroad for our use; is it right to reject the Christian religion, the only true one, merely because it comes to us from a foreign country? It is a religion which everyone ought to follow."

"You praise the foreigners' religion! Do you dare to suggest that the king and his ministers are wrong to forbid it?" "To such

words I have nothing to say in reply. It merely remains for me to die."

The magistrate then called upon him to explain his defence: "Even if your statements are correct, do you dare to call accomplices together and teach them something which the king has forbidden?" He then condemned Paul to the arm-bending torture. This torture, P'al-chu-ri, is inflicted in the following manner: the arms of the victim are tied together up to the elbows, then by means of two thick wooden bars which are used as levers, the shoulders are forced together. The executioner then unties his victim's arms, and, resting one foot on his chest, pulls them toward himself in order to bring the bones back into their proper place. When these executioners are skilful, they are able to compress the bones in such a way as only to bend them, but if they are beginners and without experience, they fracture the bones and the marrow drips out together with the blood.

The executioners who tortured this confessor of the faith knew their trade: they did not break his bones. Paul bore this horrible suffering with all patience, and to a new and more pressing order to apostatize he replied with a refusal. He was sent back to jail.

Summoned before the court again a few days later, he underwent the torture called T'op-jil or "sawing of the legs." A cord made of horsehair is passed around one of the victim's thighs, and two men, each holding one end of this cord, draw it backward and forward alternately until, biting through the flesh, it reaches the bone.

At a third interrogation, Paul was confronted with Bishop Imbert, and without hesitation confessed having helped him in his itinerancy throughout the country and in getting in touch with the Christians.

He underwent various forms of torture: a kind of acupuncture, or pricking of the living tissues with a sharp stick; the bending of his bones, and once again the sawing of the legs, but this time, instead of using a cord made of horsehair, they used a bar of wood sharpened to a triangular cross section, and "very quickly his bones were laid bare and the blood flowed to the ground. His countenance nevertheless kept its calm expression." They tried to get him to reveal the portrait of Fathers Chastan and Maubant, who had not yet been arrested, and to divulge the names of the other Christians, but he kept an unbroken silence.

In his cell he was subjected to further tortures by his jailors who overwhelmed him with questions, but he made no answer.

After the two missionaries were arrested, he was confronted with them and, together with them, transferred to the High Court of Justice. They were summoned three times before this court and on each appearance they were beaten violently on the shins and the front of the thighs.

Augustine Yu had himself also been denounced: he was arrested at his home on July 17, 1839. No sooner were they warned of this than one of his brothers and several of his relatives rushed to his house and begged him not to persist in his Christian sentiments. "Say but one word," they repeated, "only a single word."

Augustine tried to make them understand that he could not do such a thing, that his conscience would not allow it, and when they spoke of the harm that his conduct must inevitably bring to the family, he merely said:

"I am indeed deeply grieved at the sufferings you will undergo on my account, and I am very sorry for you, but once having known God, I cannot deny Him. My soul's salvation is more to me than my flesh and blood; follow my example, become Christians, and then you will learn to disdain what you now prize so highly." Bishop Imbert had also been arrested; traitors had denounced the two other missionaries. The commissioner interrogated Augustine on the reasons for their presence in Korea. The Christian replied:

"The only reason for the coming of these European scholars to our kingdom is to manifest the glory of God, and to teach people to honor Him and save their souls by keeping the Ten Commandments. In preaching this doctrine they enable people to avoid eternal punishment in hell after they die, and to go to Heaven, where they enjoy true happiness forever. Wishing as they do to teach such an excellent doctrine, how could they possibly exhort others to do good unless they practiced it themselves? Thus they strive in all purity to achieve perfection, and it is not until after they have acquired virtue that they venture to go abroad and evangelize foreign countries. If it were riches, honor and pleasure that they sought, why should they abandon their motherland of Europe, so rich and magnificent, and undertake a journey of thirty thousand miles beset by such danger that nine out of ten of them perish in the attempt? Moreover, a bishop's position is one of great eminence: what higher dignity can they covet? They bring with them funds sufficient to cover their expenses; how can they be accused of lusting after riches? After having been raised to holy orders, they swear a solemn vow before God to maintain the purity of their bodies and remain chaste until death: is there any desire for carnal pleasure in that?"

The judge said not a word in reply, but asked:

"Who brought these foreigners into our country?"

"It was I," declared Augustine.

Questioned regarding Fathers Chastan and Maubant he refused to answer, and was put to the torture.

At the sixth appearance before the court, he underwent the bending of the bones and the leg-sawing already described above. His body was as hot as if it had hot coals applied to it.

A little later he was confronted with the recently arrested Fathers Maubant and Chastan, and at once transferred to the jurisdiction of the High Court of Justice, where for several successive days he was submitted to interrogation under torture.

The perseverance of these two Christians at last earned them the supreme reward which they sought. They were condemned to be beheaded.

On September 22, 1839, at about four o'clock in the afternoon, the two confessors, whose devotion, continued efforts, and long journeys had resulted in providing the Church of Korea with priests, and had so efficaciously contributed to the spiritual welfare of the Christians, were led to the execution ground outside the Small West Gate. Paul's face wore a smile: Augustine, absorbed in contemplation, appeared already dead to the things of this world. The place still showed traces of previous executions; bones, and the trunks of criminals' bodies lay on the ground, and their decapitated heads lay near by or were hung on posts. Both law and custom in fact decreed that these remains should be left in view at the site for three days "in order to instruct the passers-by, and inspire in them a salutary terror," according to the Korean expression.

The soldiers ranged themselves around the kneeling victims, and with a swift blow of the saber beheaded them.

Paul was forty-five years old, Augustine forty-nine. Although pagan, the entire family of the latter was outlawed; his wife, his daughters, one of his sons aged twenty years, his elder brother, all strongly opposed to Catholicism, had their property confiscated and were exiled to the southern isles; twenty-six officials related to him were stripped of their rank and dismissed.

39. The Martyrdom of Nine Blessed Men and Women
(beheaded, Sept. 26, 1839)

The nine martyrs of whom we have to speak in this section were all imprisoned in 1839. The following list shows their name, age, and date of arrest:

Magdalene Hŭh Kye-im, sixty-eight years, and **Magdalene Park Pong-son,** forty-four years, imprisoned in the month of March; **Agatha Chŭn Kyŏng-hyŏp,** fifty-three years, April 18; **Perpetua Hong Keum-ju,** thirty-six years, April or May; **Columba Kim Hyo-im,** twenty-six years, June; **Juliet Kim Yu-ri-tae,**

fifty-six years, and **Charles Cho Sin-ch'ŏl,** forty-five years, in the month of July; **Sebastian Nam I-kwan,** sixty years, September 16; **Ignatius Kim Che-jun,** forty-four years, on or about the same date.

We shall recount the details regarding their life, imprisonment, interrogation, sufferings and death as the Korean witnesses have passed them down to us.

Magdalene Hŭh lived in Pong-ch'ŏn-ri, Si-heung county, with her family. She had married a pagan named Lee, whom she had not succeeded in converting, but her children were brought up in the faith. Two of her daughters, Magdalene and Barbara Lee, became martyrs, the former on July 20 and the latter on September 3, 1839.

Magdalene Park came of a pagan family and was married at the age of about fifteen to a pagan: after bearing him two daughters she became a widow, and returned to her father's home in Seoul, where she found a stepmother Cecile Kim, an excellent Christian, who shared her faith.

Agatha Chŭn was born in Seoul, to pagan parents, but losing her father in infancy fell into poverty. She was rescued by a young lady of the palace, who took her to live with her. Some years later, her brother wanted to arrange a marriage for her, but they refused to let her leave the palace, and from that time on she was given official rank in the service of her protectress. In spite of the superstitious pagan *milieu* in which she lived, helped by Lucy Park, also a young lady of the palace, whose life and death we have already recounted, she embraced the Catholic faith, but being unable to practice its precepts as assiduously as she wished, she bravely abandoned her luxurious life, and under the pretext of illness went to live with Lucy. Devoting all her time to prayer, reading, and the practice of virtue, she won the hearts of the Christians by her friendly manners, and was able to convert a large number of the pagans. Though poor and in ill health she accepted privation and sickness without ever uttering a word of complaint.

Endowed with an upright and firm character, penetrating intelligence, and with a certain virility in her attitude, her approach and her conversation, **Perpetua Hong** was a native of Seoul who, as an orphan reared by her grandmother, was married off at the age of fifteen to a pagan. She could only imperfectly follow the precepts of Christianity until, early widowed, she left the home of her husband's parents with her son, who died shortly afterward, and went to live in a servant's room in the home of Philip Ch'oe, in the Mi-na-ri-kol quarter. It was there that, in response no doubt to the exhortations of her host, she began to study the catechism with care. Her prayers were invariably accompanied with tears. Her charity has been characterized in the saying that "she used to render to her neighbors all the services of a slave."

Columba Kim was born among pagan surroundings in the village of Pam-sŏm. On her father's death her mother embraced the Catholic faith together with her six children. Columba and her two sisters Agnes and Clare resolved to take a vow of celibacy, and went to live in retirement at the home of one of their brothers named Anthony, who lived at Yong-mŏ-ri, some ten miles from Seoul. They had been living there for several years when the persecution broke out.

Juliet Kim was born in the country, to parents whom Bishop Ferréol described as "*chrétiens à gros grain*" or "Christians of Big Beads." They came to live in Seoul. They wanted to marry off their daughter: the latter, wishing to live a celibate life, refused, and in order to show that her decision was firm and irrevocable, cut off her hair. "Let it be so for the present," said her parents, "but your hair will grow again, and then we shall see."

Charles Cho, a native of Hoe-yang in the Province of Kang-won, belonged to a completely pagan family. At the age of five he lost his mother; his father squandered what little property they had. The child, not knowing which way to turn, went to live at a Buddhist monastery, stayed there several years, and then left to earn a labori-

ous living. One day someone suggested that he go into the domestic service of the ambassadors sent as envoys to Peking; this he did. He was then aged twenty-three years. His upright and disinterested character and his steadfast constancy won him the esteem of his companions who all averred that he was "the best personal servant in the whole embassy." Having saved a little money he came to the aid of his father and brother, and afterward made several more such journeys to Peking.

It was during one of these expeditions that he attracted the attention of Augustine Yu and Paul Chŭng, who resolved to try to convert him. At first Cho was astonished and could not understand the religious truths which they explained to him, so they repeated their attempt. Little by little his intelligence led him to open his mind to the doctrines which were so new to him, and his heart inclined toward the true God. It was in this disposition that he arrived at Peking. With Augustine and Paul, he went to see the Bishop and the missionaries, received the Sacraments of Baptism, Confirmation, and the Eucharist.

After the arrival of the missonaries in Korea, he devoted himself principally to the service of Father Maubant, whom he accompanied on his journeys, and, as the missionary's knowledge of Korean was imperfect, he acted as his interpreter.

Of noble family, the parents of **Sebastian Nam** had embraced the faith at the end of the century. His mother died young; in 1801, his father, denounced as a Christian, had been imprisoned and condemned to exile, where he soon died. Sebastian, then about twenty years of age, was also exiled and sent to the district of Tan-sŏng in the Province of Kyŏng-sang, where he married. He had not yet received Baptism and knew no more of the Christian religion than the Our Father and the Hail Mary which he recited regularly each evening. Being without children, he took a concubine, without realizing the gravity of the fault he committed in so doing. During an illness which attacked him in his forties he was instructed by a Christian, dismissed his concubine, received Baptism, and from that time lived a Christian life.

Some years later he was recalled from exile. A little later he went with Paul Chŭng and several Catholics to Eui-ju to seek out Father Liu there, to whom he gave shelter, and whose major-domo he became.

Grandson of the martyr Pius Kim who was beheaded in 1814, and father of the first Korean priest, Blessed Andrew Kim, who was beheaded in 1846, **Ignatius Kim** was, throughout his life, an exemplary Christian, and when his son was selected by the missionaries to be sent to study at Macao, he bravely consented to the separation and the grave danger in which his son's departure, strictly forbidden by Korean law, placed his whole family.

Let us glance for a moment at the way in which Providence led them all to this glory. Several of them had long foreseen their martyrdom: their lively faith and sincere piety led them to look on their torture as their happiest hour, since it assured them an eternity of bliss.

Perpetua Hong used to say, "What I pray for is to be robed in red." And whenever they asked her what she meant by these words she would answer, "Why, because I want to be a martyr."

Magdalene Park, Agatha Chŭn and Juliet Kim calmly went on praying in their homes as they waited for the summons which they foresaw, and which was not long in coming.

To the agents who were ill-treating her and her sister Agnes, Columba Kim said bravely: "If you arrest us, we will go with you, but why do you treat the prisoners of the government so badly?"

Charles Cho used to repeat, "I must give my life, I must bear all kinds of sufferings, and I must follow the way of the cross of Our Lord Jesus Christ."

In the spring of 1839, on his return from Peking, he had a dream. It seemed to him that he saw Jesus Christ with the holy apostles Peter and Paul appear before him standing on Mount Tabor, and that he heard Jesus say to him, "This year, I will grant you the great honor of martyrdom." Charles prostrated himself and expressed his gratitude. A second time he had the same dream. He asked himself whether he ought to attach any importance to it, and take it as some kind of warning, which seemed strange to him, for the persecution had ceased, but when he learnt, on returning home, of the arrest of so many of the faithful, he thought that his dream might well be a light from Heaven, and he prepared himself for death.

"Let us be martyrs for God," he said to his wife.

He was away from home when the police came to arrest him; he came back just as his family, some of his tenants, and even the little children were being taken to the police station: he followed them and was present at their first interrogation. When the judge ordered the court to be cleared the police tried to eject him, and when he resisted they inquired his name. "I am," he replied, "the master of the house whose inmates are imprisoned here."

They directed him to the police commissioner, who had him arrested, and interrogated him regarding himself, his family, and his ancestors, and then threw him into jail.

At the beginning of the persecution, Sebastian Nam, either from fear or from the desire to go and encourage the faithful in the provinces, left Seoul, "but," say the annalists, "fully aware of the fact that he was too well known to be able to evade arrest," he prepared himself by prayer for the sufferings of prison. He was seized at Keum-joe in the district of I-ch'ŏn.

Denounced by his son-in-law, Kwak, who came with the traitor Kim Sun-sŏng and a dozen constables to seize him, Ignatius Kim, whom the witnesses describe as possessed of extraordinary strength, and capable of overcoming five or six men, would have been able to offer resistance and take to flight, but he allowed himself to be put in irons.

The account of the interrogations of these confessors of the faith is with a few exceptions fully detailed, and it gives the readers some idea of their greatness of soul and the sincerity of their faith.

It is with regard to Magdalene Hŭh, the first to be arrested, that we are least informed. We know only that she bravely bore the torture and showed herself worthy of her two daughters, Magdalene and Barbara Lee.

Magdalene Park, bound with the red cord, was brought before the police commissioner who said, "Deny God, reveal the hiding places of the members of your family, show us where your books are and divulge the names of your accomplices, or I will have you cruelly beaten."

"I cannot deny God: the members of my family have fled without my knowledge, and I don't know where they are: I have no books and I know nothing about the subject of the Christians."

She underwent torture and dislocation of the bones and the judge insisted:

"I know all about the numbers of people who used to frequent your house: when I ask you about them, how dare you say that you don't know?"

"I really don't know," she replied, "who those persons were that came to my house."

She was put to the torture again and again, and as she would not yield she was transferred to the jurisdiction of the criminal court, the presiding judge of which told her:

"Even now, if you will only consent to apostatize, I will set you free."

"Be pleased to interrogate me no further, for it is useless to go on like this. If I had wished to be set free, I could have obtained my release at the hands of the police commissioner. If I have been brought here, it is in order to undergo martyrdom for God, for such is the law of this country; nothing remains for me but to die."

She then underwent three severe beatings on the legs and was condemned to death.

The situation of Agatha Chŭn who had been one of the palace maids of honor, brought her more numerous questions and crueller tortures than the others.

The judge repeatedly tried by both gentle

and violent means to persuade her to apostatize, but in vain. He thereupon sent her to the criminal court, the presiding judge of which addressed the same reproach to her as had the police commissioner:

"You who are one of the maids of honor at the palace, how could you dare to indulge in practices prohibited by the state? Deny God, denounce your accomplices and tell us where your books are."

"Though I were to die ten thousand deaths, I could never do it."

She was given five beatings with the sharp-edged cudgel, so that her flesh was torn off in shreds: her bones were fractured and her blood flowed to the ground. She bore this atrocious suffering without altering her demeanor, and astonished the pagans by her imperturbable courage.

After having been called upon to apostatize and denounce the Christians, Perpetua Hong was condemned to the dislocation of the bones: she bore this punishment without uttering a cry. On their own initiative the police agents put her into solitary confinement, stripped her naked, hung her from a beam and beat her with rods, but she never lost her calm demeanor. At the end of three days she was brought before the criminal court. Three times she underwent a beating on the legs at the judge's order but remained firm in her courage. She was then condemned to death and sent back to prison to await execution. Severely attacked by plague, she recovered from the disease and as soon as she was well enough she rendered the most charitable services to her Christian fellow-prisoners, helping them to rid themselves of vermin, dressing their wounds with such joy and ease of manner that all felt her to be a veritable sister.

Juliet Kim, like so many confessors of the faith, was ordered by the police commissioner to apostatize, denounce her accomplices, and reveal the whereabouts of her books, on pain of harsh torture. She answered:

"Though I should die under your blows, I could not deny God. If I were to denounce anybody, you would condemn that person to death; if I were to let you have my books, you would have them burnt: there is nothing left for me but to die." She was cruelly beaten, but maintained her courage and constancy.

She was transferred to the jurisdiction of the criminal court: the mandarin attempted to make her change her mind, at first by kindness, and then by torturing her to wring some sign of weakness from her. Juliet was cruelly beaten three times in succession, but she bore all without complaint.

It is the interrogation of Columba Kim that has come down to us most fully: her brave and intelligent answers to the magistrate are alone enough to justify this. Columba was taken with her sister Agnes into the presence of the police commissioner, who had them bound with the red cord and then asked:

"Is it true that you practice the Christian religion?"

"Yes, it is true that we worship and venerate God."

"Why aren't you married?"

"In order to cherish our body and heart in all purity, to serve and worship God, Our Supreme King and Father, Creator of Heaven and earth, of spirits, mankind and everything that exists, and to be able by this means to save our souls."

"What! Have you the audacity to practice something that destroys all social relationships, and which is prohibited by the government? Deny God, tell us where your books are, denounce your coreligionists, and divulge your brother's hiding place."

Columba then explained the motives that rendered it impossible for her to denounce the Christians or to surrender her religious books to the magistrate.

She was subjected to the double torture of dislocation of the bones and stabbing with the pointed sticks, and as she still remained firm in her resolution the judge shouted to the executioners, "Stab her harder!"

Always calm and gentle, Columba answered,

"Though we must die under these blows, we have nothing to say in reply."

Taken back to prison, the two young women were subjected to the insults of the police agents: they were stripped of their clothing, and beaten with redoubled ferocity. Columba was forced to endure a special torture: red-hot charcoal was applied to her body, but still she remained unmoved. Exhausted with their efforts to overcome their victims' determination, the executioners desisted.

After four or five days, Columba recovered her strength and her face regained its customary appearance of health: all trace of the burns disappeared. Confronted by this sudden cure, which seemed extraordinary to them, the executioners conceived the idea that she was possessed by a spirit.

In the prison, where she was confined for some time afterward, she contracted jail fever (the plague) but managed to recover.

From his journeys to Peking, Charles Cho had brought back a considerable number of articles necessary to the mission, such as books, rosaries and medals. The police found them at his home and exhibited them in court. The police commissioner asked Cho where they had come from.

"Whose merchandise is this? Who commissioned you to purchase all these things? Who are your associates?"

"These goods are the things in which I have been trading for several years on my journeys to Peking."

"Denounce their owner. Denounce your accomplices."

"The commandments of God forbid that I should harm my fellow-man; I cannot reveal their names."

"You say that you obey the commandments of God, and you refuse to answer the questions put to you by the government and the judge!"

The judge sentenced him to the dislocation of the bones both of his arms and of his legs; he ordered him to be hung up and beaten with redoubled force; and finally he resumed his interrogation.

Cho made the same replies.

As soon as Bishop Imbert had been arrested

Charles was confronted with him. The magistrate called upon him to divulge the names of those of his friends who had been at the head of religious affairs, and also the two missionaries whom the spies had not yet been able to discover: they dislocated his bones, they sawed at his flesh with the horsehair cord, and they hacked at his legs with the three-edged cudgel. Four times he underwent these atrocious tortures, silent from start to finish. In their astonishment the judges remarked to one another. "This man's body is not flesh and blood, but wood and stone."

After the arrest of Fathers Maubant and Chastan, he was summoned together with them, and like them transferred to the High Court of Justice. There for three days he was subjected to interrogation and three times received numerous blows of the cudgel.

Betrayed by a Christian who conducted the police agents to his hiding place, Sebastian Nam was also arrested and brought to Seoul.

The police commissioner made him undergo the dislocation of his bones, and ordered him to apostatize: Sebastian remained unshaken in his firm resolve to do no such thing.

On the following day he was transferred to the High Court of Justice. In three successive interrogations, he underwent severe beatings on the legs, was sentenced to be beheaded, and sent back to jail to await execution.

Now came the turn of Ignatius Kim.

Treated as a criminal on account of his religion, and as a state criminal for having allowed his son Andrew to leave the kingdom and go to Macao, he underwent a series of tortures which the witnesses do not specify but describe as "atrocious."

He wavered, gave in, and apostatized. (We twentieth-century Christians who know only the milder forms of persecution and who are always ready to adapt our convictions in the face of a smile or the slightest threat—an exaggerated timidity—let us search our heart and examine our life before we condemn

this poor prisoner for weakening under torture.) His apostasy, in any case, availed him nothing: he was condemned to death.

In the prison his fellow-prisoners exposed to him the gravity of his fault, and its uselessness as a means of obtaining release: "Don't expect to be set free," they repeated, "you are sure to be convicted: come back, then, to your true self; confess your mistake, retract your faithless words before the judge, and die a martyr."

One may stumble in the journey of life, as also on the road to Calvary, even though one is a true Christian by conviction. Saint Peter was a valiant apostle, and he fell, but under the look of Jesus he raised himself again. Ignatius Kim followed the example of Saint Peter, and rose again stronger than before his fall. He retracted his declaration of apostasy before the criminal court, and three times in succession, without yielding or weakening, he underwent cruel tortures.

And to tell the truth, to reveal our most secret thought, would not God have given this supreme courage to the father of the first Korean priest, the noblest of the martyrs of 1846?

The sentences of death were passed on the nine prisoners on September 26, 1839, and these sentences were executed on the same day.

The beheading took place at Seoul, by the Small West Gate.

When about to mount the cart that was to be for him a triumphal car, Charles Cho said to the jailor:

"My friend, I am on my way to Heaven; tell my family, I beg of you, that I am going on ahead of them, and may they all have the courage to follow me."

He then set out, radiant with joy. On the way, he appeared to have completely recovered his strength, and he never ceased praying. As soon as he was untied and taken down from his cross, he noticed several of his pagan relatives among the crowd, plunged into the deepest gloom: he greeted them with a smile.

Before consummating his martyrdom Sebastian Nam appealed to the jailor in charge of the women's prison:

"I had ardently desired to die on the same day as my wife," he said, "but as Our God disposed otherwise, tell her that I am waiting for her in the abode of eternal bliss."

Well do the martyrs of that remote "Land of the Morning Calm" deserve the tribute of the following lines composed in their honor:

C'est en ce jour, O Christ, que ta grace féconde
Les a rendus vainqueurs de Satan et du monde,
Et les a faits témoins du Testament nouveau!
En ce jour, nos martyrs ont, par droit de conquête
Pris leur place au festin, car leurs habits de fête
    Sont rougis du sang de l'Agneau!
Pour prouver ton amour, nous rendre la patrie,
Tu nous donnas ton sang, et ta chair, et ta vie;
Et jusques' à la mort, tu fus obéissant!
Nos martyrs ont voulu te servir et te plaire,
Imiter ton amour, et te suivre au Calvaire...
    Ils ont pour toi donné leur sang!

(Translation: It was on this day, O Christ, that Your abundant grace made them conquerors of Satan and the world, and witnesses of the New Testament! On this day by right of conquest our martyrs have taken their places at the banquet, for their festal robes are dyed in the blood of the Lamb!

In proof of Your love for our salvation, You gave us Your blood, Your flesh and Your life; and You were obedient until death! Our martyrs wished to serve You and please You, to imitate Your love, and to follow You to Calvary...

They have given their blood for You!)

40. Blessed Catherine Lee and Magdalene Cho

(died in prison, September 1839)

A mother and a daughter, arrested together and imprisoned in the same cell, and dying on almost the same day for Jesus Christ, such is in brief the story of Catherine Cho, née Lee, and of Magdalene Cho. It is enough of Christian glory; the details which we shall give of their life and their suffering will add

nothing more striking to their memory. In this world they lived for a few years of humble poverty: in Heaven, God has granted them an immortality of riches and grandeur.

The daughter of Catholic but poorly-educated parents, Catherine was married to a pagan: she converted him. She had several children, and brought them up in the love of God.

Of these children Magdalene was the most fervently religious: every day she rose early to pray and work hard at weaving and sewing in order to support the family. When she reached the age of eighteen they wanted to marry her to a Christian; she refused, and confided to her mother her wish to live a maiden. Catherine was pious enough to comprehend her daughter's desire but she feared the suspicions of the pagans who would find such conduct strange, and the danger, if she herself should die, of leaving her daughter without support and without family. She set forth these considerations to Magdalene, who attached no weight to them. To conserve herself for God seemed to the young woman the surest way to happiness and salvation.

Local molestation of Catholics and the fear of more pressing dangers, for there was talk of persecution, made Catherine decide to go and live with her daughter in Seoul. Bishop Imbert, having heard of their arrival, ordered several catechists to find shelter for them with a Catholic family. Their tranquillity did not last long. The persecution which Catherine had wished to avoid was more violent at the capital than anywhere else. Mother and daughter prepared themselves with all courage. One day when they were talking with a number of other Catholic women about the searches being made in order to arrest Bishop Imbert, one of them made the proposal: "If the Bishop is seized, let us all give ourselves up to the police."

"Yes!" cried Magdalene with enthusiasm. "If ever it were right to give oneself up, it would be in order to follow the footsteps of Jesus Christ and of our Bishop."

The pious women were not destined to carry out their valiant decision: a month later, at the beginning of July, five of them were arrested and imprisoned.

Catherine was fifty-seven years old and her daughter Magdalene thirty-three. They underwent a preliminary interrogation before the deputy commissioner, and a second one before the commissioner himself. The latter ordered them to apostatize.

Sent back to prison, they were left to languish there for several weeks until they fell ill, and, with an interval of only a few days, at the end of September, 1839, they both died, with the name of God on their lips. They had looked forward to martyrdom, and in fact whether burnt up drop by drop in the fever of the plague, or spilt by the stroke of the executioner's sword, their blood was indeed given for him whom Magdalene Cho called "Our Jesus" and this was what their supernatural love craved more than anything else.

41. Blessed Peter Yu Tae-ch'ŏl
(strangled, October 31, 1839)

He was only thirteen years old; his father, Augustine Yu, was a martyr; his mother was a hardened pagan, who constantly tried to break her son of a habit of praying and to bring him back to the cult of ancestor-worship. "Why," she would ask, "why don't you listen to your mother's words, and do as she asks?"

His elder sister used to say the same sort of thing. Sweetly and amiably Peter would answer that he would obey them if it were possible, but was it not right to obey the law of the Lord of Heaven, and the Master of all things? And to these dutiful words, the more touching as coming from the lips of a child, he would add expressions of tenderness toward his mother and all his family.

When the persecution broke out, he felt a lively desire for martyrdom take possession of him. The great example of his father, then in prison, and those of the confessors

of the faith inflamed his heart, and, impelled by the enthusiasm of divine love, he gave himself up to the authorities in July or August 1839.

The judge questioned him minutely about his family. Seeing that he was a Christian child, he sent him to prison. Very soon Peter was brought before the court: promises, threats, tortures, all available means were employed to force from him even a single word of apostasy. The jailors even employed methods of torture not included in the official code, which only the imagination of brutal hangmen could invent.

One evening, one of the police agents, using the bowl of his copper tobacco-pipe as a scoop, dug out a piece of flesh from his thigh and said, "Are you still a Christian?"

"Certainly," replied the child, "it's not that sort of thing that will stop me."

The agent then picked up a red-hot coal with the tongs and ordered him to open his mouth.

"There you are!" cried Peter, and opened his mouth as widely as possible. The astonished agent drew back. Some of the other Christians said to him, "You may think you are having a hard time, but all this is nothing compared with the great tortures."

"I know it well," replied Peter, "it's like a grain of rice beside a bushel."

One day, after he had suffered a protracted beating and had been brought back to his cell unconscious, he said to the surrounding Christians who were trying to revive him:

"Don't trouble yourselves so much. This won't kill me."

He was subjected to fourteen interrogations and was put to the torture fourteen times; he received over six hundred strokes of the rods and forty-five of the robbers' plank. His bones were fractured, his flesh was torn away in shreds, and, a most extraordinary thing, which we have no hesitation in calling miraculous, or at least a miraculous display of courage. The miracle was not the wounds but the joy. *Peter was joyful.* His love of God transfigured him. At times he seemed to laugh at the tortures and defy the executioners. Seizing the shreds of flesh hanging from his body he would tear them off and fling them before the judges, who quivered with hate, astonishment, admiration, and shame, and perhaps all these feelings together.

In reading the report of such tortures inflicted on a child of thirteen years one is tempted to doubt whether or not the narrator may be exaggerating. But more than ten witnesses saw these tortures and these acts of bravery, and their veracity is affirmed under oath. One can only bow in humble respect before such great-hearted firmness of character.

The magistrates no doubt hoped that Peter would die under the blows he received, but he did not die. Then they decided to have him killed. On October 31, 1839, the executioners entered his cell, seized his poor little body, which was nothing less than one great wound, for not one part of it was left unscathed. They passed a cord round his neck, and strangled the brave child. Truly in the face of such grandeur and simplicity one feels the need to go up to Calvary and contemplate the Man-God's suffering and death, and to tell oneself once again that the martyr will have Heaven for his reward, and that Heaven is an eternity of joy and glory capable of repaying one hundredfold such an admirable love.

Peter Yu is one of the most illustrious martyrs of Korea; the acts of his passion remind us of the martyr-saint Venantius, whom he resembles in more than one trait of courage and suffering patience.[1] Glory immortal to God Who enlightens the world with the marvels of His grace in all ages and in every region, and transforms humble children into unconquerable heroes!

42. Blessed Cecile Ryu So-sa
(died in prison, Nov. 23, 1839)

Cecile Ryu, whom the celebrated martyr of 1801 Augustine Chŭng had married in second nuptials, was converted by him and showed herself filled with great courage and profound piety. Imprisoned together with her three children at the same time as her husband, she regained her liberty, but her property was confiscated. Being entirely deprived of resources, she withdrew to Majae to the home of her brother-in-law, who, so far from coming to her aid, let her languish in extreme poverty. The eldest of her daughters soon died, as well as the widow and the son of the martyr Charles Chŭng, her son-in-law. No one was left to her but her son Paul and her daughter Elizabeth, who were also to give their life for Jesus Christ, the former on September 22, 1839, as we have recounted above, and the latter on December 29 of the same year.

One night, she had a dream. She heard her husband Augustine say to her, "I have built in Heaven a mansion with eight apartments, five of which are occupied while the remaining three are vacant. Bear patiently the miseries of life, and above all do not fail to come and join us."

The family did in fact consist of eight persons, five of whom were dead. This dream, which was to come true in its entirety, made a deep impression on Cecile and restored her courage.

Her son Paul, wholly given over to his grand plan to help the missionaries penetrate into Korea, had to live apart from her for years at a time. This was a severe test for the mother, and each time the young man set off for Peking Cecile's heart was torn, for she believed she was saying her last farewell to him. As soon as Paul became attached to the Bishop and the priests in

---

[1] St. Venantius, martyr, died about 250. He is said to have been a boy of fifteen, who died a martyr at Camerino, near Ancona, under Emperor Decius. Pope Clement X, (reigned 1670-76), a former Bishop of Camerino, raised the feast of St. Venantius (May 18) to the double rite and composed the hymns of his office.

their service, his mother followed him, and being too old to engage any longer in the management of the household she consecrated nearly the whole of her time to works of piety. Her charity was great, and it is told of her that more than once she went hungry in order to satisfy the needs of the poor.

During the persecution of 1839 one of her nephews offered her shelter in the country, but she declined it.

"I always wanted to be a martyr," she answered him, "and when the opportunity comes I should like to share it with my son Paul."

She was arrested on July 19, 1839. In spite of her seventy-nine years, she was bound with the red cord as a state criminal, doubtless on account of the name she bore, or of her son's relations with the foreigners. After some days of imprisonment she was brought before the police commissioner, who asked her,

"Is it true that you practice the Christian religion?"

"Yes, I practice it."

"Deny God and denounce your accomplices."

"Though I should die, I cannot deny God. Old as I am, whom could I know? I have no accomplices."

In the course of the first five interrogations she was struck two hundred and thirty times with the rod. She remained perfectly calm. This is an observation that we find regularly written down by the Korean annalists. It is fair to attribute some part of this calm to the Oriental temperament, which ordinarily does not show Occidental sensibility of soul, nor nervous susceptibility, but we must also render honor and in large part to the faith and courage of the confessors of Christ.

Cecile hoped to be beheaded, and spoke feelingly of the Passion of Our Lord, which she wished to repay in kind. But Korean law does not permit the beheading of elderly persons, so the judges tried to have her beaten to death. They had her brought before them twelve times, and redoubled their questions, threats and tortures. The intrepid woman bore all without complaint, and when her strength was exhausted, she lay on the floor of her cell, murmured for the last time the names of Jesus and Mary, and expired. It was November 23, 1839.

43. The Seven Blessed Martyrs
(beheaded, Dec. 29, 1839)

In Korea there are generations of martyrs just as there are generations of nobles, of soldiers, of laborers or of artisans. Father, mother, brothers, sisters, all give their life for Jesus Christ; their children and grandchildren succeed them in the cells and on the execution ground, which sucks up their blood as it sucked that of their forebears, and one might repeat with the poet that the golden branch does not lose its sap when it is pruned: *uno avulso, non deficit alter* (when one is lopped off, the others are not lacking.) This supreme sacrifice breeds generosity in families as well as in souls, and it redoubles the intensity of the moral life. The following lines offer indisputable proof of our affirmations:

Peter Ch'oe Ch'ang-heup, brother of John Ch'oe beheaded in 1801, and husband of Magdalene Sohn beheaded in 1840.

Benedicta Hyŭn Kyŏng-yŏn, daughter of Hyŭn Kye-heum, martyred in 1802, daughter-in-law of Ch'oe Ch'ang-hyŏn martyred in 1801, and sister of Charles Hyŭn martyred in 1846.

Magdalene Lee Yŏng-tŏk, sister of Martha Lee who was beheaded on January 31, 1840. **Magdalene Han Yŏng-i,** mother of Agatha Kwon beheaded on January 31, 1840.

Elizabeth Chŭng Chŏng-hye, daughter of the martyrs Augustine Chŭng and Cecile Ryu, and sister of the martyr Paul Chŭng.

Barbara Cho Cheung-i, wife of the martyr Sebastian Nam.

Barbara Ko Sun-i, wife of the martyr Augustine Park.

Let us prostrate ourselves before such heroism, and after having venerated from the depths of our soul these witnesses of Jesus

Christ, let us say a few words about the life of each one, in chronological order of date of their arrest in 1839.

Peter Ch'oe, Benedicta Hyŭn, Magdalene Lee were imprisoned in the month of July or August; Magdalene Han, on July 17; Elizabeth Chŭng, on July 19; Barbara Cho, in July 31 or August 1; Barbara Ko, on October 27.

Their virtues, good works and prayers had prepared these seven edifying believers for the honor, which God reserved for them, of rendering the supreme testimony of their love by shedding their blood.

Let us recount this most meritorious climax of their life. **Peter Ch'oe** appeared before the police commissioner, who asked him:

"Do you practice the perverse religion?"

"Among the truths which the Christian religion teaches, there is nothing perverse: but I do in fact practice the religion of the Lord of Heaven."

"Deny the Lord of Heaven."

"I cannot."

"How long have you been following this religion?"

"Since childhood."

The police agents shouted, "This is an old doctor of the sect," and began to insult him.

Seven times was Ch'oe subjected to the bone-bending torture and beatings. He refused to apostatize and would not divulge the name of any other Christian.

At the criminal court, he bore the same tortures, with the addition of severe beatings, with equal courage and without uttering a word of complaint.

Denounced from the very first day of the persecution, **Benedicta Hyŭn** hid for a few days. In the month of July they found out her hiding place, and she was imprisoned. She had to undergo tortures of the utmost violence while they were trying to force her to reveal the hiding place of her brother Charles, whom they knew to be the faithful companion of a European priest. She was put to the question eight times, and, on their own initiative, the police agents tormented her cruelly in order to obtain information

about the missionaries, so as to get the sum of money promised as a reward for their arrest. The firm and patient air of resignation with which Benedicta bore their ill-treatment baffled their efforts to gratify their hatred and their cupidity, and they were unable to gain a single compromising word from her.

Transferred to the criminal court, she was beaten with such violence that blood and pus flowed from her wounds, and she became incapable of moving her legs.

Cholera, which had been prevailing for a long time, came to add to her sufferings.

Magdalene Lee underwent the bone-bending torture. She endured hunger, thirst, and all the miseries of a filthy cell. She saw her mother, who shared the same sleeping mat with her, die of the plague.

From the police court she was transferred to the criminal court, and received many beatings on the legs, but she continued to profess her inviolable adherence to the Catholic faith.

Magdalene Han, her daughter Agatha Kwon, and one of their friends were denounced by an apostate, and on July 17 arrested together with a young maidservant, a Christian like themselves. The magistrate, after taking their names, had Magdalene put in solitary confinement, and left the three girls in a neighboring house, together with the guards. The reason for this strange behavior soon became clear. The traitor Kim Sunsŏng came to see them, and by promises and threats did his best to persuade Agatha Kwon to consent to go with him. The latter responded only with words of disdain.

The police agents, now touched by her youth and her beauty, agreed to rid her of the traitor's unwelcome attentions by allowing her to escape from the prison, and, a few days later, she fled with the young maidservant.

The government, however, having learned the details of this affair, cashiered the magistrate, exiled a large number of the guards, and sent police agents in pursuit of Agatha, who finally fell into their hands.

During this time, Magdalene had to under-go severe torture, principally bone-bending and beatings. From the police court she was sent to the criminal court where further tortures diminished neither her courage nor her faith.

Elizabeth Chŭng had long had a presentiment of and deep desire for martyrdom. She was imprisoned on July 19, 1839, with her mother Cecile Ryu and her brother Paul whose death we have already recounted. Part of her interrogation has come down to us:

"Where is your husband?" asked the judge.

"I have never been married."

"For what reason?"

"Who would wish to take to wife a girl like me, the issue of a disgraced family?"

She then appeared before the police commissioner, who said,

"Is it true that you follow the teaching of the Lord of Heaven?"

"Yes."

"From whom did you learn it?"

"I learnt it in infancy, from my mother."

"Deny God."

"No, I cannot."

"Your brother is condemned to death, but as for you, you need but say the word, and you and your mother will live."

"In order to leave this place and be able to live, it would be necessary to deny God: this I refuse to do."

The utmost degree of violence was employed to break down her resistance. At each interrogation she received forty-five or fifty strokes of the club; in seven appearances she was given three hundred and twenty strokes. She continued to answer,

"I cannot consent to deny God."

On November 7, she was transferred to the criminal court. She appeared six times before the magistrates, who questioned her at length; in spite of a triple beating on the legs, she remained unshaken. When asked to explain how she could remain unmoved in such an extraordinary way, she replied, "By special grace, I did not die under the blows, and I understand a little now what great sufferings Our Lord had to undergo."

During her imprisonment, she continued her prayers and meditations; she exhorted and consoled her Christian fellow-prisoners.

Arrested in the month of July, **Barbara Cho** refused either to divulge the whereabouts of her husband or to deny her faith. To all such demands she gave an absolute refusal.

"No, a thousand times no, I cannot deny my God; as for my husband's whereabouts, I know nothing."

Within a few weeks she underwent five more interrogations, always on the same subjects:

"It is for you to choose," said the judge; "either die, or renounce your religion and tell us the names of the other Christians, think it over."

Barbara answered, "I have already thought it over. Rather ten thousand deaths than commit such a crime."

The bending of the bones, and a hundred and eighty blows of the bludgeon punished her faithfulness to God and her discretion.

At the criminal court she received three further beatings.

During this time, her husband Sebastian Nam showed as much courage as his wife. Both of them longed to die for their faith.

Soon after the arrest of her husband Augustine Park, **Barbara Ko** conceived the idea of sharing his suffering by giving herself up to the authorities. The persecutors, however, forestalled her and arrested her on the following day, October 27.

"How can such a blessing be repaid?" said she. "I thank God for allowing me to under-go martyrdom for Him."

Husband and wife met in the thieves' prison: they congratulated each other, and encouraged each other to persevere.

The judge summoned them to appear together, asked them the same questions, gave them the same order to apostatize, and on their refusal inflicted the same tortures on them. Six times was Barbara tortured, and so cruelly that she lost the use of her legs and arms, but God gave her strength of spirit which never failed her even for a single moment.

Some twenty days later, she appeared with her husband before the criminal court, where she was beaten with such cruelty that her flesh fell in shreds. She aspired to martyrdom and told her companions during the last days of her captivity: "Formerly the mere mention of the tortures was enough to set me trembling, but the Holy Spirit has endowed even a poor sinner like me with grace; I have no more fear and feel only joy. I never realized before how easy it is to die."

These seven confessors of the faith obtained the fate that they had desired: they were condemned to death by beheading.

Witnesses have left us some details of their last moments and we have collected them with earnest piety.

On his departure to the execution ground, Peter Ch'oe, addressing one of the prison guards, made the following request: "Go and tell my wife and daughter, who are shut up in the same cell, that tears and sorrow come from flesh and blood: let them rather praise the Lord and thank Him for His mercies, and let them not fail to follow me."

Benedicta Hyŭn wrote to her brother Charles, one of the future martyrs of 1846, a letter which is no longer extant, but which was read and talked of by many Christians with great admiration. Some hours before her death, she enjoyed a sweet and peaceful sleep, and then set out joyfully to the suffering that she had prayed for so ardently as the gateway to eternal joy.

Magdalene Lee and Magdalene Han went to their death with the same calm and peace of soul that had never quitted them for an instant since their arrest.

Elizabeth Chŭng took leave of the faithful who remained in prison with the following words: "Above all, pray sincerely for all the poor and afflicted."

The Christian prisoners gathered around Barbara Cho and, deeply moved, expressed their sorrow. She tried to console them, and to arouse their courage with words of piety and affection, then very gently she said goodby to them. Then, lying down on the ground, she took a short sleep from which she did not awake until the time came for her to go to her death.

Barbara Ko counted on her fingers the number of days that still remained before that fixed for her execution.

This execution took place at the Small West Gate on December 29, 1839.

Thus, on the anniversary of the day on which, nearly five centuries before, Saint Thomas à Becket, Archbishop of Canterbury, had said to the knights who killed him, "*For the name of Jesus and the defense of His Church I am ready to die,*" the courage of the poor Korean martyrs was as great as that of the Primate of All England, and their love for Jesus Christ was no less grand and noble. It is the strength and the honor of the Catholic Church that it possesses sons and daughters who in all situations and in every country give their life to proclaim and sustain their faith in its divine founder.

44. Blessed Agatha Lee and Blessed Theresa Kim, Martyrs
(strangled, Jan. 9, 1840)

Agatha Lee was seventeen years old when on April 8, 1839, she was imprisoned with her father Augustine Lee and her mother Barbara Kwon, two future martyrs: she followed their examples of piety, courage, and constancy.

Theresa Kim also had the blood of the martyrs in her veins: her grandfather and her father had confessed Jesus Christ in tortures and in death. A modest and charitable young woman, she had married at the age of seventeen Joseph Sohn Yŏn-uk, who was to die for the faith in the prison of Hae-mi. She became the mother of a large family of children whom she brought up in the fear of God; on becoming a widow at the age of thirty-two she devoted the rest of her life to penitence, to the point of fasting every Wednesday and Friday each week, so that she has left us the memory of a model wife and Christian widow. After the death of her husband she went to live in Seoul, but did not stay there long, and soon returned to the province in which she had been born.

As soon as Father Liu had arrived in Korea, the first thing to do was to find suitable quarters for him, and a suitable housekeeper to look after his house. Theresa accepted the post. She joyfully complied with all the duties of a maidservant; everybody, and Father Liu, the chief among them, praised her gentle and humble manners. After the departure of the Chinese priest, she joined the household of Bishop Imbert. She had no desire to flee at the onset of danger, and was arrested on July 19, 1839, bound with the red cord, and imprisoned. She was then forty-four years old.

In the cells, Theresa found the young Agatha Lee, who had just undergone interrogations and tortures.

From the thieves' prison Agatha was transferred to the criminal court, and then sent back to her original cell. The executioners tried to persuade her that her parents had apostatized and had been set free to return to their homes: she replied in her own name and in the name of her younger brother Damian, "Whether our parents have abjured or not, is their business: as for us, we can never deny the God whom we have always served."

Three hundred blows with the rods, ninety blows with the bludgeon, hunger and thirst, and the plague were all unavailing to shake her firm and courageous stand. In order to maintain and stimulate her courage, she used to think about her father, beheaded on May 24, 1839, and about her mother, a martyr on the following September 3. The desire to follow their example was what sustained her.

Theresa Kim's sufferings were not prolonged to such an extent, yet nevertheless she had to undergo three hundred blows with the rods as a punishment for her refusal to apostatize, to divulge the names of her fellow-Christians, or to point out the hiding place of the missionaries.

After they had borne, Agatha nine months in jail and Therese six months, they were sentenced to death by strangulation: the executioners came to seize them where they lay in prison, and took them to a special cell, put the cord around their necks and tugged at it for a long time, then they tied each end of the cord around stakes which they set up firmly. It was January 9, 1840.

45. The Martyrdom of Blessed Andrew Chŭng and Blessed Stephen Min
(strangled, Jan. 23 and 30, 1840, respectively)

On January 23 and 30 two of the faithful were strangled: **Andrew Chŭng Hwa-kyŏng** and **Stephen Min Keuk-ka.** If their death was the same, their life was very different. The former, of very limited intelligence, and extreme *naïveté*, unconsciously betrayed his Bishop and many of the Christians: the latter served them with all his heart and intelligence, which was great.

Andrew Chŭng is by no means unknown to us. We have already recounted the deplorable role which he played in the arrest of Bishop Imbert. We need not repeat it in detail, this singularly depressing phase of his existence: let us content ourselves with reproducing what the *Procès Apostoliques* give us regarding the remainder of his deeds.

He was born about 1807, of Catholics in easy circumstances, in the district of Chŏng-san, in the Province of Ch'ung-ch'ŏng. His pagan friends prevented him from practicing his religion as completely as he wished, so he left his native village and led a wandering life. He often came to Seoul, "to help, within his limited means, the affairs of the Christian community."

After the seizure of Bishop Imbert, he allowed himself to be deceived by the police agents, who informed him that religious liberty would soon be proclaimed, and he revealed to them the addresses of a number of neophytes who were very soon arrested.

They also made use of him to find out the whereabouts of Fathers Maubant and Chastan; this time Andrew Chŭng clearly saw what the enemies of religion were aiming at, and realized that he had been cheated, and was about to be cheated again. He fled, and went to warn the missionaries secretly of the danger that threatened them. He made his confession, and expressed his desire to give himself up to the authorities who were conducting the persecution. The Fathers having dissuaded him from doing so, he tried to hide himself, but was seized and imprisoned.

The police commissioner commanded him to apostatize. Andrew was not an intelligent man, but was a convinced Catholic. To the persuasions of the magistrate he gave a flat refusal. He underwent with great courage the torture of bone-bending and the stabbing with the pointed rods. After five months' imprisonment borne without the shadow of any shortcoming or failure of courage, he was given a hundred strokes of the robbers' plank, and as he continued firm in his resolution he was strangled, on January 23, 1840.

Of a noble family, Stephen Min was endowed with a firm though gentle character, and a judgment both upright and well-considered. He was born into a pagan *milieu* and lost his mother in infancy. At the same time as his father and his brothers, he embraced the Catholic faith and regularly observed all its practices. He married a Christian woman who died shortly after the marriage. His friends urged him to marry again, and although he at first refused he finally decided to take their advice. Six or seven years later, his second wife died, leaving him a daughter, who very soon afterward followed her mother to Heaven. From this time on, without fixed abode, Min went wandering from one place to another, copying books in order to earn his living. Full of zeal, he was able, by means of his preaching and the example he set by his way of life, to convert a good number of pagans. After

being appointed a catechist he was able to recruit still more neophytes to Catholicism, and to edify and instruct the faithful.

Denounced toward the end of the persecution, he was sought out and arrested. The police commissioner offered him his liberty: "If you are willing to abandon the Christian religion," said he, "you may go free."

"Ten thousand times no!"

He was then subjected to the two usual tortures, namely, the bending of bones and the stabbing with the pointed sticks, and while he was undergoing these the judge and the executioners said to him,

"Only apostatize and you will be set free."

He replied with these lofty and intrepid words:

"If you set me free, not only shall I continue to practice my religion, but I shall try my best to convert others to it."

The magistrate ordered him to be beaten with the robbers' plank, and cried out at each blow:

"This is a rascal worthy of death!"

Stephen received forty blows. He spent the remaining period of his captivity in exhorting various apostates to repent. As a result, several of them, including Dominic Kim and Cosmas Yŭh, declared themselves once more Catholics and paid with their life for their courageous retractation.

Called before the court, the catechist was once again given thirty blows of the bludgeon, a torture quite unavailing for the triumph of the executioners, but which might well serve as the supreme testimony of the courage and faithfulness of this disciple of Jesus Christ. A few days later, on January 30, 1840, at the age of fifty-seven, Stephen Min was strangled in prison.

46. The Martyrdom of the Ten Blessed Men and Women
(beheaded on January 31, 1840)

On January 31 and February 1, 1840, the Church of Korea was rendered illustrious by the death of ten faithful martyrs, who nearly all belonged to families of martyrs. It is a glorious record which it is worth while to recall:

Mary Lee was the sister of Magdalene Lee;

Magdalene Sohn was the wife of the martyr Peter Ch'oe:

Agatha Kwon was the daughter of the martyr Magdalene Han;

Augustine Park was the husband of the martyr Barbara Ko;

The two brothers Hong were the grandsons and nephews of martyrs;

We shall speak of these confessors following the chronological order of the date of their arrest, which we give below together with the age of each one of them:

Name	Age	Date of Arrest
Mary Lee In-tŏk	22	June or July, 1839
Magdalene Sohn So-pyŏk	39	
Barbara Ch'oe Yŏng-i	22	
Agatha Kwon Chin-i	21	July 17
Agatha Lee Kyŏng-i	27	
Paul Hŭh Hyŏm	45	in August
Peter Hong Pyŏng-ju	42	September or October
Paul Hong Yŏng-ju	39	
Augustine Park Chong-won	48	October 26
John Lee Mun-u	31	November 11

Mary Lee had always a peaceable and upright character, with much modesty, almost to the point of self-effacement in speech and conduct. Arrested together with her sister Magdalene, whose sufferings and death we have already related, she followed the example of her sister both in prison and before the judges, in manifesting her invincible attachment to her religion.

Born in Seoul, the daughter of a father who had been exiled for his faith, and of a mother who left her an orphan early in life, **Magdalene Sohn** was brought up by her grandmother.

Her spirit having been somewhat intimidated by the misfortunes of her family, she did not dare to maintain open relations with the Catholics, and it was therefore only later that she learnt the prayers and the principal truths of the Catholic doctrine. At the age of seventeen, she married Peter Ch'oe, who

was destined to precede her on the road to martyrdom.

Her daughter Barbara Ch'oe had shown true piety in her youth. As soon as her parents spoke to her of her marriage, she replied, "I care nothing for nobility of birth or its opposite, and riches or poverty are the same to me: all I desire is to have a husband who will be a fervent and instructed Catholic." At the age of twenty she married Charles Cho, who was forty-four years old. In the following year she had a son. The two spouses exhorted each other mutually toward virtue, and observed all religious practices with the utmost fidelity.

The daughter of *Chin-sa* Kwon, who was converted on his death bed, and of Magdalene Han, who was beheaded for her faith on December 29, 1839, **Agatha Kwon** was married at the age of twelve but although all the ceremonies were duly performed her husband was unable, on account of his poverty, to take her with him, and entrusted her to one of his relations.

The family of **Agatha Lee** was a Christian one. As she had been married to a eunuch, Agatha explained her situation to Bishop Imbert who ordered her to separate herself from her husband. She obeyed, and as her mother was too poor to take care of her, she went to take refuge in the home of Agatha Kwon.

All we know of **Paul Hŭh** is that he was forty-five years old, a soldier of the *Hul-lyŏn-to-kam* (Capital Defense Force), and an excellent Catholic.

Peter Hong and his brother **Paul** were of a distinguished family; they were the grandsons of Hong Nak-min and the nephews of Protase Hong, the martyr of 1801. They lived in Yŏ-sa-ol in the district of Sŏ-san in the plain of Nae-p'o. A solid education and their faith were all that they inherited, and they made good use of them, honoring their religion by their virtues.

They were both appointed catechists and were zealous and assiduous in their instruction of the neophytes. They divided their time between the teaching of the doctrine and the care of the sick and other good works, and consequently Fathers Maubant and Chastan, impressed by their aptitude and their devotion, entrusted them with the handling of many important affairs. They provided shelter for the missionaries during the persecution of 1839, and, convinced that this courageous hospitality would cost them their life, they prepared themselves for martyrdom. In fact Kim Sun-sŏng put them on his list for banishment, among the Christians that had to be seized at all costs.

Augustine Park belonged to the middle-class of the metropolis. His character was gentle and friendly, he was fond of study and possessed remarkable talents and wide knowledge. Having lost his father in infancy he lived in extreme poverty, resigned to his station, always attentive to his mother, and faithful to all his duties. He married Barbara Ko, whose martyrdom we have already described.

Bishop Imbert soon chose him to be a catechist, and he showed himself worthy of this perilous position.

John Lee was of a noble Catholic family of Tong-san-mit in the district of I-ch'ŏn. He became an orphan at the age of five and was brought to Seoul and adopted by a pious Christian woman. His filial obedience to his benefactress was perfect. He wanted to lead a celibate life, but in deference to his adoptive mother's wishes he married. His wife and two children were now dead and he lived alone, devoted to good works and always eager to render any service to the missionaries and the Christians. He accompanied Father Maubant on some of his journeys for the administration of the Sacraments. When the persecution of 1839 broke out, he spent all his time collecting alms, which he took to the prisoners. He often went to visit the Bishop and the priests in their hiding place and took them information about what was happening. Although he was well known and the danger was increasing day by day, he would never consent to remain inactive.

After the death of Bishop Imbert, and of Fathers Maubant and Chastan, he organized a band of seven Christians and, braving the danger, he gathered up the remains of the holy martyrs and gave them Christian burial.

Let us now recount a most glorious and deserving part of their life.

Mary Lee was summoned before the police commissioner. The witnesses have left us more detailed reports of the interrogation of her sister Magdalene Lee, of whom we have already spoken, but they are unanimous in affirming the courage of Mary Lee under torture and her constancy in refusing to apostatize.

At the beginning of the persecution of 1839, Magdalene Sohn went into hiding with several of her relatives, in order to avoid arrest, but she was caught nevertheless.

In seven sessions she was subjected to the bending of the bones, and received two hundred and sixty blows of the bludgeon: her flesh fell in shreds and blood poured from her wounds.

She had with her in prison her youngest child, aged two years. Fearing the softening of resolution and possible weakness that might be induced in her at the sight of her poor child's sufferings, deprived not only of light and air but even of food, she confided it to one of her relatives to look after.

Her daughter **Barbara Ch'oe**, also the mother of a young child, followed her example.

Agatha Kwon and Agatha Lee were arrested together with a number of other Christian women and a young female slave. We have told in our account of Magdalene Han, the mother of Agatha Kwon, of the favorable treatment which the magistrate wanted to accord her, the proposals which the traitor Kim Sun-sŏng made to her, the scorn with which she received them, and the flight of the prisoners.

The government, having become acquainted with the details of this affair, cashiered the complaisant magistrate and ordered the re-capture of the fugitives.

The two Agathas were hidden in a poor

hovel in Seoul and had sent the young slave to the country. The latter, being captured first, revealed their refuge, and the police went to arrest them and took them to the police headquarters. In spite of the numerous tortures to which they were subjected they remained firm in their faith.

The five prisoners were also brought before the criminal court, where they underwent a severe beating on the legs. Their replies to the judge may be summed up in the following words spoken by Mary Lee: "I am a Christian and shall remain one until death."

It was in her cell that Agatha Kwon met for the last time her mother, whose martyrdom preceded her own by one month. One must pause a while and contemplate the scene: mother and daughter, imprisoned for their faith in the same prison, and, after having sustained the same fight and shown the same heroism, exchanging their last words of tenderness before going to shed their blood for Jesus Christ. What a farewell it must have been, as they thought of Heaven where they were to be reunited!

Now let us tell of the sufferings of the four Christians.

In spite of the insistent demands of the police commissioner and the cruel tortures, for he was given the bonebending, the stabbing and seventy blows with the robbers' plank, Paul Hŭh declared that he would remain a Catholic until the end of his life.

Some weeks later, however, he apostatized: no sooner had he done so, however, than he bitterly regretted it, and at once went to present himself before the judge.

"I have sinned," he told him, "and I repent it: my mouth pronounced the words of apostasy, but my heart was Christian, and it still is. Here I am ready to bear new tortures."

The magistrate had him thrown into jail.

Interrogated regarding the Christians whom they designated their accomplices, and pressed to apostatize, the brothers Hong underwent torture without compromising the faithful and without letting a single word of

weakness escape their lips.

They made their appearance before the criminal court. The presiding judge, a relation of theirs, did not wish to order their torture in person, and delegated this task to his subordinates, recommending them to neglect nothing that might constrain the Christians to abandon their religion. One may easily imagine how eagerly this command was obeyed. The executioners recoiled at no torture, however cruel: the other prisoners and murderers helped them to gain merit before the minister by adding to the torments. The two brothers remained inflexible.

As soon as he saw that the persecution was being intensified Augustine Park left his house to go and live with friends, but he did not give up the work which his office of catechist entailed for the welfare of the Christians, and especially of the prisoners. For eight months he was able to move about undiscovered, and he was not arrested until October 26, 1839.

Five times he was subjected to atrocious tortures to such a degree that he lost the use of his legs and arms. He remained unmoved: no muscle of his face revealed his suffering, no complaint passed his lips.

At the criminal court, where he was taken a few days later, he was given a severe beating on the legs: his flesh fell in shreds, but his constancy was unflinching.

John Lee had intended to take refuge in the country. He was spending the night of November 10-11, 1839, at the home of one of his Christian friends, when the police agents forcibly entered the house. Suddenly awakened, he was for a moment dumbfounded, but soon recovered his composure: "God is calling me," he said to himself, "God is calling me for a special benefit that He wishes to bestow on me. How can I fail to respond to His voice?"

To the criminal court he affirmed his faith as energetically as he had to the police commissioner.

On January 31, 1840, six of these confessors, Mary Lee, Magdalene Sohn, Agatha Kwon, Agatha Lee, Augustine Park and Peter Hong were taken to Tang-ko-kae, near the city walls of Seoul, and beheaded.

Barbara Ch'oe and Paul Hong, as it was forbidden by Korean law for them to suffer the death penalty on the same day as their close relatives, were beheaded on the following day, February 1, 1840, together with John Lee.

Paul Hŭh had been given one hundred and thirty strokes of the robbers' plank, and died as a result on January 31, or February 1, 1840.

47. Blessed Anthony Kim, Martyr
(strangled, April 29, 1841)

Born in 1794, Anthony Kim lived at Kwi-san and belonged to a family which enjoyed a certain affluence, and a reputation for generosity and uprightness.

"Endowed with a mild and magnanimous character," says one of the witnesses, "he gained the affection of all, even the pagans, and if his grandnephews still enjoy respect and honor in their birthplace, they owe it to the enduring reputation of their great-uncle."

As soon as Anthony Kim and his brothers heard about Catholicism they desired to learn all about it, and, later, to embrace it as their faith. Several friends and neighbors joined them, and the little village of Kwi-san soon became a flourishing Catholic community.

After the death of his mother, Anthony went to live in Seoul, where he purchased a house in the Neu-ri-kol quarter: a little later he lived at Ma-chang-an, near the Great East Gate.

His two brothers who remained at Kwi-san were arrested; the elder, Augustine, died in prison in the month of March 1841, at the age of forty-three; the younger languished in irons for several years.

His first wife having died, Anthony married a very good Christian woman. After the arrival of the missionaries, he set up a small oratory in his house, where Father Maubant used frequently to celebrate Mass.

At the end of 1839, a traitor denounced him. Seized in the month of January 1840, with all his family, and taken to police headquarters, and subsequently to the criminal court, he underwent several beatings, and also received thirty strokes of the robbers' plank. To the demands of the judge that he apostatize, he replied, "I am a Christian and I wish to die a Christian."

He settled down in prison as if he were at home, fully disposed to spend the rest of his life there, and nothing in his speech or attitude betrayed the slightest desire to go on living or to be set free.

Several pagan prisoners listened to his teaching, and two of them were converted to the faith.

At the end of April, 1841, he was summoned before the court once more, and, though given sixty strokes of the plank, he maintained his intrepid attitude. On the following night, the twenty-ninth of the same month, he was strangled. He was forty-seven years of age and had remained in prison for fifteen months.

His remains were taken to Kwi-san, his birthplace, and after solemn exequies interred near his family tomb.

CHAPTER SEVEN

THE GREAT PERSECUTION OF 1846

48. Misery Following the Persecution of 1839, and Bishop Ferréol's Plan to Enter Korea

The great persecution which began in 1838 and ended in 1841 was directed mainly against the Christians of Seoul and the four Provinces of Kyŏng-ki, Kang-won, Ch'ung-ch'ŏng, and Chŏl-la. As a result many Catholics either shed their blood or else remained imprisoned for years. It was most violent in Seoul and Kyŏng-ki Province. Among the martyrs of these two regions, who numbered more than a hundred and thirty, more than seventy were beheaded, and the remaining sixty were either hanged or died in prison as a result of cruel torture. Although the persecution diminished in ferocity after the year 1841, which heralded peace, the Korean Church was left in an indescribably miserable state from every point of view. Every Catholic village had been destroyed, and the owner of each house had met his death either by the axe of the executioner or the hangman's rope, after savage torture, or else had been exiled to a remote region. Their families were left homeless and without food, and took up an aimless wandering life, children seeking parents and parents their children, husband seeking wife and wife husband.

Almost all the Catholics became destitute, and had to seek some means of subsistence. Like their forebears in 1801 they took refuge deep in the mountains, where they began to clear land for cultivation by burning the scrub and using the ash as fertilizer. Under Providence they managed to survive: pagans who knew that the Catholics were honest people helped their new neighbors to escape starvation by lending them money and supplying them with seeds.

Although they were still in a pitiable condition without a single priest, their apostolic mission never ceased to progress. Three of the Catholics engaged in missionary work, Charles Hyŭn Sŏk-mun, lay assistant to Father Chastan, Peter Chŭng, lay assistant to Father Maubant, and Thomas Lee Sin-kyu (the third son of Lee Seung-hun), who after his wife's death became lay assistant of Bishop Imbert, all enjoyed the confidence of the foreign priests, and succeeded in evading the network of police surveillance. The three co-operated in reconstructing the Church and made preparations for the coming of a foreign missionary. The *Société des Missions-Étrangères de Paris*, unaware of the persecution in Korea, had dispatched two priests to act as assistants to Bishop Imbert. They were Father Jean-Joseph Ferréol, who later succeeded Bishop Imbert as Korea's third Bishop, and Father Joseph-Ambroise Maistre. Father Ferréol, born on December 27, 1808, at Cucurron (Vaucluse), France, had been ordained at the *Société* in 1838, and dispatched to Korea in the following year. He left France on April 28 and arrived at Macao on January 23, 1840. Father Maistre was born on Septem-

Blessed Andrew Kim Tae-kŏn
The first Korean priest and martyr (1821-1846)

The Statue of Blessed Andrew Kim
At So-ch'ŏng-do near Paek-ryŏng-do Islet

The midnight landing of
Bishop Ferréol, Fathers
Daveluy and Andrew Kim
in Korea, in 1845

A diagram showing the
chief events in the life of
Blessed Andrew Kim

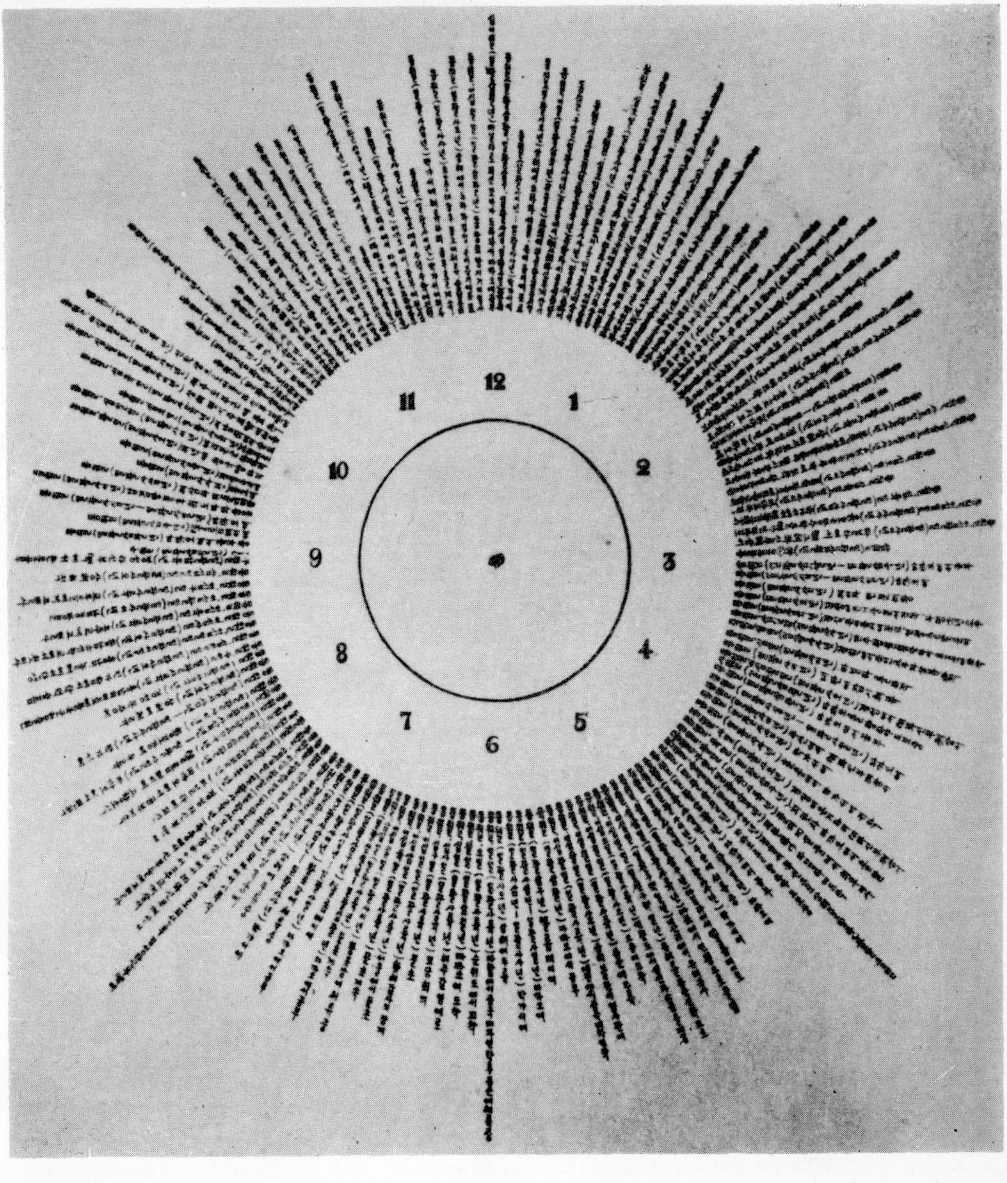

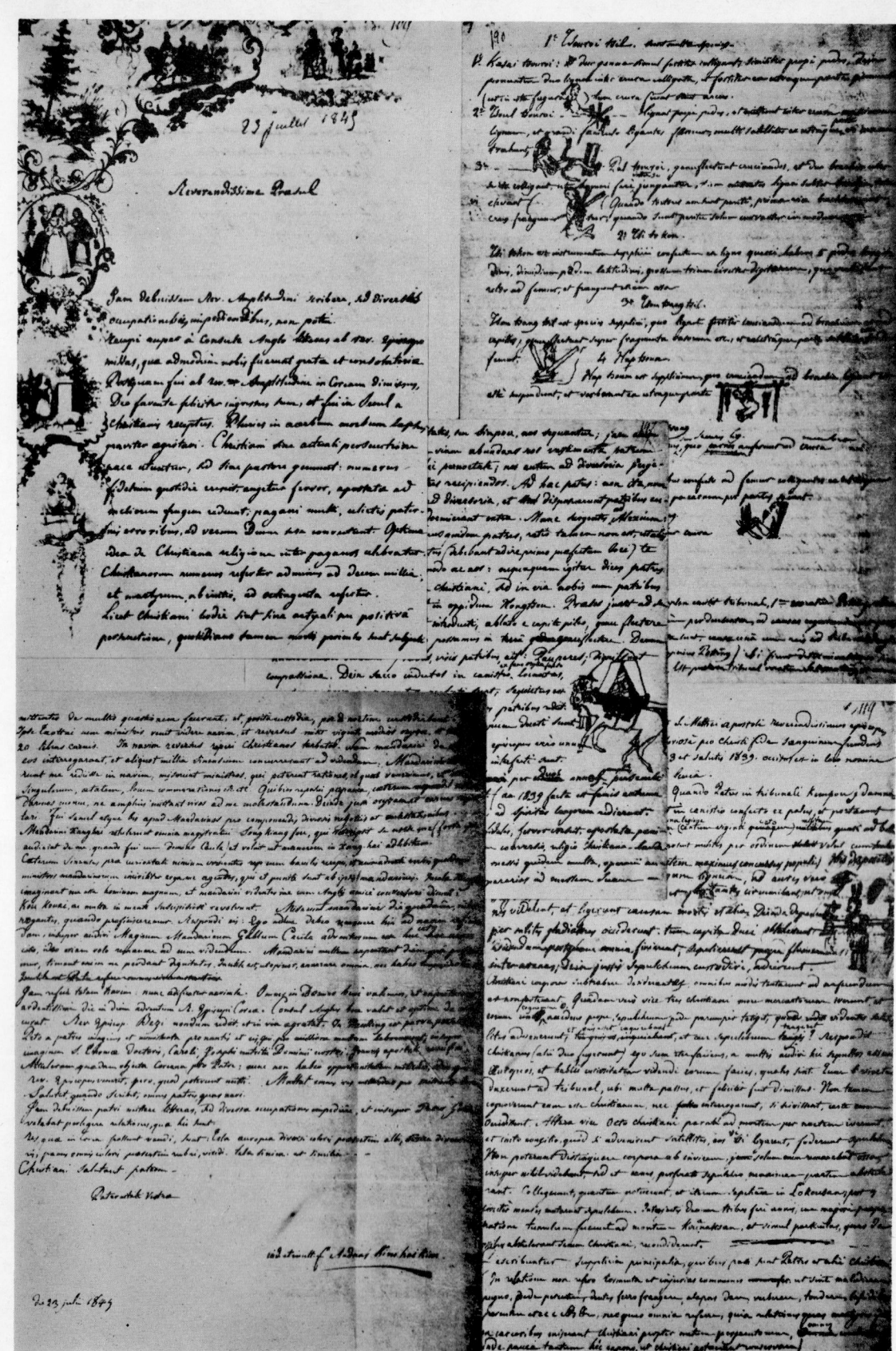

Holograph letters by Blessed Andrew Kim

With illustrations showing the tortures inflicted on the Christians during the persecution

The Mi-ri-nae Shrine at An-sŏng
Where the relics of Blessed Andrew Kim are
preserved

A pilgrimage to Mi-ri-nae Shrine

Interior of Mi-ri-nae Shrine
Showing the altar

The northern gate to Eui-ju
At the right is seen the opening in
the wall which the missioners used
to avoid detection in stealing into
Korea

*Memorial Shrine in honor of Blessed
Andrew Kim*

Bishop Devred and a priest
At the opening in the Eui-ju wall

*Tombs of Blessed Martyr Father
Andrew Kim and Bishop Jean-
Joseph Ferréol at Mi-ri-nae Shrine*

The former "Small West Gate" of Seoul
Through which the martyrs were conveyed in carts to the execution ground.

Monument in memory of the Korean martyrs
Erected at the site of their being beheaded, at the summit of Chŏl-tu-san, or the Hill of Beheading (right)

Bishop Jean-Joseph Ferréol
Third Vicar Apostolic of Korea (1843-1853)

Bishop Siméon-François Berneux
Fourth Vicar Apostolic of Korea (1854-1866)

Bishop Marie-Antoine-Nicolas Daveluy
Fifth Vicar Apostolic of Korea (1866)

ber 19, 1808 at Entremont(Haute Savoie), France, and had been ordained at the *Société* in 1839. He left Paris for the Orient on January 8, 1840. After a stay of six weeks in Macao, Father Ferréol took passage on a Chinese junk to the coast of Fukien Province and then proceeded overland via Hupeh and Chihli Provinces to Manchuria. On arriving at Mukden he found it impossible to continue any further on his journey to Korea, and went to a village in Mongolia, where he stayed for two years. He sent Chinese catechists to the Korean border at the time of the annual winter-solstice embassy in an endeavor to make contact with Korean believers, but they were unable to meet or communicate with any of them. In the meantime the Korean Catholics were doing their best to get into touch with foreign missionaries. In 1840 a Catholic was dispatched to the frontier, but he died *en route*. In the following year another was sent, but although he managed to reach the frontier he failed to meet anybody that he was looking for. The third messenger who set out in 1842 finally succeeded in meeting Father Ferréol.

Just before this meeting Father Ferréol had received papal briefs naming him Bishop of Belline and coadjutor to the Vicar Apostolic of Korea, with the right of succession. In a letter to the directors of the Theological Seminary of the *Société des Missions-Étrangères* he wrote at the time saying:

"In this way the Korean mission lacks nothing here below to make it a member of the blessed family of Our Lord Jesus Christ who was persecuted, insulted, and crucified. Let us pray to the Lord to fulfil the hope expressed by the Bishop of Capse on his deathbed, that he might soon see her people ranged under the laws of the Gospel. The blood of so many martyrs cannot have been shed in vain: it will be for this young country, as it was for our ancient Europe, the seed that will produce new converts to the faith. . . ."①

Msgr. Ferréol was consecrated Bishop by Bishop Verrolles, Vicar Apostolic of Manchuria, on December 31, 1843 and it was not until some twenty months later, on October 12, 1845, that he was able to enter Korea. Alas! He had been in the country for less than a year when persecution broke out anew, and it was Father Andrew Kim, the man who had brought him to his new home, who was destined to become its most glorious victim.

49. Inspection Along the Yalu River by the Seminarian Andrew Kim Tae-kŏn

Korea today (1964) possesses three hundred and thirty-eight priests born on her own soil. The first of this sacerdotal lineage was the martyr Andrew Kim Tae-kŏn, whose life was resplendent with faith and activity and whose death was glorified by martyrdom.

Born on August 21, 1821, at Nol-mae in the district of Nae-p'o(now Sin-chong-ri, U-kang-myŏn) in the Province of Ch'ung-ch'ŏng, Andrew was the son of Ignatius Kim, who, after a momentary weakness, gave his life for Jesus Christ on September 26, 1839.

From infancy, he showed a lively intelligence, a vigorous character, and serious piety. These qualities attracted the attention of Father Maubant. "This child," he thought to himself, "seems to be one of the chosen of God." He sent him to Macao, with two other young Koreans, to be the first of the clergy born of their motherland. This was at the end of 1836.

Five years later, in 1842, Andrew Kim and Thomas Ch'oe, the second student(the third died at Macao), were posted by the procurator of the *Missions-Étrangères* as interpreters to the commandants of the French warships *Érigone* and *Favorite*, who once had planned an expedition to Korea. They embarked with two missionaries, one of whom, Joseph-Ambroise Maistre, was being sent to Korea, and the other, Maxime de la Brunière to Manchuria. The conclusion of peace between China and England after the Opium War made the French commandants abandon

---

① Dallet, *Histoire de l'Église de Corée*, vol. 2, pp. 263-264.

their project, and the missionaries, with the two seminarians and several Christians, set sail in a Chinese junk for Manchuria, where they landed on October 25, 1842.

They were immediately detected by the neighboring customs station, the employees of which, reinforced by a troop of pagans, lost no time in surrounding them.

"At this sight," writes Father Maistre, "our terrified guides were struck dumb. They interrogated us, they seized us by the arms to take us to the magistrate and all of them excitedly pressed close around us. M. de la Brunière, who knew the language, spoke out well in good Mandarin Chinese in answer to every one of their questions, 'I am a foreigner; I don't understand you; leave me in peace; I won't talk with you. The silence of the dismayed Christians compromised us more and more.

"The young Korean student Andrew Kim, however, full of spirit and passion, made a long speech to our assailants, reproaching them for treating us like thieves, for having besmirched our reputation, for having odiously molested inoffensive persons who were emigrating from the Province of Kiangnan on business, and so on.

"While the vivacity of this speech was gaining their respect for us, a man arrived all out of breath, accompanied by a servant. The respect with which he was received by the customs official showed that he was a personage of some considerable standing in the country: he seemed moreover much upset on our account, and his eyes seemed to tell us that he had come to our aid. He then took the place of the Korean and spoke, gesticulated and shouted to such effect that the customs officials released their prey.

"I was curious to know who our liberator might be. What was my surprise when I learnt that he was an idolater, and was quite unaware of our being Europeans! But we had been recommended to him by our catechist, who was a friend of his. After all this uproar our guides seemed to have lost the use of their faculties: they couldn't think any more; they could no longer see things

for themselves. In short, instead of taking us to the cart that was waiting for us, they lost their way and took us walking at random for nearly two hours on a great highway full of pedestrians, at the risk of being recognized at every step."

With much difficulty, Father Maistre and Andrew Kim found shelter in a village some seven leagues from the coast. There they conceived the idea of diguising themselves as beggars and of trying to enter Korea, at the beginning of the year 1843. Bishop Verrolles, Vicar Apostolic of Manchuria, having decided that such a plan was lacking in prudence, they abandoned it.

It was decided that Andrew Kim, who could get about more easily and with less danger, should go alone to reconnoiter, and should set out on December 23 with two couriers.

The travelers duly started off on the date agreed on, and had gone not more than two leagues from Pienmen when they met the Korean embassy on its way to Peking: it consisted of a caravan of more than three hundred persons.

Andrew stopped and watched the Koreans filing past. He approached one of them in order to see his passport, which the envoys always carried hanging from the belt in a conspicuous position and open to the public view.

"What's your name?" he asked.

"My name is Kim," replied the Korean without stopping.

Andrew felt sad at seeing him move off. "This Korean," he said to himself, "looks better than the others, and there will not be much danger in asking him about himself. I shall not have such a good opportunity again for a long time."

Catching up with him again, he asked without preamble, "Are you a Christian?"

"Yes," replied the Korean, "I am."

"What is your Christian name?"

"Francis."

Andrew looked at him more attentively and recognized a fervent neophyte of his acquaintance. He introduced himself in his turn, and learnt that the Bishop and the two missionaries had been beheaded. More than two hundred Christians had been led to execution. His father had been beheaded, and his mother reduced to destitution and rendered homeless; the faithful were sheltering her by turns. Now the persecution had abated and a calm seemed to have succeeded that terrible storm, but the Catholics were still seized with terror and feared at every step to come upon an informer or a false brother, for the decrees proclaimed against them had not been repealed and not all the prisoners had been released.

The courier Francis also gave Andrew various papers hidden in his belt. These were a report of the persecution, written by Bishop Imbert up to the date of his arrest; the letters of the Fathers Maubant and Chastan, and a letter from the Christians expressing their wish to receive more pastors.

The intrepid Andrew Kim now resolved to enter Korea alone in order to make ready for the entry of Father Maistre in the month of February. He went to Pienmen where he spent a day preparing beggar's clothes for his disguise, in which he sewed a hundred taels in silver and forty in gold. He also procured some small loaves of bread and some salted meat. On the following day he set out at daybreak, saying goodby to the two Chinese couriers, and made his way through the waste land that lies between China and Korea. He tramped on for hours and at nightfall he saw the town of Eui-ju in the distance. His plan was to cut brushwood and load a bundle of it on his back, and so pass through the customs as a poor native woodcutter. But when he came to begin the work he discovered that he had left his knife behind at Pienmen. He lifted up his heart to God, and prayed for courage, and advanced toward the town gates. A soldier stood on the threshold ready to examine the passports of all who entered. At this moment some Koreans arrived driving a herd of oxen. The young man joined them and just as he got to the place where the passports were being examined he went to-ward the customs office and then slipped in among the cattle, whose large size hid him from the view of the sentinel.

"But all was not yet over," Andrew Kim continued, "for each person was ordered to present himself at the office and declare his name. As it was already dark, the examination was made by torchlight. There was another official standing on a raised platform in order to see that nobody slipped by unobserved. I was at my wits' end to know what to do. The first to be examined were now getting ready to go on their way, and I prepared to follow them without saying a word. But the official called me back and rebuked me for going on without showing my papers. As he kept on calling to me, I answered, 'The passports have already been given.' Then, fearing that he would pursue me I ran off hurriedly down a narrow sidestreet. I knew nobody, and there was nowhere that I could ask for shelter. It was therefore necessary for me to keep moving all night: I covered more than eight leagues.

"At dawn the cold forced me to go into a little inn, where several men were sitting. Seeing my appearance, and my clothes, and hearing me speak, they said that I was a foreigner. They caught hold of me, uncovered my head, pointed out that the socks I was wearing were Chinese; all these men, except one who took pity on me, were in favor of handing me over to the authorities, and of having me arrested as a fugitive, an illegal entrant, a spy or a malefactor.

"I replied that I was a Korean and an innocent man, and that nothing they could say would alter the nature of things, and that if I were seized, I would have nothing to worry about, for it would not be difficult for an innocent man to plead his cause.

"On hearing these words they drove me away, and as I had told them that I wanted to go to Seoul they sent someone to follow me and see which road I took. I very nearly fell into the hands of the police agents: the silver that I carried might well have been taken as proof of robbery and led to my being condemned to death, in accordance with

Korean law. I therefore waited until the spy had returned to the inn and reported that I was in fact going in the direction of the capital, and only then did I begin to make a wide detour, and take the road back to China. After sunrise I no longer dared to take the highroad, but hid in the wellwooded hills, until nightfall, when I pressed on to Eui-ju."

A serious calamity then happened. For two days Andrew had had nothing to eat. He felt his strength ebbing, fell down, and went to sleep in the snow. He was soon awakened by a voice crying "Get up and walk!" and at the same time he thought he saw a shape pointing out the way in the darkness. In recounting this fact later on, Andrew said, "I took this voice and this phantom for an illusion of my imagination, over-excited by hunger and the horror of loneliness. However, Providence rendered me a great service by it, for very probably I would have frozen to death, and would have woken up in the next world."

He went on his way again.

By daybreak he was at the banks of the Yalu River, which he could cross only with difficulty, for in several places the ice gave way beneath his feet. Finally, exhausted with hunger, cold, and fatigue, he arrived at an inn at Pienmen. There again he was in difficulty. He was refused entry, and told that he was neither Chinese nor Korean, and in fact his rags and tatters and his face, badly chapped with the cold, gave him such a strange appearance that he resembled neither the one nor the other. They wanted to hand him over to the magistrate but his presence of mind saved him. He was lucky enough to find someone who, more for self-interest than for the sake of charity, was willing to accord him a resting-place.

But he realized that this time he must give up his journey and return to Father Maistre's place of refuge.

Such was the debut of the future martyr in this life of labor and danger which from now on was to be his lot, and the tale of which was one day to wring from his judges this cry of pity:

"Poor young man! What troubles he has undergone ever since his childhood!"

These facts were reported to Bishop Ferréol who was waiting in Manchuria, at Mukden, for the Korean embassy which Francis Kim was accompanying in the guise of a trader. This embassy in fact arrived on January 24, 1844: during the night he went secretly to his Bishop, and informed him that the measures taken by the Regent Cho did not permit the entry of any missionary into Korea. "Perhaps," he added, "it may be possible next year."

While awaiting the realization of this hope, Bishop Ferréol sent Andrew Kim on a new attempt, no longer by way of Pienmen, but by Hunchun, situated in the northeast of Korea, not far from the mouth of the Tumen River. In this village, inhabited by about a hundred Manchurian families, an important fair and market was held every other year, at which, for a few hours only, the inhabitants of the adjoining countries might meet.

It had been arranged during the preceding year that the Koreans should go and make a study of the route. Andrew set out intending to get in touch with them and reconnoiter. Here, translated from the Chinese, is the principal part of the letter which he wrote to his Bishop to report on his journey:

"Your Excellency:

"After having received Your Grace's blessing and taken my leave, we mounted our sleigh and gliding rapidly over the snow we soon arrived at Kuanchengtse, where we spent the night. Next day we crossed through the palisade and entered Manchuria. (sic) The fields were entirely covered with snow, and there was nothing to break the monotony of their whiteness, except the large number of sleighs which, traveling from one settlement to another, ploughed the surface in all directions with a speed that is rarely seen in China.

"The first place we came to was Kirin, the capital of the province of the same name. The edges of the forests were not far from the city: we could see them on the horizon, raising their great black masses above the dazzling whiteness of the snow.

They lie between the Celestial Empire and the kingdom of Korea like a vast barrier, as if to prevent, it would seem, any communication between the two peoples, and to maintain this hateful separation which has existed ever since the Koreans were driven back into this peninsula. From east to west these forests occupy a space more than fifty leagues in breadth, and I have no knowledge of how far they extend north and south. If only we could penetrate them at this point and go straight on to Korea our journey would be reduced to half the distance, but they are an impenetrable rampart. We are obliged to make a long circuit and go toward Ningkuta to find a beaten path.

"Another difficulty delayed us: we did not know which road would take us to this town. Providence came to our help, and sent us as guides two merchants of our country who were returning to their motherland. In their company we would be able to travel some time still on the ice of the frozen river, which we ascended toward its source.

"We went on our way, now on the frozen river, now along one of its banks following the road that offered fewest obstacles to our progress. On our right and our left huge mountains rose up crowned with gigantic trees, and inhabited by tigers, panthers, bears, wolves, and other beasts of prey.

"Before coming to the beaten track through the forest to the Eastern Sea, we crossed a small lake six or seven leagues in breadth. Like the river which was its tributary, it was frozen. This lake is celebrated in the country for the number of pearls which are gathered from it for the emperor. It is called the Heihu or Hingchumen, "The Black Lake" or "The Jewel Gate."

"On leaving the Jewel Gate, we entered a hostelry. The first day of the Chinese New Year was drawing near, a great holiday, with much feasting and rejoicing. Every traveler was obliged to break his journey and take part in it. The innkeeper asked us where we came from and where we were going. 'From Kuanchengtse,' we said, 'and we are going to Hunchun, but we don't know the way.'

"'In this case, you will come and stay with me: now it is the New Year: in eight days, my wagons will be ready to take you to that very place; you can load your baggage and provisions on them and set out together, and while waiting for them you will be well looked after.'

"We gratefully accepted his offer. Our horses, in any case, were so tired that a stay of a few days was necessary on their account.

"We stayed eight days at Hingchumen. On the fourth day of the first lunar month, abandoning our now useless sleigh, we saddled our horses and set out with the innkeeper's wagons. His men were contracted to supply at an agreed price forage for our mounts and transportation for our provisions while we traversed the forest, for in the forest nothing could be obtained except wood for warming ourselves and cooking our food. At last we arrived at Matienho near Ningkuta, where the road began, the other end of which reached to the seashore, a distance of fifty leagues.

"When we were somewhat more than a day's journey from Hunchun, our destination, we left our heavy wagons behind and, pressing on ahead, we finally arrived, one month after leaving Your Grace, at our journey's end."

After Pienmen in the west, Hunchun is the only stopping place between China and Korea. A magistrate of the second class, of Manchu origin, commands the local police, reinforced by two or three hundred soldiers under his command.

The exchange of goods is carried out at Kyŏng-won, a small Korean town some three leagues from Hunchun.

"Once arrived at the frontier we had to wait eight days for the fair to open. How slowly they went by! How anxious I was to identify the Korean neophytes by the agreed signal, and make contact with them! But I was obliged to wait. 'Alas!' I said to myself, 'these people are in such a state of barbarism that they can only regard a foreigner as an enemy of whom they must rid themselves, and who must be expelled with horror from their country!' How well I understood this truth now, that man has no real home here below, that he is merely a traveler for a few days in this world! The only reason I had not suffered in China was that I had been taken for a Chinese, and I could only tread the soil of my own country for a moment, and only as a foreigner. Oh! When will that day come when the Father of all the great family of mankind will make all His children greet one another with a fraternal kiss in that great love which Jesus His Son came to bestow on all men!

"On the twentieth day of the first moon, the Korean mandarin of Kyŏng-won sent a message to Hunchun declaring the fair open and that trading could begin on the following day. As soon as it was daybreak we hurried, my companions and I, to reach the market. The approaches to the town were thronged with people, and we walked along in the thick of the crowd, holding our white handkerchief, and with a little red bag of tea hanging from the belt: these were the signs by which we were to be recognized: for the rest, it was for them to accost us.

"We entered into the city, we came out of it again, and nobody spoke to us. Many hours slipped by in this way and we began to feel anxious. 'Can they have missed the rendez-vous?' we asked ourselves.

"Finally, as we were watering our horses by a streamlet which flowed at a distance of three hundred paces from the city, we saw a stranger coming toward us, who had evidently seen our sign. I spoke to him in Chinese but he didn't understand a single word.

"'What is your name?' I asked him in Korean.

"'Han is my name.'

"'Are you a disciple of Jesus?'

"'I am.'

"'Here we are,' I thought to myself.

"The neophyte led us to his companions. They were a party of four in all and had been waiting for us for over a month. We could not stay together for long: the Chinese and the Koreans were pressing around us on all sides. These poor Christians looked utterly dejected. The air of mystery that reigned over our exchange of words aroused the curiosity of the pagans. When they seemed not to be listening to us we slipped in a few words about our religious matters and soon afterward went on our way to market with our horses.

"'How much do you want for it?'

"'Eighty strings of cash.'

"'It is too dear. Here you are, take these fifty strings and let me have the beast.'

"'Impossible. You can't have it for less.'

"This was the way we dealt with those pagans who were watching us and paid them back in their own coin.

"I learnt from these Christians that since the persecution the Church of Korea had been fairly quiet; that a large number of the faithful had retired to the countryside, in the southern provinces, as they were less exposed to the buffets of the storm; that many families had been converted to the faith; that it would be difficult for the neophytes to keep a missionary in the country for any length of time, but that trusting in the divine bounty they would do everything in their power to take care of him; that Pienmen would be less dangerous than Hunchun for his entry into the country because if he entered by the north, in addition to the difficulty of making a clandestine crossing of the frontier he would have to travel through the whole kingdom.

"Our meeting having been brought to a conclusion, we clasped hands in token of farewell. They sobbed and their tears ran down their cheeks.

"We got back to Hunchun where once again we saw the Korean couriers coming toward us: they could not make up their minds to leave us; they wanted to stay with us and make a final farewell. My companion leapt from his horse to exchange a few friendly words: I made a sign to him to remount for fear that the police agents who surrounded us might suspect us of having interests other than those of business, and at last, with a word of greeting to the Angel who presides over the destinies of the Korean Church, and recommending ourselves to the prayers of her martyrs, we crossed the Tumen River and re-entered Manchuria."

After this journey of exploration, Andrew Kim rejoined Bishop Ferréol in Mongolia, and some months later he was ordained a deacon.

50. The Entry of Father Andrew Kim and Bishop Ferréol

Toward the end of the year 1844, the Bishop and the new deacon retook the road to Korea. They arrived at Pienmen on January 1, 1845, at the moment when the Korean embassy was crossing the border on its way to China. Francis Kim was in the ambassadorial suite: that night he secretly presented himself at the inn where Bishop Ferréol was staying, but, as he had done the year before, he declared that it was absolutely impossible to introduce a European into Korea.

Warned of the entry of the missionaries by way of Pienmen, the government had redoubled its surveillance at this place. All those who were attached to the embassy, or who accompanied it in the capacity of traders, had to receive by way of a passport at the city of Eui-ju, a little wooden board, about three inches long and an inch broad, upon which were the name of the traveler and that of his country, together with the seal of the magistrate. This passport would not be issued until after a close interrogation, often very embarrassing, and on the return from China it would have to be handed back to the chief of the customs house that had issued it.

Soldiers were drawn up in echelon along a great part of the frontier, and the description of the three Frenchmen executed in 1839 had been circulated, with strict orders to arrest anyone who resembled them.

These precautions having been taken in order to prevent the entry of foreigners into the country, it was obviously impossible, for the time being at least, for the Bishop to pass by way of Pienmen.

Being unable to take the land route, Bishop Ferréol considered going by sea. The expe-dition offered no less danger and difficulty, for the coasts were as strictly guarded as the frontiers. The Korean fishermen were forbidden to venture on the high seas, and if their ships should be cast upon the coast of China they would be immediately handed over to the magistrate and their boat destroyed by fire.

Bishop Ferréol consented to wait for the time being, but insisted on the couriers taking Andrew Kim with them. The latter, if successful, was to attempt to get in touch with Bishop Ferréol by way of the sea route and through China, and to come himself by boat and pick up the Bishop at Shanghai.

The young deacon set out for Seoul and on March 27, 1845, he sent to Father Libois, procurator general of the *Missions-Étrangères* at Macao, a long report of his journey and his stay in the capital of Korea.

The following is a partial translation of the letter, which was written in Latin.

"Having received Your Grace's blessing I set out with the Christians in the middle of the night, and at dusk on the following day we saw in the west the city of Eui-ju. I told the couriers to go on ahead and wait for me at an appointed place. As for me, I hurried to the darkest alleys and hid myself under bushes: I was about two leagues from the town. Surrounded by a rampart of snow I waited for night and to dispel my anxiety I recited my rosary.

"As soon as darkness had covered the countryside I invoked the divine aid, and emerging from my retreat I directed my steps toward the town. In order to make no noise I walked barefoot. After crossing two streams and passing crooked and difficult roads, for the wind had piled up the snow in drifts from five to ten feet deep, I came to the appointed place: the Christians were not there. Saddened, I entered the town twice to look for them and searched everywhere without success. Finally, having returned to the rendezvous, I sat down in a field and a multitude of somber thoughts began to throng on my brain. I feared that the couriers had been arrested, for I could think of no other explanation for their absence. Sorrow for their arrest, the extreme danger to which I should be exposed if I continued in my way, the lack of money and clothing, the great difficulty of returning to China, the impossibility of receiving the missionary in Korea, all these things plunged me into deep gloom and anguish.

"I was spent with hunger and cold, fatigue and sadness. Lying down on a pile of manure so as not to be seen, I languished there deprived of all human help, trusting only in that of Heaven. Suddenly I saw a group of Christians advancing toward me. They had arrived first at the rendezvous and, not finding me there, they had left. On their return a second time they had waited a while, and then gone to search for me half a league away. Not finding me there, they had passed a great part of the night in sorrow and at last had returned once more, despairing of ever seeing me again.

"At last they found what they were seeking: then, thank God, we were all once again reunited in the name of the Lord.

"At daybreak, leaving the two Christians at Eui-ju to follow me after everything had been arranged, I set out with only one companion. I could hardly walk, and after having covered three leagues, I entered an inn to spend the night.

"Next daybreak, I bought a couple of horses and went on my way.

"On the fifth day we found Charles Hyŭn and Thomas Lee waiting for us at P'yŏng-yang with their horses. Traveling together for seven days, we finally arrived in Seoul. I was quartered in a cottage which the Christians had bought. But on account of their curiosity and indiscretion, and also because of the danger I was incurring—for the government was aware that we three had gone to Macao eight years ago, and was waiting for a chance to seize us—I wanted only the Christians who were indispensable to me to know of my presence, and I had not allowed them to announce my arrival even to my mother.

"Helped in my task by the mercy of God, I made everything ready for the reception of the eminent prelate Bishop Ferréol and his missionaries. I had bought a house in Seoul, and I had also bought a ship which cost 146 taels of silver, and now I was getting ready to sail across to the Chinese Province of Kiangnan.

"However, for fear that our Christian sailors should be terrified at the length of our voyage, I did not tell them anything about our destination. They had good reason to be afraid, for none of them had ever been on the high seas before, and most of them knew nothing about seamanship or navigation; they had conceived the idea that I was an expert pilot.

"Nevertheless I hope and trust that, remembering her goodness and love, the Blessed Virgin Mary, best of mothers, will convey us to Kiangnan and bring us back safe and sound."

A second letter written from Shanghai tells us the story of the brave seminarian's voyage.

"After having made everything ready I embarked with eleven Christians among whom only four were fishermen; the others were all landsmen with no experience of sailing. Forced to do everything hurriedly and in secret, I had been unable to engage experienced seamen or to procure proper equipment and provisions: I even had to abandon everything that was not absolutely essential. Setting sail on the twenty-fourth day of the third moon, we put out to sea. At the sight of it the astonished Christians asked one another. 'Where are we going?'

"But they didn't dare to ask me: I had forbidden them to put any questions about our destination.

"After a day's sailing with a favorable wind we were assailed by a great storm, accompanied with rain, which lasted three days and three nights, and during which, according to reports, more than thirty Kiangnan ships were lost. Our little bark, badly battered by the waves, was tossed about in a most frightening manner, and seemed on the point of sinking, for it was much too small and not built for the high seas. I cut adrift the dinghy we were towing, and at last, as the danger mounted, we also cut down the two masts, and were forced to jettison nearly all our provisions. Somewhat lightened, our ship was lifted up and carried forward by the violence of the storm, across the mountainous waves.

"Having eaten hardly anything for three days the Christians were much weakened, and had lost all hope: they gave themselves up to gloom and wailed, weeping, 'All is over, we are lost!' I showed them an image of the most Holy Virgin, who, after God, is our sole source of hope, and said to them, 'Fear not: here is the Holy Mother who is at our side and will save us.' With these and similar words, I tried to console them and give them courage.

"I too was ill, but after forcing myself to eat a little food I went on working and stifled my fears. I baptized a pagan, already a catechumen, whom I had chosen as my boatswain. A little later our rudder was smashed by the waves, for which reason we tied up all the sails in a bundle and attaching ropes to them threw them overboard, as a sort of sea anchor, but the ropes broke and we lost the sails. We then tried straw mats tied to bits of wood but, this failing, deprived of all human help, we put our sole hope in God and the Virgin Mary, said our prayers, and went to sleep.

"When I woke up the wind had dropped and there was no more rain; we felt revived and I ordered everybody to eat some food and live again in the Lord. Thus strengthened we began to try to devise some way of getting the vessel under control, but what could we do without masts, sails, rudder, or dinghy?

"Always filled with inalterable confidence in the most glorious Virgin Mary, we got together what we could of the woodwork and fashioned jury masts and rudder. At last after tacking for five days we drew near the shores of the Province of Kiangnan, and could perceive a hill in the distance. Having only jury masts and lacking everything necessary to maneuver the boat we despaired of ever reaching Shanghai. We wanted to ask the Chinese for help or at

least some information about the course to take, but we had no dinghy to go to them in, and on their part they fled at the sight of us. With no human aid we awaited only that of Heaven.

"At last a ship from Canton passed close by, and would have made off like the other; I made a signal of distress which they at first ignored but finally, moved by pity, they drew near. I went on board, and after greeting the captain I asked him to take us to Shanghai. Deaf to my prayers and entreaties he advised me to follow him to Canton, and then return to Korea via Peking in the customary way. I told him that I had no desire to go to Peking, but that it was absolutely necessary for me to get to Shanghai to repair my ship. Finally on the promise of a thousand taels of silver he agreed to take us in tow.

"After eight more days of contrary winds we had to undergo a storm which, by the grace of God, put us in no danger at all, though the junk of a friend of our captain which was sailing in company with us was wrecked, and all the crew drowned with the exception of one man.

"A little later we were approached by pirates who ordered our captain 'Stop towing that boatload of people, we want to pillage it.' At these words I gave the captain orders to fire at them, and they made off. After about seven days we arrived at Woosung."

The arrival of this junk in Woosung Roads was a startling event for the country. The way the little boat was built and the costume of the crew aroused the curiosity of the public, and as in China at this time all foreigners were enemies Andrew would have run a great risk if he had not had the foresight to anchor among the British men-of-war stationed there. The officers were astonished to hear a voice shouting in French, "I, a Korean, ask for your protection." This protection was freely given. The Chinese officials, informed of the case, sent secretaries and police agents to find out why he was there. Andrew answered them,

"We are Koreans; it was a great wind which blew us here, and we want to go to Shanghai to repair our ship."

He went to interview the mandarins of Woosung, who put many questions to him and who were forced, they said, to denounce him to the emperor and have him returned to Korea by the land route.

He replied with firmness, "I know the law well, but I don't want to return to Korea by land; much less do I want the emperor to be informed of our arrival. Don't, therefore, make any report to him. For that matter it makes very little difference to me whether you tell the emperor or not; once my ship is repaired I shall return to Korea of my own accord, so you need not worry about us. It is enough for you to know that we have landed on the coast of your empire, and for me that I have drunk the water of your land and set foot on its soil: all I desire is my full liberty. Moreover I beg you to report to the chief magistrate of Shanghai that a Korean vessel put into Shanghai for repairs. I don't wish to cause him any trouble or embarrassment, and only ask for permission to sojourn there without molestation."

With the help of the British officers, Andrew went to Shanghai: he presented himself to the British consul, who, advised by Bishop Ferréol, received him kindly and had him conveyed by palanquin to a Christian family. He then wrote to Father Gotteland, S. J., whom he had met several years before at Macao.

"At the first interview," the missionary relates, "there was the question of confession, but Andrew wanted to get his junk set to rights, so that I could say Mass on board. When it was ready, they came to tell me and I went there in the evening, prepared to stay the night in order to celebrate the Holy Mysteries next day. But I had to confess the brave Koreans at once, as it was their earnest desire."

Andrew was the first to make his confession. When he had received the Sacrament of Penance he remained kneeling supported on his heels, in order to serve as interpreter for his sailors who knelt beside him. At Father Gotteland's invitation, he explained to each of them that under such conditions nobody was obliged to confess every one of his sins. He received for reply, "I wish to tell all."

Some weeks later Bishop Ferréol arrived at Shanghai with a missionary, the future bishop and martyr, Father Daveluy. On Sunday, August 17, 1845, in the chapel of Kinchiahiang, a Christian community situated two or three leagues from the city, the Vicar Apostolic of Kiangnan conferred the Holy Orders of priesthood on Andrew Kim.

A fortnight after his ordination the new priest secretly took Bishop Ferréol and Father Daveluy on board his ship and set sail for Korea.

We shall not recount the difficulties of this voyage, the storm which nearly swallowed up the ship and all on board, and their arrival, near Quelpart Island, nearly eighty-five leagues from the place agreed upon for their landing. At last, on October 12, they were off the port of Kang-kyŏng, in the north of the southernmost province of Korea, and during the night two Christians came on board to help them to land.

How glad Bishop Ferréol was when he first set foot on Korean soil and, after six years of toil and effort, his dream came true! It was October 12, 1845, the forty-second day since he had set sail from Shanghai. Crossing the frontier without difficulty he immediately went north to Seoul, where he stayed with Catholics and administered the Sacraments. Father Daveluy decided to go into hiding in a Catholic village in order to devote himself to the study of the Korean language.

The village consisted of Catholics who had moved down from Seoul in order to escape the persecution. There were thirty or thirty-two believers, living in seven houses in the village. They were barely able to make a living by cultivating tobacco, and they thought their happiness complete when they realized that they would have a priest living among them. They attended early Mass every day, and never left the priest's side. They watched him as he ate Korean food, and were delighted to hear him speak Korean, though his speech was slow and halting. In two or three months the priest was able to understand what they said and to make himself understood by them.

51. Arrest of Father Andrew Kim and the Persecution of 1846

Bishop Ferréol, whose successful entry into Korea by the sea route owed so much to Andrew Kim's death-defying spirit of adventure, went on with his missionary work in Seoul and at the same time tried to bring in Father Maistre and Deacon Ch'oe Yang-ŏp, who were waiting in Manchuria for a chance to enter the country. Knowing that the frontier guards' surveillance in the Eui-ju area was now too strict for any missionary to be able to evade it, he decided to have them come in via Kyŏng-won, by way of the Tumen River bank, seizing the opportunity on any market day. This route had already been surveyed by Father Andrew Kim. Taking the Bishop's advice, Father Maistre and Deacon Ch'oe Yang-ŏp set off together for Hun-chun late in January 1846, accompanied by a Chinese guide. On the seventeenth day of their journey they arrived at a little border village, after an arduous trek over mountains and across frozen rivers. Here they had to wait for market day, but it was impossible for the presence of a foreigner to go unnoticed in such a small village: on the day before the market day when the frontier would be opened, Father Maistre was arrested by the officials of the Chinese Ch'ing government, and subjected to a lengthy interrogation. He was kept in jail for two days and nights and then escorted back to the Liaotung district by two police officers. There, seeing that their arduous journey had been in vain, Father Maistre and Deacon Ch'oe decided to wait for a better opportunity and in the meantime took up teaching posts at the theological seminary there.

Hearing of their failure Bishop Ferréol now had Father Andrew Kim explore the possibility of bringing them in by sea. The fishing season around Yŏn-p'yŏng Island off the coast of Hwang-hae Province began in the third month of the lunar calendar, and at this time there would be large numbers of Chinese and Korean fishing poats plying their nets in the region, which would remain there until the fifth month, attracted by the large shoals of yellow corvenia fish.

Shortly after their arrival, Bishop Ferréol tried to open up a less dangerous route for the introduction of the missionaries than that of Eui-ju. Each year in spring Chinese junks come in large numbers to the coasts of the Yellow Sea, for the fishing season.

The Bishop sent Father Andrew Kim there, with instructions to seek out ways to evade the surveillance of the soldiers and customs officers of Korea, and to get in touch with some of the fishermen.

The priest was fortunately successful in his mission, until he accidentally fell into the hands of the magistrates,[1] on the twelfth day of the fifth moon (June 6, 1946).

He has told the story himself in a letter to his Bishop, written in Latin, the translation of which is as follows:

In prison, August 26, 1846

"Your Excellency:

"Your Lordship is no doubt aware of all that has taken place at the capital since we parted. As soon as everything was ready we weighed anchor and sailed with a favorable wind until we came to the waters of Yŏn-p'yŏng: the sea was covered with the junks of the fishing fleet. The Christians bought some fish and went to sell it at the harbor on the Island of Sun-wi. Not finding a buyer they left it there in the charge of one of the crew, whom they ordered to salt it.

---

[1] Father Andrew was accompanied by Peter Park, Peter Lim, Joachim Kim, Im, Ro, Ŭm, (*Summarium super dubio: An constet de martyrio et causa martyrii*, in *Sacra Ritum Congregatione* Emo. ac Rmo. Domino Card. J. Granito Pignatelli di Belmonte relatore; *Coreana, Beatificationis seu declarationis martyrii* &c. Roma. p. 284, #498. quoted in Launay, *Martyrs Français et Coreéns*, Paris, 1925, p. 230.

"From there we went on our way around So-kang and the Islands Ma-hap, T'ŏ-chin-mot, So-ch'ŏng, Tae-ch'ŏng, and came to anchor near Paek-ryŏng Island. There I saw a fleet of about a hundred Shantung junks engaged in fishing. They came close in to the shore but the crew were not allowed to land. On the heights along the coast, and on the hill-tops nearby were soldiers posted as coast guards on the lookout, who observed them closely.

"A crowd of Koreans, attracted by curiosity, came from the neighboring islands and surrounded the Chinese. I went at night to one of them and had a talk with a junk-master. I entrusted him with the letters from Your Lordship; I wrote some to the Fathers Berneux, Maistre and Libois and to two Christians in China. To this parcel I attached two maps of Korea, with a description of the islands, rocks and other important features of the coast of the Yellow Sea. This place seemed to me a most suitable one for the introduction of missionaries and the transmission of letters, provided that one always takes precautions when making use of the services of Chinese. Each year, at the beginning of the third lunar month, they congregate here for the fishing season: they leave at the end of the fifth month.

"After having carried out the orders of Your Lordship we left and returned to the harbor of Sun-wi. Until then my voyage had taken place without incident, and I was looking forward to a satisfactory outcome. The fish we had left on the beach was not yet dry, so we had to prolong our stay in the port. My servant Veran asked me for leave to go ashore, to get back some money which he had left with a certain family, whose fear of persecution had kept them in hiding there for seven years. After he had left, the magistrate with an escort of soldiers, came on board and asked to use our vessel for dispersing the Chinese junks. Korean law does not permit the commandeering of vessels belonging to the nobility. Among the people, I don't know how, I had been taken for a *yang-pan* or noble of high rank, and in letting the mandarin use my vessel I would

lose this status, which in future expeditions would be nullified. Besides Veran had told me what to do in such a case as this.

"I told the magistrate that the vessel was for my own personal use, and that I could not let him have it. The constables overwhelmed me with insults and left, taking my pilot with them; they came back in the evening, and carried off the boatswain, and took him to the police headquarters. They interrogated them closely about me, and their answers aroused grave suspicions on my account. The magistrate was aware that the grandmother of one of them was a Christian.

"The constables took counsel among themselves, saying 'There are thirty of us; if he is really a nobleman, we shan't all be killed if we offer him violence. One or two of us will be put to death and the remainder will live; let's go and arrest him.' They came during the night accompanied by several prostitutes and hurled themselves upon me in fury; they seized me by the hair, part of which they dragged out by the roots, bound me with a cord and gave me several kicks, punches and cudgel blows. While this was going on, the remainder of the crew, under cover of night, rowed off in the skiff."

With regard to this account by Father Andrew Kim, it is interesting to read the official report made by the deputy commissioner of Teung-san who arrested the young priest:

"On the twelfth day of the fifth lunar month I went down to the beach and while I was requisitioning vessels an individual suddenly stood up on his boat and, wishing to intimidate the deputy commissioner, declared himself a noble of Seoul. He used insulting and abusive language. Hearing his words and observing his conduct, I formed the impression that he was unlike a man of our country. I had him arrested and brought to the harbor office, where, after extended questioning, he declared before me that his name was Kim Tae-kŏn, aged about twenty-five years; he was a native of Kwangtung Province in China, and practiced the European religion. In the eleventh moon of the year 1844, he had crossed the Yalu River by way of Eui-ju and come to the capital. On the eighteenth day of the fourth moon of the current year, he boarded the boat of Lim Sŏng-ryong at Ma-p'o in Seoul and came here. In examining his effects we came upon a small book written in ŏn-mun (Han-keul), the meaning of which is not clear to us; on his person he carried a small sachet of red embroidered silk, in which were two pieces of silk and cotton cloth sewn together, one of which was orna-mented with a floral pattern; he also had a small piece of blue silk. His hair showed signs of having been half shaved, and had not yet grown to its normal length again. Evidently this is a case of a foreigner, a partisan of the perverse religion. Accordingly I have impris-oned the master of the boat Lim Sŏng-ryong and the boatswain Ŭm Su in the harbor office with cangues upon their necks; as for the book in ŏn-mun, the sachet and the other writings which he surrendered to us, I have sealed them all in a package which I am sending to you together with my dispatch."

This report, addressed to governor Kim Chŏng-jip of Hwang-hae Province, was forwarded to Seoul and appeared so grave that its contents were made known to the king. Hŏn-jong shared his ministers' impression and replied with the following order, which is evidence of his deep concern:

"On examining this report it is evident that we have an emergency to deal with; the suppression of the perverse doctrine in 1839 is not yet long over, and here we have, according to this report, this foreigner who effects illegal entry into our realm; how can we defend ourselves against this grievous terror? There must be persons who aid and harbor them. Let the Grand Council of State report to us without delay the result of its investigations in order that we may come to a decision."

On June 14 the order was issued to the police commissioner at Seoul, "to send out constables to bring all the prisoners to the capital for strict examination and obtaining of evidence."

During this time, Father Kim and his companions, brought before the governor of the Province of Hwang-hae, had undergone several interrogations, a summary of which had been forwarded to the king.

This summary does not agree entirely with the declarations of the priest, but it is correct in the main, and especially in regard to the noble avowal of Catholicism on the part of the prisoner.

Let us quote a few important extracts from the two documents.

First, the governor's report:

"The criminal Kim Tae-kŏn, aged twenty-five years, has deposed to the effect that he is a native of China, of the district of Macao in the Province of Kwangtung. His name is U and given name Tae-kŏn, he was born and grew up in this district; his father is deceased, but his mother is still living, and he himself is unmarried. At the age of sixteen he began to study the European religion; at the age of twenty-three, on board a merchant ship, he made a voyage of eight hundred miles from Sungkiang, landing at Liaotung where he came ashore. In the eleventh moon of the year 1844 he came to the palisade barrier (in Manchuria) and, desirous of visiting Korea, he availed himself of the frozen condition of the Yalu River to effect an illicit entry into this country: in the eighth moon of last year, he arrived at Seoul. Wishing to visit, in order to see them, the mountains and seaways of Hwang-hae Province, he went to Ma-p'o to reserve a vessel, and as the vessel belonging to the person Lim was about to leave for Hwang-hae Pro-vince for trading, on the eighteenth day of the last fourth moon, he embarked on this vessel and came to the Island of Yŏn-p'yŏng in the district of Hae-ju, then, having visited So-kang and other places and made short stays there, he returned to the maritime fortress of Teung-san; on the same day, on account of the requisition of vessels by the fortress, he got into a dispute and his identity was revealed. His book in ŏn-mun is a summary of the doctrine of the Lord of Heaven. The human figures depicted on one of the little pieces of woven fabric are those of Saint Mary and of Jesus; on the other, it is not a floral pattern as was previously stated, but the representation of a heart; he carried them close to his body in the spirit of piety and veneration.

"In a fourth deposition, Kim Tae-kŏn declared that as to his profession he had already stated it fully in the answers he gave to the questions put to him; as to what is harmful to his country, "to do harm to one's neighbor," he said, "is expressly forbidden by our religion; on this point there is no doubt whatever; to make the map of the hills and waterways, that is for me one of my favorite pastimes; moreover, since these maps have been blown overboard and lost, there is no point in asking further questions about them; as for the letters sent, these were letters to my family; as for the rest of the questions, since there are persons who have made declarations, let these be taken as sufficient answer; what point is there in asking me all over again?"

The deposition ends with the following words of Father Kim; it is important to take notice of them, for they nobly express his acceptance of martyrdom, and under the brush-pen of the magistrate, whom they must certainly have astonished, they have especial force and significance:

"To be born once and to die once is the fate of everybody: that I should die today for the Lord of Heaven is what I prefer. No matter whether I am questioned today or questioned tomorrow, that and nothing else is my answer; whether I am beaten or whether I am killed, it is still that and nothing else that I desire. Look sharp and beat me! Look sharp and kill me!"

Here now is the part of the letter from the Korean priest which has reference to his interrogations, at first by the deputy commissioner and afterward by the governor:

"The constables having found something Chinese in my bag, believed that I was a native of that country, and on the following day the magistrate asked me whether I were a Chinese. 'No,' I told him, 'I am a Korean.'

"Giving no credit to my words, he said to me;

"'In which province of China were you born?'

"'I was brought up in Macao, in the Province of Kwangtung; I am a Christian; curiosity and the desire to spread the faith led me to these localities.'

"He had me taken back to prison.

"After five days a minor official at the head of a large number of constables conveyed me to the provincial capital, Hae-ju. The governor asked me whether I was a Chinese. I made the same answer to him as I had to the magistrate on the island. He put many questions to me on the subject of religion. I eagerly availed myself of the opportunity and told him about the immortality of the soul, about hell, Heaven, the existence of God and the necessity of worshiping Him in order to gain happiness after death. He and his people answered: 'All this that you say is good and reasonable, but the king does not want anyone to be a Christian.'

"They then asked me a lot of questions about things that might compromise the Christians and the mission. I was careful to avoid answering them.

"'If you don't tell us the truth,' they repeated, in a tone of irritation, 'we shall subject you to various kinds of torture.'

"'Do as you wish.'

"Running over to the instruments of torture I seized them in my hands and threw them at the governor's feet, saying to him 'Here I am, quite ready. Strike! I am not afraid of your tortures.'

"The constables took them away at once. The magistrate's servants came to me and told me, 'It is customary for everyone who addresses the governor to refer to himself as so-in or 'this humble person.'

"'What are you saying to me? I am great, I am a nobleman, and I know nothing of such an expression.'

"Some days later, the governor summoned me again and overwhelmed me with questions about China: sometimes he would speak to me through an interpreter to find out whether I really was a Chinese: he concluded by ordering me to apostatize. I shrugged my shoulders and gave him a pitying smile.

"The two Christians arrested together with me, overcome by the atrocious cruelty of the tortures, revealed my address at Seoul, betrayed Thomas Lee, the servant of Your Lordship, his brother Matthew and many others. They testified that I had communicated with the Chinese junks and that I had given some letters to one of them. A squad of constables was at once sent off to the junks and brought back all the letters to the governor.

"We were very strictly guarded, each in solitary confinement: four soldiers watched us day and night. We were chained hand and foot and wore the cangue. A long cord was tied to our chains, and three men would hold the end of it each time we needed to answer the calls of nature. I leave it to you to imagine what wretched treatment I had to put up with.

"The soldiers, seeing seven scars left on my chest by the leeches that had been applied during my stay at Macao, said that they looked like the constellation Ursa Major (the Great Bear) and amused themselves with thousand such pleasantries."

It has been written, based on the magistrate's declarations, that Andrew Kim declared himself to be of Chinese nationality. His own letter certifies the contrary. To the first question put to him, "Are you a Chinese?" he answered, "I am a Korean."

This reply was not recorded, and the magistrate put a second question related to the first: "In which province of China were you born?"

The priest replied, "I was brought up at Macao in the Province of Kwangtung."

And the judge inscribed him as "a native of Macao, in the Province of Kwangtung."

This apparent contradiction between the words of Andrew Kim and the evidence of the magistrate is easily explained. Either the magistrate did not believe that the prisoner was a Korean and did not think it right to record his answer, or else he was frightened to record such a declaration, extremely dangerous for himself, inasmuch as Korean law

prescribes the death penalty for those who leave the mother country, and holds the magistrates responsible for any such illicit emigration. He contented himself with altering the second reply of the prisoner, thus in lieu of putting down that he had been "brought up at Macao" he affirmed that he had been "born there."

Let us remember the remarks made shortly afterward by the Admirable Counselor Kwon Ton-in: "I hear that this person Kim seems to be a native of our kingdom, but I do not know what value to place on this rumor."

Thus even in the highest government circles they were reluctant to believe or admit that Andrew Kim was a Korean. How much more so would they be in less elevated society, in which there would be all the more reason to dread their own responsibilities.

During these interrogations and this imprisonment the constables sent from Seoul with orders to locate Andrew Kim arrived. They took him to the capital, his arms tied with the scarlet cord, his head covered with a blackish colored cloth bag, in accordance with our usage in dealing with state criminals. "On the way," says the priest, "we had to endure great hardships; the crowd beset us. I passed for a foreigner, and they climbed to trees and roof-tops to look at me."

At Seoul the prisoner was confined in the common thieves' jail.

The following day he was brought before the judges who asked whether he was a Korean or a Chinese.

The judges knew that several years earlier three young persons had been sent to Macao. One of the Christians arrested with the Andrew had testified to the fact, and had declared that the latter was one of the three.

Tergiversation and evasive replies are more or less contrary to the truth, and denote a lack of courage. What is more, before the deputy commissioner of Teung-san and the governor of the Province of Hwang-hae, Andrew had declared that he was a Korean. To the judge's question he answered as he had done before: "I am a Korean and I was brought up in China."

Thereupon, at the order of the presiding judge, he recounted a part of the travels and sufferings he had undergone in order to return to his motherland.

This narrative moved both the judges and the spectators. "Poor young man," murmured some of them, "how he has suffered ever since his childhood."

But the emotion was only transient and soon they ordered the prisoner to give up the Catholic faith. Let us listen to the confessor of the faith as he gave a summary of the interrogation:

"'Above the king,' I told them, 'there is a God who calls for my worship: to deny Him would be a crime which the royal injunction cannot justify.'

"Summoned to divulge the names of the Christians, I opposed them with the duty of charity, and the commandment of God, to love one's neighbor.

"Interrogated on the subject of religion, I spoke to them at length on the existence and the unity of God, the creation and the immortality of the soul, hell, the need to worship the Creator, the falsity of the pagan religions, and so on.

"When I had finished, the judges answered me:

"'Your religion is good, but so is ours, and that is why we practice it.'

"'If in your opinion it is as you say,' I said to them, 'you ought to let us alone and live at peace with us. Yet, far from doing so, you persecute us, you treat us more cruelly than the worst criminals: you testify that our religion is good, that it is true, and you persecute it as if it were an abominable doctrine. You are inconsistent.'

"They contented themselves with a foolish laugh at my rejoinder.

"They brought me the letters and the charts that had been seized.

"The judges read the two letters which were written in Chinese: they contained only greetings. They gave me the European letters to translate; I interpreted them so as not to cause trouble to the mission.

"They put questions to me regarding the

Fathers Berneux, Maistre and Libois; I told them that they were scholars who resided in China. Perceiving the difference between the letters written by Your Lordship and my own, they asked me who had written them. I said in a general way that they were my letters. They put yours before me and ordered me to write in the same style. They tried to trick me and I overcame them with a trick.

"'These characters,' I told them, 'were written with a steel pen; bring me one and I will satisfy you.'

"'We have no steel pen.'

"'If you haven't got one, it will be impossible for me to form characters like those.'

"They brought a quill pen: the judge presented it to me and said: 'Can't you write with this pen?'

"'That's not the same thing,' I said, 'however, I will show you how, with these European characters, one person can write in several different styles of calligraphy.'

"Thereupon cutting the quill very thin I wrote a few lines in very small letters; then cutting the tip to make it broad, I wrote some 'bold-face' letters.

"'You see,' I said, 'the characters are not the same.'

"That satisfied them, and they said no more about the letters."

The interrogations undergone by Father Kim were frequent, for the *Court Journal* mentions, on June 19, four depositions; on June 23, eleven; seven on June 26, and fourteen on June 30. They were all on the subject of the Catholic faith, on Andrew's coreligionists, and on his travels abroad.

Father Kim always and very proudly declared himself a priest of Jesus Christ. Of the Christians, he gave only the names of those who were already known to the authorities; of the foreign countries in which he lived he cited only Macao, which his judges often believed to be far distant from China.

In accordance with the desire expressed by several ministers, in spite of his chains and the darkness of his cell, the priest composed a small abridgement of geography, delineated a *mappemonde* according to the English geographers, and executed two copies of it in colors, one of which was sent to the king.

During these interrogations, one fact occurred which seemed even more extraordinary than the narratives given by Andrew Kim, and which caused an even more vivid impression: a letter from the French Admiral Cecile was sent to the Admirable Counselor.

This letter, dated June 1, 1846, reproached the government of Korea for the death of Bishop Imbert and the Fathers Maubant and Chastan, demanded an explanation of the motive for their execution, and announced that in the following year, certain men-of-war would come to Korea to receive the reply, and that the country would be visited with great calamities if such crimes should be repeated.

The prisoner learnt from his judges part of the tenor of this message and the emotion which it produced.

"The government seemed terrified," he wrote, "it recalled the death of the three French citizens martyred in 1839. They asked me if I knew why these vessels had come. I replied that I knew nothing, and that for that matter they had nothing to fear, for the French never inflict harm without good reason. I spoke to them of the might of France and the generosity of her government. They appeared to believe me. However, they pointed out that they had killed three Frenchmen with impunity."

The news of the arrival of the French ships in Korean waters caused the captive to have confused visions of his deliverance: "We shall not be put to death," he told his Christian fellow-prisoners.

"What proof have you?"

"French men-of-war are in Korea, the Bishop and Father Ahn (the Korean surname of Father Daveluy) will not fail to inform them of our situation. I know the commander-in-chief; he will unquestionably set us free."

Was it that the priest merely wished to inspire hope in his fellow-prisoners or that he himself felt it? He was not, however, without fear that in the postscript to his letter written to Bishop Ferréol he said:

"I learnt today with certainty that the French men-of-war have arrived in Korea. They can easily liberate us, but if they content themselves with threats and then go away, they will do a great deal of harm to the mission and expose me to terrible tortures before my death. My God, bring all this to a good end!"

For him, this "good end" had to be martyrdom. He soon understood this. Thus he ends his letter with a touching thought of tenderness toward his mother:

"I commend to Your Lordship my mother Ursula. After an absence of ten years, it was given to her to see her son again for a short space of time, but he was taken from her almost at once. Be good enough, I entreat you, to console her in her sadness."

So it was that neither his lengthy and perilous voyages nor the hardships of his wandering life, nor his sufferings in prison, nor his approaching death could dispel from the heart of the priest his natural affections and filial piety (so deep all over the world, but nowhere deeper than in the Far East). This is a great example added to those of his faith and his courage already demonstrated, and offered without intermission until the last day of his life.

52. The Martyrdom of Blessed Andrew Kim

After the son commending his mother to his Bishop, here is the priest addressing his final teachings to the faithful: Father Kim wrote to his Christian compatriots a letter which, by its sentiments of faith, of generosity, of the love of God and of souls, expressed with such nobility, seems to us in no way inferior to those which the scribes of the Church of the first centuries have enshrined in their annals. We give the complete translation:

"My friends,

"God, who at the beginning disposes all things, created man in His image: see what His aim and intention was in so doing. If in this tempestuous and wretched world we did not know our sovereign Master and Creator, to what end had we been born!

Our life would have been useless. Having come into the world by God's mercy, and by a still greater mercy forming, thanks to our baptism, part of His Holy Church, we bear a most precious name; but if we produce no fruit, of what use is this name? Not only will our reception into the Church prove profitless to us, but we shall prove renegades, guilty of ingratitude toward God to a degree as hateful as His graces are abundant.

"Consider the husbandman; at the proper time, he tills his field, and fertilizes it, and gives no thought to the cold of winter, the heat of summer, nor to his own hard labor. After having sown the good seed, if at harvest-time the corn is rich and plentiful, he forgets all his trouble, and his heart is full of joy. But if he doesn't see the corn grow and the ears fill with grain, if when autumn comes he reaps only straw and empty ears, he regrets the sweat, the fertilizer and the labor, and abandons the field. Alas! The field of God is this world in which we live, and mankind is the good seed which He sows. He fertilizes it with His grace; He waters and nourishes it with the blood of His Son incarnated and slain for us; He teaches us with His Holy Scriptures, exhorts us through His bishops and priests, who are our shepherds, and continually enlightens us through His Holy Spirit. How great is the care with which He educates us! When the time comes for the harvest and the judgment, if by His grace we have borne good fruits we shall enjoy the bliss of Heaven; but if we are mere barren plants, instead of being the children of God we shall become His enemies, and we shall suffer in hell the eternal punishment which we shall have deserved.

"My very dear brothers, mark this well, Our Lord Jesus having come down into this world, Himself suffered pains without number. By His sufferings, He has established His Church which must also grow amid crosses and tribulations. After the Ascension of the Saviour, from the time of the Apostles to the present day, the Church has always continued to grow amidst her manifold persecutions, but no matter what the world may do to attack and destroy her, they will never overcome her.

"In Korea, too, the Catholic religion, introduced fifty or sixty years ago, has often been roughly shaken by storms, and nevertheless there are still Christians. Today the persecution is beginning again; many of the faithful including myself are in prison, and all of you are threatened. Being of one heart with you all, can I feel anything but pain at this? Can I look at this state of things without a feeling of affliction? Nevertheless is it not written that even the number of hairs on our head is known to God, and that not one of them falls without His consent? Let us then submit to the Holy Will of the Lord, and taking up our cross like Our Master Jesus, fight always against the world and the devil.

"In these times of tumult and trouble let us like valiant warriors wear our armor on the field of battle, fight, and conquer. Above all let us never forget mutual charity, and always help one another: let us await the day when God will take pity on us and answer all your prayers.

"The twenty Christians imprisoned here are, by the grace of God, in good health: if they should be condemned to death, do not forget their families. I should like to say many more things to you, but how can they be communicated in a letter? I will end, then. As for us we shall soon enter the fray.

"I beg you all to practice virtue with sincerity, that we may all meet again in Heaven. My dear children, whom I can never forget, in these stormy times do not allow yourselves to be unduly worried; day and night with the help of God fight against the three enemies, that is to say, the three concupiscences; bear the persecution patiently and strive to save for the glory of God the souls of those who survive it. Persecution is one of God's tests: by our victory over the world and the devil we acquire virtue and merit. Do not allow yourselves to be frightened by calamities, do not lose your courage, and do not backslide in the service of God, but rather, following in the footsteps of His saints, enhance the glory of His Church and show yourselves true soldiers and subjects of the Lord. Although you are many, be of one heart; always remember charity; support and help one another, and await the moment when God will take pity on you. Time does not allow me to write more. My dear children, I hope to see you again in Heaven and to enjoy with you an eternity of bliss. I send you the tender kiss of peace."

Andrew Kim, priest

"*P.S.* Everything here below is ordained by God; everything is in its own way either reward or punishment; not even the persecution could take place except by His permission: bear it patiently for God; only, implore Him with tears to grant peace to His Church. My death will no doubt be felt by you and your souls will be in anguish; but before long the Lord will send you shepherds worthier than I. Do not be sad, but strive to serve God in all charity as He deserves to be served. Let us remain united in charity, and after death we shall be together throughout eternity, and enjoy God's love forever. I hope it, a thousand, nay, ten thousand times."

Bishop Ferréol has told us that the prisoner won the affection of his judges and the ministers, who begged the king to spare his life. "He has committed a crime deserving death," they told him, "in leaving the kingdom and consorting with foreigners, but he has expiated it by returning to his country."

We cannot be certain whether this fact is true, but an attentive examination of the documents, permits one, we believe, to think that the Bishop may have had trustworthy information. Here indeed are the words pronounced on September 5 before the king by the Admirable Counselor of the Grand Council, Kwon Ton-in:

"If Kim Tae-kŏn is not put to death, as the law prescribes, it will only provide a pretext for future discussions, without taking into account the fact that it would not fail to be interpreted as a confession of weakness on our part." In the records of the council of September 15, we find phrases which permit the same supposition: "How can we pardon him, even

for a single moment? To save this individual can only lead to later disputes." Or again these words of Heung-keun, a member of the Grand Council: "The demand of Your Majesty raises a special question: should the execution take place immediately, or should it be deferred until a later date? To grant even a temporary respite to such an atrocious criminal as this is to bring the law of punishments into contempt." The other minister expressed analogous thoughts.

However it may have been, so, the Admirable Counselor Kwon Ton-in concluded by proposing the death penalty: "My view is that to put an end to the affair by carrying out the law is really the best solution."

The Counselor of the Right Park Hoe-su expressed the same opinion succinctly: "Undoubtedly it is impossible to pardon him, and we beg Your Majesty to condemn him without further delay."

The ministers of rites, and of war.....the judge of the Royal Family Tribunal, and all the others agreed: Andrew Kim must be sentenced to death.

Then the Admirable Counselor Kwon Ton-in summed up: "Kim Tae-kŏn, in view of his crime of heresy, as also that of treason to his country, cannot be pardoned, even for a moment, and the view of His Majesty's ministers, as well as of the high officials present at the council, is unanimous and uncontradicted on this point. I therefore request Your Majesty to order that the prisoner Kim Tae-kŏn be handed over to the military authority to be decapitated and his head displayed in order to serve as a lesson to the people."

These words are followed by the supreme sentence pronounced by the king: "Let it be so."

This judgment is dated on September 15,1846.

The documents which we have just quoted, extracted from the *Annals of the Grand Council*, are corroborated by the *Annals of the Reign of Hŏn-jong* in which one may read:

"Seventh moon, twenty-fifth day (September 15, 1846).

"His Majesty, at the *Heui-chŏng-tang*(Council Hall), having convoked the Admirable Counselor and the heads of the administration of the national defense, ordained that the criminal Kim Tae-kŏn be subjected to military capital punishment."

The martyrdom of Andrew Kim took place with the same public display as that of Bishop Imbert and his two missionaries. On September 16, a company of soldiers, with rifle on shoulder, marched to the execution ground located on the banks of the river, some two or three miles from the capital. An instant later, the firing of a salute, followed by a fanfare, announced the magistrate's arrival.

During this time the condemned man was removed from his cell. A rough palanquin consisting of two long poles supporting a seat of woven straw was brought. The constables seated Andrew on this, with his arms tied behind him and, preceded, followed and surrounded by an immense crowd, he was carried to the gallows.

The soldiers had set up a flagstaff in the sands, and a flag was now hoisted, around which they stood in a ring. The circle was opened to admit the prisoner, and the magistrate read the sentence of death.

As soon as he had finished, Father Kim, in a strong voice, pronounced the following words:

"I am at my last hour; please listen to me attentively. If I have been in touch with foreigners, it was because of my religion, it was for my God: it is for Him that I die. An immortal life is about to begin for me. Become Christians, if you wish to be happy after death, for God reserves eternal punishment for those who disown Him."

After these words he was partially stripped of his clothes. According to custom, each of his ears was pierced with an arrow, which was left hanging; water was thrown at his face, which was then sprinkled with lime.

Two men, sliding bars under his arms, lifted him by the shoulders and quickly took him three times around the circle of soldiers. Then they made him kneel, attached a cord to his hair and, passing it through a hole in the flagstaff, that now served as a gibbet, they pulled it tight so as to hold his head in a raised position.

While these preparations were going on, the young priest remained perfectly calm.

"Am I in the correct position? Will it be easy for you to strike?"

"No, turn yourself a little to one side. There, that's right."

"Strike, I'm ready."

A dozen soldiers armed with sabers then ran around him in a kind of war-dance, each of them slashing at the victim's neck in turn. The head did not fall until the eighth stroke. A constable took it, placed it on a tray and showed it to the magistrate who at once left to submit his report of the execution at the royal court, and this report was published in the *Annals of the Grand Council* on the same day. The following is the translation:

"Seventh moon, twenty-sixth day (September 16, 1846).

"Verbal notice was received from the command office of the royal guard to the following effect: We have the honor to inform you that the criminal Kim Tae-kŏn has, in the presence of a large concourse of soldiers and civilians, been executed, to serve as a lesson to the people."

According to Korean law, the bodies of executed criminals must remain exposed at the site for three days; when this period has elapsed, their relatives are at liberty to remove them for burial, but the remains of Andrew Kim were, by order of the chief judge, interred at the site of his beheading. The head was replaced on the neck, and the body, clad in a short unwadded jacket of violet color, and cotton trousers, was wrapped in matting tied with thick cords, and placed in a hurriedly prepared grave.

The magistrate posted sentries around the tomb, to prevent the faithful from removing the body of the martyr. Forty days later, this surveillance ended, and the Christians could carry it away and give it honorable burial on the slopes of Mt. Mi-ri-nae, some twelve leagues from Seoul.

After having, in his letter to Father Barran, director of the Seminary of the *Société des Missions-Étrangères*, reported the foregoing details regarding the death of Andrew Kim, Bishop Ferréol added:

"You will easily understand what a cruel loss to me the death of this young native priest has been; I loved him as a father loves his son; only his present joy consoles me for his absence. He was the first and only one of his country, so far, to have been raised to the priesthood. He had gained from his clerical education ideas which put him far above his compatriots. A lively faith, a frank and sincere piety, and an astonishing mastery of public speaking won him, from the very first, the respect and love of all the Christians.

"In the performance of his holy office he surpassed our expectations and a few years of experience would have made him an outstanding priest; one could hardly perceive that he was a Korean. Business of the most diverse nature could be safely entrusted to him; his character, good manners, and general knowledge were ample warrant for its success. In the present state of the mission, his loss is an immense and almost irreparable calamity."

The first priest to penetrate into Korea, Father James Chou, and the first Korean Catholics had been martyred in 1801; the first Bishop and the first French missionaries became martyrs in 1839; the first Korean priest, a martyr in 1846. The Church of Korea, like those of Jerusalem, Antioch, Rome, like the majority of the Churches in the world, has its foundations cemented with the blood of the martyrs, joined to the blood shed on Calvary by Our Lord Jesus Christ. This is her imperishable glory, and also, we confidently hope, a pledge of complete victory and the sure promise of immortality.

The relics of Blessed Father Andrew Kim Tae-kŏn, martyr, are currently preserved in the Theological Department Chapel of Catholic College in Seoul. On November 15, 1949 he was proclaimed the Archpatron of the entire Korean clergy, inclusive of foreigners. July 5 is observed as his feast day.

53. Blessed Charles Hyŭn Sŏk-mun
(beheaded, September 19, 1846)

Three days after the execution of Andrew

Kim, Charles Hyŭn, who introduced Bishop Imbert into Korea, attended the missionaries on their journeys and assisted Father Chastan in his management of the Christian communities, was also beheaded.

He belonged by birth to the middle-class. He was born at Seoul in 1799. His father had been a martyr in 1801, his wife and son had died in prison in 1839, and one of his sisters, Benedicta Hyŭn, was beheaded for the faith in the same year. His whole life seemed to have been dedicated to helping the preachers of the Gospel and the faithful.

In the *Procès Apostoliques* ('Apostolic Processes,' records of the cause, stages and modes of procedure in the beatification and canonization of saints) he is described as "a man of merit and virtue, of gentle nature, affable and frank."

At the outbreak of the persecution in 1838, he wanted to give himself up to the authorities and declare his faith, but the missionaries dissuaded him, advising him to save his own life in order to take care of the other Christians, and to hide himself and take every precaution to avoid being arrested.

Just before death, Bishop Imbert entrusted the Church of Korea to his care. This is enough to show what place Charles Hyŭn held in the Bishop's esteem and the confidence of the Catholics. He acquitted himself of the task with care and energy, encouraging the neophytes with his counsels, helping them with alms, which he collected throughout the provinces, and assisting them to organize themselves in groups in the villages less exposed to domiciliary searches by the police.

After the calamity was over he revised and edited the documents collected by Thomas Lee, Philip Ch'oe, and others, regarding the confessors of the faith, and published a small book entitled *Ki-hae Diary* (the Persecution of 1839), which was read by every Christian.

He sent couriers to Peking on several occasions in an attempt to re-establish relations with the missionaries. He accompanied Andrew Kim on his perilous expedition to Shanghai. On his return to Seoul, he registered the house occupied by the young priest under his own name, a precaution which he knew might entail dangerous consequences to himself, but which his devotion led him to accept without hesitation.

As soon as he became aware of Father Kim's arrest, he left his house and purchased another, and took with him to his new home a part of the money and other things belonging to the mission. He had been there only a few days when the constables came to his former residence with a warrant for his arrest. They were told that his present whereabouts were unknown, but that the carriers who had helped him to move house and had even led some of the faithful to his new home would show them where he lived. That was how things turned out, so that the pursuers were able to make a bigger capture than they had hoped for.

At the moment when the police burst into Charles Hyŭn's house, there were several Christians there: Theresa Kim, Agatha Lee, Catherine Chŭng, and Susanne U. It was July 10, 1846. Hyŭn was arrested together with his visitors. In the prisons of the police headquarters his exhortations raised the courage of the Catholics held there.

He had to undergo severe beatings, stabbings, "all the tortures" as several witnesses assure us; others however say that the judges inflicted no torture on him, and treated him fairly well.

Regarding his death, which took place at Sae-nam-t'ŏ, we know only the following details, transmitted, as those of his arrest, by Catherine Kim.

"When he came to the execution ground, he raised his eyes and surveyed his surroundings; he had no fear and had retained his *sang-froid*, like a man in perfect health. Until the very moment that his head was cut off he showed the same courage."

54. The Martyrdom of the Seven Blessed Men and Women

The day after that on which Charles Hyŭn became a martyr, seven others of the faithful gave their lives for Jesus Christ.

The following list gives their name and age and the date of their arrest:

Joseph Lim Ch'i-paek, imprisoned in the month of June 1846, forty-three years.

Susanne U Sul-im, forty-four years.

Theresa Kim Im-i, thirty-six years.

Agatha Lee Kan-ran, thirty-three years.

Catherine Chŭng Ch'ŏl-yŏm, thirty years. The four were arrested on July 10 at the house of Charles Hyŭn.

Peter Nam Kyŏng-mun, forty years, at the end of August.

Lawrence Han I-hyŏng, forty-eight years, in July.

The first of these confessors of the faith, **Lim Ch'i-paek,** lived a pagan until his arrest. His wife and children had embraced the faith. When they pressed him to follow their example he would always say, "I will be converted later on."

In 1835, several Christians of his acquaintance having been arrested, he strove to protect the rest, and in order to be able to help them more effectively he got himself enrolled as one of the constables.

In 1846, one of his sons accompanied Father Andrew Kim on his expedition to the coast of the Yellow Sea, and was arrested together with him on June 5. As soon as Lim heard of this fact he went to the village where it had taken place. His son had already been carried off to the provincial headquarters. Lim went there, and protested to the governor, whose only response was to imprison him also, and a few days later to consign him to Seoul.

Susanne U was the daughter of a pagan nobleman of the district of Yang-ju. At the age of fifteen she married a Christian of In-ch'ŏn, whose faith she soon embraced. She was arrested in 1828, but as she was about to become a mother the judge released her after a detention of several weeks, during which she underwent tortures, the effects of which remained with her for the rest of her life. On becoming a widow she went, in 1841, to live at the capital, where she became a domestic servant to several Catholics, especially Agatha Lee, her future companion in suffering and in glory. She devoted herself to prayer, and through her love of God she bore patiently all ill-treatment. "My only regret," she said, "was to have missed the chance to become a martyr." Providence enabled her to regain it.

Theresa Kim, of a Catholic family, was born in 1811 at Seoul in the Kwan-u-mul-kol quarter. From her childhood she took delight in reading the lives of the saints and in imitating their virtues. At the age of seventeen she resolved to remain a maiden, and asked for nothing more than to be allowed to love God and serve her neighbor.

In 1845 she had the good fortune to enter the service of Father Kim. Having experienced the persecution of 1839 to 1841 she foresaw a renewal, and instead of fearing this she almost seemed to desire it. "If the Father is imprisoned," she told her sister, "I wish to follow his example, even if I have to give myself up voluntarily, so do not expect to keep me long in this world."

Agatha Lee was born in 1813; her parents were pagans. Married at the age of eighteen, she became a widow two years later. It was about the year 1834 that she first came to hear of Catholicism. She refused to remarry, and begged her mother to put her in touch with the Christians, a simple matter, for one of their relatives was a Catholic. The latter gave Agatha, her mother, and her brother explanations which aroused in them a sincere desire to be received into the Church. He taught them the prayers, and Father Liu baptized them. As soon as he heard of these conversions, the father of the family, an obstinate pagan, sent Agatha back to her parents-in-law, and his wife and son to the Province of Kyŏng-sang. Agatha bowed to the paternal mandate, charmed her husband's family by her sweetness of temper, and converted one of her sisters-in-law.

Born into slavery and, according to some, a cradle-Catholic, to others a convert at the age of sixteen or eighteen, **Catherine Chŭng** who was also known as Tŏk-i, had a very sweet character, average intelligence, and a heroic soul.

She was twenty when, at the winter solstice, her employer Kim, wishing to force her to take part in the traditional superstitious practices of the pagans, and infuriated at her refusal, had her arms bound behind her back and a heavy millstone attached to

her body, after which he had her thrown upon a stack of firewood to lie there until the festivities were over. At the party's end, he beat her so cruelly that she fell unconscious and did not recover till after four or five weeks.

When the spring solstice came round in its turn the same scene was re-enacted but with intensified violence.

Throughout her life Catherine bore on her body the marks of the blows received on these occasions. "Her body showed swellings and her face was yellowish; she was like an invalid and her body was hardly capable of heavy labor."

After her recovery she fled to Seoul, where she lived with some Christians in the peaceful practice of her faith. In 1845, she became a domestic servant in the household of Father Andrew Kim. These four Christian women, Susanne, Theresa, Agatha and Catherine were, as we have already said, arrested together on July 10.

Born at Seoul in 1796, **Nam Kyŏng-mun** was a soldier in the *Keum-wi-yŏng* or Capital Defense Corps. At the age of twenty-two he married Barbara Hŭh. He was converted to Catholicism by the teaching of Peter Park, whose name he was given at his baptism, and who was no doubt his godfather.

Being unacquainted with the finer points of Catholic morals, he used to lend out money at high rates of interest. He was very soon informed by Father Liu that the Church forbids such practices, and thereupon made certain restitutions, and gave up his trade in order to accompany the priest on his pastoral journeys.

Peter Nam, who is known to have been a Christian of long standing, was arrested in July 1846. As he was being taken away, his wife tried to hold him back. "How can I live without you?" she cried, seizing his arm. "It is all over," he replied, disengaging himself, "I don't think about living any more now."

Lawrence Han belonged to a noble family of Tŏk-san district. Of upright, firm, and devout character, he was instructed in the faith at the age of fourteen and showed, some years later, a really exceptional fervor. He would stay for hours on end rapt in contemplation before the crucifix, in deep contrition for his sins. On Sundays and holy days he would always go, even in bad weather, to worship and perform acts of piety and devotion at a Christian village some two or three miles from his home. At the age of twenty-one, he was married to a Christian, and went to live in the hills.

On the arrival of Bishop Imbert, he was appointed catechist. His knowledge and virtues, and the never-ceasing good examples that he gave, rendered him worthy of this position of trust, and he carried out his duties to the satisfaction of all. He lived at that time on his small estate at Eun-i in the Yang-ji district.

After the arrest of Father Kim the police decided to get hold of Thomas Lee, whom they believed to be the owner of the house where the priest had been living. They arrested one of his uncles and ordered him to reveal his nephew's whereabouts. The uncle brought them to Eun-i. All the faithful of the village had fled. Lawrence, who lived near by, was seized, insulted and beaten. The constables stripped him of his clothes, hung him from a beam, and beat him cruelly, calling upon him to apostatize and to divulge the names of the other Catholics. Upon his refusal, they tied his legs together, and passed between his feet a cord to which were tied sharp fragments of crockery, and which they pulled backward and forward so as to lacerate his flesh. Lawrence bore this torture with such patience that the executioners used to say to the converts, "If you wish to be Christians, you must show yourselves to be Christians like Han."

He was then taken to Seoul. The police offered to lend him a horse, but he firmly declined, and as his feet were so lacerated that he could not put on his shoes, he made the journey of over thirty-two miles of flinty road on his bare and bleeding feet.

These seven faithful Catholics arrested with several others during the months of June, July and August 1846 seem, to the compilers of the lists of confessors of the faith, to be the only ones deserving to be presented for the judgment of the Church.

We will now give an account of the details, scanty as they are in several cases, of their sufferings and their death.

During their imprisonment Lim had an opportunity to meet Father Andrew Kim. The sight of this young man, so full of faith and energy, endowed with a dignity before which the Christians bowed down in respect, aroused a strange feeling in Lim. Making up his mind once and for all, he exclaimed one day to his fellow-captives:

"From today on I shall practice Christianity. I have waited too long."

Father Kim explained to him that his imprisonment was a sign of God's favor, for which he should strive to respond with gratitude and faithfulness. Lim was well disposed to follow what the priest said; he began to study the prayers, and after a few days of preparation he received Baptism at the hands of the priest who gave him the name of Joseph.

After three months in prison, he learnt that the chief judge was about to summon him before the court and to condemn him to death. Radiant with joy, he spoke to his Christian fellow-prisoners in the following words:

"I hear that at today's session of the court I am to be sentenced to death. I have no merits, but if, by the especial grace of God, I may be the first to die and mount to Heaven, I will come and welcome you on your arrival there, and take you by the hand and lead you into the Kingdom of Our Father. Above all be of good heart, and take courage."

Soon afterward, seeing Peter Nam brought in torn and bleeding, he went to him and dressed his wounds. He had to undergo further interrogations and torture, but his faith and fortitude never wavered.

The four Christian women, Susanne U, Theresa Kim, Agatha Lee, and Catherine Chŭng remained in prison for more than two months.

They gave an example of patience, charity, and modesty. Theresa Kim seemed to be the bravest among them, for it was she who exhorted the others to accept the will of God with complete resignation.

All of them underwent the tortures of the robbers' plank, beating, and bone-bending. "They were questioned in every way," we read in *The Annals of the Grand Council*, "but it was never possible to wring from them a single word of apostasy."

When Peter Nam was shut up in a cell at police headquarters, one of his brothers tried unsuccessfully to visit him but managed to send him some food and clothing. "The prison food and clothes I am wearing are already too good for me, don't bring me any others," Peter told him.

The last of these captives, Lawrence Han, who had so bravely borne witness ever since his arrest, showed equal courage while being questioned under torture.

September 20, 1846, was the "Day of Glory" for these seven confessors. They were all either strangled or beaten to death. Such is the clear and definite affirmation of the juridical witnesses. Even more conclusive evidence, some consider, is that of *The Annals of the Grand Council* a translation of which follows:

"For Han I-hyŏng, the women Lee Kan-ran, U Sul-im, Kim Im-i, and Chŭng Ch'ŏl-yŏm, questioning under torture by bone-bending was repeated over and over again, but, obstinate as wood and stone, they could not be made to utter a single word of apostasy from their religion, for which reason they were beaten to death: I have the honor to inform Your Majesty of the fact."

On the subject of this kind of death a remark worthy of mention was made by Bishop Mutel to the following effect. "There is no inconsistency between what is said here and the current tradition that several of these martyrs were strangled. Once they had been condemned to be beaten to death, they would undergo a beating of atrocious severity, and if death was slow in coming the executioners would put an end to them by strangling them."

Regarding Joseph Lim and Peter Nam, *The Annals of the Grand Council* of the same date of September 20 also recorded their decease:

"Lim Ch'i-paek and Nam Kyŏng-mun have practiced the perverse religion for several years; after many applications of the bone-bending torture they resisted until death, without ever denying their religion: this is

an extremely deplorable thing, and the reason they were subjected to severe beating until they died under the blows."

As for the last moments of Joseph Lim, the *Procès Apostoliques* provide us with the following detail: "He was beaten from noon until sundown. The executioners were exhausted. As he was still breathing, he was carried back to prison and strangled."

On the following day as his two sons were bitterly mourning his death the jailors and other prisoners told them not to grieve so much, for during the previous night a mysterious light enveloped the body, and lit up the room in which it had been laid."

Impressed by this prodigy two of the guards did something which is very rarely seen in Korea: they carried away the body of this victim in a respectful manner, for "even Heaven seemed to venerate him," and buried it on a hillside about a mile from the prison.

Such were, in short, the ordeals undergone by the Bishop Laurent-Joseph-Marie Imbert, the missionaries Pierre-Philibert Maubant and Jacques-Honoré Chastan, the Korean priest Andrew Kim Tae-kŏn, and seventy-five Korean men and women, catechists and believers, with regard to whom the Church solemnly declares: that the cause of their death was imprisonment, torture, beheading or strangulation undergone for the love of God, in absolute obedience to and inviolable faith in His doctrine and precepts; that their thoughts, words and deeds reveal conclusively that their "Passion" constitutes a true martyrdom, resplendent with "nobility and courage."

In their honor, with our hearts full of holy joy, let us repeat this verse which in our Catholic Liturgy commemorates the Martyrs of the East and the West:

Poenas cucurrent fortiter,
Et sustulent viriliter,
Fundensque pro te sanguinem
Aeterna dona possident.
Who manfully their cross they bore;
And ran their race of torments sore;
For Thee they poured their blood away;
With Thee they live in endless day.

CHAPTER EIGHT

THE DEVELOPMENT OF THE CATHOLIC CHURCH
IN THE REIGN OF KING CHʻŎL-JONG (1850-1863)

55. Missionary Activities After the Persecution in the Year of 1846

At the time of the 1846 persecution there were not more than 6,000 Catholics in Korea, served by only three priests: Bishop Jean-Joseph Ferréol, Father Marie-Nicolas-Antoine Daveluy, and Father Andrew Kim Tae-kŏn. The sudden outbreak of the persecution terrified the believers, and the martyrdom of Father Kim woke memories of the horrors of the previous persecutions. Some promptly hid their sacred objects and personal property by burying them in the ground; others fled with them to the remote mountain districts, while still others entrusted them to their pagan friends for safe-keeping. It was the recently converted Catholics who were most frightened of all. Some of them abandoned their houses and land without even waiting to harvest their crops; others, who remained behind, would not dare to undress to go to bed at night, but slept fully dressed with a bundle of their most-needed possessions at their side, ready to flee at a moment's notice—often by way of holes specially made in the back walls and fences of their houses, through which they could escape at the first sound of the police pounding on the door.

By the grace of God the persecution in 1846 did not last long. For a month before Father Kim was executed, a French naval fleet had been cruising off the coast of Chʻung-chʻŏng Province. On October 14, 1846, about three months after the execution of the priest, Cho Man-yŏng, who had held the reins of government and had been the prime mover of the persecution, suddenly died. These events, and the fact that the Royal Court had grown weary of persecuting the Catholics, resulted in a period of toleration during which the reconstruction of the Church of Korea was begun.

Seven years before this persecution of 1846 the Holy See had confirmed the designation of the Blessed Virgin Mary, Mother of God, as Protectrix (Guardian) of the Korean Church. To express their gratitude to the Vatican for this mark of gracious consideration and to uphold the Vatican wishes, the Bishop and priests planned to found in Korea a branch of the "Archconfraternity of the Immaculate Heart of Mary," the center of operations of which is the Church of Our Lady of Victories in Paris. A large public gathering of Catholics was unthinkable at that time, so the ceremony was held on a reduced scale and consisted of the dedication of a devout Catholic's house in Su-ri-chʻi-kol (Sŏ-ri, Tong-myŏn, Yong-in county, Kyŏng-ki Province), to Our Lady, with only a handful of Catholics attending. The confraternity was founded and its regulations approved on November 2, 1846.

After establishing the Archconfraternity of the Immaculate Heart of Mary, Bishop Ferréol and Father Daveluy disguised themselves as usual in Korean mourners' dress and set out on a round of pastoral visitations throughout the provinces, to afford the believers the annual Sacrament of Penance and Holy Communion as prescribed by canon law. It was a deeply moving sight as the faithful risked their lives to greet their shepherd wherever his secret visitations took place. Any careless word, wrenched out by fear or torture, could become the signal for fierce and implacable searches for the missionaries, and the cause of the greatest disasters. "There we were, together," wrote Father Daveluy, "in a wretched hovel, virtually a prison. It was the month of July, the hottest time of the year. It is impossible to stay in a room constantly heated by the kitchen range. We tried several times to spend the night in the bedroom, but it was so infested with vermin that we couldn't sleep a wink: we had to sleep in the backyard. A straw mat about three feet wide was our bed for two months, day and night. It was on damp ground, and in the frequent heavy rainstorms of the season another such mat served as a screen. Food was of a quality to match the lodging. We were afraid we might fall ill, and we separated, to seek better quarters. After a few weeks, we came together again.

"Now we believe the emergency is over: our presence is not known, though perhaps suspected. However, we expect to go on our way soon, in order to complete the annual visitation of the Christians. Will we be arrested? And if we are caught, what will happen to us? Only God knows. I am in very good health. I have been making a series of fasts and abstinences which would have been beyond my endurance, even in France. It is clear then that neither leaving one's country or a change of climate is enough to kill anyone. As for me, I am getting

more and more accustomed to it: I eat rice, then rice, and then again rice. I drink all kinds of wine, made of all kinds of drugs, wine which the blind would swallow down more willingly than other people, but it doesn't matter. To tell the truth, after such a lenten fast I am tempted to believe that little by little, with patience, one could learn to live without eating. In France, this would be difficult; there's one more miracle to write down about this little known country.

"What a sweet feeling of joy came over me, when on Sundays I heard the Korean prayers of the members of our archconfraternity! I thought of the coming together of all the peoples of the world to sing this song together, each in his own language, to praise Our Lady and to pray for the conversion of sinners. May Our Blessed Mother deign to bestow on us the benefits without number that she has poured out upon so many other countries!

"But what edifies and consoles us is the eagerness of these poor people to share in the Sacraments as much as they can. This year I had to visit about five hundred Catholics, dispersed at great distances from one another. I was just setting out, when serious political troubles resulted in the roads being covered with police and spies; we had to go into hiding again, and, after waiting for a month, to postpone the visitation indefinitely. What a disappointment for these poor converts! For eight years on end they had been waiting for the Father, and at the last moment, new obstacles prevented his coming to them! A great number of them came to me where I was in hiding. Women with children at the breast, old men, young girls, all thought nothing of a four, six or even eight days' journey on foot to obtain the grace of the Sacraments, even in the dead of winter, through the mountain snows. When they arrived at my place they were tired out; often their feet were swollen, excoriated and bleeding, but that was nothing to them. Once in the presence of the Father, all their fatigue was forgotten; they fell at my feet, weeping with emotion, recovered their peace of mind, and set out on the long journey home full of joy. More than two hundred persons came in this way...."

On the whole, the fourteen years of King Ch'ŏl-jong's reign (1850-1863) were a period of tranquillity for the Catholic Church. King Ch'ŏl-jong's grandfather was the Prince Eun-ŏn whom King Sun-jo condemned to death by poisoning during the persecution of 1801. As King Ch'ŏl-jong ascended the throne during his minority, the Queen Regent Kim acted as regent during the first three years after his accession. This resulted in the downfall of the Cho clique, and the return to power of the Kim family, which had always been kindly disposed toward Catholicism. The king's grand-parents and relations who had been killed or disgraced on account of their connections with the Catholics were now rehabilitated and cleared of the charges against them. Tacit consent was also given to a certain degree of freedom for Catholics to practice their religion. This facilitated the entry of a number of French missionaries into Korea, and the number of converts to Catholicism showed a remarkable and steady increase. A Korean priest, Father Thomas Ch'oe, who had been ordained at Shanghai in 1849, returned to Korea in the same year. The French priests who arrived later were the following:

Father Ambroise Maistre	1852
Father François-Stanislas Jansou	1854
Bishop Siméon-François Berneux	1856
Father Charles-Antoine Pourthié	1856
Father Michel-Alexandre Petit-nicolas	1856
Father Stanislas Féron	1857
Father Félix-Clair Ridel	1861
Father Alphonse-Nicolas Calais	1861
Father Jean-Marie Landre	1861
Father Pierre-Marie Joanno	1861
Father Pierre Aumaître	1863

Reviewing the various ways in which these priests managed to effect their entry into Korea, the first thing we notice is the difficulty and opposition that they had to overcome. An outstanding example is that of Father Maistre who succeeded only after ten years of frustrated attempts. These priests all took the sea route first used by Father Andrew Kim.

56. Father Thomas Ch'oe Yang-ŏp

Father Thomas Ch'oe was born in Ch'ŏng-yang, Ch'ung-ch'ŏng Province and grew up in Kwa-ch'ŏn, Kyŏng-ki Province. He graduated from the seminary in Macao together with Father Andrew Kim. In February 1842 he tried to return to his country but without success. He joined Father Maistre, who was appointed to serve in the Korean Vicariate Apostolic; he made another attempt in 1846 by way of the Tumen River, but failed and decided to return to Hongkong. On July 28, 1847 he took passage on a merchant vessel leaving for his home country and arrived at a secluded island off the shore near Kun-san in Chŏl-la Province on August 10. Unfortunately the ship ran aground and he was delayed there forty days, until a rescue ship arrived and took him to Shanghai. There he found a Chinese junk, which brought him as far as Paek-ryŏng Island, Hwang-hae Province, after an arduous and stormy voyage. Here he sought in vain for a Catholic boatman to carry him to the mainland, and was forced to take the junkmaster's advice and return to Shanghai once again. Dejected at the outcome of his efforts he wrote to the then dean of the Theological Seminary of the *Société des Missions-Étrangères de Paris*, a letter from which we transcribe the following passage:

"What we are now suffering is a small price to pay for the graces of the divine mercy. How many saints have offered fervent prayers to God, made great sacrifices and undergone severe self-discipline for ten, twenty, thirty and forty years, for the conversion of one sinner or to obtain some particular grace! When I contemplate their examples, I no longer know what it is that keeps me going. Perhaps it is due to my neglect to pray for divine aid; it is due to my innumerable sins, and my too great confidence in mere human ability that God has not answered your prayers on my behalf;

I myself am the obstacle to the divine mercy. O my all-loving Lord and God, cast me into the depths of the sea if it is I who am the cause of Thy wrath, and have pity on Your faithful flock. May Thy thrice-holy will be done upon me, by me, and with me!"

Shortly after Thomas wrote these lines, he was ordained priest. His ordination took place on Quasimodo Sunday (Low Sunday) in the year 1849 at Shanghai. It was Bishop Maresca, Vicar Apostolic of the mission in Kiangnan, who performed the laying-on of hands. Now fully qualified for missionary work in his motherland, he set out for Liaotung in the month of May to make a new attempt. He spent seven months in this province under the orders of Father Berneux, coadjutor bishop of Manchuria, in visiting the sick, giving instruction on Sundays and holy days, catechizing the children and administering several neighboring Christian communities. Thus he trained himself in his holy office and acquired experience day by day. Father Maistre also arrived in Liaotung on November 3, 1849, to accompany him.

Couriers sent by Bishop Ferréol, however, warned him that it was still extremely imprudent for a foreigner to attempt to enter Korea by land. Father Ch'oe accordingly set off alone. He crossed the border, at Pienmen by the end of the year and, after an absence abroad of thirteen years, arrived safely in his homeland at the age of twenty-nine.

He began by touring the Provinces of Chŏl-la and Kyŏng-sang, preaching the Gospel with all the fervor and ardent faith of a devout and energetic young priest.

He translated the catechism of Christian doctrine into Korean, and from 1855 he undertook the great responsibility of teaching the theological students. He then took the Province of Ch'ung-ch'ŏng as his next missionary field. Soon the number of Catholics in the district rose to more than four thousands. In addition to this he went on a nationwide survey, collecting data on the martyrs killed in the persecution of 1839, which were later incorporated in *"Biographies of Martyrs Who Gave Their Life for the Faith in Korea During the Persecutions of 1839 and 1846, Compiled by Charles Hyŭn and Thomas Lee, Translated by Deacon Thomas Ch'oe from the French Text of Bishop Berneux."* The manuscript was sent to the Vatican, and resulted in the Beatification of the Seventy-nine Korean Martyrs.

On June 10, 1861, Father Thomas Ch'oe, whose missionary work had taken him to remote and almost inaccessible mountain districts, was making a journey to Seoul to report to Bishop Berneux on his work. He had got as far as Mun-kyŏng when he fell ill, but he continued his journey as far as the ferry at Chin-ch'ŏn, in Ch'ung-ch'ŏng Province, where he died, at the age of forty-one. He was buried near the Catholic seminary in the district of Pae-ron, Che-ch'ŏn, Ch'ung-ch'ŏng Province. In a letter to the *Société des Missions-Étrangères* Bishop Berneux wrote: "Father Ch'oe was fervent in faith. He gained great merit by his missionary work, and was a most kind-hearted man. He was a great pillar of the Church, and we are all proud of him."

57. Bishop Berneux and the Expansion of Church Influence

On February 3, 1853, Bishop Ferréol died, worn out by eight arduous years of unremitting missionary activity. He was the first foreign missionary in Korea to die otherwise than a violent death. He had attained a knowledge of the Korean language and the customs of the country that would have been of inestimable value to the work of the Church if only his life could have been prolonged.

As successor to Bishop Ferréol, Monsignor Berneux was appointed Vicar Apostolic of Korea and consecrated Bishop of Capse at the Vatican on August 5, 1854, and arrived in Korea on the night of Good Friday in 1856.

Siméon-François Berneux was born on May 14, 1814, in the town of Château-du-Loir, in the diocese of Mans. His parents, named Siméon Berneux and Hélène Fossé led a life of poverty and hard work, but they were good Christians and took the greatest care to bring up their son in piety and the fear of God. In 1824 one of the curates of the parish, struck by the excellent character of the child, who expressed a strong desire to study for the priesthood, gave him some lessons in Latin and then sent him to the college at Château-du-Loir, where he distinguished himself by his successful studies and good conduct. He took his degree at the College of Mans, and terminated his studies at the Minor Seminary of Précigné. One of his classmates, Msgr. Fillion, Bishop of Mans, later rendered him this touching tribute: "If we were to tell you here all about the life of this servant of God...it would be sweet to recall all the memories of a long and precious friendship, and to recount all that he taught us: at the Minor Seminary of Précigné as a model student, by his piety, regularity, and industry; at St. Vincent, as the flower of the clerical tribe, holding rank as high in the esteem of his masters as in the affection of his classmates, none of whom was surprised to learn of his great achievements."

Berneux proceeded to the Major Seminary in 1831, but as he was too young to enter Holy Orders, and as his health had been somewhat impaired by overwork, he was employed as a private tutor, at first in the home of Father Caron, cousin of the Bishop of Mans, where he remained six months, and afterward in that of Father de la Bouillerie, where he remained for a much longer period. Regarding this stage of his career, we quote the words of the Bishop of Carcassonne, brother of Berneux's pupil: "It is above all in the home that a man reveals his true personality, and your holy missionary lived with us. Kindness, piety, gentle gaiety, friendly qualities of wit and feeling, all that serves to arouse in a child a love of learning and of prayer—that is what we admired in him. We treasure the letters he wrote to his pupil, and now that he has

won such a brilliant crown, they are no longer only a good and sweet keepsake: they are a glory. That was when I came to know him personally, a tall, slightly stooping figure, with an expression of extraordinary mildness."

Berneux re-entered the seminary at Mans in October 1834 in order to complete his studies of theology. He at once felt drawn to devote himself entirely to the glory of God and the salvation of souls. For some time he dreamed of becoming a Benedictine monk at Solesmes, but later wished to join Father Moreau, who was laying the foundations of the *Congrégation de Sainte-Croix* at Mans.① But God, who was calling him to go elsewhere, prevented him from carrying out these plans. Ordained a deacon on September 24, 1836, he was appointed assistant master of philosophy in the major seminary, and, as soon as he was old enough, was promoted to the priesthood: his ordination took place on May 20, 1837. He was professor of philosophy when in 1839 after many difficulties and solicitations, he obtained permission from his Bishop to go to the seminary of the *Société des Missions-Étrangères*, where he arrived on July 27.

The first and saddest sacrifice of his missionary life was his separation from his mother, now for five years a widow, for his departure might break her heart and endanger her life. "All my family knew my plans," he wrote on August 16 to the Abbot Nouard, his early patron and first teacher. "May the Good Lord give them, especially my poor mother, the resignation and the strength to submit to the divine will, and to me the courage to bear, without being overcome, and for His glory, the assaults that I now have to endure! My mother and my sister have been surprised at my determination, and their sorrow is extreme. When will it be over, for my mother above all? When

---

① The Congregation of the Holy Cross, a society of priests and lay Brothers under simple vows, engaged on foreign missions and in the education of youth. It was formed by the fusion of two bodies, of Brothers and priests, founded in 1820 and 1835 respectively in France. The motherhouse and chief center of activity is now at University of Notre Dame, Ind., U.S.A.

will the Holy Will of God be accomplished? I am a priest in order to work for the glory and the salvation of souls—that is my object. I hope that with the help of His grace, which will not be lacking, I shall be able to carry out my intention successfully." The same day he wrote to his beloved mother: "The Good Lord is my witness that I would be willing to give the last drop of my blood to spare you such pain. That is however a sacrifice which I cannot make, for it concerns my salvation and the will of God. But there! You will not ask it of me: loving and knowing God as you do, you would not wish me to disobey Him; you would rather see me die a thousand times than see me, unfaithful to my vocation, risk my eternal salvation. If a separation of a few years gives us such pain, how much more would we suffer if we were to be separated for all eternity?"

God was not to be outdone in generosity. He did for Berneux's mother what He always does for the fathers and mothers of missionaries who sacrifice their children for His glory: He assuaged her sorrow, and filled her with His infinitely precious grace. "Dear Mother," wrote Berneux three Months later, "it is really a joy for me to see the manifold graces which God in His mercy has bestowed upon you. See, dear Mother, this vocation to go and carry the good news of the Evangel to nations that know nothing of God; this vocation, which worldly people regard as a misfortune for you and me, is already for you a source of riches infinitely superior to those of this world. Your faith has become more lively, your trust in God is now firmer, and your love for Him more ardent; I shall never cease to thank the Good Lord for all the benefits that He has poured out upon us in such profusion and liberality; I no longer feel my heart lacerated as before, now that I know you are comforted."

Toward the end of the year Berneux was able to inform the Abbot Nouard of the good news of his call to the missions, and of his forthcoming departure. "If the persecution which has ravaged and will prob-

ably continue to ravage so fiercely, should abate in Cochin-China and Tonkin we shall be sent there to repair the damage wrought on the vineyard of the Lord by the wild boar's ferocity. If the country is still closed to us we shall go either to Tartary, or to China, or to Korea. Oh! How great is the Lord's bounty to me! It is possible, as you see, that I may soon tread that soil still wet with the blood of the martyrs, that land where everything teaches holiness. ..."

Berneux left Le Havre on February 12, 1840. His traveling companions were Father Maistre who preceded him to Korea, and Father Chamaison, of the Diocese of Montauban. The journey was unpleasant for Berneux, who suffered badly from sea-sickness for more than five weeks. The missionaries arrived at Manila on June 26, where they found Msgr. Retord, Vicar Apostolic of Tonkin, who had come to be consecrated Bishop now that the persecution had mown down all the bishops of the mission. Msgr. Retord left Manila in the beginning of August, 1840, accompanied only by a Spanish Dominican Father. The other missionaries were to follow immediately, but contrary winds, and the obstacles to trade resulting from England's Opium War with China, kept them at Manila for seventy days, and they did not arrive at Macao until the end of September. During the few weeks of his stay at the Procuration, Berneux gave lessons in theology to the students there, among whom were Andrew Kim and Francis Ch'oe. Providence had already called him to the mission of Korea.

Bishop Berneux was appointed Vicar Apostolic of Korea in 1854 and on March 26, 1856, he at last succeeded in entering the country, together with the Fathers Pourthié and Petitnicolas.

His first move was to establish a theological seminary on Mt. Pae-ron in Ch'ung-ch'ŏng Province. On March 25, 1857, he promoted Father Daveluy to the rank of coadjutor Bishop, with his Vicariate at Nae-p'o. On the following day a congress of priests was held for the first time in the history of the Church in Korea. Attending the conference were Bishop Berneux, Coadjutor Bishop Daveluy, and Fathers Maistre, Pourthié, Petitnicolas, and Thomas Ch'oe. On March 28, the last day of the meeting, Father Stanislas Féron unexpectedly appeared before them: he had taken passage from China in the boat of a Catholic, and had just landed in Korea. Now the Korean Church possessed a Bishop, a Coadjutor Bishop, four French priests and one Korean priest, and was able to make steady progress with marvelous success. On November 23, 1857, Bishop Berneux wrote to the Prefect of the Sacred Congregation for the Propagation of the Faith as follows:

"Father Féron arrived unexpectedly in Korea, under divine guidance, three days after our conference, which we had convened in order to lead our priests and their flock toward the good, and to enable them to harvest an abundant crop of souls. . . . During the early period of the history of the Church in Korea there were no foreign priests, and the Church was established by Korean laymen themselves, without priestly aid. They were sincere and earnest in their faith, and were able to survive a lengthy series of cruel persecutions. Now their Church is making steady growth. Trusting in the benevolence of divine Providence, and in the far-reaching moral influence of Bishop Daveluy and his five priests, I look forward with confidence to a fruitful crop of conversions in the near future. . . .As a result of our missionary work in 1856-57, 9,981 believers received the Sacrament of Penance, 518 adults were baptized, 602 infants were baptized after recovery from illness, 804 infants were baptized *in articulo mortis*, 226 persons were confirmed, 195 couples were united in Holy Matrimony, 218 persons received the Sacrament of Extreme Unction, and 118 were prevented by circumstances from making their annual confession and communion. The total number of Catholics in Korea had now reached 15,206."

Now that the Church was making such remarkable progress, several other foreign missionaries came to work in the vineyard. Following the sea-route opened up by Father Andrew Kim, four priests, the Fathers Félix-Clair Ridel, Jean-Marie Landre, Pierre-Marie Joanno, and Alphonse Nicolas Calais, entered Korea and contributed enormously to the development of the Church. On December 20, 1857, however, the Church suffered a grievous loss in the death of Father Maistre, which took place at Hwang-mu-sil, Tŏk-san, Ch'ung-ch'ŏng Province. He had completed six years of missionary service to the Korean Church. Bishop Berneux, in a letter dated August 14, 1858, to the *Société des Missions-Étrangères de Paris* spoke of recent developments. Excerpts from his letter follow:

"...When I wrote to you last year, the outlook was unpromising; there was talk of general persecution, and already there had been some arrests. In the depth of winter, in different parts of the kingdom, Christians were seized and imprisoned. In Bishop Daveluy's district, an entire village, in order to escape pursuit, fled to the hills, abandoning their houses and lands, while neighboring families fled to an even greater distance. Large-scale persecution seemed about to begin, when all at once the prisoners were set free, without apostatizing, with one sole exception. The fugitives came down from the hills, and Bishop Daveluy, who had also taken flight, returned to his retreat. Mary, the *consolatrix* of the afflicted, had taken pity on this little band, so often and so cruelly put to the test, and the storm abated. The captives were released, whereas one of their accusers, who had presented himself before the magistrate and the royal commissioner with a list of one hundred Catholic heads of families, was bound, imprisoned and beaten unmercifully. The end of the affair amounted to a victory for us, an important victory which heartens our neophytes, and reassures the pagans, who were being held back from conversion by fear alone. The families who migrated to distant regions are now reduced to dire poverty and have many sufferings to undergo. If the number of adult Baptisms is not as great this year as it was last year, this is due to our decision to require of our catechumens a better understanding of the doctrine and a longer period of probation. But, on the other hand, the number of catechumens has almost tripled: nearly twelve hundred are inscribed on my lists. One of the highest families in the land has embraced the faith. The head of this family Kim Mun-keun, a close relative of the father-in-law of the reigning king, was baptized during the winter. Many other conversions will follow that of this family, if its members become fervent. In the town where the Japanese live, we have an able and zealous catechumen. Eight new Christian communities have been formed in Father Ch'oe's district, and seven more are announced for the coming year.

"Two years ago a Korean fishing boat was wrecked near the coast of Kwangtung, South China, during a typhoon. The crew were dying of hunger, when an English vessel hove in sight. Only one of them survived, and he was brought to Hongkong, where there was one of the Korean students. Providence made use of him to save a soul, and with that one, perhaps many others. Instructed by the student under the direction of Father Rousseille, this shipwrecked sailor was baptized. This year he returned to Korea full of joy, and has been able to meet Father Féron and Father Ch'oe, who have provided him with books and have put him in touch with me. This new Christian is a native of Che-ju Island (Quelpart Island): he is intelligent and lively, and is quite sure that his entire family, numbering about forty persons, will all be converted. May God grant that this grain of mustard seed may flourish and increase!"

We may add that Félix-Pierre (such was the name of this convert) returned to the mainland of Korea during the Christmas festivities of 1860. He had had a lot of trouble with the relatives of his traveling companions, who accused him of murdering them all. The magistrate had had the good sense to dismiss their charge. He had made some twenty converts, mostly from his own family. He had purchased a sailing boat, the crew of which were all catechumens except one, whom he hoped to win over very soon. One of them, named Peter Ko,

was baptized by Father Petitnicolas, and, with Félix-Pierre, was enroled in the work of the propagation of the faith. Bishop Berneux promised to send them a missionary as soon as possible, but was unable to keep his promise.

On a second attempt to return to the mainland they were blown off their course in a storm, and drifted to Nagasaki, where they met Bishop Petitjean and a priest, and afterward returned to Quelpart Island.

In 1866, at the height of the persecution, Félix-Pierre came to Korea once more, bringing two new converts with him, ready for Baptism.

58. Establishment of a Theological Seminary and Strengthening of the Church in the Later Years of the Reign of King Ch'ŏl-jong

It has always been the policy of the *Société des Missions-Étrangères de Paris* to train native-born priests in every country in which it engages in missionary activities. So far it had been hardly possible, with such frequent outbreaks of persecution, to do so in Korea. In the early years the only recourse at its disposal was to send the Korean students to the seminaries at Macao or Penang. Now that tacit consent to the teaching of religion was given by the government of King Ch'ŏljong, Bishop Berneux resolved to set up a theological seminary on Mt. Pae-ron, in Chech'ŏn county, Ch'ung-ch'ŏng Province, and appointed Father Daveluy dean of the institute, with Father Pourthié as teacher of some ten seminarists. In 1857, however, some pagans living in the neighborhood quarreled with Joseph Chang, the nominal proprietor of the land and buildings, and laid an information. The seminarists immediately buried their books and other objects in the ground and watched what would happen. They had almost decided to take flight when the magistrate, impressed by the purity of conduct on the part of the Catholic believers, dismissed the charge, so that they were able to continue their studies without further molestation. In this way a modern educational institution teaching Western knowledge was first set up in Korea. The site of the school in Che-ch'ŏn county was the very place where Alexander Hwang Sa-yŏng had written his famous "Silk Letter" during the persecution of 1801. Five years later Father Petitnicolas was appointed dean of the seminary.

In the years that followed, during the latter part of the reign of King Ch'ŏl-jong, Bish-op Berneux established his vicariate in Seoul with jurisdiction over the Provinces of Kyŏng-ki, Kang-won, Hwang-hae, and P'yŏng-an while Monsignor Daveluy took charge of the three southern Provinces of Ch'ung-ch'ŏng, Chŏl-la, and Kyŏng-sang. By the end of the reign the number of Catholics in Korea had mounted to more than eighteen thousand.

CHAPTER NINE

THE GREAT PERSECUTION OF 1866

59. State of the Church in the Early Years of the Reign of King Ko-jong

King Ch'ŏl-jong died on December 8, 1863, and Queen Regent Cho immediately convened a conference of elder statesmen, at which it was decided to give the succession to Lee Myŏng-pok, second son of Prince Heung-sŏn (Tae-won-kun), a boy only twelve years of age. The widowed queen was appointed regent and empowered to administer the affairs of state on behalf of the young king, who was given the royal name of Ko-jong. Actual power, however, fell into the hands of his father, Tae-won-kun, under whose rule the most horrible persecution in the history of the Korean Church took place. Before recording the six years of persecution that began in 1866, we will make a brief survey of the situation of the Catholic Church in the early years of the young King Ko-jong's reign.

Under King Ch'ŏl-jong's reign of fourteen years, during which the An-tong branch of the Kim family (which belonged to the Si clique · and maintained close and friendly relations with the Catholic Church) was in power and held the reins of office, our Church was able to make remarkable progress. On the accession of King Ko-jong there were in Korea, including Bishop Berneux, eight missionaries, who were in charge of the spiritual welfare of no fewer than twenty-three thousand believers. Among these was Martha Park, nurse of the young king,

who actually preached the Gospel in the presence of the king's mother, the Princess Min. Taking advantage of this favorable situation, the Church now published thirteen volumes of doctrinal and devotional matter in Korean, for the use of catechists and their pupils. As copies of these books passed from hand to hand throughout the country, more and more people came to believe in the Catholic religion. Bishop Berneux and his priests could travel freely throughout the countryside and were able to make visitations to the Christian communities without difficulty or danger. Non-Christians lost their former hostility and when the house of a Catholic was too small for an outstation or mass center, the pagan neighbors would willingly lend their own, while the government officials looked in the other direction. In this way the Bishop's visitations extended over a distance of 400 miles. Every day during summer five or six Catholics would come to Seoul from remote districts and return to their homes, making a round trip of about two hundred miles. On account of these extensive journeys Bishop Berneux's health gradually declined, and by 1865 he was no longer well enough to celebrate Mass. Bishop Daveluy and the six priests also became weaker, and less able to undertake strenuous journeys. The need for Korean priests became even more pressing. Bishop Berneux wrote of the theological seminary as follows:

"Our theological seminary weighs heavily

upon my mind. All of the seminarians are in poor health and should be sent home. For two years I have been trying to persuade Bishop Daveluy to establish a second seminary elsewhere, but he has been unable to select a suitable site. To the seminarist who returned from Penang four years ago, I have given the tonsure, and minor orders to Vincent Lim: the other, one of those who returned with Father Aumaître, has renounced holy orders. But these young people are feeble and sickly: I doubt whether they can live long enough to attain to the priesthood. In any case, in such a physical condition they do not give us grounds to hope for much from their ministry. It is most disheartening, for native-born priests would be infinitely more useful to us. Oh! If only I could have ten more like Father Thomas!"

At last, toward the end of May in 1865, four French priests arrived in Korea. They were the Fathers Simon-Marie-Antoine-Just Ranfer de Bretenières, Bernard-Louis Beaulieu, Pierre-Henri Dorie, and Martin-Luc Huin, all of whom were, after a sojourn of only a few months, to give their blood for Jesus Christ before having an opportunity to give their sweat, and to whom God in His infinite goodness had resolved to accord, at the very beginning, the highest reward which the missionary can desire in this world, the crown of martyrdom.

As for Prince Tae-won-kun, Bishop Daveluy wrote as follows:

"So far Prince Tae-won-kun, the father of the young king, has not bothered himself either with us or with the Christians, but how long will this state of affairs last? He has a violent and cruel nature, despising the people and placing no value on human life: if ever he attacks the religion, he will do it in a terrible manner....This will be a hard winter. The drought first of all, and then the floods, and then in autumn the violent gales have destroyed the crops and caused a shortage of food. Already many of the poor are starving. Experience teaches us that it is in times of famine that vexations and persecutions of Catholics begin to

take place. Always outlawed, we offer an easy prey to all marauders and to the pillaging hangers-on of the magistrates. Pray constantly for us...."

From the foregoing we can form an idea of the state of the Church during the two months that preceded the outbreak of the great persecution of 1866.

At the end of December 1865 a magistrate of Hwang-hae Province, a declared enemy of the Christian religion, ordered the arrest of all the Catholics in his district—it is not known for what reason. In order to force them to apostatize he tortured them so cruelly that several of them died within a few days, while others were left maimed for life. None of them having been willing to apostatize, the magistrate had them stripped of all their possessions, sold their houses and lands, and drove them out from his district naked and without any means of support, forbidding them on pain of death ever to re-enter it. Thus expelled, in the middle of a severe winter, they wandered through the neighboring districts begging their food and giving to all an admirable example of resignation.

In P'yŏng-an Province the governor had two Christians arrested, merely because they were Christians. Hearing of this, a hundred others ran to his official residence shouting "You have imprisoned two of us because they are Christians; we are too; we profess the same faith, we worship the same God; to be fair, you must imprison all of us." Fearing an uprising the governor opened the prison gates and released the detained Catholics.

The situation was much more threatening in Kyŏng-sang Province. A *yang-pan* named Hwang, in the district of Ye-ch'ŏn, who had wasted all his fortune and was now reduced to brigandage, formed a gang of robbers to pillage the Christian villages in the countryside. He knew that no one would dare complain to the authorities, for in the eyes of the latter the Christians are always in the wrong, no matter how just their cause. The Catholics defended themselves against the gang and Hwang, after being defeated once or twice, went to the magistrate, who was a friend of his, to ask for a constable to arrest a man guilty of many crimes, as he alleged, but who in reality was guilty of nothing more than being a Catholic and a fairly well-to-do one. This man, Francis Park, of the village of Pu-rŏk-i, was highly esteemed by the populace. Hwang with his companions came to the village with the constable, and, not finding Park, who had been warned and had gone away, robbed and then set fire to all the houses in the village. The alarm being given in the neighboring villages, a large number of Catholics armed with sticks came to the rescue, but it was too late. Finding nothing but smoking embers they returned to their homes, except for two, Xavier Chŭn and John Lee, who went in search of the robbers in order to rescue the kidnaped women and children, and if possible regain some of the stolen property. On finding the robbers they were astonished to see that they were accompanied by a constable. They were soon overpowered, severely beaten, and dragged off to the magistrate, who had them beaten and tortured, and then dispatched them, each with a cangue fastened round his neck, to the provincial capital of Kong-ju. It was a long and arduous journey of several days, and they suffered greatly under the brutality of the constables on the way. The governor, informed of the facts, recognized their innocence, but as they were Christians, he insisted before releasing them, that they should make the formal act of apostasy, required by law. This they stoutly refused to do, so they were put to the torture. During the interrogations that took place a few days later, Xavier and John were able to explain clearly, in the presence of a large crowd, the fundamental truths of Catholicism, the existence of God, His principal attributes, the creation, the redemption, the commandments of God, and the like. The governor wanted to save them, and earnestly pressed them to utter a single word of equivocation that might pass as an act of submission to the king. John answered calmly, on behalf

of both of them, "You may tear our four limbs from our bodies. . . .you may slice off our flesh and grind our bones to dust, and still we shall never apostatize."

"Do you speak from the depth of your heart?"

"Yes, from the depth of the heart."

"But if I have you killed, won't your parents and the other Christians take revenge on me?"

"Never!"

Thus reassured, the governor sentenced them at once, and in order to avoid tiresome formalities and long delay, he condemned them to be strangled within the prison walls.

The execution is usually carried out in the following way. A hole is made in the wall of the cell, at a height of about one foot from the floor. A running noose is put on the victim's neck, the cord is threaded through this hole, and, at a signal from within the cell, the executioner stationed outside suddenly pulls the cord with all his strength. When the victim has succumbed, the corpse is dragged out and thrown in the fields, where it remains without burial.

On the appointed day, while the final preparations were being made, the two confessors knelt for a brief space of time offering to God the sacrifice of their life, and then said to the executioner: "When you have strangled us, bury our bodies carefully, for in a few days they will be claimed, and you will be well rewarded for your pains."

Then Xavier said to John, "You are the younger, and I fear the sight of my execution may be too much for you. You go first, and I will follow you at once." Thus it was done, and a few minutes later our two martyrs reaped their heavenly reward. It was about the tenth day of the twelfth lunar month (January, 1866). As directed, the executioner interred the precious remains, and in the following month the Christians were able to redeem them and give them Christian burial.

Some months after the death of Xavier, Father Calais was passing through the village of Kŏn-a-ki to administer the Sacraments. The family of the martyr requested a Mass for the defunct, at the celebration of which the widow and the eldest son communicated. The missionary asked the second son, a little boy eight years of age, where his father was: the child, raising his hand and pointing to the sky, replied: "He is up there, in Heaven."

These martyrdoms in Provinces of Hwang-hae and Kyŏng-sang were the first of this year of 1866, ever glorious in the annals of the Korean Church. The persecution however had not yet been officially announced, and these isolated cases of violence were but the forerunners of the storm to come.

60. The Russian Invasion of Korea and the Folly of Tae-won-kun

The Russians had been steadily encroaching on Chinese territory since the end of the Anglo-Chinese War of 1839-1842, and in 1860, by a treaty with China, she came into possession of all the territory east of the Ussuri River, and all the seacoast of Asia north of Korea. In January, 1866 she invaded the northern part of Ham-kyŏng Province and demanded of the Korean government special privileges to reside and trade there. With Russian troops in occupation of the territory, the government was in great difficulty and anxiety, and it was only the Catholics, with their superior knowledge of foreign affairs gained from the Western missionaries, who were able to put forward any sensible suggestions for coping with these rapid changes taking place on the international scene.

Thomas Hong Pong-ju, the nominal proprietor of the episcopal residence, Thomas Kim Myŏn-ho, and Anthony Lee submitted a memorial to Prince Tae-won-kun making certain suggestions, as follows:

"The only way to check the Russians, we believe, is to enter into an alliance with France and Great Britain. In order to negotiate a treaty with these nations, the government of Korea should avail itself of the services of the Western bishop now residing in Korea."

The letter was delivered to the Prince Regent through Cho Ki-jin, the father-in-law of the prince's daughter. On reading the letter, the Prince tucked it away and made no comment. Thomas Kim, fearing that this silence betokened the royal anger, fled into hiding in the countryside.

Two days after his flight Martha Park, the nurse of the young king, was received in audience by the Princess Tae-won-kun, the king's mother.

"Why do you Catholics not speak out?" asked the princess. "Now the Russians are invading our country: surely your bishop could do something to help us through this crisis. Let someone write in to my husband again: I assure you it will be successful. And send for the Bishop to return to the capital at once." Martha hastened to tell Thomas Hong, who at once called in the official John Nam Chong-sam, explained the whole situation to him, and requested him to write a second letter. John Nam was a well-instructed Catholic, who had taught the Korean language to several missionaries, including Father Ridel. He was now living at the palace giving lessons in Chinese classics to the children of the court dignitaries. He consented to draw up a new request, and to present it himself to the Regent, whom he found surrounded by five or six ministers. The Regent scrutinized the letter and contented himself with a curt, "Very well. Go and speak to the minister." Next day he sent for John Nam, and talked with him at length on the subject of the Christian religion. He perceived that all was truth and beauty in this doctrine. "But," he added, "there is one thing I condemn: why do you not permit the ancestral rites?" Then, changing the subject abruptly, "Are you quite sure," he asked, "that the Bishop can prevent the Russians from taking Korea?" "Certainly, sir," answered John. "Where is he? Is he in the capital?" "No, sir, he has been gone several days. He's gone to Hwang-hae Province to visit the Christians. That's where he is." "Well now, let him know that I would like to see him."

John Nam withdrew and told several persons of the interview he had just had. The rumor that the hour of religious freedom was about to strike soon spread to every part. The Christians, transported with joy, began talking about the construction of a magnificent cathedral in Seoul, worthy of the capital of the kingdom. Thomas Kim hastened back to Seoul, and was astonished to learn that, after the Prince had expressed his desire so clearly, nobody had gone to find the Vicar Apostolic and his coadjutor bishop. They told him there were no funds for such long journeys, for they were located at places some six days' journey from the capital, Bishop Berneux at P'yŏng-san, Hwang-hae Province, and Bishop Daveluy at Nae-p'o, Ch'ung-ch'ŏng Province.

Cho Ki-jin, the father-in-law of Prince Tae-won-kun's daughter, hearing this, immediately furnished palanquins and bearers. Thomas Kim set out in search of Bishop Berneux and John Lee went to fetch Bishop Daveluy. Bishop Daveluy arrived on January 25, 1866, and Bishop Berneux four days later. On January 31, John Nam presented himself at the Un-hyŏn Palace to report their arrival to the Regent. His news was coldly received, and in an unpleasant manner the Regent demanded, "What are you still doing here in the capital at this time? Why haven't you gone down to the country to present your New Year's greetings to your father?"

"I wanted to do that," answered Nam, "but I stayed in the capital on account of this pressing matter of the...." "Yes, yes," the Regent interrupted, "I know all about that, but the matter is no longer so urgent, we will see about it later. In the meantime, off you go to your father, and give my regards to him." John's father, named Augustine Nam, was an old gentleman eighty-four years of age and an excellent Christian. Learning from his own son's mouth what was afoot, he told him:

"You have done your duty as a loyal and devoted subject of the king, but it will certainly cost you your life. When they make you sign the sentence of death, don't fail to efface any expressions in it derogatory to the Christian faith."

The reception accorded to John Nam caused some fears. Bishop Berneux, seeing that audience was being postponed on account of the impending lunar New Year's celebrations, regretted the useless interruption of his pastoral visitation, and after a few days' rest proceeded to Pu-p'yŏng and In-ch'ŏn to give the Sacraments in the Christian communities there. He was away three days, and returned on February 5. Bishop Daveluy for his part went to Nae-p'o to take up his duties again. Bishop Berneux, however, was unwilling to leave the capital, and never left his house except to visit that of Mark Chŭng (which was only five minutes' walk from his own) in order to give Confirmation and other Sacraments to several neophytes from the north.

He awaited events, and in spite of everything his heart was dominated by hope, as may be seen from the letter which he wrote to Father Féron on February 10.

61. The Progress of the Persecution of 1866

Alas! At the very moment that he was writing this letter his death, that of all his confreres, and the final suppression of Catholicism in Korea, had just been decided on. The court, as we have already remarked, was almost entirely composed of implacable enemies of the Gospel. They had already repeatedly asked in vain for edicts to be promulgated renewing the persecution. They bided their time and let no chance slip. There was no more talk of the Russians now: their warship, it was said, had left, and their troops had retired beyond the frontier. The fear they had inspired had by now almost completely vanished. On the other hand, the Korean embassy that had left for Peking in December, 1865, sent a letter on the way stating that the Chinese were putting to death all the Europeans in every part of their empire. This letter arrived at the end of January; it was like oil poured on a fire. The four ministers bitterly criticized the Regent's action regarding the Bishops. "Down with the Europeans!"

they cried, "Let us have no treaty with them, or it will mean the end of our kingdom! Death to all the Western barbarians! Death to all Christians!" The Regent reminded them of the Anglo-French expedition in China, the danger to which the country was exposed, the possible invasion of Korea, and so on. "No!" they answered, "All that is merely groundless fear! Haven't we killed several Europeans already? Did anybody try to avenge their death? What harm ever came to us as a result?" They referred to Bishop Imbert, and Fathers Maubant and Chastan, martyred in 1839, and perhaps also to the shipwrecked mariners who at various epochs in Korean history were pitilessly massacred on the coasts. Did the Regent, alone in his opinion, allow himself to be persuaded and carried away by their fanaticism? Or was he rather forced to go with the stream, for fear of losing their support and endangering his position of authority? What we know is that he sealed the death warrant of the European priests and bishops, and put in force the old laws of the kingdom against the Catholics.

Bisphop Berneux was waiting tranquilly until it should please the Regent to send for him, when, on February 14, several constables appeared at his house on two occasions, asking for contributions toward the cost of the great palace which the Regent was building. This double visit worried Thomas Hong: he began to look, without success, for some hiding place where he might conceal the money and valuables belonging to the mission. The Bishop declined to seek for a safer place to stay in. "It is I whom they are looking for," he said, "If I hide myself, they will go searching everywhere, and a general persecution will result." In the night of February 22-23 the constables came again and with the aid of a ladder climbed up on the wall and examined the whole layout of the house. This ladder was given to them by the servant of Bishop Berneux, the traitorous Lee Sŏn-i, who, not content with handing over his master into captivity, also denounced the other missionaries whose addresses he knew. At four o'clock in the afternoon of

February 23 the house was suddenly invaded by a troop of constables who, rushing straight into the Bishop's room, seized and bound him with cords. Then, seeing that he offered no resistance, they untied him again almost immediately and carried him off to the police station with a constable holding each of the sleeves of his habit. Six Christians who lived in the same house were also arrested: in the uproar and confusion, two or three managed to escape. Before going with the constables, Bishop Berneux declared to their leader that he would hold him responsible for the money that was in the house. There was in fact a fairly considerable sum, for, besides the funds that they had been collecting for some time for the building of chapels, schools, and so on, on the commencement of this liberty that had seemed so near, they had also just the received annual allowances from the Society for the the Propagation of the Faith and the Society of Holy Childhood. This official placed seals on all the doors but, four days later, the Regent had the house pillaged, and nothing was left of it but the four walls. The persecution started in the capital with the imprisonment of Peter Ch'oe Hyŏng and John Chŭn Chang-un on February 19, 1866. Bishop Berneux and Thomas Hong were arrested on February 23; two days later, Mark Chŭng Eui-pae, Father Bretnieères, and U Se-yŏng, a Catholic from P'yŏng-an Province, were arrested at Chung-rim-dong, Seoul, and also Nam Chong-sam in Ko-yang County. On the twenty-seventh Father Beaulieu was arrested in Tun-t'o-ri, Kwang-ju, Kyŏng-ki Province, where he had been engaged in missionary work, and Father Dorie in Son-kok-ri, Yong-in, Kyŏng-ki Province, the field of his intense missionary activities. They were all immediately brought to Seoul. This went on for six years, which may be divided into four periods.

The first was the persecution of the spring of 1866 which was indirectly connected with the repulse of the Russian aggressors; the second, the persecution of the autumn and winter of the same year following the arrival of the French fleet; the third was the persecution of 1868 which was touched off by the excava-

The Martyrs under the 1866 Execution

The house in Ch'akou
Where Bishop Ridel awaited for ten years to
enter Korea.

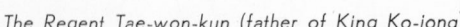

The Regent Tae-won-kun (father of King Ko-jong)

*The monument erected by the Regent Tae-
won-kun in 1871*
Bearing his edict against the Christian religion, it commemorated the expulsion of foreigners and the "Hermit Kingdom" policy,
which was demolished in 1882.

The twelve Martyrs in Korea
Of the Paris Foreign Mission Society

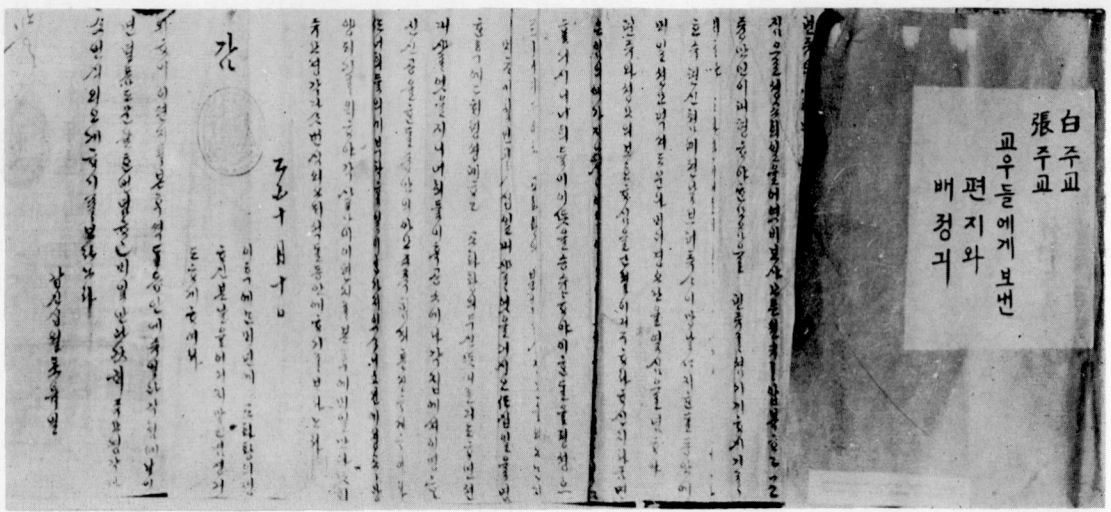

Diocesan letters
and documents
Written by the Bishops
Berneux and Blanc to
the faithful

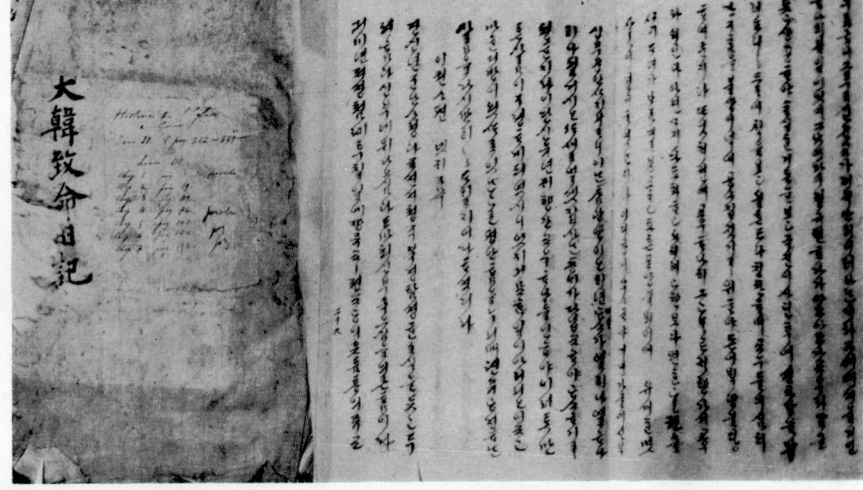

The Martyrology
of Korea
Showing *Tae-han-ch'i-myong-li-ki*, the page
referring to Father
Thomas Ch'oe Yang-ŏp

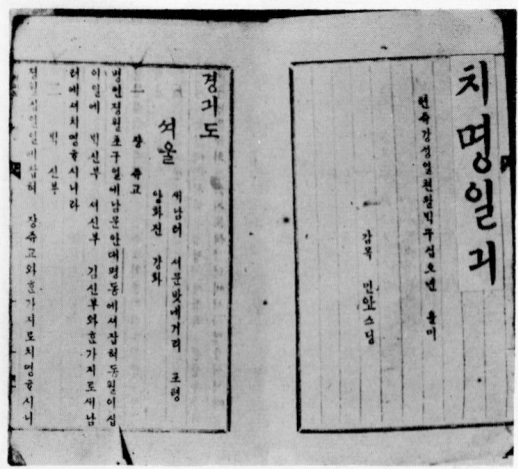

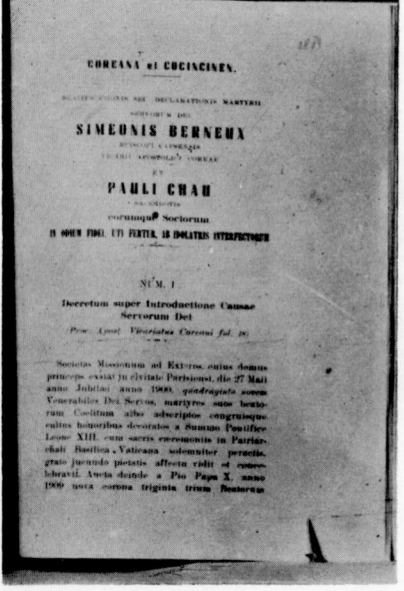

Korean version of the "Martyrology of 1866"
(left), original French text of the same (right)
Compiled by Father Chargeboeuf (877 martyrdoms are recorded)

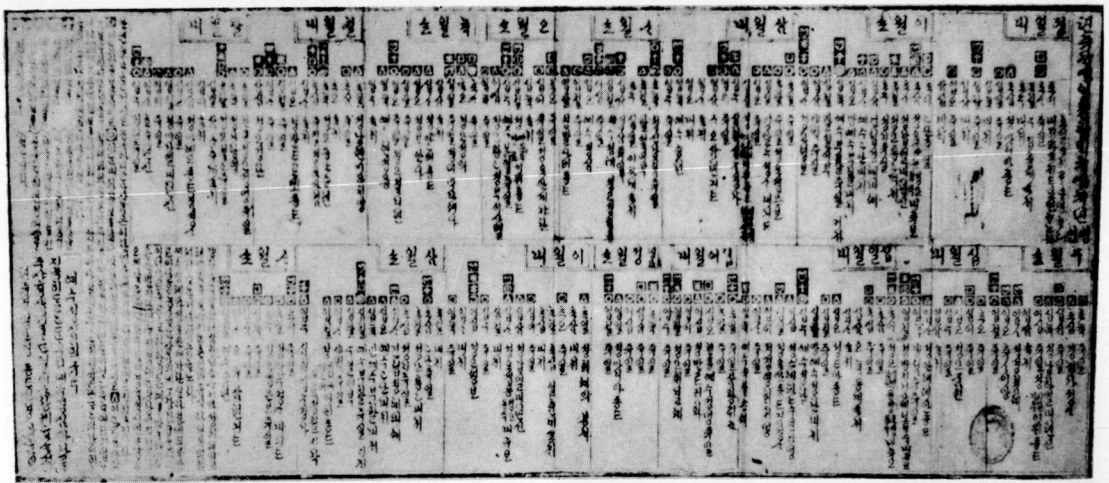

Ecclesiastical Calendar
For the year 1866

The Il-sŏng-rok (the Court
Journal)

"The Korean Grammar"
Compiled by Bishop Ridel
and other priests at
Liaotung, while awaiting
entry into Korea ↓

↑ A copy of the original
manuscript of the Ko-
rean-French Dictionary

According to an annota-
tion by Father Pichon, it
is in the handwriting of
Bishop Blanc, and was
completed on Feb. 7, 1869.

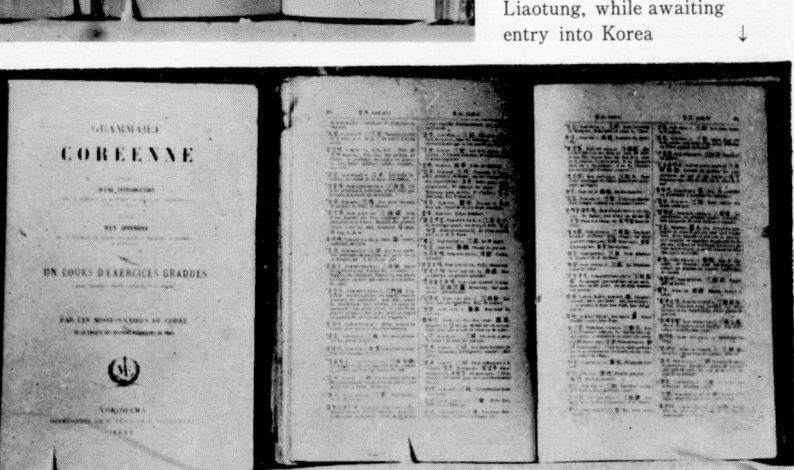

Bishop Félix-Claire Ridel, sixth Vicar Apostolic of Korea (1868-1884)

Church in Korean style at Toe-jae

Bishop Ridel's seal

The Korean-French Dictionary
Compiled by Bishop Ridel and companions while awaiting entry into Korea, printed in Japan, 1880

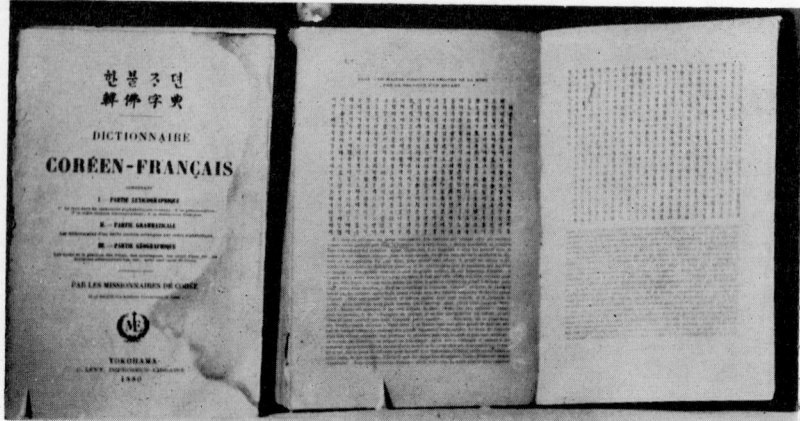

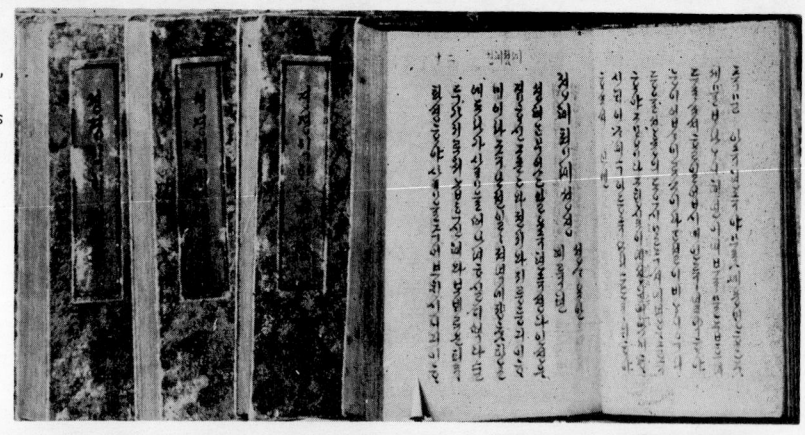

"Sŏng-kyŏng-jik-hae-kwang-ik"
(*Commentary of the Gospels and the Epistles*)
A Korean work compiled in a mountain cave during the persecution of 1866

"Sŏng-kyo-kam-ryak"
A Chinese commentary on the Old Testament. Korean ver-
↓ sion (right), published in 1886

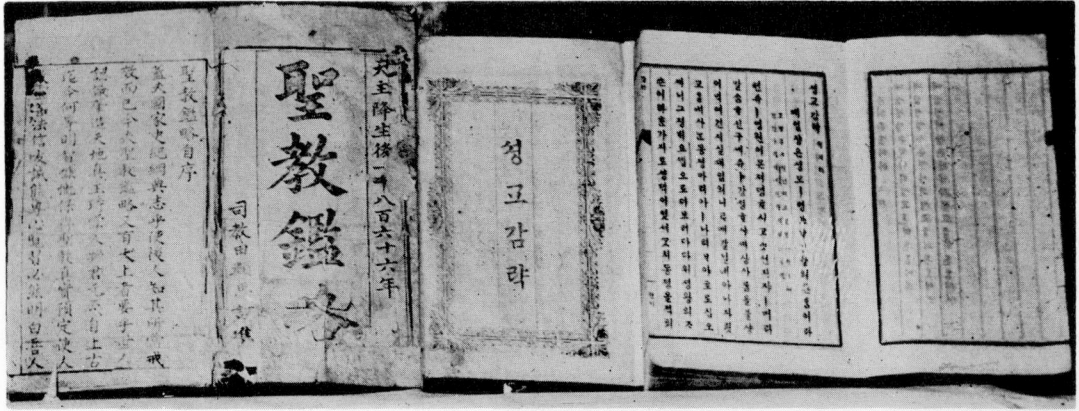

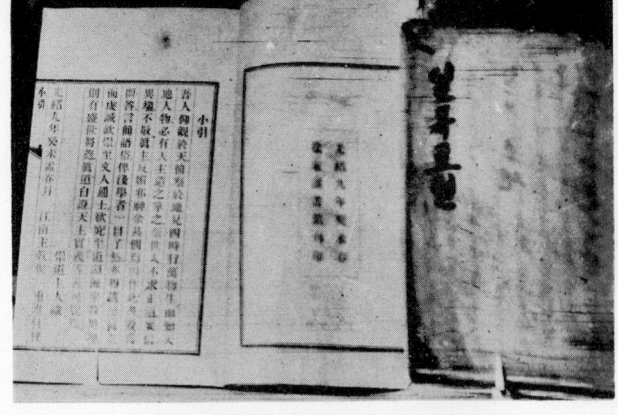

"Il-mok-yo-yŏn" (*Christianity at a Glance*)
A short exposition of Christian doctrine

"Yŏng-se-tae-eui" (*Preparation for the Sacrament of Holy Baptism*)
A Korean work by Bishop Daveluy

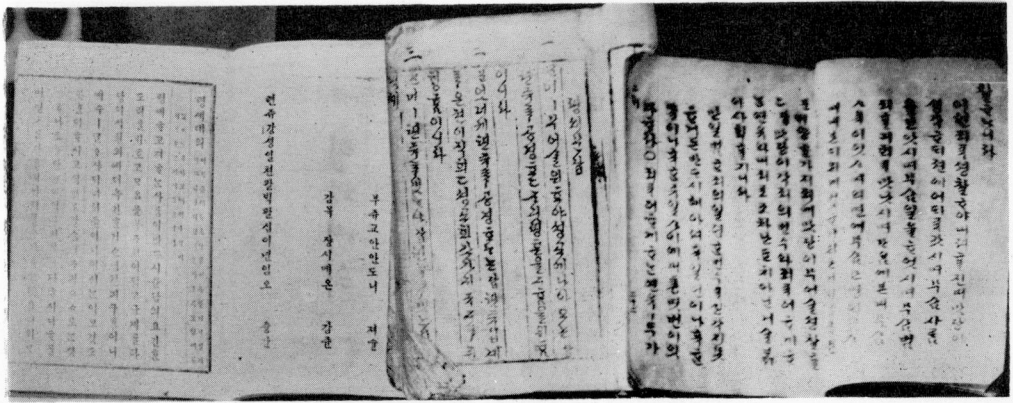

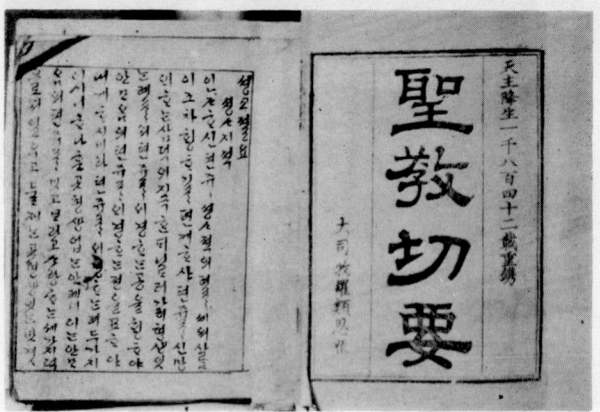

"Sheng Chiao Chieh Yao" (*Indispensable Points of the Holy Religion*)

A Catholic devotional work by Father Thomas Ortiz, in Chinese (right), 1842, and the Korean Version (left), 1837

"Sŏng-nyŏn-kwang-ik" (*Lives of All Saints Throughout the Year*)

An original text of "Sŏng-kyŏng-chik-hae-kwang-ik" by De Mailla

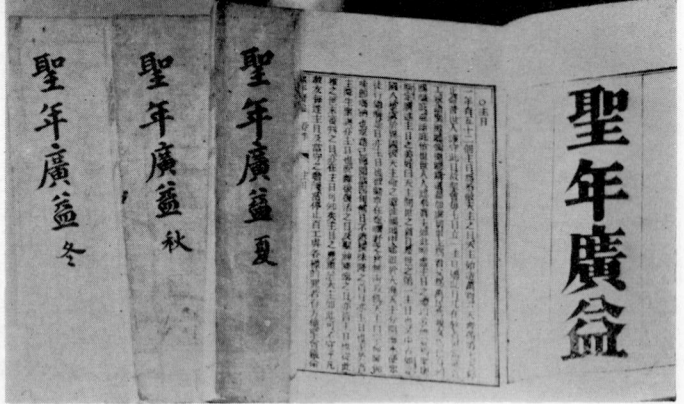

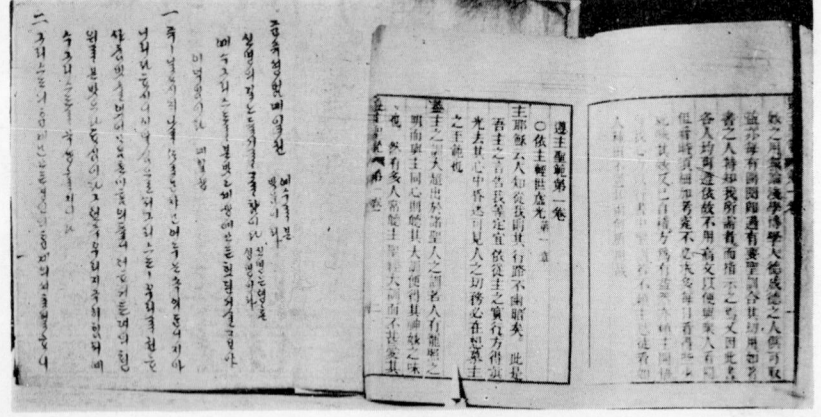

"Ch'ŏn-ju-sŏng-pŏm," a Korean version (left) of "The Imitation of Christ"

According to Father Maistre's annual letter to the Vatican for 1853, it was published in that year.

"Ch'ŏn-tang-jik-ro" (*Direct Road to Heaven*)

Korean version was published by the Korean Catholic Publication Office in 1884.

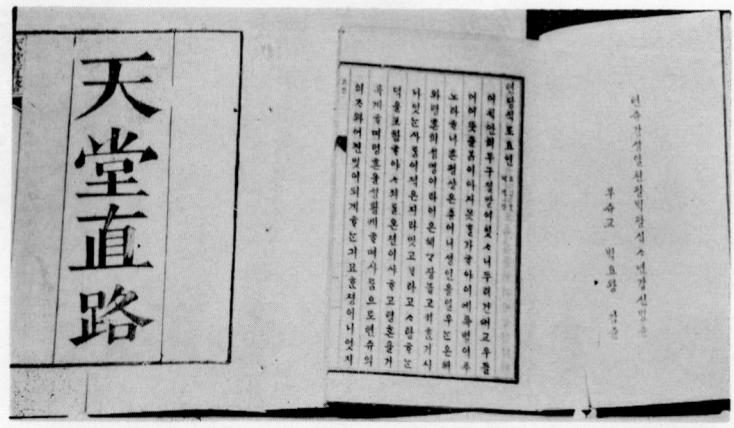

tion of Prince Nam-yŏn's grave; the fourth was the persecution of 1871 occasioned by the arrival of the fleet of the United States of America. No exact figures are available of the number of Catholics killed by Regent Tae-won-kun's orders, but his was the cruelest and most protracted of all the persecutions of Catholics in the history of Korea. Nearly four hundred Catholics were imprisoned in two police stations alone in the capital, and nearly half of them gave their lives for the faith. In view of this fact it may well be presumed that the total number of Catholics arrested and killed throughout the country must have been very large indeed.

Le Catholicisme en Corée, published by the *Société des Missions-Étrangères de Paris* (1924), the society which was in charge of missionary work in Korea, reports on the number of victims of the persecution as follows:

"By September 1868 some two thousand Catholics had already been beheaded by the persecutors. A rumor circulating in 1870 estimated that eight thousand Cathoics died in this persecution, not including those who died from exposure, starvation and other hardships while in hiding."

62. The Martyrdom of Bishop Berneux and Three Foreign Priests

Arrested and imprisoned at the second police station in Seoul with six believers, including Hong Pong-ju, on February 23, 1866, Bishop Berneux was brought before the High Court of Justice on the following day. His interrogation, in the presence of the ministers of state, began on February 26. Regent Tae-won-kun ordered the Bishop to be beaten both with the flat club and the three-edged club, until the flesh on his legs was torn to ribbons and the bones laid bare and he was at the point of death. He was finally sentenced to death on the charges of disobeying the royal decrees, refusing to abjure his faith, giving improper answers while being interrogated, and refusing to return to his own country. Capital punishment was decided on because he was the leader of the Catholics.

After four days' detention in the High Court of Justice he was taken back to the police station jail, where Fathers Bretenières, Beaulieu and Dorie had already been imprisoned.

Father Bretenières was living at the home of Mark Chŭng Eui-pae, the seventy-one-year-old catechist, in Chung-rim-dong, Seoul. The priest's servant, Paul Pʻi, a nephew of Chŭng's wife, was also his teacher of Korean.

He had made rapid progress in this language, thanks to the large number of Chinese characters that he had learnt during his stay in Liaotung, and in the months of January and February he had been able to hear nearly eighty confessions. On the same day Bishop Berneux was arrested, he had gone to a distant place, where he had heard two confessions and blessed a marriage. That evening, on his return, he heard of the Bishop's arrest. People wondered what the reason could be, for no one dreamt any more of persecution. Father Bretenières made no move to flee, but contented himself with passing on the news to Bishop Daveluy and the other confreres. On the twenty-fourth he said Mass: this was to be the last time. On the twenty-fifth his house was surrounded by constables in the early hours: Mark Chŭng was arrested and taken to police station; Paul Pʻi was absent. The missionary was not arrested: all they did was to leave a dozen constables there to keep watch on him. The next day, the twenty-sixth, he was taken to the police station. Two constables marched beside him, each holding one of his sleeves: a red cord, not used except for state criminals, was bound lightly around his arms in front of his chest. To the questions of the chief judge, he only answered in the following words:

"I came to this country to save souls. I shall die with joy." He excused himself from saying anything more on the grounds of his ignorance of the language, for although he could make himself understood by the Christians, who were accustomed to the incorrect language of the new missionaries, he was unable either to understand the pagans or to make them understand him. On leaving the police station he was taken to the High

Court of Justice and put in the same part of the building as Bishop Berneux, but in a separate cell. In accordance with custom he was subjected to four more interrogations. The Regent himself wished to ask him some questions, but he gave up the idea when he saw the difficulty he had in expressing himself. Like Bishop Berneux, Father Bretenières had repeatedly to undergo several different kinds of torture, and it is asserted that, after the Bishop's, his was the most brutal treatment. In the course of his sufferings he seemed quite impassive: with downcast eyes, he prayed, without uttering a single cry of pain.

Father Beaulieu had also made considerable progress in the Korean language, while living in a small Christian village a few leagues from the capital. He had been able to give the Sacraments to several persons and, a few days before the persecution, Bishop Berneux, considering him capable of beginning to exercise his holy ministry, had assigned him to a district where he was to make his debut. He was ready to leave: some of his new Christians had come to escort him to his post, when he learnt of the arrest of the Vicar Apostolic. He decided to wait for a while, and sent the Christians back to their homes. But some of the more lukewarm and timid among the inhabitants of the village where he lived, terrified at what was happening in the capital, begged him to take refuge elsewhere, saying that his presence there was known to too many people, and would certainly mean great trouble for everybody. He yielded to their fears and moved to a village some two miles away, at the home of a Christian named Lee. The hiding place seemed quite safe, but the missionary was betrayed, and on the morning of the twenty-seventh a band of constables came straight to Lee's house to arrest him. Public opinion has always blamed this betrayal on Father Beaulieu's servant, a man named Chang, a new Christian, baptized only two or three years earlier, who had been working for him only a few months. The fact, however, is not absolutely certain.

After having made this capture, the same constables went to the village where Father Dorie was staying, a league and a quarter from the first one. All particulars had been supplied to them, even at the capital, by the traitor Lee Sŏn-i, the servant of Bishop Berneux. Father Dorie, less proficient than his confreres in the Korean language, had accommodated himself much more easily to the customs of the country, and was very popular among the Christians. At the first news of what was happening, he ordered his servant to take flight, and waited alone in his house so as not to implicate anyone else. He was arrested at one o'clock in the afternoon of the same day, February 27.

Next day the missionaries, each carried on a stretcher or litter, their hands bound on their breast with the red cord and wearing the cap prescribed for great criminals, were taken to the capital. This cap, yellow in color, had wide cloth brims, which folded down, concealing the face and the upper part of the body so that the wearer could neither see nor be seen. This is said to be a precaution against attempts at revolt which might be provoked by the arrest of a dangerous criminal. In the presence of the judges, Fathers Beaulieu and Dorie explained in few words why they had come to Korea, and their firm resolve to die for God, excusing themselves from further response on account of their ignorance of the Korean language. Shut up for four days in the prison of the High Court of Justice, they went through the same procedures, underwent the same interrogations, and suffered the same tortures as their confreres, after which they were taken to the police station, where they met Bishop Berneux and Father Bretenières.

Who can describe the joy of the four missionaries at being together again in that filthy jail, which for them was the vestibule of Heaven? Who shall tell us of their mutual congratulations at seeing one another covered with glorious wounds received for the name of Jesus Christ? Their prayers, their hymns of joy, their transport of love as they prepared for the last sacrifice? At last came their day of triumph. On the twenty-second day of the first lunar month (March 8) they were taken to their death. An enormous crowd, eager to see the foreign priests, was assembled at the police station. Some looked at them with curiosity but the majority hurled coarse insults at them. "Do not laugh and mock at us like that," said Bishop Berneux: "You ought rather to weep. We came to bring you eternal happiness, and now, who will show you the way to Heaven? Oh, how you are to be pitied!" The confessors were each placed upon a long wooden chair, to which they were tightly bound, with their arms and legs outstretched. Each chair was then carried on the shoulders of two men by means of long poles. Above the chair, behind the head, was a signboard with the inscription: "N., rebel and recusant, condemned to death after having undergone tortures." During the journey the bearers stopped several times to rest. Then, Bishop Berneux would converse with his young confreres, or else turn his eyes to the crowd that followed them and say with a sigh "Alas! Dear God, how they are to be pitied!"

At the capital there were execution grounds in several different places. When the case was urgent or the number of victims very large, or when it was desired to keep the matter secret, the decapitation might take place even within the palace precincts, or under two bridges a few minutes' walk from the courthouse, within the city walls. But usually the condemned are taken about two miles beyond the Small West Gate, to a place called Ne-kŏ-ri, or "the crossroads." And when it is a case of high treason or the like, when it is desired to give as much publicity to the case as possible, they are taken to a place still farther away, on a wide sandy beach, by the river, near the village of Sae-nam-t'ŏ. This is where the confessors were taken.

The guard of four hundred soldiers who escorted them were ranged in a semicircle, in front of the tent of the mandarin, who also had a large escort of troops. The victims were placed on the ground, at the foot of a high flagstaff, on which hung a white flag,

and then untied from their chairs and stripped of all their clothes except a simple pair of drawers. Bishop Berneux was called first. His arms were tightly bound behind his back; an executioner folded over the upper and lower parts of each ear and passed an arrow downward through them, which remained fixed there. Two other executioners threw water over the head and face of the victim and then sprinkled powdered quicklime over them. Then they thrust wooden bars under his arms, by means of which they lifted him up, and carried him in front of the assembled people, making eight circuits of the place, each one smaller than the preceding one, so that at the end of the eighth circuit they were in the center of the ground. The victim was then made to kneel, with the head tilted forward, and with his hair tied with a cord which was held by a soldier. The six executioners, brandishing their long swords, circled round in a kind of war-dance, emitting horrible screams: each of them struck as and when he pleased. At the third blow, the head of the venerable Bishop fell to the ground and all the troops and police shouted in unison: "It is finished." The head was then taken up and in accordance with usage placed on a small stand with two sticks, and then carried to the mandarin so that he could personally verify that it was the head of the condemned person. The sticks are provided for the purpose of picking up the head and putting it down, in case the official presiding over the execution wishes to examine it at close quarters, but ordinarily they are not made use of. The head is then carried back to the trunk, and hung by the hair on a post four or five feet in height, under the signboard bearing the sentence of death.

The same procedures were repeated in the same order for each of the other missionaries. Father Bretenières came immediately after Bishop Berneux; he was followed by Father Beaulieu, and finally Father Dorie, after seeing this bloody sight enacted three times before his eyes, consummated his own martyrdom. The corpses remained exposed for three whole days, after which the pagans of Sae-nam-t'ŏ buried them together in a single grave. When an execution takes place, it is the next of kin or the friends of the victim who are responsible for the recovery of the remains; otherwise the inhabitants of whatever village the victim happened to be looking at when he died are held responsible for the burial. The Christians at the capital would have been only too glad to carry out the funeral of their shepherds by themselves, but it was absolutely impossible at that time: they could not perform this pious duty until six months later.

Bishop Berneux was nearly fifty-two years old, and had served ten years in Korea. The story of the astonishing progress of the mission during these ten years demonstrates his qualities as a vicar apostolic: a few words about his private life and his personal character will help us to know him even better. In announcing to the seminary of the *Société de Missions-Étrangères* the news of his martyrdom, Father Féron wrote:

"To an angelic piety and an ardent zeal for the salvation of souls, Bishop Berneux united a profound knowledge of theology and a rare capability in administration. His activities left him no time to rest. I have never been able to understand how he alone was able to do the work of four missionaries, how he could enter into the minutest details of matters of every kind, whether temporal or spiritual. He had a most extensive territory to look after, he carried on copious and protracted correspondence with the missionaries and the Christians; he was consulted by all, he was procurator of the mission; he gave long periods of time to prayer; nevertheless, whenever a missionary came to see him he seemed to have nothing else to do than to listen to him, to attend to his affairs, and to encourage him with his witty and friendly remarks.

"It seems that he was not naturally given either to humility or sweetness of temper. One may guess that if he had not been born a saint his strict firmness might easily have become tyranny, and his wit degenerated into sarcasm. But grace corrected everything. He

permitted himself to be contradicted upon everything; he knew how to put everyone at ease, and his letters to his missionaries always contain a word or two of tenderness and affection. His modesty he carried to a degree which might make us smile, and at which the good Bishop would be the first to smile, but without in any way diminishing it.

"As for his diet, when he was alone, rice and a few vegetables was all he took. He gave up drinking rice wine during the last years of his life. Never did meat, fish or eggs appear on his table unless he was entertaining one of us. Then he would do his best to play the host and treat his guests well and he, who would never eat bread when alone and knew that the Koreans do not make it, would take pleasure in grinding wheat into flour in a handmill, kneading the dough and baking a few loaves to present to a confrere who came to see him, or to send to the countryside for some special occasion.

"One fact will serve to show to what lengths he carried his self-denial: the cruel pains of the stone (vesical calculus) from which he habitually suffered would never make him interrupt his work until they reached such a pitch that he was lying on the floor in agony. I have seen him spend twenty-four hours on end in the confessional, and when I permitted myself to remonstrate with him, he only said, 'What do you want me to do? These pains keep me awake anyway.'"

63. The Martyrdom of John Nam Chong-sam, Thomas Hong Pong-ju, Peter Ch'oe Hyŏng and John Chŭn Chang-un

At the very moment when Bishop Berneux and his confreres were receiving the crown of martyrdom, John Nam and Thomas Hong Pong-ju were executed at "the crossroads," a smaller execution ground set up outside the Small West Gate. John, after having spent three weeks with his father, was on his way back to the capital. He was not two leagues from the city when he met a Christian named Philip Chang, who told him of the arrest of the Bishop and his missionaries, and the search which was being made for him. Seeing him change color at the news, Philip added: "I suppose that in submitting your petition to the Regent, you have made the sacrifice of your life in advance. It would be wrong for you to run away or hide: an official never hides when the constables come to arrest him." John, too upset to follow this advice, took leave of the six men who were accompanying him, tore off his official insignia, and went into hiding, two and a half leagues away, in an inn at the village of Chu-pe-tŏ-ri. The betrayer Lee Sŏn-i found out his hiding place and, with some constables, cordoned off the inn until a petty official from the capital could be sent for to effect the arrest according to the legal procedure. On March 2, John was imprisoned at the High Court of Justice. Brought before the judges he asked to be excused for running away, on the grounds that the Catholic religion does not require a believer to offer himself to be killed. He protested vigorously against the accusation of rebellion, and insisted that even the petition for which he was reproached was an act of devotion to his country and his king. For several years John, who had fallen into indifference, had not received the Sacraments, but he made reparation for his fault by a courageous affirmation of faith, and an admirable constancy under torture. He had received the Sacraments of Penance and Holy Communion at the hands of Father Petitnicolas, during his journey to Seoul.[1]

The sentence of death pronounced against Thomas Hong and John Nam was carried out on March 8. The *cortège* which was taking the Bishop and the missionaries to the execution ground had hardly started when two carts, each drawn by an ox, stopped outside the High Court of Justice prison. On each cart was a roughly-made wooden cross.

The following is the manner in which executions of this kind are carried out: the condemned man, with his feet placed on a stool, is tied to the cross with cords holding him by the arms and at the knees; his hair is lifted up and fastened by a small cord and at the top of the cross is placed the board inscribed with his sentence. As soon as the cart has passed under the Small West Gate and is outside the city walls, the stool is removed, the ox is goaded to a trot over the cobblestones and soon the unfortunate victim, already exhausted by the torture which he has undergone, is so frightfully tossed about that he loses consciousness. On arriving at the execution ground the executioners cut the ropes and let their unconscious victim fall to the ground; then they strip him naked, tie his arms behind his back, and place his head on the block. A soldier holds the head by the cord attached to the hair, and as soon as the executioner has done his work, he throws it to one side.

The bodies of John and Thomas, after having lain exposed for three days at the site of the execution, were dragged some distance to a field where they lay abandoned for fifteen days. Only then were a few brave Christians able to recover them and give them burial. John's family was treated as a family of rebels. His wife and his infant children were banished for life to separate prisons; his eldest son, aged fourteen years, and his old father were imprisoned at the police station where they were left to die of hunger. Grave doubts have arisen as to the disposition of Thomas Hong at the moment of death. It has been impossible to resolve them, in the absence of definite information. Everything leads one to believe that they are baseless, nevertheless it is our duty to mention them.[2]

The heads of John Nam and Thomas Hong were still tied to the stakes at "the crossroads" and the ground still wet with their blood, when two days later, on March 10, Peter Ch'oe and John Chŭn came to gather the palm of glory in their turn. Peter Ch'oe was one of the Christians who belonged to a good

[1] Dallet, v. ii, p. 535.

[2] Ryu Hong-ryŏl, *Han-kuk-ch'ŏn-ju-kyo-hoe-sa* (History of the Catholic Church of Korea), p. 634.

family, deserved well of the Church of Korea, by his position and above all for his devotion to the faith. His elder sister, having vowed herself to a celibate life, had died ten years before, and his younger brother Francis had been a classmate of Blessed Andrew Kim and of Father Thomas Ch'oe at Macao. His zeal and talents showed that one day he would be a worthy and holy priest, when God should call him. His elder brother was in prison for the faith at the end of 1866, when the French left Korea, and it is probable that for a long time he had followed in Peter's footsteps. When Father Maubant arrived in Korea he was struck with the enlightened piety and intelligence of Peter Ch'oe. He took him into his employ, and kept him by his side until his martyrdom. At the decline of the persecution of 1839, Peter was arrested with several other Christians, but the constables contented themselves with extorting their money. He then took service with Father Andrew Kim, went with him in the little Korean fishing boat that sailed to China to seek Bishop Ferréol and Father Daveluy, and was his faithful assistant until his martyrdom in 1846. Afterward Peter married and settled in one of the suburbs of the capital. He did a little trading, and lived in honest comfort spending his leisure hours in transcribing religious books and making rosaries. He never missed an opportunity to exhort the pagans or to teach the catechumens, and his exemplary life lent great authority to his words. Bishop Berneux cast his eyes on him for the execution of a plan he had long had in mind, to set up a printery. Peter was full of enthusiasm for the project, in spite of the danger that might arise, and during four years he distributed thousands of books among the Christians. Hence his arrest.

During the hearing of the case of Bishop Berneux, the presiding judge had been astounded at the number of religious books that the constables had confiscated, and inquired of the traitor Lee Sŏn-i where they had come from. The latter denounced Peter Ch'oe and his partner in the printery, Joseph Lim,

and at once the police were sent to arrest them. But having heard that the Bishop was to be arrested, Peter, foreseeing his own danger, had taken refuge two days before in an inn some distance away. The constables, unable to find him, cruelly maltreated his wife, but she refused to tell them anything about her husband's whereabouts. Then, although constables were on watch all night, she managed to escape, leaving only an old invalid in charge, named Matthew Lee (to whom Peter had been giving food and shelter out of charity, and of whom we shall speak later), and a young maidservant of fourteen. The constables seeing the two on their knees seized the child by the hair and with the most terrible threats forced her to lead them to the inn where Peter was hiding. They threw themselves upon him, overwhelmed him with kicks and blows of the fist, tore his hat and clothing to ribbons, and dragged him before the judge.

Joseph Lim, denounced at the same time as Peter, lived in the neighborhood. The constables could find no trace of him, for three weeks before the persecution he had sold his house and printery to John Chŭn. The latter was arrested at Joseph Lim's place and brought into court. John Chŭn, at the time of the persecution of 1839, after having been kept in prison for a whole month at the police station, had been weak enough to yield to torture and to save his life by apostasy. After he regained his liberty, the reproaches of his mother, who was a fervent Christian, and the impossibility of confessing his sin owing to the complete lack of priests in Korea, caused him to fall into deep despondency. He spent several years in this state, keeping up only the practice of certain religious observances, until the arrival of Father Andrew Kim, when he was reconverted and made a thorough general confession. The fervor of his penitence greatly edified the Christians who had been scandalized by his fall.

Peter Ch'oe and John Chŭn repeatedly underwent the customary interrogations and tortures, namely, beatings on the legs and stabbing with pointed sticks. Peter in especial had to suffer horribly. They refused to answer most of the questions which were put to them, and would reveal no names of other Christians. During their stay at the High Court of Justice, they saw Bishop Berneux several times, but it is not known whether they were able to speak to him. They were taken to execution attached to crosses in the same way as John Nam and Thomas Hong. They were beheaded in the same way, and, in compliance with the law, their bodies were left exposed at the site for three days. John's wife managed, by bribing the constables, to recover the body of her husband, and buried it near his mother's grave on the hill called No-ko-san. The body of Peter was thrown into a field to be the food of unclean beasts and birds of prey. But God watched over it, and after a few days the Christians were able to recover it and inter it in the same tomb with that of John Nam, near the scene of their final glory.

A few words now about Matthew Lee whom we left lying on the ground, almost at the point of death, in Peter Ch'oe's house. He died neither in prison nor under the sword of the executioner, yet he is nevertheless one of the primary victims of the persecution. It was he, moreover, with Francis Lee, whose martyrdom we shall recount later, who opened up the northwestern provinces of Korea to Christianity. Matthew Lee Teuk-po was of noble origin, a native of Hwang-hae, Sin-ch'ŏn district, and a scholar of great renown, well versed in Chinese literature. He taught the Chinese written language to pupils whom he prepared for the state examinations, and by this means he had acquired a small fortune.

Ambition brought him to the capital, to the 'town of delights' as the Koreans call it, but his hopes were dashed, and after having spent all his money he was, after a few months, reduced to poverty. This was what God was waiting for. While he was trying in everyway and knocking at everyone's door to find employment, he heard of the Gospel, and a few religious books chanced to fall into his hands. His naturally upright soul at once perceived the truth; he studied ardently and was soon rewarded for his efforts by the gift of the faith.

At once, like one who has found a treasure and runs to his friends crying "Rejoice with me," Matthew Lee, even before being baptized, returned to his home, some 42 leagues from the capital, begging his way along the road, and began preaching to his relatives and acquaintances. He converted a dozen of them, taught them the prayers and the catechism, and returned with them to Seoul, to receive Baptism at the hands of Bishop Berneux.

On the day of his Baptism he laid down an excessively severe rule of life for himself, from which he never afterward departed. He made the way of the Cross every day without fail; he fasted twice a week, and throughout the whole of Lent; he never ate meat, and drank wine only very seldom and very sparingly; and at all times practiced the strictest self-denial.

He had comprehended that penitence is the true way, not only to ensure one's own salvation, but to work efficiently for the salvation of others. At the capital, during the few weeks following his Baptism, this zealous neophyte converted more than ten pagans, to whom he gave the necessary instruction. On his return to his birthplace, he procured for forty more the grace of regeneration, then, in company with Francis Lee, he set out to cover the whole of the Province of Hwang-hae, and won disciples for Jesus Christ in more than ten districts where formerly there had not been a single Christian. From there he left, alone, for the Province of P'yŏng-an, the only one of the eight provinces of Korea into which the Gospel had not yet penetrated, and in which he was the first to enjoy the happiness of making a certain number of proselytes. We have recounted above how abundant the crop was which was reaped by Bishop Berneux when, three years later, he visited these provinces in which Matthew Lee had so zealously sown the seed.

Recalled to the capital later by the Vicar Apostolic, Matthew Lee was entrusted with a task as important as it was difficult; the creation, in Seoul itself, of a Christian school for the young. In a short time he succeeded in bringing together no fewer than twelve young persons, to whom he taught science and the humanities, and whose hearts and minds he trained in the study of the doctrine and the practice of religious duties. However, his health began to fail; he fell seriously ill on several occasions, and on February 19, a few days before the persecution, he had received Extreme Unction in the home of Peter Ch'oe, who supported him out of charity, for Matthew had no home of his own.

When the constables came to look for Peter, the invalid never ceased to cry out from the corner where he lay, "And I also: I am a Christian—arrest me!" "What's the poor idiot saying?" answered the constables, "In his delirium he is arguing with the members of his sect. Why bother to arrest him? Merely to have the trouble of burying him?" The next two days, he would drag himself painfully to the threshold of the front door, repeating in a plaintive voice, "Take me, I am a Christian." But there was nobody left there to pay attention to him or give him a little food; his strength, exhausted by hunger, left him entirely, and on the morning of March 1 he rendered up his soul to God. He was forty-four years old, and it had been a little more than four years since his Baptism. On the day after his death a pagan who was passing along the street saw his corpse lying there, and out of pity carried it away and gave it burial on the hill called Wa-a-ko-kae, in the place where later the remains of Bishop Berneux and the other martyrs of Sae-nam-t'ŏ were to be interred.

64. The Martyrdom of Father Pourthié, Father Petitnicolas, Mark Chŭng Euipae and Alexis U Se-yŏng

On the same day as that of the execution of Bishop Berneux and his companions, two other missionaries were brought to the capital. These were Father Pourthié and Father Petitnicolas, arrested together at the Pae-ron Seminary. On February 28 a messenger had brought them Father Bretenières' letter telling them of the Bishop's arrest, which had caused great terror among the Christians in the vi-

cinity. The missionaries, unable to believe that a persecution could begin so suddenly, decided to wait a while before leaving. Father Pourthié reassured the new Christians, and told them there was no pressing need to set about burying the sacred utensils of religion: the thick snow that covered the Pae-ron valley and the surrounding mountains seemed sufficient guarantee against an irruption of constables. Father Pourthié moreover had a long-standing chest ailment and was spitting blood, which made it impossible for him to travel. He wrote, on that very day, to one of his confreres: "I write these few lines from my sleeping mat, to which I am confined by my illness. What is to be done in these strange circumstances? If I have to go and hide in some cave in the mountains, I feel I have no strength to do so."

Next day, several constables from the capital, sent out in pursuit of John Nam, not having found him at his home, happened to spend the night at an inn only two thirds of a league from Pae-ron. There they met the local police, who were aware of the presence of the missionaries in the neighborhood, without however knowing their exact whereabouts. Their plan was soon agreed on and they set out to seize them if it were possible. On their way they saw an old woman, who ran away weeping. They realized that she was a Christian, and having beaten her with their truncheons they tied her arms behind her back and forced her to lead them to the seminary. They reached the place without anyone seeing them and giving the alarm: the two priests were arrested in their room. At first they also wanted to arrest the old catechist Joseph Chang, who was the nominal owner of the building. "What do you want with this poor old man?" said Father Pourthié to the constables, "let him die peacefully here," and he gave them the money which he happened to have. Joseph was at once released.

During the night, Father Pourthié, who had his arms tied behind his back, succeeded in creeping quietly to a corner where there were some important papers, and made signs to a Christian who was with him to hide them elsewhere, but the latter refused, out of fear, to do so, and all these papers were pillaged with the rest of the effects. The next day, March 3, at nine o'clock in the morning, the confessors were each placed on the back of an ox, the red cord was tied around their shoulders, but without binding their hands; the red cap of the state criminals was placed on their heads, and they set out on their journey to the capital. It was normally a matter of three days' travel, but Father Pourthié was so debilitated by his illness that the constables, out of consideration for his condition, consented to make the journey in shorter stages, and they took five days to get to Seoul.

On the way, the two confessors had the brim of their caps raised, and in all the villages and hamlets through which they passed an enormous crowd of pagans gathered round with eager curiosity to look at the faces and figures of the 'Western scholars.' All seemed amazed at their gaiety and the cheerfulness of their manner. At the town of Yang-ji one of the magistrate's employees looked sadly at these two young men who were being led to their death. He approched Father Petitnicolas and whispered, "Master, if you consider your soul, what you are doing is all very well, but if you think of your body, it is a deplorable thing." At these words, which sounded strange in the mouth of a pagan, the missionary, deeply moved, gripped his hand in testimony of his satisfaction, asked him who he was, and added in an affectionate tone that he hoped to meet him again one day. In another village, where they had to spend the night, a group of pagans were talking together about the Europeans who had been put to death, and particularly about the Bishop. One of them repeated, with an air of mockery, the usual calumnies against the missionaries. Father Petitnicolas drew near to them, rebuked them for thus judging and condemning, in such a reckless and unfair way, these teachers of religion who had never harmed anybody, and he was successful in making them stop their unseemly talk.

On their arrival at the capital, Fathers Pourthié and Petitnicolas were quickly brought before the presiding judge of the Second Police Station, the same judge who had interrogated their confreres. The same questions were put to them: "Your names? Your nationality? What brought you here? What have you come here to do? Do you know Bishop Chang (Bishop Berneux)? and so on. They gave answers analogous to those already given.

"What will happen if you are put to death?" was the judge's next question. "After our death," answered Father Petitnicolas, "terrible things will happen to Korea." Various witnesses have told us that Father Pourthié, owing to his illness, uttered only a very few words in the presence of the presiding judge. It was usually Father Petitnicolas who did the talking. That is probably the reason why he was beaten more often and more cruelly, and stabbed with the pointed sticks. Father Pourthié, it is said, underwent this double torture only three times. The new prisoners were excused most of the formalities required in the case of the previous confessors. They stayed at the police station, and were never sent to the High Court of Justice. Their sentence, pronounced almost at once, was carried out on the third day after their arrival. On March 11, they were taken to Sae-nam-t'ŏ, with the same ceremonies which had been performed three days earlier for the other missionaries and with a great deployment of troops: everything was done in the same way as before. Father Pourthié's head fell at the first stroke, that of Father Petitnicolas at the third.

Father Pourthié, pro-vicar of the Korean mission, spent the ten years of his apostolate at the seminary. An active ministry would have been very attractive to him, but he never hesitated to obey his bishop's wish, and sacrificed his personal tastes in order to devote himself wholeheartedly to the formation of a native-born clergy. He was also responsible for the spiritual welfare of some three or four hundred Christians living in the vicinity of the seminary, and, thanks to his zeal, this little community was one of the most edifying in the whole country. He was keen on studying the natural sciences and devoted his few leisure moments to them. He had made a series of notes on the botany, the geology, and the zoology of Korea which would have been of the utmost value to science. All this work was lost, but the most regrettable loss is that of his studies of the Korean language, for he had just completed an extensive grammar and a Latin-Chinese-Korean dictionary, the fruit of ten years' continual study and research. What his confreres admired most in Father Pourthié was his abnegation and his humility. In spite of his title of pro-vicar, he regarded himself quite sincerely as the least among the missionaries, and always behaved accordingly, without the least trace of false modesty.

Father Petitnicolas had contracted in India the illnesses that tormented the remainder of his life. In him, will power supplied what was lacking in his physical strength. The Korean language, so difficult for most people, did not seem so to him, and, thanks no doubt to his study of Indian dialects, he was, according to his colleagues, the one among them who best and most easily grasped it. He distinguished himself above all by the outstanding sagacity of his administration, and by the remarkable tact with which he overcame all difficulties. His zeal was indefatigable: long and arduous journeys over hills covered with snow, preaching, teaching the catechism, hearing the confessions of the Christians,—in these he was in his element. He had some knowledge of medicine, and a large number of the Christians, treated by him, owed their life to the medicines that he gave them. In his last years, diseases of the head, which had rendered him completely bald at the age of thirty, worsened to such a degree that he was often subject to attacks of delirium which resembled insanity. The care of souls having become an impossibility for him, Bishop Berneux sent him to help Father Pourthié in his linguistic researches. They lived together almost five years, doing the same work, caring for each other with reciprocal affection

in their frequent illnesses, and it was God's will that their friendship be consecrated by permitting that, having entered Korea together on the same day, they should also set out together on the same day, on the road to Heaven.

On arriving at the execution ground, the missionaries were joined by two Christians who gloriously followed in their footsteps: these were Mark Chŭng Eui-pae and Alexis U Se-yŏng. Mark Chŭng, of a noble family belonging to the district of Su-won, in the Province of Kyŏng-ki, was a professor of Chinese, when in 1839 he happened quite by chance to be present at the martyrdom of Bishop Imbert and the Fathers Maubant and Chastan. He was then forty-six years old, and regarded the Christian religion as a pernicious sect, justly condemned for its prohibition of the rites of sacrifice in honor of the ancestors. Nevertheless, deeply impressed by the joyful manner in which the missionaries and the Christians in all walks of life went to their death, he had the curiosity to make a study of this religion which could produce such a wonderful effect, and he bought himself some books. His naturally righteous soul soon recognized the truth: he surrendered himself, exclaiming: "I had always believed that a Christian could not possibly be a good man, but now I know that in order to be truly a good man, one must be a Christian." Bishop Ferréol, on his arrival, found in him such a lively faith and such proven virtue that he appointed him a catechist at the capital, a position which he filled, to the edification of all, until the day of his death. Bishop Berneux cherished Mark almost with veneration, and several times told his missionaries: "Look at this old man: his days are full and his ways are straight. If only I could win as good a place for myself in Heaven as he will!" His zeal was admirable: he occupied himself incessantly with the teaching of the Christians and the catechumens, with visiting the sick, and preparing them to receive the Sacraments. Always in control of himself, always with a smile on his lips, he was at all hours of the day and night at the service of those who sent for him, and no one ever saw him lose his temper or give way to anger. He was very poor, and as he was unwilling to accept anything from the Christians, his meals were more than frugal, for he had no source of income other than the work done by his wife. All the Christians loved him as a father and venerated him as a saint.

When the persecution broke out, he ordered his nephew Paul P'i to go into hiding but refused to do so himself, saying that after the arrest of the Bishop it was more necessary than ever that he should remain at his post beside Father Bretenières, and at the service of the Christians. We have spoken already of his arrest. On coming before the chief judge, he bore on his shoulders the red cord, but merely as a matter of form, for no one would tie it on, and while the two constables were holding the sleeves of his gown, the chief of the constables told them: "Let this old gentleman walk freely. Have no fear that he will escape: act merely as his escort, and don't walk too quickly." Shut up at first in a cell at the police station and then transferred to the High Court of Justice, where he remained four days, Mark had to undergo the same interrogations and the same tortures as those that we have described above. It was known that he was one of the chief leaders of the Christians, and various tortures were repeatedly employed to force him to reveal the names of his coreligionaries, but he would only give the names of persons already dead, and contented himself with repeating to the judge: "Seeing that, in your eyes, to profess Christianity is a crime worthy of death; I have committed this crime and I persist in doing so: put me to death." Sentence was pronounced and he was taken to the police station. He stayed there until March 11, and on this day had the joy of undergoing execution at Sae-nam-t'ŏ, together with Father Pourthié and Father Petitnicolas.

Mark's head did not fall until the fourth stroke of the sword. It was exposed for three days, hung up by the beard, for Mark had been bald for a long time. His wife managed to recover his precious remains later and give them honorable burial.

Alexis U, born in the district of Sŏ-heung in the Province of Hwang-hae, was the third child of a celebrated scholar who, impressed with the exceptional talent of his son, cared for his education in a special manner. He was eighteen years old and had just passed the *Chin-sa* examinations, when a catechist named John Kim spoke to him for the first time of the Christian religion, and kindled in his heart a lively desire to embrace it. Alexis at once declared to his father that he wished to proceed to the capital, in order to receive Baptism, and in spite of tears, remonstrances, and ill-treatment, he escaped from his father's house and came, with several other catechumens, to throw himself at Bishop Berneux's feet. The holy Bishop was charmed with his penetrating intelligence and his rare qualities, but, foreseeing the terrible temptations to which his faith would be submitted on the part of his family, he wished first of all to put him to the proof. He baptized all the persons who had been his traveling companions and sent them back to their homes, but he declined for the time being to baptize Alexis. The latter, bitterly disappointed, begged him with floods of tears to accord him the same grace, promising that with God's help, he would remain firm in the faith no matter what his family might do. Bishop Berneux ordered Mark Chŭng to take Alexis to live with him and observe him carefully, and, eight days later, on Mark's favorable recommendation, he baptized him. This was in 1863. "Remember," he told the neophyte when sending him back to the paternal home, "remember that you are now a child of God; take care not to become a servant of the devil; and try your hardest to get your parents to share in your joy." Alexis was very badly received by his father and his brothers. Every day he had to submit to insults, and often to blows. He bore this for several months, until, fearing his own weakness, he said to his father, "I cannot give up my faith in the religion of the Lord of Heaven. You say that I am dishonoring you by my faith in it, that I fill each moment of your life with bitterness; give me your permission to go away." "So much the better," replied his father bluntly, "and the sooner the better." Alexis returned to the capital and asked Mark Chŭng to take him into his home. He spent a whole year in Mark's house, in complete retreat, transcribing books in order to earn his keep, and never ceasing to pray to God for the conversion of his family.

His prayers were finally granted. He learnt, from two Christians of Hwang-hae Province, that his father seemed much better disposed and that he often asked for news of his son, and showed a great desire to see him again. He hastened back to him. A few days after his return his father took him aside and said to him: "You know the king and the great ones of the realm are persecuting the Christians, and that they consider them worthy of death, and that anyone who embraces this religion dishonors himself by omitting the rites of sacrifice to his ancestors; on the other hand, I believe you have sense enough not to let yourself be the dupe of any clumsy mistake, and a heart too good to allow you to deliberately bring unhappiness to your old father and all your family. Let me know the secrets of this religion; hide nothing from me." Alexis, transported with joy, began at once to explain the great Christian truths, and, the grace of God aiding him, after a few weeks his father, all his family, and several of his relatives received Baptism together. The U family was too well-known in the country to go unpunished after this conversion: they moved to the Province of P'yŏng-an, at the district of Non-sae, in order to practice their religion freely. The father of Alexis died, several months later, in an admirable state of faith.

When the persecution broke out, Alexis was arrested with sixteen other Christians. The magistrate who had just received pressing orders from the court, raged at them and treated them with the utmost rigor of the law. Alexis already had his whole body lacerated and the bones of his legs laid bare,

when at his second interrogation he had the weakness to let fall a single word of apostasy. He was immediately released. He had scarcely left the courtroom when he fell to weeping, and, hearing from the magistrate's employes the news of the arrest of Bishop Berneux and Father Bretenières, he exclaimed, "I am lost: to whom can I confess my crime now? Where can I obtain forgiveness?" Then, without a moment's delay, with the energy of sincere contrition, he had his wounds dressed, procured a horse, and rode off to the capital. "Let me go," he said to those who tried to hold him back, "let me go: perhaps it is already too late. I must confess my sin, and, at the capital, where I am well known to the Christians, I want all to be witnesses to my shame and my repentance." No sooner had he arrived at Seoul than he rushed to the house of the catechist Mark Chŭng, and found the house full of constables. In ringing words he proudly proclaimed himself a Christian. He was immediately arrested and taken to the police station, where he had the good fortune to meet Bishop Berneux. Fortified by absolution from his sin and by the exhortations of the venerable prelate who had made him a child of Jesus Christ, he bore the tortures with immovable constancy. The judge, who knew the whole story, tried over and over again to prevail upon him to recant. "A young fellow like you ought to hold on to life."—"I am holding on to it," was Alexis' naive reply. "Then live."—"I ask for nothing better."—"Yes, but to do that you have only to say one word, that word that you have already spoken once."—"Oh, no. I don't want to live at that price." Then the tortures began again more violently than ever. Alexis U was led to his death together with Mark Chŭng, immediately after Father Pourthié and Father Petitnicolas, and executed with them.

Six months later, at the beginning of September, the persecution having somewhat abated, the Christians at the capital began to consider the possibility of giving honorable burial to the martyrs of Sae-nam-t'ŏ. Always poor, they were now much poorer after the disasters of this year of terror, and they had great difficulty in finding enough money to buy coffins. Several women gave their wedding rings, their only piece of jewellery. At the appointed time, forty Christians came at night, by different roads, to the place where the martyrs had been buried. They exhumed the seven bodies, namely, those of Bishop Berneux, of the five missionaries, and of Alexis U. That of Mark Chŭng, as we have already noted, had been recovered by his wife a few days after the execution. They placed the bodies in order, one by one, each head by its trunk, and stored them for the time being out of reach of animals, and then returned to their homes, for it was nearly daybreak.

The next day but one they reassembled, bringing with them seven coffins, shrouds, holy water, and the book of prayers for the dead. They dug three wide trenches, in the form of a triangle. In the largest grave, at the head of the triangle, they placed first of all the coffin of Bishop Berneux, then at his right a little lower down, that of Father Bretenières, and on the same level with it on the Bishop's left, the coffin of Alexis U. In the right-hand grave, they deposited the remains of Fathers Pourthié and Petitnicolas, and in the one on the left, those of Fathers Beaulieu and Dorie. It seemed that the head of Father Dorie had been changed with that of Father Petitnicolas; the Christians who presided at the recognition of the remains, not having met either one or the other of these two missionaries during their lifetime, might easily have made this mistake. Near each coffin, buried in some ashes, was placed a small inverted bowl, on the bottom of which was written the name. It is there, half a league to the northeast of the capital, on the hill called Wa-a-ko-kae, that the bodies of the martyrs are lying, awaiting the day of their glorious resurrection.

65. The Martyrdom of Bishop Daveluy, Father Huin and Father Aumaître

Within a few days six missionaries had been put to death, but the rage of the persecutors was not yet sated: they wanted to put an end to the European priests. Through the denunciation of Lee Sŏn-i they had learnt that there were at least nine in Korea, and the betrayer having given the addresses where they usually lived, constables were sent out to arrest them. On the very day that Father Pourthié and Father Petitnicolas were executed at Sae-nam-t'ŏ, Bishop Daveluy was arrested in his turn. On leaving the capital, whither he had been uselessly called by the Regent, Bishop Daveluy had returned to Nae-p'o to continue his visitation to the Christian outposts in the countryside. He was still thus engaged when a letter from Father Bretenières informed him of the arrest of the Vicar Apostolic, Bishop Berneux. At first he could not believe that there would be a violent persecution, and thought that the government merely wanted to keep the Bishop and the priests in custody in order to avoid political complications with the Russians, or for some other unknown reason. Also, seeing that the constables sent in pursuit of the Europeans committed abominable acts of violence, robbing, beating, and torturing the Christians, and giving them the alternatives of death or apostasy in order to make them reveal their priests, he had for a moment the idea of giving himself up to the authorities.

He wrote to Father Féron and Father Ridel to acquaint them of his intention, without either suggesting that they should follow his example, or forbidding them to do so if they thought fit. "Do", he told them, "what the good Lord inspires you to do." On learning that Bishop Berneux was to be condemned to death he ordered a boat to be got ready, quickly wrote an account of the situation, and told several Christian seamen to put out to sea, in order to hand over the letter to the first European or Chinese ship they could find. The messengers had not yet left when he received news of the martyrdom of the Vicar Apostolic and his three companions. He wrote a second letter giving the fullest details of the danger that threatened the mission. That night the boat put out to sea, but could not find any ship and after having tacked about uselessly for a fortnight they were about to return when all at once they saw a small Chinese junk manned by smugglers who consented to forward the letters. The second letter was lost in transit, but the first eventually reached Bishop Verrolles, long after the events.

Father Aumaître was at that time in charge of the county of Su-won at Saem-kol. Rumors of the persecution having alarmed the Christians, he was obliged to discontinue his work and visit Bishop Daveluy, who lived near by, to ask him for advice and orders. Bishop Daveluy immediately summoned Father Huin, who was stationed some two leagues away, in the village of Se-kŏ-ri, and the three of them spent the day together. On parting, they told several trustworthy Christians that they entertained no hopes of escaping, for their presence was too well known, and moreover flight would be almost impossible in the flat plains of Nae-p'o. Father Aumaître went to So-teul-i, a village a league and a half away, and Father Huin returned to Se-kŏ-ri. During the next two days the villages of Kŏ-teul-i and So-teul-i were invaded and visited no fewer than seven times by bands of constables. Bishop Daveluy and Father Aumaître spent the night in a small boat, without provisions, hoping to put out to sea, but a contrary wind sprang up and for two days it was impossible to leave the shore, and finally, realizing that they were even more conspicuous by sitting in the boat than in their homes, they returned to the villages they had come from.

Bishop Daveluy lived at the house of the catechist Nicholas Sohn. A relative of the latter, who was a rather lax Catholic, wished to go to the capital in search of reliable news, and obtained from the Bishop, not without some difficulty, permission to leave and money for his traveling expenses. It was March 11. At ten o'clock in the morning he returned saying that he had met some constables who were coming to take the Europeans. Bishop Daveluy, who had no confidence in him, refused to see him. Was this man a betrayer? It is impossible to say; but a few hours after his arrival, the constables entered the village. At their head was Philip Park, a student of theology at the Pae-ron Seminary, who was at once recognized by the Christians. This unhappy young man, who, a few days earlier, had been tortured and thrown into the county prison, was he in fact playing the part of a Judas? All, and Bishop Daveluy first among them, believed it at the time. Two or three months later, Philip Park averred that they had taken him out of prison against his will, because the police did not know the way to Kŏ-teul-i, and that they had forcibly mounted him on a horse to be their guide.

However this may be, at the moment when the village was invaded, Bishop Daveluy, yielding to the insistent entreaties of the Christians, hid in a woodpile beside the basket that concealed the entrance to his chapel. The constables, ransacking every house, came to that of Nicholas Sohn, and one of them, giving a kick at the woodpile, discovered the basket. Encouraged by this first lucky strike, he gave another kick further on, and revealed the head of the Bishop. Frightened, he drew back a step, but Bishop Daveluy stood up and said, "Don't be afraid. Who are you looking for?" "The men from the West," answered the constable. "Then take me, for I am one of them." The other constables ran up, and without tying him up, they posted a guard on him in his room, although they bound the master of the house, Nicholas Sohn.

The constables, however, pressed Bishop Daveluy to reveal the hiding place of the other missionaries whom they had been sent to arrest. The prelate, convinced that repeated betrayals had destroyed all possibility of flight, and not wishing to expose the Christians to pillage, torture, and perhaps to apostasy, agreed to send for Father Huin, on the formal promise that no one would accompany the bearers of his letter. He hoped in this way to save the Christian community of Se-kŏ-ri. They gave their solemn promise to respect his wishes, but this promise was immediately broken, and from the door of his room he saw the police leave together with the two Christians he had sent. No attention was paid to his reproaches and protests.

After his interview with Bishop Daveluy and Father Aumaître, Father Huin returned to his flock and the next day continued his administration, hearing several confessions. He even intended to celebrate Holy Mass in order to distribute communion, but the wiser of the Christians prevailed upon him to move to another village. During the night he came to No-p'u-moe, Tŏk-san county, where a titled Christian named Paul Shin offered him sanctuary. There also were present several constables who, suspecting Paul of harboring a European, but not daring to violate his rights as a nobleman by forcing an entry into his house, kept up a frightful uproar outside his house all day long. One of Paul's friends, a pagan nobleman, rescued him from his embarrassment: he reprimanded the constables, slipped some money in the hands of their leaders, and managed to get rid of them. During this time Father Huin had been obliged to hide in a little closet in the wall, scarcely big enough for him to enter. He was inside it for an hour, his body doubled up, and could hardly breathe.

At nightfall he reached another village, named Soe-jae, two leagues away, and a few hours later two Christians, accompanied by five constables, entered his room. They were the messengers from Bishop Daveluy. Father Huin glanced at the letter and told them: "The Bishop was arrested this morning, and invites me to join him. That is all." The constables fired a barrage of questions at him, asking him among other matters, whether it was a long time since he had seen the other missionaries. Father Huin, convinced that Father Aumaître was already in custody, replied, "I've seen Father Oh (Aumaître)"— "Father Oh!" they answered, "Good Heavens! It looks as if there are three of them hereabouts." Father Huin remained silent. His servant, who knew all the details, then said to the constables: "The man in whose house you now find us is not a Christian. If we stay here till daybreak, this business will become public knowledge, and will cause him untold harm. Let's go at once." They agreed and at dawn on March 12, the missionary was taken to Bishop Daveluy.

On learning of the Bishop's arrest, Father Aumaître realized that he could not long escape the search that was being made throughout the neighborhood, and only tried to avoid implicating any of the Christians employed by him. Accordingly, having ascertained the route to take in order to reach Kŏ-teul-i, he took leave of them all, and set out alone. On reaching the village, he entered a Christian woman's house, and waited for Bishop Daveluy to send for him. The same morning, Bishop Daveluy, hearing the constables calling for "Father Oh" of whom Father Huin had spoken, sent him a letter telling him to give himself up. The bearers of the letter, however, had taken a different road, and had not passed him on the way. On their return, they found the three missionaries together, in the room that served as their prison.

Pleased with their success and the manner in which the missionaries had given themselves up, they did not tie them up, nor did they commit any havoc in the village, and, at their request, untied and released the Christians whom they had arrested. These were, besides Father Huin's servant, the catechist Nicholas Sohn, the seminarian Philip Park, and Luke Hwang, the servant of Bishop Daveluy. But this last refused to leave, declaring that he would follow the man who was both master and father to him.

Luke Hwang Sŏk-tu belonged to a fairly rich pagan family and had been brought up with the greatest care by his father, who counted on him to build up the family fortune. He himself recounted that at the time he would not have exchanged his prospects for an appointment to the magistracy. He did better than that. When he was nearly twenty years sof age he embraced Christianity, and won over several members of his family. His father, however, disappointed of his hopes, and frightened at the ruin that threatened him, overwhelmed him with abuse and ill-treatment. Luke bore them with admirable patience until, seeing that he could not open his mouth without provoking blasphemies on the part of his father, he resolved to take heaven by storm, and vowed not to utter another word until he had brought about the conversion of his father.

For two years he remained mute. They believed him to be ill, and dosed him with so many different kinds of medicine that they nearly killed him. But he remained steadfast and God finally granted him what he had asked for. His father became a Christian, and his conversion brought in the entire family. This took place just after the persecution of 1839. On the arrival of Bishop Ferréol, Luke devoted himself entirely to the service of the mission. Bishop Ferréol wanted to make him a priest, for his wife was willing to separate from him and live a celibate life, but as there was no properly established convent or nunnery in Korea as yet, the Bishop did not deem it opportune to give his permission.

After the death of Luke's father, his elder brother, through mismanagement, soon squandered all the family fortune, and they were reduced to poverty. Luke gave them all the property he possessed, and in an attempt to render them more substantial help, went into business, with no other capital than the goodwill of the Christians. But after several unlucky speculations, he only succeeded in ruining his partners in trade. The missionaries, fearing that their relations with him may have given him a certain standing, which Luke may have used to entrap his creditors into lending him money, closed their doors to him.

This ostracism, so to speak, lasted ten years. In 1858 Father Féron persuaded Luke to give up all his trading enterprises, and engaged him as his tutor in Chinese, after which he became, successively, catechist for Father Joanno and Bishop Berneux, and was finally assistant to Bishop Daveluy in the compilation and correction of books. He lived very frugally, and every sum that he received, whether from the missionaries or the Christians, went to pay off his debts, so that, having won the confidence of all, he even enjoyed tht respect and affection of his creditors themselves. He would not be separated from Bishop Daveluy, and indeed stayed with him until death. He was then fifty two years old.

The constables stayed two days at Kŏ-teul-i before returning to the capital. They showed themselves to be honest and considerate toward their prisoners, and seemed to listen with pleasure to the exhortations that were repeatedly addressed to them. Bishop Daveluy, pleased with their behavior, shared among them a few hundred copper coins (sapèques, Oriental coins with square hole in center) that he had in the house. Thereupon, two or three of them, who had taken part in the arrest of Bishop Berneux and had seen the large sums of money which the Regent had taken away, asked Bishop Daveluy where he kept his own funds. "All that I had," replied the prelate, "was burnt, only a few months ago, at Pang-ae-sae-kol, when my house caught fire and was burnt down." "That's right," said some of the other constables, "we heard of the conflagration in which the Bishop's house was destroyed, with everything that was in it." As some of them went on grumbling, one of their leaders cried, "Be quiet! You ought to know by now that a Christian bishop is incapable of telling a lie."

On leaving, the metropolitan constables promised to give the inhabitants of this village a document in the form of a safe-conduct, that would serve to protect them from pillage at the hands of other bands of constables, but they left without having written it, telling the provincial constables from Kong-ju to take care of the matter, but these also failed to write it. Thus this unfortunate village, one of the most important Christian communities of Korea, was later treated as a town taken by assault, and entirely ruined.

The confessors were not bound during

their journey to the capital: the red cord was laid on their shoulders, and the wide-brimmed cap placed on their heads. A holy joy shone on their faces, to the great surprise of all the pagans who flocked to see them go by. At the town of P'yŏng-t'aek, they were served with a rich and substantial meal, but it was a day of abstinence, and they would not touch it. The astonished constables asked the reason, and when they learnt that it was in obedience to the religious law, they asked to be excused for their ignorance and hastened to have Lenten dishes prepared. On their arrival at the capital the prisoners were taken to the prison at the police station.

There are no precise details extant regarding the interrogations and tortures that they had to undergo. It is known only that they were not transferred to the High Court of Justice as their predecessors were, and that when brought before the judges, Bishop Daveluy, who had achieved a mastery of the Korean language, made long and frequent speeches in defense and support of the Christian religion. Possibly for this reason, but above all no doubt because he was one of the great leaders of the Church, he had to suffer, more often and more severely than his companions, the beatings on the legs, the blows of the flat plank, and the stabbings with the pointed sticks. On the fourth day their sentence was pronounced.

But King Ko-jong was still suffering from an illness, and the palace was full of sorcerers trying to cure him with a thousand diabolical ceremonies of witchcraft, and besides, he was soon to be married. It was feared that the punishment of the Europeans might have a malign influence on the magic rites of the diviners, and that the shedding of human blood at the capital would augur ill for the royal nuptials. Orders were therefore given for the executions to take place on the naval garrison in Po-ryŏng county, Ch'ung-ch'ŏng Province, twenty-one leagues to the south of Seoul. They were taken there at once, together with another confessor, Joseph Chang, catechist of Pae-ron and Father Pourthié's landlord.

Joseph Chang Nak-so, of the village of Neung-ji-ji, in the district of Su-won, had been baptized in 1826, and had converted nearly all the members of his family. He was a pious, prudent and well-instructed Christian and Father Maubant had no sooner arrived in Korea than he hastened to appoint him a catechist, a function that he discharged until the end of his life. Four times had he been forced by the persecutions to take refuge in the hills, and to move to remote districts. He had been living at Pae-ron for twelve years when, in 1855, Father Maistre came and founded the seminary, and he was in sole charge of the first three students until the arrival of Father Pourthié in the following year. From that time on, he helped Father Pourthié in the translation of the catechism and also was catechist of the surrounding community of Christians, performing the double duty with a zeal, a patience, and a fervor beyond all praise. Father Pourthié often declared that Joseph was like his own right arm to him.

Though reduced to a state verging on poverty, he would never accept any payment for his services, and employed his spare time in manual labor to support himself and his family. We have told above how Father Pourthié, by bribing the constables, obtained Joseph's release at the time of his own arrest. But Joseph never left the house, and the following day, on the departure of the missionaries, he mounted an ox and followed them. They had gone half a league when Father Pourthié, happening to turn his head, caught sight of Joseph. He reproached the constables, and prevailed on them to send him back. Joseph obeyed in tears. He stayed five days in his house, and having nothing to eat, for the constables had stolen everything, he went to seek food at the home of a Christian in the village of No-ru-kol, two and a half leagues from Pae-ron.

The constables were in occupation: Joseph was recognized by some of them and immediately arrested. The magistrate of Che-ch'ŏn having listened to the charges against him, referred to the capital for instructions. The reply came back: "If this man is really the proprietor of the house occupied by the European priests, send him here; if not, make him apostatize and send him home." To all the questions of the magistrate Joseph replied by declaring himself a Christian and no other than the missionaries' landlord. In vain did the magistrate, touched by his venerable appearance, attempt to save him from death, trying again and again, in person and through his subordinates, to change but one word in his declaration: Joseph persisted in it. The magistrate wrote once more to the government, and four constables were sent from the capital to take the confessor there. He was imprisoned at the police station, and after undergoing the customary interrogations and tortures he was condemned to death. It was he himself, it is reported, who petitioned for and obtained the favor of being sent to his death together with Bishop Daveluy and his companions.

The five martyrs were taken to Po-ryŏng on horseback. Their legs, broken by the blows of the club, were wrapped in oiled paper tied on with scraps of cloth; on their heads were the yellow caps, and around their necks the red cord. Their hearts were overflowing with joy and several times, to the astonishment of the constables and the lookers-on, they offered up to God their fervent acts of love and thanksgiving and chanted psalms and canticles. On the evening of Good Friday they were still some distance from the execution ground. Bishop Daveluy overheard the constables planning to make a long detour so as to let them be seen in a neighboring town. "No," he cried, at once interrupting, "what you are proposing to do is quite out of the question: you will proceed straight to the execution ground, for it is tomorrow that we must die." God, who approved the pious desire of his servant to shed his blood for Jesus Christ on the very day that the Saviour shed His blood for us, gave to his words such a tone of authority that all, leaders, constables and soldiers, answered not a word,

and obeyed him exactly.

The place chosen for the execution was a sandy beach by the seaside. In addition to the customary arrangements, there were nine soldiers stationed by the magistrate's tent, with their rifles loaded and ready to fire, in case of need, at the confessors. Two hundred soldiers stood in line around the site, to keep back the crowd, which collected from every direction. A few Christians moved among the onlookers. They related that, at the last moment, the magistrate ordered the European priests to perform the "kotow" obeisance, before him, by touching the ground with their foreheads. Bishop Daveluy said that they would show their respect according to the French custom. This they did, but the magistrate, wounded in his pride, had them thrown to the ground before him. Bishop Daveluy was the first to be beheaded.

A painful scene ensued, to prolong his agony and bring it into closer resemblance to the sufferings of the Saviour. After having struck the first blow, which produced a mortal wound, the executioner refused to proceed. It was pure selfishness on the part of the wretch: the fee for his bloodthirsty work had not been agreed on, and he refused to go on with it unless it was increased. There had to be a delay while the employees of the provincial government discussed the matter. This took a long time. So possessed were the parties by their avarice that they paid no heed to their victim, whose limbs were writhing in convulsions. At last the bargain was struck, and two more saber-strokes put the martyr in possession of glory. Father Aumaître was next, and received two blows: one alone was sufficient for each of the other confessors. Prior to the execution, by a refinement of ignoble barbarity, Bishop Daveluy had been stripped completely naked. The others were allowed to wear drawers, but during the night wretches came and stole them.

The bodies lay exposed for three days, during which neither dogs nor crows, which are very numerous in this country, would dare to come near them. On the evening of the third day, the pagans of the neighborhood buried them in the sand, at the site of the execution. Several weeks later the apostate family of Luke Hwang came to exhume his remains. In the beginning of June, when the persecution had somewhat abated, several Christians went there to recover the bodies of the four other martyrs: all were intact, and only that of Father Huin bore a slight trace of corruption. They bore these precious remains to the district of Hong-san, two and a half leagues from the coast, and being without means to provide separate coffins, they made a spacious common grave, placed a thick board under each body, and buried them together.

It had been twenty-one years since Bishop Daveluy had entered Korea with Bishop Ferréol, and nine years since he had been consecrated a Coadjutor Bishop by Bishop Berneux. The latter had been put to death on March 8. Bishop Daveluy, in virtue of his title of coadjutor with future succession, had succeeded him on that day, and was Vicar Apostolic for twenty-one days. This was the fifth Bishop of Korea. We have so often had occasion to speak of this venerable prelate, to quote his letters, to describe his work on the history of the martyrs, and the compilation and correction of devotional books in the Korean language, that it is useless to return to the matter. To an ardent zeal for the salvation of souls, to an indefatigable perseverance in his work, Bishop Daveluy united his great self-denial and perfect resignation to the divine will. God, Who loves to purify and perfect His chosen ones, allowed him to be tormented not only by chronic illnesses but by violent internal pains. This final test lasted five years. He bore it with admirable patience, and availed himself of this cross to unite himself ever more closely with Jesus Christ crucified, and so deserved the honor of being put to death on the same day as his Saviour.

Father Aumaître was in the mission no longer than two and a half years, and Father Huin only eight months. In this short space of time, they had made themselves loved and esteemed by their colleagues and by the Christians, for their sincere piety, their virtues, and their eagerness in work. God, who plumbs the depths of men's heart and mind, was pleased with their good will, and found them ripe for Heaven. Father Huin said, on the way to his execution, "I don't mind dying young, nor dying by the sword, but I do deeply regret not having been able to do more for the salvation of these poor pagans."

In the month of September, 1866, a letter from Father Ridel was received at the seminary of the *Société des Missions-Étrangères*, which gave the first details of the events that we have just recounted. The candidates for the priesthood were in *villeggiatura* at the country house of the seminary at Meudon. That evening, the superior announced that in Korea, in the space of a few days, nine colleagues, two of whom were bishops and seven missionaries, had shed their blood for Jesus Christ. At this glorious news a cry of joy rose from their hearts, and at once, setting up lanterns in the branches of the great maples that surrounded the statue of the Holy Virgin, they sang a *Te Deum* as an act of thanksgiving, with the prayer, nine times repeated:

Queen of martyrs, pray for us.

What other words could more worthily celebrate such a triumph?

With what other words can we more fittingly close this account?

Yes, we praise You, O God, You Whom the army of martyrs sing in their spotless robes, You whom the Holy Catholic Church confesses and glorifies even to the ends of the earth!

Te Deum laudamus...; te martyrum candidatus laudat exercitus; te per orbem terrarum sancta confitetur Ecclesia.

66. The Martyrdom of Peter Yu Chŏng-ryul

Many Christians were sent to the provincial governor's office in P'yŏng-yang at the beginning of the first moon (about the middle of February, 1866) and being, with one exception, unable to bear the torture they gained their release by apostasy. Peter Yu Chŏng-ryul was the exception.

A monument recording the execution of this martyr by Governor Chŭng Chi-yong was erected in P'yŏng-yang in the precinct of Yŏng-myŏng-sa temple as a "memorial of the expulsion of perverse religion" and may still be seen there.

Peter Yu Chŏng-ryul was born at T'ap-hyŏn-ri (also known as Non-jae) in the district of P'yŏng-yang. He lost his parents in his childhood, and earned his living by making straw shoes. It was around 1864 that he was baptized. He had often ill-treated and beaten his wife but after his Baptism by Bishop Berneux in Seoul he would frequently beat himself with his wooden last (on which he shaped the straw shoes he made), to show his repentance for his ill-treatment of his wife, and he would go on doing this till the blood flowed.

"This is nothing," he would declare, "compared with the beatings I have inflicted on her."

Deeply moved by this proof of his sincerity, his wife also embraced the faith. Having prepared himself for martyrdom, he visited his relative's home on the second day of the first moon (February 26) to tender his New Year's greetings and said, "The village we live in is not far off, but I'm not sure whether I shall ever come back again."

He already foresaw his impending martyrdom, and was arrested that evening in the village of Ko-tun while reading the Bible with Vincent Chŭng.

Although many other Christians escaped arrest on this occasion, Peter Yu, Catechist Chŭng and four others were taken to the provincial governor's office of P'yŏng-yang the next day and put in jail in Chang-p'yŏng-ch'ŏng. One by one they underwent interrogation together with more than a hundred fellow-prisoners already imprisoned there, most of whom had the misfortune to apostatize. As Peter Yu persisted in his faith, the governor made each of the apostates beat Peter Yu three times. In this way he suffered a total of over three hundred blows.

Thus it was on the next day that he died under the torture, at the age of thirty. Chŭng Ch'ang-kyŏn, the first witness, related, "While the body was being enshrouded, it emanated a strange radiance."

The governor made the apostates throw the body into the Tae-tong River, but Peter Yu's wife bribed the magistrate to let her recover it, and, with the help of a sailor and also a relative, was able to bring the body to land, and give it burial at T'ap-hyŏn-ri.

67. The Martyrdom of Five Catholics and Persecution Throughout the Country

The persecution of 1866 since its first days raged with unparalleled severity and speed. On February 15 most of the missionaries in Korea were still counting on the liberty of religious belief; by the end of March, Christianity in Korea, crushed under a succession of unprecedented disasters, was drowning in the blood of its pastors and its leaders among the faithful. The fury of the imps of hell was unleashed, not only at the capital, but throughout the country. We have given an account of the death of the Christians who followed the missionaries to martyrdom. Here are a few details regarding five of those who, in the provinces, at the same time, imitated their constancy and shared in their triumph.

"I am sending you," wrote Father Féron, on September 25, 1866, "the following notes, unfortunately incomplete, regarding some of our martyrs:

(1) Paul Oh

"Paul Oh P'an-ji, baptized in 1857 or 1858, was of noble family but lived in great poverty at Ki-chang-kol in Chin-ch'ŏn county. Born rich, he had never troubled to study or to work, and spent his youth in idleness and dissipation, and this led to his downfall. After his conversion he bore his poverty with Christian resignation, and did his work faithfully. Arrested on March 10 or 11, 1866, by the constables of Ch'ŏng-ju, he was taken to the town prison with a young man from the same village. He had already undergone interrogation and suffered the bone-bending torture, when he saw Paul Pae brought to the prison, regarding whom I have the following details. They were interrogated together. Paul Oh P'an-ji spoke little, declared himself a Christian, refused to denounce anybody, and answered all questions about the missionaries with denials of any knowledge of them. Torture only wrung a few sighs from him: it was curtailed, because on that day the king was offering sacrifices. "While passing from the judgment-hall to the prison, one of the executioners struck him a blow on the head which drew blood. Paul merely said, 'Once I am condemned to death, let me be killed, but in the meantime what right have you to knock me about without the magistrate's orders?' These words only brought him further blows and abuse. The magistrate, however, who had no wish to put the three prisoners to death, did all he could to wring from them a formal act of apostasy. One of his secretaries, sent for this purpose, asked Paul the meaning of the words 'Jesus, Mary,' which he had uttered while undergoing torture. 'That,' replied Paul, 'is our way of calling upon God for help.' The other two prisoners had the misfortune to weaken: they were released. Paul Oh P'an-ji was strangled on Monday or Tuesday of Holy Week (March 26 or 27) at the age of more than fifty. His remains, recovered by the Christians, were interred in a piece of land belonging to his family."

(2) Hyacinth Hong

"Hyacinth Hong lived at Nong-ju in the county of Chik-san. He was sixty years old and had been blind for five years. On March 15, 1866, the constables entered his house. His first words were: 'I am a Christian.' 'But how could you learn about Christianity, seeing that you are blind? Who taught you?' 'I imbibed Christianity with my mother's milk, and it was upon her knees that I learnt the true doctrine. Moreover, I have only been blind for the last

five years.' 'If you don't apostatize, we shall tie you up, and you will be killed.' 'I cannot deny my God, and I have long desired to die for Him.' He was taken to Chik-san, where he declared himself a Christian, and refused to apostatize.

"Barbara Yun, his fellow-prisoner, told that Hyacinth was put to the torture only on one occasion, but with atrocious barbarity. After having stripped him, and tied him hand and foot, and by the hair, they beat him with extreme violence, after which he was sent back to prison with a heavy cangue fastened round his neck; he was left seven days in this state. The magistrate sent him some food, but as there were fifteen Christians in the prison, men, women, and children, to whom this favor was not accorded, and who were dying of hunger, Hyacinth shared it among them, taking hardly any of it himself. Despairing of being able to overcome his resolution, the magistrate of Chik-san sent him to Kong-ju, to the governor of the province. On the last day of the journey the constables, alleging lack of funds, left him without food, and, during the next five days, that is to say, until his death, no one even gave him a drop of water to drink.

"At the final interrogation the governor had him put to the torture. Eight executioners (four on each side) beat him without intermission, stopping only long enough for the governor to ask him this question, 'Are you still a Christian?' 'Yes,' replied the martyr. And no one heard a single groan from him. The torture was repeated on three different occasions: the answer was always the same, though from time to time it had to be interrupted because the violence of the blows made the victim lose consciousness.

"We may add that on the preceding night they had already tortured him, by pulling his head down almost to his feet in the prison chains, while his arms were still extended in the form of a cross. This torture was so painful that the victim called upon them to desist, but the constables refused to do so unless he would cease declaring that he was a Christian. Hyacinth Hong was strangled on Monday of Holy Week, March 26. His son, who had taken flight, preferred living in poverty to running the risk of apostasy in claiming his confiscated property."

(3) Thomas Song

Thomas Song known as Ch'a-sŏn, of Kŏteul-i, in the plain of Nae-p'o, Ch'ung-ch'ŏng Province, aged twenty-eight, was faithful to his duties, but of a somewhat lethargic temperament, and had given no signs of the heroism which he showed on his arrest. It took place as follows. Four or five days after the arrest of Bishop Daveluy, the constables of Tŏk-san had pillaged the houses of several Christians in Kŏ-teul-i. The magistrate had promised to make restitution of the stolen property, and Thomas was appointed to reclaim it. But, instead of keeping his promise, the magistrate interrogated him on the subject of his religious beliefs. Thomas boldly confessed them and was thrown into prison. There he was treated with such brutality by the constables that when he was sent to the provincial governor at Kongju, he had to be carried. Every day they stripped and bound him, and beat him with a club.

"Once, having hung him up by the feet, these wretches smeared dung all over his face. While undergoing this vile outrage, Thomas merely said, 'Good!' 'Why is it good?' asked the executioners. 'Because it is what a sinner deserves who has made the Lord Jesus Christ shed His blood for him. I am thirsty: what you have done is some expiation for the gall and vinegar which my sins obliged Him to drink.' On another occasion they left him hanging for such a long time that his fellow-prisoners, moved by pity, untied him, at the risk of being beaten themselves. They wanted to massage his swollen limbs and to press out the putrid blood, but he would not allow it. 'It is not worth-while,' he said, 'for that matter, Jesus and Mary have already come and laid their hands on my wounds.' And it is in fact averred that on the following day the wounds were healed and cicatrized.

"It was Lent, and Thomas scrupulously observed all the fasts and abstinences of the Church, fasts and abstinences the rigor of which was heightened both by his sufferings and by the inadequacy of the food supplied to the prisoners. Even so, nothing could make him abandon any of his customary pious practices. His uncle, an apostate and a delator, wrote to him advising him to apostatize: he rejected the letter indignantly, an act which resulted in intensified ill-treatment.

"Touched with feelings of regret at having allowed things to go to such an extreme, the magistrate wished to save Thomas Song, but as he could get from him no word or deed that would permit him to release his victim on the grounds of apostasy, he resolved to resort to a strange expedient: this was, to tell Thomas that if he did not with his own teeth bite out a bit of his own flesh, he would regard him as having obeyed his order to apostatize, and would release him. 'When I declare that I will never apostatize why do you try to pass me off as an apostate? My body belongs to God, and I am forbidden to mutilate it, but a magistrate has the authority of a father over me, and since he insists on this proof of my attachment to the faith, here you are!' and with a snap of his teeth, he tore out a morsel of flesh from each arm.

"These lesions must have been most painful, for, after his death, they were found to be dreadfully poisonous. He arrived at Kong-ju on Good Friday or Holy Saturday, and was at once brought before the governor, who put him to the question three times. He was removed unconscious, and on the same day was strangled in prison, as also were two Christian women, regarding whom I have for the time being insufficient information. Their bodies have been reverently recovered."

A letter from Father Calais gives some information about the women referred to here:

(4) Susanna Kim and Widow Kim

One of them was named Susanna Kim, of an old Christian family of Chuk-san in Kyŏng-ki, and wife of John Sim. The other, whose name is not known, was the widow of a certain Kim. When the persecution broke out, Susanna, believing herself to be too conspicuous in the village where she lived with her husband, withdrew with her three children, the youngest of which was only two months old, to stay with her brother and her aged mother in the village of Hae-sa-dong, Ch'ŏn-an, Ch'ung-ch'ŏng Province. It was there that she was arrested by the constables with her mother and the widow Kim. Some of the other Christians arrested at the same time apostatized, and were at once released. The three women were taken to the mandarin, but, on the way, the constables, seeing that the mother was not strong enough to keep up with them, got rid of her by sending her home. The two prisoners were brought before the mandarin of Ch'ŏn-an, who, moved to pity at the sight of Susanna's two babies, tried by coaxing and by threats to bring these brave Christian women to apostasy, without however putting them to the torture. Finally he had them sent to Kong-ju, the provincial capital. This meant sending them to their death. Susanna knew this, and entrusted her children to a Christian, to take back to their father. At Kong-ju the two women had repeatedly to undergo such cruel torture that their legs and several of their ribs were broken, but they uttered no cry of complaint. They were carried back to prison, and were strangled on the same day as Thomas Song. Their bodies, thrown into a field, were later buried by Christians in a common grave.

68. The Martyrdom of Peter Cho Hwa-sŏ and Six Others in Chŏn-ju

The Chŏn-ju governor's office organized its constables into two groups, and, sending one to Sŏng-chi-dong and the other to Tae-sŏng-dong, arrested the following seven Christians on December 5.

Peter Cho and his son Joseph, Peter Lee Myŏng-sŏ, Bartholomew Chŭng Mun-ho, Peter Sohn Sŏn-ji, Peter Han Won-sŏ and Peter Chŭng Won-ji.

All except the boy Joseph were beheaded on December 13; in obedience to the ancient law forbidding the simultaneous execution of parent and child, that of Joseph was put off until December 18.

Here are some accounts of their glorious martyrdom:

(1) Peter Cho Hwa-sŏ

Also known as Pyŏng-eui, he was born in Su-won and the son of Andrew Cho who was martyred in 1839.

He lived at Sin-ch'ang in Ch'ung-ch'ŏng Province and moved to Sŏng-chi-dong in the district of So-yang in Chŏn-ju. He served many years as a servant for Father Thomas Ch'oe Yang-ŏp. He was arrested at his house on December 5, 1866, together with his son Joseph Cho Yun-ho, Peter Lee Myŏng-sŏ and Peter Chŭng Won-ji. He put up for a night at a roadside inn at the crossroads of So-yang on the day of his arrest, and was imprisoned in Chŏn-ju jail the next day.

Father and son encouraged and comforted each other until their death, and we can still read of their heroic deeds in the record. "Don't change your mind. Speak only the truth before the magistrate. I'm afraid you might be weak and change your mind. Mind you do not falter in your faith!" said the father to his son. To this Joseph replied, "you need not be anxious about me. It is I who am rather anxious about you." Hearing what they were saying the jailors cursed them saying, "Are you rascals so eager to die?"

The magistrate said, "If you die at the same time with your son, you will leave your home without descendants. Does this mean nothing at all to you?" "After my death in this world," he replied, "I shall have another place to live in." He was then put to severe torture.

On this occasion he happened to be imprisoned at the jail in front of the Chŏn-ju magistrate's office, and the other Christians from Tae-sŏng-dong were at the one behind the office. The magistrate again called father and son before him and said, "You two cannot be executed together: the law forbids it. If you will only say a single word of apostasy, I will at once release you both." "How could we apostatize, considering the fact that we believe in God?" they answered in one voice, without the slightest sign of weakness. On their way to the execution ground Bartholomew Chŭng, the eldest among them, said: "Today, we are going to sit for the state examination in Heaven. Today is a day to be blessed." Peter Cho expressed his gladness saying, "You are right. Our happiness is not little. We are going to reap an abundant harvest of happiness." Having arrived at the execution ground, Peter Cho made the sign of the cross and extended his head to be cut. Seeing this the executioner struck him with his fist and said, "You rascal, even at the execution ground, do you still stick to your religion?" Peter again made the sign of the cross and said, "We persist in our holy religion to the hour of our death." He was martyred at the third blow on December 13, at the age of forty. Those servants of God who were executed together with Peter Cho were Peter Lee Myŏng-sŏ and Peter Chŭng Won-ji from Sŏng-chi-dong, and Bartholomew Chŭng Mun-ho, Peter Sohn Sŏn-ji and Peter Han Won-sŏ from Tae-sŏng-dong. Their bodies were buried by the fellow believers on the ridge of Yong-ma-ru near the site of execution.

(2) Joseph Cho Yun-ho

Joseph Cho was born at Sin-ch'ang in Ch'ung-ch'ŏng Province.

It was three years before his martyrdom in 1864 that he came to live at Sŏng-chi-dong in Chŏn-ju. He got married and, with his father who lived under the same roof, did his best to follow the Christian teaching.

He was arrested with his father, and, in accordance with the national law forbidding the simultaneous execution of father and son, he was beaten to death with sixteen blows of the cudgel, under the bridge in the market-place outside the West Gate in Chŏn-ju, on December 18, 1866, the next market-day following his father's execution. He was only nineteen years old.

At the site of his execution were his mother and a large crowd of onlookers. His body was interred in the same place as his father's. On parting from his father, his last words to him were, "You are going to the place of eternal bliss. Don't forget me when you are there." His father replied, "Of course, I am going to die. Still you should not be weak: don't fail to follow me." Joseph never yielded to the exhortation of apostasy, and said, "Whether I live or die is not a matter under your authority, so don't say anything more about it."

This brought more torture, even on his way to the execution ground. To the compelling exhortation just before his execution, he persisted in his faith answering, "Suppose one's parents commit a crime and in lieu of them one is arrested. On this occasion do you think a judge can possibly tell one to renounce and disavow one's parents? I have come to know the good teaching of Heavenly God and have followed it. Then how can I say that it is false and discard it? I can never do that, so put me to death right away." So saying, he was received into Heaven.

(3) Peter Lee Myŏng-sŏ

Peter Lee was born in Ch'ung-ch'ŏng Province, but used to travel about Chŏl-la Province, and it was at Sŏng-chi-dong in the district of So-yang in Chŏn-ju that he was arrested.

A few days earlier Peter Cho had said to a group of Christians, "We are evidently going to be arrested: hadn't we better go into hiding?" "You may do as you think best," Peter Lee had answered, "but as for me, I am a sick man, and unable to travel. Moreover it will not be long before I am called to Our Lord. When that time comes I'll be cured of my disease." (It was lung disease according to some, though others say it was a disease of the stomach.) Judging from this, he must have been completely prepared both for his liberation from every agony in this mundane world, and for glory in Heaven by martyrdom.

On his arrest he asked to be released saying that he was seriously ill and had many children to take care of, but his plea was not granted and he was carried to prison on a litter, while all the others were walking with their hands bound. He was the first to undergo interrogation at the Chŏn-ju magistrate office. The magistrate said, "Don't you think that you deserve to be called a traitor, considering you are observing a perverse religion which our country forbids? If you quit following the Lord of Heaven, your life will be spared, but if you refuse, you shall be put to death in accordance with the national law." Peter Lee replied, "Even though I should die over and over again, I cannot renounce this religion." The governor said, "Who is the head of your clique? Reveal his name at once." Peter Lee replied, "My desire is only for my own martyrdom, so I cannot denounce my fellow-believers." In spite of his illness, he underwent severe torture, but bore it with good courage. Like his fellow-prisoners, he prayed fervently every morning and evening.

On the day he was taken to the execution ground he consoled his fellow-believers with the words: "Today we are going to suffer martyrdom and then enjoy eternal happiness in Heaven." He was executed at a single blow at the execution ground of Sup-chŏng-ri outside the West Gate of Chŏn-ju, his heart full of bliss. He had reached the age of fifty.

(4) Bartholomew Chŭng Mun-ho

Bartholomew Chŭng was born at Im-ch'ŏn in Ch'ung-ch'ŏng Province and roamed about many places in Chŏl-la Province, and it was at Tae-sŏng-dong in Chŏn-ju that he was arrested.

It is supposed that the Chŏn-ju magistrate office had organized the constables into two groups and sent one to Sŏng-chi-dong and the other to Tae-sŏng-dong.

Those servants of God arrested at Tae-sŏng-dong were three: Bartholomew Chŭng, Peter Sohn Sŏn-ji and Peter Han Won-sŏ.

They put up for a night at the crossroads called Ku-chin-p'o-ri together with Peter Cho and the others arrested at Sŏng-chi-dong, and were imprisoned in Chŏn-ju jail. Once a magistrate of a certain district, Bartholomew was the eldest of the group. He was known to be a man of good behavior, was praised by the pagans for his unvarying courtesy to all, and revered by the Christians for his exemplary teaching of the Holy Gospel.

He foresaw an impending persecution and sent one Oh Sa-hyŏn (who, though a pagan, gave much assistance to the believers) to find out the situation of the Chŏn-ju magistrate, but was arrested before he received the news.

Those who had been arrested at Tae-sŏng-dong were imprisoned in a jail at the back of the magistrate's office and set apart from those who had been arrested at Sŏng-chi-dong. Bartholomew Chŭng once seemed to have weakened in the prison, but, having received the encouragement of Peter Cho Hwa-sŏ, he prepared himself for martyrdom by earnest morning and evening prayer. He was overjoyed on his way to the execution ground, and said, "We are going to sit for the state examination in Heaven. Today is a day to be blessed." He was the second to be executed, next to Peter Cho, at a single blow at Sup-chŏng-ri outside the West Gate in Chŏnju. His age was sixty-five or sixty-six. His body was interred by Oh Sa-hyŏn on the ridge of Yong-ma-ru, and on March 6, 1867, was removed to another place by his son, together with those of Peter Chŭng Won-ji and Peter Sohn Sŏn-ji.

(5) Peter Sohn Sŏn-ji

Peter Sohn had lived at Kwoe-in-tol in the district of Im-ch'ŏn in Ch'ung-ch'ŏng Province, but removed to Sin-ri-kol, Tae-sŏng-dong in Chŏn-ju and was living there when he was arrested.

This meek and faithful Christian was baptized in his childhood, and at the age of sixteen he was charged with the post of catechist by Father Chastan (martyred in the Ki-hae persecution, 1839) and fulfilled it diligently until his death.

Having put up for a night at Ku-chin-p'o-ri together with Peter Cho and companions from Sŏng-chi-dong, he was brought to the Chŏn-ju magistrate's office. When it was revealed to the authorities that he was a catechist, he underwent most severe torture.

Oh Sa-mun (who seems to have been one of his friends) sat beside the magistrate and exhorted him saying, "Just say a word, then you will be released without spending much money. Just say a word by way of renouncing the religion." Peter Sohn replied, "If you ask me ten thousand times, the answer is no." He underwent interrogation only twice before the magistrate, but the surreptitious tortures by the constables were more severe. "They say you are the chief follower of Western doctrine. Where are those Westerners who used to stay at your house, and where have you hidden those books of the Western Church?" Peter Sohn replied, "The Westerners came to my house once, but they left for Seoul and it is not known where they are now. I have no book with me." The constables twisted his arms behind him until they broke them, so that he could not feed himself and had to be fed by others. When he was taken to the execution ground, he gave his gown to his Christian cell-mates.

The executioner, who was drunk, missed his aim, striking Peter's shoulders so that he was not killed until the third blow. Before he was beheaded he prayed looking up to the sky: "Jesus and Mary! Jesus and Mary!" His body was interred on the ridge of Yong-ma-ru near the execution ground.

(6) Peter Han Won-sŏ

Peter Han was born in Ch'ung-ch'ŏng Province and was living at Sin-ri-kol, Tae-sŏng-dong in Chŏn-ju. When he was living at Chin-jam in Ch'ung-ch'ŏng Province, he used to be a catechist, but after removing to Tae-sŏng-dong, he resigned this post since Peter Sohn was holding it. Nevertheless being a man of genial character he was looked up to by others. From the time when he was living in Ch'ung-ch'ŏng Province, he was ardently looking forward to a chance to be martyred.

He was chopping wood at home, knowing nothing of his imminent arrest, when the constables rushed to his village.

Having put up for a night at Ku-chin-p'ŏ-ri together with Bartholomew and his companions, Peter Han was taken the next day to the Chŏn-ju magistrate's office. Upon his arrest his father negotiated for his son's release through the good offices of his friend, the magistrate Park, at the same time sending a letter to his son in the prison saying, "If you will only say just one word of apostasy, you will be released and everything will be settled. So I beg you to do as you are told." Peter Han rejected this entreaty saying, "What you say is unreasonable." His father made a visit to the prison and again exhorted his son to apostasy. Peter Han said, "Father, you have many children besides me, so I beg you to stop entreating me and go home." He was executed together with Peter Cho and other fellow-believers at Sup-chŏng-ri outside the West Gate on December 13, at the age of thirty-seven or eight.

His body was interred temporarily on the ridge of Yong-ma-ru, near the site of his martyrdom, by his fellow-believers, and at the beginning of March in the next year was removed by his father and brother to a place near where Peter Cho's body had been buried. That is the place which people now call Mak-ko-kae, in the district of Chŏn-ju.

(7) Peter Chŭng Won-ji

Peter Chŭng was born at Chin-jam in Ch'ung-ch'ŏng Province, removed to the Keum-ku district after having resided at Nŏl-ma-ru, Yang-ryang-su in Chŏn-ju, and was living at Sŏng-chi-dong when he was arrested.

Peter Chŭng and his wife were living under the same roof with his brother. There is not much to tell about his life, since he was quite young.

He escaped to the mountain when Peter Cho and his companions were arrested on December 5, and was trying to find out the situation in the quiet village, when he suddenly ran across the constables who were searching for his hideout in the mountains.

Having put up for a night at Ku-chin-p'ŏ-ri

together with Peter Cho and six other companions, Peter was taken to the Chŏn-ju magistrate's office and imprisoned in front of the office.

While every Christian was rejoicing at the glorious martyrdom, Peter Chŭng shed tears from time to time out of filial piety toward his old mother.

His fellow-Christians encouraged and cheered him up, and he even left a message of consolation to his family saying, "I am sure that we shall meet again in Heaven, so do not be grieved too much." He was martyred at the age of twenty-one or two, his heart full of joy as before.

His body, together with those of the others executed on that day, was interred on the ridge of Yong-ma-ru near the site of the execution ground, by Oh Sa-hyŏn, and at the beginning of March in the following year was removed to Ta-ri-sil in the district of Ko-san by his brother Chŭng Won-jip, where it still remains.

69. The Western Invasion of 1866 and Further Persecution

There were, furthermore, in the various provinces, a score of other cases of martyrdom, three of which were in P'yŏng-an, two in Hwang-hae, and the rest at Kong-ju, Song-do, and elsewhere, but it has been impossible to obtain documentary evidence as to their number, their names, and the circumstances of their death. Orders were given throughout the kingdom to burn all the books and religious objects that could be seized: the system of mutual surveillance by groups of five families, responsible to one another, was re-established and rigorously enforced, especially in the large towns: the magistrates availed themselves of all possible means to obtain the apostasy of the Christians. Most of them seized the opportunity of gratifying both their rapacity and their hatred of religion at the same time. They cruelly tortured all the neophytes who fell into their clutches, pillaged and burnt their houses, and reduced them to a shocking condition of misery. Many other magistrates, however, showed themselves by no means eager to enforce very strictly the orders that came from the royal court. Some of them, opposed on principle to persecution, even devised stratagems for evading it and relieving the Christians of their distress, and a certain number of Christians were, after a perfunctory examination, released as apostates without in reality having given the slightest evidence of apostasy.

But although they might well be disposed to close their eyes in regard to the native Christians and leave them in tranquillity, there was only the more stringency and ardor in the pursuit of European missionaries. After the denunciation on the part of the betrayer Lee Sŏn-i, it became known that there were at least nine of them in Korea, and it was suspected that there might be more. Accordingly, on the very first day of the persecution, the most stringent orders were sent to all the provincial governors and magistrates, and each week new letters were sent to stimulate them to increased activity and vigilance.

From the very beginning the government ordered sentries to be posted at every crossroads, who were to allow no traveler to pass without rigorous examination, but after a few days the soldiers grew tired of this troublesome duty and, except in the immediate neighborhood of large cities, left the sentries to look after them everywhere else. Descriptions of the Europeans, supplied by Lee Sŏn-i and other apostates, offering large rewards for their arrest, were distributed to all civil servants and government agents. As we have seen, the result of this infernal plan was the arrest, in less than a month, of nine missionaries. The other three escaped, but it is difficult to describe their sufferings during that terrible time. Hunted relentlessly from one hiding place to another, concealed during the daytime in holes, in walls or among rocks on most inaccessible mountains, wandering at night along lonely and sometimes impassable roads, heartbroken at the ruin and destruction of their Christian communities, at the lack of courage on the part of the neophytes, at the apostasy of the weaklings, and always in peril of capture, they often thought, as they themselves afterward admitted, of ceasing their efforts and giving themselves up.

"I have lost everything," wrote Father Féron to the seminary of the *Société des Missions-Étrangères*, "I have lost everything, even my breviary. I have no clothes other than those I am wearing. I can hope for no help from my Christians, who are themselves completely ruined. In addition, everyone is so terror-stricken that their faculties are numbed, which is a great danger for them, for many of them might easily have been left in peace if they had not betrayed themselves by running away. It is useless to recount how I have been living during all this time. You are well aware that we are undergoing a period of persecution: several of you have experienced it.

"But if life is hard, God is indeed kind. I can affirm that I have experienced miracle after miracle, going where I did not want to go, and not going where I wanted to go, and yet realizing after all that I have acted according to my will. I don't know, or rather I know very well, what has happened to me. And then, when I am in some dark and stifling hiding place and I feel that the good Lord is with me, I would not willingly exchange such a life for any more physically comfortable one."

For his part, Father Ridel wrote to his family:

"On hearing of the martyrdom of Bishop Berneux, I set out with several Christians for Chin-pat, Kong-ju. There was a river to cross. A government courier was waiting to cross at the same time. I got into the ferryboat last, and sat with my back to him so as not to be recognized. We got into conversation. 'As for me,' said the courier, a pagan, 'I am returning from Che-ch'ŏn on account of that business about those European rascals that have been arrested at the capital.' 'Are there any of them at Che-ch'ŏn?' 'Yes,' answered the courier, 'there

are two; I delivered a warrant for their arrest, and they have been arrested.' He went on to describe them in such detail that I realized he was speaking of Father Pourthié and Father Petitnicolas. My terrified Christians dared not say a word, and I tried to keep a straight face. The pagan went on: 'Have they arrested their wives?' — 'They haven't any.' — 'Then who keeps house for them?' — 'I don't know: go and ask them.' This brought a smile to the faces of the Christians and prevented them from betraying themselves by their sadness.

"On reaching Chin-pat I gave the Sacraments to several persons, I had my books and effects buried, and left on March 12, to go into hiding, I did not know where. Andrew, my landlord, accompanied me, with his wife Lee and children, and a few Christians. That evening, Chin-pat was invaded by the constables from the capital, with strict orders to arrest the European who usually lived there, and all the persons in his service.

"After having changed my hiding place several times, and spent all I had to feed my companions, I was obliged to send a large number of them back, and now I have come to a little hamlet in the mountains. I have shared my bed for the last fortnight with a man who has typhoid fever, and at the slightest warning, whenever my hosts have a visitor, I hide in the woodpile. It was there that, on Easter Tuesday, I heard of the death of Bishop Daveluy. That evening Andrew's children were talking among themselves of this sad news.

"I heard Anne, the eldest daughter, aged twelve years, saying to her young brothers: 'They will soon come to take the Father, with Mammy and Daddy; they'll take us too, and then they will say to us: "Give up your religion or I'll chop you to bits": what shall we do then?' — 'As for me,' answered the biggest boy, 'I shall tell them: "Do as you like, but I shall do the same as Daddy": I will never give up my faith in the Good Lord, and if they cut off my head, I shall go to His home.' — 'And I,' said the other, 'I shall say to the magistrate: "I want to go to Heaven. If you were a

Christian, you could go to Heaven too, but, as you kill Christians, you will go to hell.'" Then Anne clasped her two brothers in her arms and said, 'Good. We will all die together and we will all go to Heaven with Daddy and Mammy and the Father. But we must pray to the good Lord if we want to do that, for they will be very bad to us. They will pull out our hair, and teeth, and cut off our hands; they will beat us with a big stick, and the Father says that those who don't pray will be unable to bear it.' A few moments later, the younger of the two brothers went to look for his mother. 'Mamma, will they kill baby too? (his little brother who was only fourteen months old)...'

"I have been living nearly six weeks in this retreat, envying the good fortune of our martyrs, doing penance for my sins which have deprived me of the happiness of sharing their fate, and above all thinking over these words: 'Thy will be done on earth, as it is in Heaven!' I have been re-reading *Le Parfum de Rome*① and on going through that book again during my long hours of leisure, I found several striking descriptions of our present plight. Are we not, here in Korea, living in the time of the catacombs?...② On May 8, I at last received news of Father Féron, who is in hiding several leagues away, and on the fifteenth, after a journey by night which was not without danger, I was able to rush into his arms!"

Father Calais was, among the three missionaries, the one who was in the greatest danger. "I was in hiding," he relates, "in the pagan village of Mun-kyŏng, but one evening a slight cough on my part betrayed my presence to one of the pagans who happened to be in the house. I left the same night, and guided by the Christian who had given me sanctuary, I tried by a roundabout way to get back to the village of O-sil, where I

had been in charge some time before. We went astray and got lost in the mountains, and at midnight we could perceive O-sil three miles away. I sent back my guide (who, on his return, found his house despoiled by the pagans) and I went on alone, with my bundle on my back. I had eaten nothing since the day before, and I was dead tired. At about three o'clock in the morning, I came to a little group of Christian houses. Several women were at the door of a hut, but as I drew near I saw three constables who had just arrested them. I wanted to run away, but they seized me too, snatched away my bundle, and asked me peremptorily, 'Who are you? Where have you come from? Where are you going?' From their questions I knew that they had taken me for a Korean, so I kept silent.

"One of the Christian women then came up and told them, 'That's my father-in-law: can't you see he's stone deaf? Tell me what you want to say to him, and I'll undertake to make him understand.' The constables demanded money. There was discussion, and it was agreed to go and call the Christians hidden in the mountains. The man in charge of me tried many times to make me speak. He punched me and shouted in my ears, 'Do you understand? Then speak!' The Christians, hearing that the priest had been arrested, came in large number, and seeing that all that the constables wanted was money, and that there was no question of religion, they suspected trickery, and by questioning the impostors at length, forced them to admit that they were nothing but robbers. They punished them and let them go.

"I was still able to hear a few confessions, and to give Holy Communion on Easter Sunday. Then, warned that the constables would soon be coming to O-sil, I left on the following Friday, accompanied by the Christian

---

① A devotional work by Louis François Veuillot (1813—80), published in 1862.

② Catacombs: the subterranean cemeteries in which the Christians of Rome buried their dead during the first three centuries. They were designed like the burial places of the Jews, and at first in association with the family vaults of patrician converts, so that as burial places they enjoyed immunity from disturbance. The presence of the bodies of the martyrs caused them to be used for the celebration of Holy Mass.

Thomas Yu, to go to another village. At the town of Yŏn-p'ung we had to pass in front of an inn. Somebody shouted: 'Who are you? Where are you going?' We hastened our steps, but suspicions were aroused, and we were soon seized by five constables, who looked at me from head to foot, and in front and behind, half convinced that I was a European. We were taken into the inn to be examined more closely. Thomas, who walked in front, argued so vehemently that the constables beside me went ahead to lend their support to their companions.

"I seized the chance and ran off. 'The other one's escaping!' they all cried, and several of them started in pursuit. I was running as hard as I could when my belt, which was stuffed with copper cash, suddenly broke, and all the coins tumbled out on the cobblestones. The constables, true to their nature, threw themselves on the booty, began fighting over it, and gave no further thought to me. Up to then it had never been my custom to carry any money on my person during my travels: it was always one of my companions who was the purse-bearer; but the Good Lord, to save me from the clutches of the wicked, had allowed me to do so on that day. I managed to get to a Christian village: I did not dare to stop, and, accompanied by one or two men of good will, I hid myself in an almost impenetrable thicket in the neighboring hills, a veritable tiger's lair, where I slept eight days in the open, on the bare ground.

"Later I was able to get to Som-pa-kol, passing through entirely pagan country, sleeping every night side by side with six or eight pagans in inns along the way. God guarded me from mishap. At Som-pa-kol I carried out the annual visitation and distribution of the Sacraments, and even had the consolation of baptizing several adult pagans, who were not afraid, even in the face of death, to declare themselves Christians. I learned later that Thomas Yu, on whose person my Latin New Testament had been found, was brought before the magistrate who, on seeing this book, burst into an access of fury and anger at the constables

for having let me escape. Thomas had to undergo interrogation and beatings two or three times, but finally, finding that they could not drag out of him any denunciation against me, they let him go."

In the month of May the persecution died down a little. They went on searching for missionaries but no longer molested the Christians. The government feared that by keeping the country in such a state of turmoil they would hinder the rice-planting. Moreover, there was a severe drought; the barley, which is the staple food during summer, gave signs of dying on the stalk, and even the pagans were saying everywhere that the cruel treament of the Christians had angered Heaven and given rise to the drought. The enemies of religion therefore postponed their activities until the autumn.

Fathers Féron and Ridel were in hiding together in a little hamlet of four houses, living in the home of a poor widow in charge of six infant children. It was a safe retreat, and this woman, in spite of her privations, and in spite of the risk she ran in harboring them, had taken them in and cared for them with such friendly devotion that they stayed with her nearly two months. Famine reigned throughout the countryside; the poor Christians of the hamlet cut their barley while it was still green, so pressing was their hunger. The two missionaries tried this diet, but it immediately upset them, and made them so ill that they had to give it up. Christians pooled their last resources, sold everything they possessed, and managed to buy the missionaries two bushels of rice.

About June 15, Fathers Féron and Ridel received news of Father Calais, whom they had believed dead, and were able to correspond with him. It was then that by common accord they decided that one of their number must go to China to make known the disastrous condition of the mission, if possible, and bring help. Father Féron, the eldest of the three, was charged with the duty of selection, and chose Father Ridel to be the one to make the trip. The missionary obeyed, and departed weeping over his beloved Korean mission.

"We got a boat ready," he writes, "which was a troublesome business, but at last, on St. Peter's day, I again took leave of Father Féron. There were constables on all sides, watching all the roads, the coast-guards were more vigilant than ever, and soldiers from the capital were constantly commandeering boats to transport building materials for the construction of the new palace, all of which represented dangers to be avoided. I was hidden in the bottom of our little ship, which was manned by a crew of eleven resolute Christians, and our fears were at their height during the three days that we sailed past the numerous islands along the coast, but God came to our aid, and the *sang-froid* of our pilot brought us through safely. At last we reached the open sea: I had brought a little mariner's compass with me, and I set our course straight for the China coast. My poor seamen had never been out of sight of land before: imagine their terror when that evening they could see nothing but the sea around them!

"A gale sprang up; there was a violent squall, and for two hours it was as much as we could do to keep control of our vessel. Picture to yourself a little boat built all of fir, and fastened together with treenails (wooden pins), without a scrap of iron in her anywhere, the sails made of rush-mats, and rigged with ropes of twisted straw! But I christened her the *Saint Joseph;* I placed an image of Our Lady by the tiller, and one of Saint Anne on the lookout. Next day, no sight of land; on the third day we sighted some Chinese junks, and courage returned to the crew, but then we were becalmed. At night we had a brisk favorable wind that took us well on our way, then it began to veer and vacillate, there was a heavy swell, and the waves splashed at the gunwale. Rain began to fall in torrents. I could not but admire the courage of our pilot: he stayed on watch all night, and would not hand over the tiller till the storm was over, and he kept on course the whole time.

"Finally the wind dropped and the clouds dispersed; there was nothing but rolling, and soon the fiery light of dawn in the eastern sky announced that it would be a fine day. Where were we? Whither had the storm tossed us? That was the question we were asking ourselves, when suddenly one of the sailors spied a dark spot on the horizon, which slowly grew larger. It was land, in the right direction. There was no further doubt; it was China. Then we made out a ship, and soon saw by its sails that it was a European vessel; it was coming toward us. I gave orders to draw near to it, and hoisted a small French ensign that I had been careful to provide before our departure.

"It was a fine three-master; I learnt that it was based on Saint Malo, and was coming from Chefoo. As we passed, I dipped the ensign. The captain, who was watching us attentively, amazed at the sight of the Tricolor fluttering on an odd craft that was not even Chinese, responded courteously, and then at his orders the ensign was hoisted. I watched attentively: it was the French flag. Three times was it raised and lowered in our honor. It is impossible to describe my feelings. A poor missionary, who had not met his compatriots for six years, I was thrilled to the core. At this moment, lost at sea, and not knowing what course to steer, I should have liked to go on board that ship, but her sails, filled with a favorable wind, had already carried her to a considerable distance. Nevertheless this was a most heartening experience for us. All my crew, who had never seen a European ship before, were lost in wonder and admiration. 'Father, are they Christians? If this ship were to come to our country everyone would run away; she could conquer our country, and force the king to grant freedom of worship,' and so on.

"Soon I recognized the coast: it was the harbor of Weihaiwei, from which I had set out six years before. We were off the coast of Shantung near Chefoo, our destination. We had therefore come in a straight line, as accurately as any ship with the finest nautical instruments! What a good pilot Our Lady is!

There were only a few more leagues to go, but the head wind would not permit us to land that day. On July 7, in the morning, we sighted the port, and at noon we dropped anchor among the European ships. We were at once surrounded by Chinese, eager to look at the Koreans (whom they at once recognized as such); I landed, and was at once encircled by a mob of bowing Chinese who stared with curiosity at my strange clothing. The news which I brought caused a great sensation in the European community. I proceeded without delay to Tientsin, where I met Rear Admiral Roze, commander of the French naval expedition to the China coast. He welcomed me kindly, and promised his aid."

After the departure of Father Ridel, Father Féron rejoined Father Calais and they stayed in hiding together. Summer passed without incident. As it was a year of famine, they allowed the Christians to till their land, while letting them know that it was merely a truce, and that the persecution would begin again as soon as possible. As for the missionaries, there was always a price on their heads. On August 15 a special courier arrived from Peking, bearing a secret dispatch, so secret that the Korean ambassador, one of the chief enemies of religion, who was also in China, had no knowledge of it, for it was feared that it might come to the ears of the Christians. But nothing is secret in Korea: the dispatch and the reply of the government were soon common knowledge, and the missionaries were able to obtain copies of them. The dispatch charged the government with imprudence in putting the European priests to death; and counseled an accord with France, because this country was about to go to war with Korea.

It went on to say that, seeing that China had been unable to resist the armed forces of France, with still less reason could Korea hope to be able to defend herself. The Regent answered that this was not the first time that he had had foreigners killed, that he was within his rights, and that it was nobody's business to interfere. Deeds soon upheld

this declaration of principles. On September 2, an American schooner, having made the coast at P'yŏng-yang, was set on fire and her crew of twenty massacred. Two Shantung junks were seized and searched for Europeans on board. There were none, but some cotton cloth of European manufacture was found, and the crew were slaughtered. Stringent edicts were renewed against the Christians: order was given to put them to death, together with all their relatives to the sixth degree of consanguinity, and in general all persons were to be held as suspects; rewards were promised to all who would carry out these orders.

After the destruction of the ships which we have just mentioned, the Regent, convinced that he had struck a mortal blow at the Western barbarians, and that he had got rid of some of his enemies, would go every day to a mountain near the capital to give thanks to heaven for this brilliant success. Even then, Thomas Kim Myŏn-ho, the one who in January was most actively concerned with the approaches made to him by certain Christians on the occasion of the Russian attempt at invasion, had the untoward idea of writing to him once more. He pointed out that the ships in question had nothing to do with those that would be employed in a war with Korea, that the French vessels would not be long in demonstrating, and that the best plan would be to come to an understanding with France, primarily because she was a powerful nation, and also because her religion was true, and useful to the prosperity of nations. As one may well imagine he was, on account of his letter, immediately arrested.

Thomas belonged to a family distinguished for its elevated rank. Several of his pagan relatives held high office on the bench. His mother and his elder brother were martyrs in the persecution of 1839; another of his brothers died in prison for the faith at the same time. Thomas in his youth had been for one year in the service of Bishop Daveluy; then, drawn by ambition and the love of pleasure, he had almost entirely given up the practice of his religion. It is said that at the beginning of 1866 he was converted, and several Christians affirm that they saw him praying, and often overheard him repeating: "I heartily regret my ill conduct; I do not despair of my salvation; but for that I must undergo the martyrdom which cleanses all sins."

Nevertheless he was not seen to have received the Sacraments, which would have been an easy matter for him prior to the arrest of Bishop Berneux. Brought before the judges, he courageously averred that he was a Christian, and repeatedly underwent cruel tortures with a steadfastness that astonished the executioner. He was taken to be executed at Sae-nam-t'ŏ, together with Paul Kim Mun-won and another Christian named Lee Yŏn-sik. On the way there, and at the site, he never ceased to exhort his companions to meet their death with joy. This was on September 8 or 10.

There is no precise information about Lee: all that is known of him is that he was a domestic servant to the Regent. As for Paul Kim, he belonged to a family of the highest rank, and was always noted for his faith and his fervor. For six years one side of his body had been completely paralyzed, and he had lost the power of speech, and had to be looked after like a child. Bishop Berneux often praised the heroic patience with which Paul bore this terrible affliction. At the beginning of the persecution he lived at the house of the magistrate John Nam which he had just bought, and after John's arrest he foresaw what was going to happen and hurriedly sold it in secret. Several days later, the constables came to pillage the house, but they found it occupied by a pagan of noble rank.

Furious with frustration and disappointment, they vowed to be revenged on Paul Kim, and in September, as soon as the Regent had proclaimed the renewal of the edicts against the Christians, they dragged him before the chief justice Shin Myŏng-sun. The latter, perceiving his physical condition, (that he was crippled by hemiplegia) did not make him undergo interrogation or torture. He condemned him to death as a

Christian, and gave orders for him to be executed together with Thomas Kim. A month later his remains were given funeral honors and buried, near those of the other martyrs, on the mountain of Wa-a-ko-kae. During the next few days after the execution of Thomas and Paul, four other Christians died of hunger in the prisons of Kong-ju. Their names are not known, and no details of their martyrdom remain.

We left Father Ridel at Tientsin, whither he had gone to report the grave events in Korea to Rear Admiral Roze. The admiral was disposed to bring aid to the two French missionaries still exposed to the danger of death, when the news of an uprising in Cochin-China obliged him to change his plan. He promised Father Ridel that on his return from Cochin-China he would make a landing in Korea. The missionary returned to Chefoo, where he stayed until mid-August. Then the Koreans who had accompanied him requested him to let them go back to their country. He let eight of them go, and with the remaining three proceeded to Shanghai to await events. Three weeks later he received from Rear Admiral Roze an invitation to go to Chefoo and accompany him to Korea. He set off in all haste, and on September 10 went on board the frigate *Guerrière*. He himself tells us in full detail the story of this expedition.

"It was decided that the corvette *Primauguet*, the dispatch boat *Déroulède* and the gunboat *Tardif* would proceed to make a preliminary reconnaissance of the coasts of Korea. The admiral took me as his interpreter on this first voyage, with my three Koreans as pilots. Leaving Chefoo on the eighteenth, by the twentieth we were among a group of islands, the first of which are Ferrieres Island and Clifford Island, and we anchored in Prince Jerome Bay, near Eugènie Island. On the twenty-first the admiral sent his aide-de-camp on the *Déroulède* to reconnoiter the route to the capital: I accompanied him. Always under the direction of the Korean pilot, who had a thorough knowledge of all the ins-and-outs of the coast, we passed by Mul-ch'i Island, in front of the little town of Song-chŏng, and from there round a sharp bend we entered the strait that separates Kang-hwa Island from the mainland of Korea.

"We anchored near the island, in front of the village of Kap-ko-ji. There our mission was ended. Several officers landed, and were full of admiration at the aspect of the countryside. An enormous well-cultivated plain, full of rice fields, numerous villages, and, a league to the northwest, the town of Kang-hwa. One could see forts in the distance, very well placed, and some cannons, but not a single soldier. The terrified populace had at once fled, but a few of the more courageous individuals among them soon returned, others followed them, and when we weighed anchor, the inhabitants came down to the beach *en masse* to look at this strange ship which, without sails or oars, could proceed against the current, which is very rapid in these parts.

"Next day, we rejoined the *Primauguet* and the *Tardif*. All were enchanted with what they had seen during the voyage, and, above all, at having made certain that the channel was navigable for the fleet. The three ships immediately got under way, but the *Primauguet*, having gone wide of the course indicated by the pilot, ran on the rocks. Luckily, no serious damage was done, and only the false keel was lost. It was decided to leave her at Mul-ch'i Island. The twenty-third was a Sunday, and I said Mass on board. This was the first time that the holy sacrifice was offered, in full liberty, in the kingdom of Korea.

"The two ships then proceeded on their way toward Seoul. On emerging from Kang-hwa strait we came to the mouth of the Han River, which flows one league to the south of the capital. We would have to ascend it for a distance of five or six leagues. I was continually on duty, translating for the admiral the indications given to me by the pilot. Finally, on the evening of the twenty-fifth, we anchored in front of the capital, to the great astonishment of the enormous crowd that covered the banks of the river and the surrounding hills, to feast their eyes on this unprecedented spectacle— ships propelled by fire.

"The Korean government had attempted to stay our progress. Junks had been placed at a narrow part of the river, and a cannon shot was fired: a French shell, in reply, sank two of the junks, and others took to flight. A little further off, one or two batteries opened fire, but a few well-aimed cannon-shots and a howitzer shell, which burst a few paces from the gunners, reduced them all to silence. We spent a whole day in front of the city of Seoul, carrying out soundings, measuring heights, surveying the terrain and drawing charts and plans, taking bearings, and so on... I landed, in hopes of meeting some Christian, and getting news of my confreres and of the persecution, but nobody dared to come near us. We left the next day, and on our way down the river we made further soundings and numerous observations.

"By Sunday, September 30, we had rejoined the *Primauguet*, and we were preparing to set out on the return voyage to the coast of China, when a boat came alongside. It was my pilot and one of the sailors who had accompanied me on the voyage to Chefoo. From them I learnt of the destruction of the European vessel that ran aground in P'yŏng-yang in the month of August, the renewal of the persecution, the order for all Christians in the provinces to be put to death without sending them up to the capital, and the searches being made for the priests. I informed the admiral of my anxiety, and begged him to station one of his ships in Korea, for its presence would intimidate the Korean government, while on the other hand the departure of the whole flotilla would certainly lead to redoubled persecution. My representations were without effect, and on October 3 we were back in Chefoo. The final preparations were made, and we set out again eight days later."

While Father Ridel was re-entering China

with the warships, what had become of the two missionaries he left behind in Korea? The following letter from Father Féron will tell us:

"During the last days of September, Rear Admiral Roze sent out a reconnaissance expedition to explore the route to the capital. Father Calais had left me in order to go down to the shore, where I had had a boat made ready to take him to China. Informed before me of the arrival of the French flotilla, he wrote to ask me what he ought to do. Believing like everyone else that this was a final and definitive expedition which would set us all free, I at once got ready to join my colleague. I had ten leagues to cover; on the way I was recognized, pursued, and escaped only by miracle. The boat was not yet ready; nevertheless we leapt on board and started off that very day. We were delayed by a calm, then by a contrary wind, and it was not until the following day, in the evening, that we got to the entrance of the channel, three leagues in length, which we would have to follow to get to the French men-of-war. But at the entrance of the channel there was a town, strictly guarded. Our people took fright, but we decided nevertheless to go ahead.

" 'Let's go on, then, to the death!' they said, and we arrived in front of the town. A Korean boat emerged from the passage. 'Aren't the *barbarian* ships there?' asked our sailors. 'We shall get shot as we pass them' — 'No, they left two days ago.' We tacked about, but where were we to go? My first thought was to set our course for China. The weather was fine, the wind set fair, and we would get to Chefoo before the rear admiral left. But the proposal made everyone shudder: the boat was so small; and so badly put together! I dared not insist, and we decided to go to any Christian village in the neighborhood in search of news. We thought, Father Calais and I, that the French had only made a first reconnaissance, and that the rear admiral would soon be here in person. We wished for it all the more as we regarded it as our duty to let him know about the disaster in P'yŏng-yang, so that he could prevent its recurrence.

"As soon as we had landed I sent secretly for one of our Christians. He gave us the following news. The constables had come to arrest a Christian. As regards the reconnaissance made by the expedition, the people were in no way scared by it; they even wished for the French to come. What they were afraid of was their own government, and the bands who were organizing on the pretext of defending the national territory.

"In fact, there was great terror in Seoul. During the few days that the men-of-war had been in the river, there was in the capital no stock of rice and no supply of fuel: in eight days the whole population would have been starved to death. Everyone was taking flight: we were assured that seven thousand houses had been left empty. The Korean government having got together a large number of junks to form the nucleus of a navy, one shot, fired from a French gunboat, had been sufficient to sink two of them and put the rest to flight. The Korean artillery had done its best to return the fire, but its projectiles could not complete more than half of their trajectory. Such was the substance of the information we gathered.

"It was October 11 or 12 and our situation was becoming more and more critical. There was nothing for it but to set out for China. On that very day, Rear Admiral Roze left Chefoo for Korea. A contrary wind which carried us too far to the north prevented us from meeting him. For two days and two nights we skirted the coast as far as the latitude of Shantung, but our boat was so unseaworthy, and it would have been so imprudent to sail out to the open sea, that we were glad to meet some of the Chinese junks that carry contraband goods, and to arrange with one of them to take us to Chefoo. I will omit the account of our crossing, which was long and difficult, alternating as it did between flat calm and contrary wind. We reached Chefoo on October 26. They informed us that the *Primauguet* was expected to arrive from Korea on November 5: it would come for dispatches. We hoped to be able to avail ourselves of its departure to return to our mission, which was all the more dear to us now that we were exiled from it."

Let us now return to the expedition, and let us give first of all the official account of it which was published by the French government. It was published in the *Moniteur* of December 27, 1866:

"The Minister of the Navy and of the Colonies has received from Rear Admiral Roze, commander-in-chief of the naval division in the China seas, dispatches announcing the capture of Kang-hwa, a fortified city located on the north side of the island of the same name, and at the mouth of the river on whose banks is situated the city of Seoul, capital of the kingdom of Korea.

"Having left Chefoo on October 11, with the frigate *Guerrière*, the screw corvettes *Laplace* and *Primauguet*, the dispatch boats *Déroulède* and *Kien-chan*, the gunboats *Tardif* and *Lebrethon*, Rear Admiral Roze anchored on the thirteenth with his division, in front of Mul-ch'i Island, eighteen miles from Kang-hwa. On the following day the gunboats ascended the Salt River (to the right of Kang-hwa) towing the small boats, which carried the landing force of the *Guerrière*, and the corvettes, as well as a detachment of rifleman-marines from the Yokohama. Scarcely had they landed when our marines occupied the heights without meeting with the slightest resistance, and encamped five kilometers from Kang-hwa. On the fifteenth a reconnaissance was carried out by a column commanded by Captain Count d'Osery: on arrival at a fort that dominated the city, he was received by a rapid and well-sustained rifle-fire and by that of two small-caliber cannons. After an engagement of several minutes the fort was occupied, and the Koreans fled, leaving their flag in our hands.

"On the sixteenth, at eight o'clock in the morning, Rear Admiral Roze, at the head of all his forces, presented himself before the town, which was surrounded by a crenellated wall four meters in height. On arriving at a distance of a hundred meters from the main gate, our troops were received with a fairly vigorous fire, but the wall was soon escaladed to the cry of '*Vive l'Empereur!*' (Long live the Emperor!) and the enemy left us masters of the place.

"A large number of cannon, more than ten thousand rifles, and ammunition of all kinds was found in the immense magazines, and showed how important the place called Kang-hwa was, from the point of view of the defense of the capital of Korea. Rear Admiral Roze ordered an inventory to be carefully made of the contents of the magazines, of which he took possession in the name of the nation, and which also contained eighteen boxes filled with ingots of silver and the official archives.

"A proclamation addressed to the inhabitants informed them of the motive of the admiral in coming to chastise the Korean government, and assured them of complete protection.

"The blockade of the river of Seoul, of which the consuls of the European powers in China had been informed, and the capture of Kang-hwa, must have made a deep impression on the government of Korea. In fact, the town of Kang-hwa, being, as we have just remarked, situated at the mouth of the river of Seoul, commands the principal route which the trade of Seoul is obliged to take, especially in order to ensure the supply of rice. Thus, on the nineteenth, Rear Admiral Roze received a letter from the king, to which he was assiduous in replying, and informing him of the satisfaction that he demanded in the name of the emperor.

"The dispatch which contained these details was dated October 22; on this day, Rear Admiral Roze was still in the town of Kang-hwa, where he was awaiting the Chinese interpreters whom he had sent for from our consul at Shanghai."

The *Moniteur* of January 7, 1867, published other dispatches dated November 17, 1866.

"Rear Admiral Roze, being desirous of

assuring himself of the state of the country, a detachment, commanded by post-captain Ollivier, made a sortie from Kang-hwa and encountered, at a distance of a few kilometers from the town, Korean nationals in large numbers, entrenched in a fortified temple; the enemy, which had at first made a sortie, was repulsed and hastened to return to its entrenchments, abandoning its dead. After a vigorous fusillade, in which not one of our men was killed, but which unfortunately cost us a few casualties, the column returned the same evening to Kang-hwa.

"A few days later, Rear Admiral Roze, seeing that the Korean government did not follow up the overture as he had expected on receiving the letter from the king, decided to leave Kang-hwa: the approach of winter moreover was making itself felt, and it was to be feared that all traffic on the river of Seoul would soon cease; accordingly he ordered the destruction of all government offices as well as that of the king's palace, and our sailors returned on board the vessels anchored in front of Mul-ch'i Island.

"The boxes containing the ingots of silver, to the value of one hundred and ninety-seven thousand francs, and the manuscripts and books which might be of interest to the scientific world, were sent to Shanghai whence they will be forwarded to France.

"Rear Admiral Roze also announced that the two missionaries who had been left in Korea have succeeded in rejoining him at Chefoo.

"The destruction of Kang-hwa, an important military stronghold, of the powder magazines and the public offices in the city, must have demonstrated to the government of Korea that the murder of the French missionaries has not gone unpunished."

Such was the official version of the expedition to Korea. Here now is the more detailed account given by Father Ridel. He tells us the real story of the final engagement near the temple, which was somewhat garbled among the euphemisms of the government publication.

"Saturday, October 13. The squadron an-chored near Mul-ch'i Island. It had been decided that Kang-hwa should be captured first, so, on the fourteenth, the two dispatch-boats and the two gunboats, towing all the small boats containing the landing force, went up the strait. The frigate and the two sloops of war, which drew too much water, stayed at anchor. The landing took place near the village of Kap-ko-ji, and the companies of troops disembarked without having to fire a single rifle-shot: there was no sign of the enemy. At the approach of the French, nearly all the inhabitants had taken flight: some of them, more courageous, remained, but all they did was to make profound obeisances. The troops took possession of the village, and quartered themselves there. Two days later, they entered the town, which tried to offer some resistance. A few rifle shots, which killed three or four Koreans, put the rest to full flight: the city gates were broken open with hatchet blows. The town was almost deserted: the troops immediately occupied the governor's palace and the government magazines.

"Large stocks of arms were found, bows and arrows in great number, iron sabers which could be bent double without breaking, helmets, beautifully ornamented but excessively heavy cuirasses, about eighty brass and iron cannon of various calibers, but in very bad condition; a considerable quantity of matchlock guns of all sizes. The brass cannons were breech loaders: we saw no gun carriages. Some of the rifles were repeaters: these were provided with a series of touch holes, so that by applying the match successively to them, beginning with the one nearest the muzzle, there would be a series of discharges, which must be very dangerous to the user. There were also enormous stores of gunpowder: some of these were blown up, with explosions that rocked the ground. They found moreover textiles, various kinds of timber, brass vases, shears, aprons, brushes, well-tanned oxhides and pigskins of the best quality, beeswax, vegetable wax from south Korea, Chinese silk goods, copper ware, alum, some porcelain ware of poor quality, a great stock of dried fish, and over a hundred and eighty thousand francs worth of silver, in flat ingots.

"The library was a very rich one. Two or three thousand books printed in Chinese, with many illustrations with fine paper, bound in brass plates with covers of green or crimson silk, all carefully labeled. I noticed the ancient *History of Korea* in sixty volumes. The strangest thing was a book made of tablets of marble, folded on one another like the panels of a window-shutter, with highly-polished gilded brass hinges, and with Chinese characters incised on the marble, and each tablet protected with a cushion of scarlet silk, the whole 'book' encased in a beautiful brass box which was (in its turn) enclosed in a red lacquer box, with gilded brass fittings. These square tablets made when unfolded a book of twelve pages. These contained, according to some, the laws of morality of the country; according to others, whose opinion is more probably correct, the favors accorded to the kings of Korea by the emperor of China. The Koreans prized it very highly.

"In another box was found a marble tortoise, perfectly sculptured, on a pedestal consisting of the royal seal, that great and formidable seal which no Korean is allowed to touch or even to look at, and the possession of which has several times sufficed to transfer the royal authority and put an end to revolutions. The one which I saw was new, and looked as if it had never been used.

"Within the precincts of the governor's residence was a royal palace, for it is within the fortress of Kang-hwa that the kings of Korea take refuge in time of war. The emplacement is a well-chosen one, on a small wooded hill which overlooks the town, and from which one has a magnificent view of the island, the sea, and the mainland. The Island of Kang-hwa is very fertile, producing rice, barley, tobacco, sorghum, maize, various kinds of turnip, Chinese cabbage, chestnuts, persimmons, and sweet acorns from which the poor make a kind of broth.

"The French remained in tranquil possession of the town, and no one came to disturb them. Most of the people were too frightened to return, and we could have very little contact with them. In vain did we try to reassure them: they had no conception of this kind of warfare: they believed, in their simplicity, that the conquerors having seized the country must necessarily put all to fire and sword. What is more, they kept on asking: 'Why don't you go to the capital? What's the use of staying here? Your victory will come to nothing. You wish to avenge the murders that have been committed, and you punish poor people who are completely innocent, and who took no part whatever in them.'

"A Christian was able to get in touch with me by night at Kap-ko-ji camp. He told me that a considerable force was being got ready in the provinces of Korea, that the gunmakers were busy day and night, that all scrap iron was being collected, even the agricultural tools, to make sabers and spears, that several points, on the coast, among others at the town of T'ong-jin, on the mainland, opposite Kang-hwa, were being strongly guarded, and that the river had been blocked by sinking a number of boats about a league below Seoul. The admiral, on learning these details, resolved to reconnoiter T'ong-jin.

"A force of a hundred and twenty men was sent for this purpose: they landed on the mainland opposite the so-called 'gateway to Seoul.' This is a stone ogival arch surmounted by a flying roof in Chinese style, which commands the roadhead leading to Seoul. Around this arch there are a village and some fortifications. As soon as our marines began to disembark, they received an unforeseen volley which killed two of them. They landed nevertheless, and made themselves masters of the place, after having killed several Koreans and put the rest to flight, and then, judging it imprudent to proceed farther, they returned on board and stayed on the watch.

"That evening, part of the Korean army defiled to the further end of the plain, but a few opportune shells, to their great surprise, burst quite close to their ranks. Astonished and frightened by these hitherto unknown weapons, they soon broke their ranks and fled to the hilltops. We were told that they had manufactured some guns modeled on those seized on board the American schooner, burnt by them with her crew, some months earlier, on the banks of P'yŏng-yang. The gunboats were anchored in separate places, so as to prevent boats from passing and maintain the blockade of the waterway to the capital; a certain number of junks were burnt, but the Koreans found ways to pass through during the night in small rowing boats.

"During this time the persecution raged more fiercely than ever in the capital and in the provinces. The father of the king was furious: he had put up signboards on posts at the entrance to the palace, with notices to the effect that all persons, who spoke of making peace with the Europeans would be regarded as rebels and immediately executed. General Lee Kyŏng-ha sent the admiral a long letter on October 19, in which, after quoting some sentences from the classic philosophers, he stated that those who invaded the frontiers of another kingdom were worthy of death; that the Europeans had come to their land, and concealed themselves, disguising themselves in Korean dress and learning the Korean language, in order to carry off their wealth; that in consequence it had been quite right to put them to death; that if we did not leave, we might have the wrath of heaven to fear very soon, and so on.

"The admiral replied that he had come in the name of Napoleon, sovereign of the great empire of France, that His Majesty, whose solicitude extended to every one of his subjects, no matter how far off, wanted them to be in safety wherever they might be, and to be treated in a manner suitable for the citizens of a great empire, that having learnt that the government of Korea had just put nine French citizens to death, he had come to demand reparations, and the handing over

to him of the three ministers most active in bringing about the death of these Frenchmen, and that at the same time a plenipotentiary be sent to lay down the bases for a treaty. Otherwise he would hold the government of Korea responsible for all the calamities that war would bring in its train. This letter from the Admiral remained unanswered.

"The Koreans continued to gather at all points in the neighborhood. One day a Christian came to tell me that on the previous night three hundred Koreans, experienced tiger-hunters and crack shots, had just landed on the island, and that on the following night, they would be joined by five hundred more, and would shut themselves up in the Chŏn-teung-sa, a temple on the very island of Kang-hwa, three or four leagues to the south of the town. I hastened to warn the admiral. That same day a whaler, engaged in hydrography, had been attacked near the spot where they had effected their passage of the strait. The admiral decided to attack the temple, and detailed a hundred and sixty men for the task. At his orders I accompanied the expedition, as guide and interpreter. We set out at six o'clock in the morning. The vanguard was a few paces ahead of us, then came the commanding officer at the head of his detachment, and then the baggage and the horses that carried our lunch. We had no artillery, although the previous evening there had been talk of bringing a few small fieldpieces; I don't know why the idea was dropped. We proceeded in easy stages, stopping to rest every hour. Along the highway, which is a very fine one, we passed several small hills, and we soon sighted some walls along the ridge. Nearly all the houses along the road were deserted. A countryman told us that the night before there had been a lot of soldiers in the temple. We did in fact notice some activity in the vicinity, and several men who were clambering up the hill toward the fortress. This temple is in reality a small stronghold, usually inhabited by soldier-priests.[1]

"We did not see the actual temple, for it is situated in a ravine, surrounded by a ring of mountains, the summits of which are provided with walls four meters in height, built without mortar, with huge half-dressed stones piled up one upon another. It can be reached only by a single easy route and it was this one which we followed, after having turned to the right in order to attack from the side opposite to that by which we had come. It was half past eleven; some of us suggested having lunch, but it was found that it would be easy to make ourselves masters of the temple and lunch in the palace of Buddha itself. We left the main road to take the pathway that led to the temple. An armed Korean suddenly appeared quite close to us: two or three random shots failed to hit him: three of our men set off in pursuit, but he disappeared. We were no more than three or four hundred meters from the gate: we rested for a moment. Before us was a thick and solidly-built wall, which enclosed the ravine and extended in both directions along the slopes of the mountains.

"The gate, of dressed stone work, vaulted with a simple semicircular arch, had, as is always the case, no swinging doors to it. I made a careful survey of what was going on inside. On our arrival, I had heard several shouts; now all was silent as a tomb. The order to advance was given: a detachment took off to the right to clamber up the hill; the main body of troops, preceded by the vanguard, advanced straight toward the gateway. We had less than a hundred meters to go, and the vanguard was much nearer, when firing was suddenly heard all along the wall. The shots mingled and followed one another without stopping, and the bullets whistled by our heads and feet on all sides. I looked behind me and saw that every one was lying down and making use of whatever cover was available until the fusillade should end: I did the same.

"Our soldiers replied with a heavy and continued fire as they descended the hill in search of a more favorable position, but what effect could rifle bullets have on stone walls? The surprise had thrown our troops into disorder; the officers' commands went unheeded, and soon everyone was spread out at a certain distance, always under the enemy's fire, which was taking effect on us. Then, when the officers had rallied the men, we ambushed ourselves behind huts, fragments of rock, and woodpiles in order to prevent a sortie on the part of the Koreans, while in the meantime the wounded were carried to a hill farther back. There were thirty-two of them, and the wounds of some of them looked to be serious.

"Our position was becoming embarrassing. Deducting the wounded and those who were taking care of them, there were no more than eighty men left fit for combat. If the enemy had tried to cut off our retreat he would have been successful, or at any rate could have killed a good many of us. The men had not eaten, and the horse that carried our meal had gone over to the enemy. Stretchers were improvised for those who could not walk, and we finally managed to get back to the highway. The fit men formed a rear guard in order to keep the enemy at a respectable distance. Three times the Koreans made an attempt at a sortie,

---

[1] "There are many kinds of bonzes or priests in Korea," wrote Father Ridel, "the lettered bonzes who are engaged in such scholarly work as the writing of books and the study of the rites and ceremonies of the country; the begging priests, and the military priests whose work consists in the preparation and manufacture of arms. It is these who make the gunpowder, cast the cannon, and who build or at least supervise the building of walls (fortifications). In Korea there were formerly very many temples. Father Ridel visited a certain number of them, all of them perched on hilltops or hillsides, and always located in quiet, well-wooded places difficult of access. It is only natural, in view of their situation in the middle of rocky districts, to make them into strongholds; thus, tradition reports that several of them have served as refuges for great princesses or even queens who wished to escape the horrors of war."

but at each attempt they lost many men, and finally gave up the idea of pursuit. Besides, they were quite satisfied, and getting up on the walls, they set up a series of wild and savage yells, their cries of victory over the Western barbarians.

"I don't wish to make any critical judgment of this affair. However, wasn't it rather imprudent to send a mere hundred and sixty men, without a single field gun, against a fortress known to contain at least eight hundred enemy troops? The first landing and the capture of Kang-hwa had been so easy, that one got into the habit of going into action as if one were taking an afternoon stroll. The resistance that the Koreans put up at the so-called 'Gateway to Seoul' ought to have taught us a lesson. Luckily we had no one killed: we returned slowly to Kap-ko-ji, dispirited and thoroughly exhausted.

"All were admirable in their care for the wounded, and I could not help being moved almost to tears by the almost maternal care with which these rough-looking sailors rendered aid to their comrades. The admiral, who had had misgivings about the operation, appeared before us with some of his staff officers. He met us about half a league from the camp. He was much upset by this failure, and spoke a few words of encouragement to each one of the wounded. It was night when we got back.

"Next day, at eight o'clock in the morning, I learnt that orders had been given for our immediate evacuation. The troops who were in Kang-hwa set fire to the town and retreated to the encampment near the beach. The town was entirely destroyed. Unfortunately this precipitate departure looked very much like flight, for it was with no thought of such a prompt retreat that we had begun work on fortifying both the town and the surrounding hills. It had been planned to take away a huge bronze bell from Kang-hwa, and it was already transported halfway to the beach. It was left there, and the Koreans must have taken it back as a trophy of their victory.

"The troops embarked during the night,

and at six o'clock in the morning we were under way. At the bend in the strait, several forts fired on us, but without wounding anybody. The gunboats replied energetically. A little further on we took a last look at the temple, which is only two kilometers from the shore. Our return was a great surprise for the frigate and the corvettes. Many of the officers said that the temple ought to be bombarded from offshore; others maintained that this was impracticable. In a word, everyone felt frustrated, and vented his ill temper with unbridled tongue.

"The following night six Christian sailors came on board. They told me that the persecution was now more violent than ever, and that the Regent had solemnly sworn to exterminate all the Christians, even women and children. On the fourteenth day of the ninth moon (the end of October), the catechist John Park Yŏng-rae, a high-ranking noble of Hwang-hae, as well as the wife and son of Francis Lee Eui-song, the companion of Matthew Lee in the evangelization of the northern provinces, had been executed at Seoul, after having suffered horrible tortures. Three days later, Francis Lee himself, betrayed by his brother, who was still a pagan, went to his death in company with another Christian, whose name was Kim Chung-eun.

"The Regent, with insolence unprecedented in the history of his country, had chosen a new execution ground for these five victims. They were taken to Yang-hwa-jin, on the banks of the river, to the very place where the French warships had anchored, facing the capital, a month before. 'It is because of the Christians,' said the official proclamation, 'that the barbarians came here to this point; it is because of them that the waters of our river have been polluted by the vessels from the Occident. Their blood must wash away this stain.' I learnt also that at Yang-hwa-jin itself, there had been set up an encampment of five hundred soldiers, to whom orders had been given that if they discovered a Christian among them they were to kill him out of hand.

"I then received details about my two colleagues, Father Féron and Father Calais. At the time of the first expedition, these same sailors had been trying to bring them to our warships, but they arrived two days too late, and after having sailed about the islands for a long time, they had put them on board a Chinese junk, which should by now have brought them to Chefoo. Then there were now no more missionaries in this poor land of Korea! I looked at the coast, and could not tear my eyes away from it. When would we re-enter the country? And now, what ruin and destruction! What was to become of our poor Christians?

"The Regent, exasperated by the attack on the part of the French, bursting with pride at what seemed to him a brilliant victory, would put all to fire and sword. I spent many unhappy moments during the few days we lay at anchor: my heart was filled with grief. The prospect of soon seeing my colleagues gave me some encouragement. They arrived, in fact, on board the *Laplace*, which had been to Chefoo for dispatches. I will refrain from describing their deep grief on hearing the state of affairs.

"On leaving Korea, the flotilla dispersed. The *Guerrière* and the *Kien-chan* went to Japan; the *Laplace* returned to Chefoo, the other four ships set off for Shanghai. We ourselves arrived there on the *Primauguet*, the commander and officers of which were most obliging and attentive to us. We had brought ten Koreans with us; the three I had with me on leaving Chefoo, the one who came to rejoin me at Kang-hwa, and the six whom I have just mentioned. They are here, wearing Chinese clothes, awaiting an opportunity to return to their country, either alone or with one of us.

"The unexpected return of the expedition, after such a failure, startled the whole world, and aroused the wit of the English newspapers. I forgive them for their reflections on the subject. It was said, and repeated, that for the safety of Europeans in the Far East, to re-establish the prestige of their arms, it was absolutely necessary that the French should return to Korea in the following spring with adequate forces, otherwise the English and the Americans would consider sending an expedition themselves. When will it come? Pray, pray much for our unfortunate mission."

In this turmoil there ensued further cases of martyrdom in the various provinces.

The following Christians were beheaded on the banks of Yang-hwa-jin; on the fourth of the tenth moon, Ch'oe Su, Kim In-kil, Kim Chin and Kim Chin-ku; on the ninth of the same month, Kang Myŏng-heum, Hwang Ki-won, Lee Ki-ju and the wife of Kim Chin; on the fourteenth, Lee Yong-rae, Won Hu-jŏng and Park Sŏng-un.

The government also directed the governors of each of the eight provinces to order the arrest of every Christian, and to report every month to the Grand Council of State the numbers arrested, and the names of the officials effecting their arrest. Those officials reponsible for the arrest of twenty or more Christians were rewarded with promotion to the rank of *Pyŏn-chang*, or frontier commander, and appointed to lucrative posts.

As a result of this encouragement and pressure method, many Christians were put to death throughout the land. Let us glance at the records of their martyrdom.

Sŭng Yŏn-sun and Won Yun-ch'ŏl, who went to China and brought the Westerners into Korea, were killed at T'ong-jin on the seventeenth of the tenth moon, and Lee Chae-hyŏn, Kim Ye-ki and Kim In-ki, who had been arrested at Mun-kyŏng, were also beheaded at the command of the provincial governor.

As to John Lee Yun-il, the research papers for the process of beatification of the Blessed Twenty-six Martyrs read as follows:

John Lee Yun-il (Che-hyŏn)

John Lee Yun-il was born at Hong-ju, and was living at Yŏ-ho-mok-kol in Mun-kyŏng county, where he was arrested at the beginning of the tenth moon in 1866. Having prepared himself for martyrdom, John Lee made no effort to escape when he saw the constables coming to arrest him. When arrested he was calm and dignified.

A Christian by birth, and later a catechist, he did not reveal the names of other Christians when ordered to do so. He was severely tortured, after which, in company with some other Christians, he was sent to Mun-kyŏng.

At Mun-kyŏng, where there was no judge, he was again tortured, this time for three days. He was commanded to apostatize, and was urged to give money to the constables. On his refusal he was again tortured, being beaten with cudgels and having a double cangue fastened round his neck. He endured these tortures with a smile and even joy fulness, and his example greatly encouraged and consoled the other Christians.

He was then removed to Sang-ju, where he was again tortured. He was tortured three times every month for three months. Those Christians who renounced the faith were released, but many women and children were killed. John Lee, Catechist Kim and his brother, labelled the heads of the perverse religion, were again transferred to Tae-gu.

Three days after having been removed to Kwan-tuk-dong, outside the South Gate of Tae-gu, he was given his last meal and on the twenty-ninth day of the eleventh moon (January 21, 1867) he was beheaded, at the age of forty-five or six.

He showed a peaceful and joyful countenance when about to be executed, and greatly impressed those who were watching the proceedings. His companions, the Kim brothers, cried until the time of execution. At the place of execution he gave what money he had to the executioner, saying, "Ought I to die having this money with me? Take this money and behead me immediately." Thus he died, in a calm and composed attitude. His body was temporarily buried near the place of execution by the Christians, but three years later it was moved to Nal-mi Hill.

In the fourth year of the reign of King Ko-jong (1867) there still ensued imprisonments, and in March Kim Hong-pŏm died in the Seoul prison, when there were about thirty prisoners in the jail. On the fourth of the tenth moon, Chŭn Il-pok and Park Yŏng-su were beheaded in Seoul, and Lee Chae-hyŏn suffered the same fate on the twenty-eighth of the same month.

On the twenty-third of the first moon, 1868, Kim Kyŏng-po, Chŭn Yŏng-sŏk, Ra Ch'ang-mun, Lee Eui-tae, Kim Man-sŏng, and Ahn Heung-ju; on the thirteenth of the second moon, Kim Sŏng-sin and his wife A-ji-ryŏn, Park Kye-yong, Park Kyŏng-sŏng, Ro Sŏng-yong, and Lee Man-kil were beheaded.

On the thirtieth of the second moon, in 1868, Park Sŏng-ch'ŏl, the woman Kim, the woman Kwak, the woman Kong, Kong Hang-sŏn, Kim Paek-ch'ŏl and his wife Ko Myŏng-kil, the woman Kim, and the woman Lee Sun-i were beheaded.

On the third of the third moon, Kim-Il-tol, the woman Kim K'woe-ryŏng, the woman Lee Sŏng-sŏm, the woman Ch'oe P'il-ju, and Im Eui-kil were beheaded. On the thirtieth of the same month Ch'oe Yun-hyŏng, Cho Sŏng-no and his wife Ch'ŏe Sun-myŏng, and Park Sun-ji were also beheaded.

Among them, especially, Cho Sŏng-no and Park Sun-ji were executed on the charge of secretly burying the remains of Bishop Berneux's body in collaboration with Ch'oe Sa-kwan, father of Ch'oe Yun-hyŏng, Shin Pong-sŏk, Hong Sŏng-po, Ahn Chung-hyŏn, and Park Sŏng-un at Wa-sŏ-hyŏn, during the night. And also Pyŭn Chong-ŏk, Chang Sŏk-i, the woman Lee, the woman Lee Song-i, the woman Chang In-heui, the woman Lee In-ŏp, Pyŭn Kyŏng-kyo, the woman Pyŭn Su-ŏp, and the woman Han Sŏng-im were executed, on the fourteenth of the fourth moon, in 1868.

Thus the land of Korea was bathed with the blood of martyrs during the successive persecutions,and,when the fact became known to the world, every Christian acclaimed the glorious martyrdom of the Korean Christians, and in their pity prayed to God for the survivors. When Pope Pius IX heard of this fact, he consoled and encouraged the Korean Christians, sending the following Papal Brief dated December 19, 1866.

Letter of Pope Pius IX

My dear children, greetings and apostolic benediction!

We have been moved even to tears upon reading of the storms of evil which have torn from you the joyous beginnings of this year, and of how the wild boar from the forest has ripped up the floursihing young branches and the new shoots of the Lord's vineyard. In fact, unless the divine strength of faith had restrained in us the feelings of our faltering nature, the distress, afflictions, and slaughter of our children should have drawn naught else but tears from our paternal love. For they, deprived of their pastors, ruined and dispersed, and deprived of all the necessities of life, either wandering in lonely isolation, or, imprisoned and facing death, are persecuted by every sort of evil. But the reward of the brave not only tempers this excess of woes, but turns it to a canticle of praise. Theirs is the reward, who for the name of Christ have given all the perishable things of this world, even their lives, restoring the glory of the martyrs to the Church once more—the hope of a new and more plentiful harvest springing out of the blood of martyrs. All this compels us to a holy envy of your lot, who have been made worthy to be followers of our Divine Head and His disciples. And truly, are we not fighting for one who, although His is the Son of God, nevertheless willed to conquer the world by means of the Cross? Are we not the posterity of those who confirmed with their blood the doctrine of the Gospel handed down to the nations? Are not we, even as they, commanded to rejoice when we meet with various trials, and to exult especially when we are hated for the name of Christ, and suffer persecution for justice sake, because our reward is great in Heaven?

Abandon then, beloved sons, your sorrow; suppress your tears, and rejoice that you have received, even throughout your life, an opportunity to pay back to Christ His infinite love. For Christ laid down His life for your sake, and wholly offered Himself up for you. Remember that you were born for Heaven, not for earth, and behold those splendid thrones prepared there for the victorious, reflecting that slight tribulation, which is so short, brings eternal glory, which is great. From the bitter experience of struggle itself, raise up new vigor and spirit. We indeed are far off, but we will join in your agony in spirit. We will help you as much as possible by the liveliest prayers within our weak power. And lest you go any longer like lone sheep without a shepherd and be in even greater danger, we will, as soon as possible, take care that another, with no less courage and zeal, shall succeed to the place of him who has already received the glorious and fitting reward of his labors. We will ask God, who wished to put you to hard trials like those embraced unto Himself, that He may bestow upon you opportunities to serve Him freely, having soothed away all calamities and having restored peace in serenity. We ask God to return a bounty of good for the injuries done.

Meanwhile, as a sign of His grace to come, and as an undoubted pledge of our overflowing fatherly love, We forever impart to each and all of you Our apostolic benediction.

Given at Rome at St. Peter's on the 19th day of December, 1866; the twenty-first year of Our pontificate.

Pope Pius IX.

The text of the message was as follows:

PIUS P. P. IX.

Dilecti filii, salutem et apostolicam benedictionem.

Ad lacrymas usque commoti fuimus, cum legimus quae malorum procella exceperit apud vos laeta hujus anni exordia; et quomodo luxuriantes palmites novasque propagines vineae Domini aper de silva exterminaverit. Profecto nisi divina fidei virtus infirmae naturae sensus in nobis compescuisset, aerumnae, vexationes, caedes filiorum nostrorum, qui pastor privati, disjecti, necessariis omnibus ad vitam exuti, errantes in solitudinibus, aut etiam coacervati in ergastulis et morti devoti, malis omnibus opprimuntur, nonnisi gemitus ac lacrymas a paternâ nostrâ caritate elicere potuissent. At, profundum hunc moerorem non modo temperarunt, sed in canticum laudis converterunt palmae fortium, qui pro Christi nomine caduca omnia et vitam ipsam dederunt, instaurata rursum in Ecclesia martyrii gloria, spes novae copiosiorisque segetis e martyrum cruore erupturae; omniaque nos compulerunt ad sanctam sortis vestrae invidiam, qui digni divini capitis nostri ejusque discipulorum asseclae facti estis. Et sane, nonne illi militamus, qui licet Filius Dei esset nonnisi per crucem mundum vincere voluit? Nonne illorum progenies sumus qui traditam gentibus Evangelii doctrinam suo sanguine confirmarunt? Nonne nos, sicut et illi, jussi sumus gaudere cum in tentationes varias inciderimus, et exultare praesertim dum odio habemur pro Christi nomine et persecutionem patimur propter justitiam, quia merces nostra copiosa est in coelo?

Luctum itaque, dilecti filii, remittite, supprimite lacrymas, gaudete datum vobis fuisse, per vitam etiam, infinitum ejus amorem rependere, qui vitam suam pro vobis posuit seque totum vobis donavit. Memineritis vos coelo natos esse non terrae, intuemini fulgentes ibi sedes victoribus paratas, considerate momentaneum et leve tribulationis aeternum parare gloriae pondus. Ex ipsa acerbitate certaminis novos sumite animos. Nos licet dissiti, spiritu aderimus agoni vestro, jugibusque precibus opem, quam pro infirmitate nostra poterimus maximam, vobis feremus: ac ne diutius pastore carentes, veluti palatae oves, gravius etiam periclitemini, curabimus quamprimum, ut locum illius qui splendidam jam ac dignam laboribus suis mercedem accepit, alius non minoris fortitudinis ac zeli vir subeat. Deum vero qui vos, utpote sibi acceptos, tam dure probare voluit etiam atque etiam rogamus, ut calamitatibus omnibus aversis, reductaque pacis serenitate, plenissimam vobis faciat ei serviendi libertatem, tolerataque damna uberiore bonorum omnium copia rependat.

Auspicem interim gratiarum ejus et paternae nostrae effusaeque dilectionis pignus indubium, apostolicam benedictionem vobis universis peramanter impertimus.

Datum Romae apud S. Petrum die 19 decembris 1866; Pontificatus nostri anno vigesimo primo.

(Locus sigilli.) **PIUS P. P. IX.**

70. The Persecution in 1868

The third wave of the cruel persecution that started in 1866 assaulted the Catholics late in 1868, in connection with the alleged desecration of the tomb of Prince Nam-yŏn, the father of Prince Tae-won-kun. A great number of Catholics were sentenced to death in the Provinces of Ch'ung-ch'ŏng and Kyŏngsang during the fourth lunar month. Included among them were the descendants of Lee Seung-hun, who played a leading role in the establishment of Catholicism in Korea, and the three brave Catholics who had accompanied Father Ridel to China.

On the seventh of the fourth moon 1868, Thomas Lee Sin-kyu, son of Lee Seung-hun, and Kwon Pok, great-grandson of Kwon Ch'ŏl-sin, were beheaded outside the Small West Gate. Lee Chae-kyŏm, an adopted son of Lee Sin-kyu, was exiled to P'yŏng-an Province, and Cho Yu-sŏn to Nok-to Island in Chŏl-la Province.

On the same day, Sŭh Kun-jip died at the second police station, being unable to bear the torture. He was born at the village of Ha-tong, Yong-in and arrested at Song-tong-myŏn, Yang-ji, where he had been living for several years.

Thomas Lee Sin-kyu

Thomas Lee was born at Pan-sŏk-pang (now Chung-rim-dong), Seoul. His father was Lee Seung-hun, and his mother the sister of Chŭng Yak-yong. He removed to In-ch'ŏn, and was an old seminarian under the guidance of Bishop Imbert, together with Paul Chŭng Ha-sang.

In the Ki-hae persecution he was lucky enough to escape death, and in his hiding place he collected the biography of the martyrs, and exerted himself for the Church reconstruction, writing copies of the catechism.

At one time, in 1841, he was arrested, but soon set free, and afterward devoted himself to preaching the Gospel, together with Lee Chae-kyŏm, his adopted son, and Lee Chae-eui, his cousin.

He made friends with Lee Sa-kwan, and was still engaged in the work of evangelization, when he was arrested and martyred.

Kwon Pok

Kwon Pok was the son of Kwon Kwang, who was the grandson of Kwon Ch'ŏl-sin, a famous scholar at the time of Church establishment, and also a nephew of Lee Se-kwan. He served Bishop Berneux, made friends with Nam Chong-sam and Cho Ch'ŏl-jeung, and was engaged in the work of evangelization, when he was arrested and martyred.

Peter Kim Kye-kyo, Chang Ch'i-sŏn, John Ch'oe In-sŏ, and Anthony Kim Ch'ang-sil followed the same path. They had gone to Chefoo and Shanghai with the priests in the 1866 persecution. Among them Kim Kye-kyo and Chang Ch'i-sŏn had been arrested before the German Ernst Oppert came to Tŏk-san county. Judging from this, they were still devoting themselves to the religion, and striving to obtain the freedom of faith both at home and abroad.

The following story is a confession, from which we can get a glimpse at their history up to their martyrdom.

Peter Kim told the following story at the police station on the sixth of the fourth moon, having been arrested two weeks before Oppert's arrival.

The Confesssion of Peter Kim

"I am from Ch'ung-ju, Ch'ung-ch'ŏng Province and was taught the holy religion by Mark Chŭng Eui-pae in my childhood. In September 1866, I met Chang Ch'i-sŏn on the street of Su-p'yo-kyo when he told me, 'I am on my way to the country. I will pay you well if you carry my luggage.' So I asked, 'Where is it?' Then he said, 'It is in Su-won.'

"In the early morning the next day I presented myself at the appointed place, Su-ku-mun, where Chang was already waiting for me. He made me carry on my back clothes, sleeping gear and ten taels, and we made our way to Kŏl-mae-p'o, Su-won, where we put up for a night. Next morning he told me, 'My destination is the place where the Western boat is lying at anchor, so I am supposed to go aboard at Yong-tang-p'o. I think it best for you to follow me.' I demurred at this, and asked, 'How can we go on board when the vessel is under such strict surveillance?' He lured me on, saying, 'Don't worry about that. All on board are my subordinates, and if you go with me you will be doing a praiseworthy act, and besides, I want to know whether the general has come back or not.' I took the words in their truest sense and out of curiosity to see the Western ships, I followed him. Reaching Yong-tang-p'o, we went on Song Un-o's boat. We left Tae-jin, Su-won, together with the boatmen Lee Sŏng-eui and Lee Sŏng-jip, Song Un-o, the owner of the boat, and Park Tŏk-yŏ. Via P'al-mi Island we put up for a night at Yŏng-chong-p'o, where the seven Western ships lay at anchor. One man aboard the Western ship cried out in a loud voice to us, but we could not understand him. Only Chang understood him and replied, 'Isn't it Wang Kyŏng-ch'o?' Then the other side asked, 'Are you Chang?' To this Chang said, 'You are Father Lee (Ridel), I suppose.' Then we all went on board and set fire to the boat we had used. Aboard the ship were Fathers Ridel, Calais, Féron, Ch'oe Sŏn-il (Chi-hyŏk), Ch'oe In-sŏ, living at Ae-u-kae (A-hyŏn), the pilot Sim Sun-yŏ, and Kim Hak-i, living at Ri-mun-dong.

"I asked Ch'oe Sŏn-il and Ch'oe In-sŏ, who used to be my nodding acquaintances, 'How come you are here?' Ch'oe In-sŏ answered, 'As for me, I came from Kang-hwa; how did you get here?' I said, 'Chang asked me to follow him; where did those three priests come from?' Then Song Un-o and Lee Sŏng-eui replied, 'Father Ridel is serving on this ship; Fathers Féron and Calais were staying at the district of Mok-ch'ŏn, and we had them brought here.' Again I asked, 'I thought the men-of-war were at anchor at Kang-hwa Island; how is it that they are here?' They all replied in one voice:

" 'When they were in Kang-hwa Island they wanted to go sight-seeing to Chŏn-teung-sa Temple, but on their way they were fired on by our soldiers, and nine were killed and more than thirty wounded; so they cannot stay there any more, and want to return to their own country.'

" Then I told Chang, 'If I have any merit, I know that I shall be rewarded. This is what I am told, so I shall wait and see. However I shall not be able to go home now, and in fact I am destined to go to a faraway country. What is to be done?' Chang said, 'I have determined to go with them, so won't you go with me?' Then I became angry and rebuked him for deceiving me.

" Meanwhile the ship was about to set sail, and I had no choice but to follow them.

" After four days we reached Shanghai. The three countries of England, America, and France were building their churches, with their masters stationed there. Three priests, many other foreigners, and some Koreans were staying at the French church. I felt very sad, being so far away from my motherland and having no hope of returning. I implored Father Calais and Chang to let me go back to my country, day in and day out saying, 'I am so anxious to go back to my country that I don't feel like taking any food.' Father Calais said, 'Do as you please. Chang Ch'i-sŏn, Ch'oe In-sŏ, and you go back to your country with this seventy taels of silver, and try to help a priest enter your country.' Then he gave us nuggets of silver, and beseeched us to hold fast to the faith surreptitiously. We obeyed this advice, and carried the silver with us, dividing it into three parts.

" In the fourth moon, 1867, we got aboard a boat in Nanking, and after ten days arrived at Lientai, Peking, but we had to stay there for a while, being unable to get a boat.

"Toward the end of the seventh moon we set sail aboard a Chinese boat, and after a week arrived at Ma-eup-do, Ong-jin, Hwang-hae Province. When I arrived at Song-do (now Kae-sŏng) together with Chang and Ch'oe, Chang said, 'I can't walk any more, since my feet are swollen, so I'd better leave after my feet are cured.' Then I said, 'I am so anxious to go back to my home that I can't postpone my departure any longer, so I will proceed on my way.' Chang said, 'When can I expect to see you again?' I replied, 'I just took part in this affair of bringing a bishop into the country because the situation compelled me to do so.' Then I handed the silver nuggets over to him. Chang gave me a lump weighing four taels (liang) and said, 'This is at your disposal.' I received it and came back to Seoul. I called on Ch'oe Sa-kwan and the catechist, and told them in detail all that had happened to me. A few days later I visited Ch'oe Sa-kwan again, and met Ch'oe In-sŏ and Chang Ch'i-sŏn there. One day, I ran across the two on the street, and asked where they lived. Ch'oe In-sŏ is living at Sŏ-kang, and Chang Ch'i-sŏn at Kwang-ju, Kyŏng-ki Province. That is what they told me, but I don't know the details.

" In the eleventh moon last year, I removed to a servant's room in the home of a *Yang-ban* at Paek-dong (now Hye-hwa-dong).

"Unexpectedly Chang happened to live in an adjacent neighborhood, and, as we were on visiting terms, I came to be arrested."

The Confession of Chang Ch'i-sŏn

"I used to live at Che-ch'ŏn, and then, about the tenth moon last year, I removed to Paek-dong and engaged in business. When I was five years old, I learnt the holy religion from Oh Cha-hyŏn, who used to live at Ŏn-ri, Yang-ji district, and received Baptism.

"In spring the year before last, I heard the news that Bishop Berneux had been arrested and killed, and that many Christians also had been arrested. In the third moon I wanted to know the situation. On my way to Seoul I happened to meet Chi Cha-ik, and went to his house. Chi told me, 'The bishops and priests who came from a land so far away have been arrested and killed, together with many Christians. It is imperative for us to make known the fact to Shanghai, so that the Western ships may come and rescue fellow-Christians, and also the holy religion may become widespread in our country. Be sure to fetch Father Calais's letter.'

"I said, 'I left the letter with Park Tŏk-yŏ, living at Kal-mae-p'o, Su-won, so I'll go and get it.' Chi, much rejoiced to hear this, said, 'If we have Father Calais's letter with us, everything goes fine. Go quickly and get it.' I gladly consented to this, and went down to Su-won and got the letter. On my way back to Seoul, I met Mr. Lim at the inn of Kang-kil-ri, Su-won. I told him that I was carrying Father Calais's letter and let him know what Chi had said. Mr. Lim was re-joiced at hearing this and accompanied me to Seoul, where we proceeded to Chi's home. Chi, too, was glad to see the letter and Mr. Lim's presence and said, 'This is not a matter of mere chance. We have come into possession of Father Calais's letter, and also are joined by Mr. Lim. Moreover a family of noble class has assisted us, and we have purchased a boat, which is now at anchor at the port. Now we have nothing to worry about.'

"Then I asked, 'What is that noble family, and whose assistance is it?' Chi replied, 'He is Cho Ch'ŏl-jeung, a clerk in the Grand Council, living at Che-dong. He contributed money for us, and enabled us to buy the boat. He really deserves to be called a man of chivalrous spirit. You and Mr. Lim will see him before long.'

"Mr. Lim and I went to Cho's, guided by Chi. There we were served by a woman of about fifty with a table filled with liquor. While we were drinking, some one entered the room. Chi said, 'The man who has just entered is Cho Ch'ŏl-jeung'. We toasted each other, and then Chi said, 'The preparation of the boat and all the expenses are already furnished by Cho, so now we must get started as soon as possible.'

"Following Chi's advice we two immediately went to Yŏng-chong-p'o. Arriving there we found the boat ready, and Ch'oe Sŏn-il waiting. I told Ch'oe, 'Crossing a vast sea in such a small boat like a leaf means certain failure. How much do you estimate it would cost to build a more suitable boat?' Ch'oe replied, 'It would cost about five or six hundred taels (liang), I think, but where could we get that amount?' I suggested, 'Father Calais's money is deposited in Park Tŏk-yŏ's house. I think we'd better use this money in advance.'

"Many people were glad to hear this, and wanted me to bring it right away. Then I went to the house and told the plan to Park Tŏk-yŏ.

"Park said, 'You have now Father Calais's letter in your hands, so I don't think it will be difficult for you to borrow it.' Then Park handed six hundred taels to me.

"Having bought the timber to be used in the boat, Father Ridel and I went to Yong-tang-ri, Sin-ch'ang. There we set sail on about the eighth day of the fifth moon, together with the six boatmen—Yun Ch'i-sŏng, Sim Sun-yŏ, Lee Sŏng-eui, Lee Sŏng-jip, Park Tŏk-yŏ, Song Un-o,—and Ch'oe In-sŏ, Kim Yŏng-heui, Ch'oe Sŏn-il, and Father Ridel, and by the middle of the month we arrived at Lientai district.

"One day Father Ridel, after having gone on board the Western ship all by himself, told me, 'Several men-of-war will set sail before long.'

"I decided to come back to my country with the boatmen and arrived at Nae-p'o by way of Chang-san-kot, where many of us landed and went home. I came on alone to Seoul, and fortunately met Mr. Lim within the boundary of Small East Gate. We talked for a while and together went to Lee Yŏn-sik living at Sŏng-puk-dong.

"Lee treated me with hospitality for a month, and urged me to change my clothes, giving me a new suit. I went to Chi Cha-ik's wearing it. Chi asked me, 'How did you make out in your journey? When will the Western boats come?'

"I replied, 'I went there charged with an important mission. How can I return empty-handed? They will come within a month at the earliest, or around the eighth or ninth moon at the latest; otherwise the second or third moon next year without fail.'

"Hearing this Chi was much pleased, and afterward I met Cho, and the aforesaid woman told me, 'How would you like to stay at my home?' I accepted this offer gladly.

"Next day Cho visited me and said, full of gaiety, 'How was your voyage over thousands of miles and when will the men-of-war come?' I told him every detail. Then he asked again, 'What are the real intentions after the men-of-war come here?' I answered, 'Their only intention is to spread the Gospel. They do not have the slightest intention of killing or hurting men.' He asked again, 'Don't you think they intend to commit an aggression by means of evangelization?'

"I replied to this, 'The real intention of the holy religion does not lie in the conquest of other countries, if the holy religion comes to permeate among peoples, certain odd customs inconsistent with our religion will be changed or replaced.'

"On the ninth moon of the same year I boarded the Western boats together with Kim Kye-kyo, Song Un-o, and Park Tŏk-yŏ, and traveled to Shanghai, where I stayed until, in the ninth moon last year, I returned to my country. Hence my arrest."

At the beginning of the persecution in 1866 Chang Ch'i-sŏn reported the wretched situation to Shanghai, and helped Father Ridel flee from Korea. Chang Ch'i-sŏn was one of the leading Catholics to have tried to establish the freedom of worship in Korea, making two successive journeys to China. The police issued a warrant for the arrest of Cho Ch'ŏl-jeung, clerk of the Grand Council on the nineteenth day of the fourth moon, on the charge of helping Chang Ch'i-sŏn, by giving him money to travel to China. This was revealed by Chang Ch'i-sŏn under severe torture. Policemen were sent to Tong-myŏn, Tan-yang county, Ch'ung-ch'ŏng Province, the home town of Cho Ch'ŏl-jeung, to arrest him but it was vacant, for, knowing of the warrant for his arrest through his nephew Cho Yu-sŏn, Cho Ch'ŏl-jeung had already killed himself. Now things had come

to such a pass that a warrant was again issued for the arrest of Cho Yu-sŏn. He was soon arrested and exiled on the seventh of the fourth moon to Rok Island, Chŏl-la Province. Kwon Sŏk, who had already been arrested, was executed at the command of the police on the fourth of the fifth moon.

Chang Ch'i-sŏn and Ch'oe In-sŏ, who had been to Shanghai, were beheaded, and their heads displayed at the naval base of T'ong-jin on the twenty-second of the fifth moon; Sohn Kyŏng-ro and Kim Yang-kil, who had helped Oppert when he had appeared at Ku-man-p'o, Tŏk-san county, were also beheaded, and their heads displayed on the twenty-ninth, at Po-ryŏng, Ch'ung-ch'ŏng Province; Lee Yŏng-jung, who had been in Su-won prison, was beheaded at the naval base of Ch'ung-ch'ŏng Province, on the eighteenth of the following month.

On the thirteenth of the sixth moon, Lee Kuk-eung, an official of the Court of Censorship, submitted a petition to the king for the arrest of Cho Yŏn-seung, a former district magistrate and illegitimate nephew of Cho Cha-teung, who had already been arrested, on the charge of believing in the perverse learning. Availing itself of the opportunity, the High Court of Justice proposed the arrest of Cho Chun-seung, the younger brother of Cho Yŏn-seung, on the evidence of the other criminal's confession that he also belonged to the same religion. The king gave his consent. They were finally arrested and put to interrogation at the High Court of Justice, when another brother of Cho Yŏn-seung, Cho Nak-seung, was also arrested, and joined the brothers. The three brothers were brought to trial, and on the twenty-sixth of the same month Cho Yŏn-seung and Cho Nak-seung were sentenced to be beheaded on charge of bewitching people, teaching the catechism, and spreading rumors, while Cho Chun-seung was released.

Their execution was carried out outside the Small West Gate. While these influential Christians were shedding their blood for God, a large number of confessors were arrested in Kyŏng-sang Province. On the third of the eighth moon Lim Chŏng-t'aek in Mun-kyŏng was sent to the military fort at Chin-ju and beheaded, for having entered the room where the confessors were being tortured and having defended them.

On the fourth of the same month Ku Chu-won, the naval commander in Kyŏng-sang Province-reported to the king the decapitation of Lee Chŏng-sik, Lee Wol-ju, Park So-sa, Lee Kwan-pok, Lee Sam-keun, Ch'a Chang-teuk, Ryang Chae-hyŏn and Ok So-sa.

On the fifteenth of the same month Yun Eung-sŏn, the military commander in Kyŏng-sang Province, also reported the execution of Kim Chong-ryun, Hŭh In-paek and Lee Yang-teung. On the fourth of the ninth moon Oh Ch'i-sŏn, the governor of Kyŏng-sang Province, reported the execution of Park Su-ryŏn and others.

In this way a large number of confessors were martyred in 1868 and the land came to be dyed in their blood.

Dallet wrote, in his *Histoire de l'Eglise de Corée*, about the number of the martyrs:

"The number of the martyred in the month of September, 1868 was two thousand, five hundred of whom were executed at Seoul. Later, in 1870, it was said that the number of martyrs in Korea was no less than eight thousand, not including those who died of hunger, exposure, and destitution while hiding in the mountains.

71. Invasion of the American Naval Fleet and Ensuing Persecution, 1871

It is well known that the French did not return to Korea, nor did the English plan the slightest military action. Various United States vessels, having run aground on the coast of Korea and having been burnt and their crews massacred, a small American flotilla came in 1871, in order to negotiate a treaty for the protection of shipwrecked mariners. On June 1, while two gunboats were taking soundings in the Salt River between the Island of Kang-hwa and the mainland, the Koreans opened fire on them without warning. The gunboats replied and promptly silenced the Korean forts.

Admiral Rodgers, believing that this conflict was due to the action of some subordinate officials, waited in vain ten days for an explanation from the Korean government. On June 10, the marines landed on Kang-hwa Island and took possession of three forts, in spite of the resistance of the Koreans who, it is said, fought desperately. Official documents found in one of these forts prove that the attack on June 1 had been ordered and prepared for by the government. Negotiations were entered into. From the start the Americans offered to hand over the wounded and other prisoners, on their parole not to bear arms during the war. The minister merely answered: "Do what you like with these men: as soon as you release them we shall severely punish them." Rodgers soon understood that in order to impose a treaty the only thing to do was to seize the capital. Not daring to take such a responsibility on himself, and moreover not having sufficient forces, he had to withdraw and refer to the government in Washington. Thereafter, no further attempt was made.

A few weeks later, a missionary wrote:

"The American expedition has definitely left Korea and there is no doubt that, like that of the French in 1866, it has left the Koreans convinced that they have defeated and expelled the Western barbarians. In spite of all the explanations in the Shanghai and Hongkong newspapers, the Chinese themselves regard the American withdrawal as a defeat. It is believed that they will return to Korea, but while waiting, the poor mission is under pressure and this affair has led to an aggravation of the persecution."

The pessimistic outlook of the missionaries after the departure of the American expedition proved only too well founded. Over and over again Koreans managed to cross the frontier, and brought news from the interior. Nine Christians, who had come to the American ships in the hopes of being able to meet their priests, were sent to Shanghai by Admiral Rodgers, and have provided the following details:

"The situation is lamentable. The Christians

are all outlawed *en masse* as rebels, traitors to their country, and partisans of the foreigners: all their property has been confiscated. They no longer have the expedient of migrating to another province in order to conceal their religion, as they formerly had: a new law forbids anyone to take up residence in any district without first presenting himself to the magistrate All the Christian communities are in ruins: all the families dispersed. Numberless orphans have fallen into the hands of pagans who are bringing them up in hatred of Christianity; others, less unfortunate, are left to die of cold and hunger on the highways like outcasts from an accursed race. The persecutors, informed by traitors, have put to death all the outstanding Christians, those who by their zeal, their knowledge, their experience or their wealth, could have protected their brethren. At the capital and in the large towns, legal formalities are dispensed with in dealing with Christians: all who are recognized as being or having been Christians are dragged to the nearest prison and at once strangled. By a refinement of satanic cruelty, they try to make them apostatize before putting them to death, for the pagans are well aware of the high esteem in which the Christians hold martyrdom for the faith. If the confessor remains steadfast, they kill him in public in order to inspire terror: if, exhausted by tortures, his limbs broken, he begs for pity and pronounces a single word of apostasy they send him out as if about to release him, and kill him at the prison gates.

"In some regions they have put aside the saber and the axe, which are too slow for the executioners, and are using a new lethal instrument. It is a kind of guillotine, formed of two superposed beams: the upper beam, being allowed to drop on the lower, can crush the neck of twenty or twenty-five persons at the same time. Elsewhere, they dig wide and deep pits into which the Christians are thrown, still alive, one on top of the other, and then earth and stones are thrown in so that they are killed and buried in one operation. In the month of September, 1868, there were already two thousand victims of the persecution, five hundred of whom were of Seoul. In 1870 the rumor ran that in Korea they totalled eight thousand, not counting those who died in the hills of hunger and poverty. Naturally it is impossible to verify these figures, but, whether exaggerated or not they show that the Regent wanted to keep his word and, in less than ten years, destroy all vestiges of Christianity."

After the end of the year 1866 there were no more priests in Korea. With the glorious martyrdom of the nine missionaries and the forced exile of three others, the second period of the history of the Korean Church ends. Let us summarize it briefly.

Since Korea was raised to an apostolic vicariate there had been five bishops, three of whom were martyred; sixteen missionaries, nine of whom were martyred; two Korean priests, one of whom was martyred. All these Church workers we have seen at work, instructing the Christians, administering the sacraments to the neophytes, baptizing the pagans, multiplying the devotional books, constantly at the breach in order to repair the evils brought about by constant persecution, doing everything for everybody to win all to Jesus Christ. Their annual reports showed us with what success God vouchsafed to crown their efforts. The number of souls saved, of infidels converted, of pagan infants baptized *in articulo mortis* (on the point of death), goes on unceasingly increasing. The Gospel, better and better known in the country, spreads its conquests more and more widely, and has now penetrated to the remotest provinces, hitherto closed to its influence, and everything presages an early and brilliant triumph of the truth over error, of Jesus Christ over Satan, when God, whose ways are inscrutable, has permitted hell to make a last supreme effort. The Church in Korea has been drenched with the blood of her pastors and her faithful.

But she will rise from the tomb in which her enemies had thought to seal her for ever. Jesus Christ, constantly crucified in

His Own, is constantly resurrected. New missionaries have been sent to take the place of the martyrs. They are now working in Liaotung, a province of Manchuria contiguous to Korea, and are preparing to avail themselves of the first opportunity to penetrate to their desolated mission. To Father, now Bishop, Ridel has fallen the glorious heritage of Bishop Berneux and Bishop Daveluy. Appointed by the Sovereign Pontiff Bishop of Philippopolis and Vicar Apostolic of Korea, he came to Rome to receive the episcopal consecration, on June 5, 1870.[1]

On May 24, 1871, three days after the arrival of the American naval fleet in Korea, King Ko-jong presided in person over the trial of three Catholics, Kim Yŏ-kang, Lee Ton-ho, and Kim Ch'ang-sil at the Sam-kun-pu or Office of the Joint Chiefs of Staff. Anthony Kim Ch'ang-sil, who had accompanied Father Ridel to Chefoo in April 1866, and had returned to his country by way of Liaotung, was arrested prior to the arrival of the American fleet and interrogated in Seoul on April 1, 1871. The three Catholics were tried in the king's presence and, on May 27, beheaded outside the Small West Gate, on charges of high treason. On June 20 the Kyŏng-ki provincial governor beheaded Lee Yŏn-ku and Lee Kyun-ku at Che-mul-p'o after their arrest in In-ch'ŏn. As great-grandsons of Peter Lee Seung-hun they had attempted to approach the American fleet and guide it into Korean waters. On July 5 the Kyŏng-ki provincial governor beheaded Mrs. Chŭng, wife of Lee Chae-kyŏm; her grandson, Lee Myŏng-hyŏn, Paik Yong-sŏk, and the woman Kim Yŏ-a-ji at Che-mul-p'o. Lee Myŏng-hyŏn was the great-great-grandson of Peter Lee.

On July 17 U Yun-jip, Ch'oe Sun-pok, and Park Sang-son, who had visited the American fleet in secret, were beheaded at Kap-ko-ji, a ferry on Kang-hwa Island, and their heads displayed to the public on poles.

With these executions the persecution exerted by Tae-won-kun on the Catholics came to a temporary halt. Two years later, in 1873, the tenth year of King Ko-jong's reign, the Prince Regent, who had cruelly massacred so many Catholics, was obliged to retire to private life. On December 22 Ch'oe Ik-hyŏn a vice-secretary in the Grand Council submitted a written proposal for his retirement. Min Seung-ho, brother of Queen Min, and his colleagues supported the proposal. The prince was compelled to transfer the power of government to the king, his son, on December 24, and went to live at Kod-eun-kol, near Yang-ju.

Note:

Among the martyrs in the persecution of 1866 the following twenty-six Confessors are to be beatified after the completion of the *Procès Apostoliques*.

Bishop Berneux, Bishop Daveluy, Father Bretenières, Father Beaulieu, Father Dorie, Father Pourthié, Father Petitnicolas, Father Aumaître, Father Huin, Peter Ryu Chŏng-ryul, John Nam Chong-sam, Peter Ch'oe Hyŏng (Ch'i-jang), John Chŭn Chang-un (Seung-yŏn), Mark Chŭng Eui-pae, Alexis U Se-yŏng (Se-p'il), Luke Hwang Sŏk-tu (Chae-kŏn), Joseph Chang Nak-so (Chu-ke), Thomas Sohn Cha-sŏn, Peter Cho Hwa-sŏ (Pyŏng-eui), Joseph Cho Yun-ho, Peter Lee Myŏng-sŏ (Chae-tŏk), Bartholomew Chŭng Mun-ho (Kye-sik), Peter Sohn Sŏn-ji, Peter Han Won-sŏ (Chae-kwon), Peter Chŭng Won-ji (Won-jo), John Lee Che-hyŏn (Yun-il).

---

[1] Bishop Ridel was born at Chantenay, Diocese of Nantes, on July 7, 1830. Ordained priest in the month of December 1857, he was for eighteen months Vicar in the parish of La Remaudière. On July 29, 1859 he entered the seminary of the *Société des Missions-Étrangères*, and left for Korea on July 25 of the following year.

BOOK THREE

THE ERA OF RELIGIOUS LIBERTY

CHAPTER TEN

THE OPEN-DOOR POLICY

72. The Re-entry of Foreign Missionaries, and Their Activities

The disastrous decade of persecution under Prince Regent Tae-won-kun was now at an end. We shall recount in this chapter the efforts for the restoration and reconstruction of the Church in Korea which were made by the three surviving foreign missionaries who had succeeded in making their escape to China. On receipt of the sad news of the execution of the nine priests in 1866, the *Société des Missions-Étrangères de Paris* decided to dispatch a first group of three priests, Fathers Marie-Jean-Gustave Blanc, Pierre-Eugène Richard, and Alexandre-Jérémie Martineau to Korea to co-operate with the surviving three, and they left Paris in 1867. In the meantime the survivors, Fathers Féron, Calais and Ridel, made every effort to regain entry into Korea. Living in Shanghai, where he was diligently perfecting his knowledge of the Korean language, Father Ridel received news from Bishop Petitjean in Nagasaki that some Koreans had arrived there. He immediately went to Nagasaki to meet these Koreans and find out whether their services could be utilized in getting him into the country again. But alas! They were from Quelpart Island (Cheju-do) and knew nothing about the persecution. He decided not to pursue the matter with them, and returned to Shanghai.

Father Calais, who had moved to Manchuria in 1867 with Bishop Verrolles's assistance, to await an opportunity to re-enter Korea by land, met Fathers Richard and Martineau there on their arrival from Paris. In June, 1867, Father Ridel made an attempt to cross the Korean border, but failed. In May, 1868, Father Féron made a further attempt to enter Korea, but only incurred the hostility of the Prince Regent and returned to France in September, 1868, via Chefoo. Father Ridel now replaced him as senior missionary in the Korean Vicariate Apostolic. At the close of 1868 he went to Manchuria and held a conference, at which Fathers Calais, Blanc, Richard and Martineau were present, to decide on effective measures for prosecuting the work of the mission in Korea. As the village of Ch'akou where the conference was held was surrounded with high snow-covered mountains, they christened it "*Notre-Dame des Neiges*" (Our Lady of the Snows). A series of regulations for the mission was drawn up and approved on December 8. With the approval of Bishop Verrolles, the conference remained in session until 1874. It was decided that the Korean Christian Francis Kim should escort two missionaries as far as the Korean border and then enter Korea alone, returning to fetch them if the situation improved. Fathers Calais and Martineau volunteered to go on this mission, and while they were making preparations to leave, Father

Ridel returned to Shanghai via Chefoo, arriving there on April 24, 1869. He had planned to begin missionary work there, but hearing that Fathers Calais and Martineau were seeking a boat and crew to take them to Korea, Father Ridel returned to Manchuria, only to find that Father Calais had gone back to France for medical treatment. Father Ridel then set out on a voyage with Father Blanc and several Korean Catholics in an attempt to enter Korea, but failed, and they returned to Manchuria. On July 18, 1868, Father Ridel received information of his appointment as the sixth Bishop of the Korean Vicariate. At the invitation of Pope Pius IX he attended the Vatican conference of 1870, and on June 5 of that year he was consecrated Bishop with Cardinal Bonnechose officiating.

Bishop Ridel, charged with this heavy task, returned to Liaotung via Shanghai in the following year. He dispatched his faithful aide, John Ch'oe Chi-hyŏk, known as Ch'oe Sŏn-il, to Korea to make the necessary preparations for the re-entry of foreign missionaries into the country. In October, 1872, Bishop Ridel visited Chefoo with Father Blanc, and then returned with him to Ch'akou, in Liaotung. While awaiting a reply from Korea they spent the time compiling a Korean-French dictionary. John Ch'oe and his colleagues at last made their appearance; it was now February, 1875, and as the king of Korea had just issued an order forbidding the execution of Catholics without his own prior sanction, it seemed that the persecution had to some extent abated. Encouraged by this news Bishop Ridel left for Korea in September, 1875, with Father Blanc, instructing Father Richard to remain in Ch'akou to deal with pending issues. But the missionaries were once again destined to failure and disappointment, being successful only in escorting the Korean Catholic Thaddaeus Kwon Ch'i-mun and his party safely to the coast of Korea. The boat in which the missionaries had set out was driven back by a storm and forced to return to the coast of China. Father Martineau became ill during a trip to Intze and died there on August 10, 1875.

Bishop Ridel received a new missionary from Paris on April 27, 1876, at Ch'akou. This was Father Victor-Marie Deguette, and his arrival coincided with preparations that were being made by Bishop Ridel and Father Blanc for a renewed attempt during the fine weather of spring. Father Deguette volunteered to join them, and they went together to a certain island where, on the night of May 8, they boarded a vessel, on which Thaddaeus Kwon had come from Korea to conduct the missionaries into his country. Fathers Blanc and Deguette reached Korea safely on May 10, and entered Seoul, in disguise, on the following day. For the first time in ten years, since the outbreak of the persecution in 1866, the Korean Church had priests of its own.

Bishop Ridel now made a series of journeys to Chefoo, Shanghai, Hongkong, Nagasaki, and Peking, in an effort to pave the way for the Catholic missionaries to be admitted freely into Korea. Finally, with two more priests Camille-Eugène Doucet and Achille-Paul Robert who had been assigned to the Korean Vicariate, he left China for Korea. Drifting on the sea for eighteen days, they were finally met by John Ch'oe, who had put out in another boat to lead them into Korea. At last he was back in his beloved Korean mission; it was September 1877, eleven years since his escape, and seven since his consecration as Bishop of the Vicariate. Although Korea had concluded a treaty of friendship and commerce with Japan, which had been signed at Kang-hwa Island eighteen months before, there were no foreigners in the capital yet, and the Japanese did not establish their legation in Seoul until 1879, two years later. The attitude of the government toward Catholicism had not really changed, and foreign missionaries constantly ran the risk of arrest and renewed persecution.

Struggling valiantly against these difficulties, the Bishop and his four priests did their utmost to rehabilitate the Korean Church. The two missionaries who had preceded the others now conducted an extensive tour of the Provinces of Kyŏng-ki and Ch'ung-ch'ŏng, visiting the Catholics in those areas and bringing them the comforts of the faith. The other two settled down in Hwang-hae Province to learn the language, while Bishop Ridel stayed in Seoul in charge of the overall management of Churches throughout the Vicariate, and at the same time undertook the establishment of a theological seminary and a printing shop. The Catholics were now greatly reanimated in their morale and religious fervor, and flocked to see their Bishop and priests, visiting them constantly day and night. So great was their enthusiasm and devotion that the Bishop was kept very busy indeed. In the tenth lunar month of the year of his arrival he decided to dispatch two Catholics, Ch'oe Ch'i-hwa and Oh Ch'i-ok, to China, with letters from him and from John Ch'oe, to Fathers Coste and Mutel in Ch'akou, telling them about the situation of the Korean Church.

The two Catholics were expected to return by the twelfth lunar month, but at six o'clock in the morning of January 26, 1878, the Bishop was shocked to hear from John Ch'oe, in whose house he was living, that the two secret messengers had been arrested at the Manchurian border and under the usual harsh torture, had presumably revealed all the secret matters. "Their confession has in fact been brought to the attention of the king," he added, in great agitation, "and it is said that orders have been given for your arrest and that of all the Catholics. The apostates who betrayed the Church in 1866 have been sent for to assist the government in rounding up all of us, and I fear they will begin this very day." "Indeed," replied the Bishop, "then now is the time for us to show our faith as true Catholic believers. We have done nothing wrong; let God's will be done on earth, as it is in Heaven. I am determined to undergo arrest in an honorable manner. I have resolved to give up my life for God and for the glory of the Church. There is no more rapid way to Heaven than by dying for the faith." "As for me," answered John, "I am an old man and have no regrets about dying, but it is such a short time since you came back to Korea, and there are still so many Catholics who have not yet received the Sacraments, that it would be an irreparable loss if this should turn out to be the last day of your ministry."

Determined to go through with it, Bishop Ridel briefed his missionaries, burned all compromising documents, handed over the Church funds to a trustworthy man, and waited for the storm to burst. At four o'clock in the afternoon of January 28, the street outside was filled with approaching constables. There was a thunderous noise as they poured in through the door to make their arrests. Together with the Bishop were John Ch'oe, his faithful aide and owner of the house in which he was living, Lucy Lee, John's wife, Shin Ch'i-uk, and the nineteen-year-old boy Chŭn Sun-ryong.

In prison the Bishop remained steadfast in his resolution to die a martyr, if that should be God's will. But now that the government had been obliged to sign a treaty of amity with Japan it no longer felt free to massacre foreign missionaries as before, and delayed taking any decisive action. Finally it was decided that Bishop Ridel be expelled from Korea, and in June, 1878, he was escorted by three officials to the Manchurian border. Though he escaped with his life he was deeply disappointed at being parted from his flock, whom, at the risk of death, he had served for so long. He never returned to Korea, but lived with Father Coste in Japan, where he published doctrinal and devotional material for the Korean Church. In 1881, stricken with paralysis, he returned to France, where he died in June 20, 1884.

And what happened to the Catholics arrested together with Bishop Ridel? Rather than incur the obloquy of executing them in public, the government allowed them to starve to death in prison. Martyred in this way were the septuagenarian John Ch'oe and his wife Lucy, John Shin, Chŭn Sun-ryong, and Ch'oe Ch'i-hwa and Oh Ch'i-ok, who had been arrested at the border.

The merits of John Ch'oe are deserving of

Bishop Jean-Marie-Gustave Blanc, seventh Vicar Apostolic of Korea (1884-1890)

A Korean version of the "Histoire de l'Église de Corée" (1874)

Probably made during the last years of the nineteenth century. It was published in serial form in the "Po-kam" magazine from 1906.

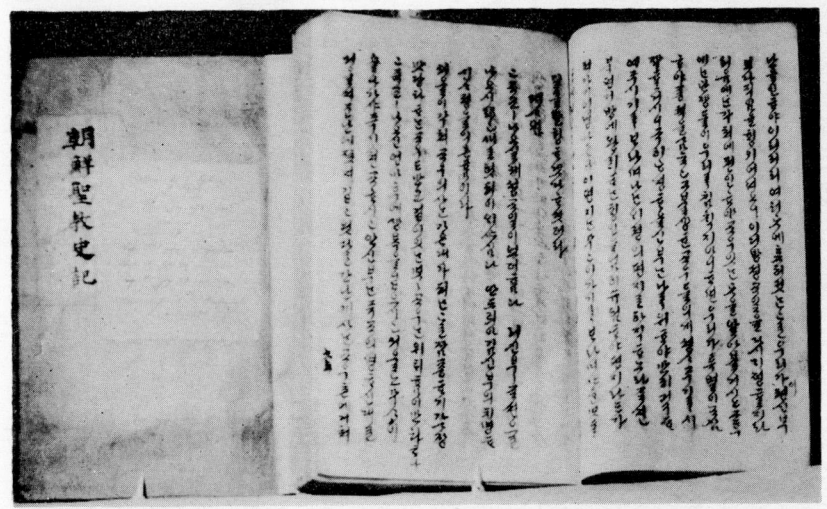

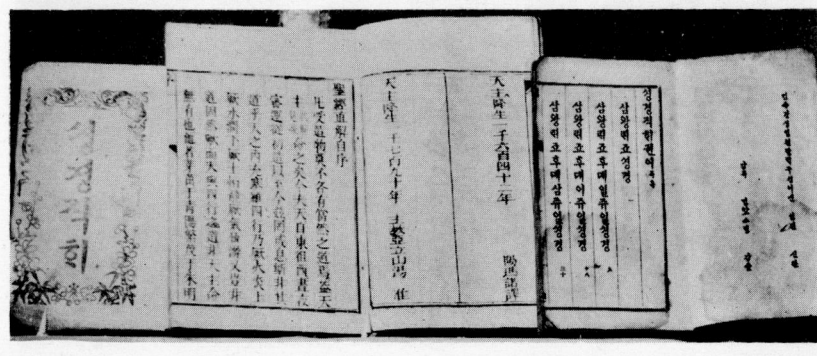

"Sŏng-kyŏng-jik-hae", a commentary of the Gospels and Epistles, (left, right) Korean version, (middle) Chinese version

Published in book form by Bishop Mutel, 1892-97

Archbishop Augustine Mutel, Eighth Vicar Apostolic of Korea (1890-1933)

The Archbishop's seal

Father Mutel in Korean costume
A photograph taken in 1885

Father Mutel (front row, center)
With clergy and laymen

CASTANIER | ROUCHOUSE | QUINTON | COMBAZ | CHAPUIS | DUCŒUR | DEMANGE | ELOY | RAYSSAC | BOURGAIN | GASPAIS
Osaka 1918 | Chengtou 1916 | Saigon 1912 | Nagasaki 1912 | Kumbakonam 1911 | Nanning 1910 | Taikou 1911 | Xa Doai 1912 | Swatow 1915 | Ningyuenfu 1918 | Chirin 1927
 | | | | | | | | | | de GOROSTARZU
FAYOLLE | SEGUIN | ROY | GRANGEON | MARCOU | RAMOND | CHOULET | BOUCHUT | FOULQUIER | PERROS | Yunnansen 1907
Soutfou 1909 | Kouy Yang 1907 | Coimbatour 1905 | Quinhon 1902 | Phat D'em 1895 | Hung hoa 1895 | Moukden 1901 | Pnompenh 1902 | Mandalay 1906 | Bangkok 1909 |
 | | | | | | | | | | CARDOT
CHOUVELLON | MUTEL | MOREL | ROBERT | de GUÉBRIANT | DELMAS F. C. | CENDREAU | BERLIOZ | Rangoon 1893
Tchun Kin?1901 | Seoul 1890 | Poudichéry 1909 | 1er Assistant | Supérieur S. S. | 2e Assistant | Hanoi 1887 | Hakodate 1891 |

The Episcopal Synod of the Paris Foreign Mission Society (Bp. Mutel, front row, second from left)

303

The Cathedral of the Immaculate Conception, Seoul

The planning and building of this Cathedral were supervised by Father Jean Coste until his death, when Father Victor Louis Poisnel (inset) took charge until the completion. The cornerstone was laid in 1892, and the consecration of the building and its dedication took place on May 29, 1898.

On the occasion of the consecration of the Cathedral

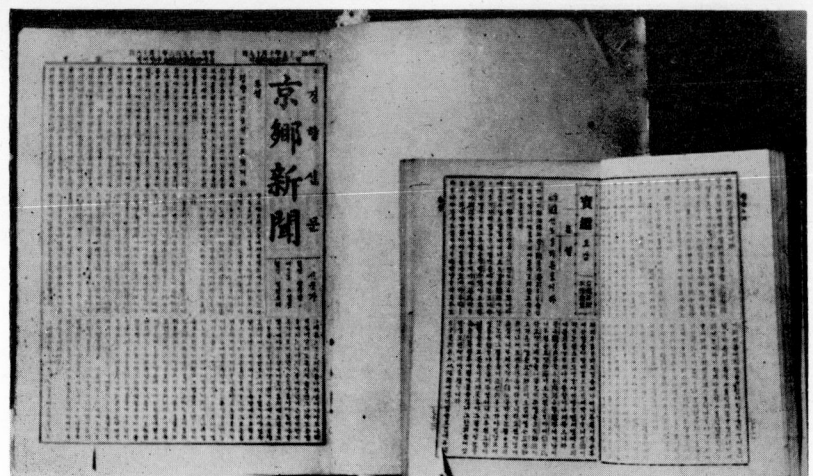

An early issue of the "Kyŏng-
hyang-sin-mun" (left)
Korea's first Catholic organ
and *Po-kam*, the Catholic magazine

"Martyrs Français et Coréens" by Launay
A book on the Seventy-nine Beatified Martyrs

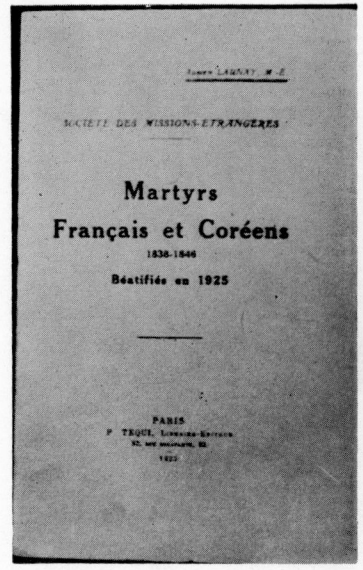

Facsimile of Archbishop Mutel's "Korean-
French Dictionary" (1878)

"The French Vo-
cabulary", with
explanation in
Korean

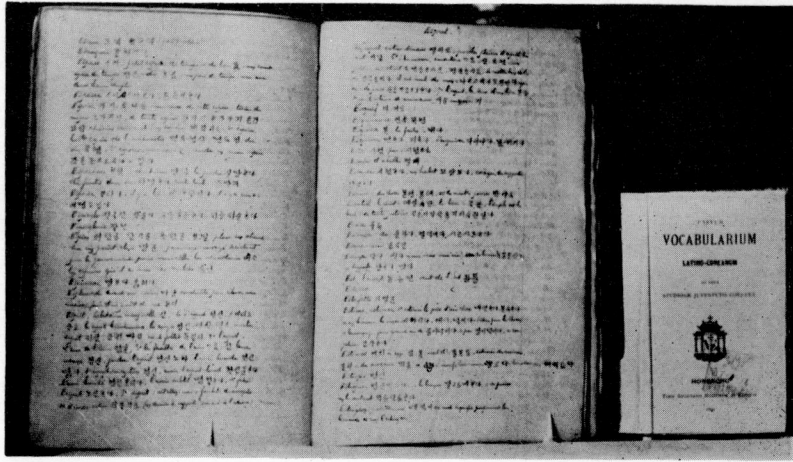

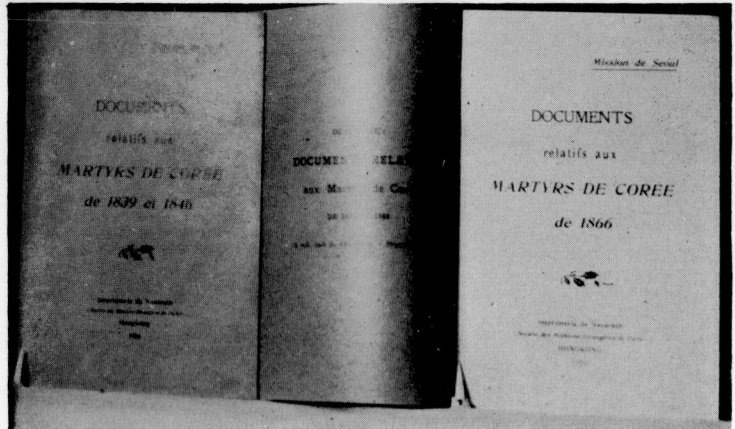

A copy of "Documents Relatifs aux Martyrs de Corée 1866"

It includes extracts from the records of the Royal Archives relating to the martyrdom of twenty-six souls, including those of Bishops Berneux and Daveluy, in 1866. Translated into French, and published in Hongkong in 1925.

Manuscript records (left, middle) and printed records (bottom) of the Diocesan Synod

Dealing with documents collected from "The Annals of the Grand Council" in the Royal Archives, by Archbishop Mutel, and containing particulars of eighty-three martyrs executed in the years 1839 and 1846

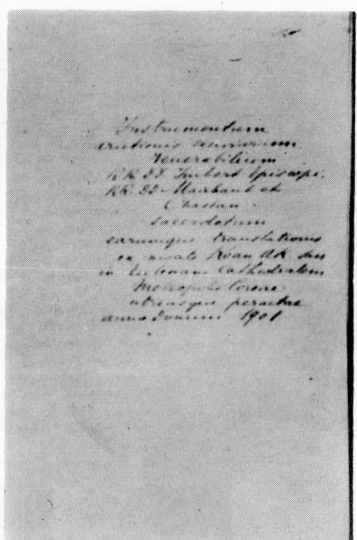

Archbishop Mutel's records of the testimony of witnesses for the beatification of Martyrs in Korea

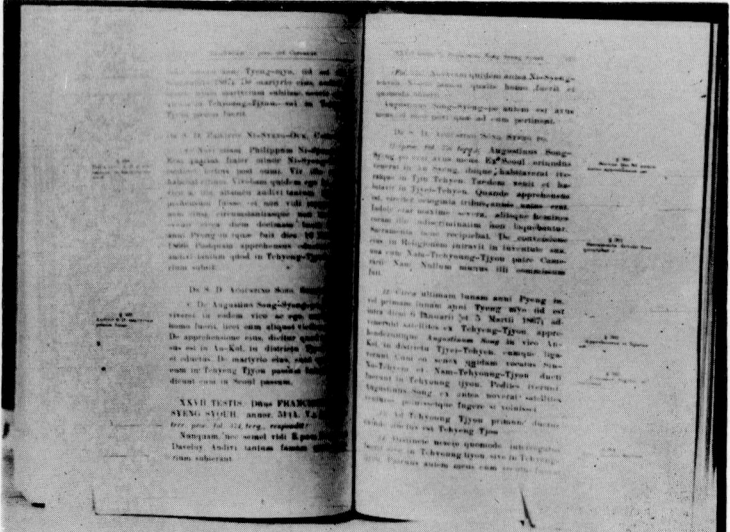

The four Bishops of Korea
(From right) Sauer, Devred,
Demange, Mutel (front)

The early Catholic Church in
Tae-gu (c. 1920)

Beatification of the Seventy-nine Martyrs of Korea in the Basilica of St. Peter by Pope Pius XI, July 5, 1925

A Painting commemorating the Martyrs of Korea, preserved in the Vatican

O. COREANI. MARTYRES
CHORIS. BEATIS. ADDITI
SALVETE. IN. ARCE. SIDERVM
DIGNA. POTITI. LAVREA

Pope Pius in procession at the Beatification of the Martyrs of Korea

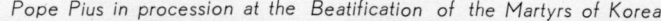

The celebration of the centenary
of the erection of the Vicariate
Apostolic of Korea, Seoul, 1931

Archbishop Mutel, officiating
at the centenary celebration

The provincial Synod with
Archbishop   Mooney,
Apostolic   Delegate   to
Japan, 1931

special notice. Born into a family of high rank in Kong-ju, he had been baptized by Father Daveluy in or about 1847. Steadfast in his faith, he had accompanied Father Ridel to China with ten other believers in 1866, when the missionary made his escape after the martyrdom of nine of his colleagues. His wife and six sons and daughters were imprisoned and severely tortured and beaten, and during his absence they all became martyrs for the faith. For twelve years he had been helping Bishop Ridel build up the Church in Korea. On several occasions he had made journeys between Korea and China bringing in new missionaries. With his superior knowledge of the language he rendered inestimable service to Father Ridel in the compilation of his French-Korean dictionary, and his Korean grammar. It was he who designed the matrices for casting the movable type for the mission press, which were first used at Nagasaki, and after 1888 in Seoul. This was indeed a significant contribution to the development of Korean typography.

After the Bishop's expulsion from Korea John's death was not long in coming.

In spite of the persecution Father Blanc was able to remain in Korea, as acting Bishop, leading his three priests, Fathers Deguette, Doucet, and Robert in the work of carrying on and building up the Korean Church. In May, 1879, however, Father Deguette was unexpectedly arrested in the Kong-ju district, together with fourteen Catholics, on information given by a betrayer. Their arrest was reported to the king, who was seriously annoyed at the news, owing to the bad impression it would make abroad. Father Deguette was expelled from Korea in September in the same way as Bishop Ridel. The missionaries now felt confident that even if arrested they would not be beheaded, but expelled, and this relieved them of a certain strain that they had been undergoing in their work. There is no record of what happened to the fourteen Catholics who were arrested together with Father Deguette, and it is to be feared that they too died in prison.

In 1880, two more missionaries arrived in Korea. One was the famous Father Gustave-Charles-Marie Mutel, who had been in Manchuria since December, 1877, the other, Father Nicolas-Lucien-Anatole Liouville, who had arrived there a year later. After one unsuccessful voyage they managed, on their second attempt, to get ashore safely at Chang-yŏn beach in Hwang-hae Province, led by Thaddaeus Kwon. They were guided to the Catholic village of Pae-ma-tang, where the villagers were mostly engaged in the craft of pottery. There they stayed at the home of Francis Park Nae-won, a wealthy Catholic. Francis Park's family were all devout Catholics: his elder brother and his sister-in-law had been martyred, and his son and grandson were later to be ordained priests. Francis looked after the new arrivals carefully and helped them get accustomed to their new life. Two months later, in January, 1881, Father Mutel was transferred to Paek-ch'ŏn to work independently on spreading the Gospel, while Father Liouville employed himself in the same way in the Chang-yŏn district. That spring, however, an ugly rumor began to spread, as a result of which Father Mutel took refuge in the capital. In March, the officials, as was to be expected, grew suspicious at the frequent meetings of large numbers of people that they noticed taking place at Father Liouville's house in Chang-yŏn. They at once sent a team of constables and the missionary was arrested.

The governor of Hwang-hae Province, however, ordered his immediate release, not only because he had received no orders to arrest foreign missionaries but also on account of the troublesome repercussions that might ensue. This unprecedented leniency caused great surprise in the neighborhood. Had the Catholics at last won liberty of worship? *Magna est veritas, et praevalebit.* (Great is the truth, and it will prevail.) The sacred blood shed by the martyrs in the past now began to produce results. The release of Father Liouville, as we shall see in the following paragraphs, marked a turning point in the history of missionary work in Korea, and, from 1882 on, the right of free entry of foreigners into Korea was tacitly acknowledged by the government.

73. The Policy of Enlightenment and the Freedom of Religion

In 1873, with the retirement from the political scene of Prince Regent Tae-won-kun, who had persistently pursued a policy of anti-Western isolationism, the Min family, led by Queen Min, rapidly rose to a position of great power. As its influence increased, this family adopted a policy in complete opposition to that of the former prince regent. Realistically appraising the international situation, the new Korean government finally concluded the Korean-Japanese Treaty of Amity, which was signed at Kang-hwa Island in 1876, the thirteenth year of the reign of King Ko-jong. The five-century-old closed-door policy came to an end, opening up the country to foreign trade. The result was rapid progress in the introduction of Occidental civilization.

As stated above, it was in 1876, the year of the signing of the Korean-Japanese Treaty at Kang-hwa, that Fathers Blanc and Deguette came to Korea. From that year the government began to abandon its postive attitude of anti-Catholic persecution. Minor persecution by ignorant officials in outlying districts still occurred sporadically, and there was a demonstration, by stubborn and narrow-minded Confucian scholars, in which they manifested their disgust in a disorderly manner. The central government still retained some hostility toward Christianity, expelling foreign missionaries instead of condemning them to death, and allowing imprisoned Korean Catholics to die of starvation in jail. At the expulsion of Bishop Ridel, it is worth noting that sixty-seven items of his personal belongings that had been confiscated were returned to him. Moreover, after Father Liouville's unconditional release from his arrest in Hwang-hae Province in 1881, he was allowed to continue his missionary work unmolested. This fact alone is enough to show the sharp contrast with previous years, when the persecution was at its height.

Reaction against the sudden change toward tolerance and liberty of worship was naturally to be expected. A book entitled *Han-kuk-ch'aek-ryak* or A Stratagem for Korea, by Hun Chün-hsin, an official of the Chinese Imperial Consulate in Japan, which advocated that Korea should conclude an alliance with the Ch'ing government of the Chinese Empire, the Japanese Empire, and the United States of America, in order to oppose further territorial expansion on the part of the Tsarist government of the Russian Empire, found its way to Korea in 1881, and shortly afterward Confucian scholars presented their "Ten-thousand-Signature Petition" to the king, staging a sit-down demonstration, in accordance with their traditional rights, outside the gates of the royal palace. This petition urged the government to adopt an anti-Western and anti-Catholic policy. These demonstrations were frequently repeated, until at last the government was obliged to take strong measures and exile many of these Confucian scholars to the provinces.

Nevertheless, in appeasement of the demands of the rank and file of the Confucianists the government also promulgated on June 11, 1881, the *Sin-sa Ch'ŏk-sa-yun-eum* or Ordinance of 1881 for the Suppression of Evil Doctrines. The ordinance, which went into effect on July 10, was the last piece of legislation against Catholicism in Korea, and merely pointed out that the best way to eliminate Christianity was by the faithful observance of the teachings of Confucius, and that the government of Korea was deeply concerned at the way in which certain Catholics had occasionally corrupted the traditional customs of Korea. The king, furthermore, issued orders to the chiefs of police not to molest or annoy Catholic believers in the practice of their religion.

The treaty with Japan was followed by similar treaties with other great powers. In 1882, the nineteenth year of the reign of King Ko-jong, Korea concluded a treaty with the United States of America; in the same year others were signed with the United Kingdom of Great Britain and Ireland, and with the German Empire; in 1884 with the Kingdom of Italy, and the Russian Empire; and in 1886 with the Third Republic of France. With the opening of trade, all these nations stationed their diplomatic representatives in the capital and the kingdom of Korea began to take part in the community of nations.

How did religion fare under this 'open-door policy'? Paragraph Two of Article Four of the treaty with the United Kingdom of Great Britain and Ireland stipulated: "British merchants shall be authorized to build their houses and set up business establishments in the places designated in the foregoing paragraphs. They shall also be permitted to practice their religion in freedom." The treaty with the Third Republic of France established a similar privilege for its citizens, and in Paragraph Two of Article One made it clear that "on their arriving at or departing from the treaty ports of Seoul, In-ch'ŏn, Won-san, Pu-san, and Yang-hwa-jin on business, the Korean government would assume responsibility for their lives and property by issuing visas." This treaty allowed, for the first time, complete freedom of movement to French missionaries, at least within the areas specified as open for trade. It was exactly one hundred and two years since the establishment of the Korean Church, fifty-five since its erection as Vicariate Apostolic, and fifty since the arrival of the first French missionary in Korea. During all these years Catholics, both Korean and French, had been carrying on their secret activities to open up Korea to the world, and now finally they saw their desire realized. This marked a great victory for the Church.

A brief look at the strength of the Church at that time would show five foreign missionaries, including Father Blanc, engaged in missionary work in Korea, though Bishop Ridel was undergoing medical treatment in Paris. There were other missionaries who belonged to the Korean Church but who resided abroad, namely, Father Deguette who

had been expelled to Manchuria, and Father Eugène Jean-Georges Coste who was engaged in the composition and publication of doctrinal and devotional works in the Korean language in Japan. The number of Catholics at that time had risen to twelve thousand five hundred. It was glaringly obvious that five missionaries could not adequately serve such a large Vicariate.

In 1882, owing to Bishop Ridel's prolonged incapacity due to illness, Father Blanc was raised to the position of Coadjutor Bishop of the Vicariate Apostolic. He proceeded to Nagasaki aboard a Japanese ship, and was formally consecrated there on July 8, 1883. On June 20, 1884, at the death of Bishop Ridel, Bishop Blanc succeeded him as the seventh Vicar Apostolic. At the same time four new missionaries arrived from France, and Fathers Deguette and Coste returned from exile. The four new priests were Fathers Victor Louis Poisnel, Jean-Baptiste Josse, Gabriel Edmond-Joseph Maraval and Calixte-Xavier Baudounet.

One of the most important results of the new freedom was the possibility of training native clergies, so as to enable the Korean people to conduct the work of their Church for themselves and by themselves. As we have already related, there had long been a seminary at Pae-ron, which had been established as long ago as 1856, when, in the reign of King Ch'ŏl-jong, Catholicism had been tacitly approved by the government of the day, and three Seminarians had been sent to the seminary in Penang in 1854 and again in 1858. The persecution in 1866 had resulted in the discontinuance of this undertaking. During the stay of Bishop Ridel at Ch'akou in Manchuria, several Korean students had been sent to him for theological studies. Father Robert, who came to Korea in 1877, taught three theological students at Paek-ch'ŏn in Hwang-hae Province. Realizing the inadequacy of these measures, Bishop Blanc resolved, in 1881, to send Korean students to the theological seminary in Penang. This was a quasi-international institution, educating students from several countries in the Far East wherein the Catholic Church had no seminary of its own. In 1881 Lawrence Kang Sŏng-sam and several other students crossed to Nagasaki, where they received preliminary instruction in a theological seminary under Father Coste. They left for Penang in 1882. Mark Kang To-yŏng and others went from In-ch'ŏn direct to Penang in 1883. They were followed by Augustine Chŭng Kyu-ha and others in 1884. In all, twenty-one Korean students had gone to Penang by 1884. Unfortunately, the tropical climate of Penang proved too much for the Korean students, and seven of the twenty-one died of disease there. It was decided to send no more students there, but to open a theological seminary in Korea, and gradually bring the students back to study theology in their native land. On May 5, 1885, the theological seminary was formally opened in Pu-heung-kol, Won-ju, now Pu-p'yŏng-ri, Kang-ch'ŏn-myŏn, Yŏ-ju county. Father Maraval took charge of this school. Its students were the four who had returned from Penang, and three freshmen. The institute was moved to Yong-san, Seoul, in 1887, and made a fresh start under its new name, "The Sacred Heart of Jesus Seminary." Its contribution to the training of Korean priests was unique, until a second seminary was opened at Tae-gu in 1914.

There had already been two Korean priests, Blessed Andrew Kim and Thomas Ch'oe. It was not until 1896 that the Church was able to welcome any successor to them, but in that year no fewer than ten were ordained to the priesthood and began to serve the Church in Korea. Of the twenty-one students who went to Penang seven died, three withdrew, and another suspended his studies on account of old age. The remaining ten who were now ordained were:

Father Lawrence Kang Sŏng-sam (1896)
Father Mark Kang To-yŏng (1896)
Father Augustine Chŭng Kyu-ha (1896)
Father Augustine Lee Nae-su (1897)
Father Alexis Kim Sŏng-hak (1897)
Father Paul Han Ki-keun (1897)
Father Luke Hong Pyŏng-ch'ŏl (1899)
Father Augustine Kim Won-yŏng (1899)

Father Joseph Kim Mun-ok (1900)
Father Augustine Kim Seung-yŏn (1900)

Another pressing responsibility the Korean Catholics had to assume after the establishment of the theological seminary was the construction of a cathedral church. A site was procured in the downtown district of the capital and on this very site, Myŏng-rae-dong, where the first Korean martyr, Thomas Kim Pŏm-u, once lived, was built the conspicuous redbrick Gothic Cathedral that now dominates the surrounding buildings near the hill called Nam-san. Another was built near the execution ground outside the Small West Gate where so many Catholics were martyred.

Three more foreign missionaries arrived in due course. These were Fathers Louis-Bon Le Merre, Arnod-Jean Lafourcade and Jean-Louis Rault. This brought the total number of foreign missionaries up to fourteen, and there were fourteen theological students attending the theological seminary. Availing themselves of the freedom of worship that they now enjoyed, a total of 14,247 believers were practicing their religion in peace and praising the glory of God.

74. The Development of the Church

Although there was not yet absolute freedom of religion, the Church flourished to such a degree that Bishop Blanc found it advisable to issue a series of directives, which were published on September 21, 1887, under the title "Guidance Book of the Korean Church." This guidance book, which served as a canon, was based on records made by Bishop Ridel in accordance with the resolution passed at the conference of priests held at "Notre-Dame des Neiges" (Our Lady of the Snows) in 1868, which remained in session until 1874. In this way the Church was, for the first time, able to possess its own unified canon with common rules applicable to all parts of Korea.

Another of Bishop Ridel's desires had to wait until a year after his retirement for its realization by his successor. This was the dedication of the Korean Vicariate to the Sacred Heart of Jesus, at a Solemn Mass at Chong-hyŏn Cathedral, celebrated by Bishop Blanc on June 8, 1888. On this occasion the Church of Korea triumphantly proclaimed to the world its victory in the long struggle for freedom of worship, and at the same time prayed for the special protection of Christ. From that day on, the Catholic priests were able to discard the traditional Korean mourning dress and fans that they had worn so long as a disguise, and to appear in public in the regular priestly garb of black silk soutane.

Now that it was enjoying full liberty of action the Church of Korea began to engage openly in social welfare, care of the aged, and care of orphans, activities which hitherto it had been able to carry on only in secret. On July 23, 1888, four French Sisters of the *Communauté de Saint Paul de Chartres* arrived in Seoul to take charge of this important relief work. This community, established in 1694, had long been engaged in such work in French Indo-China (now Vietnam, Laos and Cambodia as well as in China and Japan, in collaboration with the *Société des Missions-Étrangères de Paris* and now sent its workers to Korea, at the request of Bishop Blanc. The stages by which the relief work had progressed were as follows:

At the end of the century-old persecution, when the Church was able to emerge from hiding, the Catholics began to organize relief work for the aged, the sick, and orphans, all of whom had hitherto been neglected and abandoned by society and the state. The Church established a home for the aged and an orphanage. From 1880, Bishop Blanc had been continuously providing assistance for abandoned children, accommodating them at the home of a Catholic woman. In 1885 he bought a tile-roofed house in Kon-tang-kol, Seoul, which was fitted up as an orphanage on March 15, and the believers started taking care of orphans there. Another large tile-roofed house was also bought in Tong-kol, on Chong-ro, the main street of the capital, and there the indigent aged of both sexes were accommodated. Thus some twenty believers operat-

ed an orphanage for a hundred children, and a home for forty old people. This relief work was a heavy burden, and the Catholic lay people, in spite of their great devotion, were unable adequately to cope with it. Realizing this, Bishop Blanc, who had seen the work of the Sisters of *St. Paul de Chartres*, in Nagasaki when he went there to be consecrated Bishop in July 1883, decided, in July 1887, to write to the Superior of the Convent of *St. Paul de Chartres*, France, emphasizing the need for sacrificing, zealous, and warm philanthropical aid from the convent Sisters, on behalf of the less fortunate Koreans.

On receipt of this letter, the convent sent a team of four Sisters led by Sister Zacharie, consisting of Sister Estelle and two Chinese Sisters from Saigon, to help the Korean Church in its sacred mission. They arrived in Seoul in July 1888, and soon won an excellent reputation by their faith and works. Within a week four Catholic women knocked at their door and applied for admission into the religious life. These were Clare Francis-Xavier Park Hwang-o-ri, Maria-Joseph Kim Sun-i, Maria-Paul Kim Hae-kye-mi, and Maria-Benedicta Kim Pok-u-ji. Their sincerity won them acceptance into the novitiate. All of them were the descendants of martyrs; Clare belonged to a family that had given nine martyrs to the Church, and was only sixteen years old when she became a postulant. The convent was moved to the cathedral precinct on September 7, and the 145 orphans and the inmates of the home for the aged were also moved there, the latter under the management of Susanna Won, the daughter of Martha Park, the former nurse of King Ko-jong.

Of great importance to the Church at this time was the great increase in the publication of religious books, including Holy Scripture, Missals and devotional works and prayer books. In penal times such works could be circulated only surreptitiously and in manuscript copies, and the transcribing of these was done by zealous believers. Once the Church was free from persecution and steadily expanding, a printing-press was set up at Nagasaki in 1882 under Father Coste, with the able assistance of John Ch'oe, and this press, with Ch'oe's matrices and fonts of type, was brought to Korea by Bishop Blanc in 1888 and set up in Chŏng-dong, where it has since produced a steady flow of publications.

The next step was the erection of suitable buildings for the episcopal residence and the administration of the Vicariate. Bishop Blanc instructed Father Coste to level a site in Chong-hyŏn, and in February 1890 work was begun on a two-story Western-style house. Within the month on February 22, the Bishop, exhausted by overwork, fell ill and died, at the early age of forty-six.

When the sad news of the Bishop's death reached the Vatican, Pope Leo XIII named Father Mutel to be the eighth Vicar Apostolic of Korea. Father Mutel, on ceasing his missionary activities in Korea in 1885, had been placed in charge of a theological seminary in Paris. His consecration took place there on September 21, 1890, the fifty-first anniversary of the martyrdom of Bishop Imbert, the second Bishop of Korea, and of his companions, who had been executed at Sae-nam-t'ŏ. At the Consecration Mass Father Delpech, dean of the seminary, prayed that the Korean Church, tinged with scarlet by the blood of its martyrs, might enjoy a bright future, and offered the new Bishop the slogan: "Budding flower of martyrdom, come into full bloom!" Immediately after his consecration Bishop Mutel hurried back to Korea, on February 22, 1891, with two young priests, Fathers Léon Pierre Dutertre and Joseph-Marie Etienne Charge-boeuf, to assume his heavy responsibility. Most of the modern groundwork of the Church in Korea was laid down under his leadership. One of his first acts after his return was to dedicate the Theological Seminary of the Sacred Heart of Jesus. He urged on the construction of Yak-hyŏn Church and Chong-hyŏn Cathedral, the former being dedicated on 25 September, 1893, and the cathedral, work on which had been suspended during the Sino-Japanese War (1894-1895),

on May 29, 1898.

By this time the preaching of the Gospel had penetrated to every corner of the peninsula, and even to Chientao (Kan-to), the neighboring province of Manchuria, across the Tumen River, where Catholic believers stepped up their activities in promoting its development. In the past, missionary work had been somewhat neglected in the Kwan-sŏ and Kwan-puk districts, in the northwest and northeast respectively. Bishop Berneux had visited P'yŏng-an Province once, in 1862, and Matthew Lee Teuk-po sowed the seed of the Gospel in Sin-ch'ŏn, Hwang-hae Province, where a large Catholic community later developed as a result of his efforts. Peter Chŭng T'ae-jŏng, who was converted to Catholicism under the teaching of Matthew Lee Teuk-po, undertook missionary work in Kwan-sŏ with Matthew, reaping a great harvest of souls, including such outstanding figures as Thaddaeus Kwon Ch'i-mun, Peter Cho, Oh Ch'i-ok, John Kim Sŏng-heum, Matthew Lee, and Pius Yun Ch'ang-hyŏk, all of whom later distinguished themselves in spreading the Gospel in the Province of P'yŏng-an. Cognizant of the growth of the flock, Bishop Blanc sent Father Poisnel to P'yŏng-yang in 1884, and Father Losandre in 1895.

In 1894 Father Bret made a visit to Won-san, which resulted in a notable increase in the number of believers both in that district and in Chientao.

Playing a pivotal role in missionary work for the Chientao area at that time were Kim I-ki, a Taoist scholar, and his disciple friend Kim Yŏng-ryŏl. Kim I-ki had fled to Chientao to seek political asylum after the abortive rising of 1884. There he devoted himsef at first to the study of the Tong-hak heresy, but soon abandoned it. Hearing about Catholicism he came to Seoul to find out more about it from its adepts, but was unfortunately arrested on the charge of adhering to the Tong-hak sect, and he died under torture in prison. Though his death prevented his being received into the Church his disciples carried on his work and all became Catholics. One of them, Kim Yŏng-ryŏl, went to Won-san to study Christianity, and there met Father Joseph Vermorel, whose guidance led him into the Church. On his return to Chientao a month later John Kim devoted himself to missionary work, and made many converts. Then, in 1897, in order to be within reach of a priest, he moved to Won-san with all the members of his family and a number of friends. A cold journey they had of it: starting out in a cold wave in late winter, all heavily laden with bundles containing their belongings and household goods. Carrying John's ninety-year-old grandmother in a sedan chair or palanquin, they made the whole journey through the snow on foot. Through every hardship they were sustained by their ardor and perseverance. On their arrival they set themselves diligently to the task of learning the catechism, and many of them, including twelve of the grown men, received Baptism on Ascension Day. Impressed by the zeal of the latter, Father Bret dubbed them "the twelve disciples of Kwan-puk." Their names were:

Luke Park Yŏn-sam
Martin Cho Yŏ-ch'ŏn
Paul Kim Chin-o
Andrew Kim Chung-ryŏl
Luke Lee To-sŏn
Peter Ch'oe Ik-se
Benedict Ch'oe Mun-hwa
Thaddaeus Chi Yu-hyŏn
Joseph Han Chae-heung
Anthony Kim Sŏng-jun
Francis Kim Kye-ryŏl
Thomas Kim Ch'ang-sŏp

Some of them returned to their home towns immediately after their Baptism, while the remainder stayed in Nu-un-tal until the completion of the summer farming. On their return to Chientao they set out on a long journey through all the many districts for the propagation of the Gospel, almost all of them assuming the responsibilities of a catechist, thus laying the foundation for the later missionary work and educational projects in Chientao. Thanks to their zeal, the grace of God began to penetrate into every part of this bleak and wind-swept territory beyond the northern boundary of Korea. In 1897 Father Bret was put in charge of the missionary work in Chientao.

Magna est veritas, et praevalebit. (Great is the truth, and it will prevail.) The long years of persecution were now over, and everybody was free to worship in peace and joy. It was at this time that Princess Min, the consort of Prince Tae-won-kun and mother of the king, was converted and received into the Church. She had long cherished a feeling of affection for the Catholics and, through her son's former nurse, Martha Park, had requested Bishop Berneux to offer a special prayer on the occasion of her son's accession to the throne of Korea, as King Ko-jong, in 1864. Thereafter it was impossible for her to keep in touch with the Church owing to the fierce antagonism of her husband, Prince Regent Tae-won-kun, toward the Catholics, and his declared intention to suppress their religion. Now, however, he had long retired from the political scene; her daughter-in-law, Queen Min, was assassinated on October 8, 1895 and her son, the king, took refuge in the Russian legation four months later. All this turmoil led her to take refuge herself, but in a life of religious retirement, in which she saw her only hope of peace and happiness. On October 11, 1896, she invited Bishop Mutel to the house of a Catholic maidservant of hers named Mary Lee, situated on the outskirts of the Un-hyŏn Palace gardens, and asked to be received into the Church. Bishop Mutel baptized the eighty-year-old princess, conferring on her the name Mary. Her godmother at her Baptism was her personal maidservant, Susanna Won, the daughter of her son's former nurse, Martha Park, and later the matron of the Catholic orphanage. A year later she had the great joy of making her first Communion at the Un-hyŏn Palace. She devoted herself wholeheartedly to Jesus Christ for the remainder of her life, and later, when confined to bed with a critical illness, she begged Bishop Mutel to try to bring her husband, Prince Tae-won-kun, who was also critically ill, to accept the Christian faith as well. We can well imagine the deep emotion of Bishop Mutel on receiving such a request from the devout princess. After her death, which took place on January 8. 1898, Bishop Mutel, in compliance with her request, wrote to the prince requesting an audience. The message was kindly received, and the prince replied with a gift and a letter of acknowledgment, just before his own death on February 22 of the same year, before the audience could be granted. During the lifetime of the prince and princess Bishop Mutel was also received at the Kyŏng-un Palace by their son, the king, who received him in private audience and listened with kindness and courtesy to the Bishop's exposition of Catholic doctrine.

By 1900 the Church had made great strides, and the Vicariate Apostolic could number fifty-two priests, twelve of them Korean and the remaining forty of French nationality. There were forty-one churches, and the number of the faithful had risen to forty-two thousands. The cathedral had been completed on May 29, 1898 and was dedicated with Solemn Mass in the presence of a large congregation of Catholics from all parts of the country, and of the *corps diplomatique*. This conspicuous edifice in the heart of the great metropolis may well be considered a monument to the victory of the Church.

75. The Tong-hak Uprising and the Renewal of Persecution

The followers of the Tong-hak sect, who in 1864 had set up a Messianic cult in imitation of Catholicism at the outset of their movement, seeing the freedom and favor gained by the Church, and envying its remarkable and rapid development, now petitioned the government to clear their late founder of the charges on which he had been executed, and to declare him innocent. In February, 1893 they had their fellow-believer Park Kwang-ho and others submit a petition to the king. They lay down in front of the palace to await his reply, but their petition was not granted. In collaboration with the farmers who were suffering from pitiless exploitation, they launched a revolt in the southern provinces,

and fifteen hundred Chinese troops were brought in to suppress them. This broke an agreement with the Japanese that neither country would send troops to Korea without informing the other, and the Sino-Japanese War was started on Korean soil. The war was continued on the mainland of China, and ended in victory for the Japanese, who gained the Island of Formosa by the Treaty of Shimonoseki in 1895.

One of the slogans of the insurgents during this war was "Expel all foreigners!" and in consequence of this the Catholic Church was again exposed to sporadic private persecution, thousands of Catholics being forced to take refuge in safe areas. Priests in the western region faced grave danger. On July 24, 1894, they reported to Bishop Mutel: "Priests and laymen are in imminent danger of being killed." The Bishop authorized them to seek refuge either in the countryside or with him at the capital. Father Jean Moyse Joseau left for Seoul immediately, but, on reaching Kong-ju, he was captured by a squad of Chinese troops fleeing from the Japanese, the leader of which ordered his men to arrest the French missionary and shoot him. Two other French missionaries stationed in Chŏl-la Province, Fathers Baudounet and Marie Pierre Paule Villemot, also went into hiding and for six weeks were in great danger. A French naval vessel, the *Inconstant*, was sent to rescue them, but they failed to reach the point of embarkation until after she had left. They made their own way to the capital, by small boat and on foot, an exploit that was to be remembered in 1950 when, at the age of eighty-two, Father Villemot was forced by the Communists to take part in the barbarous "Death March" in North Korea. Father Villemot recalled his experience in the following words about five months before his death: "In the spring of 1894 I was living in Ch'a-tol-paek-i, Ko-sŏng, in Chŏl-la Province. Though the village was a tiny one, the faith of the villagers was great. Though wretchedly poor, they were firmly united in Christian fellowship. Rumors of war had reached me from adjoining districts, especially in Chŏl-la Province and the southern part of the country, but I attached no importance to them. One evening an excited member of my flock came to me and said, 'Dear Father, I hear that the government forces are now fighting a battle with the insurgents and the Tong-hak followers at Kal-mae-ul, about five miles from the market town. The rascals are fleeing in disorder and will surely assault our village and arrest you either tonight or tomorrow morning.' 'I have nothing to do with their conflict and the villagers will surely protect me,' I answered. 'When the constables and yamen-runners acted violently I submitted a detailed report to the Ko-san magistrate, who restored order at once. The villagers were so grateful that they even erected a monument in my honor. What do you think of that?

"However, they persuaded me to move, but two days later I returned home, convinced that the Tong-hak people had forgotten my existence. Late in May they occupied Chŏn-ju, and all government officials fled. Father Baudounet escaped to a safe place, and on his return twelve days later found his home completely pillaged. Father Baudounet, Father Joseau and I were in fairly serious danger in July. Bishop Mutel had recalled us all to Seoul. Father Joseau decided, in spite of his many humiliations at the hands of the Tong-hak sectaries, to remain in the province, but Father Baudounet following the Bishop's call left for Seoul. I set out to visit Father Joseau in Chŏn-ju, twenty miles away. On the journey I lodged at a wayside inn. While I was at table a group of five or six Tong-hak rioters armed with rifles, who had seen my horse outside with its European style saddle and bridle, burst into the inn shouting, 'Here is a foreigner! Kill him!' The innkeeper, an old friend of mine, told them that the owner of the horse was a merchant from Seoul, and after a long and angry dispute they departed, grumbling.

"I went on my way and arrived at Father Joseau's at nightfall. His servant told me in tears, 'The Father and his groom were killed by Chinese troops, instigated by the Tong-hak followers, two days ago. I was

walking behind them when they were captured, and ran away. The people here know nothing about it yet. Once it becomes known they will come here and kill us all. Go away, therefore, as quickly as possible, Father.' I took his advice and at once set off. Next night I reached Sŏng-pul, a village twenty miles from Chŏn-ju. Far from the highway, it appeared to be a secluded and safe retreat. However, the believers in the village advised me to hide in a cave near by. There I stayed fifteen days, with the villagers bringing me food every day. Shocking stories were related of the atrocities being committed daily by the Tong-hak adherents. An old man who had cooked food for me was subjected by them to the bone-bending torture for refusing to reveal my hiding place, which in fact he did not know. Needless to say, my home was robbed of everything that it contained...."

Father Joseau's death took place on July 29, 1894. He was only twenty-nine years old.

The Tong-hak sect, or Ch'ŏn-to-kyo, founded in 1864 in opposition to and in imitation of the Catholic religion, grew into a sinister organization that attempted, thirty years after its foundation, to suppress the Catholic religion in Korea, just at the time when complete religious liberty had been proclaimed.

76. The Growth of the Church in Che-ju-do (Quelpart Island); the Sin-ch'uk (1901) Incident

As we have related above, it was by Félix-Pierre that the seed of the Gospel was first sown in Che-ju-do, or Quelpart Island. Drifting near the coast of Kwangtung in South China he was rescued from his water-logged boat by a British ship and taken to Hongkong, where in 1856 he met a Korean student from the theological seminary of Penang, who was undergoing medical treatment there. Converted and baptized, he returned to Seoul in 1858. Before proceeding to his home he provided himself with a large supply of Catholic devotional books, and on his return soon made twenty converts among the members of his family and his friends, as well as many more among the fisherfolk. In 1860 he made a visit to Seoul and had his boatman Peter Ko baptized. After the persecution of 1866 he came to Seoul again, with two baptized believers. There are no records extant of his subsequent activities.

Thirty years later, in 1898, a Che-ju islander named Peter Ryang was baptized on the mainland, and returned to the island to carry on missionary work. This was the beginning of great activity in the evangelization of the island. The islanders, constantly facing death by water in their frail craft, with few lighthouses to guide them at night and no lifeboats to come to their aid in stormy weather, are naturally inclined to take a religious attitude to life, and as this island was the Yi Dynasty's favorite place of exile for state criminals and political offenders, many of them are the descendants of illustrious families, outstanding for their intelligence, independence of thought, and public spirit. With bitter experience of the vicissitudes of secular life and well aware of its transitory nature, they eagerly seized the hope offered by the Gospel message preached by Peter Ryang. From 1899 on, large numbers of them were converted to Catholicism, thanks largely to his indefatigable activities.

With the steady growth of the Catholic population of the island it was decided in 1899 to send Father Jean-Charles Peynet and Father Augustine Kim Won-yŏng to the island to minister to their spiritual needs. In 1900 Father Peynet was replaced by Father Marcel Laccouts. By 1901, three years after the Baptism of Peter Ryang, thanks to the close co-operation between the priests and the laity, the number of converts had risen to two hundred and forty-two, with about seven hundred catechumens. As the total population of the island was not more than forty thousand, we see that one among every forty of the islanders was a Catholic (2.5%). A church was built in the town of Che-ju and another at Han-non near Sŏ-kwi-p'o, and there were several outstations or Mass centers scattered throughout the island.

In 1901 an unprecedented incident took place on the island, an incident which is usually referred to, by the name of the year in the sexagenary cycle, as the Sin-ch'uk Incident.

The government, contrary to its convention, sent a tax-collector named Kang Pong-hŏn to the island to collect fishery taxes and to sell government-owned or public lands to private individuals. A group of Catholics, having purchased some pieces of land in this way, began to clear them of brushwood and timber, and in doing so found it necessary to fell certain old trees which had long been the object of primitive animistic veneration on the part of the pagan majority of the population, and also to remove some shamanistic shrines from their newly-acquired land, in obedience to their Catholic faith and their horror of idolatry. This inevitably aroused antagonism and indignant protests from the pagan villagers. Moreover, it seems to have been true that certain neo-Catholics and persons pretending to be Catholics attempted to use their Church as a means of obtaining personal privileges and profit in this world. Often, alas, on the strength of their close connection with the foreigners, who now enjoyed the favor and protection of the government, and who would sometimes injudiciously intercede with its local representatives on behalf of their proselytes, these misguided neo-Catholics would be able to take unfair advantage of their ignorant fellow-countrymen. This inept behavior went on until the villagers lost patience with them, and, in their resentment, forming a self-defense corps under the leadership of Oh Tae-hyŏn, assaulted the town of Che-ju. The Catholics thereupon strengthened the city walls and prepared to stand a siege. The self-defense corps, now reinforced by the islanders, pushed the siege on April 11, 1901, until they breached its defenses and massacred about two hundred believers who lived outside the walls and about five hundred who lived inside.

CHAPTER ELEVEN

THE CATHOLIC CHURCH IN KOREA UNDER
THE JAPANESE RULE AND ITS CONTINUED GROWTH

77. The Development of the Church after the Annexation of Korea to Japan

We have seen that, in spite of the severe persecution it suffered during the latter part of the Yi Dynasty, the Catholic Church in Korea never ceased to develop. After its long persecution of the Catholics, the Yi Dynasty was finally deprived of its sovereignty, and Korea fell under Japanese rule on August 29, 1910. At this time there were, in the single Vicariate that comprised the Catholic Church of Korea, fifteen native priests, forty-six foreign missionaries, fifty-nine Sisters, forty-one seminarians, sixty-nine churches, and a total of 73,517 believers.

In over fifty years that have elapsed since then, the Church has made remarkable growth. In 1964 it consisted of three Arch dioceses, namely, Seoul, Tae-gu and Kwang-ju, and of nine Dioceses viz: Pu-san, Chŏn-ju, Tae-jŏn, Ch'ŏng-ju, Ch'un-ch'ŏn, In-ch'ŏn, Su-won, P'yŏng-yang and Ham-heung with two native archbishops, two foreign archbishops, three native bishops, three foreign bishops, three hundred and thirty-eight native priests, two hundred and fifty-five foreign priests, seventy-four native monks, ninety-four aspirants and postulants, thirty-two foreign monks, one thousand and fifty-two Korean Sisters, six hundred and

ninety-two aspirants and postulants, one hundred and seventy-two foreign Sisters, three hundred and seventy-nine major seminarians, four hundred and thirty-five minor seminarians, two hundred and ninety-nine parish churches with parish priests, one thousand eight hundred and fifty-one outstation chapels, and a total of 628,546 believers, an increase which is indeed remarkable. No statistics are available for the Dioceses of P'yŏng-yang and Ham-heung in North Korea. Priests of these two dioceses are serving in various dioceses in South Korea.

78. The Erection of New Vicariates

The overthrow of the Yi Dynasty and the imposition of foreign rule proved a stimulus not only to racial pride and patriotism on the part of the Korean people, but also to their religious fervor. During the first year of Japanese rule there were three thousand converts, and the total number of Catholics in the country rose to eighty thousand souls, and this increase continued steadily day by day.

As a result Pope Pius X decreed on May 3, 1911, that the original Vicariate Apostolic of Korea erected in 1831 be divided into two, the Vicariate Apostolic of Seoul, and that of Tae-gu. Bishop Mutel retained his position of Vicar Apostolic of Seoul, and on June 11, Bishop Florian Demange, president of the *Kyŏng-hyang-sin-mun* in Seoul, was created Vicar Apostolic of Tae-gu. The Vicariate of Seoul comprised all Korea north of Seoul including Ch'ung-ch'ŏng Province, and that of Tae-gu, the Provinces of Chŏl-la and Kyŏng-sang.

Ten years later, in 1920 there were two hundred and forty-two parish churches and the number of the faithful had risen to ninety thousand.

On August 25, 1920, Pope Benedict XV decreed that the Province of Ham-kyŏng in Korea and Chientao in Manchuria, hitherto part of the Vicariate Apostolic of Seoul, be elevated to the new Vicariate Apostolic of Won-san; Bishop Bonifatius Sauer, Abbot of the Benedictine Abbey of Tŏk-won, was created Vicar Apostolic.

The Benedictine Order had first come to Korea in 1909 from St. Ottilien in Germany, at the invitation of Bishop Mutel. They founded a monastery, which was elevated as an abbey in 1913, at Hye-hwa-dong, Seoul, and began by setting up a vocational school for Korean boys. Dispatched to the mission field of Won-san, they moved the Benedictine Abbey to Tŏk-won, and erected the seminary and attached dispensary as a contribution to social welfare.

In the same year, 1920, Bishop Mutel was created Roman Count and Assistant to the Pontifical Throne by the Vatican. In March, 1925, he was consecrated as the first Titular Archbishop in the Korean mission field; he had previously ruled as Titular Bishop of Mopsueste and Vicar Apostolic of Seoul, a delegate of the Holy See like his predecessors, but from this date he, like his successors, would be Bishop in ordinary, with all the rights and duties of his office in the vicariate committed to his care.

It was due in part to his untiring efforts that after careful investigation of some fifty volumes of documents, dating from 1839, the Vatican decreed, on June 2, 1925, that the Beatification of the Seventy-nine Korean Martyrs might proceed, and on July 5 the solemnization was celebrated by Pope Pius XI in the Basilica of St. Peter in Rome.

In 1923 the Maryknoll Foreign Mission Society of America dispatched Father Patrick J. Byrne and his associate priests to Korea, and in the following year a group of Maryknoll Sisters (of the Order of St. Dominic) came to lend their help in the mission field.

On St. Patrick's day, March 17, 1927, the Prefecture Apostolic of P'yŏng-yang was created, and Father Patrick J. Byrne was appointed its first Prefect Apostolic.

In July 1928, the Yenki district of the Vicariate of Won-san was created as a prefecture, and in 1937 raised to a vicariate with Bishop Theodor Breher its Vicar Apostolic. In January 1928, as a further step in the ecclesiastical organization of the mission territory, the Vicariate Forane of Hwang-hae of the Seoul Vicariate Apostolic was established, with Father Peter Kim Myŏng-je its first Vicar Forane. In April 1931, the Vicariate Forane of Chŏl-la of Tae-gu Vicariate Apostolic was established with Father Stephen Kim Yang-hong its first Vicar Forane.

On September 26, 1931, the centenary of the erection of the Vicariate Apostolic of Korea was celebrated in the presence of Archbishop Edward Mooney, the third Apostolic Delegate to Japan. Present on this occasion were three Vicars Apostolic and three Prefects Apostolic, and a large number of Catholics from all parts of the country. After the ceremony a conference was held to consider the revision of the *"Guidance Book"* used in the Korean Church, and other matters, and it was decided to establish the central publishing committee and to start the Catholic movement in order to enable the laity, in the words of Pope Pius XI, "to participate and collaborate with the apostolic hierarchy." It was a call to Korean lay Catholics to get busy and not leave everything to the bishops and other clergy.

In October 1933 the Saint Columban Foreign Mission Society sent ten Columban Fathers South Chŏl-la Province in Korea.

They began to spread the Gospel in South Province of Chŏl-la.

On April 15, 1937, the Vicariates Forane of Chŏn-ju and Kwang-ju were raised to Prefectures Apostolic, the former with Msgr. Stephen Kim and the latter with Msgr. Owen McPolin as their Prefects respectively.

With the death of Bishop Augustine Mutel, Vicar Apostolic of Seoul, on January 23, 1933, after forty-three years of devoted service to the Church, the Catholics of Korea suffered heavy loss. He was succeeded by Bishop Adrien Joseph Larribeau, coadjutor, who became the head of the Vicariate of Seoul.

The Church of Korea now possessed three vicariates, four prefectures, three hundred and twelve parish churches, three seminaries, eighty-five Korean priests, ninety-eight foreign priests, two-hundred and sixty-three Sisters, two hundred and eighty-four seminarians, and 127,643 believers.

One of the first acts of Pope Pius XII after his election in 1939 was to proclaim before all the members of the Sacred College: "I have at heart the preservation and defense of all the rights of the Church and of all the prerogatives of the Holy See, but I desire that my first blessing, as an earnest of that peace for which humanity longs, should go forth not only to Rome and to Italy, but to the farthest limits of the earth." Soon afterward the Prefecture of P'yŏng-yang was raised to the status of Vicariate Apostolic, and Msgr. O'Shea of the Maryknoll Mission was consecrated Bishop and Vicar Apostolic of P'yŏng-yang at Rome on October 29, 1939.

In the following year, 1940, the Ch'un-ch'ŏn region of the Vicariate of Seoul was made a Prefecture Apostolic and placed in the charge of the Columban Foreign Mission Society. Father Thomas Quinlan was appointed its first Prefect Apostolic on December 8.

In January of the same year the Vicariate Apostolic of Won-san was divided into two Vicariates, that of Ham-heung and that of Tŏk-won (*Abbatia Nullius*), both of which were confided to the care of the Benedictine Order of Germany.

In January 1942 Monsignor Stephen Kim Yang-hong resigned his charge of the Chŏn-ju Prefecture, and Father Paul Chu Chae-yong was appointed his successor.

It is interesting to note that in 1941 the two Vicariates of Seoul and Tae-gu were under the jurisdiction of the *Société des Missions-Étrangères de Paris*; Tŏk-won, Ham-heung and Yenki under the jurisdiction of the German Benedictine Order; P'yŏng-yang under the Maryknoll Foreign Mission Society of America; Kwang-ju and Ch'un-ch'ŏn under the Irish Columban Mission while only the Prefecture of Chŏn-ju was ruled by a native prefect.

This was the critical period when Britain was fighting alone on the European front and China doing the same in Asia, until the Pearl Harbor incident brought in America with her mighty resources of manpower, technology, wealth, and leadership to form the ABC (America, Britain and China) alliance to overthrow the forces of German and Japanese imperialism. At this dark hour before the dawn, the Church in Korea comprised five Vicariates Apostolic, three Prefectures Apostolic and an *abbatia Nullius*, with five bishops and three Prefects Apostolic, a hundred and thirty-nine native priests, a hundred and sixty-nine foreign priests, three hundred and fifteen Korean Sisters, sixty-eight foreign Sisters, two hundred and seventy-nine seminarians and a laity of two hundred thousand souls.

79. The Japanese Oppression and the Liberation of Korea

As Japan's sphere of conquest broadened in the Pacific theater of war, her attitude toward the Korean people worsened and her government grew daily more tyrannical.

Moreover the cosmopolitan character of the clergy of Korea was used by the Japanese Governor-General as a pretext for the expulsion of many of the foreign priests as enemy aliens, the confiscation of churches, and the closure of schools run by the Church.

Thus the Cathedral of the P'yŏng-yang district with its dependencies was commandeered and used by the Japanese armed forces, the

American missionaries being driven out into the suburbs. Japanese persecution of the Church reached its height on the eve of the surprise attack on Pearl Harbor. On December 8, 1941, thirty-five American missionaries, with Bishop O'Shea at their head, were arrested in the P'yŏng-yang Vicariate; thirty-two Irish missionaries were arrested in the Prefectures of Kwang-ju and Ch'un-ch'ŏn; early in the following year the Americans were all repatriated. Furthermore, all French missionaries were placed under house arrest and, by being cut off from all contact with the people, prevented from exercising their ministry, so that in many districts the Church simply ceased to function as such. The Most Rev. Adrien Larribeau, Bishop of Seoul, being French, was prevailed upon to resign his see on January 18, 1942, and Father Paul M. Ro became his successor as Vicar Apostolic of Seoul. By an order of the Vatican dated February 4, 1942, Monsignor Paul M. Ro was appointed Administrator of the Vicariate of P'yŏng-yang, and on February 9, concurrently, Administrator of the Ch'un-ch'ŏn Prefecture.

From that time on Monsignor Paul M. Ro was under strict surveillance by the Japanese police, and held responsible for the French and Irish missionaries. On February 16, 1942, the Japanese Governor-General ordered the closure of the Major Seminary of Yong-san, on the pretext that it had not been authorized in accordance with the Educational Ordinance of the Government-General, and the whole body of seminarians was transferred to the Benedictine Seminary at Tŏk-won, in South Province of Ham-kyŏng. For one Korean priest to shoulder the responsibility for the jurisdiction of two other vicariates besides his own, and in addition undertake the other duties arising from the war, was indeed a heavy burden, and the Japanese availed themselves of this as a pretext for the introduction of Japanese priests to govern the remainder of the vicariates or prefecture, in Korea.

On September 10, 1942, the Japanese brought pressure on Bishop Jean-Germain Mousset, the French Bishop of Tae-gu, to resign his see and hand over his Vicariate to the Japanese priest, Father Hayasaka.

On November 24, 1942, Pope Pius XII appointed the Rev. Paul M. Ro Bishop, and, as the first Bishop of Korean nationality, he was consecrated at the Cathedral of the Immaculate Conception in Myŏng-dong, Seoul, on December 20, with Bishop Larribeau officiating. On Christmas day of the same year the Japanese priest Father Hayasaka was consecrated Bishop at Tae-gu.

The Irish priests all being imprisoned, the see of Kwang-ju became vacant, and was placed in the charge of another Japanese priest, Father Wakida, in April, 1942.

The Vatican next nominated the Rev. Francis Hong Yong-ho Vicar Apostolic of P'yŏng-yang, on March 21, 1943 and, as the second Bishop of Korean nationality, he was consecrated at P'yŏng-yang on April 17, 1944.

In 1944 the Japanese began to exercise even more stringent control over the Church. Priests were arrested and held in custody on the charge of failing to make the required obeisance before the Shinto shrines of the Japanese imperial religion, and both priests and seminarians were often drafted into the armed forces, or as auxiliary laborers at the front.

The Church buildings at Tae-jŏn, Yŏn-an, Yang-yang, and Sin-kye were commandeered and occupied by the armed forces, as the Cathedral of P'yŏng-yang had been.

On May 29, 1945, eleven Columban fathers, who had been interned at Mok-p'o, were transferred to the prison of Hong-ch'ŏn in Kang-won Province, on suspicion of having held communication with the Allied forces, and then came under the supervision and surveillance of the Most Rev. Paul M. Ro, Bishop of Seoul, who was held accountable for them.

At last, thanks to the might of America and the other Allied countries and the courage of their people, the Japanese imperialists were ignominiously defeated and brought to unconditional surrender, and as a result the yoke of slavery which the Korean people had worn for thirty-six years was lifted from their shoulders and their country was free once again to take her place among the nations of the world.

On this glorious day of August 15, 1945, a date that no Korean can ever forget, the Church of Korea comprised five Vicariates Apostolic, three Prefectures Apostolic, and an *Abbatia Nullius*; with six bishops and two prefects apostolic. There were one hundred and thirty-two priests of Korean nationality, and one hundred and three of foreign nationality, namely thirty-eight French, fifty-four German, ten Irish, and one Japanese; there were fifty-six monks, thirteen of whom were Korean and the remaining forty-three German; there were three hundred and eighty-two nuns, three hundred and thirty-two of whom were of Korean nationality, thirteen French, and thirty-seven German; the total number of believers at the end of 1944 had been counted at 183,666.

Regions served by priests, or quasi-parishes, numbered a hundred and sixty-three. There were many churches without priests, and over a thousand outstation Mass-centers (chapels). Of educational and social welfare institutions there were a seminary, two monasteries, six convents, nineteen infants' schools (kindergartens), fifty parochial schools, two secondary schools, three nurseries, five old people's homes, nine hospitals, nine dispensaries, and three printing plants.

CHAPTER TWELVE

THE DEVELOPMENT AND GROWTH OF
THE CHURCH AFTER THE SECOND WORLD WAR

80. The Status of the Church
After the War II

The liberation of the Korean people from their yoke of slavery to Japan, on August 15, 1945, brought with it the fundamental human rights of freedom of speech and freedom of religion, and the Church of Korea was not slow to avail herself of this God-sent opportunity for further development, both internal and external.

The United States Armed Forces landed at In-ch'ŏn on September 8, 1945, nearly a month later than those of the Soviet Union, to accept the surrender of the Japanese in Korea. They occupied the capital city of Seoul on September 9.

With their arrival we had the opportunity to express our thanks to our American benefactors, who had been rendering us such important help during the preceding ten years. One of the most outstanding among them is Francis Cardinal Spellman, Archbishop of New York.

Cardinal Spellman was consecrated Archbishop by Pope Pius XI on September 9, 1935, and was appointed by President Roosevelt his personal envoy to the Vatican City. Cardinal Spellman has traveled to almost all the countries of the world, preaching peace and goodwill. During World War II he was frequently with the U.S. Army, Navy and Air Force as one of the leaders of the chaplains to the forces. After the surrender of Japan he accompanied General John R. Hodge to Korea and set foot for the first time in our country.

On the tenth anniversary of his consecration as Archbishop, September 9, 1945, he stood beside General Hodge at the brief ceremony held in the building of the former Japanese Government-General, to watch the Japanese affix their signatures to the documents of unconditional surrender to the United States of America, and, that afternoon, he officiated at Solemn Mass and *Te Deum* in the Cathedral of the Immaculate Conception in Myŏng-dong, Seoul, to render thanks under the flags of Korea, the United States, and the Allied nations for the newly-won liberation of Korea, for the steady growth and development of the Catholic Church in Korea, and for the overwhelming victory of the Allies over the forces of Japanese tyranny and oppression.

On this occasion the Cardinal addressed the concourse of clergy and laity in the following words:

"Now that I have this opportunity to look at this picture of the Korean martyrs on the wall of your cathedral, I am reminded of the many occasions on which I have looked on the same picture in Rome, and as I listened to you singing the beautiful song dedicated

The Solemn Requiem Mass for
Archbishop Mutel (Jan. 1933)

The members of
the Order of St.
Benedict at Tŏk-
won (1932)

The graduating ordinands
of Tae-gu Seminary of St.
Justin, with the Rector
and faculty (1934)

The Maryknoll Mission Fathers
Assembled in front of the Mission center at P'yŏng-yang (1933)

The Maryknoll Fathers at P'yŏng-yang
(Front row, center) Bishop Byrne in his youth (1927)

Bishop Larribeau and clergy, Seoul (1935)

After the consecration of the first Korean Bishop, Paul M. Ro (Dec. 20, 1942)

330

On the occasion of the visit to Korea of the Most Rev. Guébrion,
Superior General of the Paris Foreign Mission Society, in 1939 (Inset)

After the consecration of Bishop Mousset
At Kye-san-dong Cathedral, Tae-gu (1939)

Bishop Paul M. Ro, Vicar
Apostolic of Seoul
Pronouncing his first be-
nediction after his consecration (Dec. 20, 1942)

The consecration of Bishop
Paul M. Ro

A composite photograph commemorating the consecration of Bishop Ro

← Bishop Florian Demange, first Vicar Apostolic of Tae-gu

→ Bishop Mousset, second Vicar Apostolic of Tae-gu

← Bishop Francis Hong, second Vicar Apostolic of P'yŏng-yang

→ Bishop O'Sea, first Vicar Apostolic of P'yŏng-yang

← Bishop Bartholomew Kim Hyŏn-pae, first Vicar Apostolic of Chŏn-ju

→ Bishop John Ch'oe Tŏk-hong, fourth Vicar Apostolicof Tae-gu

Celebration on the occasion of the liberation of Korea (Aug. 15, 1945)

Reception in honor of Francis Cardinal Spellman

Reception in honor of Bishop Byrne, First Apostolic Delegate to Korea

Memorial tablet of Blessed Andrew Kim
On the occasion of the centenary of his martyrdom (1946)

Bishop MacDonald of New York City and his party
Arriving at Kim-p'o Airport to preside over the ceremony of consecration of Bishop Byrne

to the memory of these martyrs I felt sure that you, their descendants, would prove worthy successors to them. There are many foreign missions in Korea; the *Société des Missions-Étrangères de Paris*, the Maryknoll Mission of America, and the Columban Fathers are the most prominent among them. Now that the war is over we may look forward to great strides in the progress of the Church, and I pray that their work may be successful. It may be hard for you to conceive how anxious we have been for you to achieve your independence, and how delighted we were to see you free at last. Now it is your duty to obey the laws of God and your conscience, and work hard... Thank you all for this deeply moving reception, which I shall never forget."

In 1950, after the outbreak of the Korean War, Cardinal Spellman was active in support of the National Catholic Welfare Conference, raising funds and sending supplies to the Korean war refugees. Through his good offices, vast quantities of such supplies were sent, and still are being sent, to the N.C.W.C., for distribution in Korea. Every Christmas it is the cardinal's practice to make a visit to the soldiers in the front line in Korea, bringing gifts and messages of comfort.

On June 29, 1955, His Eminence, in the presence of President Syngman Rhee and other dignitaries, dedicated eleven buildings in U-i-dong, Seoul, for use as a home for the blind war heroes.

It is fitting to recall the message of the Most Rev. Paul M. Ro, Bishop of Seoul, to the clergy and laity on August 17, 1945, urging them to maintain prudence and modesty during the chaos of the period of transition, and to make a special prayer for the gifts of the Holy Ghost, namely, wisdom, understanding, counsel, fortitude, knowledge, piety and the fear of God.

Shortly after Liberation Day Monsignor Wakida, Prefect Apostolic of Kwang-ju, resigned his post at the Kwang-ju Prefecture, and Bishop Ro was released from his concurrent post as Administrator of Ch'un-ch'ŏn. On September 28, 1945, Father Mc-

Polin resumed his post as Prefect Apostolic of Kwang-ju, and Monsignor Quinlan was restored to that of Prefect Apostolic of Ch'un-ch'ŏn. All priests in prison or under house arrest were, of course, released. On September 9, 1945, a Dutch priest and three Canadian Franciscan priests who had been detained for a long time in Kong-ju came to stay temporarily at the residence of Bishop Ro, and on September 15 more than ten Columban Fathers, released from house arrest in Hong-ch'ŏn, passed through Seoul on their way back to their posts in the Prefecture Apostolic of Kwang-ju. These Irish Fathers had been sentenced to penal servitude on charge of espionage relating to the Japanese airfield in Che-ju-do, from which flights were made to attack the Allied airfields at Chengtu, Szechwan, in China. The island forms part of the Prefecture Apostolic of Kwang-ju, and their pastoral visits had aroused the suspicions of the Japanese authorites. Father Thomas Ryan and Father Augustine Sullivan had been sentenced to two years' penal servitude, and Father Patrick Dawson to five years. From September 15 onward, two priests and a number of seminarians who had been drafted as combatants and laborers began to return. Order was gradually being restored.

On September 26, 1945, Bishop Ro celebrated Mass and *Te Deum* in commemoration of the Korean martyrs beatified on July 5, 1925, and in celebration of peace with victory. The ceremony was attended by a large number of members of the U.S. Armed Forces and several thousand Korean Catholics. Following the ceremony there was a reception in honor of the U.S. Forces in the cathedral compound, at which Major-General Arnold and other high-ranking officials were present.

General Hodge, though unable to attend, sent a message to the Bishop, congratulating the Church on the recovery of religious liberty, and pledging himself to do everything possible to maintain and safeguard it. This was a great source of comfort and confidence in those troublous days of transition, not only to the Catholics but to the people of Korea in general.

On All Saints' Day, November 1, 1945, at the Cathedral of the Immaculate Conception, Myŏng-dong, Seoul, Bishop Ro held a Solemn Requiem Mass for the repose of the souls of all members of the Allied Forces who had given their lives during World War II, General Arnold attended, as well as several thousand members of the U.S. Armed Forces.

Though free, the country was still split by the artificial frontier set up at the Thirty-eighth Parallel, and consequently exposed to Communist intrigue, infiltration, espionage and sabotage. In North Korea a puppet Communist regime was established, and there were even sporadic instances of so-called 'People's Committees' raising their ugly heads in South Korea, like toadstools after rain.

At the Moscow conference of December 28, 1945, it was decided that Korea should be put under the Trusteeship Council of the United Nations, and from that time on the people began to be divided in their allegiance, ranging themselves either on the left or on the right. In spite of this, on March 20, 1946, meetings of the Joint Committee of the United States and the Soviet Union continued to be held in the Tŏk-su Palace adjoining the British Legation (now raised to the status of embassy), at which General Arnold pressed for the unification of Korea. But the meetings of the committee were suspended, and in May the committee dissolved without coming to any agreement.

On August 1, 1945, the *Kyŏng-hyang-chap-ji* a popular Catholic magazine, resumed publication, after its suspension just before the close of the Japanese regime, and on October 6 the Catholic daily newspaper *Kyŏng-hyang-sin-mun* was started by Father Peter Yang Ki-sŏp, its president and publisher. A paper of the same name had been founded in 1906, but was suspended by the Japanese government.

In this year appeared Ahn Eung-ryŏl's Korean translation of *Martyrs Coréens*, and in February, 1947, Professor Ryu Hong-ryŏl brought out his *History of the Catholic Church in Korea*. In April 1947 the monthly magazine *Catholic Youth* made its reappearance for the first time since 1936, with a positive anti-Communist editorial policy.

As it was, at least for the time being, impossible to come to an agreement with Russia on the question of the unification of Korea, the United States Armed Forces handed over the executive power to Koreans, and Mr. Ahn Chae-hong received it from the military government as administrator. On December 12, 1946, a representative government was constituted to exercise legislative power for the preservation of social order in South Korea.

In 1947, seeing that the government of South Korea showed inclination toward democracy, the Maryknoll missionaries of P'yŏng-yang, who had been ostracized by the Japanese government, returned to Korea to carry on their work of sowing the seed of faith.

On the death of the Japanese Bishop of Tae-gu, the Most Reverend Hayasaka, on January 6, 1946, Monsignor Peter Chu Chae-yong was transferred from his post as Prefect Apostolic of Chŏn-ju, to become Administrator of Tae-gu, and on July 13, 1947, Father Bartholomew Kim Hyŏn-pae was appointed to replace him as Prefect Apostolic of Chŏn-ju.

In August 1947, the former Prefect Apostolic of P'yŏng-yang, Monsignor Patrick James Byrne, was appointed the first Visitor Apostolic to Korea with full powers of Apostolic Delegate, arriving on October 9 of the same year. On October 12, 1947, a reception in his honor was held at the Cathedral of the Immaculate Conception in Myŏng-dong, Seoul, and on October 18 the municipal government held a similar reception to welcome him in the Ch'ang-tŏk Palace. This recognition of Korea as an independent nation signified that five hundred million Catholics throughout the world would give the country their blessing and congratulations.

On May 8, 1948 the Vicariate Apostolic of Tae-jŏn was created by the Holy See, and Bishop Adrien Larribeau, the former Vicar

Apostolic of Seoul, was nominated its Vicar Apostolic.

81. The Church and the Newly-established Government of the Republic of Korea

With the complete rupture of negotiations on the unification of Korea between the United States and Soviet Russia, it was decided to hold a general election in South Korea on May 10, 1948, under the United Nations observation, and as a result 198 assemblymen were elected and began, on May 30, to draft the Constitution of the new Republic.

On June 20, 1948, the Most Reverend Paul M. Ro, Bishop of Seoul, offered Solemn Mass in the presence of all the assemblymen, as well as of many other dignitaries and distinguished foreign guests, at the Cathedral of the Immaculate Conception, Myŏng-dong, Seoul.

After the celebration of Mass a reception was held in the lecture hall attached to the cathedral, and on this occasion Dr. Syngman Rhee, speaker of the House of Assembly, made the following statement:

"The Catholic Church in Korea has over and over again proved itself capable of striving effectively for the independence of Korea in the past, and we look forward to further achievements on behalf of our country in the future."

On August 15, 1948, the Republic of Korea declared her independence to the whole world and a solemn function was held to celebrate this event, but the only response was the recognition of her independence by the Vatican City. This led the Korean people to look anxiously to the forthcoming session of the General Assembly of the United Nations in September of the same year in Paris. Representatives of the Republic of Korea, headed by Assemblyman John Chang (Chang Myŏn), were sent as delegates to the General Assembly.

Supported by delegates of the United States of America, the Republic of France, the Republic of the Philippines, and the Commonwealth of Australia, and by Ca-

tholics throughout the world, John Chang won recognition for the Republic of Korea on December 12, with 48 votes in favor, and 6 votes against, disdaining the violent protests of the delegates of states belonging to the Communist bloc.

As a special envoy of the Republic of Korea and the representative of Korean Catholics, John Chang had the honor of a private audience with Pope Pius XII, of whom he requested aid for the development of the Church of Korea.

On his way home John Chang stopped at Washington D.C. to express the gratitude of the Korean people for America's recognition of Korean independence.

During this period the Church in Korea continued to flourish. At the end of 1948 Father John Ch'oe Tŏk-hong, parish priest of Mok-p'o, was nominated Vicar Apostolic of Tae-gu and on January 30, 1949, he was consecrated Bishop, becoming the third Korean Bishop in the Korean Church. In April 1949, the Catholic fortnightly of his vicariate, the *Ch'ŏn-ju-kyo-hoe-po*, suspended since 1933, resumed publication.

On April 17, 1949, the Visitor Apostolic, Monsignor Patrick J. Byrne, was elevated to Apostolic Delegate, and at the same time was named Titular Bishop of Gazera.

His consecration took place on June 14 in the presence of Syngman Rhee, President of the Republic, and many other dignitaries and distinguished guests.

The year 1950 being a Holy Year, it was proposed to erect a monument at Sae-nam-t'ŏ in memory of the many Catholic martyrs who had been beheaded, and on February 21 a series of meetings took place at the Cathedral in Myŏng-dong, which were attended by the ecclesiastical heads of six vicariates of South Korea.

On May 15 the two bishops, Bishop Paul M. Ro and Bishop Adrien Larribeau, left for Europe, to attend the Jubilee ceremonies in Rome, and to promote the friendship of Korea with the nations of Europe.

There were many cases of conversion to Catholicism on the part of prominent Protestant ministers and other persons of distinction, and the rate of increase in the total number of Catholics in Korea was more than ten thousand every year. The statistics for 1949, the year prior to the outbreak of the Korean War, were as follows:

Church Strength: (June, 1949)

    Vicariates: 6

    Bishops: 4

    Prefect Apostolic: 3

    Priests: Korean, 144; foreign, 58

    Seminarians: 184

    Nuns: Korean, 385; foreign, 16

    Churches: parish 131 (14 in Seoul)

    Outstation chapels: 1,243

    Number of the faithful: 157,668 (excluding about 100,000 in N. Korea)

    Number of catechumens: 8,516

Social welfare institutions:

    Nurseries: 9

    Homes for the aged: 2

    Hospitals: 7

    Middle and high schools: 14

    College: 1

CHAPTER THIRTEEN

RELIGIOUS OPPRESSION DURING THE KOREAN WAR

82. The Persecution by the North Korean Puppet Regime

As already stated, freedom of worship was fully guaranteed after the national liberation on August 15, 1945, and the Church was able to make rapid progress in South Korea. In North Korea the situation was very different. There the Church was confronted by the North Korean puppet regime with cruel persecution, which grew fiercer day by day. With the invasion of the territory governed by the Republic of Korea, this persecution spread, during the early stages of the war, to South Korea as well.

(1) Yenki Diocese

Informed of Japan's impending surrender, the Soviet Army, on August 9, 1945, began its occupation of Manchuria and North Korea, and soon most of these territories were in the hands of the Reds. In this year the invading Russian troops shot and killed Father Servatius Ludwig and Brother Engelmar Zellner, in the Yenki Diocese. In May, 1946 the Communists arrested the Most Reverend Theodor Breher, Bishop of Yenki, as well as nineteen German priests, seventeen German monks, two German nuns, and one Italian nun. These were imprisoned at Yenki, Santaoku and Mu-san. Among the prisoners was Father Bonifatius Köstler, who became seriously ill in March 1947 through under nourishment. He was released and allowed

to reside at the Church in Tutaokou, under house arrest, but he died a fortnight later, on March 25, 1947.

(2) Tŏk-won—Ham-heung Vicariate

From August 15, 1945, the invading Russian troops indulged in looting and killing in North Korea. Father Witmar Farrenkopf of Hoe-ryŏng Parish was one of the first to fall victim to the Communist brutality. At the approach of the Russian soldiers toward Hoe-ryŏng, the retreating Japanese troops set fire to the Catholic church and the convent. When the Russians arrived they immediately arrested Father Witmar, and on August 23, shot and killed him without giving any reason.

After the establishment of the Republic of Korea Government in South Korea and the United Nations recognition and approval of the regime, the Russian army and the North Korean puppets started open persecution against all the Churches throughout the territory of North Korea.

On May 9th at midnight, 1949, a large number of the Communists cordoned off the precinct of the Tŏk-won Abbey and arrested the Most Rev. Bonifatius Sauer, the *Abbas Nullius* of Tŏk-won and concurrently Vicar Apostolic of Ham-heung; Father Lucius Roth, the prior; Father Arnulf Schleicher, the subprior; and Father Rupert Klingseis, professor of the theological seminary. Two days later, on May 11, the Communists raided the abbey again and arrested all the other German priests and monks in the abbey, including four Korean priests: Fathers Kim Ch'i-ho; Kim Chong-su, Kim I-sik, and Ch'oe Pyŏng-kwon. Almost simultaneously all the foreign priests and nuns throughout the *Abbatia Nullius* of Tŏk-won and the Vicariate Apostolic of Ham-heung were arrested by Communists. All these members, including Bishop Sauer, were assembled at Won-san railway station and transferred to P'yŏng-yang jail. At the same time all the Korean seminarians and monks were evicted and dispersed: the buildings were confiscated and the seminary occupied by the Sa-ri-won Agricultural College, which was renamed Kim Il-sŭng Agricultural College. They also jailed Father Ku Tae-jun of the Won-san Church.

The Won-san Convent buildings were confiscated and used as a hospital, while the Hae-sŏng School became an institute for the children of Russian soldiers.

For about a year, until the outbreak of the Korean War, only two priests were left to take charge of all the Catholics in their respective parishes throughout North Korea: these were Father Lee Chae-ch'ŏl of Ch'ŏng-jin and Father Paul Kim Pong-sik of I-ch'ŏn in the Province of Kang-won, to which he had moved from Yenki Diocese.

(3) P'yŏng-yang Vicariate

Observing the intensification of Communist persecution, Bishop Francis Hong Yong-ho of the Vicariate Apostolic of P'yŏng-yang, in his capacity of Vicar Apostolic, sent a letter of protest to Kim Il-sŭng. On May 14, 1949, Bishop Hong was arrested by the Communists, and later Fathers Kim P'il-hyŏn, Ch'oe Hwan-jun, Sŏk Won-sŏp the pastor of Kang-kye Church, and Catechist Kang Yu-sŏn, were also arrested and imprisoned. Father Han Yun-seung, of Hae-ju Church, who had moved from the Yenki Vicariate prior to Liberation Day, was also detained. In early December, 1949, six more priests were arrested,

namely:

Father Park Nong-ok
Father Sŭh Un-sŏk } P'yŏng-yang
Father Lee Chae-ho
Father Chang Tu-pong
Father Hong Kŏn-hwan   Sin-eui-ju
Father Hong To-keun   Yŏng-yu

This meant the closure of the Churches: the Catholics in P'yŏng-yang, numbering more than three thousand, were left without a single priest. In the whole Vicariate of P'yŏng-yang, there were left only five parishes with a parish priest each, namely: Chin-nam-p'o, An-ju, Ma-san (in South Province of P'yŏng-an), Eui-ju, and Pi-hyŏn.

After undergoing torture, the priests, monks, and nuns who had been apprehended by the Communists were charged with espionage and imprisoned at Kang-kye and Man-p'o-jin[1]. Many lay Catholics were also arrested on charges of reactionary activities, and their houses and property confiscated. To escape from this hell on earth, many of them crossed the Thirty-eighth Parallel and took refuge in South Korea.

83. The Outbreak of War on June 25, 1950; Massacre of Priests

Some four hundred of the Catholic refugees referred to in the above paragraph, having arrived safely in South Korea, held a rally of Catholics from North Korea at the Cathedral of the Immaculate Conception, Myŏng-dong, Seoul, on November 6, 1949, at which it was decided to raise a fund for the training and support of priests. They were deeply moved at the news of the ever-intensifying persecution of Catholics in North Korea and the stringent measures of the Red puppet regime to bring about the complete suppression of the Catholic religion. Barely six months later, the sudden outbreak of the Korean War added to their distress and indignation at the outrageous policy being carried out by the Communists.

---

[1] See Appendix A—No. II "The Sufferings of the Benedictine Mission in North Korea." and Appendix A—No. I "The Church in the Red Wave."

In the beginning of 1950 the Communists began to deploy their troops along the Thirty-eighth Parallel, at the same time pursuing their policy of ever-increasing persecution of the Church. On May 15 a convent at Sŏ-p'o near P'yŏng-yang was seized and the nuns were transferred to their daughter house, the branch convent at Yŏng-yu, where they were soon on the verge of starvation. Learning of the wretched conditions under which the Catholics were living in North Korea, a number of parish priests in South Korea held a conference on June 14, at which it was resolved to hold special Masses of intercession on their behalf in their respective parishes.

While these prayers were being offered, at dawn on Sunday, June 25, 1950, the Communist army suddenly launched a large-scale offensive along the Thirty-eighth Parallel, advancing into the territory of the Republic of Korea on the previous night (the festival of St. John the Baptist), all the Catholic priests in North Korea still at large were arrested. They were:

Father Cho In-kuk,
Father Lee Kyŏng-ho,
Father Kang Yŏng-kŏl, } P'yŏng-yang
Father Kim Kyo-myŏng, } Vicariate
Father Kim Tong-ch'ŏl, }
Father Kim Pong-sik, } Ham-heung,
Father Lee Chae-ch'ŏl, } Tŏk-won
Father Lee Ch'un-keun, } Vicariates
Father Lee Kwang-jae, Ch'un-ch'ŏn
Prefecture
Father Yun Eui-pyŏng, Eun-yul,
Hwang-hae
Father Shin Yun-ch'ŏl, Chang-yŏn
Father Yu Chae-ok, Kyŏm-i-p'o

The priests still functioning in Hwang-hae Province, North Korea, were also arrested on and after June 25. They were:

Father Lee Sun-sŏng,
Father Yang Tŏk-hwan,
Father Lee Yŏ-ku,
Father Park U-ch'ŏl,
Father Sŭh Ki-ch'ang,
Father Kim Kyŏng-mun
Father Chŭn Tŏk-p'yo,

Advancing into South Korea, the Communist army either shot and killed all Catholic priests or else arrested and imprisoned them. On June 27, Father Collier of So-yang Church in Ch'un-ch'ŏn was shot and killed.

On July 2, Father Lee Hyŏn-jong of Yŏng-dung-p'o Church was shot and killed.

In the course of their advance into the territory under the jurisdiction of the government of the Republic of Korea they arrested other priests and nuns, and confiscated all churches that they found in their path. There was soon another list of priests, either arrested or shot and killed. Monsignor Quinlan and Father Canavan of the Ch'un-ch'ŏn Prefecture and Father Crosbie of Hong-ch'ŏn Church were arrested. Father Maginn of Sam-ch'ŏk and Father Reiller of Muk-ho Church were shot and killed in July.

On and after July 11 they arrested Bishop Byrne, Apostolic Delegate; his secretary Father Booth; Father Yu Yŏng-keun, Procurator of the Seoul Vicariate; Father Villemot, Spiritual Director of the Convent of *St. Paul de Chartres;* Father A. Gombert, Spiritual Director of the Carmelite Convent; Father Coyos of the Holy Ghost Theological Seminary; and Father J. Gombert of the Convent of *St. Paul de Chartres* of In-ch'ŏn. In August, Monsignor Brennan, Prefect Apostolic of Kwang-ju, and two Irish priests were arrested. Nine French priests and one Korean priest were arrested in the Tae-jŏn Vicariate, and one of the French priests, Father Molimard of Pu-yŏ, was arrested on August 20.

This brought the total number of Catholic priests, monks, nuns, and seminarians arrested or killed by the Communist puppet army in North and South Korea to more than a hundred and fifty.

The following tables show their names and nationality, the vicariates to which they belonged, and their status.

These foreign missionaries arrested by the Communist army were at first imprisoned and interrogated in the Sam-hwa Building in So-kong-dong, Seoul. On and after July 21 they were taken to P'yŏng-yang, where they underwent a further series of interrogations. They were then interned in a school build-

Nationalities	Ordinaries	Priests	Brothers	Sisters	Seminarians	Total
Korean	1	40	—	7	4	52
French	—	13	—	2	—	15
Belgian	—	—	—	5	—	5
German	1	20	25	20	—	66
Austrian	—	1	—	—	—	1
Australian	—	1	—	—	—	1
American (including Apostolic Delegate)	2	2	—	—	—	4
Irish	1	5	—	—	—	6
Total	5	82	25	34	4	150

Vicariates / Ranks		Tŏk-won & Ham-heung	P'yŏng-yang	Seoul	Ch'un-ch'ŏn	Tae-jŏn	Kwang-ju	Total
Bishops (Monsignor)		1 (Foreign)	1 (Korean)	1 (Apostolic Delegate)	1 (Foreign)	—	1 (Foreign)	5
Priests	Korean	8	14	15	2	1	—	40
	Foreign	21	—	5	5	9	2	42
Brothers	Korean	—	—	—	—	—	—	—
	Foreign	25	—	—	—	—	—	25
Sisters	Korean	2	2	3	—	—	—	7
	Foreign	20	—	7	—	—	—	27
Seminarians	Korean	2	—	—	—	—	2	4
	Foreign	—	—	—	—	—	—	—
Total	Korean	12	17	18	2	1	2	52
	Foreign	67	—	13	6	9	3	98

ing in the suburbs of P'yŏng-yang, where they met the Minister of the British Legation in Seoul, Mr. Vyvyan Holt, and the *Chargé d'Affaires* of the French Legation in Seoul, M. Georges Perruche, and their subordinates, who were also interned there. More than a hundred of the foreign missionaries were transferred to Man-p'o-jin on September 6. Eleven of these missionaries were either killed by the Communists or died of cold or starvation. The Prioress, Béatrix Edouard, of the Convent of *St. Paul de Chartres* in Seoul was shot and killed on November 3, 1950, during the "Death March." Father Marie-Pierre Paul Villemot of the same convent died in camp on November 11, at the age of eighty-two. Father Antoine-Adeadot Gombert of

the Carmelite Convent in Hye-hwa-dong, Seoul, died in camp on the following day at the age of seventy-six. His brother, Father Julien-Marie Emile Gombert, Spiritual Director of the Convent of *St. Paul de Chartres* in In-ch'ŏn, died on the following day at the age of seventy-four. The Apostolic Delegate, Bishop Patrick Byrne died on November 25.

Mothers Marie Mechtilde Devriese and Thérèse Bastine, French nuns of the Carmelite Convent of Hye-hwa-dong, died owing to the arduous journey of the Death March on November 18 and 30, 1950, respectively. Father Francis Canavan, Irish priest of the Ch'un-ch'ŏn Prefecture, and Father Joseph Cadars, French priest of the Tae-jŏn Vicar-

June 25, 1950

On a calm Sunday morning the land of freedom was bathed with blood by the roaring thunder of the Communists. The war took a myriad toll of lives, including innumerable priests. 140,000 Korean soldiers and unknown heroes from sixteen free nations dedicated their precious lives to the freedom of this land.

The statue of Gen. Douglas MacArthur
(At the Liberty Park, In-ch'ŏn)

Landing Operation at In-ch'ŏn

A picture of the historical landing operation at In-ch'ŏn on Sept. 15, 1950 is carved on one side of the base of the statue.

The Church in North Korea was the foremost enemy of the Communists and suffered most cruel persecution.

Forcible participation of American prisoners of war in an anti-American demonstration at P'yŏng-yang. Many of them succumbed to their brutal treatment at the hands of their Communist captors.

Refugees crossing the damaged Tae-tong River bridge of P'yŏng-yang, fleeing from Communist tyranny and brutality

The U.N. Forces Cemetery, Pu-san, with the graves of those who gave their lives to preserve freedom.

Republic of Korea Armed Forces Cemetery and the graves of those who died for their country

The bereaved family

South Koreans being
forced in chains to
North Korea

Corpses of vic-
tims of the North
Korean invaders

Corpses of victims mas-
sacred by the Communists
in the Franciscan Monas-
tery at Mok-dong, Tae-jŏn.

The funeral service for Father Anthony Collier and Father Patrick Reilly, of Ch'un-ch'ŏn, killed by Communists immediately after their invasion of South Korea on June 25, 1950 (Oct. 1951)

(From left) The graves of Father James Maquine, Father Anthony Collier, and Father Patrick Reilly at Ch'un-ch'ŏn

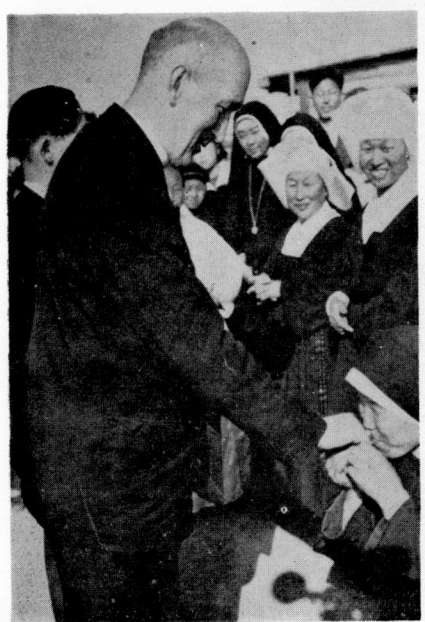

Heartfelt welcome extended to Bishop Quinlan on his return to Korea

American generals paying a call on Bishop Quinlan, Apostolic Delegate ad int. to Korea

After the Sacrament of Confirmation of the U.S. soldiers

Signor Giuseppe Brusascar, Italian Deputy Secretary of State, visiting the Italian Red Cross Hospital at Yŏng-dung-p'o, Seoul.

iate, died on December 6 and 18, 1950, respectively, at Ha-ch'ang-ri. Father Joseph Bulteau, French missionary of the Tae-jŏn Vicariate, died in camp on January 6, 1951.①

Another victim was Chaplain Emil Joseph Kapaun, a priest of the Wichita Diocese, Kan., U.S.A., who died a prisoner of war in the Communist "Hospital of Death," somewhere along the Yalu River on May 23, 1951. His heroic services for the prisoners of war has become legendary. In the Korean War there were five American chaplains who made their supreme sacrifice, including Father Kapaun, namely: Fathers Herman D. Felhoelter, Francis X. Coppens, Leo P. Craig, Lawrence F. Bounnet and Father Emil J. Kapaun.

Korean priests believed to have been killed by the Communists include:

Father Kim Pong-sik
Father Lee Kwang-jae
Father Yu Chae-ok
Father Lee Hyŏn-jong
Father Sŭh Ki-ch'ang
Father Chŭn Tŏk-p'yo

The Most Reverend Bonifatius Sauer, Bishop of the Tŏk-won *Abbatia Nullius*, died after long illness, in prison, on February 7, 1950 at the age of seventy-three. On April 6, Father Klingseis, professor at the Tŏk-won Theological Seminary, died in prison. Twenty-five other priests also died in prison at Man-p'o and Ok-sa-tok. Of the Catholic internees only twelve priests, twelve Brothers, and eighteen Sisters survived the ordeal to return to their mother country in January, 1954.

The Communist army, after advancing as far as the Nak-tong River, began to retreat under the pressure of the United Nations counterattack. On September 27, 1950, they evacuated Seoul before the advancing United Nations troops. Abandoning their capital, P'yŏng-yang, they continued to flee further to the north. On November 12, the Most Reverend Paul M. Ro, Bishop of Seoul, entered P'yŏng-yang, accompanied by Father George Carroll of the Vicariate of P'yŏng-yang. Learning that the Most Reverend Francis Hong Yong-ho, Bishop of P'yŏng-yang, had been kidnaped by Communist troops on May 14, 1949, and that his whereabouts was unknown, Bishop Ro appointed Father Carroll to take charge of the vicariate on November 20.

Within a week, however, the Chinese Communist army, numbering a million men, crossed the Yalu River into Korea on November 27, and launched an all-out attack on the United Nations Forces, driving them back from the Korea-Manchuria border in a tactical retreat. Bishop Ro had to follow the refugees southward. He arrived in Seoul on December 1, and began organizing the transfer of refugee Catholic priests and laymen to Tae-gu and Pu-san on December 12.

On January 17, 1951, learning that Tae-gu was no longer safe, Bishop Ro assembled some eighteen hundred Catholics, including priests, seminarians, lay folk, young and old, and had them transported to Che-ju Island. The Bishop returned to Pu-san on January 20, where he decided to remain for the time being.

On February 4 Bishop Ro celebrated Solemn Mass at the Holy Cross Cathedral of Pu-san, offering up prayers for the country. As soon as the United Nations Forces had driven the invaders back across the Thirty-eighth Parallel, he dispatched Father Chang Keum-ku, one of the senior priests of the Cathedral of the Immaculate Conception, Myŏng-dong, Seoul, on March 25, to take care of the Catholics there. With the Soviet Russian truce overtures on June 23, the Bishop returned to Seoul. The truce talks continued for two years until the armistice agreement was concluded on July 27, 1953. Father Yun Hyŏng-jung returned to Seoul to resume publication of the *Kyŏng-hyang-chap-ji* (*Urbi et Orbi*), the Catholic periodical which had been suspended for two years, and the first number of the new series was dated June 1953.

---

① See Appendix A—III "The Death March, from the Diary of a Kidnapped Carmelite Nun" and Appendix A—IV "The Glorious Life of Bishop Byrne."

84. Martyrs and Sufferers Before and During the Korean War

The following is a list of bishops, priests, monks, nuns, and seminarians who lost their lives or were arrested in North and South Korea as a result of Communist inhumanity during the Korean War.

TŎK-WON ABBATIA NULLIUS & HAM-HEUNG VICARIATE

Name	Rank	Nationality & Birth Year	Post	Date of Apprehension	Remarks
1) B. Sauer	Bishop	German 1877	Abbatia Nullius	May 9, 1949	Died in prison on Feb. 7, 1950
2) L. Roth	Prior	" 1890	Abbey	"	Killed at P'yŏng-yang on Nov. 3, 1950
3) A. Schleicher	Subprior	" 1906	Abbey	"	Died in prison on June 28, 1952
4) R. Klingseis	Priest	" 1890	Professor of Seminary	"	Died in prison on Apr. 6, 1950
5) A. Romer	"	" 1885	Rector of Seminary	"	Died in prison on Nov. 9, 1951
6) W. Kugelmann	"	" 1894	Professor of Seminary	"	Repatriated (Staying in Korea at present)
7) A. Brandl	"	" 1897	"	"	Repatriated
8) H. Millemann	"	" 1903	"	"	Repatriated (Staying in Korea at present)
9) D. Enk	"	" 1907	Procurator	Dec. 1, 1948	Killed at P'yŏng-yang prison on Oct. 3, 1950
10) E. Siebertz	"	" 1907	Pastor of Tŏk-won	May 11, 1949	Repatriated (Staying in Korea at present)
11) G. Frömmer	"	" 1911	Subprocurator	"	Repatriated
12) Odilo Ramroth	"	Unknown	Professor of Seminary	"	"
13) G. Sorger	"	German Unknown	Professor of Seminary	May 11 1949	Died in prison on Nov. 15, 1950
14) Benedict Kim Ch'i-ho	"	Korean Kyŏng-ki Province,1914, Ordained in 1944	Tŏk-won	"	Unknown
15) Bernard Kim Chong-su	"	Korean 1918	"	"	"
16) Martin Kim I-sik	"	Korean Sok-ch'o, Kang-won, 1920 Ordained in 1946	"	"	"
17) F. Damm	"	German 1900	Pastor of Won-san	"	Repatriated (staying in Korea at present)
18) C. Hiemer	"	" 1884	Won-san Convent	"	Repatriated
19) P. Neugirg	"	" 1894	Coadjutor of Won-san Church	"	"
20) C. Ott	"	" 1921	Pastor of Sin-ko-san	"	Died in prison on June 14, 1952

Name	Rank	Nationality & Birth Year	Post	Date of Apprehension	Remarks
21) C. Davernas	Priest	Austrian 1884	Sin-ko-san Convent	May 11, 1949	Died in prison on Nov. 6, 1950
22) G. Steger	"	German 1900	Pastor of Yŏng-heung	"	Killed at P'yŏng-yang prison on Oct. 3, 1950
23) J. Zenglein	"	" 1911	Pastor of Ko-won	"	Repatriated (staying in Korea at present)
24) E. Kohler	"	" 1899	Pastor of Ham-heung	May 15, 1949	"
25) G. Fischer	"	" 1908	Pastor of Heung-nam	"	Repatriated
26) Lawrence Lee Ch'un-keun	"	Korean Yŏn-ch'ŏn, 1915, Ordained in 1939	Sŏ-p'o Convent	June 25, 1950	Unknown
27) Maurus Kim Pong-sik	"	Korean, North Ham-kyŏng, 1913, Ordained in 1942	Pastor of I-ch'ŏn	June 24, 1950	Killed on Oct. 9, 1950
28) Matithias Ch'oe Pyŏng-kwon	"	Korean, An-pyŏn, 1908, Ordained in 1938	Tŏk-won Church	May 11, 1949	Unknown
29) Gabriel Ku Tae-jun	"	Korean, Seoul, 1912, Ordained in 1940	Hoe-ryŏng Church	"	"
30) Peter Lee Chae-ch'ŏl	"	Korean, Seoul, 1913, Ordained in 1940	Ch'ŏng-jin Church	June 24, 1950	"
31) Thomas Kim Sang-jin	Seminarian	Korean, Seoul, 1922		July 1950	"
32) Placidus Yang Ki-uk	"	Korean, South Ham-kyŏng, 1926		Aug. 1950	"
33) J. Schrötter	Brother	Germany 1880	Tŏk-won Abbey	May 11, 1949	Repatriated
34) Mark Metzger	"	" 1878	"	"	Died in prison on Aug. 3, 1949
35) E. Ostermeier	"	" 1885	"	"	Died in prison on Aug. 14, 1949
36) P. Fangauer	"	" 1882	"	"	Died in prison on Apr. 16, 1950
37) P. Gernert	"	" 1882	"	"	Died in prison on July 3, 1949
38) I. Flötzinger	"	" 1878	"	"	Died in prison on Mar. 20, 1952
39) G. Auer	"	" 1887	"	"	Died in prison on Apr. 6, 1952
40) J. Grahamer	"	" 1888	"	"	Killed in P'yŏng-yang on Oct. 4, 1950
41) H. Hoiss	"	" 1888	"	"	Died in prison on Dec. 12, 1950
42) B. Hauser	"	" 1886	"	"	Died in prison on Feb. 12, 1950

Name	Rank	Nationality & Birth Year	Post	Date of Apprehension	Remarks
43) W. Bader	Brother	Germany 1896	Tŏk-won Abbey	May 11, 1949	Repatriated
44) E. Lohmeier	"	" 1897	"	"	Died in prison on Sep. 1, 1951
45) J. Albert	"	" 1901	"	"	Repatriated
46) J. Bauer	"	" 1903	"	"	"
47. L. Fischer	"	" 1902	"	Apr. 28, 1949	Killed in P'yŏng-yang on Oct. 11, 1950
48) S. Baumgartner	"	" 1905	"	May 11, 1949	Repatriated
49) A. Sommer	"	" 1903	"	"	
50) V. Stenger	"	" 1908	"	"	"
51) A. E. Eichhorn	"	" 1905	"	"	
52) O. Bonfig	"	" 1912	"	"	"
53) G. Giegerich	"	" 1913	"	"	Died in prison on Oct. 4, 1950
54) E. Leinmüller	"	" 1912	"	"	Repatriated (Stays in Korea)
55) S. Hermann	"	" 1909	"	"	Died in prison on Dec. 13, 1950
56) Valerianus	"	" Unknown	"	"	Repatriated
57) Petrus	"	" Unknown	"	"	"
58) M. Martel	Sister	French 1906	Sin-ko-san Convent	"	Repatriated (Stays in Korea)
59) C. Link	"	German 1908	Won-san Convent	"	Repatriated
60) K. Engler	"	" 1895	"	"	"
61) M. Schmid	"	" 1892	"	"	
62) M. Gerstmayer	"	" 1898	"	"	Died in prison on Sept. 16, 1952
63) A. Gerding	"	" 1901	"	"	Repatriated
64) M. Ramsl	"	" 1899	"	"	
65) E. Schütz	"	" 1899	"	"	Died in prison on Aug. 10, 1950
66) M. Müller	"	" 1913	"	"	Repatriated
67) B. Streif	"	" 1911	"	"	"
68) L. Hopfensitz	"	" 1913	"	"	Repatriated

Name	Rank	Nationality & Birth Year	Post	Date of Apprehension	Remarks
69) M. Buggle	Sister	German 1911	Won-san Convent	May-11, 1949	Repatriated
70) M. Aigner	"	" 1917	"	"	"
71) Joanna Kim	"	Korean, Sin-ch'ŏn, Hwang-hae, Unknown	"	Unknown	Died at home in Sin-ch'ŏn on May 28, 1950
72) J. Zeller	"	German 1906	Sin-ko-san Convent	May 11, 1949	Repatriated
73) K. Grinm	"	" 1911	"	"	"
74) P. Caesar	"	" 1914	Ham-heung Convent	May 15, 1949	"
75) A. Welte	"	" 1902	"	"	"
76) L. Meffert	"	" 1909	"	"	"
77) B. Spitzlei	"	" 1915	"	"	"
78) O. Metzger	"	" 1910	"	"	"
79) Lucy Park	"	Korean, South P'yŏng-an, Unknown	Won-san Convent	Sept. 24, 1950	Killed on Oct. 8, 1950
80) Agatha Chang	"	Korean, Won-san, Unknown	Ham-heung Convent	June 25, 1950	Killed on Sept. 10, 1950

Note 1. Refer to Appendix A—II" The Sufferings of the Benedictine Mission in North Korea."

Note 2. Father Lawrence Lee Ch'un-keun, a Benedictine priest of the *Abbatia Nullius* of Tŏk-won, had served temporarily as extraordinary confessor at the Sŏ-p'o Convent, and was later arrested in Sun-an.

Note 3. On account of the Communist oppression in Kan-to (Chientao), Father Maurus Kim moved to the district of I-ch'ŏn in Kang-won Province. As the Communist oppression grew more severe. he traveled from place to place, serving Catholic communities that were without a resident priest. In the course of his travels he was arrested at Won-san, on June 24, 1950. Detained in the Wa-u-dong camp, he was killed, together with Father Timothy Lee Kwang-jae, in an air-raid shelter, on a hill in the rear of the prison camp, on October 9, 1950. Their bodies were recovered by Catholic believers of Won-san, after the recapture of Seoul by the United Nations Forces on September 28 and their subsequent advance into North Korea. The remains were given Christian burial in the graveyard situated behind the Catholic Church of Won-san.

The martyrdom of Father Kim was related by Pastor Han Chun-myŏng who narrowly escaped death at the hands of the Communists. His account is as follows:

Testimony by Pastor Han (Protestant)

I was detained, together with the youthful Father Maurus Kim Pong-sik, at a special ward at Wa-u-dong prison camp. He told me how he had been making visits to all districts left without a resident priest, and had been arrested in the course of his pastoral journeys. He was glad to receive my news of Fathers Fabian Damm and Gabriel Frömmer, by whom I had been befriended. He told me that he had been brought up at Hunch'un in eastern Manchuria. As I myself had lived in northern Chientao for twelve years we found that we had much in common to talk about during our imprisonment.

One day I saw him exchange greetings with another priest in the next room, through the door-aperture used for passing food into the cell. Thereafter I often saw him saying prayers in Latin at this aperture. Later, in the wash room, I learnt that the priest was Father Lee Kwang-jae of Yang-yang, a short balding man with a beard. Father Kim, though young, also wore a sparse beard.

After we were transferred to Wa-u-dong camp, our rations consisted of a hundred grams of millet mixed with soyabeans at each meal. Luckily we were not forced to squat during meals, as was the case during Japanese days, though they did not approve of our standing up for long. Though regarded as felons we were not subjected to violence, and the warders often allowed us to stand up for short periods to stretch our limbs. Summer passed too quickly. Our food was always very badly cooked, and far from clean.

One morning we heard a locomotive whistle sounding from about half-way between Wa-u-dong and the Won-san railwaymen's quarters. Owing to the United Nations air-raids we could never see or hear any trains during the daytime, so we knew that something special was happening. Suddenly a dark-gray plane appeared over the redbrick wall of our prison, leaving a piercing screaming noise in the air behind it. This, we learned later, was a United Nations jet bomber. The Kal-ma oil refinery was set on fire and burnt day and night, with flames soaring high into the sky. The tide of war had at last turned in our favor!

One day Mr. Lee and Mr. Park, our roommates, asked the Catholic priest and the two Protestant ministers (including me) to offer up a prayer for them. Pastor Cho and I knelt down with them and prayed aloud. Father Kim said, "I will pray for you silently in my own way. I hope you will not take it amiss if I do not join in the Protestant prayers." This was said in such a gentle and humble manner that no one could take offense.

This young priest was fond of singing, and was good at it. Every afternoon he would stand leaning against the wall, under a window that faced south-east, and sing songs, ranging from "Santa Lucia" in Italian, to "Oh, Danny Boy," which he sang quite well in English. One day a warder came and interrupted his singing, telling him not to stand up but to sit down. The priest answered very gently, "I only stood up because I wanted to sing. Please don't spoil this for us...won't you please be kind to us and leave us alone?" With a gentle smile he stood watching the warder's face and waiting for his response. The warder must have been touched with pity, for, with a brief nod, he

said, "Don't sing too loud," and marched away. These songs of his gave us great comfort, as also did the sound of the Latin prayers recited by Father Kim and Father Lee through the hole in the door.

Often we saw from the window hundreds of prisoners marched into the yard after the day's work, where the Communists vehemently exhorted them to volunteer for military service. Only those regarded by the Communists as minor offenders were permitted to volunteer.

One evening the power station near our prison camp was under attack by bombers for several minutes, and it was very surprising to us when the lights came on again within an hour. Evidently these Communists were not backward in technology!

September passed and then October, and still we were provided with no winter clothing or bedding. We repeatedly asked the warders to give us some straw at least, for it was getting very cold, but they paid no attention to our requests.

One night I heard one warder say to another: "Comrade, don't you want to be chosen as a partisan?"

"Not me! I'm going home to Keum-hwa."

I learnt from their talk that the war would soon end in defeat for the Communists, and that their main forces had probably been destroyed. Now they were organizing guerrilla warfare in order to carry on sabotage in South Korea after official hostilities had ended.

October 7. Prisoners were being carried away in trucks from the large prison building adjoining our own. We heard the sound of tramping feet, and truck engines, regularly every half hour. Later we heard that the Communists had started killing their prisoners on that very day. They were taken to the beach at Mi-ru-keut and thrown into the sea each with a heavy stone tied to his body. Another method they used was to kill the prisoners in an underground air-raid shelter, so as not to let their corpses be seen by the common people.

October 8. We were all given a special supper of K'ong-pi-ji—mashed soyabeans cooked in lard, with pork—which we all enjoyed very much, though it could be looked upon as a farewell gift from the prisoners who had been slaughtered. That night we were awakened by shouts of "All special ward prisoners, out of bed at once!" It was only ten o'clock at night, and we supposed we were going to be transferred to another prison. We asked the warders respectfully:

"What shall we do with our belongings, sir?"

"You are only going for an interrogation, and

will be back soon. Leave them where they are."

Reassured, we went with him to the office, where the first thing we saw was a white box on a table. From this box the Communists took out ropes and tied each of the prisoners with his hands behind his back, and then tied them together in groups of four. Father Kim was tied in my group, on my right side and facing me. His eyes were closed and his lips were moving in silent prayer. One of the warders shouted, "Let me inspect his mouth... he may be hiding a knife there."

"Oh, no," said Father Kim, "I am praying."

"What? Praying? Hum, you'll soon see what good that will do you. What will your God do for you this evening, eh? Ha! Ha!"

As the Communists usually expressed their scorn for religion by ridiculing us in this manner, their derision did not arouse any special foreboding in us. Father Kim, however, seemed to feel some premonition of misfortune.

"Well now, just look at that fellow! He, too, believes in Jesus," a warder shouted. Turning to the left I saw Father Lee kneeling in prayer. He too seemed to know that some evil was impending. After the prisoners had all been bound in groups of four, the Communists dragged us outside, where Red Army guards escorted us at intervals of twenty paces. After the dry and stuffy air of the prison it was refreshing to breathe once more the fresh morning air of the mountains and the seaside. Not even the thought of imminent death could destroy our pleasure in that small comfort, or our feeling of gratitude for it.

Halfway up the hill we came to a small hollow. One of the rifle-bearing soldiers, pointing to a hole in the hillside, the entrance to an underground air-raid shelter, shouted:

"In there, you dogs!"

Edging along the narrow tunnel we came to a long chamber about eight feet wide on the right. As the prisoners filed in, two Communists, holding lighted candles, accompanied them, one at the head and one following behind. Some twenty meters further on we turned to the left and, a few steps on, we were horrified to see a prison warder standing with rifle in one hand and a lighted candle in the other, and beside him another, also armed with a rifle. At their feet lay the bodies of other prisoners just killed, some still writhing in the throes of the death agony. We gazed dumbfounded at our fallen companions lying only four or five paces from us, and felt as though paralyzed.

"Get on the pile of corpses and lie down!" came the order. There was nothing to do but obey. My group sat down on the bodies, which lay four deep. The rifles were firing: the first to fall, the prisoner on the extreme left, received a bullet in the back of his head. His whole face was blown to shreds and fell a short distance away. The second prisoner also received a bullet in the back of his head, which carried away two fragments of flesh and bone. This happened in a few seconds. My turn was next. In the darkness I had noticed a close-cropped head protruding beside me from the pile of bodies below us. With his foot on my head, the warder said, "Shoot him in the head!" pointing to the close-cropped head beside me, which was probably that of a schoolboy. As the shot struck the head, blood and torn fragments of flesh showered on my face, and his brains were dashed into my mouth and nose with the force of the explosion. Coughing and choking, I could do nothing to help myself, for my hands were still tied behind my back. Gasping for breath, I pretended to be mortally wounded, and stretched out my leg in convulsive movements to simulate the death-throes. I had no means of knowing whether the Communists were convinced or not: the fact remains that I escaped the slaughter by what seemed to be a miracle.

When the massacre was concluded, the Communists withdrew. Groans and cries of agony went on in the subterranean chamber for two days. My hands were still bound behind my back, but by lifting my head I could take deep breaths in the dark. It was while I was doing this that I felt a hand touch my cheek. I perceived that it was a right hand, and a small one.

"Who are you?"

"I am a survivor."

The speaker did not disclose his name but replied that he too was still alive. I grew suspicious and sharply asked:

"Weren't you shot at?"

"I got two bullets, but they didn't kill me. We knew we were going to be killed, and provided ourselves with a knife. As we were being taken from the prison, some of us got free and escaped, but some of these were recaptured."

"Will you set me free, please?"

"Yes, I'll do that for you."

It took him about an hour to free me from my bonds. Full of gratitude I embraced him warmly. "Our Lord Jesus Christ, whom I have worshiped all my life, has sent you to my aid," I told him. "Yes, indeed," he replied, "It was Our Lord Jesus

Christ and His Mother, the Blessed Virgin Mary, whose special favor saved me." I now knew that he was certainly a Catholic believer.

"Where are you from?"

"I'm Kwon Hyŏk-ki from Ki-san-ri, Mok-Chŏn-myŏn, P'yŏng-kang county, Kang-won Province. I was a student in P'yŏng kang High School, and was arrested because they said I was engaging in reactionary activities."

I let him know that Fathers Kim and Lee had also been among the victims killed at this place, on hearing which he piously knelt and offered up prayers for them.

Among the dead around us there were still a few living whose groans and cries for help could be heard. One of them, who looked like a student, half rose from the pile of bodies and shouted, "Is there anybody here who wants to get out? I am a student of Tŏk-won Agricultural High School and am familiar with this neighborhood." His call was immediately answered from the opposite corner of the cave by another survivor, "Hey, don't go yet! Won't you set me free too?" I rejoiced at the thought that there were others who had escaped death besides myself.

"Over here!" I could hardly see him moving in the dark as he worked to set the other survivors free. As soon as one was liberated he would leave the cave. What if there were Communists lurking outside? If there were, I thought, it would certainly mean death for us. I called Kwon over to me, and we decided on a password. I heard whispering, and when we had groped our way to the sounds we found Park Myŏng-yŏn and Hwang: although Kwon had cut their bonds, they were still linked to each other by a pair of handcuffs. If there were only light enough, we might have smashed them open with a few blows of a stone. We assured them that we would take them with us, and asked them to lie down on the corpses again until we gave them the signal.

"Water! Water! Thirsty—a little water!"

Several others were groaning in the darkness.

"Help me! I am dying....."

These grief-stricken cries were suddenly answered by a quite different voice resounding from another direction:

"All right, all right. I'm bringing you water. I'll help you...." came repeatedly in a faint voice through the darkness. It was Father Lee! I made my way to him in the dark, and touching his legs and waist, and feeling his beard and bald head I knew I was not mistaken. He was lying on the bodies, himself nearly dead, and when I called to him "Father Lee!" he merely went on repeating. "All right, I will save you. I will go to your side." Though dying, and only semi-conscious, he kept on answering the agonizing cries that came to him from every direction.

Putting my lips close to his ear I called "Father Lee!" again and again.

"All right! I am coming. I am coming."

This must have been repeated about twenty times. Then his voice began to lose vitality and finally ceased. Kwon and I remained beside him long after he was dead, unable, in our sorrow, to leave him.

The cries from the prisoners became fewer, and it was getting very cold. Though I was eager to make my escape from that place of darkness, pain and death, I decided to postpone my departure. I began to look for a place among the bodies where I might shelter from the cold for a time. Groping my way along the rock wall, I thrust my hand between the bodies and discovered a living man buried among them. One of his arms was pierced by a bullet wound and it was bleeding profusely. When I moved his body slightly the bleeding increased. I could hear it. Telling him not to move, I did my best to free his hands from their bonds. I could neither cut the rope nor untie the knot. He told me his name was Song, and that he was the son-in-law of the owner of a cotton mill in Won-san. Knowing him to be a Catholic, I broke the news to him of the killing of Fathers Kim and Lee in this cave. He said that he was a friend of Father Kim, and then offered up a prayer for his soul, mentioning him by his Christian name. When we returned to the cave later, with a rescue squad, we found him dead.

Kwon and I reached safety: he is now living in Sŏ-myŏn, Pu-san.

Those who survived the massacre together with us were Sŏk Sang-pong, a woman announcer at the P'yŏng-yang broadcasting station: Park Myŏng-yŏn, physician Hwang, and two others. The bodies recovered from the cave numbered two hundred and ninety-eight, including, needless to say, those of Fathers Kim and Lee.

Note 4. The body of Sister Agatha Chang was discovered in a well in the yard of Ham-heung Prison. Her head had been struck with an axe and there were several bullet-wounds in the body. Her remains were given Christian burial in the graveyard of Ham-heung Church. The funeral ceremony was conducted by Chu Su-sŏl, and Mrs. Yu Yŏng-pok, both catechists of the Missionary Association.

Note 5. Sister Lucy Park was arrested and imprisoned by the police of Sun-an. She was taken out of prison between October 8 and 10, 1950, and killed in the vicinity of Sŏk-am Reservoir, about a mile and a half north of the old town of Sun-an. Her body was thrown into the reservoir and efforts to recover it had so far been fruitless. (Testimony given by Sister Columba Park and the aunt of the martyred nun.)

Note 6. Father Peter Lee Chae-ch'ŏl was shot and killed in the lighthouse on Ch'ŏng-jin Bay, early in October 1950, and his body thrown into the sea. It has not been recovered. Testimony of Mary Kim, woman catechist, is as follows:

"After the kidnaping of Bishop Sauer and many of the monks, Father Lee Chae-ch'ŏl took charge of the Churches in several cities, namely, Ch'ŏng-jin, Hoe-ryŏng, Ung-ki, Na-jin, and Sŏng-jin. Father Lee and we were not permitted to go out freely. We were always followed by police on his visits to these Churches to give the Sacraments. He made it a rule to make these visits once a month. Father Lee was then arrested and detained for a week, on the charge of giving the Holy Sacrament. As a result of negotiations with the Ch'ŏng-jin military command he was released. After that, contact with Hoe-ryŏng parish was maintained by Sister Olivia Ch'oe, and with Ch'ŏng-jin by me, both of us doing our best to carry out our duties.

"It was half past two in the morning of June 25, 1950. A Communist knocked at our door. We thought it was a routine inspection of citizen's identity cards, for this kind of investigation was usually carried on at night by the Communists. There was a Korean nun staying with us at the time, whose name I do not remember, as well as Deacon Ch'oe. 'Comrade!' came the shout from the gate. We opened the gate and he came in and examined the identity cards of the guests. On seeing Father Lee's card, he took possession of it, and put it in his pocket, calling upon Father Lee to get dressed. I could not but notice how pale he grew, and how he quivered in horror. Outside the gate stood two officials of the political security Bureau. They drove off with him in their car in spite of our struggle not to let him go. He had told us what to do with his important papers. Now he was kidnaped by the Red terrorists.

"In our distress we woke Deacon Ch'oe and told him what had happened. We made our way to the church and received Holy Communion from the sanctified Hosts left in the tabernacle, and without a moment's pause, we went up to the kidnaped priest's room and took charge of the church register and other important documents, which we deposited for safekeeping in the home of a Catholic layman. It was nearly dawn. Next morning we sent the deacon and a nun to Won-san. With a Catholic woman named Therese Kim and a seminarian named Aloysius, I was in the church three days later, when a number of policemen appeared calling for me. 'Comrade catechist!' Aiming their rifle at us, they sealed up all the objects in the church with red tags and called upon us to hand over the house in which we lived to the Communist Party. Soon afterward a couple of trucks drew up in front of the church gate. Then the Communists started forcibly removing the sacred objects from the church, as well as from our house. We became homeless and were forced to take refuge in the Sun-am Church. But that church had also been commandeered by the Reds, and it was all we could do to get them to let us stay in one of the rooms for only a few days. What a nightmarish life it was! On our departure we went to the prison, and the police station for inform, ation on Lee's whereabouts. Then we went to the mountain caves in search of our Father. It was all to no avail. On July 18, early in the morning, we underwent our first terrifying experience of an air raid. We took refuge in one of the highest hills in the neighborhood, Kang-nang-kol in Ch'ŏng-jin, and there we began our mountain life. It was a steep and desolate mountain, and hundreds of refugees were assembled there.

"Two months later, on September 19, we heard for the first time that Father Lee was in a cave about two miles from Ch'ŏng-jin. I rushed the his place. But, unfortunately, he was gone. On October 12, I learned from a Catholic layman who was affiliated with the Labor Party that all religious leaders, including both Catholic priests and Protestant ministers, had been executed near the lighthouse. About a week later I heard a further rumor that two persons, among the eighty religious leaders who had been shot and killed in a cave near the lighthouse, had had a miraculou escape. I braved the dangers of a long journey to gain a sight of the survivors, and asked them about the safety of our priest. They told me that he had been taken out to the seashore from the prison with many other religious leaders, aboard a truck, and that they had all been shot at about 10 p.m. These eighty or more religious leaders, according to survivors, were lined up in a single row, fastened together in pairs, and then shot. We made many attempts to recover the body of our priest, but without success, and were eventually evacuated to South Korea on board a U.S. LST transport vessel.

"I lost contact with Sister Olivia Ch'oe, with whom I used to work in the North Ham-kyŏng mission field, soon after I had taken refuge in the mountain district. I fear that she has been captured by the Communists and taken to Manchuria. Aloysius Chŭng, the seminarian, was eventually ordained a priest."

Note 7. Father Ku Tae-jun often gave the Sacrament of Penance to Allied prisoners of war, including British soldiers, imprisoned at Heung-nam during the Japanese regime. After the execution of

Father Witmar Farrenkopf of Hoe-ryŏng and the death of Father Fridolin Zimmermann, he volunteered to undertake the pastoral care of Catholics in the towns along the Korean-Manchurian border. In 1949, after long service in mission work, he went to the Won-san Convent to make a spiritual retreat, and was kidnaped together with the German priests and monks of Tŏk-won Abbey. Later imprisoned in P'yŏng-yang, he is presumed to have been killed like many of his colleagues.

Note 8. Four other priests, Father Kim Ch'i-ho, Kim Chong-su, Kim I-sik, and Ch'oe Pyŏng-kwon were also imprisoned in P'yŏng-yang together with the Germans and we have no means of finding out what happened to them. It is highly probable that they were shot and killed. (Testimony of the German Father Fabian Damm)

VICARIATE OF P'YŎNG-YANG

Name	Rank	Nationality & Birth Place	Post	Date of Apprehension	Remarks
1) Francis Hong Yong-ho	Bishop	Korean, South P'yŏng-an	Vicar Apostolic of P'yŏng-yang	May 14, 1949 (missing)	b. 1906, Ordained in 1933, Consecrated in 1943
2) Louis Kim P'il-hyŏn	Vicar General	Korean, P'yŏng-yang	Kwan-hu-ri Church, P'yŏng-yang	June 11, 1949 (missing)	b. 1907, Ordained in 1938
3) Matthias Ch'oe Hwan-jun	Priest	Korean, Sŏn-ch'ŏn, North P'yŏng-an	P'yŏng-yang Church	"	b. 1920, Ordained in 1948
4) Mark Sŏk Won-sŏp	"	Korean, Sŏng-ch'ŏn South P'yŏng-an	Kang-kye Church	July 8, 1949 (missing)	b. 1919, Ordained in 1947
5) Timothy Park Nong-ok	"	Korean, P'yŏng-won South P'yŏng-an	Sŏn-kyo-ri Church, P'yŏng-yang	Dec. 7, 1949 (missing)	b. 1912, Ordained in 1938
6) Bonifatius Sŭh Un-sŏk	"	Korean, P'yŏng-yang	Kwan-hu-ri Church, P'yŏng-yang	"	b. 1921, Ordained in 1948
7) Alexius Lee Chae-ho	"	"	Ki-lim-ri Church, P'yŏng-yang	"	b. 1917, Ordained in 1946
8) Andrew Chang Tu-pong	"	Korean, Tae-tong, North P'yŏng-an	Ki-lim-ri Church P'yŏng-yang	Dec. 8, 1949 (missing)	b. 1913, Ordained in 1943
9) Callistus Hong Kŏn-hwan	"	Korean, Eui-ju, North P'yŏng-an	Sin-eui-ju Church	Dec. 10, 1949 (missing)	b. 1912, Ordained in 1940
10) John Hong To-keun	"	"	Yŏng-yu Church	"	b. 1914, Ordained in 1941
11) Paul Cho In-kuk	"	Korean, P'yŏng-yang	Chin-nam-p'o Church	June 24, 1950 (missing)	b. 1921, Ordained in 1945

Name	Rank	Nationality & Birth Place	Post	Date of Apprehension	Remarks
12) Anselm Lee Kyŏng-ho	Priest	Korean,Kangkye, North P'yŏng-an	An-ju Church	June 24, 1950 (missing)	b. 1918, Ordained in 1947
13) Paul Kang Yŏng-kŏl	"	Korean, P'yŏng-won, South P'yŏng-an	Ma-san Church, South P'yŏng-an	"	b. 1904, Ordained in 1931
14) Benedict Kim Kyo-myŏng	"	Korean, Yang-yang, Kang-won	Eui-ju Church	"	b. 1911, Ordained in 1939
15) Mark Kim Tong-ch'ŏl	"	Korean, Ŏn-yang, North Kyŏng-sang	Pi-hyŏn Church	June 27, 1950 (missing)	b. 1915, Ordained in 1942
16) Agnetta Chang Chŏng-on	Sister	Korean, In-ch'ŏn	Superior of Sŏ-p'o Convent	Oct. 4, 1950 (missing)	b. 1906
17) Josephina Sŭh	"	Korean	Sŏ-p'o Convent	Oct. 8, 1950	b. 1919

Note 1. In the Vicariate of P'yŏng-yang, with the exception of Bishop Francis Hong and Father Paul Kang, who were somewhat advanced in age, the ages of the priests averaged about thirty years.

Father Benedict Kim Kyo-myŏng, a member of the Vicariate of Ch'un-ch'ŏn, was invited to help with the work in P'yŏng-yang, on account of the shortage of clergy resulting from the outbreak of the war in the Pacific.

A full account of their arrest is given in the appendix entitled "The Church in the Red Wave."

APOSTOLIC DELEGATION

Name	Rank	Nationality & Birth Year	Post	Date of Apprehension	Remarks
1) P. Byrne	Bishop Consecrated in 1949	American, b. 1888	Apostolic Delegate	July 11, 1950	Died during detention by Reds on Nov. 25, 1950.
2) W. Booth	Priest	American	Secretary	"	Repatriated

Note 1. For particulars, see Appendix A—IV "The Glorious Life of Bishop Byrne."

VICARIATE OF SEOUL

Name	Nationality & Birth Place	Rank & Post	Date of Apprehension	Whereabouts	Remarks Born Ordination
1) P. Villemot	French	Priest, St. Paul Convent	July 11, 1950	Died during detention by Reds on Nov. 11, 1950	1868 1892
2) Antoine Gombert	Friench	Priest, Carmel Convent	July 15, 1950	Died during desention by Reds on Nov. 12, 1950	1975 1900
3) Julien Gombert	"	" In-ch'ŏn St. Paul Convent	" Nov. 13, 1950	"	1877 1900
4) Celestin Coyos	"	" Sŏng-sin (Holy Ghost) College	"	Repatriated (Now in Korea)	1908
5) John Yu Yŏng-keun	Korean	Procurator of Seoul Vicariate	July 11, 1950	Missing	1906

Name	Nationality & Birth Place	Rank & Post	Date of Apprehension	Whereabouts	Remarks	
					Born	Ordination
6) Joseph Lee Chae-hyŏn	Korean, Sin-kye, Hwang-hae	Principal of Sŏng-sin Middle School	Sept. 17, 1950	Missing	1909	1936
7) Agapitus Paek Nam-ch'ang	Korean Sŏ-san	Sŏng-sin Middle School	"	"	1921	1946
8) Matthias Chŭng Chin-ku	Korean, Seoul	Tong-sŏng Middle School	"	"	1919	1946
9) James Lee Hyŏn-jong	Korean, Yong-in, Kyŏng-ki	Coadjutor of Yŏng-dung-p'o Church	July 2, 1950	Killed on July 2, 1950	1923	1950
10) Philip Han Yun-seung	Korean, North Ham-kyŏng	Pastor of Hae-ju Church	May 20, 1949	Missing	1911	1936
11) Paul Yun Eui-pyŏng	Korean	" Eun-yul Church	June 24, 1950	"	1890	1920
12) Andrew Lee Sun-sŏng	"	" Sin-kye Church	July 5, 1950	"	1895	1923
13) Andrew Yang Tŏk-hwan	Korean, Hap-tŏk South Ch'ung-ch'ŏng	" Chae-ryŏng Church	Oct. 5, 1950	Killed	1895	1924
14) Matthias Lee Yŏ-ku	Korean Su-won	" Mae-hwa-dong Church	July 7, 1950	Missing	1897	1925
15) Francis Yu Chae-ok	"	" Kyŏm-i-p'o Church	June 25, 1950	Killed on Oct. 5, 1950	1898	1925
16) Louis Kim Kyŏng-mun	"	" An-ak Church	June 25, 1950	Missing	1902	1931
17) Francis Sŭh Ki-ch'ang	Korean, In-ch'ŏn	" Song-hwa Church	Oct. 6, 1950	Killed on Oct. 16, 1950	1898	1925
18) Peter Shin Yun-ch'ŏl	Korean, Sin-ch'ŏn, Hwang-hae	" Chang-yŏn Church	June 24, 1950	Missing	1906	1938
19) Andrew Chŭn Tŏk-p'yo	Korean, Eun-yul, Hwang-hae	Coadjutor of Sa-ri-won Church	Oct. 12, 1950	Killed on Oct. 16, 1950	1920	1946
20) Béatrix Edouard	French	Prioress of St. Paul Convent	July 15, 1950	Killed on Nov. 3, 1950	1875	
21) Eugénie Demeusy	"	Mother, St. Paul Convent	"	Repatriated	1903	
22) Angela Kim	Korean, Seoul	"	Oct. 15, 1950	Killed on Oct. 15, 1950	1887	
23) Marianna Kim	Korean	"	"	Killed on Oct. 17, 1950	1902	
24) Regis Kang	"	"	"	Escaped, came back	1910	
25) Mechtilde Devriese	Belgian	Mother, Carmel Convent	July 15, 1950	Died during detention by Reds on Nov. 18, 1950		
26) Marie-Thérèse Bastin	"	Prioress		" Nov. 30, 1950		
27) Marie-Henriette de Lobit	"	Sub Prioress, Carmel Convent	July 15,	Repatriated		
28) Marie-Madeleine Marquier	"	Sister	"	"		

Name	Nationality & Birth Place	Rank & Post	Date of Apprehension	Whereabouts	Remarks
29) Bernedette Descayaux	Belgian	Sister	July 15,	Repatriated	

Note 1. For particulars concerning the death or disappearance of foreign priests and nuns, see Appendix A—IV "The Glorious Life of Bishop Byrne" and Appendix A—III "The Death March."

Note 2. With regard to Father Yu Yŏng-keun see Appendix No.4 "The Glorious Life of Bishop Byrne." The fact that he was arrested and taken to P'yŏng-yang was witnessed by Mother Eugénie Demeusy, Mistress of Novices at the *St. Paul de Chartres* Orphanage beside the Cathedral of the Immaculate Conception, Myŏng-dong, Seoul. On April 11, 1962, however, there appeared an article in *The Dong-A Ilbo*, contributed by the Institute for Research into Foreign and Domestic Problems, according to which he died early in November 1950, during the death march from Chung-hwa, South P'yŏng-an Province, to Kang-kye in North Province of P'yŏng-an, at a place half-way between On-jŏng and Yong-yŏn.

Note 3. Father Lee Chae-hyŏn remained in Seoul, but when the Communist army withdrew from Seoul he was arrested by the enemy at Yong-san Major Seminary, together with Father Paek Nam-ch'ang, and Father Chŭng Chin-ku, chaplain of Tong-sŏng Middle School. Nothing is known of their present whereabouts. Father Lee's work, *The Priest and the Sacred Heart*, was published posthumously.

Note 4. The story of Father Lee Hyŏn-jong's last hours is related by an eyewitness, Ahn C'hŏng-sun (eighty-two years of age, living at 160, To-rim-dong, Yŏng-dung-p'o, Seoul), and Magdalene Chŭng (fifty-seven years of age, cook at the presbytery, Mi-a-ri Catholic Church) as follows:

"Father James Lee, at the outbreak of the Communist invasion on June 25, 1950, took refuge in Kwang-myŏng-ri, together with the parish priest Father Park Il-kyu, on June 27, but returned to his own parish Church of To-rim-dong on June 29, in order to take care of it. On July 2, as he was leaving the sacristy after saying Mass, he met two Communist army men, who demanded to know who he was. "I am the priest of this Church," he answered, whereupon one of the army men drew his pistol and shot him in the chest. As he lay dying on the ground he said, "If you want to kill me, you may fire once more, but remember! Though you can kill my body, you cannot kill my soul!" The soldier fired two more shots into the priest's body, and Father Lee died at once.

"At the sound of the shots, Marino Sŭh, a servant employed to take care of the Church building, ran out in alarm. The Communist asked him, "What are you doing here?" "I work here." No sooner had he given this answer than he was shot dead by the Communist."

Ahn Chŏng-sun, the eyewitness of this scene, called Magdalene Chŭng and together they took the bodies into the sacristy to lie there for a while, afterward giving them temporary burial in the garden behind the presbytery.

After the Korean War was brought to a halt by the armistice, the remains of Father Lee were transferred to the clergy-cemetery of Yong-san, and those of Marino Sŭh, the servant, to the laycemetery.

Note 5. Father Han Yun-seung, formerly a priest of the Yenki Vicariate, was transferred to the Province of Hwang-hae prior to August 15, 1945. He served successively in the parishes of Chin-nam-p'o, Yŏng-yu, and Hae-ju. He is believed to have been killed at Hae-ju by the Communists during the Korean War.

Note 6. The body of Father Francis Sŭh Ki-ch'ang was discovered at the Political Security Bureau of Song-hwa county on October 19, 1950, and given burial at Soe-kol, Song-hwa village. Agatha Park, his Christian maidservant and housekeeper, testified as follows:

"Prior to his arrest, Father Sŭh had been repeatedly summoned to the police station, where he underwent severe interrogation under torture. After his Church buildings were taken over by the Communists, he removed the altar and sacred objects to the home of a Catholic layman, about a mile and a half away, where he used to say Mass daily.

"On October 6 at about 2 p.m., I was gathering herbs on the hillside when an old woman of the neighborhood came to tell me that our priest had been taken to the police station by some young men. I went straight to the Political Security Bureau, to ask them to release him. 'Why would a Catholic priest come to such a place as this?' they asked. I then made a search for Father Suh with the catechist, but without success.

"After his arrest we heard that he had been taken to Hae-ju, or was being held in custody by the

Political Security Bureau. Several days later, there was a heavy air-raid during the night, and the whole town became a sea of fire. At daybreak we saw the police and the taxcollectors setting fire to their buildings and hurriedly preparing to leave. 'Oh, if only our priest has found a safe place, even if it is the Hae-ju Political Security Bureau!'

Just then a woman catechist rushed up to me, saying that the Communists had begun to massacre the Christians, killing them at random wherever they happened to meet them, and urging me to run away to some safe spot with her. We went to the Yŏng-ma-reum cave and remained in hiding there for the rest of the day.

"That evening the catechist Kim came to report that they could find no trace of the body of our priest in the burnt-out police station and tax office, and that they were anxious to find out whether he was in safety or not.

"A few days later a young man came and told me that he had found a body, which he thought might be that of our priest. We ran quickly to the site where we found a pile of human bodies. Among them we were able to identify one corpse as that of 'Don Bosco,' a name given him by the Maryknoll Convent. Though all the other bodies were beginning to decay and were infested with maggots, the features of this one could be recognized as those of Father Sŭh. The two eyes were missing from the head, but the rest of the body was quite clean and free from decay.

"On the following day several catechists, including a woman, and a group of young men from the village, came to recover the remains and on closer examination marks were found on the body which showed that he had been strangled to death, with his hands tightly bound behind his back.

"We fetched floor-boards from our house to make a coffin and gave his body decent burial."

Note 7. The body of Father Andrew Chŭn Tŏk-p'yo was discovered among the piles of dead in Sa-ri-won on October 21, 1950 after the troops of the United Nations had liberated the town. The neck and hands were bound with insulated wire. The remains were given burial with military honors on the following day. The mother of Martina Kim, the late priest's maidservant, gaves the following account:

"Father Andrew Chŭn was ordained to the priesthood by the Most Rev. Paul M. Ro, Bishop (now Archbishop) of Seoul, on November 21, 1946. He arrived in Sa-ri-won on December 20 of the same year, crossing the Thirty-eighth Parallel. At his inaugural Mass on the following day he told us in his sermon that when he entered the theological seminary he chose Saint Don Bosco to be his patron saint; he went on to urge all parents to send their children to Church regularly. He was, he said, very fond of children, and was going to provide a course of lessons in Catholic doctrine for them. He told us that, on learning of his appointment to Sa-ri-won, north of the Thirty-eighth Parallel, he had felt a momentary reluctance at the thought of leaving South Korea, a feeling for which he was ashamed now that he had met his parishioners and seen their enthusiasm. He devoted himself wholeheartedly to his ministry and organized various pious unions for the different age-groups among the Christians, such as "The Children of the Little Flower of Jesus," "The Sacred Heart Youth Society," "The Society of the Immaculate Heart of Mary," and "The Saint Joseph Society for the Aged."

"In spite of Communist opposition and oppression he succeeded in strengthening the faith of the lay folk. After the confiscation of the Church school by the Communists and the departure of the nuns to South Korea, under the orders of their MotherHouse, Father Chŭn personally took over the teaching of the children in the Church kindergarten. He was confronted with added difficulty when refugees swarmed into Sa-ri-won on their way to South Korea. In spite of the strict Communist surveillance Father Chun always did his best to provide them with guides to help them to cross the Thirty-eighth Parallel zone in safety. This became known and he was arrested and taken to Hae-ju. After twenty-four hours of suffering there he was released when he promised in writing not to repeat the offense. Then Father Andrew Chŭn and Father Paul Park took over two parishes, one in Hae-ju, and the other in Sin-ch'ŏn, which had been left vacant when their respective priests were obliged to go to South Korea. Father Chŭn was forced by the Communists to undergo a physical examination for service as a military draftee, but was rejected on account of poor eyesight.

In August 1950, he was conscripted into the labor force to work in the mines at Mo-na-jĭ, but his parishioners succeeded, after tireless efforts, in persuading the Communists to release him. From September, air reconnaissance by the South Korean Air Force and oppression by the Communists grew steadily more intense. Father Chŭn sent the parish priest to take refuge in a village six kilometers away, and on the next day, October 12, decided to move there himself. As he was setting out on his bycycle after Mass, a Methodist minister from the Christian League met him, and asked him to come to a meeting which he said was about to convene. That was the last Father Chŭn saw of him, for a few moments later the whole town of Sa-ri-won was burning fiercely, and the people were fleeing. As soon as the United Nations troops entered the town, the Catholics returned to search for the body of their priest. This they found, among more than 270 indescribably mangled corpses, on October 19. The remains were buried with military honors and a salute of guns. It was said by a young novice that Father Chŭn, whose body was found with arms and neck tightly bound with copper wire, had been subjected to torture by electric shocks, but that up to the moment of his death he had exhorted his youthful torturer to be baptized and become a son of God."

Note 8. Father Lee Sun-sŏng and Father Lee Yŏ-ku were imprisoned at Hae-ju, and are presumed to have been shot on the beach there on October 5, when many other prisoners were massacred. Their bodies were not recovered.

Note 9. The Fathers Yu Chae-ok and Kim Kyŏng-mun were detained at Hae-ju prison and are believed to have been killed there. Regarding the former, a Catholic woman named Bona Lee, a former teacher at the Sin-tang-dong Sunday School, and a native of Kyŏm-i-p'o, North Korea, gave the following account:

"In May 1949, when we heard of the Communist occupation of Tŏk-won Abbey, the capture of the priests and monks, and the dispersal of the seminarians, we advised Father Yu to go into hiding. This he refused to do as long as there was a single believer left behind: when all his flock had made their way to safety, that would be time for the shepherd to leave. This was the attitude that he maintained to the end. As the Communist atrocities increased in number and intensity the priests of neighboring parishes visited him more frequently: Father Park U-ch'ŏl of Sa-ri-won on May 21, 1950; Father Lee Yŏ-ku of Mae-hwadong on May 25; Father Andrew Chŭn of Sa-riwon on May 29 and again on June 5. No doubt this was in order to receive the Sacrament of Penance, for all of them were running the daily risk of death.

"On June 6 an official from the Bureau of Political Security called on our priest, demanding the name of the representative of the Christians. As Joseph Kim Kyŏng-sik stepped forward he was immediately arrested. At the bureau headquarters they ordered him to declare the reason for the priests' visits on May 21, 25, 29 and June 5, alleging that they themselves possessed full information of the facts. Joseph Kim declared quite honestly that he knew nothing about it. The police then ordered him to render regular reports to them on everything that took place at the Church, and asked him to sign a bond on oath to co-operate with the Communists. This he firmly declined to do. When we learned this from him after his release, we again urged Father Yu to go into hiding. This he refused to do, but advised Joseph Kim to make his escape.

"It was early morning on June 25, Sunday. At six o'clock the congregation assembled for the first Mass. As our priest failed to appear we began to feel worried and went to the presbytery to look for him. We found nobody there, but on further search we saw that the back window had been broken, and then we realized' that he had been forcibly abducted during the night. Immediately Maria Han Pyŏng-tŏk (now deceased) and another Catholic woman named Lee went to the City Political Security Bureau office, and also to the Political Bureau for Industry in charge of the local foundry, to demand his release. 'Is he a close relation of yours, comrades?' asked the official. 'From the religious point of view he is as close as our real father,' they replied. The official then shouted angrily at them that they should not make the mistake of looking on the officials as kidnapers. Frustrated, they sought other means to recover their priest, but to no avail. In the meantime the Security Bureau arrested Joseph Kim and several Catholic youths and held them in prison.

"One day there was the sound of gunfire in the distance; it was the troops from South Korea marching north. At dusk the Communists escaped and were nowhere to be seen. The prisoners were released and could be heard shouting 'Man-se!' in the streets. Our Catholic youths joined the Provisional Security Maintenance Committee and organized a search for the lost priest. In the course of their search they were able to seize a hiding Communist, the one who had killed Father Yu. While interrogating him, they found the priest's watch hidden in his belt. Asked whose watch it was he admitted that it was Father Yu's. He confessed that the Political Security Bureau officials in Hae-ju had marched the prisoners to the beach on a dark night on October, 4, and had ordered each of them to dig his own grave. Next day they were interred alive in these graves and hand grenades were thrown at them. At that time Father John Lee Kye-kwang, an army chaplain, was on a visit to Kyŏm-i-p'o, and on December 3 he celebrated a Requiem Mass for Father Yu."

Note 10. Father Yang Tŏk-hwan was one of those imprisoned in Hae-ju, and killed by the Communists shortly before the liberation of the city by the South Korean Army. Although the believers made a thorough search for his body, it could not be found. Joanna Ch'oe, the catechist at Chae-ryŏng Parish, gaves the following testimony regarding Father Yang's arrest:

"Father Yang, who moved to Chae-ryŏng Parish from An-ak in 1946, was placed under strict surveillance by a Communist named Cho, head of the Social Department of the Political Security Bureau of the town, but carried on his ministry under difficulties and was able to raise the number of Catholics in the village to six hundred. Annoyed at this, Cho harassed Father Yang everyday with interrogations. With consummate tact, Father Yang dealt with these visits successfully. The year before the outbreak of the Korean War, on November 30, 1949, a jubilee ceremony was held for the twenty-fifth anniversary of Father Yang's ordination. This aroused the ire of the Communist Cho, and soon afterwards he arrested Father Yang, and charged him with holding an illegal assembly and stirring up trouble. They threatened him with the severest penalties if he should repeat the offense. Father Yang's devoted service to the Church under such arduous conditions finally broke down his health. Then the war broke out and open oppression of the Church became the order of the day.

"The Communists intruded into the Church buildings and removed the pews and furniture, and the beds and bedding from the Hospital of the Blessed Virgin Mary. They also stole his dog, to add insult to injury. Rumors circulated that priests were being kidnaped by the Communists everywhere, so we once again besought our priest to flee to South Korea as soon as possible. His reply was always the same, and delivered with the utmost composure. 'How can the shepherd run away to safety and leave his sheep in danger? It is you that I fear for, not myself. I wish you would set off for freedom as soon as possible.' He declared that he would stay with the Church until the last moment.

"Beckoning me to him he told me very solemnly, as if uttering his last words: 'Joanna Ch'oe, listen to me. I hope you will keep them carefully.' He then gave me the six rings and told me, 'I originally intended to pay back our debt to the Parish Church with these rings.' He then showed me a small notebook, which he inserted in a larger one,

and explained that the former contained the account of income accruing from private Masses he had celebrated in the past. He asked me to keep this book together with the religious register in case an unexpected mishap (such as his kidnaping or disappearance, for example) should befall him, and to hand them over to the bishop after the unification of Korea. I can still vividly recall his sorrowful countenance as he said these words, which as it turned out, were in fact his last words to me.

"On the evening of October 5, 1950, the chairman of the local Communist Party, a former elder of the Presbyterian Church, called on our priest in as kindly a manner as ever. He informed Father Yang that the Communist Party had worked out a plan to execute all priests and nuns in the near future, as well as Protestant ministers in North Korea, as active reactionaries. According to his information, the Communists had already designated the site of the execution and prepared the rifles and bayonets to be used in the execution of the religious leaders. He urged the priest to make his escape as soon as possible, and then made a hurried departure. Soon after he had left we had supper with the priest. Deeply troubled for his safety, we discussed how to convey him to a safe place. It was now about 8 p.m. The priest got up and excused himself, saying that he was going to the toilet. But he did not return, even after an hour had passed. We all felt overwhelmed with the premonition of evil, and searched all over the house for him.

"Then, in the utmost consternation, we hurried to the precinct office (*dong*) and reported his disappearance to the *dong* officials. One of them, presumably less of a leftist than the remainder, was overheard to mutter, 'Oh dear, something unfortunate may have happened to him.' He seemed to feel sorry for the missing priest. Overhearing this remark, we felt sure that Father Yang had been kidnaped, and, returning to the church, sat up all night discussing ways and means to ascertain his whereabouts. At daybreak we rushed to the Political Security Bureau and told them all that had happened the night before. Instead of being co-operative, they rather blamed us for hiding the priests and ordered us to find him at once. We were now in a quandary and did not know what to do. On the one hand we felt a strong suspicion that the Communists had killed our priest and secretly made away with his body. But on the other hand, there was the possibility that he was still alive. All the Catholic believers were mobilized to search for

God's Valiant Servants

The priests who were imprisoned and massacred by the Communists before and during the Korean War amount to more than one hundred.

Bishop Byrne, Apostolic Delegate to Korea

Bishop Sauer, Abbot of Tŏk-won Abbey

Msgr. Brennan, Prefect Apostolic of Kwang-ju

Bishop Francis Hong, Vicar Apostolic of P'yŏng-yang

Vicariates of Tŏk-won and Ham-heung

Rev. L. Roth (Prior, killed at P'yŏng-yang on Nov. 3, 1950)

Rev. A. Schleicher (Subprior died in prison on June 28, 1952)

Rev. R. Klingseis (Professor of Seminary, died in prison on April 6, 1950)

Rev. A. Romer (Rector of Seminary, died in prison on Nov. 9, 1951)

Rev. D. Enk (Procurator, killed in P'yŏng-yang prison on Oct. 3, 1950)

Rev. G. Sorger (Professor of Seminary, died in prison on Nov. 15, 1950)

Rev. Benedict Kim Ch'i-ho (missing)

Rev. Bernard Kim Chong-su (missing)

Rev. Martin Kim I-sik (missing)

Rev. C. Ott (Pastor of Sin-ko-san, died in prison on June 14, 1952)

Rev. C. Davernas (Sin-ko-san Convent, died in prison on Nov. 6, 1950)

Rev. G. Steger (Pastor of Yŏng-heung, killed at P'yŏng-yang prison on Oct. 3, 1950)

Rev. Laurence Lee Ch'un-keun (Sŏ-p'o Convent, missing)

Rev. Maurus Kim Pong-sik (Pastor of I-ch'ŏn, killed on Oct. 9, 1950)

Rev. Matthias Ch'oe Pyŏng-kwon (Tŏk-won Church, missing)

Rev. Gabriel Ku Tae-jun (Hoe-ryŏng Church, missing)

Rev. Peter Lee Chae-ch'ŏl (Ch'ŏng-jin Church, missing)

Rev. Witmarus Farrenkopf (Hoe-ryŏng Church, killed by the Soviet troops on August 23, 1945)

Br. Mark Metzger (Tŏk-won Abbey, died in prison on Aug. 3, 1949)

Br. Eugenius Ostermeier (Tŏk-won Abbey, died in prison on Sept. 14, 1949)

Br.Paschalis Faugauer (Tŏk-won Abbey, died in prison on April 16, 1950)

Br. Ildefonsus Flötzinger (Tŏk-won Abbey, died in prison on March 20, 1952)

Br. Godelibus Auer (Tŏk-won Abbey, died in prison on April 6, 1952)

Br. Josephus Grahamer(Tŏk-won Abbey, killed in P'yŏng-yang on Oct. 4, 1950)

Br. Hilarius Hoiss (Tŏk-won Abbey, died in prison on Dec. 12, 1950)

Br. Basilius Hauser (Tŏk-won Abbey, died in prison on Feb. 12, 1950)

Br. Euselius Lohmeier (Tŏk-won Abbey, died in prison on Sept. 1, 1951)

Br. Ludovicus Fischer (Tŏk-won Abbey, killed in P'yŏng-yang on Oct. 11, 1950)

Br. Solanus Hermann (Tŏk-won Abbey, died in prison on Dec. 13, 1950)

Br. Petrus Gernert (Tŏk-won Abbey, died in prison on July 3, 1949)

Seminarian Thomas Kim Sang-jin (missing)

Vicariate of P'yŏng-yang

Rev. Louis Kim P'il-hyŏn (Vicar-general of Kwan-hu-ri Church, P'yŏng-yang, missing)

Rev. Matthias Ch'oe Hwan-jun (P'yŏng-yang Church, missing)

Rev. Mark Sŏk Wonsŏp (Kang-kye Church, missing)

Rev. Timothy Park Nong-ok (Sŏn-kyo-ri Church, missing)

Rev. Bonifatius Sŭh Un-sŏk (Kwan-hu-ri Church, P'yŏng-yang, missing)

Rev. Alexis Lee Chaeho (Ki-lim-ri Church, P'yŏng-yang, missing)

Rev. Andrew Chang Tu-pong (Ki-lim-ri Church, P'yŏng-yang, missing)

Rev. Callistus Hong Kŏn-hwan (Sin-eui-ju Church, missing)

Rev. John Hong To-keun (Yŏng-yu Church, missing)

Rev. Paul Cho In-kuk (Chin-nam-p'o Church, missing)

Rev. Anselmus Lee Kyŏng-ho (An-ju Church, missing)

Rev.Paul Kang Yŏng-kŏl (Ma-san Church, South P'yŏng-an Province, missing)

Rev. Benedict Kim Kyo-myŏng (Eui-ju Church, missing)

Rev.Mark Kim Tong-ch'ŏl(Pi-hyŏn Church, missing)

Sr. Agnetta Chang Chŏng-on (Superior of Sŏ-p'o Convent, missing)

Vicariate of Seoul

Rev. P. Villemot (Priest, St. Paul Convent, died in prison on Nov. 11, 1950)

Rev. A. Gombert (Priest, Carmel Convent, died in prison on Nov. 12, 1950)

Rev. J. Gombert (Priest, In-ch'ŏn Paul Convent, died in prison on Nov. 13, 1950)

Rev. John Yu Yŏng-keun (Procurator of Seoul Vicariate, missing)

Rev.Joseph Lee Chae-hyŏn (Principal of Holy Ghost Middle School, missing)

Rev. Agapitus Paek Nam-ch'ang (Priest, Holy Ghost Middle School, missing)

Rev. Matthias Chŭng Chin-ku(Priest,Tong-sŏng Middle School, missing)

Rev. James Lee Hyŏn-jong (Coadjutor of Yŏng-dung-p'o Church, killed on the spot on July 2, 1950)

Rev. Philip Han Yun-seung (Priest, Hae-ju Church, missing)

Rev. Paul Yun Eui-pyŏng(Priest,Eun-yul Church, missing)

Rev. Andrew Lee Sun-sŏng (Priest, Sin-kye Church, missing)

Rev. Andrew Yang Tŏk-hwan (Priest, Chae-ryŏng Church, killed in Oct. 1950)

Rev. Matthias Lee Yŏ-ku (Priest, Mae-hwa-dong Church, missing)

Rev. Francis Yu Chae-ok (Priest, Kyŏm-i-p'o Church, killed on Oct. 5, 1950)

Rev. Francis Sŭh Ki-ch'ang (Priest, An-ak Church, killed on Oct. 16, 1950)

Rev. Louis Kim Kyŏng-mum (Priest, Song-hwa Church, missing)

Rev. Peter Shin Yun-ch'ŏl (Priest, Chang-yŏn Church, missing)

Rev. Andrew Chŭn Tŏk-p'yo (Coadjutor of Sa-ri-won Church, killed on Oct. 16, 1950)

Sr. Béatrix (Sister Superior of St. Paul Convent, killed on Nov. 3, 1950)

Sr. Angela Kim (St. Paul Convent, killed on Oct. 15, 1950)

Sr. Marianna Kim (St. Paul Convent, killed on Oct. 17, 1950)

Sr. Mechtilde (Carmel Convent, died in prison on Nov. 18, 1950)

Sr. Marie-Thérèsa (Carmel Convent, died in prison on Nov. 30, 1950)

Prefecture of Ch'un-ch'ŏn

Rev. P. Reiller (Priest, Muk-ho Church, killed toward the end of July, 1950)

Rev. F. Canavan (Co-adjutor of Ch'un-ch'ŏn Church, died in prison on Dec. 6, 1950)

Rev. Pt. Maginn (Priest, Sam-ch'ŏk Church, killed in July, 1950)

Rev. Timotheus Lee Kwang-jae (Priest, Yang-yang Church, killed on Oct. 9, 1950)

Rev. Damasus Paek Eung-man (Priest, P'yŏng-kang Church, died in prison at the beginning of Jan. 1950)

Vicariate of Tae-jŏn

Rev. D. Polly (Priest, Ch'ŏn-an Church, killed between Sept. 23-26, 1950)

Rev. R. Richard (Priest, Ye-san Church, killed between Sept. 23-26, 1950)

Rev. P. Leleu (Priest, On-yang Church, killed between Sept. 23-26, 1950)

Rev. J. Bulteau (Priest, Kong-se-ri Church, died during detention at Ha-ch'ang-ri on Jan. 6, 1951)

Rev. P. Perrin (Priest, Hap-tŏk Church, killed between Sept. 23-26, 1950)

Rev. M. Cordesse (Priest, Tang-jin Church, killed between Sept. 23-26, 1950)

Rev. J. Colin (Priest, Sŏ-san Church, killed between Sept. 23-26, 1950)

Rev. J. Molimard (Priest, Pu-yŏ Church, killed between Sept. 23-26, 1950)

Rev. J. Cadars (Priest, Mok-dong Church, Tae-jŏn, died at Ha-ch'ang-ri on Dec. 16, 1950)

Rev. Joseph Kang Man-su (Priest, Hong-sŏng Church, missing)

Prefecture of Kwang-ju

Rev. T. Cusack P.P. (Priest, Mok-p'o Church, missing)

Rev. J. O'Brien P.P. (Priest, Mok-p'o Church, missing)

"If any man will come after me, let him deny himself and take up his cross daily and follow me. For whoever will save his life shall lose it: for he that shall lose his life for my sake shall save it." (St. Luke, 9:23-24)

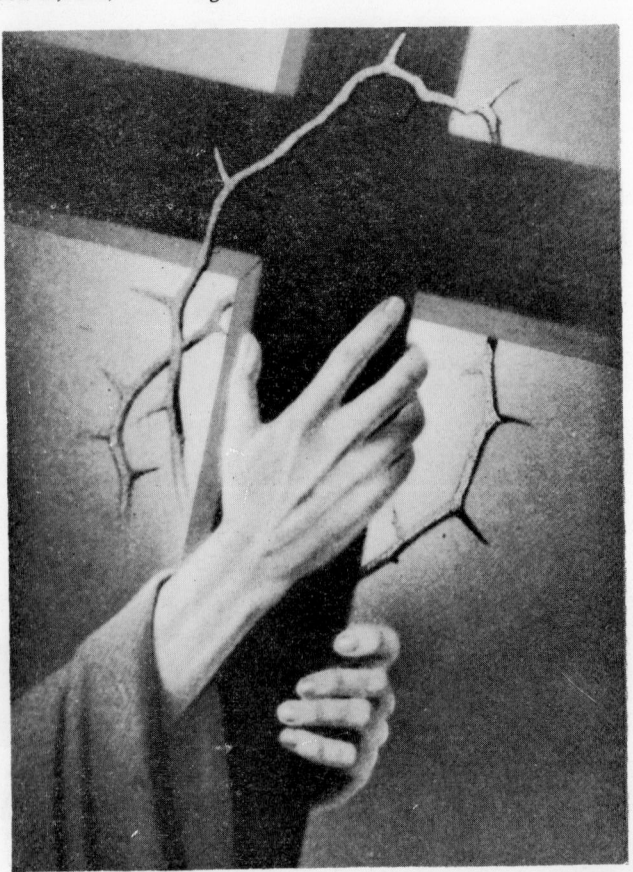

372

him. For three days we made exhaustive inquiries throughout the countryside, but without result.

"Then we reported these facts to Father Paul Park in Sa-ri-won Parish, but he was too upset to take any action. We shall never forget that ordeal of October 1950.

"At the news of the imminent arrival of the armed forces of South Korea the entire city was in an uproar: the streets were full of people shouting 'Man-se!' and the Communist troops and police were beating a hasty retreat, firing indiscriminately in their panic. We nuns all went into hiding in the basement of our church. After three days of waiting, the South Korean Army occupied the city, on October 13, 1950. There was no more gunfire to be heard. We emerged from our hiding place, to find the bodies of the victims of Communists' cruelty lying everywhere, and the ground stained with pools of blood. We renewed our search for the remains of Father Yang among the corpses on the ground, but without success. The scene at the police station jail was almost beyond description; there were piles of bodies everywhere. Hundreds of innocent people had been killed by the vicious Communists.

"Although we made a thorough search among the corpses we could not find any trace of Father Yang's remains. We decided to continue our search at Hae-ju prison. We had been told by our Catholic lay folk that the Communists in that city had shut up all the Catholic priests, and nuns, and all the Protestant ministers of religion in a room, which they set on fire before retreating from the city. On our arrival at Hae-ju we found that all had been burnt to ashes and that no identification was possible. Other Catholic informants told us that several bodies had been thrown into the sea, and several others buried. We opened recent graves in the burial ground, but could not find his body.

"During the brief period when the nation was temporarily unified, Father Peter Kim came to our parish on a visit. In accordance with Father Yang's will, I handed over to Father Kim the rings and notebooks he had left with me. One of the rings was used for the Requiem Mass that was celebrated in his honor."

Note 11. No one knew what had happened to Father Shin Yun-ch'ŏl after his arrest in Chang-yŏn. Father Yun Eui-pyŏng was arrested in Eun-yul. We had no means of ascertaining his whereabouts. It is highly probable that he, too, was killed by the Communists.

Note 12. Of the three nuns, Sister Angela Kim, Sister Marianna Kim, and Sister Regis Kang, two were stabbed to death in Mae-hwa-dong, An-ak, by the retreating Communist troops. Sister Regis Kang, who survived, gaves the following account:

"Late in the evening of October 13, 1950, the mother of P'yo Kwan-to (now an Air Force captain) called on me and asked: 'Now that the United Nations Forces have entered Sa-ri-won, a large number of rightist youths who had been engaged in underground activities have now come into the open, and wish to print some anti-Communist leaflets. May we borrow your mimeograph and a ream of paper?'

"I thought it was still too early to begin this kind of work, but she insisted that, as these anti-Communist youths were scheduled to leave for P'yŏng-yang on the 15th, they had to complete their printing of the leaflets by the 14th. I decided to let her have the machine.

"Early the following morning young men who had been in hiding for months, without enough food or sunshine, suddenly appeared all over the town. They looked pale and weak, their hair was as long as a woman's, and their faces were unshaven. A group of fifty, unarmed except for their ardent anti-Communist spirit and their bare fists, paraded through the streets in a demonstration which soon attracted a crowd of citizens, shouting slogans:

"'Down with the Reds! Kill them all!'

"The leftists, who had been lording it over the population, made themselves scarce. Everyone felt a sense of relief and happiness at being liberated from the hell of Communist slavery. Without leadership, however, they were thrown into confusion. Then a group of rightist citizens came on the scene and made a proclamation, to the following effect:

"'Fellow citizens! Tonight nobody is to stay at home or go to bed! Every household must get plenty of water ready, and everybody, including mothers with babies on their backs, should assemble at the churchyard with any tools you can rightly protect yourselves with. We must prepare to defend ourselves against the fleeing Communists, in case they attack us tonight. Stay overnight and be prepared for tomorrow.'

"Instead of rifles or swords we nuns had our rosaries, and kept vigil outside the church gate throughout the night. We shivered, not only with cold but with horror. Calling on the name of the Blessed Virgin Mary we waited for the dawn. At our usual hour for rising, half past four, we returned to our rooms for a while to wash and change our clothes, for it was Sunday. It was then that the noise of gunfire, shouting and crying suddenly burst upon us from outside the town. We were at a loss to know what to do, until Miss Yun Chae-ok, a teacher, came running to our room and announced, 'Sister! The United Nations troops are entering the town! Come out quickly and greet them!' I could hardly believe that the United Nations troops would make such a boisterous noise, but we hurried out and saw hundreds of strange-looking fellows rushing from the hills toward us. They wore a white cloth round the forehead, a thick rope round the waist, and carried rifles, swords, axes, spears, hammers, sickles and clubs in their hands, shouting 'Man-se!' over and over again. The citizens, mistaking them for the United Nations troops, approached to welcome them with similar cries of 'Man-se.' They shouted contemptuously, 'What is your "Man-se" for? You should all be destroyed!' With these cries they began to kill the citizens either by firing at them, stabbing them, or beating them. It was now about 5 a.m.

"'Although the citizens had made their preparations against attack overnight, they had no means of coping with this sudden assault. We hid ourselves at Mr. Kim's house, which was the one nearest to our own, and remained horror-struck in the inner room. We heard steps approaching, and cries of 'Where are the nuns? Nuns! Nuns!.....' They destroyed and killed as they went, and their shouts and the groans of their victims made our blood run cold.

"We heard the crash as the statue of the Blessed Virgin Mary at the door of our house was smashed to pieces, and we wondered what would happen next.

"'Hey! The women are here! I've found the nuns!' These words were suddenly screamed out in all the fury of mad dogs. The shouts outside increased in number and volume as they angrily called us to come out.

"'Well, are you going to surrender or not?' came the question in threatening tone. Turning to my two colleagues, I said, 'It is too late for us to do anything now but give ourselves up. Let us make a final sign of the cross and a fervent act of contrition.' With words of mutual encouragement, we submitted to their orders.

"'Hands up, you wicked women!' They glared at us with piercing eyes as they looked us up and down, and searched our pockets.

"'What have you got in your pockets?' they demanded. I answered that I had a copy of the Little Office of the Blessed Virgin Mary and a guide for the examination of conscience, a rosary, a handkerchief, a small pocketknife and a pair of nail scissors. 'Is that all you have?' shouted one of them, as the others gave us several blows with their rifle-butts. 'Ten steps forward!' came the order. 'What are you really, after all?'

"'I am a nun,' I answered.

"'Now we know. You are one of those wicked women who make a profession of being nuns. Ten steps forward again!'

"I obeyed, and he asked again, 'Are you really a nun? What shocking crime have you committed that you are trembling like that? Wait and see whether Syngman Rhee will come to your rescue.'

"Once more came the order to take ten steps forward. I was now in one of the streets. 'Are you really Sister Kang?' they asked. 'Yes, I am really Sister Kang. Kang has been my surname since my birth,' I replied. Turning to the crowd, the Communist who had been interrogating me shouted, 'Tie up these women! Use the thick rope!' None among the hundreds of people surrounding us made a move to obey him. Worried about what would happen to us when we were tied up, I saw two rows of about fifty or sixty persons with their hands tied behind their backs. The crowd was puzzled by the order to bind the nuns. Among those already bound I noticed several Churchmen, including Kim Kun-sam, an old man of seventy-five, who stood at the head of the line; Kwon the catechist, and Agnes Kim. Almost in tears the old man cried, 'Oh, my Sisters, my Sisters! what shall we do?' They looked almost overcome with terror and anxiety.

"They were all dragged to the mine in Tong-ch'ang-p'o, a distance of some five miles. There the Communists began to stab the people to death. As they fell, the Communists severed their heads, limbs, and breasts with blows of a steel shovel, and threw the dismembered remains over a cliff into a pond some thirty feet below. No Catholic in the group survived. Though the Communists repeatedly ordered their followers to bind us, none of them would do so.

"'Ten steps forword!' orderd the leader once more. 'No!' interrupted another Communist, 'No! These women must be stabbed to death too.' At these words, shouted in a stentorian voice, the Communists charged toward us and began striking us with their rifles, swords, sickles, spears, axes and clubs. I could no longer feel pain after so many and such violent blows, and I fell unconscious.

"Leaving us for dead, the Communists ran off. I don't know how long I lay there, but when I came to myself again, I could not believe my eyes. It seemed to me that I was in a bath, but actually I was covered in blood. My head was bleeding profusely, my left arm pierced by a spear, and my right leg crushed. I had bled so much that I was stuck to the ground by coagulated blood, and could not move. There I lay in a faint, listening to a strange noise, something like a water faucet being turned on and off. What was that noise? With an effort I tore myself from the coagulated blood that was holding me down, and got on my feet. Was I alive or dead? What of the two nuns with me at Mr. Kim's? I found Sister Angela lying on her back as peacefully as if she were asleep. Placing my hand on her forehead I felt it as cold as ice. She was dead—she had been dead nine hours. I then approached Sister Marianna: the strange noise was coming from her direction.

"What a horrifying scene I found! Her right arm had been chopped off; one of her cheeks had been hacked away with a sickle; and her temple and forehead had apparently been struck with an axe, for across it was a great wound gaping four or five centimeters between the eyes; while the nose had been dug away entirely with the point of a spear. With her nose gone, dark red blood was spouting up to a height of twenty centimeters whenever she breathed, making that strange noise which I had heard. The jet rose and fell, and the blood flowed down over her cheeks. Were the Communists satisfied with this brutality? She was unrecognizable but for her clothing. The sound became louder as she seemed to weaken. Lying down close beside her, I called loud into her ear, 'Sister Marianna! Sister Marianna!' I heard a faint groan escape from her lips. Without waiting, I urged her to make an act of contrition. 'It is the time of judgment! Let us repent! Oh, my God, I love Thee with all my heart, with all my soul and with all my strength, and with no other desire than to be inseparably united to Thee....' She answered with a faint 'Oh.' I was struck with pity and horror: I feared that the Communists would strike again as they had in the morning.

"Looking around, I saw nothing but piles of dead bodies lying on all sides, where they had fallen in the throes of death. Dogs and pigs were eagerly licking up the blood. I hurried back to town, all covered with blood as I was, to seek a hiding place in some kitchen or room. An old woman saw me and let me enter her house, where, after a short rest, I felt a strong urge to make my way back to my convent, but I found that I was now too stiff to move: though I was perfectly conscious, I seemed to have no power over my muscles. Seeing that I was unable to get up and walk, several women gathered round my bed, and carried me to the convent on a stretcher. When we arrived I decided to wait in the servants' quarters until my colleagues appeared. Now the desire came to me to have the remains of my two Sisters brought to our convent, but none of the women were willing to fetch them. Late that evening a party of more than ten women of the village came to me and I said to them, 'I hope you can bring the body of Sister Angela to our front yard, and bring Sister Marianna, who is still alive, to this room so that she can lie beside me.'

"A little later they returned exhausted, together with my other colleagues. They laid Sister Angela's body in the front yard and brought Sister Marianna into my room. It was plain that she was in great agony. As soon as they laid her on the bed she vomited a basinful of blood. Though she had lost so much blood, the jet still spouted from her nose. Unable to move, I could do nothing to relieve her. There were, I knew, hemostatic and other drugs in the church. She seemed to be in increasing pain: I shook her and called her name several times but she could no longer reply. She seemed to be unconscious. If only we had a doctor or a nurse, I thought to myself, it might be possible to save or at least prolong her life. But there was no one to whom I could appeal for help: all the visitors who came seemed terrified at the sight and smell of so much blood, and hurried away, slamming the door behind them. The nun still lay there covered with blood, and some who entered could not distinguish which was Sister Kim and which was Sister Kang.

"The fatal injuries she had received on the morning of October 15 had so weakened her that by six o'clock in the afternoon of October 17 her breathing grew irregular and the bleeding from the nose gradually decreased in volume. She grew weaker still, and now only a whitish liquid flowed from the wound. There was one long deep breath, and then all breathing stopped. No more blood or fluid came from her wounds: at last she was dead, and her soul had gone to Heaven to rest with the Lord after all her suffering.

"'O my dear Lord, may her soul rest in eternal peace. O Blessed Virgin Mary, she won her fight against the Communists! She did not fear those who can kill only the body, and so they could not kill her soul! Call her to Thee, O clement and loving Virgin!'

"Under the fiercely anti-Catholic tyranny of the Communists, we three nuns had lived in close companionship, but now, alas! the other two now lay dead beside me. We had longed to escape together across the Thirty-eighth Parallel to our Motherhouse. Now I was alone. Though I knew I must make arrangements for their funeral, I felt unable to get up, and just lay there together with them. Some one entered. It was Joanna Mun, an old acquaintance. Her visit gave me great encouragement. I explained to her how to lay out the bodies and clothe them in our religious habits. I told her not to take off the Korean dress that they were wearing when they died, but simply put the religious habit over the Korean dress.

Then the bodies were laid outside the door of the house. The next problem was coffins. An old man by the name of Ch'oe Ho-won agreed to barter his coffin for two bags of rice, and another was made from the ping-pong table in the parochial school. Two days later they were laid in these coffins, but the lack of bearers obliged me to postpone burial. Many of the townsfolk had been killed, and the youths were still in hiding for fear of the Communists. The only people to be seen on the streets were the sick, the disabled, and the aged. My only worry was that the two dead Sisters could not be buried: I myself lay on my bed with my body still covered with blood.

"Later the remains of Sister Angela Kim were interred by the grave of Father Paul Oh in the churchyard, and those of Sister Marianna Kim by that of Father Leo Nam in the same cemetery."

PREFECTURE OF CH'UN-CH'ŎN

Name	Rank & Date of Ordination	Nationality & Birth Year	Post	Date of Apprehension	Remarks
1) T. Quinlan	Prefect Apostolic 1955	Irish 1896	Prefecture of Ch'un-ch'ŏn	July 11, 1950	Repatriated (Now Bishop of Ch'un-ch'ŏn)
2) A. Collier	Priest 1938	" 1913	So-yang Church	June 27, 1950	Killed at the spot
3) P. Reiller	Priest 1941	" 1915	Muk-ho Church	July 12, 1950	Killed at the spot on July 12, 1950
4) F. Canavan	Priest 1941	" "	Coadjutor of Ch'un-ch'ŏn	July 2, 1950	Died during detention by Reds on Dec. 6, 1950
5) Pt. Maginn	Priest 1935	American 1910	Sam-ch'ŏk Church	July 1950	Killed in July 1950
6) P. Crosbie	Priest 1939	Australian 1939	Hong-ch'ŏn Church	July 6, 1950	Repatriated (Now staying in Korea)
7) Timothy Lee Kwang-jae	Priest 1936	Korean, Sin-kye, Hwang-hae, 1908	Yang-yang Church	June 24, 1950	Killed on Oct. 9, 1950
8) Damasus Paek Eung-man	Priest	Korean, I-ch'ŏn 1919	P'yŏng-kang Church	At the beginning of Apr. 1949	Died in prison at the beginning of Jan. 1950

Note 1. Father Reiller was in hiding at the house of Francis Park, then catechist, at Man-u-ri, Muk-ho, when the North Korean army captured Muk-ho. On July 12 he and Francis Park were arrested by the Red army and taken to Kang-neung Police Headquarters. A few days later Father Reiller was killed by the Communists at Pang-chae-kul mountain, about ten miles from Muk-ho. After the liberation of Ch'un-ch'ŏn city on September 28, his remains were recovered and buried in the churchyard at Chuk-rim-dong, Ch'un-ch'ŏn.

Note 2. The catechist Thomas Sŭh Chŏng-min recalls the last days of Father Maginn as follows:

"As soon as the Korean War broke out we began to be anxious for his safety, and did our best to persuade him to take refuge in a safe area. For his part he told us to do the same, and gave us some money for traveling expenses, but added: 'I shall remain here and defend the Church until death. I shall bear witness for God to the Communists who deny Jesus Christ.' One of the young neophytes, John Kim Su-sŏng, declared that he could not leave, knowing that Father Maginn was ready to face death at the hands of the Communists, and that he too would stay and dedicate his life to the Church and Father. Though Father Maginn urged him to seek refuge, this young man was not to be shaken in his resolution to die for Christ. Next day, as expected, the Red troops invaded the village, and the local Communists at once informed them of Father Maginn's whereabouts. It was not long before they came to arrest him. He received them with calmness and composure. Entering the Church he knelt before the altar for a final prayer. He was not allowed to stay here long; the impatient soldiers shouted to him from outside the church.

"When he emerged they seized and kicked him, struck him with their rifle-butts, and were about to handcuff him. With a calm smile he said, 'Make yourselves at ease: I'm not escaping. Let's go this way.' Overcome by his self-possession, they yielded to his request. He was escorted to the police station at gunpoint. A few hours later John Kim was also arrested, and detained in an adjacent ell. After an unknown period of detention, starvation and torture, Father Maginn was lying almost unconscious on the floor at midnight when a warder came and shouted to him to get up and come out of his cell. Father Maginn had already guessed the reason. He asked them to let him say a word of farewell to John Kim, who was still in the adjacent cell. The warders could not refuse the last request of a man about to die, and allowed him to see John Kim. Passing his fingers tenderly through John's hair, he gave him his final blessing.

"'John, I hope to see you again in Paradise. Whatever the pain you have to suffer, bear it patiently and never lose your faith in Our Lord Jesus Christ.' He disappeared into the pitch-black night, and John's mourning wails followed him and continued long after he had gone. Father Maginn was hustled barefooted along the rugged mountain road as far as Cha-chi-ri. There a shot echoed through the ravine and he fell. Next morning the corpse was found by villagers, who charitably buried it at the very spot. After the liberation of Ch'un-ch'ŏn city, the grave was sought on information of eyewitnesses of his last hours, and today his remains lie in Chuk-rim-dong churchyard, Ch'un-ch'ŏn, now the Cathedral Church of Ch'un-ch'ŏn Diocese."

Note 3. Father Canavan was apprehended together with Bishop Patrick Byrne, Apostolic Delegate, and died in captivity on December 6, 1950, eleven days after Bishop Byrne. (See "The Death March")

Note 4. Father Collier was captured by the Red Army soldiers on June 27, 1950, at the cross street of Ch'un-ch'ŏn city, and was shot and killed in a corn field in the vicinity of the Kong-ji-ch'ŏn River on the way to the police station. Three bullets had pierced his cheek, chest, and arm respectively. His body was given temporary burial by the believers on the same day, and reinterred in Chuk-rim-dong churchyard. The funeral ceremony was conducted by Father Chi on October 9, 1951, in the presence of priests, laity, and high-ranking U. S. military officers.

Note 5. For information regarding to the death of Father Lee Kwang-jae, see Note 3 of Tŏk-won Abbatia Nullius and Ham-heung Vicariates. (Refer to Father Maurus Kim Pong-sik)

Note 6. Father Paek Eung-man was apprehended in April, 1949, and brought to P'yŏng-yang with a hood over his head in order to conceal his identity from the public. He died after severe torture in P'yŏng-yang prison, and is interred at Yong-san Cemetery, P'yŏng-yang.

VICARIATE OF TAE-JŎN

Name	Rank & Date of Ordination	Nationality & Birth Year	Post	Date of Apprehension	Remarks
1) D. Polly	Priest 1907	French 1884	Ch'ŏn-an Church	Aug. 23, 1950	Killed bettween on Sept. 23—26, 1950
2) R. Richard	" 1929	" 1900	Ye-san Church	Aug. 3, 1950	"
3) P. Leleu	" 1930	" 1909	On-yang Church	"	"
4) J. Bulteau	" 1927	" 1901	Kong-se-ri Church	July 12, 1950	Died during detention at Ha-ch'ang-ri on Jan. 6, 1951

Name	Rank & Year of Ordination	Nationality & Birth Year	Post	Date of Apprehension	Remarks
5) P. Perrin	Priest	French 1885	Hap-tŏk Church	Aug. 14, 1950	Killed between on Sept. 23—26, 1950
6) M. Cordesse	"	" 1909	Tang-jin Church	"	"
7) J. Colin	" 1927	" 1902	Sŏ-san Church	July 10, 1950	"
8) J. Molimard	" 1924	" 1897	Pu-yŏ Church	Aug. 20, 1950	"
9) J. Cadars	" 1905	" 1878	Mok-dong Church Tae-jŏn,	Aug. 17, 1950	Died during detention at Ha-ch'ang-ri on Dec. 16, 1950
10) Joseph Kang Man-su	" 1948	Korean 1924	Hong-sŏng Church	Aug. 11, 1950	Missing

Note 1. Fathers Perrin and Cordesse were detained in the Tae-jŏn prison and Fathers Polly, Richard, Leleu, Colin and Molimard were herded into the Mok-dong Convent, which had been confiscated by the Communists and occupied by the Political Security Bureau. During the four days from September 23 to 26, the Communists massacred about 1,200 persons at Tae-jŏn Prison and about 700 at the Mok-dong Convent respectively. Among these the body of Father Molimard was identified by two young men living in Father Molimard's parish, Keum-sa-ri, Pu-yŏ county, near Tae-jŏn. The remains were interred near the convent on October 16, 1950.

Note 2. Apprehension of Father Molimard and Discovery of His Body

When the North Korean Army launched its invasion of South Korea Father Molimard, in accordance with the advice of the local police, took temporary refuge at a believer's house in the mountains. He soon returned to his church, however, and spent a few days there in peace. This peace was not to last long, for the Communists soon began to focus their attention on the Church. Although his parishioners repeatedly urged him to go into hiding he would not do so, for his only concern was for their safety. He advised them to abstain from attending Mass for the time being, and continued to celebrate Mass every morning in the empty church. In the meantime, the Communists found a revolver in a house near the church, and took this as a pretext to ransack the priest's quarters. They not only looted the sacred objects but confiscated the Church building, and at nightfall on August 20, 1950, they took Father Molimard to the Pu-yŏ Police Station.

Father Molimard offered no resistance, but quietly told them that he would go wherever they wanted him to. On the following day the Communists carried away the sacred objects they had looted. In the intervals between successive interrogations accompanied with torture, Father Molimard wrote his will in his prison cell, leaving his small personal property in Pu-yŏ and Kyu-am for the building of a church, and exhorting his flock to maintain their faith in Christ. About a month later, prior to the counterattack by the United Nations, he was transferred to Tae-jŏn prison. After undergoing great suffering he was shot and killed in a general massacre of so-called members of the *élite* or gentry, which took place in the foothills behind Mok-dong Convent in the night of September 26. An eyewitness relates that the ruthless killers battered some of the victims to death with stones and brickbats, and flung some of their prisoners one after another into a shallow well. Here, as usual in many other places, the Communists displayed their characteristic cruelty.

Father Molimard died at the age of fifty-two. His remains were recovered and given Christian burial. Two years later they were exhumed and reinterred in the cemetery of Tae-jŏn Convent, under the auspices of the Vicariate. (Declaration by the catechist Gabriel Yang of Sŏ-chŏng-ri Church)

Note 3. The last days of Father Bulteau and Father Cadars are recounted in Appendix A—III "The Death March" and Appendix A—V "Interview with Father Coyos."

Note 4. Father Joseph Kang Man-su was detained in Tae-jŏn prison, and was no doubt one of the 1,200 prisoners who were killed there. His remains, however, were not recovered.

PREFECTURE OF KWANG-JU

Name	Rank & Year of Ordination	Nationality & Brith Year	Post	Date of Apprehension	Remarks
1) P. Brennan	Prefect Apostolic 1928	American 1901	Prefecture of Kwang-ju	Aug, 1950	Unknown
2) T. Cusack	Priest 1934	Irish 1910	Mok-p'o Church	"	"
3) J. O'Brien	" 1942	" 1918	"	"	"

Note: When Mok-p'o was occupied by the Red Army, the Communists captured Father Cusack (date unknown) and paraded him through the streets all day long. He was released at nightfall. Some days later (the exact date is unknown) they arrested Monsignor Brennan, Fathers Cusack and O'Brien, and Catechist Paul Kim in the residence of Monsignor Brennan. They were taken to the police station. The Communists released Paul Kim, who is still alive at the age of eighty-two. (His son is a professor at Kwang-ju Theological Seminary.) The three foreign missionaries were last seen by believers who related that they saw them being taken to Tae-jŏn. The central figure was tall and haggard, and was being supported on either side by the other two. Sister Joanna Kim, of Puk-dong Church, Kwang-ju, says that one of the believers recognized the center figure as that of Monsignor Brennan and the others as Father Cusack and Father O'Brien. Father Anthony Kim relates that he heard of the three missionaries from a priest or believer who caught sight of them in Chŏn-ju prison, and it is therefore presumed that they were transported to Tae-jŏn and were probably among the 1,200 prisoners massacred there during September 23/26.

ADDENDA

Name	Rank & Birth Year	Nationality & Birth Place	Post	Date of Apprehension	Remarks
1) Gregory Chŭn Ki-su	Seminarian b. 1922	Korean, Na-ju, South Chŏl-la	Acolyte	Sept. 25, 1950	Killed Sept. 26, 1950
2) Peter Ko Kwang-kyu	" b. 1924	Korean, Mok-p'o, South Chŏl-la	Tonsured Ordinand	"	"

Note 1. With regard to the two seminarians Gregory Chŭn Ki-su and Peter Ko Kwang-kyu, and their death, their classmate Father Anthony Kim Chŏng-yong, who took refuge with them in Chŏn-ju, and who is now the parish priest of Nam-dong Church, Kwang-ju city, gaves the following account:

"It was September 20 when the three of us arrived at Chŏn-ju. The deserted streets of the Red-occupied city were bleak and expressionless. Through the good offices of my brother-in-law we obtained a lodging in Chŏn-dong, Chŏn-ju city. Five days later, on September 25, as the following day was both the Full Moon Festival and also that of the Beatification of the Seventy-nine Martyrs, we wanted to celebrate the occasion a little more joyously. Promising to be back in the evening, I went out to the suburbs to obtain some food and medicine. Little did I think that was to be my final farewell to them in this world! Though preparations were going on for the Full Moon Festival I sensed an ominous tension and unusual quietness in the air, and several bystanders dissuaded me from returning to the city. That very night my two friends were captured by the Reds and taken to the Jesus Hospital, which had been confiscated by the Communists and occupied by the Political Security Bureau. What I heard was that Gregory Chŭn somewhat imprudently emerged from our hideout to visit Sister Ch'oe to give her some information about her brother-in-law, Mr. Song Kyŏng-sŏp, a company owner in Seoul with whom Gregory had stayed for some twenty days. On his way to Sister Ch'oe's house he was most unfortunately captured by the Communists and made to undergo torture and interrogation. His capture brought about the subsequent apprehension of Peter Ko Kwang-kyu. Sister Kang, who had been apprehended a few days earlier, shared their sufferings in the same cell after their arrest. She told me, 'Next morning, when their morning meal was brought, Gregory prayed and said grace, and afterward added that the meal has been given by Our Heavenly Father as a viaticum, and that he was ready for death. He was perfectly calm and showed no fear.'

"On September 27, at about 5 p.m. there was exciting news. It was said that the Red Army was in flight, and had released all the detainees in Chŏn-ju prison. It was true in part, for next day the United Nations Forces arrived and the city was filled with joy—the Communists were gone. My first thought was to find the two seminarians. With a truck left behind by the Reds I went with a few young Catholics to the prison, where there was no sign of them. We then went to Han-pyŏk-tang, where many innocent people had been massacred. We examined countless dead bodies but could not find our friends among them. We then went to the Jesus Hospital in hopes that we might find them still alive. We searched the whole region including the hills surrounding the hospital, and at last came to an air-raid shelter where we saw piles of corpses, with their hands tied behind the back, and tied to one another in a row. In the middle of the row we found the bodies of the two seminarians. The bruises on their bodies and their fractured skulls showed that they had been pitilessly battered to death. After a Requiem Mass celebrated by Vicar General Bartholomew Lee, the remains were interred near the grave of Lugartha Lee, the martyr who was beheaded on January 31, 1802."

Note 2. When the Reds occupied the city of Chŏn-ju, Monsignor Bartholomew Kim, Prefect of Chŏn-ju, and the priests and Sisters took refuge in the Su-ryu Church. They were all arrested, as well as Fathers Ryu Pong-ku and Lim Eung-seung, who had come to Chŏn-ju from Seoul to escape the conflict. After suffering great hardship in the prison, all the detainees had a narrow escape from death when the Communists were forced to flee before the counterattack of the United Nations Forces.

DIOCESE OF YENKI

Name	Rank	Nationality	Post	Date of Apprehension	Remarks
1) T. Breher	Bishop	German	Ordinary of Yenki	May 20, 1946	Repatriated in Dec. 1949
2) S. Koller	Priest	"	Diocese of Yenki	"	"
3) A. Schmid	"	"	,	"	"
4) M. Schweinberger	"	"	"	"	"
5) C. Kügelgen	"	"	"	"	"
6) H. Traber	"	"	"	"	"
7) L. Ballweg	"	"	"	"	"
8) V. Zeileis	"	"	"	"	"
9) S. Ludwig	"	"	"	May 26, 1946	Killed on May 26, 1946
10) B. Köstler	"	"	"	May 20, 1946	Died in prison on Mar. 25, 1947
11) A. Hafner	"	"	"	"	Repatriated in Sept. 1950
12) G. Heigl	"	"	"	"	"

Name	Rank	Nationality	Post	Date of Apprehension	Remarks
13) K. Schräfl	Priest	German	Diocese of Yenki	May 26, 1946	Repatriated on Dec. 24, 1950 (Stays in Korea)
14) A. Müller	"	"	"	"	"
15) E. Dörfler	"	"	"	"	"
16) P. Lenz	"	"	"	"	Repatriated on Aug. 24, 1952
17) B. Appelmann	"	"	"	"	"
18) R. Egner	"	"	"	"	" (Stays in Korea)
19) A. Lenhard	"	"	"	"	"
20) M. Fütterer	"	"	"	"	"
21) A. Benz	"	"	"	"	Repatriated
22) A. Raymund	"	"	"	"	"
23) E. Zellner	Brother	"	"	Sept. 2, 1945	Killed on Sept. 2, 1945
24) A. Reis	"	"	"	May 20, 1946	Repatriated in Dec. 1949
25) B. Metz	"	"	"	"	"
26) B. Albert	"	"	"	"	"
27) D. Demharter	"	"	"	"	"
28) R. Schaub	"	"	"	"	"
29) T. Haseidl	"	"	"	"	"
30) E. Breitsameter	"	"	"	"	"
31) O. Schweiger	"	"	"	"	Repatriated in Sept. 1950
32) T. Bauer	"	"	"	"	"
33) E. Baumgärtner	"	"	"	"	"
34) L. Kimmel	"	"	"	"	"
35) S. Schlosser	"	"	"	"	"
36) A. Schiffczyk	"	"	"	"	"
37) S. Gnann	"	"	"	"	"
38) A. Gumpp	"	"	"	"	"

Name	Rank	Nationality	Post	Date of Apprehension	Remarks
39) Rita Hess	Sister	Swiss	Diocese of Yenki	May 20, 1946	Died in Ham-heung in 1947
40) L. Khun	"	"	"	"	Repatriated on Feb. 7, 1948
41) B. König	"	"	"	"	Repatriated in Dec. 1949 (Stays in Korea)
42) R. Klaus	"	German	"	"	Repatriated in Dec. 1949
43) E. Brun	"	Swiss	"	"	"
44) D. Katenkamp	"	German	"	"	"
45 F. Prozetti	"	Italian	"	"	"
46) I. Meier	"	Swiss	"	"	(Stays in Korea)
47) U. Schia	"	"	"	"	"
48) J. Weingatner	"	"	"	"	Repatriated in Sept. 1949
49) N. Fässler, Oberin	"	"	"	"	Repatriated in Sept. 1950 (Stays in Korea)
50) A. Buholzer	"	"	"	"	Repatriated in Sept. 1950
51) W. Peter	"	"	"	"	"
52) H. Kung	"	"	"	"	"
53) J. Pfiffner	"	"	"	"	"
54) S. Waldispühl	"	"	"	"	"
55) D. Füglistaller	"	"	"	"	"
56) L. Ettlin	"	"	"	"	"

Note 1. The Soviet Russian troops which advanced into Manchuria after World War II, and the Chinese Communist troops that followed them, arrested practically all the Catholic priests, monks and nuns in the Yenki Diocese, including the Most Rev. Theodor Breher, Bishop of Yenki, on May 20, 1946, and put them into jail at the headquarters of the First Constabulary Corps of the Yenki Communist Party. This touched off their persecution of Catholics. To understand the true nature of this persecution it is necessary to note that everything belonging to the Church was regarded as enemy property.

The fact that Germany had been the enemy of Russia during the war was taken as a pretext for confiscating all the movable property and landed estate of the Church as a whole in Yenki Diocese, including the sacred edifices and objects used in religious worship, and the Enemy Property Disposal Committee of the Yenki Communist Party confiscated all of them. As a result, all the Churches and presbyteries in each of the sixteen districts of Yenki and Lungching (Yong-jŏng), as well as the Yenki Monastery, its machine shops and all their equipment, and the Convent of the Immaculate Heart of Mary and its hospital, all fell into Communist hands. A Korean priest, Father Kim Sŏng-hwan, filed a protest with the Communist Army headquarters. He insisted that both by natural and international law these Church properties did not belong to the German mission, but to the Vatican, and should therefore not be regarded as enemy property by the Communists. His negotiations were fruitless.

The second step in the Communists' persecution of religion was to deny the people's liberty of worship.

The Soviet Russian Army, stationed in Yenki, had promulgated its so-called 'Eight Point Ordinance.' Article Four stated that religious services at the Catholic and other Churches shall be conducted without any restriction. In other words, the Ordinance recognized the people's right to freedom of worship. In actual fact, however, the political corps of the Eighth Route Army penetrated into every district, and began to impose its so-called land reform. It thereby revealed its anti-religious nature. Churchgoers were expelled from all organizations and denied the right to participate in the distribution of land. Catholic farmers were required to hand over their Bible and other sacred objects and to profess their determination to abandon their faith, as a condition of being admitted to the farmers' associations and of being given a share in the land distribution. Those who refused to apostatize suffered compulsory transfer to another district and confiscation of their properties, and were treated inhumanly wherever they went. In Yung-am village, Daeribja, Yenki Province, the Communists even went so far as to publicly burn all the Bibles and other religious books owned by the Catholics and to destroy the crucifixes and sacred objects. Believers who tried to defend their faith had to suffer indescribable hardships. The Communist educational policy was characterized by complete rejection of religion. On the one hand, in their school textbooks they constantly propagated the conception of religion as a kind of opium. They never ceased to insist on all students formally professing their abandonment of their religion and renunciation of belief in God. Any student who refused was severely punished. If he continued to maintain his faith he was imprisoned.

The third characteristic of their anti-God policy was the systematic wrecking of the Church organization.

As we have said, on May 20, 1946, the Communists arrested and imprisoned every Catholic priest, monk, and nun that they could lay hands on in the Yenki Diocese, but two days later they released six Korean priests, one Chinese priest, fifteen Korean Sisters, and fifteen Swiss Sisters, on the ground that they were not enemy aliens and would therefore be permitted to continue their missionary activities in accordance with the absolute guarantee of religious freedom offered by their so-called new-democracy. But their release in actual fact was the result of a strong protest on the part of Bishop Breher, at his meeting with a Communist Party representative during his imprisonment. The Bishop admitted that, as a German national, he was willing to be considered to some extent as an enemy alien because Hitler had invaded Russia. But he strongly protested that the arrest of the Sisters from Switzerland, a neutral nation and an advanced democratic country, and of Korean and Chinese priests, monks and nuns, was clearly unjustified and utterly illegal. As a result of this protest, the Korean priests were permitted to return to their respective parishes and to take charge of the spiritual leadership of their flocks. They lived in the house of one of the farmers where the church and presbytery had been destroyed. Often one priest had to take responsibility for the care of as many as four parishes, working day and night. In the meantime, the Communist persecution grew steadily more intense, until it came to the point that young men and students were forbidden to meet the priest and only the aged and the women were allowed to receive the Holy Sacraments. Their second purge began on August 1, 1947, when the Communists re-arrested the Korean priests in accordance with their so-called "thought unification" campaign. The first wave resulted in the arrest of Fathers Hŭh Ch'ang-tŏk and Reginald Egner (Wang) and four nuns and monks of Pataoku, on charges of not having taken part in the communal labor projects, and of "exploiting the blood of the believers." With placards inscribed "Exploiter" fastened to their chest and back like sandwich boards, they were forced to parade through the streets, and were so brutally beaten by the bystanders that they were almost unable to recover from their injuries. In the second wave of arrests, a Chinese priest, Father Joseph Cho Ch'ul, two Korean nuns, and a Korean monk were arrested, imprisoned and brutally beaten by the Communists, in an attempt to bring about their apostasy. On seeing that the Communist persecution had reached such an extreme of cruelty and unreason, the Catholic layfolk helped Father Vianney Ch'oe of Mutankiang, Father Maurus Kim of Domun, and Father Kim of Lungching as well as three nuns, to escape to Korea across the Korea-Manchuria border by a secret route, for they clearly saw the danger that impended.

By November 1947 there was no priest in Chien-tao who was not incarcerated.

Except for the restricted areas still occupied by the Nationalist Army of Generalissimo Chiang Kai-shek, namely, Mukden, Changchun, Kirin, and Ssupingkai, the whole of Manchuria was in Communist hands, and all churches had been converted into barracks, army halls, theaters or factories. Religion seemed to be completely eradicated and abolished.

The Tragedy of the Priests' Sufferings

After the occupation by Soviet Russian troops the first victim was Brother Engelmar Zellner. He was shot and killed in his bed about three o'clock in the morning of Septebmer 2, 1945, by Russian soldiers trespassing in the Church of Pataoku. On May 26, 1946, Father Servatius Ludwig was killed at the Chinchan Church in Yenki, to become the second victim. Father Bonifatius Köstler, who had been suffering protracted hardship at the Nanping concentration camp since his arrest in May 1946, became critically ill on account of malnutrition. After being placed under house arrest at Towtaoku Church on March 10, 1947, he died fifteen days later.

In the meantime other priests, monks, and nuns were undergoing hardship in prison. The Most Rev. Theodor Breher, Bishop of Yenki, was forcibly deprived of the crucifix and ring which he habitually wore. In a group of more than ten they were all jampacked into a single cell with barely room for them to squat day and night. Father Kim Sŏng-hwan, the Korean priest who had been released, described their sufferings.

"After about a week I was permitted to meet the Bishop. I found him pale and much weakened by his detention, during which he had been ill all the time. Our meeting lasted only ten minutes, under the strict surveillance of the Communist guards. Overwhelmed by deep emotion at the thought that we might never meet again in this world, neither of us could find much to say. The bishop exhorted me to do my best to take care of the vicariate, and to confide in the mercy of Our Lord Jesus Christ.

"A week later the priests were all transferred to the main prison in Honan, Yenki, and ten days after that they were again transferred to a temporary prison set at the Santaoku Church in Hwaryong Province.

"Although the provincial self-defense corps did their best to keep up a vigilant surveillance over the prison, it was often possible for Catholic believers to comfort the prisoners by bringing their gifts of food, in the utmost secrecy. I myself had an opportunity to spend a night with the priests in their prison. All they had to eat was a reddish-colored ball of cooked and slightly salted millet each day. Every one of them was suffering from malnutrition and indigestion. At night they tried to make themselves comfortable on a straw mat with a worn-out blanket, but on account of the fleas and mosquitoes it was impossible for them to sleep in peace.

"Two months after their transfer to Santaoku they were again shifted to the remote village of Nanping on the bank of the Tumen River, at the foot of Mt. Paek-tu, some seventy-five miles away, in an effort on the part of the Communists to put an end to their contacts with the Catholic believers. Bishop Breher, together with five priests and two monks, was, however, imprisoned separately in Yenki, and two other priests and another monk in Pataku."

In December 1949 all these imprisoned priests, monks, and nuns were released and repatriated, after a long and arduous imprisonment.

In the meantime, the eighteen nuns from the Benedictine Convent, whose Motherhouse is at Cham, not far from Zurich in Switzerland, returned home in three groups. Sister Rita Hess, who was on her way home via North Korea, died in the Ham-heung Convent Hospital of an illness contracted during her detention in Manchuria. Sister Fässler later returned from Europe, and is now Superior of the Ch'o-ryang Convent of Sisters of St. Benedict in Pu-san.

What happened to the Korean Fathers in the Yenki Diocese?

Fathers Philip Han Yun-seung, Peter Shin Yun-ch'ŏl, and Paul Kim Pong-sik were kidnapped and killed by the North Korean Communists while propagating the faith in North Korea. Six other priests made their way safely to the south, and are now doing duty in the Republic of Korea, namely, Father Matthew Han To-jun, at On-yang parish; Clement Kim Ch'ung-mu, on furlough at Wae-kwan; James Lee T'ae-jun, at Mun-kyŏng parish; Vianney Ch'oe Yŏng-ho, at T'oe-kang parish; Victorius Kim Sŏng-hwan, principal of Sŏng-eui Middle and Commercial High Schools in Kim-ch'ŏn, and Cyrus Hŭh Ch'ang-tŏk, professor of Theological Department, Catholic College.

Of the fifteen Korean nuns, only Sister Scholastica

and Sister Anna were unable to escape to South Korea: the remaining thirteen, braving various hardships, crossed the Thirty-eighth Parallel. Their headquarters is at Pu-san, and they are engaged in missionary work throughout the Republic.

85. Amazing Development of the Church After the Truce

The Korean War was one of the most tragic scourges in the history of mankind. Sixteen free nations joined in battle against the enemy, and twenty-four nations lent their help with war material. It lasted three years, from June 25, 1950 to the cease-fire on July 27, 1953. The number of casualties in the Republic of Korea, excluding combatants, was 999,998, including 128,936 killed; 84,532 kidnaped; and 308,212 missing. Not only the family and relatives of the killed but the whole populace mourned the bloodshed and loss of life, and turned their thoughts toward things of the spirit. On the conclusion of the truce people flocked to the Catholic Churches in thousands to embrace the true faith, and the number of Catholics increased year by year. In 1953, the year of the armistice agreement, the number of Catholics in the Republic of Korea was estimated at 166,471 in a population of 21,440,000. In 1954 it rose to 189,000; in 1955, 215,000; 242,000 in 1956; 285,000 in 1957; 354,000 in 1958; 417,000 in 1959; 451,000 in 1960; 492,464 in 1961, 530,000 in 1962; 576,000 in 1963; and more than 629,000 in 1964.

The number of Vicariates increased from six in 1953 to seven in 1957, eight in 1958, and nine in 1961.

Once the armistice agreement was signed missionary work in North Korea had to be suspended, though there were more than a hundred thousand Catholics north of the demilitarized zone. With the approval of the Holy See the Most Rev. Paul M. Ro, Bishop of Seoul, erected the Vicariate Forane of Ch'ŏng-ju from part of the Seoul Vicariate on September 1, 1953 and placed it in the charge of the Maryknoll Foreign Mission Society of America, which had had charge of the Vicariate of P'yŏng-yang before World War ll. On September 16, 1953, Bishop

Ro, accompanied by Father Walsh, Vice-General of the Maryknoll Mission (who was on a visit to Korea to study the situation of the Church in Korea), went to the Chang-ho-won Church, where he appointed Father James. V. Pardy Vicar Forane of Ch'ŏng-ju. Chaplain Pardy did meritorious work in converting thousands of Communist prisoners to Catholicism on Kŏ-je Island. In April 1957 when this Vicar Forane of Ch'ŏng-ju was raised to the status of Vicariate Apostolic, Msgr. Pardy was made Vicar Apostolic, and on July 4, 1958, he was made Bishop, the consecration ceremony taking place on September 16 in the United States of America.

On June 18, 1954, the Most Rev. John Ch'oe Tŏk-hong, Vicar Apostolic of Tae-gu, erected the Vicariate Forane of Pu-san, and appointed Father John Sŭh Chŏng-kil to be Vicar Forane of that territory. Six months later, as a result of Bishop Ch'oe's death on December 14, Monsignor John Sŭh was appointed Vicar Apostolic of Tae-gu on July 13, 1955, and was consecrated Bishop on September 15, 1955. This Vicariate Forane of Pu-san was raised to a Vicariate Apostolic in 1956, and Father John Ch'oe Chae-sŏn became Vicar Apostolic of Pu-san on January 26, 1957. He was consecrated Bishop on May 30 of the same year 1957.

This remarkable progress was perhaps mainly due to the positive propagation of the faith which the priests had learnt to practice during their service in the army as military chaplains. The Church of Korea, which lost almost fifty native priests by massacre during the war, trained and ordained fifty-three priests during the three years from October 20, 1950 to August 22, 1953, while their seminary was evacuated and temporarily transferred, first to Che-ju Island (Quelpart), and later to Pu-san. Most of the newly ordained priests joined the armed forces as chaplains and conducted their mission in the Army, Navy, or Air Force. As a result of their fervent and active dedication, thousands of servicemen were received into the Church. With the establishment of the

Neutral Nations Armistice Commission in 1953, consisting of representatives from Switzerland, Sweden, Poland, India and Czechoslovakia, nine priests were sent from the member countries to North Korea and to the Republic of Korea. Father Iso, who had once been coadjutor of Won-san Church, with five other priests, joined the Swiss representatives, and four Indian priests assisted in the exchange of prisoners of war in the demilitarized zone, returning to their country on January 29, 1954. In addition to these, the survivors among priests who had been kidnaped by the Communists were repatriated, and most of them returned to Korea to continue their work. Father Coyos, who had been a professor at the Holy Ghost Seminary in Seoul, was repatriated to France in May 1953, and Mother Superior Nicola Fässler of the Sacred Olivet Convent in Yenki Diocese returned to Korea via Switzerland on August 24, 1953. Monsignor Quinlan, long the Prefect Apostolic of Ch'un-ch'ŏn Prefecture, was repatriated to Ireland after three years' detention in North Korea. On October 5, 1953, he was appointed Acting Apostolic Delegate to Korea, and returned to present his credentials to the President on April 23, 1954. Twelve priests, including Father Hiemer, twelve monks and eighteen nuns of the *Abbatia Nullius* of Tŏk-won, who had lost seventeen of their confreres in North Korea, were repatriated to West Germany on January 22, 1954, after five years' detention in North Korea.

The repatriated priests returned to establish a monastery at Wae-kwan, North Province of Kyŏng-sang, in July 1955, and are now propagating the Gospel in the adjacent six counties. In 1955, Father Bitterli was appointed Administrator Apostolic of the three Vicariates of Tŏk-won, Ham-heung, and Yenki.

As soon as the fighting ceased, the armed forces of the United States and the United Nations Korean Reconstruction Agency (UN KRA) helped in repairing and rebuilding the devastated church buildings. The Maryknoll Sisters, who had formerly served in the Vicariate of P'yŏng-yang, now established a charitable hospital in Pu-san, where they cared for over two thousand poor patients every day.

On October 25, 1954, the Minister of Health awarded a letter of appreciation to Mother Mercy, director of the hospital, which had taken care of more than 430,000 patients. The Minister of Health also honored Monsignor Carroll, the Administrator Apostolic of P'yŏng-yang Vicariate and Director of the Korean Division of War Relief Services, National Catholic Welfare Conference of the American Catholic Church, who had been instrumental in obtaining over a thousand tons of relief goods on January 28, 1954. Since 1946, more than twenty-five million dollars' worth of relief goods have been sent to Korea for distribution. Father Yang Ki-sŏp of the P'yŏng-yang Vicariate, who had been in America as an envoy for many years, returned to Korea with a large quantity of relief goods presented by American Catholics, and delivered them to the Most Rev. Paul M. Ro, Bishop (now Archbishop) of Seoul.

Bishop Ro expressed his gratitude to the American Catholics for the gift, and on December 12, 1954, proceeded to America with Father Yang on a good-will visit. During the two months of his stay in the United States the Bishop visited no fewer than forty major cities, and received a whole-hearted welcome. He introduced Korea to the people of America through the American press. During Bishop Ro's absence from Korea Cardinal Spellman, Archbishop of New York, made his fourth annual Christmas visit to the servicemen in the Korean front line. On December 27 the cardinal received a hearty welcome at the Cathedral of the Immaculate Conception, Myŏng-dong, Seoul, and made a gift of $35,000 to the orphanage of *St. Paul de Chartres*.

This year of 1954, which brought so many favors to Korea, was also the centenary of the Bull *Ineffabilis Deus* of Pope Pius IX. This was his solemn definition of the Immaculate Conception of the Blessed Virgin Mary as an article of Catholic belief contained in the original teaching of the Apostles. In his edict of November 11, 1953, Pope Pius XII declared a year of Jubilee, extending from the Feast of the Immaculate Conception, December 8, 1954, to that of the following year. During this period Catholics all over the world might, after confession, communion and prayer, obtain special indulgence (remission of the temporal punishment of sin). Prayers were offered for the poor and oppressed, for world peace, and for the Pope's intentions.

The Church of Korea was rededicated to the Immaculate Conception; and the National Synod of Bishops was held on February 16~17, 1954, deciding in its edict that the jubilee celebration be held on October 8~10, in Seoul, and that the prayer for world peace be observed by children on the Children's Prayer Day, May 23.

The Most Rev. Paul Yu Pin, Archbishop of Nanking, who had also been instrumental in effecting the independence of Korea, visited Korea at the invitation of President Rhee, and in June Mr. Douglas Hyde, the former editor of the Communist *Daily Worker* of London, and now a convert to Catholicism and editor in chief of the London *Catholic Herald*, also visited Korea. Mr. Hyde left Korea on June 18 after visiting Kang-neung, Ch'un-ch'ŏn, Kwang-ju, and Mok-p'o, and observing the work of the Church in these districts.

On June 12 the Provincial of the Society of Jesus in Japan, the Very Reverend Father Alob, visited Korea and expressed his wish that the Jesuit Order might also contribute to missionary work in Korea. After his return to Japan he sent Father Theodore Geppert, S.J., a professor of Sophia University in Tokyo, to consult the prelates with a view to establishing a Jesuit college in Korea.

In January, 1955 the long-suspended monthly magazine *Catholic Youth* resumed publication. On July 7 of the same year the Catholic Committee of Korea was convened at the Bishop's Residence, Myŏng-dong Cathedral, to unify and coordinate the nation-wide activities of the Church. Prior to this conference, the several vicariates of Korea had competed

with one another in the establishment of orphanages, schools and hospitals: the Tae-gu Vicariate founded the Hyo-sŏng Women's College on April 2, 1952, and the Seoul Vicariate added a medical department to the Holy Ghost College in the spring of 1954. Father John-Baptist Janssens, Superior General of the Society of Jesus in Rome, sent a letter to Bishop Ro dated February 25, 1955, saying that the Province of Korea would be separated from that of Japan and the Wisconsin Province of the Society of Jesus was appointed to carry out the establishment of a college in Korea. On March 25, the Very Reverend Leo J. Burns, the Superior of the Wisconsin Province of the Society of Jesus, visited President Rhee, accompanied by Bishop Quinlan, the Acting Apostolic Delegate. President Rhee gratefully approved his project for the foundation of a college by the order that had done so much to combat atheistic communism.

Father Kenneth E. Killoren, S. J., came to Korea in October, 1955, and began the undertaking. The Superior General of the Order in Rome appointed Father Killoren Superior of the Society in Korea, and authorized him to proceed with the work of founding the college.

Bishop Ro left on October 15, to make a round of visits to all the countries that had sent their troops to the aid of Korea on the outbreak of the Korean War, to express the profound gratitude of Korean Catholics. His journey, which lasted almost four months until his return on February 10, 1956, took him to the Vatican, Italy, Portugal, Spain, France, West Germany, Belgium, the Netherlands, England, Ireland, and Luxemburg, and strengthened the good will existing between the Catholics of these states and those of Korea.

On November 14, 1956, His Eminence Canon Cardian, the founder of the J.O.C. movement, (*Jeunesse Ouvrière Chrétienne* or Young Christian Workers), paid a visit to Korea. Upon his arrival Monsignor Carroll, the provincial director of the movement in Korea, presided over the inaugural meeting of the sub-province of Seoul Vicariate, and appointed

Father Francis Park Sŏng-jong its spiritual director.

From October 5 to 12, 1957, a world-wide meeting of Catholic laymen was held in Rome, and on her part Korea sent Father Hyginus Lee Yŏng-sik, and Messrs. Lee Hae-nam, Ryu Hong-ryŏl, and twenty other distinguished Catholic laymen to take part in the conference.

On Christmas Eve of the same year, Cardinal Spellman made his fifth annual Christmas visit to the servicemen in the front line in Korea, and attended the ground-breaking ceremony of the Holy Mother Hospital. He made a contribution of $25,000 toward the funds for its construction.

During 1957 the National Catholic Welfare Conference (NCWC) furnished forty-five million dollars' worth of clothing, food and medicine to Korea.

At the close of the year the Vatican appointed a former councillor of the Apostolic Delegation to the United Kingdom, Bishop Lambertini, to be Apostolic Delegate to Korea in place of Bishop Quinlan, Vicar Apostolic of Ch'un-ch'ŏn, who returned to his Vicariate. Bishop Lambertini arrived in Seoul, his new post, on May 14, 1958.

It is noteworthy that in the outlying Islands of Che-ju, Ul-leung, Yŏn-p'yŏng and Heuk-san, where missionary work had been intermittent and the propagation of the Gospel not fully carried out, the number of believers actually increased. In Che-ju, or Quelpart Island, which was under the charge of the Columban Mission, of the Kwang-ju Vicariate Apostolic, the number of Catholics rose from 6,900 in 1958 to more than 10,000 in 1961. This was largly due to the zeal of Father Harold Henry, S.S.C., D.D., who became the Prefect Apostolic of the Kwang-ju Prefecture in October 1954. Monsignor Henry then erected the Vicariate Forane of Che-ju on August 21, 1956, and sent a large number of priests to propagate the faith there.

On January 26, 1957, the Vatican appointed Monsignor Harold Henry Bishop of Kwang-ju, his consecration ceremony taking place at Boston on May 11 of the same year. In March 1962, Archbishop Henry founded the Tae-kŏn Theological Seminary at Kwang-ju with gift funds which he had brought back with him after his consecration in the United States.

As a result of propagation of the faith by Father Brazil, whom Monsignor Henry had sent to Heuk-san Island in 1955, the number of the faithful rose in 1958 to 670, with more than 3,000 catechumens. In 1953 there were only three Catholics on Ul-leung Island but by the help of Bishop Sŭh, Vicar Apostolic of Tae-gu, and Monsignor George Carroll, the number was greatly increased, and by 1958 Father Francis Shin Sang-to and Father Timothy Kim Kyu-t'ae had baptized 1,430 persons and still had over five thousand catechumens. Off the west coast lie the islands of Yŏn-p'yŏng and Paek-ryŏng, where only 300 out of about 30,000 fishing inhabitants were Catholics until Father Laurent Youn Eul-su and others, including the Columban Fathers, turned their attention to them, and five years later, by 1958, the number of the faithful had risen to 1,080 in Yŏn-p'yŏng lsland alone. In June 1961, In-ch'ŏn was erected a Vicariate Apostolic and placed in charge of the Maryknoll Fathers, who are devoting all their efforts to propagating the faith in that territory, which includes the islands. The first Vicar Apostolic, Monsignor William McNaughton, D.D., was consecrated Bishop on August 24, 1961, in the United States of America.

On August 16, 1955, Prince Eui-ch'in, (Yi Kang), died, after receiving Holy Baptism under the name of Paul at the hands of Father Park of the Ka-hoe-dong Church of St. Francis Xavier, on August 9. The prince was a grandson of the Regent Tae-won-kun who was responsible for the death of almost ten thousand Catholics some ninety years before. Madame Kim Suk, widow of Prince Eui-ch'in, was baptized on August 14 at the same church, receiving the name of Maria. Seven years later Prince Yŏng-ch'in, (Yi Eun), converted himself to the Catholic faith in Tokyo on May 27, 1962.

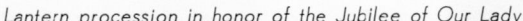

Joint Benediction by the prelates
On the occasion of the Jubilee of Our Lady, October 8—10, 1954

Lantern procession in honor of the Jubilee of Our Lady

Welcome extended to Msgr. Thomas Quinlan, Bishop of Ch'un-ch'ŏn, on his safe return to Korea after long captivity in the hands of the Reds

The Rev. Theodore Geppert, S.J. (right), treasurer of Sŏ-kang Jesuit College, on the occasion of his arrival, in Oct. 1954, for the purpose of establishing the college ↓

Arrival of the Most Rev. Paul Yupin, Archbishop of Nanking (right) April, 1954

Welcome extended to the survivors among the Benedictine Fathers of Tŏk-won and Ham-heung Vicariates on their safe return to Korea after long imprisonment in North Korea

The National Synod of the Bishops of the Church in Korea in session (Feb. 20, 1956)

Arrival of International Catholic Women Auxiliaries in Korea (Mar. 27, 1956)

Arrival of the Far East Provincial of the Society of the Sacred Heart, and the President and the Vice-President of the Sacred Heart Women's College of Tokyo on their inspection tour of the Church in Korea (Sept. 16, 1955)

Joint U.N.-Korean Catholic ceremony of Exaltation of the Korean Martyrs, held in Seoul on Sept. 29, 1957. The Guard of Honor in the playground of Holy Ghost Middle and High School

The procession of the faithful

The faithful crowded in the ground

Catholics of the ROK Armed Forces in the procession

The sacred relics of Blessed Andrew Kim Tae-kŏn carried in procession by members of the U.S. Armed Forces to the Cathedral of the Immaculate Conception, Myŏng-dong, Seoul

Francis Cardinal Spellman, Archbishop of New York, contributed both spiritually and materially for the rehabilitation of war-torn Korea.

Francis Cardinal Spellman, Archbishop of New York, on one of his frequent visits to the U.S. Armed Forces both during and after the Korean War

The Archbishop paying a call on General Arthur G. Trudeau (center), Commanding General of the U.S. First Corps

Pope Pius XII receiving
Bishop Ro in audience
(Oct. 1955)

Arrival in Korea of Cardinal
Frings, Archbishop of Köln
(May 17, 1957)

The Second World Congress of Catholic Laity, Rome, Oct. 5-12, 1957

Attended by Father Lee Yŏng-sik and twenty Korean laymen including Prof. Lee Hae-nam and Dr. Ryu Hong-ryŏl

First Asian Congress of the "Jeunesse Ouvrière Chrétienne" (Young Christian Workers)

Held at Kuala Lumpur, Malaya, in Mar. 1960

The arrival in Korea of
Bishop Lambertini, Apos-
tolic Delegate to Korea
(May 14, 1957)

Bishop Zupi, Apostolic
Delegate to Korea,
welcomed on his arriv-
al at Seoul Station
(Mar. 10, 1961)

Italian Catholic
musicians visiting
Archbishop Ro

Welcome extended to President
Ngo Dinh Diem on his visit to
Korea by Bishop Ro

Msgr. George Carroll receives the Medal of Culture
awarded in recognition of his meritorious relief work
for the refugees, through the National Catholic Welfare
Conference (Feb. 9, 1961)

Bps. Larribeau and Quinlan receive the Medal
of Culture awarded them in recognition of their
meritorious work in social welfare and culture
(Nov. 2, 1961)

First Far Eastern Conference of Bishops
With Papal Legate, Gregory Cardinal Agagianian, at the University of St. Thomas, Manila, The Philippines, December 9-17, 1958

The arrival in Korea of the Papal Legate, Gregory Cardinal Agagianian (March 5, 1959)

Gregory Cardinal Agagianian celebrating High Mass in the Cathedral of the Immaculate Conception, Seoul

The Cardinal visiting the Headquarters of the U.N. Forces in Korea

Msgr. Charles Mouton, Apostolic Delegate ad interim to Korea, handing over funds to Archbishop Harold Henry from Pope John XXIII for the relief of flood victims in the Sun-ch'ŏn area (Sept. 4, 1962)

Msgr. Mouton and Archbishop Henry inspecting the flood-stricken area

Exhibition of Relics, Books and Historical Materials of the Catholic Church in Korea

Items exhibited

Book Division: Liturgy 18; Doctrine 28; History 55; Record of Suffering 5; Guide
Book of the Korean Church 8; General History of Evangeligation 10; Books on
Protestantism 11; Magazines 8; Language 15; Others 14

Paintings and Writings Division: 15

Relics Division: 15

The opening of the exhibition
(Left to right) The Rev. Haller,
Archbishop del Giudice, Archbishop Ro

Archbishop Ro signing in the visitors'
list
(Left) Father Ch'oe, the sponsor of the
exhibition and the Director of the Institute
of the Study on the History of the Catholic
Church in Korea

Part of the exhibition hall

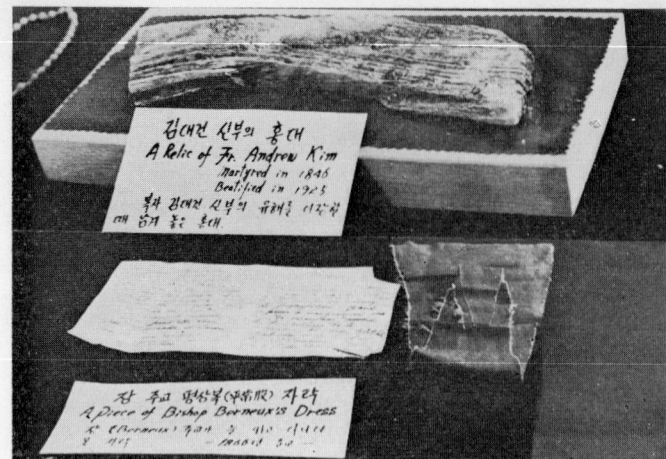

(Upper) A piece of the coffin in which Father Kim was laid in state
(Below) A piece of Bishop Berneux's dress

Crucifixes used by the Catholics in earlier days
(Right of the middle) Crucifix of Bishop Berneux

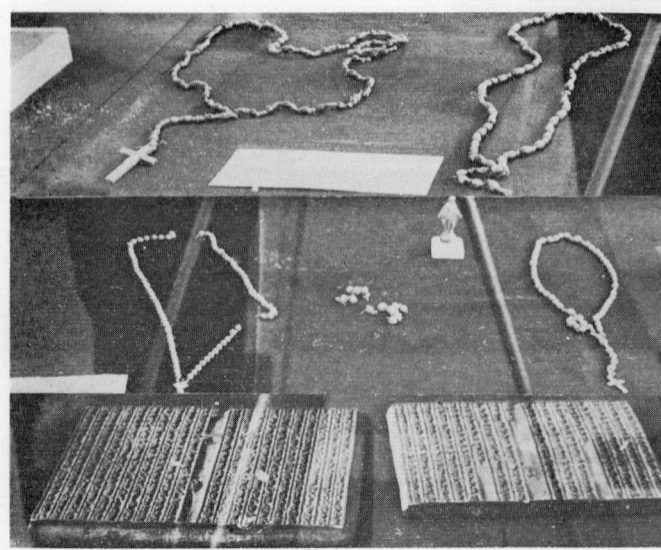

The rosaries and the engraving blocks in earlier days

Part of the exhibition

Part of the exhibition

Part of the exhibition

Part of the exhibition

"Sae-nam-t'ŏ" —
The site hallowed by the martyrdom of French and Korean Catholics on the bank of the Han River, showing the monument symbolizing the triumph of the Catholic Church in Korea

Hanging scroll of the Persecutor, Regent Tae-won-kun

86. From the Establishment of the Hierarchy to the Present

Both before and after the longed-for establishment of the Hierarchy of the Church in Korea, until recently, the political situation has been unstable and in consequence there were several changes in the regime.

During these changing years the Catholic Church in Korea has been making steady progress. The Holy Ghost Seminary in Seoul has been reorganized, and the Catholic College established. On March 1, 1958, the St. Mary Hospital attached to the medical department of the college was made a polyclinic, and on December 2, 1961, a modern ten-story building was completed.

The Jesuit Order purchased 53 acres of land in the western suburbs of Seoul, where Blessed Laurent-Marie-Joseph Imbert, Bishop and martyr, and his companions are buried, and built a four-story edifice, to house the newly-founded Sŏ-kang Jesuit College, which received its charter on February 18, 1960, with Father Kenneth E. Killoren as its first president. In July 1963, Father Killoren resigned the presidency and Father John P. Daly, M.A., S.T.L., Ph.D., was appointed the second president. On February 8, 1964, the Sŏ-kang Jesuit College held its first graduation ceremony, and produced forty-four alumni and sixteen alumnae.

Furthermore, the projected Tae-kŏn Major Seminary in Kwang-ju was placed under the charge of the Jesuits by the Holy See on October 7, 1962, and Father Andrew Bachhuber was appointed the first rector of the seminary.

The Religious of the Sacred Heart, a congregation founded by St. Madeleine Sophie Barat and Father Joseph Varin, S.J., in 1800, for the education of girls, established a middle and high school for girls at Won-hyo-ro, Seoul, in the building formerly occupied by the theological seminary. In May 1963 they opened the Sacred Heart Women's College in Ch'un-ch'ŏn. The congregation extends over almost the entire world and has over seven thousand religious. Its rules and constitutions are based on those of the Society of Jesus.

On December 9, 1958, Cardinal Agagianian, Pro-Prefect of the Sacred Congregation for the Propagation of the Faith, presided over a meeting of South-East Asian bishops in Manila, at which the Most Rev. Paul M. Ro, Bishop of Seoul, the Most Rev. Thomas Quinlan, Bishop of Ch'un-ch'ŏn, the Most Rev. Bartholomew Kim, Bishop of Chŏn-ju, the Most Rev. John Ch'oe, Bishop of Pu-san, and the Most Rev. Egaus Lambertini, the Apostolic Delegate, took part as representatives of the Church of Korea. A conference at Saigon, also presided over by Cardinal Agagianian, was attended by Bishops Ro and Kím.

On February 2, 1959, the Catholic Women's Association of Austria had initiated a movement to raise funds by observing the Lenten fast, and as a result Mrs. Pammer, the chairman of the Association, was able to bring the sum of $155,000 as a gift to Korea, in October 1961.

In December 1959 the Ministry of Education sponsored a commission for the commemoration of John Chŭng Yak-yong, (fl.c. 1780), the Catholic writer, and a monument was erected in his memory at Ma-hyŏn, Kyŏng-ki Province.

On January 28, 1960, the Most Rev. Charles Remaire, Superior General of the *Société des Missions-Étrangères de Paris*, came to inspect the mission field which his society has assiduously cultivated since 1831. He left on February 18.

As a result of the Students' April Revolution of 1960, the Catholic daily newspaper *Kyŏng-hyang-sin-mun*, which had been suspended by President Rhee's government, was able to resume publication.

The Vicariate Forane of An-tong of the Vicariate Apostolic of Tae-gu was established on June 2, 1958 under the charge of the *Société des Missions-Étrangères de Paris*, Father Haller was appointed its Vicar Forane, and on February 15, 1962, Father Coyos succeeded him in the post.

After the death of the Most Rev. Bartholomew Kim Hyŏn-pae, Bishop of Chŏn-ju, Father Peter Han Kong-ryŏl was appointed to succeed him, and was consecrated Bishop in Rome in March 12, 1961. He was inducted in April 28.

The fall of the Liberal Party, which toward the end of its long term of office, had oppressed the Catholics, meant continued progress for the Church. The new government, recognizing the Church's services to society and its contribution to the progress of Korean culture, awarded medals to several foreign bishops: in February 1961, President Yun Po-sŏn presented the highest cultural medal to Monsignor George Carroll, of the American Maryknoll Mission, and in November the Most Rev. Adrien Larribeau, Bishop of Tae-jŏn, and the Most Rev. Thomas Quinlan, Bishop of Ch'un-ch'ŏn, received the same honor.

The Most Rev. Harold Henry, Archbishop of Kwang-ju, also received the highest cultural medal from Acting President Park Chŭng-hee, in September 1962.

On the anniversary of the Liberation Day in 1963, the Government of the Republic of Korea cited the Most Reverend Paul M. Ro, Archbishop of Seoul, Father Laurent Youn Eul-su, Procurator of the Archdiocese of Seoul, Father Joseph Oh Ki-sŏn, a priest of the Diocese of Tae-jŏn, and Mother M. Martha, S.S.C., the Director of the St. Joseph Hospital in Sam-ch'ŏk, Ch'un-ch'ŏn Diocese, for their activities in the fields of education, charity, religion, and social affairs respectively.

The Most Rev. Egaus Lambertini, the Apostolic Delegate, completed his term of office and was replaced by the Most Rev. Xavier Zupi, who arrived in March, 9, 1961, and in November the Holy See appointed him an Archbishop, the consecration ceremony taking place in Italy on January 14, 1962.

On March 10, 1962, the Hierarchy was formally established by the Holy See with the appointment of residential ordinaries for three archdioceses and eight dioceses in Korea. According to the establishment of the Hierarchy, the Most Rev. Paul M. Ro, Bishop of Seoul, John Sŭh Chŏng-kil, Bishop of Tae-gu, and Harold Henry, Bishop of Kwang-ju, were raised to the dignity of archbishops. This honor for the Korean Church derives from the blood of the thousands of Koreans who died for the faith, and follows the beatification, in 1925, of the Seventy-nine Korean and French Martyrs.

The Korean Church now consists of three archdioceses; that of Seoul, with the six suffragan dioceses, In-ch'ŏn, Tae-jŏn, Ch'un-ch'ŏn, P'yŏng-yang, Ham-heung and Su-won; that of Tae-gu, with the two suffragan dioceses of Pu-san and Ch'ŏng-ju; and that of Kwang-ju, with the suffragan diocese of Chŏn-ju.

On April 18, 1962 the Most Rev. Xavier Zupi, the Apostolic Delegate to Korea, was transferred to the Republic of Pakistan, and the Most Rev. Antonio del Giudice, J.C.D., hitherto Apostolic Delegate to the Dominican Republic, replaced him and arrived in Korea on January 4, 1963.

In commemoration of the Seventy-nine Korean and French Martyrs beatified in 1925, Sister Andrea Yun Pyŏng-hyŏn founded the Convent of the Korean Martyrs, with Father Leo Pang Yu-ryong as spiritual director, at Kae-sŏng on April 21, 1946. The Motherhouse removed to Seoul on March 8, 1950, and obtained formal recognition from the Vatican on December 12, 1952. This convent possesses several precious relics and records of the martyrs. Father Leo Pang Yu-ryong founded the Brothers of the Korean Martyrs Monastery on a hillside in Sŏng-puk-dong, Seoul, in October 1953, where considerable numbers of Brothers are in training. The work of Father Leo now extends to Che-ju Island.

On October 6, 1962, the three archbishops of Korea, with their suffragan bishops, left for Rome to attend the Second Ecumenical Council of the Vatican, which opened on October 11, (the twentieth ecumenical council, which opened at Rome on December 8, 1869, was prorogued after the Italians seized Rome from the Pope on October 20, 1870).

On June 4, 1963, Pope John XXIII died.

His successor Pope Paul VI reconvened the Vatican Council: it is still unfinished.

While the second session of the Second Ecumenical Council was proceeding in the Vatican, the Church of Korea rejoiced at the news of the establishment of the Diocese of Su-won; on October 10, 1963, the Su-won Diocese, comprising nineteen counties south of the Han River, hitherto included in the Archdiocese of Seoul, was erected by the Holy See, with Father Victorinus Youn, D.D., as the Bishop of the diocese. Father Victorinus Youn Kong-hi was consecrated Bishop by Pope Paul VI at the Basilica of St. Peter, Rome, on October 20.

On February 17, 1964 the monastery of Wae-kwan was canonically raised to the status of Abbey. On April 28th, the election of the abbot took place under the jurisdiction of the Most Reverend Johannes Brechter, the Archabbot of St. Ottilien, Germany, and Father Odo Hass was elected Abbot. Afterward Abbot Odo Hass named the Reverend Augustine Ro and the Reverend Korbinian Schräfl to be the prior and Subprior of the abbey respectively.

Father Timothy Bitterli, the former prior, however, retains the post of Administrator of Ham-heung Diocese.

On April 21, 1964, the Bishop's Synod was held at the Seoul Major Seminary, and a decision was adopted to inaugurate the Committees of the Catholic Doctrine and the Liturgical Movement. The Liturgical Movement Committee, headed by the Most Rev. William McNaughton, Bishop of In-ch'ŏn, submitted the resolution of the liturgical movement to the Vatican, which was approved by the Holy See on July 12, 1964. According to the approval, the Church of Korea could soon enjoy the use of the officially prescribed liturgy in the Korean language, beginning in 1965.

In April, 1964 Bishop Adrien Larribeau retired from the See of the Tae-jŏn Diocese on account of age, and Father Émile Beaudevin, the Vicar General, was appointed Administrator of the diocese *ad interim.*

On December 11, 1963, the Holy See and the Republic of Korea simultaneously raised their diplomatic missions to the status of Legation. The Vatican raised the Most Rev. Antonio del Giudice, the former Apostolic Delegate, to the rank of Apostolic Internuncio to Korea. On February 21, 1964 he duly presented his credentials to President Park Chŭng-hee.

On the other hand the Korean Government appointed Dr. Lee Han-pin as Minister to the Vatican and Minister Lee presented his credentials to Pope Paul VI on April 20, 1964.

On March 30, 1963 Father Joseph Chang Pong-hwa, the Vicar General of the Pu-san Diocese, was given the title of Monsignor. Meanwhile Father John V. Bulaitis, the Secreatary of the Apostolic Internuncio, was also given the title of Monsignor by the Holy See on July 2, 1964. In November 18, 1962, the delegates of fifteen religious congregations of women in Korea assembled to inaugurate the Union of Religious Congregations to be placed under direct guidance of the Holy See, with the Very Rev. Monsignor Charles Burton Mouton, J.C.D., at the Convent of *St. Paul de Chartres,* Seoul. On this occasion the Rev. Mother Agnes-Therese Pang, Provincial of the Sisters of *St. Paul de Chartres,* was appointed Chairman of the Organizing Committee of the union. On December 23, 1963, the first two Sisters of the Little Company of Mary, accompanied by the Rev. Mother Mark, Mother Superior of the Australian Province, arrived in Korea, and the two nursing Sisters are now engaged in medical work at the Hospital of the Little Company of Mary, Kang-neung, Kang-won Province.

Owing to the important situation of the Korean Church in the Far East the Order of Friars Minor founded its chapter in Korea, and Father Appollinarius Van Leeuwen, the Superior of the Far Eastern region, was appointed Superior of the Korean Chapter. In September, 1964, the St. Franciscan Order opened the Korean Language Institute in Seoul.

Meanwhile, late in 1963, the missionary

Sisters of St. Columban founded their Korean Chapter at Ch'un-ch'ŏn and Mother Marie Calasanctius, the Superior of Ch'un-ch'ŏn Convent, was appointed Regional Superior of the Korean Chapter.

On June 10, 1964 five Korean and two German Sisters of the Blessed Virgin Mary, accompanied by Mother Tharasida, the Superior of the Munich Province, and Mother Agatha, the Acting Superior General of the Order at Rome, arrived in Korea. They are constructing a motherhouse and a novitiate convent at O-ryu-dong, on the south-western outskirts of Seoul, and are also planning to build a girls' middle and high school in Tae-jŏn.

The Fathers of Guadalupe, the Mexican Foreign Missionary Society, laid a stepping-stone for the evangelization of Korea by establishing the Korean Chapter of this order in early 1964. They will maintain an evangelical district in the southern part of Kwang-ju Archdiocese by 1966.

On October 9, 1962 the four-story Catholic Center building in Chŏn-ju was completed with the assistance of the Catholic Women's Society of Austria. With its social activities, the Catholic Center serves both the faithful and the other citizens of the neighborhood.

The Holy Family Hospital, a polyclinic, was built at Mi-a-dong, Seoul, with the assistance of the Eighth U.S. Army.

Meanwhile, on his eightieth birthday, May 1, 1963 the newly-built Cathedral of Saint Joseph the Worker, the largest church in Korea, was consecrated by Bishop Adrien Larribeau.

On January 26, 1964 a newly-built Salesian seminary on a hill in Tae-pang-dong, Seoul, was consecrated by the Most Reverend Antonio del Guidice, the Apostolic, Internuncio.

The two-story building of the headquarters of the Young Christian Workers' Association in downtown Seoul was also completed on December 3, 1963.

The Maryknoll Sisters Armed Forces Memorial Hospital (160 beds) in Pu-san, dedicated to Our Lady of the Rosary, was completed on March 7, 1964 with the help of the Armed Forces Assistance to Korea. At the same time the attached Catholic Nursing School was opened.

Since the epoch-making establishment of the Hierarchy in Korea, the Korean Church has made remarkable progress. According to the Vatican sources the Korean Church has established a top recorded development of evangelization in Asia.

On March 14, 1964 eighty-eight seminarians of the Seoul Major Seminary were ordained by the Most Reverend Paul M. Ro, Archbishop of Seoul. At this ceremony the Korean Church rejoiced once more at the number of ordinands, the highest recorded in the history of the Korean Church.

CONCLUSION

The Catholic Church in Korea which has toiled along a thorny path for nearly two centuries, during which it has undergone severe persecution and suffered attempts at its complete suppression, has been uniquely established by the tears and blood of fervent lay Catholics, and with the establishment of the Vicariate Apostolic of Korea on September 9, 1831 and the Hierarchy on March 10, 1962 has come to have an epoch-making moment in its glorious history.

Outstanding among the persecutions are what have been called the Four Persecutions, namely, the Sin-yu Persecution (1801), the Ki-hae Persecution (1839), Pyŏng-o Persecution (1846) and the Pyŏng-in Persecution (1866). Each period was marked by enormous sacrifice, atrocious cruelty and protracted sufferings. Korean Catholics may well take pride in the history of their Church in Korea, where it achieved glory comparable to that recorded in any other country. The blood-stained trail followed by the Seventy-nine Blessed Martyrs and the Twenty-six Martyrs to be beatified in near future, whose intrepid spirit was as steadfast as our native pine and bamboo, and whose faith was as strong as steel, was followed by many other martyrs, known and unknown. The decapitation of Korea's first Catholic priest, Father James Chou Wen-mo, in 1801 and the ensuing persecutions in the succeeding generations left the faithful without a shepherd for thirthy-three years (1801—1834), for six years (1839—1845) and again for ten years (1866—1876). Their blood and that of the other martyrs namely, members of the royal families, high-ranking officials, scholars, the common people, let alone the bishops and priests, were indeed the seed of Christians, seed which has borne abundant fruits, and by virtue of it there are now three archdioceses and nine suffragan dioceses, four archbisops, including the Apostolic Internuncio to Korea, six bishops, 593 priests and 628,542 faithful in the Church of Korea.

We can never cease to be thankful to God for endowing our martyrs with fervent faith and the grace of glorious martyrdom for His glory, and thus enabling us to have this great Church.

As our martyrs, having stood aloof from the country and the people, had sacrificed the social standing, reputation, property, parents, brothers and sisters, wives and children, even their own lives, we, taking pride not only in saying the spirit and the example of martyrdom, but also following and fulfiling them, can only hope and strive to be true Catholics, and worthy disciples of Jesus Christ, and the offspring of God.

With the door of reunion of Christianity widely opened at the Second Ecumenical Council of the Vatican by Pope John XXIII and Pope Paul VI, the problem of reunion between the Roman Catholic Church and the Protestant Churches is seriously being discussed, the dialogue is exchanged, and friendship and goodwill is being cultivated.

At this juncture we Catholics pray to God that we will be able to understand our Protestant brothers and sisters, and to promote friendship and goodwill in the bosom of Almighty God.

Jesus answered, I promise you, everyone who has forsaken home, or brothers, or sisters, or mother, or children, or lands for my sake and for the sake of the gospel, will receive, now in this world, a hundred times their worth, houses, sisters, brothers, mothers, children and lands, but with persecution; and in the world to come he will receive everlasting life. (Mark, 10:29—30)

I may speak with every tongue that men and angels use; yet, if I lack charity, I am no better than echoing bronze, or the clash of cymbals. I may have powers of prophecy, no secret hidden from me, no knowledge too deep for me; I may have utter faith, so that I can move mountains; yet if I lack charity, I count for nothing. I may give away all that I have, to feed the poor; I may give myself up to be burnt at the stake; if I lack charity, it goes for nothing.

Charity is patient, is kind; charity feels no envy; charity is never perverse or proud, never insolent; does not claim its rights, cannot be provoked, does not brood over an injury; takes no pleasure in wrong-doing, but rejoices at the victory of truth; sustains, believes, hopes, endures, to the last.

The time will come when we shall outgrow prophecy, when speaking with tongues will come to an end, when knowledge will be swept away; we shall never have finished with charity.

Meanwhile, faith, hope and charity persist, all three; but the greatest of them all is charity. (1 Cor., 13:1—8, 13)

Bishop Francis Hong, Vicar Apostolic of P'yŏngyang, pronouncing his first benediction after his consecration and enthronement (April 17, 1944)

Celebration of the one hundred and fiftieth anniversary of the foundation of the Korean Catholic Church, 1934

The old parish Church of St. Michael, Kwan-hu-ri, P'yŏngyang

Bishop Francis Hong giving the Benediction

Church of Hae-ju
In Hwang-hae Province

The Holy Mother Parochial School
At Sang-su-ku-ri, P'yŏng-yang

412

Seminarians and graduates
of Tŏk-won Major Seminary
(1938)

The Rev. Joseph Gibbon with candidates for
the Minor Seminary, at Sŏ-p'o, P'yŏng-yang
(1935)

The Rev. Joseph Connors and Sisters of
St. Paul de Chartres (1935)

Church of Sin-eui-ju by the Yalu River

Sister M. Agnetta Chang
The Rev. Superior of Sŏ-p'o Convent, Our Lady of Perpetual Help

Sisters of Sŏ-p'o Maryknoll Convent

APPENDIX

APPENDIX A

I THE CHURCH IN THE RED WAVE
II THE SUFFERINGS OF THE BENEDICTINE
   MISSION IN NORTH KOREA
III THE DEATH MARCH
IV THE GLORIOUS LIFE OF BISHOP BYRNE
V INTERVIEW WITH FATHER COYOS

APPENDIX B

ECUMENICAL MOVEMENT

Outline of Protestantism in Korea

THE CHURCH IN THE RED WAVE

Sufferings of the Benedictines
In Tŏk-won

The persecution of religion began in December 1948, immediately before the withdrawal of the Soviet Armed Forces from North Korea. In the month of December, in the first place, they laid hands on Father Dagobert Enk, and then on Brother Paschal; the former was the procurator of the Abbey of Tŏk-won, and the latter, the works-manager of the attached plant.

Whenever they ordered the arrest of priests and religious their custom was never to ascribe the fact to a religious cause, but always to a suspected political offense of some kind or other.

Just before 10 p.m. on May 9, 1949, a truck carrying several scores of men pulled up in front of the Benedictine Abbey in Tŏk-won, and cordoned off the entire premises. This was the occasion on which they planned to seize at one coup the abbey, the farm, the factory equipped with the most modern machinery, the seminary, pasture-lands, horticultural estate and other modern establishments. This abbey and its dependencies were the fruit of their efforts devoted to serving the people of this land over a period of forty years in Tŏk-won, and fifty in Korea.

These men were members of the newly-formed Political Security Bureau of province, district, and town. A few of them came forward and, knocking at the abbey gates, woke up the monk on night duty.

They demanded an immediate interview with the abbot and told us that they had come to fetch Bishop Bonifacius Sauer, the abbot, Father Lucius Roth, the prior, Father Arnulf Schleicher, the subprior, and Father Rupert Klingseis, the professor of philosophy, to the provincial headquarters of the Political Security Bureau in order to take counsel with them. It goes without saying that this was equivalent to arresting them.

All the monks who, tired after a long day of hard work, had been sleeping soundly in their beds, now, awakened by the sudden alarm-bell, gathered together in the chapel.

The aged Bishop Sauer, now in his seventies and an invalid, the sixty-year-old Prior Father Roth, and two other priests presented themselves with an air of composure and dignified respect, smiling, and turning toward the altar, gave their final benediction.

Father Roth called one of the younger Brothers to him, and gave him the following instructions: to burn the records of matters already disposed of; to place some of the remaining records in the room as before; and to bury the rest of them in the ground as soon as possible. This lasted hardly more then five minutes and the prior said,

"We are all ready."

He went out into the corridor. Father Schleicher, the subprior and Father Klingseis, the professor, had very little preparation to make.

At two o'clock in the morning, the four priests bade farewell to the sorrow-stricken monks, and acknowledging their sad words of parting, got into the truck, which at once started to move off toward the headquarters of the Political Security Bureau.

Bishop Sauer, raising his right hand, gave a final blessing to the community, saying, in the words of St. John, "Love one another." (St. John, 13:34). The truck disappeared into the darkness.

From that moment everything came to a standstill; the abbey was shut down, and contact with the outside world was cut off. The premises were encircled and watched by company-strength Red guards, and the hill at the back and all the establishments were closed to outsiders.

The rector of the seminary, Father Romer, was elected temporary head in charge of the abbey, in place of the Bishop and the prior.

On the second day after the departure of the Bishop and the three other priests, at the same hour of the night, three more trucks came. This time they took away the rector of the seminary, all the priests and monks of German nationality, and four Korean priests.

At dawn next day all the seminarians and Korean monks were moved into the seminary building, and were forbidden to leave the premises except during certain prescribed hours. Our seminary had now become a prison.

For a week we led the life of prisoners. The youngest of us was twelve years old, the eldest, sixty, and there were ninety-nine of us all told.

Fortunately we had some forty sacks of rice stored in our warehouse, which after much discussion and argument Father Romer was able to obtain for our use. Within twenty-four hours of our becoming prisoners all our remaining stocks of foodstuffs were taken over and confiscated by the Reds, and only very limited rations were issued to us.

We all expected to be arrested ourselves at any moment, just as suddenly as our Bishop, rector, and professors.

As soon as they had taken possession of the abbey, the Communists started to destroy every sacred object they could lay their hands on. Crucifixes and plaster images, valuable even from an aesthetic standpoint, were all thrown out of the fourth-floor windows: all the priestly vestments were torn to shreds and used as dusters and handkerchiefs; valuable books were torn up for toilet paper or burnt in a bonfire.

Prison life and labor kept us busy, but we realized that there were also opportunities for the vital and effective use of our reasoning powers. To witness the wanton destruction of the sacramentals was not an experience to be gone through with indifference, nor would a sensitive pagan have viewed it with equanimity. They shut down the library and sealed the bookcases with strips of paper inscribed with the insignia of their authority, but left us a couple of bedrooms, the chapel, refectory and toilet for our own use. On the one hand we kept continuous prayer in the chapel, and on the other we considered in concert how to prevent further desecration of the sacramentals at the hands of the enemies of religion.

In our seminary there was a small staff of cooks and other employes, and to them we decided that it was essential to furnish the necessary supplies of rice and other foodstuffs. One of these cooks, a woman, had a child confined to bed with a lingering illness, and in order to fulfil her duties as a mother she had to live outside the seminary precincts. We put forward a request to the Communist official to include her in the list of persons entitled to rations, and in consideration of her circumstances they quite humanely granted our request.

When she brought her rice bag to be filled in accordance with their orders sanctioning this grant, we took the opportunity to get some of our chalices and other sacred objects out of the power of the enemies of religion. Basing our actions in part upon those of our patriarch Joseph as recounted in the *Book* *of Genesis,*① we hid various chalices and other sacred objects in the rice bag that she was periodically allowed to remove from the premises. In this way we succeeded in getting several sets of priestly vestments out of their power, by having her put them on underneath her everyday blouse and skirt. This woman, showing her legitimate gate-pass to the gate-guard in a most natural manner, was able to convey these objects out of the precincts of the cordonedoff seminary to Won-san, where she handed them over to trustworthy Christians of that place.

Verifying that our operation had been crowned with success, we repeated it with other cooks and employes, until we had in the guise of almsgiving completed our self-imposed task of removing the sacramentals from the power of the enemies.

During the first week of our imprisonment we had an opportunity of learning the nature of Communist interrogations, and for the time being they had no further use for us. What was their plan? Were they going to send us to a labor camp? Or would they send us back to our parents? As long as we were confined under house arrest in what had been our seminary, there was no way for us to find out what was going to happen to us.

One of the questions they repeatedly asked during their interrogations was about our plans for the future. Our invariable answer was, "We will continue our monastic life," or "We will constantly exert all our efforts to become priests."

We packed up our personal property, each package being checked by the Communists. When examining the parcels, they deprived us of the sacramentals, monastic and priestly vestments, and certain books, and further-more seized the rosaries from our pockets and the crucifixes and medals we wore round our necks.

We were forbidden not only to lodge a protest against these seizures, but even to speak to one another, and were forced to become mutes. All we were allowed to

retain in our possession was a few suits of ordinary plain clothes.

In spite of this, however, a few of the monks and seminarians succeeded in taking out certain important books, sacramentals and vestments in their packages, by skillful evasion of the Communists' examination.

We were escorted out of the abbey precincts under guard, in single file, and only then did we realize that we were going to be allowed to return to our homes. Turning our heads toward the abbey and seminary buildings for a last farewell look, we all sang the *"Benedicite"* hymn in a loud chorus.

Driven out of the seminary we became free men on the one hand, but on the other we became homeless. Where were we to go? To our homes? To the Church? Whichever we chose, they were certain to pursue us.

As we stood there hesitating, the local people came up to us and grasping our hands, shed tears of affection and sympathy. Our natural feelings could not be repressed, for our friendship was of such long standing. They all bitterly criticized the Communists for their heartlessness and expressed the warmest sympathy for us in our troublesome predicament. Some among the villagers who had experienced monastic life for a short period affirmed that it was a life of admirable purity, humility, and devotion.

At this stage we had not yet given up our hope of returning to the abbey in the course of three or four months, for none of us believed that the Communist regime could last longer than that. How foolish we were! How we underestimated their power of survival! Even now (1951), after two years, there still seems to be little hope of our return, though we will never completely abandon all hope of doing so eventually. We firmly believe that sooner or later, when our good fortune returns, we shall be able to come back, and with no likelihood of being expelled again.

All of us now dispersed, each going his own way, some remaining in North Korea,

---

① See chapter 44, verse ii.

some crossing the Thirty-eighth Parallel to South Korea, and some going abroad to continue their studies. Those who remained in North Korea found work on farms, in factories, in towns or villages, but could obtain no official position and were kept under constant surveillance by the Communists. This, incidentally, obliged the Communists to augment their Political Security Bureau officials and their operation agency staff.

Where Was Bishop Francis Hong?

Immediately after the closure of the Benedictine Abbey and our consequent expulsion, an important case came up for trial in P'yŏng-yang. Having heard of the closure, and of the wholesale arrest of priests, monks, and nuns, Bishop Francis Hong, of the Vicariate Apostolic of P'yŏng-yang, and chief administrator of the Catholic Church in North Korea, took steps to lodge a protest against the action of the puppet government, under the following four heads:

1. Unlawful arrest of missionaries who for forty years had made a most valuable contribution toward the development of agriculture, education, science and culture in Korea.

2. Closure of all churches and general persecution of religion, in violation of the people's constitutional rights.

3. Failure to discriminate between missionary institutions and their individual members, and the consequent imputation of collective guilt to the former for the acts of the latter.

4. Prohibition of religious meetings and continued detention of those under arrest.

Requesting an interview with Park Il-u, Minister of Home Affairs, Bishop Hong forwarded his letter of protest to him with a demand for redress.

On May 14, 1949 Bishop Francis Hong spent the morning at the episcopal Residence waiting for a reply from the minister, and in the afternoon left for Sŏ-p'o, in order to pay a visit to the convent there, which he had previously planned.

At about four o'clock in the afternoon of the same day, a telephone message came from the Ministry of Home Affairs to the cathedral, to the effect that the minister wished to have an interview with the Bishop at 6:00 p.m. The message was received by the Father Louis Kim Pi'l-hyŏn, the Vicar General, who immediately set off by bicycle to the Bishop's residence, only to find, of course, that he had already left for Sŏ-p'o. Father Kim, therefore, realizing that there was no time to arrange for automobile transportation, sent off the Bishop's servant, Kim Un-sam, a seventeen-year-old boy, to Sŏ-p'o on foot, to inform the Bishop that the minister wished to see him.

About half an hour after the boy's departure another messenger, George Song Eun-ch'ŏl, an eighteen-year-old altar-boy, was also sent off to Bishop Hong at Sŏ-p'o by bicycle, accompanied by a watchdog. These two boys had orders to proceed to Sŏ-p'o and deliver the message to Bishop Hong without fail.

On receiving the message Bishop Hong promised to leave by bicycle as soon as he had finished the work he was doing, and told the two boys to return, with the watchdog, ahead of him.

Bishop Hong, however, did not appear at 6:00 p.m. for the interview, nor had he arrived by 7:00 p.m. In great anxiety, Father Kim sent several other young men to Sŏ-p'o, some by train and some by bicycle, but the Bishop was not to be found. Sister Agnita Chang informed the young men that Bishop Hong had left the convent by bicycle at a quarter to five, i.e. fifteen minutes after the two boys. Those two boys had set off straight for the Bishop's residence in P'yŏng-yang, but neither the Bishop nor the two boys and their dog had arrived.

The Vicar General, Father Kim, immediately informed the minister of this, and requested him to postpone the interview with the Bishop, as the latter's whereabouts was unknown. Father Kim then mobilized a search-party of several scores of Christians, but they could find no trace of him. The disappearance of the Bishop was confirmed, and his secretary, Father Matthias Ch'oe reported the fact in person at the police station of Sŏ-p'yŏng-yang.

The next thing Father Kim did was to call a general meeting of all priests stationed in the city of P'yŏng-yang, to consider what measures should be taken. It was resolved to request the authorities to institute a search for the missing persons.

Another day passed without news, and Father Ch'oe, the Bishop's secretary, made a second visit to the Sŏ-p'yŏng-yang Police Station, urging them to intensify their search. It was not that we had any confidence in the authorities, for we well knew it was useless to ask them to help us to find our Bishop; we made the Enquiries in order to probe their attitude toward us. Though we did not expect any cooperation, we reiterated our request several times on that day, both to the police superintendent and to the chief of the Political Security Bureau of the West Ward of P'yŏng-yang City, as well as to the Minister of Home Affairs himself.

Next day their reply exactly confirmed our expectation. It was as follows:

"Having heard of the arrest of the Bishop of Tŏk-won, you secretly made arrangements for your own Bishop of P'yŏng-yang to escape from P'yŏng-yang and go to South Korea, and now you are trying to cover up your conspiracy. If the facts that you allege were true, we would have succeeded in finding him long before this."

Wishing to avoid the obloquy of overt arrest, the hooligan-like members of the bureau captured the Bishop in a remote region away from the highway, with the deliberate connivance of the operation agents who had been constantly shadowing him for a long time. This came to light a few days later when some of our young men, making a clandestine search of the area, met an old woman who had been selling vegetables near the Kam-heung-ri police box. The old woman told them that late on May 14, she had noticed a truck waiting near by, and, a few minutes later, some hooligan-like fellows, who put three

persons, a man wearing black clothes and spectacles, and two boys, as well as a dog that refused to be loaded on the truck, and that she saw them depart. With the purpose of spying out those missing persons' whereabouts, we sent out even to the countryside, to inquire if there were any Christians who were acquainted with top ranking figures of the Communist regime. We continued our inquiries as far as the bureau's detention camp, the prison, and even checked up the list of convicts and suspects at the prosecutor's office.

It was not until much later that we found out, through an influential contact, that Bishop Hong was being held in custody in the special ward for political offenders under the jurisdiction of the People's Reformatory of P'yŏng-yang City. Since January 1950 we have not been able to find out any further information regarding his whereabouts. It is the practice of the Communist regime frequently to transfer such prisoners from place to place. Nevertheless, according to an influential source, they are still keeping the Bishop in the same prison, moving him from one ward to another within the building from time to time. There was also a rumor that he had been sent somewhere northward, together with other prisoners, on October 13, just prior to the occupation of P'yŏng-yang by the United Nations Forces.

What Became of Father Kim, Father Ch'oe, and Catechist Kang?

On June 10, 1949 a letter from Han Myŏn-su, chairman of the People's Commission of P'yŏng-yang City, arrived for Father Louis Kim, summoning him to the office of the chairman to take part in deliberations regarding the fate of the cathedral building of the Vicariate Apostolic of P'yŏng-yang.

The Vicar General, Father Kim, sent the bearer of the letter back declining to attend on the ground that the case had been closed when the matter was settled by agreement in the spring of that year. It was, he said, unnecessary to reopen the case or regard it any longer as a problem. Moreover, during the absence of the Bishop, he could not assume responsibility for any further deliberations. Nevertheless, messengers continued to press for his attendance: they came disguised as municipal government officials.

Understanding their intentions, Father Kim made up his mind what to do. This was no time to hesitate, he knew: arrest was inescapable, the affairs of the Church were still unsettled, and further delay was unnecessary and unwise. He therefore sent for Father Matthias Ch'oe Hwan-jun, the Bishop's secretary and vicariate procurator, and Catechist Kang Yu-sŏn, executive councilor of maintenance, to announce his decision to them. Father Louis Kim did not want them to be martyred together with himself, but he asked them to take over responsibility for dealing with the question of the Cathedral building from that day on.

At four o'clock in the afternoon of the same day, the three friends were gathered together and firmly resolved to undergo arrest as soon as the bureau emissaries should arrive. The general belief among the Christians was that the time had come to say goodby to Father Kim once and for all. It was a sorrowful time for them, faced as they now were with the loss of the last spiritual leader left to them in North Korea.

Owing to the fact that Father Kim was ordained in Rome, he had been arrested by the Japanese authorities on the very day that Japan declared war on the United States and Great Britain, so he had already experienced some four or five months of detention life. Now, at the hands of his fellow-Koreans, though not his compatriots but the puppets of the Soviet Union, he was obliged to take the first steps on his road to martyrdom.

Fifty or sixty devoted Christians formed a procession and, weeping and wailing, accompanied the three all the way to the city hall. On their arrival the three at once entered the vice chairman's office, and the crowd of Christians that had gathered was forcibly dispersed by the traffic police.

The next scene followed immediately: a jeep and a truck drove up to the city hall. The Vicar General got into the jeep and the remaining two into the truck, accompanied and surrounded by the Political Security Bureau officials disguised as municipal government officials.

A couple of seminarians standing near by tried to approach Father Ch'oe, but the latter made a signal to them with his hand as if to say "Everything is over; you had better go home—don't get involved." In disappointment they withdrew some fifty yards and watched the departure of the three persons with tears in their eyes.

The two cars then started up and drove off at full speed.

It was around sunset. Another young man strolling by in front of the Political Security Bureau headquarters and anxious to know the latest developments of the case, had just made up his mind to go to the city hall when the truck and the jeep pulled up at the entrance. He was able to catch sight of all three of them, Father Kim, Father Ch'oe, and Catechist Kang. He almost fainted at the sight, but quickly returning to his senses, hastened to the Bishop's residence, where he told me the whole story at ten o'clock that night.

This young man was arrested by the officials two months later as a reactionary and sentenced to five years' forced labor in the coal mines of A-o-ji, North Province of Ham-kyŏng. Since then I have heard nothing more of him.

The Abduction of Father Sŏk

Father Mark Sŏk Won-sŏp, pastor of Kang-kye parish Church, who had been indisposed for a long time, returned to his parish early in July of 1949 after three months' rest and recuperation at Bishop Hong's residence.

On the second day after his arrival at his parish his condition became worse and he became seriously ill, and was confined to his bed, exhausted after his thirty-hour railroad journey

His temperature having risen to 40 degrees it was necessary to apply ice-packs continuously. He lay completely unconscious, in the care of medical nurses who lived in the room opposite him and took attending him.

It was our practice during the state of emergency in which we were living to station five or six young men in the vestry to guard the Blessed Sacrament from desecration during the night. All the other Christians returned to their respective homes after evening prayers.

At about eleven o'clock on the night of July 8, one of the nurses on duty attending Father Sŏk came out of the rectory gate to replenish her supply of ice, which was almost exhausted. Two hooligans suddenly appeared before her barring her way. Before she could cry out for help they bound and gagged her, and then a third hooligan appeared from the darkness, and another group dashed straight into the rectory and entered the sickroom.

What could they be? A gang of robbers, or a group of petty pilferers? Her heart began to palpitate with fear. There was no one else in the vicinity except these hooligans, and though she tried to call for help the gag prevented her.

She knew that Father Sŏk was in a critical condition and had again fallen into unconsciousness, and could only offer up a silent prayer for aid. This she repeated continually until, half an hour later, the hooligans made off into the darkness without having spoken a word. She was trembling with fear and cold.

When she returned to the sickroom she found the bed empty. The nurses in the neighboring room were all fast asleep. She was too late: Father Sŏk had been abducted by the bureau officials without anybody coming to his help.

That night Catechist Ch'oe Cha-paek, who had stayed late in Father Sŏk's room earlier in the evening, did not return to his home. His wife and children were still waiting up for him when at three o'clock in the morning the bureau officials came and made a thorough search of every corner of the house. The catechist's wife, a highly-educated woman, now realized why her husband had failed to return. He had been kidnaped on his way home from visiting Father Sŏk.

St. Nicholas' Night (December 6)

The following incident occurred at P'yŏng-yang during the time when the wholesale arrest of Catholic priests was going on. At about six o'clock on the morning of December 7, 1949 I observed five or six hooligans in the waiting room of the Bishop's residence. Wearing pajamas and slippers, l was on my way back from the bathroom to my bedroom, which was located across the corridor from the waiting room. Three of them approached me and, grabbing my hand, told me to accompany them at once to their headquarters on important business. Dressed as I was, I refused.

"What is the meaning of this? Who are you?" I asked.

"We are from the bureau headquarters. Take a look at these papers." They produced an envelope and added. "Father Park asked us to fetch you. Come on, hurry up!"

There were two sheets of paper in the envelope. One was a note addressed to Father Andrew Chang Tu-pong, and the other was addressed to Alexius Lee Chae-ho, pastor of Ki-rim-ri Church, and both were written by Father Park, the parish priest of Sin-ri Church, P'yŏng-yang. The first ran as follows:

"Dear Father Andrew Chang,

I have something important to discuss with you. Will you please come to me with the bearer of this letter?

Yours sincerely, Tim Park."

I recognized the handwriting as that of Father Park. Nong-ok As his Christian name was Timothy, he usually signed as Tim Park. As soon as I had read it, I told the men:

"This note is not addressed to me. I am Chang Sŏn-heung, not Chang Tu-pong, neither am I a priest."

One of the bureau officials, a short fellow, again inquired my name and on learning that it was Chang again insisted that Father Park had told him to bring Father Chang. Another of them, a tall man, said, "This Chang is not a priest. Father Chang's name is Chang Tu-pong: where is he to be found at present?" I answered that Father Chang had left for his parish the previous day, but that Father Lee, the parish priest of Ki-rim-ri Church, might be at home. Having verified that I was not the man they were looking for, they left the corridor without further words.

I went back to my room and carefully watched their behavior from the window. One of them who seemed to be the head of the gang gave a signal, and scores of armed guards formed up before him and at his orders boarded the waiting jeeps and trucks and went off to their headquarters.

As soon as they had gone I sent for the cook and the servant and told them to go at once to Ki-rim-ri parish Church and find out what the situation was. They returned in about half an hour and reported that the Church of Ki-rim-ri was completely surrounded by Communist guards and that the interior was full of bureau officials. Nobody was allowed to enter the church.

About half an hour later a young man called on me and said that Father Lee had been captured and taken away by the bureau officials. He told how he had met an old woman who was going to attend Mass that morning and had been just in time to witness the apprehension of her spiritual director, Father Lee, at the gates of the church. With screams of horror she had cried, "Why are you arresting our priest?" Attempting to bar their way she had been knocked down and kicked. The bureau officials had then carried the priest to a jeep and driven away at full speed.

To judge from the other paper I had seen, it seemed likely that Father Park must also have been arrested by now.

At about three o'clock in the afternoon of the previous day (December 6, 1949) a member of the bureau, disguised as an official of the municipal government, came to Father Park Nong-ok of Sin-ri parish, the bishop's temporal deputy, and asked him to go to the mayor's office, on business connected with the Cathedral building. Father Park, explaining that he had no authority to deal with the matter, which should be dealt with according to formal agreement at a forthcoming conference to be held at the Bishop's residence, politely declined to accompany the official. The bureau official then left without showing any sign of dissatisfaction. According to what the sacristan said, he did not, apparently, wish to arrest Father Park, but merely to test out the priest's attitude toward him.

Assuming therefore that their priest was in no immediate danger of arrest the Christians made arrangements for a fuller attendance than usual to join in that evening's benediction of the Blessed Sacrament. It was the custom in North Korea to hold a benediction service every evening in order to dispel the constant propaganda of atheism, and to pray for the early unification of the country.

At around six o'clock in the evening a few members of the bureau entered the church and declared that they had come to escort Father Park to the People's Committee of P'yŏng-yang City. It was soon noticed that the building was completely surrounded. Immediately the benediction service ended, two young men came out of the church and declared that they could not allow their priest to go with the police. At the same time another group of young men assisted the priest to get to his bedroom.

The dispute between the Christian youths and the bureau officials grew more and more heated. and the crowd grew in number to more than two hundred, so that the bureau officials themselves became surrounded. For their part, the Christian youths declared:

"Under the plea of consulting our spiritual leaders you have already arrested our Bishop, our Vicar General, and other priests, and still not satisfied you now want to arrest our parish priest. We will not be cheated this time. If you wish to arrest him, you will have to arrest all of us as well."

They struggled bravely against the bureau officials who for their part were being steadily reinforced by new arrivals coming five or six at a time at first, and later on by truckload after truckload, till the place looked like a battlefield with two armies arrayed face to face.

The faithful surrounded the rectory two or three lines deep and prevented the bureau officials from entering to arrest the priest. Both sides went on getting reinforcements until they were more or less equal in numbers, and then began a furious hand-to-hand struggle, the stronger ones punching and kicking while the weaker resorted to biting. The situation grew from bad to worse. A young seminarian named Peter Lee began to ring an alarm on the church bell: when the bureau officials attempted to prevent him by cutting the bellrope he climbed up to the belfry and went on ringing the bell through-out the fight, for no one could dislodge him. Many non-Christians rushed to the scene to take the part of the men who were them-selves struggling valiantly to protect the priest. As however they were on the defensive, while the bureau officials thought nothing of attacking everybody with any weapon that came to their hand, they were to that ex-tent at a disadvantage. The bureau officials now began arresting all the women and children and old men, more than a hundred of whom they imprisoned in neighboring houses, after which their task became easier.

In the meantime the priest had changed from his summer clothing to the wadded winter wear that every priest in North Korea always kept ready in case of arrest, for they would get none in prison and it would be many months before they would be set free, if indeed they ever would.

He now spoke in a loud voice to the faith-ful:

"This resistance is not only useless, but it is against the spirit of the Christian religion." At first his words seemed to have no effect on his excited defenders, but soon they obeyed him. After the fighting many were found to have suffered serious injury, many were weeping either from pain or indigna-tion; some were wiping blood from nose or mouth and others bleeding seriously, while many lay unconscious on the ground, as the bureau officials continued to flog them with sticks and clubs. The children and the aged were screaming and crying in their make-shift prison where they were still confined. The faithful, unbeaten by arms or weapons or superior numbers, had shown their spirit and now either at the orders of the priest or the dictates of common sense ceased to offer further resistance.

Father Park emerged from his room and got into the waiting jeep. The bell-ringing seminarian descended from his perch, and was immediately attacked by a group of bureau officials who rushed at him, but, thanks to his knowledge of *judo* they were thrown to the ground. More of them rushed to the attack however and he was at last overcome by superior numbers and beaten uncon-scious. The Reds then hauled him into their car and sped away into the darkness. Many of his friends tried to hang on to the back of the car, but to no avail.

Almost simultaneously with this incident at Sin-ri Church another rough-and-tumble took place at Kwan-hu-ri Cathedral, as a result of which an assistant priest, Father Bonif-acius Sŭh Un-sŏk, was arrested. This free-for-all fight was not fit to look at, for the Reds savagely beat a girl student and kicked her, arousing the anger of the crowd, and then hauled the girl, together with a housemaid and the assistant priest Sŭh, to their car and drove away.

Father Park of the Sin-ri Church met his associate priest Sŭh at the office of the city council, where he had arrived about ten minutes later than Father Sŭh. The chair-man of the city council then took up the prolonged Kwan-hu-ri Cathedral building controversy and persuaded the two priests to turn over the building to the Com-munists. The priests became indignant and said,

"You have arrested our Bishop and Vicar General, and other Church leaders. You now demand that we hand over our Church building to you. Is this fair? This Church building is not our private property. It belongs to the Christians. We cannot persuade them to hand over the building to you.

"Frankly speaking, we decline to negotiate with you for the transfer of the Church building unless you release the Bishop, the Vicar General, priests, and other Christians. It is no use to try to persuade us because we have no right to handle the matter. You must approach the competent Church authority, and discuss the matter formally on a legal basis. It is not fair for you to send a horde of armed men to arrest us like criminals. Your proposal amounts to virtual expropriation, and as long as these illegal and violent practices continue, we decline to discuss the matter with you."

In this way the two priests flatly turned down the request of the chairman of the city council. They never retreated an inch from their position, though the discussion went on for nearly two hours.

When they came out from the council chamber it was around eleven o'clock at night. They returned to Kwan-hu-ri Cathedral, where many Christians were anxiouly waiting for them. On hearing what had happened they became indignant and full of resentment against the Communists, but having confirmed that the two priests were still free and unharmed they went home quietly, after thanking God for their safe return.

They went home, except for a few who were supposed to be on night duty. The two priests put out the lamp and went to bed. At three o'clock in the morning, the Communists returned in force, raided the church, and re-arrested the priests. Father Timothy Park was wearing the wadded clothes he had put on in Sin-ri, but Father Bonifacius Sŭh was very lightly clad.

This Communist trick was not a new one. They often released Christians they had arrested, in order to give them a false sense of security, and thus make the shock of re-arrest all the greater. In this way they would try to break down the confidence or morale of the people, and by subjecting them to constant strain keep them in a state of constant anxiety, too disheartened to attempt to obtain justice. The two priests probably did not expect to be re-arrested, for they had as yet had little experience of this war of nerves tactics.

In the meantime Father Andrew Chang Tu-pong, who had been convalescing at the Bishop's residence, went to Kŏm-am-ri by bus for the festival of the Immaculate Conception, and to inspect each outstation of Chung-hwa parish, and on December 7, the eve of the festival, he received news of the arrest of Fathers Park, Sŭh, and Lee.

The Reds had already thrown a police cordon around him, and the area was completely in their hands. Father Chang was immediately arrested, and taken to P'yŏng-yang, leaving the entire P'yŏng-yang district without a single priest at liberty. More than ten thousand Christians had been deprived of their spiritual leaders, of the Church buildings that belonged to them, and of all facilities for the practice of their religion.

These lambs without a shepherd would go on Sundays and feast days by the hundreds to the districts of Sa-ri-won, Sŏ-p'o or Chin-nam-p'o to hear Mass, for there were still priests there who had not yet been arrested by the Communists.

A few days after the arrest of the three priests the Cathedral buildings were seized and completely taken over by the Communists. As for the Sin-ri Church, until the autumn of 1950, when the United Nations Forces and the Republic of Korea Army captured P'yŏng-yang, this Church building was used as a theater for children, under the name of the 'children's palace'.

On December 10, 1949 two priests, Father Callistus Hong Kŏn-hwan, parish priest of Sin-eui-ju, and Father John Hong To-keun, parish priest of P'yŏng-won, were arrested by the Reds. As nobody knew of this at that time the Christians had no opportunity to manifest their indignation until it was too late. There was consequently no such violent clash between Christians and Communists as had occurred at P'yŏng-yang.

The Last Days of the Bishop's House

On December 24, 1949 we had a quiet Christmas celebration with several of the domestic staff at the Bishop's house. There were no Christmas Masses in any of the city churches, and it was one of the loneliest Christmases I ever spent. I set up a small *praesepe* or Christmas crib as a symbol of the Nativity, and surrounded it with Christmas presents for distribution among the employes. We prayed that the Savior, Who came into the world to bring peace to men who are God's friends (Luke, 2:14), might bestow that gift on the entire Korean nation this year, and save our priests from further persecution at the hands of the enemies of religion.

After the Christmas party was over and all had left, I lit the candle placed in front of the *bambino* lying in the manger and then knelt down and prayed. Tears came to my eyes. I do not remember how long I prayed, but I did not go to bed that night.

On December 26 alarming reports began coming in from all quarters: on Christmas Eve, many Protestant churches had been subject to a shower of stones thrown by Red mobs. All churches, Catholic or Protestant, had been bombarded in a similar way by members of primary-and middle-school Communist Youth Leagues. Communist policemen stood by and made no effort to stop the stone-throwing, but pretended to take no notice. The puppet North Korean government made regular use of this hypocritical procedure, ordering the organizations to demonstrate hostility to the Church and then pretending to know nothing about it. We had expected something of the kind, so on Christmas Eve we locked all the church gates and blacked out all the windows, and escaped the stoning. Some of the Protestant

Church leaders were less fortunate, and were severely beaten up by the Reds— among them several were severely injured, and others disappeared and are still missing.

At about two o'clock in the afternoon of December 29, another enemy of religion, a prosecutor of the P'yŏng-yang City Public Prosecution Department, named Kim Yŏn-tŏk, came to the Bishop's house accompanied by a number of plainclothes policemen. Producing their identification cards and credentials, they said:

"Since criminal proceedings are now being taken against Mr. Hong Yong-ho, the owner of this building, we are going to take possession of it in the name of the law, and hold it for protection until his case is decided and the verdict is announced. Kindly allow us to enter."

These words were spoken in a peremptory tone, and came as no surprise to us. Needless to say, their talk of protection was a mere pretext for expelling us from the building and seizing it for their own use. I ushered them to the third floor.

They made a close check of the Bishop's office, the furniture, bedstead and bedding, clothing and everything else in the room. I was ordered to act as caretaker of the building for the time being. They did not, however, seal the chapel, my bed-room, the kitchen or the lavatory. As I had been through all this before at Tŏk-won Abbey it did not surprise me. All our important documents and belongings had been removed to rural areas a year before; the furniture was nothing to us.

New Year's Day came and went without incident but on the following day prosecutor Kim Yŏn-tŏk returned with two policemen, who he said would replace me from then on as caretakers of the building. I would have to stay on, he said, until I had taught them their job and they were thoroughly capable of accepting the responsibility.

They had checked the inventory which they had made on their previous visit, and found that it included a number of things which they considered unnecessary. They now told me I could have these unwanted things and dispose of them as I liked. This seemed unreasonable to me, for they had previously said that I would have to keep them until the court ruling was announced. Now the two policemen said I could do as I liked with them. What a way to run a department!

They went on to say that judgment had not yet been given in the Bishop's case, and even went so far as to admit that the prosecutor had not yet lodged any definite charges against him; I could therefore dispose of the things freely, they said!

The two policemen set to work to repair the heating system. They called in workmen and discussed plans and blueprints with them. A few days later they mentioned a scheme to turn the building of the Episcopal Residence into a dormitory for a staff training school. I thought it best to be very careful in dealing with them: they made repeated promises to take care of everything till the building was returned to the Church, yet here they were setting about making radical alterations in the structure. It seemed obvious that the government had no intention of relinquishing possession.

I felt it my duty to try to prevent desecration of the sacred building, but these men did not talk like rational beings, and were plainly not to be trusted. I decided to take it upon myself to remove certain sacred things from the Episcopal Residence and store them in a safe place. I sent for a few Christians to help me, but at least a hundred responded to my call and rushed to the Episcopal Residence. Each of them took a bagful of church belongings home with him.

From that day on my freedom was restricted and I was placed under strict surveillance. There were three beds in my office; my own and the two policemen's. I was forbidden to go outdoors, and no one was allowed in to see me.

I now made up my mind to escape and go to South Korea. It was no easy task, but I decided I would make it a matter of liberty or death. Father Paul Cho In-kuk, now the only priest at liberty, sent me a secret message advising me to make my escape and go to South Korea with the help of certain intermediaries. For several days I made my arrangements. At last, through the blessing of God, my opportunity came: some Christian friends established contact with me in the dead of night, and told me what to do.

On January 19, 1950 I was to leave P'yŏng-yang for Hae-ju at 2 p.m. I played chess with the two Communist policemen all morning, and they seemed to suspect nothing. Evading their surveillance I slipped off to the railroad station, guided by two Christians. For a time I thought I was being shadowed, but I managed to elude the man I suspected of following me, and made the journey to Hae-ju without being called upon by the Communists to show my papers. Under cover of darkness I got safely to Ch'ŏng-tan, and offered up thanks to God and my Guardian Angel who had enabled me to set foot on South Korean territory.

It was good to be free in South Korea but my happiness did not last long. I learnt that many of our Church leaders in North Korea were no more, while those who still alive were suffering hardship and cruel mistreatment beyond description. How could I exult in my freedom, a butterfly in the sunshine, when my friends were still captive? The thought of them was like a thorn in my heart, and I longed to be able to liberate them.

In Seoul I was ordained to the priesthood for which I had been preparing myself for nineteen years. I urged all those who congratulated me on the occasion to pray continually for the liberation of our fellow-countrymen in the north, and in all the six hundred Masses that I have celebrated since then I have never forgotten to pray for them, both living and dead.

Secret Contact with Prisoners

The arrest and imprisonment of Catholic priests, monks, nuns and laymen went on continually and their whereabouts was kept secret. I made many inquiries among those released from prisons but to no avail. A pagan saying has it that Heaven is not without mercy and indeed this turned out to be true. Some friendly pagans tipped us off that our clergy were being held in a special political prison, and soon secret contacts were established with them. These kindly people who gave us the information never asked for payment and until now we have been unable to reward them for what they did for us. Though not Catholics, they cherished truth, justice and patriotism as much as we did, and did not lack the courage to risk their lives to help us. We are indeed deeply in their debt, for through them we could convey our news to our imprisoned clergy and receive news from them.

One lay Brother was our sole contact in maintaining this flow of intelligence, which was restricted to as few persons as possible in order that it might not be endangered by inadvertence or carelessness. The following is typical of news we received through this channel:

Early in January 1950 Father Damasus Paek Eungman, formerly parish priest of P'yŏng-kang, Kang-won Province, died in prison. His body was buried in a public cemetery at Yong-san, in the suburbs of P'yŏng-yang.

Hearing this news the Brother on liaison duty went at once to the cemetery, and located the grave, and had it marked with a wooden post inscribed 'The Grave of Paek Eung-man'. It took him several days to find it.

A month after Father Paek's death we learnt that Bishop Sauer, *Abbas Nullius* of Tŏk-won, had also died in prison. The news came as a great shock to us, for our sorrow at his death, though mitigated by our gratitude for his long and distinguished career as our prelate, was exacerbated by indignation at the cruelty and contempt with which he had been treated during life and had been continued even after his death.

Our liaison man immediately hurried to the prisoners' cemetery which had been set up at

Yong-san, in the suburbs of P'yŏng-yang. It was extremely difficult to identify the grave, for there were no name boards on any of them. He decided to open one by one all the graves that looked new. This could not be done during the day, so he decided to utilize the night hours and with the help of a nun started opening the fresh graves. The wind whistled through the sparsely wooded hills as they pursued their gruesome task in the dark, and, panting and sweating with the exertion, uncovered one by one the bodies of the unfortunate victims of the Communist cruelty. As the corpses lay on the hillside they seemed about to rise and accuse their murderers. Buried along with them were the bodies of those unjustly killed by the Communists after Korea's liberation from Japan on August 15, 1945.

At last the monk and the nun located the grave. There could be no mistake: the noble features, as of one peacefully sleeping, the snow-white beard, and the canonical garments were proof positive of identity. Hastily they dug out another grave which without affixing a marker could be identified with ease, and reinterred the body. The day was just dawning when they made their way breathlessly down the hill.

Two months later they performed a similar work of charity with the body of Father Rupert Klingseis, who had been professor of philosophy at Tŏk-won Seminary, and died on April 6, 1950. They found the face covered with the handkerchief, embroidered with his name, that he used to use at Tŏk-won Abbey. The body was clothed in black.

On the recapture of P'yŏng-yang by United Nations Forces in October 1950, I accompanied an American Army chaplain and a war correspondent to this cemetery. Only a year before, I thought to myself, Father Rupert Klingseis had, with his brilliant intellect and eloquence, impressed us all with his special lectures on the topic of Communism as an affront to human dignity. And I recalled too that my old friend Father Paek was buried here too. I thanked God for their lives, which had culminated in the glory of martyrdom.

We inspected the P'yŏng-yang People's Reformatory, and saw the cells in which Bishop Hong and the priests and monks had been incarcerated. The latter had been transferred farther north on October 14, 1950, and since then we have been unable to get in touch with them. Some of the younger priests and monks, we learnt, had been put to forced labor in the gold mines of Cha-kang-to. We tried to establish contact with them also, but were unsuccessful.

St. Mary's Convent and Sister Chang

Late in April of 1950 news came of the confiscation of St. Mary's Convent at Sŏ-p'o by the Communists. This was the first entirely Korean convent in Korea, having been founded about eighteen years previously, with a commuity of about forty Korean nuns.

Up to now it had escaped persecution by the Red tyrants, and had already sent many of its Sisters to local Churches in South and North Province of P'yŏng-an, so there were only about twenty of them there when it was seized. They lived an almost entirely enclosed life of prayer, meditation and labor. They were very poor and supported themselves by needlework and animal husbandry.

These religious women were now branded by the Reds as reactionaries—women who worked hard for their living, and who distributed every cent they could spare from their meager earnings to almshouses and orphanages, were now accused of being the tools of capitalism!

The Communists coveted their simple building and cultural facilities, and were jealous of the regard in which the nuns were held by the people of P'yŏng-yang, who were also accused of being reactionary. As a result, the Sisters dispersed to the homes of relatives and friends. Even there they could not escape Communist surveillance and persecution: caught in the Communist trap, they now became subject to what the Communists called the social purge.

On June 25, 1950, the Korean War broke

out. Planes of the Republic of Korea and the United Nations Forces, the champions of justice, freedom and democracy, now appeared over North Korea and began to subject the Communist military installations to constant bombardment.

Sister Chang, the former prioress of St. Mary's Convent, was leading a wandering life at this time. She now took refuge in a hut in the woods around Song-rim-ri near Sun-an.

There, accompanied by Sister Kang, the former subprioress of the convent, and a younger Sister, she awaited the day when all the Sisters of their community, who had been expelled by the Reds and dispersed throughout the country, might reunite and resume their monastic life.

This arduous life in the woods unfortunately brought about a breakdown in Sister Chang's health, and, suffering extreme pain, she became unable to rise from her bed.

October 4 came, the day on which the Communist forces, overpowered by those of the Free World, fled from P'yŏng-yang like rats seeking holes to hide in. The air attacks continued.

Sister Chang, who had just awakened from the first long and peaceful sleep she had enjoyed for many weeks, called Sister Kang and said:

"I feel strangely well today, perhaps because I feel so sure that our Sisters will soon be able to come together again. The United Nations planes are able to fly everywhere, even to this remote place. Surely the Communists will be unable to resist them: let us wait in patience."

Sister Kang was deeply moved at Sister Chang's words and the mysterious improvement in her condition, and hardly knew what to say in reply. Unable to share Sister Chang's optimism to the full, she said with a sigh:

"God grant you may be right. What a blessing it will be if you recover your health!"

As they were talking they saw an ox-cart approaching along the winding road that led to their little hut, and soon made out the figure of the chairman of the village chapter of the Communist Labor Party walking beside it. At first they attached little significance to the sight, and went on talking. "I don't suppose anybody knows where we are. What is your opinion, Sister Kang?"

"Why, of course they know. Don't you remember that we registered ourselves at the village office? The police must know, I am sure. You know you always reported your change of address at every move, didn't you?"

"Yes, of course I did. But I don't think they will bother us. What have they to gain by arresting us? If they had wanted to, they could have done that when they expelled us from the convent. Don't you agree, Sister Kang?"

"Well, you may be right, and I pray to God that you are. But how can we be sure what they will do? They always keep their intentions secret, and take action without warning."

Someone was shouting outside.

When Sister Kang went to the door she saw the scowling face of the village Labor Party chief. Without any greeting, he said he had orders from the Sun-an People's Committee to take Sister Chang to them. Sister Kang explained that she was confined to her bed with illness, and was too ill to be moved, and offered to go in place of Sister Chang.

The chairman replied that he already knew all about her illness, and that was why he had brought the ox-cart along. He went on to say that the committee, informed of her movements from place to place as a refugee, felt that she was undergoing excessive hardship, and wished to take care of her and all the other nuns, and provide them with houses where they could live in peace and comfort. For this reason, he went on, he must take Sister Chang with him now, to talk over the matter with the committee. His words were a series of specious promises and veiled threats.

Sister Kang was adamant and turned down his proposal, but from the interior of the hut came a call. Sister Chang wanted to tell

her that she had heard everything that they had been saying, and that she had made up her mind to sacrifice herself as the Bishop and priests had done. In fact, she pointed out to Sister Kang, there was very little choice in the matter and she could hardly do otherwise. This brought tears to their eyes as they realized that they must part.

The chief now entered the hut, with the driver of the cart and a policeman. Pushing Sister Kang aside he approached the sickbed where Sister Chang lay. He hauled her outside to the cart: at the sudden movement Sister Chang groaned with pain.

The cart started off, and Sister Kang and the younger Sister were determined to accompany it, until Sister Chang, who was still conscious, told them not to follow her, for there was no reason why they should sacrifice themselves.

"Please, please go back, dear Sisters....you must survive to carry on the work....please go back!"

The two Sisters could only obey. They stood watching the cart as it slowly moved out of sight. The last words they heard from Sister Chang were "Goodby and good luck." As the cart moved further away all they could hear was an occasional groan of pain.

They felt as if they had lost their own mother. Once in the hands of the Communists, they knew, it was very unlikely that she would ever return to them.

"What shall we do now that they have taken away our Mother?" they asked. "Ought we to curse the Communists for doing that?" Then they remembered the words of the Saint Apostle Paul:

"Do not repay injury with injury; study your behavior in the world's sight as well as in God's. Keep peace with all men, where it is possible, for your part. Do not avenge yourselves, beloved; allow retribution to run its course; so we read in scripture, Vengeance is for me I will repay, says the Lord Rather, feed thy enemy if he is hungry, give him drink if he is thirsty; by doing this, thou wilt heap coals of fire upon his head. Do not be disarmed by malice; disarm malice with kindness." (Romans, 12:17-21)

Sister Chang, like the Bishop, priests and ardent faithful, achieved the glory of martyrdom in accordance with God's will, and her own.

Almost simultaneously another Sister was arrested in P'yŏng-yang. She was the elder sister of Father Sŭh, the administrator of the Cathedral. After her arrest her whereabouts was not disclosed, and it was impossible to find out what had become of her.

"The Ever-victorious General"

11:50 a.m., October 15, 1950. Sergeant Kim, a military police guard, said:

"This is the Thirty-eighth Parallel."

The Thirty-eighth Parallel! That knife across the heart of Korea! Entrance to that inferno of the north Korea, where ten million compatriots were held in misery! The Thirty-eighth Parallel, cause of the death of hundreds of thousands of Koreans, Americans, and their allies! A line of horror, across which I had crossed to freedom in South Korea nine months before!

At that time I had crawled across like a rat, but crossing it now in broad daylight in a jeep, escorted by a military guard, my high spirits made me feel like a victorious general. I now had the honor indeed to break through this line as a member of the courageous Republic of Korea Army. I was not one of the combatants with rifle and bayonet, but as a military chaplain I shared the honor of crossing the line for the freedom of the two-and-a-half-billion inhabitants of the world.

The Republic of Korea Army had already seized Ko-rang-p'o, which was now a burnt-out waste, and was marching north in pursuit of the fleeing Communists. Onward they marched, to P'yŏng-yang, to the banks of the Yalu, to Mt. Paek-tu, They advanced at full speed, welcomed at every point by the rejoicing populace of town and village. Young and old shouted *"Man-se!"* Through flaming villages we marched on to the plaudits of the multitude.

Hundreds of villagers came to listen to my political speech. There was no public address system to amplify my voice, but my words seemed to please them, for they applauded without stopping. Some of the old grandmothers were so elated that they danced a jig.

"The Thirty-eighth Parallel has been passed—the nation must be reunited—let us build a free country!" I was surprised at the strength of my own voice as I shouted these words to them.

Under dense gun-smoke we pushed on to Sin-kye, where we put up for the night, and then early next morning on to Chŏng-pong. The shell of the Church building stood apparently undamaged, but the interior was stripped bare. The pulpit had been smashed and the priestly vestments, torn to shreds, which littered the vestry. Scores of Christians soon assembled, weeping tears of joy, and gripping our hands tight. Father Lee, the parish priest, had been arrested by the Reds just one day before the outbreak of war on June 25. I remembered him as a modest little man, and pictured him clearly in my mind's eye.

The village Christians were reluctant to let us go, but, glad as we would have been to stay with them, there was no time to spare, and we had to push on our way.

"Rest assured," I told them, "as soon as we enter P'yŏng-yang, we will break open the prison gates and release your priest without fail." That is what I thought we should be able to do, and when, on October 20, our advance party entered P'yŏng-yang, I thought it would not be long before we kept our promise. Fourteen hours later our jeep halted at the Tae-tong River and we watched the battle taking place on the gorgeous Mo-ran-pong Hill in the distance. I turned to climb the river bank and view P'yŏng-yang.

"Look, Father Chang! Our church is still standing!"

It was a miracle. After all the devastating gunfire it still stood undamaged among the surrounding ruins. Street fighting was still going on in the vicinity. The roar of heavy guns and the rattle of rifles and machine-guns went on continually. On the south bank of the Tae-tong River our artillery stood ready to open fire at any minute. Every now and then our church was obscured from view in a cloud of smoke and flames from the long-range shell explosions. Still it stood, majestic in the wreckage around it; the fruit of all the blood, sweat and tears that had been shed, of the sacrifice of our Bishop and priests; a horror to the Communists and a glory to us Christians. Was it not the very symbol of victory and peace?

At dawn on October 21 we crossed the Tae-tong River, and made all speed to the P'yŏng-yang People's Reformatory.

We found the prison gates wide open, but there were no prisoners there. The Communists had already carried them farther north.

Christians who had come out of hiding were seeking their friends; almost everyone was weeping, yearning for a sight of the Bishop and the priests and fellow Christians. On finding two of their priests, they were overjoyed: that was now the total number of priests in P'yŏng-yang.

The Cathedral building was now returned to us, together with the dependencies. Once more I sat at my desk in the Bishop's house, which had been my home and then my prison, but the other Church people who had shared it with me were gone. All the priests who had been safe up to the day before June 25 were missing. Father Benedict Kim Kyo-myŏng of Eui-ju, North Province of P'yŏng-an; Father Mark Kim Tong-ch'ŏl of Pi-hyŏn, North Province of P'yŏng-an; Father Anselmus Lee Kyŏng-ho of An-ju, South Province of P'yŏng-an, Father Laurence Lee Ch'un-keun of the Benedictine Order, who had taken refuge at Sun-an after having been

expelled from the convent at Sŏ-p'o; Father Paul Kang Yŏng-kŏl of Ma-san, South Province of P'yŏng-an; and the young priest Father Paul Cho In-kuk of Chin-nam-p'o, South Province of P'yŏng-an; all had been arrested by the Communists, and nothing was known of their whereabouts. Each had left behind the story of atrocious treatment at the hands of the Reds, borne with quiet self-control.

We discovered that all our church buildings had been secularized, some turned into theaters or tribunals, some into dance halls. On every side were buildings lying in ashes. Our culture, too, our nation's civilization, all had to be restored. It would be no easy job, I thought; to rehabilitate the Church, to reconstruct our national ethos, were the responsibility of us Christians and the whole country. It was for us Christians to give our countrymen a lead.

Onward, Christian soldiers!
Marching as to war,
With the Cross of Jesus
Going on before.

Hell's foundations quiver
At the sound of praise;
Brothers, lift your voices!
Loud your anthems raise!

Gates of hell can never
'Gainst the Church prevail;
We have Christ's own promise*
And that cannot fail.

*"Thou art Peter, and it is upon this rock that I will build my Church; and the gates of hell shall not prevail against it."
(St. Matthew, 16:18)

(From "The Sufferings of P'yŏng-yang Diocese under the Reds" by Fr. Chang Sŏn-heung)

THE SUFFERINGS OF THE
BENEDICTINE MISSION IN NORTH KOREA

The Last Benediction of Bishop Sauer

May Day, the feast of SS. Philip and James, was the anniversary of Bishop Bonifatius Sauer's consecration, and as usual we assembled with the seminarians of Tŏk-won Abbey on that day to attend the Mass offered by him. Who among us could have foreseen that our monastery was doomed to be dispersed within ten days?

It was at dead of night on the 9th of May, 1949, when the monks, tired after a hard day's work, were roused from sleep by the steady ringing of the call-bell at the front door. When the monk who was on night-duty opened the door a band of Political Security Bureau officials in plain clothes rushed in. In spite of the unusual hour they demanded an immediate interview with the Bishop (abbot), and also that the prior, the subprior, and Father Rupert Klingseis be brought to the parlor as well.

On their entering the parlor, the Bishop and the other three Fathers were arrested, and told to accompany the officials immediately to Won-san for interrogation on a case of a very serious nature. In the meantime, the corridor outside the parlor was filled with all the priests, seminarians, and monks, who were anxiously waiting for the door of the parlor to open. At last it opened, and, guarded sternly by the officials, the venerable gray-haired Bishop emerged, supporting himself with a walking stick. He was followed by Father Arnulf Schleicher, the subprior, the youngest and also the shortest man in the community. Next came Father Lucius Roth, the prior, who was a keen-witted man, and Father Klingseis, an aged professor of philosophy.

As he passed by us, the Bishop sighted Father Anselm Romer, the rector of the seminary, who was standing among us, and whispered to him,

"All authority is now delegated to you."

Then the Bishop raised his hands and, giving his last blessing to the community, proceeded to the front door. As the Bishop and the three Fathers accompanying him stepped down from the porch, all the members of the community who had gathered followed closely behind. Suddenly a certain priest moved out of the crowd toward the commander and very earnestly requested to be allowed to accompany the party, so as to be able to look after the Bishop who, besides being seventy-one years old, was suffering from constant attacks of severe and painful coughing. The cold-blooded commander refused to listen to his pleas, and gave orders to his men to drive back everybody who was following them, and make them re-enter the house.

No sooner had the kidnaped bishop and priests gotten into the car than it roared off into the darkness, leaving only the sound of its engine behind.

There was nothing we could do. Helpless,

we felt like children compelled to watch in silence while their father was taken from them.

Devastation of the Mission Headquarters

As soon as the Bishop and the three Fathers had been kidnaped in this way the commander posted Political Security Bureau officials at all the doors and gates of the abbey and seminary. He then disappeared into the parlor, calling for Father Romer, the rector, while the rest of us were confined to the refectory, to await his further orders. It would have been futile to resist, and we obeyed. Father Romer emerged after a while and conveyed the commander's orders to us. All members of the community of the Tŏk-won Abbey, whether German or Korean, were, he said, under a form of house-arrest, being forbidden to leave the precincts of the abbey grounds; no one was to be allowed to leave the house; the parlor was commandeered for the use of the North Korean troops; the cloister gate was to be kept open at all times, and the abbey farm lands were to be handed over to 'the people' and occupied by Korean farmers. That was all. For the next two days we tried to go on with our abbey life as usual. We sang hymns in the evening, and made the Stations of the Cross, and, gathered before the altar, dedicated to Our Blessed Lady our special devotions for the month of May.

On Wednesday, 11th May, a strange rumor began to circulate, though we could not find out who was responsible for starting it. The rumor was to the effect that we were all going to be transported that night. After Vespers Father Romer, in a firm, calm voice, ordered everyone he met to pack up the minimum of necessary hand baggage and wait. Amidst all this uncertainty the cool-headed Brother Wenzeslaus who was in charge of the vestry prepared two portable Mass bags. In addition he packed the pressing tool and flour required for making the Hosts, as well as a large number of ready-made Hosts for the priests, and fifteen bottles of wine. In the evening a service of Holy Communion was held both in the Cathedral and in the abbey chapel. The ciborium containing the consecrated Hosts, and the bottles of holy oils were withdrawn from the churches. After Compline each of us went to bed entrusting the future of the community and its members to the care of the Blessed Virgin Mary.

Clang! Clang! Clang! At about eleven o'clock at night the violent ringing of the bell woke us from our troubled sleep and called us out of bed. The Security Bureau officials assembled us all and made us separate into two groups, one of Germans and the other of Koreans, except that the Korean Fathers (three religious and one secular) were to go together with our German group. We were then told that we all had to go to Won-san to complete certain formal procedures, and were given an assurance that as soon as this was over we could return to the abbey at once. None of us was deceived by this barefaced lie. We shook hands for the last time with our Korean seminarians and monks, looking at one another with eyes filled with tears. A truck, well covered so as not to reveal to the public who was inside, was waiting for us, and when we were all on board it rolled down the abbey slope and sped—not to the parish of Won-san, but, at the commander's order, to the railway station.

(*Father Willibald Kugelmann*)

Devastation of Local Parishes, Won-san Parish

It was now about ten o'clock on the morning of May 10, 1949. Several Christians who had just come from Tŏk-won told me the news that the abbey was now surrounded by officials of the Political Security Bureau. I realized that the day of our own doom was also drawing near, but nothing happened on that day and night. Only one thing worried me; several high school teachers and college students, with books in their hands, kept walking up and down outside my parish church. On the evening of May 11, I called my workers to my room and distributed among them all the money I had in my possession, saying:

"Since I happen to have all this cash, I am going to pay you all several months' wages in advance."

The workers, of course, sensed my meaning. They wept and asked for my last blessing. I gave them each my blessing and asked them to give my best regards to all those fellow-Christians to whom I could not bid farewell in person.

Outside the parish church a young man and a young woman were ostensibly embracing each other and exchanging whispered words of love. With Father Placidus Neugirg I buried the books and documents belonging to the Church and the parish records that I thought would be useful if we could ever come back to this place. We thought of dispersing the vestments, clothing, and other valuables among the homes of the Christians, but gave up the idea because we realized that they might be a source of trouble to them, should their houses ever be searched by the Communists. I lay down on my bed at about ten o'clock at night, noticing that the young man and woman were still sitting outside. Their theatrical performance was really fine. However, I thought it must be rather difficult to keep watch on the enemy and pretend to make love at the same time.

Although I was lying down, I decided to keep awake for an hour or so. After a while the front of my house was lit up as if by a searchlight and there was the sound of a car coming round the curve of the road outside. There was a screech of brakes, and then the sound of my doorbell. I ignored it for a while, wishing to savor the last moments of my freedom, few though they might well be.

After a while I opened my bedroom window and looked down below. The young man and woman had moved round the corner. They were no longer arm-in-arm.

Their 'mission' was completed.

"Who is there? What's the matter?" I shouted.

Six men in plain clothes were standing below. Their leader called out in a friendly tone that they were sorry to trouble me at night, but they were from the Political Security Bureau. He asked me to open the door, as they wanted to make some inquiries. I knew I should have to go down and spend some time with them, but I didn't know that the affair was going to take five years.

I therefore came out of my upstairs bedroom and went downstairs to open the front door. At that very moment six men broke open the door and rushed toward me. The leader carried a pistol in his hand. They must have been afraid of us. He covered me with his gun and told me to wake up all my colleagues, and to hand over all the keys. With oriental courtesy I conducted them to my little office and asked them to be seated. Five of them sat down there, and one of them came upstairs with me, gun in hand. I woke up my colleagues one by one: Father Callistus Hiemer, Father Placidus Neugirg, and Brother Paschal Fangauer.

I handed over the keys to them, all except the key of the safe. I imagined their faces when they eventually managed to get it open and found nothing inside, not even a single copper coin. We boarded their car, and as we passed the convent I saw that it was brightly lit up too. There was an ambulance parked outside the main entrance. Evidently the Sisters were sharing the same fate as ourselves. The car that was carrying us off did not go to the police station, but took a quite different direction, and finally pulled up between the railway tracks beside a solitary white-curtained railway coach. The commander who had again drawn his gun ordered us to get on the coach, so up the steps we went. Ah! Inside were our colleagues from Tōk-won Benedictine Abbey! They told us they had been brought there half an hour before us. Twenty minutes later the door of the coach opened again, an, lo and behold, the white veils of our Sisters!

"*Deo gratias!*" We were not sure whether the Reverend Mother Superior was expressing her joy at being kidnaped or her delight at being with us again. From time to time the door was opened and shut during the night to admit new arrivals. Father Ku, a Korean, was the next to join us. Father Ku, who had come from Hoe-ryŏng several days before, had been conducting a retreat for the Sisters in Won-san. I had suggested to him that he stop the retreat and return home, but the Father had said that he would carry on regardless of the circumstances. I hadn't warned him when I woke the other Fathers, for he was in fact not under my roof, and I hoped to give him a chance to escape. But it seems he was picked up when he came to my house afterward while it was being searched, for he wanted to find out what had happened to us.

A fairly long time passed and then Bishop Sauer, who had been detained at the police station for three days, also came on board, with Father Roth, the prior; Father Schleicher, the subprior, Father Klingseis, and also Father Dagobert Engk, the administrator of the abbey, who had been detained for interrogation for the last five months. Everybody came forward to welcome them and exchange greetings mixed with joy and sorrow. It was indeed a deeply moving scene.

Next to arrive was Father Kunibert Ott and Father Knut of Ko-san parish, and then Father Josef Zenglein of Ko-won parish, with his catechist; Father Gregor Steger (Chŭn) of Yŏng-heung parish, with a male teacher who was a Catholic, and a woman catechist named Maria.

The train did not leave till eight in the morning, our coach coupled on to the end of a long train. Grim-looking guards came and opened the door of our coach for a moment: the buildings of Won-san were being left behind, and that church of mine that dominated the neighborhood from its little eminence. I took my last look at them and whispered a final benediction, behind the ring of grim-faced guards, to the citizens of Won-san and my faithful parishioners.

(*Father Fabian Damm*)

The Last Moment
At Won-san Benedictine Convent

So, you wish me to tell you about the last hours at the Won-san Convent? My hand trembles at the task: merely to recall the events of that last day makes me shudder and my eyes fill with tears. All that we had built up over twenty-five long years of sacrifice and toil crumbled to dust in a moment. The thought of the loss of our loved ones makes me choke with tears, yet even this is nothing in comparison to the ordeal I underwent when the Korean nuns were surrounding me and looking into my eyes for comfort and help in the terror and heartbreaking separation that lay before us. But I will do my best: like a faithful chronicler I will give an account of the events just as they occurred.

Some weeks before we were taken prisoner, our dispensary for needy patients seemed to have pose a problem, though indeed the problem had arisen as long ago as February, 1949, when the 'People's Government' sent a letter of commendation to Sister Fruktuosa in recognition of her devoted services to the destitute patients of Won-san City over a period of twenty-six years, and at the same time ordered that the dispensary be closed forthwith. Sister Diomedes, a medical doctor, who used to run a hospital in Ham-heung, was also forced to close it down, like us, and was placed under house arrest. On the night of May 7/8 I hurried to Ham-heung and consulted an influential person there to see what could be done, and find out if possible what future trouble to expect. On my way back on Tuesday, May 10, I gazed through the morning haze at the beautiful scene of the mission center, headquarters of the Brothers of the St. Ottilien Benedictine Monastery who had come to work with us, and my mind was filled with forebodings. Their fine church and monastery building had long been commandeered by the enemy, but the Brothers still stayed on peacefully, as if nothing had happened.

My first news of the trouble at Tŏk-won Abbey came from Siter Columba Park, our subprioress, as soon as I got off the train on my return from Ham-heung. She was greatly disturbed, and told me the details while we were on our why home together. We talked the matter over, but there was nothing we could do. I went through all my letters and destroyed them. After putting away a few robes, blessed rings and other things in a sale place we sat down and waited for what was coming.

I was prepared for my prospective arrest and so was Sister Fruktuosa, but neither of us imagined that we would all be expelled. Then it happened: on the night of either the tenth or the eleventh, as I lay asleep exhausted on my bed, I was awakened by the loud ringing of the doorbell. Struggling to keep calm I walked downstairs and called through the front door.

"Who is it?"

A voice from outside answered:

"We are from the Political Security Bureau, and you must come to the police station and answer a few questions. Open up! We also want to inspect the building."

I asked him to wait while I dressed. In a few moments the bell began ringing again. but I ignored it, and called all the nuns together to bid them farewell. Each of them had been told what to do in an emergency like the present, but none of use had imagined that we would all be suddenly expelled without warning.

No sooner had the bureau officials entered than they demanded all the keys and the visitors' book, so everybody in the house was summoned. (According to the new regulations enforced by the Communists, *every householder must report to the police any visitor staying overnight in his house*.) The register was checked and of course everything was found in order. The bureau officials then

separated the Korean nuns from us, and at that very moment there was the sound of heavy tramping outside the building. While we wondered if they were coming to drag us out of our home, the order was given: everyone must leave the building immediately, taking only a few personal belongings in a small bag.

Most of the nuns were extremely agitated and only half awake. We were about to leave, taking with us only the first things we could lay our hands on, when Sister Ambrosia came and whispered to me in tones of alarm:

"Mother! The Blessed Sacrament!"

I had almost forgotten the most important thing of all. How could we leave Our Blessed Lord behind? Rapidly making one excuse or another, we passed out through the vestry into the chapel, out of sight of the guards. As I searched for the key of the tabernacle I thought anxiously of the three hundred Hosts consecrated at Mass that morning. A last I found it. With trembling hands I took the pyx, the paten, and the lunette containing the Blessed Sacrament, (prepared for in sertion into the monstrance). I summoned all the nuns who vere walking about the house, evading the notice of the bureau officials, and we reverently consumed the Hosts.

"You said you'd only be gone a moment; what are you doing in there?" The voice came from outside the chapel door.

We were only just in time. As we emerged from the chapel after consuming the Hosts, we were met with a volley of abuse from the bureau officials, who drove us all out of the front door. Still, my mind was at rest. I did not mind losing my personal property.

Then there was a further delay. Sister Park collapsed with an agonizing heart attack. The cold-hearted officials cursed us again for holding up our departure. Some of the nuns carried her to the sick room and gave her what medical care they could. At this point one of the women soldiers who accompanied the bureau officials firmly barred their way into the sick room and stood on guard at the door.

Amid all this confusion Sister Eva, who was in charge of the needlework room and was anxious about the sewing work entrusted to us by a number of Russian women (work on which we relied for the greater part of our livelihood) went on calmly putting name tags on the garments so that they could be returned to their owners. This of course was done under the strict surveillance of the officials, who were deeply impressed with the exquisite needlework and fine sewing done by the nuns. We overheard words of praise passing between them, and surprise at the fact that the nuns who were capable of making such beautiful clothes for others should be content to wear such simple and austere clothing themselves. We had made a favorable impression on them at a critical moment, and they promised to return all the garments to their proper owners. Before I could complete my prayers for the safety of the Korean nuns and Sister Columba Park and bid them a heart-breaking farewell the whole house was plunged into turmoil as the bureau officials began herding everybody out and searching everywhere. Soon they began locking all the rooms one by one. We were finally driven out into the dark night without hope of return. Past the yard where the soldiers had been on guard duty, through the dispensary to which thousands of needy people used to come for relief from their sickness, and down to the main road we had to go.

A covered truck was waiting. As if afraid that the people in the neighborhood would hear what they were doing, they ordered us all to keep strict silence. When we had all got on the truck we found an official stationed in each corner, with pistols drawn.

The truck set off with a roar: we had lost our home. We were deprived of all we had built up but, far worse, separated from our loved ones who had shared our laughter and joy at the convent, and from those dear friends friends who used to frequent our house to be taught in the love and truth of God. Much later we were to learn that the Com-

munists first used our convent building as a hospital, but that later it was totally destroyed by bombing. That does not matter to us at all, for it can be rebuilt. When will our hopes be fulfilled and a new building rise on the site of the ruins?

(*Mother Gertrud*)

To P'yŏng-yang Prison

It was eight o'clock in the evening when our train drew up to P'yŏng-yang station. We had to wait about half an hour until all the passengers had got off and dispersed. High-ranking police officers and constables standing on the platform occasionally peeped in out of curiosity. The order to get off the train was given. The men prisoners were herded on to a covered truck like animals, and the one we were in bumped and jolted along the rough roads for quite a distance until it passed through a tunnel and finally drew up and sounded its horn in a long wail, as if to announce its arrival. We crawled out from under the canvas cover, and found ourselves standing in a courtyard surrounded by dark, grim-looking buildings on all sides. In the walls of the buildings were fairly large heavily-barred windows, and each building was surrounded by a fence about three or four meters in height. It was obvious where they had brought us.

Bishop Sauer and Father Rupert Klingseis were dragged off to some other place and confined separately. The rest of us checked in our few belongings, after which we were led along a corridor where three heavy iron gates stood side by side. They opened the first gate, counted off eighteen of us, and locked us up. As the bolt of the lock shot home with a loud click we became prisoners.

(*Father Willibald Kugelmann*)

Later Arrivals, Ham-heung Parish

Saturday, May 14, 1949
As parish priest of Ham-heung, I thought it best under the circumstances to take the

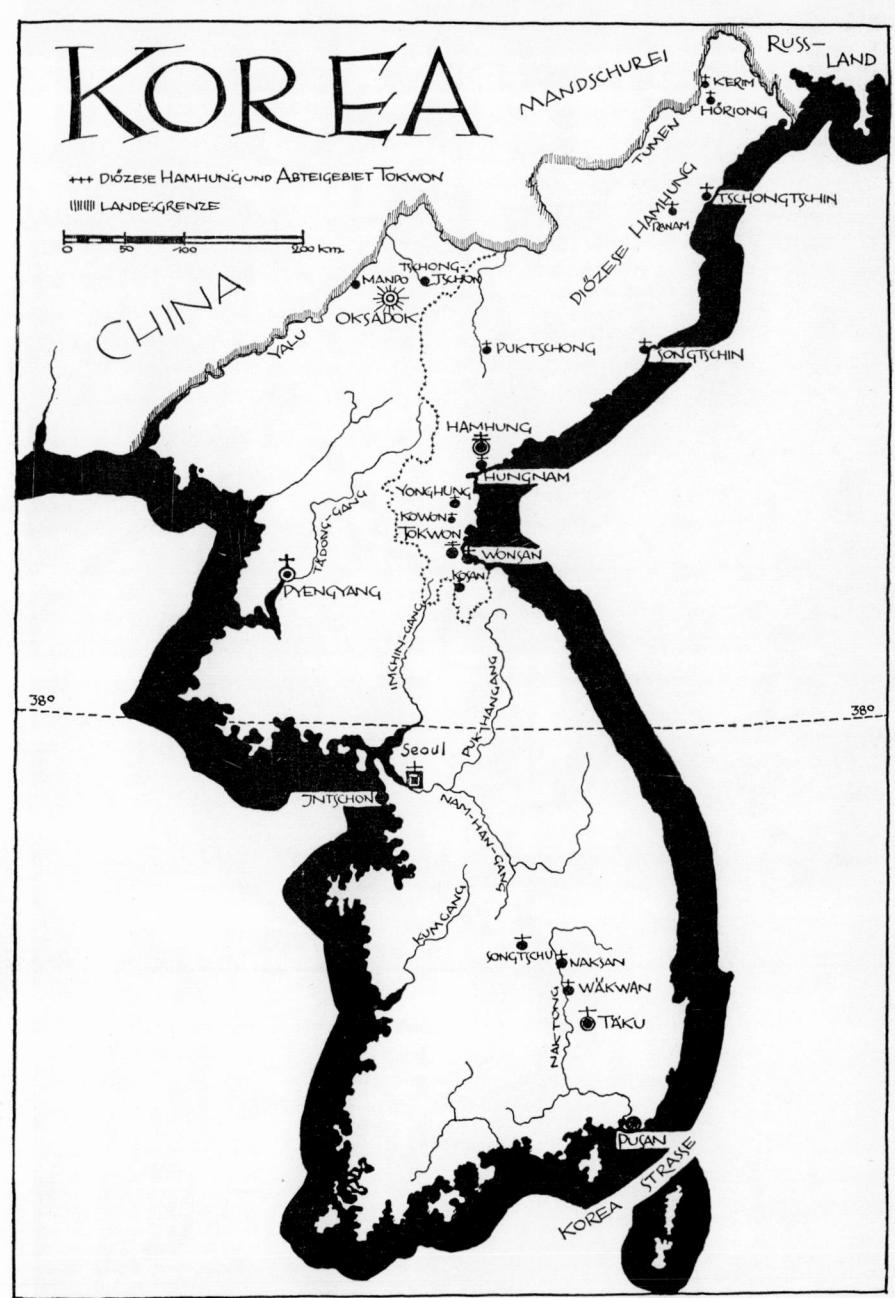

Map showing the route followed by the Benedictines of Tŏk-won during their persecution (from "Schicksal in Korea")

Ok-sa-tok Concentration Camp

Where many of the Benedictines of Tŏk-won suffered persecution and several met their death,

(from "Schicksal in Korea")

The Benedictine Abbey
at Tŏk-won

The devastated chapel of
Tŏk-won Abbey after the
Communists' incendiarism

The Communists set fire
to many Church buildings
when retreating

Bishop Sauer with priests and Brothers, Benedictine Abbey, Tŏk-won

Ordination ceremony conducted by Bishop Breher

Church of Puk-ch'ŏng

Ordination of graduates of Tŏk-won Seminary (1947)

Group of ordinands with Bishop Sauer at Tŏk-won Seminary

Father A. Romer (center) and Father Dagobert Enk (left) lost their lives during the ordeal in North Korea.

The late Father Anselmus Romer (front row, second from left) with colleague and seminarians

Survivors of the detention camp in North Korea
A photograph taken immediately after their release

Benedictines engaged in spreading the Gospel in the Wae-kwan mission field

precaution of removing the Blessed Sacrament from the church. I then went to see the Sisters in the convent, and conducted a brief service of benediction of the Blessed Sacrament in the chapel, after which I heard their confessions and offered up a prayer before the Sacrament, that we might be empowered by God's grace worthily to confront any danger that might befall us. I then administered Holy Communion to all of them.

Having urgent business to straighten out, I went home, and on my way met Dr. Bonifatius Kim, our hospital doctor, on his way back from the Political Security Bureau. The bureau chief had asked him, he said, whether the parish priest was aware of what had happened at Tŏk-won Abbey. He told the bureau chief that I was, and he was then told to deliver me a message of assurance from the bureau chief, to the effect that what had happened at Tŏk-won related only to the abbey, and that it had nothing to do with the parish in Ham-heung.

I passed this news on to the nuns and told them that they might be disturbed that night, at the same time warning them not to allow themselves to be deceived.

When I went to my room to go to bed it was ten o'clock. A little later, there were knocks at my door. Getting up to go to the window I saw that it was now eleven. I looked out of the window. There were loud shouts calling for the door to be opened. I ran to the next room and woke up my boy, Paul Kim, saying:

"I am on my way to jail."

As I opened the front gate six bureau officials stepped in. One of them drew his revolver. I showed them into the room and invited them to be seated.

"Father, you must come to the Political Security Bureau for a while. It won't take long and you needn't bring anything with you."

That was how they announced the purpose of their visit. Next they held a paper up to my eyes: it was a warrant for me to sign permitting them to search my house in my absence. I signed it for them, for I had

nothing to conceal. After that I returned to my room under escort in order to change into civilian clothes, and then followed them out. Past the parish churchyard the bureau officials took me to a place which was quite near by. There were all our nuns already assembled. They must have been arrested at the same time as I.

We were all loaded into a car together and taken to the headquarters of the Political Security Bureau.

"You people have been violating the law of the People's Republic of North Korea." The head of the Political Security Bureau greeted us with this remark.

"I am aware of no such thing," I countered.

"What do you say? Do you want me to give you a working over for a few days? Well, all right. We'll give you a day or two for you to think over what you have done."

The head said no more. From that time on I was separated from the nuns, and taken to another office, where the bureau officials were at work night and day. I was to spend days in this place, sitting on the same chair day in and day out. From time to time they would enter either to ask me a question or to make some insulting remark about religion or about our missionary activities. Sunday passed and the thought of my friendly parishioners crossed my mind. What would they think when they went to the Church on Sunday and found the gates firmly bolted? My parish workers, the man catechist and the woman catechist, what must have happened to them? Had they been taken prisoner too?

On Monday I was taken down the stairway of the bureau office. At that moment Father Gerold Fischer, who had been arrested on the same night as I, also appeared, and we were both put on board a train for P'yŏng-yang. We were not allowed to speak to each other. Utterly exhausted, I lay back against the cushion and silent tears streamed down my face.

"Ah! my Ham-heung! When shall I ever see my parish again?"

"Hey, don't cry. If you've done nothing

wrong you'll be sent back for sure."

A bureau official was standing beside me, trying to comfort me.

At about noon next day the train drew up to P'yŏng-yang station. It was May 17, 1949.

A small covered ca drew up alongside the train. We were to crawl quickly under the cover and not let outselves be seen by others.

Before long we were in the courtyard of a prison, where the bureau afficials came and led us into one of the surrounding buildions. There we surrendered all our personal belongings: it did not take long to do this, for all we had was a rosary, a belt, a hat and a pair of shoes. The jailors then came and led us to the cells. They pushed Father Fischer into one cell and me into another. Though appalled I made no attempt to argue with them but quietly greeted the Fathers, Brothers, and colleagues of Tŏk-won who were sitting on the floor. A reunion indeed, mixed with joy and sorrow! Once more we are together again, but in what a different place!

(Father Eligius Kohler)

On the Night of May 14, 1949

Missionary Fathers of Ham-heung and Heung-nam parishes arrested.

A friend from Won-san was surprised to find us totally unaware of the news. He told us that Tŏk-won Abbey had been occupied by the bureau officials since Monday, May 9, and that aow no one was allowed access to it.

It was not that we had not foreseer this very thirg, but when we heard it the news came as a great shock to us. And Won-san? The parish presbytery aïd the convent were seized during the night and the inmates taken prisoner without the knowledge of the laymen. And what was to become of us? It was Saturday night, and Father Eligius Kohler had already withdrawn the Blessed Sacrament from the parish church. After supper he came to our convent and held a service of benediction by Holy Communion. The prayers of Compline followed.

Concede, misericors Deus, fragilitate nosstrat praesidium..."

Divinum auxilium maneat semper nobiscum...."
(Grant us, O merciful God, protection in our weakness...

May the Divine aid be with us always...)
Father Kohler intoned the versicles, but ous voices were so tremulous that our responses were scarcely audible.

It was at about eleven that night, as I lay on my bed unable to sleep, when the door bell broke the silence with a shill sound that became louder and more insistent. I got up and opened the door, and about fifteen police officers swarmed in and filled small parlor.

"From onw on you people need not do any more talking here. We have orders from the Political Security Bureau to take you away."

They demanded all the keys of the building and ordered us to leave. Only after our repeated entreaties would they let us take a few toilet articles with us. Father Kŏhler. it seems, was arrested at the same time, and not allower to take either a Bible or a towel. Sister Elizabesh, a Kerean nun, begged to be allowed to accompany us but was told to stay at home. The police officers then locked up all the rooms and placed the building unPer attachment. Outside, while we were being loaded into two trucks, I saw Father Kohler. Under strict guard, we were taken to the headquarters of the Political Security Bureau, which was located in a building formerly belonging to the American Protestant mission. We were called out one by one and subjected to interrogation, some of us at considerable length and others more briefly. They demanded a list of the names of all who frequented our Church, but this we firmly declined to give them. We were then accused of operating a clandestine radio to communicate with the Vatican. A radio transmitter, they charged, had been set up in the basement of our parish church and was being used for communicating weth the Vatican for the eurpose of espionage, We denied this strenuously but they called us all liars.

Sisters Walburg Welte, Enatha Metzger, and Serva Spitzlei had to undergo interrogation for eight days, sitting on the chair until they were so exhausted that they had to lie down on the dirty floor. At this the brutes would torture them by ordering them to sit up, and the nuns could do nothing but try to obey the order and struggle to lift their exhausted bodies.

Sister Elizabeth and I received slightly better treatment on account of our illness: the two of us were allowed to sit on a wooden bench, but were kept apart from the other nuns.

For two weeks we were deprived of water for washing our faces. Kreszentia, the housekeeper of our parish presbytery, would bring us bread and jam from time to time, and we learnt that she was now cooking for the police officers living there. Occasionally she brought us each a glass of wine. Then the police officers would snatch it from her, gulp it down, and hand us the glass filled with water. Father Fischer was taken away to Heung-nam by car, leaving a message that, as he would be back by Saturday, he was not troubling to take the handbag containing his underwear and breviary.

We have not been able to find out what happened to Sister Imelda. There was a rumor that she was still detained at the bureau headquarters. After Fathers Fischer and Kohler were taken to P'yŏng-yang prison on May 18, where the Fathers and Brothers of Tŏk-won Abbey were imprisoned, four of us German nuns were taken to Hamheung prison and kept there apart from the other nuns for nearly two months.

When the rumor of our repatriation to Germany began to circulate, they came up with one condition: we must discard our Benedictine robes and wear ordinary clothes. We refused to listen, and when at length we set out on what they told us was the long journey home, it turned out that our destination was actually P'yŏng-yang prison. This time, fortunately, we were not kept in solitary confinement, but were all in one cell.

Three days later the steel door was suddenly flung open during the night, and figures could be made out in the darkness.

Our joy on learning that they were none other than our own colleagues from Wonsan and Ko-san made us forget for the moment the predicament we were in.

(*Sister Bertwina*)

In P'yŏng-yang Prison

The foregoing pages recount the circumstances in which we all became confined in P'yŏng-yang prison. We were accommodated in separate wards, each of which was occupied by eighteen persons. We were forced to sit crouched in rows on the bare wooden floor and were subjected to merciless treatment, for we were forbidden to move and the constraint, continued day after day, caused us an excruciating pain in the legs.

The Male Ward

The ward or cell in which eighteen persons had to live had a floor space of only eight square meters, which meant that we could not lie down on our backs to sleep and had to lie on our sides. If any one wanted to turn from one side to another during the night, he had to wake up every one else so that they could shift themselves to let him move.

The ceiling of the cell was very high. A massive padlock hung on the heavy barred door. Through the barred window high up in the wall came a little fresh air and, at night time, a glimpse of the stars.

Meals were brought regularly three times a day and consisted of steamed bread made from millet, and beans cooked without seasoning. They were served in dishes filled in the kitchen so that every inmate could get an equal share. When every one had been supplied, the jailor would bring round a dirty bucket of soup, and distribute a dipperful to each person. In this hot and salty soup there would be bits of potato peelings, cabbage leaves and chunks of turnip or radish.

As soon as the soup was poured out the jailor would order us to finish the meal quickly, sometimes screaming with rage at us as we struggled to swallow the scalding liquid.

"Hurry up! Other prisoners are waiting for their dinner!" he would shout.

As soon as the meal was over, three or four dipperfuls of water would be supplied for all eighteen of us to rinse our mouths, and as there was so little of it we had to ration it carefully.

We were allowed 240 grams of food a day in addition to the soup. At first we found the food so revolting that we couldn't eat it, but as time went by hunger made us change our opinion of it, and it was not long before we eagerly awaited the welcome sound of the food pails clattering along the corridor. We were all amazed at the speed with which we gobbled up our food.

So often did we complain of hunger that about halfway through the period of our detention they increased our allowance to 400 grams a day.

The spring season does not last long in Korea and by the middle of May it was already uncomfortably hot. Sitting jammed together in our cell we were kept busy wiping the sweat from our bodies day and night, and we almost suffocated. Though we wore only shirt and trousers we were dripping with sweat and we suffered greatly from thirst. The three or four dipperfuls of water supplied after meals for eighteen men seemed no more than a few drops of rain on thirsty soil. Though we begged for more, the jailors would only shout,

"No water!"
and slam the lid on the peephole in the door. Very often we could hear the sound of running water in the corridor at the very time that the jailor was shouting that there wasn't any, but as prisoners we had no choice but to make the best of it.

Among our jailors were some who took a perverse pleasure in tormenting us, and who would hurl insults and curses at us through the peephole as if they were handling untamed animals. Yet it is only fair to say that some among them were good-hearted.

On Sunday, a week after we had been thrown into the prison, we heard a church bell ringing, and we realized that the Korean Fathers were still able to continue their work in the city of P'yŏng-yang. Without any altar we were able to attend the Mass being offered by the Korean Father in the church near by: one of the priests in our cell read a dry Mass, that is to say, he read the Canon of the Mass, and when he came to the consecration, and the elevation in his text we would all turn our attention to the Church near by, to pay our tribute to Christ the King, and, at the reading of the Communion, we did our best to make a spiritual communion.

On several occasions the iron gate squeaked open and a recently-arrested Korean priest was thrown in among us. In this way we learnt several items of news about the other priests. We heard, too, that our abbey had been confiscated immediately after our arrest and was now completely in the hands of the Communists. Next, news was brought that Bishop Francis Hong, a Korean, had also been arrested, and that the Korean priests in all the parishes in North Korea had probably been rounded up by this time. This would be a great blow to the Church in North Korea.

Among the Korean Fathers sharing our confinement was Father Matthias Ch'oe (Pyŏng-kwon). He had long been stricken by tuberculosis, and two years previously had undergone an appendectomy. The scars of the operation had not yet healed completely, and pus could still be pressed out freely. Unfortunately we had nothing with which to dress the wound, but after repeated appeals we at last managed to get some toilet paper which we applied over the festering sore. As he was also suffering from semi-starvation the Father grew weaker day by day, but the merciless jailors only reviled him with curses and would not permit him to lie down, but compelled him to sit up straight just like everybody else. In his extreme pain he would often faint, or else scream and cry out in delirium. I read to him the prayer for the dead and gave him Absolution. Afterward there were times when he seemed to be getting a little better, but he was indeed unfortunate, for most of the time he really seemed to be suffering a prolonged agony of death.

The next to come was Father Benedict Kim, a member of the Benedictine abbey. This Father was also a tuberculosis patient and had only one lung to breathe with. In the foul air of the jail he had great difficulty in breathing and his affliction caused him to snore loudly in his sleep, which kept the other inmates awake at night, though no one dared to wake him up. We made repeated petitions to the authorities to have the tuberculous patients removed to hospital, or at least to another ward, for their own sakes as well as ours, but they would not listen to us.

Father Neugirg was suffering from a sore on his neck, and since there was nothing better that we could do, we dressed it with strips of cotton cloth.

Father Willibald Kugelmann had erysipelas with inflammation of the skin of his face and head. Only after days of begging did they finally consent to remove these two to another ward.

Our spiritual Father, Bishop Sauer, was confined in a small cell with Father Gabriel Frömmer. The Bishop was stripped of his golden pectoral cross. His asthma grew worse as the days wore on: he could neither sit nor lie down. The jailors, to their credit, seemed to sympathize with him in his misery, and gave him a wooden chair to sit on. The cracks of this chair were teeming with bed bugs, but it was nevertheless of great help to the sick man. He remained seated on this chair day and night, without eating or sleeping. We tried to get them to give us some milk for him, but without success. All he could take was a few spoonfuls of millet soup. To add to his sufferings, he was frequently summoned before the authorities and subjected to prolonged interrogation which left him completely exhausted. Being prisoners ourselves we could do nothing to alleviate his agony and could only remain helpless and tortured with anxiety on his behalf.

One of the nobler spirits among the jailors came to us and, noticing the plight of the Bishop, remarked that he might be liberated fairly soon. Thereafter he would from time to time convey his greetings to the Bishop, with a kindly message of good wishes.

After three months of prison life, we were all haggard and emaciated. What, we wondered, would be our end? Freedom? Transfer to another prison? Repatriation? A firing squad?

Trembling with terror and anxiety we simply kept on praying and awaited the will of God.

Occasionally the ranking jailor would make his rounds, and look at us through the barred peephole, as if to see whether we prisoners were still alive, but he never spoke to us. During a protracted interrogation one night, Father Roth, the Abbot of Tŏk-won Abbey, protested that as human beings we should not be treated like pigs. He suggested that they might as well shoot him and free all the others for he alone was exclusively responsible for the Vicariate, but they paid no attention to his words.

Many of us were frequently called out in the dead of night for interrogation, but at no time was any specific accusation made against us, and often we were not even questioned, for there was nothing that could be held against us.

At the beginning of June, Brother Eusebius Lohmeier, an architect, was called out of the ward. He was asked to design a building suitable for about sixty Occidentals to occupy. As the conversation took place in the corridor outside our ward, we were able to overhear much of it, and we came to the conclusion that we would soon be transferred to some other jail. We longed for this to come true, for our constant wish was to get out of this pit.

On June 21, 1949 the door of the ward

opened with a loud crash; the monks were ordered out, in stentorian tones. On emerging from the ward they were allowed to move about freely in the corridor, and also to speak to one another. They were all busy in recovering their belongings, and handing small sums of money to the jailors for the purchase of daily necessities. The priests however were not to enjoy this liberty, though we were glad we had more room now. The Brothers were now able to put into our wards various small articles that they had had the jailors buy for them; we were especially glad of several vests they sent in, for we had not been able to change our underwear for a long time. The Brothers also pushed in through the window bars a small rice bowl in which a number of rosaries had been placed. Of course, we carefully hid all the things which we received. We learned later that the rosaries all came from the Brothers' luggage.

On June 24, the feast of the Sacred Heart of Jesus, all the Brothers were taken out of the prison and carried away. We ran to the window and gazed at them through the bars. Ah! that sad parting! Where were the Brothers being taken? Since we knew that there was usually a train for Kang-kye, near the North Korean-Manchurian border, that left P'yŏng-yang Station in the evening, we surmised that our Brothers were being transported to some concentration camp in that region.

Late at night, several days later, a Korean catechist from the parish of Kang-kye, who had also been arrested and brought to this prison, managed to enter our ward. He told us in a low voice that he had heard from several persons the news that a large number of foreigners had been brought to a valley high up in the mountains near Kang-kye, and that they were put to work there. We guessed that these must be our Brothers who had been removed from this prison, and wished that we might be sent there too, so that we might be with them.

I should like to put on record that in spite of all the hardships we had undergone, we never lost our peace of mind. Though so closely confined in this small ward of P'yŏng-yang prison, our Father in Heaven knew what was happening to us, and we knew that we were in His hands.

The door of our ward was opened again on July 24, and we were called out by name, except for those of us who had previously been removed to another ward. From this time on the door was left open at all times, though we were not allowed to move about freely in the corridor as the Brothers had been. We felt that our lot had been somewhat alleviated, for the ventilation of our ward was now greatly improved and we could all breathe more comfortably, and our spirits rose at the thought that this slight amenity might be the first step to our eventual liberation. Furthermore, talking was now permitted, provided that we did not raise our voices, and this was also a great relief to us. The faces of the inmates now began to take on a more pleasant and cheerful expression; so much so, in fact, that the jailors must have been surprised at the change in our demeanor. The jailors were now willing to purchase daily necessities for us, though of course our funds were very limited and we could not send out for as many things as we would have liked. One of the first things we asked them to get for us was potatoes, and the next, on the following day, was tomatoes. Oh, those first potatoes! I wish I could find words to describe their delicious flavor: it seemed to us that we had never perceived the true excellence of the humble potato until then, after being restricted for so long to rice and salt water. On the third day we were able to send out for eggs.

One of our jailors was kind enough to take some of these newly purchased delicacies to our Bishop and to the seven Fathers and Brothers who were still under strict confinement. This jailor had a soft spot in his heart for our old Bishop, and always referred to him as 'Grandfather Priest,' and we were all glad that through his kind act we were able even in such a small way to alleviate the lot of our Bishop and our fellow priests.

Only now were we definitely told what had become of the Brothers who had been taken away. The jailors announced that they were now in a remote mountain valley, where they had been hard at work in a detention camp, building houses for us to live in, and now that the houses were ready, we would soon be going to join them. We could hardly bear to wait for the day of our departure, and day and night we eagerly looked forward to its coming

We did not leave, however, until the evening of August 5. Glad as we were to get out of the prison, we could not but feel sad at the thought of abandoning our Bishop and fellow priests. Bishop Bonifatius Sauer, Father Lucius Roth, Father Rupert Klingseis, Father Dagobert Engk, Father Gregor Steger, Brother Josef Grahamer, Brother Gregor Giegerich and Ludwig Fischer had to remain in confinement because in the eyes of the Communists their guilt was greater. For several days they were not allowed out of their ward, but we, with our newly-gained freedom, were able to make surreptitious visits to them. From the Mass bag we took out the Holy Chrism and handed it to Father Frömmer so as to enable him to administer Extreme Unction to the Bishop, whose debility had now reached such an advanced degree as to make this necessary.

As we bade them farewell, they responded with tears in their eyes. "Please be at ease, for you will soon be coming to join us," we said.

We tried to comfort them, but our hearts ached beyond description.

We gave them our blessings through the prison bars, and tore ourselves away. That was the last we saw of them, and though we repeatedly entreated the authorities to send them to us, or at least give us news of them, they always refused.

It was only after our return to Germany in January, 1954, that we learnt of the death of Bishop Sauer and Father Klingseis in prison, on February 7, 1950 and April 6, 1950, respectively. We still do not know whether the remaining six persons are dead or alive, but it is feared that they may have been shot by the Korean Communists during the retreat of the North Korean People's Army in October, 1950.

(Father Eligius Kohler)

The Women's Prison

On alighting from the cars after our journey we found that we were in the courtyard of a dark and gloomy prison. Since our dear Fathers and Brothers were not to be seen, we feared that we were now separated from them for good. After going through a number of tedious and vexatious formalities in connection with our entry into the prison, we were ordered to take off the veil and the dress characteristic of our religious order. We complied with the order to remove our veils, but firmly refused to give up wearing our Benedictine habits, and after that they let us continue to do so.

We were locked in cells, with five of us in each cell. The floor was dark brown and filthy with grime, and on it were laid some straw mats. The only object in the cell was a chamberpot, which gave out an offensive smell. In this cell we were to spend eighty-six days.

At first sight everything seemed frightful: it looked the sort of place where one might expect a horrible ghost to appear, and we feared that it would soon drive us mad. The woman-warders at first believed that we were all guilty of some shocking crime, and treated us with great reserve, but after the first few painful weeks had passed, they began to sympathize with us, and did not scold us without due cause. At times they were even willing to assist us with small services, even though these were no part of their duty and might even get them into trouble. They were astonished at our cheerful and playful behavior.

We often sang songs and laughed when we were not observed, and it was safe to do so. Of course, this sort of thing was an infraction of prison regulations, but we were often able to enjoy this small pleasure in secret. Moreover, we were able to find out things which we were not supposed to know, for there was a small crack in the wall through which we could see and hear something of what was going on in the prison. We learnt that there were five of our Sisters in the adjoining cell, and openly exchanged words with them. By relaying messages from that cell to the one on the opposite side we could keep ourselves informed of most of the official news. This went on for about six weeks without arousing the suspicions of the authorities, so I finally felt enough self-confidence to ask for an interview with the warden of the prison. He willingly allowed me to speak to him during what was called 'the education hour,' and I asked him on what grounds we were being detained. This, however, he was either unable or unwilling to explain, but I was successful in getting a partial relaxation of the stringent regulations and from then on we were permitted to move about inside our cells, and to take a nightly walk in the corridor, which was about fifty meters long. I also obtained permission to visit the Sisters in the other cells, which pleased me more than anything else, for I was thus enabled to see our Sisters from Ham-heung, from whom I had feared that we were entirely separated. Learning that they were in good spirits and keeping their courage up, I felt as gratified as a mother superior returning from a satisfactory inspection of her convent. Our concern for our Korean Sisters, however, remained with us.

The warden of the prison even let me know that we were to be sent to a detention camp before very long. Preparations for the move being completed we were taken to the railway station in covered cars, and there we met most, but not all, of our priests, though with their long hair and beards, and their pale and emaciated faces, it was hard for us to tell them apart at first glance. Only after looking at their faces carefully from various angles could we finally manage to recognize who was who.

(Mother Gertrud)

News Heard By Those Who Stayed Behind

On May 11, 1949, the Political Security Bureau officials left, taking with them on two trucks a total of 34 persons, comprising 8 German priests, 22 German monks, and four Korean priests. Only the Korean monks remained. Some of these latter, unable to repress their sorrow, cried out,

"Take us too, rather than separate us!"

One of the Brothers frankly expressed this desire to the Political Security Bureau officials, who answered,

"We are not so wicked as to arrest innocent men! We have come to liberate you from your exploiters, and you should be thankful."

Such brazen impudence of their part disgusted us so much that we didn't feel like speaking to them any more, though of course we had to obey their orders. They announced that we were to be expelled from the abbey which was our home.

Next morning all twenty-six of the Brothers who had been left behind were ordered to the neighboring seminary and confined there, together with the seminarians, for three days. In spite of all that had happened we still cherished our hopes of being able to continue our monastic life, and packed our Benedictine habits and prayer books in our bags. But we were disappointed, for before we left the Political Security Bureau officials inspected our luggage very thoroughly, and confiscated all clothing except underwear.

We had next to make out written personal statements giving particulars regarding name, place of birth, motive in entering the monastery, family circumstances, number of years spent in religious life, our intended destination and plans for our future. After the luggage inspection and the personal statements were completed we were all mustered together with the seminarians outside the porch, carrying only parcels containing articles of daily use. The party, numbering about a hundred persons, stood waiting under the keen eyes of the bureau officials.

" *Trium puerorum cantemus hymnum*....① Let us sing the Canticle of the Three Young Men, which these holy ones sang in the fiery furnace, giving praise to the Lord," began a seminarian, and instantly every one of us joined in with a loud ringing voice as if it were a preconcerted thing. As the plangent words rang out in majesty the keen cold eyes of the bureau officials seemed affected with emotion. Some of them bowed their heads and looked at the ground while others had a faraway look in their eyes as they gazed up at the sky.

On finishing the Canticle we marched in single file, led by the seminarians toward the monastery chapel. We could not simply pass it by, but each halted momentarily, bowing his head towards the tabernacle, even though the Blessed Sacrament was no longer there, and prayed for Our Lord's protection for ourselves and for the abbey which had been our home for so long, and where we had been brought up. We then proceeded toward the main road.

It was a tragic sight to see these deeply serious people suppressing their sorrow and setting out on a journey of unknown destination, each carrying his small package of personal belongings. Only one of the members of the group of Political Security Bureau officials that accompanied us showed any signs of sympathy for our plight.

We found the main road lined with the Christians of the neighborhood who had gathered there, with tears in their eyes, to bid us farewell. Weeping and embracing us, they begged us to spend the night at their homes. They were overwhelmed with grief at the thought of losing the Fathers and Brothers who had been their shepherds and guardians. They well knew that it was these Fathers and Brothers who had come to this obscure village thirty years before to preach the Gospel; and who had changed the desolate area around Tŏk-won into fertile fields

and covered the barren hills with forests, and had thus made Tŏk-won into a model farm village for the whole country of Korea; who had moreover built schools for the children of poor families, supplied medicine to the sick, and who had built a home for the aged.

But we could no longer remain there. We began to disperse, some leaving for Won-san and others for various places in the neighborhood of Tŏk-won.

The Communists who lived in the village near the abbey and had been engaged in systematic defamation and slander in the hope of destroying our good name now appeared to be sorry for what they had done, and looked at us with eyes of sympathy and grudging admiration.

With no definite plan in mind, I first went to the railway station. For most of the seminarians it was no great problem, for their homes lay north of the Thirty-eighth Parallel, but the monks who hailed from the other side of the Parallel were really at a loss where to go. If we had had money enough, we could have stayed for a time at an inn to make plans for our future, But the money that Father Dagobert Engk, the procurator, had distributed to us was only a small sum, barely sufficient to cover our traveling expenses.

My week's detention had prevented me from learning what had been going on in the outside world. First of all I had to find out what had happened to the parish and the convent at Won-san.

It was just as I had expected: the convent was deserted. I arranged for a fellow-monk to remain in Won-san to take care of affairs on our behalf, and decided to proceed to P'yŏng-yang.

On the Sunday following the arrest of Bishop Sauer I took a train for P'yŏng-yang, and, as the train was passing by our abbey, I saw bureau officials drive a loaded truck up the steep path to the abbey, and then drive back in an empty one.

---

① Daniel 3: 57 88, 56,

On the first day of my stay in P'yŏng-yang I read the Communists' account of evidence they said they had found in our abbey to prove what crimes had been committed in its precincts prior to its confiscation.

The accusations they had fabricated were numerous.

First, they said, the abbey printing shop had been used for the printing of reactionary handbills and other publications:

Second, secret meetings with reactionary leaders had been held in the parlor of the abbey:

Third, the nuns had held reactionary meetings in the crypt of the abbey:

Fourth, bombs to be used in an uprising were concealed in the crypt:

Fifth, a short-wave radio transmitter had been installed for purposes of international espionage.

In addition, I heard the following talk, which I thought might be based on fact:

In his detestation of the Communist Party, its principles and its practice, one of our seminarians had organized an informal, clandestine league with several others of like mind, and had printed the reactionary handbills in our printing shop. This was known only to the seminarian and to no one else in the abbey. I learnt further details: the whole affair was the work of an *agent-provocateur* working for the Political Security Bureau.

As an excuse for their confiscation of the abbey, they fabricated and made public a scandal about the so-called illegal brewing of liquor in the monastery. That attempt had proved a failure, so the Political Security Bureau then had one of their number disguise himself as an agent from South Korea and persuade South Korean sympathizers in the village near the abbey to join with him in his activties. It was he, in fact, who had associated with the young men described as "reactionaries" and who had instigated the printing of the handbills in order to provide the Communists with a pretext which they could put forward as their professed excuse

for confiscating the abbey, and to hide from the public the real purpose of their expropriation of the abbey and the abbey lands.

What I wanted most to find out was the whereabouts of the Fathers and Brothers who had been arrested in May. There were plenty of rumors, of course, but none of them reliable. Fortunately, however, I was able to obtain authentic information, to the following effect:

1. There were Germans engaged in farming in Cha-kang Province, a new province which had been constituted by the North Korean People's Government, by merging a part of the North Province of P'yŏng-an with a part of the South Province of Ham-kyŏng.

2. A Red officer of the People's Army confirmed that there were Germans in Cha-kang Province.

3. An ox-cart driver from Cha-kang Province also confirmed this information. According to him there were foreigners in Cha-kang Province who were doing hard labor in a remote coal mine among the mountains. These foreigners spoke Korean very fluently, and were "awaiting the days of their death"

I accordingly sent a woman catechist there to find out more about the matter. She returned several weeks later and reported to me as follows:

She had heard from a trustworthy Korean in Kang-kye that there were Westerners engaged in farming near the Pyŏl-ha Railway Station. She visited Pyŏl-ha and very cleverly met with her acquaintances there without arousing suspicion. What she learnt from them was to the following effect:

On proceeding from the Pyŏl-ha Railway Station beyond the reservoir one can see a steep hill surrounded by fertile fields. One day in July last year, when the corn was ripening, more than forty foreigners, both men and women, who had been in prison, were brought there. The area was now placed under strict surveillance, and only registered Communist Party members were allowed to enter it. The country people of that neighborhood had to submit reports of their reasons for living there. This place where our Fathers and Brothers were detained was called "the Pyŏl-ha Special Reformatory".

The Pyŏl-ha Special Reformatory

There was a countryman who had been there and seen the place. He had been ordered there by the authorities to work at weeding the fields there, and had seen with his own eyes how the foreign men and women lived. He gained the impression that though the men worked together with the women, they were not men and wives. They were all clad in long black clothes, and he noted with special interest that at meal times they all gathered and made certain signs with their hands in front of their faces before sitting down to eat. Two of them had died, one of old age and the other of stomach trouble brought on by eating wild berries.

At first, he went on, these people had had no houses to live in, but little by little they built houses for themselves. Several of these foreigners had gone deep into the mountains to gather mushrooms, and had lost their way. After several days they finally managed to find their way home, almost dead with hunger.

Upon hearing this news I made up my mind to send a letter secretly to them next spring, when the time for weeding came round again, through the hands of my new friend, but unavoidable circumstances caused me to give up this plan and come to South Korea across the Thirty-eighth Parallel.

What was on my mind was the fact that it was proving impossible for me to obtain authentic information as to our Bishop's whereabouts, or even whether he was alive or not. During those days rumors were circulating that the Bishop had died of some disease near Ham-heung while on his way to Siberia for transportation to his homeland. The rumors however stemmed from a report published in a Russian newspaper.

I was able to keep in touch with our fellow-monks in P'yŏng-yang prison by letters, but for obvious reasons I cannot disclose how this was effected. I thus managed to confirm, almost miraculously, that our Bishop was still alive in the prison, though seriously ill. With my letter I also sent some medicine for the treatment of his asthma, which reached him safely. The Bishop was delighted. It is unnecessary to emphasize that the persons who cooperated to make my scheme work did so at the risk of their life. Besides the Bishop there were seven others detained in the prison. According to the records of the trial which was held later, Father Roth, the abbot, was sentenced to seven years' imprisonment for crimes against the new state, while the other Fathers and Brothers were sentenced to prison terms of five years each. The crimes that were imputed to them were that the Bishop and the abbot "had viciously violated the laws of the state" that Brother Ludwig Fischer had failed to report to the authorities on the clandestine printing, though he was responsible for the management of the printing shop; that Father Dagobert Engk, who was responsible for the accounting side, was involved in the illegal brewing of liquor, while Father Gregor Steger, the parish priest of Yŏng-heung, had taught a theory refuting atheism. Father Rupert Klingseis, professor of philosophy, was found guilty of the crime of writing an anti-Communist booklet, entitled 'Is the Human Soul Material or Spiritual?' Brother Josef Grahamer, who was a doctor, was charged with causing grievous bodily harm to a nurse by beating, while Brother Gregor Giegerich, who was a truck driver, was found guilty of possessing a faked driver's licence.

(*Father Beda Kim*)

Life in the Detention Camp

It was on the evening of August 5, 1949 that we were taken away from P'yŏng-yang prison. At about one o'clock in the afternoon of August 6, our train stopped at the small railway station of the Ch'ŏng-ch'ŏn-kang.

We got off the train and walked for a while along the side of the railway embankment. We then boarded a ferry and cross-ed a river, and began climbing up a long mountain path under the hot August sun. On our way whenever we got too tired to go any further we sat down to rest, regardless of whether the guards approved or not. There was nothing to be done, however, except press on to our destination. Though weary, we pulled ourselves together and went on climbing until we came to the final resting place at about four in the afternoon. There we saw a small thatched cottage right before our eyes, on the peak of the mountain, and were told that this was our new detention camp. Several of the Brothers who had pre-ceded us came running down the hill toward us. They hugged us and greeted us with joy, relieved us of our little baggage and conducted us to our final destination.

When we arrived, the Brothers told us of the hardships they had undergone since their departure. They expressed their delight at our being reunited again in one place. They had arrived on June 25, and their life in the camp had been miserable, and had reduced them all to extreme debility. What with the poor food and the hard labor under a hot sun, they had come to feel that they would almost prefer to go back to P'yŏng-yang pris-on and live there. Their legs were swollen almost to the size of those of elephants; more and more of them fell ill, and on July 3 Brother Petrus Gernert had gone to Heaven. He had been thoroughly worn out by over-work and malnutrition, and had passed away during a coma. Brother Markus Metzger who used to be in charge of the laundry and housecleaning in the old days in Tŏk-won died on August 3. How he had longed for the Fathers to come to the detention camp!

As the health of the Brothers was deterio-rating day by day, the Political Security Bureau had sent Sister Diomedes, a physi-cian, and Sister Friedhelma, a nurse from the P'yŏng-yang prison, to this camp to render help to the Brothers, but the Sisters had been unable to obtain the medicine and nourish-ing food necessary for the proper treatment of the patients.

The place where the camp was situated was officially called Ch'on-ch'on, but the ori-ginal name of the hillside village was Ok-sa-tok, and this is the name by which we al-ways referred to it. Our camp was located in a little dell or basin high up in the moun-tains, with a little valley leading down from the camp to the plain. North Korea con-tains huge areas of primitive forest.

Since the place where we were to live was completely surrounded by high moun-tains, the Communists must have thought of it as a suitable place for the segregation of such dangerous criminals as ourselves. Dotted around the mountain sides were nu-merous small fields which had been cultivat-ed from time immemorial, and, surrounding them, high lawns and woods. A clear stream ran down through the valley wherein our new home lay, and we felt it fitting to in-augurate our residence by assembling for evening prayer and thanksgiving. We joined in singing, at the top of our voices, a can-ticle in honor of Our Lady, a thing we had not been able to do since we had left the monastery. Our first plea to the Blessed Virgin Mary on our arrival in our new home was expressed in this song.

"O Maria, help us in this valley of sighs!"

This was our first plea for help from the Blessed Virgin since we came to our new home.

August 7 was a Sunday. In the morning we donned once again our Benedictine habits which we had been carrying with us, al-though not all of us had been permitted to do so. For the first time in three months we said Mass in a small house named St. Placi-dus's. We knelt down on straw during the Mass, and there was an inspiring sermon preached by Father Schleicher, the prior of our monastery, who had been our leader during our imprisonment, and who had been appointed by Bishop Sauer. He exhorted us to make the hill to which we had climbed to build our new camp a means to heavenly glory, in spite of all poverty, exile, and physical suffering.

After breakfast a lieutenant-colonel, who

had come from P'yŏng-yang on a visit to the camp, delivered an address to us. He said that we must exert all our efforts to transform this mountain valley into a new Garden of Eden. We were, he said, neither criminals nor convicts, and were innocent of any evil acts. Our standpoint, however, in forming our 'world view' was incompatible with that of the North Korean People's Republic, and the government, therefore, had no choice but to isolate us from society. We would have to support ourselves by our own efforts, and also to live by ourselves in seclusion. He said that he could not say whether we would have to stay here six months, or a year, or even five or ten years.

Living Conditions:
Clothing, Food and Shelter

From August 8, 1949 all of us, priests, monks and nuns, began to work together. One group was assigned to weed our fields so that they might yield an abundant crop for our support. Another group was assigned to build more houses for us to live in during the coming winter, for at that time only three houses had been completed; a newly-thatched one remodeled from an old barn, which we named St. Placidus's, an old farmhouse which we named St. Maurus's, and a newly-completed building, thatched with ricestraw, occupied by the Sisters, which they named St. Gertrude's.

Autumn set in early, with chilly nights, and we found the floor very cold to sleep on. A new amenity was our refectory, a simple mess-hall in which, seated along the walls of the room, we could have our meals served by the cook from the center of the room, instead of having to eat them outdoors as we had done up to then. In conformity with our Benedictine rule, we appointed a lector to read to us at mealtimes passages from the Bible or other religious books which the Brothers had been able to slip into their pockets at the time of our arrest.

Major Chang, the warden of our detention camp, was a good-hearted military officer,

who never maltreated us, but readily approved our suggestions for the improvement of our lot. Each of us put in eight hours of work for the community every day. At mealtimes we assembled in the yard and each received a bowlful of thick porridge made from maize, millet and soybeans (i.e., a bowl of hot cereal, made from corn, broom corn, and soybeans) and in addition a bowl of vegetables. The food always tasted delicious, and we came to the conclusion that if they were going to treat us with as much consideration as we were now receiving, then detention camp held no terrors for us. How much better off we were now, working in the fresh air, and enjoying country life, than shut up in those filthy cells of P'yŏng-yang jail, where we had been compelled to squat down immobile and silent as dummies, with hardly room to move!

It was not until mid-November that we could get St. Placidus's, St. Maurus's and St. Gertrude's houses made completely weatherproof, and complete our new kitchen, which we named the 'The Help of Mary'; to this we added an annex to be used as a sick ward. We also constructed pigsties and a cowshed, and another small house for the Brothers, all three buildings standing in a row, side by side.

Spiritual Life

One of the rooms in St. Gertrude's, the Sisters' house, was used as a chapel. A simple wooden altar was set up, and we heard Mass every morning, each Father officiating in turn, while the congregation sat on the floor. The sliding doors between the Sisters' rooms were all kept wide open during Mass, so as to provide room for everybody.

We were delighted to find a fair proportion of wheat grains in the sacks of maize that were issued to us. We sifted them out carefully and ground part into flour in a small stone hand mill. Being whole-meal flour it was not quite white, but it definitely was wheat flour, and as fine as that used for making Hosts. The remaining part we were able to sow, and we grew a small patch of wheat each year so that we should not run out of flour for making hosts. In addition we gathered wild grapes and pressed out their juice by hand; this juice we allowed to ferment and made into wine for the Mass.

Our daily morning Mass was a source of great comfort and strength to us, and gave us the fortitude and confidence to bear all the hardships of our detention camp life with quietness and equanimity.

(Father Eligius Kohler)

Labor

There were of course no level roads in the mountainous region where we lived, nor was any of them paved. There were only steep winding pathways full of uneven rocks, and for this reason a cart was useless. We had a hard-working old draught-ox, which was used to draw a kind of sled up and down the steep paths. That was why some of us used to say that our detention camp was a place where one could ride sleds in summer.

Spring came, and by mid-May our work in the fields got under way with the spring sowing. We were told that in this region it was usually still too chilly at this time of the year to start putting in seeds, and indeed there had been a fall of snow during this season in the previous year.

At five each morning the guards came with loud cries of *palli, palli* (Hurry up! Hurry up!) to rouse us from our beds. We had to get to work quickly. First of all, we had to hang wooden trays from our necks, and fill these trays with manure. With backs bent almost double we made our way to the fields, and, digging small holes along the furrows left by the plough, inserted manure in them, and then placed a few seeds in each hole and covered them with earth. We worked hard at this all day for about a week, under blistering sun or piercing wind, and no one who has not gone through the experience can possibly conceive how arduous it was. By evening we were all completely exhausted. Our poor ox toiling at the plough

all day would occasionally fall down and lie on the ground exhausted, as if to protest that it could work no more, and when we saw this pitiful sight we would forget our own tiredness and get on with our work.

In spite of all our efforts, however, the crop was a poor one, and to make matters worse the crows and magpies came and robbed us of much of it. They would cluster round us with loud squawks and caws even while we were sowing, and try to steal the seeds under our very noses.

When the corn began to sprout, flocks of birds would come out of the surrounding woods and pluck them out of the ground, flying off with them roots and all. The elder Sisters were therefore put on duty to watch the fields from before sunrise until after dark. Pheasants too would raid our soybean field, delighted at their unexpected feast. Whenever we saw a flock of fine fat pheasants we wished we could catch one or two and roast them for our supper, but the pheasants only cackled in derision at the presumption of such skinny starvelings as our group of Benedictines in entertaining such a ridiculous idea. To add to our frustration, our bean fields were visited by graceful deer in groups of three or four at a time. The deer very much enjoyed nibbling the tender green shoots and leaves of the bean plants. In August, when the corn was nearly ripe, herds of wild boar came out of the woods by night and caused great devastation in the cornfields. After each foray they left the cornstalks all twisted and broken or uprooted and lying on the ground, eating many of the cobs and leaving the others, half-eaten and mangled, all over the field.

When we saw this miserable state in which they had left our corn, on which our lives depended during the coming winter, our eyes filled with tears and we choked with grief and vexation. It was already so chilly when we came to harvest the remains of our corn-crop that we had to wear gloves, and retrieve the corn and stalks from the snow that covered the ground.

The husking of the corn had to be done

outdoors, in the bitterly cold winter weather. As there was no proper threshing floor, threshing was often done on ground covered with a smooth layer of ice. We nuns squatted around the place husking the corn and removing the grains from the cobs.

Before threshing the broom-corn, or millet, we cut off the ears one by one with sickles, taking care not to lose a single grain. This also was a very cold work.

I have tried to give some idea of the suffering and disappointment that we went through, but it must not be thought that our life was one of unmitigated misery, for there were occasions when we were able to find great pleasure in it.

The clear heavens filled with bright stars at night, the delicate mists shrouding the valleys at dawn, towering cumulus clouds moving majestically through the sky at noon; these, with the masses of blossom on the well wooded hills and the music of the birds, filled our hearts with joy and hope in the midst of our sufferings.

Pleasant social evenings would often afford variety in our life, when we would sit together and sing German folk songs, and joke with one another. Our gaiety on these occasions and the reminder that we were still capable of hearty laughter a feeling of happiness gave rise to and well-being that we enjoyed more than anything else.

(*Sister Caritas*)

Special Labor

Winter was approaching: our harvest was too scanty to provide us with enough to live on—even our guards recognized the impossibility. Exhausted as we were, we needed meat and fats. The guards urged us to do everything in our power to earn some money and buy the necessary extra food. We thought of becoming charcoal burners, but we soon found that it was no easy job. The first thing we had to do was to brave the bitter cold outside and install a charcoal oven. The next thing was to climb up the narrow, steep and tortuous mountain paths

to fell trees, and then get the trunks in by tumbling them down the rocky path. On the slippery mountainside many would take a false step and tumble down like the trunks, unable to arrest their descent until they were brought up short, bruised and shaken, by the rocks below. It might be said that it was lucky that no one was killed, but we attributed our preservation to our daily prayers to God for His protection and to our guardian saints for their intercession.

By the middle of winter the snow was knee high but we were still without shoes. Those of us who were too sick to work outdoors remained at home making straw sandals for us. We tied them on our feet with straw rope and went to work on our oven beside a large rock.

This was the hardest work we engaged in during our detention. We succeeded in making and selling a lot of charcoal, but none of us ever saw any money accruing from our labor, nor did we get any meat or fats to alleviate our lot and safeguard our health. Throughout the winter the nuns were all kept hard at work, spinning cotton and weaving cloth on hand-made wooden looms, and making straw hats for the Communists. All had been led to expect payment for the work, but none of us received any reward for our labor.

Spring, summer and autumn of 1950 passed in this way, and we greeted our second winter, all of us, that is, except Sister Eva Shütz, who passed away on August 10, 1950, succumbing to the extreme adversity of camp life; Brother Eugen Ostermeier, who died on September 14, 1949; Brother Basilius Hauser who died on February 13, 1950; and Brother Paschal Fangauer who died on April 16 of the same year. The number of crosses standing in our little cemetery on the hillside had now risen to six. How can I adequately express our regret? May their souls, and the souls of the faithful departed, rest in peace!

Sacrifices for the Harvest

The harvest.... the harvest piled up in

storage in our Heavenly Father's barn. Of the 59 Brothers, six had already died by August of 1950. In the following year the total number of deaths reached 12, and at the time of our departure from the prison it had reached 17. Although they had only very small crosses on their graves, the Communists pulled them all up on the outbreak of the Korean War, on the pretext that they would be a conspicuous landmark to airplanes and help them to find out their position when flying over the camp. They ordered us to replace the crosses with name tags, as will be told in more detail later.

The Death March

July 29, 1950. On this day we saw the first plane pass over our detention camp. Planes began to pass overhead almost every day. Our guards explained to us that they were Russian planes on a regular flight between Moscow and North Korea and at first we believed them. But their number increased every day, and one morning we heard a loud explosion in a nearby valley. There was no doubt in our minds that it was a bomb dropped from a plane, but our guards explained to us in a somewhat uneasy manner, that the People's Republic Air Force were holding operational training, including bombing practice flights, over an uninhabited area around this mountain.

Soon the numbers of planes began to increase more rapidly than before, and sometimes the whole countryside was lit up at night by illuminating shells that they dropped. The sound of loud explosions in nearby places could also be heard. The guards still tried to deceive us with far-fetched explanations such as that the explosions were at a road construction site nearby, where blasting was going on. But gradually it became clear to us that war must have broken out between North and South Korea. Although our guards steadily refused to admit it, we were convinced that the time of our liberation was drawing near and we prayed to God that it would come soon. Planes flying low over the valleys sprayed villages with machine-gun bullets, and at these times we were made to take cover in the woods or lie flat on the ground. We were strictly forbidden to look up at the sky. The reason they gave was that Westerners' faces could be recognized from the air. If during an air attack one of us had merely lifted his hand to shade his eyes from the sunlight he was likely to be accused of trying to signal to the planes, and to be given three or four days' solitary confinement as a punishment.

Father Schleicher, though quite innocent, was once punished in this way.

Owing to the intensification of the air raids, our guards no longer allowed us to wear our black gowns even on Sundays, and we had to put on convicts' uniforms instead. We were also forbidden to gather at chapel for Mass on Sundays, but we assembled secretly in small groups and held our Mass separately, that is to say, one group attended Mass at St. Placidus's and another at St. Gertrude's. The small crosses at the cemetery were removed and replaced with name tags, and not more than three persons at a time were allowed to make visits to the Holy Eucharist. The guards used to get nervous and agitated when the planes appeared, but we had no fear. On no occasion was our camp ever subjected to bombing or machine-gun attacks by the planes. Perhaps the pilots recognized the site as that of a prison camp. The guards were no longer able to conceal the fact that war had broken out.

Refuge in Man-p'o

Three senior officers of the People's Army visited the camp on October 23, 1950, without warning, and announced that we must leave the camp at three o'clock that afternoon and take refuge elsewhere. They told us to carry with us only things of vital importance and promised to bring our other things by truck later on. Until that time we had been looking forward to a little relaxation during the winter, when we had expected to be able to live on the fruits of our hard labor during the year.

Now we were forced to abandon virtually all our harvested grain.

We set off at three that afternoon under the escort of People's Army troops and police officers.

On our way down the mountain we saw large numbers of North Korean and Red Chinese troops on the march. This was all that was needed to confirm in our minds that war had broken out and was being waged on a very large scale.

Our journey lasted three days, resting at farm houses during the daytime and proceeding on foot or by short train rides during the night. How cold it was! Nowhere could we find a warm place. We passed an enormous body of Chinese troops marching south, with a long convoy of heavily loaded trucks following them.

The houses and villages along the highway were in ruins, utterly destroyed by the raids, and huge crowds of refugees were slowly proceeding northward to the Korean-Manchurian border, with their belongings carried in bundles on their backs or on their heads. We thought the South Korean Army must be close behind us. It was at this time that we heard that war had broken out on June 25.

Back to Prison

On October 25, we arrived at Man-p'o on the Korean-Manchurian border. Immediately on our arrival we were taken to a building completely surrounded by a high wall, and on entering it found we were in a prison. We were greatly surprised and protested vigorously at being imprisoned, and the Communists promised that our stay there would be only temporary, and that we should be taken to a good house after a little while. We accordingly entered our cells, placing our destiny in God's hands. The prison turned out to be little different from the one in P'yŏng-yang, except that the cell doors were not fastened and we could occasionally go out on the pretext that we were going out for a smoke, or to the latrine.

On October 27, we were forced to continue our journey on foot, across the bridge over the Yalu River. We had no idea where we were being taken. Was it to a Chinese prison? Entering Manchuria we found ourselves in a large city, and spent three days sitting in the yard of a railway station. The Communists never allowed us to stand up or move about. It was very cold and we were all covered with white frost when we woke up in the morning. As they gave us nothing to eat we became exhausted with hunger. Crowds of people gathered round us jeering and laughing at us, clad as we were in convicts' uniforms. Apparently they mistook us for American prisoners of war. Though a few of the spectators showed pity for us, most of them bitterly reviled us and some went so far as to say that we deserved to die.

As we were not permitted to speak to them we could not explain our status in detail. All we could do was to whisper to some people standing near us that we were not American prisoners of war but German missionaries.

We saw another long procession of prisoners following behind us, who we learnt were kidnapees from Seoul. They looked utterly miserable: all of them were tied one to another with rope, and were dressed in thin, worn-out clothes. Most of them were sick, bowed with hunger, and, one would think to look at them, utterly incapable of proceeding any further. It was too distressing a sight to be looked at: it was the first time in our lives that we had seen people treated with such brutality.

On October 29, 1950, the Feast of Christ the King, the kidnaped South Koreans were taken to Manchuria and we were ordered to return to our prison in Man-p'o. We considered ourselves lucky.

In Man-p'o prison our diet consisted of adequate quantities of corn and soybeans, but nothing else. We were given no work to do, nor were we placed under strict surveillance. The greatest problem was the lack of water. The only water we could get was some stagnant oily water on the floor of the engine-room in the basement. We had to drink that, and needless to say all of us were soon suffering from diarrhoea. The jailors had apparently no confidence in the loyalty of their own people, and would allow no Koreans to come into contact with us. Consequently the preparation of our food and other kitchen chores were assigned by them to the nuns, who were kept hard at work from three o'clock in the morning until ten o'clock at night. Father Canut d'Avernas, who had lost much of his vigor after the three nights in the open that he was made to undergo by the Yalu River, died at last on November 6 after lying on his wretched bed unconscious for days. We were not allowed to give him Christian burial. Several convicts were brought in to take away his body and we still do not know where they buried him. Father d'Avernas's death was probably the most tragic among those of the deceased missionaries of our group.

We had brought our Mass bags to the prison with us, and wanted to hold a Mass. We all piled our bags in the corridor to serve as an altar and held a Mass early in the morning, before anybody else was up. One of the priests officiated, wearing convict's uniform, with the stole concealed under his jacket. We informed the nuns of the progress of the Mass from the Offertory, Sanctus, Consecration and Elevation, to the Holy Communion, by tapping on the wall of their adjoining cell, and in this way they were able to follow it in spirit.

Whenever the nuns brought our food from the kitchen, one of the Brothers was assigned to help them carry it, and taking advantage of this opportunity he carried the Blessed Sacrament with him concealed in a small box together with the mess-kits. The senior nun received it and allowed her juniors to approach it in her cell.

The Sea of Fire

The United Nations planes came to Man-p'o every day, dropped their bombs, and disappeared. At the first alarm we had to take refuge in our air-raid shelter. On November 9 when several bombs fell near our prison, all the windows were shattered and the roof was smashed. We all thought that it would be preferable to die at the hands of the Communists rather than meaninglessly in an airraid.

When incendiary bombs fell on the entire area of Man-p'o on November 12, the city was one vast sea of conflagration. The flames spread to our prison, and though we tried hard to take out as many things as possible, we lost half our belongings in the fire. It was while the prison itself was enveloped in flames that Father Kohler, who was in charge of the vestry, plunged into the flames crying,

"Oh, the Mass bag!"

He succeeded in bringing it out safely. This was indeed a blessing, for had he failed, we would have been unable to celebrate Mass for the next three years.

There was nothing to be done but to take refuge in the surrounding hills—nothing was left of the city but ashes.

"Out! Out! Never mind your bags, we'll bring them later," cried the police as they hustled us from the scene, grabbing our rucksacks and snatching our bags from our hands. As they had promised, they sent us our bags later, but all their contents had disappeared.

Poverty

We went on foot that evening to a new detention camp located in Kwan-mun-ri near Man-p'o. We were led to wooden barracks lying on both sides of a long valley in the hills. They looked as if they had been used as refuges by the People's Army and the Communist police. Made entirely of wood they were half hidden underground, and their roofs consisted of boards nailed on hurriedly and irregularly. There was neither glass nor paper in the windows, and there could hardly be much difference in living inside or outside them; they could only serve as places of concealment from airplanes if their roofs were properly camouflaged with grass and branches of trees. Into one of these barracks the police drove us all, priests, and nuns, and there we had to stay and share the same house. We were as crowded as beansprouts in a box. Our pains and discomfort were indescribable, but we somehow managed to cover the floor with boards and straw to keep out the cold night wind coming up from below. It was extremely cold by day and night, and many of us, frostbitten, saw their toe-nails drop off with bits of flesh attached to them. Father Gregor Sorger, who belonged to the Beuron Abbey, lost consciousness for three days after we moved into the barracks, and died on November 15 in the arms of a doctor-nun. Brother Hilarius Boiss gradually weakened and died on December 12. On the following day Brother Solanus Hermann died, unconscious, in his bed. We carried the bodies out and buried them outside at the back of the barrack under the surveillance of the police, but it was so cold that we could hardly make any impression on the frozen ground with our one blunted hoe, which was all we had. We made shallow graves and piled snow on them.

South Korean planes roared over almost every day. Then the anti-aircraft guns would rattle away with a deafening sound. We were all jampacked in our narrow building and forbidden to come out, and were on the verge of suffocation, freezing with cold, and desperately hungry. The raids grew fiercer but we were not allowed to take refuge elsewhere. On their straw beds the sick lay and died one after another, while the police with bayonets fixed in their rifles stood guard at the door. We had no opportunity for communal prayer, and were unable to hold a Mass, but ought we to be depressed or discouraged? we asked ourselves. Shall we meet our death in an air-raid or by starvation?

"Oh, merciful Father, look down on us and make haste to help us," we prayed, gasping in our agony. We were enabled by His grace to gain confidence and encouragement.

At last the police kept the promise which

they had made to provide us with warm quarters safe from air attack. They took us from the barracks on the afternoon of December 14; conducting us to a strange place in a deep ravine, they ordered us to turn to the left. What a miserable procession we looked! Pale and emaciated, clad in rags, and toiling slowly along we looked at each other without daring to speak. We hardly knew how to give each other a word of encouragement, but our Father knew our plight and was watching over us.

Bethlehem

We greeted the Christmas of 1950 in this dark air-raid shelter. In the evening we were permitted to sing several Christmas hymns in a low voice on condition that our singing should not be audible outside. Making a small fire of twigs, we gathered around it, and sang 'Silent Night, Holy Night,' which was the one we liked best, and several others. Mother Gertrud recited several Christmas poems and the nuns, returning from their work in the kitchen, brought dry boiled rice to us in secret as a Christmas present. Though we celebrated this Christmas in poverty and anxiety, it was one of the prettiest and most pleasant Christmases in our lives.

Our most fervent desire at Christmas was to be able to celebrate Mass. All religious services had been forbidden since our arrival at Kwan-mun-ri. Early in the morning as the sunlight gradually lit up our window, Father Schleicher, the eldest of us all, took his seat near the door and held the Mass bag on his knees to serve as an altar, and several others gathered round him to form a screen against any prying police outside. Then, with his stole concealed under his jacket, the priest celebrated the Mass and all present took part in silence and received the Holy Eucharist.

This was really a Holy Mass. In order to allow the nuns working in the military kitchen to share this grace of Christmas although they were prevented from attending it in person, Father Köhler, whose regular duties took him to the kitchen whenever the rice was being served out into bowls, brought the Holy Eucharist secretly to them when the time came round for him to go to the kitchen, and each nun came to him quietly and received Holy Communion without interrupting her work for more than a moment. This aroused no suspicions on the part of the guards, and we were able to celebrate in this way on several later occasions.

(*Father Eligius Kohler*)

Dark Night

We repeatedly besought the man in charge of us to let us return to our former detention camp in Ok-sa-tok. At last our request was granted, and we were allowed to return there. On January 16, 1951, we set out aboard two trucks, which continued their way through the night. On our way there we saw that all the villages and towns along the highway had been completely destroyed in the air raids. The weather was very cold and we all thought we were going to be frozen to death. One of the policemen accompanying us fell into a coma owing to the severe cold.

We foresaw our danger and decided to stop and warm up in a house in Kang-kye which lay just ahead of us. There we cooked some Indian millet we were carrying with us, and warmed ourselves at the kitchen stove. Around noon our trucks started again and it was seven in the evening and already dark when we arrived at Ch'ŏng-ch'ŏn-kang. Alighting from the trucks we began the long climb, in utter darkness, to our former home in the hill tops. We were all very glad to have finally reached Ok-sa-tok—we had led the lives of wretched refugees for 86 days, from October 23, 1950 to January 17, 1951, under conditions of indescribable hardship.

Under the Whip of 'Schleich'

We learnt that the first director of our prison had been replaced on October 21, 1949, and that he had been succeeded by several others, all of whom lived there for a brief period without taking any interest in the welfare of prisoners. On February 3, 1951, a new director with the rank of first lieutenant arrived. He stayed with us for two and a half years until October 6, 1953, as our warden. He treated us like slaves or beasts and we found it difficult to regard him as a human being. On his taking office, we began to know real slavery, though our previous experiences had been bitter enough. As he was always sneaking about and spying on us, trying to catch us out in some infraction of prison regulations which he might use as a pretext for harassing us, he gained the nickname of *Schleich*, a German word meaning 'slicky boy' or 'sneaking, cunning fellow.' He also made his men behave unpleasantly toward us, ordering them to stand guard over us with rifles no matter what work we were doing. He constantly swore at us, and heaped insults and abuses on us, so that we could not work in peace. We were indeed made into the playthings of the guards and had to submit to every hardship, just like a butterfly having its wings torn off by a cruel child, or a bird with a string tied to its leg so that it cannot escape the teasing of its captor.

With the advent of spring our farm work started. At dawn he went out to the fields with us and we worked there all day long. Tired out by evening, we wished for the order to return home, but *Schleich*, who was quite pitiless, kept on thinking up more jobs to do and made us go on working until late at night. When we finally got home we collapsed on the floor, exhausted by hunger and fatigue. Sometimes we plucked grass on our way home and made ourselves a watery gruel with it. It was no wonder that many of us fell ill. With swollen legs the sick men would struggle along, groaning at every step.

Seeing many of the sick lying on the floor in pain in the morning, the police would glare fiercely at them and shout:

"If you want to die, die and be damned, but go outside and get it over!"

You may think it impossible for a human being to behave like this, but they certainly would not have cared if we had all died.

They just drove the sick men out to work without consideration for the state of their health, whether they had swollen legs, were in the throes of fever, or on the verge of collapse.

(*Father Eligius Kohler*)

The Succession of Deaths

Many died one after another through overwork and undernourishment. Only the sick were allowed to hear Mass at home, while the other prisoners had to go out to work at five in the morning immediately after receiving Holy Communion and continue their work in the fields until eight or nine o'clock in the evening. Overwork destroyed our vigor and we fell one by one. Our food was getting even worse than before; our daily ration was reduced to 700 grams for heavy laborers, 600 grams for ordinary persons, 400 grams for the sick, and 300 grams for those confined in the jail. It was only natural that we should be incessantly sighing and groaning. What was to become of us? We asked ourselves this question despondently, and the general atmosphere of our prison grew ever more melancholy. We almost envied those fellow-Christians who had preceded us to the grave and lay buried on the hill beyond.

Our working conditions grew harder to bear day by day; our treatment grew worse, and our daily rations went on decreasing. But we bore all without complaint, only silently praying to God. We began to lose courage: some defiantly sat down on the rocks that littered the field and burst into tears like children, and some may have become temporarily unbalanced. We thought we would have been better off if we had been put before a firing squad.

On September 1, 1951, Brother Eusebius Lohmeier finally collapsed, worn out with hunger and toil. Bullied and forced by the police to go on working until just before his death, he was still accused of laziness as he lay dead in the field, and the police stepped contemptuously across his body.

In November 9 of that year Father Anselm Romer, who had been dean of the theological seminary at Tŏk-won, also passed away after a lingering illness.

Previously we had always laid the bodies of our fellow-believers to rest in a little graveyard about 200 meters away from our detention camp in reverence for their suffering and sacrifice, but now we no longer had the strength to carry their remains even such a short distance so our procedure now was to wrap the corpse in a straw bag decorated by the nuns with branches of fir and wild flowers, and have it drawn up the hill on the ox-sled. While the ox pulled his load to the graveyard, we followed the rustic hearse, praying for his eternal peace, and carried out the burial in accordance with the regulations of the Church. At each funeral we sang a hymn, and it became our custom for us to ask one another whose turn it would be next.

We had got the sledge ready to convey the body of Father Romer to the grave when it was suddenly sent for to bring home Brother Petrus, of the Beuron Abbey, who had suddenly collapsed while working in the field. We laid him down in the room under the care of the doctor-nun. Then we proceeded with the interrupted funeral of Father Romer. The garments of the deceased were always distributed among the group, and whoever received a worn-out jacket or a torn pair of trousers thought himself very fortunate.

On March 20, 1952 Brother Ildefons Frötzinger had died; he was followed by Brother Gottlieb Auer, who died on April 6. On June 14 Father Kunibert Ott, the youngest of the priests, had followed them, and now it was Father Schleicher's turn. The police had treated him with great inhumanity: immobilized by his swollen legs, he had been told to stay at home and get the night soil from the latrine ready for spreading in the fields as manure. This work made him lose his vigor completely, and he died on July 28.

Father Schleicher was an impressive preacher, and we remembered the series of sermons he had preached to us during our prison life, and his lectures explaining the rule of the Benedictine order and its application to our daughter abbey, and those on the life of Saint Paul as a missionary and as a prisoner.

On September 15, 1952, Sister Fruktuosa Gerstmayer died, the seventeenth of our group to die in captivity. As a pediatrician she had treated more than 5,000 children at the Won-san clinic. If only she and many of the other patients in our camp had been left alone by the police and given a chance to recover, and if the Communists had allowed the doctor-nuns to bring the necessary medicines with them into captivity, no doubt many of the seventeen would still be living today. They sacrificed their lives to the glory of God, and now their mortal remains lie in peace in the valley of Ok-sa-tok, awaiting the resurrection as faithful Catholic missionaries.

(*Father Eligius Kohler*)

The Prison Sewing-room

"Sister Sigeberta, please sew some buttons on these trousers."

"Is my jacket ready? For three weeks I have had no jacket to wear, for I have only the one I left with you for mending."

"It's three months now since I asked you to darn my socks, aren't they finished yet? It's getting cold now, and I want to have them back, darned or undarned."

"When may I bring my coat and trousers in for repair? I can't wear them any longer in their present condition."

These and similar requests poured into her every day. Sister Sigeberta, always gentle and affectionate, met them with a smile and did her best to repair everybody's clothes in time. She enjoyed the work, but at the same time felt frustrated. She enjoyed it because she was fond of needlework, and apart from this work of repairing the men's clothing she was not allowed to do any sewing except during her free time on Sundays. She

felt frustrated, however, for she was often unable to execute a commission for lack of a scrap of cloth for a patch, and had to disappoint her clients. Two nuns were assigned to the sewing-room, and they were responsible for the mending work for more than thirty prisoners. In addition to this they were often called out to work in the fields, to make straw bags, to launder and repair the clothing of the police, and do any odd jobs as required. It was therefore quite impossible for them to get the repairs done quickly; another point was that the material of the garments was so tattered and threadbare that they took much longer to repair than ordinary clothes.

All old clothes, no matter how badly worn, were treasured: if possible, they were repaired and made fit to wear, and, if too far gone, they would be used for patching other garments. The priests and monks tore up their black robes which they had been forbidden to wear, and gave us the shreds for wadding our winter clothes. Nobody cared if a white dress was mended with a black patch: utility came before appearance in our minds. One of the Brothers brought in his torn socks for repair and we saw that he had tried to draw the rents together by binding them with iron wire.

The Sisters spun silk yarn and wove it into material for skirts and trousers: this they did as a means of earning a little extra money. After repeated requests, the Communist guards consented to let them have their castoff remnants of cloth which the Sisters unraveled to make thread for sewing. All bits of cotton thread were carefully collected from all over the camp, and brought home by the Sisters to be used either in weaving or for sewing. Those that were knotted had to be untied. In this way the Sisters collected several balls of thread which were wound on spools and regarded as a great treasure, for which they thanked God in His divine providence.

As for needles, there was only one darning needle in a whole family of fifty or sixty coming from two abbeys. Many sighed bitterly at the lack of needles: if only they had needles, they used to say, they could mend their own clothes for themselves, and not add to the Sisters' burden. This needle which we had was really treasured by us, and whenever it got mislaid we would pray to Saint Anthony to help us find it, and when we finally discovered it everyone would rejoice. Whenever we broke one of our smaller sewing needles, through trying to sew patches on thick cloth garments stiff with dirt, all of us regarded it as a serious loss.

(*Sister Ambrosia*)

Interrogation

On Christmas Eve, December 24, 1951 a high-ranking Communist official arrived from P'yŏng-yang without warning. On the following day he started a series of interrogations, calling our priests into his office one by one, and questioning each of them for several hours. Usually this went on until midnight, but now it was protracted into the small hours. The main object of all this questioning was to find out whether any of us had kept in touch with South Korea and if so who our contacts were. The priests were taken to the guardhouse after interrogation and kept there for some time, but Father Damm was treated with even greater severity, for he was put in solitary confinement, deprived of sleep and given no food at all.

On January 1, 1952, all of the priests except Father Frömmer were confined to the guard house, but the monks and nuns were still at liberty. Father Frömmer said a Mass for the monks and nuns, and prayed earnestly for the early release of the priests from the guardhouse. It so happened that a sow that was being raised by the police farrowed during the night, and as it was bitterly cold they feared that the litter might freeze to death. The sow was accordingly taken to a small room opposite the guardhouse, but there was no room for the litter, so the priests were released from the guardhouse to make room for the little pigs. Father Damm, however, was still kept in solitary confinement. One

day Father Fischer was caught passing something secretly to Father Damm, and was forced to stand outside in the snow, wearing only an open-collared shirt, for one hour. We all thought that Father Fischer would be frozen to death. How earnestly we prayed for Father Damm! It was not until January 4 that he was released from his detention.

Life in Stockade

It was on January 30 that Brother Vitus Stenger was condemned to undergo the punishment described below.

Motivated entirely by pity for his starving fellow-prisoners, who were suffering from malnutrition and intense hunger, he attempted to remove a basket of corn cobs from a storeroom in secret, intending to make use of them to augment their daily ration of food. He was caught in the act and apprehended by the police, who immediately locked him up in solitary confinement in an unheated cell, without his overcoat and winter cap, and without a bed covering. The weather was bitterly cold at the time and he was kept there for eleven days.

In the meantime the police showered abuse and insult on all the members of our group, saying that we were all *thieves, liars* and *bitches*.

On February 9, a policeman passing by his detention room happened to peep through the window. He saw Brother Stenger lying on the floor unconscious, and blue with cold, as if dead. A physician among the nuns was immediately called in. By means of an injection she helped him to recover consciousness. With all these sufferings his punishment actually came to an end, and, in addition, he was allowed several days' rest.

Almost at the same time Brother Januarius Albert was to suffer a similar fate, for several days before the nuns had been given remnants of cloth left over from their tailoring—as a special privilege, on the understanding that these bits of cloth were to be used for needlework only with the commander's permission. One day Brother Albert appeared at the sewing-room with his trousers full of rents and asked the nuns to mend them. Of course the police had raised no objection to his having them mended with the scraps of cloth referred to, and they used some of them for mending his trousers. On the following day, however, *Schleich*, who had gone to Brother Januarius's room, saw his trousers mended with the bits of his cloth, and flew into a rage.

Screaming with fury, he ordered a thorough investigation, and had Brother Albert thrown into solitary confinement in the guardhouse in the same way as Brother Vitus.

Fortunately, however, the floor of the guardhouse collapsed and he was let out after thirteen days' detention in the bitterly cold weather.

There were a few among us who would occasionally pilfer a corncob or a potato and eat it in secret to appease their gnawing hunger. Unluckily most of them were caught, and the discovery served the police as a pretext for more angry abuse. They were especially fond of calling us all *thieves*, *liars* and *bitches*.

No matter what they called us, our pangs of hunger were so strong that we went on filching an occasional corncob from the pig feed, and making gruel of it, which we ate with as much gusto as the prodigal son who devoured the husks left by the swine (Luke, 15:13). I am afraid we never felt any pricks of conscience about doing so, nor did we consider the serious consequences that might ensue.

(Father Eligius Kohler)

The New Commander

For three and a half years we had been suffering from the persecution of the prison commander, whom we had nicknamed *Schleich* and who appeared to take delight in making us suffer, but now, on September 19, 1952, to our great surprise, a new commander suddeny made his appearance. We had never dreamed that we would be relieved of *Schleich's* presence, and had begun to look on

him as our permanent affliction, though of course we had all been longing for him to go. We had suffered cruel treatment at his hands, and knew him for the malicious brute that he was.

Until we heard of his official transfer we hardly dared to believe that he would really depart, but on October 6 of the same year he finally disappeared down the valley. No one regretted his departure, but we bore no resentment against him.

Hope and Suspicion

The new commander behaved toward us with extreme reserve for some considerable time after his arrival. His duty must have been to inspect us at least once in our place of work, but he never did so. He gave us the impression that he was either desirous of keeping us at a distance or else afraid to meet us.

We soon learned that he was a tender-hearted man who would never try to oppress us, but on the contrary was quite friendly-disposed toward us. Generally speaking, our life in captivity remained without any notable change, except that our new commander was the complete antithesis to *Schleich*. He does not only forbade his men to annoy us, but ordered them to accord us decent treatment.

From that time on the police ceased standing on guard behind us with rifles while we were at work in the fields, and let us work by ourselves.

They gave up their former practice of addressing us in vulgar and obscene language, and in general became kind and well-mannered. As their manners improved we found it possible to hold conversations and even discussions with them. They readily accepted our suggestions, and began to gather their own firewood instead of leaving all the work to us, and most of them began to till their farms too, which lightened our labor to a considerable degree.

The sick among us were also accorded generous treatment and the doctor-nun was provided with a supply of various medicines. The Communists even requested us to take good care of ourselves lest any of us should fall ill. A few of the policemen of course continued to behave as before, but their outbursts were now of no more account than a passing shower of rain.

Moreover, we were now given new clothing and jackets and even wadded blankets. Though still captive and forced to continue our coarse daily labor, we were no longer the wretched slaves that we had been.

There came a sudden shock. What had happened? On April 6, 1953, to our dismay, *Schleich* suddenly turned up again at the detention camp. Everybody was greatly surprised and troubled. But once we knew the purpose of his visit we realized that there was nothing to worry about. All he had come for, with his accompanying policemen, was to make a survey of the state of the buildings and a complete inventory of the food supply, crops under cultivation, and livestock. He also made out a complete report on the circumstances under which the deceased prisoners had died. Most busily occupied with this was Sister Diomedes, the doctress, for she was requested to report in detail on the physical condition of the deceased prisoners, and the cause of their death. She was ordered to make out an objective report, with no exaggeration, and a name plate with the name of the deceased, date of birth and date of death was set up on each grave.

The Communists promised to exhume the bodies of those prisoners who had died during our detention in Man-p'o, and bring them here for Christian burial, setting up official name plates at their graves in the same way as the others.

We could not imagine what was going on. Sister Diomedes, the doctress, had been given an ample supply of medicine and could now treat her patients more effectively. It seemed to us that the Communists' main concern now was to prevent any further deaths among the prisoners.

What seemed more strange was that one of the policemen in charge of the accounting told us a few days later that it would be quite in order for us to eat up all the grain stored in the warehouse so long as we could make it last till December 1953. Everybody in the camp now began to receive the full ration of 800 grams daily, whether he worked at heavy labor in the fields or was sick in bed. In addition to that, they allocated a large supply of vegetables to us and occasionally supplied us with meat and fats.

We were permitted to take all the sheep, goats, and chickens we had raised to our own use exclusively, and each prisoner had two suits of clothes, one for working and one for visits.

Though, as I said, we still had to go on with the heavy labor, we were no longer tortured with the pangs of hunger. The treatment of the prisoners underwent a most remarkable improvement, and we could spend our days in comparative comfort. This state of affairs continued until November 1953.

A Great Improvement

It was November 15, 1953. A high-ranking Korean police officer, a lieutenant colonel with large gold stars on his shoulders and an array of medals almost covering his chest, made a sudden appearance at our detention camp and made the following speech to us:

"Ladies and gentlemen! I am here on orders from the central government to escort you to the capital city of P'yŏng-yang. The People's Republic of Korea well understands how much you have been suffering from hardship up to this date. You will, however, never be placed in adversity again. I assure you that you will be treated from now on as honored state guests of the People's Republic of Korea."

Thus he spoke, in refined Korean. What had the Communists called us in the past? Had they not called us beggar-boys, thieves, robbers, bitches? And now we had suddenly become respectable!

"Now please take off those worn-out clothes," he said, giving us each a splendid fur cap and a thickly-wadded suit of clothes.

The next thing was that we all had to appear one by one before the lieutenant colonel for his inspection, to see whether we were presentable enough to appear in P'yŏng-yang as state guests. All this seemed like a dream to us. We could hardly believe our eyes, and carefully packed away our old clothes in case anything should go wrong.

On November 19, the day of our liberation finally arrived. In the morning we celebrated High Mass. While we were singing the *Te Deum*, our hearts were filled with joy, and our cheerful resounding voices broke the silence of the mountain valley and echoed among the hills.

Te Deum laudamus: te Dominum confitemur.
Te aeternum Patrem omnis terra veneratur....
In te Domine speravi: non confundar in aeter-
num.

> (We praise Thee, O God; we acknowledge Thee to be the Lord. Thee, the Father everlasting, all the earth doth worship.....
> In Thee, O Lord, have I trusted: let me not be confounded for ever.)

After this, we visited the graves of our fellow, prisoners, singing and praying on our way to bid farewell to the deceased.

Then we sang the *Libera Me*;
"Libera me, Domine, de morte aeterna, in die illa tremenda Quando caeli movendi sunt et terra!

> (Deliver me, O Lord, from eternal death on that day of wrath when earth and sky shall tremble!),

and the hymn *Christ Our King* which we had sung so often before. Then each of us sprinkled the graves with holy water, and we prayed for the eternal peace of our deceased fellow-prisoners lying in Man-p'o, whose memory we had kept ever green in our hearts.

"Requiem aeternam dona eis Domine: et lux per-
petua luceat eis. In memoria aeterna erit justus:
ab auditione mala non timebit.

> (Eternal rest give unto them, O Lord, and let perpetual light shine upon them. Men will remember the just for ever: no fear shall he have of evil things.)
> (Psalm, cxi 6:17)

We made a vow at their graves to carry their good wishes to their parents, brothers, sisters, relatives, all their friends and patrons when we returned home, and then left their graves.

It was really a deeply moving and sacred moment when we took our leave of our deceased friends and colleagues, who had shared our joy and sorrow. The lieutenant colonel who saw us honoring the dead was also visibly affected by the pathetic scene.

On that day we were given a good lunch, and just before leaving we sang another hymn praying for our merciful Father's protection during the long journey that awaited us. Our guards stood by and listened in a reverent manner.

At three o'clock in the afternoon we set off down the deep valley. Looking up at our detention camp perched high in the hills above us we said:

"Oh, how we toiled and suffered up there! Doubtless we were nearer to God then than before."

The train took us to the capital. It was November 20: we would leave this train as free men and women once we arrived in P'yŏng-yang—the very place where we had crawled out of that hooded truck when we first passed through on our way to captivity.

On hand to greet us warmly were representatives of the North Korean puppet regime and high police officers. They exchanged handshakes with each of us and offered us cigarettes.

At Red Paradise

A truck took us to our new home about 18 miles from P'yŏng-yang. Again it seemed a dream! We found our rooms comfortably furnished and brightly illuminated with electric lights. Each of us was provided with two blankets, a white towel, two handkerchiefs, a cake of soap, a tube of toothpaste, toothbrush, comb and mirror, and many other modern toilet articles and accessories which we could not even name.

The poor ragged nuns and Brothers had become ladies and gentlemen.

Signatures

It is against my will that I record the following: a police officer with the rank of lieutenant colonel asked us to sign a document certifying that we had been accorded good treatment during the last two months. We agreed to do so, for we were indeed grateful, but a few days later he returned and asked us to delete the words "for the last two months" from our statement. The Communists wanted to give the public the false impression that we had been well treated for the whole period of detention. We declined, explaining that the treatment we had received was often inhuman. The lieutenant colonel insisted, however, that the responsibility for this should fall on the guilty "*Schleich*" alone, seeing that his malicious acts proceeded from his own individual will and were not committed by the order of the government of the people or of any of his superior officers. We denied his assertion and presented several facts as evidence that our ill-treatment had stemmed not from him alone but from the general policy of the government at that time. We had, we showed him, evidence that we had protested and appealed to higher officialdom about the cruel treatment to which we were being subjected, and had submitted numerous petitions to the government and to its leader Kim Il-sŭng himself, the premier of the People's Republic of Korea, complaining of the shocking conditions that had in fact made it impossible for some of us to sustain life, and were undoubtedly responsible for their untimely death. We knew that these petitions had been received by the government, but it had taken no steps to alleviate them and could not now shrug off responsibility by alleging ignorance. Even if we had not protested, we said, the responsibility of the government for the acts of its official representative committed in the course of his duty would still exist, especially as they had continued over such a long period as to demonstrate that the government had countenanced them. *Schleich*, so far from being

punished, had been promoted, with the award of two stars as big as one's fist and a citation praising him for his efficiency as commander of prison and guardian of its inmates.

We furthermore rejected their assertion that we had been detained merely to protect us, as foreign residents from the dangers arising from the outbreak of the war, for our arrest had taken place more than a year before the war began. It was absurd to allege that we had been arrested for our own protection when we had been deliberately subjected to such suffering and harassment as to cause the death of several of our number.

There were many other questions that came up for discussion with the Communists. They pressed us to certify that we had witnessed the destruction by American planes of whole cities and large numbers of villages. We saw devastation, that was obvious, but in our imprisonment had no means of knowing who or what had caused it. Accordingly we objected to the inclusion of the words *American planes*.

We finally agreed to sign a statement that our sufferings, though severe, were not as great as those of the Korean people whose homes had been destroyed in the war, and that we had in fact seen American planes effect widespread destruction, on a terrible scale. We were under constraint, for we were in mortal terror of being cast back into prison if we insisted on rejecting their request.

We longed for an early release from this Red Palace, so we signed the documents without qualms of conscience.

Home!

January 7, 1954: we at last received formal notification that we would be repatriated to Germany on the following day. We were overjoyed.

Several days earlier we had each been given suits of knitted underwear. Some of these were scarlet, some bright green, and some sky blue in color. In addition we each received a white shirt and collar, a necktie, a pair of leather shoes, two pairs of socks, a suit in Western style with white stripes, a muffler, an overcoat. and a handsome fur cap.

The nuns were similarly equipped: each of them had knitted garments, a pair of leather shoes, two pairs of stockings, a grey jacket and skirt, a necktie, a hood, and a red-striped collar. In short, we all had a completely new outfit for our return to Germany.

Next morning we celebrated Mass, for the last time in North Korea, we thought. We prayed again for a safe journey to our homeland. After a sumptuous breakfast we went to the station by truck. A representative of the government came to see us off at the station, and asked us to forget about the hardships we had undergone in North Korea, to remember Korea when we returned to Germany, and try to make some contribution toward the unification of Korea. We promised him that we would do our best to do so.

A new coach had been reserved for us on the train, and we were accompanied by a police officer with the rank of lieutenant colonel. A physician and a nurse had also been sent to look after our health on the journey to the Korean border.

We crossed the border at midnight. Although we were glad to be free of our shackles, we could not help feeling sorry to leave the country. Were we leaving Korea for good? Was it not the land for the sake of whose people we had left our beloved fatherland and parents? Farewell, beloved Korea!

"Our Father, protect North Korea, the land where we worked for Thy Son Jesus Christ! Bring about peace and unification to this land and enable us missionaries to continue their work in these beloved fields!

(*Father Eligius Kohler*)

Parting

It was about 2 p.m. on January 22, 1954, that we arrived in West Germany via Soviet Russia and East Germany. Wherever we went we received an enthusiastic welcome

from everyone. We waited for transportation to a refugee camp in Friedland near Goettingen, a two-hours' journey. On our way to Friedland people lined the streets in welcome, waving to us and filling our arms with gifts and presents as we rode along. At the refugee camp there was an impressive ceremony of welcome that filled our hearts with deep emotion. Addresses of welcome were given by the representatives of the Bonn Government of West Germany, and the Hessen state, and by the director of the refugee camp and the priest in charge.

As the crowd in the plaza sang *God, Thy Power...*, tears filled our eyes so that we could not join in the singing. Who could have imagined that we should meet our fellow-countrymen with such jubilation? We had never expected such a warm-hearted reception, but rather that we should return home quietly without attracting anybody's attention.

Next morning the Archabbot of St. Ottilien officiated at a Mass of Thanksgiving in the camp chapel, which was jampacked with believers. Delivering his address of welcome, the arch-abbot often had to break off, overcome with emotion, and we were choked with happy tears while listening to him.

After the Mass we were received by our venerable Arch-abbot and Abbot Burchart, and reported our homecoming to them.

The archabbot rejoiced on the one hand at our homecoming but on the other was deeply stricken with sorrow at the news that so many of our number had died, including priests, monks and nuns. Of the total of sixty-seven who had been arrested, nineteen had died, including Bishop Sauer and Father Rupert, and six others were still missing.

"Our Father in Heaven, You protected us wherever we went and always poured out Your grace upon us. We cannot but offer our grateful thanks. May Our Father bless our beloved North Korea and have mercy upon the flock of sheep without a shepherd in North Korea, and send them peace and unification of their country!"

(*Father Eligius Kohler*)

THE DEATH MARCH

(FROM THE DIARY OF A KIDNAPPED CARMELITE NUN)

June 25, 1950, Sunday

It was the day after the feast of St. John, the Baptist, about four o'clock Sunday afternoon when our chaplain, Father Antoine Gombert, came to tell us that the North Korean troops had begun to attack along the Thirty-eighth Parallel.

His announcement set us all discussing what we had better do about it. We decided to hold the usual service of benediction of the Blessed Sacrament, after which all would offer up prayers to the Sacred Heart of Jesus and to the Blessed Virgin Mary, Guardian of Korea and Patroness of our order, for her protection against the scourge of war.

We knew that the United States of America had promised that if Korea were attacked in such strength that the army of the young republic was unable to resist, she would send military aid—but how long would it take before the American forces came to our rescue? The capital city of Seoul lay only twenty-five miles from the enemy line, while our allies were thousands of miles away on the opposite shore of the Pacific Ocean.

By next evening we could hear rapid and continuous firing, and we knew that our trial had begun.

June 27, Tuesday

Father Antoine had a brother only two years younger than he, who was chaplain of the Convent of *St. Paul de Chartres* in Inch'ŏn, and the two had been ordained together on the same day in 1900. Fifty years had passed, and we had arranged a luncheon party on the following Tuesday, June 27, to celebrate their golden anniversary, but when Bishop Patrick Byrne of the Maryknoll Mission arrived and greetings were made his first words to Mother Thérèse, our prioress, were:

"The last plane for Tokyo will leave in less than an hour. Do you want to take it? You must be ready in ten minutes."

"May our Korean Sisters come with us?"

"No, only European Sisters will be allowed to board the plane."

If we could all have gone together we might well have accepted the offer, but the idea of abandoning the Korean nuns, our spiritual daughters, was unthinkable. "When the flock of sheep is attacked, can the shepherd run away?" Our duty was clear.

Nearer and nearer came the sound of firing. So as not to show any lights after dark we decided to sing our night devotion immediately after our five-o'clock meditation period. While we were in the chapel Father Celestin Coyos, the youngest of the Fathers and professor of history at the seminary, came and told us that our convent was now under gunfire, and advised us to take refuge

The Carmelite Convent in Hye-hwa-dong, in the northeast of Seoul, had been founded in 1940, and was now a flourishing community of French, Belgian and Korean Sisters. It maintained an orphanage, schools, and a clinic near the Holy Ghost College and Major Seminary, in the parish of St. Benedict, and the parish church was only a few steps away.

at the Convent of *St. Paul de Chartres* adjoining the Cathedral downtown, rather than unnecessarily expose ourselves to danger. Father Julien of course could not return to Inch'ŏn.

Though we took his advice and went with him, the new place was even more dangerous than our Carmelite Convent, and in the meantime there were our Korean Sisters left alone to listen to the shells whistling across the grounds of the convent. Father Antoine, always careful of our safety, now led us to the basement of his presbytery. To this solidly-built crypt the faculty and seminarians had already taken the Blessed Sacrament, and we all took our seats with them and waited in silence.

The presence of the Blessed Sacrament gave us strength and confidence in the face of the growing danger, and although whenever we ventured out of the basement the deafening roar of the guns assailed our ears, not one of us showed any sign of fear. The rigors of the Carmelite life had at least taught us to subjugate our feelings.

June 28, wednesday

At dawn next morning Father Antoine said Mass without a tremor in his voice or a single sign of anxiety in his bearing, and his example showed us all how to face the new day with quietness and confidence.

Gunfire and loud explosions went on all day, and after spirited but futile resistance the Korean Army withdrew from the city. We saw one of the Korean soldiers fleeing past the gates, who pointed to his empty cartridge belt and cried in despair,

"What shall we do? What shall we do?"

At eight o'clock in the morning the victorious Communist troops came marching triumphantly along the streets, with their hand-clapping civilian admirers lining the sidewalks and shouting cries of welcome. There seemed to be an endless stream of Red troops pouring into the city. Portraits of Stalin and Kim Il-sŭng, the North Korean leader, and Russian and North Korean flags were to be seen everywhere. Now that we were under the orders of the enemy soldiers we were obliged to take emergency measures. We kept the doors of the convent closed to all but official visitors, and, taking off our Carmelite habits, put on plain clothes. Those of us who had spent the night at the Convent of *St. Paul de Chartres* returned to us during the day wearing Korean dress.

June 29, Thursday

Though the fighting continued we could perceive that the Red army was making its way steadily to the south, for without supplies or reinforcements the Korean Army could not offer any resistance.

June 30, Friday

We learned that on their entry into Seoul the Reds had killed all the soldiers undergoing treatment at the military hospital, looted the banks, and released all the convicts from the jails. There were public meetings for propaganda and indoctrination in every ward and precinct, and every family had to be represented by at least one member. To add to our distress the news came that the Bishop's House and the adjoining Convent of *St. Paul de Chartres* had now been commandeered, and that our Sisters of the convent would be permitted to stay at the attached orphanage for only a few days longer before being dispersed. It was over a week before we could get any further news of them.

July 11, Tuesday

Today Father Paul Villemot, chaplain of the Convent of *St. Paul de Chartres*, and M. Georges Perruche, the French Consul-General to the Republic of Korea, were arrested. Father Villemot was eighty-two years old and an invalid, and had long retired from active missionary work.

July 14, Friday

At last the Communists came to see us, with orders that all European Catholics must assemble at the Bishop's House. Our prioress, Mother Thérèse, made arrangements for five of our Korean aspirants, whose homes were located in Seoul, to be sent home. For the remainder of the Korean Sisters she found suitable accommodation in the homes of trustworthy Catholics whom she knew, and who would afford them seclusion and concealment where they might avoid molestation. To each she distributed clothing, some food, and a small sum of money for their traveling expenses. Every one of them dreaded the thought of leaving, and we all wondered whether we should ever meet again in this world.

July 15, Saturday

Early in the morning the two Fathers Gombert and Father Coyos said Mass in the Cathedral. The aspirants who had gone to their homes the day before were all present, and we were very glad to see them again.

The Communist cadres paid us another visit, and after making each of us answer a long questionnaire, they returned to the seminary building which they had commandeered, first locking us up in the refectory while we had our breakfast. As soon as breakfast was over, they returned with our marching orders.

"Off we go! Look sharp, and follow us!"

Hurriedly we donned our Carmelite habits and mustered with a minimum of hand baggage, ready to start. But alas! We were not allowed to take any of our things with us.

"You can't take any of that stuff with you! You're only going for a routine orientation, and you'll be back here again this evening!"

We were obliged to follow them empty-handed, as if we were merely going out for a short walk. Our Korean Sisters lay sobbing on the ground in despair. Hearing our prioress speak, Sister Marie-Madeleine, who had been completely blind for a number of years, cried in a solemn voice,

"The fullness of time has come!"

"We must do the will of Jesus," answered the prioress, and led her along by the hand. After a few steps she turned, and addressed the Korean Sisters,

"Please don't let our captors see us crying!"

As we reached the entrance, almost out of sight of the Korean nuns, the younger Korean Sisters were weeping silently: it is impossible for me to describe the sadness of the scene as we bade farewell one another.

"Bless us! Give us your blessing!" They cried and the prioress turned and whispered blessings to them, while making the sign of the Cross. The prioress then clasped the hand of the eldest Korean Sister and said to her very earnestly,

"Since you are now the senior, I place the juniors in your charge. You must be responsible for them, now that we can no longer look after them. Be always with the Lord!"

With these words she turned and led the way, while their cries of farewell rang in our ears with their repeated prayers that they might see their prioress return in safety.

Imprisonment in Seoul

(July 15—July 19, 1950)

Two jeeps were waiting for us at the top of the hill just outside the convent gates, with two soldiers in each of them. The two Fathers Gombert, Father Coyos, and the Sub-prioress Mother Henriette de Lobit went in the first, and Mother Marie Mechtilde Devriese and Mother Thérèse Bastin went with Sister Marie-Madeleine Marquier and Sister Bernadette Descayaux in the other. We drove downtown to the Sam-hwa building, opposite the Mi-do-p'a Department Store. To us, the building looked like a hotel where we might be accepted as guests, but alas! we soon learnt that it was what the Communists called the Public Security Jail.

Two Communist cadres were waiting upstairs to interrogate us. Trying to catch us in a contradiction they went over the same questions about our age, nationality, date of arrival in Korea and our Carmelite Vow again and again, until we must have answered each of them about fifty times. We became so exhausted that we began answering mechanically like parrots. Then they went on to talk of imperialism, capitalism, the Pope, and the contrasts between the precepts of Christianity and the way in which they were actually practiced by Christians. We could not help being surprised at their familiarity with the writings of André Gide (1869-1951), the French essayist, critic, novelist and dramatist who was for a short time sympathetic with Communism, but was disillusioned after a visit to Soviet Russia in 1936. How well they knew how to quote his works for their own purposes!

After two or three hours of this they took us to another room and left us in peace for a while, and we took advantage of this respite to say the Lord's prayer aloud in place of our usual evening prayers for today, which was the feast of the Scapular. In this, the beginning of our persecution, we felt the need of Our Blessed Lady's help and intercession in Heaven more than ever before, and she did not fail us.

At about six in the evening we were escorted to a large room literally crammed with people, where we were very glad to find Bishop Patrick Byrne of Maryknoll and his secretary Father William Booth, both of whom had been arrested at the residence of Bishop (now Archbishop) Paul M. Ro. Also present was Father John Yu, at that time administrator of Seoul Cathedral.

The Bishop received us kindly with words of encouragement, and the gift of a bottle of wine. Our evening meal consisted of only two cold boiled rice dumplings, wrapped in bits of newspaper, for each of us, but we remembered the days of our great Carmelite saint, Teresa of Avila, whose first Carmel was so poor that they often had to go without any supper at all. Father Yu had obtained permission from a friendly guard to bring some wine and sandwiches for the Bishop, and he secretly shared them with us while the rations of rice-dumplings were being handed out, being careful to conceal his kindness from the eyes of the other guards.

By eight p.m. there must have been over a hundred persons crowded into the room and we could hardly move even our arms. The new arrivals seemed to be persons suspected of anti-Communist activity of one kind or another, and there were so many of them that the room, large as it was, soon became jammed with people from wall to wall. That, however, was where we all had to spend the night, though of course it was impossible to lie down to sleep.

The Bishop, who at once sensed our embarrassment in trying to get settled down at night, explained that in such a time of emergency our strict rules of Carmelite discipline were no longer obligatory. We would have to learn, he said, to adjust ourselves to the new conditions, and to make the best of them. To save space, we could sleep in one another's arms without sinning. The two brothers Gombert set us an example: they had found a way to sit closely together, each with one arm round the other's waist, a sign of their brotherly affection and deep love of religion in their prison life. In the following November they would be separated from each other for a little more than twenty-four hours, and then reunited eternally in the glory of Heaven.

In the deep thought born in the darkness and silence of the first night in jail, our affection went out continually to the little Carmelites whom we had had to leave so suddenly.

"What has happened to our daughters in Christ since we parted? What will happen to them once the whole of South Korea falls into the hands of the Communists?" This problem troubled our minds hundreds of times during our imprisonment, but it would be thirty-three months before we heard of them again.

Every evening from that day on more Korean citizens were brought in on suspicion and others taken out. Shots were heard during the nights, but there was no way of knowing whether these poor people had been executed.

One morning when we woke at dawn we found that all the male Korean prisoners had been taken away. Our fellow prisoners now included a German lady, Frau Charlotte Gliese, who had been married to a Korean, a Turkish lady, Maisara Daulatsch, and a young girl named Helena, the child of a Korean father and a Polish mother.

July 16, Sunday

This morning a large number of planes roared over the city, but dropped no bombs. There was no change in the cold and cruel attitude of the Communists toward us. We Europeans were segregated in one corner of the room, the rest of which was full of other prisoners, and although they well knew that we could not sleep properly at night they forced us to keep motionless all day on our knees with feet together and sitting on our heels, a position which soon became very painful.

All windows were tightly closed and the air became sultry and polluted—our only relief from the suffocating atmosphere came from a slight breeze that entered through a broken pane in one of the windows. Mosquitoes added to our discomfort, and we found that the days were much harder to bear than the nights. None of the inmates could slake their thirst, for there were only two buckets of water a day for the whole roomful of people, not to speak of washing, which was impossible. We soon became inured to this way of life.

The afternoons were taken up with continuous and simultaneous interrogations, with one interrogator for each prisoner. From time to time one interrogator or another would lose his temper and scream in fury.

"There is nothing for it but to destroy Rome and the Vatican!" Mother Marie Mechtilde became the chief target for their insults.

"You old hag! You have done nothing for the young women of Korea but corrupt them!"

This they would shout at her, brandishing their fists in her face.

While another Sister who had come to Mother Mechtilde's assistance was attempting to answer the interrogator's questions on her behalf, one of his comrades came and said to him, just loud enough for us to hear,

"We are going to kill all the priests and nuns tonight."

They must have had some sinister reason for arresting us, we thought—or could they be playing a wicked trick on us?

That evening the room filled again with the newly-arrested persons they brought in, and from among them our guards made up one of their notorious so-called, 'people's courts.' Gesticulating and irate, they harangued this 'court.'

"You fellows, do you see these women? They are nuns of the Carmelite Convent, lazy good-for-nothings who live without working. They do nothing of the slightest good to our people, but keep sending home money and valuables, only making our country poorer and poorer. What do you think of this?"

In obedience to a prearranged signal from a cadre, they raised their fists and cried,

"Death to all nuns of the Carmelite Convent! Death!"

Human life was no more to them than that of a housefly. We well knew that they had little hesitation in decreeing the death penalty, and thought that our last hour had come. Though there were several priests present, the conditions made it impossible to administer the Sacrament of Penance individually, and Father Coyos accordingly granted us all a plenary indulgence.

In the silence of the night we often heard shots just outside the building.

One afternoon a guard came over to Father Coyos and started a lengthy debate on the institution of sacerdotal celibacy. Suddenly another of the soldiers seated at the table burst out angrily,

"We've got orders here to kill at least a hundred and twenty of them tonight." He then began calling out names from a list— first a Kim, then a Ch'oe, and so forth, one by one, and as each answered his name he was taken out and soon afterward a shot was heard outside the building. The room gradually became less crowded.

"Our turn will soon come," we said to each other. At this point the Communists brought in powerful electric lamps and shone them in our faces, watching our reactions attentively.

Hour after hour passed, and each time that

someone entered through the door we thought they had come to take us away. Just before dawn they took away the lights, and left only dim lights burning in the room. When it became light enough we saw that all our priests and nuns were still with us, and we realized that the threats of death had been merely to terrorize us. We had a feeling of being, so to speak, let down after undergoing all that nervous excitement to no definite end, as if we were momentarily disappointed at not having been called to make the supreme sacrifice for Jesus Christ: a glorious martyrdom was not to be ours after all! But this somewhat egotistic mood lasted only a few moments, for we remembered the teaching of the 'Little Way' of our other great Carmelite, St. Therese of Lisieux: one must pass through these dark nights in order to understand and benefit by them. Her 'Little Way' is a lane which, bypassing the heroic, led nevertheless to perfection. As Victoria Sackville-West, the English poet and author of novels and essays, says in her biography the saint:

"Unsensational, pierced by no swords, no arrows, broken on no wheel, roasted on no gridiron, she could have pursued her way as effectively in 'the world' as amid the severities of Carmel. 'In my Little Way,' she said, 'there is nothing but very ordinary things; little souls must be able to do everything that I do.'"

Bearing her precept and practice in mind, 'not to do extraordinary things, but to do ordinary things extraordinarily well,' we all rendered thanks to God that we were still alive, and to Our Blessed Lady for her intercession and protection.

July 17, Monday

Today we were comforted by the arrival of Father Villemot, Mother Béatrix Edouard, the Provincial Superior of the Congregation of *St. Paul de Chartres* in Korea, and Mother Eugénie Demeusy, who came to share our imprisonment. We all felt very happy to be together again, for just as troubles become easier to bear when shared, so do our

pleasures become greater. It was evident that we all had to be in jail under our new temporal masters, and we considered ourselves fortunate in that we were all in the same one.

Father Villemot had just previously been released from imprisonment in order to undergo treatment for dysentery, but now they had brought him back to prison. He was eighty-two years of age, and M. Perruche, Consul-General of France, lodged a vigorous protest against the imprisonment of such, an aged man, but in vain.

Mother Béatrix was French, and had entered the *St. Paul de Chartres* Congregation in 1899. She came to the orphanage in Seoul in 1906, and was Mistress of Novices at the convent until 1932, when she was appointed Local Superior in Tae-gu. In 1942 she was appointed Provincial Superior for Korea. Mother Eugénie, who was a trained nurse, had been Mistress of Novices in succession to Mother Béatrix since 1932. Her elder sister is Mother General of the Order. With these Sisters from the Convent of *St. Paul de Chartres* we felt in complete harmony of mind, sharing as we did the same aim and the same fears and suffering on account of our common faith.

That afternoon we were joined by Monsignor Thomas Quinlan, the Prefect Apostolic of Ch'un-ch'ŏn Prefecture Apostolic, and by two Columban Fathers, Father Philip Crosbie and Father Frank Canavan, and their presence was an added source of confidence and moral support. Father Crosbie was to become the author of an account of our imprisonment which was published in 1954 under the title *"Pencilling Prisoner,"* and we are indebted to him for much of our information about the other members of the group.

Monsignor Quinlan was about fifty-four, and back in 1920 had come to China to found the Columban Mission in that country. After twelve years' work in China he had come to Korea to open a Columban Mission in Kwang-ju. Five years later he had come to Ch'un-ch'ŏn, to open another mission there, in the mountains on the eastern side of Korea.

During World War II he had been imprisoned by the Japanese at first, but on explaining to them that the Republic of Ireland was neutral during the war he was later subjected only to house arrest. When the Americans arrived in 1945 they found him still there, smiling and ready to go on with his work. His secretary, Father Frank Canavan, was also an Irishman.

Our corner of the room became more crowded, but neither this nor the flies and mosquitoes, the hunger and thirst, or the great heat of summer troubled us so much as the daily spectacle of numbers of people being brought into the room and made to declare that from that day on they would never practice any religion, whatever it might be, that they would never permit their children to receive religious instruction, and that they would never attend any church or other place of worship, to which formal apostasy they testified by signing a document. They were thereupon given cigarettes and a sum of money, released, and allowed to go to their homes.

It became apparent to us that the room above us was being used as some sort of third-degree examination center. We tried to imagine what sort of horrors were going on over our heads: we could hear a continual mutter of questioning punctuated by screams, women sobbing, and young men crying out under what sounded like blows from a club. It was unbearably distressing to listen to, and kept us in a constant state of nervous terror.

Amid all this, by the mercy of God, came an incident to cheer us: while Sister Marie-Madeleine, the blind nun, was standing in the corridor waiting her turn to go and wash her hands,—for we were allowed out of the room for essential functions only twice a day at fixed hours—a platoon of soldiers came marching by, and one of them, as he passed the blind Sister, said in a low voice "Praised be Jesus!" We were so surprised that we did not reply immediately. In our thoughtlessness it had not occurred to us that there might be other Christians besides ourselves in that place of torment. By the time we had collected our wits, the soldier was already out of earshot.

The guards in charge of us were indefatigable, and seemed to be able to go on working all night. Occasionally one of them would lower his head and close his eyes for a few minutes, but would soon awake and go on with his bullying questions and interminable indoctrination. From the time of our arrest until we finally regained our freedom, we could always see Communist cadres working at their desks day and night, whether in the oncentration camp or in the rooms of the Red army officers. Perhaps the darkness of night is what Satan likes for his work.

That afternoon there was the noise of hammering in the room upstairs, and the sound of heavy objects being dragged across the floor. What devilish work were they engaged in? A poor enclosed Carmelite could hardly be expected to form a clear conception of the working of even such a commonplace machine as a motor-car engine or a television set, so what were we to make of all that hammering and activity going on in that terrible second-floor room? That they were installing some kind of machine we were convinced, and our nervousness led us to imagine, about nine or ten o'clock that night, that our young Korean Sisters were being led up to that room. In a nightmare we seemed to hear the cadres sternly calling the roll:

"Benedicta!"

"Agnes!"

"Michaela!"

"Gabriela!"

and so on, calling upon them to apostatize, and that some of them agreed but most of them refused to betray Catholicism. Then came the order; all who remained steadfast in the faith were to be put to the torture. The cries of the soldiers and the screams of pain nearly frightened us to death. Next we imagined that an old servant of ours who had worked many years for us was brought in and interrogated for a long time. After this a seminarian was thought to have been brought in and told to apostatize.

"I shall always remain a faithful Catholic,

no matter what you do to me."

At this they began the torture and jeered at him,

"Let us see if your Father in Heaven can save you now!"

We heard panting and sobbing, and then long-drawn-out groans. Suddenly there came loud shrieks of pain. Was it a trick? Was it a real tragedy? Or was it a nightmare?

There was so much noise that we could not make out clearly what they were saying in the upstairs room. A few words could be distinguished, but the rest of the sentence would be an unintelligible muttering.

The guards, seeing that we were listening attentively to what was going on, began coughing in unison, to prevent us from hearing. Confused noises came from the torture-machine, and we could form no definite idea of its nature. Was it not yet properly assembled and were they still trying to get it to work properly, or was it now set up and in action, inflicting pain on its victims? We could but believe the latter answer to be the true one.

Later, after our return to France, we learnt that throughout this period of our misgivings, while those terrible things were going on in the upstairs room, our beloved Sisters were still safe and sound in the Carmelite Convent.

July 18, Tuesday

At about five o'clock in the afternoon, one of the officers in charge of the guards sent one of them out to fetch five knives and then calling five soldiers forward, gave the following order:

"One of you men, kill a nun! First, stab her to the heart, then, cut off her finger-tips, her nose, and her ears, one by one! But wait till one o'clock tonight!"

When it got dark, soldiers armed with knives did in fact come in and sit down beside us. From time to time they would ask one another,

"Isn't it time yet?"

None of them seemed at all reluctant to carry out the order. However, as the time passed they made plausible excuses for post-

ponement, and when they finally left at dawn we found that we were still in the land of the living. Not one of us had been hurt.

This was the actual way in which they tried to break our spirit, by cold-blooded psychological torture, hoping that weak women would break down under the strain and beg them for mercy, but thanks to the courage we derived from our faith and the examples given by the saints and martyrs, we were at least able not to make fools of ourselves.

July 19, Wednesday

Word came that some of us were to be taken elsewhere, and we wondered where we would be sent. Some of us assumed that we were only going to be transferred to another jail in Seoul, while others thought it more likely that they were going to send us to P'yŏng-yang or some other prison in North Korea. Wherever it might be, we felt that it could hardly be much worse than staying in that stifling and overcrowded room.

Though we knew nothing about how the war was progressing, one thing we were sure of was that the sufferings of the poor Korean families must have been at least as hard to bear as our own. Driven from village to village with only what little belongings they could carry with them, deprived of their homes and separated from their loved ones, without resources, often rounded up by Communists and if not shot subjected to cruel regimentation and humiliation, or else left to die of hunger and disease, they were indeed enduring sufferings in comparison with which our own were, to use the words of St. Teresa of Avila, "Merely one night spent in a bad hostelry, that is all."

While we were standing in the filthy yard, still strewn with the garbage of weeds, a young American prisoner of war was escorted past us by a group of guards. He strode along unshaven but with chin up and a determined look on his face. We never found out who he was.

Soon a truck drove up and we helped one another to scramble up and settle ourselves for our mystery trip. Father Villemot and the two *St. Paul de Chartres* Sisters had been sent away, and our party consisted of sixteen persons: two Americans, Bishop Byrne and his secretary Father Booth; two Irishmen, Monsignor Quinlan and Father Canavan; one Australian, Father Crosbie; six French, the Fathers Gombert, Father Coyos, and Mother Henriette de Lobit, our subprioress, Sister Marie-Madeleine Marquier (the blind Sister) and Sister Bernadette Descayaux; two Belgians, Mother Thérèse Bastin, our prioress, and Mother Mechtilde Devriese; a German, Frau Charlotte Greise; a Turkish lady, Maisara Daulatsch; and the Polish-Korean girl Helena.

As we drove through the streets of Seoul we saw portraits of Stalin and Kim Il-sŭng stuck everywhere on walls and boardings, and Russian, Red Chinese and North Korean flags flying from the buildings. We had not gone far before our truck caught fire, and we all had to scramble out and wait for another, which was not long in coming. After a short ride we came to the terminus of the railway leading to the North Korean capital of P'yŏng-yang, where we were made to alight and sit beside the railway track. In no time a large crowd of people of all ages from grandmothers to little children gathered to stare at us, and our guards proclaimed to them that we were all "exploiters of the people."

Shortly afterward a soldier informed us that if we had any money we could now change it for North Korean currency and could buy some fruit and other light refreshments. This was very welcome news to us, for we were all very hungry and thirsty after our four days in that overcrowded prison room, and looked forward eagerly to a change from our diet of cold boiled dumpling with bits of newspaper stuck to them. Though we had not been allowed to bring our hand-luggage with us when we were taken from the convent, Mother Mechtilde did have a little money in her purse and we were able to enjoy some fresh fruit.

Our train arrived and we were marched to a cattle-car which of course had no steps for us to board it, so it was rather a job get-

ting in. It was very dirty, and there were a lot of Korean prisoners in it already, so by the time we had all managed to get in it was grossly overcrowded. Some of our fellow-travelers understood French, and made several attempts to enter into conversation with us, but we were not sure whether it was wise to talk freely with them, and didn't have much to say to them.

When the fruit-hawker came he said,

"Now is your chance to practice Communism. In Communist countries, everything is fair and equal. Those who don't pay also get a share!"

He then demonstrated the fairness of the Communist regime by giving two apples each to those who paid for them with their own money and four each to those who did not pay.

Although there were a lot of soldiers on the train, only one was assigned to our car to guard us, and he was only a boy of at most seventeen or eighteen years of age. Though he stood at attention with his rifle on his shoulder, he did not show any signs of tiredness, perhaps because he felt that his responsibility was so great. Our eight priests talked to him and he told them,

"In North Korea only those who have the same idea as the Communist rulers can live. Reactionaries are liable to be liquidated!"

It was as simple as that.

After dark the train started, and a few minutes later the steam heating was turned on. Jam-packed as we were we soon found it almost impossible to breathe, for the windows were tightly closed. However, the journey did not last long, and we were soon awakened. Some little time before the fighting broke out I had been reading in our convent refectory that the Russian secret police had devised a similar ordeal train for their prisoners. The magazine described overheating of the railroad cars, and false alarms of attack or breakdown as methods used to harass the prisoners being carried on long train journeys through Siberia, in an attempt to break their spirit. Underneath our car there were in fact all sorts of queer-looking attachments which, for all I knew, might be for some such purpose.

At any rate, it turned out that we too were to have the honor of riding a satanic train. There is a French proverb which says that a well-taught man is worth two men, and I would like to add to it that a well-taught woman is worth four women. I felt no fear or distress. When we heard sounds of rapid firing in the dark, cries of "Thieves, thieves!" and men running, we just smiled to ourselves in the darkness where no one could see us. Occasionally soldiers would come and shine their flashlights in our faces to see if we were frightened, and they seemed disappointed when, contrary to their expectation, none of us showed any signs of alarm.

We calmly waited for them to put on the next act: the derailment scene. Without fail, it came. Although we felt ready for anything, we couldn't help feeling a little uneasy when there came a violent jolt, and our car suddenly seemed about to subside into the ground. The train crawled slowly forward, but the act was not over: in the darkness we could catch snatches of conversation:

"We're nearly at the bridge, aren't we?"

"Yes, we shan't be long now. Another couple of minutes or so. Are you ready to drown them all in the river?"

"Yes, we're all ready."

The train crept slowly on its way. The change in the air told us that we were nearing the river; it was much fresher and there was a slight haze. One of the soldiers repeated the question,

"Are you sure everything's ready?"

"Yes, keep the train moving dead slow, please."

Slowly the train came to a halt in the middle of the bridge. But nobody was drowned, and after a while it started again. Their repertoire was not exhausted, however, for they still had a few tricks up their sleeve.

They pretended to set up an execution ground, and one of them, pointing his rifle at Father Coyos, said,

"Who's to be the first? How about this one?"

The only effect of all this mummery was to disturb our sleep, and this was our fifth night of sleeplessness.

Next morning to slake my burning thirst and to try to appease the gnawing pangs of hunger, I finished off the last few drops of water that remained in my bottle. They all jeered at me, saying,

"What, don't you know any manners? Aren't you ashamed to drink all that water of yours without offering any to your fellow-travelers?"

One of the Irish priests had some powdered milk with him. He mixed some with water in a cup and tried to have it passed to us through the crowd, but on its way it came into the clutches of one of the guards who were seated halfway between him and us. As soon as he got hold of it he drained it off at a draught. The Irish Father then mixed a second cupful, hoping that it might get safely past the guard, but he drank that one up too, in accordance with his Marxist principles, no doubt.

On the other hand some of the 'comrades' of the People's Army seemed to be trying hard to make a good impression on us and to do their best to explain their point of view. I shall never forget one young People's Army nurse, who came over to us and very kindly applied a dressing to a boil from which one of our Sisters was suffering.

At Sa-ri-won Station the train halted to pick up a number of young cadres who apparently had seats reserved for them. They had been assigned to lecture to their captive audience, and one after another they came to our car to carry out their assignment. Their speeches, though poorly composed, were delivered with fluency and spirit. Though they contained nothing worth serious consideration, we had to listen to them all from beginning to end. In due course they took up the topic of religious orders, and pointing to us, said,

"These nuns are merely parasites on society. They have been leading a life of comfort and even of luxury, shut up behind their high fence, while these men here (pointing to the priests) have been actively engaged in disseminating the idea of over-throwing Communism." I wished that I could read to him a few words from the poems of St. John of the Cross, the following stanza, for example:

> Para venir a gustarlo todo
>   No queiras tener gusto en nada.
> Para venir a poseerlo todo
>   No queiras poseer algo em nada.
> (In order to enjoy everything
>   You require to find enjoyment in nothing.
> In order to possess everything
>   You require to possess nothing).

But the mystic values of the religious life, though profound, are perhaps the most difficult of subjects to discuss in public with a hostile unbeliever, and the words would convey little meaning to the inexperienced. Knowledge about a thing is not the thing itself: instead of wanting to understand it before believing, one must believe in order to understand.

Bad as the air had been in the car during the night it now grew worse as the sun beat down on the roof during the day, and by midday we were ordered to get down and wait a while by the railroad tracks in the shade. As we left the car the cadres said,

"You people are going to be killed now, after all. We shan't have to cook so many rice dumplings this evening."

It was a great relief to breathe the fresh air, but we were so tired and thirsty that we could hardly manage to swallow the food provided for us, hungry though we were. In spite of the heat the guards moved about briskly, saying that they were going to prepare an execution ground, where we would all be shot.

The Fathers persuaded the guards to let us be taken in groups to a small well, where we could drink cool water and have a much-needed wash, and when our turn came to be marched off to the well instead of to the execution ground we really began to wonder whether our ears had been deceiving us, or whether they had been trying to tease us

with all those insults and threats.

A chance to wash! How dirty we were! We were all eager to wash the dust and sweat from our bodies, but to our embarrassment a large crowd had assembled round the well to observe how the foreign women performed their ablutions. How we would have liked to undress and take a bath, but how could we do that with all those people looking on? We Carmelite nuns have our hair cut short to the head, and over it we wear the toque ordained by St. Teresa of Avila. It is made of plain linen, and enwraps the head and throat, while leaving the forehead bare. Over the toque goes the black veil, which, thinking that we had better not miss an opportunity that might not recur for weeks, we now removed, and took off our toques. Seeing our close-cropped hair as we washed, the bystanders who had cameras took picture after picture of the ridiculous scene.

The Communists tried to annoy and embarrass us in every way, ranging from the infliction of petty inconveniences and humiliations to scurrilous abuse and threats of death, but they went no farther and we all managed to preserve an imperturbable demeanor throughout. No doubt they would have been better pleased with us if we had broken down in tears, or else lost our tempers and tried to repay them in kind, but self-control reduced all their efforts to failure.

Nightfall, and there was not a single rice dumpling for our supper. Gloatingly they told us that they hadn't thought it worth-while to give us any food, since we were all going to be killed that night. We were ordered to board the train again, and found that our car was now provided with benches, on each of which two persons could sit. But the train did not start for a long time, and we wondered what would happen next.

They began by reading aloud, in mocking and contemptuous tones, the sacred Vow of our Carmelite Order. Could we be right in suspecting that perhaps they were at heart so wretched and unhappy that their only wish was to wound? It was the idea of celibacy that seemed to infuriate them to such a pitch that they did not care what pain they inflicted. Maddened with hatred, they exchanged the foulest obscenities in our presence, in their attempt to shake our faith.

They put on a one-act play full of blasphemy, in which one Communist acted the part of a Korean nun taking the vow, while another, in his true colors, pleaded with her to abjure it for the sake of the state; finally the supposed nun agreed to do so, to the loud applause of the indoctrinated onlookers. What filthy thoughts they dragged up from the depths of their minds! We recognized the spiteful hand of Satan in their little play, for he knew well that our vow is one of his greatest stumbling blocks in his work to enslave souls, and a most efficient cause to lead them in the way of salvation. The two Sisters who knew Korean well enough to catch the meaning of the dialogue in the play sighed, and said,

"It makes us almost wish we had never learnt the Korean language!"

The leader of the cadres then brought five of his men over to us, and after earnestly explaining to them in lurid detail how to violate the chastity of the Korean nuns went away and left them in our company. The five men, grinning, said they would carry out his orders when they came back to our car after finishing some work they had to do elsewhere, and then left us. Shortly afterward the train began to move.

July 21, Friday

We arrived at P'yŏng-yang at 7 a.m. and were immediately taken to the courtroom. Some of the bystanders seemed quite friendly. Huge portraits of Stalin and Kim Il-sŭng hung on the left and right of the judge's bench. Father Crosbie told us that it might have been in this room that the Vicar Apostolic of P'yŏng-yang, Bishop Francis Hong, had knelt more than a year before to hear 'the verdict of the people.'

We were kept sitting at small desks all day; we were ordered not to move or attempt to leave the room and everyone was sunk in thought. Pens and paper were provided, and we were told to write down our personal history. Just then a plane zoomed down and a bomb crashed near by—the blast blew our papers about the room as we crouched under the desks. One of our Sisters suddenly remembered that yesterday was the commemoration of St. Margaret, Virgin and Martyr, her patron saint, and that on this day in previous years there had always been a big celebration of her feast-day at the Carmelite Convent. Unconsciously she went on asking herself,

"Where are my daughters of the Carmelite Convent? What has happened to them since we left?"

The usual interrogation began, but at 10 o'clock it was interrupted by a meal, which was better than what we had had up to now, consisting as it did of rice and good soup. The interrogation continued, interrupted during the afternoon by a second bombing and at 5 p.m. we were told that we would have to spend the night on the premises. We were taken across a yard to a small room and were served another meal. There we had begun to settle down for the night when at 10 p.m. we were suddenly told that we must leave immediately. We hurriedly got ready and boarded a worn-out old truck. The guards tossed bundles of blankets on, and we started on our way.

The truck rattled and squeaked along for some distance and then bounced along for about a mile across some fields. The bundles of blankets and other freight in the truck pressed heavily on our arms and legs, but soon it stopped and we were ordered to get off the truck and walk. It was difficult for us to walk in the dark: there was no moon and our way led along narrow paths between rice fields full of water, and across streams by stepping stones. It was easy to stumble and one of our Sisters slipped and fell into the paddy field, getting drenched to the skin and losing one of her shoes. Frau Gliese and Father Crosbie helped some of the older folk to cross the stepping stones by walking beside them barefoot in the mud.

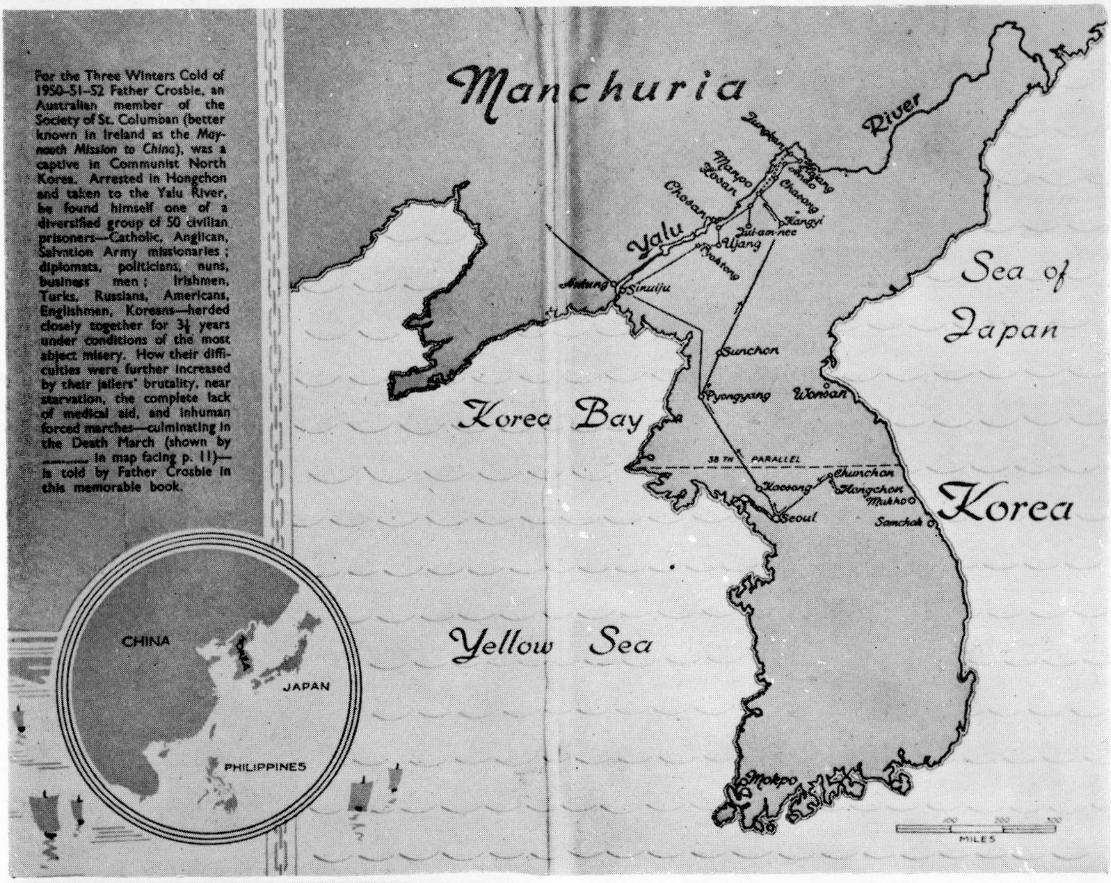

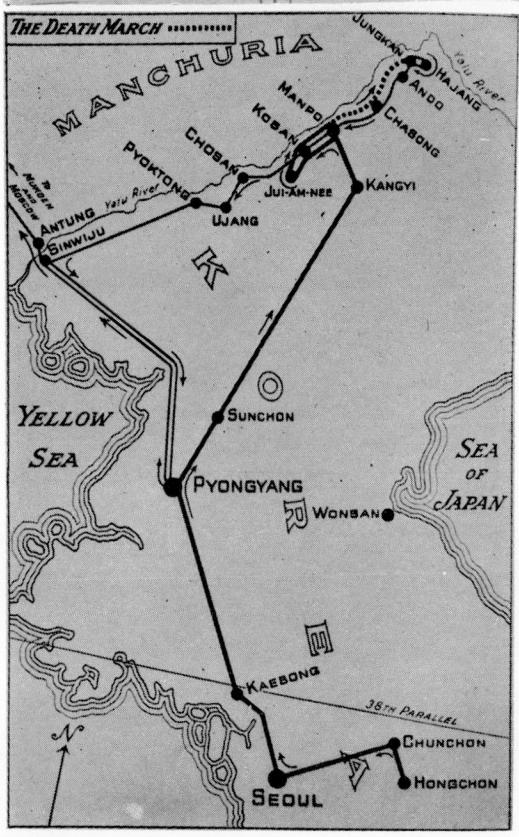

Map showing the Death March traced by Bishop Byrne and companions
(From "Three Winters Cold" by Father Philip Crosbie)

Close-up of the map

485

Scenes from the movie of the Death March, including
one of Bishop Byrne

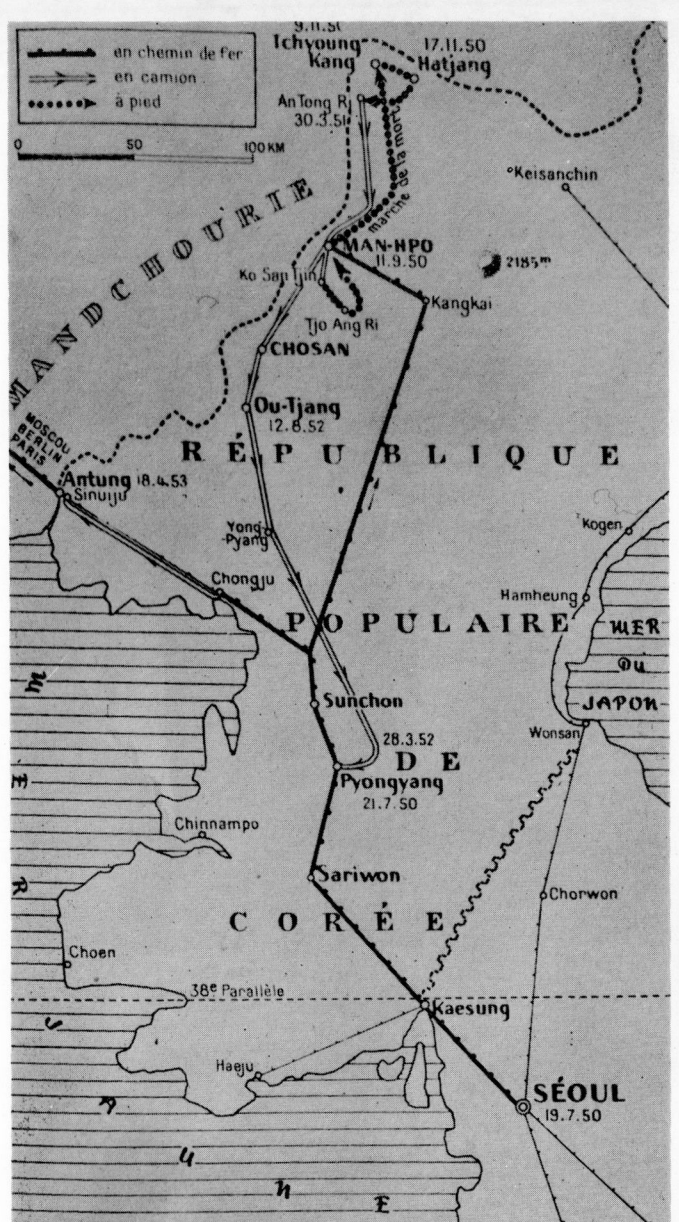

Map showing the route of the Death March traced by the kidnapees (From "Ma Captivité en Corée du Nord" by Father Coyos)

Father William Booth, one of the survivors, after his return

Bishop Thomas Quinlan, a survivor, inspecting a Tommy-gun, a reminder of things past
Father Philip Crosbie (left), Father William Booth (right)

The first group released from detention camp, taken just before on their way home

Left to right: George Blake, Bishop Cooper (Anglican), Commissioner Lord (Salvation Army), Norman Owen, Monsignor Quinlan (from "Pencilling Prisoner" by Father Philip Crosbie)

← Mother Eugénie's safe return (center)

Carmelite Sisters, after their release
The blind Sister Marie-Madeleine (left), next but one to her is Mother Eugénie

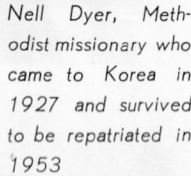

Walter Eltringham, mining engineer, ECA, who died in captivity (Nov. 17, 1950)

Nell Dyer, Methodist missionary who came to Korea in 1927 and survived to be repatriated in 1953

Commissioner Herbert A. Lord, O.B.E.
of the Salvation Army survived

Father Booth on his way home (front)

We came to a wide field and as we were exhausted we implored them to let us spend the night there, but in vain. They made us take to those slippery paths again.

At last we could see lights twinkling far ahead. We came to two large buildings and were all assembled in a large room. The Communist leader who accompanied us was treated with great respect by the guards, and we realized that he was in charge of us. But we were so tired and sleepy that we could not listen attentively to him. He started indoctrinating us on the evils of capitalism, but at last his speech came to an end and thin, worn-out blankets were distributed. Those who were lucky got an unbleached sheet as well. We were then taken to another building about a hundred yards away, and there we were divided into three groups. We women formed one group, Bishop Byrne and Father Booth, the second, and the remainder of the priests, the third. It was two o'clock in the morning.

When we came to the room assigned to our group we found three women already in occupation. We could hear some men talking in a low voice in the adjoining room and one of our Sisters was a little scared and suspicious and asked who they were. But we were so tired that we decided to forget about it and try to get a little sleep. We learned next morning that the people in the next room were M. Georges Perruche, Consul General of the French Legation in Seoul, who was usually referred to as the 'French Minister'; M. Jean Meadmore, his Vice-Consul; M. Charles Martel, the Chancelor of the Legation; and M. Maurice Chanteloup, a correspondent of the French press agency. They had all been arrested in Seoul.

We slept soundly on the bare floor. When we awoke we found a bucketful of water for washing, alongside which stood three wash basins. We washed in turn. A few days later we received a ration of toilet soap, tooth-paste and tooth-brush. Our French Minister gave us a large towel he had with him, and we cut it into five pieces, one for each Carmelite Sister.

We were now far more comfortable than we had been in our prison in Seoul. The room was spacious and light, with glass windows, and the floor was of wooden boards. The Communists still continued to watch us day and night through the windows.

The three ladies with whom we shared the room were American Methodist missionaries who had been arrested in Kae-sŏng. Their names were Miss Bertha Smith, Miss Helen Rosser, and Miss Nell Dyer. They were all very kind to us, and glad to borrow our nail-scissors to trim their nails. Like us, they had been arrested without warning and forbidden to bring even hand luggage with them. These nail-scissors of ours were really a kind of combination tool that could be used as hair- or beard-clippers as well, and all the inmates of this camp, and even the guards, were glad to borrow them from time to time. When we left the camp we asked the guards to return them to us, but each of them shifted the responsibility from himself to another 'comrade' and in the end we failed to get them back. Fortunately, Mother Marie Henriette de Lobit found a pair of embroidery scissors in her pocket and it was these that we had to use until we regained our freedom.

We had to get up at reveille, and watch the soldiers having their morning wash and singing their Communist songs at the same time. Then at six the male prisoners washed, and after them the women. Then came breakfast. Every meal was the same, one rice-ball and a bowl of soup for each meal three times a day, though the hours were irregular. Sometimes lunch was at 3 p.m. and supper as late as 9 p.m. We were thankful that the rice was well cooked, but the men felt hungry all the time because the quantity was not enough for them. Once we happened to overhear a squabble between the cook and a guard in the kitchen. The cook was angry:

"How can these people live on so little food? If you don't feed them decently I'm going to quit. I can't bear to see you starving them like this."

This benevolent cook did in fact leave soon afterward, but it made no difference to us. We went on getting one rice-ball at each meal and no more.

There was one day when a man they called the commander came to inspect the quarters, on this day we had plenty of well-cooked rice and a delicious potato soup. But from the next day on we were back on the old ration of one rice-ball each at every meal, which was really not enough for our hungry stomachs.

We were strictly forbidden to leave our room, and had to get permission even to go to the toilet. Nevertheless Sister Bernadette Descayaux did manage to elude our guards and pick some wild herbs and edible plants from the grass around our house, and cooked them for us.

A week later two more persons came to join us in our room. They were the 76-year-old Mother Béatrice Edouard, and Mother Eugénie Demeusy, of the *St. Paul de Chartres* Convent and Orphanage, and early in August, Sister Mary Clare, an Irish-born nun of the Episcopalian Church Convent, and Madame Amelia Martel and Mademoiselle Marguerite Martel, the Mother and Sister of Charles Martel, the Chancelor of the French Legation. Madame Martel opened up her bag of treasures full of needles and thread and all kinds of sewing materials and distributed them among us, and thereafter we all called her 'Mother Martel.' Hitherto all our sewing had to be done with thread unravelled from old blankets, for we could get no other for our needlework.

From now on we decided to make our life more regular. Periods during the day were set aside for meditation, rest, and daily devotion. Our daily devotion began with a recital of as many of the psalms as we could remember, and then we would offer up the Lord's Prayer as a substitute for the other prayers, followed by an Ave Maria and a recital of the Apostles' Creed, during which time we walked up and down the room. The guards did not seem to mind

our doing this, and what is more one of them went up to the American Protestant missionary women and asked,

"If these crop-haired nuns can be always saying their prayers like this, why don't you who claim to be missionaries say some prayers without getting your hair cut?"

We would sing the Anthem *Alma Redemptoris* on weekdays and on Sundays *the Canticle of the Three Young Men* in the mornings and the *Benedictus Deus* in the afternoons, concentrating heart and mind on the Blessed Sacrament in the tabernacle installed on the high altar of the Cathedral of the Immaculate Conception of Seoul.

Sister Mary Clare, the Irish-born Anglican nun from Seoul who shared our room, showed me a copy of the poem *The Dark Night of the Soul* by St John of the Cross, a book which she treasured and had kept hidden under her habit. We invited her to the Benediction of the Most Blessed Sacrament, and she seemed most impressed. One Sunday Father Celestine Coyos persuaded the guard to let him come to our room, and for our benefit he repeated and explained the Act of Contrition, pausing at intervals to explain the meaning of each part.

August 12, the Feast of Saint Clare, Virgin

The Mothers and Sisters of the two convents assembled to celebrate the feast. We paid our homage to the saint, the first Superior of the Order of Poor Clares founded by Saint Francis of Assisi, and sang some hymns in her honor. With wild flowers gathered from the yard of our prison we made little bouquets for Mother Thérèse, our prioress, for which she was very grateful. Mother Thérèse, who was formerly known as Irène Bastin, was a native of Virton in Belgium. When the Germans invaded her homeland in 1914 she was only thirteen years old, but she worked during the four years of the war as a member of "*La Dame Blanche*"—a secret group formed by the people of Virton to cooperate with the allies. Some of her friends were executed, and her own parents were imprisoned. In 1918 she herself was imprisoned, but was eventually released for lack of evidence. The strain and hardship she experienced during her years of adolescence had impaired her health, and in later life she had been affected with tuberculosis. When peace came, she entered our Carmel at Virton, and remained there till 1938, when she came to Korea as one of the foundation members for the new Carmel in Seoul. Ten years later she became prioress of our community, which now included Korean Carmelites as well as Belgian and French.

Her health which had been poor for many years began to decline during our captivity, and at this time she was evidently in the throes of a mortal illness.

We decided to introduce a little more regularity into our life in prison. In addition to our regular periods of religious meditation and daily devotions we arranged to have daily lessons in English from Madame Martel. Sister Bernadette Descayaux was permitted to help us with the kitchen chores after meals. This was her own idea: she volunteered to do the work because she thought the exercise would do her good. She was always ready to help everybody with a willing smile. There was a young Korean woman employed in the kitchen who used to bring us in our meals. One day when Sister Bernadette and a Carmelite nun were alone in the room she showed us a little crucifix that she had pinned on the inside of her blouse, and told us,

"I am a Catholic. My Christian name is Joanna." On another occasion when we were in the kitchen washing dishes after a meal a Christian soldier approached the window, pretending to bring us rice bowls to be washed, and said from outside,

"I am a Catholic. Please pray for me," and went away, making the sign of the cross on his breast.

The continued malnutrition inevitably brought about its effect. Many of us began to suffer from boils. Poor Mother Henriette de Lobit, our subprioress, had boils on her hands, feet and all over her body. Her family was a famous one in France: in World War I, it was a General Lobit who had liberated Yugoslavia, adding more luster to the family name. And at this time his niece, then in her late teens, was planning to illumine it in another and less transient way.

In the early twenties, the general's niece entered Carmel at Aire-sur-Adour, to become Sister Henriette. She volunteered, in 1938, for the Carmel in Seoul, and was assigned to the difficult task of keeping the new foundation financial. In 1948 she became subprioress. As Father Crosbie says,

"I wonder how many graces were won for our camp by the prayers of Mother Henriette. She did not have good health, and hence could not take an active part in the general life. But late at night and again early in the morning you could see her petite figure sitting quietly among the outstretched forms, and the expression on her face, so beautiful in repose, told you that her thoughts were with God."

Mother Mechtilde Devriese had given us much cause for anxiety about her health. Although at our convent she had been able to adapt herself to Korean food without much difficulty, now that she was a prisoner she could hardly bring herself to swallow even a morsel of it. To make matters worse, a large boil had broken out on her knee and she daily became weaker.

In the next room to us there was an Austrian physician, an understanding and sympathetic person named Doctor Ernst Kisch, M.D., of Vienna, who was ready to see patients.

Dr. Kisch was Jewish by race and Austrian by birth. He might have become a world-famous figure but for an extraordinary series of adversities that had dogged his career. He passed brilliantly through the medical schools of his native Vienna in the days when these schools drew students from all over the world. While still a young intern, he made the first identification of a disease which makes war on the corpuscles of the blood, and which until then had remained mysterious. The scepticism of one of his professors toward youthful learning delayed the publication of his thesis. Meantime a German professor made and announced the same discovery, and the disease was called by his name. The name of Ernst Kisch remained unknown in the world of medicine.

Hitler launched his campaign against the Jews; Dr. Kisch was herded into a concentration camp. His near relations and many of his friends perished. At length, from imprisonment he went into exile, carrying in a suitcase all that was left of his possessions. He found a post in a Methodist Mission hospital in Shanghai, and stayed there for ten years. Forced to leave them, he went to the United States and worked for a few months in a New York hospital, but found he could not remain in the country. He was offered work in the American Methodist Mission hospital in Kae-sŏng, and had been there only a few weeks when the Red invasion began. Kae-sŏng fell in the first hours of the attack.

This genius of a man, exiled from his homeland as a Jew, forced to leave China by the Communist invasion, denied permanent asylum in America, arrested with his American associates in Korea, was to end his life of disappointed hopes not many weeks after he called,

"Clinic Time!"

for the last time in Man-p'o. We knew only some of the bitterness he had tasted in life, and there would be fervor in the prayer with which we would lay his tired, worn body down: "Eternal rest grant unto him, O Lord, and let perpetual light shine upon him."

It was in Kae-sŏng that he had been captured in the service of a Protestant hospital. Arrested on the morning of June 25, 1950, he was taken to the prison where we were held in custody. He died from undernourishment in the prison in July, 1951.

He exerted his utmost efforts to help his fellow-prisoners, many of whom were suffering from undernourishment like himself. He visited our room three times, and did his best to look after Mother Mechtilde, but he could not do anything definitely helpful for her, either in the way of providing medicine or medical appliances. Not even warm water was available for him in his treatment of her.

Interrogation went on as intensively as before. They simply would not give up their constant questioning about the most insignificant details of one's past life.

The French Minister had undergone a good deal of this sort of thing and one day he answered one of their questions facetiously.

"My aunt? She was an artist, and could paint a bicycle. She was married in a carriage drawn by two horses." Stunned by the reply one of the interrogators asked,

"Excuse me, but what do you mean by that?" Everyone broke out into fits of laughter.

At the time we did not know who were occupying the other rooms of our prison, but Father Crosbie has given us a list as follows:

Room One

Captain Vyvyan Holt, Minister of the British Legation in Seoul.

Mr. George Blake, British Vice-Consul in Seoul.

Mr. Norman Owen, Secretary of the British Legation.

Room Two

Herbert A. Lord, O.B.E., Lieutenant-Commissioner in the Salvation Army, and head of that organization in Korea.

The Reverend Charles Hunt, an Anglican missionary of Seoul.

(These two fellow-prisoners were both English.)

M. Alfred Matti, manager of Cho-sŏn Hotel in Seoul. (Swiss)

Father Antoine Gombert. (French)

Father Julien Gombert. (French)

Father Francis Canavan. (Irish)

Monsignor Thomas Quinlan. (Irish)

Father Philip Crosbie. (Australian)

Room Three

M. Georges Perruche, Consul-General — of the French Legation in Seoul.

M. Jean Meadmore, Vice-Consul

M. Charles Martel, Chancelor

M. Maurice Chanteloup, correspondent of the French press agency.

Room Four

Miss Bertha Smith — of the Methodist Mission in Kae-sŏng (Americans)

Miss Helen Rosser

Miss Nell Dyer

Mother Thérèse Bastin.

Mother Mechtilde Devriese.

Mother Henriette de Lobit.

Sister Marie-Madeleine Marquier.

Sister Bernadette Descayaux.

Frau Charlotte Gliese.

Mme. Maisara Daulatsch.

Helena.

Room Five

The Reverend A. Kris Jensen, D.D., of the Methodist Mission in Seoul. (American)

The Reverend Lawrence Zellers, of the Methodist Mission in Kae-sŏng. (American)

Ernest Kisch, M.D., of the Methodist Hospital in Kae-sŏng (Austrian)

Mr. Walter Eltringham, of the American Economic Cooperation Administration staff in Seoul. (American)

Mr. Louis Dans, assistant manager of the Traders' Exchange in Seoul. (American)

Mr. William Evans, a mining engineer. (American)

Bishop Patrick Byrne, Apostolic Delegate to Korea, of the Maryknoll Mission. (American)

Father William Booth, secretary to Bishop Byrne. (American)

July 31, Monday

Father Crosbie saw a jeep drive in from the main road, and watched the passengers alighting. All were Red officials, except for one khaki-clad, bare-headed foreigner. One of his arms was in a sling and he limped as he was escorted to the other building. Commissioner Lord had been summoned to act as interpreter. Now, on his return, he told us the newcomer was Philip Deane, a war correspondent for *The Observer* in London.

In due course Philip Deane was brought to our building, and was assigned to Room Two. We learnt that he had been captured on July 23 at Yŏng-tong, in the central sector of what was then the battle line. Deane, therefore, was no more as up to date with the present situation than we were, but such news as he had, he dispensed to us with the clarity and graphic style of the trained journalist, and we heard with intense interest the account of his own experiences. We did not press him for the full story then, for he was a tired and sick man, but we heard it in detail in the days that followed.

He was a native of Greece, and was in his middle twenties. During World War II he had served in the British Navy; and when peace was restored, he had gone back to Greece to act as correspondent for *The Observer*. On the outbreak of war in Korea, he had hastened there by plane to report the fighting for the paper.

Arriving on July 10, he went at once in search of copy to the central front, which was then just north of Tae-jŏn. Having left Tae-jŏn shortly before it fell to the Reds, he reached the front line again some twenty-five miles to the southeast, just north of Yŏng-dong, on the morning of July 23. American forces were already withdrawing southward from Yŏng-tong as he moved northward out of the town by jeep. After a few miles' travel, the vehicle was immobilized by sniper fire, and he found his retreat cut off. He took shelter in a farmhouse with some American soldiers, but the thin mud walls offered little protection. Some of his companions were hit, and enemy troops were moving closer.

He crawled out to some jeeps standing near, but as he tried to get one of them moving, he was wounded in the hand and thigh, and next the vehicle itself was hopelessly crippled by bullets. Nothing to do but crawl back to the farmhouse and await the Reds. They arrived at three in the afternoon, ordered Deane and the rest to their feet, shot those who were too badly wounded to rise, and marched the others out to the road.

The prisoners were deprived of their footwear, and their hands were tied behind them. Then began for them a nightmare journey. Barefoot and bleeding, they traveled over mountain paths and country roads for days, to Communist Army headquarters near Suwon. This would be a journey of nearly ninety miles as the crow flies, but a good deal longer by ground travel.

The discovery by an interpreter that Deane was a journalist had meant the beginning of long interrogations, which were renewed when he was brought north by jeep to Seoul, and again when a truck took him to P'yŏng-yang. Eventually he had convinced his captors that he was a noncombatant, and so had been sent out to our civilian internees' camp. When he arrived he was wearing shower-slippers. These he found lying, of all places, on top of a disabled American tank which he passed during his five-day march. Both in Seoul and in P'yŏng-yang he had been ordered to broadcast over the Communist radios speeches denouncing the atrocities of the United States, but had refused. Here again he steadfastly refused to do so, and withstood all intimidation. His meager food supply was reduced in an attempt to make him consent, but though seriously weakened physically he seemed superhuman in his courage and determination.

On August 4 Philip Deane was taken away. He and the French journalist Chanteloup had both undergone lengthy spells of intimidation but to see him taken away from the camp altogether aroused great anxiety in us. Nearly a month passed. Then, on August 31 we were delighted to see him brought back safe and sound.

He had been taken to a large house in P'yŏng-yang and made to sit in a stuffy room, with a bright light close to his face, before a team of interrogators who questioned him and argued with him ceaselessly for three days and nights, till he finally lapsed into unconsciousness. Their object was still to get him to write articles or make broadcasts favorable to the North Koreans. The previous attempts had failed and this was an all-out attempt to break his resistance. He gathered that he had been taken from camp to deprive him of the moral support of the British diplomats. If the North Koreans had learnt that Deane was not British by birth, but Greek, and if they had discovered in addition that he was the son of a Greek general who had commanded anti-Red partisan forces, there is little doubt as to what his fate would have been.

"Don't you want to let your wife know over the radio that you have survived? If you'll only make a statement we will treat you well! We aren't savages, are we?"

"We're civilized people, aren't we? How can you prove that you are really a war correspondent? You may be a spy. If you don't want to talk over the radio, what about writing an article on the United States? You say you are a journalist—if you cannot write, we'll have to conclude that you are a spy."

"You rascal! You know how we deal with spies!" So it went on for three days, the interrogators working in shifts while Deane had to undergo the trial all alone.

When he recovered consciousness there was a North Korean officer of high rank standing beside him.

"All the newspapers in England are carrying the story of this man's arrest! He must be a famous correspondent, eh?" And turning to Deane he said,

"We'll help you to recover your health."

Eggs, coffee and wine were brought and from that time he was given good treatment.

Air raids were common over P'yŏng-yang during this period, and Deane was often left alone in the house while its occupants, including his guards, took shelter. During such periods he explored the rooms and discovered several radio sets. He was able to pick up various news broadcasts from the United States, Britain and Australia.

He brought back a bag of sugar, which he divided among us all in equal shares.

He was able to remember in detail the news he had picked up; he told us that Tae-gu was still safe from the enemy and that the United Nations Forces were preparing to march north. The news of the forthcoming counterattack was very encouraging to us, and gave us hope that we would soon be released.

First Stay at Man-p'o

(September 5~October 8, 1950)

On the 5th September order for our departure was issued, and we all happily began packing our belongings.

Although we tried hard to find out where we were being taken, the guards would not tell us. Two trucks took us, together with some other prisoners, including seven men, into P'yŏng-yang. On our way we picked up a Turkish couple who had been engaged in commerce in Seoul, and their six children, their uncle and aunt, and a White Russian couple and their three children. It was raining slightly when our train arrived. Now for the first time since our internment we could talk freely to all the others who had been separated from us. We were put aboard the train. The diplomats and the two journalists were put in a carriage by themselves, and the rest of us were crowded into two compartments of another carriage, women and children in one section, men in another The seats had been removed, and there was no glass in the windows. The men sealed these up as well as they could with some plywood the guards found for us. There was barely room for us all to sit down shoulder to shoulder.

We could see about seven hundred and fifty American prisoners getting into roofless coal-trucks attached to our train. Most of them were still wearing their summer uniforms, and some were barefooted and evidently had not been allowed to wash for a long time. How miserable and downcast they looked!

Soon the train came to a halt and the engine was uncoupled and driven away. It was needed elsewhere, we were told, and

our train would not be moving again till the next day. Many engines had been destroyed by bombing, and ours was no doubt required for one of the many military supply trains that were constantly going south on the other line.

The trains passing south in the night were always long, and often had two engines to haul them. They were composed chiefly of freight cars, but often included some open trucks or flat cars carrying motor lorries, tanks and artillery. On some nights they must have passed us hourly.

We spent the night in the station and at seven in the morning were able to take a little walk up the hill and enjoy the fresh air. The people of that town all looked displeased at having to provide food for about eight hundred foreigners, even though it was only rice balls. It was two o'clock in the afternoon when we had our first meal, and not long afterward the supper ration was issued.

We learnt that during the night the men, who had decided to sleep on the train, had found it impossible for all of them to lie down in the crowded compartment. Commissioner Lord, of the Salvation Army, who was the interpreter and spokesman, pressed the guard to find accommodation for some of them elsewhere on the train. The guard thought the request unreasonable, and when Commissioner Lord insisted, sent for an officer to deal with him. The officer replied to the commissioner's protest by threatening him with a pistol. The commissioner however defied the threat, and his courage was vindicated, for the officer abandoned his threatening attitude and even promised to see what he could do to meet the commissioner's demand. The other men were so greatly relieved for his sake that they regarded it as a minor matter when the officer's promise went unfulfilled.

September 6, Wednesday

The American prisoners of war were stationed on the opposite slope of the valley where we were sitting, and about three hundred yards from us. Then we saw for the first time a sight that was to become all too familiar in the days to come: four POWs carrying in a blanket the dead body of a comrade. A sergeant came across the valley and up the slope to where we were gathered.

"This lad we were burying was a Catholic, and we heard there were some Catholic priests among you. Maybe one would come and recite the funeral service."

It was agreed among the priests that Monsignor Quinlan should go, but the guard refused permission.

"We don't believe in such things," he said contemptuously, "It is not necessary for anyone to go."

The Monsignor and the American sergeant insisted on being allowed to speak to the Red colonel who was in command of the entire group of prisoners. To the credit of this officer, who was a fluent Russian speaker and presumably a confirmed Red, Father Crosbie records that he gave a sympathetic hearing to the Monsignor's appeal, and granted him permission to go with the sergeant and perform the last rites for the dead soldier.

Madame Martel had brought some holy water with her and sprinkled it on his grave, and we gathered wild flowers and made a wreath for him.

With tears in his eyes, Monsignor Quinlan offered a prayer for him. What a great sorrow for his family!

Some twenty of the American prisoners of war were in such a wretched state that we could not help crying when we caught sight of them. But there was nothing we could do for them. Some had lost an arm, some were legless. Still others could only walk by the help of their comrades. Although we were forbidden to talk to them, their sorrowful plight pierced our hearts. They were in urgent need of medical treatment, but it seemed that all they could expect was death. Some of the guards did take pity on them and gave them cigarettes, which they acknowledged with a grateful smile.

The Korean countryside is at its most beautiful in spring and autumn, and it now began to show its autumn tints—the leaves of the trees turned bright coppered, deep crimson, and warm brown. What a contrast to the cruel and heart-breaking scenes around us!

Later that day there was another air raid! Planes roared low over our train and machine-gunned it. We thought of the poor prisoners of war who were too sick or too severely wounded to leave their carriage. In the evening we returned to the train and saw the bullet holes; fortunately they were high up and there were no casualties.

That night we traveled a short distance north and at daylight had to leave the train again. We were taken as before to a valley but there were houses there, and we were billeted with their occupants for the day. They were very kind, and showed themselves as friendly as they dared.

The rest of our journey was more or less the same as the first two days. Each night the train moved on. Each day we sheltered on wooded hills or in the cabins of the country folk, except for one day when we stopped at a town and were accommodated in a school building.

Twice on the journey the colonel bought pigs and these were immediately slaughtered and cooked. For us this was the first meat we had tasted in weeks.

While we were spending the day in the school a large crowd of children and grown-ups gathered round us. One man seeing one of the priests wearing a cassock was very glad, and waited about for a chance to approach him. At last he seized an opportunity when there was no guard near and said,

"Father, I am a sincere Catholic. There are fifteen Catholics in our village."

"You are having a difficult time, I suppose?"

"Yes, you're right," he answered, "we have prayer meetings in a different Catholic's home every Sunday. For three years we have been separated from our priest, and we are unable to receive the Sacrament of Penance. May I go and bring my fellow

Catholics here?"

Bishop Byrne answered,

"If you all come together there will be fifteen of you, and it will be too dangerous; it's just impossible. But if you gather in front of the railway station when we pass this evening, and if you will each make an Act of Contrition, I'll give you all Absolution."

Later we found them all waiting there. The group consisted of men, women and children, and one old man among them bravely made the sign of the Cross, disdaining any sufferings that might befall him at the hands of the Communists. Father Booth pronounced the words of Absolution as we passed. We were deeply moved, for at no time before had we realized to the full the depth of spiritual influence as we did at that moment. Later we learnt that they had collected a small sum of money to provide comforts for the priests and Sisters. Who could possibly dare to try to sever the strong spiritual ties among the children of God?

Our journey had lasted six days.

September 11, Monday

We finally arrived at Man-p'o at daylight. We could see the broad stream of the Yalu River beyond the town. We all left the train; the prisoners of war were marched away, and two trucks came to fetch the civilians. We soon overtook the slowly-moving column of prisoners and drew up at a large building, but a guard came out and said that only prisoners of war were to be accommodated there, so we turned back, passing the weary marchers a second time. At last we came to a group of buildings destined to be our quarters. Our journey was over.

We stayed at this place from September 11 to October 8. The buildings had formerly served as a quarantine station. There were four buildings around a large yard. In the largest were quartered the guards, the six diplomats, the two journalists, and seven Korean politicians. The rest of us went to two long, low buildings, women and children and elderly men in one, the rest of the men

in the other. There were numerous rooms, and we divided ourselves up into groups by religion, nationality, and race, and the members of each group were free to live happily together. Our group consisted of nine, all in one room: the five Carmelites, and the two nuns from the Convent of *St. Paul de Chartres*, and Madame Martel and her daughter. We were able to offer up our prayers without any disturbance.

On Sunday mornings all of us including Bishop Byrne and Monsignor Quinlan gathered in our room and sang hymns and recited the rosary together. It was not possible, however, to celebrate Mass. It was beginning to get cold at night, though still warm in the day time. We used to go out and try to get rid of the lice in our clothing, while sitting in the sunshine—we must have looked very funny. Our food was satisfactory; we had three meals a day, of rice, vegetable soup rich in oil, and dried fish reconstituted in water.

In addition we got occasional issues of meat and sugar, and sometimes even soap. Monsignor Quinlan was appointed quartermaster, and was always able to distribute a generous daily allowance, including salt, red pepper and soyabean paste. Those who had money were permitted to go shopping in the market. M. Perruche, the French Minister, would sell his belongings from time to time (his wristwatch, clothes and medicines that he had brought in his bag) and buy wine and eggs for us.

The Yalu River was a twenty-minute walk from our house, and our guards used to bring us to the bank every day, so that we could wash ourselves and our clothes or else take a walk, looking across the river to Manchuria. One windy day Mother Mechtilde returned from her walk with symptoms of pneumonia. We were very anxious about her, for we had seen some fifty American prisoners of war died from this disease, mainly because there was no medicine available.

The men prisoners seemed to enjoy their daily chore of fetching water to our quarters; it was no easy task but they could meet

Korean people at the well and get news about the war from them. While they were hauling up their buckets from the well they could often get information about recent broadcasts—it was lucky the guards did not find out what they were doing. It was in this way that we learnt of the recapture of Seoul.

It is worthwhile to say something about the rest of the prisoners, many of whom died or were killed later on. There were nationals of France, Ireland, England, the United States of America, Australia, Switzerland, Austria, Germany, White Russia, Turkey, Belgium, and also seven Korean political prisoners. There were Catholics, Anglicans, Methodists, Presbyterians, Salvation Army, Russian Orthodox, Moslems and Jews. Of the seventy-four prisoners, eight were children ranging in age from 16 months to 12 years. The infant was named Benjamin. We established brotherly relations amongst ourselves, though there were cases of selfishness even during times of severe hardships.

Toward the end of September we were joined by Father Joseph Cadars, the seventy-year-old gray-bearded Paris Foreign Missionary. He had been arrested in the latter half of July when the Reds entered Tae-jŏn, ninety miles south of Seoul. On the long journey from Tae-jŏn, through Seoul and P'yŏngyang to Man-p'o, he had been given little food, little rest, and no comfort. When we welcomed him the tears streamed down his tanned old cheeks. Someone hastened to bring him a tray of food, and he soon recovered the sturdy cheeriness that we were to know, in the days to come, as his characteristic mood. Even when he first walked into the camp, weary and worn by his journey, one could not fail to be struck by the soldierly bearing of his short, stocky figure—and we were not surprised to find that he had been a soldier too. An eye injury had disfigured his face, but could not destroy his kindly and fatherly disposition.

Joseph Cadars was born in 1879 in the department of Tarn-et-Garonne in southwest France and was a novice in the Franciscans when the religious orders were expelled from France at the beginning of the century. He declined to leave France, and entered the University of Clermont. He was ordained for his native Diocese, and became a professor in a college. He resigned to join Paris Foreign Missions, and was sent to Tae-gu, Korea. Called to the colors when World War I broke out, he became a lieutenant in the French Army in Indo-China. Near the end of the war, when French troops were being sent to Siberia, some of the soldiers asked Father Cadars to go along with them as their chaplain. He went, and when released returned to Korea, and built up several parishes and erected churches in them during the years that followed. When the Korean War broke out Father Cadars was taking care of the monastery at Tae-jŏn, in the absence of its French-Canadian Community. Father Cadars was to be the last addition to our company. His arrival brought our number to seventy-four.

October 6, Friday

Late this evening we were told that we must be up early next morning. There would be news, they said.

We were dismayed. It looked as if we must be moving. If so, what of our rosy dreams of early rescue by United Nations troops? It was inconceivable that we would be taken to meet them, and if we were not to be left here, as we had hoped, to await their arrival, then a move could only be for the purpose of taking us out of their reach. Were we then going across the Yalu after all? We passed a restless night, wondering what the day would bring.

October 7, Saturday

The order was given that we were to leave the place immediately. We had no idea where we were going, except that it was to be a boat journey. Rain was falling steadily. Mother Mechtilde was quite unable to walk, and a stretcher was provided for her. Four of the able-bodied volunteered to act as bearers, and we were told to make our way, with our blankets and food supplies, to a point a couple of miles upstream. The supplies and cooking pots were carried by the able-bodied men, some of whom had to make two trips. We waited miserably on the river bank, in the rain and icy wind, for the whole day, but no boats came. Mother Mechtilde was suffering intensely from the cold, but was as cheerful as ever. We covered her with extra blankets, and although her lips were blue with cold they never lost their smile and she never uttered a word of complaint.

Toward evening we were told that the boats would not come till next day, and that we must return to the quarters we had left. We were all tired and exasperated, and to add to our discomfort we found that the glass had been removed from the windows, and that the pot in which we cooked our rice was missing. Eventually we found it and cooked some supper, and tried to get some sleep.

October 8, Sunday

The sun was shining as we all went down to the river again to wait for the boats. M. Perruche was afraid the same thing might happen again, and suggested to the commandant that a truck should be provided for us. We saw some boats coming down the river, but they were filled with some of the prisoners of war, and we were glad to know that in their pitiful condition they were not being forced to walk.

Some bread, the first and only batch the prisoners of war had cooked in their new ovens at Man-p'o, was brought and distributed to us. The afternoon passed and still no boats appeared. Finally we were told that there were no boats available and that we must go back again to our old quarters. We all became very angry, and our guards must have felt some pity for us, for they commandeered some ox-carts to help us to carry the invalids and the heavy baggages.

The proposal of M. Perruche must have been accepted for later that evening a truck came to fetch the elderly and sick people and the children, also the baggages. We saw them off, and were going to bed when another truck came and took us aboard. We went along the riverside and through the mountains in the dark, arriving at Ko-san-jin, at about midnight, after a journey of less than twenty miles.

During our stay at Man-p'o, We saw M. Perruche conversing with some of the Korean political prisoners. We learnt that one of them was a Mr. Park, who used to live in Che-ki-dong, Seoul and another was a Mr. Mun. They later joined us in the "Death March" and Mr. Park became our leader for a short time during our stay at Ko-san-jin. One day shortly after our arrival at Chŭng-kang-jin, Mr. Park visited us secretly and said that he was going to be taken away to some unknown destination. He asked for our prayers. In Man-p'o he paid us a second visit; rushing over to us, he inquired after our safety and we then asked him about himself. He said that he was working as a day-laborer and that conditions were tolerable. He then hurried away and we never saw him again.

Backward and Forward, Between Ko-san-jin and Ch'o-san

(October 8—October 31, 1950)

By the time we arrived at Ko-san-jin it was bitterly cold. Accommodation was provided for all the civilians except the Korean political prisoners, in a school building. Many of the windows were broken, and there was nowhere for us to do our cooking. The cold wind blew into our room all night, and in the morning Mother Béatrix went out into the playground to try to get warm after the freezing night. After taking a few steps, however, she fell down in a faint.

Our Turkish friends, in spite of their fatigue, worked hard at repairing the broken doors and walls and set up a small stove, in which they soon had a fire going. The men decided to build a range for our cooking pots in an old shed, and in this they were greatly helped by Mr. Ivan Nicolai Tihinoff, a white-bearded old Russian who was an expert on stoves, and a skillful craftsman. When he was arrested, Tihinoff was a cosmetics manufacturer in Seoul. He was sixty-eight when he joined us, and always cheerful.

Our guards seemed disposed to allow us more freedom now, and permitted us to read and go for walks, and even to go into the town if we had any business there. It seemed as if the Golden Age in our captivity was about to begin—our kitchen was functioning, our storeroom was well stocked with supplies and Monsignor Quinlan was in charge again; we took turns with the cooking, and stoves had arrived for the rooms. The men made plans to build a bathhouse, and began the work.

Our rooms were provided with two rows of bunks around the walls, and Sister Mary Clare, who slept in an upper berth, was unlucky enough to fall out of it one night. Luckily she broke no bones, but she suffered a severe shock, and when later she was made to take part in a forced march in her injured condition, it proved fatal to her.

October 20, Friday

The men completed the bathhouse, and the bath was filled. Early next morning the fire was lit and they proudly told us at breakfast that we could begin taking regular hot baths starting that morning.

But we never had a bath after all! An emergency order came by telephone that we were to evacuate the place at once, as it was needed for the Chinese Communist troops! We had been there only thirteen days.

We hurriedly packed up our stores and belongings, and the able-bodied members loaded pollack and onions on their shoulders and were marched off by the guards, while the old people were left sitting on the rest of the baggages by the roadside to await transport.

After a while the prisoners of war overtook us, and we were shunted off the path to let them pass. Their guards were hurrying them along, and many were finding it hard to keep up.

Our way led through an abandoned mining town called Chu-am-ri, where there was nothing but rusting machinery and abandoned ruins of buildings, and piled-up debris—a depressing sight which Father Crosbie said reminded him of sick, impoverished and doddering old age.

This ghost town contained a number of large huts, many in ruins, and we picked our way among them seeking habitable rooms. Ours was worse than anything we had ever seen before. It was in a filthy condition with cracked walls and no doors or window shutters. The only light came from the moon. We hung straw sacks over the door and windows and blocked up the holes in the wall with pieces of wood, and then went to sleep on the floor.

On the following day Father Bulteau, who was a clever craftsman, tried hard to make a door for us, but he didn't have enough wood. Father Bulteau had been arrested in his mission far south of Seoul, and his experiences had been similar to those of Monsignor Quinlan, Father Canavan and Father Crosbie. His house and church were ransacked, religious objects and pictures thrown about, and missals torn up. He was the only priest who had even one volume of the breviary, 'the Summer Quarter' and it was passed from priest to priest through the day. He was very stout, very cheerful, and possessed a magnificent beard.

There was nothing to eat and our guards had disappeared. We felt as if we had been abandoned, but later they brought us some oil, soyabeans and flour from the village and then vanished again.

M. Perruche and Captain Vyvyan Holt led a group of their fellow prisoners to the mountains to gather firewood which we badly needed. To increase our store of fuel the women also went out to gather cornstalks, twigs and leaves and whatever else they could find that would burn.

The guards disappeared again and we could see only Chinese Communist troops, and groups of North Korean people in flight. Several times throngs of these people passed through the village and went up into the mountains, and we became very apprehensive about the future.

October 26, Thursday

Orders came that we were to leave. Mr. Mun was now our camp leader, and he told us that everyone must walk or be carried, for there would be no transport. The guards confirmed this and insisted that we leave at once, but it was evening before we were ready. We improvised a stretcher for Mother Thérèse, for whom walking was out of the question; it would be very difficult too for Sister Mary Clare, who was still lame from her fall at Ko-san-jin.

It was raining, and getting dark. We could not imagine how we would ever be able to get along the slippery mountain paths, but we set out, with 82-year-old Father Villemot at our head. After we had struggled along for a while even the guards realized that it would be foolish to try to go on, and they told us to return to the camp and wait till next morning. We willingly did so, hoping it would be a fine day tomorrow.

October 27, Friday

Next morning we had to start again, but the guards had good news. There would be ox-carts, they said, for the sick and the weak. Even so, they found difficulty in staying on the cart, for there was only the flat cart with no sides, and there was nothing for them to hold on to, to prevent themselves from sliding off. The road was very steep and uneven. However, the men got within a mile of Ko-san, and there they halted for the night.

We who were accompanying the ox-carts had to stop on the way for an American prisoner of war who had been walking before us collapsed in the road. In a feeble voice he asked if he could have an egg. How could we get one for him? Mother Henriette, filled with compassion, asked the guards if they would accompany her to a nearby farm village to get an egg for him, but a farmer

among the bystanders, understanding what was needed, fetched three eggs from his hen house, refusing to accept any money for them. Though the Communists could rob these good people of their land and crops, they could never eradicate human kindness from the Korean people, so deeply it is rooted in their hearts. Mother Henriette approached the dying soldier and tried to feed him with the egg, but it was in vain, for he was breathing his last. Another soldier standing near him took the egg and ate it up. The second egg, was taken by another soldier and Mother Henriette at last realized that the dying man had no need of an egg, so she decided to give it to Mother Mechtilde, who had taken nothing since morning and had lost much of her strength.

After the soldier had passed away, we resumed our journey. We stayed the night at a village not far from Ko-san-jin, and were forbidden to go out at night, for it would be dangerous for us to be discovered by the Chinese Communist soldiers, who had already arrived there in large numbers.

Our room was far too crowded for us to be able to sleep. We had a small quantity of soyabeans for supper, and then all we could do was to sit and wait for the daybreak. The American prisoners of war in their charity sent us some porridge and after eating it we set out once more.

October 28, Saturday

It was a fine day, but the ox drawing our cart became weaker and weaker, and so slowed down our progress. When we started the guards asked us how many there were of us, and the man in charge of our group replied that there were twenty-three. But a White Russian child who had been scheduled to ride in the ox-cart had decided to accompany his father on foot. After several hours' march the guard counted us and of course the number was only twenty-two. At this he became very angry and shouted at us,

"Why did you lie to me?"

We tried our best to explain what had happened but it was useless, for he could not understand our logic.

"If you told me your group contained twenty-three persons, when there were only twenty-two, then you lied to me. If you did not lie to me then one of you must have escaped. Until you find the missing person you will not go a single step further."

And in fact he made us all sit on the grass for two hours. This we did not mind, for it gave both the ox and us a chance to rest and recover our strength.

People everywhere were in full flight. Many trucks passed us loaded with people and their baggages. There were some who threw rice-cakes to us from a truck. We saw a Chinese in a well-built two-wheeled carriage drawn by three donkeys, and we guessed that he was connected with the Chinese Army that had entered North Korea to help her in the war. At about three in the afternoon the guard ordered us to continue our journey, he said nothing more about the escapee. His anger must have cooled.

We soon joined up with the rest of the party, and volunteers were enlisted to follow us into Ko-san and help us. The party included Bishop Byrne and Father Booth, Monsignor Quinlan and Father Canavan, Bishop Cooper, Commissioner Lord, and Walter Eltringham, Ivan Kilin and Salim Salahudtin came with us, of course, to assist their wives and children. Ko-san was a dead city, and we passed through silent streets and empty houses.

Our journey had left us very tired, but we soon recovered our good spirits when our friends helped us to find rooms, lit fires for us, and brought us water from a well so that we could start cooking our evening meal.

The prisoners of war were billeted near by, and Catholics among them were able to make their confessions to one of the five priests working among them. Everybody felt free and easy, for the guards were absent

and we could forget our troubles for the time being.

Then the guards reappeared and called the able-bodied men together for the journey back. They were relieved to find that no one was missing.

October 29, Sunday

We were ordered to set off again with our ox-carts and were taken to a place about three miles from Man-p'o, where we had to stay the night in a burnt-out, roofless shell of a house where we shivered all night. The men joined us next day and helped us to carry the stones and dirt from the roofless rooms and make a shelter of beams and rice bags. There they all spent the night, crouched round the fire.

October 31, Tuesday

George Blake, the British Vice-Consul, at last had an opportunity to escape. He left his prison when the guards were absent and decided to go along the railway southward. He had not gone far when he was challenged by a sentry and marched to a house where a number of Korean officers were gathered. After questioning him they gave him a meal and sent him back to our camp without punishing him.[1]

The commandant of our guards, who was at heart a kindly man, made a farewell speech to us, shaking hands with us and apologizing in tears for his ill-treatment. He left and at five in the afternoon we were introduced to our new commander, whose nickname, "the Tiger," really suited him.

Pointing to the stars on his shoulder, he introduced himself to us in this way:

"I am a major of the People's Army." He went on to announce that we would all have to make a journey of 250 kilometers over the mountains, and that we must keep on walking to our destination, no matter

---

[1] Some of us wondered at their leniency, but it was not until eleven years later that we learnt he was a Soviet spy. The British Court sentenced him 42 years in prison, the heaviest term handed out by the court. (*TIME*, May 12, 1961)

how great the difficulty. Commissioner Lord protested:

"But they will die if they have to march."

"Then let them march till they die! This is a military order."

M. Perruche begged him to provide some sort of transportation, no matter what, for the sick, the children, and the elderly people. But at this the Tiger pointed his pistol at the *chargé d'affaires*' breast and threatened him:

"No complaints! This is a military order. Choose one of the alternatives: either going on foot or death!"

We were horrified at what this would mean for Mother Mechtilde, who was still in a very enfeebled condition after her recovery from pneumonia. It would be utterly impossible for her to walk such a long distance. Conscious of our deep concern she was as courageous as ever and said:

"Don't worry. I'll walk."

The new officials of Political Bureau let us start only after they had confiscated all our belongings, our food supplies and cooking pots, even our pencils and pocket knives.

He told us that we had a long walk before us, and must proceed in military formation. His orders were to be obeyed as military commands. They would be conveyed to us through leaders whom he would now appoint. He asked us to suggest a group leader, and we named Commissioner Lord, who had been our leader up to Mr. Mun's appointment to that post by the major.

"I have other work for him. Suggest another."

Though he did not say so at the time, the Tiger had already decided to use Commissioner Lord as interpreter for the entire party, prisoners of war as well as civilians. We nominated Monsignor Quinlan, and the Tiger acquiesced. Who would be the leader of the women? Miss Nell Dyer's name was mentioned by several of us, and again the Tiger agreed. Did he expect such people as those in our group to march along in military formation? Did he expect it of the

tottering octogenarian Father Villemot? Of the frail and aged Mother Béatrix? Of Sister Mary Clare, still lame from her fall? Of consumptive Mother Thérèse? Of mothers with babies in arms?

Commissioner Lord stepped foward to voice the consternation we were all feeling. He pointed out that many of the party would find it impossible to march like soldiers, and that for some the attempt must surely be fatal.

"Then let them march," said the Tiger, "till they die! That is a military order."

We formed up in such a way that the weak would have, as far as possible, the help of the strong. Father Villemot was between Monsignor Quinlan and Father Bulteau. Mother Eugénie supported frail Mother Béatrix. Sister Bernadette gave her arm to blind Sister Marie-Madeleine, and Larry Zellers and Nell Dyer helped Sister Mary Clare. Father Canavan and Father Crosbie took charge of the Carmelite Superior, Mother Thérèse, who had risen from a sick bed to take her place in the line.

First came a long line of ox-carts piled high with supplies. Then came the long line of prisoners of war, some with bare and already bleeding feet.

Our civilian group fell in at the end of the column. On our way through Man-p'o we passed our old home, the quarantine station. It was then that M. Perruche recognized a man standing beside an expensive car as a Soviet diplomat he had known in Peking. When the Russian saw us he concealed himself behind his car. At about ten that night we reached a small village and they made us turn off the road into a field and rest. The farmers had already harvested their corn, and only the leaves remained in the field. We gathered them to sleep on, but we did not sleep much. Mother Mechtilde did not seem to be in any serious trouble so far. God had mercy on the prisoners in distress, and we were able to make a fire to keep ourselves warm. Next morning when we woke we saw icicles on the beards of the men prisoners.

November 1, Wednesday

All Saints Day. This was the day on which our Holy Roman Catholic Church proclaimed the dogma of the Assumption of Our Lady, though we were not to hear about it until after our liberation. A moment of grief and tragedy was approaching. With our guards continually shouting,

"Palli! Palli!" (Hurry up! Hurry up!)

We had gone two or three miles when there was a sudden halt. None of us will ever forget the scene.

At the head of the halted column, the Tiger, a group of guards and some POWs were talking. Commissioner Lord was there, interpreting: presently they moved over to the side of the road.

We saw a prisoner singled out, and guards put a bandage over his eyes. We gasped as we stared, rigid and breathless, unwilling to believe it....The Tiger drew his pistol and stepped behind the prisoner....A shot rang out, and its echoes died among the hills.

The Tiger had given strict orders that no one was to be allowed to fall out. Five officers stood before him:

"Why did you allow men to fall out against my orders?"

"We asked the guards what should be done, and that is the advice they gave us."

"Who were these guards? Bring them forward."

The guards could not be produced.

"I will shoot these five men," said the Tiger, "for disobeying my orders."

Commissioner Lord pointed out that they had acted in good faith, that the Tiger's decision was quite unjust. The Tiger reconsidered.

"Then I will shoot the man from whose section most men were allowed to fall out. Who is he?"

Lieutenant Thornton, of Texas, stepped forward. He was calm, master of himself. He merely whispered to Commissioner Lord,

"Save me if you can, sir."

The commissioner tried, but the Tiger turned on him in fury.

"You shut up," he snarled, "or I'll shoot you, too! You're only the translator."

As he stood there muttering to himself, as if in doubt, a band of soldiers passed along the road. He called to them:

"What should be done to a man who disobeys the People's Army?"

"Shoot him!" they shouted back....

So a guard blindfolded Lieutenant Thornton, the Tiger drew his pistol, cocked it, and stepped behind his victim. Then he flicked up the back of the lieutenant's cap, and shot him through the head.

A brave man fell dead. In the frightened hush that followed the shot, another brave man walked calmly from the ranks and began to dig a grave. It was the same sergeant we had watched as he dug a grave two months before. He had come to us as we sheltered in the valley, to have his dead comrade buried by a priest.

The march was resumed.

We kept on hour after hour, knowing that it would be inviting further tragedy to fall out now.

Our guards told us,

"Put on good shoes: the road ahead is very rough."

But where could we get good shoes? Mother Mechtilde could endure the march with less difficulty than others, for she wore somewhat better shoes. Mother Thérèse had cloth shoes made by herself and Mother Béatrix wore the summer sandals of the Carmelites, which were mere slippers. Some Sisters wore shoes made with wire which pricked their feet. One had wooden *geta* or clogs. They suffered indescribable pain in climbing the steep and rocky mountain tracks. Bishop Cooper and Father Hunt were suffering from a severe attack of neuralgia, and each step forward was an act of heroism for them. Sister Mary Clare was a pitiful sight as she limped stooping along. Father Bulteau though robust had to bear the weight of Father Villemot on his arm, and was also exhausted. Sister Marie Bernadette, with a heavy load on her back, was leading the blind Sister Marie-Madeleine. The Fathers

Gombert walked well but were beginning to fail. Father Cadars bore up well but was suffering from an infected wound in the hand.

These three, moreover, were suffering from dysentery, which increased their weakness. Bishop Byrne and Dr. Jensen helped each other but were finding it difficult to keep going. Walter Eltringham helped Mother Mechtilde and Sister Mary Clare and others as long as he could, but he was already weak before the march began, and now could hardly keep moving himself. Seventy-six-year-old Madame Martel was still able to walk, but with great difficulty, and the same was true of the elderly Russians, Madame Funderat, Tihinoff and Leonoff. The Anglican Missionary Charles Hunt was still suffering from gout. Among the younger ones the worst sufferer was Madame Hoang, whose plumpness was telling against her as she toiled along, hour after hour, with her young son.

But it was Mother Béatrix who was in the worst condition of all. It became obvious that she could not go on much longer. Mother Mechtilde was feeling the increasing cold badly. The French diplomats came upon Mother Béatrix and Mother Eugénie halted by the wayside with a guard trying to bully them. The Frenchmen had tried to carry Mother Béatrix for a while, but they became exhausted themselves. The guards jabbed them in the back with their bayonets and drove us along as if we were animals, shouting,

"Quicker! Quicker!"

Why did they drive us so mercilessly? We still do not know the reason. Was it because the United Nations Forces were approaching to set us free?

Mother Mechtilde was being dragged along by two of the less weakened Sisters. She looked frozen to death, but did her best to keep on to the end.

Sister Eugénie called at a house in one of the villages we passed through, to ask for a little hot water, explaining that it was needed for a seventy-seven-year-old woman. The heartless woman who answered the door, after a tirade of abuse, slammed the door in her face shouting,

"Why did she come to Korea, the hag?"

The house was a local Communist center, so it is no wonder they were treated like that.

Straw rice bags were precious things to us, but it was pitiful to see how the poor American prisoners were throwing them away on the road—light as the bags were, the men no longer had the strength to carry them.

We too felt the need to jettison every ounce of unnecessary weight. Knowing that we would miss them very much, we unfastened our rosaries and secretly buried them. Our guards had repeatedly exhorted us to save our lives by throwing away everything, even our food supplies. Countless American prisoners were dying along the road.

November 2, Thursday

Arriving at the next town late at night we were forced to listen to a speech by the Tiger, women sitting upright and men taking off their hats as a gesture of respect. He made a powerful speech, as if to show off his ability as a People's Army commander, and talked a great deal about atrocities on the part of imperialistic countries, and their wrongdoings.

Commissioner Lord translated his speech into English.

During the march the Carmelite Sisters and those from the Convent of *St. Paul de Chartres* constantly recited, in a whisper, the *De Profundis* and the rosary prayers.

"Oh, Holy Mother of God, please help us. Help your unfortunate sons and daughters. Pray for us now and at the hour of our death."

On the following day we spent the night on a mountainside or in a cornfield, and the third and fourth days in a school, but it was so crowded that we had no room to sleep.

Coming out with our Mother Henriette in the morning to collect leaves, we saw white objects which, as we approached nearer turned out to be the bodies of American prisoners, frozen to death in the night.

November 3, Friday

We shall never forget this day.

Shortly before departure M. Perruche sought out the Tiger to tell him that many of the old people, including several French citizens, for whom, as chargé d'affaires, he was responsible, could walk no further, and it was imperative to get transport for them. The Tiger climbed on a box and made a speech. He assured us that we need have no anxiety about people who fell out on the march. They would be taken to 'People's hospitals' and well cared for. This comforted us all, especially Mother Eugénie who knew that Mother Béatrix could not walk much more.

When the time came for departure the able-bodied men were told to start off at once, except Commissioner Lord, who would be our interpreter. Some of the other men wanted to stay behind to help the women and children and elderly men, but they were told angrily that their help was unnecessary, as transport would be provided.

No sooner were they out of sight than we women were told that we would have to walk as before, but without the help of the men! Their talk of hospitals seemed to be about hospitals equipped with execution grounds, for if we could hardly manage to get along the road yesterday even with the men to assist us, what was to happen to us today?

Mother Béatrix's arms and legs were swollen and she showed symptoms of a heart attack. Brave as ever, she took a few steps but was soon forced to sit down on the ground.

"I cannot walk any more," she said calmly to the guard who began forcing her to get up.

"I really cannot go any further, though I should like to," she said. Mother Eugénie told the guards that Mother Béatrix was seventy-six, had spent nearly fifty years caring for the sick and the poor and the orphans of their country. They tore Mother Eugénie's arms away from her. Calmly Mother Béatrix said,

"Go, my Sister, go!"

Thus she met her glorious death, that

morning of November 1950. Anne Marie Edouard had wished from early girlhood to devote her life to God's poor, but she had duties first to her young brothers and sisters. By 1899, when she was twenty-four, she was free to follow her chosen vocation, and in that year she entered the *St. Paul de Chartres* Congregation in her native France. After her religious profession, she was assigned to a home for the aged. Her missionary career began in 1906 with an appointment to the orphanage maintained by her congregation in Seoul.

Before long the sick and the lowly in the poorer quarters of the city were familiar with her slim, upright figure, her dark oval face, her brilliant black eyes; they soon learnt to appreciate the thoughtfulness and generosity that lay behind her shy expression. This shyness of hers made the learning of her adopted people's language a slow task, but meantime she would not let this difficulty keep her from her poor. With a Korean Sister for companion and interpreter, she went day by day on her errands of mercy to the sick and needy.

Recognition of her exceptional qualities brought her successive appointments as mistress of novices in Seoul till 1932; as local superior in Tae-gu till 1942; as provincial superior then for the whole of Korea. She still held the latter office at the time of her arrest. She had received instructions from her Superior-General to leave Seoul in the event of a Red invasion, but had written pleading to be allowed to stay with her Korean Sisters no matter what befell This permission had been granted.

The second victim was Madame Funderat, the Russian widow. With her swollen legs she had somehow managed to get to the midday resting place, where she ate some corn for her lunch. That was the last we saw of her, but Father Crosbie has related how he saw Commissioner Lord come into the camp, shortly after Mother Eugénie's arrival, towing her along on a rope.

Madame Funderat was nearly seventy years old, and childless She had been left alone in the world by the death of her husband, just a few days before the invasion began, and had been arrested in her home when the Reds arrived in Seoul. Commissioner Lord had helped her that morning, when she could walk no further on her own, and finally the guard had got a length of rope which he bade the commissioner tie around her waist and pull her along after him.

The march resumed, shortly after our lunch, and the guard insisted now that the commissioner leave her behind. When we last saw her the guard was helping her along. We never saw her again.

That afternoon Father Villemot, weakened by three months of hardship and semi-starvation, found it almost impossible to continue the march. Supported by Monsignor Quinlan and Father Crosbie, who were themselves beginning to weaken, he stumbled along: as they prayed aloud, he would try to join in whenever he could catch his breath. There was no skin on his heel, and his shoe was sticky with blood. What weariness and pain he endured!

Life had begun for Paul Villemot in 1868, in the neighborhood of the Novan Mountains in central France. In 1892, at the age of twenty-four, he was beginning his missionary career in Korea as a newly-ordained priest of the Paris Foreign Mission Society. At that time the Church in Korea was slowly rebuilding her strength after a series of persecutions that had left her, two decades before, without a single priest for her 17,000 Christians, and without a single Church building.

The first known effort to introduce Christianity into Korea was made by a Spanish Jesuit at the end of the sixteenth century during the period of Japanese occupation, but the seed was not successfully planted till nearly two centuries later. Korea in those times had to send a delegation each year to Peking, with tribute for the Chinese emperor, and it was from books and information brought back by members of theses delegations that the first Korean Christians got their knowledge of the faith. The knowledge was imperfect, and was soon overlaid with error. But when the first priest, Father James Chou, arrived at the end of the eighteenth century, he found a priestless Christian community that had developed in less than a score of years to a membership of more than 4,000, and already had its roll of martyrs. This newly arrived priest was soon added to the roll, and thousands of Korean Christians were to die for their faith in the waves of persecution that swept over the country till late in the nineteenth century.

The whole country—which today has ecclesiastical divisions—had, then, but a single bishop, who lived in Seoul. There were no native priests, and only about a score of foreign missionaries.

Korea had but very recently been forced —by Japan, by the United States, by Britain, by Germany, by France and others—to permit the entry of foreigners, and she was still seething with resentment against foreigners during Father Villemot's early years as a missionary. To add to his troubles, Korea became a battleground between China and Japan two years after his arrival in the country, and he narrowly escaped the execution suffered by one of his confreree when the vanquished Chinese armies retreated through his district in the southwest. The Bishop recalled all the missionaries to Seoul at this time, and Father Villemot eventually arrived there after a hazardous journey that involved—like this other—a walk of a hundred miles.

In Seoul he had been procurator—no sinecure in those days, when many pioneering works, including the completion of Seoul Cathedral, put a heavy strain on mission coffers. He retained this responsibility till 1918. For twenty-five years he was in charge of the Cathedral parish. He handed over his post to a Korean priest in 1942, to retire from active missionary life and become chaplain to the Convent and Orphanage of the St. Paul de Chartres Sisters.

He had come, indeed, a long and glorious journey through life With Father Crosbie, we all wondered whether it was going to end now, this November afternoon of 1950.

"Leave me here," said Father Villemot, "and these people will surely let me die in their yard, and then bury me."

The guard levelled his rifle.

"If you don't go on, I'll kill you."

"I'm ready," the old man replied. "You may shoot me if you wish." The guard looked at Monsignor Quinlan and Father Crosbie.

"You can't leave him here. You'll have to go further."

They struggled on another half a mile, and rested again. The farmhouse was now out of sight.

"You can go now," said the guard.

They begged the guard to give them a little more time. They managed another quarter mile, half a mile, a mile. Then they came round a bend of the road where they saw an ox-cart surrounded by a group of our people. They found the Tiger talking with the French diplomatic group. Madame Martel had collapsed there, and the Tiger had come upon the scene. He had agreed to stop a supply cart and let her ride it. Monsignor Quinlan appealed to him, and he agreed that Father Villemot could ride too.

That evening the whole party assembled in a field until the stragglers arrived; then the prisoners of war were marched to a school for the night, and we civilians were taken to a small church.

Again we had to take turns at sitting up, to allow the others to sleep for a while.

November 4, Saturday

It was snowing when the guards came at dawn to call us, but they forced us to continue our march in spite of the bad weather. There was a mountain pass to cross, and we were told we must hurry to get there before it was blocked with snow. Here on the foothill it was already ankle deep, and was falling steadily.

Now, without breakfast, we began a hurried, uphill march through the snow. Mercifully, Father Villemot and Madame Martel were allowed to ride on a supply-cart. The rest of us struggled along, panting and gasping. We could see the prisoners of war ahead of us, and it was evident that they were being pressed hard.

Mother Thérèse was being helped by Father Crosbie, and already they were lagging behind the rest. Sister Bernadette was toiling along through the thickening snow leading the blind Sister Marie-Madeleine.

We passed by many prisoners lying on the mountainside.

"No vehicles coming?" they would ask with groans of pain. As our priests passed these men they would give them plenary indulgence. A platoon commander fired a shot at one of them who was still alive, and the Tiger kicked their bodies over a cliff.

Father Crosbie heard two shots, but thought little of it till he and Mr. Zellers, who was supporting Sister Mary Clare, saw an officer and some guards returning to the road, laughing. Ahead of us more shots sounded—I, for one, remember hearing eighteen in all.

We passed one exhausted prisoner of war sitting by the roadside and then another. Beside each of them a guard was standing. As soon as we had passed round the bend two shots rang out behind us. At last we realized what was happening. Our hearts ached with helpless pity as we saw more and more prisoners of war sitting or lying helpless by the roadside, attended always by guards who waited ominously till the stragglers passed. Then, each time, we listened in dumb anguish for the sound that always came—the sound of a shot behind us on the road.

Father Crosbie goes on to tell how, while the priests were speaking words of comfort to these men, of God's mercy, His love, His forgiveness, some would nod understandingly, while one boy sang *God Bless America* as he waited for death by the roadside, but his voice was stilled before he reached him. It was one of the women who told him later.

Twenty-two men fell out that morning. Knowing what had been their fate, we had no doubt now of what had happened to Mother Béatrix and Madame Funderat and the eighteen soldiers who had fallen out the day before, and the men who had been left on previous days.

And we now knew that in fact People's hospitals meant 'Execution Grounds' in the Tiger's language.

An ox-cart came along, but Mother Mechtilde was unable to ride it as it was already fully loaded with passengers.

Tired and unhappy children were doing their best to keep up with their parents. The sturdy and resolute Turkish and White Russian ladies, with their babies tied on their backs, crossed the rugged peak full of determination; their babies were crying with cold and hunger. How we longed to rest! But no rest came, and heavy gunfire from far behind us reminded us of the approach of the United Nations Forces.

One of the Carmelite Sisters, owing to an injury to her foot, could no longer continue to walk. She was preparing for death, confident that her fate would be the same as that of Mother Béatrix. At that time many of us awaited death almost as one would await the visit of a kind friend who would put an end to our pain.

Among our guards we occasionally found good-hearted soldiers, who showed kindness and compassion toward us. One of them came to us in the afternoon and said,

"When you get back to your country after the war, please don't tell anybody how we massacred the American prisoners of war this morning."

On another occasion when a Carmelite Sister asked him to help her carry her bundle of belongings as she climbed a steep ascent, he was willing to do so, and when another asked for permission to rest for an hour on the snow-covered bank of a mountain stream, he acquiesced.

We assembled at the top of the pass, waiting for stragglers and worried about what might have happened to them. But at last they turned up, Sophia and Sultan riding on a supply-cart, and then Madame Martel and

Father Villemot on another. Some others were allowed to join them for the steep descent on the other side; the tortuous route through slippery snow was difficult and dangerous and Mother Thérèse became faint before we reached the bottom.

We arrived at Cha-sŏng by mid-morning, about ten o'clock, and were told we need march no more that day. We were taken to a classroom of a school, where straw was laid out in bed-size lots on the floor. At last we could rest our aching bodies. That evening four trucks came to carry off the women, the children and the old men, and five very sick prisoners of war, but the able-bodied would have to continue their journey on foot the following day. Mother Mechtilde and blind Sister Marie-Madeleine and Sister Mary Clare were allowed on the first truck.

We arrived in downtown Chung-kang-jin at one in the morning. Our guards seemed to have no idea where to take us. First they took us some distance in one direction, then made us go back to our starting-point and continue in the opposite direction. Mother Mechtilde fell down and severely injured her knee. For about two hours we wandered about the dark streets here and there, until at last we reached a large school. The men on night-duty at the school were at first astonished to see us, but finally gave our guards the key of the building.

Next morning the second truck with Sister Henriette, Sister Bernadette, and Mother Eugénie arrived. We could not move around at all, for we were forced to sit in pairs in boxes of straw which were only just wide enough for us. Discipline was strictly enforced, and we were not allowed to get down from the boxes, but had to remain there throughout the day. We were also forbidden to lie down or to speak. Because one of the little children had helped himself to a few vegetables without permission, one meal was withheld from us as a punishment, and we were also deprived of the comfort of a fire.

The bitter hardship to which we had been subjected began to take its toll. Sister Mary

Clare passed away from a heart attack as she lay on the straw during the night.

She had given up teaching to become an Anglican nun, and had begun her career as a missionary in Korea during World War I. There she had founded a Korean Sisterhood: she trained the novices, and became the first superior of the congregation. She was an expert in handicrafts, and taught them to her spiritual children. In her spare moments she devoted herself to the translation of prayers and spiritual books into Korean. During World War II she was forced to leave Korea, but her congregation survived under a Korean superior, to whom she returned as adviser after the war.

November 8, Wednesday

The men prisoners arrived here after completing their journey on foot. We were glad to see them but our joy was cut short when we saw the Tiger accompanying them. He was still the Tiger, and said he would be even stricter with us now, since we had not obeyed his orders on the march as well as we should have. He told the sick that their afflictions were due to their failure to take care of their health.

To that insult he proceeded to add further injury: he gave orders that everyone must turn out for physical exercise before breakfast. We protested how sick many of our folk were, but we could get exemption for only three, Mother Thérèse, Mother Mechtilde, and Father Villemot, and even he had to be brought out into the yard on a stretcher, in the bitter cold. Bishop Byrne, Father Canavan, and Walter Eltringham were on the verge of pneumonia, but they too were ordered out into the freezing air of the yard. So, too, were the septuagenarian Gombert brothers, both of whom would be dead in a few days. Father Antoine was unable to walk alone. Someone helped him to his feet and brought him as far as the outer door. There he collapsed, and had to be carried back. The temperature dropped to thirty degrees below zero that morning.

We had begun our forced march from Man-p'o on October 31. Our arrival at Chung-kang-jin on November 8 completed a journey of more than a hundred miles. We had left almost a hundred dead along the way.

November 9, Thursday

The death march was over, but its toll of lives was not closed. It had cost the prisoners of war ninety-six of their number. We had lost Madame Funderat and Mother Béatrix, and now Sister Mary Clare had died of its effects. Fourteen more deaths in the civilians' party were soon to follow.

In the afternoon of November 11, while we were gathered round him reciting the rosary, Father Villemot exclaimed:

"We cannot enter the Kingdom of Heaven without many trials."

Shortly afterward his soul passed quietly away. After fifty-seven years of faithful service he was released from all his burdens and entered the glory of God in Heaven.

Some of the prisoners of war buried him, and Monsignor Quinlan was permitted to go along. During the burial the United Nations Forces heavily bombed the school in which we were quartered, and all taking part in the funeral were forced to flee for shelter to the woods near by. It was bitterly cold, and Monsignor Quinlan, exposed to the freezing wind, contracted both bronchitis and pneumonia, so that we were afraid we were going to lose him too.

November 12, Sunday

Father Antoine Gombert died at 4 p.m. today. In his last moments he had received a request from his younger brother:

"When you are with God, call me."
The call came for Father Julien at 8 p.m. next day. Even death couldn't keep apart those whose lives had been practically one.

The Gombert brothers belonged to a family of seventeen children. They entered the Paris Foreign Missionary Seminary together, and were ordained together in 1900. They left France on the same ship for Manchuria, but before the ship reached Hongkong, the Boxer Rebellion had broken out, and they were diverted to Korea.

Father Antoine, stationed at An-sŏng for thirty-three years, had built up a flourishing parish by the time he was transferred to the Major Seminary in Seoul, first as spiritual director and later as procurator. From active missionary work he at length retired to become chaplain to the Carmelite Sisters of Seoul.

Father Julien had developed two districts into fine parishes when, with the outbreak of war, he was called into Seoul Cathedral in 1942. In 1946 he went to In-ch'ŏn, as chaplain to the Convent and Orphanage of the Sisters of *St. Paul de Chartres.*

The districts that these men took over are now prefectures embracing a dozen large parishes. Yet in those pioneering days, each of them made regular visitations of all the territory under their care, traveling sometimes on horseback, but mostly on foot.

Mother Mechtilde, conscious of Father Antoine's long and loving care of the Carmelites, wanted to be at his bedside, but could not leave her own bed, owing to her exhaustion. Mother Thérèse asked for his intercession on our behalf when he should be in Heaven. He looked around with his blue eyes as simple as a child and seemed to understand. Father Julien announced a visitor from the adjoining room:

"Brother, M. Perruche is here. Isn't it just like seeing France?"

Father Antoine quietly breathed his last.

We then took his cassock and crucifix to hold in memory of him.

Father Julien, apart from his dysentery, had seemed healthier than many of the others after the Death March. It really seemed to us that his death was a result of his brother's entreaty to God while he was enjoying bliss in His presence after passing through purgatory. In other words, it seemed that God had granted the prayer of His servant who had served Him faithfully throughout life.

We had a small fire in a stove, and were fed by small quantities of half-cooked corn, or maize. Mother Mechtilde could not eat much because of her constantly bleeding gums, and was in fact, like others, starving through inability to eat hard foods. Her pneumonia returned and she kept on coughing painfully day and night. What could be more heart-rending than to see our beloved one suffering and be unable to relieve her from pain?

The water supply too was inadequate. The well in our backyard was almost dry from the demands on it for washing the sick people's clothes. M. Perruche and others drew water in a wooden tub by cart from a river about three kilometers away, but it froze on the way home, and when it arrived it was needed by the hundreds of prisoners of war, each of whom got only half a bowl of water. They could use this either for washing or for drinking, but it was insufficient for either purpose.

One American lady decided to use her water ration for drinking, and her cabbage soup for washing.

Late on the evening of November 15 a Red officer came to say that we must be ready to leave at five o'clock next morning. The women had to go to the kitchen and make things ready for getting breakfast before snatching a few hours' sleep. Then in the early hours they faced the cold of the kitchen again. They had breakfast ready for us by 3 a.m. The able-bodied were all lined up in the courtyard with their packs before daylight, but the very sick could remain at the school, we were told, while the rest of us took shelter in the hills for the day, returning to the school at evening.

Bishop Byrne, Mother Mechtilde and Sister Marie-Madeleine were among those who stayed behind, but Mother Thérèse, the Prioress of the Carmelite Convent, set out with Mother Henriette and Sister Bernadette. We had not gone far when we were told to halt the day's journey. We were taken to a derelict building, and not allowed to go outside during our stay.

November 16, Thursday

Mother Mechtilde and Mother Thérèse spent the whole day together talking over their work for the Carmel. The two spent the sweet hours recollecting happy times together. Born in 1888 at Ypres in Belgium, Godelieve Devriese became Sister Mechtilde in the Carmelite Convent in her home town. When the Germans invaded her country in 1914 she had to return to her family, but three years later was able to re-enter Carmel at Aire-sur-Adour, in southwest France. Then, from the Middle East, came a call for Sisters, and she was soon pacing the cloisters of the Carmel in Smyrna. During the uprising of 1922-3, when Turkey became a republic, and many foreigners were killed, the Sisters managed to escape on a French vessel. Back in Aire-sur-Adour, and now prioress, Mother Mechtilde listened to Bishop Larribeau of Seoul as he pleaded for Sisters to open a Korean Carmel.

The prioress resigned, and volunteered for Korea. Her first convent was washed away by a flood and another had to be built. Then came the difficult years of World War II, and now the Communist invasion of Korea.

Talking over the past, the two friends would occasionally remain silent, but it was then that they could communicate with each other more intimately than when they talked. Leaving everything in the hands of God the two souls could tell each other their thoughts more eloquently in these moments than they could in words.

During the evening a nurse came in to give Mother Mechtilde an injection, after which she passed a quiet night.

November 17, Friday

Orders had come for all, including the sick, to leave. Mother Mechtilde spoke to Mother Thérèse:

"I shall die on the roadside."

"I, too, can walk no more," was the answer.

The two made their preparations for death.

Mother Mechtilde, since her retirement from the office of prioress, had often been addressed as "Grandmother" by the Sisters.

"My grandmother, are you afraid to die?"

"No, I am not afraid, though I have often done wrong. I feel like a child returning to its father. I know His love and mercy are infinite. If you see my Mother Thérèse and the little Sisters, please ask them to forgive me my faults. If you survive this ordeal, unlikely as it seems at present, and enjoy the happiness of seeing our children again, please convey my deepest love to them."

Even the guards might have been moved to see the pitiful emaciated figures of the two Carmelites scarcely able to stand as they stepped into the garden supported by American soldiers on either side. They were allowed to ride on a supply-cart, but they were so weak and the road was so rough that they had to be tied on to the cart where they lay on the bags of millet. Mother Mechtilde groaned softly as the cart, bumped along the rugged road in the bitter cold.

Life at Ha-ch'ang-ri

(November 18, 1950—March 30, 1951)

On our arrival at our destination she was on the point of death. She could no longer speak. We cleared a space for her to lie down but she was no longer conscious, no longer able to hear the turmoil around her. We gathered round her bed for her passing, and the priest whose turn it was to have the breviary read the Miserere and the Absolution. At 11 p.m. on November 18 she at last passed away after a spotless life, to enjoy that everlasting peace in Heaven for which she had always confidently hoped.

Next day Mother Thérèse spoke of pain in her side: she looked very tired and was a little feverish. To make matters worse, she could not eat. This made us all very worried about her. All the food we could get at this time was a little boiled millet, without salt or side dishes of any kind. We tried our best to think what we could do to arouse her appetite and strengthen her weak stomach. The pain in her side made her groan heavily. One of the priests who had studied medicine, Father Bulteau, examined her and asked us not to worry so much, as he was sure she was not suffering from pleurisy. We were told to give her aspirin if we could get any, but none was available. Mother Thérèse told us that her end was nearing, but we tried to comfort her by denying it. But she repeated it and gave us her final instructions regarding our work in Seoul, if we should ever return there.

We tried to keep her warm in bed with our clothes and any other covering we could get, but our efforts were in vain. Already she was unable to move, and showed no sign of consciousness.

On the morning of the 25th Monsignor Quinlan announced to us that Bishop Patrick Byrne had gone to Heaven. There was not a soul in the camp who heard this news without a deep sense of personal loss. He was buried close to our other dead, in a cassock of black silk, with red buttons and piping. Monsignor Quinlan had been wearing this when he was arrested, and with it he now clothed the body of the Apostolic Delegate. The red, hard buttons, Monsignor hoped, might afterward help to identify the remains.

Father Canavan who had been suffering from pneumonia now seemed out of the crisis, but now Father Crosbie came down with the same disease. Fortunately the Korean doctor gave him some sulphadiazine, and, under the careful and devoted nursing of Monsignor Quinlan, he too recovered. Father Coyos, though terribly emaciated by tuberculosis and suffering from a throat infection that made it almost impossible for him to speak, also managed to survive as also did Father Booth, who suffered a long time from a spreading carbuncle which, however, gradually disappeared.

But there was no such good fortune in store for our beloved Mother Thérèse. We called to her repeatedly.

"Our Mother, if you hear us, try to clasp our hands!"

There was no reply. Like Mother Mechtilde, she received Absolution while unconscious. We continued praying by her bedside, our only recourse for consolation in our grief. She seemed to be already in another world.

We were weeping silently in the darkness, when we heard her gasping for breath. Her breathing gradually become slower and weaker, and she died quietly, without a groan escaping from her lips.

It was the night of 30th November, and on going out to ask the time, for our watches had been taken from us, we learnt that it was 2 a.m. She lay in death with a calm expression on her face; her lips and eyes were closed, though none of us had touched them. She looked as if she lay in meditation.

The doctor declared that her death was due to tubercular meningitis, but we were not sure how much confidence we could place in his judgment.

The earth was frozen so hard that we could not dig a deep grave for her. She was buried beside Mother Mechtilde on the far side of Ha-ch'ang-ri, overlooking Manchuria.

After our two Mothers had ascended into Heaven our little community, which they had led for so long in their chosen field of missionary work, and which they had loved so much, began to seem quite empty, and we often felt very lonely.

Then Father Cadars, who had been suffering from an infection of the hand sustained during the Death March, began to get worse. The infection developed into necrosis, and to make matters worse he also contracted dysentery and soon became very weak. He passed away on December 18.

Father Bulteau, who had helped to nurse him was finally in need of nursing himself. He looked very strong, a bearded giant of a man, but now his endurance was quite worn down, and Our Lord took him home on the feast of the Epiphany.

Born in 1901 in the province of Vendée, in France, he was ordained for the Paris

Foreign Missions in 1927. He went to the Vicariate of Tae-gu, and was sent to Pu-san, where he built the church. He served in the French Army during World War, II, and was taken prisoner by the Germans and subsequently released because of illness. He took a brief course in medicine after the war, and returned to Korea just before the invasion. In those few months he had begun a flourishing dispensary. The Church lost a very zealous member when Father Bulteau was laid in that lonely grave in Ha-ch'ang-ri.

Monsignor Quinlan never missed a single funeral service and always joined in the work of grave-digging. Though he was often urged by the guards to return as soon as the body was covered with earth, he never failed to complete his prayers for the dead before coming away from the grave.

Mother Eugénie was also indefatigable in her care of the sick. As it was strictly forbidden for the Sisters to enter any of the men's rooms, she tried hard to get special permission to do so, on grounds of humanity, and at last this was granted. Though she was allowed only two visits a day to her patients, it was generally thought that in several cases, including that of Father Coyos, who had been given up as incurable by Dr. Kisch, their recovery was largely due to her devoted care. She used to go outside in freezing weather to wash the patient's clothes in an old broken jar which was all she could find for the purpose. But before she had been long at this work, the water would be frozen solid. Then she would secretly beg for warm water from the others, and go on with her washing.

What she did for the sick French priests at Ha-ch'ang-ri is beyond telling, but she never spoke of it, nor asked for help, nor complained. In later camps there were few for whom she did not wash or sew at one time or another. Hour after hour she would sit making socks and gloves, patching and altering garments. When thanked her for a service she would say simply,

"*A votre service.*"

The water supply was never adequate, for it had to be brought a long way and there was never enough for our needs.

The physical exercises before breakfast were continued, but the civilian prisoners were not kept out so long as the prisoners of war. These had to go on after we were dismissed, and with their enfeebled bodies, clad in many cases only in their summer uniforms, they braved the intense cold and for more than an hour we could hear the shouts of "one, two, three, four" coming from the yard. No wonder so many of them contracted pneumonia! There were four or five funerals every morning: the bodies, with the hands tied together, were tied to a pole and carried away.

What a pitiful sight it was to see these thinly-clad prisoners of war staggering along, supporting themselves against the wall! One Turkish lady said to me in tears,

"Those poor men! Their legs are thinner than those of my six-year-old son! How can the Communists bear to treat their fellow men with such extreme cruelty?"

Many of them were not draftees, but volunteers who had enlisted full of high spirits. If they had felt that there was any hope of alleviating their lot they might have endured their hardships with greater fortitude, but they seemed to have lost hope completely, and between sixty and seventy per cent of them succumbed.

Seeing this high death rate among the prisoners of war, the People's Army commander one day called in representatives of the prisoners and pressed them to sign a false statement that the reduction in their number was due not to death but to transfer of prisoners to other villages, for he feared that the ill-treatment might come up for discussion at any future international conference for the exchange of prisoners.

On one occasion Sister Bernadette saw a prisoner of war who had been chosen, as the fittest among them, to carry a small bag of food rations. As he was too weak to lift it to his shoulder he asked the Communists to help him lift it up, so that he could carry it, but they only sneered at him in contempt.

We were visited by Red Chinese Army soldiers nearly every day. Stationed in this village, they came out of curiosity. They jeered at us. One of our civilian prisoners, a woman of French and Korean parentage, was put in solitary confinement in an ice-cold cell for twenty-four hours for declaring that it was not the United States of America that was the aggressor in the war. A Russian lady was punished with face-slapping for a similar statement. Commissioner Lord was also placed in solitary confinement in an unheated house. The Tiger would repeatedly badger him, pistol on table, with interrogations and demands for a "confession." When, after a fortnight, Commissioner Lord returned to us he could barely stand with the aid of a stick.

Toward the end of January the diplomats were all taken away by bus, and the rumor spread that we would follow them in a few days. An officer told us that they had gone by train from Kang-kye to P'yŏng-yang, and we had no more news of them till we met them again twelve months later in Man-p'o.

Before leaving, Madame Martel gave us her English missal, and Father Coyos secretly translated the Sunday Mass for the faithful every week. We hid the book in a hole. We let the American prisoners of war use it too, but one day it disappeared and could not be found. We heard nothing more of it.

Sister Marie-Madeleine, the blind Sister, bore her affliction with gentleness, patience and fortitude. She had been much affected by the death of Mother Béatrix, Mother Mechtilde, and Mother Thérèse, but now she began to teach French to Sagida Salahudtin, the second child of the Turkish family, who was then about seventeen. In addition to her own Turkish language, she could speak English and some Russian. Other children soon flocked around the Sister for lessons.

With the advent of spring it began to get warmer, and, disappointed of our hopes of liberation by Christmas, we began to hope it would come at Easter. We missed our French diplomats for although we could only exchange a word with them from time to time when they were here, it was some comfort to us living with the representative of our country. After their departure some of us were moved to their house and everybody could have enough room to sleep outstretched at night.

We would often ask Monsignor Quinlan: "When shall we take a nice long trip?"

"At the end of the month," he would always answer with a smile. Though he would never say which month, his prediction proved true. It was at the end of March we were ordered to pack our things.

Though it was a bright and sunny day, it cost us a pang to leave the place where our two Mothers were buried and not to go and say a prayer at their graves before leaving.

Our destination, however, turned out to be a house at a distance of about 7. 4 miles. The short journey was almost like a picnic excursion compared with our former experiences, and we all began to believe they were going to liberate us. We arrived at Chung-kang-jin, and passed the school where we had stayed for a week last time we were here. A little further on was the church that had been built by Father Cleary when the Maryknoll Fathers had charge of this area. We kept on through Chung-kang-jin and out along the Man-p'o road and soon came to a cluster of buildings at the foot of a mountain. Later we learnt that these had been barracks, built by the Japanese. They were afterward used as a school.

Sojourn at Chung-kang-jin

(March 30—October 8, 1951)

Most of the American prisoners of war had already arrived, and the sick ones arrived next day on ox-carts. We were not supposed to talk to them, but they told us that the B29s we had seen flying over had successfully bombed one of the Yalu River bridges. Later the civilian men were put together with the American officers, and they could talk more freely.

Our group consisted of thirteen grownups and seven children. Although we were not allowed to talk to the American prisoners, the food we ate was cooked by them. It was a mixture of corn with a very little rice and millet. The corn was not well ground nor sufficiently cooked, and the soup was very thin, and too highly seasoned, so that not one of us could finish it.

One day the commander inspected the kitchen; tasting the soup he said,

"This isn't soup. This is nothing but water. Put in some oil and vegetables."

From that time on we got better soup. The few prisoners assigned to kitchen duty could eat twice as much as the others and in consequence looked healthy and energetic. They occasionally played football after supper and the Communists would take pictures of them for publication in their newspapers and magazines, but they never took pictures of the pale and emaciated men lying on the ground, or of those with frost-bitten hands and feet.

The commander seemed to be impressed by the deaths among us, and ordered that in future only those who volunteered should do field work. Since he himself was consumptive, he could understand and sympathize with others. He kept a rooster and a hen in the front yard of his house for the sake of the eggs. One day the rooster was not to be found. The widowed hen looked lonesome without the rooster, so in due course she disappeared too, but the commander was too tender-hearted and sagacious to make a fuss about it. Indeed, as Father Crosbie said, the prisoners of war were recovering their spirits, and a quiet battle was going on between them and the guards.

Sister Bernadette, one lucky afternoon, found a peppermint plant growing wild in the yard. She boiled it with sugar and made a refreshing drink with it which she distributed to the prisoners of war lying on the floor. The first one to taste it exclaimed with delight.

"Oh! How sweet it is!," and after a few sips passed the glass to a comrade. In this way a glassful was shared among three men. Sister Bernadette was moved to tears at their gratitude for this small comfort she was able to bring to them.

We tried in every way to bring them what little comfort we could, but it seemed unlikely that we should be able to provide them with anything very substantial, so we asked them to select four Catholics who could speak French among them so that through these men we might be able to render more service.

One American prisoner, Mr. Hebbel, told us wistfully that he had a little blue-eyed daughter named Joanne at home, and invited us to visit him in California after the war. He said he was a good shot and could provide us with plenty of wild duck.

Mr. Rolan was a devout Catholic who said he was sorry he could not attend Mass daily. He was not afraid of death, and said:

"The day of one's death is the day of success and arrival."

He also went on to say that he had become acquainted with a girl in the city of Angers (Maine-et-Loire) when he was touring France during World War II.

"What beautiful letters she used to write to me! If only I could show you her letters!"

Mr. Nebenan was an impressionable and sensitive type. He at once became sad when he heard others talk of going home after their liberation. He told us.

"My mother died when I was four years old. I was brought up by my grandmother, who kept house for us. How I wish I knew whether she is still alive!"

He had learned to speak French a little, but could not read it, but one of the Carmelite Sisters secretly taught him to read when the guards were not present.

Mr. Bultred was a Canadian who aroused our interest because he spoke the old-fashioned French of the *habitants* or descendants of the original French colonists of Canada.

He asked the Sisters to teach him some of the more refined expressions of modern French, for he felt that the *habitant* or Acadian dialect was too rustic.

We often set aside half of our supper for the prisoners of war. Called in secretly to receive it, some of them would take it away in their caps, but Mr. Rolan, who would never be separated from his towel for fear it might be appropriated by a room-mate, would take his portion in his towel. Evading the guards he would often drop in for a chat on his way back from field work, and he valued that even more than food. What he appreciated was to be in a friendly atmosphere by our side where he could get rid of his sorrow after being abused, beaten and humiliated by the guards, for it was friendship that gave him encouragement to endure with fortitude.

On the anniversary of their Saint's days we made handkerchiefs for them out of worn-out cotton cloth, embroidered with their initials in threads which they had pulled from their worn-out blankets. Given these handkerchiefs as keepsakes they were very grateful. Poor prisoners! What good would a piece of cloth be to you who had no proper clothing! We believe however that they would keep them until the day of their liberation.

Our interrogation continued. When the interrogators asked us if we were desirous of remaining in North Korea after the war we unanimously replied "No!" A little displeased, they said:

"Very well. You may return to South Korea with the American prisoners of war. We'll see what happens to you."

Occasionally prisoners with good voices were allowed to sing. We also had propaganda shows of films and lantern slides, about Communism. There was also a play acted by poor North Korean actors which the American prisoners of war were shown. The play contained scenes representing the murder of a Korean woman by American soldiers, and their attacking young Korean women. All the American prisoners gave loud whistles of contempt and left the theater before the play was over.

The priests had at least the satisfaction of preaching the Gospel and administering the Holy Sacraments. They made clandestine visits to the officers' quarters and preached sermons and read the May devotions. They succeeded in converting some of the prisoners to Catholicism. The Protestant ministers also preached to them. This preaching must have been noticed by the Communist commanders, for soon after, in the middle of May, they removed all the male civilian prisoners to a small valley called An-to-ri in the mountains on the other side of the river.

Shortly afterward the Turkish and Russian families were sent to the same place. This may have been on account of their friendliness with the Americans, and the care they took to help them. Soon Sister Eugénie and the German lady shared the same segregation, for Sister Eugénie started taking English lessons with the prisoner Nebenan and the latter was caught exchanging her pocketknife for some of the prisoners' tobacco.

Father Coyos, regardless of his own fatigue, came whenever anyone was on the point of death, to give Absolution, and to inquire whether Sister Marie-Madeleine was still alive. The sick nun in accordance with the rule of the Carmelite Order prepared for death by asking pardon for her wrongdoings. She took an overdose of some medicine, which caused her acute pains in the stomach, but she recovered and was soon out of danger.

While we were still with the prisoners of war we witnessed a tragic scene. There was a well in an area where we were allowed to go without asking permission. Early one morning an American prisoner, Lieutenant Sirman, went there to draw some water. Suddenly a shot rang out and we saw him lying dead. Whether he had failed to hear or had ignored the guard's order to halt we did not know. The commander later told the prisoners:

"My man made a mistake. But you must

all refrain from walking outside when it is dark. Everyone is on edge about the P'an-mun-jŏm talks."

On another occasion the commander made an announcement to us about these talks:

"You sick prisoners need not worry about next winter. You will be on your way home by then."

Our pale faces began to light up with joy as we talked over the matter in the evening. Who of us was to know that these talks would go on for more than two years before we could be liberated?

One of the American prisoners, Louis Dans attempted to escape. He was extremely fool-hardy to attempt such a thing, for he knew nothing of the terrain nor the language, and had no means of disguise. Soaked by the rain, he wandered along a narrow mountain path until it came to a village, where he asked for food. The astonished police immediately arrested him and brought him straight back to prison. The commander sent him to the sick prisoners' ward and ordered him to be given medical treatment. After presenting a written apology he was granted a pardon.

An officer brought him to the male prisoners and made him tell them his story. His plan, he said, had been to keep to the mountains away from frequented roads. But he had encountered country that was far more rugged than that around us, and found peaks he couldn't climb, and precipices that forced him to turn back. He had spent a couple of nights in pouring rain, and he grew weak. In three days he had gone thirty miles. The officer knew this unsuccessful attempt at escape would deter others.

August 8, Wednesday

Again we were ordered to depart. We were sent across the river to the valley where the other civilians had been since the middle of May. We waded across at a ford. The water was waist-deep and the current very strong. Faithful Sister Bernadette was anxious for the safety of blind Sister Marie-Madeleine. Just as I was taking off my shoes

a pair of strong arms snatched my bundles of food and carried them across the river for me, pressing them to his breast like a mother carrying a baby. Before I could thank him he disappeared from sight. I suppose he was an American soldier, but I never found out his name. It was good to be with Sister Eugénie and Father Coyos again.

We called our new prison 'the Fruit House,' for there were all kinds of wild fruit to be picked in abundance on the hillside near by.

"O mountain!," we said, "You are indeed our friend. May you stand by us till the end of our captivity!"

These wild fruits soon brought about a great improvement in our health. We could eat our fill of strawberries, walnuts, and grapes, as well as wild onions, chives, and leeks. After climbing around the mountain with the agility of a goat, Sister Bernadette brought back baskets full of fruit and delicious mushrooms. From one of these trips she returned a little downcast, for in climbing a tree she had somehow managed to lose her shoes.

Potatoes were now issued to us for the first time, and with them supplies of Welsh onions were delivered. The children got madly excited at the first sight of the potatoes, but the Welsh onions were too much for their self-control: with cheers of joy they grabbed them all and ran off with them. After this little incident Monsignor Quinlan made a rule that all new deliveries were to be kept out of the children's reach until he had distributed them in fair shares all round.

The men felled plenty of trees for winter fuel, and were kept very busy chopping them up, and also plastering the walls of the houses with clay in preparation for the winter. But alas! As soon as everything was ready, orders came for us to move again. It was October 8. Experience had taught us, as Father Crosbie remarked, that when we had made a camp comfortable, it was time to move on to the next.

This had been the first camp where we had been able to walk about freely and enjoy the fresh air and beautiful scenery, and where we could rest and recuperate from our hardships and the sickness that had resulted from them. We learnt that we were being sent down the river to Man-p'o, where we were to rejoin our compatriots and the other diplomats who had been imprisoned there.

October 9, Tuesday

Our commander bade us farewell and tried to promote our morale with his words and behavior. Sister Bernadette was on the verge of tears at the thought of leaving behind the store of wild fruits that she had gathered, and started to eat them up. Another nun began to help her. Father Coyos was firmly convinced that the Communists were about to release us, but seemed a little displeased when he found that the Carmelite Sisters did not share his optimism.

Although we rode in a truck it was a most enjoyable journey, and all were willing to endure the discomfort of the lengthy trip in the hope that Father Coyos might be right and that we should soon be set free. Eleven of our party had been left behind as there was no room in the truck for them, and among those was Father Crosbie.

The journey took three days. We spent the nights in thatched cottages, which were always so crowded that we could not sleep well. The food too was very poor.

We were going back over the very scene of our forced Death March. We had no eyes for the clear autumn sky and the beautiful scenery surrounding us on every side, for cruel memories were awakened at many points: the place where Mother Béatrix had been killed, and the cliff over which the Communists had kicked the dead bodies of the American prisoners of war were the most poignant.

The Second Stay at Man-p'o

(October 11, 1951—August 12, 1952)

Unloading us from the truck at a distance of some two and a half miles, outside the town of Man-p'o, our guards wasted some hours without telling us to proceed. They forestalled our inquiries with the bleak announcement:

"The quarters we prepared for you are now occupied by Chinese Communists."

We could hardly believe this, for it would not be the first time they brought us to a place without making preparations for our lodging.

Leaving the highway we were led along a mountain path. It seemed to wind up the mountainside quite aimlessly: what our guards seemed to be doing was getting us concealed from passers-by, or perhaps aircraft. They ordered us to stay on the mountain, so we all sat down on our packs: a Korean doctor (if he was in fact a doctor) was sent to us, with a nurse who examined the sick prisoners and took notes of what medicine they would require. In spite of this impressive beginning, none of us ever received any medicine at all.

It grew cold and dark. They had to fix us up for the night somehow, and they finally led us to a thoroughly repulsive dugout, the entrance to which was nothing more than a yawning hole in the ground. We looked at each other in consternation, and the terrified children burst into tears, one of them clinging to his mother's arm in a paroxysm of fear. We decided that the best thing to do was to collect some bundles of straw for bedding and get ready to spend the night underground. We received a little rice and cabbage in small bowls, but were told that there would be no soup till the following morning. Though drizzling rain was falling we lay down on our straw bedding, hoping things would be better next day.

It was sunny the following morning, which was a great help to us. But they had done nothing to make our wretched straw-roofed dugout fit for habitation, nor had they found a more suitable place for us. We were being treated in the same way as the Korean convicts near by, about 95 per cent of whom were anti-Communist prisoners.

We were strictly forbidden to speak to them, but we ventured to have a short talk with some of them. We asked one of the pitiful prisoners what had brought him to his captivity. He replied that he had been sentenced to thirty years' imprisonment for anti-Communist remarks. If everyone who criticized the president or the government of France were to be jailed in this way, what enormous prisons we should need! Women prisoners were treated in the same way; among them we saw well-educated women from Seoul who had been imprisoned as 're-actionaries' in order to undergo 're-education.' They were assigned to laundry and other menial work. Still clad in summer wear and bare-footed, the men prisoners were weaving straw bags in the yard. Prison food in North Korea is three small meals a day consisting of millet, cabbage and radish, and it was not surprising that during our stay we saw funerals everyday.

But it was not only their poor food and quarters that aroused our pity, it was the shameful destruction of the prisoners' morale by constant spiritual bullying. The Communist lecturers never ceased their attacks on the prisoners' self-respect, attempting to destroy in them every trace of individualism and transform them into docile and uncritical tools of their regime, who would themselves prevent any independent thinking on the part of any single member by denouncing him as 'deviationist' in their periodical sessions of so-called 'self-criticism' and 'mutual criticism,' where under the guidance of a cadre they would examine their fellow prisoners' minds and hearts until no trace remained in them of anything but sheep-like action and parrot-like speech.

Our guards seemed to have realized that it was impossible for us to go on living in those dugouts any longer, and allowed us to move to a shed located on the western slope of the mountain, if we wished, but they placed all responsibility for repairs on Monsignor Quinlan. When he and some other men went to inspect it, they at first thought of rejecting it, but finally decided that it was perhaps a slight improvement compared with the dugouts.

This building was about fifty by fifteen feet, with walls about three feet high and a very steep roof. At one end there was a kitchen, with sunken floor, and down the center ran a corridor, with built-up *ondol* floors on each side. These *ondol* were heated by the kitchen fires. Men and women were put in there together, the men on one side and the women on the other. We lined the room with thick straw mats which we got from the prison, but even so it was cold and draughty. All agreed however that it was better to be cold than to be suffocated underground.

The men of our party were kept busy gathering firewood on the hillside in all weather under the leadership of Monsignor Quinlan. The guards at first would not let them fell trees, but made them gather only deadwood and twigs and fallen leaves, but they were not always strict about this and sometimes they were able to cut down pine trees and chop them up. Later a coal-burning stove was set up in our shed, which was stoked with coal dust by Mr. Ilian Kijikoff. It was a sooty affair, and blackened not only the straw mats covering the walls of our room but also the faces of the sleepers during the night, so that we all looked like coal miners just up from the pits.

With the deep snow and slippery ice on the steep mountain paths it was extremely dangerous to go out of the building after November, but fortunately no one incurred any serious injury.

Christmas came round again, and with merry carols we gathered in our 'Bethlehem House' in a friendly and peaceful atmosphere, united in prayer with our loved ones at home who were anxious for news of our safety. We saw the New Year with a little feast of broiled soyabeans and corn and began the year in a happy mood.

It had been customary in the past for the International Red Cross, with its headquarters in Geneva, to send comfort boxes and food parcels to prisoners of all nationalities, but we had not received anything so far. The Soviet Russian Red Cross, though it ought to have helped, pretended to know nothing about us and consequently sent us nothing.

But one day we were informed that a consignment of relief goods had arrived from Czechoslovakia. Some of the men hurried to the station while rest of us waited expectantly, guessing what the contents might be. With a smile, Monsignor Quinlan opened up the packages and asked us to draw lots. What a strange collection of things it was! Father Coyos drew a pair of chestnut-brown woolen socks and a pair of white ones. Our Carmelite Sisters drew a hat, a pair of children's worn-out shoes, a child's dress and pieces of cloth of various colors.

We tried hard to think of ways in which to make use of these things. Sister Henriette proposed to offer the goods for sale in the local market, but it was hard to get permission. The Communists however made no objection to our sending Sisters Henriette and Eugénie. Sister Eugénie had repaired the child's dress expertly, and they left light-heartedly on their mission. On their way they met a policeman who ordered them back to barracks, but after their repeated entreaties he allowed them to proceed on their way.

They first tried a shop, but the Man-p'o shopkeepers would not buy them because they were worn out. Rather than return home penniless, Sister Henriette decided to auction them then and there in the street. A group of amused bystanders soon gathered: a countryman tried the shoes on his little son's feet, liked them and bought them, and a woman bought the pretty dress for her daughter. The children were delighted, and so were we at Sister Henriette's success as a trader. They grossed thirteen hundred won, which seemed a lot of money at the time, and they immediately laid out the money on toilet-soap, stationery, and eggs for a forthcoming christening party.

With the advent of spring we were able to gather edible herbs from the hillside; allowed as we now were to wander freely about we could gather wild garlic, and various other plants from which we could cook fresh vegetable soup.

Sister Bernadette, the Carmelite lay Sister, came into her own again. She had worked on her parents' farm in France, before entering Carmel at Aire-sur-Adour in the Landes, on the upper reaches of the river that runs down from the Hautes-Pyrénées through Dax to Biarritz. She had come to Seoul from that convent, with other Sisters, in 1938, and had been given charge of the kitchen. So Korean kitchens were no mystery to her, and she could perform wonders with very little equipment and material. Sister Bernadette never raised her voice or became involved in an argumemt, but she did what she wanted and got what she wanted. Her efforts were directed solely toward making things pleasant for others, with never a thought for herself.

The hillsides were now covered with wild flowers and blossoming trees. Violets and lilies of the valley perfumed the air, and the countryside soon turned into beautiful flower gardens with golden-ball flowers, various species of roses and strange-looking orchids, the work of nature and beyond the power of man to imitate. Whenever Sister Bernadette went up to these little valleys among the mountains she was filled with awe and admiration. Soon our dreary room was brightened with pots of flowers gathered by her, and constantly renewed with fresh supplies of different varieties. She set a good example by sharing out all the fruit she gathered among her colleagues in the kitchen. By June the mulberries were in season, and others followed her example. We were able to make steamed mulberry bread or ordinary bread for the Americans when they brought us flour.

A most interesting discovery was made by a member of our group, who came across human bones half exposed in the ground near a winding mountain path. Making his way through tall, thickly growing grass, he found five European-style graves side by side. The villagers told us that the monks of the Benedictine Abbey of Won-san had once had a house near our prison. Deeply moved, we weeded the site and planted a row of golden-ball trees on each side, and, cleaning up the graves, covered them with leaves.

As Sister Marie-Madeleine could not climb up the mountain paths, she kept to the level ground as best she could. But she liked and enjoyed our mountain-villa life as much as anybody else. She had been staying with us since early summer when it grew warm enough for us. The one who deserves most credit for designing our little summerhouse or flower-villa, as we sometimes called it, was Father Coyos, who not only thought out plans for beautifying the place but worked as hard as a team of army engineers, making use of whatever materials were at hand. The words of the Gospel,

"Seek and ye shall find," (St. Matthew, 7:7) came true in the case of our flower-villa.

Father Coyos collected boards and nails here and there and constructed stools and a reclining chair for the comfort of our fellow prisoners. The reclining chair, covered with a blanket, made a most welcome resting-place for men tired out with gathering kindling, or other chores. He also made a small desk—a most useful addition to our furniture. He also repaired the leaking roof with straw bags and sand.

The little summerhouse was finished in a day (like the 'Ling-t'ai' of Wenwang described by Mencius).

(Wenn rex) mensus est (locum) et inchoavit (aedificationem) Spirituum turris; mensus est ejus locum, delineavit eum. Totus populus adlaboravit ad eum; non die (integro consumpto) perfecit eam.

     (Trans. by S. Couvreur, S.J., 1896)

"When he built the Magic Tower,
When he planned it and founded it,
All the people worked at it;

In less than a day they finished it."
     (Trans. by A. Waley, 1937)

Father Coyos blessed it with special prayers, and named it "Carmelite Villa." Standing by a little gurgling brook that flowed through the valley, with a waterfall near by, the little arbor resounding with the noise of the cataract and the twittering of birds seemed to encourage us to offer up our own fervent prayers of thanksgiving.

Later Father Coyos also fitted up a bathing and drying room behind the summerhouse.

The Journey—from Man-p'o to U-jang— And Sojourn at Hu-ch'ang-ri

(August 12, 1952—March 27, 1953)

It was on August 12 that we received orders to get ready to leave the following morning. The commander told us that we need take nothing with us, for everything would be provided at the new camp specially prepared for us. We rejoiced very much for we all expected our liberation, but we remembered that there had been so many broken promises before and did not place too much faith in his words.

"Probably we are going to P'yong-yang," we said.

Hearing our words, the commander said,

"Even if matters don't turn out as you wish, I hope you will not lose courage, but keep up your spirits."

He was at times of a melancholy disposition, like many North Korean people, but at heart he was of a kindly nature. He went to a lot of trouble trying to get supplies for us, and was often absent till late at night on journeys to various places for this purpose, and we thought that it was probably owing to the impossibility of feeding us properly here that they had decided to remove us to some other place.

Next morning we were taken by trucks to a place called U-jang between Ch'o-san and Pyŏk-tong, where we were told we must stay the night. We were still waiting six months later.

Our commander explained that thenceforth the Chinese Communists would supply rations and medical care to us, while the Korean troops would be responsible for quarters and guards. These new quarters consisted of a group of Korean cottages three miles from town, each of which was occupied by four of us. We had never expected that we could enjoy such happiness. For the first time we four—three Carmelite Sisters and Mother Eugénie, the *St. Paul de Chartres* nun—could be together and have a room of our own. Joyfully we moved in and began to make the place comfortable. There were two doors, one on the south side and one on the north and we could get plenty of sunshine even in winter. By the north door was a wooden floor where we could eat our meals when the weather was warm. Our surprise and gratitude were not for those things alone, for the mayor of the town came to pay his respects, and brought us a present of fuel and soybean sauce.

It seemed too good to be true. One day a horse and cart drew up with a load of rice, flour, fresh vegetables, and wooden chests containing other supplies. Monsignor Quinlan, our experienced quartermaster, ran out to take charge of the goods. This happened regularly every month, the driver waving his whip, the horse-bells jingling merrily, and the children cheering his arrival.

A Chinese doctor visited us frequently at U-jang, and Monsignor Quinlan, who knew the language, could have lengthy talks with him. Once when they were alone together he bowed to Monsignor Quinlan and said,

"Salve Pater!"

Astonished, Monsignor Quinlan could only gaze silently at him.

"I am a Catholic," he went on, "I am a graduate of the *Aurora* University of Shanghai, Zikawei, operated and maintained by the Jesuit Fathers."

Monsignor Quinlan asked if he could do anything to alleviate our lot, but he answered.

"No, Father, I'm sorry to say I cannot do a thing. I am only in charge of the medical work, and have no authority."

He did his best however to give us the best medical care and medicine that he could. He cured Sister Marie-Madeleine of an intestinal complaint which had been troubling her, and did his best to cure Sister Henriette's neuralgia, but told her,

"I cannot cure you of this disease without certain drugs that are quite impossible to get nowadays, I am sorry to say."

He seemed quite regretful that Sister Henriette would have to go on trying to walk on her almost paralyzed legs.

On another occasion two young men called on Father Coyos and said:

"We are Catholics, and have firmly resolved to keep the faith and remain Catholics till death, no matter what happens to us."

Life at U-jang

The men resolved that this year they would not leave all the woodcutting to Monsignor Quinlan, and day after day they spent all their available time on the hillside up to the beginning of December, cutting and hauling firewood.

The food improved enormously; there was no more millet, but plenty of rice and enough flour to provide bread once a day, and we had pork as long as the cold weather lasted. They also gave us clothes—a summer and winter issue—and smokers received a ration of tobacco every month.

The surroundings of our house were very beautiful, with pleasant walks along winding pathways, but we were forbidden to go more than two hundred yards or so from our cottages. Occasionally American prisoners of war would pass us in trucks, and would always greet us and shout 'Hurrah!' and wave gaily to us. We understood this as their expression of fellowship in adversity. Their Chinese guards were lenient, and allowed them considerable freedom. We found it very heartening to meet these Americans: how much more heartening it would have been if we had ever met French prisoners! But we never did.

Commissioner Lord borrowed our copy of

the *Imitation of Christ* and read it with piety and zeal every day. Deeply impressed with the book, he recommended it to the Methodist missionaries. This was a book that Sister Bernadette had casually put in her pocket when she left Seoul, and was the only spiritual reading matter we possessed. At every reading our eyes were opened to some new discovery. Bishop Cooper, listening to an explanation of Catholic doctrine, began to reflect, discovering that he had been following a false tenet.

"Have I been teaching a false doctrine for fifty years?" he murmured, sceptical of himself.

The soul can find the light of truth more easily when it is in darkness.

Monsignor Quinlan earned the respect and admiration of all, for his moral courage was as great as his dignity of bearing—he was every inch a leader, both spiritually and in practical life. Tall and impressive in appearance, he had the mind of an innocent child, and a strength of character that could bring peace to the troubled. His presence radiated love. Whenever any hard labor was required of us, he was always the first to lead the way to the job and begin work on it.

He never wasted time in religious controversy, or in casting aspersions on non-Catholic doctrines, but preached his doctrine in silence by putting into practice the commandment to love and serve others without self-interest. He made friends with all, regardless of their faith. His winning smile gained the confidence of all, and when he left our prison in March, 1953, everyone grieved over his departure as the loss of a friend, and our prison seemed as if it had lost its sunshine.

The young Turkish girl Sagida was deeply influenced by Monsignor Quinlan. What temptations beset a pretty and sentimental young girl! Monsignor never spoke much, but whenever he happened to meet her outdoors he would say:

"Dear Sagida, always follow the right path. Be always right."

And this was enough. Long after, she wrote to him saying:

"I will never forget you, my dear Father. As long as your memory stays with me, I will never fall into sinful ways."

Winter came and the ground lay deep in snow, but the men had nothing to worry about for their forethought and hard work now began to pay off. Thanks to them we all had plenty of fuel for the winter, and probably enough for the early spring as well.

On New Year's Eve the English in accordance with their national custom all clasped one another's hands and sang the Scottish song by Robert Burns called "*Auld Lang Syne*." The Turks carried out their national custom by having a whitebearded old man go out from one door, while a very young man entered through another. One of the Carmelite Sisters and Mother Eugénie remained in their room, where they silently greeted the New Year by praying God to protect all their fellow prisoners in every future adversity, and by leaving everything at His merciful disposal. The Chinese Communist troops went on feeding as regularly, but the day longed for of our deliverance did not come. We all began to grow anxious, and, I am afraid, sometimes bored and irritable. The mood of the inmates grew gloomier day by day.

"How much longer must we put up with this prison life?"

Everyone mutely asked himself this question, and grew more and more discontented and anxious.

We began to be subjected to further repeated interrogation, which at least dispelled the monotony of our life. Though we often answered them very frankly, and gave what must have seemed to them very unsatisfactory and often displeasing replies, they never lost their temper or took revenge on us by inflicting punishments. This was an entirely new departure, quite contrary to our former experience.

Two Communist officers came to us from P'yŏng-yang on March 19. They summoned Monsignor Quinlan and the two Englishmen, Commissioner Lord of the Salvation Army and the Anglican Bishop Cooper. When they began to examine the color of their hair, the shape of their noses, ears, and so on, and taking measurements we were all struck with amazement. Father Coyos, who acted as barber, laughed and said:

"If they get their hair cut tomorrow, the measurements will be wrong."

The Communist officers patiently replied:

"We are taking these measurements because their friends have come to P'yŏng-yang and have been asking for them.

We all laughed heartily that evening, and sang an anti-Communist song.

On March 6 we noticed that all North Korean and Chinese troops were wearing black armbands, and that the portrait of Stalin in the commander's room was draped with black cloth. The death of Stalin was confirmed in the newspapers sold in the street. We wondered whether the death of this Communist ringleader would affect our position, and in what way.

On March 21, the two Communist officers called again and sent for the two Englishmen and the Irishman, and told them to get ready to leave within an hour. They packed up and a truck came for them carrying high-ranking officers. Monsignor Quinlan gave us a last benediction and we all waved them out of sight. There were some tears at their departure. We had never expected to be set free by nationality, but had thought we should all go together when the time for liberation came, and we even doubted whether it was really in order to be set free that they had been taken away.

Most of us had been whispering to one another, "It will be the Frenchmen's turn next!."

March 27, Friday

Officials in civilian clothes came again and sent for all the French citizens, but did not take any physical measurements. They seemed concerned about the French who had died, and had statements about their death drawn up.

"Don't get excited! We are not here to free you!" they told us. Nevertheless we all

got ready, and that evening a truck arrived. We boarded it and waved our hands in farewell to those remaining.

Journey to P'yŏng-yang Again

(March 27—April 17, 1953)

There were seven of us aboard the truck, and where they were taking us no one knew. Everyone was quiet, until Father Coyos, who was keeping a sharp lookout, pointed to a highway which led to P'yŏng-yang and another leading to Manchuria. There was snow to be seen still in many places. The road we took was very steep and slippery, and our driver had to reverse several times and try a second time to get up the hills. It became very cold and we were without blankets, for the Korean guards would not let us bring the blankets that the Chinese Communists had given us, though we promised to send them back to the prison later on. At midnight they allowed us to alight and warm ourselves in a police station.

Off we started again at three o'clock in the morning. The roads were so bumpy and we were all shaken up so much by the jolting of the truck that everyone of us suffered from attacks of vomiting and nausea. By ten o'clock the following morning we reached a little village but by six in the afternoon we had to set out again. We were told that it was extremely dangerous to attempt to use the roads during the daytime, for the United Nations air attacks were becoming fiercer day by day and any moving vehicle was likely to be bombed.

Along the road we saw signs of the devastation. Countless houses stood abandoned, some roofless and some with only part of the walls left standing. We now began to understand why the Communists had concealed us prisoners in those wretched underground mountain dugouts.

P'yŏng-yang! But what a different P'yŏng-yang!

Nothing remained of its former beauty, its charm that had so attracted us on our first visit on July 21, 1950. Every building had been demolished by the repeated bombing, and not one was left standing in the city.

We were told that even Kim Il-sŭng and his immediate subordinates lived in dugouts deep underground. We keenly realized the horrors of the aftermath of war.

The guards who had accompanied us seemed to have received no instructions about where to take us. They telephoned the authorities to ask for definite orders. One of the senior officers spoke to a subordinate in Korean, saying:

"We won't put them together with the diplomats." As we knew enough Korean to understand what he said, we realized with much satisfaction that M. Perruche, our French chargé d'affaires from whom we had parted two years ago, was still somewhere in the city, and that we would probably have an opportunity of seeing him again. As we all sat waiting in a spacious garden several high-ranking Communist officials approached us at a rapid pace (a sign of respect in the Orient) and gave us a cordial welcome. Their commander personally conducted Sister Marie-Madeleine, the blind nun, with every sign of respect and consideration in his manner. How had this transformation been brought about? We were led to a large and well-furnished room glittering with electric lights, and were seated at a long table beautifully decorated with vases of artificial flowers. Courteously the commander began to express his anxiety about our fatigue after our long and arduous journey.

"You must be awfully tired!" he remarked.

"In a few minutes, we shall ask you to have dinner with us. In all sincerity we have done our best to prepare a satisfactory meal for you. Then, after dinner, we will conduct you to the bedrooms we have made ready for you."

We really felt as if it were all a dream. With an affectionate smile a young woman-soldier brought in dishes—two kinds of meat, prawns of the highest quality, bread made

with eggs, various kinds of fruit, biscuits, and vegetables.

"You'll have soup tomorrow. I'm sorry that we weren't able to provide soup today."

He even apologized to us for the inadequacy of the entertainment. Several officers stood at a short distance from the table, watching our delighted appreciation of the delicacies on the table. As soon as we had made a hearty meal we were led downstairs to the basement of a large building, fairly deep underground. There we found our beds all in order as they had told us. On each bedstead were a straw mattress and clean blankets.

"They are just like our beds at Carmel," we thought. We still felt as if we were dreaming.

For the first time in thirty-three months we could lie down without our undergarments. Privacy is a blessing indeed! But it was very damp in those underground rooms. Each of us rendered fervent thanks to God, and lay down to rest.

Next morning we were awakened by the reveille. The bugler played the same tunes that we were so familiar with in France. Every event of the day was signaled by bugle calls. The soldiers' food was wretchedly poor and consisted of nothing but millet and soup. During our meals they used to hold parades to the accompaniment of much bugle-blowing outside our dining-room windows: it seemed as if they were showing off to us Europeans.

Our meals were all completely Western in style, and very well cooked, but there was not much variety in them. The toast and butter was always of the highest quality, and we had tea and biscuits at four in the afternoon.

Up till now we had been wearing the Chinese dresses provided for us by the Chinese Communists, and this may have been somewhat displeasing to our Korean hosts, for they replaced our Chinese clothes with new, lightly wadded garments. They took away our soiled towels and gave us new and clean ones in exchange. Several days later they brought in a dressmaker, who took our measurements for European-style dresses which they said they were going to have made for us.

Ever since our arrival in the city a doctor had visited us every day, and given us a thorough examination. A nurse came every day too, to bring medicines and to inquire whether we needed anything. We could think of nothing that we lacked: it was plain to us that this generous treatment on the part of our captors meant that the day of our liberation must be drawing near.

Nevertheless they would not commit themselves to any definite date. We also found the enforced idleness irksome, and thought we might feel more at ease if only we had some work to do to occupy our minds.

As soon as we came they had asked us to fill in our place of birth and other personal particulars, which had to be done in French, English, and Korean. Then came their request for a written report on the circumstances under which six members of our group (Mother Mechtilde Devriese, Mother Thérèse Bastin, Mother Béatrix Edouard, Father Antoine Gombert, Father Julien Gombert, and Father Paul Villemot) had met their deaths, leaving eleven survivors.

The report on those who died between November 3 and January 6 raised an issue. The director of the North Korean Red Cross paid a courtesy call on us and apologized for the failure of his organization to provide us with better treatment. He read our report, and frowned with embarrassment and perplexity, for it revealed to him all that had befallen us. When we told him that we were prevented from attending Mother Béatrix he seemed greatly confused.

"Why did you leave her?" he asked.

"Because the Communist soldiers forced us to choose between leaving her and being killed," we replied.

"Where did this happen?"

We told him in exact detail what we had seen, but still he seemed to be unable to understand what had happened to her.

Although this inquiry lasted several hours, no definite conclusion was reached. He therefore resolved to bring it to an end. In the course of conversation with us, he seized upon the fact that Mother Béatrix had suffered from a heart condition prior to her arrest and detention by the Communists.

"As she had this heart condition, it was no doubt this that caused her death," he declared.

He put pressure on us all to confirm this decision with our signatures. On hearing the detailed statements regarding the death of the five priests, he also forced us to place our signatures to a document to the effect that we recognized that they had all died of a disease. Copies were made in three languages, and he withdrew.

Every day we had to attend movie shows. They were all Soviet propaganda films showing a paradise of farmers and laborers in Soviet Russia. The films concerned their daily life on the collective farms, ploughing, harvesting, and dancing.

"Now I have something definite to tell you," a Communist officer announced one day. We all got very excited expecting that he had come to inform us of the date of our liberation. But he had nothing to say on that subject, but began beating about the bush with such remarks as:

"You have all suffered great hardship during your period of detention. It must have been doubly hard for you to bear since you are accustomed to such a high standard of living. But for our part we always did our best to treat you well."

He then proposed that it would be fitting for us to write a letter of thanks to Kim Il-sŭng, the leader of the North Korean puppet government, for the good treatment he had provided for us so far, adding that this was not an order.

We all did as he requested. What he had said was not entirely false. The North Korean farmers we met had to live on nothing but corn and edible grasses. Reduced to utter poverty by the war, they led a bitter life of extreme hardship and distress. It was only fair that we who had come to live with them and serve them should share their sufferings.

The attitude of these Communists toward us underwent a very remarkable change. The populace too looked upon us with sympathy and friendliness as they saw us in public. A simple fisherman showed his feelings by depositing, at the feet of Monsignor Quinlan, a basket of fish that he had been carrying. On another occasion when he was out for a walk a countryman gave him an egg, and on another somebody left a packet of cigarettes for him to pick up.

Except for the Tiger, his men, and several others who were mentally unbalanced, all the guards in charge of us prisoners did their best to provide us with as good treatment as was possible under the circumstances. It was the supply system that failed, and rendered them unable to do as much for us as they wished.

At the last prison in which we were detained the relations between the commander and the prisoners' representatives were particularly cooperative, and in P'yŏng-yang they became even more so.

April 10, Friday

Today we were told to expect visitors of high rank. About four o'clock in the afternoon they brought in the luggage of our Chargé d'Affaires M. Perruche, and Madame Martel. Guessing that these were the persons we were to receive, we looked out of the windows and very soon saw the chargé d'affaires and Madame Martel approaching with calm and deliberate mien, as if they were taking an afternoon stroll. We were overjoyed to see them again, and to learn how they had been getting on since our separation. They had been living in an underground apartment similar to the one we were now occupying, and located only a hundred meters away.

April 15, Wednesday

The Communist authorities finally made public the date of our release.

"The President of the Republic of France, through the Government of the Union of Soviet Socialist Republics, has requested the Government of the People's Republic of North Korea to release you, and our government, acceding to this request, had decided to repatriate you immediately, via the Trans-Siberian Railway."

This announcement, welcome as it was, caused us all considerable vexation. M. Perruche, for one, had urgent business to attend to at his legation in South Korea. Madame Martel also wanted to be allowed to proceed directly to Seoul. M. Maurice Chanteloup, the war correspondent, was also longing to go to Seoul and thence to Tokyo where his wife and children were waiting for him. Mother Eugénie and the three Carmelite Sisters asked for nothing more than to be allowed to return to their convents in Seoul. At the thought of a journey of thousands of miles in the opposite direction we were all disappointed and many could not repress their tears.

Our liberation coming in this form so different from what we had expected seemed much less gratifying to us. But it was our duty to obey the providence of God, and it was not for us to repine at His decree.

Preparations for our departure began. First of all we were taken to a bomb-damaged public bathhouse. Then our Western-style dresses for which we had been measured were brought to our quarters. My skirt was a little too short for my taste, and the overcoat was a very heavy one. They brought us a large assortment of shoes and asked us to take our pick. When we had all put on our new attire, we felt very strange at first, and laughed at one another and at ourselves.

After dinner we were requested to go out into the garden where there was a long table spread with a profuse display of refreshments, cakes and fruit. We were shown to seats at the table and tea was served. Two North Korean pressmen and two Soviet Russian correspondents also took their seats, and a group photograph was taken. We willingly posed for the camera as this would probably be their last request.

The questionnaire began, and was addressed principally to M. Perruche. They put several questions to us too, and we were careful to think before answering. At the conclusion of the interview they expressed their satisfaction at the tone and content of the M. Perruche's replies. Now that he had answered all their questions M. Perruche thought it was his turn to speak, and he began by asking,

"May I now ask you a question?"

"Of course," they answered.

"Why then did you prevent the minister of the Republic of France from communicating either with his president or with his family for nearly three years, in direct contravention of the provisions of International Law?"

The newspapermen were at a loss and unable to reply. After some hesitation the answer came.

"We are nothing but reporters: it is not for us to comment on or criticize the actions of the heads of state."

They then hurried off as if to avoid further embarrassment.

April 17, Friday

Before leaving, Madame Martel once again tried to find out where her daughter was being detained. The latter, a Sister of the Benedictine Convent of Won-san, had been arrested by the Communists in 1949, but her whereabouts was unknown. Her mother, Madame. Martel, was a woman of strong character who during her own long tour of Communist prisons in captivity, had never relaxed her efforts to find out what had become of her daughter, and carefully questioned everyone she met who might be able to give her some information. When one Communist officer told her that her daughter's liberation would be delayed pending the completion of certain necessary documents, she retorted:

"A few days ago another of your officers said that she had already been released and was on her way to France. You people all contradict yourselves. How can I place any trust in your words?"

At their final propaganda lecture the Communist speaker said in an ingratiating way:

"Once you get back to your country, I hope you will all do your best to promote peaceful relations between our two countries."

They were fond of posing as pacifists: another remark was:

"Your country has long been renowned for its high achievements in the arts, and I earnestly hope our two countries will soon establish friendly relations."

The lecture was over, and we set out on our long journey.

From P'yŏng-yang to Paris: From Paris to Montmartre Carmel

(April 17—May 3, 1953)

It was still the rule to travel by truck and only at night. M. Perruche and the 76-year-old Madame Martel were allowed to ride in a jeep.

An official who introduced himself as the Foreign Minister of the Republic of North Korea, and a Russian doctor accompanied us. In spite of the presence of these high-ranking officials the atmosphere was as chilly as when we had made our journeys by horse and cart. On the way more Korean fellow-travellers got on board. What with the crowding and the violent jolting, the trip was most unpleasant.

At about five in the morning we saw the city of Sin-eui-ju spread out ahead, and were told that rooms in the city's best hotel had been reserved for us. After a short rest and a well-cooked, satisfying dinner, we had to board the truck again and proceed to the customs office. There we were subjected to a very rigorous search. Our copy of *The Imitation of Christ* which had nourished our souls throughout our detention was seized, precious though it was in our eyes. All our personal writings, consisting of little notebooks in which we had jotted down a rough diary, little poems and songs, and miscellaneous memoranda, had to be torn into shreds by us in the presence of the inspectors, and thrown to the winds. Worst of all, we had to destroy the letter which Mother Thérèse had written to her family shortly before her death.

Soon we were crossing the great bridge that spans the Yalu River between Korea and Manchuria. Facing in the direction of the graves of our colleagues in Ha-ch'ang-ri we offered prayers for the repose of their souls, and for God's protection for each of our nuns in Seoul. We bade farewell to this country that had fallen into the clutches of the cruel Communists. Our truck jolted us over the border and deposited us at Antung, where the Chinese customs examination was even more rigorous than the one we had just undergone at Sin-eui-ju. Female inspectors took the Sisters to a separate room and made a thorough examination of all parts of our bodies. Sister Eugénie, who wears her hair in a bun, had to let them undo her hair and make sure that she was not carrying anything concealed in it.

M. Perruche, who had been stationed at the French Embassy in Peking some years previously, had made a collection of pictures of scenic interest in the Orient. Consisting of an album of 260 pictures, it was his constant companion throughout his captivity, and he valued it much more highly than all the rest of his baggage. We could easily understand his indignation when the customs officers, abusing their authority, attempted to seize them.

"Bring the Russian ambassador here! How dare you confiscate the personal belongings of a French minister?"

It was the first time we had ever seen him angry, and we were deeply impressed. The Chinese must have been impressed too, for they brought back the album of pictures and returned it to him.

The North Korean Army officer and the military doctor who had accompanied us as far as Sin-eui-ju were now replaced by two officials from the Waichiaopu, or Chinese Ministry of Foreign Affairs in Peking; the two Russians still remained with us.

Our train took us to Mukden, the ancient capital of Manchuria, scene of the great Japanese victory in 1905, during the Russo-Japanese War, and also of the 'incident' of September 18, 1931, which led the creation of Manchukuo by the Japanese. We learned that its name had been changed to Shenyang and that its population was now more than three million. From there we proceeded to Manchuli, now called Lupin, where we changed to the Trans-Siberian Railway.

At first M. Perruche was very unwilling to spend much of the money that had been allotted to us as traveling expenses, but when he learned that the French Government had purchased special class tickets for our journey from Antung to Paris he told us not to worry about money any more. Thanks to the generosity of our government we were freed from further anxiety on that head, and able to order anything on the menu that we thought we would like to taste after our three years of austerity.

The scenery all the way to Moscow was monotonous: broad frozen steppes, forests of bare pine and silver birch trees, tractors in operation in the fields of the collective farms, and small log-cabins dotted about the countryside. The windows of our carriage were provided with double panes, between which pink geraniums were blooming, and it was very warm in the train. Leaving China behind we skirted Lake Baikal where we saw many crosses standing in a distant graveyard, and the roofs of a group of buildings which we conjectured must have been a monastery in bygone days. Our next stop was at Irkutsk, a city of two hundred thousand inhabitants; at Omsk, which we were told has a half million, we were allowed to get out and stretch our legs on the station platform for an hour and a half.

We were surprised to see that very few of the Russian passengers made use of the dining-car, and we French had it to ourselves most of the time. Most of them seemed to prefer to buy snacks from the train vendors or milk from the milkwomen, or else they had brought their own home-cooked food with them. We were interested to see that whenever the train pulled up at a wayside village, too small to have a station, the country people would come on board and shop for supplies with the train vendors. We noticed that heavy maintenance work on the permanent way was being done by women workers, which we thought only men could be able to do in France. But for all we knew, even in France this heavy labor may have been taken over by women during the war. There was much that we had to learn about the outer world after our long seclusion!

There was of course at this time no single station along the route that did not display a huge portrait of Stalin, and we were not to know that a few years later he would be in posthumous disgrace.

April 30, Thursday

"You are not far from Moscow now," said our conductor. "We shall arrive at about eleven tomorrow morning." When we assembled at the women's table to take our places for our last dinner aboard the train we found cakes and chocolates of the most expensive brand set for each of us, a present from M. Perruche, who had also placed gift-boxes of cigarettes on the men's table. We decided to eat only a very few of the chocolates and take the rest back to El Carmel with us.

Our reception at the Moscow station was unforgettable. We were welcomed on the platform by virtually the whole of the French community of Moscow, led by His Excellency the French Ambassador, his embassy staff, and their families. Their enthusiasm was overwhelming and all found it difficult to control their emotion.

A long procession of flag-bedecked cars followed that of the ambassador through the city. With us in our car was his pretty young woman secretary, who pointed out the buildings of interest as we passed them.

"That is the Kremlin," she explained, "and that black marble stone over there marks the place where many people shed their blood during the revolution... That mausoleum is Lenin's tomb, now shared by Stalin," she went on, though neither of us imagined that Stalin's tenancy of it would be so short. The enormous Cathedral of St. Basil, with its ex-

traordinary agglomeration of onion-shaped domes, had survived the revolution, we saw, but it was now being used as an anti-religious museum.

The Tricolor of France waved vigorously over the French Embassy, symbol of the hearty welcome the French residents had been busily preparing for us since early in the morning.

It was our earnest desire to receive the Blessed Sacrament at the Mass celebrated by the only Catholic priest in Moscow but as our departure was scheduled for four o'clock that afternoon it was, to our great regret, impossible for us to do so.

This priest was a Canadian Father, permitted to reside in Moscow for the purpose of ministering to Catholic diplomats, and we had heard that he could speak French very well. The Catholic Church that formerly existed in Moscow had disappeared, and its site was now occupied by a Russian Orthodox Church. The priest therefore had no parish church but as chaplain of the embassy he celebrates Holy Mass in the embassy reception room every Sunday. On weekdays he holds a private Mass in his house. Who shall say that this daily offering of the host and chalice may not be a seed that will grow into a tree of salvation for the people of Russia?

Our departure was after all delayed, for the French plane that had been booked for us was out of order. But on Sunday, May 3, we boarded a well-equipped Russian plane with very comfortable seats. At the Russian border we landed at an airport and had lunch at about eleven o'clock. By three in the afternoon we were in East Berlin, in the Russian sector.

Here again we were given a warm welcome by the French community. They escorted us across the quietly flowing River Spree to the residence of French High Commissioner of West Berlin. As we drove through the streets of Berlin with the Tricolor flying proudly on our car they pointed out places of historic interest: the destruction and devastation wrought by aerial bombing however needed no pointing out. Nevertheless there had been great progress in reconstruction: fine new skyscrapers and residential buildings surrounded by gardens full of flowers were to be seen on every side.

We were given a welcome as warm as that we had received in Moscow: it was like coming back to the arms of our brothers and sisters. Military officers conducted us to our hotel, where a table beautifully decorated with flowers was laid for dinner.

"My dear Sister, what would you like, lemonade or champagne? We have *poulet en aspic* here; I hope you haven't forgotten the flavor of *poulet*? Which Carmel do you come from? We know the Carmel in Versailles very well. May I offer you an orange?"

Neither brothers nor friends could be kinder, we thought, as they filled our pockets with oranges. We realized the deep affection that exists between French people all over the world.

At two o'clock a milling horde of newsmen pressed around us popping their flashlight bulbs and taking picture after picture. Seeing our embarrassment before this battery of cameras one of the French ladies said to them,

"Please have some consideration for the Sisters; they have come such a long way and have been through so much hardship. Surely they would like to rest a little now. Come, now, you are really too inconsiderate! No more picture-taking now!"

One of the French gentlemen assiduously attended to Sister Marie-Madeleine, describing the scene to her and bringing her nice things to eat and drink.

A French plane was ready and waiting for us at the airfield and it was time for us to leave. After affectionate farewells we boarded it and found it not very luxurious, but of course we didn't mind that. We took our seats on steel stools, and the time passed rapidly in joyful talk until at seven p.m. Someone announced in a voice filled with emotion, "We are now flying over France."

Overwhelmed with joy, we all became silent. M. Perruche, who always knew how to handle every situation, said in tone of repressed excitement,

"We must not fail to toast the occasion!"

Kind and shrewd M. Perruche! Our ambassador at Moscow had specially provided him with several bottles of wine for our toasts on flying across the French border. M. Chanteloup, the war correspondent, pulled out from his socks the manuscript of the detailed account of our life in North Korea which he had been writing so that it could be published as soon as we arrived in Paris. This made us all burst into laughter.

"We were already free in Moscow. Why did you go on taking these precautions?"

"I can feel safe only on French soil," he replied.

At about eight we were told that the heights of Paris could be seen below us. There they lay, a brilliant network through which the Seine wound its tortuous way past Neuilly and the Bois de Vincennes and plunging northwest embraced the Cathedral of Notre Dame on the Île de Cité, closing its arms below the old Pont Neuf to flow on past the Palais Royal and the Tuileries and Île de St. Germain. Again it seemed like a dream that had at last come true.

As we emerged from the plane at 9 p.m. there was a barrage of flash-bulbs from the newsmen. The Acting President of the Republic was there to greet us on behalf of M. Vincent Auriol, and the crowd was so dense that we could hardly make headway through it. The police tried to clear a way for us but they complained:

"We have been waiting at the airport to see them for three days!"

Mother Henriette, our subprioress, walked at the head of our group. Her family rushed to embrace her. The Bishop of Paris was there, and he gave us a gracious welcome on behalf of all the Carmelite Sisters. There were telegrams from Carmelite Convents in all parts of the world congratulating us on our safe return. M. Perruche embraced his wife and children and introduced us to them. Mother Henriette, our Mother Superior, was conveyed immediately to hospital.

The Bishop took blind Sister Marie-Madeleine by the arm to conduct her through the crowd. On our way to the cars, which were to take us to the Montmartre Carmel the newsmen followed closely on our heels.

As we came to the gate of the Carmel the Bishop granted us all a special dispensation from our Carmelite vow of the great silence, adding laughingly that he was sure we had so much to say that we would break it anyway.

After we had all chanted Compline before the altar the Mother Superior and four other Sisters received us with sisterly love. They brought more congratulatory telegrams, including two from El Carmel and Al Carmel, and, to crown our joy, a letter from our Carmelite daughters in Korea. Our gracious God had so determined that it should be here waiting for us. This letter dispelled our dark and vexing anxiety and put fresh strength into us. We could hardly bear the bright lights, or was it the light of God's favor that was blinding us? Happy tears welled into our eyes.

"They are growing up vigorously," we said to ourselves, "by faithfully observing the sacred Carmelite discipline. They are in the southern most part of Korea, in the city of Pu-san. Our younger Sisters, under the leadership of the seniors, are courageously and faithfully spreading the Gospel of love and glorifying God in their devastated and poverty-stricken homeland." For the first time we could feel at peace.

When we retired to the private room which had been allotted to us, we found a large package from El Carmel. In spite of our fatigue we could not go to bed without opening it. Imagine our joy to find that they had sent us three new Carmelite habits, made to our measure, neatly stitched by hand as a mark of their devotion. Once more our eyes overflowed with happy tears.

The Montmartre Carmel Convent faces, across the narrow Rue de la Bonne, Rue Azais, the famous Byzantine-Romanesque Cathedral of the Sacré-Coeur. As the Cathedral grounds expanded, the adjoining convent became closer to it, and now occupies a site that gives it the appearance of being embraced by the great Sacré-Coeur as Saint John the Apostle was by our Lord Jesus Christ at the Last Supper. The Church of St. Pierre was only a few steps away.

Now at last we could receive the Holy Eucharist for the first time in thirty-three months. How could I express in words my infinite joy? I could only remain silent. As we rendered thanks to God, it seemed to me as if our Master were gently whispering, as He had done to Saint Peter.

"Why didst thou hesitate, man of Little faith?" (St. Matthew, 14:31)

Return to Korea

(December 4, 1953—January 29, 1954)

December 4, Wednesday

Mass was celebrated this morning by the vice-general of our order for the special intention of prayers for our safe return to Korea. In the Lady Chapel we could pray undisturbed with all our hearts and unite ourselves with the holy sacrifice of Jesus Christ. After a brief prayer the priest heard our confessions and gave us Absolution, with words that, arising from his ardent faith, increased our courage.

We began to set our cabin in order. The Assistant Mother Superior cried in mock despair,

"Where can we stow all these packages?"

Finally we got everything properly stowed away after a few hours of work. Our journey was going to be fun with all those little Vietnamese nuns chatting away like larks.

January 3, Sunday

No sleep last night. It was not that the weather was stormy, but due merely to my intense emotion at the thought of landing a few hours later in Japan.

After early Mass we sat waiting for the immigration officials at the foot of the stairway, when the ship's dignified old black cat came to say goodby to us.

Three old friends, Mr. Kim and Mr. and Mrs. Salbarrelli, were on board.

The immigration officials took so long to clear us that we began to feel uneasy, but a Franciscan Father approached us, and when he asked,

"What! Are you going to Korea again? Are you going back there with no guarantee that you won't have to go through those hardships all over again?"

"Where are you going, Father?" was our rejoinder.

"Well, after thirty years in China I couldn't stand the life in France, so now I am going to Japan, so as to be ready to return to my parish in China as soon as there is the slightest opportunity for me to do so, no matter what difficulty there may be in re-entering the country."

"What, then, is your attitude to the trials that await you?" We laughed merrily.

During the voyage we heard many missionaries' remarks:

"I lived more than twenty years in China," or "How good-hearted and lovable the believers were in China!"

No doubt the long-persecuted China missionary society will soon reap a bountiful harvest.

Once ashore we went straight to our Carmel in Tokyo, staying there for a few weeks, while the formalities for our entry into Korea were being completed. Then we took a plane from the great Haneda Airfield, and flew smoothly and swiftly across the Sea of Japan to Pu-san.

Awaiting us at the airport were Monsignor Carroll, the Korean Sisters of the Convent of Our Blessed Lady, and a woman doctor. Tears of deep emotion were in their eyes, and we could well understand their feelings when they saw us return without their Mother Superior, whom we had lost in North Korea.

Bouquets of fragrant flowers were presented to us, but a cold January wind was blowing, and it reminded us of the bleak winds that blew across the wild and boundless wastes of the Siberian steppes when we passed there after our release from captivity.

The beautiful flowers in our arms and the bitter wind seemed to symbolize the message of the Gospel in this country which though full of devastation and distress still had this hope to cling to.

The nuns of the Maryknoll Convent received us with true sisterly love. We thanked them from the depths of our hearts, and soon established close bonds of friendship with them. When our spiritual daughters took refuge in Pu-san in their flight from the Communist invaders who occupied Seoul, it was the Maryknoll Sisters who received them warmly, comforted and sheltered them, and gave them medical care with true maternal love. They spared neither time nor money in looking after them and providing them with necessities.

Monsignor Carroll had booked a plane to take us to Seoul two days later, so we thought we would be able to make a short spiritual retreat near the beautiful Church of Our Lady in Pu-san, but there were so many aspirants clamoring for admission to the Carmelite Convent and beseeching us to accede to their requests that we had to leave the Church and meet them. It was our sad duty to break the news to them that our convent was full, and that they must wait.

"You say we must wait, Reverend Mother, but you do not tell us how long!"

We thought to ourselves that if so many young women felt that they had a vocation, and wished to respond to the summons of our Father, we ought to try to establish another convent, for there was every sign that it would prosper. We decided that this matter should be offered to our Patron, St. Joseph, for his intercession.

January 28, Thursday

This morning Monsignor Carroll conducted us to the residence of Father Connors. We were most happy and grateful to meet the priest who had been the spiritual director of our Daughters and guided and supervised their spiritual life so closely for two years, during their stay at a poor little house on a hillside near that of Father Connors. This house, facing south, enjoyed sunshine and there was a beautiful view of the sea.

In the afternoon we went to pay our respects to the French Minister at our legation in Pu-san.

January 29, Friday

This was one of the most unforgettable days in our life. The weather was bright and sunny all morning, and just after lunch Monsignor Carroll called with a young Korean girl to take us to the airport. What a kindness! He tried to help us in every way. Though the plane was delayed and there was a long wait before it finally took off, he kept us company right up to the time of our departure. With his kind send-off we two old birds were again airborne, on the last lap of our journey to Seoul! Were we awake or dreaming?....

It was announced that we would be flying over Yŏng-dung-p'o in ten minutes. Overwhelmed with deep emotion, and enjoying that peace which it is beyond the power of words to describe, we looked back in self-reproach at the numerous occasions during our captivity when we had asked ourselves that melancholy question.

"Oh, Seoul! When shall we see you again?" Look! There was the answer, below us!

As we slowly descended the steep stairway from the plane, we were suddenly clasped in a tight embrace by someone. Oh! Here were our Sisters, our outdoor workers, welcoming us so enthusiastically.

They wept and laughed at the same time. We had expected to see them at the airport, but who were all these other people? Why were there so many? There were Korean Fathers, there were chaplains of the United Nations Forces, there were Sisters from the Convent of *St. Paul de Chartres*, and a countless number of the faithful. As we made our way through the assembly, they greeted us with thunderous applause. Photographs of us were being taken on every side. We were welcomed by a Civic Reception Committee presided over by the Mayor of Seoul, where a group of beautifully dressed little girls pre-

sented us with bouquets and floral wreaths. How could we express our joyful thanks? Next, the Commander of the United States Armed Forces in Korea made a congratulatory address, followed by another from Father Thomas Lee, and others. We could hardly manage to make adequate speeches of acknowledgement and thanks for so much kindness. Unfortunately, Bishop Ro, unaware of our prospective arrival, had flown to Pu-san that morning.

Our Daughters had borrowed a car from a Catholic friend and decorated it with flowers and bunting, and as we made our way to it a choir of Catholics sang the Song of the Korean Martyrs in vigorous tones.

This song and the loud cheers that resounded around us we dedicated to our two Mothers, Mother Mechtilde and Mother Thérèse, who, though they left no written record of their spiritual life, had crowned a long life in the service of our holy Church with martyrdom as surely as those Korean martyrs who died in the 1839-1866 persecutions and before.

It is beyond our power to express the deep gratitude to our Father and to all the faithful in Seoul that we felt as we stepped into the car. The priests, Brothers and the faithful all boarded buses and cars, and the long procession slowly wound its way through the shell-pocked streets and bombed buildings to the Cathedral. Passers-by, their curiosity aroused, stared and inquired of one another what it was about, and young men ran alongside peeping into the car windows to see who we were.

As we entered the Cathedral close, all the bells began to ring. We were led into the brilliantly lit Cathedral, and the noble words and music of the *Te Deum* well expressed our thoughts as we entered. After the adoration of the Blessed Sacrament we were conducted to the Convent of *St. Paul de Chartres*. It called up happy memories of 1939 when, as young Carmelite nuns, we had received our first welcome in the same house. We were all agog to proceed to our own convent and see our Sisters as soon as possible, so after exchanging greetings we took our leave of our gracious hosts and boarded a car to go to Hye-hwa-dong with Father Han, the Assistant Superior of our convent. As we entered the convent grounds the faint but familiar sound of our Carmelite bell came to our ears. Our small chapel was filled to capacity with the faithful, and all the doors were wide open so that those who could not get in could take part in the Benediction of the Blessed Sacrament. The service began with a hymn sung by the Minor Seminary Choir. The *Te Deum* renewed our praise of God.

Permitting ourselves only a brief moment to say a few words of greeting and thanks to our kind Catholics, we opened the longed-for gates of our convent and at last we could give our dear Sisters an embrace so lovingly firm and prolonged that it seemed to express our wish never to be parted from them again.

Mastering their deep feeling, our Sisters sang the Magnificat for us. We passed through the rest room, the main floor, and the refectory, where they had set up an arch of welcome beautifully constructed of pine branches, we finally rejoined our family. We felt as if Mother Mechtilde and Mother Thérèse were still with us, and we were still dominated by our loving memory of them.

The minutes flew by as we recounted our experiences to them, and it was past midnight before we realized how late it was, and went to bed. How lovingly my room had been prepared for me! They had been careful to arrange everything exactly as it was when I left, and I could not find the slightest change in it, all was quietude, seclusion and tranquillity. Peace reigned over our house, and our three-year absence was a thing of the past.

Our Blessed Lady in her delicate understanding had determined that our first conventual Mass after our safe return should be, as it was a Saturday, the Mass of the Will of the Blessed Virgin. The joy that filled our minds was most eloquently expressed in the words of the introit:

Gaudeamus omnes in Domino diem festum celebrantes sub honore beatae Mariae virginis: de cujus solemnitate gaudent Angeli, et collaudant Filium Dei: Eructavit cor meum verbum bonum: dico ego opera mea Regi....

(Let us all rejoice in the Lord, celebrating a festival day in honor of the Blessed Virgin Mary, on whose solemnity the Angels rejoice, and give praise to the Son of God: My heart hath uttered a good word: I speak my works to the King.)

(From the *Diary of a Kidnaped Carmelite Nun*)

THE GLORIOUS LIFE OF BISHOP BYRNE

(1888—1950)

THE GREAT MARTYR IN KOREA WHO WAS BORN IN THE U.S.A.

"There have been many martyrs in Korea, heralded to the world; but there have been a great number of those 'unknown saints' of whom the world will never hear… men who, by living for Christ, have done what was perhaps harder than dying for Him. It is the privilege of Maryknoll to follow where these pioneers have led.

"After the privilege of my priesthood, the greatest privilege of my life is to suffer for Christ with all of you."

These words were said by Bishop Patrick James Byrne, who met his glorious death in North Korea in 1950.

Born in 1888 in the city of Washington, D.C., U.S.A., Patrick James Byrne graduated from St. Mary's Seminary, Baltimore, in 1915, and was ordained to the priesthood forthwith.

In 1922, the Maryknoll Society was asked to staff a mission in a territory which was then part of the Vicariate of Seoul, but which would later become the Prefecture of P'yŏng-yang. Among the first Maryknollers to reach the Korean mission was Father Pat Byrne. He had joined the newly-formed society soon after his ordination, and had already been entrusted with major tasks of adminis-tration. His priesthood in Korea started in 1923 as pastor of Eui-ju parish to 1924. In 1927 he became the first Prefect Apostolic of P'yŏng-yang, but in 1929 he was elected as an assistant to the Superior General in the central administration of the Maryknoll So-

ciety, and the Holy See allowed him to resign his office to take up this appointment in the United States.

Six years later, Father Byrne led a pioneer group of Maryknollers to Kyoto in Japan. When the area was made a Prefec-ture in 1937, he became its first Prefect Apos-tolic. Again he resigned his office, this time as a tactful gesture to enable the Holy See to appoint a Japanese. This was in antici-pation of the hostility soon to be shown by the Japanese Government toward any re-ligious activity which could be shown to be under the direction of a foreigner.

It is a signal proof of the respect Father Byrne commanded among the Japanese as a man devoted only to his work, and above all suspicion of self-interest, that in spite of his nationality he was not arrested after Pearl Harbor. When other American nationals, after a period of internment, were repatriated in exchange for Japanese nationals held by Japan's enemies, Father Byrne was allowed, at his own request, to remain on in the Maryknoll House in Kyoto, and was still there when American troops arrived in 1945. After a holiday visit to the United States, he returned as Superior of Maryknoll's personnel in Japan.

In 1947 he was sent as Visitor Apostolic to Korea, to study the problems which had been created for the Church by the change in civil administration, and to advise on any necessary adjustments to the new situation.

In this delicate task he was eminently successful, and in April 1949 he was made Apostolic
Delegate to Korea, with headquarters in
Seoul. In June of that year he was consecrated Bishop in Seoul Cathedral.

When the invasion from North Korea
was approaching Seoul, a year later, Bishop
Byrne had to choose between staying to meet
the Reds or moving south. His only concern
was with the question of where he could
serve the Church best...north or south of the
battle line. He decided that a Church overrun
by Communists would have more need of
such aid as he could offer, and, in the hope
that he might be allowed to give it, he remained at his headquarters in Seoul.

As events turned out, his hope of giving
any direct help to the Church under the
Reds was not fulfilled. On the contrary, his
decision had cost him his freedom, and was
soon to cost him his life. But in the wider
and longer view, the choice he made will
not be balked of its noble purpose: the greater
good of his beloved Korean people. No one
who knew this Christ-like man can have
any doubt that the sacrifice he made of himself in the interests of Christ's Church will
bring grace upon grace, in the years to come,
to countless souls in this land where his
earthly relics are laid to rest.[1]

We cannot help revering the late Bishop
Byrne for his spirit of martyrdom and for his
conception of following the steps of the
Korean martyrs as a privilege of Maryknoll.
Clad only in summer wear he endured temperatures as low as thirty degrees below zero
on the so-called Death March. Deeply
mourning we make the same prayer as Monsignor Quinlan recited at his grave:

"May the Angels lead thee into Paradise;
may all the Martyrs receive thee at thy
coming, and take thee to Jerusalem, the Holy
City. May the choirs of Angels surround thee,
and mayest thou, like the once poor Lazarus,
have rest everlasting."

When Monsignor Byrne arrived in Korea

in 1947 as Visitor Apostolic, with full powers
to act as Apostolic Delegate, one of the local
newspapers commented: "The coming of
Monsignor Byrne means that Korea, a country without a government, divided in half,
occupied by the American Army in the
south and by the Russian Army in the north,
has at last been given a degree of diplomatic
recognition. The Korean people are grateful."

All along the roadside from Kim-p'o Airport
to Chong-hyŏn Cathedral countless Catholics
bearing banners in their hands ceaselessly
shouted, "Hurrah! Apostolic Delegate!" while,
in his car, Father Byrne at each shout would
say *sotto voce "Domine non sum dignus!"* (Lord,
I am not worthy!).

His appointment as Apostolic Delegate was
announced by the Holy See in April 1949,
and the ceremony of his consecration took
place on June 14. The procession from the
rectory to the Cathedral was led by the band
of the ROK Marine Corps, followed by seminarians, priests and prelates. Several triumphal arches had been erected along the route,
inscribed with congratulatory words and
greetings, such as *"Ad Multos Annos"* and
"Congratulations, Bishop Byrne." The ceremony of consecration was presided over by
Bishop McDonnell. In his first official statement as Apostolic Delegate to Korea, Bishop
Byrne rebuked the Communists of North
Korea for their apprehension and imprisonment of ministers of religion. This brought
threats broadcast by the Communist radio
of P'yŏng-yang that if the Bishop should be
captured by them he would be the object of
a severe reprisal. Despite these threats from
the Communists Bishop Byrne remained at
his post discharging his diplomatic and spiritual duties day by day.

On the morning of Sunday, June 25, 1950,
the Korean War broke out and the Red
troops of the north invaded the Republic of
Korea. Everyone expected Bishop Byrne to
flee south like most of the citizens of Seoul.
As the danger of the capital falling into the
hands of the Reds grew more acute, officials

---

[1] Crosbie, Fr. Philip: *Pencilling Prisoner*. Melbourne, The Hawthorn Press, 1954, pp. 39-41

from the American Embassy urged him to seek safety in flight, together with the remainder of the American civilian community. He declined to do so, but stated that while other American priests might be evacuated he would remain at his post. On June 27 Bishop Byrne went to Kim-p'o Airport to see off the other priests, and then returned to the rectory with his secretary, Father William Booth.[1] There he found Father Lee Sŏn-yong, the priest of Se-chong-ro Church, waiting for him. Father Lee had called on the Bishop to get information about the situation, and when the Bishop saw him he greeted him as cheerfully and calmly as if there was nothing to worry about in the world.

"You are really welcome, Father Lee."

"How is the situation developing, Bishop?"

"Oh," he replied, almost indifferently, "Seoul City is to be occupied by the enemy either this evening or tomorrow morning. It is really very stupid of America to let the Republic of Korea be overrun so easily. But—God's will be done!"

"But what about you? What are you going to do, Bishop?"

"I have nothing to worry about. All the other American priests have been safely evacuated. I have made up my mind not to leave Seoul. At first I wanted Father Booth to leave, but he insists on staying with me, live or die."

Father Lee stayed to lunch, and Bishop Byrne gave him all the information he sought: how many divisions, tanks, planes, and so on, had been mobilized by the Reds, the power and range of their artillery,—and, on the other hand, the weakness of the ROK Army, and the unpreparedness of the U.S. Armed Forces. In the Bishop's judgment of the situation, in the first stage of the war the whole territory of the Republic of Korea would be occupied by the Reds, and the ROK Government would consequently have to seek refuge abroad, and return when the U.S. Forces had prepared defenses and were ready to begin their counterattack. "There is," he concluded, "nothing to get worried about."

Father Lee was not satisfied and questioned Bishop Byrne's assumption that the Red occupation would not last long. "What will happen to you under the Communists?" he asked.

"As I was sent to Korea as Apostolic Delegate my first duty is to keep in touch with the ROK Government, and as I am not the Vicar Apostolic of any Vicariate Apostolic in Korea, I am free to move anywhere together with the ROK Government, of whose *corps diplomatique* I am an accredited member. Nevertheless, as Bishop Ro, the Bishop of Seoul, and Bishop Larribeau, Bishop of Taejŏn, are both away from their sees on their *ad limina* visit to Rome,[2] I fear the moral effect of my departure on the faithful might be one of disquiet, and I feel it is my duty to remain here. Moreover I came to Korea for the sake of the Korean people and it is my desire to stay here until death, and if I were obliged to leave Korea in order to be with the ROK Government, I would return at the earliest opportunity. I dislike the idea of leaving Korea even to take temporary refuge from the Reds."

Father Lee took leave of the Bishop with a firm handclasp, and promised to return very soon. That night the rattle of machine-guns grew louder and the thunder of guns sounded nearer. Next morning there was heavy firing around the delegation and when it ended a jeep filled with North Korean

---

[1] Father Booth, like Bishop Byrne, was one of Maryknoll's pioneer missionaries in Korea. Repatriated when the civilian internees were exchanged in 1942, he worked as a missionary in Chile till re-entry to Korea was made possible by the surrender of Japan. Maryknoll's mission territory, however, was now behind the Iron Curtain, so Father Booth offered his services in the Vicariate of Seoul, and was engaged in pastoral work there till he joined Bishop Byrne. (v. ibid. p. 41)

[2] *Ad Limina Apostolorum* "to the threshold of the Apostles", i.e. the graves of St. Peter and St. Paul at Rome. The expression is generally used of a bishop's obligatory quinquennial visit to the Holy See.

soldiers drove into the delegation courtyard.

"I want to *borrow* your jeep," the officer said, pointing at the garage where the Bishop's car and Father Booth's jeep were parked. The officer ordered his driver to take the jeep without waiting for permission, and they drove off. Moments later, three more North Korean soldiers came to *borrow* the Bishop's car.

"Look, if some general comes along and wants my car, what am I to say to him?"said Bishop Byrne to them. The Red soldiers, confused by this reply, could say nothing more for the moment and left, but half an hour later they were back again with an official order for the car. This was going on all over the city—cars and trucks were being commandeered everywhere. As soon as the soldiers had gone off with the car, fellow-travelers and fifth columnists who had been planted in the city began to come in. They were all dressed in civilian clothes, and wore an armband.

They began to pillage the delegation, stripping it of everything movable. Bishop Byrne sent a boy to Father Lee Sŏn-yong to ask him to come over to the delegation. This boy, about ten years of age, lived near the delegation and Bishop Byrne had befriended him, allowing him to play in the delegation compound, and sometimes taking him for a ride in his car.

When Father Lee arrived the Reds were trying to frighten the Bishop, by firing their rifles into the air. The Bishop introduced Father Lee to the Reds, saying, "This is my closest friend, and you will surely understand if I give him all the vestments and sacred objects in the delegation." The Reds, however, who were looting the building, forbade him to remove anything from the premises. "Why not?" demanded the priest. "Aren't we all under the people's government? These things belong to you as much as they belong to us." The Reds were without an answer, and watched the brave little priest walk away with his pushcart.

Bishop Byrne jokingly held out his miter in his hand, and offered it to Father Lee, saying "Here, you can wear this miter if you become a bishop: if you don't, and I am still alive, you can give it back to me." The Reds absent-mindedly looked on as the brave priest walked away with it in his pushcart. Then they returned to their looting, and by evening there was hardly anything movable left in the house. With even their wrist watches confiscated Bishop Byrne and Father Booth made their way on foot to the Myŏng-dong Cathedral in their shirt-sleeves. There the Korean priests kept him informed of what was going on in the city.

At about five o'clock in the evening of July 11, Bishop Byrne stepped out on the balcony to get some fresh air. It had been a hot and stifling day, and he had just taken a turn around the balcony when Monsignor Carroll's jeep roared into the Cathedral compound with North Korean soldiers behind the wheel. Before Bishop Byrne could withdraw, the Reds had seen him. A soldier hurried into the rectory and demanded to know who it was that he had seen.

To avoid an unpleasant scene, Bishop Byrne and Father Booth came downstairs, still in their shirt-sleeves as they had no cassocks left to them. In this attire they were taken out of the house by the Reds. Father John Yu volunteered to accompany them, so as to render any help that he could. The Reds motioned him into the jeep. The jeep with Bishop Byrne, Father Booth, and Father Yu in it drove off out of sight and nobody knew where they were being taken, until another jeep came roaring into the compound, and there was Father Yu in it with some officials of the Political Security Bureau; he had come back to fetch their bedding. Father Chrysostomus Chang who was present tells us that Father Yu quickly wrapped up the bedding and a change of clothes in a bundle and got back into the jeep, waving a silent farewell without a word.

In order to trace where the jeep went, Father Chang had asked several young men beforehand to station themselves in the various streets and keep the lookout. The jeep with Father Yu in it had pulled up outside the Sam-hwa commercial building opposite the Mi-to-p'a Department Store. The Reds had commandeered the Sam-hwa building and turned it into a jail. Bishop Byrne, Father Booth and Father Yu were immediately led to the foul-smelling, fly-ridden basement where, under a dim electric light, Communist officials were questioning Korean civilians.

The newly-arrested were herded into a dark corner of the basement, a room about fifteen by twenty feet in area. The basement was like a Turkish bath, and the Red interrogators were soaked with sweat. They were to spend the next eight days in this fetid basement, allowed to move from it only once in the morning and once at night to go to the wash-room. They were served twice a day with a ball of cooked barley and a little rice wrapped in a scrap of news-print, and given a small cup of water.

Among their fellow prisoners in the basement were other missionaries and foreign civilians. Father Paul Villemot, the eighty-one-year-old French priest, spiritual director of the *St. Paul de Chartres* Convent adjoining the Cathedral, was there, and the two elderly Gombert brothers, both priests, one seventy-six years old and the other seventy-four, who had just celebrated the fiftieth anniversary of their ordination; Father Coyos, another French priest, was also brought in. Mother Béatrix Edouard, the Superior of the Sisters of *St. Paul de Chartres*, arrived later with her companion, Mother Eugénie Demeusy, the mistress of novices. There were also five Carmelite nuns; two Belgians, Mother Thérèse Bastin, the prioress, and Mother Mechtilde Devriese, and three French, Mother Henriette de Lobit, the subprioress, Sister Bernadette Descayaux, and Sister Marie-Madeleine Marquier, who was totally blind. Monsignor Thomas Quinlan, the Superior of the Columban Fathers in Ch'un-ch'ŏn was brought in; he had been arrested at the altar while saying Mass. With him was Father Crosbie, an Australian Columban, and Father Canavan, an Irish Columban.

The basement soon became so crowded that there was hardly room enough for the prisoners to lie down at night. Bishop Byrne welcomed the new arrivals with kind words and consolation. Since his arrest he had been unable to take any food, and Father Yu obtained special permission to go out and fetch him a little meat and a bottle of wine. The Bishop, however, would not take these delicacies for himself alone, but insisted on sharing them with Father Villemot, the senior priest, and Mother Béatrix Edouard.

According to the record kept by these Sisters, Father Yu made his last appearance at their convent on the afternoon of July 23, Sunday. Asking for some food and toilet requisites for the prisoners, he informed them of the conditions in which they were living, and said that the Bishop and Mother Béatrix were growing weaker every day, on account of the poor food they were getting: a single ball of cooked barley with a little salt, which they could not eat. "I wonder how much longer they can go on like this," said Father Yu, and his words brought tears to the eyes of the listening nuns. They provided him with some bread and other things, and, dressed in ordinary civilian clothes, he hurried back to the basement prison of Sam-hwa Building. This was the last they saw him.

After several days of interrogation, insult and maltreatment, the Bishop and the other priests were brought before what the Reds called the 'People's Court.' Old Father Villemot, now much weaker, and in great suffering, once asked for a cup of water. Father Yu passed on the request to the guard and at once brought on himself a torrent of abuse from the mob.

"Why are you sucking up to this foreigner? Are you one of the running dogs of the imperialists?"

The court asked Bishop Byrne why he had come to Korea. He replied that he had come to teach religion. "Kill the American!" shouted the crowd, as it had been taught beforehand by the indoctrinators. The Bishop then said, "I am here not as an American but as the diplomatic representative of a sovereign state, the Vatican: I am the Apostolic Delegate."

When Father Booth was interrogated by the court, all he would say was that as his Superior, the Apostolic Delegate, had already testified, he had nothing to add. At the conclusion of the 'trial' the chairman declared that unless Bishop Byrne would broadcast, over the Communist radio, a denunciation of the United States of America, the United Nations and the Vatican, he would be sentenced to death. The Bishop's only reply to this was: "There is only one course open to me, that I die."

After eight days of ceaseless questioning by relays of interrogators, deprived of sleep, in stench and heat, and constantly plagued by flies, Bishop Byrne and his companions were taken from the basement and loaded aboard trucks. In his weakened state, while trying to climb onto the truck, Bishop Byrne collapsed and fell unconscious. He was lifted on board and when his companions had succeeded in bringing him round, his first words were an apology for the trouble he had caused "I have never fainted before in my life," he added. As the main railway terminus of Seoul had been bombed they were taken to a station north of Seoul, and loaded on to a train which took them to P'yŏng-yang, the scene of Bishop Byrne's pioneering work for the Maryknoll Mission in the twenties.

The prisoners were marched to a school building on the outskirts of the city, where they found many other captives. They were herded into rooms by nationalities, with other missionaries, diplomats, businessmen and other civilians,① and here the Bishop was to remain from July 19 to September 5. The food supplied to the prisoners at P'yŏng-yang was even worse than what they had been given in Seoul. The unvarying daily ration consisted of rice, watery soup made of radish leaves, and two drinks of water. Here, too, the interrogation continued unceasingly. Bishop Byrne's state of

health grew worse: he contracted diarrhoea and dysentery, and his skin broke out in sores due to malnutrition.

Every day the prisoners could see the United Nations planes bombing the City of P'yŏng-yang, and although all news of the war was kept from them, they realized that the counterattack was under way. When the prison treatment grew harsher the prisoners attributed it to the Communists' resentment at the Red Army's inability to withstand the forces under General MacArthur, which were steadfastly holding their ground in the south, and when orders came for a further move, they correctly surmised from the attitude of the guards that General MacArthur's counterattack was successfully under way, and that the Reds had been robbed of easy victory.

They prayed for deliverance, but there was worse in store: late in the afternoon of September 5, during a heavy air attack on the city, the Bishop and his companions were marched from the school building and put on board a train for Man-p'o, a journey that took less than ten hours in peace time, but which was to take them almost a week of hard travel. The railway traffic could move only at night, and the trains were kept hidden in tunnels during the day whenever possible.

One day, however, when they were sitting on the hillside with the empty train below them, American planes appeared and strafed it, as it was unmarked, but no one was hurt. Bishop Byrne met American soldiers for the first time on this train: they were prisoners of war captured in the south and many of them were suffering from wounds and exhaustion. No medical facilities were available to them, but Bishop Byrne did what he could for them, and grieved over the pain which they were enduring.

One day on the way to Man-p'o instead of taking shelter in the bushes on the hillside the prisoners were dragged through the

---

① For a list of names of these fellow prisoners, see *The Diary of a Kidnaped Carmelite Nun*, Appendix A—III (The Death March)

streets of a small town to a school building. Father Booth remarked to the Bishop that the place looked familiar to him, and, entering one of the classrooms, sat down at one of the desks and fell asleep. He was awakened by a hand on his shoulder.

"Aren't you Father Booth?" asked a young man in civilian clothes.

"Yes," answered the priest, in surprise.

"Don't you remember me?" asked the young man.

"I am sorry, I don't think I do."

"I am John Lee. You confirmed me here almost twelve years ago."

Father Booth remembered. As temporary administrator of the territory during Monsignor Byrne's absence on a visit to America, he had come to this country town to administer the Sacrament of Confirmation. John was about twelve years old at the time.

"You will get into trouble talking to me," said Father Booth.

"The guard probably thinks I am trying to sell you these," said John, as he showed Father Booth a string of eggs packed in straw that he was carrying behind him. John also pressed a package of tobacco on the priest, and gave him a sum of about five dollars that the local Catholics had collected after they had seen the priests marched through the village.

John told him that there was now no priest in the village but that the Catholics met regularly in his house. He told Father Booth that the Catholics would be at the station when the priests were leaving and asked if the priest would give them Absolution when he walked by. "We do not know when we shall be able to see a priest Again," John concluded. When Bishop Byrne and Father Booth returned to the train, the little group of Catholics were gathered close to the station. They made no sign of recognition in order not to attract the attention of the Red guards. As Father Booth walked past he made the sign of the cross close to his breast and uttered the Absolution in a low voice.

The eyes of the Christians sparkled with joy as they understood and appreciated the blessing.

The train pulled in at Man-p'o on the morning of September 11.

The group of prisoners at that time consisted of fifty-nine civilians, seven hundred and twenty-five American prisoners of war, and some foreign diplomats. The civilians were marched into a long building divided along both sides into cubicles. Winter was approaching and it was already cold; a bitter wind was blowing steadily across the Yalu River from Manchuria. Six weeks later orders came to leave for Ko-san; the war was developing badly for the North Koreans and they wanted to retreat further before the advancing troops of the United Nations. Mother Mechtilde had fallen ill with bronchial pneumonia and had to be carried by the other prisoners on an improvised stretcher. Mother Béatrix also became ill on the march. At Ko-san the prisoners were herded into wretched little hovels with no heat: they gathered a few cornstalks to provide a little warmth, but all suffered intensely from the piercing cold. Three American prisoners of war attempted to escape, but two of them were shot dead and the third was recaptured.

The North Korean Army was by now in full retreat before the counterattacking forces of General MacArthur, and everything was in a state of demoralization and confusion. Red officers ordered that the prisoners be taken to a remote and deserted mining village far away in the mountains, so that the United Nations soldiers would be unable to find and liberate them. The prisoners reached the place but the guards, in their panic, abandoned them completely. At the time the United Nations Forces were only a short distance away, but as the prisoners did not know how to find them they decided to make their way back to Man-p'o in the hope of meeting them.

Bishop Byrne's sixty-second birthday anniversary came round during the return journey, and Father Booth bought a couple of chickens with the money given by John Lee. Those provided the last decent meal that Bishop Byrne was ever to have.

Father Booth recalls the occasion as follows:

On the way back to Man-p'o, instead of meeting the United Nations Forces, we met Chinese 'volunteers' by the hundreds, who were pouring across the Yalu in an incessant flood, called by the Chinese the "*Jen-hai*" (Sea of Men). They were armed to the teeth with modern weapons and equipment and were pressing forward to attack the United Nations Forces, so that instead of being liberated we were recaptured, and at Man-p'o we were put into a burned-out building for the night. The building had no roof and the weather had turned bitterly cold: we spent a wretched and painful night.

We were luckier than the American prisoners of war, however, for they had to lie out in the open on the bank of the river, and ten of the poor soldiers were frozen to death during the night. I shall never forget that date: it was October 31, and on that very day we met the "Tiger." This was the nickname by which we referred to the North Korean commandant who now took charge of all the foreign prisoners. He was full of bitterness at the Americans who had frustrated the ambitions of the North Koreans, and he was ready to vent his fury on his captives. He had the prisoners lined up before him and barked:

"We are going to march about two hundred and fifty kilometers to Chung-kang-jin by a mountain path: it is a long walk that we have before us, and we must proceed in military formation. All orders are to be obeyed as military commands." It was pointed out to him that many of the party would find it impossible to march like soldiers, and that for some of them the attempt must surely be fatal.

"Then let them march," said the Tiger, "till they die! That is a military order."

So began their march of death. (Father Crosbie has given a memorable account in his *Pencilling Prisoner*, of which we have already made liberal use.) Eight days' march from Man-p'o to Chung-kang-jin was indeed an ordeal, almost beyond description. During this journey ninety-eight POWs perished, and Mother Béatrix was also killed. Of the thirteen members of the *Société des Missions-Étrangères de Paris* only one priest survived to be repatriated two years later.

After their arrival at Chung-kang-jin on November 17, 1950, the exhausted survivors were again called upon to march.[①] Several of the sick, shivering with cold and fever, stepped forward a few feet, fell down in the snow, and on trying to rise, collapsed again. At all costs they had to get to Ha-ch'ang-ri, where they could get shelter in a few straw-thatched shacks, one of which was assigned to Bishop Byrne and his group.

On November 18, Monsignor Quinlan and Father Booth were sharing the room with Bishop Byrne, who was in a critical condition, and there was nothing that they could do to help him. The village was devastated, and no supplies were available. Bishop Byrne was dying.

At midnight, three Communist guards entered and ordered the immediate removal of Bishop Byrne, and also of Father Coyos, who was afflicted with tuberculosis, to their so-called "People's Clinic," or "People's Hospital," which the prisoners referred to as "the morgue," a filthy hut without heat, without beds, and without attendants. It was a mere empty shack with a mud floor over which some straw had been strewn. It was really a place to which dying prisoners were taken and left unattended, until God in His mercy should call them to Him.

Monsignor Quinlan and the other missionaries asked the guards to allow them to take care of Bishop Byrne in their own shack. This the guards stubbornly refused, insisting that if the Bishop had to die, he must do so in the People's Hospital. Realizing that it was no use arguing with them, Monsignor Quinlan and I volunteered to help the sick man to "the morgue." I was able to give the Bishop the Sacrament of Penance

---

① Refer to Appendix A—III, The Death March, from *The Diary of a Kidnaped Carmelite Nun*.

Glimpses of Bishop Byrne as a Great Leader and Martyr

On his return to Korea as Apostolic Delegate

"Next to the grace of the priesthood, I look on it as the greatest privilege of my life to have been able to suffer with you for Christ."
(Bishop Byrne's words during the Death March)

"There have been many martyrs in Korea, heralded to the world; but there have been a greater number of those 'unknown saints' of whom the world will never hear—men who, by living for Christ, have done what was perhaps harder than dying for Him. It is the privilege of Maryknoll to follow where these pioneers have led."

Patrick J. Byrne.

Consecration of Bishop Patrick Byrne (June 14, 1949)

Bishop Byrne in his younger days as ordinary of P'yŏng-yang Prefecture (Front row, fourth from left)

Bishop Byrne's sixty-first birthday anniversary
Wearing a traditional Korean official costume

Prelates at the consecration of Bishop Byrne

and Absolution.

As they were helping him across the snowy fields, Bishop Byrne whispered to Monsignor Quinlan, "Don't feel bad about me, Tom: it has always been my hope to give my life for the faith. Now the good Lord has granted me this privilege. Look out for yourself and keep your eyes on the others now." When I saw the so-called hospital he almost broke down. The scanty scattering of straw on the filthy floor, the walls that could not keep out the bitter wind, and the icy interior, as cold as a refrigerator, with only a tattered straw mat hung over the broken doorway were enough to daunt anyone, but Bishop Byrne, as we laid him on the cold floor, only turned to us and said, "Next to the grace of the priesthood, I regard it as the greatest privilege of my life to have been allowed to share your sufferings for Christ."

Father Booth goes on to describe the next few days as follows:

"Miss Helen Rosser, a Methodist missionary from Georgia, U.S.A., was an excellent trained nurse. Although the Communists would not permit her to attend the sick in "the morgue," as we called it, she was indefatigable in attending the prisoners. She made some thick bean soup and I carried some of it over to the Bishop. That was the only medicine available for the sick. The Bishop was now so weak that I had to feed him. Day and night the sick man lay in the cold, wrapped only in his single blanket.

"For four days he endured this, and then his condition grew worse. Father Coyos gave the Bishop Absolution on November 24, and shortly afterward, the Bishop fell into a trance, and finally became delirious. He never complained or seemed dissatisfied.

"On the morning of the twenty-fifth, Monsignor Quinlan, who had gone to visit him, returned to announce that Bishop Pat had gone to Heaven. There was not a soul in camp who heard the news without a leaden sense of personal loss.

"Bishop Byrne was buried that day, close to the other dead, in a shallow grave which Monsignor Quinlan and his companions dug

with painful labor in the hard, frozen ground. The guards ordered the funeral group to return to their shack, but Monsignor Quinlan proceeded without haste. Standing bareheaded in the cold he recited prayers beside the grave:

" 'May the Angels lead thee into paradise; may the martyrs receive thee at thy coming; and take thee into Jerusalem, the Holy City. May the choirs of Angels receive thee, and mayest thou, with the once poor Lazarus, have rest everlasting.' "

Bishop Byrne's remains lie just outside the little village of Ha-ch'ang-ri, north of Chung-kang-jin.

Monsignor Quinlan furnishes a further note on the funeral, as follows:

"The Bishop had no cassock so I placed my own around him. I left it with him in the hope that in the years to come the remains might be identified from the red bone buttons, which will not decay. We marked his grave with rocks laid out in the form of a cross. I still have his rosary. It was not his own: his own had been taken away from him, but the Carmelite nuns with us gave the Bishop one of their own. I saw him use it, and when he died I took it and have been using it myself. I shall forward it to Bishop Lane, his Superior General at the Maryknoll Mission."

People living on the east coast of the United States of America remember November 25, 1950, as the day on which a hurricane of exceptional ferocity ravaged the Atlantic coast, flooded towns, and left the countryside strewn with uprooted trees and debris, cutting off the supply of light, heat and power from every community for several days.

While this storm was at its height, the cloistered nuns at Maryknoll kept up a *triduum* of prayer, day and night, with exposition of the Blessed Sacrament, as an act of reparation for the blasphemous acts committed by the Communists in North Korea. Constant prayers were offered for the safety of Bishop Byrne, Father Booth, Sister Agnita and their fellow-sufferers in Korea. On the second day of this *triduum*, Bishop Byrne died. This was not known in America until two years later, when Monsignor Quinlan and Father Booth were freed and repatriated.

Postscript:

On hearing of our intention to publish the present work, Father Booth, the former secretary of the late Bishop Byrne, wrote to us a letter, extracts from which we publish as follows:

"From the time of the arrest of Bishop Byrne by the Communists in Seoul on July 11, 1950 to the last moment of his martyrdom in North Korea on November 25 of the same year, this period was a *via crucis* for Bishop Byrne on his way to the glorious sacrifice of his life for the faith.

"Bishop Byrne was never physically strong; he had a keen mind and a strong will, in a somewhat weak body. During this period he endured extreme hunger and cold, and was reduced to the utmost physical exhaustion, yet he never complained, but thought only of how he might help the others, and his usual cheerful manner never deserted him.

"The last fortnight of his life, while he was suffering from pneumonia and dysentery, was a period of increasing weakness and suffering. He died in utter destitution in the presence of those other dying men, lying on a bare earthen floor.

"The thing that I would like to stress in the life and death of Bishop Byrne is that everything he did was for the building up of the Church in Korea.

"From the time of his appointment as Visitor Apostolic to the Republic of Korea, in August 1947, until his death on November 25, 1950, Bishop Byrne devoted all his time and talents to the sole object of helping the Korean people in every possible way, and particularly towards strengthening and advancing the Catholic Church in Korea.

"Bishop Byrne was a dedicated foe of atheistic Communism. He was the foe of Communism in Japan, immediately after the close of the World War II in 1945, and he was the foe of Communism in Korea, from his arrival in 1947 until the outbreak of the Korean War in 1950.

In Korea, during his detention in the prison camps of the Communists, there were two incidents that demonstrated his charity toward his fellow-men. The first occurred when we arrived at Man-p'o on September 11, 1950, when Bishop Byrne volunteered to serve out the rations, three times a day, to each of the fifty-nine civilian prisoners, a duty which he shared with the Anglican Bishop Cooper. In view of the fact that he was not robust, this was an arduous and by no means obligatory task. The second occasion was on the fifth unforgettable night of the death march. We came to a small wooden building (formerly a chapel for Protestant worship) and there was hardly room for all of us to enter and find a place to lie down and rest. Bishop Byrne with the help of another civilian measured and marked out sleeping spaces for everybody so that all could lie down, but omitted to mark out any space for himself, so that he had to spend the whole night either sitting, standing, or walking about outside.

"In spite of his sufferings, Bishop Byrne never complained or showed any resentment toward his captors. He remained cheerful to the end, and always tried to help others. This I believe is what I ought to emphasize in writing of Bishop Byrne—namely, his generosity, forgiveness of injuries, in short, his great charity, which, after all, is more important than miracles. Bishop Quinlan was present at the burial of Bishop Byrne and he can tell you more by word of mouth than I can in writing. Father Coyos, too, was in the room when Bishop Byrne died.

"When at last we were released in April 1953, we were taken by truck from a small village near the Yalu River through Yŏn-p'yŏng to P'yŏng-yang. We remained there for ten days. Then we were taken by truck to Sin-eui-ju, and thence to Antung. From Antung we went by train to Manchuli, and then we made a seven-day train journey to Moscow. After twenty-four hours in Moscow we took a plane to Frankfurt in Germany, and from there we went by plane to New York.

"My recollection of those two years and ten months of captivity is that I gained great help and comfort through the intercession of our Lady, the Blessed Virgin Mary. Whenever possible I did my best to say the fifteen decades of the rosary, especially when I was sent to the mountainside to gather fuel and kindling. Every day I would try to say one or two rosaries, and when I was incapacitated with that tiresome carbuncle, I remember particularly reciting the *Memorare*. (A popular prayer to Our Lady, attributed to St. Bernard of Clairvaux, so called from its first word in Latin. Its use was greatly popularized by a French secular priest, Claude Bernard, in the early seventeenth century).

"I left the United States again in October 1955, and arrived in In-ch'ŏn on October 24:

I remained there until 1961 On May 31, 1961 I left for the U.S.A., and have been living there until now. Though my health is somewhat improved I am not quite well, and am suffering from failing eyesight, for which reason my return has been postponed. I look forward to return to Korea again when my health permits."

(Based upon the testimonies of the captured priests, Sisters, and others; Fr. Booth's Letter; *Ambassador in Chains* by Bp. Lane; *Interview with Father Coyos* by Fr. Hwang; *Ma Captivité en Corée du Nord* by Fr. Coyos; *Three Winters Cold*, and *Pencilling Prisoner* by Fr. Crosbie; *The Diary of a Kidnaped Carmelite Nun*.)

APPENDIX A—V

INTERVIEW WITH FATHER COYOS

Father Coyos, of the Paris Foreign Missions, accompanied the Carmelite Sisters during their imprisonment, and after their return to Paris toward the end of April in 1953, Father Peter Hwang, a Korean priest studying in Paris, was asked to interview him on behalf of *the Kyŏng-hyang-chap-ji*, a Catholic monthly, Seoul.

—Written by Father Hwang in Paris—

Informed that Father Coyos had returned to Paris, I immediately went to call on him at the Paris Foreign Missions Seminary. There I found him surrounded by newspapermen, so after a few words of greeting, I left. The next time I went to see him he was in hospital, but I could not speak to him at length because he was too exhausted. When I went a third time he was in high spirits and, though still tired, willing to tell me about his ordeal during the war, and the sufferings of Korean Christians.

"On June 27, 1950," he began, "we had gathered at a luncheon party in the Carmelite Convent in Seoul to celebrate the fiftieth anniversary of the ordination of Father Antoine Gombert, Father-confessor at the convent. (Born in 1875, he was formerly parish priest at An-sŏng.) Present at the gathering were his brother, Father Julien Gombert (born in 1877, and formerly parish priest of Non-san), who was ordained together with his brother on the same day, and who was Father-confessor at the Convent of *St. Paul de Chartres* in In-ch'ŏn as well as several Korean priests of Seoul.

"Although we had heard of the incidents along the Thirty-eighth Parallel, none of us took them very seriously, nor did most of the people of Seoul. At dusk, however, the city was in a great turmoil and on the following morning the citizens saw the Communist troops advancing into their city. Father Julien was unable to return to In-ch'ŏn and the three of us lived together.

"On the morning of July 15 the Communist police came to us and ordered us to go to the Carmelite Convent. After lunch at the convent, the police came and ordered us, together with the five foreign Sisters, to go for an interrogation. We were taken by a truck to a large building (Editor's note: the Sam-hwa Building, opposite the Mi-to-p'a Department Store) in the vicinity of the Cho-sŏn Hotel.

"We were led into the building and underwent an interrogation that lasted the whole day long. In the evening we were told that the interrogation was over, and released. On leaving the room, however, we were met by another group of young men, who took us to another room where we found Bishop Patrick James Byrne, the Apostolic Delegate; his secretary, Father William Booth; Father Paul Villemot, Father-confessor at the Convent of *St. Paul de Chartres* in Seoul (81 years old); Mother Béatrix (Anne Marie Édouard, 76 years old), the Provincial Superior of the convent and Mother Eugénie Demeusy.

"Bishop Byrne and Father Booth, we were told, were apprehended on July 11; Father

Villemot was again brought into the building on July 17 after a temporary release on account of his poor health on July 13; and Monsignor Thomas Quinlan (54), Father Philip Crosbie and Father Francis Canavan, Columban Fathers of the Vicariate Apostolic of Ch'un-ch'ŏn, had arrived there on July 16."

"How did you suffer while you were confined there?"

"We were given only one rice-ball each in the morning and one in the evening. We were accused everyday of being tools of the imperialists, capitalist lackeys, and blood-suckers of the people.

"In the meantime the police must have searched my house high and low, for one day they confronted me with several letters, a radio, and a chalice which they had brought from my house, and a rifle which I do not know where they found. They shouted at me that my return to Korea was evidently for some evil purpose. With the radio I communicated with the enemy; with the golden chalice I indulged in luxurious living; and with the rifle I massacred the helpless and innocent people. Then they brought in a young man, whom I had never seen before, to serve as witness. They repeatedly beat the young man in a terrible fashion until he confessed it was all true."

"How many people were confined in the cell?"

"Besides ourselves there were many others. In the suffocating heat we were packed in these like bean-sprouts in a container."

"Were there any Sisters in the room?"

"No, the women were confined separately. Every evening several of the detainees were taken away. No one of us knew what would happen to them afterward. At around 3 a.m. on July 19, I was suddenly awakened by a strong light shining in my face. I saw several Communist soldiers with their bayoneted rifles standing before me. Realizing that my hour was about to come, I woke up my colleagues and gave them Absolution. The soldiers, however, disappeared and then, after returning for a moment half an hour later, went away for good. I have no idea why

they did so. On the afternoon of July 19 the Communist police came to us in a truck and ordered us on board. One group, consisting of Bishop Byrne, Father Booth, Monsignor Quinlan, Father Crosbie and Father Canavan, the Fathers Gombert, myself and the Carmelite Sisters went on this truck. Father Villemot and the two nuns of the *St. Paul de Chartres* Convent were permitted to remain there and I assumed that they would soon be released.

"My assumption proved to be false, for we met again at P'yŏng-yang a few days later. After a short ride we changed to a truck which took us to the first station north of Seoul. After a wait in the station we got into a train."

"Was it a passenger train?"

"No, it was not. How could we be considered worthy of such a privilege? It was a freight car used for carrying cattle. Proceeding northward the whole night long, we arrived at Sin-mak Station on July 20. We got off the train and spent the day having a wash and strolling about the station. At night we were put on a train and reached P'yŏng-yang Station at about 8 a.m. on July 21. We were immediately taken to the appellate court, where we spent the whole day. In the meantime the Communists asked each of us for particulars as to our nationality, date of birth, date of arrival in Korea, the purpose of our coming to Korea, and our means of support.

"Bishop Byrne was asked if he was really a Papal ambassador. As he declared that he was, they demanded the document of accreditation. Always with a gentle smile on his face, Bishop Byrne replied that he had nothing but his canonical dress that he was wearing, and had not been able to bring any documents with him.

"On the night of July 21 we were put on a truck again and taken to a kindergarten near the Kim Il-sŭng University, in the suburbs of P'yŏng-yang. There we were divided into groups according to our nationality and detained in separate rooms. Women were accommodated separately as before. There was no distinction between clergy and laymen in grouping the detainees.

"We were informed of the presence of Captain Vyvyan Holt, the British Minister, and M. Georges Perruche, Chargé d'Affaires of the French Legation in Seoul, and immediately went to see them, and agreed that we would act together in the future.

"Father Bulteau, parish priest of Kong-se-ri, South Province of Ch'ung-ch'ŏng, formerly parish priest of Pu-san-jin, had been taken to Seoul by truck on July 19, and was brought to P'yŏng-yang on July 29 along with Father Villemot, and the two nuns, Mother Béatrix Edouard and Mother Eugénie Demeusy."

"What kind of treatment did you receive at the kindergarten in the vicinity of Kim Il-sŭng University?"

"We stayed there until September 6. The worst thing was the continual hunger. We cooked for ourselves, but often could get nothing to eat the whole day because of the continual air raids. Our food consisted only of bread and soup, with a paper-thin slice of pork added once a week. We were indeed on the verge of starvation. We slept on an earthen floor with only a single blanket on us. Four guards watched us night and day. We had to get permission before we could go to the toilet at night.

"We were not obliged to do any work, nor were we beaten or subjected to any punishment. On rising we were forced to take physical exercise. On the whole we were treated in a fairly gentlemanly fashion, and they even gave us newspapers to read, though of course, they were Communist organs and quite untrustworthy."

"To which place were you taken from there?"

"On September 6, we left for Man-p'o along the Manchurian border. It seemed that P'yŏng-yang was in danger, but we had no means of finding out. Bishop Byrne and the diplomatic group went by truck and the rest rode in a train. In the daytime the train would stop and take refuge in a tunnel, while we would take ours on the hillside. Father Crosbie looks back on these days as

'picnics' but it was hard work getting up those hills. We arrived at Man-p'o on September 11, and were accommodated in a building which seemed to be a night duty shelter for customs officials. The diplomats were housed separately from the others. For the first time we came under the regular surveillance of Communist army soldiers as well as police. Our rations improved and we were given meat two or three times a week. We could get our hair cut and buy cigarettes. The treatment improved considerably.

"We hoped that this improvement meant that our liberation would come soon.

"On October 8, however, we were told that we had to move.

"No notable change took place in our life in Ko-san-jin except that the Fathers Antoine and Julien Gombert were afflicted with malaria.

"We had to do our own cooking there. Bishop Byrne and the Methodist missionaries were assigned to water-carrying. Father Cadars, whom I have not yet mentioned, had been arrested in Tae-jŏn on August 17. He left Tae-jŏn on the 19th and arrived in Seoul on the 21st, in P'yŏng-yang on the 29th, and in Man-p'o on September 18. We welcomed him with great delight.

"The weather at Ko-san-jin in the morning and evening became very cold in October, but several of us, including Bishop Byrne, wore wadded clothes, and up to now the officers of the Communist army treated us very kindly."

"How long did you stay there?"

"How could we expect that happiness to last? On October 22 we were removed to Chu-am-ri. The Fathers Gombert and the Sisters went by truck, and the Sisters Mary Clare and Mechtilde, who were very ill, were carried on a stretcher. The rest of us went there on foot. In Chu-am-ri we were housed at the local laborers' hall, called Kim Il-sŭng Hall.

"The days grew colder, and there were no stoves or *ondol* floors for us. The air raids grew fiercer and more frequent, and our new guards were very hostile and cold-hearted. Our sufferings increased. Our guards would complain:

"'What a miserable job this is, protecting these foreigners from the heavy bombing which never misses even the remotest cottage in these ravines!'

"Lying before us was a veritable Way of the Cross. Before describing it I must say a few words about the North Korean Catholics. A flock of the Lord's sheep with no shepherd, they clung tenaciously to their faith under the most horrible Communist persecution. I could perceive in them the true spirit of the glorious Catholic martyrs of Korea of the nineteenth century. The spirit of Blessed Andrew Kim is still alive in their hearts.

"On the day we were taken to the school building in Ko-san-jin I saw a young stranger prowling about our house. On seeing me he said without hesitation,

"'My dear Father, I am the catechist here. In this town we have more than a hundred and fifty Christians, sheep who have lost their shepherd. Our priest was arrested, but we still cherish our faith with great fervor. Dear Father, do give us the Sacrament before you leave!'

"Deeply moved, I replied after a moment's thought:

"'I cannot do that now. If we were discovered not only we but you also would incur severe punishment.' At this the young man wept like a child."

Father Coyos broke off his narrative as the tears welled up in his eyes at the memory. It seemed as if he could still see the young catechist's grief-stricken face.

I could not suppress a deep sigh as I thought of the plight of our poor fellow-Christians in North Korea, their adversity, and of the possibility of their souls' salvation. Outside the window was Paris decked in the green of May under the bright sun. This glorious month of May must have visited Korea, too, I thought. After waiting for Father Coyos to regain his composure, I asked him:

"How did you deal with him?"

"'Please don't cry,' I begged him. 'We are leaving tomorrow: gather outside the railroad station as we pass by, and we will pronounce Absolution over you all.'

"As I promised they gathered at the place and we gave them Absolution.

"Afterward we occasionally met other Catholic believers. They could easily recognize us as we were all wearing soutanes. Although we were under strict surveillance to prevent us from communication with any of the Christians, we noticed many of them weeping when they saw us in captivity, and I shall never forget those tears."

After a slight pause, he continued.

"On October 28 we set out on our journey from Ko-san-jin, where we had spent the night. The older priests rode ox-carts and the rest went on foot. We arrived at Man-p'o on the 30th and were accommodated in a roofless house. We spent the night in utter cold. Our guards, with intimidating looks, stared at us and told us:

"'From now on you have only two alternatives! Either keep on marching, or die! If any of you fails to keep up with us and lags behind he will be shot.'

"This was on October 31. At that time our group consisted of about 800 prisoners, and all of us now had to begin that terrible Death March that almost destroyed us.

"This Death March which began on October 31 was indeed a Way of the Cross. It was a long forced march, which would have been tough even for soldiers in perfect condition and training, though well within their powers, but all of us were physically weak and exhausted by months of malnutrition, and many of us were elderly and sick. Provided as we were with only a ball of millet and cup of cold water twice a day, and in this severe cold, how could we be expected to come through?

"As the Sisters failed in their last efforts to keep on walking, and collapsed, the heartless guards showered them with abuse. We and they supported the Sisters and tried to help them to walk; Father Villemot, the oldest among us, collapsed and was carried by Father Cadars on his back. Father Antoine Gombert and his brother Father Julien kept on for three days, but Mother Béatrix came to the end of her strength on the second day. She was left behind alone, for none of us had the strength to carry her, though all knew well what a horrible thing it was to leave her in that desolate mountain area. Hurried along by the Communists with threats and curses we had to go on marching like automata. I presume that she was shot at that spot."[1]

Father Coyos continued his story.

"On the third day we arrived at Cha-sŏng, completely exhausted. The Communists had no choice but to bring in a truck for the sick. Bishop Byrne and his group, Father Cadars and Father Bulteau had to walk. Father Cadars fell on a rock and injured his hand badly, but received neither medical treatment nor the privilege of riding in a truck.

"November 7, many prisoners were shot, for they couldn't keep up with the march because of their extreme exhaustion.

"Upon arriving at Chung-kang-jin we were led into the former Japanese army barracks. Father Villemot was in a critical condition and could not move his body. The two Fathers Gombert were in a state of extreme debility due to dysentery. On November 11 Father Villemot beckoned me to his side. He was dying.

" 'I am leaving,' he murmured, his eyes full of tranquil tears. After receiving the Sacraments from Bishop Byrne, Father Villemot shook hands with each of us in a last farewell, and closed his eyes. He was 81 years old, and he had suffered extremes of hunger, cold and fatigue."

Father Coyos paused again and his eyes filled with tears. I myself had vivid recollections of him from the time when I was a youngster in the Minor Seminary of Paekdong, and of Father Villemot. At Solemn Mass, he would take his seat to the left of the High Altar, clad in white short habit, I too wept. After a while he opened his eyes, looked at me, and continued:

"In the evening we placed his body in the cold outside.

"On the following day Monsignor Quinlan and I tried hard to dig a grave, but the frozen earth did not yield to us, so we placed his body in a depression and covered it with twigs, over which we piled a cairn of stones. On the following day, November 12, the elder Father Gombert, returning from the compulsory physical exercises in the early morning, suffered a severe heart attack and we all feared he was going to die. He recovered consciousness for a short space of time but died at 4 p.m. Physical exercise is no doubt a good thing for people confined in jail, but I cannot see why it should be forced upon the old and frail who are suffering from undernourishment and extreme exhaustion. Bishop Byrne administered the Sacraments to him before his death. Beside him lay his brother who was also in a critical condition. When informed that his brother was dying, he turned slightly toward him and said,

" 'Your merit is indeed splendid. After death, do not forget your brother; I will follow you tomorrow.'

"As he had foretold, he died the following day.

"Their bodies were buried by the Communists.

"On November 16 we were all removed to Ha-ch'ang-ri like a herd of cattle under the goads of the Communists, who feared a massed paratroop attack from the United Nations Forces. Almost all of us were ill. Bishop Byrne caught pneumonia, and I also had a second attack of the same disease. I could not make headway any more, so with four others,—Bishop Byrne, a Protestant minister, a Swiss, and an American—I decided to remain where we stood.

---

[1] As for the execution of Mother Béatrix, see *The Diary of a Kidnaped Carmelite*, Appendix A—III (The Death March).

"On November 17, however, strict orders were issued that we must continue the march. It took us several hours to cover a mere couple of kilometers, for we fell down at every tenth step or so, and got up again, throughout the whole journey. At last the Communist soldiers realized that there was nothing for it but to hire some ox-carts to carry the sick. I, however, was not among those permitted to ride, so I said to them,

" 'As you see, I really cannot go any farther.'

"In cold derision they shouted back:

" 'As you believe in God, you had better ask Him to perform a miracle for you. What have you to worry about? If you die, you'll go to Heaven, won't you?'

"Fortunately enough however, the British Minister, Captain Vyvyan Holt, came to my aid and half supporting, half dragging me along, enabled me to keep up with the rest until the end. I am sorry to say that as a reward for his compassion he only caught pneumonia from me.

"In Ha-ch'ang-ri, on November 18, Mother Mechtilde died.

"The cold was becoming more intense up there in the mountains. Most of us were ill, with body temperatures of over 40°C (104°F), clothed in rags and bitten by lice. In spite of her own sufferings, Mother Eugénie did her best to take care of the sick. On the day of Mother Mechtilde's death, the Communists sent to hospital the four who were most seriously ill among us—Bishop Byrne, Father Canavan, an American soldier, and me.

"At first we vigorously opposed the idea of being sent to hospital, for we had no confidence in the ability of the Communists to provide us with proper medical treatment, but they pressed us earnestly to go there, and we gave in. The hospital turned out to be a shabby thatched house, in which we were put at the part farthest from the heated *ondol* floor. The roof was full of holes and the doors and windows unpapered. It was as cold inside as outside, but we laid a blanket on the cold floor and lay and shivered there.

"For the first two days we were fed on thin millet gruel, but from the third day on, we received a millet ball and a cup of cold water each, and nothing more.

"Bishop Byrne, who was the most critically ill among us, always kept a cheerful smile on his face. In this severe suffering, he told us:

" 'Next to the grace of the priesthood, I regard it as the greatest privilege of my life to have been allowed to suffer with you for Christ.'

"His words still resound in my mind.

"On November 24, Bishop Byrne became delirious, and then fell into a coma. Looking closely at him, I saw that his breathing was irregular and intermittent. I immediately gave him Absolution and shortly afterward he died—it was November 25.

"Others among those hospitalized followed him in quick succession. Father Canavan of the Columban Fathers died of pneumonia on December 6."

Father Coyos paused to offer a silent prayer for the deceased as their memory flashed upon him. Then he continued:

"Left alone, I moved over to the vacant places beside Father Cadars and Father Bulteau. I learnt that Mother Thérèse had died on November 30. Father Cadars died on December 16 after a long period of suffering from diarrhoea and hernia. Father Bulteau died on January 6, 1951 after suffering from intense pain of a wound to his hand which he received on falling against a rock, a wound which afterward became infected and inflamed, and also from his hernia."

"How did you manage to survive this ordeal?" I asked.

"I was immensely encouraged by the devoted care and words of consolation from Mother Eugénie. On one occasion, a Communist army doctor passing by, saw Mother Eugénie at my bedside and ejaculated the merciless words:

" 'Let him alone. He'll die before nightfall.'

"When I heard his words, I felt an access of strength and joy. I woke next morning: I was still alive! The Communist doctor passed again and jeered at me:

" 'What long life you are enjoying! But we

have no medicine or ability to serve you. For you it's either God's miracle or death!'

"At this, the thought flashed upon me that I must use all my will power to survive this ordeal in order to bear witness to all that had happened to us. I made a vow to Our Blessed Lady that if she would help me to survive, I would make a pilgrimage to Lourdes on foot though my home is located not far from there.

"Strangely enough, I seemed to get better from that day. Under Mother Eugénie's care my health steadily improved. By March, I was able to walk. I remained there until October. After that I was allowed to take short walks. Together with Monsignor Quin-lan, we would go up the mountain paths, gathering firewood, wild fruit, and mush-rooms.

"In this way we passed the years of 1951 and 1952. Then we greeted the year of 1953.

"On April 5, 1953, we were taken to P'yŏng-yang. Nothing could have been more sur-prising than the changed attitude of the Com-munists toward us. They allowed us to take frequent baths and showed us movies every evening. They even offered us such Russian delicacies as caviare, butter, and vodka. Of course, we had to listen to a lot of Commu-nist propaganda about peace.

"Up to now, we had been isolated from the outside world and we were eager for news of recent happenings. We knew that some-thing unexpected must have taken place, so we asked our guard,

" 'Are you going to set us free?' He replied:

" 'We, too, have been told nothing. We are in the same position as you. I am just obey-ing orders to treat you kindly.'

"A few days later we heard on the radio that the Englishmen had been released. When we asked the Communists whether they were going to release us too, he looked at his com-mander for a nod of approval and said:

" 'You are going to be released.'

"On the next day they gave us new clothes. They then led us into a garden, where they had arranged chairs and desks for a press conference. What had we to say? The time passed in silence. The next thing was that we were rushed off to Sin-eui-ju, where after a few formalities at the station, we were taken to Sin-eui-ju's best hotel, as if we had been invited to a wedding banquet. We were given the opportunity to taste many delicacies that we had almost forgotten; eggs, chicken, beef and fruit, and we were also able to drink some beer, a drink which we had almost forgotten too. Best of all, we were allowed to have a good long sleep.

"On the following day, we were put on board a special observation car heading for Moscow. The high Russian officials who es-corted us were so hospitable that they al-most made us forget the agony we had passed through during our captivity. Once we had traversed the wilds of Siberia and entered Russia Proper, the people received us not as prisoners of war but as special en-voys from France. We were accorded all privileges.[1]

"We arrived at Moscow at 11:20 a.m. on April 30, and were received by high-ranking Russian officials. We were conducted to the French Embassy. The plane which we were supposed to take at 3:30 p.m. was out of order and we had to stay overnight in Mos-cow.

'On May Day, we took a sightseeing trip and saw magnificent parades. Outwardly, the Russian people gave no sign of their po-litical leanings, but just took the occasion as an opportunity for merrymaking.

"Those who stood at my side, perceiving that I was a foreigner, stopped the passers-by and made them sing and dance for me. It was really wonderful. I went to see the Stalin's tomb, where there was a long queue of people waiting to go in. I also visited the National Museum, where the splendid collection of

---

[1] The Russians, when they were in North Korea, always made it their policy to have the Koreans do their dirty work for them, while they hypocritically pretended to be full of sympathy and understanding.

fifteenth-century art attracted me more than anything else. Noticing a church on my way I went in, and was surprised to see that many of the graves in the churchyard were marked with a cross on the tombstone.

"At 9:30 a.m. on May 3 our plane left for Berlin, and by 5 p.m. we were in Berlin. We arrived at Paris at 8:45 p.m. on the following day."

My last request to Father Coyos was that he would give me, on behalf of the Fathers who had been victimized in North Korea, a message to the Korean Christians.

Father Coyos was plunged in thought for a while with closed eyes.

Finally he spoke.

"This was not the first time that French missionaries in Korea underwent great suffering and sacrificed their lives. They made this sacrifice out of their great love for Korea and her people, and wanted to help them to accept the truth and hold fast to the faith at any cost. The missionaries of today are teaching you with the same spirit as those who made the supreme sacrifice in bygone days.

"I trust, therefore, that Korean Christians, the posterity of those martyrs who brought glory to the Church in the nineteenth century, will never allow themselves to be deceived by materialism. I am confident that the Korean Christians of today will inherit this spirit of the past, and march forward to the ultimate goal of the establishment of the Kingdom of Christ in this world, and will be able, through the intercession of the Blessed Korean Martyrs in Heaven, to overcome all obstacles.

"As we have been promised the final victory by Our Lord Christ, I earnestly hope and pray that all Korean Christians will hold fast to the faith, and, following the example of St. Paul, spread it among the peoples of the world."

INDEX

(OF APPS. III, IV AND V)

Army, Indo-China 1918, chaplain to French expedition to Siberia 1917-18, d. December 18, 1950.

Canavan, Rev. Fr. Francis (Frank), b. 1912, Columban missionary, 1950 arrested by Communists, d. December 6, 1950.

Chanteloup, Maurice, French war correspondent, French Press Agency, 1950 arrested by Communists.

Clare, Sister Mary, Irish-born Anglican nun, Seoul, school-teacher.
    during World War I came to Korea as novicemistress.
    during World War II left Korea (First Superior of Anglican Convent).
    after World War II returned as adviser to her successor.
    d. November 1950 during the Death March.

Collier, Rev. Fr. Anthony (Tony), Columban missionary.
    1939: arrived at Korea.
    1950: at Ch'un-ch'ŏn, missing from June 27, 1950.

Cooper, Right Rev. Cecil, Anglican Bishop of Korea, b. c. 1880.
    1930: succeeded Bishop Trollope.
    a poet and apiarist, High-Church, mild and gentle in manner.
    1950: arrested by Communists.

Coyos, Rev. Fr. Celestine French Basque Paris Foreign Missions.
    1933: came to Korea.
    1936: returned to France on sick leave.
    1946: professor of philosophy and ecclesiastical history at Seoul Major Seminary.

Crosbie, Rev. Fr. Philip, Columban Mission.
    1936: to Columban Seminary, Galway.
    1940: came to Korea.
    1950: arrested with Monsignor Quinlan.
    author of *Pencilling Prisoner* (Melbourne 1954).

Dans, Louis, American former professional acrobat. assistant Manager, Traders' Exchange, Seoul.
    1950 arrested by Communists.

Daulatsch, Maisara, Turkish lady in detention camp.

Deane, Philip, British, of Greek extraction, son of Greek general, war correspondent for 'The Observer' (London).
    1950: arrested at Yŏng-dong.

De Lobit, Mother Marie Henriette, French Carmelite.
    1920's: entered Carmel at Aire-sur-Adour.
    1938: came to Korea to found Seoul Carmel.

1948: Subprioress of Carmelite Convent.
1950: arrested, by Communists. after Mother Thérèse's death, was addressed by the Carmelites as 'Mother Superior.'

Demeusy, Mother Eugénie, French, formerly Yvonne. *St. Paul de Chartres* Convent and Orphanage, Seoul.
1932: Mistress of Novices.
1950: arrested by Communists.
1952: celebrated silver anniversary of entrance into religion.
    Her elder sister is Mother General of the Order (1954).

Devriese, Mother Mechtilde, b. 1889 at Ypres, Belgium.
1906: entered Carmel Convent of Ypres.
1914: returned home by German invasion.
1917: re-entered Carmel at Aire-sur-Adour, Soon afterward became a member of Carmel in Smyrna, Turkey.
1923: back again Aire-sur-Adour, escaping from insurrection of Turkey, and now Prioress.
1939: came to Korea as a foundation member of Carmel Convent.
1940: elected Prioress till 1949.
1950: arrested by Communists, d. November 18, 1950.

Dyer, Miss Nell, American, Methodist missionary, Kae-sŏng.
1927: appointed teacher in Methodist school, Seoul
1950: arrested by Communists.
    chosen as their leader by the women, in the Death March.

Edouard, Mother Béatrix (Beatrice, formerly Anne-Marie) French, b. 1874.
1899: entered *St. Paul de Chartres* Congregation, France.
1906: appointed to *St. Paul de Chartres* Orphanage, Seoul, Mistress of Novices to 1932.
1932-1942: Local Superior of *St. Paul de Chartres* Convent, Tae-gu.
1942: Provincial Superior for Korea.
1950: arrested by Communists.
    executed on the Death March, November 3, 1950.

Eltringham, Walter, American, mining engineer, E.C.A., Seoul.
1950: arrested by Communists.
    d. November 17, 1950.

Eugénie, Mother, see Demeusy.

Evans, William, American, b. 1900.
    1950: arrested by Communists, d. December

1950.

Funderat, Mme, French, widow, childless, b. *c.* 1880,
    1950: arrested by Communists.
        d. (on the Death March) November 3, 1950.

Gliese, Charlotte (Lotte) German, b. Berlin, wife
    of Korean businessman in Berlin. on fall
    of Berlin sent by Russians via Siberia to
    Korea with husband. Professor of German
    at Seoul National University.

Gombert, Rev. Fr. Antoine, French, b. 1874, Paris
    Foreign Missions.
    1900: ordained at same time and place as
        younger brother Julien (see below), 1901:
        came to Korea. at An-sŏng for 33 years.
    1934: Spiritual Director, Seoul Major Seminary,
        Procurator of Seminary.
        chaplain to Carmelite Sisters.
        (on June 27, 1950, celebrated the golden
        anniversary of his ordination, together,
        with his brother, at Carmelite Convent.)
    1950: arrested by Communists, d. 4 p.m.,
        November 12, 1950.

Gombert, Rev. Fr. Julien, b. 1876, younger brother
    of preceding, Paris Foreign Missions, Or-
    dained 1900.
    1901: came to Korea, built up 2 parishes.
    1942: appointed to Seoul Cathedral.
    1946: to In-ch'ŏn, as chaplain to Sisters of *St.
        Paul de Chartres* Convent there.
    1950: arrested by communists, d. 8p.m., Novem-
        ber 13, 1950.

Hebbel, POW

Helena, a Polish-Korean girl with the detainees in
    camp for a short space of time.

Henriette, Mother, see De Lobit.

Hoang, Mme. Simone, b. at Paris, w. Korean scholar
    Sohn Nan-sŏng there.
    1950: arrested by Communists.

Holt, Captain Vyvyan, Minister at the British
    Legation, Seoul.
    1950: arrested by Communists.

Hong, Right Rev. Bishop Francis.
    1949: kidnaped by Communists at P'yŏng-
        yang, and missing since then.

Hunt, Rev. Charles, F.R.G.S., English, Anglican
    missionary in Seoul.
    1947: chaplain in the Royal Navy.
    1915: came to Korea, under Dr. Trollope, first
        Anglican Bishop in Korea, President of
        Royal Geographic Society, Korea Branch.
    1950: arrested by Communists, d. 1952.

Jensen, Rev. Kris, D.D., American, b. Denmark,
    Methodist Mission.

1927: came to Korea.
1950: arrested by Communists.

Kijikoff, Ilian, White Russian, in detention camp.

Kilin, Ivan, & wife, White Russian, in the detention
    camp.

Kisch, Ernst, M.D., Austrian (Jewish), doctor in
    Methodist hospital, Kae-sŏng.
    1950: arrested by Communists, d. June 29, 1951.

Leer Kamp, Henry, American POW buried victims
    of Death March en route.

Lord, the Herbert A., O.B.E., English, married,
    Lieutenant-Commissioner in charge of
    Salvation Army in Korea, came to Korea
    before 1910.
    1936: Singapore.
    1942: captured by Japanese, interned 3 1/2 years.
    1945: awarded O.B.E.
    1945: in charge of Salvation Army in Korea.
    1950: arrested by Communists at British Legation,
        interpreter in the prison camp.

Marie-Madeleine, Sister, see Marquier.

Marquier, Sister Marie-Madeleine, (formerly
    Henriette), Carmelite nun.
    b. *c.* 1892 at Marmande, Agen, s.w. France.
    Influenced by Psichari, joined Universitaires
    Catholiques.
    entered Carmel at Aire-sur-Adour, Novice
    Mistress.
    1948: became completely blind, constantly
        attended by Sister Bernadette.
    1950: arrested by Communists.

Martel, Mme. Amelia, widow of professor Martel of
    Seoul National University, professor of
    French, mother of Charles Martel (see
    below) and of Marguerite and another
    d., a Benedictine nun long at Won-san,
    arrested in 1949. b. 1874.

Martel, Charles, French. Chancelor, French Lega-
    tion, Seoul.
    1950: arrested by Communists.

Martel, Marguerite, sister of Charles Martel (see
    above).
    1950: arrested by Communists.

Mary Clare, Sister, see Clare, Sister Mary.

Matti, Alfred, Swiss, b. 1902.
    manager, International Red Cross, Shang-
    hai, 1939-1945. manager, Cho-sŏn Hotel.
    1950: arrested by Communists, d. December 1952.

Meadmore, Jean, French, Vice-Consul, French Le-
    gation, Seoul, served in China.

Mechtilde, Mother, see Devriese.

Nebenan, POW

Owen, Norman, secretary, British Legation, Seoul,

1950: arrested by Communists.

Perruche, M. Georges, French, Chargé d' Affaires, French Legation, Seoul. long service in China. 1950: arrested by Communists.

Quinlan, Monsignor Thomas, Irish, b. 1896 at Thurles, Tipperary.

1918: joined Columban Mission Seminary, Galway, Ireland.

1920: came to Hanyang in China.

1930: to Kiangsi.

1934: to Kwang-ju, Korea.

1950: 27 June, fall of Ch'un-ch'ŏn. 2 July, arrested with Father Crosbie.

Roaln, American POW in camp.

Rosser, Miss Helen, American, Methodist Missionary and trained nurse, Kae-sŏng.

1950: arrested by Communists.

Salahudtin, Salam, and wife Paiza; Sagid (b. 1932) son: Sagida, b. 1933; daughter, Farid (b. 1937), Shaucat (b. 1941), Morat (b. 1944), sons; Hamid, son, b. 1949; and Sultan Ahmet, b. 1921, a former boxer, brother of Paiza, and Sophia Ahmet, sister of Paiza. Turkish family in camp.

Smith, Miss Bertha, American, Methodist missionary, Kae-sŏng, 1950: arrested by Communists.

Thérèse, Mother, see Bastin, Mother Thérèse.

Thornton, Lieutenant, American, one of the first to be shot on the Death March, November 1, 1950.

Tihinoff, Ivan Nicolai, White Russian, b. 1882, arrested by Communists 1950.

Villemot, Father Paul, French, b. 1868, Paris foreign missionary, 1892: began missionary career in Korea. to 1918 Procurator of Paris Foreign Missions in Korea. In charge of Cathedral parish for 25 years.

1942: retired from active missionary life, chaplain to St. Paul de Chatres by Communists Orphanage.

1950: arrested by Communists, d. November 1950.

Yu, Rev. Fr. John, Seoul Cathedral.

1950: visited internees in Seoul, missing.

Zellers, Laurance (Larry) Rev. American Methodist missionary, Kae-sŏng, English teacher.

1950: arrested by Communists.

APPENDIX B

The Ecumenical Movement

Introduction

The Christian Ecumenical Movement was given an epoch-making momentum with the opening of the Second Ecumenical Council of the Vatican in 1962 under the auspices of the late Pope John XXIII, to which for the first time Protestant leaders were invited as observers since Protestantism had been separated from the Roman Catholic Church in the 16th century. This paves the way for the Roman Catholic Church to push through the long-hoped-for unity drive.

In the meantime both Catholic and Protestant leaders in Korea have come in contact with each other in earnest through dialogues and open discussions over the radio or in the press, baring mutual grievances, discussing advantages or disadvantages and agreement or disagreement on points of doctrine and trying their level best to effect a rapprochement.

In this domain lies our real purpose in inserting here a brief history of Protestantism in our country.

The Outline of Protestantism in Korea

1. Its Foundation

In June 1832, the first Protestant missionary ever to visit Korea came to the country. He was a German named Karl A.F. Gutzlaff, who for some forty days propagated the Gospel in the vicinity of the Keum-kang River estuary in the west coast. His activities should be appreciated in the light of Korea's internal situation of that date which, unlike China and Japan, accepted no religious undertakings, let alone the entry of foreign missionaries.

Thirty-three years later, in 1865, the missionary Robert J. Thomas, a native of Wales, was engaged in the propagation of the Gospel for over two months along the Ong-jin coastal islands, Hwang-hae Province. He had been led into Korea from Chefoo, in the Province of Shantung in China, by a Korean refugee Catholic Kim Cha-p'yŏng and his companions, who were living in the home of Alexander Williamson, agent of the National Bible Society of Scotland, and by a Chinese Catholic named Yu Wen-tai. The former attracted Thomas to the Korean religious mission by revealing the historical and unforgettable scenes of sanguinary martyrdom of Catholic priests and laymen.

In August 1866 Thomas was ashore again in Korea, availing himself of the voyage of the American merchant ship "General Sherman," which mistakenly sailed up the Tae-dong River to P'yŏng-yang, where he was beheaded on September 3. The ineradicable Protestant influence which long prevailed in the neighborhood indeed owed its origin to his martyrdom.

Thereafter many Western missionaries stationed in China were eager to get to Korea. A Northern Presbyterian missionary Hunter Corbett succeeded in propagating the Gospel in Mok-po-dong on the Hwang-hae coast for some two weeks in January 1867, and later that year, Alexander Williamson undertook the holy project at the northern "Korean Gate" area, on his arrival overland.

The immortal efforts of the Christian propagation in the early Korean Protestant era were also shared by John Ross of the Presbyterian Church of Scotland in Manchuria and his brother-in-law John McIntyre. Spreading the Gospel from the U-chang village near the "Korean Gate" area since 1873, they gave Baptism in 1874 to four young Korean scholars Lee Ung-ch'an, Paek Hong-chun, Lee Sung-ha and Kim Chin-ki of Eui-ju, and subsequently spent more than twenty years there in translating the Bible and propagating the Gospel.

Around 1881 they completed the full translation of the first part of the New Testament, comprising the Four Gospels and the Acts of the Apostles, and in 1887 published an edition of 3,000 copies of the Bible at their printery which had been set up in Mukden (now Shenyang), Manchuria, in 1882. In the meantime the first Korean Protestant church was built in Eui-ju, in 1883 and the next year they gave Baptism to 75 Koreans in the Chientao district of Manchuria, when the first Chientao Protestant church was built.

In 1881 in Japan, Lee Su-jŏng, a Korean student in Tokyo, embraced Christianity, influenced by three American missionaries in Japan, Henry Loomis of the American Bible Society, Northern Methodist Robert S. Maclay and George W. Knox, Northern Presbyterian. Lee later translated the Gospel of St. Mark.

It was not until 1882, when the Korea-U.S. Treaty of Commerce and Amity was signed and the closed-door policy of the former was abandoned for good, that the propagation activities of Protestantism as well as Catholicism were legally permitted in Korea.

In 1884 the Methodist missionary Robert S. Maclay received permission from the Korean Government for educational and medical projects, and the medical missionary Dr. Horace N. Allen of the Northern Presbyterian Mission in China became the first resident Presbyterian missionary in Korea.

In 1885 William B. Scranton, a medical missionary of the Northern Methodist Mission, landed on Korea in the wake of the Rev. Horace G. Underwood of the Northern Presbyterian Mission and Henry D. Appenzeller of the Northern Methodist Mission. They were promptly followed by other Protestant sects. In October 1889, the Rev. J. Henry Davies and his sister Miss M.T. Davies, both of the Presbyterian Church of Victoria, Australia, took the missionary field in the Pu-san and South Kyŏng-sang Province areas; in December 1889 Mr. Malcolm C. Fenwick of the Canadian Baptist Church, as an independent missionary, in the Wonsan area: in 1890 Bishop John Corft of the Anglican Church, in Seoul and Kyŏng-ki Province area: in 1893 the Rev. L.B. Tate and Miss Marris S. Tate, Miss Linnie Davis, the Rev. and Mrs. B. Reynolds and the Rev. and Mrs. W.B. Junkins, of the Southern Presbyterian Church, in Chŏl-la Provinces; on August 10, 1896, the Rev. C.F. Reid of the Southern Methodist Church was invited together with his family to Kae-sŏng by Yun Ch'i-ho; in 1898 Dr. and Mrs. Robert G. Grierson, the Rev. and Mrs. W.R. Foote, and the Rev. D.M. MacRae of the Canadian Presbyterian Church, in the Ham-kyŏng Provinces; in 1904 Korean residents in Hawaii, Sohn Heung-jo and Lim Ki-pan and the Japanese Seventh-Day Adventist missionary Hideshi Kunitani, in the Sun-an and Kang-sŏ areas of South P'yŏng-an Province; in 1907 Mr. and Mrs. C.E. Cowman and Mr. E.A. Kilbourne of the Oriental Missionary Society came to Korea and established the Oriental Mission, the predecessor of the Holiness Church, and in September, 1908, the Salvation Army was organized under the guidance of "Colonel" Hoggard.

The American Northern Presbyterian Mission had as missionary areas Seoul and Provinces of Kyŏng-ki, South Ch'ung-ch'ŏng, North Kyŏng-sang, Hwang-hae and South and North P'yŏng-an, whereas the American Northern Methodist Mission held Seoul and Provinces of Kyŏng-ki, South Ch'ung-ch'ŏng, Kang-won, Hwang-hae, North and

South P'yŏng-an, and South Ham-kyŏng.

The Protestant sects which were engaged in the missionary works in Korea in the closing era of the 19th century, were very cautious in their activities, as Korea in those days was not ripe for full-fledged propagation, though nominally the open-door policy had been ushered in. They directed their efforts instead to the fields of education, culture, and medical affairs, at the sacrifice of proper and original missionary works.

2. Progress

The following are the schools set up by missionary sects in those days: the American Northern Methodist Mission established Pae-chae Hak-tang and Ewha Hak-tang in Seoul in 1886 and Kwang-sŏng School and Chŏng-eui Girls' School in P'yŏng-yang in 1894; the Southern Methodist Mission, Pae-hwa Girls' School in Seoul in 1898 and Hoston Girls' School in Kae-sŏng in 1904. On the other hand the American Northern Presbyterian Mission built Kyŏng-sin School in Seoul in 1905, Sung-sil School in P'yŏng-yang in 1898, and Sung-eui Girls' School in 1901 in the same city. According to the 1920 tabulation the Methodist Mission was administering 11 boys' schools and 15 girls' schools all over the nation.

The Presbyterian Mission also set up a theological seminary in P'yŏng-yang in 1900 and four years later another was established in Seoul by the Methodist Mission.

In February 1885 the Kwang-hye-won Hospital was authorized to be opened in Seoul, the first Western-style hospital. Doctor Allen treated Prince Min Yŏng-ik, who, nephew of the Queen and the Commandant of the Royal Guards, was seriously wounded during the Kap-sin Coup d'État of December, 1884.

This resulted in his being granted authorization to receive hospital patients. Since then the missions have followed his example by establishing hospital facilities provided with a medical doctor and dispensary in all missionary local headquarters, e.g. Seoul, P'yŏng-yang, Sŏn-ch'ŏn, Chae-ryong, Won-

san, Ch'ŏng-ju, Tae-gu, Pu-san, Kae-sŏng, Kwang-ju, etc.

The establishment of the Severance Hospital took place in 1904. Dr. Oliver R. Avison, financed by Mr. Louis Severance, built the hospital, with which later he incorporated smaller hospitals in Seoul, and where he began the training of native medical students. The Severance Hospital is at present a part of Yon-sei University.

In 1893 the Presbyterian Council was organized with the participation of the four aforementioned Presbyterian sects, to meet the demand for more united and prearranged religious activities in Korea. In 1901 the council was reorganized into the Joint Council which was inaugurated including Korean priests. In 1912 the Korean Presbyterian General Assembly came into being.

The two aforementioned Methodist sects were incorporated into one organization under the name of the Korean Methodist Church in December 1930.

Previously in 1905 the Korean Association of the General Council of Evangelical Missions in Korea was organized, comprising all Presbyterian and Methodist sects in Korea and holding its regular annual meetings in September. Its chief aims are to discuss and coordinate the friendly relations, propagation activities, documental correspondence, medical projects, education and training works, allocation of mission areas, compilation of the Bible, and missionary programs among Koreans resident in Japan. The body was developed in 1919 into the Federal Council of Evangelical Missions absorbing the remaining Protestant Churches and Missions, which in turn was renamed in 1924 the National Christian Council, and given its international importance.

In 1910, the Bible Revised-Translation Board, previously set up by the Rev. John Ross and Lee Su-jŏng, completed the revised translation of the Bible with the efforts of Drs. Underwood, and J.S. Gale both of the Northern Presbyterian Mission, and the Rev. W.D. Reynolds of the Southern Presbyterian Mission. In 1925 Dr. Gale published a new edition of the Bible, translated into the more easily understood spoken Korean.

In 1919, the Korean Christian Literature Society came into being, succeeding the Korean Religious Tract Society which was set up in June 1890 by the Rev. Horace Underwood and other missionaries in Korea. The institute puts out regularly "Sunday School Lessons", "The Christian News", a Presbyterian organ "The Methodist Christian Advocate", a Methodist organ "Ki-tok Shin-po", and "the Korea Mission Field," and also publishes Interdenominational "Union Hymn Books".

3. Trials

Meanwhile the progress and development of Protestantism in Korea was confronted with the Japanese policy of suppression and extermination of religion. In 1911 the so-called Terauchi Assassination Plot, fabricated by the Japanese themselves, served as an excuse for the Japanese to hamper and molest religious activities in Korea, and sporadic persecutions continued until in 1945 Korea recovered her full national independence.

Korean Christendom sent 15 of its leaders among the 33 patriots who masterminded the famous Samil Independence Movement on March 1, 1919. This was motivated by the then U.S. President Woodrow Wilson's Fourteen Points Policy, which postulated the self-determination of small nations. The tense internal atmosphere after World War I was also brought nearer to the exploding point by the death of Emperor Ko-jong.

Japanese atrocities and despotism were climaxed by the Su-won Incident when the Japanese gendarmes herded the Korea faithful into a church and massacred them, setting the church afire and bayoneting the fleeing Christians.

The Japanese, realizing that the attempted suppression had rather the reverse effects, changed their Korea policy. The Korean Church benefited by the lull and continued its development.

During the 1930's the Japanese military leaders put great emphasis on spiritual re-armament based on Shintoism, which they alleged should be embodied in the worship in the Shintoist shrines.

The worship was enforced on the Korean people as well as on foreigners, regardless of their religious beliefs.

In 1935 the Japanese governor of South P'yŏng-an Province expelled two foreign educators, Dr. George S. McCune and Miss V.L. Snock, on the pretext that they refused to abide by Japanese law, by boycotting the Shintoist shrine worship.

The Japanese suppression and atrocities grew more and more severe until in 1938 the Japanese authorities commanded the clergy to resolve in favor of Shintoist shrine worship against the clergy's will. Nevertheless hundreds of true Christians never submitted to the Japanese gendarmes' unparalleled tactics of oppression, and were crowned with the glory of martyrdom. Their resolute, self-sacrificing and genuine deeds culminated in the Rev. Chu Ki-ch'ŏl's death in P'yŏng-yang prison.

With the outbreak of the Pacific War, which was touched off by the Japanese surprise attack on Pearl Harbor, Hawaii Islands on December 8, 1941, the Japanese banished almost all foreign missionaries from Korea, and put all Christians under police surveillance thus bringing about the suspense of religious activities in this country.

The Japanese blood-mad policy closed in all 200-odd religious centers of worship and commandeered all the clergy for military industries or put them under systematic tortures.

In 1942 all religious sects were deprived of their historical, proper denomination, and grouped under an overall name the "Religious Group" and in 1943 the Holiness, the Seventh-Day Adventist and the East Asia Christian Churches were banned in Korea. The Protestant believers decreased to a half in number from 700,000 to 350,000.

The strength of the main Protestant sects in Korea on the eve of the outbreak of the Pacific War is shown below:

	Churches	Ministers	Missionaries	Constituency
Presbyterians	3,262	3,315	48	276,108
Methodists	876	414	2	56,642
Anglicans	136	129	23	7,955
Adventists	196	181	1	9,462
Holiness	183	231	—	12,765
Salvation Army	140	155	—	6,923

4. After Liberation

On August 15, 1945 Korea became an independent and free nation after her 36-year subjugation under Japanese rule, according to the Cairo and Postdam Declarations. But alas! The joy and hope of the Korean people was instantly brushed aside by the land's division along the 38th-Parallel. The Korean Churches could not escape this unexpected harsh reality. Rehabilitation and development began at once, though bearing the seeds of other misfortunes.

The Korean Presbyterian Church held a general assembly in Seoul in June 12, 1946, having completed the reconstruction of all local Church leaders' assemblies by the spring of that year. At the meeting of the general assembly it declared null and void the previously enforced resolution for the worship of Japanese Shintoist shrines.

On the part of the Korean Methodist Church, it resolved on the reconstruction of the Church and the re-establishment of the Methodist theological seminary at the joint annual Methodist meeting held at the Chŭng-dong Church, Seoul, on January 14, 1946. Subsequently this Church was split into two factions—one opting for the Church reconstruction and the other for the maintenance of the Church status—factions which were later reunited to form the Korean Methodist Church.

Three Protestant Churches which had been banned by the Japanese—the Holiness Church, the Salvation Army and the Baptist Church—were all reconstructed shortly after the emancipation of Korea. The Holiness Church approved the establishment of a theological seminary in Seoul at a general assembly held on November 9, 1945. The Salvation Army's Headquarters in Seoul were

reconstructed on October 18, 1945 and in 1947 the Salvation Army Academy was reopened.

The Churches in the northern areas occupied by the Communist (Soviet) Army have been exterminated by ruthless oppression and antireligious policy.

In September, 1945, in Sin-eui-ju, North P'yŏng-an Province Christian leaders, including the Revs. Han Kyŏng-jik and Yun Ha-yŏng organized the Korean Christian Social-Democratic Party, comprising a large number of Christians in North Korea. The inevitable strife between the Communist Party and the Christian party produced many victims and illegal arrests of Christians in November of that year.

The resulting unrest was utilized as a pretext for the Soviet occupation authorities to deploy their strongest oppression measures toward all Churches in North Korea.

About this time 40 Christian leaders, inclusive of the Rev. Kim Hwa-sik, were apprehended, on the allegation of preparing to organize a democratic party, to be known as the Christian Liberal Party. Most of them met death in the Communist prisons or are now missing and presumed dead.

The Christians in North Korea, at a meeting of the Joint Presbytery held on October 20, 1946 prior to general elections of North Korea, resolved in favor of a strong request for religious freedom. The Communist authorities, in order to counter the pressure from the freedom-loving and democratic Christians, organized a pseudo-religious organ named the "Christian League General Assembly" under the control of the former minister Kang Nang-uk, the secretary of Kim Il-sung, the dictator of North Korea. The Christians in North Korea who refused to joint the Red organ as well as those leaders affiliated with the leaders of Joint Presbytery were all deprived of their posts and imprisoned.

5. After the Korean War

Another round of Korean Christians' sufferings was started with the invasion of the Republic of Korea by Communist armed forces of North Korea on June 25, 1960. During the hostilities innumerable Christian leaders in South Korea alone, not to mention North Korea, have perished. In Seoul many a valuable Christian library as well as Christian buildings, e.g. those of the Seoul Young Men's Christian Association, The Korean Bible Society and the Korean Christian Literature Society were reduced to ashes by Communist incendiaries.

Following the Red invasion a refugee Christian organ named the Korean Christian National Salvation Association was formed at Tae-jŏn, South Ch'ung-ch'ŏng Province, consisting of Protestant sect leaders. The organ, with its 30-odd branch sections throughout the nation, embarked on projects such as pacification and propaganda, relief, broadcasting, and the enlistment of Army volunteers in collaboration with the Ministries of National Defense and Social Affairs. In January 1951, the Korean Christian Wartime Emergency Measure Council was organized for the purpose of cooperation and relief for the people, together with the foreign missionaries' assistance.

The armistice on July 27, 1953, between the United Nations Forces and the Communist Armies, signaled a period during which the refugee Christians who thronged in the Pu-san and Tae-gu areas could return to their prewar posts and re-erect their war-torn Churches.

As of 1955, 1,200 Presbyterian, 500 Methodist, 250 Holiness, and 100 other churches had been newly built since the retreat of the Communist armed forces from South Korea.

Sung-sil College, now the Union Christian College, Sung-eui Girls' Middle and High School, and Po-sŏng Girls' Middle and High School, previously all operated in P'yŏng-yang by the Korean Presbyterian Church and Kwang-sŏng Middle and High School of the Korean Methodist Church in P'yŏng-yang were revived in South Korea. Hoston Girls' Middle and High School in Kae-sŏng has been transplanted in Tae-jŏn, South Ch'ung-ch'ŏng Province.

New educational institutions have also been established by the Churches; Kye-myŏng Christian College in Tae-gu, the Christian College in Tae-jon and the Christian Women's College in Seoul, by the Presbyterian Church, and Kuk-che College in Seoul by the Methodist Church.

As of 1957 the educational institutions operated by the Korean Protestant Churches included Yŏn-sei University, Ewha Women's University, three colleges, more than 30 middle and high schools, and some 15 girls' middle and high schools.

Theological seminaries operated by the Korean Protestant Churches number 8 in Seoul, 2 in Tae-gu and 1 each in Pu-san, Tae-jŏn, and Yang-ju county of Kyŏng-ki Province.

World Protestant sects which made Korea their propagation areas after Korea's liberation from Japan, and in particular, since the 1953 Armistice, are as follows:

The Baptist Church—introduced by the Rev. Malcolm C. Fenwick of the Canadian Baptist Church in 1889. After World War II the American Southern Baptist Church sent the Rev. and Mrs. John Abernathy, and the Church was reorganized under the name of the Korean Baptist Church in 1950. It has 192 churches, 168 ministers and 8,365 constituency as of 1963, with headquarters at Yŏng-dung-p'o, Seoul.

Assemblies of God—organized early in 1953 by a Korean ministers educated in Japan, and headquartered in Se-jong-no, Seoul, with 44 churches, 34 Church workers and 8,762 constituency as of the end of 1955.

Church of Christ Mission—set up in 1934 by the Rev. John T. Chase and headquartered in Song-wol-dong, Sŏ-tae-mun-ku, Seoul, with 17 churches, 19 Church workers and a constituency of 1,550 as of 1959.

The Nazarene Mission—reorganized in 1954

by itsfi rst missionary the Rev. Donald D. Owens and his wife with its headquarters at Sa-jik-dong, Chong-no, Seoul. It has 31 churches, 53 Church workers and a consituency of 2,352 as of 1962.

The Church of God—headquartered in P'il-dong, Chung-gu, Seoul, with 3 churches, 4 Church workers and a constituency of 186 as of 1962.

the Mennonite Doopers—introduced into Korea in 1953 and now headquartered in Sam-dŏk-dong, Tae-gu. They are engaged in protection and relief projects for war orphans and deformed children in Kyŏng-sang Province areas.

The Baptist Bible Fellowship—headquartered in Haeng-tang-dong, Sŏng-dong-ku, Seoul, since its introduction into Korea in 1955. Propagating the Gospel mainly among Korean children.

The American Seoul Clinic—propagating through the monthly organ "Seoul Clinic" since its introduction into Korea in 1955.

The Team Mission—introduced in February 1953 and engaged in the propagating of the holy books and documents and in relief projects, with its headquarters in Won-san-dong, Chong-no-gu, Seoul.

The Friends' Service Unit—engaged in medical assistance and relief aids. Introduced into Korea in 1953 and headquartered in Kun-san City, Nŏrth Chŏl-la Province.

The Jehovah's Witnesses—introduced into Korea in 1950 and headquartered in the 2nd Street of Ch'ung-chŏng-no, Sŏ-tae-mun-ku, Seoul. They have 30 churches, 164 Church workers and a constituency of 1,427.

The Greek Orthodox Church found its way into Korea in January 1900 with Patriarch Hritsanpo and in 1903 built the Orthodox Church on its present site. During the Korean War Father Kim Eui-han was abducted to the north by the Communists and the church building was gutted. Later the church was reconstructed by the Greek Forces stationed in Korea. The incumbent Father Mun Richun has been ordained and placed in charge of the church by the Greek Army Chaplain, His Beatitude Patriarch Andrei in Korea.[1]

6. Institutes and Present Conditions

The Protestant Churches in Korea maintain a large number of important organizations societies as shown below:

The Korean Bible Society
The Christian Literary Society
The Korean Christian Education Society
The Christian Books Propagation Society
The Christian Broadcasting Society (HLKY)
The Christian Andio-Visual Propagation Society
The World Vision
The Young Men's Christian Association
The Korean Student Christian Federation
The Young Women's Christian Association
The Korean Youth Christian Federation
The Korean Church World Conference
The Christian Children's Welfare Association
The Christian Self-Restraint Society
The Amputee Rehabilitation Center
The St. Bede's House (Church of England)
The St. Michael's Church of England Seminary

---

[1] The Greek Orthodox Church, though not a sect of Protestant, is included here for covenience sake.

THE STATISTICS OF PROTESTANT CHURCHES

December 31, 1963

Classifications / Sect	Number of Churches	Protestant People Constituency (the Baptized)	Church Workers			Educational Institute		
			Priests	Presby-terians	Deacons	Colleges	High Schools	Middle Schools
Presbyterians	4,490	605,785 (125,145)	1,869	4,905	28,271	6	45	46
Methodists	1,208	247,613	645	1,133	3,237	6	12	14
Holinesses	615	139,035 (28,000)	280		6,528	1	3	3
Baptists	192	8,365	168	217		1		
Lutherans	1	50	1					
Anglicans (Episcopalians)	53	5,694	168					
Salvation Army	135	34,800 (13,200)	225	78	1,350			2
Assemblies of God	44	7,293	37					
Disciples of Christ	20	2,000	20			1		
Evangelical Church	11	1,446	41					
Nazarenes	31	2,352	53					
Eschatological St. Apostle	38	4,458	128					
Church of God	3	186	4					
Immanuel Jesus Church	16	1,321	35					
True Jesus Church	9	1,191	12					
Pentecostals	11	961	21					
Reconstruction Church	58	4,845	244					
Adventists	278	30,454	553					
Jehovah's Witnesses	30	1,427	164					
Grand Total			6,333					

Up to the ninth line the statistics are based on those of the National Council of Churches on Dec. 31, 1963, and the rest on the Religious Handbook issued by the Ministry of Education, Republic of Korea Government, on December 31, 1963.

Reference Books

Clark, C.A., *Digest of the Presbyterian Church of Korea*, The Korean Religious Tract Society, Seoul, 1918.
Stokes, C.C., *The History of Methodist Missions in Korea (1885—1930)*
Paik, L.G., *The History of Protestant Missions in Korea (1832—1910)* YMCA Press, Seoul, 1929.
Kim, Y.S., *The History of the Korean Church*, Seoul, 1956.
Clark, C.A., *The Korean Church and the Nevius Methods*, Revell, New York, 1928.
Clark, C.A., *The History of the Korean Church* Seoul, 1961.

THE CATHOLIC CHURCH
IN KOREA
TODAY

THE APOSTOLIC INTERNUNCIATURE

The Apostolic Internunciature was established in the month of August, 1947, by His Holiness Pope Pius XII, with the nomination of the late Bishop Byrne as the first Apostolic Delegate.

On the occasion of the proclamation of the foundation of the autocratic Government of the Republic of Korea to all the nations of the world, on August 15, 1948, Bishop Patrick J. Byrne, Apostolic Delegate to Korea, made public to all the letter from the Holy See, which mentioned that the Republic of Korea is recognized as an independent state. Thus the Holy See was the first among the many countries of the world to recognize Korea as an independent nation.

Because the Apostolic Delegate, Bishop Byrne was arrested in the month of July, 1950, by the invading Communist Forces and martyred in North Korea, on November 25 of the same year, Archbishop De Furstenberg, Internuncio to Japan, was in addition to this post appointed temporarily as Acting Apostolic Delegate to Korea.

On his visit to Korea in the month of May, 1951, the Most Reverend Maximilian De Furstenberg, appointed Msgr. George Carroll, the present Administrator Apostolic of the P'yŏng-yang Diocese, as his personal substitute.

Msgr. Thomas Quinlan of the Ch'un-ch'ŏn Vicariate, who was repatriated to his native home, after having experienced abduction and prison life under the Communists, was nominated as Regent of the Apostolic Delegate on October 5, 1953, in addition to his task as ordinary and arrived once again in Korea on April 23rd of the following year.

In December, 1957, the Holy See then appointed Monsignor Lambertini, Papal Chancelor in Britain, as the second Apostolic Delegate to Korea, and, accordingly, Bishop Quinlan was released from his concurrent position and assumed exclusively his task as Ordinary of the Vicariate Apostolic of Ch'un-chŏn.

After his arrival in Korea on May 14, 1958, the Apostolic Delegate, Msgr. Lambertini made a great contributicn to the Church of Korea, which was overcoming the postwar disasters of the June 25th conflict.

Upon Msgr. Lambertini's transfer to another country in 1961, Monsignor Xavier Zupi was appointed as the third Apostolic Delegate to Korea. He arrived in March of 1961. Monsignor Zupi was consecrated an Archbishop in Rome in November, 1961 and in January, 1962, while still in Rome, he was appointed as Apostolic Internuncio to Pakistan.

On April 18, 1962, Archbishop Antonio del Giudice was appointed as successor to Archbishop Zupi. The present Apostolic Delegate arrived in Korea on January 4, 1963.

During the period after Archbishop Zupi's departure in November, 1961, and Archbishop del Giudice's arrival, the functions of the Apostolic Delegation in Korea were carried out by Msgr. Charles Burton Mouton, Chargé d'Affaires *a.i.* Thus Msgr. Mouton presided on the occasion of the establishment of the Hierarchy in Korea on June 29, 1962.

On December 11, 1963 the Holy See elevated the Apostolic Delegation to the status of the Apostolic Internunciature, and at the same time the Most Rev. Antonio del Giudice was raised to the Apostolic Internuncio. Prior to this occassion, in September 1963 Monsignor Mouton, Secretary to the Apostolic Delegation, was replaced by Father John V. Bulaitis, who was promoted to Monsignor on July 1, 1964.

The Most Rev. Antonio del Giudice, J.C.D.,
Apostolic Internuncio to the Republic of Korea

The Right Rev. John V. Bulaitis, Secretary to the
Apostolic Internunciature in Korea

The front gate of Apostolic
Internunciature

The Apostolic Internunciature

After Archbishop Antonio del Giudice, Apostolic Internuncio to Korea, presented his credentials to President Park Chung Hee at the Blue House

President Park Chung Hee (center), Apostolic Internuncio Antonio del Giudice (left), and Foreign Minister Chung Il Kwon

After Dr. Lee Han-pin Minister to the Vatican, presented his credentials to Pope Paul VI at the Vatican

Pope Paul VI (center), Minister Lee Han-pin (left) and his attendant Kim T'ae-ji

The late Bishop Patrick Byrne, First Apostolic Delegate to the Republic of Korea (1947-1950)

The Most Rev. Thomas Quinlan, Regent of the Apostolic Delegation ad int. (1953-1957)

The Most Rev. Maximilian de Furstenberg, Apostolic Delegate ad int. (1950-1953)

The Most Rev. Egano Righi Lambertini,
Second Apostolic Delegate to the Republic
of Korea (1957-1961)

The Most Rev. Xavier Zupi,
Third Apostolic Delegate to the Republic
of Korea (1961-1962)

The Very Rev. Msgr. Charles Burton Mouton, J.C.D.,
Chargé d'Affaires a.i. to the Apostolic Delegation

THE SHORT HISTORY
OF
THE DIOCESES OF KOREA

THE SHORT HISTORY OF THE DIOCESES OF KOREA

THE PROVINCE OF SEOUL

THE ARCHDIOCESE OF SEOUL

In 1784 Peter Lee Seung-hun, having received the Sacrament of Baptism in Peking, returned to his native land of Korea bringing with him a large number of Catholic books and consecrated objects. Using the house of Thomas Kim Pŏm-u located in Myŏng-rae-pang, Seoul, as his chapel and headquarters, he began to spread the faith widely among the people. Thomas Kim eventually won the crown of martyrdom at Tan-yang, in North Province of Ch'ung-ch'ŏng.

The first Mass to be offered on Korean soil was celebrated by Father James Chou Wen-mo, the Chinese priest, who had succeeded in penetrating into Korea on the night of December 23, 1794. Father Chou also achieved martyrdom, being sentenced to death and beheaded on April 19, 1801.

From this time on the number of believers has begun the steady increase that has marked the history of the Korean Church right up to the present year. Although they had no ordained priest to administer the Sacraments, they taught one another the catechism, baptized the neophytes, and held regular meetings for prayer and worship.

Their sincerity and enthusiasm moved Pope Gregory XVI to create the Vicariate Apostolic of Korea in 1831, and to request the *Société des Missions-Étrangères de Paris* (French Foreign Mission Society) to send a bishop and missionaries to Korea. Bishop Barthélemy Bruguière was appointed Vicar Apostolic of Korea, but on his way to korea he died in Manchuria, on October 20, 1835.

In December, 1837, Bishop Laurent-Joseph-Marie Imbert, his successor, at last managed to penetrate into Korea and became the first Bishop to govern the Vicariate Apostolic.

In 1839, during the so-called Ki-hae Persecution, Bishop Imbert, together with his missionaries Father Maubant and Father Chastan, achieved martyrdom, being executed on September 21 of that year.

Once again the Church was left without a shepherd, until in August 1845 she acquired her first priest of Korean nationality with the ordination of Andrew Kim Tae-kŏn, who, however, was soon crowned with martyrdom, being executed at the age of 26 at Sae-nam-t'ŏ, together with many other Christians, on September 16 in the following year.

The third Vicar Apostolic was Bishop Jean-Joseph Ferréol, who succeeded in entering Korea in October 1845, and died in 1853.

Bishop Siméon Berneux was the fourth Vicar Apostolic, and arrived in March 1856, and, after ten years in office, he too was honored with martyrdom, during the persecution known as the Pyŏng-in Persecution.

Bishop Marie-Antoine-Nicolas Daveluy who had been coadjutor since March 1857 was appointed to succeed him, but only three weeks later he also was martyred.

Thenceforth the Catholic Church in Korea was left without priests for ten years, during which it underwent severe persecution and oppression. Attempts at suppressing the Christian faith continued until the day of religious liberty at last dawned in Korea with the signing of a treaty between Korea and the United States of America in 1882.

In 1884 Bishop Jean-Marie-Gustave Blanc was appointed the seventh Vicar Apostolic. He died in 1890, and his successor, Bishop Augustine Mutel, was appointed in the same year.

In 1911 the original Vicariate Apostolic of Korea was divided into two, the Vicariate Apostolic of Seoul, and that of Tae-gu. And in 1920, the Vicariate Apostolic of Seoul was divided into two, that of Seoul remaining in the care of the *Missions-Étrangères de Paris* while the newly created Vicariate of Won-san was entrusted to the Benedictine Order of St. Ottilien, of Germany.

On January 18, 1942, Father Paul-Marie Ro Ki-nam was appointed Vicar Apostolic of Seoul and his consecration took place at Cathedral of Immaculate Conception in Seoul on December 20 of the same year. Bishop Paul M. Ro is the tenth Vicar Apostolic of Seoul and the first Bishop of Korean nationality.

The consecration of a Korean Bishop marked a significant stage in the progress toward placing the Korean Church in the charge of a Korean shepherd.

In 1942, moreover, Japan decreed the suspension of all foreign missionary work in Korea and as a result Bishop Paul M. Ro was given the additional responsibility of administering the vicariates vacated by the expulsion or internment of their ordinaries, a situation which lasted until the surrender of Japan in 1945.

Although the Japanese government-general in Korea did not put Christians to death or inflict serious bodily injuries on them, their attitude in continually interfering in Church affairs and frustrating Church work caused almost intolerable distress, the details of which are too numerous to relate.

After Japan's surrender Korea became an independent nation, and Bishop Paul M. Ro called for nationwide prayers on behalf of the newly-founded state and the newly-chosen representatives of the people entrusted with its government. He carried out extensive reforms in the organization and management of Church affairs, and there was a rapid increase in Church membership, but unfortunately, this blissful atmosphere of promise was rudely shaken by the outbreak of the Korean War on June 25, 1950.

Bishop Paul M. Ro, who was abroad at the time, broke off his journey and hastened home to organize relief work.

In spite of the upheaval and destruction of war and the heavy loss of life the Church steadily continued to grow in numbers.

On March 10, 1962, Pope John XXIII erected the Hierarchy of Korea, as a result of which the Vicariate Apostolic of Seoul was raised to an archdiocese and on June 29, 1962 the ceremony announcing the execution of Papal Brief Establishing the Hierarchy of the Church in Korea was held under the presidence of the Acting Apostolic Delegate, the Very Rev. Msgr. Charles Burton Mouton, together with the enthronement ceremony of Archbishop Ro. No greater proof could be shown of the action of Divine Providence.

The Chronological List of Ordinaries of Seoul Archdiocese

1. Barthélemy Bruguière (Ist Vicar Ap.) 1831-1835
2. Laurent-Joseph-Maire Imbert (2nd Vicar Ap.) 1836-1839
3. Jean-Joseph Ferréol (3rd Vicar Ap.) 1843-1853
4. Siméon-François Berneux (4th Vicar Ap.) 1854-1866
5. Marie-Antoine-Nicolas Daveluy (5th Vicar Ap.) 1866-1866
6. Félix-Clair Ridel (6th Vicar Ap.) 1868-1884
7. Jean-Marie-Gustave Blanc (7th Vicar Ap.) 1884-1890
8. Augustine Mutel, Abp., (1925) (8th Vicar Ap.) 1890-1933
9. Adrien Larribeau (9th Vicar Ap.) 1933-1942
10. Paul M. Ro Ki-nam, (10th Vicar Ap.) 1942-1962
11. Paul M. Ro Ki-nam (lst Archbishop) 1962—

Statistics of Seoul Archdiocese, 1964

1. Faithful	111,194
2. Priests	112
3. Religious Brothers	55
4. Religious Sisters	795
5. Parishes	40
6. Outstation Chapels	47
7. Hospitals	9
8. Orphanages	4
9. Kindergartens	8
10. Parochial Schools	2
11. Middle Schools	4
12. High Schools	4
13. Vocational Schools	4
14. Colleges	3
15. Magazines	3

1. Thomas Quinlan (1st Prefect Ap.)	1940-1942
2. Paul M. Ro (Administrator)	1942-1945
3. Thomas Quinlan (1st Prefect Ap.)	1945-1955
4. Thomas Quinlan (1st Vicar Ap.)	1955-1962
5. Thomas Quinlan (1st Bishop)	1962-

Statistics of Ch'un-ch'ŏn Diocese, 1964

1. Faithful	46,433
2. Priests	52
3. Parishes	28
4. Outstation Chapels	181
5. Religious Sisters	101
6. Parochial School	1
7. Vocational Schools	2
8. College	1

THE DIOCESE OF CH'UN-CH'ŎN

The Prefecture Apostolic of Ch'un-ch'on was erected on December 8, 1940: it consists of part of the territory formerly included in the Vicariate Apostolic of Seoul. Father Thomas Quinlan, of the Columban Fathers, was appointed the first Prefect Apostolic.

From 1942 to 1945 Msgr. Quinlan and all his foreign missionaries were held in custody by the Japanese government-general. The Prefecture came temporarily under the rule of Bishop Paul M. Ro during World War II but after Japan's surrender on August 15, 1945 Msgr. Quinlan resumed his see.

In 1950, on the outbreak of the Korean War, Msgr. Quinlan was kidnaped and taken to North Korea by the Communists, where he remained a prisoner for three years. After the armistice he was repatriated via Russia, and after a short stay in Ireland returned to Korea to resume his see again and at the same time occupy the regency of the Apostolic Delegate to the Republic of Korea. His consecration took place in December, 1955 at the Cathedral of Immaculate Conception and in accordance with the erection of the Hierarchy of Korean Church, his enthronement ceremony was held at Sacred Heart Cathedral on July 26, 1962.

The Chronological List of Ordinaries of Ch'un-ch'ŏn Diocese

THE DIOCESE OF TAE-JŎN

South Province of Ch'ung-ch'ŏng, in which the city of Tae-jŏn is located, has won acclaim for the number of martyrs it has produced.

Blessed Andrew Kim Tae-kŏn, the first Korean priest, was a native of this province. In the seventeen-nineties Louis-Gonzaga Lee Tan-won was the apostle who brought the Gospel to this region, and Columba Kang Wan-suk also lived here. Louis-Gonzaga Lee Tan-won, a native of Yŏ-sa-dong, Ch'ŏn-an (now Sin-ch'ŏng-ri, Sin-am-myŏn, Ye-san county) received the Gospel message brought by Peter Lee Seung-hun from Peking in 1784, and began preaching, with Francis-Xavier Kwon Il-sin in the district of Nae-p'o (now Sŏ-san, Tang-jin, Hap-tŏk, Ye-san and Hong-sŏng) with such success that the area became one of the principal theaters of Christian martyrdom in Korea.

Korea's first two native-born priests, Father Andrew Kim Tae-kŏn and Father Thomas Ch'oe Yang-ŏp, both counted Louis-Gonzaga Lee Tan-won among their ancestors. Louis-Gonzaga Lee Tan-won was martyred at Hwang-sae-pa-wi (now, Kong-ju prison) near Sŏng-kyo, of Kong-ju district, in 1801.

James Kwon Sang-yŏn after a life devoted to the apostleship, was martyred at Chŏn-ju in 1791.

It was in this diocese that the Regent Tae-won-kun put to death more than two thousand Christians in 1866, including Bishop Daveluy and many other priests, leaving the Korean Church without priests for ten years.

On the site of their martyrdom there is now the Chapel of Sin-ri, Hap-tŏk Parish, where many of their relics are preserved. Near by at Hwang-mu-sil are the tombs of Father Landre and Father Maistre.

In 1882, religious liberty was granted and previous to this, on November 2, 1846, Bishop John Ferréol founded the Fraternity of the Immaculate Heart of Mary at Pong-sin-ri, Sin-ha-myŏn, Kong-ju county. In 1895 a parish church was established at Kong-se-ri, Hap-tŏk, and at thirteen other parishes in the same province, previous to the establishment of the Vicariate Apostolic of Tae-jŏn.

On May 8, 1948, Pope Pius XII approved the erection of this district as a Vicariate Apostolic with Bishop Adrien Larribeau as the first Vicar Apostolic.

In April 1964 the Most Rev. Adrien Larribeau, the Bishop of Tae-jŏn Diocese, retired on account of age, and Father Émile Beaudevin was appointed Administrator *ad interim* of the Tae-jŏn Diocese.

The Chronological List of Ordinaries of Tae-jŏn Diocese

1. Adrien Larribeau (1st Vicar Ap.) 1948-1962
2. Adrien Larribeau (1st Bishop) 1962-1964
3. Émile Beaudevin (Adiministrator) 1964—

Statistics of Tae-jŏn Diocese, 1964

1. Faithful	49,925
2. Priests	40
3. Religious Brothers	14
4. Religious Sisters	54
5. Parishes	22
6. Outstation Chapels	251
7. Hospitals	3
8. Orphanages	3
9. Home for the Aged	1
10. Kindergartens	7
11. Parochial Schools	11
12. Middle Schools	4
13. High Schools	3
14. Vocational School	1

THE DIOCESE OF IN-CH'ŎN

In October 1958 the In-ch'ŏn region of the Vicariate of Seoul was made a Vicariate Forane. As the Church grew rapidly in this district it was soon made a Vicariate Apostolic with Msgr. William J. McNaughton as the first Vicar Apostolic of In-ch'ŏn in June, 1961. With the establishment of Hierarchy in Korea the region took rank with other dioceses.

The Chronological List of Ordinaries of In-ch'ŏn Diocese

1. William J. McNaughton (1st Vicar Ap.) 1961-1962
2. William J. McNaughton (1st Bishop) 1962—

Statistics of In-ch'ŏn Diocese, 1964

1. Faithful	36,567
2. Priests	26
3. Religious Brothers	11
4. Religious Sisters	96
5. Parishes	12
6. Outstation Chapels	84
7. Hospitals	2
8. Orphanages	3
9. Homes for the Aged	3
10. Kindergartens	2
11. Parochial School	1
12. Middle Schools	2
13. High Schools	2

THE DIOCESE OF SU-WON

As the Church grew rapidly in Su-won district this region of the Archdiocese of Seoul was made a diocese, and Father Victorinus Youn, S.T.D., Administrative Assistant of the Catholic Committee of Korea, was appointed a Bishop dated October 7, 1963. His consecration ceremony took place at the Basilica of St. Peter on October 20 of the same year.

Statistics of Su-won Diocese, 1964

1. Faithful	48,253
2. Priests	36
3. Religious Sisters	47
4. Parishes	24

5. Outstation Chapels   254
6. Orphanages   2
7. Home for the Aged   1
8. Kindergartens   6
9. Middle Schools   3
10. High Shools   2
11. Vocational School   1

THE DIOCESE OF P'YŎNG-YANG

The P'yŏng-yang Prefecfure was erected in 1927, and consists of North and South Provinces of P'yŏng-an, formerly included in the Vicariate of Seoul. It was placed in charge of the Maryknoll Foreign Mission Society of America, and Monsignor Patrick J. Byrne was appointed the first Prefect Apostolic. On his appointment as the first Assistant to the Superior General of the Maryknoll Mission, Msgr. Byrne was permitted to resign this post, but after the surrender of Japan in 1945 he returned to Korea as the first Visitor Apostolic to the Republic. He died in a Communist prison camp on November 25, 1950. He was succeeded in the P'yŏng-yang Prefecture by Father John Morris, who was followed by Father William Booth. In 1939 Bishop O'Shea was appointed to the post, and the Prefecfure was elevated to the status of a Vicariate Apostolic, and in 1942 Bishop Francis Hong Yong-ho, Korea's second native-born Bishop, succeeded him. During two years under the Japanese rule and the following four years under the antireligious Communist regime, he did his best to guide the destiny of the faithful, but he was kidnaped by the Communists and since then nothing has been heard of him.

With the retreat of the Communist forces in the Korean War Bishop Paul M. Ro and Father George Carroll entered P'yŏng-yang on November 12, 1950 and, in the absence of Bishop Hong, nominated Father Carroll as Administrator of the Vicariate of P'yŏng-yang. Msgr. Carroll quickly began to rebuild the ruined churches and gather the scattered survivors of the faithful, but, on the withdrawal of the United Nations Forces to the south of the Thirty-eighth Parallel, the Christians of P'yŏng-yang Vicariate made their base in Seoul where Msgr. Carroll took care of the refugees from the Vicariate.

The Chronological list of Ordinaries of P'yŏng-yang Diocese

1. Patrick J. Byrne (1st Prefect Ap.) 1927-1929
2. John E. Morris (2nd Prefect Ap.)   1930-1936
3. William R. Booth (3rd Prefect Ap.) 1936-1938
4. W.F. O'Shea (1st Vicar Ap.)   1938-1942
5. Francis Hong Yong-ho(2nd Vicar Ap.)1943-1949
6. George M. Carroll(Administrator)   1950—

THE DIOCESE OF HAM-HEUNG

In 1908 Bishop Mutel, Vicar Apostolic of Korea visited the Archabbot of the Benedictine Order of St. Ottilien in Germany and requested him to dispatch some of his monks to help in the work of education in Korea. As a result Father Bonifatius Sauer was dispatched to Seoul as the head of a group of Benedictine monks, but, lacking Japanese academic qualifications they were not allowed to do more than establish a monastery in Paek-dong, Seoul, and open a vocational school, where they taught carpentry, light engineering, and horticulture.

On May 15, 1913 the monastery was raised to the canonical status of abbey, with Father Sauer as the first abbot. After World War I they were commissioned to open the mission fields of Ham-kyŏng Provinces in North Korea and Chientao in Manchuria.

On August 25, 1920 the Vicariate of Won-san was canonically erected and on May 1, 1921 Msgr. Sauer was appointed and consecrated Bishop. An abbey, a seminary, and attached manufacturing plants were built and completed on November 17, 1927. The entire property of the Benedictine monastery in Seoul was transferred to the *Société des Missions-Étrangères de Paris* (Paris Foreign Mission Society).

The Vicariate of Won-san prospered and the converts became so numerous that it became too large for one Bishop to rule, and it was accordingly divided into three parts: in 1928, the Prefecfure Apostolic of Yenki and that of Ilan were erected by the Holy See with the territory beyond the Korea-Manchuria border, and the territory of North and South Provinces of Ham-kyŏng was remained under the jurisdiction of Won-san Vicariate Apostolic. On January 12, 1940, the abbey became the Abbatia Nullius of Tŏk-won and the Won-san Vicariate was replaced by that of Ham-heung.

On May 9, 1949, the entire property of the Abbey was confiscated by the Communist government of North Korea, and Bishop Sauer was arrested together with all the foreign monks and nuns and confined in a prison camp under conditions of extreme hardship. There he and many of his companions died, the survivors being repatriated after the armistice in 1953.

On May 9, 1952, Msgr. Timothy Bitterli was appointed concurrently to be Administrator of the Abbatia Nullius of Tŏk-won and Ham-heung Vicariate, and on July 7 the monastery was built at Wae-kwan in North Province of Kyŏng-sang, and Msgr. Bitterli also assumed the post of Administrator of Yenki on April 9, 1955.

On January 3, 1956, the monastery was raised to the status of cathedral priory and separated from the Vicariate of Tae-gu and the Vicariate Forane of Wae-kwan was canonically erected to include the six counties of Ch'il-kok, Sŏng-ju, Sŏn-san, Keum-neung, Sang-ju, Mun-kyŏng, and the city of Kim-ch'ŏn.

On February 17, 1964 the monastery of Wae-kwan was raised to the status of Abbey, and the election of the Abbot took place on April 28th. Father Odo Hass was elected the Abbot of Wae-kwan Abbey. Father Timothy Bitterli, however, remained in charge of the Administratorship of Ham-heung Diocese.

The Chronological List of Ordinaries of Ham-heung Diocese

1. Bonifatius Sauer (1st Vicar Ap.) 1920-1950
2. Timothy Bitterli (Administrator) 1952—

Statistics of the Vicariate Forane of Wae-kwan

1. Faithful	27,000
2. Cathedral Priory	1
3. Priests	30
4. Seminarians	23
5. Religious Brothers	33
6. Parish Churches	15
7. Schools	2
8. Teachers	77
9. Students	2,637

The Diocese of Yenki: The Vicariate of Won-san was canonically erected in 1920 but with the growth of the Church it became necessary, in 1928, to erect the Prefecture Apostolic of Yenki in that part of Won-san Vicariate that extended beyond the Korean border into the Manchurian territory of Chientao. The first Prefect Apostolic was Father Theodor Breher.

In 1937 the Prefecture Apostolic of Yenki was raised to the status of Vicariate Apostolic, and in 1946 to that of a Diocese. The strenuous efforts of Bishop Breher resulted in the construction of an abbey, a church, and a school, and thanks to his cultural and welfare work the number of converts steadily increased. All looked promising until the occupation of Manchuria by the USSR in 1945, which brought about the closure of the abbey and the Church, the confiscation of all Church property by the Red Army, and the imprisonment of foreign priests and religious. The Korean priests and religious were dispersed and were forced to take refuge in South Korea, while the faithful were left scattered like sheep without a shepherd.

Bishop Breher after long suffering in prison was repatriated and died in West Germany on November 2, 1950. Some of the survivors are now working in the Vicariate Forane of Wae-kwan in South Korea.

The Chronological List of Ordinaries of Yenki Diocese: 1. Theodor Breher (1st Prefect Ap.) 1928-1937 2. Theodor Breher (1st Vicar Ap.) 1937-1946 3. Theodor Breher (1st Bishop) 1946-1950 4. Raymond Ackermann (Administrator) 1950-1955 5. Timothy Bitterli (Administrator) 1955-

THE PROVINCE OF TAE-GU

THE ARCHDIOCESE OF TAE-GU

On May 3, 1911, Pope Pius X erected the Vicariate Apostolic of Tae-gu and appointed the Rev. Florian Demange, then publisher of the Catholic newspaper *Kyŏng-hyang-sin-mun* ("*Urbi et Orbi*"), to be the first Vicar Apostolic. His consecration was solemnized on June 12, and assumption of his post followed on June 26.

Bishop Demange's motto was "Trust and Work." By 1913 he had completed the building of the episcopal residence; by 1914 that of the Seminary of St. Justin; by 1915 the Convent of *St. Paul de Chartres* was completed, and in 1918 the Cathedral was enlarged and the Hall of the Confraternity of Christian Doctrine was built.

After these great strides, the Vicariate Forane of Chŏl-la Provinces was erected on May 9, 1931 in order to pave the way for the establishment of an autonomous prefecture. On April 10, 1934 the South Province of Chŏl-la was separated from the Chŏl-la Vicariate Forane and entrusted to the Columban missionary Fathers of Ireland.

On April 15, 1937, the Vatican published the erection of two Prefectures that of Chŏn-ju, in North Province of Chŏl-la, and that of Kwang-ju, South Province of Chŏl-la. Father Stephen Kim Yang-hong was appointed the first Prefect Apostolic of Chŏn-ju, and Father McPolin was appointed Prefet Apostolic of Kwang-ju.

On February 9, 1938, Bishop Demange died and was succeeded by Father Mousset, whose consecration as the second Vicar Apostolic of Tae-gu was solemnized by Archbishop Chambon in the Cathedral of Tae-gu.

In December 1941, with the outbreak of the Pacific War, the Japanese forced Bishop Mousset to resign and his successor, the Japanese Father Hayasaka, was appointed Ordinary of Tae-gu Vicariate on August 30, 1942. Bishop Hayasaka died on January 6, 1946, and on January 16 the Vatican appointed Msgr. Paul Chu Chae-yong, then Prefect Apostolic of Chŏn-ju, to be Administrator *ad interim* of Tae-gu Vicariate. His assumption of the post took place on February 27 of the same year.

He resigned his see on May 21, 1948, and on June 1, 1948 the Vatican appointed the Most Rev. Paul M. Ro, Vicar Apstolic of Seoul, to be concurrently Administrator *ad interim* of the Vicariate of Tae-gu. For eight months Bishop Ro traveled to and fro between Seoul and Tae-gu, until a successor would be appointed.

On December 9, 1948 the Vatican announced the appointment of Father John Ch'oe Tŏk-hong as Vicar Apostolic of Tae-gu. Msgr. John Ch'oe Tŏk-hong, adopting the motto, "*Charitas est Omnia*" and emulating his predecessor, promoted the training of ardent Catholics, intelligentzia, inviting foreign religious orders to come to Korea and found religious communities, and initiating new projects for the development of the Vicariate. The Catholic Youth Union was founded in Tae-gu in September 1948, and the fortnightly magazine *Ch'ŏn-chu-kyo Hoe-po*(Catholic Church Reporter) began publication on April I, 1949. Bishop John Ch'oe, taking over the journal, made it the official organ of his Vicariate in May 1951, under the new title of *The Catholic Times*.

In December 1950 the Vicariate of Tae-gu had already taken over the *Tae-gu Mae-il Sin-mun* (Tae-gu Daily News).

On March 12, 1952, the second postwar National Ecclesiastical Synod or Council of the Korean Church opened in the Bishop's residence, Tae-gu.

On April 2, 1952 the Ministry of Education granted a charter for the foundation of the Hyo-sŏng Women's College of Tae-gu Vicariate, which thenceforth would possess educational institutions of all grades from kindergarten up to college.

As already stated above, the Benedictines from Tŏk-won and Yenki re-established themselves during and after the Korean War in the district of Wae-kwan, and Father Bitterli, the Prior of the Wae-kwan Monastery, became Vicar Forane of six counties of the Vicariate of Tae-gu.

The Benedictine Sisters of Won-san settled in Tae-gu, while those of Yenki went to Pu-san.

On June 18, 1954 the Vicariate Forane of South Province of Kyŏng-sang was erected with Father John Sŭh Chŏng-kil as Vicar Forane, On December 14, 1954 Bishop John Ch'oe Tŏk-hong died and was succeeded by Msgr. Bernard Sŭh Chŏng-to as Administrator *ad interim.*

On July 13, 1955, Pope Pius XII appointed Msgr. John Sŭh Chŏng-kil, then Vicar Forane of South Province of Kyŏng-sang to the Vicar Apostolic of Tae-gu. Bishop John Sŭh Chŏng-kil appointed Rev. Joseph Chŭng Chae-sŏk as the second Vicar Forane of South Province of Kyŏng-sang.

On January 26, 1957, this Vicar Forane of South Province of Kyŏng-sang, was canonically raised to the status of Vicariate Apostolic of Pu-san, and Father John Ch'oe Chae-sŏn became the first Vicar Apostolic.

On June 2, 1958 the Vicariate Forane of An-tong was erected and entrusted to Rev. Francis Haller, Director of the Korea Branch of the Foreign Mission Society of Paris. The Archdiocese of Tae-gu was raised on March 10, 1962 and Bishop Sŭh Chŏng-kil was enthroned as Archbishop.

The Chronological List of Ordinaries of Tae-gu Archdiocese

1. Florian Demange (1st Vicar Ap.) 1911-1938
2. Gelmans Mousset (2nd Vicar Ap.) 1938-1942
3. Hayasaka (3rd Vicar Ap.)   1942-1946
4. Paul Chu Chae-yong (Administrator)
                                   1946-1948
5. Paul M. Ro Ki-nam (Administrator)
                                   1948-1949
6. John Ch'oe Tŏk-hong (4th Vicar Ap.)
                                   1949-1954

7. John Sŭh Chŏng-kil (5th Vicar Ap.)
                                   1955-1962
8. John Sŭh Chŏng-kil (1st Archbishop)
                                   1962—

Statistics of Tae-gu Archdiocese, 1964

1. Faithful	94,500
2. Priests	113
3. Religious Brothers	52
4. Religious Sisters	322
5. Parishes	52
6. Outstation Chapels	301
7. Hospitals	5
8. Orphanages	2
9. Homes for the Aged	2
10. Kindergartens	18
11. Parochial School	1
12. Middle Schools	5
13. High Schools	5
14. College	1
15. Printery	1
16. Newspapers	2

THE DIOCESE OF PU-SAN

On June 18, 1954 the Vicariate Forane of South Province of Kyŏng-sang was canonically erected and Father John Sŭh Chŏng-kil was appointed the first Vicar Forane.

With the death of the Most Rev. John Ch'oe Tŏk-hong, Bishop and Vicar Apostolic of Tae-gu, the Vatican appointed Msgr. John Sŭh Chŏng-kil to be the Vicar Apostolic of Tae-gu, and the Father Joseph Chŭng Chae-sŏk succeeded him as the second Vicar Forane of South Province of Kyŏng-sang.

As the number of the faithful continued to increase more churches were built and on January 21, 1957 the Vicariate Apostolic of Pu-san was erected with Father John Ch'oe Chae-sŏn as its first Vicar Apostolic. On May 30, 1957, he was consecrated Bishop and took charge of the new Vicariate, now separated from the Vicariate of Tae-gu. As a result of the establishment of the Hierarchy in Korea, the Pu-san Vicariate Apostoilc was raised to the status of a Diocese.

The Chronological List of Ordinaries of Pu-san Diocese

1. John Ch'oe Chae-sŏn (1st Vicar Ap.)
1757-1962
2. John Ch'oe Chae-sŏn (1st Bishop) 1963—

Statistics of Pu-san Diocese, 1964

1. Faithful	90,299
2. Priests	54
3. Religious Sisters	216
4. Parishes	43
5. Outstation Chapels	204
6. Hospitals	4
7. Orphanages	5
8. Kindergartens	10
9. Parochial School	1
10. Middle Schools	6
11. High Schools	6

THE DOCESE OF CH'ŎNG-JU

The seeds of the Gospel were first sown in the Ch'ŏng-ju region in the years prior to the Sin-yu (1801) Church persecution.

After the royal proclamation of religious liberty in 1882 the surviving Christians were able to practice their religion openly and began to build for themselves numerous outstation chapels in many localities, all of which came under the jurisdiction of the Vicariate of Seoul.

In 1896 Father C. Bovillon arrived from France and founded the first parish in the district and built the first parish church.

In 1906 the second parish church of the region was built at Ok-chŏn, and in 1932 the third, at Ch'ŏng-ju. The fourth was at Cheung-p'yŏng, which was completed in 1936, the fifth, at Che-ch'ŏn, in 1940, and the sixth, at Ya-hyŏn, in 1945. These six parishes flourished until 1950, when that of Cheung-p'yŏng had to be abolished after the devastation caused by the Communist invasion in South Korea. The remaining five parishes, however, are still flourishing, and in September 1953, at the request of the Most Rev. Paul M. Ro, Vicar Apostolic of Seoul, the Maryknoll Foreign Mission Society took charge of this mission field, and the Vicariate Forane of Ch'ŏng-ju was erected. with Father James Pardy as the Vicar Forane of the district. At this time there were only five priests, and the number of the faithful was estimated at about eight thousand.

As a result of the strenuous efforts and material help of the Maryknoll missionaries under the leadership of Msgr. Pardy, more parishes were founded and the number of converts grew rapidly.

In August 1958 Msgr. Pardy was permitted to resign his post of the Vicar Forane in order to accept the Vicar General of the Maryknoll Mission, and was succeeded by Father Joseph Connors.

Pope Pius XII had erected this Vicariate Forane to the status of Vicariate Apostolic in July 1958, and appointed Father James Pardy the first Vicar Apostolic of Ch'ŏng-ju; his consecration was solemnized on September 16, 1958.

With the establishment of the Hierarchy in Korea, his enthronement was held in his Cathedral of the Holy Family, at the same time the Vicariate of Ch'ŏng-ju was raised to the status of the Diocese of Ch'ŏng-ju.

The Chronological List of Ordinaries of Ch'ŏng-ju Diocese

1. James Pardy (1st Vicar Ap.)   1958-1962
2. James Pardy (1st Bishop)   1962-

Statistics of Ch'ŏng-ju Diocese, 1964

1. Faithful	40,131
2. Priests	40
3. Religious Brothers	3
4. Religious Sisters	61
5. Parishes	21
6. Outstation Chapels	160
7. Hospitals	4
8. Orphanages	2
9. Home for the Aged	1
10. Parochial School	1
11. High School	1
12. Vocational Schools	2

THE PROVINCE OF KWANG-JU

THE ARCHDIOCESE OF KWANG-JU

In 1911 the Vicariate of Tae-gu was canonically erected to cover the southern districts of the Vicariate of Seoul.

On May 9, 1931, the Vicariate Forane of Chŏl-la Provinces was erected, consisting of a group of parishes in the Vicariate Apostolic of Tae-gu. And on April 10, 1934, this Vicariate Forane was divided into two parts to form the Vicariate Forane of South Province of Chŏl-la, which was entrusted to the Columban Father, and the original Vicariate Forane was named the Vicariate Forane of North Province of Chŏl-la. On April 15, 1937, these Vicariates Forane were canonically raised by the Holy See to the status of Prefectures Apostolic, the Prefecture Apostolic of Kwang-ju and that of Chŏn-ju, and Father Owen McPolin was appointed the first Prefect Apostolic of Kwang-ju.

During the Pacific War the Japanese government obliged Msgr. McPolin to resign the post, and a Japanese priest, Father Wakida, was appointed acting temporal head of the prefecture. On the surrender of Japan to the Allies in 1945 Msgr. Wakida was repatriated and Msgr. McPolin resumed his former position.

In 1949 Father Patrick T. Brennan became the third Prefect Apostolic of this Prefecture, but was almost immediately kidnaped and killed by the Communists. It was not until 1954 that the fourth Prefect Apostolic, Msgr. Harold W. Henry, was appointed.

On January 26, 1957, Pope Pius XII raised the status of the Prefecture to that of Vicariate, after which Msgr. Henry's consecration as Bishop was solemnized.

On March 10, 1962 Pope John XXIII established the Hierarchy of Korea and raised the Vicariate Apostolic of Kwang-ju to the Archdiocese of Kwang-ju.

The Chronological List of Ordinaries of Kwang-ju Archdiocese

1. Owen McPolin (1st Prefect Ap.)	1937-1942
2. Wakida (acting temporal head)	1942-1945
3. Owen McPolin (2nd Prefect Ap.)	1945-1948
4. Harold W. Henry (acting ordinary)	1948-1949
5. Patrick Brennan (3rd Prefect Ap.)	1949-1950
6. Harold W. Henry (Acting ordinary)	1950-1954
7. Harold W. Henry (4th Prefect Ap.)	1954-1957
8. Harold W. Henry (1st Vicar Ap.)	1957-1962
9. Harold W. Henry (1st Archbishop)	1962-

Statistics of Kwang-ju Archdiocese, 1964

1. Faithful	65,489
2. Priests	85
3. Religious Brothers	65
4. Religious Sisters	134
5. Parishes	32
6. Outstation Chapels	139
7. Hospital	1
8. Orphanages	3
9. Kindergartens	7
10. Parochial School	1
11. Middle Schools	6
12. High Schools	4
13. Vocational School	1
14. Major Seminary	1

THE DIOCESE OF CH'ŎN-JU

In 1911, with the erection of the Vicariate of Tae-gu, Chŏl-la Provinces was transferred from the jurisdiction of Seoul to that of the new vicariate, but the seven parishes of Chŏn-ju, An-tae-dong, Kang-kyŏng, Su-ryu, Chŏng-eup, Mok-p'o, and Che-ju-to (Quelpart Island) retained their local identity under two native priests, Father Stephen Kim Yang-hong and Father Bartholomew Lee Sang-hwa, and five foreign missionaries stationed there.

In 1931 the centennial of the Vicariate of Korea was celebrated, and in order to pave the way for the erection of an independent Prefecture in North and South Provinces of Chŏl-la the Vicariate Forane of Chŏl-la was canonically erected with Father Stephen Kim Yang-hong as the first Vicar Forane.

In 1934 the Vicariate Forane of South Province of Chŏl-la was erected and placed in the charge of the Columban Fathers, with Father McPolin as the first Vicar Forane.

On April 15, 1937, the two Prefectures Apostolic of Chŏn-ju and Kwang-ju were formally recognized, with Msgr. Stephen Kim Yang-hong, Prefect Apostolic of the Chŏn-ju and with Msgr. McPolin that of Kwang-ju.

On January 5, 1942, Msgr. Stephen Kim Yang-hong resigned and was succeeded by Father Paul Chu Chae-yong, and in 1946, the year following Japan's surrender to the Allied Powers, Msgr. Paul Chu was transferred to the Vicariate Apostolic of Tae-gu.

On January 16, 1946, Father Bartholomew Kim Hyŏn-pae was appointed the third Prefet Apostolic of Chŏn-ju.

In 1950 on the outbreak of the Korean War the whole of Chŏl-la Provinces was under Communist occupation, and all clergy and religious in the Prefecture of Chŏn-ju were arrested and imprisoned, including the head of the Prefecture, but fortunately they were soon released.

On March 7, 1957, the Prefecture Apostolic of Chŏn-ju was canonically raised to the status of Vicariate Apostolic and Msgr. Bartholomew Kim Hyŏn-pae was appointed the first Vicar Apostolic of Chŏn-ju, but on

April 30, 1960 he died and was succeeded by Father Peter Han Kong-ryŏl, Rector of Seoul Major Seminary, who became the second Vicar Apostolic of Chŏn-ju. His consecration having taken place in Rome on March 12, 1961, he assumed office on April 28 of the same year. With the establishment of the Hierarchy in Korea the Vicariate Apostolic of Chŏniju was elevated fo the status of Diocese of Chŏn-ju.

The Chronological List of Ordinaries of Chŏn-ju Diocese

1. Stephen Kim Yang-hong (1st Prefect Ap.)
1937-1942
2. Paul Chu Chae-yong (2nd Prefect Ap.)
1942-1946
3. Bartholomew Kim Hyŏn-pae (1st Vicar Ap.)
1947-1960
4. Peter Han Kong-ryŏl (2nd Vicar Ap.) 1961-1962
5. Peter Han Kong-ryŏl (1st Bishop)   1962-

Statistics of Chŏn-ju Diocese, 1964

1. Faithful	45,755
2. Priests	35
3. Religious Sisters	27
4. Parishes	25
5. Outstation Chapels	230
6. Hospitals	2
7. Kindergarten	1
8. Middle Schools	2
9. High Schools	2

Editor's Note: In the Chronological List of Ordinaries of each Diocese we mentioned the following terms as follows.

Prefect Ap.: Prefect Apostolic
Vicar Ap.: Vicar Apostolic
Bishop: Residential Bishop
Archbishop: Residential Archbishop

The Most Rev. Paul M. Ro, D.D., Archbishop of Seoul

The Cathedral of the Immaculate Conception, Myŏng-dong, Seoul

The Cathedral stands on the site of the former Myŏng-rye-pang or House of Manifest Propriety, the residence of the first Catholic martyr of Korea, Thomas Kim Pŏm-u, which was used as a secret chapel and Mass center in the early days of the Catholic Church in Korea.

The foundation stone of the Cathedral was laid on August 5, 1892 and the building was consecrated and the first Mass offered on May 29, 1898.

The architects were successively the Rev. John Coste and the Rev. Victor Poisnel.

The enthronement of
the Most Rev. Paul
M. Ro, Archbishop
of Seoul

The faithful in front of the Cathedral
on the occasion of Archbishop Paul
M. Ro's enthronement

A view of the enthrone-
ment ceremony

After the spiritual retreat (1962)

A procession of the Holy Eucharist at the Holy Ghost Middle and High School

The congregation assembled at the open-air Mass

Church of St. Joseph, Chung-rim-dong, Seoul (1893)
The church is one of the earliest examples of church architecture in Korea

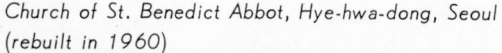
Church of Ch'ŏn-ho-dong, Seoul (1958)

Church of St. Benedict Abbot, Hye-hwa-dong, Seoul (rebuilt in 1960)

Church of Our Lady of Peace, Myŏng-su-tae, Seoul

The Parish Church of Myŏng-su-tae and Mr. Zweber

An American flower has fallen on the land of Korea—courage, compassion matinaled Hero's life—sergeant Zweber laid down his life for the glory of God. There is a light-brown colored statue of B.V.M. at the right hand of the altar of the Parish Church of Myŏng-su-tae in the quarters of Heuk-sŏk-dong and on the base of the statue of this modern sculptured work is inscribed in English, "In memory of Medard Zweber, by the employees of U.S. Economic Co-ordinator, October I, 1956". How did this American heroic youth come to be related with the Parish Church of Myŏng-su-tae? One winter afternoon in 1954 the Rev. Alexander Lee, Pastor of Myŏng-su-tae Church of Our Lady of Peace, was visited by an American G.I. His military rank was that of a non-commissioned officer. With a smiling eyes, he introduced himself, saying that he had come to Korea on military service, that his elder brother was a priest, his three sisters were nuns and his younger brother, a seminarian. This is the prelude of the story of how he was related with the parish Church of Myŏng-su-tae. It was at this very juncture that the Rev. Alexander Lee, having started the construction of the Church building, had been obliged to stop the work owing to lack of funds. On hearing of Father Lee's predicament this young hero said: "I am going to do my best to help you." From then on, every day, Sergeant Zweber used to come to Father Lee's aid, after his daily routine of the 181st Signal Battalion.

In the meantime, he wrote to his father in his homeland to the effect that a young Korean priest had been stopped in building a church by lack of money. His father, a faithful Catholic, deeply moved, sent some remittances to him, to be used for building the church.

Medard Zweber often said that his most rewarding project was the Church in Heuk-sŏk-dong. The pastor, Fr. Alexander Lee, needed money to hire workmen. Medard's regular salary, which was now that of a staff sergeant, was insufficient. So he volunteered for the job of detonating unexploded mines and shells left in the aftermath of the Korean War. With the increased pay that he earned in his hazardous work, he was able to contribute more money. Furthermore accompanied by Fr. Lee, he used to travel round from unit to unit of the U.S. Army raising funds for the Church building.

With his unceasing efforts, the Church building was completed in the month of July 1955, and he rejoiced to hear the first Mass solemnized in this new church.

He rallied GIs around him, collected their contribution and led them on "expeditions" to refugee centers, and hospitals. There they did what had to be done: painting, roofing, carpentry, and plumbing. He often told a supply sergeant from whom he "borrowed" surplus electrical supplies that could do more for Korea than American guns. The pity was, he said, that most GIs know only how to use guns.

In September 1955, Zweber was discharged from the Army. However in January 1956, he returned to Korea as an employee of the U.S. Economic Co-ordinator.

On the afternoon of August 6, he saw two boys swept downstream in a treacherous current of the Han River. He dove into the water, but unable to battle against the strong current, was swallowed up by the waves. He lost his life but we are sure he feels no regrets. His death was the symbol of his blazing love—great and golden and immensely human.

At present, we presume the Rev. Alexander Lee is wiping away the tears of the late Medard Zweber's parents in the U.S.A. His brother, the Rev. Benedict Zweber (four priests and four Sisters in his family), has volunteered to work in ecclesiastical territory in Korea and is working in high spirits as the pastor of Yŏn-p'yŏng Island Parish Church in the Diocese of In-ch'ŏn.

Rev. Alexander Lee and the late Medard Zweber

(Below) The family of the late Medard Zweber. At the right of the back row is his brother, the Rev. Benedict Zweber, who is now serving in Korea.

The Theological Department
of Catholic College

As the Church has been bereft of many priests as a result of the Korean War, and yet the number of the faithful continues to grow, it is urgently necessary to train Korean priests to take their place. In this institute the future leaders of the Church obtain spiritual and intellectual training to qualify themselves for Holy Orders.

A bird's-eye view of the Theological Department, Catholic College, Hye-hwa-dong, Seoul

Main hall of the Theological Department, Catholic College

The Rev. John Lee Mun-keun, Rector of the Theological Department

The Rev. Mark Chŭng Kyu-man
Dean of the Graduate School of the Theological
Department

Interior of the Seminary Chapel,
showing the High Altar

The faculty and seminarians of the Theological Department, Catholic College (center: Archbishop Ro)

The newly-built library of the Theological Department

The Most Rev. Dr Herrman Schäufele, Archbishop of Freiburg-Br. im-Breisgau, Germany.

He contributed greatly both materially and spiritually to building the library.

Thanksgiving service after the ceremony

A reading room in the library of the Theological Department

One of the stack rooms of the library

The Holy Ghost Middle and High School, Hye-hwa-dong, Seoul

The Rev. Peter Cho In-hwan, Principal of the Holy Ghost Middle and High School

Benediction of Blessed Sacrament
(the students of Holy Ghost Middle and High School)

Ringing the bell

Prayers offered by the students

The Main Hall of the Medical Department of Catholic College

The Rev. Isidore Park, Dean of the Medical Department

St. Mary Hospital
Catholic Medical Center attached to the Medical Department of Catholic College

The Main Building of the Tong-sŏng Middle and High School

Morning drill, Tong-sŏng Middle and High School

The Diocese of Ch'un-ch'ŏn

The Cathedral of the Sacred Heart of Jesus, Chuk-rim-dong, Ch'un-ch'ŏn

The Most Rev. Thomas Quinlan, S.S.C., D.D., Bishop of Ch'un-ch'ŏn

The Bishop's Residence

*Bishop Quinlan
receiving the
Order of Ap-
pointment*

*Bishop Quinlan
and Cardinal
Frings on the
occasion of the
latter's visit to
Korea (May
1957)*

Bishop Quinlan, awarded the Medal of Merit (Nov. 2, 1961)

Bishop Quinlan with Father Philip Crosbie (right)

Bishop Quinlan giving Benediction to the members of U.S. Armed Forces in Korea

A bird's-eye view of the
Church of St. Patrick,
So-yang, Ch'un-ch'ŏn

Church of St. Anthony,
Sang-dong

Church of the Holy
Rosary, In-jae

Church of St. John the Apostle
at Tan-ku-dong, Ch'un-ch'ŏn

Church of Immaculate
Conception, Hong-ch'ŏn

Church of Holy Trinity, Sam-ch'ŏk

The Diocese of Tae-jŏn

The Right Rev. Emile Beaudevin, Administrator of Tae-jŏn, ad int.

Cathedral of St. Joseph The Worker, Tae-heung-dong, Tae-jŏn

The Enthronement of the Most Rev. Adrien Larribeau, Bishop of Tae-jön, at Tae-jön Cathedral (July 24, 1962)

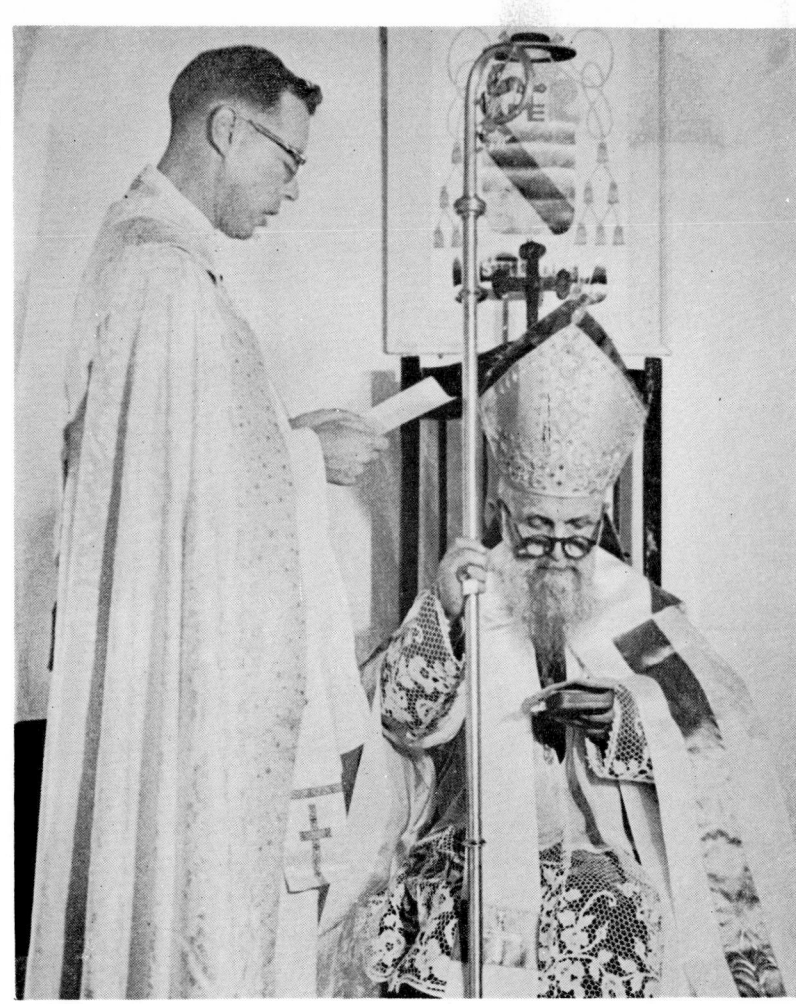

The ceremony of Induction of the Most Rev. Adrien Larribeau as Bishop of Tae-jön

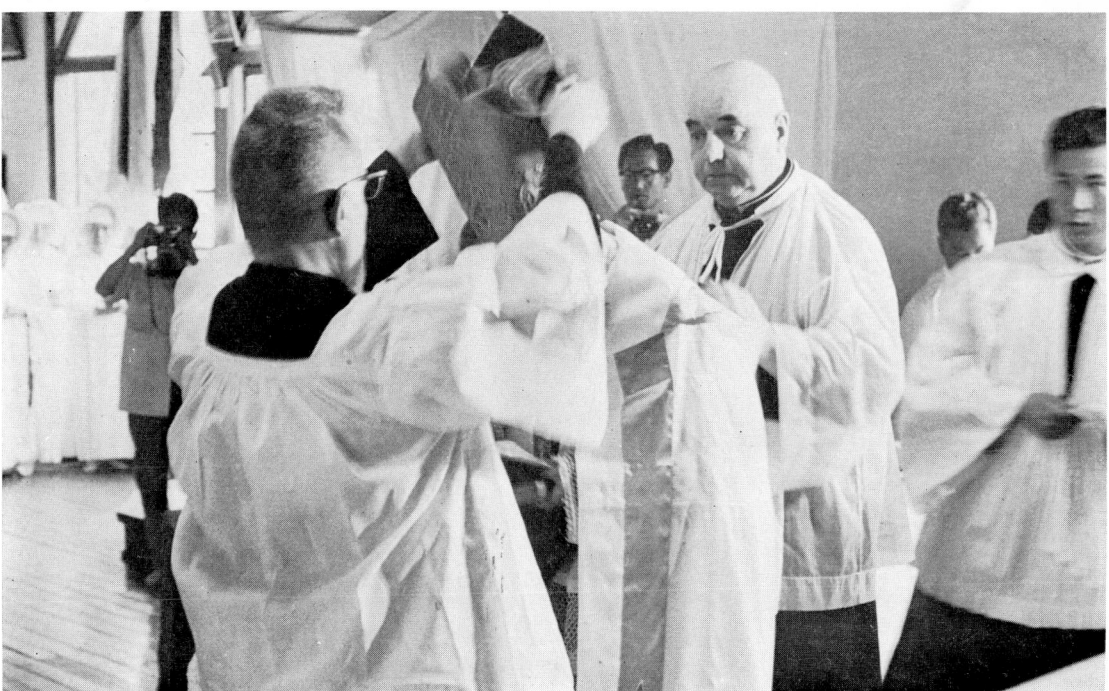

The Most Rev. Adrien Larribeau, received in audience by Pope John XXIII

(left to right) Rev. Paek, Rev Haller, Pope John XXIII, Bishop Larribeau, Rev. Cuny, Rev. Pyŭn

The Most Rev. Bishop Adrien Larribeau celebrating Mass

In the catacomb of SS. Nereus, Achilleus and Domitılla on the Via Ardeatina, Rome, in the presence of Korean seminarians (Oct. 1960)

The Golden Jubilee of
Bishop Larribeau's ordination to the priesthood

The Rev. Celestin Coyos
after being awarded the
Cultural Medal of the
Republic of Korea

The celebration of the
eightieth birthday anni-
versary of Father Jules
Bermond, Pastor of the
Church of the Immacu-
late Heart of Mary,
Kang-kyŏng

The Rev. Joseph Oh Ki-sŏn, after
being decorated with the Cultural
Medal of the Republic of Korea

Church of the Sacred Heart, Ye-san

Church of the Immaculate Heart
of Mary, Kang-kyŏng

Church of St. Joseph, On-yang

The Tae-kŏn Middle and High School, Non-san (dedicated to Blessed Andrew Kim)

Children of the Guardian Angel Kindergarten, Sŏ-san

Children of the Guardian Angel Kindergarten, Sŏ-san
With the Rev. Jean Olivier (right) and the Rev. Armand Martin

The Diocese of In-ch'ŏn

The Most Rev. William J. McNaughton, M.M., D.D., Bishop of In-ch'ŏn

The Episcopal residence

Cathedral of St. Paul,
Tap-dong, In-ch'ŏn (1889)

Enthronement of Bishop McNaughton at St. Paul's Cathedral, In-ch'ŏn (July 1, 1962)

The Most Rev. William McNaughton, Bishop of In-ch'ŏn, after his enthronement

After the Enthronement of Bishop McNaughton

(from left) Bp. McNaughton, Msgr. Mouton, Abp. Ro, Bp. Larribeau

Church of the Holy Rosary,
Kim-p'o

The Rev. Michael Bransfield, M.M.,
parish priest of Kim-p'o, before the
altar

The Rev. Fernand Paquet, the former parish priest of the Church
of Most Holy Trinity at Yŏn-p'yŏng-do

The parish Church of Christ the King, Kang- hwa Island (1958)

The parish Church of Immaculate Heart of Mary, Pu-p'yŏng (1952)

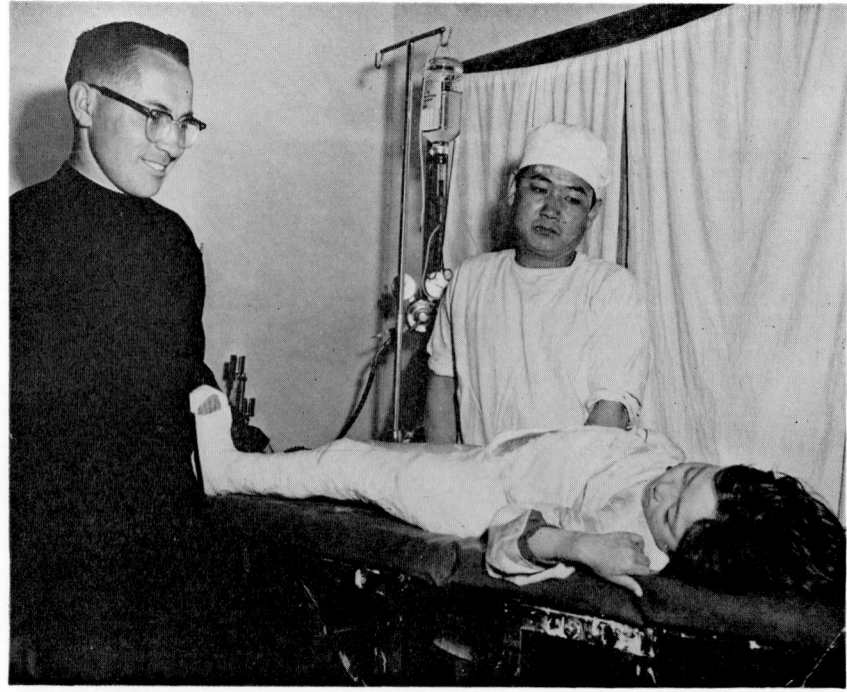

The Rev. Benedict Zweber visiting sick children in the clinic

The Rev. Roman Theisen M.M., Chancellor of the Diocese of In-ch'ŏn, with Catholic children

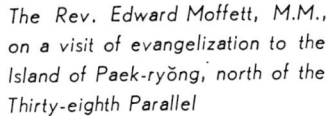

The Rev. Edward Moffett, M.M., on a visit of evangelization to the Island of Paek-ryŏng, north of the Thirty-eighth Parallel

Father Edward Moffett, Pastor of St. James Church at Paek-ryŏng-do (front row, third from left), Father Donald Dentinger, pastor of the Holy Name of Jesus Church at In-ch'ŏn (front row, third from right) and the catechists

*The Yŏng-hwa Boys'
Middle and High School,
In-ch'ŏn*

*The Pak-mun Girls'
Middle and High
School*

*The Charity Hospital of Our
Lady of Mercy, In-ch'ŏn*
(Affiliated to the Medical
Department, Catholic College)

The Most Rev. Victorinus Youn, D.D., Bishop of Su-won

The Diocese of Su-won

Cathedral of St. Joseph, Su-won

Bishop Youn, with twelve other bishops, being consecrated by Pope Paul VI at the Basilica of St. Peter (Oct. 20, 1963)

Bishop Youn (second from left) received in audience by Pope Paul VI with other bishops

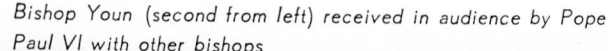

Bishop Youn being consecrated by Pope Paul VI

The Enthronement of Bishop Youn

Prelates and priests at the enthronement

Church of St. Therese, the
Little Flower, Sŏ-chŏng-ri

Church of the Sacred Heart
of Jesus, Yang-p'yŏng

Church of the Immacu-
late Heart of Mary,
An-yang

Church of St. Francis
Xavier at Pal-an-ri

Church of Our Lady of Good
Counsel, An-sŏng

The auditorium (left) and the Main Building
of An-pŏp Middle and High School, An-sŏng

The Diocese of Ham-heung

(sede vacante)

The Right Rev. Msgr. Timothy Bitterli, O.S.B.,
Vicar Forane of Wae-kwan, and Administrator Apostolic of Ham-
heung Diocese

After the capture and imprisonment of Bishop Sauer, Vicar Apostolic of Ham-heung, and all the clergy and religious of the Vicariate in 1949, and the death in prison of Bishop Sauer in February 1950, the Right Rev. Msgr. Timothy Bitterli, O.S.B., at Wae-kwan, assumed the position of Administrator Apostolic of the Vicariates of Ham-heung and the Abbatia Nullius of Tŏk-won and Yenki Diocese in July of the same year

The Right Rev. Msgr. George Carroll, M.M., Administrator Apostolic of P'yŏng-Yang Diocese

The Most Rev. Francis Hong was consecrated second Vicar Apostolic of P'yŏng-yang in 1943, and after valiantly resisting Communism for five years from 1945, and striving to develop the Church in North Korea, was kidnapped by Communist agents on May 14, 1949, and is still missing. Msgr. George Carroll's appointment as Administrator Apostolic of the Vicariate of P'yŏng-yang dates from November 1950.

The Most Rev. John Sŭh, D.D., Archbishop of Tae-gu

The Cathedral of Our Lady of Lourdes, Kye-san-dong, Tae-gu (1886)

The Archiepiscopal Residence
(left) and the Shrine of Our
Lady of Lourdes (right)

The Enthronement of Archbishop Sŭh at the Cathedral of Our Lady of Lourdes, Tae-gu, July 5, 1962

Archbishop John Sŭh leaving the Cathedral, after his enthronement

The Jubilee procession of the
Holy Eucharist, Tae-gu (1961)

Another view of the Jubilee
procession

The same

The same

Church of Sts. Peter and Paul, Ch'il-sŏng-dong, Tae-gu

Church of St. Joseph at Nam-san-dong, Tae-gu

Church of the Resurrection, Chŏm-ch'on

Church of Our Lady of Lourdes, Wae-kwan

Church of St. John the Baptist at Tae-pong-dong, Tae-gu

Church of St. Therese, the Little Flower, P'o-hang. (In the foreground, the Rev. Pierre Bertrand, M.E.P., P.P.)

The Shrine of the Immaculate Conception of Our Lady of Lourdes, erected ex voto in the grounds of the archiepiscopal residence

The Very Rev. James Lee, Vicar General, saying Mass at the Shrine of Our Lady of Lourdes

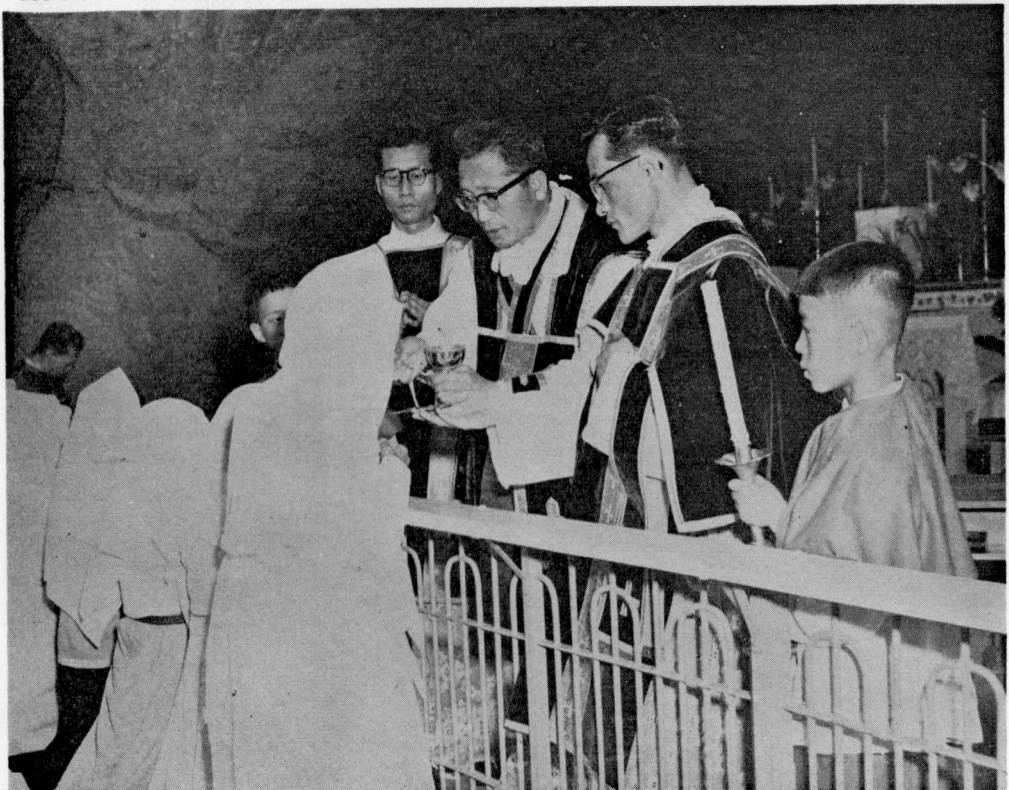

Archbishop Sŭh welcoming the Sisters of Discalced Carmelites on their arrival at Tae-gu

Mme. P. Pammer, President of the Austrian Catholic Women's Association, receiving a letter of appreciation and gifts, presented by the Governor of North Kyŏngsang Province (Oct. 1961)

Mme. Pammer, in Korean dress, at a party in her honor in Tae-gu

The statue of Our Lady in front of the Hyo-sŏng Women's College, Tae-gu

The Hyo-sŏng (Morning Star) Women's College is fulfilling its function in the higher education of women in North and South Kyŏng-sang Provinces.

The main hall of the College

The Rev. Ignatius Chŭn Sŏk-jae, Dean of the College

The Dean and Faculty of the College

The Housekeeping Department

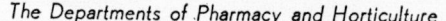

The Departments of Pharmacy and Horticulture

The Auditorium

The Dormitory

Hyo-sŏng Women's College students engaged in horticulture

Hyo-sŏng Women's
College boarders

General view of the Tae-kŏn Middle and High School, Tae-gu

The Hyo-sŏng Girls' Middle and High School, Tae-gu

The Ha-yang Holy Family Clinic, Ha-yang, North Kyŏng-sang Province

The Holy Family Home for the Aged
In Ch'il-kok County, North Kyŏng-sang Province

The Tong-ch'on Farm of the Holy Family Home

The Editorial Room of the Tae-gu Catholic Weekly Times

The Most Rev. John Ch'oe, D.D., Bishop of Pu-san

Cathedral of the Holy Cross, Pu-san

647

The Enthronement of
Bishop Ch'oe in the
Holy Cross Cathedral
(July 17, 1962)

The Right Rev. Msgr. Joseph Chang,
Vicar General of Pu-san Diocese

Msgr. Chang taking the habit

Bishop Ch'oe received in audience by Pope Pius XXIII

A view of the large congregation of the faithful commemorating the establishment of the Vicariate Apostolic of Pu-san and the consecration of Bishop Ch'oe

The clergy of the Vicariate Apostolic of Pu-san (May 25, 1961)

The Very Rev. Joseph Chang, Vicar General of Pu-san, welcoming Mme. Pammer, President of the Austrian Catholic Women's Association, on the occasion of her visit to Pu-san

New messengers of the Gospel on their arrival on board SS. Panama, to serve in the Vicariates of Tae-gu, Wae-kwan and Chŏn-ju

Bishop Ch'oe visiting the Friars Minor Conventual

(left to right) The Rev. Francisco Faldani, Superior; the Rev. Joseph Kim; Bishop Ch'oe; the Rev. Andrew Hŭh

The Procession of the Holy Eucharist after the reception ceremony to welcome Bishop Lambertini, Apostolic Delegate (at Pu-san, Sept. 28, 1959)

The outdoor altar erected for the U.S.-Korea Joint Procession of the Holy Eucharist (Sept. 30, 1962)

The vanguard of the procession of the Holy Eucharist

The procession of the Holy Eucharist

Church of Our Lady, Queen of
Heaven and Earth, Kŏ-je Island

Church of Christ The King, Ŏn-yang

Church of Our Lady, Help
of Christians, Chin-ju

Church of the Sacred Heart
of Jesus, Ch'o-ryang, Pu-san

Church of the Immaculate
Conception, Kim-hae

Church of Our
Lady of Fatima,
Ch'ung-mu and
its vicinity

*The Tae-yang Middle and
High School, Pu-san*

The Ch'ung-yŏl Girls' Middle and Commercial High School, Ch'ung-mu

The Rev. Joseph Kim Chae-sŏk, Principal of the School

The Theresa Girls' Middle and High School, Pu-san

The Sŏng-ji Girls' Middle and High School, Sin-ma-san

The Sŏng-ji Girls' Middle and High School

The Rev. Bartholomew Lee Chong-ch'ang, Director of the kindergarten
at Ham-an and the children

In commemoration of the Graduation of the Ch'ŏn-sin Kindergarten
(Inset) Father Constantius Giupponi, Director

The Diocese of Ch'ŏng-ju

The Most Rev. James V. Pardy,
M.M., D.D., Bishop of Ch'ŏng-ju

The Holy Family Cathedral, Nae-tŏk-dong

The Episcopal Residence

The Enthronement of
Bishop Pardy at Holy
Family Cathedral (July
25, 1962)

The Very Rev. Msgr. Mouton,
Secretary of the Apostolic
Delegation, proclaiming the
appointment of Bishop Pardy

Bishop Pardy, after his
enthronement

Tree-planting to commemorate Bishop Pardy's enthronement:
Msgr. Mouton, Archbishop Sŭh, and Bishop Pardy

Bishop Pardy, after conferring Holy Orders

Peter Cardinal Agagianian's visit to Ch'ŏng-ju (1959)

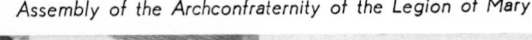

Assembly of the Archconfraternity of the Legion of Mary

Church of St Therese
of the Child Jesus,
Ok-ch'ŏn

Church of Queen of
All Saints, Mu-keuk

Church of the Holy
Name of Mary, Pu-kang

Church of St. Joseph, Ya-hyŏn-dong

Church of Our Lady of Fatima, Ch'ŏng-san

Church of Our Lady Queen of Angels, O-song

At the Gate of Heaven Home for the Aged,
Ok-ch'ŏn, on the feast of Sister Boaventura's
patron saint

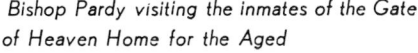

Bishop Pardy visiting the inmates of the Gate
of Heaven Home for the Aged

The Chi-kok School for the
Blind, at Ch'ŏng-ju.

The Archdiocese of Kwang-ju

The Most Rev. Harold W. Henry, S.S.C.,
D.D., Archbishop of Kwang-ju

Cathedral of Sacred Heart of Jesus
Puk-dong, Kwang-ju

The Archiepiscopal Residence

The Enthronement of Archbishop Henry at the Sacred Heart of Jesus Cathedral (July 4, 1962)

Archbishop Henry proceeding to the Cathedral

Archbishop Henry conferring the Sacrament of Holy Orders on a new priest

The Sixty-first birthday anniversary of the Right Rev. Msgr. Paul Kim, Vicar General of Kwang-ju Archdiocese

After taking the habit

(Left to right) The Superior General of the St. Columban's Foreign Mission Society; Peter Cardinal Agagianian; Archbishop Henry (in the U.S.A.)

Msgr. Martin J. McDonna, Regional Superior of the Archdiocese of Philadelphia, of the Sacred Congregation of the Propaganda of the Faith, extending congratulations to Archbishop Henry. (Right) The Rev. Herbert Henry, younger brother of the Archbishop

Assistant Superior General of the Society of St. Francis de Sales (right), in conversation with Archbishop Henry

Clergy at a retreat conducted by Archbishop Henry

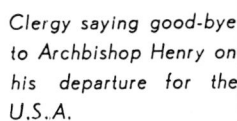

Clergy saying good-bye to Archbishop Henry on his departure for the U.S.A.

Archbishop Henry at Sang-mu-tae, Kwang-ju, on a visit to the chaplain and friends

Church of St. Martin,
Hwa-sun

Church of the Holy
Cross, Mok-p'o

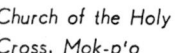

Church of Our Lady Comforter of the Afflicted, So-rok-do

The No-an Asylum and Provisional Chapel, attached to Hyŏn-ae Sanatorium

The parish Church of the Immaculate Conception, Che-ju

Statue of Our Lady inside the Church of Immaculate Conception, Che-ju

Church of St. Patrick, Che-ju
Island, and the Parish Priest

Church of Sts. Peter and Paul
Sin-ch'ang, Che-ju Island

Church of the Immaculate Heart
of Mary, Han-rim, Che-ju

Church of Our Lady of Fatima
Mo-seul-p'o, Che-ju Island

Reading the Divine Office in his breviary

Talking to a Catholic child

Enjoying a Korean meal

Repairing the engine of a jeep

The Statue of Our Lady of Fatima in the grounds of the Sacred Heart Cathedral

On the base of the statue is inscribed a prayer that "the Souls of Msgr. Brennan and Fathers Cusack, O'Brien and Malimard may rest in peace."

Procession of the Holy Eucharist, Mok-p'o

Tae-kŏn Major Seminary at Kwang-ju

Where the spirit of Blessed Andrew Kim, Priest and Martyr, is handed down to succeeding generations of clergy.

The symbol of Blessed Andrew Kim
It bears on the right side a sailing boat, and on the left a palm leaf.

The Main Building

The Very Rev. Andrew Bachhuber, S.J., Rector of the Seminary

Archbishop Henry welcoming the rector on his arrival at the Seminary and assumption of his post

The Rev. Clement De Muth, S.J., in his office at the Seminary

Seminarians paying homage to the Most Rev. John Sŭh, Archbishop of Tae-gu, on visit to Tae-kŏn Major Seminary in the company of the Most Rev. Harold W. Henry, Archbishop of Kwang-ju

Factulty and seminarians

The Sin-sŏng Girls' Middle and High School, at Che-ju

Sin-sŏng students welcoming Msgr. Mouton and Archbishop Henry on their visit to the School, June 10, 1962

The visit of the Superior General of the Columban Foreign Mission and Archbishop Henry to the School, May 19, 1960

The Diocese of Chŏn-ju

The Most Rev. Peter Han, D.D.,
Bishop of Chŏn-ju

The Episcopal
Residence

Cathedral of Sacred Heart at Chŏn-ju

Interior of the Cathedral, showing the west end of the nave (left) and the High Altar (right)

682

Bishop Han giving his first benediction after his consecration, at Rome, March 12, 1962

Bishop Han received in audience by Pope John XXIII (March 3, 1961)

Bishop Han (left) with Cardinal Agagianian (center) and Archbishop Pietro Sigismondi at the auditorium of Urbanian Seminary

Clergy, religious and lay guests including Koreans attending the consecration ceremony at Rome

A procession of the
Holy Eucharist at
Chŏn-ju

A scene of the
procession

A scene of the
procession

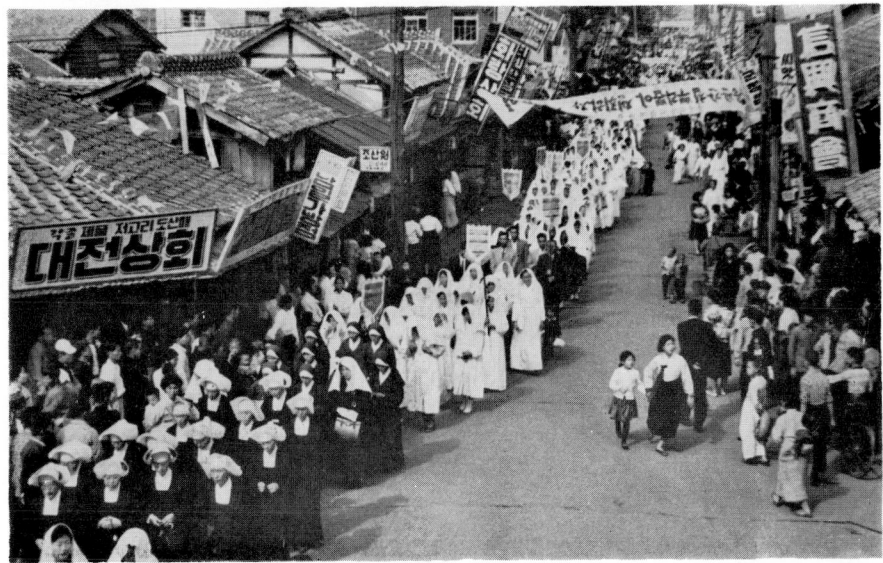

The monument in memory of Lugartha Lee, martyr

The monument in memory of Blessed
Andrew Kim, martyr

Archbishop Zupi, the
Apostolic Delegate,
in prayer before the
tomb of Lugartha
Lee and her spouse
in spiritual wedlock,
John Ryu Chong-sŏn

Prelates and priests
before the Martyr's
Monument on the
sacred site of their
martyrdom, Sup-jŏng,
Chŏn-ju

Church of St. Francis Xavier, Chŏn-ju

Church of the Holy Rosary, Chang-kye

Church of the Sacred Heart, Nam-won

*Church of St. Joseph,
Mu-ju*

*Church of Christ the
King, Ham-yŏl*

*Church of Immaculate
Heart of Mary, Kim-je*

The Sacred Heart Girls'
Middle and High School,
Chŏn-ju

Students of the Sacred
Heart Girls' Middle and
High School at Mass

THE CATHOLIC COMMITTEE OF KOREA

The Most Rev. Victorinus Youn, President of the C.C.K.

The Rev. Nicholas Chŭng (left)
the Rev. J.R. Heisse

A general definition of National Catholic Committees has been approved by Rome: "A National Catholic Committee is a voluntary association of the Catholic Bishops of a country for the purpose of organizing, coordinating and unifying the efforts of the Catholic people in education, social welfare and other national activities in character. The priests of the national office, under the direction of the Bishops make plans and studies, gather and publish information, books and booklets, develop facilities and offer them to the ordinaries. It is for each ordinary to decide whether and how he wishes to use these facilities in his own diocese."

In November, 1948, Msgr. Patrick Byrne, the Apostolic Delegate in Korea, asked Fr. Hugh Craig, M.M., to plan the organization of such a committee. The Korean conflict interrupted the work of the committee but it was reactivated in the spring of 1952 when Archbishop De Furstenberg, Acting Apostolic Delegate to Korea, called a meeting of the Bishops in Tae-gu. Fr. Craig remained as

Director until 1955 when he was replaced by Fr. Benedict Sŭh Sŏk-t'ae, O.S.B.

Fr. Craig had purchased a house in the Chang-ch'ung-dong section of Seoul which served as headquarters for the committee. The committee has gone through several reorganizations. Until 1959 it was more or less attached to the Apostolic Delegation, but in 1959 it was reorganized and again became a committee of the hierarchy.

In June, 1960 Fr. J. R. Heisse, M.M., and Fr. Victorinus Youn, S.T.D., were appointed to the Catholic Committee office as Executive Secretary and Administrative Assistant, respectively. In October, 1963 Father Youn was canonically raised to a bishop and appointed to the Bishop of Su-won Diocese, and Father Nicholas Chŭng succeeded him. In April 1964, on the occasion of Diocesan Synod, the Most Rev. Victorinus Youn was elected as president, and the Most Rev. William McNaughton as vice-president, succeeding to the Most Rev. James V. Pardy and the Most Rev. Paul M. Ro, respectively.

THE MISSIONARY SOCIETIES, THE RELIGIOUS ORDERS AND OTHERS

THE MISSIONARY SOCIETIES

THE PARIS FOREIGN MISSION SOCIETY
(La Société des Missions-Étrangères de Paris)

This Society was founded in 1658 by Msgr. François Pallu and Msgr. Pierre de la Motte Lambert to prepare priests for missionary work. It was authorized by Louis XIV in 1664, by Louis XI in 1775, then suppressed in 1791, re-established in 1805, again suppressed in 1809; it was restored in 1815 and serves 37 missions in the Far East. It has over 1,000 French missionaries and 1,500 native priests. These Fathers are responsible for numerous schools, orphanages and hostels, workshops and dispensaries, hospitals and leprosaria.

In 1812, the Christians of Korea, being unable to obtain priests on account of the deplorable state to which the Church of Peking had been reduced by persecution, wrote a touching letter to Pope Pius VII, which he received in his prison at Fontainebleau. For the time being he could do nothing more than resort to prayer and wait for better times.

When peace was restored and the Pope re-entered Rome in triumph, better days dawned for the Church. Not only did she rise again from the ruins to which her enemies had attempted to reduce her, but, as if to console her, there was a powerful movement of apostolic zeal for the conversion of the whole world. Vocations multiplied and the Sacred Congregation was kept busy regulating these generous efforts. Korea was not forgotten, but the deplorable state of the mother-mission in Peking and superannuated pretensions of Portugal to the *"Padroado do Oriente"* (patronage of the missions in the Orient) prevented a definite solution until in 1825 another letter from Korea arrived at Rome. The letter is too long to cite here, but, as a result, the Sacred Congregation, on September 1, 1827, wrote to the *Société des*

Missions-Étrangères de Paris (MEP) to ask whether they could accept the charge of supplying priests to Korea for the future. It was not easy to answer at once, for Korea had always followed a rigid policy of isolation and it was as hard for a missionary to enter the country then as it is for a South Korean to cross the Demilitarized Zone into North Korea today. Bishop Bruguière was the first to make the attempt, but he died in Manchuria, and it was Bishop Imbert who first succeeded in penetrating into the country, with the aid of two other MEP missionaries, Fathers Maubant and Chastan, in 1837.

In this way the MEP began its long years of missionary service to Korea, laying a firm foundation for the future prosperity of the Korean Church with the blood of the loyal priests who gave their lives for her.

When persecution began in 1839 these French missionaries, patterning their lives after example of Christ, died for the Faith. A monument stands on the Han River bank today at the site of their martyrdom. The MEP not only furnished a steady supply of foreign priests, but also provided for the training of Korean priests, sending young men to Macao and Penang for their seminary studies and eventual ordination. Without these native priests the Church could never have risen from its initial status, that of a foreign body in Korea. The first native Korean priest, Father Andrew Kim Tae-kŏn, was trained by the MEP and died a martyr in 1846, to glorify Christ and His Church in Korea.

From 1850, young MEP missionaries began to arrive in numbers, and more Korean priests were ordained. Many of them shared the glory of martyrdom with Blessed Andrew Kim, Blessed Laurent Imbert, and their companions. The holocaust of 1866, when it became known in the theological seminary of the MEP, only served to stir in the hearts of the young seminarians the ardent desire and firm resolution to follow the martyrs' example. A secret seminary in Kang-won district was set up to serve the Korean youths who for their part were no less determined that the Church should thrive in Korea. Soon this was superseded by the seminary publicly established in the Yong-san district near the site of the early martyrs' execution ground. Saint Joseph's Church, the first brick building to be erected in Korea, was built on Yak-hyŏn hill, near the Small West Gate. Next to be built was the Cathedral of Myŏng-dong, dedicated to the Immaculate Conception, near Nam-san hill dominating the Seoul skyline. The Most Rev. Mutel was another great MEP leader of the Korean Church. His Apostolic Vicariate extended over the whole of the kingdom of Korea and even included part of the territory of Manchuria.

On January 18, 1942, Bishop Larribeau handed over his see to Korea's first native-son Bishop, the Most Rev. Paul M. Ro Ki-nam, (now Archbishop of Seoul). The bodies of the martyrs were enshrined in the crypt of the Cathedral of the Immaculate Conception, and their desire for the Church to be firmly established on Korean soil was realized.

The MEP missionaries also handed over all their facilities and plant to their Korean counterparts. Were the French Fathers leaving Korea? No; in accordance with the special wishes of the Pope, they remained to help the Korean priests in whatever fields they required their assistance. Their common effort over a period of a hundred and fifty years and the blood they had shed established a close bond between the Korean Church and the MEP, a bond which will grow ever stronger as the priests of the two countries continue their humble efforts to glorify the Lord Christ.

THE COLUMBAN FATHERS

(The St. Columban Foreign Mission Society)

The original work of the Columban Fathers, a society of secular priests founded for work on the foreign missions, was among the Chinese people and peoples having a Chinese cultural background.

The Columban Fathers Society was founded by an Irish Priest, Father Edward J. Galvin, in 1918. Ordained in the National Seminary at Maynooth, Ireland, in 1909, Father Galvin went to work in Holy Rosary parish, Brooklyn, New York City. In 1912 he met a Canadian priest, Father Frazer, who was enlisting support for foreign missions in China. Father Galvin volunteered for China and left at once. Four years in China convinced him that individual priests could do very little on their own, and that they needed an organized society behind them to support their efforts. In 1916 he returned

to Ireland and obtained permission from the Irish bishops to start a foreign mission society.

The new society got off to a good start when several seminary professors resigned their chairs and joined Father Galvin. In 1918 the Holy See gave temporary canonical approval with the "decree of praise" and named Saint Columban as the patron of the society.

In 1918 Father Galvin went to Omaha, Neb. and obtained permission from Archbishop Harty to found a house of the society in that city. Father Galvin also began publication of the society's magazine, *The Far East.*

In 1919 Father Edward Maguire went to Australia and founded a house of the society there.

The first group of sixteen Columban Fathers sailed for China in March 1920 and went to work in Hanyang in central China. Among them was Father Thomas Quinlan, now Bishop of Ch'un-ch'ŏn. In 1925 the Holy See gave final approbation to the society and assigned them the Apostolic Vicariate of Hanyang, and in 1927 Father Galvin was consecrated Bishop and appointed Vicar Apostolic.

In 1931, at the request of the Holy See, the Columban Fathers went to the Philippines, and in 1933 they came to Korea for the first time. The first group of ten priests arrived in Pu-san on the feast of Christ the King, October 29. They took charge of the mission territory of Kwang-ju in southwest Korea, which in 1937 was raised to a Prefecture Apostolic with Msgr. Owen McPolin in charge.

In 1938 the Holy See allotted the Columban Fathers another mission in Korea. This time they moved north to Kang-won Province. In March 1939 the first priests took over the parishes in the new territory. Msgr. Thomas Quinlan was the Superior of the new mission. In December 1940, the district was made a Prefecture Apostolic with Msgr. Quinlan as Prefect.

In 1936 the Columban Fathers accepted a region in northern Burma which has since been raised to a diocese with a Columban Bishop.

After World War II the Columban Fathers accepted a third mission in China in addition to Hanyang (Bishop Galvin) and Kiangsi (Bishop Cleary).

In 1948 the first priests of the society went to work in Japan. They now have a hundred priests there, working in four districts.

In 1949 the Columban Fathers went for the first time to South America, where they took charge of parishes in Peru, Chile, and Argentina.

In 1951 the society accepted a mission in the Fiji Islands.

During World War II missionary activity was suspended in many countries. In Korea the Columban Fathers of American and British nationality were sent home in an exchange of prisoners. The Irish Fathers were first imprisoned and later placed under house arrest. In August 1945 they resumed their missionary work in Korea. When the Korean War broke out on June 25, 1950 the Columban Fathers had forty-two priests in the country working in Kwang-ju and Ch'un-ch'ŏn. During the war seven priests of the society lost their lives. The first foreigner killed was Father Antony Collier in Ch'un-ch'ŏn on June 27. Later Fathers James Maguin, Patrick Reilly, John O'Brien, Thomas Cusack, Francis Canavan, and Msgr. Patrick Brennan lost their lives. Msgr. Thomas Quinlan and Father Philip Crosbie survived three years in a North Korean prison camp and returned to Korea in 1954.

In 1955 the Columban Fathers opened the Parish of St. Patrick's in Ton-am-dong, Seoul, and in 1959 they opened another at Wang-sip-ri, Seoul, the Sacred Heart of Jesus.

In 1962 the Columban Fathers had in Korea 60 parishes with 110,000 Catholics and 12,000 catechumens. They have one Archbishop, (the Most Rev. Harold Henry, Archbishop of Kwang-ju) and one Bishop (the Most Rev. Thomas Quinlan, Bishop of Ch'un-ch'ŏn) and 121 priests of the society assigned to Korea. It is the largest Catholic missionary organization in Korea.

The society has missons in the Philippines, Japan, Burma, Korea, the Fiji Islands, and South America. The community has 314 parishes and 1,888 mission stations caring for 1,600,000 Catholics and 25,000 catechumens.

There are 1,060 members of the Columban Fathers, including 820 priests. The society has two Archbishops (the Most Rev. John Dooley, formerly Apostolic Delegate to Vietnam and the Most. Rev. Henry of Kwang-ju) and five Bishops, one in Korea, two in the Philippines, one in Burma and one in Ireland, (Bishop Cleary, formerly Bishop of Kiangsi, China)

Bishop Galvin was expelled from China by the Communists in 1954, and died in Ireland in February 1956.

Msgr. Patrick Brennan first came to Korea in 1937 to work in Kwang-ju. He went to

Kang-won in 1938, was repatriated in 1942, joined the United States Army as a chaplain and left the Army in 1945. In 1947 he was appointed director of the Columban Fathers in Asia, and in 1949 was named Prefect Apostolic of Kwang-ju. He was arrested by North Korean Communists in July 1950, and taken by them to Tae-jon, where he was last seen alive in September 1950.

THE MARYKNOLL FATHERS

(*The Catholic Foreign Mission Society of America*)

Maryknoll, a congregation of priests for the foreign missions, whose full name is the Catholic Foreign Mission Society of America, was founded at the Maryknoll Seminary, New York, in 1911 by Bishop J.A. Walsh and Father T.F. Price, especially for work in China.

If these founders could return to this uneasy world today, they would be sorely disappointed to note that fifty years after their foundation there are no missionaries in China, their first love and hope, and astonished to observe the large number of Maryknoll missioners in South America and Africa, countries to which they scarcely gave a thought. For China and the Far East were their constant preoccupation. Perhaps they might have envisaged eventual extension of the mission to cover India but in their wildest dreams they could not have imagined that in the year 1961, one hundred and sixty Maryknoll missionaries would be found in South America and over one hundred others deep in the continent of Africa.

The old Oriental adage, "Head winds blow hard at the start," indicating that calm would soon follow, was hardly verified in the experience of the first Maryknoll missioners in China. Periods of banditry were followed by civil wars and the invasion by Japan, culminating in the overthrow of the Nationalist government of Generalissimo Chang Kai-shek and the complete domination of that vast country by the Communists. Today the Church of China is the Church of Silence, and oddly enough the only remaining missioner in that oppressed land is Bishop James Walsh, the first Maryknoll missioner to arrive in China in 1918, and now languishing in a Shanghai jail.

The Maryknoll Fathers' effort in Korea began in 1923 when Father Patrick Byrne (later to become the first Apostolic Delegate) took up residence in Sin-eui-ju on the Yalu River. The French Fathers withdrew and the Maryknollers assumed the task of evangelizing the Provinces of North and South P'yŏng-an. These were the days when Korea was ruled by the Japanese Governor-General and every civilian official of importance was the Japanese. These were the days when the Japanese program called for the gradual elimination of the Korean customs and language and the studied effort to impress upon their subjects the glorious privilege of Japanese people. Had it not been for World War II the Korean language would have been suffocated, and Japanese would have become the required medium not only for the Korean people but for the foreign missioners too. Such was the program envisioned and such was the atmosphere in which the missioners lived in those uncertain days. No movement, no activity escaped the vigilant and suspicious eyes of the Japanese police.

The Maryknoll Fathers built on the solid foundation laid by those grand pioneers of the Faith in Korea, the priests of the *Société des Missions-Étrangères de Paris*, whose sweat and blood had continued to hallow the soil of Korea for over a century and a half. The record of the French Fathers is one of the glories of the universal Church. From their day to the present moment, the Korean Faith has not only not faltered, but a constant influx of new converts has brought the number of Catholics almost to the half-million mark.

The Maryknoll Fathers have two Bishops, seventy-three priests and six Brothers laboring in the Dioceses of Ch'ŏng-ju, In-ch'ŏn, and Pu-san, caring for more than 45,000 Catholics in 35 parishes. There are no outstanding humanitarian or social projects such as they would desire. A medical clinic, schools for the blind, the deaf and dumb, two primary schools, two high schools, a home for the aged and several orphanages constitute the works of charity, along with the relief efforts in each parish carried on in conjunction with the National Catholic Welfare Conference, but the hearts of all Maryknoll missioners are gladdened by the constant stream of adults, both men and women, who are drawn to the Faith, and it is an open secret that the Maryknoll Superior, who resides in New York, rejoices most of all because of the vigorous character of the Church in Korea and its thousands of catechumens.

Maryknoll Fathers in Korea rejoice too in their pleasant relations with the Korean clergy, the French missionary priests, the Columban Fathers, the Jesuits, the Salesians, the Benedictines and the Franciscans just as they rejoice too in their increasing personnel and their numerous conversions. The Lord alone knows the future, but at this point the Catholic Church in Korea is no longer the Church of the Catacombs, but the Church Triumphant, giving promise of development undreamed of a few years ago, when short and stocky soldiers stationed in every railroad station and every hamlet proclaimed the awesome power of the Japanese Emperor. Few who were living in that humiliating era can have foreseen that the day was so near when the shackles would be broken and the Korean people once again breathe as free men.

It is the fervent prayer and hope of every missionary in Korea that temporal and economic advances will be accompanied by sound moral development, for progress based on clear-cut moral principles alone will make for a strong and enduring nation.

History shows that no nation can long endure as a force for good and in tranquillity without the support of religion. Toward that objective the Maryknoll Fathers hope to make a not unworthy contribution.

The Paris Foreign Mission Society

The main building of the M.E.P. in Paris

On the occasion of the visit of the Most Rev. Le Merre, Superior General of the M.E.P., to Korea (Feb. 9, 1960)

The main hall of the
M.E.P. in Paris

The Very Rev. Francis Haller, Superior of the Korean
Chapter of the M.E.P., with Bishop Adrien Larribeau

The Rector of the M.E.P.
Seminary

A group of M.E.P. priests
after a retreat

The Columban Fathers

Father Neil Boyle, the Superior

The Chapel

Main Building of the Korean Chapter

The Maryknoll Fathers

A bird's-eye view of the Catholic Foreign Mission Society of America (Maryknoll Fathers) Headquarters and the Society's attached Seminary at Maryknoll

It is located 35 miles from New York City, near Assining, with conspicuous 'flying roof' in the Chinese style.

The Most Rev. John W. Comber, Superior General of the Maryknoll Mission

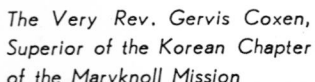

The Very Rev. Gervis Coxen, Superior of the Korean Chapter of the Maryknoll Mission

Celebration of the fiftieth anniversary of the founding of the Catholic Foreign Mission
Society of America (Maryknoll) (June 29, 1961)

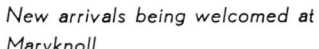

The Very Rev. Gervis Coxen (center,
front row) with newly-arrived priests

New arrivals being welcomed at
Maryknoll

Maryknoll Fathers assembled in front of the Episcopal Residence at Ch'ŏng-ju, after their conference

Maryknoll Fathers in the Korean mission field

Maryknoll Fathers with Bishop Lambertini, Apostolic Delegate to Korea, Archbishop Ro and Msgr. Carroll

THE RELIGIOUS ORDERS AND OTHERS

THE CONGREGATION OF THE SISTERS
OF ST. PAUL DE CHARTRES

1. FOUNDATION

In Chartres, France, a place now known as "Saint Mary's village," there stands the massive magnificent thirteenth-century cathedral full of beautifully carved reliefs, with its two greatbelltowers rising high to the skies. In the shadow of this cathedral stands the Motherhouse of the community of the Sisters of *St. Paul de Chartres*, center of the hopes and love of all the Sisters of St. Paul scattered throughout the world.

The community dates from 1694, when Father Louis Chauvet decided that the sufferings of the people during the time of plague, famine, and foreign invasion in the wake of the Reformation must be alleviated. So clearly did he realize the necessity of the services of devoted women in the relief of their suffering that, on April 20, 1699 he obtained a small building where they could begin their work. Four young girls from different walks of life formed the nucleus of the movement.

2. ITS SPIRIT

Such was the beginning of the Congregation of the Sisters of St. Paul, which was founded in the tiny village of Levesville. For more than three hundred years she has gone on extending her warm and self-sacrificing hands to all who are unhappy, neglected, forgotten, and ill.

This was the spirit that animated our founder, and our first Mothers, who cheerfully put up with poverty, sickness and oppression, in whole-hearted devotion to the relief of the homeless and the poor, in their struggle against heartbreaking odds throughout the eighteenth century.

We see here the very embodiment of the sublime teaching of Christ when He said:

"Believe me, when you did it to one of the leat of my brethren here, you did it to me." (St. Matthew, 25:40)

Thus it is that we Sisters of the Congregation of *St. Paul de Chartres* gain lofty inspiration from the words of St. Paul the Apostle:

"It is now no longer I that live, but Christ lives in me." (Gal., 2:20)

Bearing these words in mind, the Sisters make all efforts, by close contact with Our Lord through their three vows of Poverty, Chastity, and Obedience, to try to be as perfect as Our Heavenly Father is perfect.

In order that we Sisters of St. Paul may realize our sublime aim, it is imperative for us to cease entirely to live for ourselves. We have to live a life of continual self-sacrifice in accordance with our three principles of (1) Regularity (2) Austerity (3) Industry, as embodied in the words of St. Paul:

"You must be heavenly-minded, not earthly-minded, Christ is your life . . . there is nothing but Christ in any of us." (Colossians, 3:10)

3. OVERSEAS EXPANSION

From the four grains of wheat which were sown and which took root in Levesville there have sprung a great many new lives.

Since the Sisters were first summoned to go and serve in Guiana, South America, to help the poor and sick, the number serving abroad has steadily grown, and today there are four thousand of us working in fifteen different countries: namely, Belgium, Switzerland, England, Italy, Maskelyne Island, the Antilles, China, Vietnam, Japan, Korea, Thailand, Laos, the Philippines, Canada, Africa and Madagascar.

4. IN KOREA

Day by day as Catholicism gains ground in Korea the number of religious congregations increases with the growth in the number of believers. Only seventy years ago there were no nuns in this country.

Our congregation, the Sisters of *St. Paul de Chartres*, has undergone all kinds of hardship and difficulty: feudalism and the policy of seclusion; the confused phases of life at the end of the Yi Dynasty; the Sino-Japanese and the Russo-Japanese War; the long despairing period of thirty-six years under Japanese occupation; disorder and confusion after the liberation from Japanese rule and the recent Korean War. This congregation has now well and truly laid her firm foundation as an independent religious community.

As Christ said:

"Believe me when I tell you this; a grain of wheat must fall into the ground and die, or else it remains nothing more than a grain of wheat; but if it dies, then it yields rich fruit." (St. John, 12:24)

So, with the grace of God, we have stood the tests successfully. The following is a brief account of the history and the spirit of our congregation.

Our Catholic Church in Korea, whose foundation was cemented with the blood of the three martyrs, Blessed Laurent Imbert, Bishop, and his companions Jacques Chastan and Pierre Maubant, beheaded on September 21, 1839, had, by the end of Yi Dynasty, undergone eighty years of persecution. As it became easier for missionaries to spread the faith, Bishop Blanc, the seventh Vicar Apostolic of Korea, who had come to Japan for his consecration ceremony in 1883, personally visited the Sisters in that country and inspected their work. Impressed by what he saw, he invited them to Korea. Of the four who came, two were French and two Chinese, and they landed at In-ch'ŏn on July 19, 1888. On July 29 five Korean aspirants were accepted and our first convent was opened with Sister Zacharia as foundress and Mother Superior.

At first everything was so new and unfamilar to them that the troubles and hardships they had to face seemed almost insurmountable. Nevertheless they succeeded in overcoming them and accomplishing the successful development of their work, as may be seen today.

It is a most delightful and heart-warming fact that two of those five founding aspirants are still alive and with us today. They are Sister Paul Kim, who is ninety-three years old, and Sister Xavier Park, who is ninety-two. They are the living history of our foundation in Korea, who hand down to us the spirit of our foundress and the real situation of the past.

"The Lord is my light and my deliverance, whom have I to fear? The Lord watches over my life; whom shall I hold in dread?" (Psalm, 26:1)

The Korean War was an unforgettable experience! How can we ever erase from our minds the memory of those days when the "Land of the Morning Calm" was steeped in blood? It was like a nightmare. We cannot repress our feelings of grief at the sight of the ruin and destruction in the country.

We could not expect dignity of life on the part of the invaders, and our reverend and beloved Provincial Superior, Mother Béatrix, who had lived all her long life in the love of God, died a martyr for Him in this strange land on November 3, 1950, during the Death March enforced by Communists.

"By a single offering, he has completed his work, for all time, in those whom he sanctifies." (Hebrews, 10:14)

Our Lord Who has said, "I will never leave thee or forsake thee," (Joshua, 1:5) kept His promise, and helped our beloved Mistress of Novices, Mother Eugénie Demeusy to survive.

"No, we do not play the coward; though the outwad part of our nature is being worn down, our inner life is refreshed from day to day. This light and momentary affliction brings with it a reward multiplied every way, loading us with everlasting glory; if only we will fix our eyes on what we can see." (II Corinthians, 4:16-18)

She was treated like a beast by them, but now she is freed from their snares and among us in the free world.

Two of our Mothers were tortured to the point of death by the enemy and offered themselves as sacrifices.

"The Lamb will guide them to the fountains of the waters of life, and God will wipe away every tear from their eyes." (Apocalypse, 7:17)

Now there is no more death, sadness, grief or suffering in His eternal and blessed abode.

5. ACTIVITIES

The Sisters of St. Paul in Korea manage one Mother house, in Seoul, and forty-seven branch convents, and the members of the congregation consist of 372 professed Sisters, sixty-five novoices and thirty postulants and aspirants. The present condision of the activities of the Sisters is outlined in the following note:

1. The Kye-sŏng Girls' Middle and High School in Seoul
2. The St. Paul Girls' Middle and High School in Non-san
3. The Keun-hwa (Rose of Sharon) Girls' Middle School in Kyŏng-ju
4. Paek-hap (White Lily) Kindergarten in Yong-san, Seoul
5. St. Paul Orphanage, Seoul
6. Star of the Sea Orphanage, In-ch'ŏn
7. White Lily Orphanage, Tae-gu
8. St. Paul Hospital, Ch'ŏng-ryang-ri, Seoul
9. St. Mary Dispensary, Che-ki-dong, Seoul
10. Star of the Sea Hospital, In-ch'ŏn
11. St. Joseph Hospital, Tae-gu

6. FOR THE APPLICANTS

In order to be eligible, applicants must be:
1. born in wedlock,
2. sound in mind and body,
3. of lofty and irreproachable character,
4. graduates of schools higher than girls' high school,
5. between seventeen and thirty years of age.

And the training courses are:
Probationary Period   (1 or 2 years)
Novitiate   (2 years)
Period of Temporary Vows (5 years)
Period of Perpetual Vows (for the term of life)

THE ORDER OF ST. BENEDICT

1. FOUNDATION

St. Benedict, the founder of the Benedictine Order, was born at Norcia (about 480), in Umbria, Central Italy. The Italy of St. Benedict was the Italy of the Ostrogoths and Theodoric, of Belisarius and Justinian's war of recovery—his seventy years or so of

life spanned the abyss that separates Romans from Italians. He himself is one of the last of the Romans and it may be safely said that the spirit of Rome, baptized now, is the inspiration of all that is new, revolutionary even, in his work. His family were wealthy country landowners. At the age of seventeen he fled from Rome, where he was educated, to live as a solitary, thirty miles away in the wild mountain district that is now Subiaco (about 497). Disciples gathered round him, whom he organized in communities. After twenty years or so he moved to Cassinum, half way between Rome and Naples (now Montecassino). It was there that his Holy Rule was written, and his monasteries became the cradle of the Benedictine Order and the model for Western monasticism in general. The date of his death is not accurately known; the year which used, traditionally, to be considered correct—543—is almost certainly wrong and the latest, well-reasoned, theory would place it between 555 and 557.

Montecassino afterward underwent several devastations in successive wars, but reconstruction and rehabilitation followed soon after each disaster, and it retained its position as the headquarters of the Benedictines. This may well be taken as a manifestation of Divine Providence, and justify our trust that the Benedictines will survive for the glory of God until the end of the world.

2. OVERSEAS EXPANSION

It was the Benedictine who took up the work of the earlier Irish missionaries in evangelizing countries north of the Alps such as England and Germany during the Middle Ages, and enabled them to become what they are today. They preserved Christian documents through the ages, as oases of civilization; they advanced the arts and sciences, and especially contributed to the development of the sense of propriety.

The Fourth Lateran Council legislated for the formation of associations of Benedictine houses and these congregations are in effect each one a true and separate order. According to the Holy Rule of St. Benedict, manual work is the principal occupation and the celebration of the Divine Office in choir the most important duty of monks. The Divine Office is celebrated daily in every monastery; but with the custom of ordaining all monks, (established since about 1,000) and the appearance of lay-Brothers, manual labor for

choir-monks has almost disappeared. Instead, Benedictines have occupied themselves as missionaries, in study, and as schoolmasters, and education is their most characteristic activity today. The congregations of Belgium and St. Ottilien are concerned with foreign missions. At present there are sixteen congregations, more than two hundred monasteries, and upwards of 12,000 monks. St. Ottilia was founded in Germany in 1884 for foreign mission work: it first made its way to Africa, and in 1909 to Korea.

3. IN KOREA

At the request of the Most Rev. Mutel, eighth Vicar Apostolic of Korea, Father Bonifatius Sauer came to Seoul and established a monastery at Hye-hwa-dong. In 1913 the monastery was raised to the status of Priory, and he became the first Abbot. When World War I broke out, the liberty of the German monks was entirely suppressed and the functioning of the monastery virtually suspended, but these monks continued to conduct their engineering school and their prestige was high among the Korean people.

For more than a century, missionary work in Korea had been entirely dependent on the *Société des Missions-Étrangères de Paris* and as the Church grew in numbers and influence St. Ottilien was given the charge of mission work in Ham-kyŏng Provinces of Korean and the Chientao Province, Manchuria, which had formerly belonged to the Vicariate Apostolic of Seoul, an area extending from Won-san to Khabarovsk and to the Amur River, extending 1,200kms. Later the part of this area covering the Sungari River basin was placed in the charge of the Franciscan missionaries, and the Yenki Vicariate in southeast Manchuria remained in the care of the Benedictines. For twenty years from 1921 to 1941 their mission activities developed and prospered, with sixty priests and forty Brothers belonging to the abbey, supported by Benedictine nuns from Lutzen (East Germany) and Cham (Switzerland). They gained some 35,000 converts, in the vicariates where there was little stability and order for the promotion of Catholicism, and devoted themselves to education and social welfare. Abbey-operated hospitals at Won-san, Tŏk-won, Ham-heung and Yenki helped to relieve many sufferers in these districts. A seminary was set up, and a printing shop in which the first Korean translation of the Bible was published. Devoted Korean priests, catechists, and lay-men co-operated enthusiastically with the German missionaries in the spread of the faith. All this was swept away and almost totally destroyed when the area north of the Thirty-eighth Parallel was placed under Com-munist control on the surrender of Japan in 1945. In 1948 the Russian forces withdrew and the conditions became even worse for the missions. On May 9, 1949 it was com-pletely suppressed. By then all church build-ings had been either destroyed or confiscated, and all foreign priests, monks, and nuns and Korean priests were imprisoned at P'yŏng-yang. There Bishop Bonifatius Sauer, five priests and three Brothers lost their lives. The others spent four years of cold, hunger, and forced labor in a camp near Kang-kye, where five priests, ten monks and two nuns died of starvation and ill treatment. Bishop Breher of Yenki and his clergy were deported to Germany as 'unwelcome guests' in 1949. The other German priests, monks and nuns who managed to survive in North Korea were finally rescued from Communist tyranny in 1953—a bitter-sweet experience, for the re-covery of their liberty meant departure from their beloved Korea, a severe separation for them.

Despite the loss of a third of their number by death and another third by protracted sickness and infirmity in their homeland, twelve of the deported returned to Korea after two years' rest and recuperation. In 1956 the Benedictines took charge of the missionary work in one city and six counties in the north of the Vicariate Apostolic of

Tae-gu: namely, Kim-ch'ŏn, Ch'il-kok, Sŏn-san, Sang-ju, Mun-kyŏng, Sŏng-ju and Keum-neung Counties, and Kim-ch'ŏn City, North Province of Kyŏng-sang. This meant the establishment of Vicariate Forane of Wae-kwan with Father Timothy Bitterli as Vicar Forane. Six years before, this district had only five churches for ten thousand believers. Now, with the Wae-kwan monastery plying the leading part it was soon (in June 1962) to possess fifteen churches, and a total num-ber of believers surpassing 30,000. A beautiful modern-style monastery has been erected at Wae-kwan, with dormitory, and both a boys' middle and high school, and a girls' middle and high school. There are now also five leprosaria where about five hundred victims of leprosy are receiving treatment. The Wae-kwan monastery runs an up-to-date Ger-man typographical installation in which the printing shop is putting out good books even more efficiently than the Tŏk-won printing shop did. Farming, carpentry, and metal-working projects are under way and ex-panding. Already the number of Benedictines is over one hundred and ten, not counting the nuns at Pu-san and Tae-gu, and most of them are native sons of the Republic of Korea.

In February 1964 the Benedictine monas-tery of Wae-kwan, which until then be-longed to the Tŏk-won Abbey, was raised to the status of Abbey, and Father Odo Hass was elected Abbot of Wae-kwan Ab-bey in the following April. The newly elected Abbot appointed Father Augustine Ro Prior, and Father Korbinian Schräfl Subprior. Msgr. Timothy Bitterli, the former Prior, continued to hold the post of Admini-strator of Ham-heung Diocese.

Conditions required of applicants:
1. Six months' training as Aspirant
2. One year's training as Postulant
3. One year of Novitiate
4. Period of temporal vows, three years.

THE SISTERS OF OUR LADY OF PERPETUAL HELP

1. FOUNDATION

The Maryknoll Fathers' effort in Korea begin in 1923 when Father Patrick J. Byrne took up residence in Sin-eui-ju on the Yalu River. Following the establishment of Prefecture Apostolic of P'yŏng-yang in 1927, covering the South and North Province of P'yŏng-an, the activities of the Maryknoll Fathers were increased remarkably.

Due to those increasing takes of evangelization Monsignor J. Morris, the second Prefect Apostolic of P'yŏng-yang, requested the Maryknoll Sisters of St. Dominic to undertake the training of Korean native Sisters. This resulted in the foundation of our congregation.

On the feast of Our Lady of Perpetual Help, June 27, 1932, our congregation was founded at Sang-su-ku-ri, P'yŏng-yang. At the beginning we underwent the training of novitiate under the guidance of Maryknoll Sisters. Mother Mary Geneviève, of the Maryknoll Sisters, engaged in the mission work at the time in Eui-ju and Yŏng-yu in North and South P'yŏng-an Province, was the first to take charge of our training, and Novice Mistress Mary Silvester took charge of our novitiate, with another Sister teaching handicrafts, and Sister Francisca Theresa specializing in the teaching of music and English. These American Sisters could not help returning on account of the repatriation to their native country, on the outbreak of World War II. After their departure from Korea, another Korean, Sister Mary Agnetta Chang Chŏng-on of the Maryknoll Sisters was appointed Novice Mistress. She had finished her own noviciate and training in New York, and had studied in the Sacred Heart University in Tokyo. From this time, we had elected Sister M. Peter Kang Song-hyo our representative, and Sister M. Famula

counselor, and were treated as an entity separated from the Maryknoll Sisters.

Once the approval of the Vatican had been conferred on us, on March 19, 1938, six years after the foundation of our congregation, sixteen postulants were formally admitted. Some of them had been waiting for six years. In 1940 eleven novices professed simple vows and were dispatched to the countryside for mission work. The number of novices showed a steady annual rate of increase.

Liberation from Japanese rule on August 15, 1945, brought us much joy, which was followed by bitterness and severe suffering. Nine of our Sisters were now preparing to take solemn vows of perpetual poverty, chastity, and obedience and had gathered at the Motherhouse for their second novitiate, and a spiritual retreat. A synod was held to elect the one of our number who would be Mother Superior of our congregation as soon as we had full members who had taken solemn vows.

On May 14, 1949, Bishop Francis Hong, Vicar Apostolic of P'yŏng-yang gave final tests to the expectant nuns but was taken captive by the Communists on his way home after completing our examination. Communist persecution was so violent that we were obliged to abandon our plan and disperse each to her own parish or to a friend's family. Prevented from taking perpetual vows, we renewed our temporary vows for a further period of one year. On May 25, 1950 our convent building was confiscated by the Communists. On October 4, Mother Agnetta Chang was taken captive, and is still missing, the first victim in our congregation. Her death only bound us survivors together more strongly.

2. IN SOUTH KOREA

On December 2, 1950 we made our way

to South Korea, and in Pu-san strove to rebuild our convent. At last, in 1955, we were able to establish our new headquarters in Heuk-sŏk-dong, Yŏng-dung-p'o, Seoul, and now it has 115 Sisters. In April, 1962, we have acquired a piece of woodland about 18,000 *p'yong* (about 59,400 square meters) in area in Chŏng-neung, Seoul and are putting heart and soul into the construction of our Motherhouse and novitiate house.

Our aspirant house is now located in Hyo-cha-dong, Ch'un-ch'ŏn, Kang-won Province, and the Most Rev. Quinlan, Bishop of Ch'un-ch'ŏn Diocese, has been our benefactor in providing us with quarters as well as a spiritual director.

At present we are running a foundling hospital in Pu-san, an orphanage in In-ch'ŏn, and a vocational guidance house and hospital in Seoul.

The total numbers of 115 Sisters includes twenty-five aspirants, fifteen postulants and 25 novices as of September 1962.

3. ITS SPIRIT

Our motto is *Sursum Corda* (Lift Up Your Hearts), a constant reminder to us to make persevering efforts to achieve unity with God through noble-mindedness and generosity in word and deed.

We take the three vows of religion, namely, poverty, Chastity and Obedience, according to the Augustinian rule. Our aim is to help others to salvation as well as seeking it for ourselves as follows:

1. Direct mission of giving assistance to parish priests.
2. Indirect mission of educational work, especially the education of women.
3. The salvation of souls through works of charity, including the institution of orphanages, almshouses, hospitals, and so on.

In order to foster the above work we have the more talented of our Sisters specially trained and educated in Korean universities or the Regina Mundi International Sisters' College in Rome, after they have taken their perpetual vows.

4. FOR APPLICANTS

Training Terms:
1. Aspirant Term: one year
2. Postulant Term: six months
3. Novitiate Term: two years

Qualifications:
1. Daughters born in wedlock.
2. Education up to the high-school level at least.
3. Sound mind and body, without congenital disease.
4. Women of at least three years' standing as baptized Catholics.
5. Aged from sixteen to twenty-six years on entry, with exceptions in special cases necessitated by studies.

THE MISSIONARY BENEDICTINE SISTERS

1. FOUNDATION

The Congregation of St. Ottilien Benedictine Houses was founded in 1884, and is concerned especially with foreign missions. The Motherhouse of the Benedictine nuns of this congregation, erected also at St. Ottilien, was moved in 1904 to Tutzing, near Munich. Though our Motherhouse is located in Germany, our Sisters come from at least twelve different nations, so that our congregation is international in character. The highest authority for our congregation in all countries and seat of our Mother General is therefore in Rome at Grotta Ferrata. There are more than 1,300 Benedictine Sisters in Germany, Switzerland, Italy, East Africa, South Africa, South-west Africa, North Brazil, South Brazil, North America, in the Philippines and in Korea, and recently a new foundation has been established in Portugal. All of them are trying to do their best to propagate the Kingdom of God in this world.

Though the convents at Tutzing and the other houses in Germany and Switzerland conduct hospitals and schools, their first and most important task is the education of missionary Sisters for work abroad, where they carry on schools, hospitals, orphanages, leprosariums, boarding schools, teacher-training colleges, and music conservatories.

2. IN KOREA

In Korea, since their arrival in 1925 at Won-san in response to the call from Bishop Bonifatius Sauer, O. S. B., our first Sisters overcame all the difficulties that confronted them as strangers in the land, and succeeded in establishing a novitiate for native Sisters, a hospital, several dispensaries, kindergartens and primary schools at Won-san, Ko-san, Hoe-ryong, Ch'ŏng-jin, Ham-heung, and Heung-nam, and operated them until May 1949 when the entire missionary personnel of priests, monks, and nuns were taken prisoner by the Communists, and all mission buildings either confiscated or destroyed.

The German Sisters, together with the priests and Brothers, lived for four years and eight months in prison and labor camp until by diplomatic intervention they were sent back to West Germany in 1954. Since 1955, after having recovered from their imprisonment, most of them returned to Korea.

After severe questioning, the imprisoned Korean Sisters were released and dispersed. During 1950 several of them succeeded in making their way to South Korea, where they took refuge with the Sisters of *St. Paul de Chartres.*

Suddenly war broke out on June 25, 1950 and they were forced to hide in the houses

of Christian friends. When the United Nations Forces recaptured Seoul and pushed northward, the Sisters planned to return to their beloved home. Several Sisters living in Won-san hastened to reopen our kindergarten there, living monastically and dedicating themselves whole-heartedly to their missionary work. They sent for the Sisters who were still at P'yŏng-yang and Seoul to come back to Won-san and help them as soon as possible. Then came the frightening news of the retreat of the United Nations troops. Just as the four Sisters in Seoul were about to flee to Pu-san on December 6, 1950, five Sisters from P'yŏng-yang suddenly appeared. The nine reached Pu-san safely on December 9 and went to the Chung-ang Church.

That evening the last steamer from Won-san had brought four of our Sisters and several candidates, together with hundreds of refugees to Pu-san. We could only thank God for His merciful Providence in bringing all our Sisters together from there such distant places.

Four had been unable to flee. Sister Agnetta Chang had been killed as a martyr for the faith in the prison at Ham-heung. Sister Lucia Park is still missing after her imprisonment at Sun-an near P'yŏng-yang, and presumed killed also.

The Sisters at Pu-san were kept busy. Six of them became nurses at the army hospital and cared for the wounded. The others worked as laundresses and seamstresses for the army. By the grace of God there were American priests there to help and encourage them. At the end of June, 1951, Msgr. Henry sent for seven of the Sisters to work at two locations in the Kwang-ju Prefecture, where they operated a kindergarten and were able to do very successful missionary work.

When the Sisters at Pu-san eventually got in touch with our Mother General, she dispatched Sister Othmara Ammann as their Superior to Korea. The Sisters selected Tae-gu as the site of their new Motherhouse. At Sin-am-dong, Tae-gu, a novitiate was erected and the education of native Sisters was begun.

3. ACTIVITIES

Today there are about eighty candidates, postulants and novices studying under the direction of their Sister-teachers and striving to perfect themselves so as to be able to spread the Kingdom of God in their own country.

The Sisters work at six different parishes and carry on missionary work at the Army and Air Force hospitals.

The Sisters also operate a kindergarten besides doing all kinds of missionary work. They make frequent visits to the jail to bring to the poor prisoners the knowledge and the love of Christ.

At Sŏng-ju, a branch house in the North Province of Kyŏng-sang our Sisters work in the same manner. They also make a tour to the rugged mountain districts to visit the widely-scattered families of farmers living there, and have been very succesful in their activity.

Our Sisters in Seoul, besides engaging in general missionary work, specialize in educational work for the deaf and dumb. They help them to earn their living, teach them a trade, and settle them in a colony.

Our developing congregation is full of hope for the future. There are now more Sisters than before the war. There are now forty-two Sisters, eighteen novices, twenty-eight postulants and about thirty candidates. Though our congregation has not been in Korea for very long, it has been through two wars, and has known life in a labor camp, flight, and refugee life.

Today missionary work is our first goal.

But in order to develop our hospital work, we have just completed the building of our Fatima Hospital with forty beds which will eventually be increased to seventy.

Our congregation in Korea is being well prepared for missionary and hospital duties, but education is also specifically one of its aims. This remains a problem for future solution and belongs to our extensive long-term plans. In the meantime we are taking pains to train Sisters who will be able to teach at home and abroad.

Under the Benedictine motto that "God Be Glorified in All Things," our congregation on the one hand praises God by a cloistered secluded life, the celebration of the Divine Office, spiritual reading, meditation, and the sanctification of self. On the other hand, it undertakes every work that may glorify God at every opportunity that He may grant to propagate the Kingdom of Christ. With the strict but mild rule of St. Benedict as our mirror we offer everything to Christ: "Thy Kingdom come!"

Training Terms:

Postulant: Two years.

Novitiate: One year.

Profession of Temporary Vows: Three Years.

Number of Professed Sisters: Forty-two.

Prioresses:

Mother Mathilde Hirsch	1925-1933
Mother Huberta Ilg	1933-1939
Mother Amberosia Engler	1939-1948
Mother Gertrude Link	1948-1954
Mother Othmara Ammann	1956-1961
Mother Immaculate Martel	1961-
	U.I.O.G.D.

THE SISTERS OF ST. BENEDICT

1. FOUNDATION

The Benedictine Sisters who in 1946 were banished by the Red Regime from Yenki, Manchuria, and later newly established in Ch'o-ryang, Pu-san, have their Motherhouse in Cham, Switzerland.

Our order is spiritually affiliated with the Olivetan Congregation whose founder, St. Bernardo Tolomei, through the disposition of Divine Providence and a vision of the Blessed Virgin Mary who revealed to him the Holy Rule of St. Benedict, and the white Benedictine habit they were to wear in her honor, established in 1313 an Abbey-nullius at Monte-Oliveanto near Siena, under an Abbot General, where they were to follow a strict interpretation of the Holy Rule. The Olivetan Benedictine Sisters not only observe this Holy Rule, but also strive to realize in their daily life the Benedictine motto: Ora et Labora (Work and Pray).

In view of the great importance of the part played by Mothers in social development, the teaching of girls and women has been, from the beginning, one of our major activities. In Switzerland, where our Motherhouse is located, there are many kindergartens, primary schools, high schools, and colleges conducted by our Sisters. Besides teaching, charitable work is another of our major activities. We maintain children's relief organization, hospitals, and tuberculosis sanatoriums.

2. IN YENKI, MANCHURIA

The history of our Pu-san Convent goes back to 1931 when the Benedictine Sisters came to Yenki Vicariate in Manchuria with the Benedictine Fathers from St. Ottilien. There were seventeen Swiss Sisters, two German Sisters and one Italian Sister until 1945, when we were joined by nineteen Korean Sisters. We worked at eight parishes teaching catechism and doing charity work in our own small hospital and several dispensaries. Our work there was successful in line with the development of Yenki Vicariate until the end of World War II and occupation by the Russian Army in 1945, which dealt the death blow to All our activities. Living in Communist territory, we awaited guidance from Almighty God. In 1946 all Church property was confiscated or destroyed and all foreign

priests, monks, and Sisters were jailed. The Swiss Sisters were fortunately released after a single night in jail when it was known that they were citizens of a neutral nation. In announcing that we were free they added that we would have to live under house arrest, and this we did, supporting ourselves by the skills we had been taught, such as tailoring, knitting, factory labor, painting and nursing. Since we could not earn much in this way, kind-hearted Korean Catholics used to give us help. Our restrictions became more stringent in the last two years of the war, and we were not permitted to meet Catholic laymen. The Catholics were kind to the point of heroism, risking their lives to bring us food and clothing. We still vividly remember how their gifts of a few eggs, corn on the cob, and vegetables helped us to survive.

In November 1949 four of our Sisters were permitted to return to Switzerland via Tientsin and Hongkong. The rest of the Sisters also returned their homelands in 1950 and 1951. The Korean Sisters left Manchuria for South Korea by disguising themselves as house-wives and so on.

Two years after our departure from Manchuria, fourteen Sisters met in South Korea. Two Sisters were unable to escape and three Sisters died in Manchuria.

3. IN SOUTH KOREA

We paid a visit to the Most Rev. Paul M. Ro, then Bishop of Seoul, and he helped us to get to an orphanage in Ch'ŏng-ju which was being run by Father Philip Kim. There we worked for our keep. Our first duty was to become self-supporting in our daily life. Mother Aloysia Yu started to raise chickens because that was the only kind of business we could engage in without much working capital. To get a good breed of hen, she tramped many miles through the countryside from village to village until she finally became lame. Since we were not experienced chicken farmers, we made lots of mistakes and failed over and over again, and often laughingly compared ourselves to Bouvard and Pecuchet.

Since the Korean Church had no money to spare at the time and we could not get in touch with our Motherhouse, there was no way for us to raise funds enough to build a new convent. However, in 1949, the Motherhouse found means to send us some money and with this we bought a small house and orchard at So-sa, on the outskirts of Seoul city. We set to work to repair it ourselves and worked hard throughout the summer.

Disaster never left us for long. Even before we could celebrate our first anniversary there, the Korean War broke out in June 1950 and our project was nipped in the bud. In December 1950 we had to take refuge in Pu-san. We borrowed a room from a Catholic in Pu-san, and lived there together. the Most Rev. Paul M. Ro, then Bishop of Seoul, and Monsignor George Carroll helped us with our daily needs.

4. ACTIVITIES

In November 1951, Dr. Yu Eul-jun asked us to join him in taking care of the poor sick refugees. We were then able to borrow two rooms in Ch'o-ryang-dong, Pu-san, one for a doctor's consulting room and the other for a dispensary. The number of patients increased day by day, so that it became impossible to carry on in such restricted quarters. It was imperative for us to find more spacious quarters, and to get an ampler supply of medicines. In both aspects we received considerable help through the generosity of the Korea Civil Assistance Command (KCAC) and Army chaplains of all religious denominations. The more medicines we received, the more patients we were able to deal with, and the more we were obliged to extend our operations by purchasing other small buildings in the vicinity, one by one. In 1952, fifty patients were treated in their homes free of charge, and the number of patients treated in the clinic increased to between four and six hundred a day. In due course we set up a surgical clinic, dental clinic, eye clinic, and ENT (Ear, Nose and Throat) clinic. The

number of patients now sometimes rose to a thousand a day. Though the different sections were housed in separate buildings, none of them was adequate to cope with such a large number of daily patients. A large, properly equipped and hygienic hospital building was now a *sine qua non*.

When 1953, Mother Superior Nicola Faessler and Sister Irementrud Meier came to Korea, we were indeed relieved and delighted. In 1954, through the generous assistance of AFAK (Armed Forces Assistance to Korea), we were able to establish a polyclinic in a four-story building on a site of 588 *p'yŏng* in area (one *p'yŏng*=3.3058 square meters). The Army supplied the building materials free of charge, and our Motherhouse supplied the funds to pay for the labor and the equipment. In March 1958, Sister Beda, who was Mistress of Novices in Manchuria, and Sister Ursula, a nurse, arrived in Korea. As the necessity to start a new young Sisterhood was now evident, we had much reason to rejoice and thank God for His merciful guidance.

While the clinic was being built, the department for the treatment of in-patients and surgical cases was still functioning in the old barracks. On September 17, 1959, there was a severe typhoon which seriously threatened the stability of this old barracks in which the inpatients were being treated. We were therefore obliged to begin the construction of another building, a five-story edifice for about sixty patients, with financial aid supplied by voluntary contributions from Swiss individuals and a gift and loan from the German *Misericordia*.

In 1961 our Sisters were invited to teach in the new girls' middle and high school at Kim-ch'ŏn. A small convent had to be built for the school Sisters.

In May, 1962, we could finally say with St. Benedict: "Let us establish a school in the Lord's service;" *i.e.* "Let us build our Motherhouse and novitiate in Korea for the many vocations in this country!" In Kwang-an-dong near Pu-san, we bought a piece of land 1,900 *p'yŏng* in area and a Swiss architect worked on the plans for its construction. Now, sixteen years after our expulsion from the convent in Manchuria, after a series of inconveniences and frustrations, we give thanks to God and look forward to moving into our long-desired monastery at an early date. At present we have fifty-two Korean Sisters, four foreign Sisters, six training Sisters, and eighty aspirants and postulants. "Lord,

we will praise Thy blessing for ever and ever."

The Benedictine tradition is pre-eminently a family tradition. Our apostolate grows from prayer and family life. Through the peace, joy, and security of our family life, we try to show by example what family life should be in the world.   U.I.O.G.D.

THE HANDMAIDS OF THE SACRED HEART OF JESUS

1. FOUNDATION

Some years ago in a small Korean village eleven young girls from old Catholic families met together one Sunday afternoon. They wanted to make better use of their lives by doing something outstandingly beautiful . . . what was this to be? They were going to hold a meeting to see if they could find the answer. They had very little money, but were rich in good will and faith. They decided that they would make their faith live by charitable works. One of them spoke of a lonely old man who lived nearly in extreme poverty and without help from friends. Another mentioned the orphan boy of the village, who also led a miserable life, neglected and often hungry. Still another proposed teaching the catechism. There was no lack of ideas.

This was in the village of Yong-p'yŏng, Hwa-sam-myŏn, Yŏng-ch'ŏn, North Province of Kyŏng-sang, and the year was 1934. Though they arrived at no definite program at this inaugural meeting, their group became nucleus of a society which grew in importance. Their timid but generous initiative was the beginning of their apprenticeship in the apostolate.

One day one of these young women baptized a very old lady who seemed to be at the point of death. But the old lady didn't die, and they were concerned about her future, and whether she would keep her faith.

They had brought her into the Church and felt responsible for making her understand what this meant. They acquired a small cottage for her and helped her with material and spiritual support. This was the beginning of their old folks' home.

Shortly afterward a poor Catholic woman, whose husband had been sent to a leprosarium, abandoned her child one night and disappeared, and the young women brought up the child. That was the beginning of the orphanage, which now takes care of 380 children. Soon the village of Yŏng-p'yŏng was no longer able to afford them scope for their work, and they began to visit the neighboring villages, bring help and comfort, and teach the catechism.

On December 8, 1935, six of these eleven girls decided to consecrate their lives to God. Thus was born the first Korean congregation of Sisters, later to be known as The Handmaids of the Sacred Heart of Jesus.

Their spiritual director was a missionary priest of the *Société des Missions-Étrangères de Paris* (the Paris Foreign Mission Society), Father Louis Deslandes, or "Nam *Sin-pu*" as he was known in Korean. He already had twelve years of fruitful apostolic work behind him, in Nak-san, Pu-san-jin and Tae-gu, and now he was assigned to the Yong-p'yŏng district.

2. EXPANSION

In May 1940 this small group, which had now grown to sixteen, with their spiritual director, Father Deslandes, moved to Yŏng-ch'ŏn, taking the orphans and old people with them. Several of the Sisters were sent to Japan to study; the rest had to work hard, even tilling the fields and doing the work of men.

As their work of making Christ known extended, the Japanese authorities then governing Korea grew suspicious. They were always on the lookout for 'secret societies' that might be agitating for Korean independence. Eventually they arrested twelve of the Sisters on account of their 'suspicious correspondence with their colleagues in Japan. Japanese jailors are well-known for their cruelty, but they were impressed with the holy lives of these prisoners. The Japanese promised to set free any of the Sisters who would renounce their vows and get married. Some of them did, including the Sisters in Japan. Most of them, however, persevered in their vocation, and bore the hardships of imprisonment for five months. Father Deslandes was himself arrested on December 8, 1941, but was released three weeks later, but both he and the Sisters were kept under close surveillance until Liberation Day, August 15, 1945. When that day arrived, the Sisters were kept busy caring for the refugees and the sick.

In 1948, when the Vicariate of Tae-gu passed from the care of the *Société des Missions-Étrangères de Paris* to that of Korean priests, Father Deslandes had to leave Yŏng-ch'ŏn. A small group of the Sisters went to Chuk-to-dong village in P'o-hang to teach, but the main group went to Song-jŏng, a village several miles from P'o-hang. There they acquired some woodlands and rice fields totaling 100,000 *p'yŏng* in area (one *p'yŏng*=3.3058 square meters) along the bay. When Father Deslandes's parents died, he received an inheritance, which he used to give the congregation a firm financial standing.

In 1952, when Bishop John Ch'oe was in Tae-gu Vicariate, Archbishop Maximilian de Furstenberg, the Apostolic Delegate to Japan, satisfied that the congregation had spread and given evidence of its vitality, requested the Holy See to grant its approval of the order. Father Deslandes then asked two of the Sisters of the Congregation of *St. Paul de Chartres* to come from Seoul and direct the infant organization. Seven of the ten young women took the veil as postulants.

On September 8, 1952, these seven received their new habits. The number of aspirants went on growing, until now there are ninety-four Sisters who have taken vows, eighty-four novices, and about ninety-five postulants and aspirants. In 1959 a dependent house was founded at Song-jŏng.

The Sisters occupy themselves mainly with parish work. They are working in fifteen mission stations spread throughout North and South Ch'ung-ch'ŏng, North and South Kyŏng-sang, and North Chŏl-la Provinces, and many of the Sisters are engaged in apostolic work in these districts. Others at the main convent care for 400 orphans, babies, and old folks.

3. ITS SPIRIT

The aim of the congregation is twofold. to labor for those forsaken by society, and to assist the priests by prayer, penance, and work. They look after anyone who has no home or who cannot look after himself. They pray for the priests and offer up their lives of penance for the work of the priests. They do not aim at spectacular objectives, but try to lead a spiritual life without worrying about the future. "Do not fret, then, over tomorrow; leave tomorrow to fret over its own needs; for today, today's troubles are enough." (St. Matthew, 6:34)

The order differs from other congregations in that it receives all who have the desire to be a Sister, even though they have had little or no education. There are many convents in the world for educated people, but few for the uneducated. Father Deslandes wanted to start one for just such women. Hence the name: The Handmaids of the Sacred Heart of Jesus

Actually there is no definite limit to the work of the congregation. The Sisters will undertake the most difficult tasks as Handmaids of the Lord. As their number grows

they will be able to do more and more in compliance with the requests of many of the bishops. Small and weak an instrument as it may appear now, with God's grace it will flourish and live for His greater glory.

THE ORDER OF FRIARS MINOR

(Province of Canada)

1. FOUNDATION

Saint Francis of Assisi (Giovannie Francesco Bernadone 1182-1226) experienced as a young man a spiritual crisis while on a military expedition, as a consequence of which he lived for a time in solitude and prayer and devoted himself to the relief of the poor, the sick, and the lepers. He was joined by disciples, the first of the Franciscan Order of Friars Minor, for whom he drew up the rule in 1209. He preached in Italy and went to the Holy Land and Spain. The special note of his teaching was joyousness and love of Nature. His rule was approved by Pope Innocent III and his life and message received a direct sanction from Christ in 1224 when on September 14 Francis received the Stigmata of the Passion on Mount Alverno.

There are three Franciscan rules: for the friars, the nuns (Poor Clares) and the lay tertiaries. The definitive rule for the Friars is that of the year 1223. Various interpretations and constitutions in regard to it have been made from time to time by the Holy See. It is followed by the Friars Minor and the Capuchins. The Conventuals keep it according to the constitutions of Pope Urban VIII (1628) which sanctioned certain modifications especially with regard to poverty. In accordance with it, boots and shoes may be worn only in case of necessity, the Divine Office is said daily in choir, all Fridays are fasting days. There must be corporate as well as individual abandonment of all property, the particular evangelical work of the

Brothers is preaching, and provision is made for the conduct of missions to the heathen. Franciscan life is summed up as being "to observe the Holy Gospel of Our Lord Jesus Christ by living in obedience, without goods, and in chastity." Pope Nicolaus III in 1279 decreed that the clause about property should be understood in the sense that the Brothers were to have no more than the "moderate use" of things necessary, without any ownership therein.

2. ORGANIZATIONS

The Franciscans are the Friars Minor founded by St. Francis of Assisi in 1209. They form one Order of Friars Minor, divided into three distinct and independent branches, of which one is known simply as Friars Minor (O.F.M. *Observantium*), another as Friars Minor Conventual (O.F.M. *Conventualium*) and the other as Friars Minor Capuchin (O.F.M. *Capucinorum*). The Friars Minor and Capuchins are the second and the third largest orders in the Church and were known as Grey Friars in England.

The nuns are called Poor Clares, and there are several congregations of Sisters of the Third Order Regular. There are two branches of the Poor Clares, the Colettines and the Urbanists. There is also a branch of the Poor Clares called the Capuchinesses, having the Capuchin constitutions and in some cases subject to the Minister General of that order. Other Capuchin Sisters are engaged in active work. The Colettines are strictly cloistered. They rise for night office at midnight, and again at 5 a.m. Fasting and abstinence are perpetual; the Divine Office is recited, not sung; 6 hours of work a day; one hour's recreation; bed at 8 p.m. The habit is brown, and they go barefoot except out of doors when they wear sandals. The Urbanists follow Pope Urban's modification of this rule, and some of their convents undertake external work. There are many other congregations following the rule of the Third Order of St. Francis in all parts of the world, most of which have no other connection with the order. They are principally women. The most important are the Third Order Regular of Carmelites; Dominican Sisters, who combine the contemplative with the active life, teaching school, nursing, etc., and Franciscans, priests, Brothers, and Sisters, all engaged in active work.

3. IN KOREA

In September 1937, the Franciscans of Friars Minor came to Korea. They set up a monastery at Mok-dong, Tae-jŏn, in October 1939. Due to the outbreak of Pacific War the monastery was temporarily suspended from December 8, 1941 to September 26, 1945. In July 1950 the monastery was forced by the Korean War to disperse its members; however, they reopened the monastery in April 1955.

In 1955 two priests of the Friars Minor came to Korea from the Italian Province, and are devoting themselves to evangelization and charity work in Chin-ju district, South Province of Kyŏng-sang. In October 1958 two Franciscans of Friars Minor Conventual came to Korea, and are devoting themselves to preaching the Gospel both in Pu-san and Tae-gu. They set up the Whasŏng Seminary at Pŏm-ŏ-dong, Tae-gu in September 1964.

Training Terms:
  Aspirant Term: Three Years
  Postulant Term: One Year
  Novitiate Term: Three Years
  Membership: Four Priests, four Brothers and ten aspirants.
Priors:
  Fr. John Joseph (Founder)
  Fr. Justin Bellerose (Second Prior)
  Fr. Peter Ahn Sŏn-o (Third Prior)
  Fr. Jean Berchmans Prévost (Present Prior)

THE MARYKNOLL SISTERS OF ST. DOMINIC

1. FOUNDATION

The Maryknoll Sisters were founded by a small group of women who came to help with the *Field Afar* magazine, then edited by Father James Anthony Walsh and Father Frederick Price, cofounders of the Maryknoll Fathers, in 1911. This group felt a religious desire to form a congregation of women for the foreign missions, and under the guidance and leadership of Mary Rogers, later to be known as Mother Mary Joseph, they began training for the religious life and were approved by the Holy See on February 14, 1920, to be known as Maryknoll Sisters. Since all new congregations have to be affiliated with an already established rule, that of the Dominicans was chosen and the Sisters' training was begun by a Dominican Sister from Sinsinawa, Wisconsin. Being part of the Dominican Order, the Congregation was called Foreign Mission Sisters of St. Dominic but in 1954, with the approval of the Holy See, this was changed to Maryknoll Sisters of St. Dominic.

The foundress, Mother Mary Joseph Rogers, was Superior General of the congregation until 1946. She died in 1955. Mother Mary Columba Tarpey was the second Mother General and served two terms. The present and third Mother General is Mother Mary Colman who visited Korea in May 1961. The Motherhouse of the Maryknoll Sisters is at Maryknoll, New York, on the Hudson River, thirty miles above New York City. The name Maryknoll is taken from the site at which the foundation was first made, a hill top on the countryside, and the founders wishing to call the mission group after Our Lady, named it Mary's knoll—Maryknoll.

As an integral part of the congregation there is the Maryknoll Cloister, founded in 1932. The cloister is not an end in itself but a means reserved for certain Sisters representing the entire congregation to glorify God and, remembering the petition of Christ, "Thy Kingdom come, Thy will be done on earth as it is in Heaven," to draw His paternal solicitude on all Maryknollers and their works in particular, and on all mission endeavor in general, by a life of living comtemplation, prayer, fasting, and penance. The Sisters follow the rule of Second Order Dominicans. A Sister must complete her novitiate in the active branch before requesting permission to enter the cloister.

2. OVERSEAS EXPANSION

The first venture in foreign lands of Maryknoll Sisters in spreading the Gospel was the mission opened in Hongkong in 1921. At the time of expulsion from South China the Sisters there numbered sixty. In 1962 there are 114 Maryknoll convents, eighty-one of which are on the missions. Maryknoll Sisters number close on 1,600. From China, missions spread to Manchuria, Korea, Japan, the Philippines, and Hawaii. When the Orient was closed to missionaries during World War II, missions were opened in Central and South America and in Africa. Work is also done with various racial groups within the United States. After the war, work in the Orient was resumed except when the Sisters were expelled by the Communists from Manchuria in 1948 and China in 1950. Work in Ceylon has closed out because the activities of religious communities are at a standstill there.

There are novitiates for Maryknoll Sisters at Maryknoll, New York; St. Louis, Missouri; and Topsfield, Massachusetts. A new novitiate for Asian candidates was opened in 1961 in Manila, the Philippines, with five aspirants, two from the Philippines, one from Hongkong, one from Japan and one from Ceylon. Another group of eight postulants entered in 1962. The training period for the novitiate in the United States is nine months' postulancy, two years novitiate, and six years temporary vows preceding perpetual vows.

The work of the Maryknoll Sisters is varied, covering parish and catechetical, home visiting, social service, medical, educational, secretarial, and training of native novitiates. The work on many of the missions is carried on in cooperation with the Maryknoll Fathers.

3. IN KOREA

The Mission in Korea was first opened in Eui-ju, North Korea, with houses in Yŏng-yu, Sin-eui-ju, and P'yŏng-yang. At the request of the Maryknoll Fathers the training of a Korean community was undertaken. This group later became known as the Sisters of Our Lady of Perpetual Help. The work of the various missions in Korea fructified until 1942, when the priests and Sisters were put under house arrest and later repatriated by Japanese.

In 1949 three Sisters returned to Korea to operate an outpatient clinic in Pu-san. In 1950, when the Communists came down from North Korea, the Sisters were evacuated to Japan but with the permission of General Douglas MacArthur, the Commander-in-Chief of the United Nations Command were allowed to return again in 1951 when they resumed the clinic work taking care of sick refugees from North Korea. The original three Sisters were joined by two more and each year has seen more Sisters coming so that there were thirty-eight, in 1962, working in Korea, among whom are doctors, nurses, medical technologists, pharmacists, social service workers, and catechetical Sisters.

In those days our clinic was treating an average of five hundred outpatients a day, in cooperation with Korean doctors, and nurses, and the total staff numbers over eighty.

The clinic has an Adult and Pediatric Department, Cardiac Clinic, Orthopaedic and Physio-therapy Department, Social Service Department, and Home Visiting TB Program. An integral part of the program is the Catechetical Department where one Sister works with five lay catechists who do home visiting to patients who have received Emergency Baptisim or became interested in the Church through contact with the clinic. The clinic and the entire work of the Maryknoll Sisters in Pu-san is maintained largely by the charity of Catholics and friends in America through whose faithful generosity we are able to contribute to the care of the sick-poor here.

In conjunction with the parish Church the Sisters conduct doctrine classes for poor children, and Baptism and Confirmation classes for women. Literacy classes are also given for those women and children who are not able to read.

Credit Union work, begun in Pu-san two years ago with the employes of the Maryknoll Clinic, has expanded to five groups in Pu-san numbering over five hundred members, and a Credit Union or Seminar in each of the provinces in South Korea. The program now includes a leadership training course and in general has been accepted as a constructive self-help project by all the leaders and members.

As part of the Maryknoll Fathers' work in North Province of Ch'ung-ch'ŏng, Ch'ŏng-ju Diocese, a small dispensary was opened in Cheung-p'yŏng in 1956. There are five Sisters doing medical, home visiting, and catechetical work there, taking care of 150-200 patients a day together with their Korean staff.

On March 7, 1964 a 160-bed hospital which was known as Maryknoll Sisters Armed Forces Memorial Hospital was opened to the public. The hospital was constructed with the help of the Armed Forces Assistance to Korea (AFAK), and dedicated to Our Lady of the Rosary. On the occasion the desired Catholic Nursing School was also opened. They are planning a program for internes and a school for medical technicians (hospital technicians).

It is hoped that, through our prayers and works and in union with other priests and Sisters working here, we may help to extend the Kingdom of God in Korea so that we may all be made one in Christ.

THE DISCALCED CARMELITES OF THE ANNUNCIATION

1. FOUNDATION

The Carmelites, or Brothers of the Order of the most blessed Mother of God and ever Virgin Mary of Mount Carmel, have claimed descent from hermits living on that mountain under the direction of Elias and Eliseus. For practical purposes their history may be said to begin in 1150, when a hermitage of western men was founded there by St. Bert-hold. Their hermits spread to Europe, and under an Englishman, St. Simon Stock, modified their life and became mendicant friars. The reforming activities of St. Theresa of Avila (1515-1582) and St. John-of-the-Cross (1542-1591) resulted in two independent branches of the order. (a) The Calced or Shod Carmelites, (properly called "of the Old Observance") are the parent stem. They have modified their original rule, e.g. as regards fasting, abstinence, night office, and the like, but retain their medieval liturgy. (b) The Discalced, Barefooted, or Teresian Carmelites say the Divine Office daily in choir, rising from bed for the night office, and mental prayer is also made in common, twice a day. Abstinence is perpetual and there are special fasts. The Motherhouse on Mount Carmel is peopled by the Discalced.

The nuns of the order, founded in 1452 with papal sanction under the "mitigated" rule then in force, spread rapidly, producing among other saints Maria Magdalena de' Pazzi (1566-1607). From 1562 St. Theresa of Avila founded convents under the primitive non-mitigated rule, which are now far more numerous than the others. Among them, two kinds of constitutions are in force, differing but slightly, both approved by the Church, and both recognized as Theresian. The nuns live in poverty and have strict enclosure, limited numbers, perpetual abstinence and silence (except two hours' recreation), choir office, mental prayer, and manual work.

2. IN KOREA

In 1940 the Carmelite Convent was opened in Korea. The pioneeress was Mother Mechtilde Devriese, then the Prioress of Carmelite Convent of Aire-sur-Adour in southwest France. Several members of the Carmelites followed soon after Mother Mechtilde. Their first convent was washed away by a flood, and another had to be built. Then there came the difficult years of World War II and, after ten years devotion in Korea they met the disastrous Korean War in 1950. When the Communists invaded South Korea, Mother Mechtilde and her four European companions were arrested by the Communists in Seoul together with a large number of foreign priests and Sisters including Bishop Byrne, the first Apostolic Delegate to Korea.

Mother Mechtilde and Mother Thérèse Bastin, the Prioress, died during the Death March in the northernmost region of the Korea-Manchuria border, in November, 1950.

After their three years' miserable life in the prison camp in North Korea, three survivors of the Carmelites, Sisters Henriette de Lobit, Bernadette Descayaux and Marie-Madeleine Marquier, were repatriated to their home country. Nevertheless they returned to their own convent in Seoul January 1954.

They built an elegant convent at Su-yu-ri, in the northern outskirts of Seoul, and moved there in August 1964.

Training Terms:
Aspirant: One year
Novice: Four years
Profession of Temporary Vows: Three years
Membership, regular nuns: Fifty-seven
souls

Prioresses:
Mother Mechtilde Devriese, martyr, died on Nov. 18, 1950 in prison camp, from 1940 to 1949.
Mother Thérèse Bastin, martyr, died on November 30, 1950 in prison camp, from 1949 to 1950.
Mother Henriette de Lobit, from 1950 to 1960.
Mother Mary Clare of the Trinity, from 1960 to present.

THE ORDER OF DISCALCED CARMELITES IN PU-SAN

This convent received the approval of the Holy See on July 8, 1955. It was founded in Pu-san, with the assistance of Monsignor George Carroll, and Fathers Andrew Ch'oe Sŏk-u and Joseph Chŭng Chae-sŏk, by Mother Marie Elizabeth Park and a Belgian Sister. There are four postulants who have taken the veil. On October 13, 1961 the cloister was formally consecrated by Monsignor Joseph Chŭng Chae-sŏk, Vicar General of Pu-san, in the absence abroad of the Vicar Apostolic of Pu-san, Bishop Jone Ch'oe.

THE HOLY FAMILY SISTERS

1. FOUNDATION

This Korean congregation was founded on Christmas day, 1943, under the spiritual direction of a French priest, Father Peter, in the precincts of Saint Benedict's Church, Hye-hwa-dong, with the Most Rev. Paul M. Ro, Bishop (now Archbishop) of Seoul as Superior General, and Father Peter as spiritual director. It began with the reception of three aspirants who took the veil with the intention of leading the life of nuns. In 1945 Sister Thecla Chang was appointed provisional Superior. On July 1, 1947, a dependent house was established in Hap-tŏk, South Province of Ch'ung-ch'ŏng, together with an orphanage. On February 3, 1949, it received the formal approval of the Vatican.

On October 1, 1949, another dependent house was opened at P'yŏng-t'aek, Kyŏng-ki Province.

With the outbreak of the Korean War on June 25, 1950, the convent was moved to Pu-san, where it established its provisional headquarters in Tae-ch'ŏng-dong.

On April 15, 1952, a branch was established in Hu-am-dong, Seoul and another at Tang-jin in South Province of Ch'ung-ch'ŏng, and received charge of the Old Folks' Home from Father Laurent Youn Eul-su.

On Novenber 21, 1952, Mother Immanuel Kim became Superior of the Motherhouse and stepped-up efforts were made to further development of the congregation.

On January 9, 1954 the convent took over the management of an orphanage in Chung-rim-dong, Seoul, from a Belgian, M. Pales.

On April 2, 1954 the convent was assigned the management of the Saint Joseph Hospital in Chung-rim-dong. On the same day it formally opened another branch at Eui-Chŏng-pu and began to operate a kindergarten school attached to it.

The Holy Family Orphanage in Chung-rim-dong was moved to more commodious quar-

ters in So-sa, where a farm, an orchard and land were acquired for the purpose.

In June 1955 another branch was opened at Che-ch'ŏn, and in June 1956 another at Mi-a-dong.

On July 20, 1957, a branch was opened in A-hyŏn-dong, and on September 2, 1957 another in Tae-pang-dong showing steady development during the five years of Mother Immanuel's tenure of office.

On November 21, 1957, Mother Simon Ko was elected the second Superior of the Motherhouse.

On August 23, 1958, the congregation opened the new Holy Family Hospital in Mi-a-dong, and on March 16, 1959, 563 *p'yŏng* of adjoining land was acquired for additional hospital building. On April 28, 1959, the Saint Joseph Hospital was transferred to the Catholic Medical College.

On May 6, 1959, the Old Folks' Home in Hu-am-dong was moved to So-sa.

On November 27, 1959, a branch was opened at On-yang.

In July, 1960, the first phase of construction of a Holy Family Hospital started.

On December 20, 1960, the Widows' Home was dedicated in Tong-ja-dong, Seoul. In the same year the congregation accepted the management of a dressmaking school for widows, from the Chung-rim-dong Church.

On July 12, 1961, the formal opening of a branch took place in the precincts of the Cathedral closure of Chŏn-ju Vicariate. On July 14, 1961, the congregation opened a branch in Puk-sŏ-dong, Su-won. In the same year, the congregation's Nazareth Vocational Institute received formal approval. On June 1, 1962, a branch was set up in Tang-san-dong, Seoul.

The Holy Family Sisters now operate nineteen branch convents throughout the country, and total number of 172 Sisters consists of seventy-two professed Sisters, twenty novices, fifty-five postulants and four students studying abroad.

2. INSTITUTES UNDER DIRECT CONTROL

School: So-myŏng Girls' Middle and
               High School
Kindergarten: Holy Family Kindergarten,
               Mi-a-dong
Orphanage: Holy Family Orphanage,
               Seoul
Old Folks' Home: So-sa Old Folks' Home
Hospital: Mi-a-ri Hospital, Seoul
Dressmaking School for Widows: Chung-
               rim-dong, Seoul
Vocational School for Widows: Nazareth
               Vocational School for Wi-
               dows, Chung-rim-dong, Seoul

3. FOR APPLICANTS

Training Terms:

Postulants: Two years
Novices: Two years
Profession of Temporary Vows: Five years.

Qualifications:

1. Women between the ages of 20 and 30
   years.
2. Possessed of rightful aspiration, and determination to serve the poor, upholding
   the spirit of Lord Jesus Christ.
3. Of good conduct, and willing to obey
   the rule and regulations of the Convent.
4. Born in wedlock.
5. Docile.
6. Free of hereditary disease.

THE BROTHERS OF THE BLESSED KOREAN MARTYRS

1. FOUNDATION

A Religious Society established by our own
efforts in the land where our forefathers embraced the Faith of their own accord.

This Religious Society was founded in 1952,
and after having proved its viability received
the approval of the Holy See in 1956.

For four years, or five, to be exact, we led
an underground life, in cellar, closet, or tent.
Our aim was to walk the Way of the Cross
which our predecessors had followed in the
eighteenth century and after, as Our Lord
showed us.

We came to this decision in accordance
with the historical fact that Korea is the only
country in which the people went abroad
and fetched the faith to the nation of their
own accord without waiting to have it
brought to them by foreign missionaries. As
one of the latter smilingly said "I always
think of the Koreans as 'do-it-yourself' Catholics." Our postulants therefore realize
that they must make every effort to accom-

plish our end no matter what cost in hardship and difficulties.

"Where there's a will, there's a way." God
helps those who help themselves, and by His
grace we are able to report the following
development.

Our membership, including postulants,
novices and monks who have taken the vow,
now numbers more than three score and
ten, and they are working in the Motherhouse and in monasteries scattered throughout the country.

2. ACTIVITIES

To the Motherhouse are attached a ma-
chine-shop, a carpentry, a light industry
plant, and an architectural department. In
the countryside we are running two hospitals,
a vocational school, a civic school, and
farming over two hundred thousand *p'yŏng*
of arable land and pasture. (one *p'yŏng*=
3,3058 square meters). We have been able
to carry on these activities on a self-support-

ing basis, proof enough that those who work for the sake of their love of God will receive His blessings in abundance.

Our Motherhouse was founded in November 1957 at Sŏng-puk-dong, Seoul. Its present members number forty-one, and the majority of them are engaged in various handicrafts. In October 1957 the Sae-nam-t'ŏ branchhouse was opened at I-ch'ŏn-dong, Seoul, with two members. They are now managing the Martyrs School. The Che-ju branchhouse was opened in August 1959 at Sŏ-kwi-p'o, Che-ju Province, with three members. They are engaged in farming; horticulture, persimmons and orchards. In March 1961, the In-ch'ŏn branchhouse was also opened at Man-su-dong, In-ch'ŏn, with eight members engaged in livestock raising.

The fact that we could achieve so much in such a short space of time is due entirely to God's bounty. "Unless the Lord build the house, they labor in vain that build it", (Psalms, 126:1) We believe that we monks, who are the descendants of the martyrs, are continuing their work, assisted by the Blessed Martyrs in Heaven, without which we could not have had such a conspicuous success.

3. ITS SPIRIT

Sanctification, or justification is the main purpose of our society: in the first place, to sanctify ourselves by the faithful fulfilment of our duty and by following the teaching of the Gospels, the Sacred Constitution, and the Manual of the Catholic Church, and cultivating the Three Virtues; and in the second place, to train religious priests, to spread the faith, and to preach the Gospel.

With regard to the mystic principle and practice of sanctification, we exercise the ascetic spirit in theory and practice, separating ourselves from the temporal world. We resolve to apply the principle of asceticism in all the situations of time, place, matter and circumstances of the world, without exception.

The rule is so strict that it may not be relaxed for a single moment, therefore all the monks realize that the degree to which they approach perfection depends largely on their own efforts.

4. CONDITIONS OF ENROLLMENT

As our society is one of Clerks Regular, it consists of priests and Brothers. In the course and period of training, the aspirants must undergo a period of probation before being admitted to the two-year aspirants' course.

After the two-year postulants' course, they take the novitiate course which also lasts two years, and it followed by a four-year period of profession of temporary vows, after which they make perpetual vows.

The requirements for applicants are as follows:

1. Applicants must have been baptized at least three years before they can be accepted.
2. Those who contemplate taking Holy Orders must have completed their high-school education. Others wishing to be Brothers must have completed middle school education.
3. Applicants must be between the ages of fourteen and thirty years.
4. In exceptional cases older candidates may be considered for admission if there is no subsisting impediment of marriage.

5. MEMBERSHIPS

Professed Monks:	One (perpetual vows)
	Seven (temporary vows)
Novices:	Thirty
Aspirants:	Nine
Postulants:	Seven

THE SISTERS OF THE BLESSED KOREAN MARTYRS

1. FOUNDATION

On April 21, 1946, the centennial of the death of the Korean martyr, Blessed Andrew Kim Tae-kǒn, the Convent of the Korean Martyrs came into being in Kae-sǒng under the aegis of the first Korean Bishop, (now Archbishop of Seoul), the Most Rev. Paul M. Ro, promoted by Father Leo Pang, with the aim of filling the gap left in the number of Korean nuns, and at the same time to uphold and perpetuate the veneration of the Seventy-nine Beatified Korean Martyrs and to spread the Gospel.

On March 8, 1950 the Motherhouse moved from Kae-sǒng to the present site at Ch'ǒng-p'a-dong, Seoul. The congregation was approved by the Holy See on December 12, 1952.

2. ORGANIZATION

Still pending are a Contemplative Order, and an Active Order to be responsible for missionary activities and simple labor. The preparations include a two-year postulancy, a novitiate of eighteen months, and two years in temporary vows, renewable for a further period of two years, after which come perpetual vows. It therefore takes ten years before a nun is permitted to take perpetual vows.

3. PROGRESS

Under the supervision of the Most Rev. Paul M. Ro, Archbishop of Seoul, who has expressed his gratification at our silent growth and the work of our founder, Father Pang, one hundred members of us and our Mother Superior manage the main cloister and a dozen convents, a hospital, a girls' school, two

kindergartens, and another kindergarten at the Motherhouse, and thus participate both directly and indirectly in missionary endeavors.

Ours is a small convent of "little sisters" and it observed its fifteenth anniversary last April. Since it is still so young we are all working together as hard as we can to make it grow up quickly. Our Mother Superior knows that there are still shortcomings, but these are due to our youth, and we hope it is not too early to present this little vignette to the public.

4. ACTIVITIES

We are Koreans and should remain so. It is for this reason that we wish to conserve the best of our national tradition, to guard it as a treasure. We wear the traditional Korean multi-colored costume and a long ribbon in our hair when we observe the clothing ceremony at our formal admission to canonical novitiate. We are also taught to bow low in accordance with Korean court etiquette observed in the loyal palaces.

We also have replicas of the instruments of torture and the executioners' tools under which our Korean martyrs suffered. Whenever we look at them we feel our veneration for the martyrs increase. There are also ancient court costumes and formal attire used long ago. We hope these treasures may be given greater publicity, so that the world may learn about the Blessed Martyrs of Korea and their unconquerable faith. Our Sisters take great care of those relics.

Ours is a "little sister" convent. The general opinion is that it is a very poor one. Yes, it is. Poverty is our friend. We have sworn to live with her all our life.

THE SALESIAN SOCIETY

1. FOUNDATION

On December 8, 1841, in the sacristy of a parish church in the industrial metropolis of Turin (Turino) in Northern Italy, the providentially arranged meeting of an impoverished boy and a zealous priest was the seed which was to blossom forth into one of the largest religious congregations in the Church. The priest was Don Bosco. The boy was the orphaned and abandoned Bartholomew Garelli.

Don Bosco was the youngest son of a poor peasant family. His father died when he was only two, and from that time on the family struggled to eke out their daily existence from the meager plot of land that was theirs. By dint of sheer will power and with the simple confidence in Divine Providence which he learned from his saintly mother, the young Don Bosco managed to educate himself to the extent that he was able to enter the ecclesiastical seminary at Chieri in 1835.

After ordination, according to the directives of his confessor, St. Joseph Cafasse, Don Bosco entered the Ecclesiastical College in Turin in order to perfect his knowledge of moral theology. While he attended this college, Don Bosco would often say Mass on Sunday and feast days at the Church of St. Francis of Assisi, in which the above incident occurred. From his earliest years, Don Bosco had been guided by the gentle hand of Our Blessed Lady by means of various visions and revelations which Don Bosco humbly referred to as dreams. It was no wonder then that the work which was to occupy the saint's whole life and every energy began on December 8, 1841.

From that day on Don Bosco gave himself completely to the moral and material welfare of poor and abandoned boys. He didn't wait for them to come to him, but went to search them out in order to care for them. It was the heyday of the Industrial Revolution in Europe. Young people were flocking to the cities to find work and a means to go on living. Oftentimes their parents were dead, victims of disease and famine.

They were poor, simple boys, forsaken by all, unaware of the depravity of their perilous surroundings, prey to the unscrupulous and to companions already corrupted. Boys similar to those who wander out streets today, deserted and left alone by all, trying to scratch out the barest existence, deprived of true love and the advantages of home and religion.

At first Don Bosco gathered jobless boys only on Sundays and holidays in order to play together, hear Mass, and receive the Sacrament. This was the beginning of the modern Catholic Youth Movement. Afterwards seeing the need of caring for his boys in a more complete way, he found a fixed abode in Valdocco, Turin. From this modest work emerged numerous vocational and classical schools, as well as Youth Centres, and almost every other active and apostolic work on behalf of youth, especially the poor and abandoned; and in later years the Saint was to begin that missionary movement which has grown to be one of the largest mission efforts in the Church today.

As the years went on, Don Bosco's modest beginnings multiplied rapidly. At his death, in 1888, the tiny society which he had founded to perpetuate the work which Our Lady had entrusted to him had grown to 863 members and 276 novices. At present the Society numbers 21,480, including novices. There are houses on every continent in which the members continue the work of their holy founder; the running of schools of all types, the printing and distribution of books, periodicals and pamphlets, and the care of abandoned boys and of the children of the working class.

2. IN KOREA

The growth of the Salesian Society in Korea has been no less miraculous. In 1954, at the invitation of the Monsignor (now Archbishop) Harold W. Henry, Prefect Apostolic of Kwang-ju, Monsignor Tassinari, then Provincial of the Japanese Province of Salesians, agreed to erect a school for the education of Korean youth at Kwang-ju South Province of Chŏl-la. The youthful and energetic Father Archimedes Martelli was called on to plan and execute the work and eventually take over the direction of the new school so generously endowed by the Columban Fathers. Funds to build the school were found only with the greatest difficulty and materials necessary for a permanent structure were extremely scarce and very slow to arrive. Nevertheless, March 19, 1956 was the beginning of the first Salesian School in Korea, with 280 students, 4 Salesians and 7 lay teachers. At present the school has grown to embrace the high school division and now numbers 1,452 students, 12 Salesians and 38 lay teachers.

In 1958 the Salesian Society undertook its second work in Korea, the direction of St. John Bosco Parish in the Yŏng-dung-p'o section of Seoul(To-rim-dong). Father Joseph Suarez, one of the pioneers of the Kwang-ju expedition, was appointed pastor. The parish is located in the poorest and most industrial section of Seoul. In addition to the ten praesidia of the Legion of Mary and the ordinary parish activities, there are five groups of J.O.C. and a large turn-out of more than 400 pagan children for Sunday School. Moreover there is a dispensary in which 3 Catholic doctors of the parish give medical care to the poor once a week. The priests of the parish have also been entrusted with the spiritual care of the prison, in which there are now more than a hundred cate-chumens. At present a new church is under construction. When completed, it will be the second largest Catholic church in the capital. At that time, the present church building will be used as a primary school.

In the very near future we plan to begin construction of a new technical school in Seoul. Teachers for such a school are now being trained at the foundation in Kwang-ju.

One of the first counsels received at the beginning of the new work in Korea was to search out native vocations at once. Therefore, from the very beginnings of the work in Korea a nucleus was already being formed to perpetuate the congregation in Korea. Moreover, at the request of Bishop Henry, the members undertook to train the junior seminarians for the Kwang-ju Vicariate. In one of his famous visions Don Bosco was counseled to begin the training of young men who were beyond high school age, but who had felt the call to a more perfect life. In gratitude to Mary Immaculate for this counsel, Don Bosco called this special group the Sons of Mary. This special vocation movement has already produced results here in our own nation.

On Janually 26, 1964 a newly built seminary building at Tae-pang-dong, Seoul was consecrated by Archbishop Antonio del Giudice, the Apostolic Internuncio to Korea.

In another vision, Don Bosco was made to envision the spread of the Salesian Congregation throughout the world. He was made to understand that if the Salesians always cultivated the virtue of Mary, the congregation would have a great triumph. There was also a promise of Salesian centers all around the world and especially in South America and Asia. In one vision Don Bosco was greeted by large groups of children who ran to him saying, "At last, you've come! We've waited so long for you." The saint's unique objection was "Where shall I get the personnel to care for so many people?" Since Divine Providence is supplying the congregation with many native vocations in almost all of its mission centers, and most especially in Asia, it seems that the answer is obvious.

Since the first group of Salesian novices gathered under the direction of St. John Bosco, a hundred years have passed. Here in our own Korea the first group of ten Korean young men have begun their year of novitiate, and two Korean novices who took their training in Japan have made their first vows, as, so to speak, the fulfilment of the first hundred years of work. In a hundred years such progress is not the work or genius of one man, nor is the great influx of native vocations to the society, established here in Korea a scant six years, to be attributed to the work of the members here in Korea. All this is merely the fulfilment of the promise which Our Lady made to Don Bosco about the work she had entrusted to him, a promise which Don Bosco inscribed on the walls of the church which he built in her honor as the center of the Salesian work in Turin—INDE GLORIAM MEAM—"from here will spread my glory."

THE SOCIETY OF JESUS

1. FOUNDATION

One year before the discovery of America, a boy named Ignatius was born in Loyola, Spain. As a young boy he became a page at the court of the Spanish kings. The turning point of his life came in 1521 when he was wounded during the war with France. During convalescence the readings on Christian Faith and the lives of the saints led him to a decision of becoming a soldier of Christ.

He started to study for the priesthood right after his return from a trip to Palestine. He later met his six associates when he was at the University of Paris. They organized a religious order in 1534. The order was officially recognized as the Society of Jesus by Pope Paul III in 1540.

The members of the Society of Jesus are generally known as "Jesuits," ever since the early days of the society's foundation. The Jesuits initiated many different kinds of work for the glory of God wherever they were asked to go.

2. PROGRESS

The Catholic Church was in great need of good educators when the so-called "Religious Reformation" started. Educational work in the Society of Jesus began in 1547 with the opening of a college. Within nine years, thirty-three colleges were approved by St. Ignatius and opened before his death in 1556. Today, the Jesuit Fathers own and operate 337 colleges and universities all over the world. They also own and operate numerous elementary, middle and high schools, graduate schools, and many other educational institutions. The mission work (largest among the Catholic orders), parishes, seminaries, retreat houses, science research institutes, broadcasting stations, educational publications, credit unions, co-ops, religious services at the armed forces, prisons, and leprosaria are some of the activities carried out by the Jesuits. The work of the Jesuits can be summarized by saying that any work which will bring greater glory to God can be carried out by the Jesuits.

Francis Xavier was sent to India and Japan by the order of St. Ignatius. However, he did not reach China on his mission to the Orient. Today there are thousands of his followers engaged in the mission work all over the world.

Saints Ignatius, Xavier, Stanislaus Kostka, Francis Borgia, Peter Claver, Peter Canisius, Robert Bellarmine, Isaac Joques, and Alphonsus Rodriquez are some of the twenty-seven saints of the Society of Jesus.

According to 1961 statistics there are thirty-five thousand Jesuit Fathers, Brothers and scholastics in the Society. They belong to one of the sixty provinces in seventy-eight countries with headquarters in Rome.

3. IN KOREA

The Jesuits were invited to Korea at the request of the Korean Catholic Church for the purpose of the establishment of a Catholic higher educational institute. In 1955, the Wisconsin Province of the Society of Jesus was appointed to carry out the establishment of a college in Korea. In the same year, Father Theodore Geppert, a German Jesuit working in Japan, was sent to Korea for the preparations for the college charter and the land for the school buildings. Many other Jesuits came to Korea afterward.

In 1957 a sixty-acre lot for the college buildings was purchased at No-ko-san(hill), Ma-p'o-ku, Seoul, and the construction of the first classroom building was initiated. Sŏ-kang College opened its doors to the first class of freshmen in April of 1960. In 1962, there are 350 men and women students in the freshmen, sophomore and junior classes. About one third of the students are Catholics. There have already been more than thirty converts among the students during its 2 1/2 years of operation.

Sŏ-kang College does not intend to enroll a large student body. Sŏ-kang is operated under the long tradition of the Jesuit educational system of high quality rather than quantity. Thus the consideration for admission to Sŏ-kang was given only to those applicants who had graduated in the upper half of their high school class.

Since Sŏ-kang has been following the high scholastic standard for its students, there was no need for educational reform at Sŏ-kang in contrast to many other colleges and universities as was urged by the new military government of Korea.

The first Catholic missionaries to Korea found well-educated coreligionists. Korean

Jesuit Fathers Thomas Park, Tobias Kim, Peter Chin, and Simon Yun started Jesuit training long before the first Jesuit assignment in Korea. After their long training in Japan, Europe, and the United States, they came to Korea to help our people grow in love and knowledge of Christ.

Since the arrival of Father Geppert in Korea in 1954, six Korean youths entered the Society of Jesus for priesthood, and two for the Brotherhood. The six are at present in the United States as part of the fifteen-year training program for the Jesuit priesthood. The two candidates for the Brotherhood are in Japan for their training.

At the present time, there are nine Jesuit Fathers, two Brothers, and five scholastics (Jesuit seminarians under vows and Minor Orders) working at Sŏ-kang. Fathers Simon Yun, Tobias Kim, Clement Demuth, and Andrew Bachhuber are engaged in the Kwang-ju Seminary where they operate a Latin school and have now taken in the first year of philosophy. In March of 1963, they accepted a new philosophy class, and so on until three years of philosophy and four of theology are in operation.

On October 7, 1962 the Sacred Congregation for the Propagation of the Faith decreed that the projected Tae-kŏn Major Seminary in Kwang-ju would be placed under the jurisdiction of the Holy See and the management of the seminary under the charge of Wisconsin Province of the Society of Jesus. Father Andrew Bachhuber was appointed its first rector.

Father Kenneth E. Killoren, the first President of the Sŏ-kang College, resigned the presidency on completion of his term of office, and Father John P. Daly succeeded him as the second president in July 1963. Father Daly was also nominated Superior of the Korean Province of Society of Jesus in June 1964.

On February 8, 1964, the Sŏ-kang College held its first graduation ceremony, producing forty-four alumni and sixteen alumnae, in the presence of the Superiors of the Far Eastern Provinces of the society. Prior to this occasion they held a week-long annual conferance of the Superiors of the Far Eastern region of the Society of Jesus.

The Jesuits in Korea are requesting the full cooperation of the Korean Catholics for the better education of Korean youth for the leadership needed in Church and country for the glory of God.

THE COLUMBA INSTITUTE AND THE CARITAS SISTERS OF THE BLESSED SACRAMENT

The Columba Institute

1. FOUNDATION

The Columba Institute came into being during the Korean War on the initiative of of Father Laurent Youn Eul-su, now the Vicar General of Seoul Archdiocese, who was moved by the vivid scenes of hordes of orphans and aged people, wandering aimlessly on the war-torn streets, deprived of daily necessaries, and often suffering under the rampant epidemics, with nobody to take care of them. The Columba Children's Home, built in Su-won, Kyŏng-ki Province in March, 1951, was moved to Hu-am-dong, Seoul in May of same year, with its housing capacity increased to 120. Later in April, 1935, the institute put under its management another children's home, the Friendship Children's Home, in Ch'ŏng-p'yŏng, Kyŏng-ki Province. As a result of increasing activities the institute set up its headquarters building at So-sa, Kyŏng-ki Province, and registered formally with the provincial authority of Kyŏng-ki Province in August, 1953.

2. PURPOSE

The institute is intended for promoting such projects as education, protection of orphans, support of aged people, leprosy works, assistance to self-support and settlement, relief, and medical aids, in compliance with the Children's Welfare Law and the Law on Protecting National Living. Since its inception the institute has been developed into the present huge institution, comprising six departments, fourteen bureaus and forty-one sections.

3. ACTIVITIES

1. Educational Work

In the wake of the International Social Worker's Conference of 1956 held in Munich, West Germany, Father Youn established the Ku-san Welfare School in November, 1965, in So-sa, with the agreement of the Right Reverend Ferrondi Baldelli, the Right Reverend Carld Bayer, and the Right Reverend Edward Swanstrom of the Caritas Internationalis.

Six years after, in Columba Village in the same town, the Caritas Vocational School was inaugurated with the purpose of teaching the techniques on livestock breeding, forestation, and cultivation, to the grown-up orphans and destitute students of the neighborhood, thus imbuing them with the idea of self-support and regional development.

In 1961 the institute set up the Ch'ung-ryŏl Middle and Commercial High School in Ch'ung-mu city, South Kyŏng-sang Province.

2. Congregations

In the meantime two congregations have been affiliated with the institute, one of which is the Caritas Sisters of the Blessed Sacrament, and the other the St. John Caritas Monastery. The later was established on December 27, 1961, under the patronage of St. John the Apostle, and is currently engaged in propagating the faith with twenty-one members at home and abroad.

3. Medical Work

The mobile medical unit, set up in cooperation with the Korean Association of Voluntary Agencies, makes annual circular consultations in the doctorless country district, so far having made 34 stops and given treatments to 16,736 patients.

In 1958 the St. Columba Hospital was dedicated by the institute in Pu-am-dong, Seoul, for the purpose of dealing with tuberculosis patients, heretofore having treated 11,408 patients.

4. Lepra Work

According to the lepra work policy of the institute St. Lazarus House was opened south of Seoul, in order to improve the protection of deformed persons, and the treatment of positive patients and secluded persons. In addition, in April, 1963, with the assistance of the German Leprosy Association, St. Lazarus Hospital was built with the capacity to accommodate 200 in-patients.

Cognizant of the importance of protecting non-infected children in possibly contaminated areas, the institute during the last five years has transferred and put the secluded children under the protection of the Sin-saeng Non-infected Children's Home in Tŏk-san, South Ch'ung-ch'ŏng Province, the Yong-saeng Non-infected Children's Home in So-sa, Kyŏng-ki Province, and the Paek-ryŏng Non-infected Children's Home on the West Coast. The institute has also made an authorized Annex of the St. Lazarus within the Ko-ch'ŏn Primary School in Kyŏng-ki Province. Furthermore the institute has, with the government help, successfully settled 490 families of former leprosy patients in 14 local areas.

5. Land Reclamation and Re-forestration

Besides the projects above mentioned the institute, in order to contribute to the national policy toward increased food production, has claimed 40,172,175 square meters of land from 1956 through 1962, and is now working on another reclamation project covering 7,551,925 square meters in 9 areas. At the same time the seedling beds for reforestation begun in 1958 by the institute have resulted in transplanting 715,000 seedlings in 1960 and at present are bringing up 98,680 seedlings.

6. Micro Promotion Projects

The Micro Promotion Projects forwarded by the institute purport to aid the needy with funds collected among the members, each donating a trifling sum. The beneficiaries of the projects are 495 lepers, 240 non-infected children, 27 orphans, 86 vocational trainees and 15 others, totalling 762. The projects also maintain branches abroad.

The Caritas Sisters of the Blessed Sacrament

1. FOUNDATION

The Congregation of the Caritas Sisters of the Blessed Sacrament was founded on June 5, 1956 by Father Laurent Youn Eul-su, then President of Caritas Koreana, with the particular aim of helping the needy. Late in 1960 it was approved by the Holy See.

Since then the Congregation of the Caritas Sisters of the Blessed Sacrament has made remarkable progress in various fields such as increasing its membership, establishing many branch houses in various localities.

The Sisters depend entirely upon charity and work entirely among the lepers. They are able to support themselves on a three dollars a month allowance, ten percent of which is pledged to the needy. Of the 305 Sisters, some 153 are working in various social centers, institutions and parishes, covering the whole of Korea from distant islands in the north near Communist territory down to the most southerly islands, taking in some forty-seven locations.

The congregation at present has 305 sisters, including the members in the overseas house. Among them, about 110 are postulants.

2. ACTIVITIES AND ITS FIELDS

Up to the present forty-two Sisters and postulants have been sent to various universities and professional institutions to be trained in the fields of medicine, nursing, pharmacy, school-teaching, and social work under the educational program of the congregation.

As the projects under the Columba Institute are greatly in need of doctors, nurses, school teachers as well as social workers, training the specialists is one of the most important tasks of the congregation.

A considerable number of the Sisters have been trained in special institutions in the past, and they are now engaged in various projects under the Columba Institute.

At present the total number of 153 Sisters and postulants are distributed in five different districts in seven provinces, and four coastal islands, as follows:

District	Numbers	Type of Service
Kyŏng-ki Province	42	Hospital, Leprosarium, Non-infected children of leper, Land reclamation and forestry, Parish and mission work
Kang-won Province	13	Parish work
South Province of Ch'ung-ch'ŏng	5	Parish work and Orphanage
North Province of Ch'ung-ch'ŏng	11	Parish work
South Province of Chŏl-la	12	Parish work
Paek-ryŏng	37	Hospital, Parish work, Protection of non-infected children of lepers Care for the aged, Kindergarten, Missionary work
South Province of Kyŏng-sang	33	School and Parish work

The activities of Sisters in local areas are many and varied, and include care for the physical needs of the patients and the relief of their psychological strain and mental anguish.

1. Religious Work:

This involves the education of personnel in the religious way of life. The Sisters strive in all possible ways to assist the priests in spiritual matters. This work is mainly centered in the institutions, and has resulted in approximately a thousand conversions during the last three years.

2. Educational Work:

This includes the provision of well-trained school teachers for work in the institutions under the management of the Columba Institute. There are now twenty Sister-teachers and administrative staff members engaged in educational work at the Madonna Girls' School (Ch'ung-ryŏl Girls' Middle and Commercial High School) in Ch'ung-mu city, South Province of Kyŏng-sang, and the Caritas School of Vocational Training in So-sa, Kyŏng-ki Province.

Aside from these institutions the Sisters of the Blessed Sacrament are also engaged in various institutions such as kindergartens, an orphanage, and a home for grown-up orphans under the management of local parishes.

Institutions in which the Sister-teachers are serving are: The Mount Columba School of Social Service, The Caritas School of Vocational Training, The Madonna Middle and Commercial High School, Yŏn-ch'on Kindergarten, Yang-jang Kindergarten, Tong-nae Kindergarten, Won-dong Public Nursery, Home for Grown-up Orphans.

3. Leprosy and Orphanage Work:

The Sisters of the Blessed Sacrament began to help the Columba Institute in the work of lepra rehabilitation when the institute undertook the lepra rehabilitation project in 1958.

Much assistance has been rendered to the Columba Institute as a result of their efforts and sacrifices over the past three years. The following is a list of homes for non-infected children of leper parents under their protection: An-yang Non-infected Children's Home at An-yang, Kyŏng-ki Province; Sin-seang Non-infected Children's Home at Tŏk-san, South Province of Ch'ung-ch'ŏng; Yŏng-sŏng

Non-infected Children's Home at So-sa, Kyŏng-ki Province; Paek-ryŏng Non-infected Children's Home in Paek-ryŏng Island off the West Coast.

The Sisters also render assistance to the Columba Institute in the work of orphanages. Many orphans, after being cared for by the Columba Institute, grow up under the special guidance and education of the Sisters. The following is the list of the orphanages: The Columba Children's Home in So-sa, The Columba Children's Home in Seoul, The Friendship Children's Home in Ch'ŏng-p'yŏng, The New Life Children's Home in Tŏk-san, The Home for Grown-up Orphans in So-sa.

4. Land Reclamation and Re-forestration

Even since the Columba Institute undertook the project of land reclamation and re-forestration, the Sisters of the Blessed Sacrament have played a significant role in bringing the project to a successful issue. Much waste land has been reclaimed and rendered arable, and extensive hill areas have been planted with trees with the cooperation of the Sisters of the Blessed Sacrament. Many of the Sisters have taken part in the work in some cases actually working in the fields and hills together with the poor farmers.

They have also helped in the distribution of NCWC relief goods and other daily necessities to the needy farm population. The Sisters are now continuing their help to the farmers in the newly-undertaken projects in Tae-sŏng-ri, Paek-ryŏng, and Im-ch'o-ri, Kyŏng-ki Province.

5. Medical Work

The Medical Service was initiated by the Columba Institute in 1961, with personnel supplied by the Sisters, who also serve in the following locally established institutions.

Name of Hospital or Dispensary	Type
St. Lazarus Hospital	Leprosy
St. Columba Hospital	Tuberculosis
I-t'ae-won Hospital	Medical Care for Needy Patients
St. Andrew's Hospital	Ordinary Hospital

THE MISSIONARY SISTERS OF ST. COLUMBAN

1. FOUNDATION

On February 1, 1922, at the request of the priests of the Society of St. Columban, a few experienced Sisters were sent to a small house in Cahiracon, County Clare, on the banks of the River Shannon, to undertake the formation of a new religious institute, the Missionary Sisters of St. Columban. The Very Reverend John Blowick, then Superior General of the Society of St. Columban, had resigned his professorship at Maynooth, the National Seminary (founded in 1795: a society of missionaries "of Saint Columbanus," for work in China, was founded there in 1916) to join the newly-formed missionary society, and it was he who wrote the constitutions for the new Sisterhood and who explained the Sacred Canons on which they were based.

In 1947, when the congregation celebrated its Silver Jubilee, it finally received the approval of the Holy See and was raised to the status of a Pontifical Institute.

The little town of Cahiracon proved too small to accommodate the Motherhouse, even though, as a specifically missionary congregation, it sent many of its Sisters abroad as soon as they had completed their training. A larger building in a more convenient situation near Dublin was acquired in 1956, and the Motherhouse was moved to St. Columban's Convent, Magheramore, Wicklow.

It was fitting that Father Edward Galvin, an Irish priest who had left his native land to labor for Christ, first in America, and later in China, where he was eventually consecrated Bishop of Nanyang, Hupeh, should choose St. Columban as the patron of the new missionary society of priests which he founded in 1916 and of the Sisterhood founded in 1922 to cooperate with the Fathers in their missionary work.

2. ITS SPIRIT AND FORMATION

Motto: CHRISTI SIMUS NON NOSTRI, (Let us be Christ's, not our own), is the high ideal set before the Missionary Sisters of St. Columban.

The congregation of the Missionary Sisters of St. Columban has for its general end the sanctification of its members by the observance of the simple Vows of Poverty, Chastity, and Obedience, and of the Constitutions. Its special end is to labor for the salvation of souls, especially in pagan countries; to minister to the spiritual and corporal needs of Christians in the missions into which they are sent; to conduct schools for Christians and pagans; to succor the poor and the afflicted; to teach Christian doctrine, especially to women and girls. The Sisters may also undertake the care of the domestic arrangements in the colleges and seminaries of the Society of St. Columban. They may labor among Oriental Catholics and, if need be, embrace the Oriental rite.

The Sisters follow the Rule of St. Ignatius. After a postulancy of six months and a novitiate of two years, members are admitted to temporary profession for three years, followed by renewal of a profession for a further two years. After this probationary period of at least seven and a half years, Sisters make profession of final and perpetual vows. Those destined for specific works such as teaching, medicine, nursing and so on receive suitable preparation.

3. OVERSEAS EXPANSION

In September 1924 after completing their novitiate the first Sisters made their vows and the Bishop appointed the first Superior General and her Council and the local Superior. The Irish Sisters of Charity remained with the infant congregation for another six years acting as Novice Mistress but before the First General Chapter in 1930 they withdrew, thinking that the congregation was now capable of self-governing. Other groups of aspirants quickly followed the pioneers, so that by October 1926 there were six Sisters ready to sail for China.

Another six followed them in 1929. A clinic was opened for the poor of Nan-yang, China, and the Sisters went out on house-visitation to treat those who were too ill to attend the clinic. In the disastrous floods which inundated the Yangtse valley in 1931, the Sisters gave up their new Convent to the refugees, and went out daily to the hundreds of thousands of refugees encamped on the hills outside the city, taking food, clothing and medicine, in the terrible cholera epidemic which followed the flood. The Catholic Church had proved that it was a friend in need, a friend indeed. In some parishes, as many as five thousand baptisms annually were recorded.

By 1935, a second Vicariate in the Province of Kiangsi had been entrusted to the Columban Fathers and they requested Sisters to take charge of the orphanage and open a clinic and a small hospital.

In 1937, a school for White Russian girls, refugees from the Soviet Union, was opened in Shanghai and the Sisters there followed the Byzantine Rite.

When, during the Sino-Japanese War, the invading army approached Hupeh, and it became unsafe to keep young women in the catechumenate, they returned to their homes in the country and the Central Catechumenate was converted into a hospital for wounded soldiers.

Later, just before the Japanese captured the city of Nanyang, it was reconverted into a Doctrine School for local Catholics and continued to function as such until, when the American Forces were retaking the city, the constant bombings rendered it impracticable. It was then opened as a hospital for air-raid victims. After the emergency, it continued as a General and Maternity Hospital, until the Communists compelled the Sisters to leave in 1951.

In the meantime the Sisters were requested by the Hongkong Anti-tuberculosis Association to staff the Ruttonjee Sanatorium. Early in 1949 the former Royal Naval Hospital, which had been damaged during the war, was donated by the government and opened by the Sisters of St. Columban as the Tuberculosis Center for the colony. Besides attending the patients there, the Sisters also lecture in the University of Hongkong and provide tuberculosis training for graduates from government hospitals. A training school for Cantonese nurses has been opened and the students have achieved good results in their examinations.

An appeal for Sisters came from the Philippines, and in 1938 a few Sisters opened a school and a clinic there. The latter was not in operation for long, but the educational work has increased and flourished over the years, and now the Sisters have kindergartens, grade and high schools, and colleges, in various parts of the islands.

In 1930 a few Sisters undertook the care of the domestic arrangements in the Preparatory College in Silver Creek, N.Y., on the shores of Lake Erie.

In 1946 at the request of the late Cardinal Mooney, Columban Sisters commenced the training of a new missionary Sisterhood in Detroit.

In 1947 the American novitiate was opened, first, in Silver Creek and later near Boston. Two schools were also opened in California, one for Mexican refugees in Los Angeles, and the other a grade school in Westminister. The Sisters attended various colleges, as there was no Central House of Studies until in 1954, through the generosity of the late Bishop Galvin, who had been expelled from China by the Communists, a House in Chicago was acquired.

In 1946 the Sisters were sent to Myitkyina, Burma, near the Chinese border, to open an English-speaking Grade and High School. It is hoped to open a much-needed clinic and hospital there in the near future.

4. IN KOREA

In 1955 Monsignor Harold Henry, now Archbishop of Kwang-ju, offered to give his central house in Mok-p'o if the Sisters would open it as a hospital and clinic. Two Sister-doctors, some nurses and technicians came from Ireland and America, and founded the hundred-bed general and tuberculosis hospital and clinic, where up to four hundred patients are treated daily. They also visit the Catholic leper settlement in Na-ju once a fortnight.

Shortly after the Mok-p'o foundation was made, a similar project was inaugurated at Ch'un-ch'ŏn in Province of Kang-won. Two years later, the original clinic proved too small to accommodate the patients who flocked to it at the rate of up to five hundred a day.

A second clinic housing the X-ray department and laboratory was added but that failed to relieve the overcrowding, so further extension is under way.

Ch'un-ch'ŏn being only two hours' journey from Seoul is fortunate in having the additional services of the National Medical Center staffs. These doctors visit Ch'un-ch'ŏn every other month to examine specially selected patients and arrange for their admssion to the medical center.

A special tuberculosis clinic is held three times a week but patients who cannot attend so frequently are given one or two months' supply of medicine to take home, returning to the clinic for periodic check-ups. It is planned to have a mobile clinic so that the Sisters may take comfort and healing to the outlying villages.

A further development in the Province of Kang-won is the recent opening of a large clinic, St. Joseph Clinic, in Sam-ch'ŏk on the east coast. This was made possible by a grant from the German Bishops' Campaign against Hunger and Disease, and completed with funds from the Bishops and people of

America and Ireland. This clinic will serve the fishing and mining communities, especially in winter when the mountain roads to Sam-ch'ŏk are impassable.

In Che-ju Island the Columban Fathers introduced the Four-H Club plan, and better crops and livestock were the result. Sheep, pig, and cattle were imported, wool was sheared and spun into yarn: knitting and textile machinery was installed, and the priests sought buyers for the island's products, and

since these are excellent a prosperous future is assured. The Sisters of St. Columban were asked to cooperate and a few specially trained ones have been put in charge of the wool-weaving section at Hal-lim, Che-ju.

Increasing the activities, the Korean Chapter of the Missionary Sisters of St. Columban was founded in December 1963, and Mother M. Calasactius was appointed the Superior of the Korean Chapter.

THE SOCIETY OF THE SACRED HEART

1. FOUNDATION

At about eleven o'clock at night on December 12, 1779, in the little town of Joigny about ninety miles from Paris, while a fire was raging not far away, a girl was born to Jacques and Madeleine Barat, who was destined to enkindle the flame which Christ came to cast on earth. Next morning she was baptized Madeleine Louise Sophie, her brother Louis being godfather.

Sophie, as she was called, early showed remarkable intelligence, and when Louis, who was studying for the priesthood, came back to Joigny he undertook her education. Not only did he prescribe studies far beyond what were usual for a girl at that time but he also endeavored to form her character and to train her spiritually. After his ordination he took her with him to Paris where he met Father Varin, who wished to found a society of religious women under the title of 'The Society of the Sacred Heart' for the education of girls. On November 21, 1800, the feast of the presentation of Our Lady, Sophie and three companions pronounced their consecration. In 1801 they moved to Amiens, where a modest little house became the first convent of the society. In 1802, Sophie was made Superior; in 1805 a second convent was founded at Grenoble, and the

following year she was elected Superior General. As the nuns do not take the names of saints she was now known as Mother Barat. From that time on, throughout her long life, she traveled constantly, founding houses all over Europe.

Her two distinctive virtues were humility and charity. Her charity not only embraced her nuns and their families, but showed itself in sympathy with suffering, care of the sick, forgiveness of those who had wronged her, love of the poor, love of children, and it went out to every soul in the entire world. She died on Ascension Thursday, May 25, 1865, and was canonized on May 24, 1925. Since then she has been called St. Madeleine Sophia Barat.

2. OVERSEAS EXPANSION

At the time of her death there were fifty convents of the society in eight countries of Europe, in Egypt, and in America where at her suggestion Blessed Philippine Duchesne (1769—1852, beatified in 1940) had founded the first house in 1818 at St. Charles, Missouri. At the present time there are nearly 7,000 nuns in the society in 188 convents in eleven countries of Europe and in North and South America, Egypt, the Congo, Uganda, India, Australia, New Zealand and the Far East. The foundation in Tokyo was made in 1908 (there are now four convents in Japan and a fifth will be opened in near future in Sapporo). The school and college in Shanghai (founded in 1926 and closed by Communists) have lately been replaced by a school in Taipei. The convent in Seoul was opened in 1956.

3. ORGANIZATION

The Society of the Sacred Heart is governed by a Superior General who is elected for life. The present Superior General, who resides in Rome, is the Very Reverend Mother Sabine de Valon, who visited Korea in April 1961. She is aided in her task by an assembly composed of the Assistants General who form her private council, and of the Superiors Vicar corresponding to provincials in other orders. There are at present four Assistants General of different nationalities: Belgian, American, Italian and Spanish.

The nuns are divided into Mothers and Sisters. The Mothers say the office of Our Lady and are, for the most part, engaged in teaching, while the Sisters usually perform household duties: cooking, washing, cleaning, and so on. Both have the same religious duties and the same spiritual and common life.

4. FOR APPLICANTS

Of those who present themselves as candidates the society expects a solid vocation, an open character, legitimate birth, and good health. No dowry is necessary. For the Sisters, primary education is expected and good will to be formed for work.

For the Mothers, at least high school education is expected and college education is a great asset. Here in Korea it is found advisable for these girls to spend a year at the convent before entering, so that they may see and be seen. When they enter, there is a postulantship of from six months to a year, followed by a novitiate of two years, at the end of which the religious vows of poverty,

chastity and obedience are taken. These are simple perpetual vows. At the end of five years, six months of a second novitiate are given as a last probation to prepare for profession when the vows are taken again solemnly, the choir nuns adding to them a vow to consecrate themselves to the education of youth. Both choir nuns and Sisters add a vow of stability. This vow of stability is closely connected with the maintenance of enclosure which is as strict as it compatible with the work to be carried on.

The end of the Society of the Sacred Heart is to glorify that Heart by aiming at the perfection of its members and by working for the salvation of souls. The life of the nuns is, then, partly contemplative and partly active, prayer and interior life taking first place. The works undertaken for the glory of the Sacred Heart consist in the education of youth, the work of retreats, and intercourse with persons living in the world. The scope of the work of education extends from kindergarten to university and colleges and includes the very important work of training colleges.

5. IN KOREA

The nuns of the Sacred Heart first came to Seoul in 1956 when seven, of six different nationalities, took up residence in one of the buildings on the property then owned by the *Société des Missions-Étrangères de Paris*. Later the French Fathers left and through the kindness of the Most Rev. Paul M. Ro Ki-nam, Vicar Apostolic of Seoul (now Archbishop of Seoul), the whole property was donated to the nuns. In April 1957 a middle school was opened with thirty pupils. Each year a class has been added. Beside the Korean school there has been added an International School so the premises have grown too small. A new building was added to house the International School and dormitory, thus leaving the other buildings free for the Korean school. The community has increased to thirty-one in 1964. The nuns come from South Africa, Australia, Belgium, China, Cuba, Germany, Ireland, Malta, and the United States, as well as Korea.

The highlight of recent year was the visit of the Very Reverend Mother General. About a hundred parents went to meet her at Kimp'o Airport and she was deeply touched by the welcome she received and full of admiration for the lovely dresses of the ladies. Her visit was a time of joy for all concerned. She entered fully into the ideals of the Korean people and promised to do all she could for the advancement of the work of education in Korea. The society made great strides with the establishment of an elementary school in Seoul and a women's college in Ch'unch'ŏn. The former, Sacred Heart Elementary School, was opened early in 1963 and the latter, Sacred Heart Women's College, on May 23. Schools of the society have been requested in four other dioceses and it will be a great joy to the nuns if they are able to comply. At present there are three Korean Mothers and two Sisters, who have made their first vows, while twelve others are undergoing training in the Japanese Novitiate.

THE INTERNATIONAL CATHOLIC AUXILIARIES

1. FOUNDATION

The idea of a society of laywomen who would dedicate themselves to the service of nascent Christian communities in the mission territories finds its origin in two major currents of thought that influenced the Church during the period between the two world wars. The first was renewed consciousness of the vital role of lay-people in the apostolate, the second, the improved understanding of the nature and importance of the missions that was aroused by the appeals of Popes Benedict XV and Pius XI.

In 1937, Yvonne Poncelet laid the first foundations for the society, guided by Father André' Boland and following the inspiration of Father Vincent Lebbe. From the first handful of young women preparing for their apostolate in wartime Belgium, the society has grown to number more than two hundred members from twenty-three Asian, African, American, and European countries. Teams of Auxiliaries are at work in nineteen different countries, mainly in Africa and the Far East, in Europe and in America. In 1957, the Church accorded final approval to the statutes of the society.

The Auxiliaries' specific field of the Apostolate is in those parts of the world where the Church has not yet reached its full stature or where it is not yet able to play its full part in the development of the country concerned. The Auxiliaries become members of the human community in which they live and work. They try to enter into the mentality of the people and share their hopes and aspirations. They respect their values, learn to speak the same language, and as far as possible adopt the same manner of living. Their role, as "auxiliaries," is to be at the service of the local community, not directing, but collaborating with the Christians of the country in the development and strengthening of Catholic leadership. Their goal is to assist the local people and to hand over to them as soon as they are ready to take on their social and apostolic responsibilities.

2. ITS SPIRIT AND ACTIVITIES

The Auxiliaries live in small teams of at least three members, sharing the same aims and working in coordination under a team leader. This is not merely a convenience for the work and a preventive of loneliness.

It has also a profound spiritual meaning. The team is intended to be a dynamic cell of the Mystical Body. Its members who are normally of different nationalities and backgrounds, should be united in a life of mutual charity evident to all those who come in contact with it.

Since the Auxiliaries are lay-people at work in the temporal order the quality of their professional service is important. Each member is required to have adequate training, suited to her own interests, but on the needs of the country and of the local Church. It is usually in one or more of the following fields: medicine, nursing, teaching, social service; secretarial, administrative, or research work; as well as catechetical work and various forms of Catholic action. The society, when providing teams, endeavors to send Auxiliaries with qualifications corresponding to the requests of the local, religious, governmental, or private organizations concerned.

The Auxiliaries are called to live a life of selflessness in the service of their fellowmen, and to be in the world a witness to the infinite love of God. Each of them must ensure the authenticity of her apostolate by a deep and personal union with Our Lord, maintained and strengthened by the traditonal means: prayer, chastity, the spirit of poverty, and the practice of obedience. The spirituality of the Auxiliaries is simply Catholic in the fullest sense, based on the teachings of the Gospels and of St. Paul, and marked by an intense love of the Church. Their spiritual program is expressed in the triple motto given to them by Father Lebbe:

    TOTAL renunciation
    TRUE   charity
    CONSTANT joy

"The force of it lies in the words in capital letters. Try sincerely and you will soon see that the Gospel is contained therein," (Fr. Vincent Lebbe).

Until now Auxiliaries have been trained at one of the society's training centers, in Brussels, Chicago, or Montreal. The society is now starting training centers in Korea and Japan since many girls of these countries wishing to work for the Church with the same objective, have applied to join the society.

At the end of the first year's training the new Auxiliary promises to live the life of an Auxiliary during her period of training. In the final year, taken at a training center, the Auxiliary prepares herself to take the oath at the end of the year and to begin work in her given field of the apostolate. The first oath is subject to renewal after five years but is taken with the explicit intention of total dedication for life.

The Auxiliaries are working in Jordan, Syria, Lebanon, India, the Congolese Republic, Ruanda, Upper Volta, Brazil, Formosa, Vietnam, Japan, and Korea. In Europe and North America, the Auxiliaries have the direction of the Crossroads Students' Centers, the aim of which is to facilitate mutual friendship and understanding between young people of all races, creeds, and nations and to stimulate and assist them to discover and take up, in a spirit of service, their social, political and religious responsibilities.

3. IN KOREA

At the beginning of 1956, the Most Rev. Paul Ro Ki-nam, Archbishop of Seoul, then Vicar Apostolic of Seoul, being in Brussels, asked the International Catholic Auxiliaries to send a team to his vicariate. The first two Auxiliaries arrived in Korea in March 1956. After a short time to study the language, they were put in charge of the Catholic Students' Center. This center was opened to the girls of the countryside who were in the capital studying in the numerous colleges and universities in Seoul. The main purpose of the center is to assist in the religious and apostolic training of the undergraduates.

THE SALESIAN SISTERS OF ST. JOHN BOSCO

1. FOUNDATION

Twenty years after founding the Salesian Society[1] Saint John Bosco had a dream in which Our Blessed Lady appeared to him and told him that she wanted him to begin the same work for girls as he was doing for boys. Don Bosco protested to Our Lady that he did not know anything about girls, and that he was interested only in boys, but Our Blessed Lady was emphatic, and Don Bosco, bewildered, set about performing this Heaven-sent task.

His search was soon rewarded. About three hours' journey by motor-coach from Turin lay the poor little village of Mornese. Here in poverty lived people whose virtue was their simplicity, and here in 1872 Don Bosco found the Co-foundress he needed to begin the Society of the Daughters of Mary, Help of Christians, or, to give the title they are better known under, Salesian Sisters of Don Bosco. She was Saint Maria D. Mazzarello.

She had a simple and pure nature, rich with wonderful endowments of humility and leadership. It is to her that the credit should go for the vast growth of the society. These Sisters, following the example of the Mother, are working for the salvation of souls in every corner of the world and we hope with the same zeal and love as their Mother had before them.

The number of professed Sisters in the congregation is now about 19,000. There are about two thousand novices.

2. HOUSES IN VARIOUS PARTS OF THE WORLD

Italy	Holland	Africa
England	Brazil	Thailand
Ireland	Hongkong	Japan
Spain	France	Germany
Argentina	India	Burma
America	Ecuador	Chile
Belgium	Mexico	Korea

3. IN KOREA

In 1956 Monsignor Henry, now Archbishop of Kwang-ju, invited the Salesian Sisters of Don Bosco to begin work in Korea. It was due entirely to his help and encouragement that in the following year the Sisters were able to arrive in their new mission center.

They arrived in Seoul on April 24, 1957. There were five of them, and in this small number there four different nationalities, two Italian, one Korean, one German, and one Philippine Sister. This variety of nationalities shows clearly how diverse the origins of the Sisters are and yet how closely united they all are under the one banner, the pink-and-blue banner of Our Lady Help of Christians, their one aim being the salvation of souls.

The twenty-fourth of the month was purposely chosen because on the twenty-fourth of each month the Salesians honour Our Lady in a special way, commemorating her special feast day which is March 24.

In 1958, again through the courtesy and kindness of Monsignor Henry, the Sisters were invited to start a school in Kwang-ju, and three Sisters were sent out to begin this new work.

Now, after only four years in Kwang-ju, the Sisters have a flourishing Middle and High School. God has certainly blessed their efforts no doubt through the intercession of Our Blessed Lady whom they love so much.

There are aspirants and boarders at Kwang-

[1] For an account of the Salesian Society, see p. 725.

ju, and hope for further vocations in the near future. Seoul is catering for aspirants at the moment and the Sisters are taking an active part in parish activities.

In Kwang-ju there are now five Sisters; three Italian, one Korean, and one Irish. In Seoul there are six; three Italian, one Filipino, one Korean, and one German. There are also three Korean postulants in Japan. That is all they number at present, but they hope to increase the number soon, especially with Koreans. Their hope is strong and well-founded, for in the heart of

each Salesian and Daughter of Mary, Help of Christians, is echoed the prayer of Don Bosco:

DA MIHI ANIMAS, CETERA TOLLE. (Give me souls: take away everything else).

That is their motto, and their rule of life. May they always keep this program before their eyes and with the help of Our Heavenly Mother bring many souls to the feet of Jesus. And when their earthly days are ended may they be able to say, "Lord, we have finished the work which Thou gavest us to do."

THE ST. JOHN OF GOD BROTHERS

1. FOUNDATION

Juan de Dios—St. John of God—lived in times when the world was going through the pangs of revolution in many fields: religion, arts, and geographical discovery. It was his destiny to start a revolution in hospital care.

St. John of God was born in Portugal in 1495. At the age of nine he disappeared mysteriously from the home of his devoted parents. After a long and difficult journey he arrived at Oropesa in Spain where he fell under the helpful influence of the parish priest. As a young man he had felt the urge to offer himself, like many others, as ransom for Christians held captive by the Moors. Yielding, however, to the advice of his confessor, he settled in Gibraltar where he carried on a work of the apostolate surprisingly modern in its conception and execution, that of the printed page. Printing was still a new invention then but this young man managed to procure a supply of prayer books and missals and traveled around the countryside distributing them in an effort to spread knowledge of God and His Church.

It was at this time that John of God re-

ceived the vision of the Child Jesus, Who is reported to have given him the name by which he was to be known from that time on. The turning point of his life came as he was listening to the sermon of his namesake, Blessed John of Avila, at Granada, when he felt himself so inflamed with divine charity towards his neighbor that he distributed all he possessed to the poor and consecrated his life to their service, performing public penance in the streets of the city. A pilgrimage to the distant shrine of Our Lady of Guadaloupe brought him to greater emotional balance and broadened his view of the purposes of the works of mercy.

Returning to Granada in 1537 he established his first hospital and introduced a number of innovations. He provided transportation for the sick. There were no ambulances in those days, so he carried them to hospital on his back. He washed his patients, though cleanliness was not regarded as very important then. He cleaned their rooms and he mended their clothes. He begged for their food. His way of begging was to walk through the streets crying out, "Who wants to do good to himself? Do good to yourselves, brothers, do good!" He was trying to make the people realize that in asking for alms for the sick he was offering them the opportunity to do good to their own souls.

Other hospitals used to let three or four patients suffering from different contagious diseases all sleep together in one bed. John was the first to allot a separate bed to each patient and to attempt the segregation of diseases. Other hospitals used to treat the patients no better than animals. John treated them with love and respect. So many sick and poor people flocked to his hospital that he became known as the Vincent de Paul of Granada①. Cripples, paralytics, lepers, deaf and dumb people, lunatics, old men and women, poor children and vagrants, all found food and shelter there.

He was already in his forties when he started his great order for works of charity. His only legacy to them was that they would see in the sick and the poor the person of Jesus Christ. He died on March 8, 1550.

During his lifetime, John of God gave no formal rule to his followers. His own virtues set the example which they faithfully imitated. Six years after his death, the rule which bears his name was written and decreed. Pope Saint Pius V gave canonical approval to the Order of Charity in a Papal Bull of January 1, 1571. In this Bull he imposed upon the members of the order the obligation to follow the Rule of Saint Augustine. He also stated the form of habit to be worn, adding to the original tunic and cincture the scapular and hooded cowl, and authorized the members to take solemn vows. Four vows are observed: Poverty, Chastity, Obedience, and Hospitality. Pope Urban VII declared John of God beatified in 1630, and in 1690, Pope Alexander VIII canonized him. In 1886 Pope Leo XIII declared Saint John of God the Patron Saint of Hospitals and the sick, with Saint Camillus de Lellis, and in 1930 Pope Pius XI named Saint John of God the Heavenly Patron of nurses.

2. OVERSEAS EXPANSION

Today the Order the Brothers Hospitals of Saint John of God is divided into twenty-six provinces with a total membership of over three thousand Brothers, having in all more than two hundred and thirty hospitals and clinics in more than thirty countries.

Of these, forty-nine members are behind the Iron Curtain and many of our hospitals have been confiscated and our Brothers sent to labor in the mines of Siberia. During the Spanish Revolution seventy-seven of our Brothers were murdered by the Communists. Practically all our Brothers are qualified nurses and some are doctors. We use the initials OH after our name which signify: Order Hospitaller.

Our Motherhouse is now at St. John Calybit Hospital, Isola Tibernia, Rome, where our Brother General, with his five counsellors, lives and governs the whole order. He is elected for six years, and the Superior of each hospital or clinic for three. We have the privilege of nursing the Popes and it is our Brothers that attended on our late Holy Father Pope John XXIII. We also run the Vatican Pharmacy. At first our Brothers had to chant the Divine Office in common, but on account of our nursing duties it was found impossible to continue this, so we now chant the Little Office of the Blessed Virgin Mary in common everyday.

3. IN KOREA

At the invitation of the Most Rev. Harold W. Henry. D. D., now Archbishop of Kwang-ju, five Brothers from the Irish province came to serve in Kwang-ju in November 1958. Since our arrival we have purchased a five-acre property, built a twenty-two room outpatients' clinic, and a community house. Our clinic opened in January 1960 and over five thousand patients were treated during its first year of operation. There were 20,429 patient-visits,

---

① Saint Vincent de Paul(1581-?1660) French priest, born at Dax, who founded the Lazarists and the Sisters of Charity, proclaimed special patron of all charitable associations by Pope Leo XIII.

and fifty-one major operations and seventy-three minor ones were performed.

Our plan is to build a general hospital and open a novitiate where young Korean boys will be admitted and trained to be future nursing Brothers.

THE FRANCISCAN MISSIONARIES OF MARY

1. FOUNDATION

The Servant of God, Mother Mary of the Passion, Helene de Chappotin de Neuville, died at the age of 65, at San Remo, Italy, November 15, 1904. The Institute of the Franciscan Missionaries of Mary was founded January 6, 1877.

The Foundress, Helene de Chappotin de Neuville (Name in religion: Mary of the Passion) was born at Nantes, Britanny. She went to Rome to visit the Pope (the Vicar of the Christ) and to receive his approval of the congregation she had planned and organized. On the Feast of the Epiphany (the day on which the Gentiles first adored the Savior) Pope Pius IX gave his canonical approval to the order she had founded for the special purpose of serving in the foreign missionaries. It was an auspicious day, as is shown by the results achieved. Her choice of site for the drawing up of the rule, namely the Roman amphitheater, so often flowing with the blood of the martyrs in ancient times, is also of great significance.

2. ITS SPIRIT AND ACTIVITIES

The Institute of the Franciscan Missionaries of Mary after the example of the Blessed Virgin Mary and based on the spirit of St. Francis follows the contemplative life and at the same time devotes itself to many kinds of work. The Sisters seek in prayer for the blessing of their apostolate, and in their apostolate they seek the object of their prayer.

Over and above this the special purpose of this institute is that the members, by complete and voluntary self-sacrifice, should unite themselves to the sacrifice of Christ on the Cross, offering themselves as victims to God for the Church and for souls.

The special characteristic of the institute's contemplative life is devotion to the Blessed Sacrament. The Sisters make a daily adoration before the Blessed Sacrament exposed. They kneel in turn for thirty minutes, praying in sight of the Blessed Sacrament radiating in the monstrance. In this way, they are continuously imploring through prayer for the salvation of sinners and pagans.

The name of the institute shows that it was founded in the spirit of the Franciscan Order and honors St. Francis of Assisi as its Father. The members of the Institute, following their constitutions, must show forth the characteristics of Saint Francis by abandonment to Divine Providence, apostolic zeal, and by a pure love of God, to initiate Saint Francis' perfect love of God, shown by his words, 'My God and My All!'

It would be difficult to enumerate all the works given by God to this institute—it is devoted to all kinds of charitable work—orphanages, day nurseries, schools for the poor, boarding schools, shelters, industrial training workrooms, clinics, homes for the aged, hospitals, leprosariums, and so on. The Sisters render especial help to the priests in the spheres pertaining to women, and one of the important purposes of the institute is to raise the status of woman in the mission fields. Since the foundation of the institute, there have been 13,600 Sisters at work in sixty-four different countries.

3. FOR APPLICANTS

Those wishing to become Sisters of the Franciscan Missionaries of Mary must enjoy good health, have a serious piety, deep faith, and a solid and special vocation for the duties of the institute. Aspirants must be virgins who have been baptized for at least three years, must at least have finished high school, be from eighteen to twenty-eight years of age, and have been born in wedlock.

Aspirants who are of the age must bring their parents' written consent. After this point has been confirmed, application may be made. From the very beginning of the religious life, following the capacities and qualities of each person's character they should make progress by means of the most suitable and authorized rules.

For the first twelve months the postulants wear a black dress and short black veil, after which, previous to receiving the religious habit, the "pros and cons" are carefully discussed so as to make sure that it is entirely of their own free will that the novices wish to take the veil.

During their two-year novitiate, the novices must apply themselves exclusively to their training in the community life of the institute. In the religious life, their love for God will never be easy or comfortable. The novices are trained in and are devoted to every kind of work in turn. In this life of prayer and work, truly the spirit of self-sacrifice is necessary.

4. IN KOREA

Twelve Sisters of the Institute of the Franciscan Missionaries of Mary, who may be sent anywhere in the world and who are known for their brilliant activities in many fields, after receiving an invitation from the Bishop of Pu-san, first set foot in Korea somewhat tardily on June 26, 1958. They rested from their travels in a small house belonging to the Catholic Church in Tong-hang near the harbor of Pu-san and prepared their temporary home. Even in this small and inconvenient temporary location, in the charitable spirit of their institute, they set up a small dispensary and helped the poor.

On May 19, 1961, through the kind efforts of their Mother Provincial for the Far East they moved to their new four-story convent built in Yang-chŏng-dong, Pu-san, and on October 12 of the same year opened the "Saint Francis Dispensary" where they render service in their mission by treating patients afflicted with various maladies.

On April 7, 1961, the Holy Mother Girls' Middle and High School, a five-story building with modern facilities, was started, and is contributing to the education of Korean girls, who have an intense desire for learning. There is a thoroughly equipped boarding school.

THE SOCIETY OF MARY (MARIANISTS)

"With Mary—to do the work of God:
By Mary—in her name:
For Mary—under her auspices." (Fr. Chaminade)

1. FOUNDATION

William Joseph Chaminade, the founder of the Marianists, was born in Perigueux, France, in April, 1761 and died on January 22, 1850. Proof of the holiness of the Chaminades is that four of their six children became priests. William learnt his theology under the Sulpicians, a society of secular priests founded by the Abbé Olier in 1642 to undertake the direction of Seminaries, named from their headquarters, the seminary of St. Sulpice in Paris (now at Issy). He was ordained priest while attending the Sorbonne.

Early in his ministry, he aided his two brothers, also priests, in directing a college in Mussidan. During the French Revolution Father Chaminade continued his priestly duties in secret. In 1797 he was exiled and went with his brother, Father Louis, to Saragossa, Spain. There, before the famous shrine of Our Lady of the Pillar, Father Chaminade was inspired to his future work.

Father Chaminade's works all have a definite purpose:

Sodalities: in 1801, Father Chaminade began training apostles in the fundamental principles of multiplying Christians.

Daughters of Mary Immaculate: in 1816, Father Chaminade founded an order of Sisters devoted to this apostolic mission.

Society of Mary in 1817, Father Chaminade began his order for men with three categories: priests, teachers, and working Brothers.

2. ITS SPIRIT

The Blessed Mother showed Father Chaminade a new type of leader. Each leader he envisioned was pursuing the same objective trying under the inspiration of a filial devotedness to Mary to develop in himself and in others the fullness of Christian life while engaged in the many occupations and preoccupations of the ordinary day.

It is by such new types of leadership that world problems must be solved. The founder of the Marianists worked out a plan whereby Catholic leadership might successfully combat modern errors. Under the leadership of the Blessed Virgin Mary, Marianist priests, teaching Brothers, and working Brothers pass on Father Chaminade's doctrine to their pupils and sodalists, and these in turn, together with the affiliates, immediately influence the world about them.

The Marianist *prays* with the knowledge that the great victory of our days is reserved to the Blessed Virgin, and so he dedicates all to the service of Mary.

The Marianists *works* so that all he does will bring the designs of Mary to fruition.

The Marianist *plans* to save and sanctify himself by saving others. Total consecration to Mary is devoted to but one object: the faithful imitation of Christ, Who became the Son of Mary in order to save mankind.

3. ACTIVITIES

More than three thousand Marianists dedicate their lives to works throughout the world. Members from various countries make up the provinces—Italian, French, Japanese, American, Austrian and so on, eleven in all. In America there are four provinces since the total number of Marianists there is over 1,700. The Pacific Province, one of the four in the United States, supplies personnel and supervises the new establishment in Korea. The St. Louis Province has missions in South America, while the Cincinnati Province has schools in Africa.

Brothers from Europe came to Japan in 1888. The Morning Star School was founded in Tokyo in 1888 and another foundation, "The Star of the Sea," was made in Nagasaki in 1892. A Marianist Novitiate was founded in Tokyo in 1895 and the first two Japanese Marianists made their first profession of vows the following year. Today the Japanese Province numbers 150 Marianists, 32 of whom are foreigners. Additional houses are in Fukuoka, Osaka, Oiso, Sapporo, and Yokohama.

Two attempts to start work in China were made, one in Junghsi-las, Tsinan, in 1903, and again in 1933. In each case the Marianists were forced to leave.

The principal works of the society have been in the field of education. The other works of zeal to which the Society of Mary devotes itself are Sodalities of the Blessed Virgin, retreats, and missions, and also the different functions of the sacred ministry.

The priests and Brothers teach in educational institutes, specialize in the various arts and sciences, conduct sodalities, supervise athletics, speech and dramatics, engage in research projects, and acquire advanced college degrees. Priests may also help in parishes and preach retreats.

Brothers who are not directly engaged in classroom teaching may be in manual arts and crafts. Such employment includes mechanics, cooks, carpenters, business supervisors, farmers, printers, builders, and so on. The working Brother category is an integral part of the Society of Mary in Korea.

4. IN KOREA

The first community of Marianists in Korea numbered three, two Brothers and one priest. The date of arrival in Kwang-ju was September 20, 1960. The first few years are being spent in studying the language. At present the Marianists supervise minor seminarians.

The Most Rev. Harold Henry, Archbishop of Kwang-ju, has expressed his desire for a Catholic boys' school in Mok-p'o. Preparations for this are now under way.

THE MIYASAKI CARITAS SISTERS

1. FOUNDATION

Our convent was founded in Miyasaki, Japan in 1938, by Father Antonio Cavarri, a Salesian missionary who had come from Italy with the ardent apostolic hope of saving souls, especially those of the sick and destitute. As parish priest of Miyasaki, he first founded a group of the St. Vincent de Paul Sisters, and was thus able to provide help for the sick and needy of the parish. Their convent afterwards developed into our present society. Though there were many old folks with no one to care for them, and the Japanese government was not yet conscious of its duty to help them, so, realizing the impossibility of raising funds in Japan, he returned to Italy and after a strenuous campaign succeeded in collecting a substantial sum. On his return to Japan, he set up the Yoshimura Old People's Home, in Yoshimura city. The foundation grew and soon there were a crèche and nursery, and a clinic. The next requirement was personnel, so he sought among the most virtuous and devout of the Catholic laywomen for aspirants willing to sacrifice themselves for the glory of Christ and the service of their less fortunate fellow citizens.

2. ITS SPIRIT

Bearing in mind the wishes of his superiors for "an indigenous convent in every parish," and the expressed wish of Pope Pius XI he resolved to found a society for Japanese Sisters. To convey the purpose of the society to the minds of the people, he named it the Caritas Sisters, a society that out of love for mankind modelled itself on the Sacred Heart of Jesus and practised charity to all. Remembering His pardoning of sinners, His consolation of the poor, and His healing of the sick, culminating in the redemption of mankind, they were to try to follow in His footsteps.

Like other congregations, it aims at holiness, but it has a further purpose. It aims at spreading the Gospel in pagan lands. Sisters of our congregation are engaged in parish work under the supervision of the parish priest, and in taking care of novices, of the sick, of the believers, and the destitute. Visits are made to the homes of the poor. Their work is always based on the infinite love of Christ for mankind, and the benevolence that springs from His Sacred Heart.

The Caritas Sisters, whose congregation is now more than twenty years old, have twenty-five branch convents in Japan and Korea. Every one of them operates a crèche, a nursery, a kindergarten, a school, and an old folk's home. These attached institutes help the Sisters to promote their missionary work. The Sisters number 240.

3. IN KOREA

The Korean convent was founded in October 1956 with three Korean Sisters, in accordance with the instructions of the incumbent Archbishop of Kwang-ju. In December, four nursing Sisters were added, making a total of seven. They work in Nam-dong, Kwang-ju, and the Na-ju Church, under the supervision of the parish priests. A novitiate was opened for the first time in Na-ju in March 1957. Continued help from the Archbishop enabled the convent to construct a new building in Hak-dong, Kwang-ju. Now that six years have passed since our convent was founded in Korea, it has, by the grace of God, ten Sisters, scores of novices, and postulants, and scores more of aspirants.

Current projects include missionary work in Nam-dong Parish, Kwang-ju, Na-ju Parish, and Puk-kyo-dong Parish, Mok-p'o under the parish priests, education of non-infected children of leper parents on So-rok Island in the leprosarium which was opened in October 1961, and the management of a sewing center at Hak-dong.

The Sisters plan to extend their work as soon as their novices complete the training and make their profession of vows. They are ready to go wherever they are required.

THE SISTERS OF CHARITY OF MOTHER SETON

1. FOUNDATION

In the year 1805 a woman in America made a momentous decision which was destined not only to change her whole way of life but also to affect many other people from that time until the present day and no doubt for many generations to come. What was this far-reaching decision, and who was the woman?

Elizabeth Ann was born in 1774, the daughter of a New York doctor and devout Episcopalian named Richard Baily. She grew into a very beautiful young woman, always kind and gracious to others, and, at the age of nineteen, she was married to a young merchant named William Seton, to whom she bore five children. She was the very pattern of daughter, wife, and mother, and took excellent and loving care of her husband and children and aged father, employing her spare time in prayer and visits to the sick of the neighborhood. Sadness entered her life when it was found that her husband was suffering from consumption and had probably not long to live. They decided to go to Italy in the hope that it might prolong his life and at least sweeten what years remained to him. Husband and wife set out with their eldest daughter Annina, now nine years old. Three days after their arrival he passed away.

Her acceptance of God's will bore witness to her faith and piety.

During her six months' stay in Italy she had the opportunity of becoming acquainted with Catholic doctrine, and soon conceived a desire to approach Holy Communion with a Catholic friend.

On her return to New York, when it became known in 1805 that she had been received into the Catholic Church, she had to endure obloquy and insult, contempt and estrangement and the loss of all her former friends.

She entered upon a six months' course of prayer and meditation, and, realizing that she had five children to support, decided to open a small school. But New York in those days was a stronghold of Protestant bigotry and anti-Catholic prejudice and she could get very few pupils.

On the advice of Father Dubuque she moved to the more tolerant milieu of Maryland, and before long she had a flourishing school well attended by many young girls whose parents were impressed by the piety and intelligence of the still beautiful young widow and convert, who led an ascetic but gracious life and taught their daughters with such kindness and efficiency. Soon they formed a small religious congregation with Mrs. Seton as their head. This was the beginning of the Caritas Sisters in America.

2. PROGRESS

The little congregation increased and Bishop Carroll, their spiritual director, guided them carefully along the way to canonical recognition and approval. In 1809 they adopted the Rule of St. Vincent de Paul in a slightly modified form and inaugural ceremonies, in which the nuns took the veil, were held on the Feast of the Holy Sacrament.

About a year later the Sisters of Caritas founded a second school and dedicated it to Saint Joseph. Sorrow visited Mother Seton again, however, when her two daughters Annina and Rebecca died shortly afterwards.

Elizabeth, still Mother Superior, lived until January 4, 1821 when she succumbed to consumption. At her death the congregation had grown into an important organization, spreading to New York and Philadelphia.

They are still working in the fields of education and medical nursing, and are now divided into five groups. The following is an outline of the rule adopted by Mother Seton for the Congregation, based on that of St. Vincent de Paul.

The groups are located at Seton Hill in Greensburg; and in Pennsylvania, Maryland, Louisiana, Arizona, California, and Korea.

The Sisters of Caritas of Seton Hill are engaged in education and medical nursing. Seton Hill Women's University is a private institution with schools of Liberal Arts and Sciences, and many foreign students come from all parts of the world to pursue their studies there.

For special training they maintain the St. Vincent de Paul Institute for deaf-mutes and quite recently they have started a school for the blind. Sisters teach in thirteen high schools, forty-five primary schools, two nursing schools, three kindergartens and run three polyclinics, one sanatorium, and one foundling hospital, and in Pittsburgh they have been carrying on social welfare work for more than twenty years.

3. IN KOREA

In 1960 Bishop Henry, now Archbishop of Kwang-ju, visited the Motherhouse at Seton Hill and informed the Sisters of the devotion and fidelity manifested by Korean neophytes, expounding the pressing need for Sisters to be sent for teaching work to Korea. The Sisters of Charity had never entertained the idea of sending Sisters abroad but at Bishop Henry's insistence, they felt it their duty to contribute their share towards strengthening the Church of Korea. The year 1960 marks the sesquicentennial of Mother Seton's death and the Sisters unanimously felt that it was fitting to commemorate the occasion by initiating this new development of her foundation. Four Sisters were sent to Mok-p'o to start a new school there, and they arrived in Korea on November 3, 1960.

It was decided however that they should begin by founding a small school at Kang-jin while undergoing language training, which will take a year, before building a school at Mok-p'o. Kang-jin school is dedicated to St. Joseph, and known as St. Joseph's Middle and High School for Girls. The principal of the school is Mother Thomas Aquinas Carey, the Superior of the congregation in Korea.

The Mother Superior of the Sisters of Charity of Mother Seton, remembering that the Legion of Sisters of Caritas are teaching young American Catholics, is offering her sincere prayers that the Sisters may be successful in preaching the Gospel to Korean women who have to defend freedom for the sake of God and even lay down their lives for His sake.

THE DAUGHTERS OF ST. PAUL

1. FOUNDATION

The congregation of the Daughters of St. Paul was founded in Alba, Italy in 1915, by an Italian priest, Father James Alberione, who is at present the Superior General of the congregation.

The scope of Father Alberione's original plan in founding the congregation extended to the provision of a new body of religious who would dedicate themselves exclusively to the Apostolate of the Press, an apostolate which until then had been realized by laymen who, for one reason or another, had had very little success.

By the Apostolate of the Press, Father Alberione means the diffusion and penetration of Catholic Doctrine into society, and into souls, so as to render the family and the individual, as well as general education and legislation and every other phase of society truly Christian.

The spirit which animates the Daughters of Saint Paul is indeed the same as that with which their patron St. Paul was imbued—to spread the Gospel throughout the world.

The Daughters of St. Paul form one unique family without distinction of class or person. They hold everything in common, pray in common, and each one applies her talents in the common exercise of the one apostolate.

2. OVERSEAS EXPANSION

The Motherhouse is in Rome. In the more advanced countries, the congregation has established provincial houses. At present there are seven provinces, namely: Italy, the United States of America, Argentina, Brazil, Chile, the Philippines, and Japan. In these provinces there are 179 houses in all, 93 in Italy and 86 in the other provinces. All depend upon the Superior General at Rome. In every nation every effort is concentrated on the intelligent application of those powerful media of mass communication, the press, the cinema, and radio, in order to bring the divine teaching to everybody.

The Sisters are taught not to look back on past achievements but always to press on to new ones in the boundless fields of the apostolate that awaits them. A Pauline Sisters is characterized by initiative, promptness, and simplicity.

3. IN KOREA

The Pauline Congregation sent its first representatives to work in Korea in the month of December 1962. Since that time they have accomplished little for their time has been taken up with learning the language. They have, however, taken a few initial steps; they have opened a library, a center where Catholic publications in Korean and Japanese, and even a few in English and French, are made available to the public. They have had a new translation of the Gospel printed, and recently another book entitled "*My Ideal*" has been published, which aims at spreading devotion to Our Lady.

The small community consists at present of thirteen members, six of whom are professed Sisters and seven aspirants. There is a waiting list of applicants whose admission will become possible when the new convent building now under construction at Mi-a-dong, Seoul is completed. In this vocational house space will be reserved for the accommodation of a bindery workshop equipped with bookbinding machinery. A Sister specially trained in the technique of bookbinding will instruct the aspirants in the work.

4. FOR APPLICANTS

The period of aspirancy lasts two years, and is followed by a year of postulancy and another year of novitiate. Perpetual vows are professed after five years of temporal vows.

The admission conditions to aspirantship are:
1. The aspirant should possess, in addition to the vocation for religious life, an active desire for the apostolate.
2. She should not be more than 24 years of

age, though in exceptional cases she may be admitted at the age of 25.
3. She must be a high school graduate.
4. She must submit all the necessary documents required by the rules and regulations.

THE SOCIETY OF ST. PAUL

1. FOUNDATION

The Society of St. Paul was first established on August 20, 1914, by Father Giacomo Alberione, D.D., in the town of Alba in Italy. Father Alberione's aim was to deliver the message of Jesus Christ to all the people of the world through mass media such as publications, movies, radio and television. His first step was to engage two young men to help him in the work. Such were the humble beginning of this society, whose Japanese branch now contains eight native priests and ten native Brothers, working along with many members who are in training.

2. IN KOREA

On December 2, 1961 an aged priest arrived at Seoul railroad terminal, and was met by the personal representative of the Most Rev. Paul M. Ro Ki-nam, now Archbishop of Seoul, and members of the Society of the Daughters of St. Paul stationed in Seoul, who braved the cold weather to welcome the venerable Father.

This aged priest was Father Paul Marcellino, and he had come all the way from Italy especially for the purpose of establishing the Korean Branch of the Society of St. Paul.

Three weeks later, Father Testi, another Italian priest, also arrived in Korea to assist Father Marcellino. These two Fathers were joined by Brother Kim Si-ŏk, a Korean who came from Japan a month later to complete the team which was to carry out the above

mission.

Consultations with the Most Rev. Paul M. Ro immediately followed, out of which came the agreement that a building belonging to the Korean Blessed Martyrs Monastery would be lent to the above mission. This building is located at Ton-am-dong, Seoul. Thus were the foundations laid for the Korean Branch of the Society of St. Paul.

In the autumn of 1963 the Korean Branch hopes among other things to set up a monastery and printing shop in the Mi-a-dong district of Seoul, and to recruit aspirants for the religious life.

3. FOR APPLICANTS

Application may be made for either of two divisons of religious life. The first is for Brothers, and the second for priests, and the qualifications required of candidates are as follows:

Brothers: Preferably high-school graduates, but middle-school graduates will not necessarily be excluded. They must enjoy good health and should not be more than twenty-five years of age, and their military service must be completed before application.

Priests: High shool graduates who are eligible for admission to Seoul Major Seminary this autumn. The number of applicants to be admitted into the society is ten for the Brothers and five for the priests. Those who are admitted will be required to lead a religious life and to dedicate themselves to the work of the society.

Applicants should submit a letter of recommendation from their parish priest along with documents certifying to Baptism, Confirmation, first Communion, school records, good health, good behavior, and parents' consent.

Successful applicants should provide themselves with bedding and personal effects at their own expense, but if possible, the applicant's family should make a contribution toward the cost of tuition and books.

It is hoped that many candidates and supporters will join with the Society of Saint Paul in carrying out its activities in Seoul, activities that are sublime and worthy, and in the spirit of the times in which we are living.

THE FRATERNITY OF THE LITTLE SISTERS OF JESUS

1. FOUNDATION

The Fraternity of the Little Sisters of Jesus was founded at Touggourt, Algeria, on September 8, 1939 and was recognized as a diocesan congregation by the Most Rev. de Provencheres, of Aix-en-Provence, on June 13, 1947.

Since then the congregation has grown rapidly and now has 800 Sisters, 650 of whom have taken vows.

The congregation has some 200 Fraternities established in the ecclesiastical territories of over a hundred dioceses. Founded among the poorer classes in a non-Christian environment, the congregation makes it a rule that at least a quarter of the fraternities and a quarter of the total number of Sisters, must be stationed in Moslem countries. This is to commemorate our precursors, Father Charles de Foucald, who laid down his lives for the Moslems of Touggourt, though the intention of the congregation is to extend the activity of the fraternities to cover the entire world.

The fraternities are united in a national organization obeying the Rule, so as to form one group characterized by adaptability and universality, in opposition to all forms of racial, national, or class prejudice.

2. ITS SPIRITS

The principal devotion of the fraternities is to the adoration of the Blessed Sacrament and to prayers for special intention. Some of the fraternities engage in agriculture, handicrafts, and manual labor; others in welfare work among the nomads, in care of the sick, and of prisoners; the remainder of the fraternities work as artisans.

The Little Sisters are capable of taking on any organized work that they may be entrusted with, at the same time performing acts of charity toward their neighbors.

Wherever they are stationed, they help one another in their daily life, and help to spread a Christian atmosphere in society in preparation for the preaching of the Gospel. In earning their living, they imitate the hidden life of Jesus of Nazareth and are willing to earn their daily bread by manual labor, whether in the factory, or in the hospitals or on the land.

However, in order to obtain funds for the establishment of a new fraternity, or of study centers, they are permitted to solicit donations from external sources. The Little Sisters, as regards their personal standard of living, prefer to live in the same way as the common laboring classes, with a preference for extreme simplicity in their quarters.

In this way they try to keep the Church alive, by living in the humblest environment. Cradled in the Sahara, our fraternities continue to grow and spread, and now include Sisters of forty-five nationalities.

The two books written by Father René Voyaume, *To the Heart of the Masses* and

Letters to the Fraternities, convince the reader of the value of what the Little Sisters of Jesus are doing. They have already been translated into six languages.

3. IN KOREA

In June 1955, the Little Sisters of Jesus arrived in Korea and began their work in Tae-gu and Wae-kwan. The Sisters engaged themselves party in manual work in the sock-factory and also in attending the leper patients. In July 1957 the Little Sisters of Jesus moved their houses to Hye-hwa-dong, Seoul for the purpose of founding the Korean Chapter of the Little Sisters.

4. CONDITIONS FOR ENROLLMENT

1. Judgment and understanding, sound common sense, well-balanced temperament, open and loyal character, piety in thought, word and deed.
2. Sound bodily condition, strength of nerves, and strength of body sufficient for sustained manual labor: adaptability to every kind of climate from tropical to sub-arctic.
3. Potential intellectual development adequate for dealing with human problems.
4. Right intention, perfect goodwill, pure motivation and flexibility adequate for the exercise of childlike obedience.
5. Desire to share the hardships and poverty of the under-privileged manual laborers.
6. Understanding capacity for religious love

without proselytism.

7. Simplicity of heart and soul adequate for the reception in the spirit of childlike innocence, the message of the Infant Jesus in the cradle which is one of the principle sources of the Little Sisters' spirituality.
8. Ability to carry out a life of prayer in the midst of the violent struggle for life going on around one.
9. Readiness to be sent on any mission and to do any work allotted.
10. Tolerance of emergent difficulties inevitable in a young congregation founded barely twenty years ago.
11. Firm desire to follow Jesus in self-abasement and humility.

No enrollment can be considered until after a trial period of at least fifteen days, without obligation on either side.

The Fraternities of the Little Sisters of Jesus are working throughout the world, as follows:

Group (or Arch-Confraternity)	Number of Countries	Number of Fraternities
1 North Africa	6	24
2 South and Central Africa	7	19
3 North America and West Indies	4	9
4 South America and Mexico	6	14
5 Oceania and South Asia	7	9
6 Northern and Central Europe	6	15
7 Western and Southern Europe	8	45
8 Far Eastern Asia	4	10
9 Middle East	4	8
10 The East	6	18
11 The Motherhouse	3	22

Delegates of fifteen religious congregation of religious women in Korea, assembled at the inaugural meeting of the Union of Religious Congregations, with Msgr. Mouton (Nov. 18. 1962)

The Sisters of St. Paul de Chartres

Motherhouse of the Sisters of St. Paul de Chartres, at Chartres, France

Mother Michaella, Third Superior of the Convent

Mother Agnes-Therese Pang, Fourth Provincial Superior of the Convent

Mother Marie John Hŭh, Eighth Local Superior of the Convent

An early photograph of the Sisters of this Convent (c. 1890)

Mother Béatrix Edouard, First Provincial Superior of the St. Paul de Chartres Order in Korea

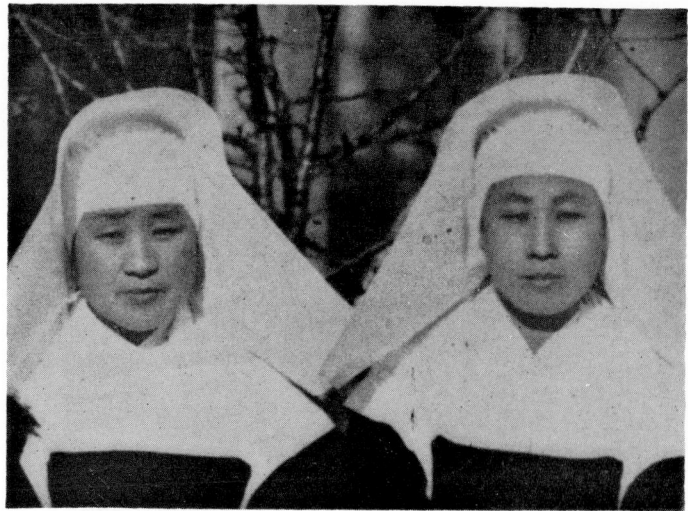

Sister Angela Kim (left) and Sister Mariana Kim (right) killed by the Communists at Mae-hwa-ri, Hwang-hae Province, Oct. 15, 1950

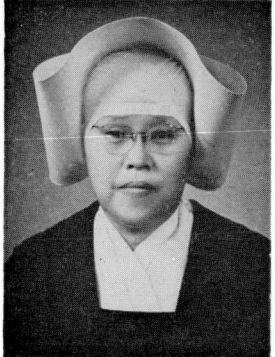

Sister Marie Regis Kang

Beaten by the Communists till at the point of death, while Sisters Angela and Marianna Kim were killed. She eventually recovered and returned to South Korea.

Mother Eugénie Demeusy, Third Provincial Superior of the Convent

The Convent of the Sisters of St. Paul de Chartres, Seoul, Korea

The Chapel of the Seoul Convent
of the Sisters of St. Paul de
Chartres

Veneration of the relics of Blessed Andrew Kim,
priest and martyr, at Mi-ri-nae Shrine by the
Sisters of St. Paul de Chartres

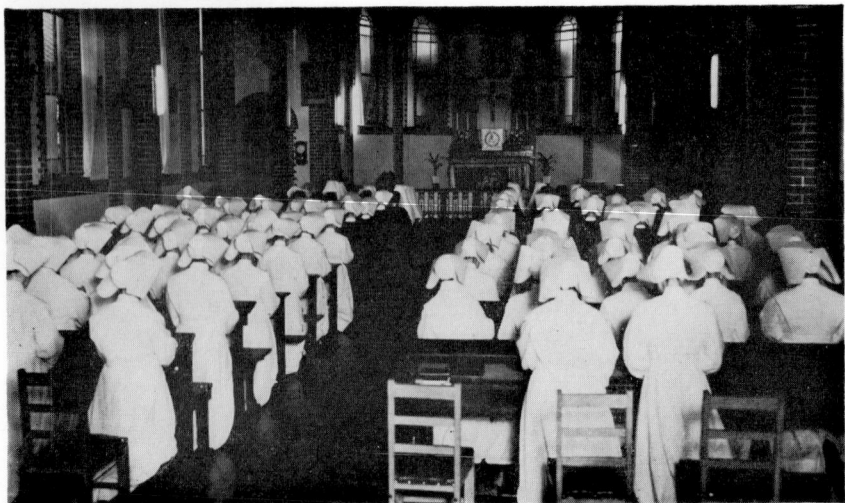

The Sisters at prayer

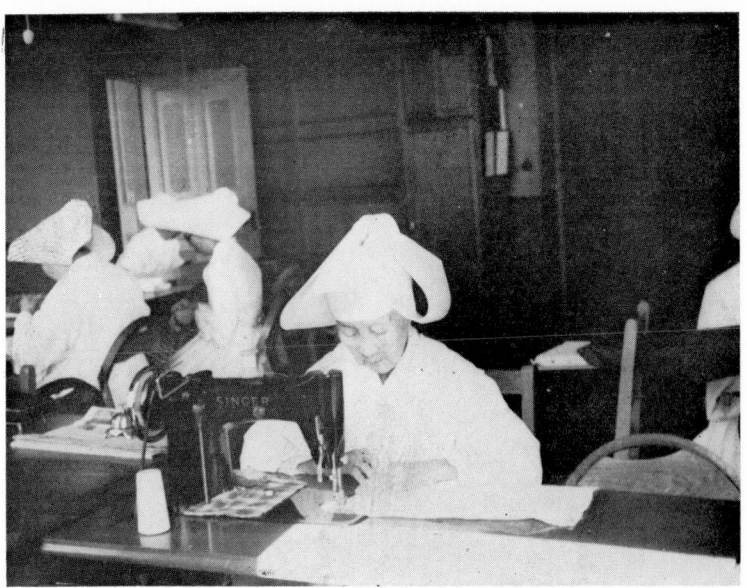

The nonagenarian Sister Paul Kim giving a lesson in fine needlework

Sisters ironing clothes and embroidering priestly vestments

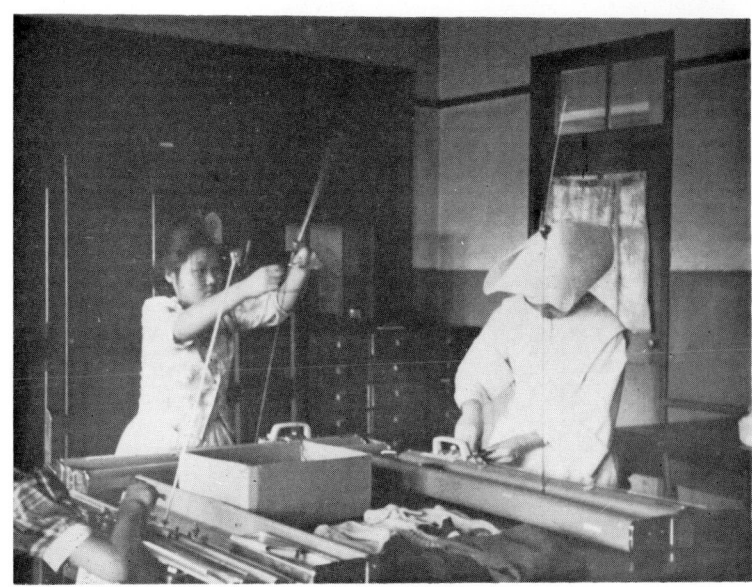

A Knitting Lesson

Kye-sŏng Girls' Middle and High School, Seoul

Schoolgirls praying before Masabiel

Keun-hwa Girls' Middle School, Kyŏng-ju

St. Paul's Hospital,
Ch'ŏng-ryang-ri, Seoul

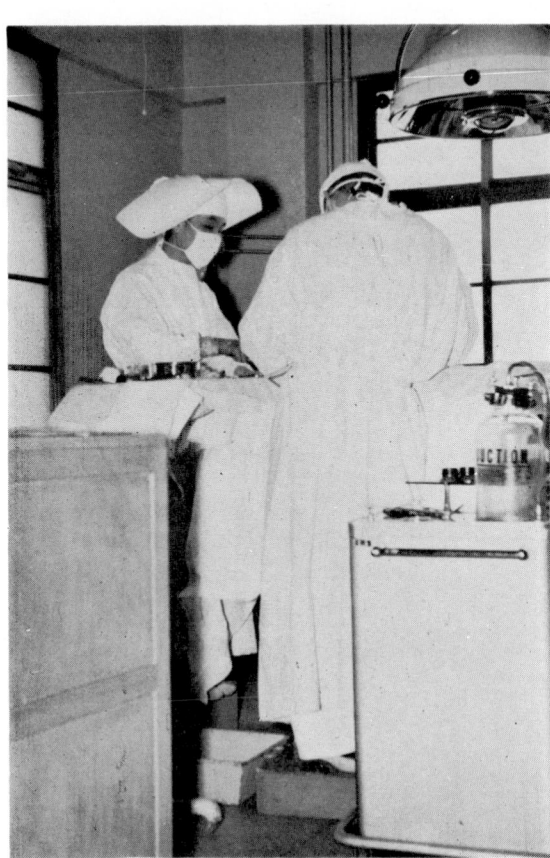

The surgery at St. Paul's Hospital

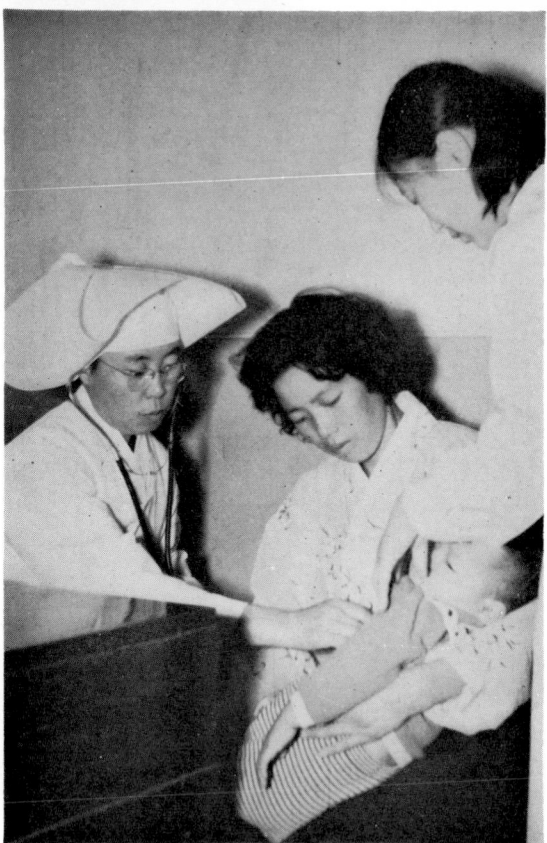

A Sister-doctress diagnosing

In-ch'ŏn Branch Convent, Sisters of St. Paul de Chartres

Orphan children in the Star of the Sea Orphanage run by the Branch Convent

Star of the Sea Clinic, the Branch Convent

Star of the Sea Orphanage, the Branch Convent

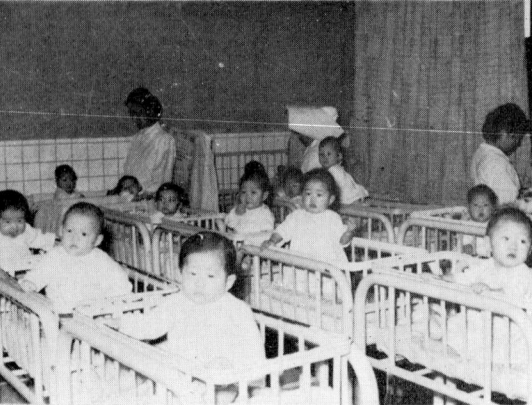

The aged enjoying the Sisters care

The St. Joseph's Home for the
Aged at Non-san

The Convent of St.
Paul de Chartres in
Tae-gu

Children at the Lily
Orphanage, conduct-
ed by the Sisters of
St. Paul de Chartres

The Order of St. Benedict

The Most Rev. Abbot Odo Haas, O.S.B.,
St. Benedict Abbey of Wae-kwan

The St. Benedictine
Abbey at Wae-kwan

The Most. Rev. Abbot Odo Haas, O.S.B.,
being consecrated by Archbishop Sŭh

His first blessing
after his being consecrated

After his being consecrated

The visit of the Most Rev. Brechter, Archabbot of the Benedictine Order, to Korea, September 1958

Retreat of Korean priests of Wae-kwan Vicariate Forane

The interior of St. Benedict Abbey Chapel at Wae-kwan

Printing plant of the Benedictines at Wae-kwan

The Silver Jubilee celebration of Msgr. Timothy Bitterli's ordination to the priesthood

Welcome accorded to the Benedictine Fathers on their safe return to Korea, after imprisonment by the Communists from 1949 to 1953

The sixty-first birthday anniversary celebrations for the Rev. Olaf Graf, O.S.B., Ph.D., May 1960

The Sŏng-eui Middle and
Commercial High School
for Boys at Kim-ch'ŏn

The Sun-sim (Immaculate)
Middle and High School
at Wae-kwan

The Sŏng-eui Middle and
Commercial High School
for Girls at Kim-ch'ŏn

The Sisters of Our Lady of Perpetual Help

The Motherhouse at Heuk-sŏk-dong

Our motto is "Sursum Corda" (Lift up Your Heart): Constant effort to achieve unity with God

Mother Maria Famula, the Superior

The Hospital of Our Lady of Perpetual Help, managed by the Sisters

Orphan children at the In-ch'ŏn
Orphanage

Orphan children

Orphan children taking a bath

Hospital of the Ch'un-ch'ŏn
Branch Convent

Ceremony of taking the Vow and the Habit (1961)

The same ceremony (1960)

The Missionary Benedictine Sisters

The Benedictine Motto: That God Be Glorified in All Things.

The Missionary Benedictine Sisters. This Order, whose Motherhouse is in West Germany, came to Korea for the first time in 1925 and founded a convent at Won-san, South Ham-kyŏng Province. There they spread the Gospel until 1949, when they were dispersed or held captive. Later sixteen Korean Sisters reassembled, received the authorization of the Mother General of the Olivetan Generalate, and regrouped at Tae-gu, establishing the new headquarters at the present site.

The Convent of the Missionary Benedictine Sisters in Tae-gu

Reception in honor of Sister Chrysostom and Sister Gertrud
On their safe return to Korea after their release from Communist imprisonment

Hospital of Our Lady
of Fatima

Sr.M. Edeltrud Weist, Directress
of Fatima Hospital

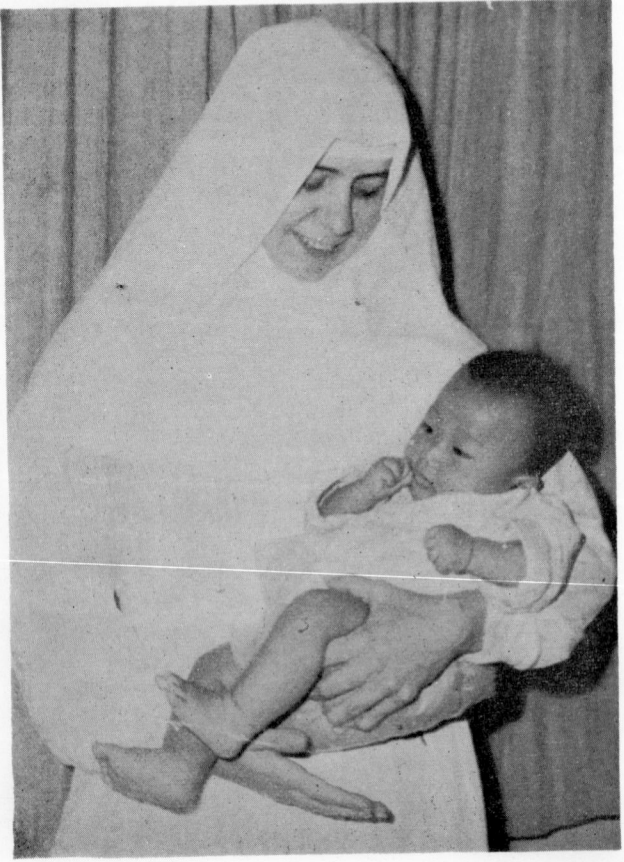

Sister in charge of pediatric
department

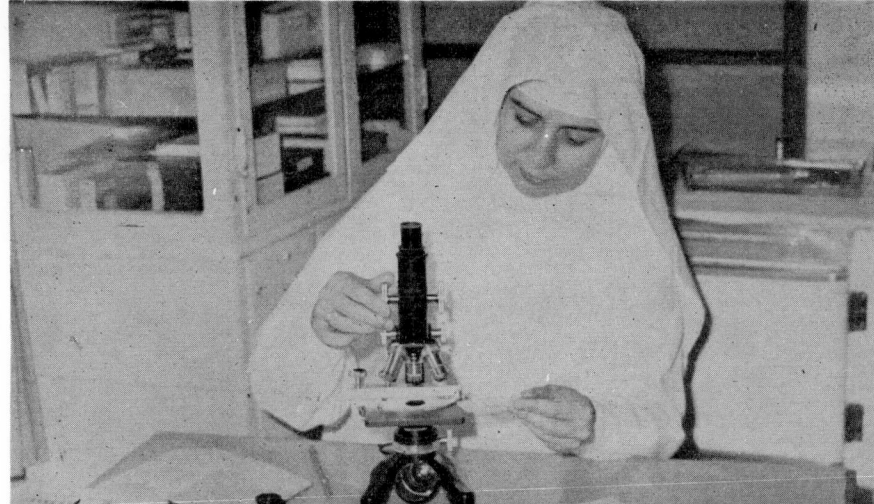

The bacterioscopy room

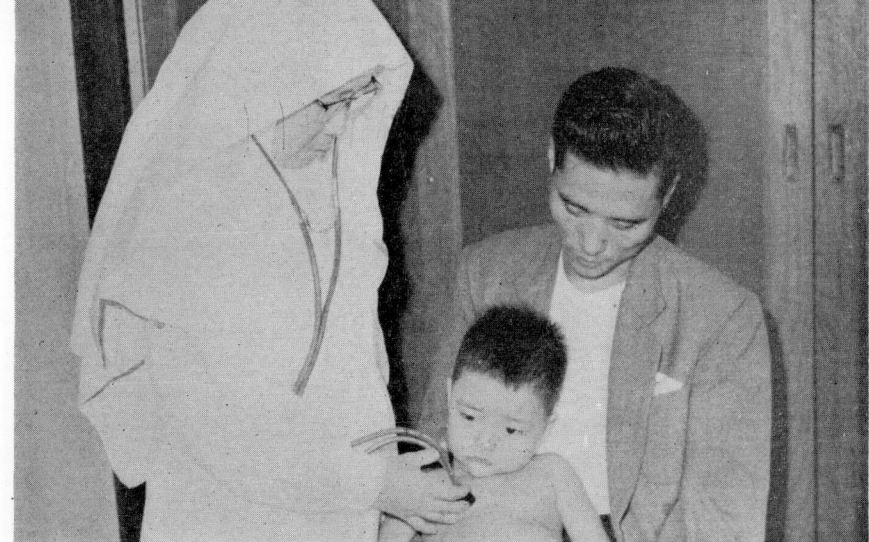

The Korean Sister-doctress, Mary Luke, diagnosing

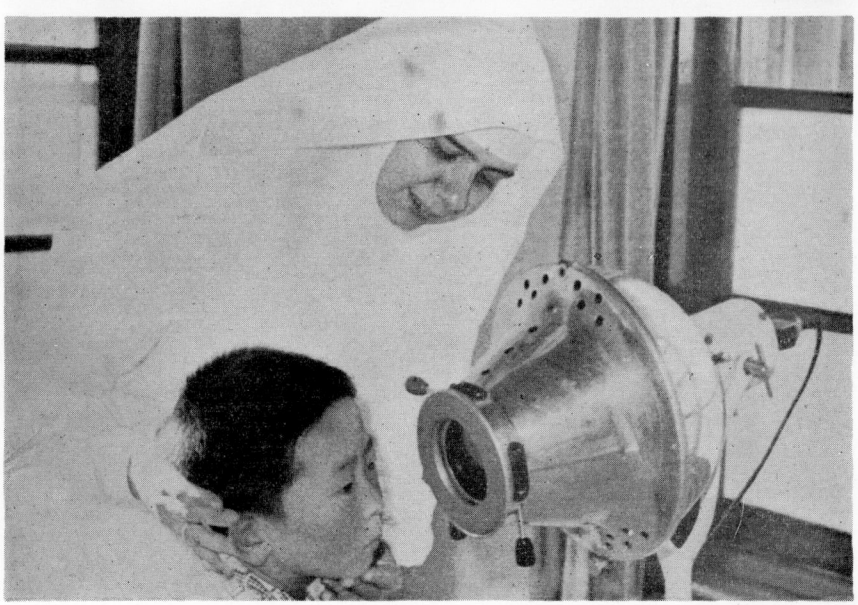

The electro-therapy room

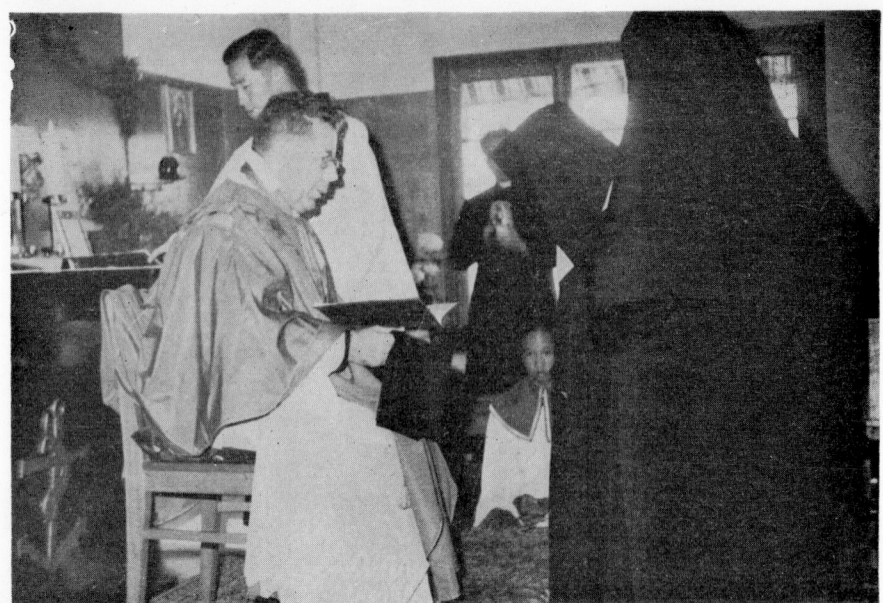

Ceremony of Taking
the Habit

The Seoul Branch
Convent at Ton-
am-dong

The School for Deaf
and Dumb at Ton-
am-dong, under the
Branch Convent

Sister Caritas, Superior of Seoul Convent, teaching her pupils to play the flute

In the flower garden

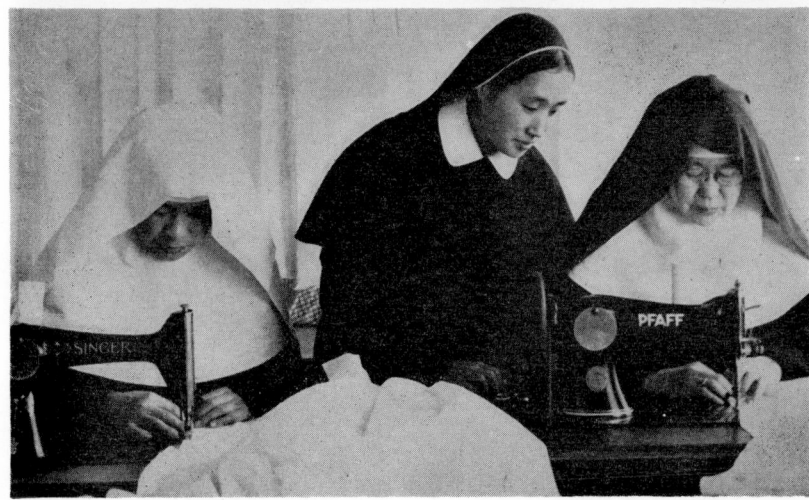

Sewing lessons for the postulants

The Sisters of St. Benedict

This Order, whose Motherhouse is in Switzerland, came to Korea in October 1934 and founded a convent. This was confiscated by the Soviet army. The Sisters were dispersed, but in April 1955 they reassembled and established a new convent in Pu-san.

The Motherhouse, Olivet, Switzerland

Novices at Yenki

Novices leaving Yenki for the free world

St. Benedict Hospital in Pu-san
(Inset) The Rev. Mother Nicola Faessler, Director of the Hospital

The Sisters of the Convent of St. Benedict

Recreation after a busy day of work, prayer and meditation, at Yŏng-do, Pu-san

The Branch House of the Benedictine Charity
Hospital at Tong-ja-dong, Seoul

The Kim-chòn Branch Convent

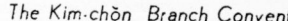

Chicken rearing at the So-sa
Branch Convent

A Sister inspecting the beehives,
at the So-sa Branch Convent

The Handmaids of the Sacred Heart of Jesus

The motto of the Handmaids of the Sacred Heart of Jesus
is "Tamquam Instrumentum in Manu" (As an Instrument
in His hands).

The symbol of the Congregation

*Father Louis
Deslands, the
Founder*

The headquarters of the Congregation, in Yŏng-il County, South Kyŏng-sang Province

The new Convent

The children in the
nursery

A postulant amuses
the children

Fostulants and novices after taking the veil and vows
In front of the statue of Our Lady of Fatima

The nursery and orphanage

Children brought to receive the blessing on Holy Innocents' Day

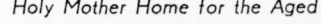

Holy Mother Home for the Aged

The Order of Friars Minor (Canadian Province)

The Monastery of the Order of Friars Minor at Tae-jŏn

The Very Rev. Father Jean-Berchmans Prévost, O F.M., the Superior

The Rev. Father Apollinarus Van Leeuwen, O.F.M., Superior of the Branch in Seoul

The Monastery Chapel

The Most Rev. Adrien Larribeau,
former Bishop of Tae-jŏn, blessing
the new church building

Monks after a retreat at
Tae-jŏn

Hwa-sŏn Minor Seminary
of O.F.M. Conventual at
Tae-gu

The Brothers moulding
cement-blocks

New Building

The Rev. Francisco Faldani,
O.F.M. Superior (right) and
the Rev. Daniel No

The Rev. Francisco Faldani, with Little Brothers

The Inauguration of the Little Brothers
of O.F.M., Third Order (Lay Tertiaries)
at Tae-gu

The Maryknoll Sisters
of St. Dominic

"Meditate, and propagate the result of it to others"

The Rev. Mother Mary Joseph
Rogers, Foundress

The Rev. Mother Mary
Coleman, Superior General

Sister M. Augusta, the
Superior

The Very Rev. Mother
Mary Coleman, Superior
General, visiting Korea

Newly-arrived Sisters

The visit of Sister Mercy, Vicaress-general and former Superior in Pu-san, to the Maryknoll Sisters (1962)

The mobile clinic serving
doctorless districts

Rush hour at the out-patients' clinic

Sisters busily mimeographing

Maryknoll Convent Chapel, Ch'ŏng-ju

Maryknoll Sisters engaged in medical
service at Ch'ŏng-ju

The Maryknoll Convent
in Ch'ŏng-ju

The Order of Discalced Carmelites

The Carmelite Convent at Su-yu-ri, Seoul

The Discalced Carmelite Convent, Pu-san

The Discalced Carmelite Convent, Tae-gu

The Holy Family Sisters

The Rev. Peter Singer, the Founder

Mother Simon Ko,
Superior

The Convent of the
Holy Family Sisters,
Hye-hwa-dong, Seoul

Postulants in the classroom

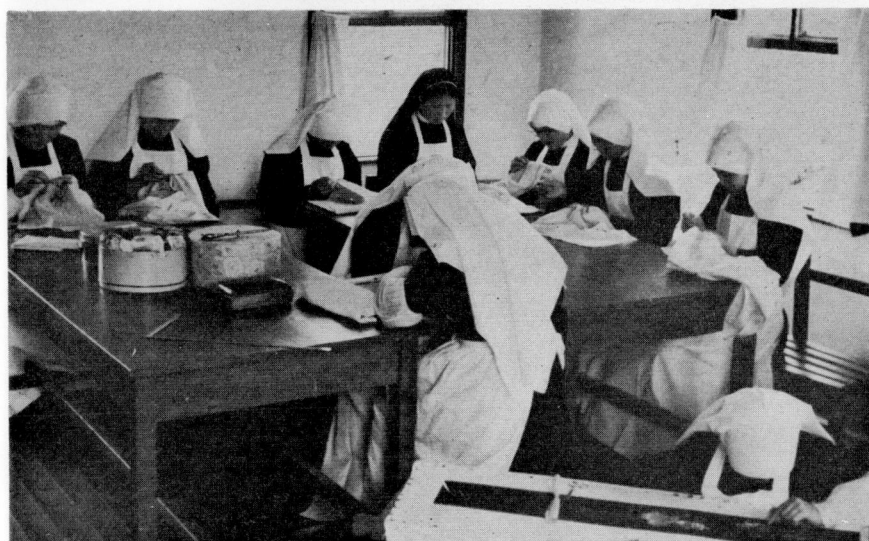

Postulants working

Sisters engaged in horticulture

The Branch Convent at So-sa (Novitiate, Orphanage, and Schools)

In front of the Convent Chapel

Taking the Vow

Sisters at work on the farm in So-sa Branch Convent

The Brothers of the Blessed Korean Martyrs

" The Monastery we built in the land to which we brought the faith of our own accord"

The Rev. Leo Pang Yu-yong, the Founder

The Monastery at Sŏng-puk-dong, Seoul

Professed Brothers and aspirants of the Order

Assembled before the statue of Blessed Andrew Kim, priest and martyr

In the library

Brothers at prayer during Compline

Brothers in the workshop

Brothers making
suitcases

The Sisters of the Blessed Korean Martyrs

The Convent Chapel

The Ch'ŏng-p'a-dong Convent in Seoul

Gardening

Floriculture

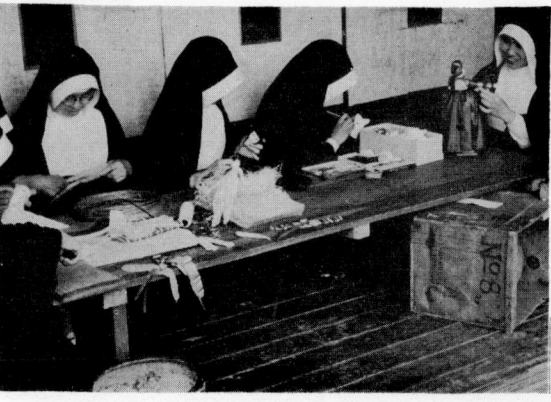

Making Artificial Flowers

Making dolls

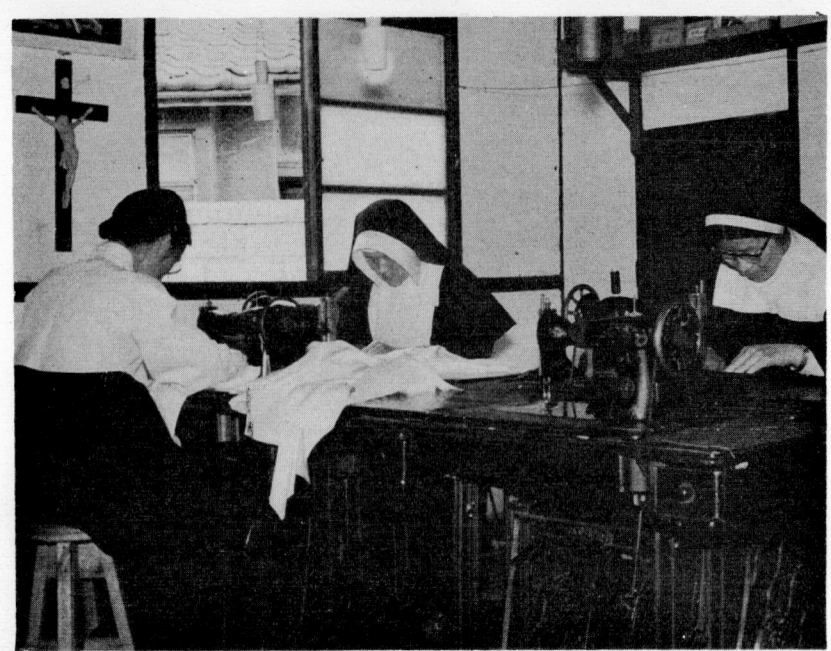

The Sewing Room

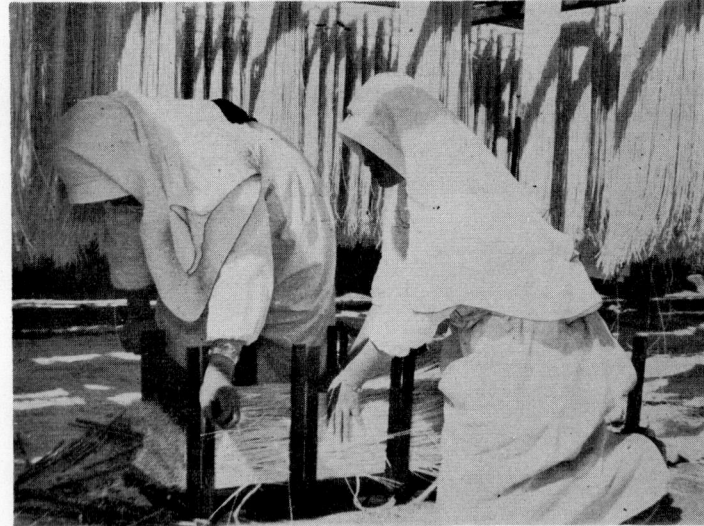

Making noodles

The kitchen-garden

Lay Sisters after taking the Habit
at Pu-san Branch Convent

Pu-san Branch Convent

The Blessed Kindergarten at
Pu-san Branch Convent

The Salesian Society

S. JOANNES BOSCO

St. Don Bosco, the Founder

Beatus Dominicus Savio

St. Dominic Xavier, Juvenile
apostle of peace

The Very Rev. Rinaldo
Facchinelli, S.D.B.,
Superior of the
Monastery

The Salesian Middle and
High School and attached
Lecture Hall

Archbishop Harold Henry welcomed by boy scouts at the Salesian Middle and High School

Brothers of the Society of Don Bosco

Novices of the First Enrollment

*A novice of the First Enrollment
taking the Vow*

*High Mass, celebrated by Archbishop
Harold Henry*

In memory of the centenary of the
apparition of the BVM at Lourdes

High Mass in the Salesian Middle and High School Chapel

Blessing of the Statue of St. Dominic Xavier

The baseball team

807

The Rev. Victor Miller, Rector
of the Salesian Seminary

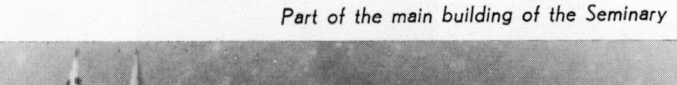

Part of the main building of the Seminary

Baseball training of the Salesian members

The Rector with
the Brothers and
the Seminarians

The Society of Jesus

St. Ignatius Loyola and St. Francis Xavier, the
Founders (at Paris University)

The Main Building of Sŏ-kang College

The Rev. John P. Daly,
M.A., S.T.L., Ph. D.,
President of the College

Bird's-eye view of Sŏ-kang
College, at No-ko-san Hill

The Rev. Theodore Geppert, the former treasurer of Sŏ-kang College

Korean Jesuits in the U.S.A.

A group of Jesuit fathers

The Dean of Studies and the
Provincial of Wisconsin Province
(second from left)

Dean of Marquette University on
a visit of inspection (third from
right)

The Rev. Kenneth Killoren,
the first President, in his
office

The College Library

The Laboratory

On the lawn of the Campus

Blessing of the New Building presided over by the Most Rev. Antonio del Giudice, Apostolic Delegate (now Internuncio) to Korea

The New Building

The Columba Institute and the Caritas Sisters of the Blessed Sacrament

The Congregation is affiliated with St. Columba Institute and engaged in many fields of social welfare which the Institute operates.

The Very Rev. Father Laurent Youn Eul-su, Ph.D., President of the Columba Institute, the Founder of the Congregation, and Vicar General of Archdiocese of Seoul

View of the Motherhouse of the Congregation of the Blessed Sacrament of Charity

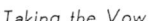

After Retreat

Taking the Vow

St. Lazarus Hospital at An-yang

Yang-su-ri Leper Settlement
of the Negative Patients

The happy faces
distribution of clothing
at An-yang St. Lazarus
Leprosarium

After being decorated with the Medal of Culture

Traveling clinic of the Institute

Exerting himself to build new houses

Sisters playing with orphans

The poultry farm

Sisters at work in the garden

The Missionary Sisters
of St. Columban

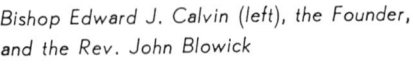
"Christi Simus Non Nostri" (*Let us be Christ's, not our own.*)

Bishop Edward J. Calvin (left), the Founder, and the Rev. John Blowick

Mother Mary Lucy, the Superior

St. Columban Hospital, Mok-p'o

Archbishop Zupi, Apostolic Delegate
to Korea, visiting the Sisters of the
St. Columban Order

Archbishop Harold Henry visiting
St. Columban Hospital with foreign
guests

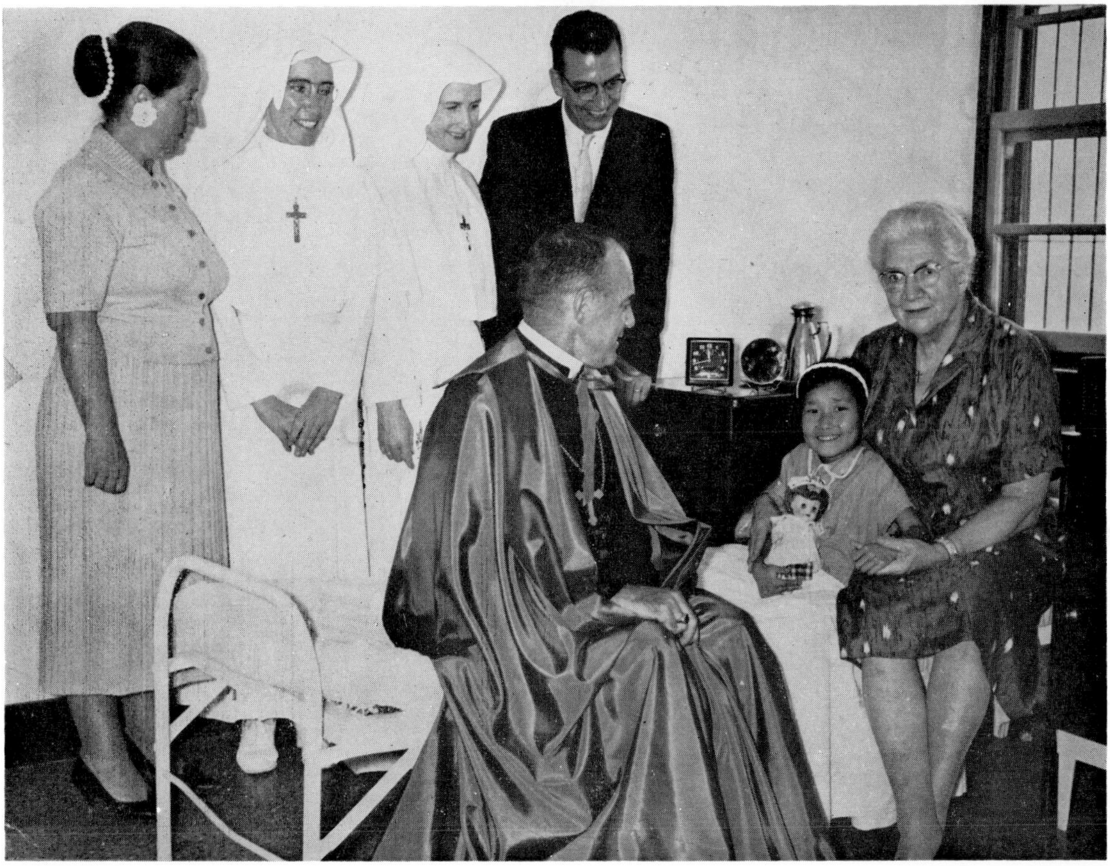

A Sister nursing a baby

A Sister and a nurse attending and comforting a child suffering from poliomyelitis

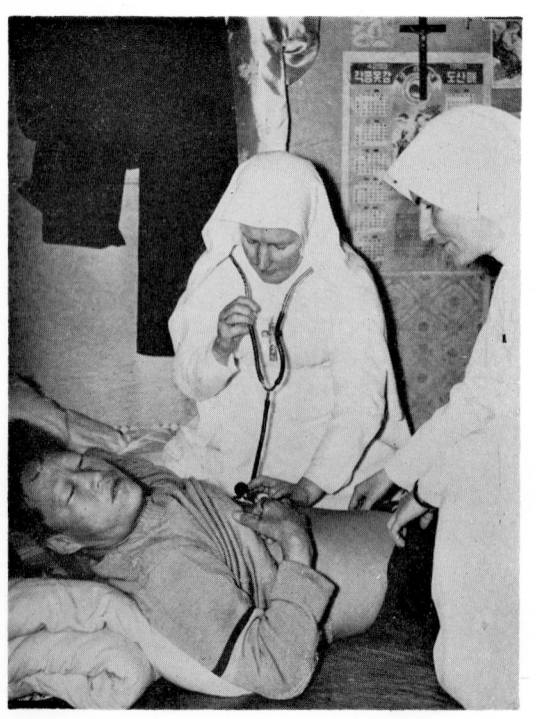

A Sister examining a patient suffering from leprosy

The St. Columban clinic at Ch'un-ch'ŏn

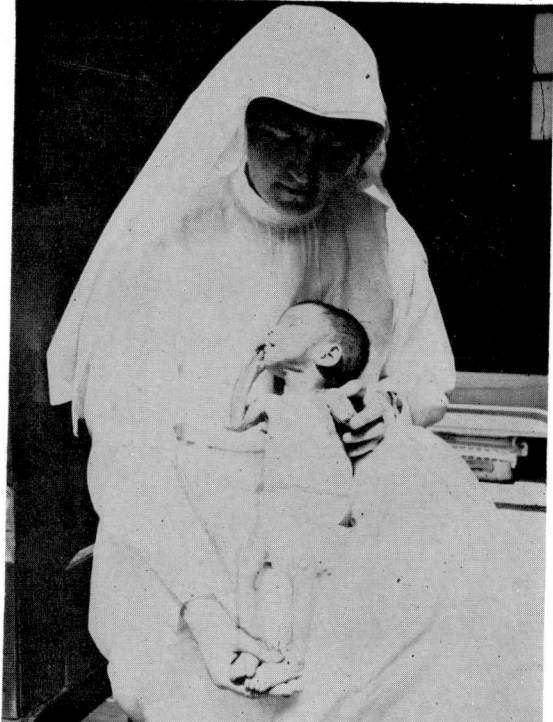

Mother Mary Calasantius nursing an
undernourished child

The St. Joseph Clinic at
Sam-ch'ŏk

The Society of the Sacred Heart

"Love the Sacred Heart of Jesus and make Him known and loved."

The Motherhouse of the Society of the Sacred Heart, in Rome

The Very Rev. Sabine de Valon, Mother General of the Society, arriving at Yŏ-eui-do Airport (1961)

Sister M. Chu (left), Principal of the School, with Mother Cora McHardy-Flint, Superior of the Convent

The Convent Chapel

Mother Superior Cora McHardy-Flint and the nuns

The Main Building of the Sacred Heart Girls' Middle and High School

An athletic display by the girls of the School

Mother Nicholls, President of Sacred
Heart Women's College

Nuns of the Society of the Sacred Heart

Main Building of Sacred Heart Women's College

The Interior of the chapel

The lesson at physics

The Interior of the library

Sacred Heart International
Primary School

Children of the School

The Noviciate

Archbishop Henry and Sisters of the Salesian Order: (left to right) Mother Ancilla; Mother Provincial Therese; Sister Milta; Mother Superior Carmela; Sister Antoinette

Group of Sisters photographed after taking the Vow

Mother Ancilla Gritti, the
Principal

Morning drill of Eung-se
Salesian Girls' Middle and
High School

After the baptism of the
students

Physician Brothers, assistant doctors and nurses

A physician Brother giving treatment to an infant

A physician Brother treating an elderly patient

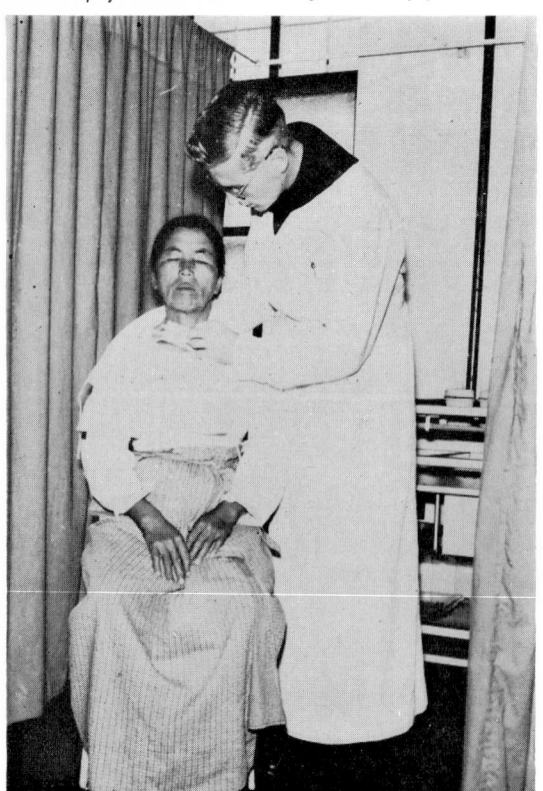

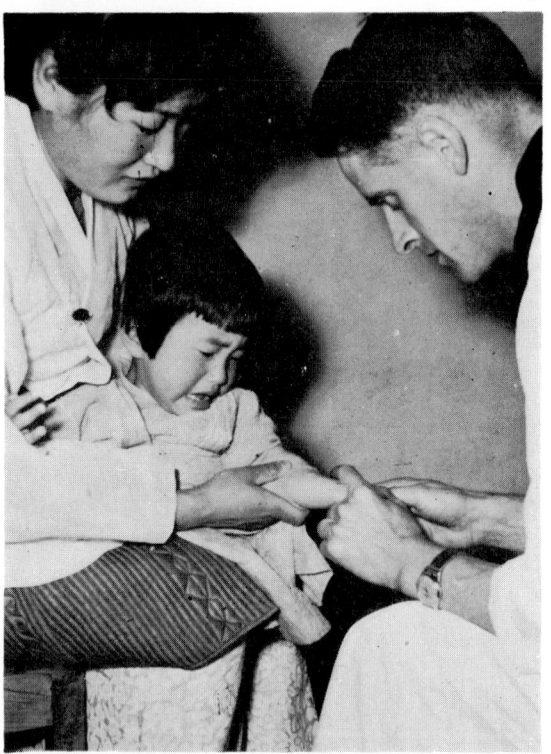

When the first Korean youth enrolled in this Order completes his course of training in medical science and becomes a nursing Brother, Korea may be enlisted as one of the provinces of the Salesian Congregation.

The Franciscan Missionaries of Mary

Mother Mary of the Passion,
Helene de Chappotin de
Neuville, the Foundress

The Convent of the
Franciscan Sisters
of Mary at Pu-san

The first group of
Franciscan Sisters
of Mary to arrive
in Korea

A Sister-pharmacist at work

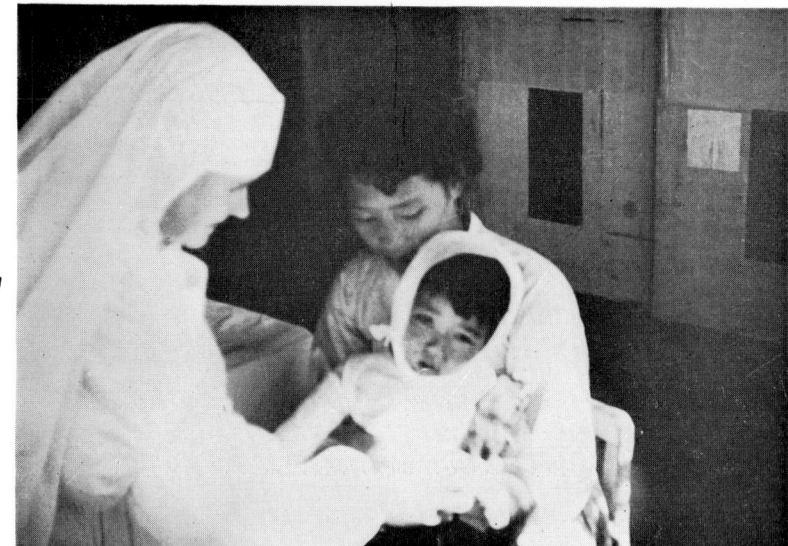

A Sister-physician diagnosing

St. Francis Dispensary,
Pu-san

Holy Mother Girls' Middle and High School in Pu-san

Vanguard of education for Korean women

A Sister giving a lesson

The Society of Mary (Marianists)

With Mary.........to do the work of God:
By Mary ....in her name:
For Mary............under her auspices.
                              (Fr. Chaminade)

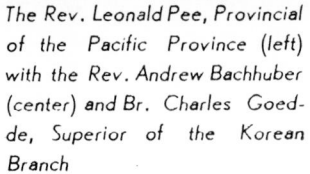

The Rev. Leonald Pee, Provincial of the Pacific Province (left) with the Rev. Andrew Bachhuber (center) and Br. Charles Goedde, Superior of the Korean Branch

(From left) The Rev. Peter Chu, the former Spiritual Director of the Monastery; Brother Charles Goedde; Brother Melvin Silva

Newly-arrived Brothers

The Miyasaki Caritas Sisters

The symbol of the Order

Archbishop Harold Henry with the
Superior Sister (second from left,
front row) and aspirants

Mother Marcelina Hua, Superior Sister

General view of the Convent

The Noviciate house

Designing and
Knitting School

A Sister giving a lesson
in dressmaking

The Sisters of Charity of Mother Seton

"The love of Christ encourages us"

The Blessing of St. Joseph's Girls' Middle and
High School at Kang-jin

General view of St. Joseph's Girls' Middle and
High School

Thomas Aquinas Carey, Superior Sister

Archbishop Harold Henry with the first Sisters of Charity of Mother Seton to arrive in Korea (1960)

Teachers of St. Joseph's Girls' School, Kang-jin

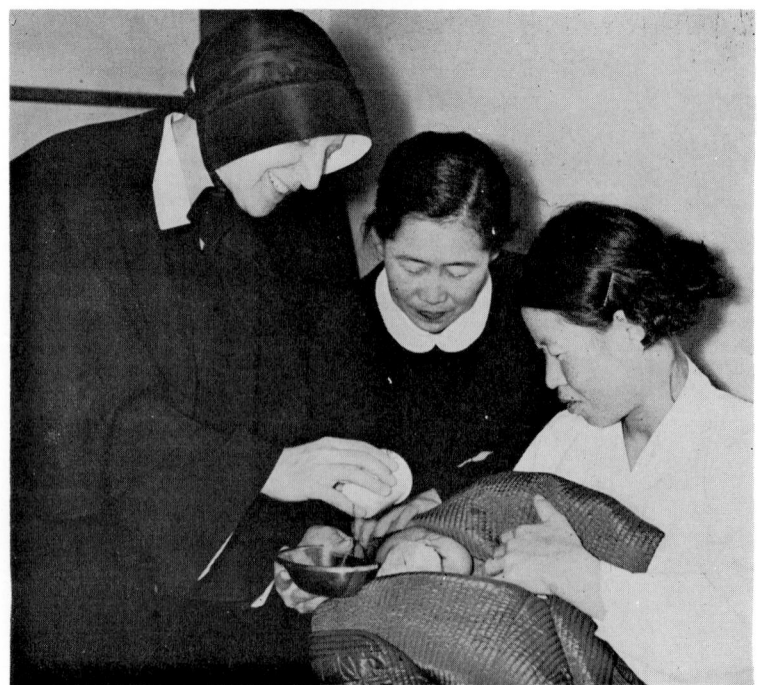

The Superior Sister baptizing an infant

The Daughters of St. Paul

"Oh, learned men, men of parts, possessors of strong will, possessors of mild mind, practical men, the incarnates of self-sacrifice, the flame-bearers of sanctification, those who thirst for the salvation of souls; come, all of you, to us in the field of the apostleship of publication, and view with joy the wide horizon that awaits your fulfilment of God's vocation!"

St. Paul the Apostle, the Society's Guardian Saint

The Rev. Alberione, the Founder

Maria Ignazia Balla, the Mother General

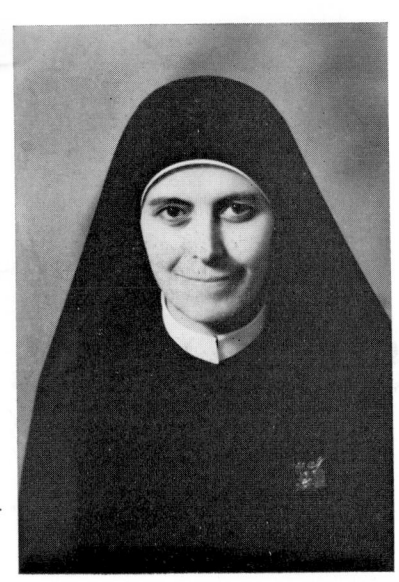

Mother Eulalia D'Ettorre, the Superior

The Convent

The composing room of Printing Office. "Truth is spread by each piece of type."

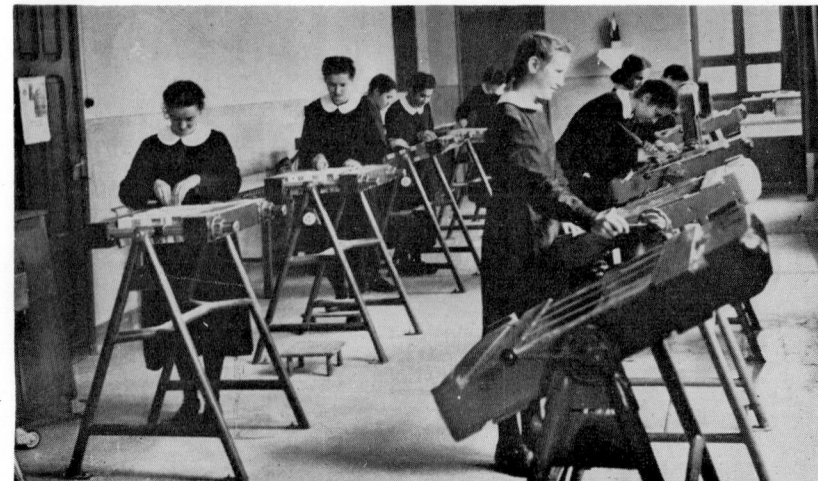

Postulants learning the technique of bookbinding

The Blessing of St. Paul's Book Store on opening day, Myŏng-dong, Seoul 1962

Customers buying books

Sisters visiting homes with pamphlets

Mother Superior Eulalia D'Ettorre (second from left) received by the Rev. James Lee (right), Vicar General of Tae-gu and the Rev. Melchior Kim, former Publisher of the Tae-gu Daily News (left)

The visit of the former Mother General Maria to all novices in Korea

Some of the Sisters in front of their newly-built Convent in Mi-a-dong, Seoul

The Society of St. Paul

The Rev. Paul Marcellino, the Superior

The monastery of the Society of St. Paul

The first Brothers of the Society to come to Korea

Brothers of the Society of St. Paul

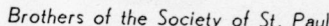

The Fraternity of the Little Sisters of Jesus

"Charles de Jesus." This beautiful name was chosen by Father Charles Foucauld himself. It transcends all classes, races and nations.

Charles de Jesus (Charles Foucauld)
who founded the fraternity, imitating our Lord Jesus Christ and preaching universal brotherhood, and who laid down his life for the Moslems of Touggourt

Welcome accorded to the Little Sisters of Jesus
(front row) Sr. Anne Antoinette of Jesus, Sr. Therese Noemie, Archbishop Ro. Sr. Joseph Regine

The Institute of the Blessed Virgin Mary

Motherhouse of Munich Province

Mother Elizabeth Park, Superior of the Institute

The Noviciate House

Bishop Larribeau visiting the Motherhouse of Munich Province (1962)

Korean Military Chaplains Corps

Father John Chang Pyǒng-yong, the Superior

The Chapel of the R.O.K. Military Academy at T'ae-neung

Benediction of the Chapel

Mass attended by cadets of the R.O.K. Military Academy

The Retreat Center of the U.S.
Armed Forces in Korea

U.S. chaplains' retreat. The Rev. Gilbert Zlatar (left), Spiritual Director, and the Rev. Joseph Raggier, former Superior of Military Chaplains Corps

U.S. chaplains' retreat, Sept. 10-14, 1962

U.S. Army Personnel at a retreat conducted by Bishop (1961) Murphy

The Five Chaplains Martyred in the Korean War

These five martyrs gave their lives,
>fulfilling their duties as priests and as soldiers
in the love of God,
>on the bloody battle field
and in Communist prison camp.

The Catholic Chaplains' Memorial Chapel

This Chapel, erected under the supervision of the St. Columban Fathers and paid for by the contributions of American soldiers, was dedicated on November 4, 1953 in Seoul, Korea, by the local Bishop, the Most Rev. Paul M. Ro. The Chapel honors the five American priests who made the supreme sacrifice in the Korean theatre of war. There were many distinguished guests at the dedication including President Syngman Rhee, Ambassador Ellis Briggs and General Maxwell D. Taylor. In the vestibule of the church is a beautiful marble plaque with this legend:

> DEDICATED TO THE MEMORY
> of
> Father Herman D. Felhoelter
> Father Francis X. Coppens
> Father Leo P. Craig
> Father Emil J. Kapaun
> Father Lawrence F. Brunnert
>> And to all who gave their lives
> in the cause of justice, freedom
> and peace in Korea.

Chaplain (Capt) HERMAN D. FELHOELTER, OFM (1913—1950)

Father Felhoelter was born on 17 July 1913 in Louisville, Kentucky. A member of the Order of Friars Minor, Father Felhoelter attended Duns Scotus College, Detroit, Michigan and Holy Family Seminary, Oldenburg, Indiana. He was appointed 1st lieutenant in the Army Chaplains' Branch 11 April 1944. He served with the 19th Infantry Regiment of the 24th Infantry Division in Korea. Father Felhoelter was killed in action north of Tae-jŏn, Korea on 16 July 1950 when "without regard for his own personal safety, voluntarily remained behind to give his wounded comrades spiritual comfort and aid." For his "extraordinary heroism" he was awarded the Distinguished Service Cross and the Purple Heart.

Chaplain (Capt) FRANCIS X COPPENS (1914—1951)

Father Coppens was born 2 January 1914 in Brighton, Massachusetts. He was an alumnus of Canisius College, Buffalo, New York, Boston College and St John's Seminary, Boston, Massachusetts. Before entering the Service he was the Assistant Pastor at Our Lady of the Presentation Parish, Brighton, Massachusetts and the St Francis of Assisi Parish, Braintree, Massachusetts. He was appointed 1st lieutenant in the Army Chaplains' Branch 3 August 1945. While chaplain of the 21st Infantry Regiment of the 24th Infantry Division, Father Coppens was killed in action on 27 May 1951 by attacking Chinese Communists. He was awarded the Purple Heart posthumously.

Chaplain (Capt) LEO P CRAIG, OP (1913–1951)

Father Craig was born in Everett, Massachusetts, 27 October 1913. A member of the Dominican Order, Father Craig studied at Providence College, Providence, Rhode Island, St Thomas Aquinas Seminary, River Forest, Illinois and Immaculate Conception College, Washington, D.C. He entered the Service as 1st lieutenant in the Chaplains' Branch of the Army on 17 January 1949. Father Craig, as Catholic Chaplain of the 1st Calvary Division Artillery, was killed by a mine at Sa-p'yŏng, Korea, "while disregarding his own personal safety, he moved through a mine-infested field to give comfort to the injured." For his heroism he was awarded the Bronze Star and Purple Heart posthumously.

Chaplain (1st Lt) LAWRENCE F BRUNNERT

Father Brunnert was born on 22 September 1917 in St Louis, Missouri. He attended St Louis Preparatory Seminary and Kenrick Seminary, St Louis, Missouri. He served as assistant pastor in various parishes of St Louis before entering the Army as 1st lieutenant in the Chaplains' Branch on 29 October 1948. He was taken prisoner on 2 December 1950 near Hagaru-Ri, Korea while Catholic Chaplain of the 32d Infantry Regiment of the 7th Infantry Division. Officially, Father Brunnert is still listed as missing in action. Returning prisoners of war, during Little and Big Swith, testified to his heroic service in prisoner of war camps. They also expressed the conviction that he had died while a prisoner.

Chaplain (Capt) EMIL J KAPAUN (1916–1951)

Father Kapaun was born in Marion, Kansas, 20 April 1916. He studied at Conception Junior College and Seminary and Kenrick Seminary, St Louis, Missouri and the Catholic University, Washington, D.C. He was ordained 9 June 1940 at Sacred Heart Academy, Wichita, Kansas. Before entering the Service on 9 August 1944, he was in four parishes in the Diocese of Wichita, Kansas. While with the 8th Cavalry Regiment of the 1st Cavalry Division, he was awarded the Bronze Star for his heroism in action against the enemy near Kumchon, Korea. Father Kapaun was taken prisoner on 2 November 1950 when "although fully aware of the great danger, he voluntarily remained behind and when last seen was administering medical treatment and rendering religious rites wherever he found need." Father Kapaun died 6 May 1951 while in the hands of the enemy, after his heroic services for the prisoners of war had become legendary. He was awarded the Distinguished Service Cross posthumously.

Towering in heroism and self-sacrifice on the bloody battlefield of Korea, the full stature of Father Kapaun as a priest, as a soldier, reached majestic maturity as a captive of the Chinese Reds. Marching and carrying the wounded over the rugged frozen terrain of Korea—housed in primitive barracks, slowly starving, lacking medicines and the bare necessities of life—this devoted chaplain, emaciated and sick himself, rallied, comforted, cheered his fellow prisoners—tired men who no longer wanted to live. Father Kapaun became the counselor, the nurse, the leader, the provider, the defender of this fellow prisoners, even their thief—for he "stole" food to keep his buddies alive.

His example of exquisite charity to all prisoners welded his men into a closely knit group, both before and after his death, revived in despondent hearts the will to live and kept alive the hope of liberation. He resisted calmly but firmly the brain-washing tactics of the Communists, dared to hold daily religious services, gave his men a deep faith in themselves and in the providence and mercy of God. The following letters speak eloquently of the multifold, untiring services of Father Kapaun. He was not to come back, but his fortitude in every trial was the chief factor in the survival and ultimate freedom of hundreds of his fellow P.O.W.s.

From Lt. Walter Mayo, Jr. to Father Tonne:

"Always with his pipe or a cigar in his mouth, he was an inspiration to everyone, being so calm and cheerful in a difficult situation.

"Wherever and whenever there was action, he was always there to help the wounded and give solace and the last rites for the dying. It was the same all the way up from Tae-jŏn to Seoul to Kae-sŏng to P'yŏng-yang to An-ju and then to Un-san.

"His pipe was shot out of his mouth but he put adhesive tape on it and continued to smoke. He must have dragged about fifteen or twenty men out of that field into our trenches.

"When night was approaching, he told us he was going back to the dugout which was about 150 yards from our outposts. He said he had to be with those 50 wounded. And back he went.

"That night the Chinese attacked us in force and it was hand to hand fighting at times. We knew that they must have gotten into the dugout.

"The next day was the third of November and we were still surrounded on the valley floor. We could not get out of our positions and find out what happened to Father. We held out, about 250 of us plus 150 more wounded, that day and next day.

"On scouting a way out of the trap, I went to the dugout and the wounded who were left told me what happened to Father.

"Being Dead, He Yet Speaketh"
by Helen Stewart

Being dead, this hero-chaplain has spoken
To my wakened heart as I sit and meditate
Upon his ordeal across the sea. As with a pen
Of gold, it has winged its spirit-way to me!

The padre with the broken pipe

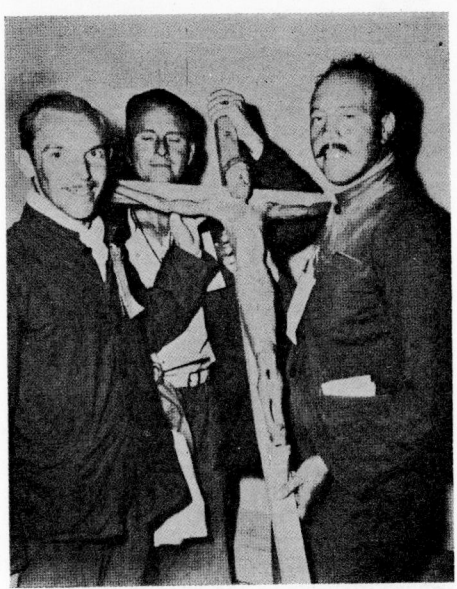

Capt. O'Connor (left), Warrent Officer McCool (middle) and Capt. Nardella (right), carrying the crucifix into Freedom Village

Could it be that I who've sat at home in ease
Surrounded by all comfort— heard the best of
Sermons too me— no! I've never known what
Sacrifice or, suffering is, until, this Saintly,
Soldier brushed aside all shame and shown me
By his fortitude, upon the bloody battlefield,
And in that filthy prison-camp, the beauty of
The Lamb of God!

"During their prison camp life Father would get out and sneak down to the sick and wounded first and then to see the men and say prayers.

"When they died he would get on the burial detail and dig the grave out of the rocky, frozen ground. He did that continuously.

"We were pretty hard up for food and were starving, so Father would go on ration run to get our cracked corn, millet and soy-beans. Before he went, he would say prayers to Saint Dismas, the Good Thief. They helped, because Father would steal, or get away with, sometimes two one-hundred-pound sacks of grain plus pocketfuls of salt which was very scarce. Pretty soon all of us were praying earnestly to St. Dismas, but Father succeeded much better than the rest of us."

A second letter from Lt. Walter Mayo, Jr:

"This was in February of 1951, when it was bitterly cold, about 20 below zero F. He would be up at five or six every morning in the dark and when the whistle blew for us to get up at 7:00 a.m., he would stick his head in the door and holler 'hot coffee' and hand us a nice hot cup of boiled water. People were dying at the rate of ten to twenty a day in the camp. As soon as he could he would sneak down past the guards to the enlisted men's section of the camp.

Oh God! to think that I could ever murmur
More upon this earth, when he unwavering,
Walked in mud and mire, in snow and sleet
Holding to his breast the dying, as Father,
As Shepherd, 'til the very last. He's earned his
Heavenly rest! Being dead, he yet speaketh.

Capt. Dolan (left), and Chaplain Kapaun (right), leading an exhausted soldier out of the line

"Lord it is true thy yoke is easy, thy burden light. I have often experienced that it is pleasant and comforting to bear the burden of duty. I would rather die for the true values of life than live for the false."

"After the Easter Services we noticed that Father was limping badly and had difficulty moving around. We found that he had a blood clot in his leg and that it was swollen from above the knee to the toes and had turned yellow and black."

"One day, about a month later, the Communists forced him to move to the 'hospital of death', and several days later he died there."

Unsolicited testimony comes from Peter V. Busatti:

"Is Father Kapaun a Saint? As far as I am concerned, he is. If I were able to send a note to Heaven, I would say, 'thanks to a great priest, a great soldier, and a great man way up there in Heaven. If anyone deserves Heaven, it certainly is you, Father—I shall never forget you."

From another prisoner, Felix McCool comes this letter to Father Tonne:

"He was a MAN of God. He ministered to all—Catholics, Protestants, Mohammedans, and Jews. He would hold evening prayers, wash the clothes of the sick and hear confessions. All this while he was slowly being eaten by disease caused by lack of proper food, sanitation and clothing."

"Father Kapaun began physically to look like Christ," is the surprising statement made by Major David MacGhee, in an article in COLLIER'S MAGAZINE for January 22, 1954. Major MacGhee, American airman, prisoner for thirty months, described Chaplain Kapaun as "by far the great man I ever met," and adds that "he came close to saintliness."

A Korean correspondent for the Associated Press sent the following dispatch to the United States—part of it runs as follows:

"His Regiment had recommended Father Kapaun for the Distinguished Service Cross, the second highest award for valor. Whether he received this award or not, all who knew him are agreed that he was Distinguished in the Service of Christ."

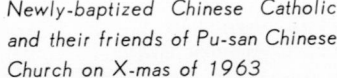

Father Matthias Ho, former Pastor
of Seoul Chinese Catholic Church

The Chinese Catholic
Church in Korea

Father Peter Liu, Pastor of
Pu-san Parish

Pu-san Chinese Catholic Church
(Sacred Heart of Jesus)

Newly-baptized Chinese Catholic
and their friends of Pu-san Chinese
Church on X-mas of 1963

Father Donald Haven,
Pastor of Seoul Chinese
Church

Newly-built Tae-gu Chinese Catholic Church (Sept. 21, 1964)

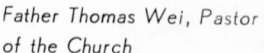

Father Thomas Wei, Pastor of the Church

Interior of the Church

The ceremony of laying cornerstone of the new Chinese Church in Tae-gu was blessed by Msgr. Carlo Van Melckbeke, Apostolic Visitor for Overseas Chinese Catholics

After the conceration of the Church (Center) Msgr. John V. Bulaitis, Secretary to Apostolic Inter-nunciature in Korea

The Legion of Mary

Reunion of confraternities at the Archconfraternity Center, Seoul

The Kwang-ju Legion

The Young Christian Workers' Association (J.O.C.)

Archbishop Zupi, attending a conference of the J.O.C. (1961)

The Rev. Joseph Cardian, Conductor of the Jeunesse Ouvriere Chrétienne

The Catholic Central Credit Union

After a lecture for the leaders of the C.C.C.U. in Pu-san

Korean Catholic Students' Association

The 10th Congress of National Delegates of K.C.S.A.

Dialogue on the Ecumenical Movement By Anglicans, Protestants and Catholics sponsored by K.C.S.A. The speaker (right) is the Rev Augustine Rah Sang-jo, Spiritual Director of K.C.S.A.

The Korea Center of the National
Catholic Welfare Conference,
Catholic Relief Service

*Msgr. George Carroll, Director of
the NCWC, Catholic Relief Service*

The warehouse of the Korea Center

*Msgr. Carroll receiving
the relief goods*

*Members of the
NCWC visiting
disabled soldeirs
with relief goods*

TABLE OF 79 KOREAN AND FRENCH BLESSED MARTYRS

No.	Social Position	Name	Age	Date of Arrest	Date of Martyrdom	Place of Martyrdom	Classification of Death	Kinship	Birthplace
1	Bishop	Laurent-J.-M. Imbert	43	Aug. 11, 1839	Sept. 21, 1839	Sae-nam-t'ŏ	B. & G.		France
2	Father	Perre-P. Maubant	35	Sept. 6, 1839	〃	〃	〃		〃
3	〃	Jacques-H. Chastan	〃			〃	〃		〃
4	Catechist	Augustine Lee Kwang-hŏn	53	Apr. 7, 1839	May 24, 1839	O.S. W.G.	B.	H. of 5, Br. of 16	Seoul
5	Woman	Barbara Kwon Heui	46	〃	Sept. 3, 1839	〃	〃	Wife of 4	〃
6	Virgin	Agatha Lee	17	〃	Jan. 9, 1840	〃	G.	Daughter of 4	〃
7	Catechist	Damian Nam Myŏng-hyŏk	38	〃	May 24, 1839	〃	B.	Husband of 8	〃
8	Woman	Maria Lee Yŏn-heui	36	〃	Sept. 3, 1839	〃	〃	Wife of 7	〃
9	S.T.Maker	Peter Kwon Teuk-in	35	Jan. 16, 1839	May 24, 1839	〃	〃		〃
10	Widow	Agatha Lee So-sa	56	Feb. 1836	〃	〃	〃	Sister of 58	〃
11	〃	Magdalene Kim A-ji	66	Oct. 1836	〃	〃	〃		〃
12	〃	Barbara Han A-ji	48	〃	〃	〃	〃		〃
13	Woman	Anna Park A-ji	57	Apr. 1836	〃	〃	〃		〃
14	Widow	Agatha Kim Ŏp-i	50	Oct. 1836	〃	〃	〃		〃
15	C.L. & V.	Lucy Park Heui-sun	39	Apr. 15, 1839	〃	〃	〃	Sister of 28	〃
16	Virgin	John Lee Kwang-yŏl	45	Apr. 7, 1839	July 20, 1839	〃	〃	Brother of 4	〃
17	〃	Magdalene Lee Yŏng-heui	31	Apr. 11, 1839	〃	〃	〃	Daughter of 18, Sister of 20	Si-heung
18	Woman	Magdalene Hŭh Kye-im	67	〃	Sept. 26, 1839	〃	〃	Mother of 17	〃
19	〃	Theresa Lee Mae-im	52	〃	July 20, 1839	〃	〃	Aunt of 17	Seoul
20	Widow	Barbara Lee Chŏng-heui	41	〃	Sept. 3, 1839	〃	〃	Sister of 17	Si-heung
21	Virgin	Barbara Lee	15	〃	May 27, 1839	〃	D.P.	Niece of 17	〃
22	Widow	Martha Kim Sŏng-im	50	〃	July 20, 1839	〃	B.		Pu-p'yŏng
23	Virgin	Lucy Kim Nu-si-a	22	〃	〃	〃	〃		Seoul
24	Widow	Anna Kim Chang-keum	51	Apr. 7, 1839	〃	〃	〃		〃
25	〃	Rose Kim No-sa	56	Jan. 16, 1839	〃	〃	〃		〃
26	Virgin	Maria Won Kwi-im	21	Apr. 7, 1839	〃	〃	〃		〃
27	Shoes Vd.	John Park Hu-jae	41	May 3, 1839	Sept. 3, 1839	〃	〃		〃
28	Woman	Mary Park Tae-a-ji	54	Apr. 15, 1839	〃	〃	〃	Sister of 15	〃
29	Sem.	Paul Chŭng Ha-sang	45	July 19, 1839	Sept. 22, 1839	〃	〃	Son of 47	〃
30	Catechist	Augustine Yu Chin-kil	49	July 17, 1839	〃	〃	〃	Father of 61	〃
31	Md.	Charles Cho Sin-ch'ŏl	45	July 1839	Sept. 26, 1839	〃	〃	Husband of 56	Hoe-yang
32	Catechist	Sebastian Nam I-kwan	60	Sept. 16, 1839	〃	〃	〃	Husband of 41	Seoul
33	Priest's Fr.	Ignatius Kim Che-jun	44	Sept. 1839	〃	〃	〃	Father of 71	Myŏn-ch'ŏn
34	Court Lady	Juliet Kim Yu-ri-tae	56	July 1839	〃	〃	〃		
35	〃	Agatha Chŭn Kyŏng-hyŏp	53	Apr. 15, 1839	〃	〃	〃		Seoul
36	Widow	Magdalene Park Pong-son	44	Apr. 1839	〃	〃	〃		〃
37	〃	Perpetua Hong Keum-ju	36	Apr. 1839	〃	〃	〃		〃
38	Virgin	Columba Kim Hyo-im	26	May 3, 1839	〃	〃	〃	Sister of 39	〃
39	〃	Agnes Kim Hyo-ju	24	〃	Sept. 3, 1839	〃	〃	Sister of 38	〃

40	Mty's Br.	Peter Ch'oe Ch'ang-heup	53	July 1839	Dec. 29, 1839	O.S. W.G.	B.	Uncle of 45	Seoul
41	Woman	Barbara Cho Cheung-i	58	July 1839	″	″	″	Wife of 32	″
42	Widow	Magdalene Han Yŏng-i	56	July 17, 1839	″	″	″		″
43	Woman	Agatha Kwon Chin-i	21	″	Jan. 31, 1840	Tang-ko-kae	″	Daughter of 42	″
44	Virgin	Agatha Lee Kyŏng-i	27	″	″	″	″		
45	Woman-Catechist	Benedict Hyŭn Kyŏng-yŏn	46	July 1839	Dec. 29, 1839	O.S. W.G.	″	Sister of 72	″
46	Virgin	Elizabeth Chŭng Chŏng-hye	43	July 19, 1839	″	″	″	Sister of 29	″
47	Widow	Cecile Ryu So-sa	79	″	Nov. 23, 1839		D. P.	Mother of 29	″
48	Woman	Barbara Ko Sun-i	42	Oct. 27, 1839	Dec. 29, 1839	″	B.	Wife of 51	″
49	Virgin	Magdalene Lee Yŏng-tŏk	28	July 1839	″	″	″	Sister of 50	″
50	″	Mary Lee In-tŏk	22	″	Jan. 31, 1840	Tang-ko-kae	″	Sister of 49	″
51	Catechist	Augustine Park Chong-won	48	Oct. 26, 1839		″	″	Husband of 48	″
52	″	Peter Hong Pyŏng-ju	42	Sept. 1839	″	″	″	Brother of 53	″
53	″	Paul Hong Yŏng-ju	39	″	Feb. 1, 1840	″	″	Brother of 52	″
54	Woman	Magdalene Sohn So-pyŏk	39	July 1839	Jan. 31, 1840	″	″	Wife of 40	″
55	Catechist	John Lee Mun-u	31	Nov. 11, 1839	Feb. 1, 1840	″	″		I-ch'ŏn
56	Woman	Barbara Ch'oe Yŏng-i	22	July 1839	″	″	″	W.of 31,Dr.of 40	″
57	Soldier	Paul Hŭh Hyŏm	45	Aug. 1839	Jan. 30, 1840		D.P.		″
58	Catechist	Peter Lee Ho-yŏng	36	Feb. 1836	Nov. 25, 1838		″	Brother of 10	″
59	Widower	Joseph Chang Sŏng-jip	54	May 18, 1839	May 26, 1839		″		Seoul
60	M.I. Maker	Protase Chŭng Kuk-po	41	May 12, 1839	May 21, 1839			″	″
61	Boy	Peter Yu Tae-ch'ŏl	13	July 1839	Oct. 31, 1839		G.	Son of 30	″
62	Widow	Barbara Kim	35	Apr. 1839	May 27, 1839		D.P.		″
63	Woman	Lucy Kim	71	″	Sept. 1839			″	″
64	Widow	Catherine Lee	57	July 1839	″			Mother of 65	″
65	Virgin	Magdalene Cho	33	″	″			Daughter of 64	″
66	Catechist	Francis Ch'oe Kyŏng-hwan	35	July 31, 1839	Sept. 12, 1839				Hong-ju
67	Ll. of Bp.'s House	Andrew Chŏng Hwa-kyŏng	33	Sept. 1839	Jan. 23, 1840		G.		Chŏng-san
68	Widow	Theresa Kim	44	July 19, 1839	Jan. 9, 1840		″	Aunt of 71	Ch'ung-ch'ŏng-do
69	Catechist	Stephen Min Keuk-ka	53	Jan. 25, 1840	Jan. 30, 1840		″		″
70	Ll. of O.	Anthony Kim	47	Jan. 1840	Apr. 29, 1841		″		Kwang-ju
71	Father	Andrew Kim Tae-kŏn	26	May 5, 1846	Sept. 16, 1846	Sae-nam-t'ŏ	B. & G.	Son of 33	Yong-in
72	Catechist	Charles Hyŭn Sŏk-mun	50	July 10, 1846	Sept. 19, 1846	″	″	Md. of 3	Seoul
73	Soldier	Peter Nam Kyŏng-mun	40	July 1846	Sept. 20, 1846		B.D.		
74	Sailor	Lawrence Han I-hyŏng	48	Aug. 1846	″		″		Tŏk-san
75	Seaman	Joseph Lim Ch'i-paek	43	June 1846	″		G.		Seoul
76	Virgin	Theresa Kim Im-i	36	July 10, 1846	″		B.D.		″
77	Widow	Agatha Lee Kan-ran	33	″	″		″		″
78	″	Susanna U Sul-im	44	″	″		″	Ss. of 77	Yang-ju
79	Maid-Servant	Catherine Chŭng Ch'ŏl-yŏm	30	″	″		″	Maid of 71	

TABLE OF 26 MARTYRS TO BE BEATIFIED

No.	Social Position	Name	Age	Date of Arrest	Date of Martyrdom	Place of Martyrdom	Classification of Death	Kinship	Birthplace
1	Bishop	Siméon-F. Berneux	52	Feb. 23, 1866	Mar. 8, 1866	Sae-nam-t'ŏ	B.		France
2	″	M.A.N. Daveluy	48	Mar. 11, 1866	Mar. 30, 1866	Po-ryŏng	″		″
3	Father	S.M.A.J.R. de Bretenières	28	Feb. 26, 1866	Mar. 8, 1866	Sae-nam-t'ŏ	″		″
4	″	B.L. Beaulieu	26	Feb. 27, 1866	″	″	″		″
5	″	Pierre-Henri Dorie	28	″	″	″	″		″
6	″	Charles A. Pourthié	36	Mar. 8, 1866	Mar. 11, 1866	″	″		″
7	″	Michel A. Petitnicolas	38	″	″	″	B.&.G.		″
8	″	Pierre Aumaître	29	In the middle of March, 1866	Mar. 30, 1866	Po-ryŏng	″		″
9	″	Martin-Luc Huin	30	″	″	″	″		″
10		Peter Yu Chŏng-ryul	30	Feb. 16, 1866	Feb. 17~18, 1866	″	B. D.		P'yŏng-yang
11	Govenment Official	John Nam Chong-sam	54	Feb. 25, 1866	Mar. 8, 1866	O.S. W.G.	B.		Che-ch'ŏn
12	D. Books' Maker	Peter Ch'oe Ch'i-chang (Hyŏng)	57	Feb. 19, 1866	Mar. 10, 1866	″	″		Kong-ju
13	″	John Chŭn Chang-un	58	″	″	″	″		Seoul
14	Catechist	Mark Chŭng Eui-Pae	71	Feb. 25, 1866	Mar. 11, 1866	Sae-nam-t'ŏ	B.&.G.		Yong-in
15	Yang-pan	Alexis U Se-yŏng	21	″	″	″	″		Sŏ-heung
16	Md.	Luke Hwang Sŏk-tu	52	Mar. 12, 1866	Mar. 30, 1866	Po-ryŏng	″		Yŏn-p'ung
17	Catechist	Joseph Chang Nak-so	65		″	″	″		Su-won
18		Thomas Sohn Cha-sŏn	27	″	Mar. 31, 1866	Kong-ju	G.		Nae-p'o
19	Md.	Peter Cho Hwa-sŏ	40	Dec. 5, 1866	Dec. 13, 1866	Chŏn-ju	B.	Fr. of 20	Su-won
20		Joseph Cho Yun-ho	19	″	Dec. 18, 1866	″	B. D.	S. of 19	Sin-ch'ang
21		Peter Lee Myŏng-sŏ	50	″	Dec. 13, 1866		B.		
22	Yang-pan	Bartholomew Chŭng Mun-ho	65-66	″	″	″	″		Im-ch'ŏn
23	Catechist	Peter Sohn Sŏn-ji	48	″	″	″	″		″
24	″	Peter Han Won-sŏ	37-38	″	″	″	″		Chin-jam
25		Peter Chŭng Won-ji	22	″	″	″	″		″
26	Catechist	John Lee Yun-il	45-46		Jan. 21, 1867	Tae-gu	″		Hong-ju

Guide to Abbreviations: B.=Beheaded; B.D.=Beaten to Death; Br.=Brother; C.=Court; D.=Devotional; D.P.=Died in Prison; Dr.=Daughter; Fr.=Father; G.=Gibbeted; H.=Husband; I.=Instrument; L.=Lady; Ll.=Landlord; M.=Musical; Md.=Major-domo; Mty.=Martyr; O.=Outstation; O.S.W.G.=Outside of the Small West Gate; S.=Son; Sem.=Seminarian; Ss.=Seamstress; S.T.=Sacred Things; Vd.=Vendor; W.=Wife

STATISTICS OF THE CATHOLIC CHURCH IN KOREA 1964

No statistics are available for the Dioceses of Pyŏng-yang and Ham-heung in North Korea. Priests of these two Dioceses are serving in various Dioceses of South Korea.

Classifications	Divisions	Archdiocese of Seoul	Diocese of Ch'un-ch'ŏn	Diocese of Tae-jŏn	Diocese of In-ch'ŏn	Diocese of Su-won	Archdiocese of Tae-gu	Diocese of Pu-san	Diocese of Ch'ŏng-ju	Archdiocese of Kwang-ju	Diocese of Chŏn-ju	Total
Archbishops	Korean	1	—	—	—	—	1	—	—	—	—	2
	Foreign	1	—	—	—	—	—	—	—	1	—	2
Bishops	Korean	—	—	—	—	—	—	—	—	—	1	3
	Foreign	—	1	—	1	1	—	1	1	—	—	3
Monsignors		1	—	—	—	—	1	—	—	1	—	4
Priests	Korean	99	13	20	2	36	79	39	4	16	30	338
	Foreign	13	39	20	24	—	34	15	36	69	5	255
Brothers	Korean	13	—	14	10	—	32	—	—	5	—	74
	Foreign	5	—	—	1	—	6	—	3	17	—	32
	Novices	16	—	—	1	—	4	—	3	16	—	36
	Postulants	21	—	—	—	—	10	—	—	27	—	58
Nuns	Korean	371	40	54	91	39	210	100	56	64	27	1,052
	Foreign	37	23	—	5	—	22	46	5	34	—	172
	Novices	113	25	—	—	—	85	30	—	16	—	269
	Postulants	274	13	—	—	8	68	40	—	20	—	423
Major Seminarians		89	20	21	24	36	66	48	22	25	28	379
Minor Seminarians		85	18	45	32	42	37	54	19	71	32	335
Catechists	Male	313	167	392	44	326	370	50	143	89	319	2,213
	Female	447	63	77	38	47	69	40	28	23	18	850

	Total									
Teachers — Male	1,286	—	—	19	115	262	107	245	83	64	391
Teachers — Female	747	—	—	15	60	107	95	207	48	125	90
Religious Societies											
Priests — Benedictines	30	—	—	—	1	28	—	—	—	—	1
Columbans	111	—	54	—	—	—	—	—	—	39	18
Conventuals	4	—	—	—	2	2	—	—	—	—	—
Franciscans	13	—	—	—	5	—	—	—	3	—	5
Guadalupe	6	—	6	—	—	—	—	—	—	—	—
Jesuits	15	—	4	—	—	—	—	—	—	—	11
Korean Martyrs	1	—	—	—	—	—	—	—	—	—	1
Marianists	1	—	1	—	—	—	—	—	—	—	—
Maryknoll	73	—	—	36	5	—	—	24	—	—	8
Paris Foreign Mission	32	—	—	—	—	14	—	—	17	—	1
Paulists	2	—	—	—	—	—	—	—	—	—	2
Salesians	10	—	5	—	—	—	—	—	—	—	5
TOTALS	**298**	—	**70**	**36**	**13**	**44**	—	**24**	**20**	**39**	**52**
Brothers — Benedictines	85	—	—	—	—	72	—	—	—	—	13
Franciscans	16	—	—	—	—	—	—	—	14	—	2
Jesuits	2	—	—	—	—	—	—	—	—	—	2
Korean Martyrs	57	—	3	—	—	—	—	10	—	—	44
Marianists	5	—	5	—	—	—	—	—	—	—	—
Maryknoll	6	—	—	3	—	—	—	1	—	—	2
Paulists	6	—	—	—	—	—	—	—	—	—	6
Salesians	17	—	8	—	—	—	—	—	—	—	9
St. John of God	6	—	6	—	—	—	—	—	—	—	—
TOTALS	**200**	—	**22**	**3**	—	**72**	—	**11**	**14**	—	**78**
Benedictines (Pu-san)	63	—	—	—	44	9	—	—	—	—	10

Classifications	Archdiocese of Seoul	Diocese of Ch'un-ch'ŏn	Diocese of Tae-jŏn	Diocese of In-ch'ŏn	Diocese of Su-won	Archdiocese of Tae-gu	Diocese of Pu-san	Diocese of Ch'ŏng-ju	Archdiocese of Kwang-ju	Diocese of Chŏn-ju	Total
Sisters											
Caritas (So-sa)	149	9	5	30	—	6	8	—	3	15	225
Caritas (Kwang-ju)	—	—	—	—	—	—	—	—	31	—	31
Carmelites	25	—	—	—	—	18	14	—	—	—	57
Columbans	—	13	—	—	—	—	—	—	18	—	31
Daughters of St. Paul	24	—	—	—	—	—	—	—	—	—	24
Fran. Miss. of Mary	—	—	—	—	—	—	12	—	—	—	12
Holy Family	159	3	2	—	26	—	—	3	—	3	196
Handmaids of Sac. Heart.	—	—	11	6	—	204	4	30	13	—	268
Korean Martyrs	56	3	15	13	—	6	21	7	—	—	121
Little Comp. of Mary	—	2	—	—	—	—	—	—	—	—	2
Little Sisters of Jesus	3	—	—	—	—	4	—	—	—	—	7
Loretto	7	—	—	—	—	—	—	—	—	—	7
Maryknoll	4	—	—	4	—	—	27	5	—	—	40
Missionary Benedictines	8	—	—	—	3	30	—	—	—	—	41
Perpetual Help	38	22	—	3	—	—	4	5	—	—	72
Sacred Heart	20	11	—	—	—	—	—	—	—	—	31
Salesians	40	—	—	—	—	—	—	—	8	—	48
Seton Hill	—	—	—	—	—	—	—	—	6	—	6
St. Paul de Chartres	248	—	21	40	10	170	17	6	17	9	538
TOTALS	791	63	54	96	39	447	151	56	96	27	1,820
Scholastics											
Jesuits	4	—	—	—	—	—	—	—	1	—	5
Salesians	12	—	—	—	—	—	—	—	—	—	12
TOTALS	16	—	—	—	—	—	—	—	1	—	17
Vicariates Forane	—	3	—	—	—	2	—	—	1	—	6
Parishes	40	28	22	12	24	52	43	21	32	25	299

Secondary Stations	47	181	251	84	254	301	204	160	139	230	1,851
Churches: Capacity 400	35	26	20	20	16	53	44	21	41	30	306
Chapels: less than 400	64	133	89	48	36	17	4	85	95	73	644
Catholics: 1964	111,194	46,433	49,925	36,567	48,253	94,500	90,299	40,131	65,489	45,755	628,546
Population	3,972,842	3,000,000	2,820,714	726,609	1,336,742	4,230,000	4,299,958	1,464,697	3,896,782	2,401,063	28,149,407
Bapt.: Adult	7,401	2,632	2,177	4,267	3,347	7,462	7,625	3,637	1,562	2,299	42,409
Bapt.: Cath. Infants	3,537	1,750	1,861	1,176	2,247	2,907	2,718	1,419	1,957	1,639	21,211
Bapt.: Danger of Death	1,610	1,104	574	769	1,112	3,013	3,298	970	854	429	13,737
Immigrants	12,049	3,018	1,598	2,888	2,709	6,917	6,709	2,288	2,937	802	41,915
Deaths	558	367	405	272	385	550	508	237	491	281	4,054
Emigrants	9,469	3,110	2,444	2,808	2,377	7,102	9,533	2,807	3,452	2,131	45,233
Tepid	6,420	3,101	1,944	1,647	2,023	5,034	3,661	1,867	5,776	1,658	33,131
Increase in Cath. Pop. 63~64	*-33,270	3,612	3,104	5,251	*48,253	9,634	7,011	4,632	1,767	2,808	52,802
Catechumens	5,946	3,737	2,940	6,494	2,685	9,705	9,790	6,185	4,037	7,180	58,699
Conf.: Annual	51,151	21,119	24,119	20,105	25,961	46,346	43,754	19,994	28,423	21,538	302,510
Comm.: Easter	50,819	21,109	24,004	20,138	25,746	53,472	44,514	20,267	28,851	21,524	310,444
Conf.: Devotional	401,493	186,541	137,312	202,873	152,961	363,570	334,607	185,041	293,863	132,371	2,390,632
Comm.: Devotional	1,661,984	501,082	464,037	510,859	522,436	1,271,990	999,765	585,317	985,113	364,743	7,867,326
Marriages { Catholic	820	224	293	208	376	376	380	166	147	242	3,262
Marriages { Mixed	289	202	115	120	173	370	230	187	276	54	2,016
Doctors	196	4	5	15	2	18	30	2	5	2	279
Nurses	257	27	12	39	4	59	66	8	50	8	530
Hospitals	9	—	3	2	—	5	4	4	1	2	26
Beds	600	—	20	110	—	92	250	—	100	25	1,197
Dispensaries	1	2	2	6	—	1	3	2	2	1	20

Classifications	Archdiocese of Seoul	Diocese of Ch'un-ch'ŏn	Diocese of Tae-jŏn	Diocese of In-ch'ŏn	Diocese of Su-won	Archdiocese of Tae-gu	Diocese of Pu-san	Diocese of Ch'ŏng-ju	Archdiocese of Kwang-ju	Diocese of Chŏn-ju	Total
Patients	280,000	39,768	35,400	135,792	—	141,298	297,550	28,359	97,568	23,809	1,079,544
Orphanages	4	—	3	3	2	2	5	2	3	—	24
Orphans {Boys	199	—	70	22	48	150	103	22	243	—	857
Orphans {Girls	185	—	150	343	62	220	353	33	145	—	1,419
Homes for Aged	—	—	1	3	1	2	—	1	—	—	8
Residents	—	—	50	52	35	560	—	35	—	—	732
Leper Colonies	—	—	1	—	1	6	3	—	1	—	12
Patients	—	—	160	—	167	746	300	—	333	—	1,706
Kindergartens	8	2	7	2	6	18	10	—	7	1	61
Children {Boys	338	65	173	77	117	482	466	—	175	78	1,971
Children {Girls	292	90	174	46	92	478	484	—	185	47	1,887
Primary Schools	2	1	1	1	2	1	1	1	1	—	11
Pupils {Boys	50	63	—	177	359	—	17	396	106	—	1,168
Pupils {Girls	101	61	83	445	344	630	9	368	75	—	2,116
Middle Schools	4	—	4	2	3	5	6	—	6	2	32
Pupils {Boys	1,053	—	1,026	528	525	2,842	586	—	1,114	537	8,211
Pupils {Girls	1,260	—	420	1,028	526	3,068	3,239	—	1,498	1,085	12,124
High Schools	4	—	3	2	2	5	6	1	4	2	29
Students {Boys	727	—	493	436	177	1,830	673	171	753	255	5,515
Students {Girls	903	—	499	546	262	1,882	2,034	—	988	865	7,979
Professional Schools	4	2	1	—	1	1	1	2	1	—	13

	Total										
Students {Boys	903	—	—	50	15	27	727	—	40	1	58
Students {Girls	431	—	40	37	—	—	—	—	40	128	171
Colleges	6	—	1	—	—	1	—	—	—	1	3
Students {Male	1,357	—	94	—	—	—	—	—	—	—	1,263
Students {Female	1,469	—	—	—	—	1,121	—	—	—	99	249
Sunday Schools	647	48	32	68	40	51	30	60	80	54	184
Children {Boys	28,255	929	2,310	3,015	4,500	2,350	1,345	3,557	3,114	2,135	5,000
Children {Girls	33,766	2,121	2,675	3,430	5,500	2,560	1,742	3,981	3,777	2,535	5,445
Printing Presses	2	—	—	—	—	1	—	—	—	—	1
Newspaper Companies	2	—	—	—	—	2	—	—	—	—	—
Magazine Offices	3	—	—	—	—	—	—	—	—	—	3
Birth	—	2. 3.1913	7.11.1909	3. 9.1898	1. 7.1912	5. 1.1911	11. 8.1924	12. 7.1926	—	9.13.1896	12.13.1901
Ordination	—	6.24.1939	12.21.1932	1.26.1930	6.12.1938	6.11.1938	3.20.1950	6.13.1953	—	2. 2.1920	10.26.1930
Ordinaries {Appointment	—	1. 3.1961	1.26.1957	7. 4.1958	3. 7.1957	7.13.1955	10. 7.1963	6. 6.1961	—	9.20.1955	1. 3.1940
Ordinaries {Consecration	—	3.12.1961	5.11.1957	9.16.1958	5.30.1957	9.15.1955	10.20.1963	8.24.1961	—	11.23.1955	12.20.1942
Catholics in 1954	189,408	24,504	13,575	—	—	59,388	—	—	23,954	9,875	58,112
Catholics in 1961	492,464	38,955	60,953	28,768	72,268	73,879	—	—	43,689	37,584	136,368
Catholics in 1962	530,217	40,949	61,961	31,612	76,398	76,864	—	28,107	45,017	40,764	128,545
Catholics in 1963	575,789	42,992	63,722	35,499	83,288	84,866	—	31,316	46,821	42,821	144,464
Catholics in 1964	628,546	45,755	65,489	40,131	90,299	94,500	48,253	36,567	49,925	46,433	111,194

* OCT., 1963, SUWON DIOCESE (42,648) CUT OFF FROM ARCHDIOCESE OF SEOUL.

※ THIS IS BASED ON THE STATISTICS AS OF JUNE, 1964 OF C.C.K

1253-1255 Guillaume de Rubruc, a Franciscan, made the round journey to Karakoram, the Mongol capital.

1294 Joannes a Monte Corvino, a Franciscan, arrived in Cambaluc (Peking), engaged in missionary work for 30 years and made 30,000 converts.

1342 Joannes a Marignolli, Papal Legate, arrived in Peking.

1520 Thomas Pires, envoy of the king of Portugal, arrived in Peking.

1534 Foundation of the Society of Jesus (S.J.) by St. Ignatius de Loyola and St. Francis Xavier in Paris.

1540 The S. J. was recognized as a foreign mission by Pope Paul III.

1542 St. Francis Xavier began his missionary work at Goa, India.

1552 Dec. 3: St. Francis Xavier died at Sancian Island near Macao.

1567 Fr. Gaspar Vilela, S.J., attempted to penetrate into Korea from Japan.

1568 Certain Catholic books were banned by the government of Korea (Yi Dynasty).

1582 Fr. Matteo Ricci, S.J., arrived in China (Ming Dynasty).

1592 Hideyoshi, Regent of Japan, invaded Korea, and rapidly conquered three quarters of the country.

1593 Many Korean prisoners, including Blessed Vincent Kwon, were taken to Japan.

1594 Fr. Gregoris de Cespedes, S.J. came to Korea and was stationed at Ung-ch'ŏn, Kyŏng-sang Province.

1595 Fr. Cespedes returned to Japan. Korean prisoners baptized in Japan.

1597 Br. Carletti took five Korean boys, including Anthony Corrêa, to Goa, India.

1601 Fr. Matteo Ricci arrived at Peking. Vincent Kwon became a Jesuit in Japan.

1603 Fr. Matteo Ricci published *True Doctrine of God*, in two volumes, at Peking.

1606 The Korean Anthony Corrêa went to Rome.

1610 Hŭh Kyun went to Peking and after reading *Kye-sip-i-jang* (Twelve Hymns) became a Christian.

1614 Lee Su-kwang published his *Chi-pong-yu-sŏl*, (The Essays of Chi-pong).
Bro. Vincent Kwon, S.J., attempted to enter Korea via Peking, but failed.

1616 Fr. Juan de S. Dominic, accompanied by two monks, attempted to penetrate into Korea from the Philippines, but was not permitted to land.

1618 The Korean Catholic Hŭh Kyun was assassinated.

1619 Nov. 18: Blessed Cosmas Takeya, Korean layman, martyr, burnt alive, at Nagasaki, Japan. Beatified in 1867.

1620 Paul Hsu Kwang-chi, Ming Dynasty scholar and official, friend and colleague of the Jesuit Fathers, petitioned the emperor to dispatch him to Korea as a special envoy to advise the Korean government in its struggle against the Manchus, but the petition was disallowed.

1626 June 20: Blessed Vincent Kwon, S. J., martyr, burnt alive at Nagasaki, Japan. Beatified in 1867.

1644 Fr. Johann Adam Schall von Bell, S.J., (1591-1666), the leading missionary in Peking, became friendly with the Korean Prince So-hyŏn. The prince returned to Korea taking with him to the royal court of Korea three maids of honor and five eunuchs, but on his death they returned to China.

1650 Fr. Anthony de Santa-Maria, a Franciscan, attempted to enter Korea by the land route, but failed.

1686 The government of Korea ordered the expulsion of foreigners and displayed hostility to Christianity.

1693 For their service at court the French missionaries were given a piece of land inside the Forbidden City.

1703 Fr. D. Noel attempted to establish a Christian mission in Manchuria.
The Emperor Kang Hsi issued an edict legalizing and protecting Catholic missionary work in the empire.

1704—1710 Pope Clement XI sent his first Papal Legate to Peking, Msgr. Charles Maillard de Tournon, to settle the 'Rites Controversy.'

1713 Completion of the *Peitang* (Catholic church in north Peking).

1715 Pope Clement XI forbade the Chinese Christians to observe ancestral rites.

1719—1720 Pope Clement XI sent a second Papal

Legate to Peking, Msgr. Jean Ambrose Charles Mezzabarba, in an attempt to convince the Emperor Kang Hsi, who favored toleration.

1720 Lee I-myŏng visited the *Nantang* (Catholic church in south Peking), and discussed Catholicism with European Catholic missionaries.

1758 Christians in Hae-sŏ (Hwang-hae Province) and Kwan-tong (Kang-won Province) destroyed ancestral shrines and abandoned ancestor worship.

1766 Hong Tae-yong met foreign Catholic missionaries at South and East Churches (*Nantang* and *Tungtang*) at Peking during January.

1777 Kwon Ch'ŏl-sin, Chŭng Yak-jŏn, Chŭng Yak-yong and Lee Pyŏk opened a class for the study of Christian doctrine in an abandoned Buddhist temple (Chu-ŏ-sa, Mt. Aeng-cha-pong, in the district of Yŏ-ju) and practiced religion there.

1783 Lee Pyŏk, Chŭng Yak-jŏn and Chŭng Yak-yong met on a boat on the Han River, and made further researches into Christian doctrine in the month of April. Lee Seung-hun left for Peking on Oct. 14.

1784 Jan.: Lee Seung-hun baptized in Peking by Fr. Louis de Grammont, S.J., with the name of Peter, returning to Korea on Mar. 24.
Lee Pyŏk and Kwon Il-sin embraced the faith. The Emperor Kang Hsi displayed animosity toward Christianity and persecution arose in Peking.

1785 Bp. Alexander de Gouvéa arrived at Peking. In spring, 20 or 30 Christians met at the house of Kim Pŏm-u and organized the "False Ecclesiastical Hierarchy," of the Korean Catholic Church, without validly ordained priests.
Apr.: Kim Pŏm-u was arrested and exiled to Tan-yang in the Province of Ch'ung-ch'ŏng, Ryu Ha-won petitioned the government to suppress the Catholic religion.
Temporary apostasies of Lee Seung-hun and Lee Pyŏk.

1786 Import of books from Peking prohibited. Yun Chi-ch'ung baptized, with the name Paul. Lee Pyŏk died.

1787 Francis-Xavier Kwon Il-sin was appointed "bishop," and Lee Seung-hun, Lee Tan-won, Ryu Hang-kŏm, and Ch'oe Ch'ang-hyŏn were appointed "priests."
Martyrdom of Kim Pŏm-u, at Tan-yang, his

place of exile.

1788 Christian Catechism was translated into Korean by Lee Ka-hwan and his companions. Official order issued for the burning of all Catholic books.

1789 Oct.: Yun Yu-il conveyed a secret letter sewn in his clothing to the Catholic Church in Peking.

1790 Feb. 5: Yun Yu-il baptized by Fr. Nicholas Joseph Raux with the name of Paul.
The members of so-called "False Ecclesiastical Hierarchy," realizing its invalidity, disbanded and ceased to function.
May: Paul Yun Yu-il and John U conveyed second secret letter from Peter Lee to Peking in May; Bp. de Gouvéa promised to send a priest to Korea. Rise of persecution of Christians in Korea, owing to their refusal to participate in the rites of ancestor worship.

1791 Fr. John dos Remedios, a Chinese, reached the Korean border but failed to enter Korea. Outbreak of the *Sin-hae* persecution, in the month of November.
Paul Yun Chi-ch'ung and James Kwon Sang-yŏn executed. Kwon Il-sin died in prison.
Public burning of Catholic books in the capital and countryside.
Korean catechism book published, printed, from wooden blocks.

1792 The Most Rev. Alexander de Gouvéa, Bishop of Peking, reported the foundation of the Church in Korea to Pope Pius VI.

1793 Jan.: Peter Won Si-jang tortured to death. Paul Yun Yu-il and Sabas Chi Hwang conveyed a secret letter to the Catholic Church in Peking. Fr. James Chou Wen-mo, a Chinese, dispatched to Korea.

1794 Number of Catholics in Korea reached over 4000.
Fr. Chou left Peking in Feb. to spread the faith in Korea. He arrived in Korea on Dec. 23.

1795 Jan.: Fr. Chou established his residence at the home of the widow Columba Kang Wan-suk.
June 27: Warrant for Fr. Chou's arrest issued.
June 28: Matthias Ch'oe In-kil, Sabas Chi Hwang and Paul Yun Yu-il tortured to death in prison,
Lee Tan-won, captured at the end of 1795, was sentenced to six years' house arrest.

1796 Sept.: Fr. Chou sent a letter to the Church in

Peking, mentioning the situation of the Church in Korea, through Hwang Sim.

The British man-of-war *Providence* arrived off the South Coast of Korea and a Korean Christian named Hyŏn Kye-heum went on board to look at it.

Decree issued by King Chŏng-jo suspending the death penalty for Christians.

1797 Jan. 28: Hwang Sim arrived safely in Peking, and reported to the Catholic Church on the situation of the Church in Korea.

1798 June: Martyrdom of Lee To-ki, of Ch'ŏng-yang, in the Province of Ch'ung-ch'ŏng.

1799 Martyrdom of James Won, cousin of Won Si-jang, and that of Lawrence Park, of Hong-ju.

1800 June 28: Death of King Chŏng-jo. King Sun-jo succeeded at the age of eleven.

Total number of Catholics reached 10,000.

Dec. 17: Re-arrest of Thomas Ch'oe P'il-kong.

Dec. 19: Arrest of Peter Ch'oe P'il-je.

Outbreak of persecution of the Church.

1801 Government decrees suppression of Catholic religion (*Sin-yu* persecution). Many Christians arrested, through the system of collective responsibility in five-family groups.

Feb. 21: Martyrdom of Kwon Ch'ŏl-sin, Lee Ka-hwan tortured to death: and Lee Seung-hun, Chūng Yak-jong, Ch'oe P'il-kong, Ch'oe Ch'ang-hyŏn, Hong Nak-min, and Hong Kyo-man all decapitated outside the Small West Gate. Feb. 28: Martyrdom of Lee Tan-won (decapitated)

Mar. 13: ″ ″ Lee Chung-pae ″
Apr. 20: ″ ″ Kim Kŏn-sun ″
 ″ ″ ″ ″ Kim Paek-sun ″

Apr. 19: ″ ″ Fr. James Chou Wen-mo decapitated at Sae-nam-t'ŏ, and head exposed to the public.

May 23: Martyrdom of women Christians Columba Kang Wan-suk (41), Kang Kyŏng-pok, Kim Yŏn-i, Han Sin-ae, Mun Yŏng-in, all decapitated.

May 25: Martyrdom of the virgins, Chūng Sun-mae and Yun Chŏm-hye, both decapitated.

Sept.: Capture of Hwang Sa-yŏng and the secret silk letter.

Oct. 9: Martyrdom of John Ryu Chong-sŏn (son of Ryu Hang-kŏm), by hanging.

Nov. 5: Martyrdom of Hwang Sa-yŏng, outside the Small West Gate, by decapitation.

Dec. 26: Martyrdom of Charles Lee Kyŏng-to (brother of Lugartha Lee) decapitated.

Dec. 28: Martyrdom of Lugartha Lee (lifelong virgin spouse of John Ryu Chong-sŏn) and of Matthew Ryu(18) both decapitated.

1802 Jan.: Official ban for the "Suppression of Evil Doctrine" promulgated throughout the country. John Kwon, Shin Tae-po, Lee Yŏ-jin and Maurus Ch'oe met to plan rebuilding of the Korean Church.

1811 Mar.: Enforcement of the prohibition of the Catholic religion throughout the nation.

Oct. 24: John Kwon sent a secret letter through John Lee Yŏ-jin to Bishop of Peking appealing for missionary priests.

1812 Outbreak of persecution of Catholics in Ch'ung-ch'ŏng Province.

1813 At the end of year: John Lee Yŏ-jin took another secret letter to Peking.

1814 Feb. 20: Pius Kim Chin-hu (grandfather of Blessed Andrew Kim Tae-kŏn, first Korean priest, and martyr) died in prison after ten years' incarceration, at the age of 76.

1815 Feb.: Outbreak of the *Eul-hae* persecution of Catholics in Kyŏng-sang Province, 300 arrests, 100 imprisoned at Tae-gu.

1816 Martyrdom of twenty-nine Catholics in the prison of Tae-gu.

July 14: Captain Basil Hall, commanding the British merchantman the *Lyra*, and Captain Murray Maxwell the *Alceste* visited the coast of Ch'ung-ch'ŏng Province to engage in trade, but without result.

Oct. 24: Paul Chūng Ha-sang left for Peking to interview the Most Rev. Cajetani Pires Pereira, Bishop of Nanking and ask for missionary priests to be sent to Korea.

1817 Oct.: Arrest and inprisonment of more than 30 Catholics at Hae-mi, in Ch'ung-ch'ŏng Province.

1819 May: Martyrdom of Peter Cho Myŏng-su and two companions, at Seoul.

1823 A party of Catholics went to the border to receive a priest, but without result.

1824 Paul Chūng Ha-sang, Augustine Yu Chin-kil and Charles Cho Sin-ch'ŏl went to Peking.

1825 Paul Chūng Ha-sang, Augustine Yu Chin-kil, and Lee Yŏ-jin addressed a joint petition to Pope Leo XII. Fr. Sim attempted to enter Korea, but died of sickness on the journey. Enrolment of Msgr. Barthélemy Bruguière in the M.E.P.

1826 Government of Japan reports flight of Japanese Christian refugees to Korea.

1827 Outbreak of the *Chŏng-hae* Persecution of the Church. Arrest and imprisonment of 240 Catholics at Kok-sŏng pottery works, Chŏl-la Province. Martyrdom of seven of these prisoners at Chŏn-ju.

Sept. 1: Pope Leo XII received the letter from Korean Christians and requested the M.E.P. to send missionary priests to Korea.

1830 Lee Yŏ-jin died.

June: The British ship *Adamastor* commanded by Captain Basil Hall appeared off the coast of Hwang-hae and Ch'ung-ch'ŏng Provinces.

Sept. 9: Erection of the Vicariate Apostolic of Korea by Pope Gregory XVI.

1831 The Protestant missionaries Gutzlaff and Lindsay attempted to open their mission field in Korea.

1832 Sept.: The Most Rev. Barthélemy Bruguière, Bishop of Capse, a priest of the M.E.P., was appointed Vicar Apostolic of Korea, and left Penang for Korea, accompanied by Joseph Wang.

1833 Dec.: Frs. Maubant and Chastan left Fukien, China, for Korea.

Fr. Pacificus Liu Fang-chi, a Chinese priest, succeeded in entering Korea with the help of Chŭng Ha-sang.

1834 Bp. Bruguière and Fr. Maubant, accompanied by the seminarian Joseph Wang, made an unsuccessful attempt to enter Korea.

1835 Jan.: Augustine Yu Chin-kil, Charles Cho, and Francis Kim met Joseph Wang in Peking and sent letters to Bishop Bruguière and Pope Gregory XVI promising to do their best to help the Bishop to enter Korea.

Oct. 20: Bp. Bruguière died in Manchuria, on his way to Korea.

1836 Jan. 13: Fr. Pierre-Philibert Maubant crossed the border after a narrow escape from discovery at Eui-ju.

Jan. 25: Fr. Maubant arrived in Seoul. Arrest of eight Catholics in Seoul and two at On-yang.

Feb.: Death of Chŭng Yak-yong, at the age of 74.

Dec.: Fr. Pacificus Liu, the Chinese priest, returned to China, taking three Korean youths, Andrew Kim Tae-kŏn, Francis-Xavier Ch'oe Pang-je, and Ch'oe Yang-ŏp to study theology at the seminary of Macao. The total number of Christians in Korea reached 6,650.

1837 Jan. 15: Fr. Jacques-Honoré Chastan arrived in Seoul via Eui-ju.

May 14: The Most Rev. Laurent-Joseph-Marie Imbert consecrated Bishop of Capse by the Vicar Apostolic of Szechuan, Bp. Fontana, in succession to Bp. Bruguière.

July: The three youths including Andrew Kim Tae-kŏn, arrived at Macao.

1938 Jan. 1: Bp. Imbert arrived in Seoul via Eui-ju.

In this year 1,237 souls were baptized.

Francis-Xavier Ch'oe, seminarian, died at Macao.

Nov.: Peter Lee Ho-yŏng died in prison at Seoul.

1839 Outbreak of the great *Ki-hae* Persecution. (79 of the martyrs were beatified in 1925.)

Mar. 5: Lee Chi-yŏn, the Counselor of the Right of Korea, proclaimed the edict for the total eradication of *Sŏ-hak* (Western Learning, Roman Catholicism). 20 or 30 Christians had already been arrested by the Police Commissioner.

Apr.: Seventeen Christians tortured to death in the prisons of Seoul, Chŏn-ju, Sang-ju and Tong-nae.

July: Eight Christians including Lee Kwang-ryŏl tortured to death outside the Small West Gate.

Aug. 10: Arrest of Bp. Imbert at Su-won.

Sept. 6: Two priests, Maubant and Chastan, were arrested at Hong-ju.

Sept. 21: Martyrdom of Blessed Laurent-Joseph-Marie Imbert, Jacques-Honoré Chastan and Pierre-Philibert Maubant at Sae-nam-t'ŏ by decapitation, and 20 days later, these three bodies were buried on No-ko-san (hill).

Sept. 22: Martyrdom of Chŭng Ha-sang and Yu Chin-kil at Sae-nam-t'ŏ and nine companions including Cho Sin-ch'ŏl, Nam I-kwan, Kim Che-jun, etc. by decapitation, and the heads of Chŭng and Yu were exposed to the public.

Oct. 18: Promulgation of royal decree "for the Exclusion of Perverse Religion."

1840 Mar.: The envoys of the winter-solstice embassy to Peking returned, headed by Lee Ka-u, who brought news of the persecution of the Church in Peking.

Dec.: Arrival in Macao of Msgr. Jean-Joseph Ferréol.

1842 Hyŭn Sŏk-mun completed his compilation of the *Ki-hae Diary* (of the Persecution of 1839).

Dec.: Andrew Kim Tae-kŏn explored the Korean-Manchurian border for several miles along the Yalu River in preparation for the entry of Fr. Ferréol.

1843 The remains of Blessed Laurent Imbert, Bishop and martyr, and companions Jacques Chastan and Pierre Maubant, priests and martyrs, interred at Sam-sŏng-san or "The Three Saints' Hill," Kwa-ch'ŏn district.

Fr. Ferréol's appointment as Third Vicar Apostolic of Korea announced.

1844 Jan.: Andrew Kim met Korean Christians at Kyŏng-won and withdrew to Pachiatsu in Manchuria.

1845 Jan.: Deacon Andrew Kim entered Korea via Eui-ju, returning to Shanghai in March.
Aug.: Deacon Andrew Kim's ordination as Korea's first 'native-born' priest.
Oct.: Bp. Ferréol, Fr. Marie-Antoine-Nicolas Daveluy and Fr. Andrew Kim entered Korea at Kang-kyŏng-ri, Ch'ung-ch'ŏng Province.

1846 Outbreak of the great *Pyŏng-o* Persecution of the Church.
Unsuccessful attempt by Father Maistre and Ch'oe Yang-ŏp to enter Korea, via Hunchun, Manchuria. Fr. Andrew Kim's arrest at Sun-wi Island on May 12, and his martyrdom at Sae-nam-t'ŏ, on Sept. 16.
July 26: Martyrdom of Hyŭn Sŏk-mun.
Nov. 2: Inauguration of the "Society of the Immaculate Heart of Mary" by Bp. Ferréol at Su-ri-ch'i-kol.

1847 Jan.: Fr. Ambrose Maistre and Thomas Ch'oe Yang-ŏp returned to Hongkong.

1848 Fr. Maistre and Deacon Thomas Ch'oe Yang-ŏp reached Paek-ryŏng Island in the second attempt to enter Korea, but failed to land and returned to Shanghai.
Aug.: Two French warships *La Gloire* and *La Victorieuse* wrecked at Sin-ch'i Island, on the west coast.

1849 Apr.: Deacon Thomas Ch'oe Yang-ŏp ordained to the priesthood at Shanghai as Korea's second 'native-born' priest.
May: Arrival of Fr. Thomas Ch'oe in Manchuria.
Dec.: Arrival of Fr. Thomas Ch'oe in Seoul.

1852 Jan.: Fr. Ambroise Maistre and Fr. François Stanislas Jansou arrived at the west coast of Korea and attempted to help two youths to leave for study at the Seminary of Penang, but failed.
Aug. 29: Fr. Maistre succeeded in landing at Kun-san in Korea, after trying for ten years.

1853 Feb. 3: Bp. Ferréol died of sickness at Seoul and was buried at Mi-san-ri. Total number of Christians reached 12,165.

1854 Mar.: Three youths sent to the Seminary at Penang. Fr. Janson entered Korea, but died at Kwa-ch'ŏn, Kyŏng-ki Province, on June 18. Fr. Antoine Daveluy compiled his *Korean-French Dictionary* (destroyed during the 1866 persecution).
Fr. Daveluine founded a school an dtaught six students.
Dec. 23: Msgr. Siméon-François Berneux, Bishop of Capse, appointed as Fourth Vicar Apostolic of Korea, in Liaotung, Manchuria.

1856 Mar.: Entry of Bp. Berneux, Fr. Petitnicolas and Fr. Pourthié into Korea and arrival at Seoul.
Foundation of seminary at Pae-ron, Che-ch'ŏn, in Ch'ung-ch'ŏng Province. A shipwrecked Korean fisherman from Quelpart Island (Che-ju-do) drifted to Hongkong and received Baptism with the name Félix Peter.

1857 Mar. 25: Fr. Daveluy consecrated Coadjutor Bishop, and charged with compilation of *The History of the Korean Martyrs.*
Mar. 26–28: First Diocesan Synod of the Korean Church summoned by Bp. Berreux, to discuss the maintenance of the faith in the vicariate.
Mar. 28: Arrival of Fr. Féron in Seoul.
Dec. 20: Death of Fr. Maistre.

1858 The seminarians Vincent Lim, John Kim, and Paulino Lee left Korea to pursue their study at Penang. Coadjutor Bp. Daveluy, sent the manuscript of his *History of the Korean Church* to Paris. Catechism published from engraved wooden blocks. 43 orphans adopted by the orphanage.

1859 Outbreak of the *Kyŏng-sin* Persecution of the Church, at the end of December.

1860 Aug.: Persecution of Church ceased.

1861 Mar.: Four priests, Frs. Joanno, Landre, Ridel and Calais landed at Kang-hwa Island from a French boat and were received by the brother of the two virgin martyrs, Blessed Columba and Agnes Kim, and arrived at Seoul.
June 10: Death of Fr. Thomas Ch'oe Yang-ŏp. Number of Catholics in Korea reached 18,035. Outbreak of the Tong-hak, or Eastern Learning Civil War.

1862 Matthew Lee Teuk-po evangelized Hwang-hae and P'yŏng-an Provinces.

Oct.: Coadjutor Bp. Daveluy forwarded the Manuscript of his seven-volume *History of the Korean Church* to Paris.

1863 Death of Frs. Landre and Joanno, from illness. Fr. Aumaître returned to Korea bringing the two seminarians Vincent Lim and John Kim from Penang. Bp. Berneux made his episcopal visitation to the Province of Hwang-hae.

Dec.: The Prince Regent Tae-won-kun, father of the king, became the ruler of Korea. Princess Min (his wife) became a catechumen under the spiritual direction of Bp. Berneux.

1864 First year of the reign of King Ko-jong, under the regency of the Prince Tae-won-kun.

1865 May 27: Arrival in Korea, via Nae-p'o, Ch'ung-ch'ŏng Province, of four French priests, Frs. Bretenières, Dorie, Beaulieu, and Huin.

Winter: Arrest and imprisonment of Alexis U Se-yŏng, in P'yŏng-an Province. Total number of Catholics reaches 23,000, with 12 missionaries.

1866 Outbreak of the *Pyŏng-in* persecution of the Catholic Church, which lasted for 6 years.

Jan.: Martyrdom of Francis-Xavier Chŭn and John Lee, tortured to death in Kong-ju prison.

Mar. 8: Martyrdom of John Nam Chong-sam and John Hong Pong-ju, beheaded outside the Small West Gate.

Martyrdom of Bp. Berneux, and companions, Frs. Bretenière, Dorie, and Beaulieu, beheaded at Sae-nam-t'ŏ.

March 10: Peter Ch'oe Hyŏng and Matthew Chŭn Chang-un beheaded at Sae-nam-t'ŏ.

Mar. 11: Martyrdom of Frs. Pourthié and Petitnicolas, with Mark Chŭng (73), Alexis U, and companions, beheaded at Sae-nam-t'ŏ.

Mar. 30: Martyrdom of Bp. Daveluy, Fr. Huin, and Fr. Aumaître, Luke Hwang (clerk of the Bp). Joseph Chang (landlord of Pae-ron School), beheaded at Po-ryŏng.

June: Ernest Oppert, a Shanghai businessman, a German, sailing under the Union Jack, arrived at Hae-mi to ask for permission to trade.

July: Arrival of the U.S.S. General Sherman, and its burning near P'yŏng-yang.

July 7: Departure of Fr. Ridel and Ch'oe Chi-hyŏk for China by sea, and arrival at Chefoo, Sept: Unauthorized reconnaissance visit of three French warships to the Han River estuary, under Admiral Roze.

Oct.: Departure of Frs. Féron and Calais, to China by sea, and arrival at Chefoo.

Oct. 13: Arrival of seven French warships under Admiral Roze, with Fr. Ridel on board as interpreter; occupation of Kang-hwa town by French troops.

Oct.: Exchange of gunfire between Korean forts and the French warship at Mun-ju. Defeat of French by the garrison of Chŏng-chok-san, followed by withdrawal of French forces from Korean soil.

1867 Escape of Frs. Blanc, Richard and Martins to Manchuria, establishing the Korean Church headquarters at Ch'akou.

1868 Return of Ernest Oppert to Korea, his attempt to desecrate the tomb of Nam-yŏn-kun (father of the Regent Tae-won-kun); his retreat leaving the bodies of his crew killed in exchange of fire with the fortress of Yŏng-chong-do near In-ch'ŏn.

Apr. 27: Msgr. Ridel appointed Bishop of Philippopolis and Sixth Vicar Apostolic of Korea.

1869 Dec.: Bp. Ridel attended the Vatican Ecumenical Council, which adjourned one month after the Italians seized Rome from the Pope on Oct. 20, 1870.

1870 June 5: Bp. Ridel consecrated Bishop, at Rome.

1871 Apr.: Five American warships arrived to protest the burning of the S.S. General Sherman, but withdrew after a month's stay.

Apr. 25: The Regent Tae-won-kun erected a monument to commemorate the exclusion of the "Perverse Learning of the Occident."

1873 Nov. 4: The Regent Tae-won-kun handed over the reins of government to the king and retired to private life.

Bp. Ridel continued to conduct the training of seminarians for the Korean priesthood at Ch'akou in Manchuria.

1874 John Ch'oe Chi-hyŏk returned to Korea from Shantung.

Dallet's *Histoire de L'Église de Corée* published in Paris, by *Victor Palme, Rue de Grenelle-Saint-Germain* 25, in two volumes.

1876 Feb.: Treaty of Friendship between Korea and Japan signed.

May: Frs. Jean Blanc and Victor M. Deguette succeeded in penetrating into Korea.

1877 Sept.: Bp. Ridel met John Ch'oe Chi-hyŏk

in Chang-yŏn, Hwang-hae Province and assisted Frs. Eugéne Doucet and Achille Robert
to penetrate into Korea.

1878 Jan. 28: Arrest of Bp. Ridel and John Ch'oe
Chi-hyŏk.
June: Expulsion of Bp. Ridel to Manchuria.
July: Death of John Ch'oe Chi-hyŏk in
prison.

1879 May: Arrest of Fr. Deguette at Kong-ju, and
his expulsion to Manchuria.

1880 Dec.: Frs. Augustine Mutel and Lucien
Liouville penetrated into Korea via Paek-
ryŏng Island by Thaddaeus Kwon Ch'i-mun's
good offices.
Dec.: Publication of *Korean-French Dictionary*
at Yokohama.

1881 Spring: *Korean Grammar with Explanation in
French* published at Yokohama.
June 11: Promulgation of "the Ordinance for
the Suppression of the Evile Doctrine."

1882 Apr.: Treaty of Commerce and Amity signed,
between Korea and the U.S.A.
June: Fr. Blanc raised to Coadjutor Bishop.
Aug. 5: Demolition of the "Antiforeign Monument." Seminarians sent to study for the
priesthood at Penang.

1883 July: The Right Rev. Marie-Jean-Gustave
Blanc consecrated Bishop in Nagasaki.
Oct.: Conclusion of Anglo-Korean Agreement. Treaty between Korea and Germany
concluded. Purchase of site at Chong-hyŏn
in Myŏng-dong. School founded.

1884 June 20: Death of Bp. Ridel. Bp. Blanc
succeeded him as the seventh Vicar Apostolic.

1885 Bp. Blanc founded the seminary at Pu-
heung-kol, Won-ju.

1886 May: Treaty of Commerce and Amity signed
between Korea and France.

1887 Spring: Foundation of Sacred Heart Seminary
at Yong-san. Seminarians transferred from
Won-ju to Yong-san.
Sept.: Publication of *The Catechists' Manual.*

1888 June 8: Solemn dedication of the Korean
Church at High Mass. Korean clergy adopted
cassock (*vestis talaris*) as ecclesiastical uni-
form in place of the mourning garments in
former use as disguise.
Catholic printery moved from Nagasaki to
Seoul.
July 19: Entry of the Sisters of *St. Paul de
Chartres* into Korea, and foundation of the
Orphanage of St. Paul in Myŏng-dong.

1890 Bp. Blanc celebrated High Mass, dedication

of the Church of Korea to the Immaculate
Conception of the Blessed Virgin Mary.
Feb. 21: Death of Bp. Blanc.
Sept. 2: Father Mutel consecrated Bishop
and appointed the eighth Vicar Apostolic of
Korea.

1891 Two-storey building of the seminary of the
Sacred Heart at Yong-san dedicated.

1892 Aug.: Cornerstone of the cathedral laid at
Myŏng-dong, Seoul.

1893 Sept.: Completion of first Western-style Church
building at Yak-hyŏn in Seoul.

1894 Outbreak of civil war between the Tong-hak
faction and the government of Korea, followed by outbreak of the Sino-Japanese War.

1895 Aug.: Death of Matthew Lee Teuk-po at
P'yŏng-yang. Fr. Doucet founded a school, in
the Yak-hyŏn Church compound.

1896 Oct. 11: Baptism of Princess, Min, wife of
the Regent Tae-won-kun, with the name of
Mary.

1897 Oct. 12: Enthronement of King Ko-jong as
Emperor of Korea.

1898 May 29: The edifice of the Cathedral of
the Immaculate Conception, Seoul, was dedicated.
Fr. Peter Yang launched his missionary work
in Quelpart Island.

1900 Under the rule of Bp. Gustave Mutel, Vicar
Apostolic of Korea, the total number of
Catholics in Korea rose to 42,441, with 40
missionary priests, 12 Korean priests, and 26
seminarians.

1901 Spring: Uprising in Quelpart Island against
Catholics, many of whom were killed.

1904 Outbreak of the Russo-Japanese War.

1905 Korea becomes a Japanese protectorate.
Freedom of faith officially recognized.

1906 Catholic weekly newspaper *"Kyŏng-hyang-sin-
mun"* inaugurated.

1909 Monks of the German Benedictine Order
were admitted into Korea through the good
offices of Bp. Mutel, and founded their
mission at Hye-hwa-dong, Seoul.
Catholic monthly magazine *"Kyŏng-hyang-
chap-ji"* inaugurated.

1910 Korea's annexation to Japan effected.
Number of Catholics rises to 73,517, with 46
missionary priests, 15 Korean priests, 59
nuns, 41 seminarians and 69 parish churches.

1911 May 3: Erection of the Apostolic Vicariate
of Tae-gu, embracing the Provinces of
Kyŏng-sang and Chŏl-la, by Pope Pius X.

June 11: Fr. Florian Demange, publisher of the Catholic weekly newspaper *Kyŏng-hyang-sin-mun*, appointed the First Vicar Apostolic of Tae-gu.

1920 Aug. 25: Erection of the Apostolic Vicariate of Won-san, embracing the Provinces of Ham-kyŏng, Korea, and Chientao, Manchuria, by Pope Benedict XV.

Bp. Bonifatius Sauer, Abbot of Tŏk-won, appointed the first Vicar Apostolic of Won-san. Bp. Mutel, Vicar Apostolic of Seoul, was honored with the Pontifical title of Count by the Pope.

1921 Mar. 1: Fr. Devred was appointed and consecrated Bishop in charge of assistant to Bp. Mutel.

1923 Arrival of Fr. Patrick J. Byrne in Korea, from the Catholic Foreign Mission Society of America (Maryknoll Fathers).

1924 Entry of the Maryknoll Sisters of St. Dominic into Korea.

1925 Mar.: Bp. Augustine Mutel, Vicar Apostolic of Seoul, was raised to the rank of Titular Archbishop by Pope Pius XI.

July 5: Beatification of Seventy-nine Martyrs of Korea at the Basilica of St. Peter, at Rome, by Pope Pius XI. Entry of Sisters of the German Order of St. Benedict into Korea.

1926 Jan. 18: Death of Bishop Devred, Vicar General of Seoul.

1927 Mar. 17: Erection of the Prefecture Apostolic of P'yŏng-yang, consisting of part of the territory formerly included in the Vicariate Apostolic of Seoul.

May 1: Consecration of Fr. Adrien Larribeau as Bishop charged with Vicar General of Seoul. Nov. 26: Appointment of Fr. Patrick Byrne as the first Prefect Apostolic of P'yŏng-yang.

1928 Jan.: Erection of the Vicariate Forane of Hwang-hae, with the Fr. Kim Myŏng-je appointed the first Vicar Forane of Hwang-hae of the Vicariate of Seoul.

July: Part of the territory of the Vicariate Apostolic of Won-san was erected into the Prefecture Apostolic of Yenki by Pope Pius XI and placed in the charge of the German Benedictine Order.

Fr. Breher was appointed the first Prefect Apostolic of Yenki.

1929 Msgr. Byrne was elected as Assistant to Superior General in the central administration of the Maryknoll Society, and the Holy See allowed him to resign his office to take up this appointment in the U.S.

1930 Jan.: Fr. John Morris was appointed the second Prefect Apostolic of P'yŏng-yang.

1931 May.: The Vicariate Forane of Provinces of Chŏl-la was erected and Fr. Kim Yang-hong was appointed the fi1st Prefect Apostolic. First National Council or Synod of the Korean Church convened. Catechists' Manual revised. Central Catholic Committee of Korea established. "Catholic Action", or the participation and collaboration of the laity with the apostolic hierarchy, was inaugurated.

Sept.: Celebration of the centenary of the erection of the Vicariate Apostolic of Korea, under the leadership of the Apostolic Delegate to Japan, Abp. Mooney.

The remains of the late Most Rev. Barthélemy Bruguière, Bp. of Capse and Vicar Apostolic of Korea, who died in Manchuria on Oct. 20, 1835, on his way to assume office in Korea, were translated from their resting place in Liaotung, Manchuria, to their new shrine in the ecclesiastical cemetery of Yong-san, Seoul.

1933 Jan. 23: Death of the Most Rev. Augustine Mutel, Titular Archbishop and Vicar Apostolic of Seoul.

Appointment of Bp. Adrien Larribeau as Vicar Apostolic of Seoul.

Oct. 29: Ten missionaries of the Columban Order arrived at Tae-gu from Ireland, and established their mission in South Province of Chŏl-la.

1937 Apr. 15: The Chŏn-ju region of the Vicariate Apostolic of Tae-gu was formally set up and given canonical status as an autonomous Prefecture and Fr. Stephen Kim Yang-hong was appointed its first Prefect Apostolic.

The Kwang-ju territory of the Vicariate Apostolic of Tae-gu was canonically erected Prefecture, and Fr. Owen McPolin was appointed the first Prefect Apostolic of Kwang-ju.

1938 Feb. 9: Death of Bp. Demange of the Tae-gu Vicariate Apostolic.

Dec. 13: Fr. Mousset was appointed the second Vicar Apostolic of Tae-gu.

1939 Oct. 29: Msgr. O'Shea was appointed the Vicar Apostolic of P'yŏng-yang and consecrated Bishop at St. Peter's, Rome.

1940 Jan. 12: The Vicariate Apostolic of Won-san was divided into two parts, the Ham-heung Vicariate Apostolic and the Abbatius

Nullius of Tŏk-won.

Dec. 8: The Prefecture Apostolic of Ch'un-ch'ŏn was erected and placed in the charge of the Columban missionary priests. Fr. Thomas Quinlan was appointed the first Prefect Apostolic of Ch'un-ch'ŏn.

The Japanese Government confiscated the Cathedral of P'yŏng-yang for military purposes, and expelled the foreign missionaries to the suburbs.

1941 Dec. 8: On the outbreak of war in the Pacific the Japanese authorities arrested 35 American missionaries including Bp. O'Shea. In Kwang-ju and Ch'un-ch'ŏn, two Irish Prefects Apostolic and 30 priests were arrested and held in custody.

1942 Jan.: In Chŏn-ju, Msgr. Stephen Kim Yang-hong resigned his post of Prefect Apostolic and was succeeded by Fr. Chu Chae-yong.

Jan. 18: Bp. Adrien Larribeau obtained permission from the Holy See to resign his post as Vicar Apostolic of Seoul and was succeeded by Fr. Paul M. Ro.

Feb. 4: In P'yŏng-yang, Bp. O'shea likewise resigned his post and Msgr. Paul M. Ro. assumed the function of Vicar Apostolic *pro tempore* of P'yŏng-yang concurrently.

Feb 9: In Ch'un-ch'ŏn, Prefecture Apostolic Msgr. Quinlan resigned his post and Msgr. Paul M.Ro assumed the function of Prefect Apostolic *pro tempore* of Ch'un-ch'ŏn concurrently.

Feb. 16: The Major Seminary in Yong-san was ordered to close and the seminarians were obliged to continue their studies in the seminary of the Benedictine *Abbatius Nullius* of Tŏk-won.

Apr.: In Kwang-ju, Msgr. McPolin was obliged to vacate his post and a Japanese Catholic priest, Fr. Wakida, was appointed to succeed him as acting head of Kwang-ju Prefecture.

Sept. 10: In Tae-gu Bp. Mousset was similarly obliged to vacate his post, and was succeeded by the Japanese priest, Fr. Hayasaka, as Vicar Apostolic of Tae-gu.

Dec. 20: Consecration of Msgr. Paul M. Ro as Korea's first "native-born" Bishop.

1943 Mar. 21: Fr. Francis Hong Yong-ho appointed Vicar Apostolic of P'yŏng-yang, and consecrated on April 17, 1944.

1944 Catholic priests and seminarians arrested and conscripted by the Japanese as combatants and laborers in the battle zone: Church buildings at P'yŏng-yang, Tae-jŏn, Yŏn-an,

and elsewhere confiscated.

1945 May 29: Eleven Irish priests under house arrest in Mok-p'o taken to Hong-ch'ŏn in Kang-won Province and imprisoned.

Aug. 15: As a consequence of the surrender of Japan to the Allied Powers, Father Wakida resigned his post as acting head of Kwang-ju Prefecture.

Aug. 15: the Church of Korea numbered 183,666 souls, with eight vicariates (six of which were administered by bishops).

Sept. 26: High Mass was celebrated in Seoul Cathedral in the presence of U.S. Armed Forces in thanksgiving for the restoration of peace.

Dec. 8: A reception was held to welcome the members of the Provisional Government, including Kim Ku and Kim Kyu-sik, and High Mass was solemnized in thanksgiving for their safe return.

1946 Jan. 6: Bp. Hayaska, Vicar Apostolic of Tae-gu, died.

Jan 16: Fr. Bartholomew Kim Hyŏn-pae appointed Prefect Apostolic of Chŏn-ju.

Feb. 22: Msgr. Paul Chu Chae-yong, Prefect Apostolic of Chŏn-ju, was translated to the Vicariate of Tae-gu. The Catholic Church was given the Chŏng-p'an-sa plant and set up the Tae-kŏn Printing Office.

With the Communist army occupation, all priests and ministers of religion in Vicariate Apostolic of Yenki, Manchuria, including Bp. Theodor Breher, were arrested, and all Church property was confiscated.

Aug. 1: The Catholic monthly magazine *Kyŏng-hyang-chap-ji* suspended since the end of the Japanese regime, resumed publication.

Sept. 16: Centenary of the Martyrdom of Blessed Andrew Kim: 'Society for the Veneration of Korean Martyrs' formed.

Oct. 6: The Catholic weekly newspaper *Kyŏng-hyang-sin-mun*, suspended during the Japanese regime, resumed publication.

1947 Apr.: The Catholic monthly magazine "*Catholic Youth*," suspended during the Japanese regime, resumed publication.

Aug. 12: Fr. Patrick J. Byrne appointed Visitor Apostolic to Korea.

Oct. 9: Arrival of Msgr. Byrne in Seoul.

1948 May 8: The Tae-jŏn territory of the Vicariate Apostolic of Seoul was formally set up and given canonical status by Pius XII, and Bp. Adrien Larribeau was appointed the First

Vicar Apostolic of Tae-jŏn.

May 21: Msgr. Chu Chae-yong resigned his post of Administrator of the Tae-gu Vicariate; the Most Rev. Paul M. Ro, Bp. of Seoul Vicariate, was appointed concurrently Administrator *pro tempore* of Tae-gu.

Aug. 15: Foundation of the Republic of Korea.

Msgr. Quinlan resumed his post of Prefect Apostolic of Ch'un-ch'ŏn.

1949 Jan. 30: Fr. Ch'oe Tŏk-hong was appointed Vicar Apostolic of Tae-gu.

May 9: Arrest by the Communists of 11 clergy, and confiscation of all Church property at Tŏk-won.

May 14: Arrest and imprisonment of the Most Rev. Francis Hong, Bishop of P'yŏng-yang Vicariate, and many other priests, and closure of many Churches.

June 14: Msgr. Byrne, was appointed Delegate Apostolic, and consecrated Bishop.

Nov. 12: Father Patrick Brennan appointed Prefect Apostolic of Kwang-ju.

1950 Feb. 7: Death of Bp. Bonifatius Sauer in P'yŏng-yang prison.

Feb. 21-23: First postwar plenary Ecclesiastic Council, or Synod, held at Seoul.

June 25: Outbreak of Korean War. Arrest and imprisonment in North Korea of Bp. Byrne, Msgr. Quinlan, and many priests, monks, nuns, and seminarians.

Nov. 20: Father Carroll appointed Administrator of the Vicariate Apostolic of P'yŏng-yang.

Nov. 25: Death of Bp. Byrne, in captivity, at Ha-ch'ang-ri.

1951 The Most Rev. Maximilian de Furstenberg, Apostolic Delegate to Japan, was appointed concurrently Apostolic Delegate *ad interim* to Korea.

1952 Apr. 2: Foundation of the Hyo-sŏng (Morning Star) Women's College, in Tae-gu.

The Vicariate Forane and Monastery of Wae-kwan was established and placed in the charge of the Benedictine Order.

Father Timothy Bitterli was appointed Vicar Forane of Wae-kwan, and concurrently Administrator of the Ham-heung and Yenki Vicariates, *Abbas Nullias* of Tŏk-won.

1953 Sept.: Arrival of Fr. Walsh, Vice Superior General of the American Maryknoll Society. Erection of the Vicariate Forane of Ch'ŏng-ju in North Province of Ch'ung-ch'ŏng, formerly part of the Seoul Vicariate. Appointment of Fr. James Pardy, of the American Maryknoll Fathers, as Vicar Forane of Ch'ŏng-ju.

July 27: Armistice Agreement signed by the commander-in-chief of the United Nations Forces and the commanders of the North Korean Army and the "Chinese People's Volunteers."

Oct. 5: Release of Msgr. Quinlan from prison, and his return to Korea.

Msgr. Quinlan appointed Regent Apostolic Delegate to Korea and concurrently Prefect Apostolic of Ch'un-ch'ŏn.

1954 June 18: Erection of the Vicariate Forane of Pu-san, South Province of Kyŏng-sang, formerly part of the Tae-gu Vicariate.

Fr. Sŭh Chŏng-kil appointed the first Vicar Forane of Pu-san.

Oct.: Fr. Harold W. Henry appointed Prefect of Kwang-ju.

Dec. 14: Death of the Most Rev. Ch'oe Tŏk-hong, Bishop of Tae-gu Vicariate.

1955 Oct. 15: Return of the Most Rev. Paul M. Ro, Vicar Apostolc of Seoul, from goodwill visit to 11 nations which dispatched their armed forces to aid Korea during the war.

1956 Nov. 16: Foundation of the Korea branch of the *Jeunesse Ouvrière Chrétienne* (Young Christian Workers), at Seoul Cathedral, Myŏng-dong, Seoul.

1957 Jan. 21: Canonical erection of Pu-san Vicariate Apostolic.

Jan. 26: Msgrs. H.W. Henry, Bartholomew Kim Hyŏn-pae and Fr. John Ch'oe Chae-sŏn were appointed Bishops.

May 30: Bp. John Ch'oe Chae-sŏn, Vicar Apostolic of Pu-san, consecrated Bishop.

Oct. 5-12: the second World Congress of Catholic Laymen held at Rome, at which Korea was represented by Fr. Hyginus Lee Yŏng-sik, and Messrs. Ryu Hong-ryŏl, Lee Hae-nam and companions.

Oct. 18: General Assembly of the Jesuit Order held in Rome. Fr. Kenneth Killoren appointed Superior of the Korean Province of the society, and concurrently president of the prospective Jesuit College in Korea.

Dec.: Bp. Quinlan, Vicar Apostolic of Ch'un-ch'ŏn, was released from his concurrent post of the Regent Apostolic Delegate to Korea. Bp. Lambertini was appointed the second Apostolic Delegate to Korea.

1958 Mar. 1: The Holy Mother Hospital of Seoul

was developed into a polyclinic.

May 14: Arrival of Bp. Lambertini, Apostolic Delegate to Korea.

June 2: Canonical erection of the Vicariate Forane of An-tong. Fr. Francis Haller appointed the first Vicar Forane of An-tong.

July: Canonical erection of Ch'ǒng-ju Apostolic Vicariate.

Msgr. Pardy, Assistant to Superior General of the Maryknoll Foreign Mission, appointed Vicar Apostolic of Ch'ǒng-ju.

Sept. 16: Consecration in the U.S.A. of Msgr. Pardy as Bishop.

Oct. 9: Death of Pope Pius XII.

International Congress of the Blessed Virgin Mary Institute at Lourdes, attended by over thirty Korean representatives, led by the Most Rev. Paul M. Ro, Vicar Apostolic of Seoul.

Bp. Paul Ro assisted at the funeral service of Pius XII and Enthronement of Pope John XXIII.

Dec. 9: Bp. Paul M. Ro attended the Southeast Asia Congress of Bishops conducted by the Most Rev. Cardinal Agagianian in Manila.

1959 Feb. 16-21: Asian Area Congress of the 'Society of Maria' conducted by Cardinal Agagianian, opened in Saigon, and attended by the Most Rev. Paul M. Ro, Vicar Apostolic of Seoul, and the Most Rev. Kim, Vicar Apostolic of Chǒn-ju.

Mar. 5-12: His Eminence Cardinal Agagianian, Vice-Secretary of the Sacred Congregation De Propaganda Fide visited Korea.

Sept. 2: The Most Rev. Paul M. Ro, Vicar Apostolic of Seoul, left to attend the seventh World Congress for Liturgical Worship and Propaganda held in the Netherlands Republic, and also the centenary celebrations at Lyons, France, commemorating St. John Mary Vianney, Confessor, (Curé d'Ars for nearly forty-two years), who died August 4, 1859, was beatified in 1905 by Pope Pius X, and canonized by Pope Pius XI in 1925.

Nov. 21: In the village of Ki-san, Sǒ-ch'ǒn county, thirty members of the Protestant 'Holiness Church' or Oriental Mission, embraced the Catholic faith and were received into the Church en bloc.

Dec. 12: Erection of a monument in honor of Chǔng Yak-yong (Ta-san, 1762-1836) at Ma-hyǒn, Yang-p'yǒng county, Kyǒng-ki Province, under the auspices of the Chǔng Ta-san Society.

1960 Feb. 18: Sǒ-kang (Jesuit) College opening ceremony held.

Apr. 30: Death of Bp. Bartholomew Kim Hyǒn-pae, Vicar Apostolic of Chǒn-ju.

1961 Mar. 1: Bp. Xavier Zupi, Apostolic Delegate to Korea, arrived, and in November was consecrated Archbishop.

Mar. 12: Consecration at Rome of Msgr. Peter Han Kong-ryǒl, Vicar Apostolic of Chǒn-ju.

June: Fr. Andrew Bachhuber appointed Rector of Tae-kǒn Seminary, Kwang-ju.

Erection of the Vicariate Apostolic of In-ch'ǒn.

Aug.: Msgr. William J. McNaughton consecrated in America as Bishop of In-ch'ǒn. A bookstore was opened in Seoul by the Congregation of the Daughters of St. Paul.

1962 Feb. 15: Fr. Célestin Coyos, of the Société des Missions-Étrangères de Paris, appointed Vicar Forane of An-tong.

Mar. 1: Pope John XXIII raised the Most Rev. Paul M. Ro, Bishop of Seoul, the Most Rev. John Sǔh, Bishop of Tae-gu, and the Most Rev. Harold W. Henry, Bishop of Kwang-ju, to the rank of Archbishop, and instituted the new Hierarchy of Korea.

May 27: Prince Yi Eun (Prince Yǒng-ch'in) received Holy Baptism in Japan.

June 29: The Vicariates of Seoul, Tae-gu and Kwang-ju received the status of archiepiscopal dioceses in a ceremony held at the Cathedral of the Immaculate Conception of Seoul.

Oct. 6: The episcopate of Korean Church including three archbishops, left Kim-p'o Airport to participate in the Second Ecumenical Council in the Vatican Council beginning on Oct. 11.

1963 Jan. 4: Arrival of Apostolic Delegate, the Most Rev. Antonio del Giudice at Seoul, Korea.

June 4: Death of Pope John XXIII.

June 21: Election of Pope Paul VI.

June 30: Coronation of Pope Paul VI.

Oct. 7: The Su-won district of the Archdiocese of Seoul was canonically erected a diocese, and Fr. Victorinus Youn was appointed the first Ordinary of Su-won.

Tae-kǒn Major Seminary in Kwang-ju was placed under the charge of the Jesuit Order of Wisconsin Province, U.S.

Oct. 20: Consecration of Bishop Youn at St. Peter's in Rome.

Nov. 18: The delegates of fifteen religious congregations of women in Korea assembled at the Convent of *St. Paul de Chartres* to inaugurate the Union of Religious Congregations.

1963 Nov. 23: The first two Sisters of the Little Company of Mary arrived in Korea accompanied by Mother Mark, Mother Superior of the Australian Province.

Dec. 5: The Franciscan Order of Friars Minor founded Korean Chapter with Fr. Appollinarius van Leeuwen as Superior.

Dec. 11: The Apostolic Delegation to Korea was raised to the status of the Apostolic Internunciature, simultaneously Abp. Antonio del Giudice was raised to Apostolic Internuncio.

1964 The Fathers of Guadalupe, the Mexican Foreign Mission Society, founded the Korean Chapter early in 1964.

Feb. 7: The monastery of Wae-kwan was canonically raised to the status of Abbey. Fr. Odo Hass was elected Abbot on April 28.

Apr.: Bp. Adrien Larribeau of Tae-jŏn Diocese retired on account of age, Fr. Emil Beudevin, the Vicar General, was appointed Administrator *ad interim.*

Apr. 21: Bishops' Synod was held at Seoul Major Seminary and the Committees of Liturgical Movement and Catholic Doctorine was formed.

May: The Sacred Heart Women,s College in Ch'un-ch'ŏn was opened.

June 10: The first five Sisters of the Institute of the Blessed Virgin Mary arrived in Korea accompanied by Mother Terasia Konstantin, Superior of the Munich Province.

BIBLIOGRAPHY

Ch. Dallet: Histoire de l'Église de Corée, 2 vols, Paris, 1874.

La Catholicisme en Corée, Hongkong, 1924.

The Catholic Church in Korea, Hongkong, 1924.

Klemens Tilmann: Todesverächter, ein Tatsachenbericht aus der Geschichte der Kirche in Korea, Freiburg, 1955.

Documents Relatifs aux Martyrs de Corée de 1839~1846, Hongkong, 1924.

Documents Relatifs aux Martyrs de Corée de 1866, Hongkong, 1924.

E. Fourer: La Corée, Martyre et Missions, Nancy, 1895.

Adrien Launay: Les Missionaires Français en Corée, Paris, 1895.

Adrien Launay: Mémorial de la Société des Missions-Étrangères, 2 vols, Paris, 1916.

Adrien Launay: Martyrs, Français et Coréens (1838-1846), Béatifiés en 1925.

Reinhold Hoch: Die Koreanischen Märtyrer, 1929.

Adrien Launay: Les Bienheureux Martyrs des Missions-Étrangères, 1929.

Lettre de Alexandre Hoang à Msgr. de Gouvéa, Évêque de Pékin, 1801, Hongkong, 1925.

H.P. Jourdan: Travaux et Martyre de Msgr. Imbert et ses Deux Compagnons M.M. Maubant et Chastan, Paris, 1855.

Ch. Salmon: Vie de Msgr. Daveluy, Paris, 1888.

Pichon: Vie de Msgr. Berneux, Le Mans, 1867.

Lady Herbert: Life of Msgr. Berneux, 1872.

F. Baudry: Vie de Henri Dorie.

F.M. Bouquet: Fleur de Vendée, Pierre Henri Dorie, Lucon, 1925.

Renard: Un Martyre en Corée, Petitnicolas, Tours, 1874.

P. Desire: Vie de Michel Alex, Petitnicolas, St. Die, 1891.

Leandre Poutuo: Vie de M. Pierre Aumaître, Paris, 1879.

D'Hulst: Vie de Just de Bretenières, Paris, 1888.

C. Appert: Pour la Foi, Just de Bretenières, Lyon, 1910.

Florence Gilmore: For the Faith, Just de Bretenières, Ossing, New York, 1918.

L. Bocat: Sang Versé en Corée, Just de Bretenières, Paris, 1951.

Théophile Baumaget: Vie de Martin Luc Huin, Langres, 1893.

Deydou: Vie de Bernard Louis Beaulieu, Bordeaux, 1893.

Arthur Piacentini: Msgr. Ridel, Évêque de Philippopolis, Vicaire Apostolique de Corée, Lyon, 1890.

Relation de la Captivité et de la Délivrance de Msgr. Ridel de la Société des Missions-Étrangères, Paris, 1879.

Msgr. Ridel: Ma Captivité dans la Prisons de Séoul, Paris, 1901.

Le Chanoine Jean Vandon: Histoire Générale de la Communauté des Filles de Saint-Paul de Chartres, de 1880 à nos Jours, Paris, 1931.

Raymond A. Lane: Ambassador in Chains, Bishop Byrne, New York, 1955.

Ernst Oppert: Reisen nach Korea, ein Verschlossenes Land (A Forbidden Land), London, 1880.

W.E. Griffis: Corea, the Hermit Nation, New York, 1902.

J. H. Longford: The History of Korea, London, 1911.

Dictionnaire Coréen-Français, Yokohama, 1880.

Grammaire Coréene, Yokohama, 1881.

Bulletin de la Société des Missions-Étrangères de Paris, Hongkong.

The Catholic Church in Korea, Hongkong, 1924.

Annals de la Propagation de la Foi, 106 volumes, Paris et Lyon, 1827-1928.

St. Ottilien: Schicksal in Korea, Benediktiner-Missionäre-Berichten.

Philip Crosbie: Pencilling Prisoner, the Story of an Australian Prisoner in North Korea, Melbourne, 1957.

Trois Ans de Captivité d'une Religieuse dans le Nord-Corée, Chartres, 1953.

Sr. M. Gertrud Link O.S.B.: Seele Du, in Sturm und Nacht——Lieder aus der Verbannung in Korea, St. Ottilien, 1954.

Carmels de Séoul, Bouvines, 1950-1954 (Polycopie).

Sessiones Collationis Processus Informativi super Epo. Simeone Berneux et Sociis Ejus.

Coreana. Beatificationis seu Declarationis Martyrii Ven. Servorum Dei Laurentii Imbert......, positio super Validitate Processuum, Romae, 1910.

Coreana. Beatificationis seu Declarationis Martyrii Ven. Servorum Dei Laurentii Imbert Episcopi Capsensis et Sociorum in Odium Fidei ab Idolatris Interemptorum. Positio super tuto, Romae, 1925.

Sanctissimi Domini Nostri Pii Drvina Provi Dentia Papae XI, Litterae Apostlicae quibus Ven. Dei Famuli Laurentius Imbert Ep. Capsensis et Socii Beati Renuntiantur, Romae, 1925.

Coreana et Cocincinen. Beatificationis seu Declarationis Martyrii Servorum Dei Simeonis Berneux Epi Capsensis Vicarii Ap. Coreae Eorumque Sociorum in Odium Fidei, uti Fertur, ab Idolatris Interfectorun.

Instrumentum Erutionis Exuviarum Venerabilis Andreae Kim Sacerdotis Earumque Translationis ex Monte Mirinai in Seminarium Ryongsan Utriusque peractae Anno Domini 1901.

Instrumentum Erutionis Exuviarum Simeonis Berneux, Epi. Tit. Capsensis et Vicarii Aplici Coreae Sacerdotumque Missionariorum aptlicorum Justi Ranfer de Bretenieres, Henri Dorie, Ludovici Beaulieu, Antonii Pourthie et Michaelis Petitnicolas Necnon et Alexii Ou Syei Hpil, Christiani Coreani Peractae die 30a Octobris 1899.

Acta Visitationis Sepulchri Servorum Dei Simeonis Berneux, Epi. Tit. Capsen. et Vic. Aptlici Coreae, Antonii Daveluy, Epi Aconen. Ludovici Beaulieu, Sac. Henrici Dorie, Sac. Antonii Pourthie, Prov. Michaelis Petitnicolas, Sac. Petri Aumaitre, Sac. Lucae Huin, Sac. Alexii Ou Syei-hpil, Joannis Baptistae Nam Tjyong-sam, Petri Tchoi Tchi-tchang, Josephi Tjyeng Nak-sye, Catechistae, die Quarta Mensis Decembris Anni 1925 Peractae in Crypta Ecclesiae Quasicathedralis de Seoul in Corea.

A. Launay: LXXIX Martiri Corani Mons. Lorenzo Imberte Compagni (1839-1846). Versione del Dott. A. Verghetti Milano, 1925.

F. Ollivier, Notice sur Monseigneur Imbert, Évêque de Capse, Vic. Apostolique de Corée, Aix, 1880.

P. Souillac: La Famille du Bienheureux Imbert, Évêque et Martyr, Aix, 1925.

L. Lecolley: Panégyrique du Bienheureux Pierre Maubant, Prononcé le 18 Juillet 1926 en l'Église de Champ-du-Boult.

F. Trochu, Le Serviteur de Dieu, Siméon-François Berneux, Paris, 1937.

Ch. Salmon: Vie de Monseigneur Daveluy, Évêque d'Acones, Vicaire Apostolique de Corée, Mort pour la Foi le 30 Mars, 1866, 2 tomes, Paris-Amiens, 1883.

Renard: Vie de Michel Alexandre Petitnicolas, Décapité pour la Foi en Corée le 12 Mars 1866, Paris-Bordeaux, 1891.

Msgr. Larribeau: Un Grand Évêque Missionnaire, S. Exc. Gustave Mutel, Archevêque Titulaire de Ratiaria, Vicaire Apostolique de Séoul (Corée) de la Société des Missions-Étrangères de Paris, Paris.

Pro Corea. Docunenta Collecta a L. Pichon, Seoul, 1938.

Pour la Corée. Traduction Française, Documents 1 et 2, Seoul, 1938.

A. Choe. L'Érection du Premier Vicariat Apostolique et les Origines du Catholicisme en Corée, 1592—1837, Suisse, 1961.

The Royal History of Yi Dynasty: The Volumes of Kings Chŏng-jo, Sun-jo, Hŏn-jong Ch'ŏl-jong and Ko-jong. (朝鮮王朝實錄＝正祖, 純祖, 憲宗, 哲宗, 高宗編)

The Annals of the Grand Council: The Annals of the Privy Council and the Annals of the Secretariat. The Parts of Kings Chŏng-jo, Sun-jo, Hŏn-jong, Ch'ŏl-jong and Ko-jong. (承政院日記〔承宣院日記, 秘書院日記〕＝同上)

The Transcripts of the Border Defense Command: The Parts of Kings Chŏng-jo, Sun-jo, Hŏn-jong, Ch'ŏl-jong and Ko-jong. (備邊司謄錄＝同上)

The Court Journal: The Parts of Kings Chŏng-jo, Sun-jo, Hŏn-jong, Ch'ŏl-jong and Ko-jong. (日省錄＝同上)

The Transcripts of Criminal Records of the 1st and 2nd Police Headquarters. (左右捕盗廳謄錄)

The Transcripts of High Court of Justice Records (The Journals of Royal Hearings). (義禁府廳謄錄〔親鞫日記〕)

The Journals of Investigations. (推鞫日記)

The Verdict Records of the Ministry of Census. (秋曹決獄案)

Kim Chae-ch'an: The Diaries of Hae-sŏk, 30 volumes, 15 books. (金載瓚：海石日錄, 30 卷, 15 册)

The Draft Records of Hwang-hae Province: one volume (The Verdict Drafts for Father Kim Tae-kŏn by the Governor of Hwang-hae Province in the Year Pyŏng-o, the 12th Year of King Hŏn-jong). (海西文牒錄一册〔憲宗 12 年丙午 黃海監司의 金大建神父에 대한 獄案〕)

Chŭng Hyŏn-yu: The Journals of Tong-san (from the 12th Year of King Ch'ŏl-jong till the 3rd Year of King Ko-jong). (鄭顯裕：東山日記〔哲宗 12 年서 高宗 3 年까지〕)

The Leisure-Time Records of Yong-Ho (the author unknown) (龍湖閑錄〔著者未詳〕)

The Journals of Japanese Ambassadors (the official records). (倭使日記〔官撰〕)

The Negotiations of Foreign Relations Compiled by the Government: The Dialogues of Japanese Ambassadors. (外務交涉衛門編：倭使問答)

The Hand-Book on the Royal Court of Yi Dynasty. (國朝寶鑑)

Chŭng Ha-sang: The Letters to the Admirable Counselor. (丁夏祥：上宰相書)

Lee Su-kwang: The Analogues of Chi-pong. (李晬光：芝峰類說)

Lee Kyu-kyŏng: The Essays on the Five Continents Written on Long Scrolls. (李圭景：五洲衍文長箋散稿)

Lee Man-ch'ae: The Confucian Ban on Christianity, 7 volumes, 2 books, 1931. (李晩采：闢衛編, 1931 年刊)

Yun Chong-eui: The New Confucian Ban on Christianity. (尹宗儀：闢衛新編)

Kim Yun-sik: The Subsequent "Eum-ch'ŏng" Journals. Volume I, Seoul, 1959. (金允植：續陰晴史上, 1959 서울)

Lee Neung-hwa: The History of the Korean Christianism and Diplomacy, Seoul, 1928. (李能和：朝鮮基督教及外交史, 1928, 서울)

Hyŭn, Sŏk-mun: The Ki-hae Diaries, Seoul, 1905. (玄錫文：己亥日記, 1905, 서울)

Onosaburo Kusuda: The Short History of the Korean Catholicism, Pu-san, 1933. (楠田斧三郎：朝鮮天主教小史, 1933, 釜山)

Kazusaburo Uragawa: The Korean Martyrology, Osaka, 1944. (浦川和三郎：朝鮮殉教史, 1944, 大阪)

Masayuki: Yamaguchi: A Study on Hwang Sa-yŏng's Silk Letter, Osaka, 1946. (山口正之：黃嗣永帛書의 研究, 1946, 大阪)

Tr. by Lee Neung-sik: L'Introduction de l'Historie de l'Église de Corée, Seoul, 1947. (李能植譯：달레의 朝鮮教會史序說, 1947, 서울)

Tr. by Ahn Eung-ryŏl: Martyrs Français et Coréens, Séoul, 1946. (安應烈譯：朝鮮殉教福者傳, 1946, 서울)

Tr. by Han U-kun: The Korea Travelogue by Ernst Oppert, Seoul, 1959. (韓沽劤譯：읍페르트의 한국기행, 1959, 서울)

Ryu Hong-ryŏl: The History of the Korean Catholic Church, Volume I, Seoul, 1949. (柳洪烈：朝鮮天主教會史上卷, 1949, 서울)

Ryu Hong-ryŏl: The Story of Lee Lugartha, Seoul, 1955. (柳洪烈：李누갈다傳, 1955, 서울)

Ryu Hong-ryŏl: The History of the Korean Catholic Church, Seoul, 1962. (柳洪烈：韓國天主教會史, 1962, 서울)

Ryu Hong-ryŏl: The Study on Persecutions of the Christianity During the King Ko-jong's Reign, Seoul, 1962. (柳洪烈：高宗治下西學受難의 研究, 1962, 서울)

Kim Ku-jŏng: The Biography of Kim Tae-kŏn, Seoul, 1961. (金九鼎：金大建傳, 1961, 서울)

Kim Ku-jŏng and Kim Yŏng-ku: The History of Catholic Development in the Ho-nam Region, Chŏn-ju, 1964. (金九鼎・金榮九：天主教湖南發展史, 1964, 全州)

Hong I-sŏp: The Study on Chŭng Yak-yong's Political-Economic Ideology, Seoul, 1959. (洪以燮：丁若鏞의政治經濟思想研究, 1959, 서울)

Chu Chae-yong: On Catholic Ideologies and Rites of Ancestral Worship of Confucianist Elders, Seoul, 1958. (朱在用：先儒의 天主思想과 祭祀問題, 1958, 서울)

The Hand-Book Attached to the Magazine Kyŏng-hyang-sin-mun: The Translation of l'Histoire de l'Église de Corée of Ch. Dallet, the monthly issues of from 1907 till 1913, Seoul. (京鄉新聞〔雜誌〕附錄寶鑑：대한〔조선〕성교사기〔달레교회 사번역〕1907~1913 每月連載, 서울)

The Guidance Books (3) of the Christianity, Seoul, 1862. (天主聖教工課〔三册〕, 1862, 서울)

The Outline of Baptism, Seoul, 1864. (領洗大義, 1864, 서울)

The Essence of the Catholicism, Seoul, 1864. (主教要旨, 1864, 서울)

The Catholic Liturgy Book, 1865. (天主聖教禮規, 1865)

Masasuke Sugimoto: The Modern History of Korea, Compiled by the Korean Historians Association. (朝鮮史學會編纂杉本正介述朝鮮最近史)

Sim Yong-Je: The Excerpts of Korean Martyrdom, Shanghai, 1900. (沈容齊：高麗致命事略, 1900, 上海)

Chargeboeuf: The Diaries of the Korean Martyrology, Seoul, 1895. (宋神父致命日記, 1895, 서울)

Park Che-hyŏng: The Hand-Book of the Politics of Korea, Volume I, Tokyo, 1886. (朴齊炯：朝鮮政鑑〔上〕1886, 東京)

Adrien Larribeau: The Short History of the Korean Catholic Church, Seoul, 1934. (元亨根：朝鮮天主公教會略史, 1934, 서울)

Kim Ch'ang-mun and Chŭng Jae-sŭn: The History of the Korean Catholic Church—Yesterday and Today, Seoul, 1963. (金昌文・鄭宰善 編：韓國가톨릭 어제와 오늘, 1963, 서울)

Philip Crosbie: Three Winters Cold, Dublin, 1955.

Célestin Coyos: Ma Captivité en Corée du Nord, Paris, 1954.

Arthur Tonne: The Story of Chaplain Kapaun, Emporia, Kan., U.S.A., 1954.

The Catholic Liturgy Book, 186-, C... 1888.

Matsuda Sugimoto. The Modern History of Korea, Compiled in the Korean Historian Aburamoto. (?)

Sin Yong Je. The Exercise of Korean Martyrdom. Shanghai, 1900.

Changbaeof. The Diaries of the Korean Martyrology. Seoul, 186...

Park Cuchwang. The Head-Book of the Politic of Korea. Vohnon, Totem, 1886.

Adilor Poytheana. The Short History of the Korean Catholic Church, Seoul, 1931.

Kim Changnam and Chang Jae-sun. The History of the Korean Catholic Church—Yesterday and Today. Seoul, 1963.

Philip Crosnie. Three Winters Cold. Dublin, 1955.

Gaston Cayron. Ma Captivité en Corée du Nord. Paris, 1954.

Arthur Tanner. The Story of (Chaplain Kapaun) Emporia, Kan., USA, 1954.

INDEX
to
Martyrology

M

N

Q

R

KOREA

Glancing Through Pictures

The coastal scenes near Ch'ong-sŏk-
chŏng at Mt. Keum-kang

Another view of the above

The three midstream peaks in the Han River near To-tam, North Ch'ung-ch'ŏng Province

The Paek-ma River flowing by Pu-yŏ, South Ch'ung-ch'ŏng Province

The cliff around Pŏm-sŏm (Tiger-Island) in Che-ju Island

The Hong-kyo (Rainbow-Bridge) in the precinct of the Sŏn-am-sa Temple, South Chŏl-la Province

The coastal scenes of
Tu-mo-jin on Paek-ryŏng
Island in the West Coast

The Ch'ŏn-ji-yŏn Fall seen
from the air in southern
Che-ju

The P'al-tam (Eight-streams) Cascades in a valley of Mt. Keum-kang (The Diamond Mountains), Kang-won Province

Haeng-hwa village in Springtime, by Mt. Puk-han, north of Seoul

An autumn scene, near Seoul. Reeds are a common feature of the landscape

Mt. Sŏl-ak in Kang-won Province. One of the country's most celebrated tourist resorts is located here.

Part of the rampart around Mt. Nam-han, Kyŏng-ki Province

The Hwa-hong (Bright-Rainbow) Gate in Su-won, Kyŏng-ki Province

The magnificent Pul-kuk (Buddhist-Land) Temple near Kyŏng-ju, North Kyŏng-sang Province

The nine-storied octagonal pagoda on the Wol-chŏng-sa (Moon-Spirit-Temple) in Mt. O-tae, Kang-won Province

The cherry-blossoms in their full
bloom in Chin-hae, the country's
southwestern port town

The scene of the Kwang-han-lu in
Nam-won, North Chŏl-la Province.
The site is the birthplace of
Korea's most romantic story
"Ch'un-hyang-jŏn."

A pathway through fir-
bedecked slopes of Mt.
O-tae, Kang-won Province

The scene of Tong-ku-
neung (East-Hill Tombs),
royal tombs east of
Seoul

Ancient Palaces

The Hyang-won-jŏng (Perfume-Distant-Kiosk) Pavilion in Kyŏng-pok Palace in Seoul

A general view of In-chŏng-jŏn (Gracious-Administration-Edifice), the main building of Ch'ang-tŏk Palace in Seoul

The Sŏk-cho-jŏn (Stone-Edifice) inside Tŏk-su
Palace in Seoul

The Kyŏng-hoe-ru (Joyful-Meeting-Pavilion)
in Kyŏng-pok Palace in Seoul

The Tae-cho-jŏn (Great-Edifice) in Ch'ang-tŏk Palace in Seoul

The Ae-ryŏn-jŏng (Love-Lotus) Pavilion near the lotus pond in the Secret Garden in Seoul. The highlight of Ch'ang-tŏk Palace

The Ok-ryu-ch'ŏn (Clear-Stream), waterway in the Secret Garden in Seoul

The Myŏng-chŏng-jŏn (Wise-Administration-Edifice) in Ch'ang-kyŏng-won of Seoul

The Ch'ong-sŏ-kak Library (Stack Rooms) in Ch'ang-kyŏng-won of Seoul

The Tae-sŏng-jŏn in the compound of Sŏng-kyun-kwan University, the nation's centuries-old Confucian Academy

Seoul

Seoul, the capital, seen from atop Nam-san Hill toward the Capitol
(background, middle center)

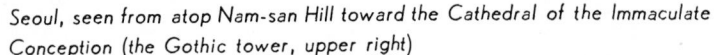

Seoul, seen from atop Nam-san Hill toward the Cathedral of the Immaculate
Conception (the Gothic tower, upper right)

The Nam-tae-mun (South-Great-Gate) near Seoul Railroad Station.
The Gate is designated as The Nation Treasure No 1.

The 13-storied pagoda in the park of
the same name in Seoul

The monument for the Buddhist saint
Won-kak (Complete Enlightenment) in
the Pagoda Park

The Su-chŏng-kak (Water-Kiosk) seen across the lotus pond in Ch'ang-kyŏng-won (Botanical and Zoological Gardens) of Seoul

The P'al-kak-jŏng (Octagonal Pavilion) in the Pagoda Park in Seoul. At this pavilion the famous Declaration of Independence was publicly read on March 1, 1919.

The Tok-rip (Independence) Gate in western Seoul. The gate commemorates the expulsion of Chinese influences.

A snowy scene of Tŏk-su Palace, Seoul

Government buildings (housing economic ministries) along Se-jong Street.
The building in the background is the Capitol.

Ban-do Hotel

Korea House, an entertainment center for foreign guests

The National Museum in Tŏk-su Palace of Seoul

Education and Culture

College of Liberal Arts and Sciences,
Seoul National University

Bird's-eye view
of Han-yang
University

Korea University

Kyŏng-hi University

Students of Ewha Women's University parading on the occasion of the "May Queen" Nomination

The open-door concert ground in the compound of the Capitol Building

A joint performance by the Korean Broadcasting System Orchestra,
the Seoul Municipal Symphony Orchestra and choruses

The opening ceremony of the National Athletic Meeting in Seoul

An aerial view of the Seoul Stadium. The vacant near-circular ground on the upper left is for baseball games.

A member of the National Classic Music Association playing a Ka-ya-keum.
Korea's age-old unique string instrument

Korean women playing Chang-ko (drum) and performing classic dancing

Korean handicrafts. Lacquerware exhibited in a Seoul department store. Korean lacquerware has recently gained importance in the domain of foreign trade.

Korean dolls

The atelier of a painter of the
Oriental school

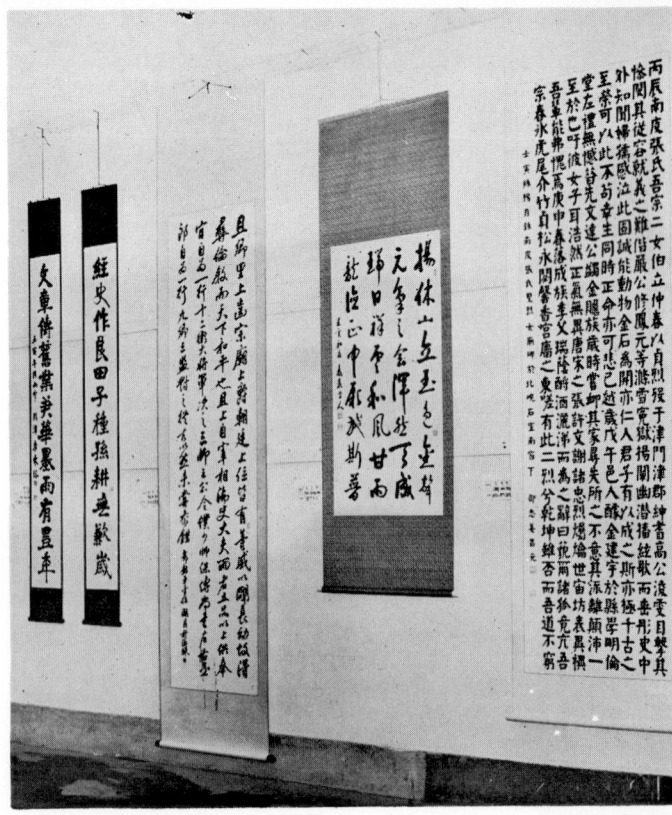

A caligraphical exhibition (on
the occasion of a National
Art Exhibition)

Korean People and
Their Customs

A happy grin

Korean children riding a seesaw. Seesawing
is very popular at holiday time.

The Swing

Swing in particular is prevalent in the season including the Tan-o Festival (the fifth day of the fifth lunar month).

The Yut Game

The game, played with four short sticks by both sexes, is especially popular in the winter months.

Korean archers competiting in a contest

Archery is being revived throughout the country.

Kite-flying

Together with archery, kite-flying is said to have originated in Northeastern Asia. Contests are held yearly, and attract many contestants and spectators.

Classical Dance

Mother and her girl

Women in the traditional costume

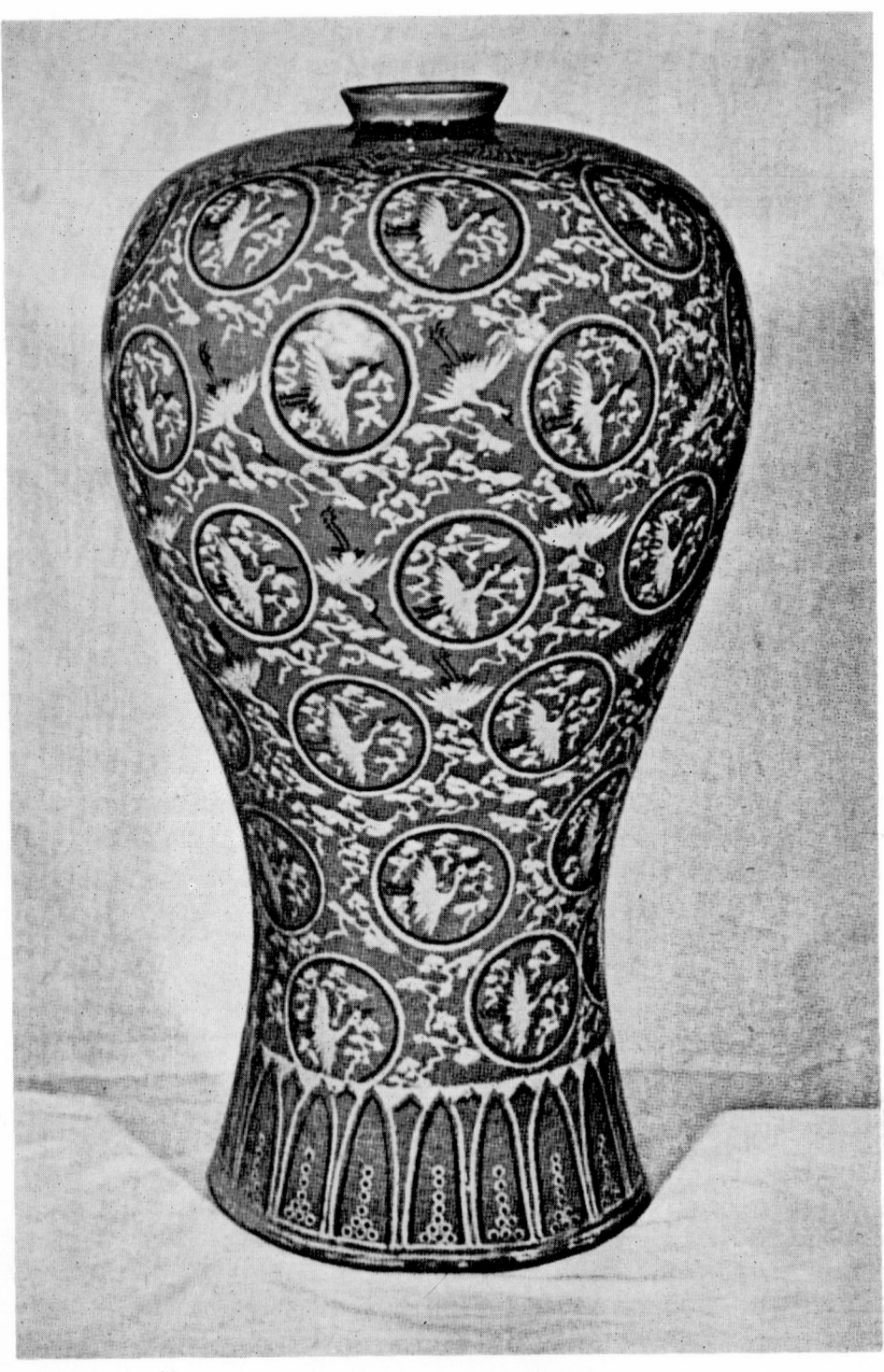

Vase
Celadon glaze, incised decoration filled with white and black slips
(height 42.1cm, diameter 25.1cm), Ko-ryǒ Dynasty (late 12th century)

A porcelain figurine of a mounted warrior of the Lolang Period (height 21.5cm, length 26.5cm). It is much influenced by the Han Dynasty of China. (c. 200 BC-c. 200AD)

Gold Crown (height 35 cm.) Sil-la Dynasty (5~6th century)

Gold Earrings (length 8.4cm.)
Excavated from the Pu-pu (man and wife) Tomb of the Sil-la Dynasty, Kyŏng-ju (5~6th century)

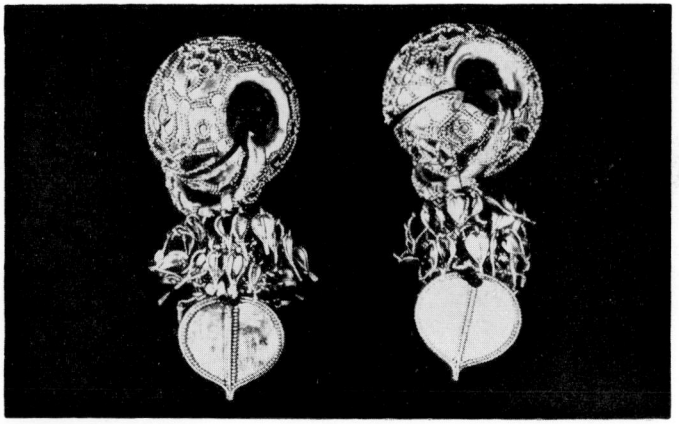

Buckle
Gold with turquoise ornaments excavated from Tomb No. 9, Pyŏng-yang (height 6.6cm, width 94.5cm), Lolang Period (1st-2nd century)

Incense Burner with a Reticulated Ball Cover
Celadon glaze, modeled, incised and under glaze iron and white slip decoration (height 15.2cm, width 12.2 cm), excavated 12-13th century.

Water Pot, Cover and Bowl
Celadon glaze, reticulated, modeled and incised decoration (pot height 17.8cm, diameter at base, 10.3 cm and bowl height 8-9cm, diameter at mouth, 19cm), Ko-ryŏ Dynasty (12th century).

Incense Burner
Celadon glaze, modeled, incised and under glaze iron decoration (height 21.3cm, width 16cm), Ko-ryŏ Dynasty (11-12th century).

Vase
Celadon glaze, painted peony design in under glaze iron (height 27cm, diameter at shoulder, 16.5cm), Ko-ryŏ Dynasty (mid-13th century).

Vase
Celadon glaze, modeled and incised decoration filled with white and black slips (height 25.6cm, diameter at base, 9.4cm), Ko-ryŏ Dynasty (12-13th century)

Jar with Slightly Flattened Sides
Celadon glaze stamped and incised decorations filled with white and black slips (height 27cm, diameter at base, 19,9 cm), Ko-ryŏ Dynasty (mid-13th—early 14th century).

Water jar
Celadon glaze, modeled and incised decoration filled with white and black slips (height 20cm, diameter at base, 15.2 cm), Ko-ryŏ Dynasty (12-13th century).

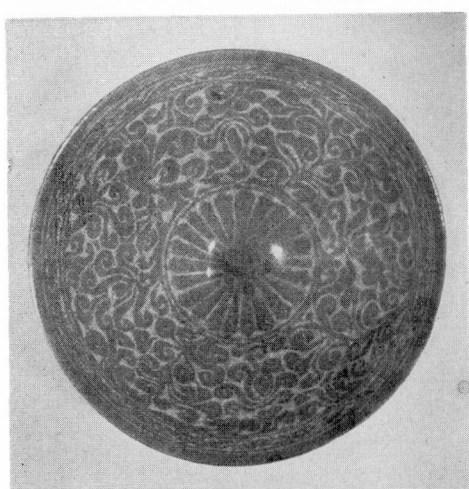

Drinking Bowl

Celadon glaze, incised and with incised decoration with white and black slips (height 6.2cm, diameter 6.9cm), Ko-ryŏ Dynasty (12th century). The interior (upper) is also decorated with a white chrysanthemum design.

Wine Pot with Lid

Celadon graze, incised decoration filled with white and black slips (height 21.1cm, diameter at base, 7.6cm), Ko-ryŏ Dynasty (late 12th century).

Rounder Cosmetic Box and Cover with Five Boxes Inside

Celadon glaze, incised decoration filled with white and black slips (height 7.6cm, diameter 19cm), Ko-ryŏ Dynasty (late 12th—early 13th century)

A Painting by Kang Heui-an (1419∼1465)

A Man watching the waters in a leisurely mood

Butterflies, painted on silk, by Shin Myŏng-yŏn (1809~?)

"The Dharma," painted by Kim Myŏng-kuk (?-?)

A colored painting of a cow, by Kim Tu-ryang (1696~1763)

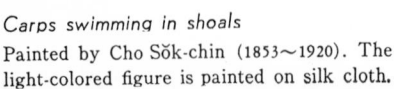

Carps swimming in shoals
Painted by Cho Sŏk-chin (1853~1920). The light-colored figure is painted on silk cloth.

Cats and Sparrows
Painted by Pyŏn Sang-pyŏk (early 18th century)

The light-colored painting
By Kim Ung-hwan (1742~1789), showing the riverside landscape in which
people are enjoying themselves with flute sounds.

A savage tiger
Painted by Sim Sa-jŏng (1707~1770). The figure
is painted in black Indian ink.

*A painting of a pair of magpies and a
group of cats*
The painter is unknown.

Fluttering Butterflies
(watercolor)
By Lee Kyo-ik (1807)

The light-colored summer landscape
painted on silk
By Hǔh Yu (1809~1892)

Bunches of grapes in the
moonlight
By Lee Ke-u (1574~?)

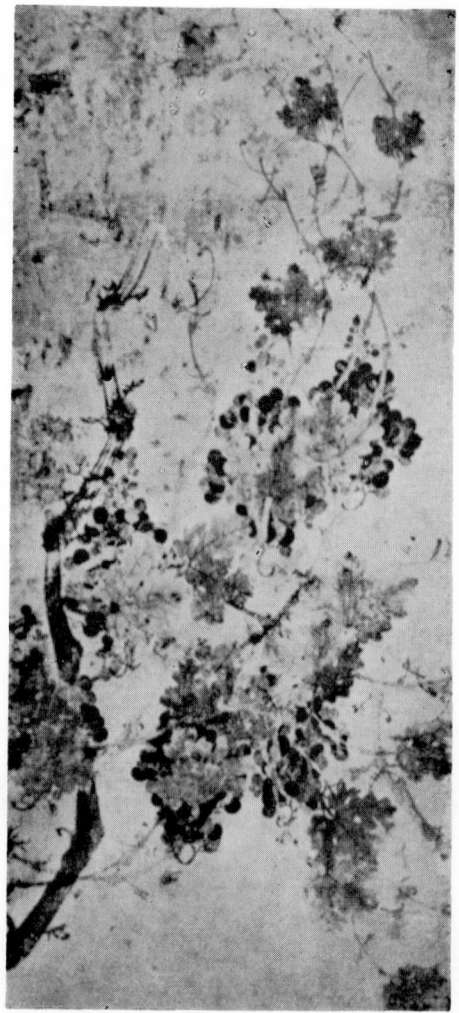

Wild Ducks (watercolor)
By Kim Hu-sin (?~?)

A colored painting on silk. Women enjoying themselves merrily by the waterside during the Tan-o (Dragon Boat) Festival
By Shin Yun-pok (1758~?)

A light-colored painting of mounted woman
By Yun Tŏk-heui (1685~?)

A colored painting of a bunch of grapes
By Lee In-mun (1745~1821)

NIHIL OBSTAT

Paulus Kim, Censor

IMPRIMATUR

die 15 Aug. 1964
+Paulus M. Ro
Archiep. Seoulensis

CATHOLIC KOREA
YESTERDAY AND TODAY

1964年 12 月　1日　印刷
1964年 12 月 25日　發行

編　者　金　昌　文・鄭　宰　善

發行者　金　　　昌　　　文

發行處　가톨릭코리아社

서울特別市 城東區 新堂洞 406—4 番地
登　錄：1963年 9 月 30日　第 1253 號

印刷所　三 和 印 刷 株 式 會 社
製本所　二　　　友　　　社